THE OXFORD HANDBOOK OF

COMPARATIVE
POLITICS

THE OXFORD HANDBOOKS OF POLITICAL SCIENCE

GENERAL EDITOR: ROBERT E. GOODIN

The *Oxford Handbooks of Political Science* is a ten-volume set of reference books offering authoritative and engaging critical overviews of all the main branches of political science.

The series as a whole is under the General Editorship of Robert E. Goodin, with each volume being edited by a distinguished international group of specialists in their respective fields:

POLITICAL THEORY
John S. Dryzek, Bonnie Honig & Anne Phillips

POLITICAL INSTITUTIONS
R. A. W. Rhodes, Sarah A. Binder & Bert A. Rockman

POLITICAL BEHAVIOR
Russell J. Dalton & Hans-Dieter Klingemann

COMPARATIVE POLITICS
Carles Boix & Susan C. Stokes

LAW & POLITICS
Keith E. Whittington, R. Daniel Kelemen & Gregory A. Caldeira

PUBLIC POLICY
Michael Moran, Martin Rein & Robert E. Goodin

POLITICAL ECONOMY
Barry R. Weingast & Donald A. Wittman

INTERNATIONAL RELATIONS
Christian Reus-Smit & Duncan Snidal

CONTEXTUAL POLITICAL ANALYSIS
Robert E. Goodin & Charles Tilly

POLITICAL METHODOLOGY
Janet M. Box-Steffensmeier, Henry E. Brady & David Collier

This series aspires to shape the discipline, not just to report on it. Like the Goodin–Klingemann *New Handbook of Political Science* upon which the series builds, each of these volumes will combine critical commentaries on where the field has been together with positive suggestions as to where it ought to be heading.

THE OXFORD HANDBOOK OF

COMPARATIVE POLITICS

Edited by

CARLES BOIX

and

SUSAN C. STOKES

OXFORD

UNIVERSITY PRESS

Great Clarendon Street, Oxford, OX2 6DP,
United Kingdom

Oxford University Press is a department of the University of Oxford.
It furthers the University's objective of excellence in research, scholarship,
and education by publishing worldwide. Oxford is a registered trade mark of
Oxford University Press in the UK and in certain other countries

© The several contributors 2007

The moral rights of the author have been asserted

First published 2007
First published in paperback 2009

Published in the United States of America by Oxford University Press
198 Madison Avenue, New York, NY 10016, United States of America

British Library Cataloguing in Publication Data
Data available

Library of Congress Control Number: 2007003069

ISBN 978-0-19-956602-0

Contents

PART VI   MASS POLITICAL MOBILIZATION

PART VII   PROCESSING POLITICAL DEMANDS

PART VIII   GOVERNANCE IN COMPARATIVE PERSPECTIVE

ABOUT THE CONTRIBUTORS

James E. Alt is Frank G. Thomson Professor of Government at Harvard University.

Robert H. Bates is Eaton Professor of the Science of Government at Harvard University.

Pablo Beramendi is Assistant Professor of Political Science at Duke University.

Carles Boix is Professor of Politics and Public Affairs, Princeton University.

Matthew E. Carnes is a Ph.D. candidate in Political Science at Stanford University.

Helma G. E. de Vries teaches in the Department of Government and Law at Lafayette College.

Raymond M. Duch is Professor in Quantitative Political Science and a Professorial Fellow at Nuffield College, Oxford.

Jonathan Eastwood is Assistant Professor of Sociology at Washington and Lee University.

John Ferejohn is Carolyn S. G. Munro Professor of Political Science at Stanford University, a senior fellow at the Hoover Institution Graduate School of Business, and a regular visiting professor at New York University Law School.

Robert J. Franzese, Jr. is Associate Professor of Political Science at the University of Michigan, Ann Arbor.

Timothy Frye is Professor, Department of Political Science, Columbia University.

Barbara Geddes is a Professor of Political Science at University of California, Los Angeles.

John Gerring is Associate Professor, Department of Political Science, Boston University.

Liah Greenfeld is University Professor and Professor of Political Science and Sociology, and Director of the Institute for the Advancement of the Social Sciences, at Boston University.

Frances Hagopian is Michael P. Grace II Associate Professor Latin American Studies in the Department of Political Science at the University of Notre Dame, and a Faculty Fellow of the Kellogg Institute for International Studies.

Russell Hardin is Professor of Politics at New York University.

Ronald Inglehart is a Professor of Political Science at the University of Michigan and President of the World Values Survey Association.

Stathis N. Kalyvas is Arnold Wolfers Professor of Political Science and Director of the Program on Order, Conflict, and Violence at Yale University.

Philip Keefer is Lead Research Economist in the Development Research Group of the World Bank.

Herbert Kitschelt is George V. Allen Professor of International Relations in the Department of Political Science, Duke University.

Mark I. Lichbach is Professor in the Department of Government and Politics at the University of Maryland.

Kenneth M. McElwain is a Post-Doctoral Fellow, Division of International, Comparative, and Area Studies, Stanford University.

James Mahoney is an Associate Professor of Political Science and Sociology at Northwestern University.

José María Maravall is Director of the Centre for Advanced Studies in the Social Sciences (Juan March Institute, Madrid).

Isabela Mares is Associate Professor of Political Science at Columbia University.

Pippa Norris is Director of Democratic Governance at the United Nations Development Programme in New York and the Maguire Lecturer in Comparative Politics at Harvard University.

Benjamin Nyblade is Assistant Professor of Political Science at the University of British Columbia, Canada.

Elinor Ostrom is Arthur F. Bentley Professor of Political Science; Co-Director of the Workshop in Political Theory and Policy Analysis, Indiana University; and Founding Director, Center for the Study of Institutional Diversity, Arizona State University.

Steven Pincus is Professor of History, Yale University, specializing in early modern British history.

G. Bingham Powell, Jr. is Marie C. and Joseph C. Wilson Professor of Political Science at the University of Rochester, Rochester, New York.

Adam Przeworski is Carroll and Milton Petrie Professor in the Department of Politics, New York University.

Shanna S. Rose is an Assistant Professor at New York University's Robert F. Wagner Graduate School of Public Service.

Frances Rosenbluth is a Professor of Political Science and Director of the Georg W. Leitner Program in Comparative and International Political Economy at Yale University.

Filippo Sabetti is Professor of Political Science, McGill University, Montreal, and Affiliated Faculty, Workshop in Political Theory and Policy Analysis, Indiana University, Bloomington, Indiana.

David Samuels is Benjamin E. Lippincott Associate Professor in the Department of Political Science at the University of Minnesota.

Charles Shipan is the J. Ira and Nicki Harris Professor of Social Science and Professor of Public Policy at the University of Michigan.

Hendrik Spruyt is Norman Dwight Harris Professor of International Relations and Chair, Department of Political Science, Northwestern University.

Susan C. Stokes is John S. Saden Professor of Political Science, Yale University.

Kaare Strøm is Professor of Political Science at the University of California, San Diego.

Rein Taagepera is Research Professor, University of California, Irvine and University of Tartu.

Sidney Tarrow is Maxwell M. Upson Professor of Government and Professor of Sociology at Cornell University.

Charles Tilly is Joseph L. Buttenwieser Professor of Social Science at Columbia University.

Ashutosh Varshney is Professor of Political Science, University of Michigan, Ann Arbor.

Celso M. Villegas is a graduate student in the Department of Sociology, Brown University.

Christian Welzel is Professor of Political Science at the Jacobs University Bremen (JUB) and a member of the Executive Committee of the World Values Surveys Association.

Ronald Wintrobe is Professor of Economics at the University of Western Ontario.

Elisabeth Jean Wood is Professor of Political Science at Yale University and Research Professor at the Santa Fe Institute.

Anne Wren is Assistant Professor of Political Science, Stanford University, and Senior Research Fellow, Institute for International Integration Studies, Trinity College Dublin.

PART I

INTRODUCTION

CHAPTER 1

....

INTRODUCTION

....

CARLES BOIX
SUSAN C. STOKES

Why do authoritarian states democratize? What accounts for the contours, dynamics, and ideologies of the nation-state? Under what conditions do civil wars and revolutions erupt? Why is political representation channeled through political parties in contemporary democracies? Why do some parties run on policy programs, others on patronage? Can citizens use elections and courts to hold governments accountable?

These are some of the crucial questions that comparative political scientists address. And they are the questions, among others, around which this volume is organized. We asked a set of top scholars in the field of comparative politics to write critical surveys of areas of scholarship in which they are expert. We assembled the volume with two guiding principles. First, we are committed to the possibility (and desirability) of generating a systematic body of theoretical knowledge about politics. The discipline advances, we believe, through theoretical discovery and innovation. Second, we embrace a catholic approach to comparative methodology. In the following paragraphs we offer an overview of our authors' contributions, with occasional critical commentary of our own or additional thoughts on the directions in which future research should go.

1 THEORY AND METHODS

....

The questions posed above and others that our contributors raise are too complex, and too important, to restrict ourselves to one or another methodology in our attempts to answer them. It is not that, metholodogically speaking, "anything goes;" some research designs and methods for gathering and analyzing evidence are not fruitful. But our contributors explain the advantages and pitfalls of a wide range of techniques deployed by comparativists, from econometric analysis of cross-national datasets and observational data to extended stints of field-work. They employ a variegated toolkit to make sense of political processes and outcomes.

Among the starkest shifts in comparative politics over the past two decades is the rise of statistical studies of large numbers of countries. Most graduate students in comparative politics who studied in leading departments in the 1960s through the 1980s were trained to conduct research in a single region or country. Indeed, the very term *comparative* was in most cases misleading; comparative politics frequently entailed not making comparisons but studying the politics of a foreign country. With slight exaggeration one could think of this as the State Department approach to comparative politics, where one scholar staffs the "Japan desk," another the "Chile desk," etc. Of course there were important exceptions. One was Almond and Verba's *The Civic Culture*, which compared citizens' attitudes in five countries. Still, it would have been hard to predict circa the 1970s or even 1980 the degree to which comparative politics would come to prominently feature large-N cross-national studies.

Our volume, significantly, includes two studies that take stock of what we would lose should the traditional comparative enterprise, with its emphasis on close knowledge of the language, history, and culture of a country or region, be abandoned altogether, and should the activity supporting that approach, the extended period of work in the field, be lost along with it. John Gerring contends that neither case studies nor large-N comparisons are an unalloyed good; rather, both entail tradeoffs, and we are therefore well advised as a discipline to retain both approaches in our collective repertoire. Where case studies are good for building theory and developing insights, Gerring argues, large-N research is good for confirming or refuting theory. Where case studies offer internal validity, large-N studies offer external validity. Where case studies allow scholars to explore causal mechanisms, large-N comparisons allow them to identify causal effects.

Elisabeth Wood's chapter alerts us to what we are in danger of losing should we as a profession give up on field research. To the rhetorical question "Why ever leave one's office?" she gives several answers. Interacting personally with subjects in their own setting may be the only way to get a handle on many crucial research questions, such as which of many potential political identities subjects embrace and what their self-defined interests are. Fieldwork is not without perils, Wood explains, both intellectual and personal. Interview subjects may be evasive and even strategically dissimulating; field researchers may have strong personal reactions, positive or negative, to their subjects, reactions that may then color their conclusions; and fieldwork is a lonely endeavor, with predictable highs and lows. Wood suggests strategies for dealing with these pitfalls.

James Mahoney and Celso Villegas discuss another variant of qualitative research: comparative historical studies. The aims of this research differ from those of cross-national studies, they contend. Comparative historical scholars "ask questions about the causes of major outcomes in particular cases," and hence seek to explain "each and every case that falls within their argument's scope." By contrast, large-N researchers "are concerned with generalizing about average causal effects for large populations and . . . do not ordinarily seek to explain specific outcomes in particular cases." Mahoney and Villegas discuss recent methodological developments in comparative historical research, such as the identification of necessary and sufficient conditions, the use of Boolean algebra to uncover inter-active causal effects, and fuzzy-set logic. They also address some of the criticisms of comparative historical research, such as the reliability and generalizability of the historical record. They tout both secondary and primary source research.

One might press Mahoney and Villegas to go a step further in their definition of primary historical research. They cite as primary sources "government documents, newspapers, diaries, and bulletins that describe past events at roughly the time they were occurring." Yet, with the exception of diaries, these printed documents fail to meet the historian's criterion of a manuscript source. Unpublished manuscript or archival sources—internal memos, individuals' notes on organizational debates, correspondence among political actors, spies' accounts—are the functional equiva-lent for historians of personal interviews for field researchers, which (as Wood explains) can be the best window into an actor's identity, strategic calculations, and interests. Government documents, newspapers, and published bulletins, while useful, represent a version of "events as they were occurring" that has been produced for public consumption. This particular critique raises broader questions about the adequacy of training of many social scientists who undertake historical research.

Robert Franzese's chapter defends large-N, quantitative techniques against some of the critiques that other contributors level against them. Comparative political scientists, like empirically oriented sociologists and economists, are bedeviled by four problems: a tradeoff between quantity and quality in the collection of data; multi-causality; context-conditionality, that is, the fact all the effects of our variables are conditional on other variables; and endogeneity. Yet, as Franzese argues, these obstacles, which are in fact inherent in our trade, should not lead us to dodge quan-titative strategies of research. On the contrary, a simple, back-of-the-envelope calcula-tion shows that the plausible loss of precision involved in measuring large numbers of observations does not justify retreating to qualitative studies of a few cases—even if we attain very precise knowledge about small samples, they fail to yield robust inferences. Similarly, the presence of multiple and conditional causality cannot be solved easily by case studies (although good process tracing may alleviate these problems). Finally, qualitative case study research does not necessarily escape from problems of endogene-ity. To move from correlational analysis to causal propositions, Franzese contends, we need to employ more sophisticated techniques, such as variable instrumentation, matching, or vector autoregression. But even these techniques are not sufficient. Here we would like to add that, influenced by a few macroeconomists and political econo-mists, part of the discipline seems on the verge of uncritically embracing the use of instrumentation to deflect all the critiques that are leveraged against any work on the grounds that the latter suffer from endogeneity. It turns out that there are very few, if any, instruments that are truly exogenous—basically, geography. Their use has extraordinary theoretical implications that researchers have either hardly thought about (for example, that weather determines regime, in a sort of Montesquieuian manner) or just avoid (when they posit that the instrument is simply a statistical artifact with no theoretical value on its own and then insist that it is the right one to substitute for the variable of interest). Thus, we want to stress with Franzese that only theory building can truly help us in reducing the problem of endogenous causation.

Adam Przeworski offers a less optimistic perspective on observational research, large-N or otherwise. Observational studies, ones that do not (and cannot fully) ensure that the cases we compare are matched in all respects other than the "treatment," cannot deal adequately with problems of endogeneity. "We need to study the causes of effects," he writes, "as well as the effects of causes." Some covariates (traits of a unit that it has prior to the application of a treatment) are unobserved. These unobserved covariates may determine both the likelihood of a unit's being subjected to the treatment and the likelihood of its evincing the effect. Because these covariates are unobserved, we cannot test the proposition that they, rather than the treatment or putative cause, are actually responsible for the effect.

Przeworski discusses traditional as well as more novel approaches to dealing with endogeneity, but his chapter leans toward pessimism. "To identify causal effects we need assumptions and some of these assumptions are untestable." His chapter will be essential reading for comparativists as they assess the promise and limitations of observational versus experimental or quasi-experimental designs.

But perhaps the mood of the chapter is more pessimistic than it need be. Theory should help us distinguish cases in which endogeneity is plausibly present from ones in which it is not. One way of reading Przeworski's chapter is that a crucial research task is to shift key covariates from the unobserved to the observed category. This task is implied by a hypothetical example that Przeworski offers. A researcher wishes to assess the impact of governing regime on economic growth. Future leaders of some countries study at universities where they become pro-democratic and learn how to manage economies, whereas others study at universities that make them pro-dictatorial and teach them nothing about economic management. Both kinds return home to become leaders and govern their societies and economies in the manner consistent with their training. It therefore appears that democracy produces economic growth. The training of leaders is a variable that we cannot observe systematically, in Przeworski's view. But there is a difference between unobserved and unobserv*able*. It is not obvious to us why this variable could never be systematically observed, should our theory—and, perhaps, our close, case study-informed knowledge—tell us that we should worry about it.

Whether one studies a large or small number of cases, and whether one employs econometrics or other techniques, Robert Bates argues that one should do theoretically sophisticated work informed by game theory. Indeed, the use of game-theoretical models, of varying degrees of formalization, is a strong recent trend in comparative politics. Illustrating his methodological claims with his recent research on the politics of coffee production and commercialization, Bates offers a strategy of comparative research that, in a way, revisits all of the chapters that constitute Part II of the volume. The first step of research is apprehension: a detailed study and understanding of a particular time and place. *Verstehen* is then followed by explanation: the researcher apportions the things she knows "between causes or consequences" and attempts to develop "lines of logic to link them." In Bates's view, the explanatory drive should begin with the assumption (or principle) of rationality and use game theory to impose a structure on the phenomena we observe. The structure of the game allows us to push from the particular to the construction of broader theories, themselves susceptible of validation. The construction of theoretical explanations must be then subject to the test of confirmation: this implies progressively moving from small-N comparisons to much larger datasets in which researchers can evaluate their theories against a broad set of alternatives and controls.

The final contributor to our theory and methodology section also explores the role of rationalist assumptions in comparative research. Elinor Ostrom takes as her point of departure the proposition that "the theory of collective action is *the* central subject of political science" and that the problem of collective action is rooted in a social dilemma (or, in game theory terms, a prisoner's dilemma) in which, as is well known, rational individuals in pursuit of their optimal outcome may end up not cooperating even if it was in their interest to do so. Ostrom assesses the first generation of studies of collective action, which stress the structural conditions (number of players, type of benefits, heterogeneity of players, the degree of communication among them, and the iteration of games) that may increase the likelihood of achieving cooperation. She finds these studies wanting. Ostrom recognizes that the rationalist model only explains part of human behavior. Hence she calls for a shift towards a theory of boundedly rational, norm-based human behavior. Instead of positing a rationalistic individual, we should consider agents who are inherently living in a situation of informational uncertainty and who structure their actions, adopt their norms of behavior, and acquire knowledge from the social and institutional context in which they live. In this broader theory of human behavior, humans are "adaptive creatures who attempt to do as well as they can given the constraints of the situations in which they find themselves (or the ones that they seek out)." They "learn norms, heuristics, and full analytical strategies from one another, from feedback from the world, and from their own capacity to engage in self-reflection. They are capable of designing new tools—including institutions—that can change the structure of the worlds they face for good or evil purposes. They adopt both short-term and long-term perspectives dependent on the structure of opportunities they face." All in all, her approach encompasses a broader range of types of human action, from instances in which individuals exhibit "complete rationality" (normally in those environments in which they live in repetitive, highly competitive situations) to more "sociological agents" for which their rules of action are derived from shared norms. To some extent, the discipline seems to come full circle with this contribution: moving from cultural approaches under the aegis of modernization theory to the rationalist assumptions of institutionalist scholars and now back to a richer (perhaps looser but certainly closer to the way our classical thinkers thought about human nature) understanding of human agency. This journey has not been useless. On the contrary, as we traveled from one point to the other we have learned that a good theory of politics must be based on solid microfoundations, that is, on a plausible characterization of interests, beliefs, and actions of individuals.

2 STATES, STATE FORMATION, AND POLITICAL CONSENT

The institutional and ideological foundations of the modern national state are central concerns of comparative politics. Hendrik Spruyt considers the institutional dimension of state formation. Spruyt provides a bird's-eye overview of recent contributions to our understanding of state formation, an area of research that has grown exponentially in the last three decades. He reviews the ways in which the modern state, with its absolute claims of sovereignty over a particular territory and population, formed and displaced all other forms of governance. This change came in response to a shift in war technology, the growth of commercial capitalism, and new ideas about legitimate government. Spruyt also examines several influential and still-unsettled debates about what caused the emergence in the modern period of distinct types of constitutional and administrative regimes. Most studies of state building have focused on Europe in the modern period; the recent emergence of independent states outside of Europe in the last centuries is not adequately explained by these accounts. As Spruyt notes, state formation in the twentieth century allows us to evaluate the extent to which the international system, the economy, and the colonial legacy affect how sovereignty and legitimacy have expanded across the globe.

Other chapters consider the ideological dimensions of state formation and of intrastate identity conflict. Russell Hardin's chapter lays bare the difficulties in positing legitimacy as the ideological foundation of national states. Hardin warns against the fallacy of assuming that the existence of a political arrangement means that those subject to it deem it to be "legitimate." Hardin's reflections on legitimacy as a positive and normative concept underscore the limitations of the concept, at least in the ways it has been deployed by comparativists. Social scientists and political theorists typically ascribe legitimacy to a regime, Hardin explains, based on "how it came into existence, what it does for us, or our relationship to it both historically and now." But none of these grounds for assessment is firm. In Hardin's view, the dominant, Weberian definition amounts to equating legitimacy with a state's capacity to stay in power. But this coding would have us attribute legitimacy to regimes which, from the vantage point of both those who live under them and those who examine them from a distance, fall far short of legitimacy.

The ideological underpinnings of the modern state are also the subject of Liah Greenfeld and Jonathan Eastwood's contribution. They define national identity as a secular understanding of the self and its attachments, the vision of the world as partitioned into separate communities, and a notion of popular sovereignty. In contraposition to well-known arguments that stress either the perennialism of nationalism or its modern emergence, they claim that nationalism arose in modern times as a response to an upsetting of traditional hierarchies. Faced with the dissolution of the old concepts of status, individuals reinterpreted their position as one of belonging to a nation of equals. Within this shift in ideas, Greenfeld and Eastwood explore the distinct dimensions of nationalism: the criteria for membership in the nation and the images that a community creates about the relationship between the collectivity and each individual. The authors use these dimensions to develop a typology of nationalisms.

Nationalist states in the contemporary world are sometimes riven with conflict, and these conflicts have stimulated much theory building and research in comparative politics. Assessing the literature of ethnic identity and conflict, Ashutosh Varshney describes how a very young field of research has grown and progressed by taking seriously both the need to look for causal mechanisms and the need to explain empirical variation. His chapter tracks the fruitful dialogue among scholars through several sequential theoretical layers: essentialism, which initially dominated the field and now has been mostly superseded by the idea that nations are modern constructs; instrumentalism, which posits ethnic groups and nations as concepts that derive from material benefits and self-interest; constructivism; and institutionalism. Varshney's essay engagingly describes the advances as well as the limits of each school and offers ideas about how a blending of elements from each may help advance our research agenda.

3 POLITICAL REGIMES AND TRANSITIONS

Given the democratic revolution of the past quarter-century, it is scarcely surprising that democracy has been a central concern—perhaps the central concern—of comparative politics. Christian Welzel and Ronald Inglehart aim to restore a role for mass beliefs in the process of democratization. In so doing, they offer an important methodological insight. They contend that certain kinds of mass beliefs make democratization (and authoritarianism) more likely, especially "societal-led" democratization. Evidence that this is true can be found in surveys applied to mass publics in countries which vary in their degrees of democratization. Yet because they fear committing an ecological fallacy, social scientists have been wary of drawing inferences from these data. The fear, Welzel and Inglehart suggest, is based on an equally debilitating "individualist fallacy." Researchers commit an individualist fallacy when they (1) find that correlations that hold at the aggregate level do not also hold at the individual level and then (2) infer that these correlations are therefore meaningless.

This, they insist, is a mistake: the discovery of a potential ecological fallacy may itself be theoretically illuminating. The disjuncture between correlations in democratic values among individuals and in societies is illuminating in just this way. Welzel and Inglehart contend that the presence of certain values in high levels in a population creates a pro-democracy climate in the population as a whole, even though these values do not covary strongly at the individual level. The presence of these values in aggregate is predictive of effective democracy. Although some readers may remain skeptical about the last link, between mass beliefs and democratic institutions, the authors' methodological point, as well as their substantive claims, will be thought provoking for many students of comparative democratization.

Mass attitudes or beliefs of an undifferentiated kind play little role in Barbara Geddes's theories of democratization, or in the theories she reviews. Instead, these theories focus on more narrowly defined actors: rich people and poor people, or regimes that seek to maximize their own political control versus regimes that act as perfect agents of the wealthy. Despite comparativists' near-obsession with democratization, Geddes argues, we have few firm and uncontested conclusions about democracy's causes. Our empirical results in this area, furthermore, are less robust than one would like, changing in theoretically important ways depending on the sample of countries studied, on the time frame considered, and on the nature of specifications (e.g., does the model include or exclude country fixed effects?). The problem is not an absence of theory; our theories of democratization have become increasingly sophisticated and explicit. Rather, Geddes suggests, the problem may lie in heterogeneity of the explanandum, democratization. Transitions from absolutist monarchy to constitutional monarchy or to republics may be fundamentally different than transitions from modern military dictatorship to mass democracy. Separating these distinct phenomena, analyzing them—and, more to the point, developing distinct theories of them—is the key, in her view, to gaining firmer knowledge of why countries democratize.

With the exception of Hobbes, the relationship between civic culture and political regimes has been one of the central preoccupations of all modern political theorists. Embracing the new methods that characterized the new, self-consciously empirical political science that emerged after the Second World War, Almond and Verba in the 1960s tackled this secular concern in their highly influential book on civic culture. Yet, as Sabetti aptly explains, this attempt to put the study of the relationship on solid empirical grounds proved unsuccessful. The problem with this research agenda had less to do with the (still) very contentious notion of culture than with the ways in which researchers categorized democracy and political culture. They entertained too limited a conception of democracy, restricted to the institutional mechanisms that determine governance at the national level. They thus disregarded the vast number of democratic practices that operate at the local level and in intermediate social bodies. They defined political culture, in turn, as a set of beliefs and dispositions toward certain political objects. But this notion proved to be unsatisfactory: the role that these beliefs and attitudes played in sustaining democratic life and practices was unclear; their origins remained unknown; and, from a purely empirical point of view, there was no clear proof that democratic stability was bolstered by a particular democratic culture. Yet, it was precisely at the time when the political culture approach had gone down "a degenerative path" that researchers rescued the concept of culture and hence the problem of its political effects by stressing its eminently relational nature. In the late 1980s, Gambetta put trust back into the research agenda. Several researchers emphasized the need to understand interpersonal networks to explain particular behaviour. Coleman drew on game-theoretic concepts to develop the notion of social capital. And Putnam then transformed our way of understanding governance and culture in his famous study of Italian regional politics. This new approach is, as Sabetti insists, still in its infancy—we know little (both theoretically and empirically) about the mechanisms that go from social capital to good governance and next to nothing about the dynamics that create, sustain, or deplete civic virtue. And some of us doubt that trust, as opposed to an engaged skepticism, is the appropriate posture of citizens in democratic polities. But the new approach may well be putting us in the right path to "untangle the complex relationship between democracy and civic culture."

More than thirty years ago, Juan Linz wrote a highly influential piece on dictatorships for the *Handbook of Political Science*, edited by Fred Greenstein and Nelson Polsby. Linz's approach was mostly conceptual and sociological and drew on the literature on totalitarianism and authoritarianism that had been developing since the Second World War II. Non-democratic regimes, according to Linz, could be defined by their degree of internal pluralism, their ideology, and the level of political mobilization which they demanded of their subject populations. Preoccupied with the mechanisms that sustained dictatorships and the choices dictators and their subjects made, Ronald Wintrobe offers here a different account that starts from economic or rationalist assumptions. To rule, dictators have to combine some degree of repression with the construction of political loyalty. Given the two variables—repression and loyalty—and the objective functions dictators may have, Wintrobe distinguishes between tinpot dictators (who maximize consumption and minimize repression levels), totalitarian dictators (intent on maximizing power), tyrants (who repress without achieving much "loyalty"), and timocrats (who invest in creating loyalty and gaining their citizens' love). Wintrobe presents evidence about the behavior of dictators that is supportive of this typology, and explores the ways in which democracies and dictatorships compare in terms of economic growth and economic policy making.

4 POLITICAL INSTABILITY, POLITICAL CONFLICT

Revolutions, civil wars, and social movements are central objects of study in comparative politics. Blending his training as a historian with a keen interest in comparative analysis, Steven Pincus examines the historical conditions that generate revolutionary episodes. He asks, why do revolutions occur and why do they have dramatically different outcomes? Scholars have argued that revolutions occur exclusively as a result of social and economic modernization (Skocpol, Huntington). More recently, an influential line of argument, brought forth by Goldstone, has framed revolutions as the outbreak that follows a Malthusian imbalance between a growing population and its environment. By contrast, according to Pincus, the necessary prerequisite for revolution was always state modernization. State modernization programs simultaneously bring new social groups and new regions into direct contact with the state, and legitimize ideologies of change. These two developments create a social basis and a language on which to build revolutionary movements. Revolutions lead to very different political outcomes. In part following in the steps of Barrington Moore, Jr., Pincus argues that revolutions lead to open, democratic regimes when the state relies on merchant communities and foreign trade. Absent the latter, however, revolutions typically result in the imposition of an authoritarian regime.

Where Przeworksi alerts us to the omnipresence of endogeneity problems, Kalyvas alerts us to their centrality in a subject that reality has placed centrally on the agenda of comparativists: civil wars. Kalyvas reviews a plethora of studies of civil wars that offer a plethora of independent variables: features of the societies before the civil war broke out, or features of combatants in their pre-war incarnations. These pre-war-outbreak features of societies and combatants ostensibly explain the likelihood of civil wars occurring, their duration once they occur, or the intensity of the violence they unleash. But such exogenous explanations, Kalyvas explains, may be wrong-headed: much changes as civil wars unfold, including the distribution of populations, the preferences of key actors, and the value of resources over which combatants seek control. These new, war-driven conditions are themselves likely to shape the outcomes of interest. "Collective and individual preferences," he writes, "strategies, values, and identities are continuously shaped and reshaped in the course of a war, while the war itself aggregates all kinds of cleavages from the most ideological to the most local."

Sidney Tarrow and Charles Tilly examine contentious politics (episodic public collective action) and social movements (sustained challenge to holders of power). They analyze the ways in which these contentious politics and social movements happened in a dynamic sequence. The authors observe that modernization and the spread of democracy spawned the invention of social movements. Yet, at the same time, the time and location of social movements (that is, their interaction with political institutions, society, and cultural practices) determined the form in which they emerged. Tarrow and Tilly conclude by reflecting on the impact that globalization may have on the processes of political and social mobilization as we know them. They ask whether globalization may "more or less automatically connect potential activists across the world, present them with similar challenges, and thus move social movement collective action away from local and national concerns." There answer is, probably not: domestic political factors and involvement of national states in international organizations are the best predictors of participation in "transnational contention."

Lichbach and de Vries's chapter complements that of Tarrow and Tilly by surveying theories of contentious politics in light of recent global protest movements. To fully understand the phenomenon of contentious politics, they remind us that we need to operate at three levels. At the macro level researchers have developed a vast array of explanations that span from precise economic structural theories (such as the impact of trade on the welfare of populations) to cultural hypotheses (for example, the impact of modernization on the perception of elites in underdeveloped countries) to the emergence of a global civil society or global institutions that permit generalized protest and act as focal points. These macro-level stories must be complemented with meso-level causes, in particular the insights of strategic political opportunity theory, that make protest feasible. Finally, understanding contentious politics involves comprehending the micro-level components of action: the motives that bring individuals to the fore, their resources, their prior commitments, and the networks that rear them in political action.

5 MASS POLITICAL MOBILIZATION

Why do party systems look the way they do? How do their origins help explain their contemporary dynamics? What explains dramatic differences in the strategies that parties deploy in their efforts to mobilize electoral support? These questions animate the contributors to this section of the volume.

Carles Boix presents a multi-stage yet compact account that helps explain how parties and party systems developed in Western Europe and North America from rather loose networks of politicians, catering to small and strictly delimited electorates, in the early nineteenth century to mass-based, well-organized electoral machines in the twentieth century. This chapter does not limit itself to explaining, as in most analyses, how many parties effectively compete, but what kinds of parties espouse which ideologies. Boix traces the nature of parties and party systems back to the underlying structures of preferences, which could be either uni- or multidimensional. But, he then shows how these preferences or political dimensions were mobilized as a function of several additional key factors: the parties' beliefs about which electoral strategy would maximize their chances of winning, and the electoral institutions that mediate between voters' choices and the distribution of seats in national parliaments. (These electoral institutions, as Boix has shown in earlier work, were themselves the product of strategic action of parties.) In a way, the chapter may be read as a response to two types of dominant approaches in the discipline: those institutionalist models that describe political outcomes as equilibria and that, somehow trapped in static applications of game theory, hardly reflect on the origins of the institutions they claim constrain political actors; and those narratives that stress the contingency and path dependency of all political phenomena while refusing to impose any theoretical structure on them. By contrast, Boix thinks it should be possible to build historical accounts in which we reveal (1) how political actors make strategic choices according to a general set of assumptions about their beliefs and interests and (2) how their choices in turn shape the choice set of future political actors.

Where Boix develops an integrated model of the origins of distinctive party systems, Herbert Kitschelt offers a broad review of the questions that scholars ask about party systems and the way they answer them. Why do democracies feature parties in the first place, as almost all do? Why do many parties compete in some democracies whereas in others competition is restricted to two major parties (or two major and one minor one)? Why do some parties compete with the currency of programs, others with valence issues, and still others with clientelism and patronage? Why are elections perennially close in some systems, lopsided in others? Kitschelt reviews the measures that scholars find helpful in answering these questions—party system fractionalization, the effective number of parties, electoral volatility, and cleavages. The problems afflicting party politics are regionally specific: whereas scholars of advanced industrial systems worry, as Kitschelt notes, about the decay of party–voter linkages, scholars of new democracies worry about whether such linkages will ever take shape.

Several contributors to our section on mass political mobilization explore the question, under what conditions do political parties adopt distinct political strategies? Strategies may vary from appeals to identity and nationalism, to personalistic and media-centric campaigns, to programmatic offers, to clientelistic linkages. Ann Wren and Kenneth M. McElwain identify a shift toward personalistic and media-heavy campaigns in Western Europe, a shift from the more organizationally grounded strategies of parties during the periods analyzed by Boix and by Kitschelt. One of the central insights of the comparative work done in the 1960s was that partisan attachments and party systems had remained frozen since the advent of democracy in the West. Yet, as this chapter explains, in the last forty years party–voter linkages have substantially thawed. Economic growth, the decline of class differences, and the emergence of postmaterialist values lie in part behind this transformation. In the wake of changes in the electorate and its preferences, it took party bureaucracies some time to adjust. Taking advantage of the slow rate of adjustment of the older parties, new parties sprang up to lure away dissatisfied voters.

Yet party dealignment and electoral volatility have not diminished, even after new parties that should have stabilized the electoral market have entered these party systems. Therefore, to explain continued volatility, we must look beyond changes in the structure of voter preferences. As Wren and McElwain stress, weakening party–voter ties must be put in the context of a shift in the educational level of the population and new technologies (radios and TV). As parties became less important as informational shortcuts, politics has grown more candidate centered and party elites have been able to pursue electoral campaigns without relying on the old party machinery. If Wren and McElwain are right, our old models of, and intuitions about, party-centered democracy should give way to a more "Americanized" notion of democracies, where personal candidacies and television campaigns determine how politicians are elected and policy made.

Chapters by Frances Hagopian and by Susan Stokes consider the origins and effects of clientelistic linkages between parties and voters. Hagopian addresses questions such as why do some parties build loose and heterogeneous coalitions of voters, or narrow constituencies that are linked by religious affiliations or programmatic preferences? And what effects do the parties' choices have? "Is there a relationship," she asks, "between who is mobilized, how they are mobilized, and how stable or successful the voter mobilization strategy is?" Her highly suggestive answers raise questions about the prospects for stabilization of party systems and electoral processes in developing democracies.

In the last two decades, democracy has become the dominant system of government across the world, both as a normative ideal and as a fact. But not all nominal democracies generate accountable, clean governments. Susan Stokes addresses one of the possible causes of malfunctioning democracies by looking at the practices, causes, and consequences of clientelism. Clientelism, or the "proffering of material goods [by the patron] in return for electoral support [by the client]," was a hot topic of research in the 1960s and 1970s, buoyed by the emergence of new nations. Shaped by a sociological approach, researchers at that time explained clientelism as a practice underpinned by a set of norms of reciprocity. Yet, as Stokes claims convincingly, clientelism must be rather seen as a game in which patrons and clients behave strategically and in which they understand that, given certain external conditions (such as a certain level of development and the organizational conditions that allow for the effective monitoring of the other side), they are better off sustaining a pattern of exchange over the long run. Such a theoretical account then allows us to make predictions, which are beginning to be tested empirically, about the institutions underpinning clientelistic practices, the electoral strategies pursued by patrons, and the potential economic and political effects of clientelism: whether it depresses economic development and political competition.

Pippa Norris surveys the very large literature on political activism. She reviews the social and psychological model of participation developed by Verba and Nie, as well as the critiques generated from a rational choice perspective. She then examines how key developments in the research community and the political world have affected the ways in which we evaluate this subfield. She notes a growing interest in the role of institutions in shaping participation in general and turnout in particular. Echoing Wren and McElwain, she draws our attention to changes in party membership, which was widespread and hence instrumental in many advanced democracies but has progressively shrunk, with consequences that are still widely debated among scholars. The constructs of trust and social capital, pioneered by Coleman and Putnam, are also relevant to our expectations about levels of participation. Norris also identifies cause-oriented forms of activism as a distinct type of participation, activism that includes demonstrations and protests, consumer politics, professional interest groups, and more diffuse "new" social movements and transnational advocacy networks. All of these, she notes, have expanded and in a way marginalized the more institutionalized, party- and union-based mechanisms of participation that dominated in the past.

6 Processing Political Demands

In the magisterial five-volume *Handbook of Political Science* mentioned earlier, published thirty years ago, the term *accountability* appears not once. The term representation appears sporadically and, outside of the volume on political theory, only a handful of times. Thirty years later, in our volume, accountability appears as an organizing concept in comparative politics, and representation is not far behind. The chapters in the current volume in the section "Processing Political Demands" are deeply engaged with the concepts of accountability and representation.

In democracies, how do citizens' preferences get translated into demands for one public policy over another? This is the fundamental question that G. Bingham Powell takes up. If everyone in a society had the same preferences, the problem would not be a problem at all. But never is this the case. And scholarship on preference aggregation, as Powell notes, must come to grips with social choice theory, which should lead us to doubt that citizens in any setting in which politics is multidimensional can evince any stable set of policy preferences. The dominant strains of research, some of which come to grips with the social choice challenge and others of which ignore it, include examinations of the congruence of various sorts. One kind of congruence study looks at the fit between constituents' preferences and the issue positions of their representatives. Another looks at the fit between electoral outcomes and the allocation of elected offices, treating, as Powell notes, citizens' policy preferences as though they were fully expressed by their votes. Another sort of congruence study examines the coherence of issue positions among co-partisans, both political elites and citizens who identify with parties, and tends to find a good deal more coherence among the former than among the latter. Yet another deals with the congruence between electoral platforms and campaign promises, and government policy. Powell's overarching concern is about the potential for accountability and representation in democratic systems, and how this potential is best realized by certain institutional arrangements and political contexts.

Rein Taagepera goes at the question of the expression of citizen preferences through elections from a more institutional vantage point, focusing on electoral rules. After offering a typology of electoral systems, he reviews the "Duvergerian agenda" of electoral rules, that is, the analysis of the ways (mechanical and psychological) in which electoral systems affect the voting behavior of electors and, as a result, the election of candidates, the structure of parties and party systems, and the politics of coalition building in democracies.

Shifting from voting behavior and elections to institutional politics, David Samuels reviews what we know about the impact of the separation of powers on accountability. The conventional view in the United States is that a separation of powers is so central to democratic accountability that this separation is nearly definitional of democracy. Samuels evaluates this proposition empirically. His own research and that of other authors which he reviews address questions of accountability and representation, as well as the effects of a separation of powers on the policy process and on regime stability. Among his central findings is that presidentialism has several deleterious effects; a separation of executive from legislative powers increases the chances for policy deadlock and for the breakdown of democracy.

The institutional design of judiciaries and of their relations with other branches of government is meant to produce horizontal, if not vertical, accountability (O'Donnell 1994). John Ferejohn, Frances Rosenbluth, and Charles Shipan's contribution on judicial politics considers the institutional and political settings in which the courts attain independence, especially from executives but also from legislatures, independence which O'Donnell and others consider a necessary condition for vertical accountability. Ferejohn, Rosenbluth, and Shipan also explain other aspects of cross-national variation, such as why courts everywhere are not enabled to carry out judicial review and why courts are sometimes more active in the legislative process, other times less.

Assessing judicial independence, as these authors acknowledge, is not always straightforward. They advocate two measures: the frequency with which courts reverse governments, and the frequency with which they reverse governments that nationalize parts of the economy (or attempt to do so). The authors note that a drawback of either approach is that courts, which seek (among other objectives) not to have their decisions reversed, may rule against governments only when they anticipate not being reversed, in which case these measures would tend to overestimate their independence. Another difficulty is that courts may rule in favor of governments when they find governments' actions to be lawful or when they spontaneously agree with governments' actions. Hence, whereas rulings against governments probably indicate independence, rulings in their favor are less certain indications of dependence (see Helmke 2002, 2005).

The two final contributions in this section consider aspects of government structures that may have significant impacts on accountability, both vertical and horizontal. Pablo Beramendi provides an overview of the concept of federalism. He shows that federalism was first introduced to accommodate the interests of the periphery in the military and economic affairs of a union. Yet federalism is necessarily a complex, fluid institutional form. This insight then shapes the rest of the review. The relationship between democracy and federalism seems to be conditional, as far as we know, on the particular internal structure of federalism. The effects of having a federal structure on the economy, in turn, depend on how the federal institutions allocate power and responsibilities between the center and regional governments. Naturally, this opens up the question about the origins of federalism. Without a strong theory of how and when federal institutions are adopted, it is difficult to identify the independent effects of federalism.

Kaare Strøm and Benjamin Nyblade critically assess the literature on coalition making, particularly regarding the formation of governments in parliamentary democracies. Drawing on neo-institutionalism and, more specifically, on the trans-action costs literature, they show how the costs of negotiation and the demands of the electorate, interested in monitoring parties' performance, reduce cycles and push politicians to strike relatively stable pacts. They note that theories of coalition formation began with William Riker's application of the "size principle," which predicted that parties would try to minimize the number of actors in a coalition. Although influential theoretically, this approach proved to be rather unsatisfactory empirically. In response, Strøm and Nyblade relax Riker's fundamental assumptions about payoffs, about the role of information, and about the effects of decision rules and institutions, to reach a much richer theory, and one that fits the data more closely.

7 GOVERNANCE IN COMPARATIVE PERSPECTIVE

The "discovery" of economic voting several decades ago transformed the fields of comparative voting behavior and party competition. It was thought to depict a simple rule of thumb that voters could—and did—apply when deciding whether to vote for incumbents: if the economy had performed well on their watch, retain them, if it hadn't, turn them out. Recent scholarly developments place economic voting in institutional contexts and present more nuanced stories about what voters need to know to carry off "simple" economic voting. Raymond Duch's chapter reflects and advances this new agenda. Duch develops a series of propositions about how varying institutional contexts, coalition governments, and informational settings will mediate between economic conditions and voters' appraisal of them. Factors that Duch suggests will influence economic voting include party system size, the size of government, coalition governments, trade openness, and the relative strength of governing and opposition parties in the legislature. Duch offers empirical evidence that sheds light on these mediating factors.

Ever since a seminal paper published by Nordhaus in 1975 launched research into the political business cycles, the study of the effect of elections on policy making has had to contend with substantial theoretical inconsistencies—why should voters accept policy manipulation and leave governments unpunished?—as well as considerable empirical disagreements. What scholars tend to agree about most is that the presence of politically induced economic cycles is rather irregular. With these problems in mind, James Alt and Shanna Rose's essay pursues dual objectives. They argue that political business cycles must be understood as a particular instance of the broader phenomenon of political accountability in democratic regimes. Political business cycles are not merely the result of a signaling game in which politicians try to build their reputation as competent policy makers. Rather, the manipulation of economic policy and outcomes is an inevitable result of voters' willingness to accept the transfer of some rents to politicians in exchange for the election of competent policy makers. In their empirical analysis of American states, Alt and Rose implement a model that predicts that political manipulation of the economy will occur under certain institutional and social conditions: when elections are close, when voters are not very well informed, and in the absence of budgetary rules constraining policy makers' room for maneuver.

Matthew Carnes and Isabela Mares examine the evolution of the certainly very crowded field on the welfare state. Echoing the well-known essay Amenta and Skocpol wrote two decades ago, Carnes and Mares masterfully review the different theoretical contributions in the area. After the first papers and books on the topic were written within the framework of modernization theory, welfare state scholars moved to assess the impact of power politics (through parties and unions) on the construction of different types of welfare states. That class-based orientation, however, had limited validity beyond some archetypical cases with high levels of union mobilization and strong left-wing parties. Accordingly, researchers switched to explore the impact of cross-class coalitions—hence dwelling on the role of middle classes, agricultural producers, and employers. In doing so, they have shifted our attention from the pure redistributive components of the welfare state, which were the keystone of pure class-based, power politics accounts, to social policies as insurance tools that address the problem of risk and volatility in the economy. Related to this change in perspective, welfare state scholars have progressively spent more time on mulling over the impact of the international economy on social policy. Two path-breaking pieces by Cameron and Katzenstein showing economic openness and the welfare states to be positively correlated have been followed by a very stimulating scholarly debate that has alternatively related the result to a governmental response to higher risk (due to more economic volatility in open economies), denied the correlation completely, or called for models that take openness and social policy as jointly determined. As Carnes and Mares's essay reveals, the welfare state literature has indeed traveled a long way from its inception. Yet it still has a very exciting research agenda ahead of it: first, it should become truly global and extend the insights (and problems) of a field built around Europe and North America to the whole world; second, it should offer analytical models that combine the different parameters of the successive generations of research in the area; third, it should take seriously the preferences and beliefs of voters across the world (and the cultural differences we observe about the proper role of the state); and, finally, it ought to integrate the consequences of welfare states (something about which we know much less than we should) with the forces that erect them.

Whether the transition to democracy in many developing countries in recent decades has meant a shift to accountable, effective government is a question that has concerned many scholars of comparative politics. Reviewing the burgeoning literature on development and democracy, Philip Keefer notices that, although both the number of researchers and the theories on the topic have multiplied considerably, we still know little about the relationship between growth and political regimes. In particular, he points to the fact that policy and performance vary considerably across democracies. Poor democracies show lower growth rates and worse public policies than rich democracies. In a nutshell, in spite of having formal mechanisms that should have increased political accountability and the welfare of the population in poor democracies, the provision of public goods and economic performance remain thoroughly deficient in those countries. Since the key parameters of democracy and redistribution (inequality and the struggle for political control between elites and non-elites) cannot explain that outcome (since low development and democratization are cast as contradictory), Keefer turns to political market imperfections to explain the failure of governments to deliver in democracies. In young, poor democracies, politicians lack the credibility to run on campaigns that promise the delivery of universal benefits and public goods. Accordingly, they shift to building personal networks and delivering particular goods. This type of electoral connection, compounded by low levels of information among voters, who can scarcely monitor politicians, results in extreme levels of corruption and bad governance.

The promise of economic voting was that voters would be able to use economic conditions as a measure of the success or failure of governments; the anticipation of being thus measured would induce politicians to improve economic conditions on their watch. Economic voting would enforce accountability. Yet, as José María Maravall shows in his contribution to this volume, "in parliamentary democracies losses of office by prime ministers depend in one-half of the cases on decisions by politicians, not by voters." This fact would not be so dire if prime ministers were removed from office by colleagues who anticipated bad electoral outcomes—if, as Maravall puts it, "voters and politicians...share the same criteria for punishing prime ministers." But they do not. Whereas prime ministers are more likely to be turned out by voters when economic times are bad, they are more likely to be turned out by their colleagues when economic times are good. Hence politicians who hold their comrades to account seem to practice a reverse kind of "economic voting." Maravall's chapter cautions us against excessive optimism regarding democracy, accountability, and economic voting.

If (as economic voting implies) office holders who produce bad economic outcomes will face the wrath of voters, why would they ever risk a costly transition to liberalized economy? Whether asked in the context of post-communist countries undertaking a "leap to the market" or in developing countries elsewhere in the world under pressure to move away from statist policies, the question has preoccupied comparative politics and political economy for more than a decade. Reviewing the literature on economic transitions in Eastern Europe, Timothy Frye identifies a number of factors, from the quality of domestic governance to membership in the European Union, that make governments more likely to undertake reforms and then stick with them. Yet serious gaps remain in our understanding of the determinants of market reforms, including what role is played by institutional legacies from the past, and by contemporary social institutions—networks, business associations, reputational mechanisms—state institutions—courts, bureaucracies, legislatures—and the interaction of the two.

8 Looking Ahead

By critically assessing the existing literature in their area of expertise, most, if not all, of the contributors to this volume already point toward the research questions and gaps that our discipline still has to address. Thus, we will refrain from paraphrasing and summarizing them again. We just want to invite the reader to read them and mull over their suggestions carefully. That should be enough to push many a scholar to plunge into yet-to-be-discovered waters. Still, we wish to close this introduction by writing briefly about the broad issues raised to us by the rather long preparation and shepherding of this volume.

The scientific enquiry of comparative politics has certainly shifted in the last decades, or, one may say, over the course of the last three generations of scholars devoted to this field, in at least two ways. First, the ways in which theory is built have changed markedly. Probably influenced by the then dominant approaches of structural sociology and Marxism, in the past comparatists relied on systemic, broad explanations, to explain political outcomes. Just think of the initial theories of political modernization, the first articles relating democracy to development, or the work on party formation laid out in the 1960s. Today, theory building very often proceeds (or, perhaps more modestly, claims to proceed) from "microfoundations," that is, it starts from the individual, and her interests and beliefs, to then make predictions about aggregate outcomes. We found this to constitute a truly forward step in political science. Making us think hard about the final unit of analysis of the model, that is, about each individual (and his motives and actions), allows us to have theories that are more transparent (i.e. where one can truly probe the consistency and plausibility of assumptions) and easier to falsify.

At this point it is important, however, to pause to stress that embracing the principle of methodological individualism does not necessarily mean accepting a purely instrumental or rationalist model of human action. As is well known, our increasing reliance on microfoundations has been triggered to a considerable degree by an influx of mathematical and game-theoretic tools and by the influence of economic models in the discipline. But, as Moon already discussed in the Greenstein–Polsby handbook thirty years ago, models built on propositions about how individual actors will behave under certain circumstances may well employ a variegated set of assumptions about the interests and beliefs of the actors themselves. In fact, his claim (and our hunch) is that the only way to show that rationalistic assumptions do not work is to build models that are populated by intentional actors (with goals that are not strictly instrumental) and that these models perform better than those developed by rational choice theorists. To sum up, building theories of intentional actors and constructing models of (strictly) rationalist individuals are two different enterprises. The latter needs the former but the reverse is not true. Realizing that difference should save all of us from what has been a considerable source of conflict and confusion.

Coming to appreciate the role of individuals and their motives has also had a very beneficial effect on comparative politics. It has moved it closer to our forefathers in the discipline. Each classical theory of politics, from Aristotle and Machiavelli to Hobbes, Locke, Rousseau, and Nietzsche, starts from a particular conception of human nature. With different tools and with a different dataset (for one, we have some information about how real democracies work in practice), all these different (micro) models are, at the end, grounded on specific assumptions about human behavior. These assumptions are still deeply contested in comparative politics: they span from a purely instrumental conception of political actors intent on securing survival and maximizing power to a notion of individuals that may consent to particular structures contingent on others cooperating to, finally, visions of politics that appeal to the inherent sociability of humans. This contestation is unavoidable. Our guess is that as we all move to build intentional models of politics, it should become easier to adjudicate between different points of departure.

The second way in which the discipline has changed has to do with the gradual acceptance among most researchers about the need to develop broad, general propositions about politics and about the value of employing standard scientific practices to provisionally validate them (until they are disconfirmed). Interestingly, this growing consensus has come with an equally increasing and valuable skepticism about how much it can be accomplished by employing quasi-experimental methods of the kind comparatists usually employ. The problem is perhaps compounded by the fact that comparative politics cannot rely on something like microeconomic theory to keep building models (while empirically oriented researchers battle over what and how to test any of their propositions). (We say "perhaps" because not having something akin to a microeconomic theory makes our work less constrained and therefore less forgetful about all the traits of human behavior that violate the strict assumptions of rationality.)

For the provisional solutions to this question, which has mostly to do with endogeneity issues, we again refer the reader to the essays of the first part. Here we wish to present this question as an opportunity rather than as a problem. In recent years, the field of comparative politics has progressed substantially in modeling certain political outcomes, mostly as equilibria. Duverger's law has become clarified and formalized through models of strategic coordination. Civic virtue has given way to models of trust sustained by repeated interaction. Patronage politics can be profitably thought of as a game in which patrons and clients are interlocked. But, we still know little about the ways in which political institutions, social practices, norms, and arrays of political interests originate and collapse. History was important in the broad, sociological literature written a few decades ago. Yet, the way in which it was tackled was messy or unsystematic. Institutionalists altogether abandoned historical work. We think that, with the new tools we have in our hands, the right time has come to deal with that question again. To some extent, given the problems of endogenous causation we are confronted with, engaging in this type of work is now becoming inevitable.

References

HELMKE, G. 2001. The logic of strategic defection: judicial decision-making in Argentina under dictatorship and democracy. *APSR* 96 (2): 291–30.
—— 2005. *Courts under Constraints: Judges, Generals, and Presidents in Argentina.* Cambridge: Cambridge University Press.
O'DONNELL, G. 1994. Delegative democracy. *Journal of Democracy,* 5: 55–68.

PART II

THEORY AND METHODOLOGY

CHAPTER 2

....

MULTICAUSALITY, CONTEXT-CONDITIONALITY, AND ENDOGENEITY

....

ROBERT J. FRANZESE, JR.

1 INTRODUCTION

....

MODERN scholarly reviewers characterize[1] the pre-war and immediate post-war study of comparative politics as legalistic, favoring categorical enumeration over positive-theoretical analysis of constitutional details, and as parochial and, indeed, as non-comparative, exhibiting Western (often specifically US) bias in the topics studied and in normative conclusions and rather lacking in theoretical or empirical comparison.

From the mid-1950s, Gabriel Almond (1956) and contemporaries, applying a Parsonian approach to social science, led a political sociology revolution in comparative politics. Sparked by the catastrophic rise of fascism and dictatorship that plunged the globe into war, and by democracy's failure to advance and secure its initial post-war successes, the central question for these scholars was what conditions fostered

---

[1] The ensuing intellectual historiography of comparative politics as a field of enquiry is likely more caricature than characterization. It serves here merely to provide background for how the notion that *context matters* is and always has been a core tenet of the field.

stable, democratic political development. Inspired by contemporary scientific sociology, they sought answers in the polity's social structure: e.g. its homogeneity and stratification (Almond 1956), its socioeconomic development, or the cross-cutting or reinforcing nature of its sociopolitical cleavages (Lipset 1960). Perhaps most notable about this revolution was the movement it signaled from configurative description toward a positive science of comparative politics that asks theoretical research questions (e.g. what societal characteristics may contribute to democratic development and stability, and how?) and not merely descriptive (e.g. what does the French constitution say?) or historical-factual (e.g. who voted for Hitler?) ones and that proposes positive theories about causal relationships in answer rather than unadulterated parochialism or bias or normative judgement. Empirical evaluation of these positive theories, however, remained depressingly impressionistic and, perhaps, too often as parochial and biased as earlier configurative descriptions had been.

The political culture and political behavior revolutions of the 1960–1970s completed the movement in comparative politics from configurative description to positive social science. Almond and Verba's (1963) classic *Civic Culture* perhaps initiated and still best exemplifies both revolutions in following the posing of *a positive question*—what fosters stable, well-functioning democracy (which they defined precisely enough)—with *logically argued, positive-theoretical, hypothetical answers*—crudely: a citizenry with beneficial cognitive, affective, and evaluative orientation toward the political system (which they defined precisely enough)—*and empirical evaluation* based on equally sufficiently precise and objective measurement of key components (variables) in the argument. *The Civic Culture*, however, suffered a critical limitation that its ultimate explanandum (dependent variable), stable, well-functioning democracy, remained impressionistically measured and in only five contexts (nations). For this reason, the book more solidly established the extent and content of the *Civic Culture* in these five nations than it did the posited theoretical (causal) relationship between *Civic Culture* and well-functioning democracy. Later work in the cultural-behavioral tradition, e.g. Inglehart's (1990) *Culture Shift*, reduced these limitations, in the process perhaps cementing the case, begun by pioneers like Karl Deutsch (1971), for the utility of large-sample statistical analysis to the positive study of comparative politics.

By the 1980s, social structure, political culture, and public opinion and behavior had become the main sources of likely independent variables in the modern, positive, political science of comparative politics, and statistical analysis of comparative-historical data had become one important tool in empirical evaluation of those positive arguments. However, this tool also enabled scholars to discern that, in fact, social structure seemed to determine political outcomes—e.g. social homo- and heterogeneity related to (in)stability (Powell 1982), societal fractionalization and polarization related to party system (Sartori 1976), etc.—less fully, universally, and surely than previously thought. Spurred by the weakness or incompleteness of such social-structural explanations for macro-political outcomes and perhaps also unsatisfied with the immediacy and causal proximity with which culture, beliefs, attitudes, and opinion linked to each other and to micro-behaviors like, say, vote choices, Sartori, Powell, Smith (1972), Berger (1981), Lehmbruch and Schmitter (1982), Lijphart (1984), and others returned institutions—political, social, and economic—to the center of analysis. Building from earlier work that theoretically and empirically linked, e.g. electoral law to party system outcomes (Rae 1967) and party and governmental systems to coalition politics (Riker 1962; Dodd 1976), these authors argued socioeconomic structure *works through* political, social, and economic institutions to shape the incentives of political actors: voters, workers and employers, and policy-making and party elites. Comparative-historical statistical analysis again helped establish these claims empirically, showing that, *in addition to* or *controlling for* socioeconomic-cultural conditions, presidential, majoritarian-parliamentary, and representative-parliamentary institutions affect participation and social and governmental stability (Powell 1982), institutional structures of labor help determine political-economic performance (Cameron 1984), majoritarian or consensual institutions shape democracies' performance (Lijphart 1984), etc. This effectively added sociopoliticoeconomic institutions to the growing list of (classes of) key explanatory variables. However, the full recognition of the implications of socio-economic-cultural conditions *working through* institutions, which implies that the effects of institutions *depend on* these conditions and, vice versa, that the effects of socioeconomic-cultural conditions in turn depend on those institutions, went largely unexplored in statistical empirical work for some time.

The modern, positive-theoretical study of comparative politics thus emphasizes the societal structure of interests, political culture and public opinion, and socio-politicoeconomic institutions, in explaining the intranational, cross-national, inter-national, and/or cross-temporal variation observed in political outcomes. In this regard, the field has come full circle. The central tenet of modern comparative politics is, as that of classical pre- and post-war comparative politics was, that *context*—structural, cultural, institutional, and strategic; social, economic, and poli-tical; international, domestic, and local—matters. More precisely, *context matters* in at least three ways. First, the outcomes we seek to explain, understand, or predict have multiple causes, so the values of the many potential causes in any given context affect the outcomes: *multicausality*. Second, the effects of each cause on outcomes tend to vary across contexts, which is to say that the effects of each cause tend to depend on the values of one or more other potential cause(s) present in that context: *context-conditionality*.[2] Third, the many outcomes and many putative causes in the political world that we seek to understand tend, in fact, to cause each other to some degree rather than some factors being only causes and others being only effects: *endogeneity* (synonyms: simultaneity, reverse causality, bi- and multidirectional causality).

These three aspects of the *"context matters"* central tenet of comparative politics—*multicausality, context-conditionality,* and *endogeneity*—also represent three of the most ubiquitous and severe challenges to empirical inference in political science. Indeed, although perhaps most directly implied by the *context matters* mantra of

---

[2] This includes history, and so context-conditionality subsumes historical path and state dependence.

comparative politics, *multicausality, context-conditionality,* and *endogeneity,* along with the relative paucity of information—that is, too few observations: we typically have, after all, only the one comparative history of the world from which to infer anything—are perhaps the central challenges to empirical evaluation across all of social science (and in many if not all natural sciences as well).[3]

In short: first, almost everything matters (i.e. many X's cause most of the Y's studied throughout social science); second, how each X matters depends on almost everything else (i.e. the effects of each X on some Y typically depends on many other X in that context); and, third, everything pretty much causes everything else in sociopoliticoeconomic reality (i.e. almost everything in society, polity, and economy is endogenous to almost everything else in and across those spheres). Finally, to make matters worse, we usually have precious little empirical information with which to sort through all this complexity.

That *context matters* in these ways is sometimes taken as a challenge for statistical methods of empirical evaluation of theory in particular, but the challenges are logically inherent to the substantive propositions of multicausality, context-conditionality, and endogeneity and do not inhere, therefore, to the particular empirical-methodological approach taken to (partially) redress them. Stated differently, these challenges do not arise because specifying a statistical model, i.e. writing one's empirical arguments formulaically, highlights and clarifies them mathematically, and they do not go away simply because one neglects to do so. Likewise, the challenges do not arise because some scholar records the information she observes numerically and analyzes them statistically as observations in a dataset, and they do not disappear if some other scholar instead records the information he observes qualitatively and analyzes it in some manner as "causal-process observations" (Brady and Collier 2004; *Political Analysis* 2006: 14 (3)). Furthermore, as shown below, the challenges are not necessarily surmounted, nor indeed are they often surmountable even in principle, solely by analyzing some available empirical information more closely or simply by gathering more empirical information. This is because the challenges are logical and theoretical as much as, or more than, empirical. Thus, these are the challenges of empirical evaluation in social science, and not those of quantitative or qualitative methods, and, insofar as we manage to learn something from our empirical analyses,[4] quantitative or qualitative, we must somehow have redressed these challenges to some degree.

That quantitative and qualitative empirical studies face the same logical challenges is now widely accepted, and some very useful works (e.g. King, Keohane, and Verba 1994; Brady and Collier 2004) have begun to consider how the approaches may be understood from this perspective and how analyses of each sort may be improved by understandings gained from the other. Relatively missing from these useful

---

[3] *Comparative Politics,* as a colleague is fond of (correctly) saying, is a subject matter and not a methodology (W. Clark: personal communications); that a chapter on methodology in a handbook of comparative politics should address methodological concerns of at least social scientific breadth is therefore wholly fitting.

[4] "Learn something" and similar such phrases below mean "learn something helpful in general empirical evaluation of positive theory." One can of course learn many useful things on many other dimensions from empirical description that is useless for general empirical evaluation of positive theory.

discussions, contributions, and debates, however, has been explicit statement from the statistical perspective of these fundamental challenges[5] that both approaches face and discussion of the choices each must make as necessary conditions to learn from comparative history. The rest of this chapter offers such explicit discussion so that the formal statement of the challenges from this perspective will help researchers from both perspectives understand more fully the challenges they face and the choices and tradeoffs they make in redressing them.

2 THE PROBLEM OF TOO FEW OBSERVATIONS/TOO LITTLE INFORMATION: QUALITY VS. QUANTITY

Before proceeding to consider multicausality, context-conditionality, and endogeneity, an abstract consideration of the terms of the tradeoff between the quality and the quantity of information brought to bear upon a question of empirical inference may be enlightening. Given the constraints of time, competencies, and the availability of information, researchers often must choose between observing more pieces of information more cursorily and fewer pieces of information more fully and accurately.[6] The terms of this tradeoff are impossible to determine with great precision as a general proposition, but we can offer some help to gauge those terms broadly by considering the tradeoff between the accuracy of some measures and the number of such measures used to estimate some quantity of interest.

Suppose, for example, that some researcher is interested in the empirical relation between the quality of democracy and the level of economic development in some society. Suppose further that the actual relationship between economic development, *EcDev*, and the true quality of democracy (in whatever meaningful sense), *QualDem**, is the following:

$$QualDem^* = \beta \times EcDev + \epsilon \qquad (1)$$

where ϵ is some random noise, with variance σ_ϵ^2, since the relationship is not deterministic and exact.[7] Now suppose, realistically, that the researcher can measure

---

[5] Certainly, formal statements of statistical models or discussion of their use and implementation are not in short supply. What is missing has been an explicit formal statement from the statistical perspective of the challenges for empirical analysis of comparative politics and discussion of the terms of tradeoffs researchers in that substantive area must make.

[6] The phrase *pieces of information* intentionally replaces the more common *observations, cases,* or *countries,* because the issues raised and discussed do not hinge in any way on the comparative-historical analysis under consideration being within or across countries or cases and because whether the information gleaned is labeled a dataset or a causal process observation is likewise irrelevant to the present discussion.

[7] We use an extremely simple bivariate and linear model with additively separable error component here strictly for expositional convenience. The results of this consideration of weighing quality vs. quantity would be complicated but not changed in upshot if these simplifications were abandoned.

the true quality of democracy, $QaulDem^*$, only with some error, γ, whose variance, σ^2_γ, he can reduce by focusing his empirical studies on fewer contexts. This means that the researcher can only evaluate empirically the following relationship:

$$QualDem = QualDem^* + \gamma \Rightarrow QualDem = \beta \times EcDev + \epsilon - \gamma \tag{2}$$

Under the usual conditions, the researcher obtains the best[8] estimate of β by:

$$\hat{\beta} = \frac{Cov(QualDem, EcDev)}{Var(EcDev)} \tag{3}$$

and this best estimate of the relationship between economic development and the quality of democracy will have a variance (i.e., uncertainty) of

$$V(\hat{\beta}) = \frac{\sigma^2_\epsilon + \sigma^2_\gamma}{Var(EcDev)} = \frac{\sigma^2_\epsilon + \sigma^2_\gamma}{(n-1) \times \sigma^2_x} \tag{4}$$

Thus, to characterize the terms of the tradeoff between the quantity of information and the accuracy of the measurement of that information requires that one be able to gauge the relative contributions to uncertainty regarding the relationship of (a) measurement error, σ^2_γ, (b) the inherent uncertainty in the actual relationship, σ^2_ϵ, and (c) the variation in the explanatory variable, σ^2_x, which last determines the (expected) contribution to the certainty of the estimate of each piece of information.[9] Researchers wondering how to trade quantity for quality will not know the values of these crucial quantities a priori, of course—indeed, absent further theory or assumption, distinct estimation of σ^2_γ and σ^2_ϵ is impossible—but a sense of the expected variation in the explanatory factor, $\sigma^{\pm 2}_x$, might be obtained from data (plus assumptions) in some cases. Researchers could, in any event, profit from considering the equation, inserting their own substantive-theoretical senses of the relative magnitudes of explanatory variable variation, inherent variance (i.e. uncertainty or randomness) in the outcome (given their model), and measurement error variance.

Table 2.1 gives some examples where inherent uncertainty in the relationship, σ^2_ϵ, is one, and measurement uncertainty varies across the columns from one-tenth of that, so that lack of information quality is just less than 10 percent of the total numerator

---

[8] *Best* here means BUE, the best unbiased estimator, under the usual conditions (and the restriction to the class of linear estimators being unnecessary because we have stipulated that the true relationship is indeed linear).

[9] The example simplifies matters dramatically by confining measurement error to the dependent variable, by considering only one explanatory factor, by omitting an intercept from the true relationship, and by finessing the difference between the variance of a random variable and the sample variation in a regressor. The insights generated hopefully merit the simplifications, but, for the record: (1) including a constant would add nothing of interest to the discussion; (2) considering error in the explanatory factor(s) would add a bias cost to the inefficiency discussed in the text, but its magnitude would simply parallel that of the inefficiency; although (3) the magnitudes of the bias and efficiency costs of measurement error(s) where more than one explanatory factor enters would be far more complicated to determine (see Achen 1985, 2002); and (4) the finessing merely allows the discussion to sidestep explicit consideration of the expected contribution of an additional observation, which would require a long discussion before arriving to the $(n-1) \times \sigma^2_x$ denominator as given.

uncertainty, to ten times that, so lack of quality is just over 90 percent of that total. The top section of the table considers a case with relatively little variation to be gained from greater quantities of information, $\sigma_x^2 = .5$, so independent variable variation is only half the variance of the dependent variable's true stochastic component, ϵ, to a case at the bottom with relatively much to gain, $\sigma_x^2 = 2$, so independent variable variation is twice the true stochastic component's true variance, with a case in between where independent variable variation equals the true stochastic component's variance. Down the rows, the table lists quintuplings of the sample size (i.e. amounts of information) from 2 to 10 to 50 to 250. The cell entries give the uncertainty (namely, the variance) of the estimated relationship between the independent and dependent variables. The table reveals, e.g. that, under the most extremely low-quality information conditions considered (the last column, $\sigma_y^2 = 10$), to compensate for an 80 percent reduction in information quality from 50 to 10, one would need a 90 percent improvement in information quality (to $\sigma_y^2 = 1$), which might seem reasonable. To compensate for a further 80 percent reduction in information from 10 to 2, however, would require a ninety fold enhancement of information quality.

Table 2.1 Example terms of quality vs. quantity tradeoffs

	Variation of explanatory variable (σ_x^2): 0.5						
	$\sigma_y^2 = 0.1$	$\sigma_y^2 = 0.25$	$\sigma_y^2 = 0.5$	$\sigma_y^2 = 1$	$\sigma_y^2 = 2$	$\sigma_y^2 = 4$	$\sigma_y^2 = 10$
n=2	2.200	2.500	3.000	4.000	6.000	10.000	22.000
n=10	0.244	0.278	0.333	0.444	0.667	1.111	2.444
n=50	0.045	0.051	0.061	0.082	0.122	0.204	0.449
n=250	0.009	0.010	0.012	0.016	0.024	0.040	0.088
	Variation of explanatory variable (σ_x^2): 1						
	$\sigma_y^2 = 0.1$	$\sigma_y^2 = 0.25$	$\sigma_y^2 = 0.5$	$\sigma_y^2 = 1$	$\sigma_y^2 = 2$	$\sigma_y^2 = 4$	$\sigma_y^2 = 10$
n=2	1.100	1.250	1.500	2.000	3.000	5.000	11.000
n=10	0.122	0.139	0.167	0.222	0.333	0.556	1.222
n=50	0.022	0.026	0.031	0.041	0.061	0.102	0.224
n=250	0.004	0.005	0.006	0.008	0.012	0.020	0.044
	Variation of explanatory variable (σ_x^2): 2						
	$\sigma_y^2 = 0.1$	$\sigma_y^2 = 0.25$	$\sigma_y^2 = 0.5$	$\sigma_y^2 = 1$	$\sigma_y^2 = 2$	$\sigma_y^2 = 4$	$\sigma_y^2 = 10$
n=2	0.550	0.625	0.750	1.000	1.500	2.500	5.500
n=10	0.061	0.069	0.083	0.111	0.167	0.278	0.611
n=50	0.011	0.013	0.015	0.020	0.031	0.051	0.112
n=250	0.002	0.003	0.003	0.004	0.006	0.010	0.022

To restate it more strikingly from the other side, an increase in sample size from the lowest possible, 2,[10] to a still relatively small 10 would increase the quality of the inferences the researcher could draw as long as the quality of information worsened by no more than 9,000 percent (i.e. $90\times$) or so, from a very high-quality $\sigma_\gamma^2 = .1$ to a situation where measurement error was about 90 percent of total uncertainty about the dependent variable ($\sigma_\gamma^2 \approx 9$). Judging from the table, further increases in sample size, from 10 to 50 and from 50 to 250, likewise merit undertaking as long as information quality does not diminish by too much more than 4,000 percent ($40\times$) to something over $\sigma_\gamma^2 = 4$, i.e. greater than 80 percent of the total uncertainty of the researcher about the relationship (but not to nearly as close to $\sigma_\gamma^2 = 10$ and over 90 percent as in the first case). Furthermore, the comparisons would look dramatically worse again for quality if reductions in quantity entailed also a reduction in useful independent variable variation (movements up the table). Yet further, these comparisons assume just one quantity of interest (parameter) to estimate; the reported relationship between information quality and quantity and the certainly of inference are *per parameter*. Likewise, the relationships in the table assume each new piece of information is independent; if, e.g. information sets correlated (overlapped) at .9 (90%), the comparisons would need to be multiplied by (roughly) 10. In short, over the ranges of σ_γ^2, σ_ϵ^2, and σ_x^2 that comparativists likely typically travel, information quality in larger samples must be abysmal and represent overwhelming proportions of researchers' total uncertainty (i.e. many times the uncertainty related to shortcomings in theory plus the inherent randomness of outcomes), and reductions in the quantity of information must come at quite benign costs in lost variety (i.e. useful variation) and quite high gains in quality, if trades of quantity for quality are to offer gains in researchers' certainty about the relationships they wish to explore empirically. Clearly, then, a case for narrowing one's focus to fewer contexts solely on the basis of enhancing the quality of the information from those fewer contexts is extremely difficult to sustain.[11]

Proponents of pursuing greater depth of observation from fewer contexts, therefore, must see advantages beyond simple quality-of-information improvements. Potentially valid candidates are not lacking; indeed, as we will conclude and explain later, *qualitative analysis is an essential and valuable part of the scientific enterprise.* The above discussion simply demonstrates that one cannot easily sustain an argument that researchers should confine their attention more deeply to fewer contexts on the *sole* basis of the greater quality of information that surely affords. Certainly, e.g. the greater breadth of information that researchers may obtain when looking more closely at fewer contexts can essentially multiply observations within contexts (King, Keohane, and Verba 1994), although we should now reiterate that these extra

---

[10] Inference about the relationship between 2 variables from 1 piece of information on the pair is obviously impossible. Graphically, that corresponds to drawing a line through one point; infinite such lines exist.

[11] This conclusion, moreover, does not depend on the simplicity or linearity of the model, nor to any great extent on the particulars of the tabulated examples (see n. 9).

pieces of information from within one context may not offer as much useful variation in explanatory factors (σ_x^2) as would the same quantity of additional information from other contexts. (Traversing contexts may raise other challenges, though, as discussed later.) Many scholars, however, have not much appreciated King et al.'s view of qualitative research in fewer contexts, which stressed efforts and attention to multiplying observations within those contexts (and to case selection), as it might seem to have relegated qualitative empirical analysis to the role of a necessarily inferior substitute when statistical empirical analysis is truly not possible, a substitute whose inherent inferiority is to be minimized by the former better approximating the latter.[12] Accordingly, numerous other advantages, such as some usefully greater ability to trace processes, and possibly thereby to grapple with multicausality and/or context-conditionality or to identify causality better, have also been claimed (Hall 2003; Brady and Collier 2004; *Political Analysis* 2006, 14 (3)).

Deferring discussion of such arguments until we turn, as we will next, to consider multicausality, context-conditionality, and endogeneity in sequence, let us first consider how, in light of foregoing considerations, we might interpret claims sometimes made (e.g. Rogowski 2004) for the empirical power and utility of single-case studies over and above any intra-case multiplying of observations. First, of course, empirical *utility* encompasses more than precise estimation of relationships. Single-case studies clearly can serve to raise theoretical conjectures and hypotheses for further exploration, for example, as has long been recognized (Przeworski and Teune 1970). Notably in this regard, e.g. Rogowski is careful to express all the empirical claims derived from his considerations of prominent single-observation studies in the conjunctive tense. Moreover, the points he makes that these studies of anomalies challenge previously held views of the empirical support for particular theories rest on knowing where the single observations in question lie relative to the rest of an implicit sample, either decidedly off the pattern of independent and dependent variables set by those only implicitly referenced others or far from the centroid (i.e. the multidimensional mean) of the independent variables in those others but not with dependent variable taking values where simple (usually linear) extrapolation of the theory to those extremes would predict. Discovering an extreme case that does not remotely fit implicitly referenced patterns from prior studies or that lies far from where extrapolation of the theories under consideration would predict is just what Rogowski argues it is: *potential* empirical anomaly[13] that should motivate theoretical refinement. As such, it is indeed potentially

---

[12] Noting that statistical analysis is always possible, just as qualitative analysis is, if the *logically* necessary conditions for revealing empirical analysis have been met, would surely only heighten these sensitivities.

[13] So-called *critical cases* do not exist unless one believes the socioeconomic-political world deterministic, i.e. as long as one considers outcomes at least partially driven by chance. In general, in a stochastic world, any one observation, no matter how extreme, could always have arisen by chance (unless the chance is bounded more tightly than the apparent anomaly in the outcome's extremity). This also means that two observations would suffice for Mill's method of determining causality by comparing observations alike in every detail but one putative cause and (potentially) one putative effect only in a deterministic and not in a stochastic world.

empirically powerful and useful, but it is not (nor does or should it claim to be) general empirical evaluation of theory in the same sense as would be discovering statistical unlikelihood that the pattern across several contexts follows the theoretical predictions.[14]

3 MULTICAUSALITY: ALMOST EVERYTHING MATTERS

We turn now to the first of the three fundamental challenges for empirical analysis raised by the mantra that context matters (after the "too little information" problem which pervades and exacerbates them all): *multicausality,* or the conviction that many possible causal factors potentially operate in any given context. In one (not so extreme) example, Huntington (1991) identifies at least twenty-seven explanatory factors in democratization accounts in the literature before naming five most compelling: (1) deepening legitimacy problems of authoritarian systems as democratic norms are becoming increasingly globally accepted; (2) economic growth and expanded middle classes; (3) transformation of churches (especially the Catholic Church) from defenders of the status quo to opponents of authoritarianism; (4) changes in the policies of external actors (USA and Europe in particular); and (5) snowball effects (i.e. diffusion). Dahl (1971) lists eight (pre-)conditions for democracy: the peaceful evolution of democracy (yielding clean transfer of legitimacy from the old to new regime), decentralized economy (avoiding economic power concentration), economic development, economic equality, social homogeneity, elite pro-democratic beliefs (ideally with authority structures similarly democratic across societal institutions), popular beliefs in democratic efficacy and in the sincere intentions of adversaries, and passive or supportive international conditions. Even leaving for the next section the complex *context-conditionality* inherent in several of these contentions, democratization theories, taken together (plus controls)—and taking them separately (or omitting important controls) would be dangerous for omitted variable reasons discussed below—offer quite an array of putative causes and so quite a complexly contextual account of the causes of democratization.

Let us again follow a strategy of discussing from an econometric perspective a simple example illustrating the challenges such multicausality raises for empirical

---

[14] The more apt analogy in statistical methodology is to outlier detection and sensitivity analyses, which may serve to begin to justify the contention above that qualitative analysis is an essential part of the scientific enterprise. The process and product of these statistical analogs, however, also help explain how and why the reliance on a single case and only implicit reference to some background empirical information set leaves the researcher reliant on discovering *extreme* departures from predictions or from the mean elsewhere for any reasonable confidence that the perceived anomaly is indeed anomalous.

evaluation: those of controlling potentially confounding covarying factors and determining their relative (partial) explanatory impact, and those of omitted variable bias, "included-variable bias,"[15] and Achen's (2002) "rule of three." Let us assume for simplifying expositional purposes that the researcher determines that just two factors should favor democratization (*Dem*): the level of economic development, *EcDev*, and of equality in its distribution, *EqDist*. Furthermore, development and equality matter simply linear additively (e.g. they do not interact), no other factors enter, and the inherent randomness in democratization outcomes is additively separable from the systematic component that depends on *EcDev* and *EqDist*:

$$Dem = \beta_1 EcDev + \beta_2 EqDist + \epsilon \tag{5}$$

In such a case, a simple Venn diagram can usefully—if incompletely, imperfectly, and not fully generally (see e.g. Ip 2001)—depict the challenge of discerning and distinctly gauging the effects of economic development and of equality. In Figure 2.1, e.g. the areas of the oval labeled X_1 could depict the total variation observed across cases in democratization outcomes, and the ovals X_2 and X_3 those of *EcDev* and *EqDist* respectively. The overlapping sections reflect covariation of the corresponding variables. So, for example, the coefficient relating X_1 to X_2, following the formula from (3) above is given by the area of [2]+[3], depicting covariation of X_2 and X_1, divided by the area of the oval depicting X_1's variation, [1]+[2]+[3]+[4]. In multicausal contexts, generally, this will not be a good description of the variation in X_2 "due to" X_1 because [3] reflects the extent to which the outcome associates also with X_3—called shared covariation (and in a different way because [4] is variation in X_1 "not available to be associated with" X_2). If information sets that isolate just one single potential cause cannot be created—and they cannot as long as multicausality exists[16]—then some strategy of isolating the shares of covariations and variations due to each potential cause net of those due to others must be adopted. An important aspect of the challenge here is that no empirical information exists to inform allocation of [3], the covariation with X_2 shared by X_1 and X_3, across those latter two covariates. One can theoretically impose an ordering or an allocation—as in path analysis or stepwise regression—and this may sometimes be useful and informative, but one cannot determine how to allocate [3] from empirics alone.

Multiple regression and related statistical analyses resolve this by basing estimates of the relationships only on the unique variation and covariation of the

---

[15] The term, explained below, is borrowed from lectures by Gary King the author was privileged to hear.

[16] This is so to some extent even in the social-science laboratory because the experimental subjects inherently bring with them potential explanatory factors the researcher cannot control. The researcher can randomize (or match) but even then can only evaluate empirically the efficacy of the randomization (and adequacy of the sample variation and size) across observables (see Przeworski, this volume, and Section 5 below).

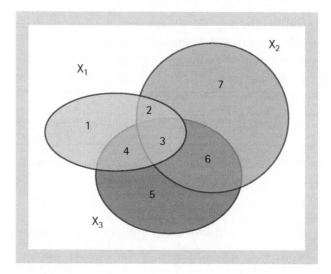

Fig. 2.1 Stylized representation of variation, covariation, and partial coefficients in multiple regression

variables. That is, the partial association of X_1 with X_2 (i.e. the *partial coefficient* on X_2 in this model and, under the current assumptions, the *effect* of X_1 on X_2 *controlling for* X_3, i.e. after netting the relationship between X_3 and X_2) is $[2]/([1]+[2])$. This seemingly simple procedure is one crucially important contribution of multiple regression to comparative empirical analysis. Since, for the most part, we have only comparative history as our database, i.e. we have only the world as it is and was, to control for multiple possible causes by holding all potential causes exactly fixed except the one of central interest is rarely possible. We can, however, partial away the shared covariation of the dependent and independent variables with other explanatory factors, *conditional upon a theoretical model* like (5) that explicitly states how these other explanatory factors relate to the outcome, thereby obtaining an estimate of the relationship between one factor and the outcome holding other factors constant even though we cannot and have not exactly held those other factors constant.[17] In other words, given that most everything varies most of the time, we can only gauge the partial association of any one independent variable with a dependent variable if we know how our independent variable covaries with other possible causes and how those others relate to the dependent

---

[17] Propensity-score matching and related non- and semi-parametric techniques attempt to relax this need to leverage a particular specified empirical model of the relations between controls and outcomes in obtaining estimates for some particular variable's effect. They achieve this by replacing parametric model assumptions with others related, *inter alia*, to the distributions of the observed and unobserved controls (see Przeworski, this volume, and the discussion below). In either case, then, we can redress multi-causality in the social scientific context only by adding theoretical information. Again, social-scientific experimentation, laboratory or, a fortiori, field, can only partially evade this need because it can only partially control possible causes.

variable. Furthermore, to net away the latter we must know, estimate, or be willing to stipulate some model of how controls (as well as independent variables of interest) relate to the dependent variable (see also n. 17). If *EcDev* and *EqDist* both relate to *Dem*, e.g. we cannot ascertain the effect of one without having some way of netting the effect of the other, regardless of whether we analyze the available information qualitatively or quantitatively.

Equation (6) below shows explicitly how this "partialing away" of shared covariation is done in the simple linear, trivariate regression case of (5).[18] Jumping to the last lines of each open brace (after the first), we see that to gauge the partial association of one independent variable, say *EcDev*, with the dependent variable, *Dem*, controlling for the other, *EqDist*, one must assess the covariation of *EcDev* with dependent variable, *Dem*, net away the partial association of *Dem* with the other independent variable, *EqDist*, times the covariation of the two independent variables, *EcDev* and *EqDist*, and then divide by the variation in *EcDev*. (This appears toward the middle of equation (6).) Alternatively, if one cannot or prefers not to stipulate or assess a priori the partial association of the other independent variable, then one must multiply the covariation of *Dem* with *EcDev* by the variation of *EqDist*, subtract the covariation of *Dem* and *EqDist* times the covariation of *EcDev* and *EqDist*, and divide all that by the product of the variations of *EcDev* and *EqDist* minus their covariation squared.

$$Min_{b_1,b_2} \sum_{i=1}^{n} (Dem_i - b_1 EcDev_i - b_2 EqDist_i)^2$$

$$\Rightarrow \begin{cases} (i) & \dfrac{\partial \sum_{i=1}^{n} (Dem_i - b_1 EcDev_i - b_2 EqDist_i)^2}{\partial b_1} = 0 \\[4mm] (ii) & \dfrac{\partial \sum_{i=1}^{n} (Dem_i - b_1 EcDev_i - b_2 EqDist_i)^2}{\partial b_2} = 0 \end{cases}$$

$$(i) \Rightarrow \begin{cases} \sum_{i=1}^{n} EcDev_i(Dem_i - b_1 EcDev_i - b_2 EqDist_i) = 0 \Rightarrow \sum_{i=1}^{n} EcDev_i Dem_i \\[3mm] = b_1 \sum_{i=1}^{n} EcDev_i^2 + b_2 \sum_{i=1}^{n} EcDev_i EqDist_i \\[3mm] \Rightarrow b_1 = \left(\sum_{i=1}^{n} EcDev_i Dem_i - b_2 \sum_{i=\pm1}^{n} EcDev_i EqDist_i \right) / \sum_{i=1}^{n} EcDev_i^2 \\[3mm] \Rightarrow b_1 = \dfrac{Cov(Dem, EcDev) - b_2 \times Cov(EcDev, EqDist)}{Var(EcDev)} \end{cases}$$

[18] Indeed, we simplify yet further by assuming *EcDev* and *EqDist* each have sample mean zero so the last lines of each open brace (after the first) may be written in terms of sample variations and covariations.

$$(ii) \Rightarrow (analogously) \begin{cases} b_2 = \left(\sum_{i=1}^{n} EqDist_i Dem_i - b_1 \sum_{i=1}^{n} EcDev_i EqDist_i \right) / \sum_{i=1}^{n} EqDist_i^2 \\ b_2 = \dfrac{Cov(Dem, EqDist) - b_1 \times Cov(EcDev, EqDist)}{Var(EqDist)} \end{cases}$$

$$\Rightarrow \begin{cases} b_1 = \dfrac{\left(\sum_{i=1}^{n} EcDev_i Dem_i \right)\left(\sum_{i=1}^{n} EqDist_i^2 \right) - \left(\sum_{i=1}^{n} EqDist_i Dem_i \right)\left(\sum_{i=1}^{n} EcDev_i EqDist_i \right)}{\left(\sum_{i=1}^{n} EcDev_i^2 \right)\left(\sum_{i=1}^{n} EqDist_i^2 \right) - \left(\sum_{i=1}^{n} EcDev_i EqDist_i \right)^2} \\ b_1 = \dfrac{Cov(Dem, EcDev) \times Var(EqDist) - Cov(Dem, EqDist) \times Cov(EcDev, EqDist)}{Var(EcDev) \times Var(EqDist) - [Cov(EcDev, EqDist)]^2} \end{cases}$$

and, analogously:

$$\Rightarrow \begin{cases} b_2 = \dfrac{\left(\sum_{i=1}^{n} EqDist_i Dem_i \right)\left(\sum_{i=1}^{n} EcDev_i^2 \right) - \left(\sum_{i=1}^{n} EcDev_i Dem_i \right)\left(\sum_{i=1}^{n} EcDev_i EqDist_i \right)}{\left(\sum_{i=1}^{n} EcDev_i^2 \right)\left(\sum_{i=1}^{n} EqDist_i^2 \right) - \left(\sum_{i=1}^{n} EcDev_i EqDist_i \right)^2} \\ b_2 = \dfrac{Cov(Dem, EqDist) \times Var(EcDev) - Cov(Dem, EcDev) \times Cov(EcDev, EqDist)}{Var(EcDev) \times Var(EqDist) - [Cov(EcDev, EqDist)]^2} \end{cases}$$

$$(6)$$

I remind the reader that this is the simplest possible case: purely linear additive, only two independent variables (each with sample mean zero), and an additively separable stochastic component. The expression becomes (exponentially) more complicated, not less, as we relax these extremely restrictive assumptions, for example by entertaining non-linear and/or interactive relationships or non-separable stochastic components (such as common in binary or other qualitative outcome models). Notice also that to gauge two parameters of interest, b_1 and b_2, we need at least three observations (i.e. to observe three contexts, three sets of information). This just reflects the obvious point that positive degrees of freedom are necessary to learn anything empirically (as elaborated next section).[19]

Thus, whether one works by qualitative or quantitative analysis, if more than one cause possibly operates and if each of those potentially varies across the contexts considered, then one must gauge all of these quantities and perform the calculations in (6) at least loosely if one is to claim comprehension of the association of a variable with an outcome, controlling for others. Of course, qualitatively, working (implicitly) with Figure 2.1 would be preferred, but the figure is imperfect and not generally applicable as a representation of multivariate analysis and one must at least loosely

---

[19] Actually, in (6), just two will suffice to gauge the parameters because we stipulated rather than estimated the sample means of the variables, although to gauge their certainty would still require at least one more.

gauge all of the above variations and covariations (or partial covarations) to draw it with appropriately sized and positioned ovals and overlaps anyway. Drawing such figures properly with more than two independent variables or for non-linear or other more complexly context-conditional cases is, to state it mildly, extremely difficult. We can clearly see from this exposition why such heavy premium is rightly placed in qualitative traditions on selecting contexts for close observation that literally fix as much as possible apart from a single or very, very few potential causes of interest. To state the conclusion more baldly and boldly, one simply cannot manage the complexity of partialing shared covariation in one's head, at least not easily or well, and certainly not with more than two moving potential causes, so, given multicausality, qualitative empirical analysts must (and rightly do in most cases) strive carefully and determinedly to isolate for analysis episodes from within their contexts in which only one potential cause at a time moves, preferably by a lot because only few instances of an uncertain effect will be observed; in short: seek contexts with big effects and single or very few moving causes.

We can also see from Figure 2.1 and equation (6) the intuitions behind the important and powerful omitted variable results from statistical analysis.[20] Suppose, for example, that, in addition to or instead of *EcDev* and *EqDist*, a cross-cutting rather than a reinforcing ethno-religio-linguistic social cleavage-structure, *CCut*, fosters democratization. Some theories suggest, moreover, that *CCut* would also foster *EcDev* and *EqDist*. Accordingly, estimation of (5) or qualitative analysis of democratization that considered only *EcDev* and *EqDist* and did not or could not control for *CCut*, i.e. "partial away" its effects quantitatively or hold it fixed in qualitative analysis, would tend to overestimate the importance of *EcDev* and *EqDist*. We can see this most easily from the following line of equation (6):

$$b_1 = \frac{Cov(Dem,\ EcDev) - b_2 \times Cov(EcDev,\ EqDist)}{Var(EcDev)}$$

$$= b_1^{\text{bivariate}} - b_2 \times b_{EqDist.on.EcDev} \tag{7}$$

The first term in the numerator divided by the denominator is the bivariate coefficient from a regression of *Dem* on *EcDev*. The term after the minus sign thus gives the bias in that bivariate coefficient relative to the corresponding partial coefficient from

---

[20] Figure 2.1 can also illustrate the oft-noted problem of multicolinearity. As the overlap of X_2's and X_3's ovals increases, gauging their partial relations with X_2 increasingly relies on mere slivers of unique covariation with X_2. Thus, multicolinearity induces greater uncertainty and larger standard errors, *but it does so correctly and without any associated bias*, in general. The researcher really is less certain of the association of X_1 with X_2 holding X_3 constant as X_1 and X_3 correlate more. The problem of multicolinearity is the uncertainty it correctly leaves about partial associations, not bias. It is an unfortunate fact of the information one has and not a failure of model specification or estimation strategy. Only more information, preferably new information in which the covariance of potential causes is lower, can help. On the other hand, this is one area where relatively greater emphasis on quality could also be very productive. With random and uncorrelated measurement error, those slivers of unique variation, and perhaps some of the covariation in limited samples, would comprise largely noise as measurement error and correlation among the true explanatory factors increased.

the (assumed correct) multivariate regression. The bias of the bivariate regression coefficient in the truly trivariate case is simply the (correct) partial coefficient on the omitted variable times the coefficient one would obtain regressing the omitted variable on the included one. Thus, the signs of omitted variable biases in the trivariate case are easily determined given some assumptions, argument, or theory about how the omitted factor relates to the dependent variable and the included independent variable.

The logic is intuitive: empirical analysis omitting some factors will attribute to factors that are included and that relate to the omitted ones a share of the associations of those omitted variables with the dependent variable proportional to the covariations of the omitted with the included variables. In our example, the omitted *CCut* was expected to relate positively both to the independent variables and to the dependent variable. If these former statements intended positive partial covariations with the included variables, then we would expect its omission to bias the researcher's conclusions about the effects of each *EcDev* and *EqDist* positively. However, if the statement intended only that *CCut* covaried with each positively, but that its partial covariation with each controlling for the other might be negative, this logic actually establishes only that the sum of the effects of the included, *EcDev* and *EqDist*, will be overestimated due to the omission of the third, *CCut*.

The general formula for omitted variable bias in the k-regressor multivariate case is:

$$\left[(\mathbf{X}_1'\mathbf{X}_1)^{-1}\mathbf{X}_1'\mathbf{X}_2 \right]\mathbf{b}_2 \equiv \mathbf{F}_{1,2}\mathbf{b}_2 \tag{8}$$

where $\mathbf{F}_{1,2}$ is a $k_1 \times k_2$ matrix of partial coefficients obtained from regressing the vector of k_2 omitted factors on the vector of k_1 included factors and $\mathbf{b}_2$ is the vector of partial coefficients on those omitted factors. Thus, in our example, $\mathbf{b}_2$ is just the single partial coefficient on the omitted *CCut*, which was assumed positive, and $\mathbf{F}_{1,2}$ is the vector of two partial coefficients obtained from regressing *CCut* on *EcDev* and *EqDist*. Thus, if partial coefficients on *EcDev* were positive and on *EqDist* negative,

Table 2.2 Sign of omitted-variable bias from bivariate analysis of trivariate relationship

		Sign of partial coefficient on omitted factor from trivariate regression of dependent on independent variables		
		Positive	Zero	Negative
Sign of coefficient from regression of omitted on Included variable	Positive	Positive Bias	No Bias	Negative Bias
	Zero	No Bias	No Bias	No Bias
	Negative	Negative Bias	No Bias	Positive Bias

then the association of *EcDev* with *Dem* would be overstated and that of *EqDist* with *Dem* understated if *CCut* were omitted or ignored.

The potential biases from omitted variables, and the inherent difficulty discussed above in gauging the partial association of multiple included and omitted variables, represent the first of the fundamental challenges for empirical evaluation in the complex, multicausal world of social science. As readily noted from Table 2.2 and equations (6) and (8), the signs and magnitudes of omitted variable biases are relatively easily determined and gauged, qualitatively or quantitatively, in the trivariate case, but they grow exponentially more complicated to assess, especially qualitatively, as the number of potentially important causal factors grows. Moreover, if information on the omitted potentially relevant factors can be obtained, then including them seems at first blush relatively costless for quantitative analyses. (For qualitative empirical analysis, the difficulty of partialing the associations due even just two moving explanatory factors already suffices to place extremely high premium on choosing contexts across which just one or as few as possible potential explanatory variables vary.) Return to equation (7) or Table 2.2, and notice that if the hypothetical omitted factor in them, *EqDist*, were actually irrelevant to the dependent variable, then the middle column of Table 2.2, the case where $b_2 = 0$ in (7), would apply and bias from including or excluding such an irrelevant factor is zero.[21] This line of reasoning has generally led to a predisposition among quantitative empirical researchers "to err on the side of caution" and include any and all reasonably plausible controls in their estimation models.

The seemingly cautious strategy of considering and controlling many factors, however, has its own serious perils. First is *overfitting*. When one includes too many explanatory factors (or too flexibly includes some number), then one tends to find in limited samples associations of those independent variables with the random component that just happens to have realized in that sample. Oversized models in this sense do correspondingly poor jobs of out-of-sample prediction.[22] Second is what might be termed *included variable bias*. In short, control should be applied only for causal priors and not causal posteriors. If, for example, economic development affects democratization through the effect of development on equality, then controlling for equality will induce understatement of development's democratization effect. In Figure 2.1, the areas [3]+[6] reflect X_2's and X_3's shared covariation, but stem solely from variation in X_2, and so should not be partialed away if one

---

[21] This assumes the included irrelevant (in this sense) factor is exogenous. If endogenous, then its relationship with the dependent variable may be misgauged (as non-zero), inducing biases in other variables' coefficient estimates (see e.g. Franzese and Hays 2006).

[22] Many or most quantitative empirical analyses are likely overfit thusly. Many or most qualitative empirical analyses probably are as well, although for different reasons. Namely, when describing in qualitative detail events and circumstances in a limited set of contexts, one often feels almost compelled to explain everything about those contexts. If the sociopoliticoeconomic world is partly random, then complete explanation in this sense necessarily includes erroneously systematic seeming accounts of non-systematic (i.e. random) aspects of those events and circumstances. The caution against overfitting therefore, like almost everything discussed in this chapter, applies to quantitative and qualitative empirical analyses alike.

seeks to gauge the total impact of X_2 on X_1.[23] Third, even quantitatively, the complexity with which various sources of incorrect inference tend to interact in multicausal models, especially if we add mismeasurement or misspecification possibilities, should lead researchers to place great weight on parsimony. After discussing some of these important and complex difficulties, Achen (2002) suggests restraining research questions to a narrower range of contexts, leaning more heavily on theory to help specify empirical models and explorations, and, famously, "ART: a rule of [no more than] three [explanatory factors]." Unfortunately, the first piece of advice is not applicable for comparativists who seek empirically helpful general theory rather than an unconnected set of partial theories that may be empirically helpful each in their narrow context.[24] The third, as stated in the catchy ART, is clearly not helpful if understood too simplistically and rigidly (which was not the intent). The problems and complexities Achen discusses are real and very important, but, unfortunately, so are the problems of omitted variables, even though Achen is also correct to argue that the omitted variable problems are often overemphasized to the exclusion of the equally difficult problems he stresses. Parsimony is certainly to be valued, and Achen's second admonition, that we rely more heavily and directly than currently common on our theoretical models and arguments (and substantive knowledge) to specify our empirical models and explorations, is certainly to be followed, but no rigid rules or limits will ever suffice to encapsulate those valuable guides, and three will often prove too few, sometimes way too few, to capture even just the most important potential causes.[25] Unhelpful as the following may be, the only general advice one can offer on the number of factors to include in empirical models and the proper way to specify their inclusion is "the right number, the right way." The importance and full meaning of the latter part of that banality, attention to empirical

---

[23] Notice, however, that, as the example is drawn, simply omitting X_3 would be inefficient—more exactly, the estimated variance of the estimated coefficient on X_1 would be higher than it could (correctly) be—because some share of the dependent variable, X_2, would be treated as stochastic (random) whereas in fact, it is systematic in X_3. In such a case, we might wish to include $X_3|X_1$, i.e. X_3 net of X_1, as a regressor. Notice then, too, that this would stipulate a priori that all shared covariation of X_1 and X_3 with X_2 is attributed to X_1. In the more complicated (and probably more common) case where we are unable or do not wish to make such stipulation, we are back in the original multicausal case where no empirical information, quantitative or qualitative, can determine how to allocate the shared covariation. Any specific allocation can only be imposed a priori by theory or assumption. The interested reader should reference a good text on structural equations, e.g. Duncan 1975, however because the issues involved are more complex than this note can fully relay.

[24] See also the discussion in Section 2 about the empirical uses of and strategies for "single-case" studies. Moreover, paradoxically, the latter "empirical [helpfulness] each in their narrow context" may often prove difficult to adjudge with information only from that narrow context, especially given multicausality. One problem is that, typically, a great many potential causes will be held constant or not vary much by the narrowed focus; accordingly, if they are indeed causes, means of gauging their impact relative to those that do vary within the narrow context will not exist. Again, see also the discussion of "single cases" in Section 2.

[25] Huntington's discovery of twenty-seven in the democratization literature is probably too many, but illustrative. A model of democratization that omitted history (the previous state of the regime), economic development, social structure, or international conditions would almost certainly be badly misspecified, for example (and the important aspects of each of those, especially social structure, almost certainly number more than one).

specification, will become manifest as we turn now to the second of the fundamental challenges for empirical evaluation in social science, the one most central to comparative politics' core tenet that *context matters*: the effect of everything depends on pretty much everything else.

4 CONTEXT-CONDITIONALITY: THE EFFECT OF ALMOST EVERYTHING DEPENDS ON ALMOST EVERYTHING ELSE

The contention that *context matters* perhaps means most centrally that how particular causes operate, and perhaps the entire structure of the causal process, is highly contextual; the causal process varies across contexts: it is context conditional. Such contentions and the concerns they raised regarding the prospects for successful general empirical evaluation of theoretical propositions may have underlain the parochialism and non-comparativeness of the pre-war comparative politics that is generally viewed (probably unfairly) by all modern comparativists as pre-scientific. In the extreme, *context matters* means that processes and outcomes differ uniquely, each specific substantive venue in each place at each time having its own unique processes relating to outcomes. If this is so, *any* comparison, within or across cases, times, or venues, would always be unwarranted or unhelpful. Under these conditions, as I show formally below, one simply could not and cannot learn any more than description from comparison, history, or comparative history. Some scholars may have realized this, and some may even have appreciated and intended it, but many seemed (and some seem) to think one could hold simultaneously that each context was unique in this sense and that one could learn from comparative history. That is not logically possible.

Such contentions and concerns were also foundational to early cultural and behavioral approaches to comparative politics, in which the meaning and effect of various objective circumstances and factors (e.g. deprivation) depend on cultural and sociopsychological context (e.g. perceived or relative deprivation). However, with this wave of theoretical progress, contextual variation became something to be understood better by comparison, rather than something debarring it. Likewise in institutional approaches, the effects of societal interest structures *manifest through*, are *shaped by*, and therefore *depend upon* the institutional structure of the society, economy, and polity. Institutions, in other words, became a key to understanding context-conditionality. At least by the 1980s, perhaps all comparativists could agree, scholars had also established that statistical analysis of comparative-historical data could help evaluate and fruitfully inform positive theories relating social structure, culture, and institutions to political outcomes. The early empirical work, quantitative and qualitative alike, on these two theoretical approaches did not often reflect as well and fully as one might like the multicausality, and rarely reflected at all the context-conditionality and endogeneity, of comparative-politics arguments and reality. For example, culture matters, if it does, in complex ways and often by modifying the relations between other objective conditions, like poverty and underdevelopment, and outcomes, like democratic stability. Individuals' interpretations of poverty and appropriate responses thereto, a cultural argument might contend, hinge on cultural symbols and understandings. Likewise, institutions matter mostly by altering the relationships between objective interests and the institutionally shaped set of actions perceived as possible and most effective by individuals or groups with those interests. For example, the extent to which some polity's cleavage structure will induce (i) leaders to form political parties mirroring the societal groups drawn by that structure and (ii) voters to support such parties depends upon the electoral rules and party-systemic strategic-structure that shape the relationships from votes to representation and from representation and governmental power.

Complex, context-conditional propositions of this sort are now the hallmark of positive comparative politics; the effect of X (e.g. institutions) on Y (outcomes) *depends on* Z (culture, structure, etc.): formally, $\partial Y/\partial X = f(Z)$. Early empirical work that established that institutions matter *in addition to* culture and structure (and vice versa) by controlling for the latter in regressions of outcomes on the former, reflected multicausality, and so faced the challenges to empirical inference thereof as discussed above, but they did not reflect such context-conditionality. They showed only that the effect of X (institutions) on Y (outcomes), given or controlling for Z (culture, structure, etc.) is not zero, not that the effect of X on Y *depends on* Z: formally, they showed $\partial Y/\partial X|_Z \neq 0$ and not (necessarily) that $\partial Y/\partial X = f(Z)$.

Critics of statistical analysis in comparative politics often cite this concern (*inter alia*) that regression coefficients impose a *constant* effect for each independent variable, albeit controlling for others, not effects that differ depending on context. That is, they object that broad statistical comparison neglects the context-conditionality that lies at the very heart of comparative politics. This criticism, however, applies only to the simplest linear-additive regression. Nor does it follow that other approaches necessarily evade this or any other limitation simply because one has discovered or claims a weakness in one approach. Hall (2003), e.g. offers perhaps the most careful, nuanced, and best statement of this concern (among others to which the next section returns):

Regression analysis is more flexible. It is well-adapted to an ontology that envisions probabalistic causation and, given enough cases, it can cope with some interaction effects (cf. Jackson 1996). However, the types of regression analyses commonly used to study comparative politics…assume unit homogeneity, which is to say that, other things being equal, a change in the value of a causal variable x will produce a corresponding change in the value of the outcome variable y of the same magnitude across all the cases. It assumes no systematic correlation between the causal variables included in the analysis and other causal variables omitted from it. It assumes that all the relevant interaction effects among the causal variables have been captured by interaction terms in the regression…[26]

---

[26] The last two sentences in the quotation refer to the multicausality and omitted variable bias discussed in Section 3; we need re-emphasize here only that the potential problem is not one of regression

As Hall notes, the statistical device most frequently used to evaluate theoretical claims that the effect(s) on some dependent variable(s), Y, of some independent variable(s), X, depend upon or are moderated by a third (set of) independent variable(s), Z, is the linear-interactive, or multiplicative, term. One simply includes one or more $X \times Z$ terms among the regressors. Interaction terms are hardly new to comparative politics. Indeed, their use is now common, yet, especially with current and growing attention to the roles of institutions in comparative politics, they should perhaps become more common still. Moreover, as we will elaborate later, many statistical devices exist to incorporate the context-conditionality of comparative phenomena (of any complexity) into empirical models. In fact, if one can make a logically consistent claim that theory predicts some relationship between Y and X (and chance), $Y=f(X,\epsilon)$, then one can write a statistical model to reflect that proposition, and, if the necessary empirical information actually exists, estimate and evaluate it. And, again, the challenges to redress in doing so are not a function of the empirical methodology chosen, but rather logically inherent in the attempt to infer complex context-conditionality from comparative history. They do not arise just because we write the problem formally, and they do not disappear just because we do not.

As Table 2.3 (from Kam and Franzese forthcoming) shows, 54 percent of articles 1996–2001 in leading political science journals use some statistical methods,[27] and 24 percent of those employ interactions. Among exclusively comparative journals, *Comparative Political Studies* had 49 percent and 25 percent and *Comparative Politics* 9 percent and 8 percent. The other journals all have many comparative publications also, and statistical analyses comprise 25–80 percent of those articles, with interactive analyses representing a relatively fixed 20–5 percent. Thus, about half of top journal political science articles employ some statistical methods, and about a quarter of those and over an eighth of all articles use interaction terms.[28] Comparative politics, using *CPS*, *IO*, and *WP* to gauge that, operates somewhere between the discipline's mean and half that on these dimensions. Trends in comparative politics and the broader discipline likely continue mildly upward in both regards. Notwithstanding this widespread and expanding usage of interactions, still more empirical work should contain them than currently does, given the substance of many comparative politics arguments. Consider the gist of most institutional arguments, for example. In one influential statement, Hall (1986, 19) states:

institutional analysis of politics...emphasizes institutional relationships, both formal and conventional, that bind the components of the state together and structure its relations with

---

analysis but of empirical evaluation of social science. Qualitatively or quantitatively, valid empirical inference rests on assumptions or arguments that one has controlled for or has randomized over other potential causes (and has observed sufficient and sufficiently independent information sets for randomization to be effective). We have already discussed also the relative efficacy of quantity and quality in making such control or randomization.

[27] That is, they report some certainty estimate(s) like standard errors, confidence intervals, or hypothesis tests.

[28] Moreover, the denominator includes formal theory and political philosophy, and implicitly interactive functional forms, like logit or probit, are not counted in the numerator. These are very conservative estimates.

Table 2.3 Types of articles in major political science journals, 1996–2001

Journal (1996–2001)	Total articles	Statistical analysis		Interaction-term usage		
		Count	% of tot	Count	% of tot	% of stat
American Political Science Review	279	274	77	69	19	25
American Journal of Political Science	355	155	55	47	17	30
Comparative Politics	130	12	9	1	1	8
Comparative Political Studies	189	92	49	23	12	25
International Organization	170	43	25	9	5	21
International Studies Quarterly	173	70	40	10	6	14
Journal of Politics	284	226	80	55	19	24
Legislative Studies Quarterly	157	104	66	19	12	18
World Politics	116	28	24	6	5	25
TOTALS	2,446	1323	54	311	13	24

society... [I]nstitutions... refers to the formal rules, compliance procedures, and standard operating practices that structure the relationship between individuals in various units of the polity and economy... Institutional factors play two fundamental roles... [They] affect the degree of power that any one set of actors has over policy outcomes [...and they...] influence an actor's definition of his own interests, by establishing his... responsibilities and relationship to other actors... With an institutionalist model we can see policy as more than the sum of countervailing pressure from social groups. That pressure is mediated by an organizational [i.e. institutional] dynamic....

Thus, in this approach to institutional analysis, and, as we argued above, inherently in all approaches, institutions are intervening variables that *funnel, mediate,* or otherwise *shape* the political processes that translate the societal structure of interests into effective political pressures, those pressures into public policy-making responses, and/or those policies into outcomes.[29] For example, one prominent line of research connects the societal structure of interests to effective political pressure on policy makers through institutional features of the electoral system: plurality-majority versus proportional representation, etc. (e.g. Cox 1997; Lijphart 1994). Another emphasizes how governmental institutions, especially the number and polarization of key policy makers (veto actors) that comprise it, shape policy-making responses to such pressures (e.g. Tsebelis 2002). A third stresses how the institutional configuration of the economy, such as the coordination of wage–price bargaining, shapes the effect of certain policies, such as monetary policy (e.g. Franzese 2002*b*, ch. 4). In every case, and at each step of the analysis from interest structure to

---

[29] Extending the list of synonyms might prove a useful means of identifying interactive arguments. When one says *X alters, modifies, magnifies, augments, increases, moderates, dampens, diminishes, reduces,* etc. some *effect* (of *Z*) on *Y*, one has offered an interactive argument.

outcomes (and back), the role of institutions is to mediate, shape, structure, or condition the impact of some other variable(s) on the dependent variable of interest. That is, institutional arguments are inherently interactive, yet, with relatively rare exceptions—see e.g. Ordeshook and Shvetsova 1994; Franzese 2002b, ch. 3; Franzese 2002b, ch. 4, respectively, regarding the above topical examples—empirical work on institutional arguments has ignored this interactivity.

Another example further reveals the ubiquity of the interactive, i.e. context-conditional, implications of comparative-institutional theories. Scholars consider principal–agent (i.e. delegation) situations interesting, problematic, and worthy of study because, if each had full control, agents would determine policy, y_1, in response to some (set of) factor(s), X, according to some function, $y_1 = f(X)$, whereas principals would respond to some perhaps different (set of) factor(s), Z, perhaps differently according to, $y_2 = g(Z)$. (For example, the principals might be the current government, responding to political-economic conditions X, and the agents unresponsive central banks, giving $Z=\emptyset$, as in Franzese 1999.) Theorists then offer some arguments about how institutional and other environmental conditions determine the monitoring, enforcement, and other costs, C, principals must incur to induce agents to enact $g(Z)$ instead of $f(X)$. In such situations, realized policy, y, will usually be given by some $y = k(C) \cdot f(X) + [1-k(C)] \cdot g(Z)$ with $0 \le k(C) \le 1$ and $k(C)$ weakly increasing. Thus, the effects on y of each $c \in C$ generally depends on X and Z, and those of each $x \in X$ and $z \in Z$ generally depend on C. That is, the effect on y of *everything* that contributes to monitoring and enforcement costs generally depends on *all* factors to which the principals and agents would respond differently, and, vice versa, the effect on y of *all* such factors depends on *everything* that affects monitoring and enforcement costs. In fact, policies and outcomes in all situations of shared policy control, through delegation or otherwise (e.g. presidents and legislatures), will usually be describable as convex combinations like these, implying the corresponding multiple and complex interactions. Most empirical applications of principal–agent and other shared-policy-control models seem to have missed this point.

A rough quantification of the magnitude of such institutional interactions omissions from empirical specifications is startling. Of Table 2.3's 1,012 articles with non-interactive statistical analyses, half or so offer some sort of institutional argument. Even if only half of all institutional effects actually reflect the interactivity argued here to be inherent, then almost as many articles, $\frac{1}{2} \cdot \frac{1}{2} \cdot 1012 = 253$, incorrectly employ non-interactive empirical techniques to evaluate interactive hypotheses as actually employ interactive terms (311). If, instead, all institutional arguments are inherently interactive, and many other arguments are also (e.g. contextual effects in cultural-behavioral theories), say half, that would imply that roughly 2.5 times as many articles made interactive arguments but empirically evaluated them non-interactively ($\{1/2 + 1/4\} \cdot 1012 = 759$) as actually employed interactions.

The theoretical and substantive interestingness of such complex context-conditionality is readily apparent in comparative political economy. For example, in a recent review, Franzese (2002a) argued that venerable electoral and partisan cycles may merit theoretical and empirical revisit to explore the institutional, structural, and strategic conditionality:

Policymakers in democracies have strong partisan and electoral incentives regarding the amount, nature, and timing of economic-policy activity. Given these incentives, many observers expected government control of effective economic policies to induce clear economic-outcome cycles that track the electoral calendar in timing and incumbent partisanship in character... until recently, both rational- and adaptive-expectations electoral-and-partisan-cycle work underemphasized crucial variation in the contexts—international and domestic, political and economic, institutional, structural, and strategic—in which elected partisan incumbents make policy. This contextual variation conditions policymaker incentives and abilities to manipulate economic policy for electoral and partisan gain, as well as the effectiveness of such manipulation, differently across democracies, elections, and policies. Although relatively new, research into such context-conditional electoral and partisan cycles seems to offer much promise for resolving anomalies and an ideal substantive venue for theoretical and empirical advancement in the study of political economy and comparative democratic politics more generally. (2002a, 369)

For example, in small, open economies, domestic policy makers may retain less autonomy over some policies, or some policies may be less economically effective, so that electoral and partisan cycles in those policies and outcomes are less pronounced than in larger, less-exposed economies. Some polities, moreover, concentrate policy-making control in fewer, more disciplined partisan actors, which may induce sharper cycles in, e.g. Westminsterian than in other democracies. Furthermore, some policies may have more effect and so be more useful and so more used for electoral or partisan purposes, and this too varies with institutional, structural, or strategic context. For instance, political benefits of geographic relative to demographic targeting of spending may vary by electoral system, e.g. single-member plurality favoring the former and proportional representation the latter. These and other contextual variations condition policy makers' incentives and abilities to manipulate policies and outcomes for electoral and partisan gain, and modify the political and economic efficacy of such manipulation, in manifold ways across democracies, elections, and policies, all of which suggests exciting opportunities for interactive models that inform comparative politics. Another obvious locus of interactive effects lies in recent studies of *Varieties of Capitalism* (Hall and Soskice 2001) or of globalization, the comparative political economy approach to which stresses that the domestic response to international economic integration varies, depending critically on domestic political and institutional context (e.g. Boix 1998; Garrett 1998; Swank 2002). Similar examples from outside political economy are not hard to imagine. The propensity for (apparent) directional voting versus proximity voting in individual electoral behavior, for example, depends on electoral and party systems and the types of government they tend to produce (see e.g. Kedar 2002).

With so many opportunities, some currently being taken but many as yet ignored, to explore interactions—indeed, with the logically inherent interactive nature of comparative politics theory—the good news is that quantitative empirical modeling of such context-conditionality can be quite simple (Brambor, Clark, and Golder 2006 and Kam and Franzese forthcoming, discuss more thoroughly). First, one must understand empirical models that embody interactive hypotheses. For example, one typical theoretical argument might be that X generally reduces Y and does so more in the presence of or the larger is Z. Note that this is actually *two* hypotheses: (a) that $\partial Y/\partial X$ is negative (X reduces Y) and (b) that $\partial^2 Y/\partial X\partial Z$ is negative (and increasingly so with Z). In a model containing regressors X, Z, and $X\times Z$, such as $Y = \ldots aX + bZ + cX \times Z \ldots$, the interpretation of results regarding (b) is straightforward. $\partial^2 Y/\partial X\partial Z = c$, so the coefficient c simply and directly tells us how the effect of X changes per unit increase in Z and, vice versa, how the effect of Z changes per unit increase in X.[30] Thus, the standard t-test on coefficient c corresponds to hypothesis (b). The effect on Y of X, $\partial Y/\partial X$, however, is not simply a, nor is the effect on Y of Z, $\partial Y/\partial Z$, equal to b; nor, even, are these the "main" effects of X or Z. The effect of X on Y, $\partial Y/\partial Z$, equals $a + cZ$, which depends, as the hypothesis said, on the value of Z (and vice versa: $\partial Y/\partial Z = b + cX$). The effects of X and Z each depend on the other variable's value, and the coefficient a or b is just the effect of an increase in X or Z when the other variable equals zero (which need not be "main" in any way, and could even be out of sample or logically impossible). In interactive models, as in any models beyond the strictly linear additive, the *effects* of variables do not correspond directly to just one *coefficient*; effects of each variable depend on the values of their interacting variables, which is what the interactive argument argued in the first place. Nor do the standard errors (or t-tests) of these *effects* correspond directly to those of any one coefficient; just as the effects of X and Z vary depending on the value of the other, so too do the standard errors of those effects. The best approach for researchers presenting interactive results is to graph or tabulate the *effect* of each variable as a function of the value of its interacting variables, along with the standard errors or confidence intervals of those effects. Even with a relatively firm understanding of interactive models, some scholars express considerable reservations over them or question how far they can go toward reflecting and evaluating the complex context-conditionality of comparative politics.

Some note, correctly, that the empirical task of distinguishing not just a single, constant effect for X, but one that varies (albeit only linearly) depending on Z, imposes much heavier burden on the data. This is also the substantive meaning of concerns expressed regarding the high multicolinearity (i.e. correlation) among regressors X or Z and $X\times Z$ in interactive models.[31] Efficiency (but not bias) concerns over multicolinearity are quite valid, as we discussed already above. The empirical task that interactive analyses set *is* very demanding, and these demands will heighten

---

[30] These converses are logically identical, and this identity is logical, not a result of regression modeling.

[31] Moreover, one must discard the notion that "centering" the interacting variables (subtracting their means), as some methodological texts advise, eases this empirical task. *Centering alters nothing important mathematically and nothing at all substantively.* Likewise, the oft-raised concern that multiplicative terms cannot distinguish, for example, $XZ=12$ with $X=3$ and $Z=4$ from $XZ=12$ with $X=2$ and $Z=6$, is incorrect because the model, that is the model of the effect of X and Z on Y, can and will distinguish those cases insofar as they actually do differ logically. Incidentally, under the heading of potentially misleading common admonitions, that one should include both X and Z if the model contains an XZ term is usually a highly advisable philosophy of science guideline (Occam's razor), and typically soundly cautious and conservative scientific practice at least to explore, but it is neither a logical nor a statistical necessity (see Kam and Franzese forthcoming).

sharply as the number and complexity of interactions increase, as the complex context-conditionality of comparative politics suggests they should. However, this concern too is unavoidable *logical necessity*, and not a function of the empirical methodology chosen. Indeed, the difficulty of the task increases with the number and complexity of the interactions *relative to the number of—more exactly, the useful total variation in—the sets of information used to evaluate them.*

Comparative researchers seem to have four options, each with characteristic perils. (i) Ignore the context-conditionality of their arguments by omitting interactive terms. Judging by Table 2.3, most analysts do this, but this does violence to the inherently (and interestingly) interactive nature of comparative politics and plagues those effects actually estimated with omitted variable bias and inefficiency. (ii) Reduce context-conditionality by allowing only one or few of the hypothesized interactions in their empirical model. This enables more exclusive focus on those included interactions and reduces the omitted variable biases and inefficiencies relative to excluding them altogether, but it does not eliminate these problems and it ignores the likely complexity of the context-conditionality in comparative politics. (iii) Constrain the empirical model of context-conditionality to follow a specific functional form suggested by theory (see e.g. the above regarding principal–agent models; Franzese 1999, 2003). This reduces the empirical-inferential demands on the data to reveal more of the theorized complex, context-conditionality in comparative phenomena, thereby reducing further the misspecification and inefficiency issues of the previous approaches, but many comparative theories may not be sufficiently precise to determine the form of inter-actions, the gained strength arises from leaning more heavily on theory, and the multi-colinearity concerns re-emerge, albeit at a lesser pace, as the allowed complexity increases. (iv) Conduct closer (i.e. qualitative) analysis (of fewer contexts) to supple-ment or substitute for quantitative analysis. This may partly counteract the information deficiency that is the multicolinearity problem by enriching the detail and depth of the empirics, but it typically enhances the quality of the information thusly at the cost of severely reducing the quantity, a tradeoff Section 2 showed is unfavorable in many circumstances. Furthermore, the ability to discern complex interactions qualitatively, i.e., without precise numerical measurement and statistical control of independent variables, is inherently more difficult. Indeed, Section 3 showed that qualitative analysis of contexts in which more than one or two potential explanatory factors vary was exceedingly difficult already, without adding interactive context-conditionality, and even a single linear interaction will generally require variation in three explanatory factors, X, Z, and $X \times Z$, and so at least four information sets.

The third of these options, therefore, seems most promising. Ultimately, the problems raised by complex context-conditionality are logically inherent, so qualita-tive recourse cannot evade them and the other two options evade them only to the degree they suppress the (interesting) conditionality. To see the promise of this third approach, return to the principal–agent (i.e. delegation) situation described above. Generally, in such situations, we argue that, if each had full control, agents would act according to some function, $y_1 = f(X)$, while principals would act differently, $y_2 = g(Z)$. We then argue that some institutional and other contextual conditions determine the monitoring, enforcement, and other costs, C, principals must incur to force agents to enact $g(Z)$ instead of $f(X)$. Realized policy, y, will then typically be given by some $y=k(C){\cdot}f(X)+[1-k(C)]{\cdot}g(Z)$ with $0{\leq}k(C){\leq}1$ and $k(C)$ weakly increasing as noted. If the comparative theory can identify $k(C)$, that is, the function $k(\cdot)$ and contextual conditions, C, that determine the degree to which principal or agent has effective control, and the functions $f(\cdot)$ and $g(\cdot)$ and factors X and Z that state to what and how principal and agent would respond if wholly (hypothetically) in charge, and if these functions and/or factors are not identical, then non-linear regression techniques (as, e.g., in Franzese 1999, 2003) can gain leverage on *all* the complex conditional effects predicted in that comparative context. Moving beyond delegation to other situations of shared policy control, researchers might also fruitfully apply this approach to study the relative weight in policy control of, e.g. executive and legislative branches in (semi-)presidential systems, or of different chambers in multicameral systems, or of prime, cabinet average, cabinet median, and portfolio ministers in parliamentary systems, or of committees or cabinets and legislature floors or backbenchers or oppositions, or, even, of the degree to which elected representatives act legislatively as if they represent the residents of their electoral district, those therein who support them, or their national party constituency. Finally, even more generally, researchers can apply similar non-linear approaches to any situation in which some factor or set of factors modify the impact of several others proportionately, thereby bringing many more of their highly interactive theoretical propositions under empirical scrutiny than perhaps previously thought possible. Indeed, institutions often operate in this way. For example, institutions that foster greater party discipline may induce legislators to behave less geographically distributively and more class/ideological redistributively, implying a proportionate modification in their response to a range of political-economic conditions. Similarly, institutions that facilitate voter participation tend to broaden the distribution of interests represented in the electorate (and so in policy), again suggesting that such electoral institutions will proportionately modify the effect of many political-economic conditions on government policies (see e.g. Franzese 2002, ch. 2).

Non-linear regression is simple to describe, given an understanding of linear regression. As noted above, the empirical implications of positive theory will usually amount to some statement that an outcome, y, depends on random chance, ϵ, and some explanatory factors, x, perhaps including multiplicative interactions or other complex terms, according to some function, $y = f(x,\beta,\epsilon)$, involving parameters β that relate x to y following f$(\cdot)$. In linear regression, we assume the function is linear additive and separable, with β being simple coefficients on x, giving $y = x\beta + \epsilon$. The ordinary linear regression problem and solution is thus:

$$Min_\beta \sum_{i=1}^{n} (y_i - x_i\beta)^2 = Min_\beta (y - X\beta)'(y - X\beta) = Min_\beta y'y - y'X\beta - \beta'X'y + \beta'X'X\beta$$

$$\Rightarrow \frac{\partial(y'y - y'X\beta - \beta'X'y + \beta'X'X\beta)}{\partial\beta} = o \Rightarrow -2X'y + 2X'X\beta = o$$

$$\Rightarrow X'y = X'X\beta$$

$$\Rightarrow \hat{\beta}_{OLS} = (X'X)^{-1}X'y \tag{9}$$

If we instead continue to assume the random component is additively separable but allow explanatory factors, x, and associated parameters, β, to determine the systematic component of y according to some nonlinear function, $E(y) = f(x, \beta)$, specified by theory, we have the following non-linear regression problem and solution:

$$Min_\beta (y - f(X, \beta))'(y - f(X, \beta)) = Min_\beta S$$

$$\equiv y'y - y'f(X, \beta) - f(X, \beta)'y + f(X, \beta)'f(X, \beta)$$

$$\Rightarrow \frac{\partial S}{\partial\beta} = 0 = -2\left(\frac{\partial f(X, \beta)}{\partial\beta}\right)'y + 2\left(\frac{\partial f(X, \beta)}{\partial\beta}\right)'f(X, \beta)$$

$$\Rightarrow \left(\frac{\partial f(X, \beta)}{\partial\beta}\right)'y = \left(\frac{\partial f(X, \beta)}{\partial\beta}\right)'f(X, \beta) \tag{10}$$

If $f(x, \beta)$ is the linear-additive $x\beta$ as in the ordinary regression problem, then the last expression solves analytically to the familiar OLS formula in (9). However, if $f(x, \beta)$ is non-linear in parameters β, then the last expression in (10) cannot in general be simplified further. $\hat{\beta}_{NLS}$ may be found numerically (i.e. computer search) though, either by finding the values for β that satisfy that last expression or by finding the values that minimize the sum of squared errors, S, given the data, y and X. Effectively, the *derivatives*[32] of $f(x, \beta)$ with respect to β, which are just x in the linear-additive case, serve as the regressors (and play a like role in estimating the variance of the estimated parameters). In short, our basic understandings about ordinary least squares regression, its necessary assumptions, and its properties under those assumptions, applies to non-linear regression with the *derivatives* of $f(x, \beta)$ replacing x.[33] The crucial change lies in interpretation and is the one that comes with any move beyond strictly linear-additive models—even just to simple linear interaction models, dynamic models (i.e. models with time or spatial lags of the dependent variable in them), or the familiar logit or probit models of (probabilities of) binary outcomes— namely, that *coefficients* are not *effects*. The effect of X on Y is, always and everywhere, the derivative or difference of (change in) Y with respect to (over the change in) X,

---

[32] Actually, the correct term is *gradient* because β is a vector, so the slope is multidimensional.

[33] All the usual additional complications of numerical optimization as opposed to analytical solution—such as possibility of local maxima, flat areas or ridges, or "nasty" surfaces to search and the concomitant need to explore multiple starting values and search sensitivities and procedures—apply also.

dY/dX, but only in purely linear-additive-separable models are these effects, these derivatives, equal to the coefficient on the variable in question. In other models, effects of one variable generally depend on other variables' values and usually more than one coefficient—that is, the effects of X are context conditional. The important point here is that, if we can theorize how Y depends on X with logical consistency, then we can write a function[34] that describes that relationship, and then we can specify our empirical model by that function. Finally, provided the specified equation is identified and has positive degrees of freedom so that empirical evaluation from comparative history is logically possible, and if comparative history has actually given us sufficient useful variation, we can estimate, evaluate, and interpret that model. In other words, complexity hardly debars statistical empirical analysis; in fact, as the discussions throughout this chapter suggest, complexity tends rather to argue strongly for such analysis. (Furthermore, the statistical software packages that political scientists commonly use now possess user-friendly NLS procedures.[35])

The approach is not magic, of course; it does have prerequisites and limitations. Most importantly, researchers must have sufficiently precise theory to specify empirical models usefully sharply. In the principal–agent situations described previously, for instance, the suggested approach requires that researchers can adequately specify policy determination under the hypothetical extremes of principal and agent full control, that the inputs to these policy response functions and to the function describing monitoring and enforcement costs vary empirically in sample, and it gains the empirical leverage to produce revealing estimates of those parameters only to the degrees that they do so with explanatory power. Then, too, tests of hypotheses regarding the parameters estimated generally tend to weigh that the x matter in the way specified against x does not matter. The same is true in linear regression or any parametric-modeling approach as well, but linear-interactive models containing X, Z, and $X \times Z$, for example, will have the linear-additive model nested in them, so empirical evidence could favor that X matters linear interactively, linear additively, or not at all. Non-linear models may not always have such intermediate complexity models nested within them. Still, many important substantive problems in comparative politics, and in political science more generally, involve complex, context-conditional relationships, and this approach seems to offer a more theoretically, methodologically, and empirically promising way to address those issues than do alternatives.

The conclusion here can be stated thus: *context matters, so model it!* Before leaving that statement as the terse conclusion of this section, let us again adopt the strategy of writing formally the simplest possible reflection of that broad substantive proposition of complex context-conditionality to explore what is logically possible and what is not with regard to gaining empirical leverage upon it. We start from the most general, broadest interpretation to show why that interpretation of *context matters* thoroughly debars any possibility of learning anything (beyond pure description) from comparative history, by any empirical methodology. From there we work down-

---

[34] Or, minimally, a *correspondence* (where E(y) has several values for a single given set or sets of values).
[35] See *nl.ado* in Stata™. E-Views™ least squares algorithm, LS, accepts any $f(\mathbf{x}, \beta)$ desired.

ward to illuminate what sorts of assumptions, theories, or arguments are necessary or useful in altering that situation, along the way discussing some conjectures about what qualitative empirical analyses do or might do in these regards and mentioning very briefly some statistical procedures of germane utility.

The most general formal expression of the proposition that *context matters* might be:

$$y_{it} = f_{it}(\mathbf{x}_{it}, \boldsymbol{\beta}_{it}, \epsilon_{it}); \; \epsilon \sim (0, \Sigma_{it}); \; i = 1..N, \; t = 1..T, \; n = NT \tag{11}$$

In this model, an outcome, y, at time t in place i (jointly, in context it) is a function, f_{it}, which is not necessarily linear or additively separable and which may differ across i and/or t, of explanatory factors, $\mathbf{x}_{it}$, which may differ and at least potentially vary across i and/or t, and which relate (not necessarily linear additively or separably; rather, according to f_{it}) to the outcome by parameters, $\boldsymbol{\beta}_{it}$, which may also differ across i and/or t, and of a random component, ϵ, drawn from some probability distribution, not necessarily independently, although with mean zero and some defined variance-covariance across information sets, Σ_{it}, although that (multivariate) distribution could also differ across i and/or t. Note that $\mathbf{x}_{it}$, the explanatory factors, could include temporal and/or spatial lags of any complexity, so, e.g. strategic interdependence and/or path dependence are subsumed as possibilities. Thus, (11) interprets *context matters* fully generally and broadly. From this formulation, we see that this broadest interpretation gives K (the number of β's) plus $\frac{1}{2}(NT)^2 + \frac{1}{2}NT$ (the number of unique parameters in each variance-covariance matrix for the random component) total parameters *per function* to learn **from each information set observed**. If this is our understanding of *context matters*, then we simply cannot learn anything from comparative history because each piece of information observed empirically would come with many, many times that unit of information to learn. Social scientists therefore must reduce this parameterization, i.e., impose tighter structure on this formulation.[36] The imposed additional structure would ideally come from theory and/or substance or, failing that, practicality, but in any event some assumptions must be made, regardless of empirical methodology, no matter how many contexts we analyze or how closely we analyze them.

To begin, we usually assume $f_{it}(\cdot) = f(\cdot) \; \forall i,t$, i.e. the same function relates $X_{it,it}$, and ϵ_{it} to y in all contexts, opting instead to parameterize variations in the effects of variables across contexts as we described doing previously in this section. Note that this subsumes (i) allowing the effects to vary across but not within certain groups of contexts (e.g. across countries but not over time, or vice versa) and (ii) allowing the set of relevant factors to vary across contexts. Likewise, we always assume $\Sigma_{it} = \Sigma \; \forall i,t$, i.e. that the random component of the outcome in each context is a draw from a distribution with some variance-covariance across contexts, but this variance-covariance across contexts is itself fixed across contexts. Either

---

[36] Indeed, even though historians might say that those who do not learn from history are doomed to repeat it, they would simply be wrong about that if they also believed "each context is unique" to this full extent because, then, any historical episode would, as this formulation shows, be entirely *sui generis*.

assumption may be relaxed somewhat if other restrictions open sufficient degrees of freedom to do so. This still leaves $K(NT) + \frac{1}{2}(NT)^2 + \frac{1}{2}NT$ per NT contexts, or $K + \frac{1}{2}(NT + 1)$ per context, which is still way, way too many to learn anything from comparative history. We must, of course, get to less than NT things to learn per NT contexts before we can learn anything (beyond description of a now-irrelevant past) from empirical observation of any kind.

Next, we can assume the β constant across contexts. This still leaves $K/(NT) + \frac{1}{2}(NT + 1)$ per context, which is still much larger than one; however, this also may be stronger than needed and definitely is stronger than desired given the centrality of context-conditionality to comparative politics. We can, in fact, allow $\beta_{it} = g(z, \gamma, \eta_{it})$, that is, we can model the contextual variation in the effects of variables as a function, g, of other variables, z, with parameters, γ, which is what we discussed above. We could even allow a random component, η_{it}, i.e. stochastic variation, in the effects of variables, which produces the random effects or random coefficients model that we will mention again below (see e.g. *Political Analysis* 2005: 13 (4)). We can do these things, though, only provided the parameters to learn in g, including those in the variance-covariance of the random effect component(s) if any, remain less than the number of contexts, NT, minus K, the number of β, minus the number of parameters involved in specifying Σ^γ and Σ^ϵ.

Alone or together, these steps will not suffice, however, because even a single variance-covariance of the stochastic components across the NT contexts, Σ^ϵ, by itself contains up to $\frac{1}{2}(NT)^{\pm 2} + \frac{1}{2}NT$ unique parameters, which far exceeds NT. (That's $\frac{1}{2}(NT+1)$ per context!) The structure of this variance-covariance gives our explicit statement as to how each context is related to and informed by all other contexts at different times and/or places. In an annual, cross-national information set, e.g. if how France 1972 relates to France 1971 may differ arbitrarily from how 1971 relates to 1970, and how France 1986 relates to Germany 1986 from how France 1987 relates to Germany 1987, etc., then degrees of freedom are negative, and comparative history can offer nothing beyond description of exclusively photographic interest. One must at this point emphasize once again that the challenge, and the inability of gathering more empirical information or of considering some contexts more closely to redress it, and so the necessity of restrictive assumptions, do not arise because we have written the proposition down formally, and do not go away if we do not. Thus, for example, when a scholar claims to have learned something useful for contexts beyond those now past and irrelevant episodes in some one or few closely studied context(s), s/he may be correct, but, if so, that must be because some assumptions restraining the generality of the allowed variance-covariance across contexts have been imposed (at least implicitly). Empirical inference was not logically possible otherwise. Perhaps seeing explicitly some of the common restrictions in standard statistical analyses would be helpful here. We begin by describing the contents of the variance-covariance matrix, Σ^ϵ, for a generic time series cross-section of information (a structure befitting comparative politics):[37]

---

[37] For tractability, (12) shows just a small, 2-unit-T-time-period example; more generally, the block structure of the variance-covariance would expand horizontally and vertically for N units.

$$V(\epsilon) \equiv V(y|X) \equiv \Sigma = \sigma^2 \Omega$$

$$= \sigma^2 \times \begin{bmatrix}
\omega_{1,1}^2 & \omega_{1,12} & \omega_{1,13} & \cdots & \omega_{1,1T} & \omega_{12,11} & \omega_{12,12} & \omega_{12,13} & \cdots & \omega_{12,1T} \\
\omega_{1,21} & \omega_{1,2}^2 & & \vdots & & \omega_{12,21} & \omega_{12,22} & & & \vdots \\
\omega_{1,31} & & \omega_{1,3}^2 & \vdots & & \omega_{12,31} & & \omega_{12,33} & & \vdots \\
\vdots & & & \ddots & \vdots & \vdots & & & \ddots & \vdots \\
\omega_{1,T1} & \cdots & \cdots & \cdots & \omega_{1,T}^2 & \omega_{12,T1} & \cdots & \cdots & \cdots & \omega_{12,TT} \\
\omega_{21,11} & \omega_{21,12} & \omega_{21,13} & \cdots & \omega_{21,1T} & \omega_{2,1}^2 & \omega_{2,12} & \omega_{2,13} & \cdots & \omega_{2,1T} \\
\omega_{21,21} & \omega_{21,22} & & \vdots & & \omega_{2,21} & \omega_{2,2}^2 & & & \vdots \\
\omega_{21,31} & & \omega_{21,33} & \vdots & & \omega_{2,31} & & \omega_{2,3}^2 & & \vdots \\
\vdots & & & \ddots & \vdots & \vdots & & & \ddots & \vdots \\
\omega_{21,T1} & \cdots & \cdots & \cdots & \omega_{21,TT} & \omega_{2,T1} & \cdots & \cdots & \cdots & \omega_{2,T}^2
\end{bmatrix}$$

(12)

Let us describe the elements of this matrix to understand better that about which we must make assumptions. We first underscore that this is the variance-covariance matrix of the stochastic component, i.e. of the residual after netting our model of the systematic component. If one theoretically or substantively expects some covariation of observations, the first move usually should be to try to model this *systematic* expectation in the *systematic* component. Given that, note next that the two blocks on the prime diagonal (top left to bottom right) are the variance-covariance matrices for units one and two respectively. The prime-diagonal elements of those submatrices give the relative variances of information sets *1* to *T* within that unit. The off-diagonal elements of these prime-diagonal blocks give the covariances of the corresponding time period observations; e.g. $\omega_{2,4}$ is the covariance of the second-period with the fourth-period observation. The entire matrix and each block submatrix are symmetric (mirrored above and below their prime diagonals) because, e.g. $\omega_{2,4} \equiv \omega_{4,2}$. The off-diagonal blocks give cross-unit covariances. The prime diagonals of these blocks give the contemporaneous (same time period) covariances, and their off diagonals give the cross-temporal cross-unit covariances. For example, $\omega_{21,11} = \omega_{11,21}$ is contemporaneous covariance in the first period across these two units, and $\omega_{21,13} = \omega_{13,21}$ is the covariance of the second unit's first period with the first unit's third period. If we leave each of these $\frac{1}{2}NT(NT+1)$ elements to differ arbitrarily, then, to put it in simple language: no time and place could offer empirical information relevant to any other time and place.

The most stringent of the common assumptions to redress this is *sphericity*, i.e. that we have sufficiently modeled in the systematic component all sources of covariation and non-constant variance across contexts, which is what ordinary least squares regression assumes: $\sigma^2 \Omega = \sigma^2 I$. This reduces the parameterization from $\frac{1}{2} NT(NT+1)$ terms to just one term to learn per NT pieces of information and thereby earns us $NT-1$ degrees of freedom to spend on enriching the model of the systematic component with interesting multicausality and context-conditionality.[38] However, such a stark assumption—it amounts to a claim that, net of our systematic-component model, each observation is an independent draw from one constant distribution[39]—may often seem implausible. Another common assumption is *panel heteroskedasticity*, which holds that sources of covariation are sufficiently modeled, but variances of the distributions from which observations are (conditional-) independently drawn may differ across contexts; e.g. one common assumption is that they may differ across units but not over time within units: $V(\epsilon_{it}) = \sigma_i^2$. This eats N degrees of freedom, leaving $NT-N$ for enriching the systematic-component model. In the temporal dimension, a common parameterization is that stochastic components correlate directly from one observation to the next, giving $\epsilon_{it} = \rho\epsilon_{i,t-1} + v$ and two parameters if this correlation, ρ, is assumed the same across units or $\epsilon_{it} = \rho_i\epsilon_{i,t-1} + v$ and $N+1$ parameters if it is assumed to differ arbitrarily, leaving $NT-2$ or $NT-N-1$ degrees of freedom. The Parks–Kmenta procedure that Beck and Katz (1995) so influentially exiled from comparative-politics practice added contemporaneous correlation of the form $\sigma_{ij} = \sigma_{ji}$, one such for each dyad ij, to unit-specific ρ_i and σ_i^2. This gives $2N+\frac{1}{2}N(N-1)$ parameters, meaning that positive degrees of freedom require $T>N$. To obtain reasonable estimates of parameter estimate uncertainty, $T \gg 2N$ seems necessary.[40]

Many other plausible parameterizations are imaginable and feasible. Researchers can in fact structure Σ however they like—that is, they can assume about the relative covariances and variances of their observed information whatever follows theoretically substantively—provided (i) that these assumptions, combined with stances taken on the other elements of their model as discussed above, yield fewer parameters to learn than pieces of information available and (ii) that researchers understand and accept that increased uncertainty and greater demand for more numerous and usefully variant information sets is unavoidably concomitant with allowing greater complexity. As always, writing the model formally clarifies, but does not create, the logical requirements for empirical evaluation just noted. A question, neither rhetorical nor intended as implicit jibe, then, is what sorts of assumptions are qualitative analysts offering about, e.g. the amount of novel information contained in each of temporally adjacent episodes from with a single context? The answers are not always clear, yet such assumptions logically must be being held whenever inferences about the empirical validity or utility of theoretical propositions are being drawn, by whatever methodological approach, from what is observed. Methodological research seeking to close qualitative-quantitative divides needs to provide better answers to such questions.

Working from the most general model downward, as we just did, counters a parsimony favoring method of theoretical development and empirical evaluation

---

[38] As our parents would say, however, don't spend it all enriching the substantive component because we will need a large number to spare to endow our estimates with any appreciable certainty!

[39] More exactly, drawn independently from one distribution or from distributions all having the same variance.

[40] The latter is because Parks–Kmenta, like any standard FGLS procedure, ignores parameters estimated in $\hat{\Sigma}$.

that would work from simplest upward. As guides to empirical practice, the latter requires evidence to sustain increasing model complexity; the former requires evidence to support reducing it. Franzese (2005, 2006) offer discussions of the possible in general empirical evaluation of positive theory in political science working from simplest models upward that are similar in motivation and spirit to the present discussion, but more technical. Conclusions therein can be summarized thus. If one can model the theoretical/substantive reasons for deviation from the classical linear regression model (CLRM), do so, and, if and insofar as one does so successfully, the strategy is optimal in all regards. Insofar as possible, "Model It!" thusly in the first-moment, $E(y)$, i.e. the systematic component, for two reasons: (i) most usually, theoretical/substantive information regards the systematic, not the stochastic, components and (ii) observationally, the only information one may obtain on the stochastic component (i.e. second moment) is conditional on information from the first moment, i.e. on one's model of the systematic component. So insufficiencies in the first-moment model will seem incorrectly to be violations of second-moment CLRM assumptions, and creditworthiness of empirical results regarding second-moment relationships is governed by that of the first-moment model. However, some theoretical propositions and substantive information do directly regard second moments (variances and covariances); e.g. education or lack thereof may induce survey respondents to answer more variably (second moment) rather than, or as well as, differently (first moment). In such cases, "Model It!" is still the advice; in second moment, this means to model a reduced parameterization of Ω. Finally, insofar as one fails to model sufficiently the theoretically/substantively expected deviations from the CLRM, problems arise essentially as omitted variable bias in worst cases, but as "just" inefficiency and incorrect standard errors in many other cases. Redresses, mostly partial and/or imperfect, of deficiencies in implementation of the "Model It!" strategy include sandwich estimators of the variance-covariance of parameter estimates (e.g. so-called *robust* standard errors, such as Beck and Katz's famous PCSE), FGLS (e.g. Parks–Kmenta), fixed-effects estimators (aka dummy variable regression), shrinkage estimators (like random effects or random coefficients, aka hierarchical, models).

The upshot of this section is that complex context-conditionality not only does not debar quantitative approaches to *general* empirical evaluation, but rather tends to demand them because empirical evaluation of theories that nest complex context-conditionality within general models that explain the nature of the conditionality across contexts logically necessarily places greater demands on precise calculation of multiple partial associations and requires greater variation across more numerous sets of information. The advantages of closer scrutiny of fewer contexts likely lie more in exploration and (potential) discovery of such conditionality, a process closer to theoretical development and refinement and, empirically, to sensitivity analysis than to general empirical evaluation.

5. ENDOGENEITY: ALMOST EVERYTHING CAUSES ALMOST EVERYTHING ELSE

The third, final, and in many ways largest of the fundamental challenges for empirical evaluation of positive theory in social science, the third way in which *context matters*, is the ubiquitous issue of endogeneity (aka, simultaneity, selection, bi- or multidirectional causality);[41] i.e. more often than not, X's cause Y's and Y's cause X's: $X \Leftrightarrow Y$. Section 2, for instance, used an example of the relationship of economic development to democratic quality, being careful to speak of association rather than cause and effect because correlation between the two could as easily derive from a causal relationship from development to democracy, from democracy to development, or both (not to mention the spurious possibilities). The likelihood of coups, social instability, and regime change, too, may increase in economic inequality or hardship, but sociopolitical instability, or expectation thereof, also hinders investment and so development (e.g. Przeworski et al. 2000; Londregan and Poole 1990). Theorized vicious or virtuous circles are another class of examples common in comparative politics. For example, trust or social capital begets well-functioning sociopolitical institutions, and such effective functionality renders rational any popular expectations of cooperation from others and the public, i.e. social capital (e.g. Putnam 1993). In a relatively neglected political-economy example, the temporal proximity of an election may induce incumbents to manipulate policies in various ways to cultivate current favor from informationally disadvantaged publics, yet public support (or trends expected therein) can strongly affect the timing of elections in some parliamentary systems (e.g. Smith 2004). Further examples are easy to amass since most everything causes most everything else in society, polity, and economy, but suffice it to note how often one study's dependent and independent variables reverse roles in another study (or later in the same study, and sometimes even simultaneously), even if direct references to bi- or multidirectional causality are not made.

We adopt once more the strategy of formalizing the positive propositions inherent in core tenets of comparative politics as a means of understanding better possible empirical leverage on them and alternative empirical-methodological approaches thereto. Let us start with a simple, two variable system: $X \Leftrightarrow Y$. Suppose a researcher only knows or is willing to argue that democracy, X, spurs development, Y, and development favors democracy; simplifying (inconsequentially for the conclusions) that both relations are linear, this gives:

$$Y = a \times X; \ X = b \times Y$$
$$\Rightarrow Y = a \times (b \times Y)$$
$$\Rightarrow ab = 1 \text{ or } a = b^{-1} \tag{13}$$

---

[41] NB, sets of definitions and usages of these terms are not entirely consistent across texts, even just within the formal statistics literature. One commonly used and useful set defines endogeneity as any covariance-of-regressor-with-residual problem, of which simultaneity and its exact synonym bi-/multidirectional causality, and selection, which is very nearly synonymous as well, are subsets. All four are used synonymously here.

If the first line were all we could say about this system, i.e., that Y is a function of (depends on) X and vice versa, then we could not say much or learn much from comparative history about this simultaneous relationship because its parameters, a and b, are *unidentified*. The last line of (13) reveals this; absent some further information, *any a* and *b* such that $a=b^{-1}$ is equally consistent with the circular proposition $X \Leftrightarrow Y$. An infinite set of (a,b) satisfies this relation, although not just any a and b. Valid (a,b) must satisfy $a=b^{-1}$; the specifications in the first line of (13) plus $X \Leftrightarrow Y$ get us this far, at least. However, without more theory, we cannot get any further toward establishing the (causal) *effect* of X on Y or of Y on X, i.e. toward gauging a or b, no matter how many sets of information we might obtain or how closely we might explore any given set(s) of information. We (logically) necessarily require *extra-empirical* information (from the usual candidates: theory, substance, or assumption).

We can see the situation graphically if we consider, e.g. a scatterplot of "democracy" (Freedom House political plus civil liberties) and "development" (real GDP per capita). In Figure 2.2, the long, downward-sloping line gives the simple linear association (regression) of democracy with (on) development. This association, however, reflects neither the effect of development on democracy, $Dem=f(Dev)$, nor the effect of democracy on development, $Dev=g(Dem)$, but rather the particular mix as of those two causal relationships that happen to have manifested across this set of contexts (sample). That is, each data point (context) gives the intersection of the two lines that happens to have occurred in that country in 1980—Figure 2.2 shows a hypothetical pair of these lines crossing through Uganda 1980—and both lines likely shift, for many reasons (multicausality and context-conditionality), from one datum to the next. As drawn in Figure 2.2, the inferential error made by

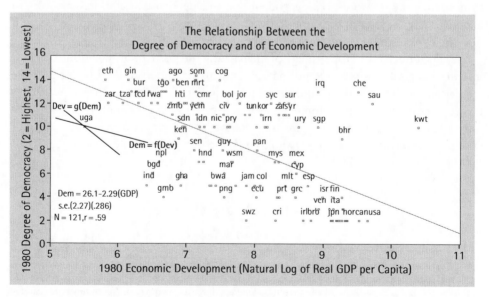

Fig. 2.2 Empirical vs. causal relationships of democracy and development

interpreting the observed association of democracy with development as the effect of development on democracy (i.e. the simultaneity bias) is appreciable. As drawn, one overestimates the impact of development on democracy, which is rather small in this example, by neglecting the rather sizeable (in this example) effect from democracy on development. The bias could be much larger still if disparity between the slopes of the multiple causal relationships were greater (going in opposite directions, for example, such as in situations paralleling supply and demand as a function of price). Biases from interpreting observed association as causal effect is not a function of how one observes the association, nor does it depend on how closely or how often one observes it. Accordingly, all of the strategies that social (and other) scientists have brought to bear upon identifying causality—(i) from imposing theoretically derived structure (assumptions) on the empirical estimation model; (ii) to experimentation in lab, survey, or field; (iii) to (propensity score) matching; (iv) to vector autoregression; to (v) "process tracing" or "causal process observations" and the like—ultimately work by adding/imposing and succeed only insofar as they add/impose (correct) *extra-empirical* information on the empirical analysis.[42] Furthermore, the correctness of the logically necessary *extra-empirical* information cannot be empirically tested directly. Przeworski (this volume) discusses causal analysis in general and most of these five broad classes of strategies for identifying causal effects in particular sufficiently for most of our present purposes, so we focus here on issues receiving less attention there. Let us, then, characterize more formally the general challenge of ubiquitous endogeneity—most everything causing most everything else—to clarify how much extra information is needed and in what forms it can come, briefly discussing these five broad classes of strategies for identifying causal effects along the way.

Consider a system of M endogenous outcomes, $\mathbf{y}$, that depend—linear additively and separably for the sake of simplicity—on each other and on K exogenous explanatory factors, $\mathbf{x}$, plus a stochastic error, ϵ, for each. In matrix notation, we can write such a system of M equations *for one empirical observation of a context, i*, as follows:

$$\begin{bmatrix} y_1 \\ y_2 \\ \vdots \\ \vdots \\ y_m \end{bmatrix}_i' \begin{bmatrix} \gamma_{11} & \gamma_{12} & \cdots & \gamma_{1M} \\ \gamma_{21} & \gamma_{22} & \cdots & \gamma_{2M} \\ \vdots & \vdots & \vdots & \vdots \\ \vdots & \vdots & \vdots & \vdots \\ \gamma_{mn} & \gamma_{m2} & \cdots & \gamma_{mm} \end{bmatrix} + \begin{bmatrix} x_1 \\ x_2 \\ x3 \\ \vdots \\ x_k \end{bmatrix}_i' \begin{bmatrix} \beta_{11} & \beta_{12} & \cdots & \beta_{1M} \\ \beta_{21} & \beta_{22} & \cdots & \beta_{2M} \\ \vdots & \vdots & \vdots & \vdots \\ \vdots & \vdots & \vdots & \vdots \\ \beta_{k1} & \beta_{k2} & \cdots & \beta_{km} \end{bmatrix} = \begin{bmatrix} \epsilon_1 \\ \epsilon_2 \\ \vdots \\ \vdots \\ \epsilon_m \end{bmatrix}_i$$

In matrix notation, the system may be written compactly as:

$$\mathbf{y}_i'\Gamma + \mathbf{x}_i'\mathbf{B} = \epsilon_i \tag{14}$$

In (14), Γ is an $M \times M$ matrix of up to M^2 coefficients on each y in each y's equation; $\mathbf{B}$ is an $K \times M$ matrix of each of the K exogenous variables' coefficients in each of the M equations; and ϵ is an $M \times 1$ vector of stochastic components of the endogenous

---

[42] Whether the extra-empirical information is added in Bayesian or Classical manner affects our discussion little, so we can safely side step that involved discussion.

variables, with a corresponding $M \times M$ matrix of variances and covariances across the equations. Variance-covariance matrices are symmetric, so $V(\epsilon) \equiv \Sigma$ has $\frac{1}{2} M^2 + \frac{1}{2} M$ unique elements. So, with each information set an empirical researcher observes on a set of M endogenous variables, she has, at most general, up to $M^2 + KM + \frac{1}{2} M(M + 1)$ parameters to learn. Luckily, the associations observed between the variables in that one information set, while not the causal effects sought (rather, some complicated mix of them as, e.g. Figure 2.2 illustrated in a simple, two-variable case), will nonetheless reduce the amount of extra information she needs to bring to the system to "tie it down" (i.e. identify it). In particular, if she simply regressed the M y's on the K x's, she would find some $\mathbf{y} = \mathbf{x}' \Pi + \mathbf{v}$, with $V(\mathbf{v}) = \Theta$, which provides $KxM + \frac{1}{2} M(M+1)$ pieces of information— namely, observed associations, variances, and covariances across equations, which are useful information, but not the causal effects sought. So, in general, for a system of M endogenous variables, we need M^2 additional, *extra-empirical* pieces of information to get valid estimates, qualitative or quantitative, of effects. The first M of those are essentially automatic. The diagonal elements in Γ are the coefficients on each y in its own equation, and so amount to arbitrary scaling coefficients, which we always set to one (because explaining y is more direct than explaining, e.g. $4y$).

Practically, then, a system of M equations requires $M(M-1)$ *extra-empirical* pieces of information, i.e. theoretical or substantive (and empirically untestable) restrictions.[43] For example, our system of two endogenous variables, democracy and development, requires two extra-empirical pieces of information. In what forms can these come? *Identities:* If some things are true for certain, say as accounting or other identities, then one can impose these facts rather than attempt to estimate them. *Exclusions:* factors from among the set of x or y that are excludable (by assumption) from some equation— identically, whose coefficient in those equations can be fixed to zero. Such "instrumental variables" assumptions are the most common econometric strategy. *Coefficient restrictions:* Exclusions can be generalized to any sort of parametric restrictions on possible coefficients for x or y variables, such as that two or more coefficients must be equal or proportional across equations. *Functional form:* the intuition is complicated for how functional-form information can help identify systems and how much applications of such strategies can buy empirical researchers. In essence, if one is willing to impose that some variable matters according to a specifically shaped function in one equation and (a) differently shaped one(s) in others, then one can leverage the difference between the imposed shapes of these relationships to help identify the system (instead of or in addition to other restrictions). *Stochastic-component variance-covariance restrictions:* How this sort of additional information, which, in different ways, is what experimentation and matching, on the one hand, and vector autoregression on the other primarily employ, works is also complicated. Experimentation and matching methods randomize on unobservables as Przeworski (this volume) describes. If such match or randomization is achieved, which, as he also notes, is not directly testable, this amounts to restricting the

---

[43] This is just the rank condition; it ensures that enough information has been added to identify M equations. The more complicated order condition ensures that *each* equation is identified. Jointly, the rank and order conditions are necessary and sufficient for identification.

variance-covariance matrix to the single parameter of the variance of that *independent* random component. Experiments also manipulate potential causes, ensuring safe exclusion of treatments applied in one equation from other system equations. The general rule for what imposition of the extra-empirical pieces of information buys empirical researchers is that each immovable fact or each fact rendered immovable by assumption yields one parameter identified.

Graphical intuition for how exclusions (and other coefficient restrictions) work may be seen by imagining in Figure 2.2 that one had another variable, say climate, that affected, say, economic development but that did not affect democracy except insofar as it affected development. Such an explanatory factor would enter the equation for development, but not directly that for democracy. As such, variation across contexts in climate would shift the $Dev = g(Dem)$ function around, but would not shift the $Dem = f(Dev)$ functions, thereby tracing out for the researcher that $Dem = f(Dev)$ causal function. Conversely, if something could be found that in parallel manner entered the $Dem = f(Dev)$ but not the $Dev = g(Dem)$ function, then the $Dev = g(Dem)$ causal function could be traced. The two extra-empirical pieces of information required to identify both equations of the system would be these untestable exclusion assumptions. Practically, in brief, one would regress development on climate and then use that prediction rather than development itself as a regressor in the democracy equation (this is the instrumental variables by two-stage least squares method).

Vector autoregression and related techniques, for their part, amount to sophisticated applications of what might be called the "poor man's exogeneity:" history. Namely, things that happened in the past are assumed exogenous to what happened later. In the strictest sense, this must be true. However, in social-science practice, expectations of the future can cause outcomes today, and, if the empirical model does not capture these expectations sufficiently, then future values of outcomes can seem to cause present ones. Similarly, expectations of contemporaneous outcomes or actions of others can shape one's own actions contemporaneously, so time lag is not always necessary for cause to induce effect in social science. Contemporaneous response can occur. Similarly, if the empirical models insufficiently capture temporal dynamics, then those inadequacies can leave future observations conditionally correlated with present ones, and so induce endogeneity. Many applications of instrumental variables strategies employ this poor man's exogeneity (i.e. endogenous variables are time-lagged and declared exogenous), as do many qualitative strategies, one suspects. The sophisticated way in which vector autoregression uses time, though, to describe its practice briefly, is to regress each endogenous variable on some number of its own time lags and of all other endogenous variables. The residuals from these regressions are then, by construction, (linearly) inexplicable by lags of any of the endogenous variables. One could in principle then use these dynamic models as estimated to trace responses (called *impulse-response functions*) of all the endogenous variables to these "inexplicable shocks" (called *innovations*). The remaining problem, though, is to determine to which variables to allocate the covariation across the equations' residuals/innovations. VAR resolves this by temporally ordering the responses, i.e., positing that some variables adjust more quickly than others.

This restricts the temporal feedback between the jointly endogenous variables and thereby identifies, not the system directly, but these impulse responses and related estimation outputs such as Granger-causality test statistics or explained-variance decompositions.

Przeworski describes how experimentation and matching achieve randomization and the issues involved therein. One might only add emphasis on two aspects of his discussion for our purposes. First, randomization requires large samples to achieve its beneficial effects reliably. That is, even if, in making causal comparisons, we believe that unobserved factors are drawn independent-randomly, having just one or very few such comparisons would render the estimate's unbiasedness (being correct on average or in expectation *across many draws*) cold comfort and would not suffice to draw any solace from the consistency (being exactly right with no uncertainty *as the number of draws approaches infinity*). Thus, "quasi-experimental" and matching-like logics are problematic bases for drawing causal inference from small numbers of information sets. Second, the stable unit treatment value assumption (SUTVA) underlying matching methods, in particular (but not solely) the implication of SUTVA that one unit's receipt of the treatment does not affect the receipt by, or the value of the treatment to, other units, seems implausible for many comparative politics applications. One could hardly imagine, for instance, that the nature of the regime in one country had no effect on regimes or their effects in others, as matching methods would require for valid estimates from an observational study of the effects of regime type.

Tracing episodes through "causal-process observations" (e.g. Brady and Collier 2004; Bennett and Elman 2006) or similar methods of close and careful qualitative analysis (e.g. Hall 2003) have been advocated as particularly effective strategies for assessing (complex) causality. All of the potential sources of additional information logically necessary to evaluate and gauge causality are as available to qualitative as to quantitative empirical methods, so this may be. Indeed, since the necessary information is *extra-empirical*, whether one employs qualitative or quantitative approaches while imposing that extra information is largely irrelevant; conversely, though, the choice of qualitative or quantitative approach will not *ipso facto* provide the logically necessary extra-empirical information. Simply tracing some process (set of episodes) through time to establish which movements or episodes occur in what order, for example, would seem to be familiar assertion of the poor man's exogeneity, and so to come with that instrument's drawbacks or caveats regarding expectations and the need to specify very precisely and sufficiently the dynamics of the process. Process tracing may also involve analogs to experimental or matching analyses if, for example, closer scrutiny enables the researcher to hold with greater substantive-theoretical certainty that particular moving factors in their account could only have moved exogenously.[44] However, notable relative weaknesses plague qualitative analogs

---

[44] Empirical certainty, on the other hand, that some factors have moved exogenously should probably be seen as problematic if not impossible to ascertain because any observed associations, seen closely or distantly, in numerous or in scant contexts, can be misleading about causality and so endogeneity and exogeneity.

to experimental and instrumental strategies: namely, the precision in model specifi-cation necessary to effective instrumental strategies is not a relative strength of the approach, and the randomization that undergirds experimental and matching ap-proaches provides only very weak basis for confidence in comparisons of few contexts. More promisingly analogous, therefore, may be the vector autoregression approach of distilling innovations from that which is predictable from raw dynamics of the endogenous variables, imposing a temporal ordering to the incidence of those impulses, and tracing responses thereto. If so, considerable work translating the logic of that identification strategy to something understandable in qualitative analysis terms remains. Finally, note that the issues discussed in previous sections regarding quality–quantity tradeoffs, multicausality and the difficulty of ascertaining partial associations, and the challenge of modeling and assessing (complex) context-conditionality—all pervade and compound this already thorniest of challenges for empirical evaluation of social science theory, ubiquitous (and perhaps complex) endogeneity. To evaluate causality and gauge causal effects from comparative history, in other words, requires effective redress of all these challenges. Once again, then, vis-à-vis general empirical evaluation, writing explicitly the logical challenges for empirical evaluation associated with this central tenet of *context matters*—most everything causes most everything else—seems to indicate that, far from debarring quantitative analysis, ubiquitous and complex endogeneity tends to demand it.

6 CONCLUSION: CONTEXT MATTERS, SO MODEL IT!

In an influential critique of empirical practice in comparative politics that similarly emphasizes that *context matters*, Hall (2003) argues for close empirical analysis of several (i.e., more than the one or very few of one end of current practice, less than the many of the other), raising these concerns about regression analysis in comparative politics:

... [1] the types of regression analyses commonly used to study comparative politics provide valid support for causal inferences only if the causal relations they are examining meet a rigorous set of assumptions (see Wallerstein 2000). [2] In general, this method assumes unit homogeneity, which is to say that, other things being equal, a change in the value of a causal variable x will produce a corresponding change in the value of the outcome variable y of the same magnitude across all the cases. [3] It assumes no systematic correlation between the causal variables included in the analysis and other causal variables omitted from it. [4] It assumes that all the relevant interaction effects among the causal variables have been captured by interaction terms in the regression. [5] It assumes that the cases are fully independent, such that [6] the values of the causal variables in one case are unaffected by the value of the causal variables or outcomes in other cases. [7] Although instrumental variables can sometimes be used, most regression analyses assume that there is no reciprocal causation, i.e. that the causal variables are unaffected by the dependent variable...

Here we have engaged and continued the discussion by expressing formally the specific multicausal, context-conditional, and ubiquitous-endogeneity propositions entailed in the *context matters* central tenet of comparative politics. We have done so to clarify the logical requirements of empirical evaluation from comparative history in general, and some of the specific approaches to fulfilling those requirements that quantitative methods employ. That, in turn, may help clarify what the corresponding moves to fulfill those requirements might be in qualitative methods and help to define and to characterize more sharply the terms of any tradeoffs between the approaches. Thus, we have seen that, regarding Hall's concerns: [1] rigorous assumptions are necessary to valid support for causal inferences by any methodology; moreover, any set of assumptions chosen must achieve the same things in terms of parameter reduction and the like to allow meaningful empirical inference from comparative history. [2] Context-conditionality, regardless of complexity, can be modeled, estimated, and interpreted quantitatively provided the context-conditional propositions are logically consistent and that sufficient empirical information logically could exist to gauge them;[45] if insufficient information actually exists in comparative history to estimate these relations well, it is unlikely that restriction to narrower sets of contexts will add the needed further contextual variation, and increased quality of information is unlikely to compensate sufficiently. [3], [4] If potential causal factors, whether interactive or simple causes, are omitted from analysis, whether qualitative or quantitative, inferences will be biased if the omitted are indeed causal and also correlate with the included. Likewise, however, equally valid concerns should be considered regarding excess complication of empirical analyses (Achen 2002). [5], [6] One need not assume independence of outcomes[46] across contexts (e.g. time and/or place), but, by any method of analysis, one must assume some pattern of correlation across contexts that reduces the information needed to gauge and account for that interdependence of outcomes sufficiently to leave enough free information from the available comparative history to infer something also about the systematic aspect of the proposition being analyzed empirically.[47] [7] The severe challenge that reciprocal

---

[45] Later, Hall lists some manifestations of contextual complexity seen as challenges for regression analysis in particular. *"i. We find instances in which an increase in x (level of economic development) causes an increase in y (movement toward democracy) in some cases but does not have this effect in others, where y is caused by an entirely different set of variables, w. ii. We find cases in which an increase in x (social democratic governance) is associated with an increase in y (social spending) at one point in time, t1, but not at another point in time, t2. iii. We find instances in which an increase in x (social protest) causes an outcome y (government turnover) in some cases but an entirely different outcome (repression) in other cases. iv. We find instances in which an outcome y (successful wage coordination) depends on the value of many other variables, v (union density) w (social democratic governance), and x (social policy regime), whose values are in turn jointly dependent on each other. v. We find cases in which increases in x (support for democracy) increase y (the stability of democracy) and in which increases in y also tend to increase x."* Each of these, e.g., is easily written as an estimable empirical model. The open-endedness of some qualitative analysis may allow researchers to discover signs of such context-conditionality, but whatever systematically context-conditional propositions may emerge cannot be well evaluated empirically in the same discovery process.

[46] The dependence or independence of explanatory factors is not an issue (for any method of analysis) unless these explanatory factors are also endogenous to outcomes.

[47] Moreover, assumptions of identical data-generating processes or independence in statistical analysis, if the analyst does make such assumptions, regard Y|X and not Y. That is, these assumptions apply to the outcome and scenarios being compared *controlling for* the actual empirical model on offer. If one thinks context alters the effects of some X, for example, then one can and should model this modification of effects in Y|X.

causation raises for empirical evaluation requires *extra-empirical* information to resolve; therefore, no particular empirical methodology or approach brings such information by itself or enjoys any inherent advantage in generating it. Using such extra-empirical information effectively to explore endogenous relationships, however, does seem to require a certain mathematical precision in processing the empirical and extra-empirical information that may favor quantitative strategies. The same seems true regarding the partialing of evidence related to multicausal and/or context-conditional relationships in general.

The biggest and fundamental challenges for empirical evaluation in comparative politics—multicausality, context-conditionality, endogeneity—inhere logically in the nature of the theoretical processes argued to be present and being considered for empirical evaluation: *context matters.* That implies that any approach we may offer for obtaining useful empirical leverage on such propositions must somehow address these same logically inherent challenges. By any approach, if we believe we have learned something useful as anything more than a photograph of some specific scenario(s), a photo that is wholly useless in any other scenario (tomorrow in the same exact geographic, cultural, strategic, etc., context, for example), then we must have offered, implicitly or explicitly, some redress of those challenges—and always and everywhere, it will be partial redress. In other words, if one claims to have learned something from the comparative historical record that is of use for anything beyond solely describing that now-gone situation—and explaining that situation is as beyond describing it as is understanding by that analysis of that situation something useful in other, related situations—and regardless of whether one has used that comparative historical record in statistical or some other kind of analysis to get this *understanding-beyond-description*— then one must assume, implicitly or explicitly, something about how these multicausal, context-conditional, and/or endogenous relations in this scenario relate to those in other scenarios. (Indeed, even photographic description may be impossible without some minimal stands on these issues.)

One can tell what these necessary parameter-reducing assumptions are in a given statistical model—e.g. that the effect of X is a constant in all contexts like those in the sample, or that the effect of X depends on (only) Z (linear additively), etc. These sorts of necessary assumptions tend to be similar but—more flatteringly put: *flexible*; pejoratively put: *arbitrary*; perhaps fairly put: *subjective*—in qualitative methods. In any event, this sort of flexibility is not a virtue in providing general empirical evaluation. Moreover, we have increasingly found over the course of our discussion here that contextual complexity, far from arguing for closer analysis of narrower sets of contexts, tends almost universally to argue strongly against it *for purposes of general empirical evaluation.* We hasten here to reiterate, as we had at the start, that qualitative analysis is an essential part of the scientific enterprise. These methods have particular advantages that seem, however, to have little to do with general empirical evaluation of multicausal, context-conditional, and ubiquitously endogenous relationships. Their great advantages seem instead to lie most heavily in ascertaining and validating conceptualization and measurement quality, in exploring applicability, sensitivity, and robustness, and in developing and refining theory. The advantages lie in those equally essential parts of the iterative continuum of theoretical development and empirical analysis rather than in general empirical evaluation—after all, narrower deeper focus is precisely *not* broad and general. This theory-building/empirical-evaluation iteration is also more continuous in qualitative and more discrete in quantitative analyses, which greater merging of the acts of theory building and empirical evaluation in the former is also not a virtue in terms of general empirical evaluation. Conversely, the weaker points tend to lie precisely in the areas of empirical evaluation of those theories given those given concepts and measures, in fact especially in empirical evaluation of multicausal, context-conditional, endogenous relations. Put more crudely than perhaps it should be: qualitative empirical analyses tend to be robustness checks, sensitivity analyses, stress tests, and field tests—after having built a new power tool and tested it in the lab to show its general safety and efficacy, one also gives it to some carpenters to use in the field to discover whether it is ultimately useful!—more than general tests. Far greater strengths for the approach lie in its potential for theory building and refinement.

Viewing this comparison of the relative effectiveness of the approaches in different aspects of the broader scientific endeavor as a competition is rather pointless, though. Provided that we all share the same or very similar overarching goals—"theoretically and empirically useful understandings" may perhaps be reasonably uncontroversial—and that we all (reasonably accurately, in our own way) understand and accept the tradeoffs along the frontier of the achievable (certainly we will, and to a certain extent should, continue to argue about the precise terms of the tradeoffs and location of the frontier though), then we can also perhaps agree that the particular vector one takes to that frontier is more a matter of taste, and that good and productive work is defined by its proximity to, and perhaps furthering of, that frontier rather than the vector it chooses. *A* probably needn't worry so much what vector *B* chooses; if *B* pushes the frontier out along her particular vector, then *A* can get further along his vector and vice versa. That is, this rosy scenario would obtain *if* we have some means of communicating, a common goal, and perhaps some common understanding of/standards for progress, toward which end hopefully this chapter has been of some utility to at least one researcher other than its author.

REFERENCES

ACHEN, C. 1985. Proxy variables and incorrect signs on regression coefficients. *Political Methodology*, 11 (3–4): 299–316.

—— 2002. Towards a new political methodology: microfoundations and ART. *Annual Review of Political Science*, 5: 423–50.

ALMOND, G. 1956. Comparative political systems. *Journal of Politics*, 18 (3): 391–409.

—— and VERBA, S. 1963. *The Civic Culture*. Princeton: Princeton University Press.

BECK, N., and KATZ, J. N. 1995. What to do (and not to do) with time-series cross-section data. *American Political Science Review*, 89: 634–47.

BENNETT, A., and ELMAN, C. 2006. Complex causal relations and case study methods: the example of path dependence. *Political Analysis*, 14: 250–67.

BERGER, S. ed. 1981. *Organizing Interests in Western Europe*. Cambridge: Cambridge University Press.

BOIX, C. 1998. *Political Parties, Growth, and Equality*. Cambridge: Cambridge University Press.

BRADY, H., and COLLIER, D. 2004. *Rethinking Social Inquiry: Diverse Tools, Shared Standards*. Lanham, Md.: Rowman & Littlefield.

BRAMBOR, T., CLARK, W. R., and GOLDER, M. 2006. Understanding interaction models: improving empirical analyses. *Political Analysis*, 14 (1): 63–82.

CAMERON, D. 1984. Social democracy, corporatism, labor quiescence and representation of economic interest in advanced capitalist society. Pp. 143–78 in *Order and Conflict in Contemporary Capitalism*, ed. J. Goldthorpe. Oxford: Clarendon Press.

COX, G. 1997. *Making Votes Count*. Cambridge: Cambridge University Press.

DAHL, R. 1971. *Polyarchy*. New Haven: Yale University Press.

DEUTSCH, K. 1971. Social mobilization and political development. Pp. 384–401 in *Political Development and Social Change*, ed. J. Finkle and R. Gable. New York: Wiley.

DODD, L. 1976. *Coalitions in Parliamentary Government*. Princeton: Princeton University Press.

DUNCAN, D. 1975. *Introduction to Structural Equation Models*. New York: Academic Press.

FRANZESE, R. J., Jr. 1999. Partially independent central banks, politically responsive governments, and inflation. *American Journal of Political Science*, 43 (3): 681–706.

—— 2002a. Electoral and partisan cycles in economic policies and outcomes. *Annual Review of Political Science*, 5: 369–421.

—— 2002b. *Macroeconomic Policies of Developed Democracies*. Cambridge: Cambridge University Press.

—— 2003. Multiple hands on the wheel: empirically modeling partial delegation and shared control of monetary policy in the open and institutionalized economy. *Political Analysis*, 11 (4): 445–74.

—— 2005. Empirical strategies for various manifestations of multilevel data. *Political Analysis*, 13 (4): 430–46.

—— 2006. Models for time-series-cross-section data. Lectures at Academia Sinica, Taipei, Taiwan.

—— and HAYS, J. C. 2006. Spatio-temporal models for political-science panel and time-series-cross-section data. Paper presented at the 2006 Summer Meetings of the Political Methodology Society, Davis, California. **http://polmeth.wustl.edu/retrieve.php?id=626**

—— and NOORUDDIN, I. 2002. Geographic and partisan bases of representation: distributive politics and the effective number of constituencies. Department of Political Science, University of Michigan—Ann Arbor.

GARRETT, G. 1998. *Partisan Politics in the Global Economy*. Cambridge: Cambridge University Press.

HALL, P. 1986. *Governing the Economy*. Oxford: Oxford University Press.

—— 2003. Aligning ontology and methodology in comparative research. Pp. 333–72 in *Comparative Historical Analysis in the Social Sciences*, ed. J. Mahoney and D. Rueschemeyer. Cambridge: Cambridge University Press.

—— and SOSKICE, D., eds. 2001. *Varieties of Capitalism*. Oxford: Oxford University Press.

HUNTINGTON, S. P. 1991. *The Third Wave: Democratization in the Late Twentieth Century*. Lincoln: University of Oklahoma Press.

INGLEHART, R. 1990. *Culture Shift in Advanced Industrial Society*. Princeton: Princeton University Press.

Ip, E. 2001. Visualizing multiple regression. *Journal of Statistics Education,* 9 (1): **www.amstat. org/publications/jse/v9n1/ip.html**

Jackson, J. E. 1996. Political methodology: an overview. Pp. 717–48 in *A New Handbook of Political Science,* ed. R. Goodin and H.-D. Klingemann. Oxford: Oxford University Press.

Kam, C. D., and Franzese, R. J., Jr. Forthcoming. *Modeling and Interpreting Interactive Hypotheses in Regression Analysis.* Ann Arbor: University of Michigan Press. **www.press. umich.edu/titleDetailDesc.do?id=206871**

Kedar, O. 2002. Policy balancing in comparative context: institutional mediation of voter behavior. Ph.D. dissertation. Cambridge, Mass.: Harvard University.

King, G., Keohane, R., and Verba, S. 1994. *Designing Social Inquiry.* Princeton: Princeton University Press.

Lehmbruch, G., and Schmitter, P. eds. 1982. *Patterns of Corporatist Intermediation.* Beverly Hills, Calif.: Sage Publications.

Lijphart, A. 1971. Comparative politics and the comparative method. *American Political Science Review,* 64 (3): 682–93.

——1984. *Democracies.* New Haven: Yale University Press.

——1994. *Electoral Systems and Party Systems.* Oxford: Oxford University Press.

Lipset, S. M. 1960. *Political Man.* Garden City, NY: Doubleday Press.

Londregan, J. B., and Poole, K. T. 1990. Poverty, the coup trap, and the seizure of executive power. *World Politics,* 42 (2): 151–83.

Ordeshook, P., and Shvetsova, O. 1994. Ethnic heterogeneity, district magnitude, and the number of parties. *American Journal of Political Science,* 38 (1): 100–23.

Political Analysis. 2005. Special Issue: Multilevel modeling for large clusters. 13 (4).

——2006. Special Issue: Causal complexity and qualitative methods. 14 (3).

Powell, G. B., Jr. 1982. *Contemporary Democracies.* Cambridge, Mass.: Harvard University Press.

Przeworski, A., and Teune, H. 1970. *The Logic of Comparative Social Inquiry.* New York: Wiley.

——Alvarez, M. E., Cheibub, J. A., and Limongi, F. 2000. *Democracy and Development: Political Institutions and Well-Being in the World, 1950–1990.* Cambridge: Cambridge University Press.

Putnam, R. 1993. *Making Democracy Work: Civic Traditions in Modern Italy.* Princeton: Princeton University Press.

Rae, D. 1967. *The Political Consequences of Electoral Laws.* New Haven: Yale University Press.

Riker, W. 1962. *The Theory of Political Coalitions.* New Haven: Yale University Press.

Rogowski, R. 2004. How inference in the social (but not the physical) sciences neglects theoretical anomaly. Pp. 75–84 in *Rethinking Social Inquiry: Diverse Tools, Shared Standards,* ed. H. Brady and D. Collier. Lanham, Md.: Rowman & Littlefield.

Sartori, G. 1976. *Parties and Party Systems.* Cambridge: Cambridge University Press.

Smith, A. 2004. *Election Timing.* Cambridge: Cambridge University Press.

Smith, G. 1972. *Politics in Western Europe.* New York: Holmes & Meier Publishers.

Swank, D. 2002. *Global Capital, Political Institutions, and Policy Change in Developed Welfare States.* Cambridge: Cambridge University Press.

Tsebelis, G. 2002. *Veto Players: How Institutions Work.* Princeton: Princeton University Press.

Wallerstein, M. 2000. Trying to navigate between Scylla and Charybdis: misspecified and unidentified models in comparative politics. *APSA-CP: Newsletter for the Organized Section in Comparative Politics of the American Political Science Association,* 11 (2): 1–21.

CHAPTER 3

HISTORICAL ENQUIRY AND COMPARATIVE POLITICS

JAMES MAHONEY
CELSO M. VILLEGAS

HISTORICAL enquiry has always been central to the field of comparative politics. Scholars from Alexis de Tocqueville and Max Weber to Gabriel Almond and Seymour Martin Lipset to Theda Skocpol and Margaret Levi have explained political dynamics by comparing the historical trajectories of two or more cases. In doing so, they have suggested that the roots of major political outcomes often rest most fundamentally with causal processes found well in the past. Moreover, they have maintained that to elucidate these causal processes one must look closely at the unfolding of events over substantial periods of time.

Comparative analysts who engage in historical enquiry have explored topics almost as varied as those that characterize contemporary political science. And they have developed explanations that cross the full gamut of theoretical orientations in the field. One cannot therefore delimit historical analysis by subject matter or theoretical orientation. Nevertheless, comparativists who practice historical analysis do employ a distinctive approach to asking and answering questions. Most basically,

* James Mahoney's work on this project is supported by the National Science Foundation under Grant No. 0093754. We thank Carles Boix and Susan Stokes for helpful comments on a previous draft.

these analysts ask questions about the causes of major outcomes in particular cases. The goal of their analyses then becomes explaining adequately the specific historical outcomes in each and every case that falls within their argument's scope (Mahoney and Rueschemeyer 2003). By adopting this approach, historical researchers differ from cross-national statistical analysts, who are concerned with generalizing about average causal effects for large populations and who do not ordinarily seek to explain specific outcomes in particular cases. Whereas a cross-national statistical analyst might ask about the average causal effect of development on democracy for a large population of cases, a historical researcher will ask about the causal factors that make possible or combine to produce democracy in one or more particular cases (Mahoney and Goertz 2006). Or, to cite actual research, historical analysts ask about the causes of contrasting state-regime complexes in specific early modern European cases (Downing 1992; Ertman 1997; Tilly 1990); the factors that wrought different kinds of welfare states in the advanced capitalist countries (Esping-Andersen 1990; Hicks 1999; Huber and Stephens 2001); the origins of social revolution in certain types of historical and contemporary countries (Foran 2005; Goldstone 1991; Skocpol 1979); and the sources of democracy and dictatorship in regions such as Central America (Mahoney 2001; Paige 1997; Yashar 1997). In each of these research areas, the goal of analysis is to explain specific outcomes of interest in the particular sets of cases under investigation.[1]

This orientation to asking and answering questions is associated with at least three other methodological traits which also help us to recognize historical research as a singular approach within comparative politics. First, historical analysts employ their own distinctive tools of causal analysis. Some of these tools involve techniques for analyzing necessary and/or sufficient causes, whereas others entail procedures for assessing hypotheses through within-case analysis. Both kinds of techniques contrast in major ways with statistical methods (Brady and Collier 2004; George and Bennett 2005; Mahoney 2004; Mahoney and Goertz 2006). Second, historical analysts are centrally concerned with the temporal dimensions of political explanation. To account for the occurrence of specific outcomes, they attribute great causal weight to the duration, pace, and timing of events (Pierson 2004; Thelen 2003). Finally, historical researchers develop a deep understanding of their major cases and establish a strong background in the relevant historiography. This kind of case expertise is essential for the successful explanation of particular outcomes in specific cases, and it is achieved through the mastery of secondary and/or primary source material (Skocpol 1984; Ragin 1987). Here we explore each of these three traits in turn.

---

[1] It bears emphasis that historical researchers often generalize their explanations across all cases that fall within their theory scope. However, the scope of their theory—defined as a domain in which assumptions of causal homogeneity are valid—is usually restricted to a small to medium number of cases. For a discussion, see Mahoney and Rueschemeyer (2003, 7–10); Mahoney and Goertz (2006).

1 METHODS OF CAUSAL ANALYSIS

1.1 Cross-Case Analysis

Early discussions of cross-case analysis and hypothesis testing in historical research usually focused on Mill's methods of agreement and difference (e.g. Skocpol and Somers 1980) and Przeworski and Teune's (1970) most similar and most different research designs. In more recent periods, however, the methodology of necessary and sufficient conditions, Boolean algebra, and fuzzy-set logic have superseded earlier formulations (e.g. Goertz and Starr 2003; Ragin 1987, 2000).

Mill's methods of agreement and difference are tools for eliminating necessary and sufficient causes (see Dion 1998; George and Bennett 2005; Mahoney 1999). The method of agreement is used to eliminate potential *necessary* causes, whereas the method of difference is used to eliminate potential *sufficient* causes. The methods usually operate deterministically, such that a single deviation from a hypothesized pattern of necessary or sufficient causation is enough to conclude that a given factor is not (by itself) necessary or sufficient for the outcome of interest. While this deterministic approach is controversial,[2] methodologists agree that it is essential to the ability of the methods of agreement and difference to systematically eliminate rival hypotheses when only a small number of cases are selected.

Methods designed to test necessary and/or sufficient causes need not be deterministic, however. One can easily evaluate causes that are necessary or sufficient at some quantitative benchmark, such as necessary or sufficient 90 percent of the time (e.g. Braumoeller and Goertz 2000; Dion 1998; Ragin 2000). And if a modest number of cases is selected (e.g. $N = 15$), scholars can achieve standard levels of statistical confidence for their findings. Likewise, there is no reason why one needs to use dichotomous variables when testing hypotheses about necessary or sufficient causation. For example, necessary causation can mean that the absence of a particular range of values on a continuously coded independent variable will always (or usually) be associated with the absence of a particular range of values on a continuously coded dependent variable.

In comparative politics, a widely used method of cross-case analysis is typological theory (George and Bennett 2005). With this technique, one treats the dimensions of a typology as independent variables; different values on the dimensions reflect alternative values on independent variables. The categories or "types" in the cells of the typology represent the values on the dependent variable. The dimensions of the typology are thus hypothesized to be jointly (not individually) sufficient for particular values on the dependent variable. There are numerous examples of works

---

[2] Statistical methodologists usually assume that determinism is wholly inappropriate for the social sciences (e.g. Lieberson 1991; Goldthorpe 1997). Some qualitative methodologists share this view. However, determinism can be justified on the grounds that, when one is *not* generalizing from a sample to large population, but rather explaining particular cases, it is meaningless to say that a cause exerts a probabilistic effect. For any particular case, a cause either exerts a given effect or it does not.

in comparative politics that implicitly or explicitly employ this kind of typological theory—Downing's (1992) study of political regimes in Europe, Goodwin's (2001) work on revolutions, and Jones-Luong's (2002) analysis of party and electoral system dynamics, for example.

Other methods evaluate necessary and sufficient causes with more formal techniques. Perhaps the best known of these is Boolean algebra (Ragin 1987), which is used to test whether combinations of dichotomous variables are jointly sufficient for an outcome. Because several different combinations of factors may each be causally sufficient, this method allows for multiple paths to the same outcome, or what is sometimes called equifinality. More recently, Ragin (2000) has introduced fuzzy-set analysis to assess continuously coded variables within a probabilistic Boolean framework. Dozens of comparative studies have now used Ragin's techniques for testing hypotheses about necessary and sufficient causes (see the citations at **www.compasss.org/**).

To conclude, cross-case analysis usually involves the assessment of hypotheses about necessary and/or sufficient causation, and a whole class of methodologies exists for testing these kinds of hypotheses. By contrast, as multiple methodologists (both qualitative and quantitative) have pointed out, mainstream statistical techniques are not designed for the analysis of necessary and sufficient causes (Braumoeller 2003; Goertz and Starr 2003; but see Clark, Gilligan, and Golder 2006).

1.2 Within-Case Analysis

Writings on within-case analysis have a distinguished pedigree in the field of qualitative methods (e.g. Barton and Lazarsfeld 1969; Campbell 1975; George and McKeown 1985). In recent years, there has been considerable effort to formally codify the specific procedures entailed in different modes of within-case analysis (e.g. George and Bennett 2005; Brady and Collier 2004; Mahoney 1999). We briefly discuss some of these procedures.

First, some historical researchers use insights from within their cases to locate the intervening mechanisms linking a hypothesized explanatory variable to an outcome. These scholars follow methodological writings that suggest that causal analysis not only involves establishing an association between explanatory variables and an outcome variable, but also entails identifying the intervening mechanisms that link explanatory variables with the outcome variable (Hedstrom and Swedberg 1998; Goldthorpe 2000). Intervening mechanisms are the processes through which an explanatory variable produces a causal effect. The effort to infer causality through the identification of mechanisms can be called "process tracing" (George and McKeown 1985; George and Bennett 2005) and the data thereby generated are "causal-process observations" (Brady and Collier 2004).

Process tracing is often used to help analysts who work with a small number of cases avoid mistaking a spurious correlation for a causal association. Specifically, mechanisms that clearly link a presumed explanatory variable and outcome variable increase one's confidence in the hypothesis. For example, Skocpol's (1979, 170–1) work on the origins of social revolutions employs process tracing to reject the hypothesis that ideologically motivated vanguard movements caused social revolutions. Although ideologically motivated vanguard movements were active in her three cases of social revolution, she contends that they were not responsible for triggering widespread revolts against landlords and states. Rather, the movements were marginal to the central political processes that characterized social revolutions in France, Russia, and China, appearing on the scene only to take advantage of situations they did not create.

Other scholars use process tracing not to eliminate causal factors but to support their own explanations. For example, Collier and Collier (1991) identify mechanisms linking different types of labor incorporation periods with different types of party systems. In their analysis of Colombia and Uruguay, Collier and Collier systematically identify the processes and events through which the incorporation pattern of "electoral mobilization by a traditional party" led to the party system outcome of "electoral stability and social conflict." These processes included: a period in which the party that oversaw incorporation briefly maintained power, the gradual emergence of conservative opposition, a period of intense political polarization, a military coup, and, finally, the creation of party system marked by stable electoral politics and social conflict. Each of these events acts as a mechanism linking labor incorporation with a particular party system outcome. Indeed, although any work can potentially benefit from process tracing, it is an especially important tool for those studies such as Collier and Collier's in which explanatory and outcome variables are separated by long periods of time.

A given hypothesis might suggest specific features of a case besides the main outcome that should be present if the central hypothesis is correct. These features need not be intervening variables. Thus, some historical researchers use within-case analysis not to identify intervening mechanisms, but to evaluate whether certain hypothesized features are in fact present. This is how Marx (1998) proceeds in his comparative study of racial orders in the United States, South Africa, and Brazil. He asserts that where whites were divided, as in the US and South Africa following the Civil War and Boer War, white unity and nationalist loyalty were forged through the construction of systems of racial domination that systematically excluded blacks. Where no major intra-white cleavage developed, as in Brazil, whites did not have to achieve unity through exclusion and thus a much higher degree of racial harmony could develop.

Marx supports this argument using within-case evidence that confirms implicit and explicit predictions about other things that should be true if this argument is valid. For instance, Marx suggests that, if intra-white conflict really is decisive, efforts to enhance black status should produce increased white conflict along the North–South fault line in the US and between British and Afrikaners in South Africa. By contrast, progressive racial reforms should not generate similar intra-white divisions in Brazil. Likewise, if intra-white divisions really are the key, then Marx suggests that we should see evidence that more progressive white factions view political stability as more important than racial equality. His historical narrative then backs up these propositions. Overall, he suggests that it is highly unlikely that these auxiliary facts are accidental; rather, he contends that they are symptoms of a valid main thesis.

2 METHODS OF TEMPORAL ANALYSIS

....

Historical enquiry in comparative politics is sensitive to temporal processes. Researchers often understand cases as spatial units within which one observes patterns of temporally ordered events, such as sequences, cycles, and abrupt changes. While statistical researchers will sometimes develop hypotheses that consider temporal dimensions, the focus of historical researchers on specific outcomes in particular cases calls central attention to temporality. At the level of particular cases, issues of timing and sequencing often seem paramount in a way that may not be true when one wishes to generalize about averages for large populations using available quantitative data. Hence, when a historical researcher hypothesizes that "X is causally related to Y," it is quite likely that variable X is defined in part by temporal dimensions, such as its duration or its location in time vis-à-vis other variables. In this sense, "history matters" to comparative-historical researchers in part because temporally defined concepts are key variables of analysis. We can examine here three temporal concepts that historical researchers use frequently: path dependence, duration, and conjuncture.

2.1 Path Dependence

The concept of path dependence is associated with the effort of researchers to understand the repercussions of early events on subsequent and possibly historically distant outcomes. A quite significant literature in economics, political science, and sociology now exists to codify the various tools of analysis used to study path-dependent sequences (Arthur 1994; David 1985; Goldstone 1998; North 1990; Pierson 2000, 2004; Mahoney 2000; see also Clemens and Cook 1999; Collier and Collier 1991; Thelen 2003). For our purposes, two examples illustrate the breadth of the use of this concept.

Goldstone (1998, 2007) argues that the industrial revolution in England was the result of path-dependent process. He contends that "there was nothing necessary or inevitable" about England's breakthrough to modern industrialism (1998, 275). Rather, the outcome was a product of a number of small events that happened to come together in eighteenth-century England. Perhaps most importantly, the industrial revolution depended on the advent of Thomas Newcomen's first steam engine in 1712—it made possible the subsequent creation of more efficient steam engines that dramatically improved the extraction of coal. Efficient coal extraction reduced the price of coal. In turn:

Cheap coal made possible cheaper iron and steel. Cheap coal plus cheap iron made possible the construction of railways and ships built of iron, fueled by coal, and powered by engines producing steam. Railways and ships made possible mass national and international distribution of metal tools, textiles, and other products that could be more cheaply made with steam-powered metal-reinforced machinery. (1998, 275)

Thus, the sequence of events leading to the industrial revolution ultimately depended on the advent of the first steam engine. Yet, Newcomen did not pursue his invention in order to spur an industrial revolution. Instead, he was trying to devise a means to pump water from deep-shaft coal mines: the steam engine removed water by turning it into vapor. It was necessary to remove water from the mine shafts because the surface coal of the mines had been exhausted, which had led the miners to dig deeper, which had caused the mines to fill with water. And of course the surface coal of the mines was exhausted in the first place because England was exceptionally dependent on coal for heating. Going even further back, as Goldstone does, England was dependent on coal (rather than wood) because of its limited forest area, its cold climate, and its geology, which featured thick seams of coal near the sea.

Orren's (1991) study of *Belated Feudalism* offers a different kind of example of path dependence, one in which path dependence involves the stable reproduction of a particular outcome. Orren calls attention to the remarkable persistence of status-based labor legislation in the United States. From its inception until well into the twentieth century, the United States legally defined all able-bodied individuals without independent wealth as workers who could be subject to criminal charges for not selling their labor in the marketplace. This "law of master and servant" was originally established in feudal England, but it managed to carry over into the United States, and it then persisted for more than 150 years despite the supposed liberal orientation of American culture.

To explain this specific outcome, Orren emphasizes the key role of American courts in upholding the law. In her view, judges enforced the law because they believed it was legitimate, even though it increasingly clashed with American mores and norms. Specifically, "the judges believed that what was as stake was no less than the moral order of things," and hence upheld the law (Orren 1991, 114). Orren emphasizes that American judges did not follow precedent simply because of personal gain (1991, 90). Likewise, she contends that judges did not simply support legislation on behalf of the interests of economic elites, even though the employment legislation clearly benefited employers (1991, 91). Rather, she argues "that the law of labor relations was on its own historical track, and that it carried protection of business interests along for the ride" (1991, 112).

In both examples of path dependence, Goldstone and Orren identify "critical junctures" where events early in the process have lasting effects, even after those initial causes have disappeared. Scholars using the critical juncture concept emphasize how such events are contingent—that is, they are unpredictable by theory or perhaps truly random (Mahoney 2000; David 1985)—and focus on how these events, at that time, were hardly an indication of the path to follow. The invention of the Newcomen steam engine in England affecting the industrial revolution is a case in point: Newcomen did not intend to begin an industrial revolution, nor was his machine heralded at that time as the harbinger of the tremendous transformation to come, yet it spurred a series of events that led England down an unrepeatable path towards industrialization.

Other scholars have focused on important political choices during critical juncture periods whose institutional implications were unforeseen, but would have significant results in the future. Collier and Collier's (1991) study of labor incorporation provides the iconic example of critical junctures—the means by which political elites managed the introduction of labor into the political sphere had lasting, long-term effects on party dynamics far removed from the initial decision to forcibly exclude labor or incorporate it through populist, traditional, or radical parties. Certainly political elites in Chile and Brazil did not assume that through their repression of labor in the 1930s they would precipitate the political conditions for military coups in 1973 and 1964, respectively.

Goldstone's argument in particular shows how path dependence may involve reaction–counterreaction dynamics, such that an initial event triggers a reaction and thereby logically leads to another quite different event, which triggers its own reaction, and so on, until a particular outcome of interest is reached. Mahoney uses the phrase "reactive sequence" to characterize these "chains of temporally ordered and causally connected events" (2000, 526). The narrative mode of analysis used in historical analysis generally describes sequences characterized by tight causal linkages that are nearly uninterruptible, such that A leads to B, which leads to C, which leads to D, and so on until one arrives at Z, or the logical termination point of the sequence.

By contrast, Orren's argument focuses on a kind of path-dependent sequence in which a particular outcome happens to occur at a critical juncture, and then this outcome is subject to self-reproducing mechanisms, causing it to repeatedly exist across time, even long after its original purposes have ceased. Scholars use the label "self-reproducing" to describe these sequences in which a given outcome is stably reinforced over time (Thelen 2003; Pierson 2004; Mahoney 2000). Self-reproducing sequences are also the norm in work on increasing returns, which models processes in which each step in a particular direction induces further movement in that same direction (Arthur 1994, 1989; Pierson 2000).

In some cases, however, self-reproduction and lock-in capture only part of a path-dependent process; scholars may look to ideas such as institutional layering and conversion to explain why and how certain aspects of institutions persist and why some aspects change. According to Thelen, "institutional survival is often strongly laced with elements of institutional *transformation* to bring institutions in line with changing social, political, and economic conditions" (2003, 211, emphasis in the original). Through institutional layering, actors choose not to remake existing institutional configurations, but instead add new components that bring the institution in alignment with their needs. For example, the Bill of Rights and subsequent amendments to the US constitution altered pre-existing arrangements while leaving the core the same. In addition, institutions initially set up to foster a certain social or political arrangement are often "converted" to suit other purposes. Orren's analysis of the law of master and servant is a good example of this: while the law in its English form fostered feudal ties between landlord and serf, as American judges reinterpreted it, the law was converted to support free labor policy.

2.2 Duration and Conjunctural Analysis

Historical researchers also evoke duration as a key temporal variable by exploring the causes of the length of a given process for a particular outcome (Aminzade 1992, 459). According to Mickey and Pierson, "attending to duration can both help scholars more clearly specify the mechanisms by which independent variables affect outcomes of interest, and can help generate new causal accounts" (2004, 7). Some duration arguments refer to repeated processes over a long time period. For example, Huber and Stephens's (2001) work on welfare states in advanced industrial countries highlights the importance of "electoral success over *an extended period of time*" to the maintenance of long-lasting welfare state institutions (Pierson 2004, 85, emphasis in the original). Other duration arguments explore the importance of slow-moving processes that may take years to unfold. For instance, Tilly's (1990) analysis of state making is centrally concerned with explaining the pace at which modern states were formed in Europe across perhaps centuries of time.

The fact that many sequences of events have a typical or normal duration allows one to speak of processes that are "too short" or "too long" or "just right" (Mickey and Pierson 2004, 15). Compressed processes often lead to significantly different outcomes because they entail a particularly rapid sequence of events. Karl notes that oil booms spur compressed processes of economic and social development. "The restraint inherent in more limited revenues . . . is abruptly removed, both psychologically and in reality" (1997, 66). As a result:

Policymakers, once torn between their preoccupations with diversity and equity, now think they can do both. The military demands modernized weapons and improved living conditions; capitalists seek credits and subsides; the middle class calls for increased social spending, labor for higher wages, and the unemployed for the creation of new jobs. (Karl 1997, 65)

Bureaucracies expand uncontrollably and "ultimately contribute to growing budget and trade deficits and foreign debt" (1997, 65). For Karl, oil booms accelerate processes that eventually overwhelm states and produce economic busts.

Historical researchers also often develop hypotheses about the intersection of various causal processes (see Aminzade 1992; Pierson 2004; Zuckerman 1997). If and when two or more processes meet in time and/or space can have a large impact on subsequent outcomes. Conjunctural analysis considers specifically the intersection point of two or more separately determined sequences, or as Pierson puts it, "the linking of discrete elements or dimensions of politics in the passage of time" (2004, 55).

In his classic work *Modernization and Bureaucratic-Authoritarianism*, O'Donnell (1979) notes certain social conditions that gradually came into being and then remained as "constants" throughout subsequent Argentine history. Each such condition worked to "load the dice more and more against an effectively working political system" (1979, 118). By the 1960s, three historical constants came together: political traditions and social processes for national unification, international economic integration, and political mobilization (O'Donnell 1979, 119–31). The conjuncture or coming together of these processes served to limit the political choices available to actors in a way that would not have been true if the sequences did not intersect at this particular time. Ultimately, the conjuncture had the effect of stimulating a determined effort by established sectors "to close any significant political access to a politically activated urban popular sector" (O'Donnell 1979, 131). In turn, this outcome set the stage for the emergence of harsh bureaucratic-authoritarian regimes.

3 USING HISTORICAL DATA

If they are to be successful, historical analysts must develop a deep knowledge of the cases they study. This is true most obviously because the effective explanation of outcomes in specific cases cannot be achieved if the analyst lacks good information about those cases. Indeed, all of the various methods of causal and temporal analysis described above can go awry if they are used in conjunction with poor data about the cases. To achieve case expertise, historical researchers read a lot about their cases— always many secondary sources and sometimes significant numbers of primary sources as well. Let us weigh in on key methodological issues and debates raised by the use of these kinds of historical sources.

3.1 Secondary Sources

Scholars who produce excellent works of historical enquiry in comparative politics always become experts in the "secondary" literature relevant to their research questions—i.e. they become quite familiar with the published books and articles by historians and area specialists who work on their cases. In some instances, this expertise requires attempting to master a vast historiography covering a large range of topics and huge time periods. An extreme example of this engagement would be Wallerstein's project on the *Modern World System*, whose first three volumes cover global economic history from 1450 to 1850, and whose bibliographies cite some 4,300 secondary sources (Wallerstein 1974, 1980, 1989). But other excellent studies in this field also reflect a deep reading of the secondary literature, as can be seen in Table 3.1

Table 3.1 Number of bibliographic references for ten historical works

Historical work	Number of bibliographic references
Bates 1981	249
Collier and Collier 2002	1,176
Downing 1992	959
Ertman 1997	695
Esping-Andersen 1990	273
Karl 1997	701
Moore 1966	431
Rueschemeyer, Stephens, and Stephens 1992	596
Skocpol 1979*	778

* Select bibliography

The extensive use of secondary sources by historical analysts in political science and sociology has been the subject of concern by some methodologists (Goldthorpe 1991; Lustick 1996; Isacoff 2005; see also Thies 2002). Critics point out that the historiography is not an unbiased accounting of past events; rather, it is a series of potentially contestable inferences by historians who construct the past in light of often underspecified theoretical frameworks. The historiography therefore does not offer one "true" version of the past, but rather several different, potentially evolving, and potentially contradictory inferences about what occurred.

Skeptical methodologists argue that the potential for faculty inference from secondary sources is large. Goldthorpe contends that historical researchers have "to treat the facts . . . that they find in secondary sources *as if they were* relatively discrete and stable entities that can be 'excerpted' and then brought together in order that some larger design may be realized" (1991, 221–2, emphasis in the original). For Lustick (1996), the problem is specifically bias in the selection of secondary sources: historical analysts may only use those sources that support their particular theories, downplaying or ignoring the rest. Indeed, he points out that the field of historical analysis lacks explicit rules for deciding what sources to use in the face of inevitable contradictions in the secondary literature.[3]

Scholars who pursue historical work in fact do often explicitly acknowledge that the historiography presents competing interpretations of events. For example, in their introductory chapters, comparative researchers often consider alternative explanations that reflect competing strands of the historiography and the theories associated with those strands (e.g. Gorski 2003; Mahoney 2001; Marx 1998). Likewise, in the course of their narratives, historical researchers frequently acknowledge

---

[3] Lustick (1996) offers his own rules for using secondary sources, but these ideas are themselves highly problematic (see Thies 2002 for a nice discussion). See also Isacoff (2005) for potential solutions.

differences among historians in the interpretation of particular events or processes. This is as true of classic works of historical research such as Skocpol (1979, 174–9) and Wallerstein (1974, various footnotes) as more recent studies in the field such as Collier and Collier (1991) and Rueschemeyer, Stephens, and Stephens (1992, 96). Indeed, we are convinced that *most* comparative-historical books call attention to differences in the historiography, and they usually use these differences to help animate their own arguments.

Historical researchers also often state explicitly how they try to resolve differences in the historiography. In some cases, the researcher simply follows the bulk of the recent historiography, which itself responds to and addresses shortcomings in earlier historical interpretations. For example, in her critique of the "bourgeois revolution" interpretation of the French Revolution, Skocpol (1979) uses the evidence marshaled by historians critical of the traditional Marxist account to support her claims. Similarly, in her work on Central American political regimes, Yashar (1997) takes note of one strand of the older historiography that viewed Costa Rica as having a democratic political system in the nineteenth century, but she rejects this historical interpretation by drawing on a large number of more recent and careful historical studies that highlight fatal flaws in the earlier view. A related strategy used by historical scholars is to side with the historical interpretation that appears to be grounded in the more careful and thorough research. For example, the footnotes of both Skocpol's (1979) and Yashar's (1997) books suggest that they take note of the primary sources used by historians and on smaller issues they sometimes side with that historian who carried out more rigorous and meticulous archival work.

Another common strategy is to explore the implications of a particular contradiction in the historiography for the specific argument being advanced. With some contradictions, the alternative sides in the dispute do not have important implications for the argument at hand. Here researchers may note the different interpretations in the literature, and then assert essentially that "Regardless of which view is taken as correct, the implication for the present argument is the same" (e.g. Mahoney 2001, 152; Skocpol 1979, 313–14 n. 146, 318 n. 4). In other cases, of course, the contradictions may have major implications, which in turn might lead the researcher to pursue his or her own primary source research to reach an informed decision about the validity of the alternative accounts, which we will discuss below.

It also bears emphasizing that historical work in political science relies significantly on "basic information"—i.e., information about well-known events that is relatively free of interpretation and not subject to a high level of contestation (Thies 2002, 353–4). In many studies, historical researchers use mostly basic information—or at least not highly contested information—to make inferences about causal processes. The validity of the arguments constructed with such information may depend less on the facts themselves than on the specific methods that are used to make inferences. This helps explain why the most important debates in historically oriented comparative analysis are often less about the historical facts themselves and more about what causal inferences can be legitimately made given these facts.

3.2 Primary Sources

Many historical researchers also use "primary sources" in their work—i.e. historical material such as government documents, newspapers, diaries, and bulletins that describe past events at roughly the time they were occurring.[4] However, the degree to which and the ways in which this primary source material is incorporated vary a great deal from study to study.

The most extensive use of primary sources occurs when a social scientist seeks to make a contribution to the historiography by drawing heavily on undiscovered or underutilized primary sources. The resulting social science work may receive as much attention from historians as from social scientists. For example, in *Labor in Latin America: Comparative Essays on Chile, Argentina, Venezuela, and Colombia* (1986), Bergquist uses primary sources that illuminate the specific cultural, institutional, and political experiences of workers and how those experiences shaped the development of their movements. For Bergquist, "twentieth-century Latin American historiography suffers from two very grave deficiencies. It has failed to recognize the decisive historical role of organized labor and the labor movement in the evolution of the societies of the region... [and] it has failed to account for the very different ideological and political trajectories of the various Latin American labor movements" (1986, 1). To remedy these problems, Bergquist draws on primary sources— often from the workers themselves—that describe in contextualized detail the daily lives of workers. With this base of information, *Labor in Latin America* looks very much like an analytically informed work of history.

A less extensive engagement with historical documents occurs through "targeted" primary source research. With this strategy, the analyst uses primary sources to investigate selected issues relevant to his or her research question. In some instances, the primary source research may involve an effort to resolve certain specific contradictions in the historiography. For example, Mahoney (2001) pursued this kind of primary research to resolve differences in the historiography regarding Marxist and non-Marxist interpretations of five major liberal reform leaders in nineteenth-century Central America. In particular, he attempted to read the key documents that were usually cited in leading works on these leaders, retracing the steps of previous historians to develop an informed opinion of his own. In other instances, targeted primary research may entail filling in specific gaps on topics not adequately covered by the secondary literature. For example, in *The Price of Wealth* (1997), Chaudhry "uses heretofore unexamined archives... [and] two years of fieldwork" (1997, 38) in Saudi Arabia and Yemen to gather information on the workings of state institutions in these countries that is not available in the secondary sources. She in particular draws from government documents, royal decrees, and interviews with key officials to test theories regarding the development of state agencies.

---

[4] The distinction between primary and secondary sources is not always clear. For example, scholars sometimes comment that good ethnography becomes history, thus suggesting how what was originally conceived as a secondary source is later treated as a primary source.

Initial research on a topic may also lead a historical researcher to explore certain primary sources; in turn, this exploration may inspire the researcher to a new research question, whose answer requires still more primary source research. For example, in *Protecting Soliders and Mothers* (1992), Skocpol was "inspired by fresh descriptions of what did and didn't happen in the development of social policies [in the United States] from the 1870s to the 1920s" (1992, 7). Doing background research for a proposed comparative project on European and US welfare states, she uncovered a study of turn-of-the-century pension policy by Isaac Max Rubinow, *Social Insurance, With Special Reference to American Conditions.* Rubinow noted the possibility of using the pension program for Civil War veterans as a means to develop a national pension system like those in Europe. "Fascinated by his description of the breadth and experience of these old-age benefits," Skocpol writes, "I asked myself how historians of U.S. social welfare could have overlooked them" (1992, p. vii). Rubinow led Skocpol to other Progressive Era writers on the Civil War pension system and spurred her to study of the effects of Civil War pensions as an impediment to the development of a European-style system for social insurance.[5]

4. CONCLUSION

Students of comparative politics will always be attracted to history because the outcomes they seek to explain and the causal processes they find most compelling are often located in the past. Yet this chapter has emphasized that historical analysis is hardly simply the study of the past. Rather, historical analysis embodies a distinctive set of techniques for the assessment of causal hypotheses, for the study of temporal processes, and for the analysis of data. It is these traits along with the pursuit of the valid explanation of particular outcomes in specific cases that distinguish historical analysis as a leading orientation in the field of comparative politics.

REFERENCES

AMINZADE, R. 1992. Historical sociology and time. *Sociological Methods and Research*, 20: 456–80.

ARTHUR, W. B. 1989. Competing technologies and lock-in by historical events. *Economic Journal*, 99: 116–31.

[5] Like Skocpol, Orren launched a research project based on her serendipitous discovery of unexplored primary sources. In the preface to *Belated Feudalism* (1991), she writes that "I had no inkling of what I would find when I probed beneath the surface, to the legal precedents on both sides of the ongoing controversy" (Orren 1991, p. ix).

——1994. *Increasing Returns and Path Dependence in the Economy*. Ann Arbor: University of Michigan Press.

BARTON, A. H., and LAZARSFELD, P. 1969. Some functions of qualitative analysis in social research. Pp. 163–205 in *Issues in Participant Observation*, ed. G. J. McCall and J. L. Simmons. Reading, Mass.: Addison-Wesley.

BATES, R. H. 1981. *States and Markets in Topical Africa: The Political Basis of Agricultural Policy*. Berkeley and Los Angeles: University of California Press.

BERGQUIST, C. 1986. *Labor in Latin America: Comparative Essays on Chile, Argentina, Venezuela, and Colombia*. Stanford, Calif.: Stanford University Press.

BRADY, H. E., and COLLIER, D. eds. 2004. *Rethinking Social Inquiry: Diverse Tools, Shared Standards*. Lanham, Md.: Rowman & Littlefield.

BRAUMOELLER, B. F. 2003. Causal complexity and the study of politics. *Political Analysis*, 11 (3): 209–33.

——and GOERTZ, G. 2000. The methodology of necessary conditions. *American Journal of Political Science*, 44 (4): 844–58.

CAMPBELL, D. T. 1975. "Degrees of freedom" and the case study. *Comparative Political Studies*, 8: 178–93.

CHAUDHRY, K. A. 1997. *The Price of Wealth: Economies and Institutions in the Middle East*. Ithaca, NY: Cornell University Press.

CLARK, W. R., GILLIGAN, M. J., and GOLDER, M. 2006. A simple multivariate test for asymmetric hypotheses. *Political Analysis*, 14: 311–31.

CLEMENS, E. S., and COOK, J. M. 1999. Politics and institutionalism. *Annual Review of Sociology*, 25: 441–66.

COLLIER, R. B., and COLLIER, D. 1991. *Shaping the Political Arena: Critical Junctures, the Labor Movement, and Regime Dynamics in Latin America*. Princeton: Princeton University Press.

DAVID, P. A. 1985. Clio and the economics of QWERTY. *American Economic Review*, 75: 332–7.

DION, D. 1998. Evidence and inference in the comparative case study. *Comparative Politics*, 30 (2): 127–45.

DOWNING, B. M. 1992. *The Military Revolution and Political Change: Origins of Democracy and Autocracy in Early Modern Europe*. Princeton: Princeton University Press.

ERTMAN, T. 1997. *Birth of the Leviathan: Building States and Regimes in Medieval and Early Modern Europe*. Cambridge: Cambridge University Press.

ESPING-ANDERSEN, G. 1990. *Three Worlds of Welfare Capitalism*. Cambridge: Polity.

FORAN, J. 2005. *Taking Power: On the Origins of Third World Revolutions*. Cambridge: Cambridge University Press.

GEORGE, A. L., and BENNETT, A. 2005. *Case Studies and Theory Development in the Social Sciences*. Cambridge, Mass.: MIT Press.

——and McKEOWN, T. J. 1985. Case studies and theories of organizational decision making. *Advances in Information Processing in Organizations*, 2: 21–58.

GOERTZ, G., and MAHONEY, J. 2005. Two-level theories and fuzzy-set analysis. *Sociological Methods and Research*, 33: 497–538.

——and STARR, H. eds. 2003. *Necessary Conditions: Theory, Methodology, and Applications*. Lanham, Md.: Rowman and Littlefield.

GOLDSTONE, J. A. 1991. *Revolution and Rebellion in the Early Modern World*. Berkeley and Los Angeles: University of California Press.

——1998. The problem of the "early modern" world. *Journal of Economic and Social History of the Orient*, 41: 249–84.

——2007. *The Happy Chance: The Rise of the West in Global Context, 1500–1800*. Cambridge, Mass.: Harvard University Press.

GOLDTHORPE, J. H. 1991. The uses of history in sociology: reflections on some recent tendencies. *British Journal of Sociology*, 42: 211–30.

GOLDTHORPE, J. H. 1997. Current issues in comparative macrosociology: a debate on methodological issues. *Comparative Social Research*, 16: 1–26.

—— 2000. Causation, statistics, and sociology. Pp. 137–60 in *On Sociology: Numbers, Narratives, and the Integration of Research and Theory*, ed. J. H. Goldthorpe. Oxford: Oxford University Press.

GOODWIN, J. 2001. *No Other Way Out: States and Revolutionary Movements, 1945–1991*. New York: Cambridge University Press.

GORSKI, P. S. 2003. *The Disciplinary Revolution: Calvinism and the Rise of the State in Early Modern Europe*. Chicago: University of Chicago Press.

HEDSTROM, P., and SWEDBERG, R. eds. 1998. *Social Mechanisms: An Analytical Approach to Social Theory*. New York: Cambridge University Press.

HICKS, A. 1999. *Social Democracy and Welfare Capitalism*. Ithaca, NY: Cornell University Press.

HUBER, E., and STEPHENS, J. D. 2001. *Development and Crisis of the Welfare State: Parties and Politics in Global Markets*. Chicago: University of Chicago Press.

ISACOFF, J. B. 2005. Writing the Arab–Israeli conflict: historical bias and the use of history in political science. *Perspectives on Politics*, 3 (1): 71–88.

JONES-LUONG, P. 2002. *Institutional Change and Political Continuity in Post-Soviet Central Asia: Power Perception, and Pacts*. Cambridge: Cambridge University Press.

KARL, T. L. 1997. *The Paradox of Plenty: Oil Booms and Petro States*. Berkeley and Los Angeles: University of California Press.

LIEBERSON, S. 1991. Small N's and big conclusions: an examination of the reasoning in comparative studies based on a small number of cases. *Social Forces*, 70: 307–20.

LUSTICK, I. 1996. History, historiography, and political science: multiple historical records and the problem of selection bias. *American Political Science Review*, 90: 605–18.

MAHONEY, J. 1999. Nominal, ordinal, and narrative appraisal in macrocausal analysis. *American Journal of Sociology*, 103 (4): 1154–96.

—— 2000. Path dependence in historical sociology. *Theory and Society*, 29: 507–48.

—— 2001. *The Legacies of Liberalism: Path Dependence and Political Regimes in Central America*. Baltimore: Johns Hopkins University Press.

—— 2004. Comparative-historical methodology. *Annual Review of Sociology*, 30: 81–101.

—— and GOERTZ, G. 2006. A tale of two cultures: contrasting quantitative and qualitative research. *Political Analysis*, forthcoming.

—— and RUESCHEMEYER, D. 2003. Comparative historical analysis: achievements and agendas. Pp. 3–38 in *Comparative Historical Analysis in the Social Sciences*, ed. J. Mahoney and D. Rueschemeyer. Cambridge: Cambridge University Press.

MARX, A. W. 1998. *Making Race and Nation: A Comparison of South Africa, the United States, and Brazil*. Cambridge: Cambridge University Press.

MICKEY, R. W., and PIERSON, P. 2004. As long as it takes: duration and the explanation of political outcomes. Paper presented at the Workshop on Comparative Politics, Yale University.

MOORE, B. 1966. *Social Origins of Dictatorship and Democracy: Lord and Peasant in the Making of the Modern World*. Boston: Beacon Press.

NORTH, D. C. 1990. *Institutions, Institutional Change and Economic Performance*. Cambridge: Cambridge University Press.

O'DONNELL, G. 1979. *Modernization and Bureaucratic-Authoritarianism*. Berkeley: Institute of International Studies.

ORREN, K. 1991. *Belated Feudalism: Labor, the Law, and Liberal Development in the United States*. Cambridge: Cambridge University Press.

PAIGE, J. M. 1997. *Coffee and Power: Revolution and the Rise of Democracy in Central America*. Cambridge, Mass.: Harvard University Press.

PIERSON, P. 2000. Increasing returns, path dependence, and the study of politics. *American Political Science Review*, 94: 251–67.

——2004. *Politics in Time: History, Institutions, and Social Analysis*. Princeton: Princeton University Press.

PRZEWORKSI, A., and TEUNE, H. 1970. *The Logic of Comparative Social Inquiry*. New York: Wiley.

RAGIN, C. C. 1987. *The Comparative Method: Moving beyond Qualitative and Quantitative Strategies*. Berkeley and Los Angeles: University of California Press.

——2000. *Fuzzy-Set Social Science*. Chicago: University of Chicago Press.

RUESCHEMEYER, D., STEPHENS, E. H., and STEPHENS, J. D. 1992. *Capitalist Development and Democracy*. Chicago: University of Chicago Press.

SKOCPOL, T. 1979. *States and Social Revolutions: A Comparative Analysis of France, Russia, and China*. Cambridge: Cambridge University Press.

——ed. 1984. *Vision and Method in Historical Sociology*. New York: Cambridge University Press.

——1992. *Protecting Soldiers and Mothers: The Political Origins of Social Policy in the United States*. Cambridge, Mass.: Harvard University Press.

——1999. How Americans became civic. Pp. 27–80 in *Civic Engagement in American Democracy*, ed. T. Skocpol and M. P. Fiorina. Washington, DC: Brookings Institution Press and Russell Sage Foundation.

——and SOMERS, M. 1980. The uses of comparative history in macrosocial inquiry. *Comparative Studies in Society and History*, 22: 174–97.

THELEN, K. 2003. How institutions evolve: insights from comparative historical analysis. Pp. 208–40 in *Comparative Historical Analysis in the Social Sciences*, ed. J. Mahoney and D. Rueschemeyer. Cambridge; Cambridge University Press.

THIES, C. G. 2002. A pragmatic guide to qualitative historical analysis in the study of international relations. *International Studies Perspectives*, 3: 351–72.

TILLY, C. 1990. *Coercion, Capital, and European States, AD 990–1990*. Cambridge: B. Blackwell.

WALLERSTEIN, I. 1974. *The Modern World-System: Capitalist Agriculture and the Origins of the European World-Economy in the Sixteenth Century*, vol. i. New York: Academic Press.

——1980. *The Modern World-System II: Mercantilism and the Consolidation of the European World-Economy, 1600–1750*. New York: Academic Press.

——1989. *The Modern World-System III: The Second Era of Great Expansion of the Capitalist World-Economy, 1730s–1840s*. New York: Academic Press.

YASHAR, D. J. 1997. *Demanding Democracy: Reform and Reaction in Costa Rica and Guatemala, 1870s–1950s*. Stanford, Calif.: Stanford University Press.

ZUCKERMAN, A. S. 1997. Reformulating explanatory standards and advancing theory in comparative politics. Pp. 277–310 in *Comparative Politics: Rationality, Culture, and Structure*, ed. M. I. Lichbach and A. S. Zuckerman. Cambridge: Cambridge University Press.

CHAPTER 4

....

THE CASE STUDY: WHAT IT IS AND WHAT IT DOES

....

JOHN GERRING

Two centuries after Le Play's pioneering work, the various disciplines of the social sciences continue to produce a vast number of case studies, many of which have entered the pantheon of classic works. Judging by the large volume of recent scholarly output the case study research design plays a central role in anthropology, archeology, business, education, history, medicine, political science, psychology, social work, and sociology (Gerring 2007a, ch. 1). Even in economics and political economy, fields not usually noted for their receptiveness to case-based work, there has been something of a renaissance. Recent studies of economic growth have turned to case studies of unusual countries such as Botswana, Korea, and Mauritius.[1] Debates on the relationship between trade and growth and the IMF and growth have likewise combined cross-national regression evidence with in-depth (quantitative and qualitative) case analysis (Srinivasan and Bhagwati 1999; Vreeland 2003). Work on ethnic politics and ethnic conflict has exploited within-country variation or small-N cross-country comparisons (Abadie and Gardeazabal 2003; Chandra 2004; Posner 2004). By the standard of praxis, therefore, it would appear that the method of the case study is solidly ensconced, perhaps even thriving. Arguably, we are witnessing a movement away from a variable-centered approach to causality in the social sciences and towards a case-based approach.

----

[1] Acemoglu, Johnson, and Robinson (2003), Chernoff and Warner (2002), Rodrik (2003). See also studies focused on particular firms or regions, e.g. Coase 1959, 2000.

Indeed, the statistical analysis of cross-case observational data has been subjected to increasing scrutiny in recent years. It no longer seems self-evident, even to nomothetically inclined scholars, that non-experimental data drawn from nation-states, cities, social movements, civil conflicts, or other complex phenomena should be treated in standard regression formats. The complaints are myriad, and oft-reviewed.[2] They include: (a) the problem of arriving at an adequate specification of the causal model, given a plethora of plausible models, and the associated problem of modeling interactions among these covariates; (b) identification problems, which cannot always be corrected by instrumental variable techniques; (c) the problem of "extreme" counterfactuals, i.e. extrapolating or interpolating results from a general model where the extrapolations extend beyond the observable data points; (d) problems posed by influential cases; (e) the arbitrariness of standard significance tests; (f) the misleading precision of point estimates in the context of "curve-fitting" models; (g) the problem of finding an appropriate estimator and modeling temporal autocorrelation in pooled time series; (h) the difficulty of identifying causal mechanisms; and last, but certainly not least, (i) the ubiquitous problem of faulty data drawn from a variety of questionable sources. Most of these difficulties may be understood as the by-product of causal variables that offer limited variation through time and cases that are extremely heterogeneous.

A principal factor driving the general discontent with cross-case observational research is a new-found interest in experimental models of social scientific research. Following the pioneering work of Donald Campbell (1988; Cook and Campbell 1979) and Donald Rubin (1974), methodologists have taken a hard look at the regression model and discovered something rather obvious but at the same time crucially important: this research bears only a faint relationship to the true experiment, for all the reasons noted above. The current excitement generated by matching estimators, natural experiments, and field experiments may be understood as a move toward a quasi-experimental, and frequently case-based analysis of causal relations. Arguably, this is because the experimental ideal is often better approximated by a small number of cases that are closely related to one another, or by a single case observed over time, than by a large sample of heterogeneous units.

A third factor militating towards case-based analysis is the development of a series of alternatives to the standard linear/additive model of cross-case analysis, thus establishing a more variegated set of tools to capture the complexity of social behavior (see Brady and Collier 2004). Charles Ragin and associates have shown us how to deal with situations where multiple causal paths lead to the same set of outcomes, a series of techniques known as Qualitative Comparative Analysis (QCA) ("Symposium: Qualitative Comparative Analysis" 2004). Andrew Abbott has worked out a method that maps causal sequences across cases, known as optimal sequence matching (Abbott 2001; Abbott and Forrest 1986; Abbott and Tsay 2000).

---

[2] For general discussion of the following points see Achen (1986), Freedman (1991), Kittel (1999, 2005), Kittel and Winner (2005), Manski (1993), Winship and Morgan (1999), Winship and Sobel (2004).

Bear Braumoeller, Gary Goertz, Jack Levy, and Harvey Starr have defended the importance of necessary-condition arguments in the social sciences, and have shown how these arguments might be analyzed (Braumoeller and Goertz 2000; Goertz 2003; Goertz and Levy forthcoming; Goertz and Starr 2003). James Fearon, Ned Lebow, Philip Tetlock, and others have explored the role of counterfactual thought experiments in the analysis of individual case histories (Fearon 1991; Lebow 2000; Tetlock and Belkin 1996). Colin Elman has developed a typological method of analyzing cases (Elman 2005). David Collier, Jack Goldstone, Peter Hall, James Mahoney, and Dietrich Rueschemeyer have worked to revitalize the comparative and comparative-historical methods (Collier 1993; Goldstone 1997; Hall 2003; Mahoney and Rueschemeyer 2003). And scores of researchers have attacked the problem of how to convert the relevant details of a temporally constructed narrative into standardized formats so that cases can be meaningfully compared (Abell 1987, 2004; Abbott 1992; Buthe 2002; Griffin 1993). While not all of these techniques are, strictly speaking, case study techniques—since they sometimes involve a large number of cases—they do move us closer to a case-based understanding of causation insofar as they preserve the texture and detail of individual cases, features that are often lost in large-N cross-case analysis.

A fourth factor concerns the recent marriage of rational choice tools with case study analysis, sometimes referred to as an "analytic narrative" (Bates et al. 1998). Whether the technique is qualitative or quantitative, scholars equipped with economic models are turning, increasingly, to case studies in order to test the theoretical predictions of a general model, investigate causal mechanisms, and/or explain the features of a key case.

Finally, epistemological shifts in recent decades have enhanced the attractiveness of the case study format. The "positivist" model of explanation, which informed work in the social sciences through most of the twentieth century, tended to downplay the importance of causal mechanisms in the analysis of causal relations. Famously, Milton Friedman (1953) argued that the only criterion of a model was to be found in its accurate prediction of outcomes. The verisimilitude of the model, its accurate depiction of reality, was beside the point. In recent years, this explanatory trope has come under challenge from "realists," who claim (among other things) that causal analysis should pay close attention to causal mechanisms (e.g. Bunge 1997; Little 1998). Within political science and sociology, the identification of a specific mechanism—a causal pathway—has come to be seen as integral to causal analysis, regardless of whether the model in question is formal or informal or whether the evidence is qualitative or quantitative (Achen 2002; Elster 1998; George and Bennett 2005; Hedstrom and Swedberg 1998). Given this new-found (or at least newly self-conscious) interest in mechanisms, it is not surprising that social scientists would turn to case studies as a mode of causal investigation.

For all the reasons stated above, one might intuit that social science is moving towards a case-based understanding of causal relations. Yet, this movement, insofar as it exists, has scarcely been acknowledged, and would certainly be challenged by many close observers—including some of those cited in the foregoing passages.

The fact is that the case study research design is still viewed by most methodologists with extreme circumspection. A work that focuses its attention on a single example of a broader phenomenon is apt to be described as a "mere" case study, and is often identified with loosely framed and non-generalizable theories, biased case selection, informal and undisciplined research designs, weak empirical leverage (too many variables and too few cases), subjective conclusions, non-replicability, and causal determinism. To some, the term case study is an ambiguous designation covering a multitude of "inferential felonies."[3]

The quasi-mystical qualities associated with the case study persist to this day. In the field of psychology, a gulf separates "scientists" engaged in cross-case research and "practitioners" engaged in clinical research, usually focused on several cases (Hersen and Barlow 1976, 21). In the fields of political science and sociology, case study researchers are acknowledged to be on the "soft" side of hard disciplines. And across fields, the persisting case study orientations of anthropology, education, law, social work, and various other fields and subfields relegate them to the non-rigorous, non-systematic, non-scientific, non-positivist end of the academic spectrum.

The methodological status of the case study is still, officially, suspect. Even among its defenders there is confusion over the virtues and vices of this ambiguous research design. Practitioners continue to ply their trade but have difficulty articulating what it is they are doing, methodologically speaking. The case study survives in a curious methodological limbo.

This leads to a paradox: although much of what we know about the empirical world has been generated by case studies and case studies continue to constitute a large proportion of work generated by the social science disciplines, the case study *method* is poorly understood.

How can we make sense of the profound disjuncture between the acknowledged contributions of this genre to the various disciplines of social science and its maligned status within these disciplines? If case studies are methodologically flawed, why do they persist? Should they be rehabilitated, or suppressed? How fruitful *is* this style of research?

In this chapter, I provide a reconstructed definition of the case study approach to research with special emphasis on comparative politics, a field that has been closely identified with this method since its birth. Based on this definition, I then explore a series of contrasts between case study and cross-case study research. These contrasts are intended to illuminate the characteristic strengths and weaknesses ("affinities") of these two research designs, not to vindicate one or the other. The effort of this chapter is to understand this persisting methodological debate as a matter of tradeoffs. Case studies and cross-case studies explore the world in different ways. Yet, properly constituted, there is no reason that case study results cannot be

---

[3] Achen and Snidal (1989: 160). See also Geddes (1990, 2003), Goldthorpe (1997), King, Keohane, and Verba (1994), Lieberson (1985: 107–15, 1992, 1994), Lijphart (1971: 683–4), Odell (2004), Sekhon (2004), Smelser (1973: 45, 57). It should be noted that these writers, while critical of the case study format, are not necessarily opposed to case studies per se (that is to say, they should not be classified as *opponents* of the case study).

synthesized with results gained from cross-case analysis, and vice versa. My hope, therefore, is that this chapter will contribute to breaking down the boundaries that have separated these rival genres within the subfield of comparative politics.

1 DEFINITIONS

The key term of this chapter is, admittedly, a definitional morass. To refer to a work as a "case study" might mean: that its method is qualitative, small-N; that the research is holistic, thick (a more or less comprehensive examination of a phenomenon); that it utilizes a particular type of evidence (e.g. ethnographic, clinical, non-experimental, non-survey based, participant observation, process tracing, historical, textual, or field research); that its method of evidence gathering is naturalistic (a "real-life context"); that the research investigates the properties of a single observation; or that the research investigates the properties of a single phenomenon, instance, or example. Evidently, researchers have many things in mind when they talk about case study research. Confusion is compounded by the existence of a large number of near-synonyms—single unit, single subject, single case, N=1, case based, case control, case history, case method, case record, case work, clinical research, and so forth. As a result of this profusion of terms and meanings, proponents and opponents of the case study marshal a wide range of arguments but do not seem any closer to agreement than when this debate was first broached several decades ago.

Can we reconstruct this concept in a clearer, more productive fashion? In order to do so we must understand how the key terms—case and case study—are situated within a neighborhood of related terms. In this crowded semantic field, each term is defined in relation to others. And in the context of a specific work or research terrain, they all take their meaning from a specific inference. (The reader should bear in mind that any change in the inference, and the meaning of all the key terms will probably change.) My attempt here will be to provide a single, determinate, definition of these key terms. Of course, researchers may choose to define these terms in many different ways. However, for purposes of methodological discussion it is helpful to enforce a uniform vocabulary.

Let us stipulate that a *case* connotes a spatially delimited phenomenon (a unit) observed at a single point in time or over some period of time. It comprises the sort of phenomena that an inference attempts to explain. Thus, in a study that attempts to explain certain features of nation-states, cases are comprised of nation-states (across some temporal frame). In a study that attempts to explain the behavior of individuals, individuals comprise the cases. And so forth. Each case may provide a single observation or multiple (within-case) observations.

For students of comparative politics, the archetypal case is the dominant political unit of our time, the nation-state. However, the study of smaller social and political units (regions, cities, villages, communities, social groups, families) or specific institutions (political parties, interest groups, businesses) is equally common in other subfields, and perhaps increasingly so in comparative politics. Whatever the chosen unit, the methodological issues attached to the case study have nothing to do with the size of the individual cases. A case may be created out of any phenomenon so long as it has identifiable boundaries and comprises the primary object of an inference.

Note that the spatial boundaries of a case are often more apparent than its temporal boundaries. We know, more or less, where a country begins and ends, even though we may have difficulty explaining *when* a country begins and ends. Yet, some temporal boundaries must be assumed. This is particularly important when cases consist of discrete events—crises, revolutions, legislative acts, and so forth—within a single unit. Occasionally, the temporal boundaries of a case are more obvious than its spatial boundaries. This is true when the phenomena under study are eventful but the unit undergoing the event is amorphous. For example, if one is studying terrorist attacks it may not be clear how the spatial unit of analysis should be understood, but the events themselves may be well bounded.

A *case study* may be understood as the intensive study of a single case for the purpose of understanding a larger class of cases (a population). Case study research may incorporate several cases. However, at a certain point it will no longer be possible to investigate those cases intensively. At the point where the emphasis of a study shifts from the individual case to a sample of cases we shall say that a study is *cross-case*. Evidently, the distinction between a case study and cross-case study is a continuum. The fewer cases there are, and the more intensively they are studied, the more a work merits the appellation case study. Even so, this proves to be a useful distinction, for much follows from it.

A few additional terms will now be formally defined.

An *observation* is the most basic element of any empirical endeavor. Conventionally, the number of observations in an analysis is referred to with the letter N. (Confusingly, N may also be used to designate the number of cases in a study, a usage that I shall try to avoid.) A single observation may be understood as containing several dimensions, each of which may be measured (across disparate observations) as a variable. Where the proposition is causal, these may be subdivided into *dependent* (Y) and *independent* (X) variables. The dependent variable refers to the outcome of an investigation. The independent variable refers to the explanatory (causal) factor, that which the outcome is supposedly dependent on.

Note that a case may consist of a single observation ($N=1$). This would be true, for example, in a cross-sectional analysis of multiple cases. In a case study, however, the case under study always provides more than one observation. These may be constructed diachronically (by observing the case or some subset of within-case units through time) or synchronically (by observing within-case variation at a single point in time).

This is a clue to the fact that case studies and cross-case usually operate at different levels of analysis. The case study is typically focused on within-case variation (if there a cross-case component it is probably secondary). The cross-case study, as the name suggests, is typically focused on cross-case variation (if there is also within-case variation, it is secondary in importance). They have the same object in view—the explanation of a population of cases—but they go about this task differently.

A *sample* consists of whatever cases are subjected to formal analysis; they are the immediate subject of a study or case study. (Confusingly, the sample may also refer to the observations under study, and will be so used at various points in this narrative. But at present, we treat the sample as consisting of cases.) Technically, one might say that in a case study the sample consists of the case or cases that are subjected to intensive study. However, usually when one uses the term sample one is implying that the number of cases is rather large. Thus, "sample-based work" will be understood as referring to large-N cross-case methods—the opposite of case study work. Again, the only feature distinguishing the case study format from a sample-based (or "cross-case") research design is the number of cases falling within the sample—one or a few versus many. Case studies, like large-N samples, seek to represent, in all ways relevant to the proposition at hand, a population of cases. A series of case studies might therefore be referred to as a sample if they are relatively brief and relatively numerous; it is a matter of emphasis and of degree. The more case studies one has, the less intensively each one is studied, and the more confident one is in their representativeness (of some broader population), the more likely one is to describe them as a sample rather than a series of case studies. For practical reasons—unless, that is, a study is extraordinarily long—the case study research format is usually limited to a dozen cases or less. A single case is not at all unusual.

The sample rests within a *population* of cases to which a given proposition refers. The population of an inference is thus equivalent to the breadth or scope of a proposition. (I use the terms *proposition, hypothesis, inference,* and *argument* interchangeably.) Note that most samples are not exhaustive; hence the use of the term sample, referring to *sampling* from a population. Occasionally, however, the sample equals the population of an inference; all potential cases are studied.

For those familiar with the rectangular form of a dataset it may be helpful to conceptualize observations as rows, variables as columns, and cases as either groups of observations or individual observations.

2   What is a Case Study Good For? Case Study versus Cross-Case Analysis

I have argued that the case study approach to research is most usefully defined as the intensive study of a single unit or a small number of units (the cases), for the purpose of understanding a larger class of similar units (a population of cases). This is put forth as a minimal definition of the topic.[4] I now proceed to discuss the *non-definitional* attributes of the case study—attributes that are often, but not invariably, associated with the case study method. These will be understood as methodological affinities flowing from a minimal definition of the concept.[5]

The case study research design exhibits characteristic strengths and weaknesses relative to its large-N cross-case cousin. These tradeoffs derive, first of all, from basic research goals such as (1) whether the study is oriented toward hypothesis generating or hypothesis testing, (2) whether internal or external validity is prioritized, (3) whether insight into causal mechanisms or causal effects is more valuable, and (4) whether the scope of the causal inference is deep or broad. These tradeoffs also hinge on the shape of the empirical universe, i.e. (5) whether the population of cases under study is heterogeneous or homogeneous, (6) whether the causal relationship of interest is strong or weak, (7) whether useful variation on key parameters within that population is rare or common, and (8) whether available data are concentrated or dispersed.

Along each of these dimensions, case study research has an affinity for the first factor and cross-case research has an affinity for the second, as summarized in Table 4.1. To clarify, these tradeoffs represent methodological *affinities*, not invariant laws. Exceptions can be found to each one. Even so, these general tendencies are often

Table 4.1   Case study and cross-case research designs: affinities and tradeoffs

	Affinity	
	Case study	Cross-case study
Research goals		
1. Hypothesis	Generating	Testing
2. Validity	Internal	External
3. Causal insight	Mechanisms	Effects
4. Scope of proposition	Deep	Broad
Empirical factors		
5. Population of cases	Heterogeneous	Homogeneous
6. Causal strength	Strong	Weak
7. Useful variation	Rare	Common
8. Data availability	Concentrated	Dispersed

[4] My intention is to include only those attributes commonly associated with the case study method that are *always* implied by our use of the term, excluding those attributes that are sometimes violated by standard usage. Thus, I chose not to include "ethnography" as a defining feature of the case study, since many case studies (so called) are not ethnographic. For further discussion of minimal definitions see Gerring (2001, ch. 4), Gerring and Barresi (2003), Sartori (1976).

[5] These additional attributes might also be understood as comprising an ideal-type ("maximal") definition of the topic (Gerring 2001, ch. 4; Gerring and Barresi 2003).

noted in case study research and have been reproduced in multiple disciplines and subdisciplines over the course of many decades.

It should be stressed that each of these tradeoffs carries a ceteris paribus caveat. Case studies are more useful for generating new hypotheses, *all other things being equal.* The reader must bear in mind that many additional factors also rightly influence a writer's choice of research design, and they may lean in the other direction. Ceteris are not always paribus. One should not jump to conclusions about the research design appropriate to a given setting without considering the entire range of issues involved—some of which may be more important than others.

3. HYPOTHESIS: GENERATING VERSUS TESTING

Social science research involves a quest for new theories as well as a testing of existing theories; it is comprised of both "conjectures" and "refutations."[6] Regrettably, social science methodology has focused almost exclusively on the latter. The conjectural element of social science is usually dismissed as a matter of guesswork, inspiration, or luck—a leap of faith, and hence a poor subject for methodological reflection.[7] Yet, it will readily be granted that many works of social science, including most of the acknowledged classics, are seminal rather than definitive. Their classic status derives from the introduction of a new idea or a new perspective that is subsequently subjected to more rigorous (and refutable) analysis. Indeed, it is difficult to devise a program of falsification the first time a new theory is proposed. Path-breaking research, almost by definition, is protean. Subsequent research on that topic tends to be more definitive insofar as its primary task is limited: to verify or falsify a pre-existing hypothesis. Thus, the world of social science may be usefully divided according to the predominant goal undertaken in a given study, either hypothesis *generating* or hypothesis *testing.* There are two moments of empirical research, a lightbulb moment and a skeptical moment, each of which is essential to the progress of a discipline.[8]

---

[6] Popper (1969).

[7] Karl Popper (quoted in King, Keohane, and Verba 1994, 14) writes: "there is no such thing as a logical method of having new ideas . . . Discovery contains 'an irrational element,' or a 'creative intuition.'" One recent collection of essays and interviews takes new ideas as its special focus (Munck and Snyder 2007), though it may be doubted whether there are generalizable results.

[8] Gerring (2001, ch. 10). The tradeoff between these two styles of research is implicit in Achen and Snidal (1989), who criticize the case study for its deficits in the latter genre but also acknowledge the benefits of the case study along the former dimension (1989, 167–8). Reichenbach also distinguished between a "context of discovery," and a "context of justification." Likewise, Peirce's concept of *abduction* recognizes the importance of a generative component in science.

Case studies enjoy a natural advantage in research of an exploratory nature. Several millennia ago, Hippocrates reported what were, arguably, the first case studies ever conducted. They were fourteen in number.[9] Darwin's insights into the process of human evolution came after his travels to a few select locations, notably Easter Island. Freud's revolutionary work on human psychology was constructed from a close observation of fewer than a dozen clinical cases. Piaget formulated his theory of human cognitive development while watching his own two children as they passed from childhood to adulthood. Lévi-Strauss's structuralist theory of human cultures built on the analysis of several North and South American tribes. Douglass North's neo-institutionalist theory of economic development was constructed largely through a close analysis of a handful of early developing states (primarily England, the Netherlands, and the United States).[10] Many other examples might be cited of seminal ideas that derived from the intensive study of a few key cases.

Evidently, the sheer number of examples of a given phenomenon does not, by itself, produce insight. It may only confuse. How many times did Newton observe apples fall before he recognized the nature of gravity? This is an apocryphal example, but it illustrates a central point: case studies may be more useful than cross-case studies when a subject is being encountered for the first time or is being considered in a fundamentally new way. After reviewing the case study approach to medical research, one researcher finds that although case reports are commonly regarded as the lowest or weakest form of evidence, they are nonetheless understood to comprise "the first line of evidence." The hallmark of case reporting, according to Jan Vandenbroucke, "is to recognize the unexpected." This is where discovery begins.[11]

The advantages that case studies offer in work of an exploratory nature may also serve as impediments in work of a confirmatory/disconfirmatory nature. Let us briefly explore why this might be so.[12]

Traditionally, scientific methodology has been defined by a segregation of conjecture and refutation. One should not be allowed to contaminate the other.[13] Yet, in the real world of social science, inspiration is often associated with perspiration. "Lightbulb" moments arise from a close engagement with the particular facts of a particular case. Inspiration is more likely to occur in the laboratory than in the shower.

The circular quality of conjecture and refutation is particularly apparent in case study research. Charles Ragin notes that case study research is all about "casing"— defining the topic, including the hypothesis(es) of primary interest, the outcome, and the set of cases that offer relevant information vis-à-vis the hypothesis.[14] A study of the French Revolution may be conceptualized as a study of revolution, of social revolution, of revolt, of political violence, and so forth. Each of these topics entails a different population and a different set of causal factors. A good deal of authorial

---

[9] Bonoma (1985: 199). Some of the following examples are discussed in Patton (2002, 245).

[10] North and Weingast (1989); North and Thomas (1973).

[11] Vandenbroucke (2001, 331).

[12] For discussion of this tradeoff in the context of economic growth theory see Temple (1999, 120).

[13] Geddes (2003), King, Keohane, and Verba (1994), Popper (1934/1968).

[14] Ragin (1992).

intervention is necessary in the course of defining a case study topic, for there is a great deal of evidentiary leeway. Yet, the "subjectivity" of case study research allows for the generation of a great number of hypotheses, insights that might not be apparent to the cross-case researcher who works with a thinner set of empirical data across a large number of cases and with a more determinate (fixed) definition of cases, variables, and outcomes. It is the very fuzziness of case studies that grants them an advantage in research at the exploratory stage, for the single-case study allows one to test a multitude of hypotheses in a rough-and-ready way. Nor is this an entirely "conjectural" process. The relationships discovered among different elements of a single case have a prima facie causal connection: they are all at the scene of the crime. This is revelatory when one is at an early stage of analysis, for at that point there is no identifiable suspect and the crime itself may be difficult to discern. The fact that A, B, and C are present at the expected times and places (relative to some outcome of interest) is sufficient to establish them as independent variables. Proximal evidence is all that is required. Hence, the common identification of case studies as "plausibility probes," "pilot studies," "heuristic studies," "exploratory" and "theory-building" exercises.[15]

A large-N cross-study, by contrast, generally allows for the testing of only a few hypotheses but does so with a somewhat greater degree of confidence, as is appropriate to work whose primary purpose is to test an extant theory. There is less room for authorial intervention because evidence gathered from a cross-case research design can be interpreted in a limited number of ways. It is therefore more reliable. Another way of stating the point is to say that while case studies lean toward Type 1 errors (falsely rejecting the null hypothesis), cross-case studies lean toward Type 2 errors (failing to reject the false null hypothesis). This explains why case studies are more likely to be paradigm generating, while cross-case studies toil in the prosaic but highly structured field of normal science.

I do not mean to suggest that case studies never serve to confirm or disconfirm hypotheses. Evidence drawn from a single case may falsify a necessary or sufficient hypothesis, as discussed below. Additionally, case studies are often useful for the purpose of elucidating causal mechanisms, and this obviously affects the plausibility of an X/Y relationship. However, general theories rarely offer the kind of detailed and determinate predictions on within-case variation that would allow one to reject a hypothesis through pattern matching (without additional cross-case evidence). Theory testing is not the case study's strong suit. The selection of "crucial" cases is at pains to overcome the fact that the cross-case N is minimal. Thus, one is unlikely to reject a hypothesis, or to consider it definitively proved, on the basis of the study of a single case.

Harry Eckstein himself acknowledges that his argument for case studies as a form of theory confirmation is largely hypothetical. At the time of writing, several decades ago, he could not point to any social science study where a crucial case study had performed the heroic role assigned to it.[16] I suspect that this is still more or less true.

---

[15] Eckstein (1975), Ragin (1992, 1997), Rueschemeyer and Stephens (1997).   [16] Eckstein (1975).

Indeed, it is true even of experimental case studies in the natural sciences. "We must recognize," note Donald Campbell and Julian Stanley,

that continuous, multiple experimentation is more typical of science than once-and-for-all definitive experiments. The experiments we do today, if successful, will need replication and cross-validation at other times under other conditions before they can become an established part of science... [E]ven though we recognize experimentation as the basic language of proof... we should not expect that "crucial experiments" which pit opposing theories will be likely to have clear-cut outcomes. When one finds, for example, that competent observers advocate strongly divergent points of view, it seems likely on a priori grounds that both have observed something valid about the natural situation, and that both represent a part of the truth. The stronger the controversy, the more likely this is. Thus we might expect in such cases an experimental outcome with mixed results, or with the balance of truth varying subtly from experiment to experiment. The more mature focus... avoids crucial experiments and instead studies dimensional relationships and interactions along many degrees of the experimental variables.[17]

A single case study is still a single shot—a single example of a larger phenomenon.

The tradeoff between hypothesis generating and hypothesis testing helps us to reconcile the enthusiasm of case study researchers and the skepticism of case study critics. They are both right, for the looseness of case study research is a boon to new conceptualizations just as it is a bane to falsification.

4. Validity: Internal versus External

Questions of validity are often distinguished according to those that are *internal* to the sample under study and those that are *external* (i.e. applying to a broader—unstudied—population). Cross-case research is always more representative of the population of interest than case study research, so long as some sensible procedure of case selection is followed (presumably some version of random sampling). Case study research suffers problems of representativeness because it includes, by definition, only a small number of cases of some more general phenomenon. Are the men chosen by Robert Lane typical of white, immigrant, working-class, American males?[18] Is Middletown representative of other cities in America?[19] These sorts of questions forever haunt case study research. This means that case study research is generally weaker with respect to external validity than its cross-case cousin.

The corresponding virtue of case study research is its internal validity. Often, though not invariably, it is easier to establish the veracity of a causal relationship pertaining to a single case (or a small number of cases) than for a larger set of cases. Case study researchers share the bias of experimentalists in this regard: they tend to be

---

[17] Campbell and Stanley (1963: 3).   [18] Lane (1962).   [19] Lynd and Lynd (1929/1956).

more disturbed by threats to within-sample validity than by threats to out-of-sample validity. Thus, it seems appropriate to regard the tradeoff between external and internal validity, like other tradeoffs, as intrinsic to the cross-case/single-case choice of research design.

5. CAUSAL INSIGHT: CAUSAL MECHANISMS VERSUS CAUSAL EFFECTS

A third tradeoff concerns the sort of insight into causation that a researcher intends to achieve. Two goals may be usefully distinguished. The first concerns an estimate of the causal *effect*; the second concerns the investigation of a causal *mechanism* (i.e. pathway from X to Y).

By causal effect I refer to two things: (a) the magnitude of a causal relationship (the expected effect on *Y* of a given change in *X* across a population of cases) and (b) the relative precision or uncertainty associated with that point estimate. Evidently, it is difficult to arrive at a reliable estimate of causal effects across a population of cases by looking at only a single case or a small number of cases. (The one exception would be an experiment in which a given case can be tested repeatedly, returning to a virgin condition after each test. But here one faces inevitable questions about the representativeness of that much-studied case.)[20] Thus, the estimate of a causal effect is almost always grounded in cross-case evidence.

It is now well established that causal arguments depend not only on measuring causal effects, but also on the identification of a causal mechanism.[21] X must be connected with Y in a plausible fashion; otherwise, it is unclear whether a pattern of covariation is truly causal in nature, or what the causal interaction might be. Moreover, without a clear understanding of the causal pathway(s) at work in a causal relationship it is impossible to accurately specify the model, to identify possible instruments for the regressor of interest (if there are problems of endogeneity), or to interpret the results.[22] Thus, causal mechanisms are presumed in every estimate of a mean (average) causal effect.

---

[20] Note that the intensive study of a single unit may be a perfectly appropriate way to estimate causal effects *within that unit*. Thus, if one is interested in the relationship between welfare benefits and work effort in the United States one might obtain a more accurate assessment by examining data drawn from the USA alone, rather than crossnationally. However, since the resulting generalization does not extend beyond the unit in question it is not a case study in the usual sense.

[21] Achen (2002), Dessler (1991), Elster (1998), George and Bennett (2005), Gerring (2005), Hedstrom and Swedberg (1998), Mahoney (2001), Tilly (2001).

[22] In a discussion of instrumental variables in two-stage least-squares analysis, Angrist and Krueger (2001: 8) note that "good instruments often come from detailed knowledge of the economic mechanism, institutions determining the regressor of interest."

In the task of investigating causal mechanisms, cross-case studies are often not so illuminating. It has become a common criticism of large-N cross-national research—e.g. into the causes of growth, democracy, civil war, and other national-level outcomes—that such studies demonstrate correlations between inputs and outputs without clarifying the reasons for those correlations (i.e. clear causal pathways). We learn, for example, that infant mortality is strongly correlated with state failure;[23] but it is quite another matter to interpret this finding, which is consistent with a number of different causal mechanisms. Sudden increases in infant mortality might be the product of famine, of social unrest, of new disease vectors, of government repression, and of countless other factors, some of which might be expected to impact the stability of states, and others of which are more likely to be a result of state instability.

Case studies, if well constructed, may allow one to peer into the box of causality to locate the intermediate factors lying between some structural cause and its purported effect. Ideally, they allow one to "see" X and Y interact—Hume's billiard ball crossing the table and hitting a second ball.[24] Barney Glaser and Anselm Strauss point out that in fieldwork "general relations are often discovered *in vivo*; that is, the field worker literally sees them occur."[25] When studying decisional behavior case study research may offer insight into the intentions, the reasoning capabilities, and the information-processing procedures of the actors involved in a given setting. Thus, Dennis Chong uses in-depth interviews with a very small sample of respondents in order to better understand the process by which people reach decisions about civil liberties issues. Chong comments:

One of the advantages of the in-depth interview over the mass survey is that it records more fully how subjects arrive at their opinions. While we cannot actually observe the underlying mental process that gives rise to their responses, we can witness many of its outward manifestations. The way subjects ramble, hesitate, stumble, and meander as they formulate their answers tips us off to how they are thinking and reasoning through political issues.[26]

Similarly, the investigation of a single case may allow one to test the causal implications of a theory, thus providing corroborating evidence for a causal argument. This is sometimes referred to as pattern matching (Campbell 1988).

Dietrich Rueschemeyer and John Stephens offer an example of how an examination of causal mechanisms may call into question a general theory based on cross-case evidence. The thesis of interest concerns the role of British colonialism in fostering democracy among postcolonial regimes. In particular, the authors investigate the diffusion hypothesis, that democracy was enhanced by "the transfer of British governmental and representative institutions and the tutoring of the colonial

---

[23] Goldstone et al. (2000).

[24] This has something to do with the existence of process-tracing evidence, a matter discussed below. But it is not necessarily predicated on this sort of evidence. Sensitive time-series data, another specialty of the case study, is also relevant to the question of causal mechanisms.

[25] Glaser and Strauss (1967, 40).

[26] Chong (1993, 868). For other examples of in-depth interviewing see Hochschild (1981), Lane (1962).

people in the ways of British government." On the basis of in-depth analysis of several cases the authors report:

We did find evidence of this diffusion effect in the British settler colonies of North America and the Antipodes; but in the West Indies, the historical record points to a different connection between British rule and democracy. There the British colonial administration opposed suffrage extension, and only the white elites were "tutored" in the representative institutions. But, critically, we argued on the basis of the contrast with Central America, British colonialism did prevent the local plantation elites from controlling the local state and responding to the labor rebellion of the 1930s with massive repression. Against the adamant opposition of that elite, the British colonial rulers responded with concessions which allowed for the growth of the party–union complexes rooted in the black middle and working classes, which formed the backbone of the later movement for democracy and independence. Thus, the narrative histories of these cases indicate that the robust statistical relation between British colonialism and democracy is produced only in part by diffusion. The interaction of class forces, state power, and colonial policy must be brought in to fully account for the statistical result.[27]

Whether or not Rueschemeyer and Stephens are correct in their conclusions need not concern us here. What is critical, however, is that any attempt to deal with this question of causal mechanisms is heavily reliant on evidence drawn from case studies. In this instance, as in many others, the question of causal pathways is simply too difficult, requiring too many poorly measured or unmeasurable variables, to allow for accurate cross-sectional analysis.[28]

To be sure, causal mechanisms do not always require explicit attention. They may be quite obvious. And in other circumstances, they may be amenable to cross-case investigation. For example, a sizeable literature addresses the causal relationship between trade openness and the welfare state. The usual empirical finding is that more open economies are associated with higher social welfare spending. The question then becomes why such a robust correlation exists. What are the plausible interconnections between trade openness and social welfare spending? One possible causal path, suggested by David Cameron,[29] is that increased trade openness leads to greater domestic economic vulnerability to external shocks (due, for instance, to changing terms of trade). If so, one should find a robust correlation between annual variations in a country's terms of trade (a measure of economic vulnerability) and social welfare spending. As it happens, the correlation is not robust and this leads some commentators to doubt whether the putative causal mechanism proposed by David Cameron and many others is actually at work.[30] Thus, in instances where an intervening variable can be effectively operationalized across a large sample of cases it may be possible to test causal mechanisms without resorting to case study investigation.[31]

---

[27] Rueschemeyer and Stephens (1997, 62).
[28] Other good examples of within-case research that shed light on a broader theory can be found in Martin (1992); Martin and Swank (2004); Thies (2001); Young (1999).
[29] Cameron (1978).
[30] Alesina, Glaeser, and Sacerdote (2001).
[31] For additional examples of this nature, see Feng (2003); Papyrakis and Gerlagh (2003); Ross (2001).

Even so, the opportunities for investigating causal pathways are generally more apparent in a case study format. Consider the contrast between formulating a standardized survey for a large group of respondents and formulating an in-depth interview with a single subject or a small set of subjects, such as that undertaken by Dennis Chong in the previous example. In the latter situation, the researcher is able to probe into details that would be impossible to delve into, let alone anticipate, in a standardized survey. She may also be in a better position to make judgements as to the veracity and reliability of the respondent. Tracing causal mechanisms is about cultivating sensitivity to a local context. Often, these local contexts are essential to cross-case testing. Yet, the same factors that render case studies useful for micro-level investigation also make them less useful for measuring mean (average) causal effects. It is a classic tradeoff.

6 SCOPE OF PROPOSITION: DEEP VERSUS BROAD

The utility of a case study mode of analysis is in part a product of the scope of the causal argument that a researcher wishes to prove or demonstrate. Arguments that strive for great breadth are usually in greater need of cross-case evidence; causal arguments restricted to a small set of cases can more plausibly subsist on the basis of a single-case study. The extensive/intensive tradeoff is fairly commonsensical.[32] A case study of France probably offers more useful evidence for an argument about Europe than for an argument about the whole world. Propositional breadth and evidentiary breadth generally go hand in hand.

Granted, there are a variety of ways in which single-case studies can credibly claim to provide evidence for causal propositions of broad reach—e.g. by choosing cases that are especially representative of the phenomenon under study ("typical" cases) or by choosing cases that represent the most difficult scenario for a given proposition and are thus biased against the attainment of certain results ("crucial" cases). Even so, a proposition with a narrow scope is more conducive to case study analysis than a proposition with a broad purview, all other things being equal. The breadth of an inference thus constitutes one factor, among many, in determining the utility of the case study mode of analysis. This is reflected in the hesitancy of many case study researchers to invoke determinate causal propositions with great reach—"covering laws," in the idiom of philosophy of science.

By the same token, one of the primary virtues of the case study method is the depth of analysis that it offers. One may think of depth as referring to the detail,

---

[32] Eckstein (1975, 122).

richness, completeness, wholeness, or the degree of variance in an outcome that is accounted for by an explanation. The case study researcher's complaint about the thinness of cross-case analysis is well taken; such studies often have little to say about individual cases. Otherwise stated, cross-case studies are likely to explain only a small portion of the variance with respect to a given outcome. They approach that outcome at a very general level. Typically, a cross-case study aims only to explain the occurrence/non-occurrence of a revolution, while a case study might also strive to explain specific features of that event—why it occurred when it did and in the way that it did. Case studies are thus rightly identified with "holistic" analysis and with the "thick" description of events.[33]

Whether to strive for breadth or depth is not a question that can be answered in any definitive way. All we can safely conclude is that researchers invariably face a choice between knowing more about less, or less about more. The case study method may be defended, as well as criticized, along these lines.[34] Indeed, arguments about the "contextual sensitivity" of case studies are perhaps more precisely (and fairly) understood as arguments about depth and breadth. The case study researcher who feels that cross-case research on a topic is insensitive to context is usually not arguing that *nothing at all* is consistent across the chosen cases. Rather, the case study researcher's complaint is that much more could be said—accurately—about the phenomenon in question with a reduction in inferential scope.[35]

Indeed, I believe that a number of traditional issues related to case study research can be understood as the product of this basic tradeoff. For example, case study research is often lauded for its holistic approach to the study of social phenomena in which behavior is observed in natural settings. Cross-case research, by contrast, is criticized for its construction of artificial research designs that decontextualize the realm of social behavior by employing abstract variables that seem to bear little relationship to the phenomena of interest.[36] These associated congratulations and critiques may be understood as a conscious choice on the part of case study researchers to privilege depth over breadth.

7 THE POPULATION OF CASES: HETEROGENEOUS VERSUS HOMOGENEOUS

The choice between a case study and cross-case style of analysis is driven not only by the goals of the researcher, as reviewed above, but also by the shape of the empirical

---

[33] I am using the term "thick" in a somewhat different way than in Geertz (1973).
[34] See Ragin (2000, 22).
[35] Ragin (1987, ch. 2). Herbert Blumer's (1969, ch 7) complaints, however, are more far-reaching.
[36] Orum, Feagin, and Sjoberg (1991, 7).

universe that the researcher is attempting to understand. Consider, for starters, that the logic of cross-case analysis is premised on some degree of cross-unit comparability (unit homogeneity). Cases must be similar to each other in whatever respects might affect the causal relationship that the writer is investigating, or such differences must be controlled for. Uncontrolled heterogeneity means that cases are "apples and oranges;" one cannot learn anything about underlying causal processes by comparing their histories. The underlying factors of interest mean different things in different contexts (conceptual stretching) or the X/Y relationship of interest is different in different contexts (unit heterogeneity).

Case study researchers are often suspicious of large-sample research, which, they suspect, contains heterogeneous cases whose differences cannot easily be modeled. "Variable-oriented" research is said to involve unrealistic "homogenizing assumptions."[37] In the field of international relations, for example, it is common to classify cases according to whether they are deterrence failures or deterrence successes. However, Alexander George and Richard Smoke point out that "the separation of the dependent variable into only two subclasses, deterrence success and deterrence failure," neglects the great variety of ways in which deterrence can fail. Deterrence, in their view, has many independent causal paths (causal equifinality), and these paths may be obscured when a study lumps heterogeneous cases into a common sample.[38]

Another example, drawn from clinical work in psychology, concerns heterogeneity among a sample of individuals. Michel Hersen and David Barlow explain:

Descriptions of results from 50 cases provide a more convincing demonstration of the effectiveness of a given technique than separate descriptions of 50 individual cases. The major difficulty with this approach, however, is that the category in which these clients are classified most always becomes unmanageably heterogeneous. "Neurotics," [for example], . . . may have less in common than any group of people one would choose randomly. When cases are described individually, however, a clinician stands a better chance of gleaning some important information, since specific problems and specific procedures are usually described in more detail. When one lumps cases together in broadly defined categories, individual case descriptions are lost and the ensuing report of percentage success becomes meaningless.[39]

Under circumstances of extreme case heterogeneity, the researcher may decide that she is better off focusing on a single case or a small number of relatively homogeneous cases. Within-case evidence, or cross-case evidence drawn from a handful of most-similar cases, may be more useful than cross-case evidence, even though the ultimate interest of the investigator is in a broader population of cases. (Suppose one has a population of very heterogeneous cases, one or two of which undergo quasi-experimental transformations. Probably, one gains greater insight into causal

---

[37] Ragin (2000: 35). See also Abbott (1990); Bendix (1963); Meehl (1954); Przeworski and Teune (1970, 8–9); Ragin (1987; 2004, 124); Znaniecki (1934, 250–1).
[38] George and Smoke (1974, 514).
[39] Hersen and Barlow (1976, 11).

patterns throughout the population by examining these cases in detail than by undertaking some large-N cross-case analysis.) By the same token, if the cases available for study are relatively homogeneous, then the methodological argument for cross-case analysis is correspondingly strong. The inclusion of additional cases is unlikely to compromise the results of the investigation because these additional cases are sufficiently similar to provide useful information.

The issue of population heterogeneity/homogeneity may be understood, therefore, as a tradeoff between N (observations) and K (variables). If, in the quest to explain a particular phenomenon, each potential case offers only one observation and also requires one control variable (to neutralize heterogeneities in the resulting sample), then one loses degrees of freedom with each additional case. There is no point in using cross-case analysis or in extending a two-case study to further cases. If, on the other hand, each additional case is relatively cheap—if no control variables are needed or if the additional case offers more than one useful observation (through time)—then a cross-case research design may be warranted.[40] To put the matter more simply, when adjacent cases are unit homogeneous the addition of more cases is easy, for there is no (or very little) heterogeneity to model. When adjacent cases are heterogeneous additional cases are expensive, for every added heterogeneous element must be correctly modeled, and each modeling adjustment requires a separate (and probably unverifiable) assumption. The more background assumptions are required in order to make a causal inference, the more tenuous that inference is; it is not simply a question of attaining statistical significance. The ceteris paribus assumption at the core of all causal analysis is brought into question. In any case, the argument between case study and cross-case research designs is not about causal complexity per se (in the sense in which this concept is usually employed), but rather about the tradeoff between N and K in a particular empirical realm, and about the ability to model case heterogeneity through statistical legerdemain.[41]

Before concluding this discussion it is important to point out that researchers' judgements about case comparability are not, strictly speaking, matters that can be empirically verified. To be sure, one can look—and ought to look—for empirical patterns among potential cases. If those patterns are strong then the assumption of case comparability seems reasonably secure, and if they are not then there are grounds for doubt. However, debates about case comparability usually concern borderline instances. Consider that many phenomena of interest to social scientists are not rigidly bounded. If one is studying democracies there is always the question of how to define a democracy, and therefore of determining how high or low the threshold for inclusion in the sample should be. Researchers have different ideas about this, and these ideas can hardly be tested in a rigorous fashion. Similarly, there

---

[40] Shalev (1998).

[41] To be sure, if adjacent cases are *identical*, the phenomenon of interest is *invariant* then the researcher gains nothing at all by studying more examples of a phenomenon, for the results obtained with the first case will simply be replicated. However, virtually all phenomena of interest to social scientists have some degree of heterogeneity (cases are not identical), some stochastic element. Thus, the theoretical possibility of identical, invariant cases is rarely met in practice.

are long-standing disputes about whether it makes sense to lump poor and rich societies together in a single sample, or whether these constitute distinct populations. Again, the borderline between poor and rich (or "developed" and "undeveloped") is blurry, and the notion of hiving off one from the other for separate analysis questionable, and unresolvable on purely empirical grounds. There is no safe (or "conservative") way to proceed. A final sticking point concerns the cultural/historical component of social phenomena. Many case study researchers feel that to compare societies with vastly different cultures and historical trajectories is meaningless. Yet, many cross-case researchers feel that to restrict one's analytic focus to a single cultural or geographic region is highly arbitrary, and equally meaningless. In these situations, it is evidently the choice of the researcher how to understand case homogeneity/heterogeneity across the potential populations of an inference. Where do like cases end and unlike cases begin?

Because this issue is not, strictly speaking, empirical it may be referred to as an *ontological* element of research design. An ontology is a vision of the world as it really is, a more or less coherent set of assumptions about how the world works, a research *Weltanschauung* analogous to a Kuhnian paradigm.[42] While it seems odd to bring ontological issues into a discussion of social science methodology it may be granted that social science research is not a purely empirical endeavor. What one finds is contingent upon what one looks for, and what one looks for is to some extent contingent upon what one expects to find. Stereotypically, case study researchers tend to have a "lumpy" vision of the world; they see countries, communities, and persons as highly individualized phenomena. Cross-case researchers, by contrast, have a less differentiated vision of the world; they are more likely to believe that things are pretty much the same everywhere, at least as respects basic causal processes. These basic assumptions, or ontologies, drive many of the choices made by researchers when scoping out appropriate ground for research.

8 CAUSAL STRENGTH: STRONG VERSUS WEAK

Regardless of whether the population is homogeneous or heterogeneous, causal relationships are easier to study if the causal effect is strong, rather than weak. Causal "strength," as I use the term here, refers to the magnitude and consistency of X's effect on Y across a population of cases. (It invokes both the shape of the evidence at hand and whatever priors might be relevant to an interpretation of that evidence.) Where X has a strong effect on Y it will be relatively easy to study this relationship. Weak

---

[42] Gutting (1980); Hall (2003); Kuhn (1962/1970H); Wolin (1968).

relationships, by contrast, are often difficult to discern. This much is commonsensical, and applies to all research designs.

For our purposes, what is significant is that weak causal relationships are particularly opaque when encountered in a case study format. Thus, there is a methodological affinity between weak causal relationships and large-N cross-case analysis, and between strong causal relationships and case study analysis.

This point is clearest at the extremes. The strongest species of causal relationships may be referred to as *deterministic*, where X is assumed to be necessary and/or sufficient for Y's occurrence. A necessary and sufficient cause accounts for all of the variation on Y. A sufficient cause accounts for all of the variation in certain instances of Y. A necessary cause accounts, by itself, for the absence of Y. In all three situations, the relationship is usually assumed to be perfectly consistent, i.e. invariant. There are no exceptions.

It should be clear why case study research designs have an easier time addressing causes of this type. Consider that a deterministic causal proposition can be *dis*proved with a single case.[43] For example, the reigning theory of political stability once stipulated that only in countries that were relatively homogeneous, or where existing heterogeneity was mitigated by cross-cutting cleavages, would social peace endure.[44] Arend Lijphart's case study of the Netherlands, a country with reinforcing social cleavages and very little social conflict, disproved this deterministic theory on the basis of a single case.[45] (One may dispute whether the original theory is correctly understood as deterministic. However, if it *is*, then it has been decisively refuted by a single case study.) *Proving* an invariant causal argument generally requires more cases. However, it is not nearly as complicated as proving a probabilistic argument for the simple reason that one assumes invariant relationships; consequently, the single case under study carries more weight.

Magnitude and consistency—the two components of causal strength—are usually matters of degree. It follows that the more tenuous the connection between X and Y, the more difficult it will be to address in a case study format. This is because the causal mechanisms connecting X with Y are less likely to be detectable in a single case when the total impact is slight or highly irregular. It is no surprise, therefore, that the case study research design has, from the very beginning, been associated with causal arguments that are deterministic, while cross-case research has been associated with causal arguments that are assumed to be minimal in strength and "probabilistic" in consistency.[46] (Strictly speaking, causal magnitude and consistency are independent features of a causal relationship. However, because they tend to covary, and because we tend to conceptualize them in tandem, I treat them as components of a single dimension.)

---

[43] Dion (1998).

[44] Almond (1956); Bentley (1908/1967); Lipset (1960/1963); Truman (1951).

[45] Lijphart (1968); see also Lijphart (1969). For additional examples of case studies disconfirming general propositions of a deterministic nature see Allen (1965); Lipset, Trow, and Coleman (1956); Njolstad (1990); discussion in Rogowski (1995).

[46] Znaniecki (1934). See also discussion in Robinson (1951).

Now, let us now consider an example drawn from the other extreme. There is generally assumed to be a weak relationship between regime type and economic performance. Democracy, if it has any effect on economic growth at all, probably has only a slight effect over the near-to-medium term, and this effect is probably characterized by many exceptions (cases that do not fit the general pattern). This is because many things other than democracy affect a country's growth performance and because there may be a significant stochastic component in economic growth (factors that cannot be modeled in a general way). Because of the diffuse nature of this relationship it will probably be difficult to gain insight by looking at a single case. Weak relationships are difficult to observe in one instance. Note that even if there seems to be a strong relationship between democracy and economic growth in a given country it may be questioned whether this case is actually typical of the larger population of interest, given that we have already stipulated that the typical magnitude of this relationship is diminutive and irregular. Of course, the weakness of democracy's presumed relationship to growth is also a handicap in cross-case analysis. A good deal of criticism has been directed toward studies of this type, where findings are rarely robust.[47] Even so, it seems clear that if there *is* a relationship between democracy and growth it is more likely to be perceptible in a large cross-case setting. The positive hypothesis, as well as the null hypothesis, is better approached in a sample rather than in a case.

9 USEFUL VARIATION: RARE VERSUS COMMON

When analyzing causal relationships we must be concerned not only with the strength of an X/Y relationship but also with the distribution of evidence across available cases. Specifically, we must be concerned with the distribution of *useful variation*—understood as variation (temporal or spatial) on relevant parameters that might yield clues about a causal relationship. It follows that where useful variation is rare—i.e. limited to a few cases—the case study format recommends itself. Where, on the other hand, useful variation is common, a cross-case method of analysis may be more defensible.

Consider a phenomenon like social revolution, an outcome that occurs very rarely. The empirical distribution on this variable, if we count each country-year as an observation, consists of thousands of non-revolutions (0) and just a few revolutions (1). Intuitively, it seems clear that the few "revolutionary" cases are of great interest. We need to know as much as possible about them, for they exemplify all the variation that we have at our disposal. In this circumstance, a case study mode of analysis is

---

[47] Kittel (1999, 2005); Kittel and Winner (2005); Levine and Renelt (1992); Temple (1999).

difficult to avoid, though it might be combined with a large-N cross-case analysis. As it happens, many outcomes of interest to social scientists are quite rare, so the issue is by no means trivial.[48]

By way of contrast, consider a phenomenon like turnover, understood as a situation where a ruling party or coalition is voted out of office. Turnover occurs within most democratic countries on a regular basis, so the distribution of observations on this variable (incumbency/turnover) is relatively even across the universe of country-years. There are lots of instances of both outcomes. Under these circumstances a cross-case research design seems plausible, for the variation across cases is regularly distributed.

Another sort of variation concerns that which might occur *within* a given case. Suppose that only one or two cases within a large population exhibit quasi-experimental qualities: the factor of special interest varies, and there is no corresponding change in other factors that might affect the outcome. Clearly, we are likely to learn a great deal from studying this particular case—perhaps a lot more than we might learn from studying hundreds of additional cases that deviate from the experimental ideal. But again, if many cases have this experimental quality, there is little point in restricting ourselves to a single example; a cross-case research design may be justified.

A final sort of variation concerns the characteristics exhibited by a case relative to a particular theory that is under investigation. Suppose that a case provides a "crucial" test for a theory: it fits that theory's predictions so perfectly and so precisely that no other explanation could plausibly account for the performance of the case. If no other crucial cases present themselves, then an intensive study of this particular case is de rigueur. Of course, if many such cases lie within the population then it may be possible to study them all at once (with some sort of numeric reduction of the relevant parameters).

The general point here is that the distribution of useful variation across a population of cases matters a great deal in the choice between case study and cross-case research designs.

10 DATA AVAILABILITY: CONCENTRATED VERSUS DISPERSED

I have left the most prosaic factor for last. Sometimes, one's choice of research design is driven by the quality and quantity of information that is currently available, or

---

[48] Consider the following topics and their—extremely rare—instances of variation: early industrialization (England, the Netherlands), fascism (Germany, Italy), the use of nuclear weapons (United States), world war (WWI, WWII), single non-transferable vote electoral systems (Jordan, Taiwan, Vanuatu, pre-reform Japan), electoral system reforms within established democracies (France, Italy, Japan, New Zealand, Thailand). The problem of "rareness" is less common where parameters are scalar, rather than dichotomous. But there are still plenty of examples of phenomena whose distributions are skewed by a few outliers, e.g. population (China, India), personal wealth (Bill Gates, Warren Buffett), ethnic heterogeneity (Papua New Guinea).

could be easily gathered, on a given question. This is a practical matter, and is distinct from the actual (ontological) shape of the world. It concerns, rather, what we know about the former at a given point in time.[49] The question of evidence may be posed as follows: How much do we know about the cases at hand that might be relevant to the causal question of interest, and how precise, certain, and case comparable is that data? An evidence-rich environment is one where all relevant factors are measurable, where these measurements are relatively precise, where they are rendered in comparable terms across cases, and where one can be relatively confident that the information is, indeed, accurate. An evidence-poor environment is the opposite.

The question of available evidence impinges upon choices in research design when one considers its distribution across a population of cases. If relevant information is concentrated in a single case, or if it is contained in incommensurable formats across a population of cases, then a case study mode of analysis is almost unavoidable. If, on the other hand, it is evenly distributed across the population—i.e. we are equally well informed about all cases—and is case comparable, then there is little to recommend a narrow focus. (I employ data, evidence, and information as synonyms in this section.)

Consider the simplest sort of example, where information is truly limited to one or a few cases. Accurate historical data on infant mortality and other indices of human development are currently available for only a handful of countries (these include Chile, Egypt, India, Jamaica, Mauritius, Sri Lanka, the United States, and several European countries).[50] This data problem is not likely to be rectified in future years, as it is exceedingly difficult to measure infant mortality except by public or private records. Consequently, anyone studying this general subject is likely to rely heavily on these cases, where in-depth analysis is possible and profitable. Indeed, it is not clear whether *any* large-N cross-case analysis is possible prior to the twentieth century. Here, a case study format is virtually prescribed, and a cross-case format proscribed.

Other problems of evidence are more subtle. Let us dwell for the moment on the question of data comparability. In their study of social security spending, Mulligan, Gil, and Sala-i-Martin note that

although our spending and design numbers are of good quality, there are some missing observations and, even with all the observations, it is difficult to reduce the variety of elderly subsidies to one or two numbers. For this reason, case studies are an important part of our analysis, since those studies do not require numbers that are comparable across a large number of countries. Our case study analysis utilizes data from a variety of country-specific sources, so we do not have to reduce "social security" or "democracy" to one single number.[51]

Here, the incommensurability of the evidence militates towards a case study format. In the event that the authors (or subsequent analysts) discover a coding system that provides reasonably valid cross-case measures of social security, democracy, and

---

[49] Of course, what we know about the potential cases is not independent of the underlying reality; it is, nonetheless, not entirely dependent on that reality.

[50] Gerring (2007b).   [51] Mulligan, Gil, and Sala-i-Martin (2002, 13).

other relevant concepts then our state of knowledge about the subject is changed, and a cross-case research design is rendered more plausible.

Importantly, the state of evidence on a topic is never entirely fixed. Investigators may gather additional data, recode existing data, or discover new repositories of data. Thus, when discussing the question of evidence one must consider the quality and quantity of evidence that *could* be gathered on a given question, given sufficient time and resources. Here it is appropriate to observe that collecting new data, and correcting existing data, is usually easier in a case study format than in a large-N cross-case format. It will be difficult to rectify data problems if one's cases number in the hundreds or thousands. There are simply too many data points to allow for this.

One might consider this issue in the context of recent work on democracy. There is general skepticism among scholars with respect to the viability of extant global indicators intended to capture this complex concept (e.g. by Freedom House and by the Polity IV data project).[52] Measurement error, aggregation problems, and questions of conceptual validity are rampant. When dealing with a single country or a single continent it is possible to overcome some of these faults by manually recoding the countries of interest.[53] The case study format often gives the researcher an opportunity to fact-check, to consult multiple sources, to go back to primary materials, and to overcome whatever biases may affect the secondary literature. Needless to say, this is not a feasible approach for an individual investigator if one's project encompasses every country in the world. The best one can usually manage, under the circumstances, is some form of convergent validation (by which different indices of the same concept are compared) or small adjustments in the coding intended to correct for aggregation problems or measurement error.[54]

For the same reason, the collection of original data is typically more difficult in cross-case analysis than in case study analysis, involving greater expense, greater difficulties in identifying and coding cases, learning foreign languages, traveling, and so forth. Whatever can be done for a set of cases can usually be done more easily for a single case.

It should be kept in mind that many of the countries of concern to anthropologists, economists, historians, political scientists, and sociologists are still terra incognita. Outside the OECD, and with the exception of a few large countries that have received careful attention from scholars (e.g. India, Brazil, China), most countries of the world are not well covered by the social science literature. Any statement that one might wish to make about, say, Botswana, will be difficult to verify if one has recourse only to secondary materials. And these—very limited—secondary sources are not necessarily of the most reliable sort. Thus, if one wishes to say something about political patterns obtaining in roughly 90 percent of the world's countries and if one wishes to go beyond matters that can be captured in standard statistics collected by the World Bank and the IMF and other agencies (and these can also be very sketchy

---

[52] Bollen (1993); Bowman, Lehoucq, and Mahoney (2005); Munck and Verkuilen (2002); Treier and Jackman (2005).

[53] Bowman, Lehoucq, and Mahoney (2005).   [54] Bollen (1993); Treier and Jackman (2005).

when lesser-studied countries are concerned) one is more or less obliged to conduct a case study. Of course, one could, in principle, gather similar information across all relevant cases. However, such an enterprise faces formidable logistical difficulties. Thus, for practical reasons, case studies are sometimes the most defensible alternative when the researcher is faced with an information-poor environment.

However, this point is easily turned on its head. Datasets are now available to study many problems of concern to the social sciences. Thus, it may not be necessary to collect original information for one's book, article, or dissertation. Sometimes in-depth single-case analysis is more time consuming than cross-case analysis. If so, there is no informational advantage to a case study format. Indeed, it may be easier to utilize existing information for a cross-case analysis, particularly when a case study format imposes hurdles of its own—e.g. travel to distant climes, risk of personal injury, expense, and so forth. It is interesting to note that some observers consider case studies to be "relatively *more* expensive in time and resources."[55]

Whatever the specific logistical hurdles, it is a general truth that the shape of the evidence—that which is currently available and that which might feasibly be collected by an author—often has a strong influence on an investigator's choice of research designs. Where the evidence for particular cases is richer and more accurate there is a strong prima facie argument for a case study format focused on those cases. Where, by contrast, the relevant evidence is equally good for all potential cases, and is comparable across those cases, there is no reason to shy away from cross-case analysis. Indeed, there may be little to gain from case study formats.

11 CONCLUSIONS

At the outset, I took note of the severe disjuncture that has opened up between an often-maligned methodology and a heavily practiced method. The case study is disrespected but nonetheless regularly employed. Indeed, it remains the workhorse of most disciplines and subfields in the social sciences. How, then, can one make sense of this schizophrenia between methodological theory and praxis?

The torment of the case study begins with its definitional penumbra. Frequently, this key term is conflated with a set of disparate methodological traits that are not definitionally entailed. My first objective, therefore, was to craft a narrower and more useful concept for purposes of methodological discussion. The case study, I argued, is best defined as an intensive study of a single case with an aim to generalize across a larger set of cases. It follows from this definition that case studies may be small- or large-N, qualitative or quantitative, experimental or observational, synchronic or diachronic. It also follows that the case study research design comports with any

[55] Stoecker (1991, 91).

macrotheoretical framework or paradigm—e.g. behavioralism, rational choice, institutionalism, or interpretivism. It is not epistemologically distinct. What differentiates the case study from the cross-case study is simply its way of defining observations, not its analysis of those observations or its method of modeling causal relations. The case study research design constructs its observations from a single case or a small number of cases, while cross-case research designs construct observations across multiple cases. Cross-case and case study research operate, for the most part, at different levels of analysis.

The travails of the case study are not simply definitional. They are also rooted in an insufficient appreciation of the methodological tradeoffs that this method calls forth. At least eight characteristic strengths and weaknesses must be considered. Ceteris paribus, case studies are more useful when the strategy of research is exploratory rather than confirmatory/disconfirmatory, when internal validity is given preference over external validity, when insight into causal mechanisms is prioritized over insight into causal effects, when propositional depth is prized over breadth, when the population of interest is heterogeneous rather than homogeneous, when causal relationships are strong rather than weak, when useful information about key parameters is available only for a few cases, and when the available data are concentrated rather than dispersed.

Although I do not have the space to discuss other issues in this venue, it is worth mentioning that other considerations may also come into play in a researcher's choice between a case study and cross-case study research format. However, these additional issues—e.g. causal complexity and the state of research on a topic—do not appear to have clear methodological affinities. They may augur one way, or the other.

My objective throughout this chapter is to restore a greater sense of meaning, purpose, and integrity to the case study method. It is hoped that by offering a narrower and more carefully bounded definition of this method the case study may be rescued from some of its most persistent ambiguities. And it is hoped that the characteristic strengths of this method, as well as its limitations, will be more apparent to producers and consumers of case study research. The case study is a useful tool for some research objectives, but not all.

REFERENCES

ABADIE, A., and GARDEAZABAL, J. 2003. The economic costs of conflict: a case study of the Basque Country. *American Economic Review*, 93: 113–32.

ABBOTT, A. 1990. Conceptions of time and events in social science methods: causal and narrative approaches. *Historical Methods*, 23 (4): 140–50.

—— 1992. From causes to events: notes on narrative positivism. *Sociological Methods and Research*, 20 (4): 428–55.

—— 2001. *Time Matters: On Theory and Method*. Chicago: University of Chicago Press.

——and FORREST, J. 1986. Optimal matching methods for historical sequences. *Journal of Interdisciplinary History*, 16 (3): 471–94.

——and TSAY, A. 2000. Sequence analysis and optimal matching methods in sociology. *Sociological Methods and Research*, 29: 3–33.

ABELL, P. 1987. *The Syntax of Social Life: The Theory and Method of Comparative Narratives*. Oxford: Clarendon Press.

——2004. Narrative explanation: an alternative to variable-centered explanation? *Annual Review of Sociology*, 30: 287–310.

ACEMOGLU, D., JOHNSON, S., and ROBINSON, J. A. 2003. An African success story: Botswana. Pp. 80–122 in *In Search of Prosperity: Analytic Narratives on Economic Growth*, ed. D. Rodrik. Princeton: Princeton University Press.

ACHEN, C. H. 1986. *The Statistical Analysis of Quasi-Experiments*. Berkeley and Los Angeles: University of California Press.

——2002. Toward a new political methodology: microfoundations and ART. *Annual Review of Political Science*, 5: 423–50.

——and SNIDAL, D. 1989. Rational deterrence theory and comparative case studies. *World Politics*, 41: 143–69.

ALESINA, A., GLAESER, E., and SACERDOTE, B. 2001. Why doesn't the US have a European-style welfare state? *Brookings Papers on Economic Activity*, 2: 187–277.

ALLEN, W. S. 1965. *The Nazi Seizure of Power: The Experience of a Single German Town, 1930–1935*. New York: Watts.

ALMOND, G. A. 1956. Comparative political systems. *Journal of Politics*, 18: 391–409.

ANGRIST, J. D., and KRUEGER, A. B. 2001. Instrumental variables and the search for identification: from supply and demand to natural experiments. *Journal of Economic Perspectives*, 15 (4): 69–85.

BATES, R. H., GREIF, A., LEVI, M., ROSENTHAL, J.-L. and WEINGAST, B. 1998. *Analytic Narratives*. Princeton: Princeton University Press.

BENDIX, R. 1963. Concepts and generalizations in comparative sociological studies. *American Sociological Review*, 28: 532–9.

BENTLEY, A. 1908/1967. *The Process of Government*. Cambridge, Mass.: Harvard University Press.

BLUMER, H. 1969. *Symbolic Interactionism: Perspective and Method*. Berkeley and Los Angeles: University of California Press.

BOLLEN, K. A. 1993. Liberal democracy: validity and method factors in cross-national measures. *American Journal of Political Science*, 37: 1207–30.

BONOMA, T. V. 1985. Case research in marketing: opportunities, problems, and a process. *Journal of Marketing Research*, 22 (2): 199–208.

BOWMAN, K., LEHOUCQ, F., and MAHONEY, J. 2005. Measuring political democracy: case expertise, data adequacy, and Central America. *Comparative Political Studies*, 38 (8): 939–70.

BRADY, H. E., and COLLIER, D. eds. 2004. *Rethinking Social Inquiry: Diverse Tools, Shared Standards*. Lanham, Md.: Rowman & Littlefield.

BRAUMOELLER, B. F., and GOERTZ, G. 2000. The methodology of necessary conditions. *American Journal of Political Science*, 44 (3): 844–58.

BUNGE, M. 1997. Mechanism and explanation. *Philosophy of the Social Sciences*, 27: 410–65.

BUTHE, T. 2002. Taking temporality seriously: modeling history and the use of narratives as evidence. *American Political Science Review*, 96 (3): 481–93.

CAMERON, D. 1978. The expansion of the public economy: a comparative analysis. *American Political Science Review*, 72 (4): 1243–61.

CAMPBELL, D. T. 1988. *Methodology and Epistemology for Social Science*, ed. E. S. Overman. Chicago: University of Chicago Press.

—— and STANLEY, J. 1963. *Experimental and Quasi-experimental Designs for Research*. Boston: Houghton Mifflin.

CHANDRA, K. 2004. *Why Ethnic Parties Succeed: Patronage and Ethnic Headcounts in India*. Cambridge: Cambridge University Press.

CHERNOFF, B., and WARNER, A. 2002. Sources of fast growth in Mauritius: 1960–2000. Center for International Development, Harvard University.

CHONG, D. 1993. How people think, reason, and feel about rights and liberties. *American Journal of Political Science*, 37 (3): 867–99.

COASE, R. H. 1959. The Federal Communications Commission. *Journal of Law and Economics*, 2: 1–40.

—— 2000. The acquisition of Fisher Body by General Motors. *Journal of Law and Economics*, 43: 15–31.

COLLIER, D. 1993. The comparative method. Pp. 105–19 in *Political Science: The State of the Discipline II*, ed. A. W. Finifter. Washington, DC: American Political Science Association.

COOK, T., and CAMPBELL, D. 1979. *Quasi-experimentation: Design and Analysis Issues for Field Settings*. Boston: Houghton Mifflin.

DE SOTO, H. 1989. *The Other Path: The Invisible Revolution in the Third World*. New York: Harper & Row.

DESSLER, D. 1991. Beyond correlations: toward a causal theory of war. *International Studies Quarterly*, 35: 337–55.

DION, D. 1998. Evidence and inference in the comparative case study. *Comparative Politics*, 30: 127–45.

ECKSTEIN, H. 1975. Case studies and theory in political science. Pp. 79–133 in *Handbook of Political Science, vii: Political Science: Scope and Theory*, ed. F. I. Greenstein and N. W. Polsby. Reading, Mass.: Addison-Wesley.

—— 1975/1992. Case studies and theory in political science. In *Regarding Politics: Essays on Political Theory, Stability, and Change*, by H. Eckstein. Berkeley and Los Angeles: University of California Press.

ELMAN, C. 2005. Explanatory typologies in qualitative studies of international politics. *International Organization*, 59 (2): 293–326.

ELSTER, J. 1998. A plea for mechanisms. Pp. 45–73 in *Social Mechanisms: An Analytical Approach to Social Theory*, ed. P. Hedstrom and R. Swedberg. Cambridge: Cambridge University Press.

FEARON, J. 1991. Counter factuals and hypothesis testing in political science. *World Politics*, 43: 169–95.

FENG, Y. 2003. *Democracy, Governance, and Economic Performance: Theory and Evidence*. Cambridge, Mass.: MIT Press.

FREEDMAN, D. A. 1991. Statistical models and shoe leather. *Sociological Methodology*, 21: 291–313.

FRIEDMAN, M. 1953. The methodology of positive economics. Pp. 3–43 in *Essays in Positive Economics*, by M. Friedman. Chicago: University of Chicago Press.

GEDDES, B. 1990. How the cases you choose affect the answers you get: selection bias in comparative politics. Pp. 131–52 in *Political Analysis*, vol. ii, ed. J. A. Stimson. Ann Arbor: University of Michigan Press.

—— 2003. *Paradigms and Sand Castles: Theory Building and Research Design in Comparative Politics*. Ann Arbor: University of Michigan Press.

GEERTZ, C. 1973. Thick description: toward an interpretive theory of culture. Pp. 3–30 in *The Interpretation of Cultures*, by C. Geertz. New York: Basic Books.

GEORGE, A. L., and BENNETT, A. 2005. *Case Studies and Theory Development*. Cambridge, Mass.: MIT Press.

——and SMOKE, R. 1974. *Deterrence in American Foreign Policy: Theory and Practice*. New York: Columbia University Press.

GERRING, J. 2001. *Social Science Methodology: A Criterial Framework*. Cambridge: Cambridge University Press.

——2005. Causation: a unified framework for the social sciences. *Journal of Theoretical Politics*, 17 (2): 163–98.

——2007a. *Case Study Research: Principles and Practices*. Cambridge: Cambridge University Press.

——2007b. Global justice as an empirical question. *PS: Political Science and Politics* (forthcoming).

——and BARRESI, P. A. 2003. Putting ordinary language to work: a min-max strategy of concept formation in the social sciences. *Journal of Theoretical Politics*, 15 (2): 201–32.

——and THOMAS, C. 2005. Comparability: a key issue in research design. MS.

GLASER, B. G., and STRAUSS, A. L. 1967. *The Discovery of Grounded Theory: Strategies for Qualitative Research*. New York: Aldine de Gruyter.

GOERTZ, G. 2003. The substantive importance of necessary condition hypotheses. Ch. 4 in *Necessary Conditions: Theory, Methodology and Applications*, ed. G. Goertz and H. Starr. New York: Rowman and Littlefield.

——and LEVY, J. eds. Forthcoming. Causal explanations, necessary conditions, and case studies: World War I and the end of the Cold War. MS.

——and STARR, H. eds. 2003. *Necessary Conditions: Theory, Methodology and Applications*. New York: Rowman and Littlefield.

GOLDSTONE, J. A. 1997. Methodological issues in comparative macrosociology. *Comparative Social Research*, 16: 121–32.

——GURR, T. R., HARFF, B., LEVY, M. A., MARSHALL, M. G., BATES, R. H., EPSTEIN, D. L., KAHL, C. H., SURKO, P. T., ULFELDER, J. C., Jr., and UNGER, A. N. 2000. State Failure Task Force report: phase III findings. Available at **www.cidcm.umd.edu/inscr/stfail/SFTF%20 Phase%20III%20Report%20Final.pdf**

GOLDTHORPE, J. H. 1997. Current issues in comparative macrosociology: a debate on methodological issues. *Comparative Social Research*, 16: 121–32.

GRIFFIN, L. J. 1993. Narrative, event-structure analysis, and causal interpretation in historical sociology. *American Journal of Sociology*, 98: 1094–133.

GUTTING, G. ed. 1980. *Paradigms and Revolutions: Appraisals and Applications of Thomas Kuhn's Philosophy of Science*. Notre Dame, Ind.: University of Notre Dame Press.

HALL, P. A. 2003. Aligning ontology and methodology in comparative politics. In *Comparative Historical Analysis in the Social Sciences*, ed. J. Mahoney and D. Rueschemeyer. Cambridge: Cambridge University Press.

HEDSTROM, P., and SWEDBERG, R. eds. 1998. *Social Mechanisms: An Analytical Approach to Social Theory*. Cambridge: Cambridge University Press.

HERSEN, M., and BARLOW, D. H. 1976. *Single-Case Experimental Designs: Strategies for Studying Behavior Change*. Oxford: Pergamon Press.

HOCHSCHILD, J. L. 1981. *What's Fair? American Beliefs about Distributive Justice*. Cambridge, Mass.: Harvard University Press.

JERVIS, R. 1989. Rational deterrence: theory and evidence. *World Politics*, 41 (2): 183–207.

KENNEDY, P. 2003. *A Guide to Econometrics*, 5th edn. Cambridge, Mass.: MIT Press.

KING, C. 2004. The micropolitics of social violence. *World Politics*, 56 (3): 431–55.

KING, G., KEOHANE, R. O. and VERBA, S. 1994. *Designing Social Inquiry: Scientific Inference in Qualitative Research.* Princeton: Princeton University Press.

KITTEL, B. 1999. Sense and sensitivity in pooled analysis of political data. *European Journal of Political Research,* 35: 225–53.

—— 2005. A crazy methodology? On the limits of macroquantitative social science research. Unpublished MS. University of Amsterdam.

KITTEL, B., and WINNER, H. 2005. How reliable is pooled analysis in political economy? The globalization–welfare state nexus revisited. *European Journal of Political Research,* 44 (2): 269–93.

KUHN, T. S. 1962/1970. *The Structure of Scientific Revolutions.* Chicago: University of Chicago Press.

LANE, R. 1962. *Political Ideology: Why the American Common Man Believes What He Does.* New York: Free Press.

LEBOW, R. N. 2000. What's so different about a counterfactual? *World Politics,* 52: 550–85.

LEVINE, R., and RENELT, D. 1992. A sensitivity analysis of cross-country growth regressions. *American Economic Review,* 82 (4): 942–63.

LIBECAP, G. D. 1993. *Contracting for Property Rights.* Cambridge: Cambridge University Press.

LIEBERSON, S. 1985. *Making it Count: The Improvement of Social Research and Theory.* Berkeley and Los Angeles: University of California Press.

—— 1992. Einstein, Renoir, and Greeley: some thoughts about evidence in sociology: 1991 Presidential Address. *American Sociological Review,* 57 (1): 1–15.

—— 1994. More on the uneasy case for using Mill-type methods in small-N comparative studies. *Social Forces,* 72 (4): 1225–37.

LIJPHART, A. 1968. *The Politics of Accommodation: Pluralism and Democracy in the Netherlands.* Berkeley and Los Angeles: University of California Press.

—— 1969. Consociational democracy. *World Politics,* 21 (2): 207–25.

—— 1971. Comparative politics and the comparative method. *American Political Science Review,* 65 (3): 682–93.

LIPSET, S. M. 1960/1963. *Political Man: The Social Bases of Politics.* Garden City, NY: Anchor Books.

—— TROW, M. A., and COLEMAN, J. S. 1956. *Union Democracy: The Internal Politics of the International Typographical Union.* New York: Free Press.

LITTLE, D. 1998. *Microfoundations, Method, and Causation.* New Brunswick, NJ: Transaction.

LYND, R. S., and LYND, H. M. 1929/1956. *Middletown: A Study in American Culture.* New York: Harcourt, Brace.

McKEOWN, T. J. 1983. Hegemonic stability theory and nineteenth-century tariff levels. *International Organization,* 37 (1): 73–91.

MAHONEY, J. 2001. Beyond correlational analysis: recent innovations in theory and method. *Sociological Forum,* 16 (3): 575–93.

—— and RUESCHEMEYER, D. eds. 2003. *Comparative Historical Analysis in the Social Sciences.* Cambridge: Cambridge University Press.

—— and GOERTZ, G. 2004. The possibility principle: choosing negative cases in comparative research. *American Political Science Review,* 98 (4): 653–69.

MANSKI, C. F. 1993. Identification problems in the social sciences. *Sociological Methodology,* 23: 1–56.

MARTIN, C. J., and SWANK, D. 2004. Does the organization of capital matter? Employers and active labor market policy at the national and firm levels. *American Political Science Review,* 98 (4): 593–612.

MARTIN, L. L. 1992. *Coercive Cooperation: Explaining Multilateral Economic Sanctions*. Princeton: Princeton University Press.

MEEHL, P. E. 1954. *Clinical versus Statistical Predictions: A Theoretical Analysis and a Review of the Evidence*. Minneapolis: University of Minnesota Press.

MULLIGAN, C., GIL, R., and SALA-I-MARTIN, X. 2002. Social security and democracy. MS. University of Chicago and Columbia University.

MUNCK, G. L., and SNYDER, R. eds. 2007. *Passion, Craft, and Method in Comparative Politics*. Baltimore: Johns Hopkins University Press.

—— and VERKUILEN, J. 2002. Measuring democracy: evaluating alternative indices. *Comparative Political Studies*, 35 (1): 5–34.

NJOLSTAD, O. 1990. Learning from history? Case studies and the limits to theory-building. Pp. 220–46 in *Arms Races: Technological and Political Dynamics*, ed. O. Njolstad. Thousand Oaks, Calif.: Sage.

NORTH, D. C., ANDERSON, T. L., and HILL, P. J. 1983. *Growth and Welfare in the American Past: A New American History*, 3rd edn. Englewood Cliffs, NJ: Prentice-Hall.

—— and THOMAS, R. P. 1973. *The Rise of the Western World*. Cambridge: Cambridge University Press.

—— and WEINGAST, B. R. 1989. Constitutions and commitment: the evolution of institutions governing public choice in seventeenth-century England. *Journal of Economic History*, 49: 803–32.

ODELL, J. S. 2004. Case study methods in international political economy. Pp. 56–80 in *Models, Numbers and Cases: Methods for Studying International Relations*, ed. D. F. Sprinz and Y. Wolinsky-Nahmias. Ann Arbor: University of Michigan.

ORUM, A. M., FEAGIN, J. R., and SJOBERG, G. 1991. Introduction: the nature of the case study. Pp. 1–26 in *A Case for the Case*, ed. J. R. Feagin, A. M. Orum, and G. Sjoberg. Chapel Hill: University of North Carolina Press.

PAPYRAKIS, E., and GERLAGH, R. 2003. The resource curse hypothesis and its transmission channels. *Journal of Comparative Economics*, 32: 181–93.

PATTON, M. Q. 2002. *Qualitative Evaluation and Research Methods*. Newbury Park, Calif.: Sage.

POPPER, K. 1934/1968. *The Logic of Scientific Discovery*. New York: Harper & Row.

—— 1969. *Conjectures and Refutations*. London: Routledge and Kegan Paul.

POSNER, D. 2004. The political salience of cultural difference: why Chewas and Tumbukas are allies in Zambia and adversaries in Malawi. *American Political Science Review*, 98 (4): 529–46.

PRZEWORSKI, A., and TEUNE, H. 1970. *The Logic of Comparative Social Inquiry*. New York: John Wiley.

RAGIN, C. C. 1987. *The Comparative Method: Moving beyond Qualitative and Quantitative Strategies*. Berkeley and Los Angeles: University of California Press.

—— 1992. Cases of "what is a case?" Pp. 1–17 in *What Is a Case? Exploring the Foundations of Social Inquiry*, ed. C. C. Ragin and H. S. Becker. Cambridge: Cambridge University Press.

—— 1997. Turning the tables: how case-oriented research challenges variable-oriented research. *Comparative Social Research*, 16: 27–42.

—— 2000. *Fuzzy-Set Social Science*. Chicago: University of Chicago Press.

—— 2004. Turning the tables. Pp. 123–38 in *Rethinking Social Inquiry: Diverse Tools, Shared Standards*, ed. H. E. Brady and D. Collier. Lanham, Md.: Rowman & Littlefield.

ROBINSON, W. S. 1951. The logical structure of analytic induction. *American Sociological Review*, 16 (6): 812–18.

RODRIK, D. ed. 2003. *In Search of Prosperity: Analytic Narratives on Economic Growth.* Princeton: Princeton University Press.

ROGOWSKI, R. 1995. The role of theory and anomaly in social-scientific inference. *American Political Science Review,* 89 (2): 467–70.

ROSS, M. 2001. Does oil hinder democracy? *World Politics,* 53: 325–61.

RUBIN, D. B. 1974. Estimating causal effects of treatments in randomized and nonrandomized studies. *Journal of Educational Psychology,* 66: 688–701.

RUESCHEMEYER, D., and STEPHENS, J. D. 1997. Comparing historical sequences: a powerful tool for causal analysis. *Comparative Social Research,* 16: 55–72.

SAMBANIS, N. 2004. Using case studies to expand economic models of civil war. *Perspectives on Politics,* 2 (2): 259–79.

SARTORI, G. 1976. *Parties and Party Systems.* Cambridge: Cambridge University Press.

SEKHON, J. S. 2004. Quality meets quantity: case studies, conditional probability and counterfactuals. *Perspectives in Politics,* 2 (2): 281–93.

SHALEV, M. 1998. Limits of and alternatives to multiple regression in macro-comparative research. Paper prepared for presentation at the second conference on The Welfare State at the Crossroads, Stockholm.

SMELSER, N. J. 1973. The methodology of comparative analysis. Pp. 42–86 in *Comparative Research Methods,* ed. D. P. Warwick and S. Osherson. Englewood Cliffs, NJ: Prentice-Hall.

SRINIVASAN, T. N., and BHAGWATI, J. 1999. Outward-orientation and development: are revisionists right? Discussion Paper no. 806, Economic Growth Center, Yale University.

STOECKER, R. 1991. Evaluating and rethinking the case study. *Sociological Review,* 39: 88–112.

SYMPOSIUM: QUALITATIVE COMPARATIVE ANALYSIS (QCA). 2004. *Qualitative Methods: Newsletter of the American Political Science Association Organized Section on Qualitative Methods,* 1 (2): 2–25.

TEMPLE, J. 1999. The new growth evidence. *Journal of Economic Literature,* 37: 112–56.

TETLOCK, P. E., and BELKIN, A. eds. 1996. *Counterfactual Thought Experiments in World Politics.* Princeton: Princeton University Press.

THIES, M. F. 2001. Keeping tabs on partners: the logic of delegation in coalition governments. *American Journal of Political Science,* 45 (3): 580–98.

TILLY, C. 2001. Mechanisms in political processes. *Annual Review of Political Science,* 4: 21–41.

TREIER, S., and JACKMAN, S. 2005. Democracy as a latent variable. Department of Political Science, Stanford University.

TRUMAN, D. B. 1951. *The Governmental Process.* New York: Alfred A. Knopf.

VANDENBROUCKE, J. P. 2001. In defense of case reports and case series. *Annals of Internal Medicine,* 134 (4): 330–4.

VREELAND, J. R. 2003. *The IMF and Economic Development.* Cambridge: Cambridge University Press.

WARD, M. D., and BAKKE, K. 2005. Predicting civil conflicts: on the utility of empirical research. MS.

WINSHIP, C., and MORGAN, S. L. 1999. The estimation of causal effects of observational data. *Annual Review of Sociology,* 25: 659–707.

—— and SOBEL, M. 2004. Causal inference in sociological studies. Pp. 481–503 in *Handbook of Data Analysis,* ed. M. Hardy and A. Bryman. London: Sage.

WOLIN, S. S. 1968. Paradigms and political theories. Pp. 125–52 in *Politics and Experience,* ed. P. King and B. C. Parekh. Cambridge: Cambridge University Press.

YOUNG, O. R. ed. 1999. *The Effectiveness of International Environmental Regimes: Causal Connections and Behavioral Mechanisms.* Cambridge, Mass.: MIT Press.

ZNANIECKI, F. 1934. *The Method of Sociology.* New York: Rinehart.

CHAPTER 5

....

FIELD RESEARCH

....

ELISABETH JEAN WOOD

A SCHOLAR of comparative politics need not leave her office to have at her fingertips
an astounding array of information about most countries. In addition to compil-
ations of economic data, readily available information includes recent proclamations
by many insurgent groups, internal debate within some social organizations via
email lists and online fora, public opinion data from most poor as well as rich
countries, texts of parliamentary proceedings, local electoral results, and many
national, regional, and local newspapers. Even if a source is not available online,
networking among libraries increasingly makes the resources of the best research
libraries available to scholars working elsewhere.

This unprecedented access to information sharpens the focus on the question this
chapter addresses: Why ever leave one's office? Given the declining cost of non-field
methods, should researchers not invest more in those methods? What does field
research contribute to scholarly understanding? Are there particular questions or
settings for which field research is particularly suited? Or particularly not suited?
How might we practice it better? What are the challenges typically confronted in field
research?

By "field research," I mean research based on personal interaction with research
subjects in their own setting.[1] Field research includes research with residents of
one's own neighborhood or organization; one need not go abroad to be in "the

  * The author gratefully acknowledges support from Yale University and the Santa Fe Institute and
comments from Carles Boix, Stathis Kalyvas, Evan Lieberman, Susan Stokes, and Jeremy Weinstein, as
well as from the members of the Laboratory on Comparative Ethnic Processes.
  [1] Thus field research contrasts with research carried out in the laboratory. "Field" is defined as "used
attributively to denote an investigation, study, etc., carried out in the natural environment of a given
material, language, animal, etc., and not in the laboratory, study, or office" *OED* (2nd edn.).

field."[2] Field research methods include carrying out surveys, interviews both informal and structured, field experiments, and the activities known as participant observation (which often includes living in a community alongside residents, ongoing observation of community life or organization meetings, and working alongside workers). Archival research is excluded, although some similar practical issues arise where archives are not located in universities or other easily accessible sites. Also excluded is the analysis of survey data gathered by others, newspapers or other compiled sources, or other types of databases. Some "natural experiments," the interpretation of exogenous sources of variation as a quasi-experimental method, draw on field research; where there is no personal interaction between the researcher and the participants they do not count as field research as discussed here. "Narratives" may be based on field research, but need not be as they may be based on sources such as newspaper articles or databases not compiled through field research.

The methodological challenges confronting field researchers are well known (King, Keohane, and Verba 1994). Data gathered in interviews with political actors are often difficult to interpret and verify, particularly their stated reasons for doing what they did. Without careful attention to research design, field research may merely confirm preconceptions with which the researcher went to the field. Causal inference is often difficult from data gathered in the field and generalization to other settings often problematic. To randomize an experimental "treatment" or to draw a randomized sample is difficult in societies where demographic characteristics are not well defined due to inadequate statistical services or to population movements not captured by those statistics due to poverty, war, or fear of state authorities.

Despite these challenges, field research can and often does make contributions to social science that could not occur via other methods of analysis and data collection. Field research is often the only source of adequate description of social, economic, or political processes that are not evident in other documents. Close familiarity with a well-chosen case may not only identify what appear to be key processes but also central concepts and relevant actors. Field researchers often develop better measures of key concepts (Adcock and Collier 2001) or new analyses of rare events (Mahoney and Goertz 2006).

Field research contributes to causal inference in several ways (George and Bennett 2005; Brady and Collier 2004). Works that focus on a single case often take the preliminary form of theory generation, the positing of a causal relationship that appears to hold in the case investigated, with the suggestion that it may hold for others as well. Field research on a single case may also disconfirm a theory or model

---

[2] In anthropology the "field" in "field research" refers to research in communities "in the field," that is, in communities other than one's own. Historically, anthropological field sites were usually isolated culturally to some degree from markets and the state, and were often in another country. Beginning in the late 19th century, field research was increasingly also carried out in indigenous communities in researchers' own countries. Sociologists of the Chicago school of urban ethnography extended "the field" to include domestic urban sites defined by neighborhood or occupation. Today field "sites" include institutions, organizations, bars, occupations, and street corners.

when it shows that the sequence of events does not match that predicted by theory, when the salient events were driven by actors other than those identified in the theory, or when an alternative mechanism appears to be doing more causal "work" than the postulated one. In particular, the analysis of contingent events and path dependency often depends on "process tracing" impossible without data gathered through field research (Bennett and Elman 2006). Field researchers often identify causal mechanisms and the conditions for their occurrence through comparison of cases chosen for that purposes. As a result of their close understanding of political processes, many field researchers endorse a view of social causation as conjunctural (an antecedent may have causal effect only in the presence of another causal effect) and sometimes also s multiple (more than one set of causal antecedents may bring about the outcome), a view that is increasingly given a probabilistic rather than deterministic case (Ragin 1987, 2000; Mahoney and Goertz 2006).

In part to address the tradeoff between depth of knowledge of a few cases and the stronger causal inference possible with more, research designs in comparative politics are increasingly sophisticated as scholars attempt to widen their work's descriptive or inferential power. Scholars who do field research increasingly combine field methods with one another and also with non-field methods such as formal modeling and statistical analysis of data not gathered in the field. Field researchers may identify potential causal mechanisms that underlie a statistical regularity, or explore alternative mechanisms that may account for outliers in the statistical analysis (Lieberman 2005). And the identification of the mechanism may contribute to the subsequent development of a formal model. The relationship between field research and a formal model may be reversed: field research may confirm (for a particular case) the presence of a causal mechanism developed via a formal model. If the causal process unfolded as posited by the model in the sequence prescribed, via the mechanisms proposed, by the actors claimed, and with appropriate perceptions on their part, field research adds to the plausibility of the model.

One indication of the abiding contributions of field research comes from the surprises that field researchers often report. Such surprises often come from the realization that research findings contradict the presuppositions with which the researcher went to the field: for example, the crucial question turns out to be different from that originally posed, the actors not those anticipated, or the relevant constraints or opportunities not those identified earlier. Thus experience in the field may correct initial bias on the part of the researcher and lead to the recognition that existing theory is inadequate and the recognition of new empirical patterns or causal mechanisms. In particular, many field researchers report learning enormously from their subjects, ranging from the surprise expressed by respondents at a particular question to themes that subsequently become central to the researcher's analysis. Sometimes such insight comes from self-reported data in interviews, sometimes from the data conspicuously missing in interviews.

An important category of data often unavailable except through observation or face-to-face interaction with subjects is the preferences and beliefs of political actors. How actors varied as union members (Lipset 1956), local elites (Dahl 1963), parliamentarians

(Fenno 1978), and lobbyists and activists (Graetz and Shapiro 2005) understand their identities and interests is often best approached through interviews, observation, and surveys designed specifically for that purpose. General public opinion surveys may be useful for some questions but often do not ask the right questions or do not ask them such that the results are relevant for scholarly analysis. In particular, how political actors perceive their strategic interactions with other actors in real settings—what choices they confronted, their beliefs concerning the likely consequences of different choices, their analysis of paths not taken—is often unavailable except through face-to-face interaction with the actors themselves, that is, through field research.

This is especially the case in four circumstances. The first is when the political actor is at a permanent disadvantage as a result of repression or domination or lack of education severe enough that its access to global media is severely limited. Although insurgent and social movement organizations increasingly publish material on the internet, it is rarely sufficient for scholarly investigation. The second is when the scholar seeks to disaggregate actors such as organizations into their constituent factions or individuals whose beliefs and preferences may be quite distinct from the official line available in publications. The third is when the scholar seeks to understand the internal processes of a group, which may become available only through participant observation and interviews. The fourth is when the actors have reasons to obscure their preferences and beliefs from public view, as when they are engaged in strategic interactions with other actors and thus stand to lose advantage should they reveal their preferences and beliefs, as in nearly all political and economic negotiation processes. Surprisingly often, such actors are nonetheless willing to talk with academic researchers.

To understand why political actors make the choices they do the researcher often must evaluate the relevance of their own reports of why they made those choices. Self-reported motivations are best evaluated in face-to-face interactions, that is via field research, so that the strategic context can be discussed, inconsistencies probed, and alternative motivations raised. Of course those interviewed, surveyed, or observed may well interact strategically with the field researcher. The reasons may vary from a desire to obscure a belief that is believed to be illegitimate, to exaggerate or minimize one's own role, to mislead the researcher concerning rivals, and so on. And first-hand reports may be subject to various other kinds of distortion. A good field researcher does not take reports and observations as true per se nor as a complete report of the causal forces at work, but as data reported within a particular context. In order to develop an interpretation of self-reported data, the field researcher typically seeks to interview, observe, or survey other people concerning the same subjects to explore whether some pattern seems general or particular to specific people or setting. Where available, the researcher may also "triangulate" with other sources, by comparing reported data to judicial, newspapers, human rights reports, and other records of relevant events. The purpose may be to prod the memory of those interviewed or to assure them that the interlocutor already knows quite a lot and thus a superficial answer is not desired and a fallacious one unsustainable.

The alternative to considering self-reported reasons relevant is the assumption that observed behavior reveals the actor's reasons. But even in markets settings it is difficult to construct economic preference orderings, for example, to construct demand functions by observing economic choices as relative prices vary. And even in the controlled laboratory settings of experimental economics, the interpretation of motives is highly contested as in the current debate about social preferences. It is difficult to see how motivations can be imputed in complex political settings without consideration of self-reported reasons.

In addition to subjects' preferences and beliefs, researchers in the field often identify, locate, or generate other kinds of data that would not be available without personal interaction. It is frequently the case that face-to-face interaction plays a role in persuading informants to pass on data judged sensitive. For example, persons interviewed a second or third or tenth time often provide previously withheld names, documents, photographs, archives, maps, or budgets. Similarly, personal interaction may persuade an actor to generate new data for the researcher in the form of hitherto unexplored statistical analysis of databases unavailable to the researcher, newly drawn maps, or the inclusion of new questions in their own survey.

In this essay, I address these "why leave the office" questions principally through discussion of exemplary works that draw on field research. I begin by considering a classic work of field research in comparative politics, James Scott's *Weapons of the Weak,* and then turn to some recent works that explore related topics using some combination of interviews, surveys, and participant observation. I then discuss other field research methods, illustrating with selected recent works the trends toward natural and field experiments and combinations of field methods with non-field methods.[3] I discuss the challenges that field researchers confront irrespective of their particular method, including some ethical and practical dilemmas. In concluding, I recommend that graduate training for students in comparative politics include more in-depth training in field research than usually occurs.

1 JAMES SCOTT'S *WEAPONS OF THE WEAK*

James Scott's *Weapons of the Weak: Everyday Forms of Peasant Resistance* draws on extensive field research to discredit the theory that in class societies ruling groups ideologically dominate subordinate groups in the sense that subordinate groups believe that social structures that favor superordinate groups are immutable, inevitable, natural, legitimate, and perhaps just.

---

[3] I do not restrict the discussion to works by political scientists but describe works based on exemplary field research by other types of social scientists as well. I do not attempt to summarize practical advice for the variety of field methods discussed here but provide some references for the interested reader.

Scott spent two years (1978–80) living in a Malaysian village in the Muda region of north-western Malaysia. In 1971, several years before Scott's fieldwork, the village began harvesting two crops of paddy rice a year rather than one, thanks to a recent irrigation scheme and other "green revolution" policies. As a result, most residents of the region were better off than before (Scott 1985: 64). The site was a crucial case for the exploration of class relations: if the dominant ideology was contested even in such a propitious setting, it was all the more likely to be contested in settings where average income was declining. Among Scott's explicit criteria for the selection of a particular village was that it had been studied before the advent of double-cropping.

Scott gathered a wide range of data concerning the perceptions of class relations through participant observation, including passing time at the gathering places of different village factions, threshing paddy fields, and attending ritual gatherings such as weddings and funerals. Through more structured interviews he also gathered data on land tenure, farm size, land use, production costs, income, and political affiliations (party affiliation and whether or not the household head belonged to the farmers' association) for each of the seventy-four households in the village. And he collected a variety of relevant documents and quantitative data from government and other sources. Comparing his data with the (far less detailed) data gathered by a development economist a dozen years before, Scott found that for the first six or seven years after double-cropping began, nearly all households increased their income substantially (essentially double the work was available for those reliant on wage labor and two harvests for those with access to land). For a brief period, even poor households held ritual feasts, a significant rise in their local status. However, by 1978 or so poor families began to experience several negative consequences of the increased productivity of the land. Because large farmers began farming more land themselves and because outsiders also began to farm land in the village, less land was available for rent and contracts increasingly required a large lump sum up front (sometimes for several years' rent). Many of the owners and larger tenants began harvesting their crop with combines and some began broadcasting paddy seed rather than transplanting seedlings, resulting in a drastically reduced demand for local labor. The result was a sharp increase in inequality in the village and a severing of the traditional economic interdependence between rich and poor families that undergirded traditional social relations.

Scott documented in great detail the very different interpretations of these changes by distinct social groups, the claims made by each, and the strategies they employed. The village poor sought to persuade the rich to continue traditional patterns of employment and charity through various strategies, the "weapons of the weak." While deferential in direct interactions with the particular rich, in private settings some poor men attacked the reputations of rich individuals as stingy, condemning their abandonment of ethnic and religious notions of fellowship. Some teams of women laborers delayed transplanting seedlings for farmers who had harvested with combines (but did not announce a boycott as that would have been to run the risk of direct retaliation). While Scott did not hear of attacks on combines in the village, such attacks were rumored to have occurred elsewhere in the region. Several poor heads of household refused to join the ruling party despite the material benefits they would have received. In contrast, rich individuals generally sought to legitimize their new practices by identifying and holding up for emulation "good" workers and scorning others as lazy and incapable. And in public they maintained that due to the high costs they confronted they themselves were poor despite their access to abundant land.

Scott concludes that the poor actively resisted the ideological domination of the rich, despite their deference in public interactions with their well-off neighbors. The poor contested the claim of the rich to have to do things in new ways and asserted the moral superiority of the old ways through indirect channels that nonetheless circumscribed (to a limited extent and for a limited time) the behavior of the rich. Thus Scott argues that the theory of ideological hegemony does not generally hold. The ideas of the dominant class do not persuade subordinate groups that class relations are inevitable, much less legitimate and just. Rather, subordinate classes actively resist the ideology of the dominant, often through appeal to traditional ideologies of reciprocity or to millenarian interpretations of religious tradition. Scott asserts a sweeping claim: resistance by peasants, slaves, and workers pervades history; class relations are contested even where no overt rebellious activity is observed.

Scott thus challenged a theory with meticulous ethnographic field research and suggested an alternative theory of subordinate resistance. The persuasiveness of the work also comes from its descriptive depth, its accumulation of information about social dynamics in the village as experienced by various factions. Importantly, the combination of quantitative and qualitative methods lends it a particular authority: it is hard to imagine Scott being misled by his informants given the detailed knowledge of local conditions he commanded. Scott's ability to carry out the survey, in particular the gathering of sensitive quantitative data (such as household income), depended on the trust and acceptance developed through participant observation methods (1985, 202–3). That Scott is explicit about the limits to his research (he found he could not gather data on thefts or violence and had no way to evaluate the chilling effect of repression on discontent in the village) strengthens the reader's confidence in the data Scott did gather.

Thus the book's persuasive power rests in large part on the internal validity of Scott's ethnographic data, supported by relevant statistics and documents. I consider below a variety of strategies to increase the external validity and replicability of participant observation research, include randomized surveys to test findings, choosing field sites on more explicitly theoretical or statistical grounds, and conducting experiments in the field.

2 COMPARISON OF CASES
IN FIELD RESEARCH

Scott's research design is a classic one in comparative politics: a single case chosen as a test of a theory is analyzed in great depth against a background of theory and other cases using a variety of field methods; the theory is shown to be false; and a new theory suggested. A single case can of course only refute a theory that asserts a pattern should hold deterministically rather than as a tendency, and can only suggest an alternative theory. Thus Scott's book set a theoretical and comparative agenda: whether consent to class hierarchy occurs in other cases and the conditions for covert resistance to become overt collective action.

Susan Stokes (1995) addresses the first question, whether subordinate classes ever consent to domination. Stokes combined in-depth participant observation with a survey in a single community, a shanty-town in Lima, Peru. After a year of partici- pant observation in the community during which she developed relationships with local leaders, Stokes carried out extended interviews with two dozen leaders. She identified two broad patterns of political culture, one that replicated traditional clientelistic relations and a new one that challenged such traditional relations. She then carried out a survey of nearly a thousand residents of the shanty-town (ran- domly chosen from the list of voters) and confirmed that ordinary people also tended to have one of these two political cultures. Contrary to the elite interviews, the survey found that women were in general less mobilized and more conservative than men.

Stokes argues that, contra Scott, the clientelistic pattern was founded on consent to core aspects of the dominant ideology. This finding together with Scott's suggest that in some settings the rich ideologically dominate the poor while in others they do not. But neither work articulates in any depth the conditions under which elites will or will not ideologically dominate the poor; nor is any inference of the frequency of domination possible from their work. Stokes's analysis of non-clientelist politics does explore the sources of ideological change among the poor, namely, unions, new religious teachings, and schooling under Peru's reformist military regime.

The literature on collective action frequently addresses the second question raised by Scott (and others before him), the conditions for mobilization in hierarchical societies. Drawing on a comparative research design in the tradition of Barrington Moore, Jr., Deborah Yashar (2005) explains the emergence of indigenous social movements in the late twentieth century in some Latin American countries but not others. She argues that increasing challenges to local autonomy, combined with the opportunity in indigenous communities to organize and their capacity for collective action, led to the emergence of powerful indigenous movements in Bolivia, Ecuador, and to a lesser extent in Mexico and Guatemala. Despite similar challenges to indigenous autonomy, a movement did not arise in Peru as the ongoing civil war closed local associational space and destroyed local capacity. In classic Millian fashion, Yashar compares and contrasts her cases (including in some cases comparison within a case) to show that her theory explains the observed levels of indigenous mobilization whereas rival theories do not. Her analysis drew on field research in all five countries (with a particular focus on the core cases of Ecuador, Bolivia, and Peru), including interviews with 150 movement leaders, observation of dozens of meetings, and the collection of a wide array of documents. Developing networks of contacts in social movements in a single country is a challenge; the scope of Yashar's work testifies to her skill in persuading activists to talk with her.

In my own work (Wood 2003), I explored why some peasants supported insurgent groups during El Salvador's civil war despite the high risks they thereby ran. In this setting where few police records were kept and the data compiled by human rights organizations were quite incomplete, I relied on extended, often repeated, interviews with local residents (both those who supported the insurgency and those who did not) of five case study areas. The interview took the form of oral histories of their family and the local community. (I also interviewed field-level insurgent commanders and military officers, government and UN officials, and landlords.)

I found that support for the hitherto small insurgency dramatically escalated in the wake of extreme violence by state agents against a non-violent social movement whose legitimacy was deeply rooted in liberation theology, a Catholic movement that taught that social justice was God's will. In areas where the grip of the state was relatively weak (rural peripheries and near insurgent bases), this support evolved from covert individual activities such as the provision of military intelligence to overt collective action, including a wave of land occupations that spread across three of the case study areas. I documented the land occupations by a particular method: I asked insurgent activists from four of the case study areas to draw maps showing property rights and land use in their neighborhoods before and at the close of the war. Drawn collaboratively by at least two and usually several members in a process interspersed with much discussion of the history of the area as well as gossip, jokes, and teasing of one another (and of me), the resulting maps document how cooperatives of insurgent supporters literally redrew the boundaries of class relationships through their collective action.[4] Drawing maps was not a familiar task; only a few said they had ever seen a map (insurgent commanders had a few, well-worn maps held together with tape). One non-literate elderly leader traced property lines with his forefinger while his grandson drew the line in its wake. Each pair took two days to draw, an unpaid sacrifice of time that I understood as an indication of their enthusiasm that the history of the war in their area be documented.

In accounting for why about a third of the residents of four of the case study areas actively supported the insurgency, I took seriously the reasons for their activism evident in the oral histories and supported by details they included in the maps. I argued that reasons for this high-risk collective action were threefold: the meaningfulness of

---

[4] The accuracy of the claims by these cooperative leaders to occupy extensive areas of land in 1992 was confirmed by my own travel and observation in the case study areas and by examination of the land claims data held by the insurgent group, the government, and the United Nations during the post-war land transfer process.

participation in the building of God's Kingdom, defiance of unjust authority in the wake of state violence, and pleasure in historical agency—the remaking of class relations, culture, and history through own's own efforts. I cleared the way for this argument by showing that alternative explanations did not account for the observed pattern of mobilization across the case study areas: mobilization occurred both in areas of tenancy and large commercial estates; class position did not predict which individuals participated; nor did pre-war community structure account for the pattern. And while acknowledging the difficulties in interpreting self-reported reasons for collective action (Wood 2003, ch. 2), I also argued that the particular elements of this insurgent political culture required explanation and that my interpretation of those elements was more parsimonious than alternatives.

Both Yashar and I base our findings on analysis of five cases, sacrificing ethnographic depth of analysis for analytical traction through comparison of cases that vary in the extent of mobilization observed. Comparison of subnational units has some advantages over comparison of national units, allowing a narrowing of likely explanatory variables as those shared across subunits cannot account for the different outcome observed. There are often practical advantages as well: subnational comparison often requires skills in only one language, one local affiliation, and one research approval. And of course travel between sites is usually less demanding. However, there are two distinct problems with subnational comparison (in addition to a frequent pattern of inadequate variation within a single state). As Richard Snyder (2001) pointed out, distinct subunits may not be independent cases, undermining the supposed power of the observed pattern of similarity and differences. And the assumption of national-level similarity may not hold, particularly in just the types of settings that at first glance might appear ideal for this design such as large federal states with great internal diversity whose constituent states may in fact differ significantly in the factors often supposed constant across the federation.

3 NATURAL AND FIELD EXPERIMENTS

The findings of such comparative research designs rest on the assumption that the cases vary in the causally relevant variables in ways well understood by the researcher. Yet whether that is in fact the case is often asserted rather than demonstrated. An alternative design is that of the so-called "natural experiment," in which cases that were once indistinguishable (except in trivial ways) diverged because of an exogenous event whose consequences are analyzed.

Daniel Posner (2004) used the arbitrary nature of colonial boundaries in Africa as the setting for a complex natural experiment. Posner compared the cultural relationship between two ethnically distinct groups (the Chewa and the Tumbuka) on the Malawian side of the border with their relationship on the Zambian side. Posner conducted an open-ended questionnaire and focus groups in two pairs of very similar villages located on either side of the border. In one pair, both villages were homogeneously Chewa but one was in Zambia and the other in Malawi; in the other pair, both villages were homogeneously Tumbuka. Posner found that while, in Zambia, relations between the two groups were very cordial ("we are brothers"), in Malawi, the same cultural difference had high political salience. Because he had picked the pairs of villages ingeniously to control for confounding alternative explanations (such as different exposures to markets or levels of modernization), Posner showed that the demographic importance of the ethnic groups within each country is a hitherto-neglected mechanism that explained the difference in the political salience of the same cultural difference.[5] In Malawi, both the Chewas and the Tumbukas comprised relatively large fractions of the population (28 and 12 percent, respectively), while in Zambia together the two groups comprise only 11 percent of the population. The two groups compete for political resources in Malawi, aligning with different political parties, but join the same coalition in Zambia.

Raghabendra Chattopadhyay and Ester Duflo (2004) analyze a very different type of natural experiment that explores the effect of a particular institutional innovation, mandated female representation, on the provision of local public goods in India. Beginning in the 1990s, a third of the seats on the village council and a third of the chiefs of the councils in each village-level election were reserved for women. The councils that were reserved were chosen randomly, which should control for differences other than reservation. Chattopadhyay and Duflo carried out a survey of public investment in a sample of both reserved and unreserved village councils in two districts, one in West Bengal and the other in Rajasthan, in order to analyze whether the type of local public good depended on whether the council headship had been reserved for a woman. They first confirmed that reserved villages had indeed been chosen randomly and that the villages did not in fact differ significantly other than in being reserved or not. They found that mandated representation made a difference in the provision of public goods: in villages reserved for women heads, public investment was significantly more likely to target the concerns of women such as provision of drinking water.

Both works test the observable implications of social science theory, in the first case the theory of political identity developed by Posner in his dissertation (and later book) and in the second the classic claims of representative democracy. The analytical power of the natural experiment method relies on exogenous events (the drawing of a colonial boundary across an ethnic group or the requirement that women hold particular offices in randomly chosen sites) to generate distinct "treatments" across groups who are supposed otherwise similar in all relevant ways. Thus the exogenous event effectively randomizes the subsequent "treatment" (which polity a subset of the previously identical population joins or the application of a policy to a particular

---

[5] Posner 2005 further explores the relationship between political institutions, group size, and ethnic identity in Zambia using another natural experiment, the switch from a multiparty regime to one-party rule and back again.

site or not). The inferential power of the method is of course undermined when the exogenous event was not in fact entirely exogenous (as when the population varies with the treatment in some way) or when subsequent processes in addition to the hypothesized one occur with different causal force on distinct sides of the border.

In contrast to the reliance on exogenous events to randomize treatment in natural experiments, randomized variation for the purpose of experimental control in field experiments is achieved through the research design itself. In the most common design, groups are randomly selected to receive particular treatments or none (the control group); the randomness of the selection allows the presumption that the groups are otherwise indistinguishable (the differences "cancel out").[6]

Leonard Wantchekon carried out a field experiment in Benin to explore the determinants and consequences of clientelistic appeals to voters. With the cooperation of the four major political parties running candidates in the 2001 presidential election, Wantchekon compared voting behavior in randomly selected, ethnically homogeneous villages that received clientelistic appeals ("vote for candidate X as he will bring goods Y to this district") and those that received public goods appeals ("vote for candidate X as he will bring goods Y to all people of Benin") to that in control villages which received the usual mix of appeals. (In order to avoid affecting the outcome of the election and to secure the parties' cooperation, the treatment groups were all in districts dominated by one party or another.) Wantchekon's research team gathered the data on voting behavior via a representative survey carried out in all districts that also gathered data on respondents' demographic characteristics and the degree of exposure to the campaigns. He found that clientelistic appeals had an effect everywhere, but were significantly more effective in some regions than in others, were more effective for incumbent candidates than for challengers, and that men responded to clientelistic appeals more than women. Thus voters' response to clientelistic or public goods appeals depends on political and demographic factors, not just ethnicity.

In a research project that compared the results of experimental games across radically different field settings, an interdisciplinary group of anthropologists and economists carried out a series of experiments in fifteen "small-scale" societies including hunter-gatherer groups in Latin America and Africa and pastoral groups in African and Mongolia (Henrich et al. 2003, 2005).[7] The project grew out of the puzzling findings by experimental economists that many students played economic games in controlled laboratory settings in ways not predicted by standard economic theory: they did not play selfishly. For example, consider an interaction called "the ultimatum game," in which one randomly chosen player is given a stake, say ten

---

[6] Green and Gerber 2002 and Harrison and List 2004 review the role of field experiments in political science and economics respectively. Not all field experiments fall within "field research" as defined in this essay.

[7] These experiments might be understood as laboratory experiments in that the researchers attempted to some extent to establish laboratory conditions in the cultural settings of each society. However, the games are better understood as involving interactions between members of a small-scale society in their own cultural setting and hence I discuss them here.

dollars, and makes an offer to a second student of some part of the stake, say two dollars; the second player may accept the offer, in which case they divide the stakes accordingly, or reject it, in which case neither gets anything. In the laboratory, respondents typically rejected low offers, apparently seeking to punish (at a sacrifice to themselves) unfair offers, and proposers typically made offers much higher than the minimum (perhaps anticipating the rejection of low offers). Experiments in university laboratories across the world had confirmed this (and related findings).

Realizing that these findings were nonetheless limited to university student populations in market societies, the group decided to radically vary the type of society and see if members replicate the way university students play the games. Ethnographers with long experience in different hunter-gather, pastoral, and other small societies were recruited to ask residents in their field sites to play the ultimatum and other games, suitably adjusting the stakes appropriately, e.g. tobacco rather than cash in some societies. As in the university settings, the roles were assigned randomly.

Compared to the limited variation in the play of students across diverse university settings, the findings across these populations were extremely diverse. In some societies, respondents accepted even low offers; in others, proposers made hyperfair offers (more than half of the initial stakes), which were sometimes rejected; and so on. Because fifteen societies were included in the study the patterns of play could be analyzed statistically both by individuals and by small-scale society—a key innovation of the project. Individual characteristics such as gender or wealth did not predict how individuals played; rather, the different patterns of play corresponded to group-level characteristics. The group's findings draw on its collective ethnographic knowledge as well as the game results. In particular, the group found that the average ultimatum game offer in each society was significantly and positively correlated both with the degree of market integration and the degree of cooperation in everyday life.

To be persuasive, field experiments face similar challenges to natural experiments and laboratory experiments, including whether the treatment was truly random, whether subjects differed in relevant ways other than the treatment, and whether the interpretation has external validity. In the case of the fifteen societies, whether the experiment was understood as the same game in the different societies is problematic: the researchers used a variety of methods to operationalize the game (Henrich et al. 2005, 805–6).[8] Whether anonymity is possible in such intimate societies is also a question; if not, the comparability with the university-based findings is lessened. And a variety of other interpretations of the findings have also been proposed.[9]

---

[8] The project is now in its second phase with ethnographers asking residents of a wider range of field sites to play a wider variety of games (with stricter controls for divergent cultural interpretations) and measuring more precisely apparently important factors such as market integration and everyday cooperation.

[9] See the various commentaries on Henrich et al. (2005) in the succeeding pages of the journal.

4 COMBINING METHODS

In comparative politics, researchers are increasingly combining a variety of field methods with non-field methods in order to more powerfully confirm apparent factual findings, to establish the relative causal force of distinct mechanisms, and to parry alternative explanations. For example, case studies are sometimes identified in tandem with statistical analysis of many cases (Lieberman 2005). An anomalous case "off the regression line" may be chosen to explore why the observed statistical regularity does not hold in that case, perhaps identifying a new mechanism. Or a crucial case "on the regression line" is chosen to verify whether the observed regularity appears to occur via a posited mechanism.

In his analysis of communal violence in India, Steven Wilkinson (2004) combined statistical analysis of a large dataset of Hindu–Muslim riots since 1900 that he and Ashutosh Varshney collected based on a close reading of Indian newspapers and police reports with field research in a case study area chosen to explore the relationship between elections, mobilization, and policing. Wilkinson tests with these data not only his own hypotheses but several others. Such explicit hypothesis testing is unusual in the field of ethnicity and politics, which usually relies on only narrative analysis. Wilkinson shows that elections comprise an incentive to violence in a divided society under democratic government when local elections are close *and* when the level of government that controls police forces (in India, the state government) values the votes of the aggressor group more than minority votes and thus does not order police forces to prevent and stop ethnic violence. Thus the work circumscribes the frequent claims that in a divided society politicians will "outbid" each other and that ethnic polarization and mobilization are thus unavoidable. Wilkinson shows that this claim is sometimes, but not always, true.

Yet further, these comparisons assume just one quantity of interest (parameter) to estimate; the reported relationship between information quality and quantity and the certainly of inference are *per parameter*. Likewise, the relationships in the table assume each new piece of information is independent; if, e.g. information sets correlated (overlapped) at .9 (90%), the comparisons would need to be multiplied by (roughly) 10. For example, Jeremy Weinstein (2006) gathered data to test the observable implications of his informal model of the organizational challenges that insurgent groups confront. His model suggested that groups tend to recruit distinct types of members (opportunistic or committed) depending on whether their endowment is economic or social, and that the type of member shapes distinct patterns of rebel organization and violence. Nascent groups with access to significant economic endowments will attract opportunistic members and will thus exhibit a lack of discipline evident in excessive violence, looting of civilian resources, and an inability to punish abuses by those within their ranks. In contrast, only individuals highly committed to the goals of the organization will join organizations with only social endowments. The idea is that committed individuals find credible the promised long-term gains of the insurgency; their interaction with one another supports this as a common belief. Such long time horizons and common expectations support cooperative relations with civilians and a high level of discipline within the organization, making possible selective use of violence and a degree of co-governance with civilian leaders.

Weinstein tests this theory by tracing its observable implications in the trajectories of four rebel organizations, the National Resistance Army in Uganda, Renamo in Mozambique, Sendero Luminoso in Peru, and a distinct faction of the latter in the Upper Huaullaga Valley. Weinstein carried out several months of field research on each case, interviewing former guerrillas, military leaders, and civilians in conflicted areas, gathering documents from a wide range of archives (some hitherto unavailable), and compiling data from newspaper articles for statistical analysis. Weinstein shows that the groups varied significantly in the form and extent of the violence they deployed and that initial patterns of endowment shaped subsequent rebel choices concerning recruitment, governance, and the use of force. Weinstein argues that his theory illuminates as well two out-of-sample cases, rebel groups in Colombia and Angola. He also carried out multivariate analysis of patterns of violence in all civil wars since 1945 with an explicit assessment of four cases not lying on the regression line.

In a work that in its methodological and theoretical contribution sets a high standard for research in comparative politics, Stathis Kalyvas (2006) presents a new theory of violence in civil war. His theory begins from the insight that civil wars are nearly always fought as irregular wars in which control of territory depends not on the preferences of civilians living there but rather on their behavior, namely, whether or not they give information to the opposing force. The degree of control an armed group exercises compared to its rival determines its interaction with civilians and therefore its use of violence. Thus patterns of violence follow from patterns of control, rather than vice versa. Kalyvas develops this relationship between control and violence in a formal model that predicts a counterintuitive pattern of selective violence, namely that it will be *low* in areas where the parties exercise approximately equal control.[10]

Kalyvas shows the general plausibility of the argument through anecdotal evidence from dozens of civil wars. He then tests the predictions with data on patterns of violence during the Greek civil war. During his field research in the Argolid, an area in eastern Peloponnese, he compiled data on approximately 750 civilian deaths in the sixty-one villages of the case study area for the year beginning in September 1943, drawing on archives of the Greek Army, the Greek Communist Party, the regional criminal courts, memoirs and autobiographies, and a variety of European archives. This diversity of archival sources enabled Kalyvas to prod the memories of the 200 residents of the area in interviews. He compiled a database for most of these civilian deaths, recording the identity of the victim and perpetrator, the ties between them, and whether it occurred as a result of selective or indiscriminate violence. He also constructed measures of incumbent and insurgent control, which were clearly

---

[10] Kalyvas also analyzes the frequent (and counter-productive) use of indiscriminate violence: actors kill indiscriminately when they do not have access to local information to identify combatants and supporters of the other side.

independent of his observations of violence. His multivariate analysis of the resulting database largely confirmed his theory: the model's predictions proved significant and the predictions of alternative explanations for civil war violence were not borne out. Kalyvas then carried out a number of out-of-sample tests, including multivariate analyses of a second, ethnically divided area and of a dataset of civil war deaths from 136 villages across Greece based on various types of local histories.

An additional strength of the work is Kalyvas's explicitness about the way in which his initial research on the Greek case (interviews but not in the Argolid, which he later chose as his field site) informed the development of his theory and model (2006, 14–15; see also the methodological appendix). The data gathered in his subsequent research in the field site then served as a test of the theory. Thus the reader is able to trace the dialogue between theory and data and evaluate the overall claims of the work.

5 SOME CHALLENGES OF FIELD RESEARCH

The field researcher confronts some particular challenges in the course of her work due to the personal interaction with research subjects. In this section I discuss some of the challenges involved in face-to-face research but do not address the many practical challenges of field research or the methodological challenges discussed above.[11]

Because field research depends on personal interaction, field researchers may gather data that suffer from unrecognized selection bias by cultivating ongoing contact with individuals with whom they are more comfortable, for example, individuals who are more educated or hold similar values to those of the researcher. Even if the researcher starts out in the field with such dangers in mind, an element of selection bias may creep into the sample without the researcher's being aware of it. For example, the enthusiasm of some of those interviewed for the project may render their views or ongoing participation more acceptable, more accessible, or simply more fun to gather. Their enthusiasm is itself data: why they see the research project as interesting rather than as some alien chore is important to understand. But the lack of enthusiasm on the part of others is also of course data, but data more difficult to gather. Purely personal likes and dislikes may mean that the views of some individuals weigh more heavily than others, thereby shaping the field researcher's evolving understanding of the topic in ways not always recognized.

Thus the field researcher must manage her own subjectivity, attempting to be aware of how her own proclivities shape her interactions with her research subjects.

---

[11] On field research methods, see Lofland et al. (2006); Emerson, Fretz, and Shaw (1995); Bernard (2002); Rubin and Rubin (2005); PS Symposium (2002); Qualitative Methods Symposium (2004). On interviews, see PS Symposium (2002), especially the articles by Leech (2002); Goldstein (2002); and Berry (2002). See also Weiner (1964); Whyte (1986); Sieber (1986); Bernard (2002, especially chs. 9 and 13). On the practical challenges of field research, see Barrett and Cason (1997); Devereux and Hoddinott (1993).

The keeping of field diaries and logs, as well as more formal notes of interviews and observations, is one way not only to manage one's subjectivity but also to comprehend one's own evolving understanding of interactions and findings as field research data (Emerson, Fretz, and Shaw 1995; Bernard 2002, ch. 14).

Field researchers also face ethical challenges in the field. At a minimum, for field research to be ethical, research subjects must consent to their participation in full understanding of the potential risks and benefits (Kelman 1972; Belmont Report 1979[12]). In the procedures for ensuring informed consent, field researchers must state the purpose of the project in understandable language, inform the subjects of any potential risks (and benefits) of the research, and assure the subjects that their participation is entirely voluntary and that their privacy will be respected. Consent procedures usually include information intended to ensure that the researcher is accountable to his subjects, such as contact information for the institutional review board responsible for the project. Yet whether the research subjects understand the purpose and risks to the extent needed for informed consent is often difficult to determine.

Ensuring the security of field data (important both for practical and ethical reasons) may be difficult, particularly if the research design requires either extended stays in one community, where private spaces may not be respected, or frequent travel between field sites, which increases the risk of theft, inadvertent loss, or confiscation by authorities or others.[13] Field researchers increasingly protect electronic data with encryptions or passwords, but some types of field data (artifacts or maps, for example) are less amenable to such safeguards in the field. A related dilemma concerns the inclusion of sensitive field materials in publications. Some decisions are dictated by the conditions given by individual respondents, who may specify some material as not for publication. But sometimes the field researcher should decide not to use some material even if given permission, because it may in the researcher's own judgement nonetheless seem too sensitive to publish, for example, likely to identify or implicate the interviewee.

Scholars based in the USA carrying out research involving human subjects must submit their research protocols (including detailed procedures for obtaining informed consent and securing confidential data) to a mandatory review by their local institutional review board, which must either approve project procedures or rule the project exempt.[14] Researchers in comparative politics are increasingly often required also to submit their protocols for review in the country where they will carry out the research. Review of protocols is of course particularly important in contexts

[12] See National Commission for the Protection of Human Subjects of Biomedical and Behavioral Research (1979), known as the Belmont Report.

[13] On field notes, see Emerson, Fretz, and Shaw (1995); Bernard (2002, ch. 14).

[14] Review board standards evolve in response to the emergence of new research issues and also the development of new legal standards and research norms. Issues currently under discussion include whether review boards should specialize in particular kinds of research (e.g. social science or medical research), whether informed consent protocols have become too formal and legalistic (providing institutional cover but obscuring comprehension by the research subject), the risks and opportunities provided by new information technologies, and the interpretation of a key phrase in the process, "minimal risk." See National Research Council 2003 and National Science Foundation n.d.

(such as conflict zones) where the degree of risk to the research subject needs particularly careful evaluation.[15] An unintended consequence of the requirement that changes to research protocols (such as interviewing a new group of people or addressing subjects not anticipated before going to the field) must also be approved by the review board is that the process constrains innovation in the field, as approval may take several weeks.

But approved protocols are rarely sufficient to meet the ethical challenges of field research. The researcher may well confront ethical dilemmas whose resolution depends on her judgement of issues in a particular context.

Lesser dilemmas also arise in the course of field research. For example, field researchers often have to decide whether or not to challenge lies that they are told in the course of their work. This is a practical dilemma but one that may have ethical implications (for example, challenging lies may lead to greater hostility toward the project and perhaps toward research subjects). My personal resolution of this dilemma was not to challenge lies but to invite elaboration in a bland and naive way, which often leads to extremely useful material reflecting the speaker's ideology, values, analysis of events, and so on.

A challenge many field researchers confront is how to thank those individuals or groups whose cooperation has made the research possible. For many field researchers, this is a source of ongoing discomfort as there may be no acceptable way to do so. Anthropologists and other ethnographers endorse a particular form of reciprocity: materials gathered in the field should be returned to the community of origin. Some years ago this was understood as making publications available to the academic communities of the countries where field research was conducted. Increasingly, however, many ethnographers hold that the field researcher's obligations extend far beyond the dissemination of publications to include the return of the field materials themselves. But the norm says both too much (not all material should be returned; for example, confidential material should not be) and too little (returned to whom and when?).[16]

Some field researchers may find that sustaining their research role is difficult for emotional reasons. In the field, researchers often go through predictable periods of depression during which they question the meaning and feasibility of their project and whether they are adequate to the task. Such field research "blues" typically occur a few months after entry to the field site, often after the first excitement has worn off, and again after exit (whether or not "the field" is near one's home institution). These periods often reflect the stress and loneliness of making a transition between cultural settings and of leaving family members or friends behind. For example, the absence of privacy is particularly stressful in many field settings. For many researchers the necessary balance between engagement and observation is another source of stress as

---

[15] For a more extended discussion of the ethical dilemmas confronted in conflict zones, see Smyth (2001); Bell (2001); Wood (2006); for field research generally, see Wilson (1993).

[16] See the essays collected in Jaarsma 2002 for extended discussion of the difficulties in implementing this norm.

they come to feel there is an element of deception in the scholarly reserve necessary to observe as well as participate.

Those carrying out research in conflict zones, who may experience intense emotions of fear, anger, outrage, grief, and pity, often wonder why research is worth pursuing over purely humanitarian relief work. And in sharply polarized settings where research objectives require the researcher to work with all parties, researchers may find it stressful to "manage" information from both sides and to engage empathetically with everyone, especially when one side is clearly responsible for much of the violence. The challenges of doing so in some settings may preclude the attempt, leading the researcher to focus her work on only one party to the conflict, with the resultant narrowing of perspective and possible bias.

I mention these emotional dynamics because I am persuaded that inadequate attention to them may lead field researchers to make errors in judgement that may have significant consequences for their research subjects as well as for their research and possibly for themselves personally (Wood 2006).[17] In the emotionally challenging circumstances of field research, most people endure extended periods of doubt about their project and their ability to complete the anticipated work on what often comes to seem an impossible timetable. As a result, the researcher may decide, on the one hand, to curtail the original research design in ways that undermine its scholarly value, or on the other hand, persist in an overly ambitious design that results in superficial understanding. Or the researcher may be susceptible to flattering invitations to share their experiences (and inevitably their data) or to take on policy jobs or consultations that offer the comfort of an immediate work product. On a more personal level, the researcher may find it enjoyable to entertain new friends with stories (and data) from their field site (which may compromise the confidentiality of the research subjects) or to embark on relationships that someone may see as compromising the project (and perhaps lead to their no longer sharing information with the researcher). Or the researcher may become frustrated with the research role and decide to "make a difference" by passing on field data "confidentially" to some (supposedly responsible) organization.

Good field researchers find ways to manage these challenges and take care to shelter their ongoing research from their own emotional vagaries, sometimes in the form of close friendships with those similarly positioned as "outsiders" and sometimes through interim visits to their academic institution for consultations but also to reaffirm a sense of engagement with the academic community. In contrast to the usual immersion for a year or two in field research that is typical in comparative politics, some research designs themselves provide for periods away from the field, as when the researcher carries out a sequence of visits to different field sites that allows for a return to her home university along the way.

---

[17] Which is not to say that the emotional vagaries of field research should be inflicted on the reader. See Ellis (1995) for her analysis of how her personality shaped her fieldwork in a fishing village on Chesapeake Bay. See also Clark (1975) and Gans (1986).

6. CONCLUSION

It is hard to imagine how the data and the findings of the works discussed in this chapter could have been gathered and supported without field research.

But given the declining cost of non-field methods, should researchers not invest more in those methods? Because data and analysis that depend on field research and those that depend on other types of research are usually *complements* in the production of useful knowledge, not substitutes, the declining price and growing availability of non-field data raises, rather than lowers, the marginal productivity of investment in field research. Whether or not researchers should shift relative investment toward non-field methods cannot be decided in the abstract, as it depends entirely on the strength of this complementarity for the particular topic. Where this complementarity is strong, the case for increasing the share of scholarly resources going to field research is compelling.

But the obstacles to making valid causal inferences based on field data are of course formidable. In particular, research based in large part on participant observation is not easily amenable to replication in part because so much follows from the quality of the relationship between the researcher and the subjects. For example, an ethnographer less skilled than Scott might well have missed the significance of the "weapons of the weak" entirely and argued that class relations in the village confirmed the theory of ideological hegemony. Studies of the same ethnographic setting by different ethnographers within a relatively short period of time are not common, however.[18] Much more common are studies of the same community after a lapse of a few decades (by the same ethnographer or a different one); differences between the resulting ethnographies may reflect either different skills and experiences or social processes in the interim.[19] While the subjectivist turn in recent anthropological writing often obscures the research subjects from view, the tendency for ethnographers to provide more details of their engagement with the research subjects does allow the reader to judge the quality of the ethnography, a process often difficult for ethnographies written as though the observer were a fly on the wall whose presence had no effect.

If the scholarly community is to realize the promise of field research, better training in field research methods should become part of graduate training in social science. For all too many students, the first encounter with the challenges of

---

[18] One example of an ethnographic "restudy" was carried out in the central Mexican village of Tepotztlán. Oscar Lewis, whose field research occurred seventeen years after that of Robert Redfield, confirmed some of Redfield's findings, but argued that Redfield's work did not report adequately the degree of conflict and violence in the village, perhaps because of his theoretical and normative proclivity toward understanding rural culture as idealized "folk culture" (Lewis 1970).

[19] Some examples that are often cited as restudies were not based on significant new field research within a reasonable period of time. Derek Freeman argued that Margaret Mead had misrepresented key aspects of Samoan culture, in particular, the degree of sexual freedom of adolescent girls (see Orans 1996 for a review of the debate). However, Freeman's work was published more than half a century after Mead's, raising the possibility that the discrepancy in findings was due to the changes in the culture. For examples and discussion, see Kemper and Peterson Royce (2002) and Carmack (1988).

field research is in their field site where the consequences of practical, ethical, or methodological mistakes may not only undermine the project but may undermine or endanger the research subjects. Where resources are not sufficient to offer courses focused on field methods, provision should be made for students to attend the course offered every January by the Consortium on Qualitative Research Methods (**www.asu.edu/clas/polisci/cqrm**).

However, training should go beyond the standard seminar discussion of research design to include the hands-on trying out of various methods. Instructors should consider having students practice fieldwork techniques by carrying out a local research project during the course.[20] Many field researchers hold that field techniques can only by learned by doing them but that is no reason such learning need take place in the dissertation field site. Participants in the class would think through issues of entry to the field site, the identification of key respondents and sample frames, and the minimization of selection bias. They would practice particular skills, including participant observation, formal and informal interviews, and oral histories. The class would together brainstorm over the problems and opportunities encountered, in part by reviewing various types of field notes. And class discussion might include explicit consideration of the emotional dynamics of research in the field.

Urban sociologists often teach such practice-based courses. The challenge for the comparative politics student is to define a project within reach of her university that is nonetheless engaging and that hopefully has some relation to her core interests. For example, a student who intends to analyze the evolution of police policy in Rio de Janeiro could study police policy in her university town. While such semester-long projects are unlikely to serve as comparative cases, the student will at least have carried out a field research project and will carry that experience to the "real" field site.

References

ADCOCK, R., and COLLIER, D. 2001. Measurement validity: a shared standard for qualitative and quantitative research. *American Political Science Review*, 95 (3): 529–46.

BARRETT, C. B., and CASON, J. W. 1997 *Overseas Research. A Practical Guide*. Baltimore: Johns Hopkins University Press.

BELL, P. 2001. The ethics of conducting psychiatric research in war-torn societies. In *Researching Violently Divided Societies: Ethical and Methodological Issues*, ed. M. Smyth and G. Robinson. London: UN University Press and Pluto Press.

BENNETT, A., and ELMAN, C. 2006. Complex causal relations and case study methods: the example of path dependence. *Political Analysis*, 14: 250–67.

BERNARD, H. R. 2002. *Research Methods in Anthropology: Qualitative and Quantitative Approaches*, 3rd edn. Walnut Creek, Calif.: Altamira Press.

BERRY, J. M. 2002. Validity and reliability in elite interviewing. *PS: Political Science and Politics*, 35 (4): 679–82.

---

[20] For an example of such a course, see the syllabus for my Qualitative Field Research course, available on my website, **pantheon.yale.edu/~ejw33**

BRADY, H. E., and COLLIER, D. 2004. *Rethinking Social Inquiry: Diverse Tools, Shared Standards.* Savage, Md.: Rowman & Littlefield.

CARMACK, R. ed. 1988. *Harvest of Violence: The Mayan Indians and the Guatemalan Crisis.* Norman: University of Oklahoma Press.

CHATTOPADHYAY, R., and DUFLO, E. 2004. Women as policy makers: evidence from a randomized policy experiment in India. *Econometrica*, 72 (5): 1409–43.

CLARK, M. 1975. Survival in the field: implications of personal experience in field work. *Theory and Society*, 2: 63–94.

DAHL, R. A. 1963. *Who Governs? Democracy and Power in the American City.* New Haven: Yale University Press.

DEVEREUX, S.,, and HODDINOTT, J. eds. 1993. *Fieldwork in Developing Countries.* Boulder, Colo.: Lynne Rienner.

ELLIS, C. 1995. Emotional and ethical quagmires in returning to the field. *Journal of Contemporary Ethnography*, 24 (1): 68–98.

EMERSON, R. M., FRETZ, R. I., and SHAW, L. L. 1995. *Writing Ethnographic Fieldnotes.* Chicago: University of Chicago Press.

FENNO, R. 1978. *Home Style: House Members in their Districts.* Boston: Little, Brown, and Company.

GANS, H. J. 1986. The participant observer as a human being: observations on the personal aspects of fieldwork. Pp. 53–61 in *Field Research: A Sourcebook and Field Manual*, ed. R. G. Burgess, 2nd edn. London: George Allen & Unwin.

GEORGE, A. L., and BENNETT, A. 2005. *Case Studies and Theory Development in the Social Sciences.* Cambridge, Mass.: MIT Press.

GOLDSTEIN, K. 2002. Getting in the door: sampling and completing elite interviews. *PS: Political Science and Politics*, 35 (4): 669–72.

GRAETZ, M. J., and SHAPIRO, I. 2005. *Death by a Thousand Cuts: The Fight over Taxing Inherited Wealth.* Princeton: Princeton University Press.

GREEN, D. P., and GERBER, A. S. 2002. Reclaiming the experimental tradition in political science. Pp. 805–32 in *Political Science: State of the Discipline*, ed. I. Katznelson and H. V. Milner. New York: W. W. Norton.

HARRISON, G. W., and LIST, J. A. 2004. Field experiments. *Journal of Economic Literature*, 42: 1009–55.

HENRICH, J., BOYD, R., BOWLES, S., CAMERER, C., FEHR, E. and GINTIS, H. 2003. *Foundations of Human Sociality: Economic Experiments and Ethnographic Evidence from Fifteen Small-Scale Societies.* Oxford: Oxford University Press.

—— et al. 2005. "Economic man" in cross-cultural perspective: behavioral experiments in 15 small-scale societies. *Behavioral and Brain Sciences*, 28: 795–855.

JAARSMA, S. R. ed. 2002. *Handle with Care: Ownership and Control of Ethnographic Materials.* Pittsburgh: University of Pittsburgh Press.

KALYVAS, S. 2006. *The Logic of Violence in Civil War.* Cambridge: Cambridge University Press.

KELMAN, H. C. 1972. The rights of the subject in social research: an analysis in terms of relative power and legitimacy. *American Psychologist*, 27 (11): 989–1016.

KEMPER, R. V., and PETERSON ROYCE, A. eds. 2002. *Chronicling Cultures: Long-Term Field Research in Anthropology.* Walnut Creek, Calif.: Altamira Press.

KING, G., KEOHANE, R. O., and VERBA, S. 1994. *Designing Social Inquiry: Scientific Inference in Qualitative Research.* Princeton: Princeton University Press.

LEECH, B. 2002. Asking questions. techniques for semi structured interviews. *PS: Political Science and Politics*, 35 (4): 663–88.

LEWIS, O. 1970/1953. Tepoztlán restudied: a critique of the folk-urban conceptualization of social change. Originally published in *Rural Sociology*, 18 (2): 121–36. Republished in *Anthropological Essays*, by O. Lewis. New York: Random House.

LIEBERMAN, E. S. 2005. Nested analysis as a mixed-method strategy for comparative research. *American Political Science Review*, 99 (3): 435–52.

LIPSET, S. M. 1956. *Union Democracy. The Internal Politics of the International Typographical Union*. Glencoe, Ill.: Free Press.

LOFLAND, J., SNOW, D., ANDERSON, L., and LOFLAND, L. 2006. *Analyzing Social Settings: A Guide to Qualitative Observation and Analysis*. Belmont, Calif.: Wadsworth.

MAHONEY, J., and GOERTZ, G. 2006. A tale of two cultures: contrasting quantitative and qualitative research. *Political Analysis*, 14: 227–49.

NATIONAL COMMISSION FOR THE PROTECTION OF HUMAN SUBJECTS OF BIOMEDICAL AND BEHAVIORAL RESEARCH (The Belmont Report). 1979. *Ethical Principles and Guidelines for the Protection of Human Subjects of Research.*

NATIONAL RESEARCH COUNCIL. 2003. *Protecting Participants and Facilitating Social and Behavioral Sciences Research*. Panel on Institutional Review Boards, Surveys, and Social Science Research, ed. C. F. Citro, D. R. Ilgen, and C. B. Marrett. Committee on National Statistics and Board on Behavioral, Cognitive, and Sensory Sciences. Washington, DC: The National Academies Press.

NATIONAL SCIENCE FOUNDATION (n.d.). Interpreting the common rule for the protection of human subjects for behavioral and social science research. **www.nsf.gov/bfa/dias/policy/ hsfaqs.jsp.**

ORANS, M. 1996. *Not Even Wrong: Margaret Mead, Derek Freeman, and the Samoans*. Novato, Calif.: Chandler and Sharp Publishers.

POSNER, D. N. 2004. The political salience of cultural difference: why Chewas and Tumbukas are allies in Zambia and adversaries in Malawi. *American Political Science Review*, 98 (3): 529–46.

—— 2005. *The Institutional Origins of Ethnic Politics: Regime Change and Ethnic Cleavages in Africa*. Cambridge: Cambridge University Press.

PS SYMPOSIUM. 2002. Symposium: interview methods in political science. *PS: Political Science and Politics*, 35 (4): 663–76.

QUALITATIVE METHODS SYMPOSIUM. 2004. Symposium: discourse and content analysis. *Qualitative Methods Newsletter*, 2 (1): 15–39.

RAGIN, C. C. 1987. *The Comparative Method*. Berkeley and Los Angeles: University of California Press.

—— 2000. *Fuzzy-Set Social Science*. Chicago: University of Chicago Press.

RUBIN, H. J., and RUBIN, I. S. 2005. *Qualitative Interviewing: The Art of Hearing Data*, 2nd edn. Beverly Hills, Calif.: Sage.

SCOTT, J. 1985. *Weapons of the Weak: Everyday Forms of Peasant Resistance*. New Haven: Yale University Press.

SIEBER, S. D. 1986. The integration of fieldwork and survey methods. Pp. 176–88 in *Field Research: A Sourcebook and Field Manual*, ed. R. G. Burgess, 2nd edn. London: George Allen & Unwin.

SMYTH, M. 2001. Introduction. In *Researching Violently Divided Societies: Ethical and Methodological Issues*, ed. M. Smyth and G. Robinson. London: UN University Press and Pluto Press.

SNYDER, R. 2001. Scaling down: the sub-national comparative method. *Studies in Comparative International Development*, 36 (1): 93–110.

STOKES, S. C. 1995. *Cultures in Conflict: Social Movements and the State in Peru*. Berkeley and Los Angeles: University of California Press.

WANTCHEKON, L. 2003. Clientelism and voting behavior: evidence from a field experiment in Benin. *World Politics*, 55: 399–422.

WEINER, M. 1964. Political interviewing in social research. Pp. 102–33 in *Studying Politics Abroad*, ed. R. Ward. Boston: Little Brown.

WEINSTEIN, J. 2006. *Inside Rebellion: The Politics of Insurgent Violence*. Cambridge: Cambridge University Press.

WHYTE, W. F. 1986. Interviewing in field research. In *Field Research: A Sourcebook and Field Manual*, ed. R. G. Burgess, 2nd edn. London: George Allen & Unwin.

WILKINSON, S. I. 2004. *Votes and Violence: Electoral Competition and Ethnic Riots in India*. Cambridge: Cambridge University Press.

WILSON, K. 1993. Thinking about the ethics of fieldwork. Pp. 179–99 in *Fieldwork in Developing Countries*, ed. S. Devereux and J. Hoddinott. Boulder, Colo.: Lynne Rienner.

WOOD, E. J. 2003. *Insurgent Collective Action and Civil War in El Salvador*. Cambridge: Cambridge University Press.

—— 2006. The ethical challenges of field research in conflict zones. *Qualitative Sociology*, special issue on Political Ethnography, 29: 307–41.

YASHAR, D. J. 2005. *Contesting Citizenship in Latin America: The Rise of Indigenous Movements and the Postliberal Challenge*. Cambridge: Cambridge University Press.

....

IS THE SCIENCE OF COMPARATIVE POLITICS POSSIBLE?

....

ADAM PRZEWORSKI

1 INTRODUCTION

....

THE chapter is an overview of issues entailed in making causal inferences when the data are generated by processes that are not under the control of the researcher. As all overviews, this one is just an introduction to issues that have been studied in greater depth by others. No part is original, but hopefully the whole is greater than their sum.

Many research questions in comparative politics concern the impact of some institution, policy, or event on some outcome, result, or performance. I will generically refer to the former as "the (potential) cause" and to the latter as "the effect." Examples include:

(1) The impact of political institutions on economic development.
(2) The impact of political regimes on the initiation of wars.
(3) The impact of electoral systems on the number of parties.
(4) The impact of trade strategies on economic performance.
(5) The impact of signing particular international treaties on some performance, say of signing the Kyoto protocol on carbon emissions.

* With apologies to MacIntyre 1972 for stealing the title. I appreciate comments by Neal Beck, Fernando Cortés, Gösta Esping-Anderson, Jennifer Gandhi, David Laitin, and the editors of this volume.

(6) The impact of revolutions on subsequent social change.

(7) The impact of peace-keeping missions on peace.

The list is endless: I just want to emphasize that the causes may include institutions, policies, and events. Moreover, problems of this form are not limited to the cross-national level. For example, in the aftermath of the 2004 elections, some people noted that the Bush vote was higher than expected in those Florida counties that used electronic machines while it was about what one would expect in those countries that used traditional punch card machines. Did the type of voting machine affect the outcome? This is again a question about the effect of a cause.

These are then the kinds of questions that are considered below. We will find, however, that at least in one view such questions cannot be answered without enquiring where the causes come from. To identify the impact of political regimes on growth, we need to learn how political regimes come about and die. To identify the impact of peace-keeping missions on peace, we need to know when such missions are undertaken. To identify the impact of voting machines on the Bush vote, we need to know under what conditions different machines were in place. Hence, we need to study *causes of effects* as well as *effects of causes*. And this means that we face almost all problems generic to comparative politics.

2 THE PROBLEM

Suppose we have a data matrix that looks like this.[1] T stands for the potential cause, where $T = 1$ indicates "treatment" and $T = 0$ "control" (or a different treatment).[2] X and V are "covariates," that is, traits of an individual unit prior to the application of the treatment. X is the vector of covariates observed by the researcher, V are covariates not observed. NA stands for "not available." $Y = \{Y_0, Y_1\}$ is the variable subject to the potential effect of the cause, where Y_0 stands for states of the units not exposed to treatment and Y_1 of those exposed to it, so that for each unit i we observe either Y_1 or Y_0:

$$Y_i = T_i Y_{1i} + (1 - T_i) Y_{0i}. \tag{1}$$

A "unit" is an opportunity for the cause to operate. It may be an individual, a country, or what not. Moreover, it may be the same individual or a country in a different state: say Sweden in 1950 and in 1951. Hence, the "unit" is a full set of observable and unobservable covariates: i is coextensive with the vector of "back-ground conditions" $(\mathbf{x}_i, \mathbf{v}_i)$.

---

[1] A comment on notation. As conventional in this literature, capital letters denote variables; small letters particular values. Bold letters represent vectors. $E()$ is to be read as "the expected value," $Y|X$ as "the value of Y conditional on the value of X," so that $E(Y|X)$ is "the expected value of Y given X." To simplify the notation, I implicitly use throughout the law of iterated expectations.

[2] Although for simplicity I assume that the cause is a binary variable, everything said here holds for any discrete or continuous values of T.

Table 6.1 Experiments and quasi-experiments

i	T	X_1	X_2	$\ldots$	X_k	V_1	V_2	Y_0	Y_1
1	0	1	1	1	1	NA	NA	y_{01}	NA
2	1	1	1	1	1	NA	NA	NA	y_{12}
3	0	1	1	1	1	NA	NA	y_{03}	NA
4	1	1	1	1	1	NA	NA	NA	y_{14}
5	0	3	5	1	6	NA	NA	y_{05}	NA
6	1	3	5	1	6	NA	NA	NA	y_{16}
$\ldots$	$\ldots$	$\ldots$	$\ldots$	$\ldots$	$\ldots$	NA	NA	$\ldots$	$\ldots$
$\ldots$	$\ldots$	$\ldots$	$\ldots$	$\ldots$	$\ldots$	NA	NA	$\ldots$	$\ldots$
$N-1$	0	17	14	6	9	NA	NA	$y_{0,N-1}$	NA
N	1	17	14	6	9	NA	NA	NA	y_{1N}

Now, let U stand for the effect of V on Y and assume linear separability. Then

$$E(Y|X, V) = E(Y|X) + U. \qquad (2)$$

Substituting into (1) (and dropping the i subscript) yields

$$Y = E(Y_0|X) + T[E(Y_1 - Y_0|X)] + \{T(U_1 - U_0) + U_0\}$$
$$= \beta_0(X) + \beta(X)T + U, \qquad (3)$$

where $\beta(X) = E(E(Y_1 - Y_0)|X) = E(Y_1 - Y_0|X)$ is the average causal effect, discussed further below, and $U = T(U_1 - U_0) + U_0$.

I introduce all this notation abruptly just to show the basic concern in identifying causal effects, namely, whether $E(U) = 0$. Whether it does equal 0 is unknowable in general, but there are different identifying assumptions that imply this property. These assumptions, in turn, are not testable but we can intelligently argue whether they are reasonable. I will let the reader decide whether what we practice is science or art.

3 KINDS OF DATA

3.1 Experimental Studies

To fix ideas, assume that we do know that $E(U) = 0$. This will be true if the treatment is randomly assigned to units.

The most important aspect of random assignment is that it matches on unobserved as well as on observed covariates. Note that in Table 6.1 the observed covariates are exactly matched, meaning that for each vector x there is an equal number of observations with $T = 0$ and $T = 1$, so that the means of each X are identical for the treatment and control groups. Most of what is said below, however, also holds when the observations are sufficiently well "*balanced*," meaning that the means of each X are sufficiently similar for units with $T = 0$ and $T = 1$. Under random assignment the unobserved covariates should be balanced as well. And since random assignment means that the value of the causal variable is independent of all characteristics of a unit, T is independent of U and $E(U) = 0$.

Now, what is the causal effect of treatment on the particular unit i, the Individual Treatment Effect? This effect is *defined* as the difference between the states of an individual unit when it is subjected and not subjected to the operation of the cause, say the difference in the intensity of Joe Smith's headache after he did and did not take aspirin or the extent of social change in France as a result of the revolution of 1789 and without it. Formally,

$$ITE_i = y_{1i} - y_{0i} \equiv \beta_i \tag{4}$$

But for all odd-numbered units in Table 6.1 we observe only their state under control and for all even numbered only under treatment. Hence, even under random assignment, this question cannot be answered without making some assumptions about hypothetical situations that would have occurred had an individual who did not get treatment (had not been exposed to the potential causes) received it or had an individual who did receive treatment not received it. Since these states did not occur, they are contrary to fact, *counterfactual*.[3] And since counterfactuals cannot be observed, assumptions about counterfactuals cannot be directly tested.[4] Hence, we arrive at the first conclusion.

Conclusion 1: *The effect of a cause on an individual unit cannot be determined without making assumptions about counterfactuals. These assumptions cannot be tested.*

What assumption would identify the individual treatment effect under random assignment?

Assumption 1: *Unit homogeneity (Holland 1986).*
For any $i, j \in N$,

$$if \ (\mathbf{x}_i, \mathbf{v}_i) = (\mathbf{x}_j, \mathbf{v}_j), \ then \ y_{0i} = y_{0j} \ and \ y_{1i} = y_{1j}.$$

This assumption says that if any two individuals have the same values of covariates, they would have the same states under control and the same states under treatment. When this assumption is true, the process of selection can be ignored: it does not matter which of two identical units is subject to treatment and which serves as control.

---

[3] The idea of counterfactuals goes back to Pascal 1669, section 162: "*Le nez de Cléopâtre: s'il eût été plus court, toute la face de la terre aurait changé.*" On the distinctions among different types of conditional propositions, see Edgington 2001. On the logical problems with counterfactuals, see Quine (1953); Lewis (1973); Mackie (2002/1973); Goodman (1979); Stalnaker (1987).

[4] For a statistical view of causality without counterfactuals, see Dawid (2000), who rejects them as metaphysical.

This assumption *identifies* the causal effect of treatment. Applying the homogeneity assumption to the $(i + 1)st$ unit in Table 6.1 yields

$$ITE_{i+1} = y_{1,i+1} - y_{0,i+1} = y_{1,i+1} - y_{0,i},$$

where now both $y_{1,i+1}$ and $y_{0,i}$ are observed.

What does "*identify*" mean? While econometrics textbooks use this term technically in many contexts, intuitively "to identify" is to be able to infer relations among variables (or the parameters of multivariate distribution) on the basis of all the possible observations (Koopmans 1949; in Manski 1995, 6). But often identification is possible only by assuming something that may or may not be testable. As Manski (1995, 18) observed, "Theories are testable where they are least needed, and are not testable where they are most needed. Theories are least needed to determine conditional distributions $P(y|x)$ on the support of $P(x)$. They are most needed to determine these distributions off the support." We have seen that since each unit can be observed only in one state at one time it is not possible to identify the individual causal effect without making some assumptions. Hence, we need *identifying assumptions*, such as unit homogeneity. This assumption is not testable. But it seems reasonable.

Now we can ask about the Average Treatment Effect, *ATE*. Specifically, under what assumptions

$$\beta_{ATE} = E(Y_1 - Y_0|X) = E(\beta|X) = \bar{y}_1 - \bar{y}_0 = \bar{\beta},$$

so that the observed mean difference identifies the *average* treatment effect? The answer is "conditional mean independence:"

Assumption 2: *Conditional Mean Independence.*

$$E(Y_1|X, T = 1) = E(Y_1|X, T = 0) = E(Y_1|X)$$
$$E(Y_0|X, T = 0) = E(Y_0|X, T = 1) = E(Y_0|X)$$

This assumption says that conditional only on *observed* covariates we can expect the units not exposed to treatment to react to it identically to those observed under treatment and the units exposed to treatment not to differ in their control state from those observed under control.[5] For example, let the treatment be central bank independence and the effect the rate of inflation. This assumption says that if a country where the central bank is not independent had an independent bank, it would experience the same inflation rate as the country where the bank was in fact independent as long as the two countries are identical in all the observed aspects. Conversely, the country where the bank is independent would experience the same rate of inflation as the one where it is not independent, again conditional on the two countries being identical in all the observed covariates.

---

[5] Again, to help with the notation, $E(Y_1|T = 1)$ is to be read as "the expected value of the outcome under treatment, given that the units have been observed as treated," while $E(Y_1|T = 0)$ as "the expected value of the outcome under treatment, given that the units have been observed as not treated."

Under random assignment this assumption is trivially true. And it implies that the observed difference identifies the average causal effect:[6]

$$\bar{\beta} = E(Y_1|X,\ T = 1) - E(Y_0|X,\ T = 0) = \bar{y}_1 - \bar{y}_0.$$

Conclusion 2: *If the assignment to treatment is random, then the difference of the observed means identifies the average causal effect of treatment.*

3.2 "Quasi-experiments" and Historical Studies

Suppose now that the data in Table 6.1 were generated by some process unknown to the researcher. Note that "unknown" does not preclude random assignment: even if the researcher did not randomly assign treatments, history may have.[7] If it is possible to make a plausible case that assignment by history was in fact random, we have a "natural experiment" and everything established above applies; specifically the observed difference identifies the average causal effect.[8] But suppose that the claim of randomization cannot be supported. History generated observations by some process and all the researcher did was to rearrange the data into the form of Table 6.1, perhaps dropping observations without an exact or a close match (or including only the common support). Some people would want to qualify such data structures as "quasi-experiments," which "lack random assignment of units to conditions but otherwise have similar purposes and structural attributes to randomized experiments" (Shadish, Cook, and Campbell 2002, 104). Yet quasi-experiments are not natural

---

[6] According to a theorem by Rosenbaum and Rubin 1983, if the conditional mean independence holds in the form specified in the text, then it also holds in the form in which $p(X) = \Pr(T = 1 \mid X)$ is substituted for X, where $p(X)$ is the "propensity score."

[7] The distinction between randomization by the researcher and by nature goes back to Haavelmo 1944; cited in Angrist and Krueger 2001: 80, who drew an analogy between the experiments "we should like to make" and "the stream of experiments that nature is steadily turning out from her own enormous laboratory, and which we merely watch as passive observers."

[8] To see what is entailed, consider a beautiful study by Banerjee and Iyer (2002). When the British were conquering India, they implanted different tributary systems in different areas: during one period they delegated tax collection to landlords, during another they either charged tax collection to the village as a community or collected taxes themselves from individual peasants. Since these tributary systems depended on the date of conquest, rather than on the characteristics of particular districts, these institutions were exogenous with regard to local climate, endowments, and presumably the unobserved characteristics of the districts. The identification strategy adopted by Banerjee and Iyer was to construct a restricted sample of districts that are geographical neighbors, but which happened to have different tax systems. They observed that "Our strategy might give biased results if the British decision of which land tenure system to adopt depended on other characteristics of the area in systematic ways." (2002, 10–11). But using this strategy allowed them to assume that "there is no reason to think that the choice of land tenure system at the district level was closely tied to the characteristics of the district.... It is therefore probably reasonable to assume that when two districts lying directly across from each other on either side of the boundary between two settlement regions ended up with different types of tenure systems, it was for reasons mostly unrelated to their innate differences." Since institutions were exogenous with regard to background conditions and since (until independence) they remained the same regardless of the consequences they generated, the observed differences in development can be attributed to institutions.

experiments. *Even if units can be perfectly matched on observed covariates, there is nothing to guarantee that they are also randomized with regard to unobserved ones.*

In most studies in the social sciences, and generically in comparative politics, the researcher cannot control the assignment of causes to units. We cannot randomly assign political regimes, trade policies, revolutions, or civil wars to countries. Such studies, in which the investigator cannot control the assignment of potential causes to background characteristics, are generically referred to as "observational studies." Yet the type of research that bears this label, reviewed in Rosenbaum's (2002) magisterial treatise, is characterized not only by the sources of data but also by a methodological approach. The method of medical research on the causes of disease is to emulate experiments by treating the data as quasi-experimental. The assignment of causes to units is generated by nature: people are given to the researcher with the number of cigarettes they smoke and with their covariates. Observational studies seek to balance the smokers and non-smokers (or smokers of different intensity) on their observed characteristics. Having reached a satisfactory balance, they then invoke mean independence assumption, thus assuming in fact either that balancing on the observed covariates is sufficient to balance on the unobserved ones or that unobserved factors do not affect the outcome, say the incidence of lung disease. Needless to say, this is a venerated research design in comparative research, going back to J. S. Mill's "method of only difference," and dubbed "the most similar systems design" by Przeworski and Teune (1970).

Yet, following Heckman (2004),[9] I think that analogies with experiments are misleading.[10] The crux of the matter is how to identify causal effects *in the absence of random assignment.* Even if they look "quasi-experimental," treating historical data as experiments "but for random assignment" is to hide the central problem under the proverbial rug. The most inane example I recently read was a study which found that women who do not work are more likely to become sick. Suppose that we have matched the working and non-working women on all the observed covariates. Might it still not be true that women who are more prone to sickness are less likely to work?

Assignments of causes to units have two distinct features. Randomization naturally matches units on covariates, so that all the exogenous characteristics of the units are controlled ex ante, while assignment by "nature" or "history" may or may not generate such matches, so that the covariates must be controlled ex post, by calculating means conditional on their values. But this difference—whether "controlling" for the covariates occurs ex ante or ex post—would have no consequences for identification if all the covariates could be controlled for ex post. The crucial difference is that when assignment is not random, unobserved covariates may differ between the units exposed and not exposed to a cause even if values of all the observed covariates are "balanced." Consider a beautiful study by Posner (2004) of the relations between the same two ethnic groups on the two sides of the border between Malawi and Zambia. While Posner provides persuasive arguments that members of each of the two groups do not differ otherwise than by being on different

---

[9] Heckman refers to what I call "observational" studies as "statistical" and juxtaposes them to "scientific" or "econometric." While my terminology is more neutral, the substance of the distinction is the same.

[10] For a lucid discussion of natural experiments in political science, see Dunning (2005).

sides of the border, rival hypotheses entailing unobserved differences are always plausible. They may be more or less plausible but, as Dunning (2005) emphasizes, assessments of their plausibility are inevitably subjective.

While students of history, which is what we are, share with experimentalists the goal of identifying causal effects and the conceptual apparatus relying on counterfactuals, they need to justify the counterfactual hypotheses. Experimental justification of counterfactuals is that the assignment of causes is generated by a mechanism that *could have* assigned a different treatment to the same unit. The properties of this mechanism—randomization—are known, as is the probability that a particular value of treatment is assigned to any set of covariates. But the observations given to us in comparative politics, the *data*, are generated by some obscure processes, to which we agnostically refer as "history." And if we invoke counterfactuals, we must be assuming that history could have generated a world different from the one in which we live, that realizations of history other than the actual one are possible. To construct counterfactuals. we must specify the mechanism by which history assigns causes to units.

How can we justify such assumptions? They must be somehow disciplined; otherwise we could fantasize in any way we please. As Hawthorn (1991, 168) posed the issue, "Are the alternatives to any actual given only by the facts of that actual, or by possibilities that were can vassed at the time, or by very close comparisons? Are there not also theories to suggest possibilities that we would not otherwise have been able to see?" While there is no general answer to such questions, the point is that to engage in practical counterfactual inferences we need some systematic criteria. Without such criteria, "the possibilities we would be entertaining would be possibilities not for an actual, but for what would itself be merely a possible. And at the point, our History or social science would have dissolved into a literature of the imagination" (Hawthorn 1991, 167; see also Kundera 2003).

If we are to be guided by the "facts of the actual," we need to use the world we observe to identify the mechanisms by which history produces observations, specifically, by which it assigns causes to covariates. "Historical studies" are studies that analyze data generated by history and, as distinct from observational studies, enquire into the causes of effects as well as the effects of causes.

4 POTENTIAL BIASES

We have seen that to identify causal effects, we need to ensure that

$$E(U) = E[T(U_1 - U_0) + U_0] = 0,$$

where U is the impact of unobserved factors in $Y = \beta_0(X) + \beta(X)T + U$ and $\beta(X)$ is the average causal effect conditional on X. There are various reasons why this condition may be violated.

4.1 Baseline Bias

Note first that the causal effect of interest need not be the effect on the average unit but on those units that are actually observed as treated.[11] This *estimand* is typically referred to as the Average effect of Treatment on the Treated, *ATT*, defined as

$$\beta_{ATT} = E(Y_1 - Y_0 | X, \ T = 1). \tag{5}$$

The value of this parameter tells us how the treatment changes the outcome for those units that were observed as treated. Note that $E(Y_1 | T = 1)$ is observed, while $E(Y_0 | T = 1)$ is the missing counterfactual. Now consider the bias of the observed difference, $\bar{\beta}$, as an estimator of β_{ATT}:

$$\begin{aligned}
\bar{\beta} - \beta_{ATT} &= E(Y_1 | X, \ T = 1) - E(Y_0 | X, \ T = 0) - E(Y_1 - Y_0 | X, \ T = 1) \\
&= E(Y_0 | X, \ T = 1) - E(Y_0 | X, \ T = 0) \\
&= E(U_0 | T = 1) - E(U_0 | T = 0),
\end{aligned} \tag{6}$$

where the last expression is the difference in the control state between those units that were treated and those that were not, typically referred to as the "baseline bias." Suppose, for example, that an omitted variable, say human capital, H, is correlated with the treatment and it affects the development prospects of a country, so that $E(U_0 | H = high, \ T = 1) > E(U_0 | H = low, \ T = 0)$. Since countries observed under $T = 1$ would have developed faster under $T = 0$ than those actually observed under $T = 0$, the observed difference overestimates the causal effect of T. This bias is sometimes referred to as "the" selection bias, but we will see that there are other potential selection biases than the baseline bias.

4.2 Self-Selection Bias

Now, return to *ATE*. The bias of $\bar{\beta}$ as the estimator of β_{ATE} is

$$\bar{\beta} - \beta_{ATE} = E(Y_1 | X, \ T = 1) - E(Y_0 | X, \ T = 0) - E(Y_1 - Y_0 | X). \tag{7}$$

Adding and subtracting $E(Y_0 | T = 1)$ yields

$$\begin{aligned}
\bar{\beta} - \beta_{ATE} &= \{E(Y_0 | X, \ T = 1) - E(Y_0 | X, \ T = 0)\} + \\
\{E(Y_1 - Y_0 | X, \ T = 1) &- E(Y_1 - Y_0 | X)\} = \\
&\{E(U_0 | T = 1) - E(U_0 | T = 0)\} \\
&+ \{E(U_1 - U_0 | T = 1) - E(U_1 - U_0)\}.
\end{aligned} \tag{8}$$

---

[11] This effect is of particular interest in remedial policy programs. As Heckman repeatedly points out, it makes no sense to ask what would be the effect of manpower training programs on millionaires. In turn, we want to know the effectiveness of such programs for the people who need them and get them.

The term in the first curly brackets is the by now familiar baseline bias. The term in the second brackets, in turn, is best thought of as "self-selection" bias. This term is the difference between the effect of treatment on those who were actually treated and on the average unit. But why would the effect of the treatment on the treated differ from its effect on those who are not? One reason is that recruitment to treatment depends on something unobserved by the researcher but anticipated by the unit. This will occur if individuals seek treatment for some reasons other than the X's observed by the researcher or if they comply differently with the treatment depending on the X's. Suppose—I am not asking you to believe it—that political elites which opt for democracy also know how to make the country develop faster. Then the effect of democracy on development for the countries observed as democracies will differ from the effect on the average country: a self-selection bias.

4.3 Post-treatment Bias: "Manipulability" and "Attributes"

Thus far we have assumed that the X's and the V's, called here "covariates," do not change with treatment. The assumption was that causes can be manipulated one at a time. But suppose that some of the covariates—call this subset A for "attributes"—change as the effect of treatment: this is called "post-treatment effect" by King and Zeng (2002). Now the treatment may have two effects: a direct one and an indirect via A. We need some identification assumptions to tell these two effects apart.

Can we always make such assumptions? Here we enter into a complex and subtle issue. According to Holland (1986), to qualify as a potential cause, the particular variable must be vulnerable to (potential) *manipulation*. The critical feature of the notion of cause is that different values of the cause can be realized under the same background conditions. This is why attributes, such race or gender, cannot be causes. "Causes," Holland says, "are only those things that could, in principle, be treatments in experiments" (1986, 954). What distinguishes statistical association from causation is manipulability: "the schooling a student receives can be a cause, in our sense, of the student's performance on a test, whereas the student's race or gender cannot." It makes no sense to say "Joe earns $500 less than Jim *because* Joe is black," since skin color (called "race" in the United States) cannot be manipulated. Causal inference is concerned with the effect of causes under specific background conditions ("on specific units") and attributes cannot be manipulated without changing these conditions.

Note that this argument confounds two propositions: (1) T cannot be manipulated and (2) T cannot be manipulated without changing A. The first one says that we cannot change the skin color of an individual. The second says that we can change it but if we change it, we will also change other characteristics of this individual (or the treatment of this individual by others). The confusion becomes apparent when we read that "An attribute cannot be a cause in an experiment, because the notion of *potential exposability* does not apply to it. The only way for an attribute to change its value [so it can be changed!] is for the unit to change in some way and no longer be the same unit" (Holland 1986, 954). Now, if (1) holds, it may still be true that there are other units that have the same background conditions but a different value of T and we can use the conditional mean independence assumption to identify the causal effect. Only if (2) is true does identification become impossible.

Consider an example closer to our practice: the location of a country in Africa, which in many analyses appears to affect civil strife and economic growth. Does it make sense to say that "the effect of Africa on growth is β"? "Africa" is clearly an attribute by Holland's definition, a set of related unobserved characteristics. If history had placed Zimbabwe in Latin America, it would have no longer been Zimbabwe: it would differ in various ways that make Africa distinct from Latin America. Hence, relying on the Africa dummy to generate counterfactuals would generate a "post-treatment bias."

King and Zeng (2002, 21) emphasize that controlling (matching) for variables that are endogenous with regard to treatment generates bias. This can be seen as follows. For simplicity, suppose that assignment is random, so that there is no baseline or self-selection bias, but $X_1 = X_0 + \delta T$. Then conditioning on X,

$$
\begin{aligned}
E(Y_1 - Y_0 | X) &= E(Y_1 | X_0 + \delta T) - E(Y_0 | X_0) \\
&= E(Y_1 - Y_0 | X_0) + \{E(Y_1 | X_0 + \delta T) - E(Y_1 | X_0)\},
\end{aligned}
\tag{9}
$$

where the last term is the "post-treatment bias." For example, Przeworski et al. (2000) found that labor force, a source of economic growth, increases faster under dictatorships. Conditioning on the growth of labor force would then generate post-treatment bias.

4.4 Non-independence Bias: "SUTVA"

One final implicit assumption concerns independence of the Y variables across units. This assumption is called SUTVA, for "stable unit treatment value." Suppose that the units are individuals and that they learn from one another, so that $y_i = f(y_j)$. This means that the performance of the treated may affect the performance of the untreated, or vice versa. In Lucas's (1988) growth model, a young plumber learns from the experienced one. Hence, if we take the difference in their productivity as the effect of experience, it will be underestimated because of the externality. Or take T to be "export-oriented" development strategy. South Korea adopted this strategy early and had high growth rates. Brazil adopted it late. But suppose that Brazil had adopted it early: would the growth rate of Korea been the same? If it would not have been the same, the values observed for Korea under treatment depend on the realization of the treatment variable for Brazil: hence the Korean values are not "stable." One needs some kind of an equilibrium model to identify the causal effect when this assumption is violated.

5   HISTORICAL STUDIES

5.1 An Example

Let us look at an example, concerning the effect of political regimes, dichotomized as democracies ($T = 0$) and dictatorships ($T = 1$), on economic development between 1950 and 2000.[12]

Here the cause is the political regime. The observed covariate X is GDP/cap lagged one year. The unobserved variable V is the "quality of leadership." The outcome (performance) variable Y is the rate of growth of total GDP.

The country-year observations are sorted from the lowest to the highest per capita income. Note that nine observations with the lowest GDP/cap are dictatorships. Indeed, there are only four democratic years until the 155th poorest observation: they

Table 6.2 Fragments of data concerning political regimes and economic development

n-th lowest GDP/cap n	Country	Year	GDP/cap	Quality	Regime	Growth under DEM	Growth under DIC
1	Zaire	1997	310	N.A.	DIC	N.A.	−5.90
...	...	...	...	...	DIC	N.A.	...
10	Uganda	1981	443	N.A.	DEM	44.36	N.A.
13	Uganda	1980	451	N.A.	DEM	0.47.	N.A.
69	Malawi	1995	545	N.A.	DEM	26.38	N.A.
155	Uganda	1982	630	N.A.	DEM	6.90	...
...	...	...	...	N.A.	DEM	...	N.A.
...	...	...	...	N.A.	DIC	N.A.	...
4,589	Taiwan	1995	14,036	N.A.	DIC	N.A.	6.19.
...	...	...	...	N.A.	DEM	...	N.A.
...	Singapore	...	...	N.A.	DIC	N.A.	...
...	...	...	...	N.A.	DEM	...	N.A.
5,079	Singapore	1996	22,642	N.A.	DIC	N.A.	14.22
...	...	...	...	...	DEM	...	N.A.
5,161	Luxembourg	2000	41,354	N.A.	DEM	7.68	N.A.
Average						3.68	4.27
N						2,459	2,702

[12] The economic data are combined from Penn World Tables Release 5.6 and Release 6.1. They are in 1995 purchasing power parity dollars. Regime classification is due to Cheibub and Gandhi (2004). Six Middle Eastern oil countries are excluded.

are listed in the table. In turn, eighty-two observations with the highest GDP/cap are all democracies: the wealthiest dictatorship, Singapore in 1996, ranked 5,079th. The wealthiest dictatorship outside Singapore was in Taiwan in 1995: it ranked 4,589th. Between Uganda in 1982, with per capita income of $630, and Thailand in 1995 with income of $14,036, there are dictatorships as well as democracies, but their distribution is still not the same. Dictatorships are heavily bunched in poor countries, democracies are frequent in rich ones. Indeed, 90 percent of observations of dictatorships are below $6,000, while only 42 percent of democracies are below this level. Figure 6.1 shows the density of per capita incomes for the two regimes.

We see in Table 6.2 that $\bar{y}_0 = 3.68$ and $\bar{y}_1 = 4.27$, so that $\hat{\beta} = 0.59$. At these rates, total income doubles in 16.2 years under dictatorships and in 18.8 years under democracy. Hence, it looks like dictatorships grow faster.

5.2 Types of Estimators

How can we identify causal effects when the data are generated by history?[13] Basically, we can adopt two approaches: drop the observations that are not "comparable," restricting identification of causal effects to those that are, or keep all the observations and generate hypothetical matches for each of them. Using only "comparable"

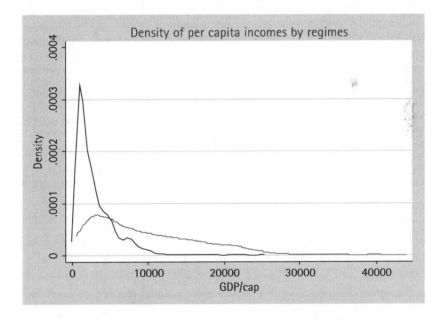

Fig. 6.1 Density of per capita incomes by regimes

[13] For overviews of estimators see Angrist and Krueger (1999); Berk (2004, ch. 5); DuFlo (2002); Persson and Tabellini (2003, ch. 5); or Winship and Morgan (1999). For reasons of space, I do not discuss difference-in-difference estimators, for which see Woolridge (2002) and Bertrand, Duflo, and Mullainathan (2004).

cases would eliminate (or give almost zero weights to) all the observations in Table 6.2 that do not have close matches, while procedures generating hypothetical counterfactuals would fill all the growth cells for which history did not generate the information.

5.2.1 Matching

One way to proceed is to *match on observables*.[14] Say we want to examine the effect of guaranteed income programs on labor supply. We observe some wealthy countries with such programs (*Revenue minimum d'insertion* in France) and many countries, rich and poor, without them. We would not want to match the wealthy treatment cases with controls from poor countries. Hence, we use as controls countries with comparable per capita income, and restrict our causal inference to such countries.

Matching takes the assignment of causes as given and calculates causal effects conditional on the assignment of causes realized by history, relying on the conditional mean independence assumption

$$E(Y_j|X, \ T = j) = E(Y_j|X) \forall j, \tag{10}$$

which says that the value of *Y* in any state *j* does not depend on the state *T* in which a unit is observed once it is conditioned on the observed covariates. This is the same assumption as conditional mean independence introduced above, but written more generally to emphasize that the cause may assume any set of values.

Matching estimators are vulnerable to two problems:

1. Dropping observations reduces the scope of generality. Sometimes, as in the example of minimum income programs, this is not a loss. It is not a loss because the probability that a poor country would institute these programs is zero: poor countries cannot afford such programs, so that the question how these programs would affect labor supply in poor countries is moot. But how should we proceed when this probability is positive under all conditions, yet very differently distributed with regard to these conditions, as in the case of political regimes? What to do with observations without a close match? You know from Table 6.2 that there are poor dictatorships without a close democratic match and rich democracies without a close autocratic match. We can throw these observations out. Alternatively, and almost equivalently, we can keep them in but assign them very low weights.[15] In either case, we have to worry whether the causal effect is the same for those observations with close matches and those without them. If we are matching on GDP/cap, we have to be concerned about the shape of the function that relates this covariate to the effect variable, the rate of growth. And observe in Figure 6.2 that this relation is non-linear:

---

[14] On matching estimators, see Rosenbaum (2002); Imbens (2002); Becker and Ichino (2002); and, more critically, Heckman (2004).

[15] Depending on the algorithm, matching estimators treat differently observations that cannot be matched exactly. When matching is restricted to common support or when it is confined to balanced strata, observations without a match are ignored. When some kind of distance measure is employed, distant matches obtain weights approaching zero.

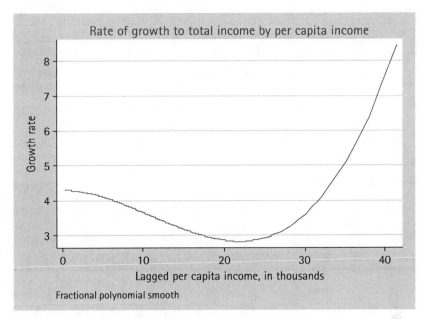

Fig. 6.2 Rate of growth of total income by per capita income

Consider the upper tail of distribution of GDP/cap. There are only 10 country-years of dictatorships with incomes above $14,036, all from Singapore which grew at the spectacular rate of 7.86, while 562 observations of democracies in this range have mean growth of 2.82. Moreover, there are 82 observations of democracies that are wealthier than the wealthiest dictatorship. Are we willing to believe that dictatorships grow faster in this range? As King and Zeng (2002) emphasize, extrapolations out of range of common support are highly sensitive to the form of the function.

2. We can match on observables. But should we not worry about unobservables? Suppose that leaders of some countries go to study in Cambridge, where they absorb the ideals of democracy and learn how to promote growth. Leaders of other countries, however, go to the School for the Americas, where they learn how to repress and nothing about economics. Dictatorships will then generate lower growth because of the quality of the leadership, which is "Not Available" in Table 6.2. Since this is a variable we could not observe systematically, we cannot match on it. And it may matter. Conditional mean independence—the assumption that unobserved factors do not matter—is very strong, and likely to be often false in cross-national research.

All that was said about matching applies to regression models that control for the observables. Matching is just non-parametric regression: both generate means of Y conditional on X and T. Moreover, as observed respectively by Manski (1995) and Achen (1986), both matching and parametric regressions that control for observables may in fact exacerbate the biases due to selection on unobservables.

Both matching and parametric regression estimates can be subjected to sensitivity analysis. Given assumptions about the unobservables, one can calculate the range of estimates that are compatible with the observed data (Manski 1995). Rosenbaum (2002, ch. 4) presents methods for quantifying the sensitivity of the estimates of causal effects under different assumptions. Obviously, the more plausible the assumption and the narrower the bounds, the more credible is the estimate.

5.2.2 *Instrumental Variables*

Instrumental variables estimator is based on the assumption of conditional mean independence in the form:

$$E(Y_j|X, Z, T = j) = E(Y_j|X, Z)\forall j. \tag{11}$$

The idea is the following. Suppose that after conditioning on X, Y_j still depends on j, in other terms that $cov(T, U) \neq 0$. Now, suppose that there is a variable Z, called an "instrument," such that

$$cov(Z,T) \neq 0 \tag{12}$$

and

$$cov(Z,U) = 0. \tag{13}$$

Then conditioning on X and Z satisfies (11). Thinking in regression terms, let $\hat{Y} = f(Z)$ and $\hat{T} = g(Z)$. Then, by assumption (13), β in $\hat{Y} = \beta\hat{T}$ is that part of the causal effect of T on Y which is independent of U.

To qualify as an instrument, a variable must be related to the cause and only to the cause, so that its entire effect is transmitted by the cause. Note that while the assumption that the instrument is related to the cause (conditional on all exogenous variables) can be and should be tested, the assumption that it is independent of the conditions that also shape the effect is not testable.

Instruments must be correlated with the cause. Weak instruments (those weakly correlated with the treatment) can generate biased estimates even with very large samples. But instruments cannot be too strongly correlated with the cause. In the limit, if the instrument and the cause are the same, the instrument is as endogenous as the cause: this is "the curse of strong instruments." The causal effect cannot be identified, because it is impossible to separate the impact of the cause from that of the conditions that give rise to it.

In turn, the "exclusion restriction" (13) requires that the instrument have no effect that is not mediated by the cause. Moreover, given that $U = T(U_1 - U_0) + U_0$,

$$cov\,(Z, U) = cov\,(Z, U_0) + cov\,(Z, T(U_1 - U_0)). \tag{14}$$

Hence, the exclusion restriction has two parts, and Heckman (1996, 2004) repeatedly makes the point that, even if $cov(Z, U_0) = 0$, in the presence of unobserved self-selection the second covariance will not be zero.

Since the exclusion restriction is not testable, it necessitates conjuring and dismissing stories about rival channels through which the instrument may affect the outcome. For example, Acemoglu, Johnson, and Robinson (2001), who use settler mortality at the time of colonialization as the instrument for institutions, have to argue that the natives were not vulnerable to the same sources of mortality as the settlers: otherwise the causal impact of settler mortality would be transmitted by the productivity of the natives in addition to the path via institutions. Yet Djankov et al. (2003) pointed out that settler mortality does not qualify as an instrument since it has an impact on economic performance via the human capital of the settlers. (See also Glaeser et al. 2004).

Justifying instruments entails rhetoric: one has to tell a story and it better be a good one. Identification is sometimes aided by the structure of the data. But proponents of instrumental variables often overstate their case. Angrist and Krueger (2001, table 1), for example, distinguish between "natural experiments," which they never define, and "randomized experiments" as aids in identification. In turn, according to Woolridge (2002, 88), "A natural experiment occurs when some (often unintended) feature of the set up we are studying produces exogenous variation in an otherwise endogenous explanatory variable." The search for natural experiments is motivated by the hope that "nature" or "history" would have randomized not only with regard to observable but also with regard to unobserved covariates. Yet as long as the assignment is not random, at best we have "quasi-experiments," in which the units are matched on observables, but with no guarantees about unobservables.[16] Finding such data makes the story better, but it is still a story.

5.2.3 *Selection on Unobservables*

Both matching and instrumental variables estimators condition on observed covariates and both are vulnerable to the influence of unobserved variables that are correlated with the treatment. Another approach conditions on unobserved as well as on observed covariates. One way to think of these estimators is that they emulate experiments, but differently than matching: not by eliminating observations that do not have an observed match but by creating observations to match all the observed values. The assumption is that if the conditioning is correct, then the resulting data have the same structure as if history had performed a random experiment assigning different values of treatment to each unit. Since the conditional mean independence of the form

$$E(Y_j|X, Z, V, T = j) = E(Y_j|X, Z, V) \forall j \qquad (\pm 15)$$

holds whenever assignment is random, the only issue with regard to these estimators is whether they correctly emulated random assignment.

The basic idea is the following. We first describe the process by which the observed assignment of causes was generated by history:

---

[16] Instrumental variables estimators are also vulnerable to the critique that they identify as best the "local" effects. For a discussion of this issue in political science, see Dunning (2005).

$$T^* = Za + V, T = 1(T^* > 0), V \sim (0, 1). \tag{16}$$

This equation says that the propensity toward being observed under treatment depends on observable variables Z and unobserved factors V and that we observe $T = 1$ if $T^* > 0$. Second, we exploit the possibility that $\sqrt{cov}(V, U) \neq 0$, by expressing $E(U_j|T = j)$ in

$$E(Y_j|X, T = j) = E(Y_j|X) + E(U_j|T = j), \tag{17}$$

as

$$E(U_j|T = j) = \theta_j E(V|T = j), \tag{18}$$

where the latter expectation can be estimated from (16). Finally, we substitute, to obtain

$$E(Y_j|X, T = j) = E(Y_j|X) + \theta_j E(V|T = j), \tag{19}$$

which can be now estimated by least squares. The OLS coefficients of $E(Y_j|X) = X\beta_j$ can be then used to generate counterfactual values of Y_j for the cases in which it is not observed, thus filling all the missing values in Table 6.2. Finally, for $j = \{0, 1\}$,

$$\hat{\beta}_{ATE} = E(Y_1|X) - E(Y_0|X) = (\hat{\beta}_1 - \hat{\beta}_0)X,$$

is the estimator of the average causal effect.

Note that we still have to be concerned about strong endogeneity of treatment. In principle, it has to be true that $0 < \Pr(T = 1|Z) < 1 \forall Z$. Otherwise, the counterfactuals cannot be realized given the mechanism by which history assigns treatments, so that the entire exercise is moot. The main vulnerability of this class of estimators stems from the untestable assumption about the joint distribution (V, U_1, U_0).

5.3 Back to the Example

To illustrate these methods, let us return to our example, arbitrarily taking the "treatment" to be dictatorship. We will test the robustness of the estimators with regard to (1) the specification of the selection mechanism and (2) the functional form of the outcome equation. The model to be estimated is

$$p = \Pr(REGIME = 1) = \Pr(Za + V > 0) = F(Za). \tag{20a}$$

$$GROWTH = f(GDP/cap) + \beta * REGIME + U. \tag{20b}$$

Table 6.3 contains all the results.

We specify the selection mechanism (20a) in two ways. The "static" specification includes three variables: lagged per capita income, lagged proportion of countries in the world that were democratic in a particular year, and lagged number of completed

Table 6.3 Estimates of causal effects of regimes

6.3a Estimates of causal effects of regimes on the rate of growth of total income

Estimator	Static linear	Dynamic linear	Static cubic	Dynamic cubic
OLS	−0.20	−0.24	−0.22	−0.23
	(0.60)	(0.60)	(0.60)	(0.60)
Match	0.63	0.44	0.74	0.66
	(0.39)	(1.06)	(0.39)	(1.08)
IV (pscore)	0.31	0.33	0.33	0.35
	(0.23)	(0.23)	(0.24)	(0.24)
Heckman	0.63	0.59	1.11	1.04
	(0.01)	(0.01)	(0.07)	(0.07)

Note: Match is Imbens nnmatch with one match. IV with the probability of dictatorship (pscore) as the instrument. (2SLS with separate instruments generates almost identical results.) Heckman is the Heckman two-step estimator, with separate regressions for each regime. In the static specification, the probit used to generate pscore and to estimate the first stage of Heckman procedure uses GDP/cap (and its higher powers, as indicated), ODWPlag (proportion of other countries that are democracies in a given year), and STRAlag (the number of completed spells of democracy in the history of the country). These variables are used as controls in OLS and as instruments in IV. The dynamic specification adds to this list the lagged regime and its interactions with all the exogenous variables. Standard errors in parentheses.

3b. Detailed estimates of causal effects of regimes, dynamic cubic specification

		Hypothetical as					
		Dic	Dem		Heckman	Match	N
Observed as	Dic	4.39	4.25	ATT	0.14 (0.01)	−0.84 (1.42)	2,702
	Dem	5.74	3.72	ATC	2.02 (0.14)	2.01 (1.46)	2,459
	All	5.04	4.00	ATE	1.04 (0.07)	0.69 (1.08)	5,161

Note: The cell entries are the rates of growth predicted by the second stage of the Heckman estimator.

spells of democracy in the history of a country. The "dynamic" specification adds to this list the lagged regime and its interactions with the three covariates. The static version assumes that regimes are generated each year anew according to the values of the covariates. The dynamic version presupposes that regime are generated by a Markov process in which the transition probabilities depend on the covariates (Przeworski 2004a). In both cases, we estimate by probit the probability p that a regime is a dictatorship conditional on the covariates.

The static version fits reasonably well: all the variables are highly significant and pseudo $R^2 = 0.33$. Moreover, there are relatively few observations for which the probability of dictatorship is lower than 0.05 or higher than 0.95. In other words, under most conditions, as characterized by the values of the covariates, almost all countries have some positive probability of having both a democratic and a dictatorial regime during a particular year. This is not true under the dynamic specification, which predicts regimes much better: pseudo $R^2 = 0.86$. Now there are many observations for which the probability of dictatorship is almost zero or almost one. We are thus back to a philosophical question: should we entertain counterfactuals when the mechanism by which history assigns causes to covariates is almost deterministic? Obviously regimes are highly endogenous. Yet as long as $0 < p < 1$, history may have realized regimes that have a very low probability: in fact, even among the observations that are almost certain to be dictatorships, we observe some democracies (India!).

As Table 6.3a shows, for the matching (Imbens's nnmatch in Stata, with one match) and the Heckman two-step estimators (but not OLS and IV) the specification of the selection mechanism makes some difference for the estimate of the causal effect of regimes. Under the static specification, dictatorships appear to grow somewhat faster, while the difference between regimes is lower under the dynamic specification.

Both the matching and the Heckman estimators are also sensitive to the form of the function that relates per capita income to the rate of growth. Note first that a non-parametric regression (fractional polynomial smooth) of the rates of growth on lagged per capita income, shown in Figure 6.2, suggests that the function is cubic, with a maximum around $1,500 and a minimum around $23,000. Columns 3 and 4 of Table 6.3a show estimates of the average causal effect with a cubic specification of the function. It is apparent that the estimates are higher when higher-order terms are introduced.

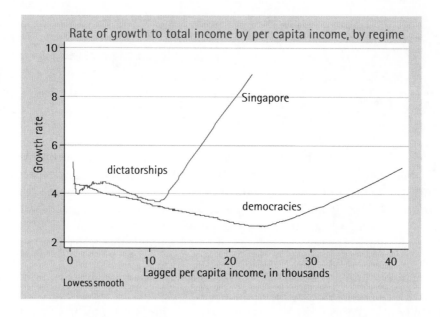

Fig. 6.3 Rate of growth of total income by per capita income, by regime

Why would it be so? Inspect Figure 6.3, which shows lowess smooths separately for the two regimes and recall that the sharply upward segment of the dictatorial line is due almost exclusively to Singapore. Now, albeit in different ways, all the estimators compare the developed democracies to these observations of Singapore, which is their closest match. They predict that if the developed countries which are observed as democracies were dictatorships, they would have grown like Singapore.[17] The effect of fast-growing wealthy dictatorships is evident when we consider separately the effect of dictatorship on the cases actually observed as dictatorships (*ATT*) and those actually observed as democracies (*ATC*). Table 6.3b, which details the dynamic cubic specification, shows that if the cases observed as democracies had been dictatorships, they would have grown much faster, while if the cases observed as dictatorships had been democracies they would have grown somewhat slower (Imbens) or at about the same rate (Heckman).

I present this exercise to show the basic issues entailed in estimating causal effects. Estimates of causal effects are likely to be sensitive to assumptions used to identify the models and to correct the potential biases. Specifying better the determinants of causes affects the estimates of their effects. The non-linearity of the relation between GDP/cap and the growth rates plays havoc even when we match for the observables or generate counterfactuals by studying selection on unobservables.

6 CONCLUSION

When we cannot control the assignment of the potential causes, we are at the mercy of history. The information we can squeeze from the data is a matter of luck. And luck may vary from context to context. History may be very kind and in fact randomize the unobserved, as well as the observed, background characteristics, thus generating a "natural experiment." Unfortunately, most historical data may have the structure illustrated by our example, where dictatorships were more likely to occur in poor countries and democracies in wealthy ones. What this means is that political regimes are endogenous with regard to the level of development. Suppose that this relation were perfect: that high income were a necessary and sufficient condition for a country to be democratic. All dictatorships would be poor and all democracies rich, so that we could never tell whether their rates of growth were due to their income or their political institutions. Alternatively, suppose that political institutions survive only if they generate development, so that they are endogenous

---

[17] Note, however, the different estimators do it differently. Consider the wealthiest observation in the dataset: Luxembourg in 2000. Matching will assign it to it the rate of growth of the wealthiest dictatorship, Singapore in 1996. But Heckman, which estimates the parameters separately for the two regimes, will multiply the income of Luxembourg by the cubic coefficient of the dictatorial regression, hence generating a larger difference.

with regard to growth rates. Identification would not be possible. Hence, endogeneity makes identification difficult. And there are good reasons to think that institutions, policies, and events are endogenous.

The motor of history is endogeneity (Przeworski 2004b). From some initial circumstances and under some invariant conditions ("geography"), wealth, its distribution, and political institutions are mutually interdependent and evolve together. Since we can never completely specify this process, we observe some randomness. Indeed, we exploit this randomness to identify the particular models of this process: for identification, we need to observe different values of causes under the same background conditions. And here we face a paradox. The better we specify our models, the more endogenous loops we consider, the more difficult it becomes to identify their causal structure. As Mariscal and Sokoloff (2000, 198) observe, "When variables are mutually reinforcing or simultaneously determined, discerning what is exogenous and what is endogenous is not transparent."

Suppose that history is perfectly path dependent. From some initial conditions all variables evolve over time in a unique way. This means that X, U, and T vary together and there is no way to isolate the effect of T on Y. Given the importance of this topic, the most dismaying example is the answer given by Banerjee and Duflo (2003) to the question "Inequality and growth: what can the data say?," which is "Not much." It seems that in spite of numerous attempts, the relation between inequality and development just cannot be untangled. We can still engage in descriptions, in the sense that we can say that all these features come together. But we cannot isolate the effect of T independent of X (and perhaps U). This may be the most we can do, but I suspect that the temptation to entertain counterfactuals is irresistible: would Latin America have developed at the same rate as the United States had it been more equal? We may be hurling ourselves against the impossible, but hurl we do and hurl we will.

The difficulty presented by endogeneity is to distinguish the effects of causes from the effects of conditions under which they operate. Do democracies grow more slowly because they are democracies or because they tend to occur under conditions under which economies grow more slowly regardless of political institutions? Did the French Revolution generate little social change, as Tocqueville (1964/1856) would have it, because revolutions result in little change or because they occur only in countries resistant to change?[18]

A necessary condition for identification is path *independence*: situations where historical paths diverged at some time from the same background conditions.[19] In India, random assignment of different tributary systems to identical underlying conditions resulted from the ignorance about these conditions by the colonizing force. The political institutions of Costa Rica and Guatemala, which according to Yashar (1997) shared almost identical historical conditions until the 1940s, diverged as the result of policies adopted during democratization of the late 1940s–early 1950s.

---

[18] As argued by Fearon (1991), small-N does not change the logic of inference.

[19] Note that "path dependence" is not, as some would have it, an approach but a historical fact, to be determined.

The question posed in the title is not rhetorical. Obviously, if by science we mean following justifiable procedures when making inferences and examining evidence, if science is no more than an agreement about how to disagree, comparative politics can be a science. We can and do generate reproducible results, arrived at through reasonable procedures. But to identify causal effects, we must rely on some assumptions that are untestable. In Heckman's (2004, 51) words, "There is no assumption-free method of causal inference." The reason is that even if we observe marginal distributions of outcomes separately under different values of the potential cause, by construction we cannot observe their joint distribution. And since no single estimator can correct for all the potential biases, we cannot be certain that the conclusions would be robust.

What, then, can we do in the presence of endogeneity? All we can do in my view is to try different assumptions and hope that the results do not differ: Persson's and Tabellini's (2003) study is exemplary in this respect. If they do not differ, we know that the conclusions are at least robust with regard to different potential biases. If they do differ, all we can do is to throw our hands up in the air. Where history was kind enough to have generated different causes under the same conditions we will know more and know better. But history may deviously generate causes endogenously and this would make our task next to impossible.

References

ACEMOGLU, D., JOHNSON, S., and ROBINSON, J. A. 2001. The colonial origins of comparative development. *American Economic Review*, 91: 1369–401.

ACHEN, C. 1986. *The Statistical Analysis of Quasi-experiments*. Berkeley and Los Angeles: University of California Press.

AMEMYIA, T. 1994. *Introduction to Statistics and Econometrics*. Cambridge, Mass.: Harvard University Press.

ANGRIST, J. D., and KRUEGER, A. B. 1999. Empirical strategies in labor economics. Ch. 23 in *The Handbook of Labor Economics*, vol. iii, ed. O. Ashenfelter and D. Card. Amsterdam: North Holland.

—— —— 2001. Instrumental variables and the search for identification: from supply and demand to natural experiments. *Journal of Economic Perspectives*, 15: 69–85.

BANERJEE, A. V., and DUFLO, E. 2003. Inequality and growth: what can the data say? *Journal of Economic Growth*, 8: 267–99.

—— and IYER, L. 2002. History, institutions and economic performance: the legacy of colonial land tenure systems in India. MS. Department of Economics, MIT.

BECKER, S. O., and ICHINO, A. 2002. Estimation of average treatment effects based on propensity scores. *Stata Journal*, 7: 1–19.

BERK, R. A. 2004. *Regression Analysis: A Constructive Critique*. Thousand Oaks, Calif.: Sage.

BERTRAND, M., DUFLO, E., and MULLAINATHAN, S. 2004. How much should we trust differences-in-differences estimates? *Quarterly Journal of Economics*, 119: 249–75.

CAMPBELL, D. T., and STANLEY J. C. 1963. *Experimental and Quasi-experimental Designs for Research*. Chicago: RandMcNally.

CHEIBUB, J. A., and GANDHI, J. 2004. Classifying political regimes. MS. Department of Political Science, Yale University.

DAWID, A. P. 2000. Causal inference without counterfactuals. *Journal of the American Statistical Association*, 95: 407–24.

DJANKOV, S., LA PORTA, R., LOPEZ-DE-SILANES, F., and SHLEIFER, A. 2003. The new comparative economics. *Journal of Comparative Economics*, 31: 595–619.

DUFLO, E. 2002. Empirical methods. Class notes. Department of Economics, MIT.

DUNNING, T. 2005. Improving causal inference: strength and limitations of natural experiments. Paper presented at the Annual Meetings of the American Political Science Association, Washington, DC.

EDGINGTON, D. 2001. Conditionals. Pp. 385–414 in *The Blackwell Guide to Philosophical Logic*, ed. L. Goble. Oxford: Blackwell.

FEARON, J. 1991. Counterfactuals and hypothesis testing in political science. *World Politics*, 43: 169–95.

GLAESER, E. L., LA PORTA, R., LOPEZ-DE-SILANES, F., and SHLEIFER, A. 2004. Political institutions and human capital in economic development. MS. Department of Economics, Harvard University.

GOODMAN, N. 1979. *Fact, Fiction, and Forecast*, 4th edn. Cambridge, Mass.: Harvard University Press.

HAAVELMO, T. 1944. The probability approach in econometrics. *Econometrica*, 12 (suppl.): 1–115.

HAWTHORN, G. 1991. *Plausible Worlds: Possibility and Understanding in History and the Social Sciences*. Cambridge: Cambridge University Press.

HECKMAN, J. J. 1992. Randomization and social policy evaluation. Pp. 201–30 in *Evaluating Welfare and Training Programs*, ed. C. Manski and I. Garfinkel. Cambridge, Mass.: Harvard University Press.

—— 1996. Instrumental variables: a cautionary tale. Technical Working Paper 185. Cambridge, Mass.: National Bureau of Economic Research.

—— 1997. Instrumental variables: a study in implicit behavioral assumptions used in making program evaluations. *Journal of Human Resources*, 32: 441–62.

—— 2004. The scientific model of causality. Working Paper. Department of Economics, University of Chicago.

HOLLAND, P. W. 1986. Statistics and causal inference. *Journal of the American Statistical Association*, 81: 945–60.

IMBENS, G. W. 2002. Semiparametric estimation of average treatment effect under exogeneity: a review. Working Paper. Department of Economics, University of California at Berkeley.

KING, G., and ZENG, L. 2002. When can history be our guide? The pitfalls of counterfactual inference. **http://GKing.Harvard.edu**

KOOPMANS, T. C. 1949. Identification problems in economic model construction. *Econometrica*, 17: 125–44.

KUNDERA, M. 2003. *The Art of the Novel*. New York: Perennial.

LEWIS, D. 1973. *Counterfactuals*. Cambridge, Mass.: Harvard University Press.

LUCAS, R. E., Jr. 1988. On the mechanics of economic development. *Journal of Monetary Economics*, 22: 3–42.

MACINTYRE, A. 1972. Is a science of comparative politics possible? Pp. 8–26 in *Philosophy, Politics and Society*, ed. P. Laslett, W. G. Runciman, and Q. Skinner. Oxford: Basil Blackwell.

MACKIE, J. L. 2002/1973. The logic of conditionals. Pp. 106–14 in *Philosophy of Science: Contemporary Readings*, ed. Y. Balashov and A. Rosenberg. London: Routledge.

MANSKI, C. F. 1995. *Identification Problems in the Social Sciences*. Cambridge, Mass.: Harvard University Press.

Mariscal, E., and Sokoloff, K. L. 2000. Schooling, suffrage, and the persistence of inequality in the Americas, 1800–1945. Pp. 159–217 in *Political Institutions and Economic Growth in Latin America*, ed. S. Haber. Stanford, Calif.: Hoover Institution.

Pascal, B. 1669. *Pensées*.

Pearl, J. 2000. *Causality: Models, Reasoning, and Inference*. Cambridge: Cambridge University Press.

Persson, T., and Tabellini, G. 2003. *The Economic Effects of Constitutions*. Cambridge, Mass.: MIT Press.

Posner, D. N. 2004. The political salience of cultural difference: why Chewas and Tumbukas are allies in Zambia and adversaries in Malawi. *American Political Science Review*, 98: 529–45.

Przeworski, A. 2004a. Economic development and the transitions to democracy. MS. Department of Politics, New York University.

—— 2004b. The last instance? Are institutions the primary cause of economic development? *European Journal of Sociology*, 15: 165–88.

—— and Teune, H. 1970. *The Logic of Comparative Inquiry*. New York: John Wiley and Sons.

—— Alvarez, M. E., Cheibub, J. A., and Limongi. F. 2000. *Democracy and Development*. New York: Cambridge University Press.

Quine, W. V. 1953. *From the Logical Point of View*. Cambridge, Mass.: Harvard University Press.

Rosenbaum, P. R. 2002. *Observational Studies*, 2nd edn. New York: Springer-Verlag.

—— and Rubin, D. B. 1983. The central role of the propensity score in observational studies. *Biometrika*, 70: 41–55.

Shadish, W. R., Cook, T. D., and Campbell, D. T. 2002. *Experimental and Quasi-experimental Designs for Generalized Causal Inference*. Boston: Houghton Mifflin.

Stalnaker, R. C. 1987. *Inquiry*. Cambridge, Mass.: MIT Press.

Tocqueville, A. de 1964/1856. *L'Ancien Régime et la Révolution*. Paris: Gallimard.

Winship, C., and Morgan, S. L. 1999. The estimation of causal effects from observational data. *Annual Review of Sociology*, 25: 659–707.

Woolridge, J. M. 2002. *Econometric Analysis of Cross Section and Panel Data*. Cambridge, Mass.: MIT Press.

Yashar, D. J. 1997. *Demanding Democracy: Reform and Reaction in Costa Rica and Guatemala, 1879s–1950s*. Stanford, Calif.: Stanford University Press.

CHAPTER 7

....

FROM CASE STUDIES TO SOCIAL SCIENCE: A STRATEGY FOR POLITICAL RESEARCH

....

ROBERT H. BATES

In writing this essay, I have several audiences in mind: area specialists, comparativists, and those drawn to the use of game theory in political research. To encompass these diverse audiences, I cast this article as an exploration of the ways in which we comprehend. One theme of this chapter is that comprehension implies several different things:

* This chapter builds upon the works of Eckstein 1975; Stinchcombe 1968; and Przeworski and Teune 1970; and the later contributions of George and Bennett 1998; King, Keohane, et al. 1994; and Geddes 2003. Influential arguments by Achen 1986 and Sekon 2003 also shape the argument. To a great degree, the essay arises from discussions with Scott Ashworth while training graduate students in Gov. 3007 at Harvard University and with Avner Greif, Margaret Levi, Jean-Laurent Rosenthal, and Barry Weingast while writing *Analytic Narratives* 1998. The author alone is to be blamed for its shortcomings.

The chapter was written with financial support from the National Science Foundation (Grant SES 9905568), the Carnegie Corporation, and the Center for International Development and the Weatherhead Center for International Affairs of Harvard University. I wrote it while a Moore Distinguished Scholar at the California Institute of Technology.

Presentations of earlier drafts were made at Duke University, Durham, NC, April 28, 2005, and at the Workshop in Political Theory and Policy Analysis, Indiana University, Bloomington, May 5, 2005. I acknowledge with deep appreciation the extensive comments of Arun Agrawal, Carles Boix, Geoffrey

- Apprehension, or *verstehen*.
- Explanation.
- Confirmation.

I shall briefly address each form of comprehension and demonstrate its role in the process of political research.

A second theme of this chapter is that comprehension, explanation, and confirmation interact; the product of the one influences the production of the other. Fieldwork and formal modeling; interpretation and statistical inference; deductive reasoning and empirical estimation—these emerge from the discussion as complementary activities.

In support of these arguments, I draw upon some of my own research into the role of agriculture in the political economy of development.

1 FORMS OF COMPREHENSION

The first form of comprehension is what I call apprehension and others *verstehen*. It is formed through experience, mobilizes intuition, and yields insights that lay the foundations for causal argument.

1.1 Apprehension

Importantly for social scientists, not only do we possess intellects, capable of abstraction and reasoning, but also social intelligence, capable of sympathy and insight. To explain political outcomes, we must employ both endowments.

Phrased in common language, we must "scope out" situations, see "where people are coming from," and "decode" their verbal expressions and body language. In the words of one political scientist, we must "soak and poke," or immerse ourselves in the lives of those we study (Fenno 1990). Anthropologists embrace this method: thus their use of ethnography (e.g. Amit 2000; Brizuela 2000) and their stress on interpretative methods (Geertz 1993). So too do historians, as they delve into the material, social, and cultural worlds of those they study.[1]

As with other forms of intelligence, social intelligence can—and must—be trained. It requires immersion. In some instances, this immersion comes naturally: those who study their "own" polities tend to be well attuned to their own cultures. But even in such

Brennan, Michael McGinnis, Lesa Morrison, Roger Parks, Michael Schoon, Suzanne Shanahan, and Lihua Yang. The excellent editing of Patty Lezotte and David Price has been of great help.

[1] Especially those of the annaliste school. I leave out the majority of modern social historians since, unlike Braudel 1980 they appear unwilling to entertain such additional steps as testing or modeling, as in the use of game theory.

instances, a more sophisticated understanding can be acquired through the use of ethnographic methods. To illustrate, consider the "new institutionalism," one of the most important innovations in the contemporary study of politics. A major variant of this approach emerged from the "Rikerian-side" of the Department of Political Science at the University of Rochester, with its emphasis on formal theory. But those who pioneered the approach were also students of Richard Fenno, who instilled in them an intimate knowledge of the folkways and byways of the committee system—knowledge he acquired from fieldwork on the United States Congress (Fenno 1966).

Fenno's field research targets a political arena, but one lodged within a culture of which he himself is a member. Immersion is even more necessary for those who study politics in cultures other than our own. We "foreigners" must virtually be trained in the same manner as have the adults of that culture. We must be infused with the collective memories and taught the shorthand allusions that inform the controversies that animate the politics of those that dwell within it.

The argument thus far constitutes a defense of "soft" approaches to learning, variously labeled intuition, insight, or *verstehen*. These approaches target the particular, be it a village, a committee, or a specific event. They are often counterpoised against "systematic" forms of understanding that seek general and therefore more abstract accounts. But rather than constituting rivals, the two approaches are complements.

The argument, like the research process, proceeds in stages. The first step comes in the field itself, when the researcher starts to find that she is less frequently surprised. Behavior that once seemed inexplicable now appears ordinary; fewer interactions jar or unsettle. These changes suggest that the researcher is beginning to understand. The second step takes place as the researcher begins to separate from the field, both physically and emotionally. At that moment she begins to move from apprehension to explanation.

While moving toward explanation, the comprehension acquired during fieldwork continues to play a significant role. It informs judgement and sharpens intuition. Phrased crudely, it provides a "bullshit meter"—something useful for all academics and perhaps essential for graduate students. The study of politics is no less immune to the pathologies of discourse than are other academic fields, whether in the form of polemical exaggeration or scientific pretension. The best corrective is a confident mastery of a body of evidence and a sense of authority derived from having "been there." Such grounding yields an ability to discriminate between arguments that offer traction and those that are merely clever. It provides a means for discriminating between the trendy and substantial, and between those who simply want to score in debates and those who seek to contribute to knowledge.

1.2 Explanation[2]

The movement from apprehension to comprehension is marked by the recoding of what has been learned into an account that instills a sense of "*therefore*." The

---

[2] This section represents an extension and critique of Wedeen (2002).

researcher begins to apportion the things now known to be true between causes or consequences and to develop lines of logic to link them.[3] To illustrate, consider one form of explanation: that derived from game theory.[4]

Some games—indeed, some highly important ones—have been constructed solely to advance a theoretical argument. The prisoner's dilemma, for example, highlights the self-defeating properties of rationality in choice and the distinction between individual and social rationality (Barry and Hardin 1982). But game theory is also employed to model, i.e. to capture the logic that structures human interaction. Such explanations can and should be shaped by the understandings achieved through fieldwork and by the materials mobilized in thick descriptions. Grounded in the realities as experienced by other human beings, explanations move the researcher toward a sense of "therefore." The "therefore" to which game theory gives rise is a recognition that the behavior one seeks to explain is what one must of necessity expect, given one's understanding of the political setting.

Peopling this setting are actors with preferences and expectations who can make choices but who also face constraints. A key feature of a game is the presence and influence of other actors; the decision makers are not the atomistic actors of market economics. These actors are locked in patterns of interaction, so that the outcomes they achieve are the product not only of their own decisions but also of the conduct of others.

What is the identity of the actors? What are the values that inform their decisions? Given the stations they occupy, to what outcomes might they reasonably aspire? What ambitions might they seek to fulfill? What expectations do they hold, particularly of the conduct of others? If based upon the theory of games, the movement from apprehension to explanation requires that these questions be answered. This mode of explanation therefore demands a level of intimacy with the subject similar to that achieved by an ethnographer who has immersed herself in the life of "her" village or by a historian who has worked through the family papers of a politician or the archives of a bureau chief.

In game theory, the logic of explanation appeals to rationality in choice. The actions observed have been chosen strategically, i.e. knowing the sequence that will be followed and anticipating the behavior of others along the path of play. To account for the choices made, the analyst must demonstrate that the actor could credibly expect these choices to yield the best of the outcomes attainable, given what the actor could control, the constraints under which she labored, and the information then available. The re-creation of the world in which the actor is choosing, of how she operates within it, of the sequence of actions, and of beliefs about the consequences of her decisions provides the necessary data. The data may best come from observation, reading, interviewing, and thereby acquiring an intimate knowledge of the key players and the strategic environment that they inhabit.

The thick description provided by anthropologists, sociologists, and historians thus provides the underpinnings for the abstract, mathematical logic that moves the

---

[3] Note that the argument calls for logical—indeed, nomothetic—accounts. It is not sufficient to point to causal mechanisms (McAdam, Tarrow, et al. 2001) or to engage in "process tracing" (George and Bennett 1998).

[4] Among several excellent reviews, turn first to Dixit and Skeath (2004).

researcher from apprehension to explanation. Knowledge of key features of political life is essential to its recoding in the form of game. The theory of games provides a means of extracting explanations from such knowledge. Once the analyst has constructed the game, she then can begin to comprehend why outcomes occurred, i.e. why people behaved in the fashion she observed. Once formally modeled, the strategic situation captured by the game may yield equilibria; and these equilibria contain the choices that should be expected to prevail, if the model correctly captures the incentives that drive choices in the strategic setting.

In arguing for complementarities between abstract and qualitative methods, it is useful to point out that the kinds of reasoning employed in the process of "explanation" also contribute to the process of "apprehension." The assumption of rationality provides a source of empathy that enables the analyst to occupy the position of those whose behavior she seeks to understand.

The assumption of rationality imposes no requirements on the *content* of the values or preferences of the people being studied; in many instances they will possess values and aspirations far different from those of the analyst. But latent in the assumption is an acceptance of the possibility that were the analyst herself embedded in the structures and constraints that define the strategic setting, she too, if rational, would have made the same choices and suffered the same consequences as did those whose behavior she seeks to comprehend. In some settings, the result is confrontation with the question: "could I have possibly behaved with such humanity?" In others, it is the recognition that, "yes, in such a situation, I too might have killed." The premise of rationality thus transforms the relationship between the analyst and those being studied, imbricating it with sympathetic identification. It enhances the capacity to apprehend.

Many in the social sciences favor interpretation over explanation. Shunning the use of deduction and logic, they instead offer evocative accounts in which comprehension is achieved by appealing to preferences and mental states. Basing explanations on individual values is equivalent to asserting that a person behaves the way he does because that is the kind of person that he is. If the choice is irrational, then so too must he be. An advantage of game theory is that it offers a way of avoiding such tautology. In situations of strategic interdependence, people may easily become trapped: strategic interaction may yield outcomes that no rational individual would desire. Assuming that it is a harsh fate that we seek to explain, the researcher can then seek to identify the reasons people fail to transcend it. Given that the people are rational and capable of behaving in a sophisticated manner, why, then, do they continue to suffer? Driven by this question, the researcher will move from a study of the individuals and their preferences to a study of the game form, and focus on the forces that generate perverse results as equilibrium outcomes.

This discussion is of particular importance to those who study the politics of violence or underdevelopment. Observation suggests that many who are engaged in fighting or living in poverty are neither thugs nor incompetents but are nonetheless living in misery. The challenge posed is thus to isolate the features that divorce the qualities of the individuals from the properties of the lives they lead. In contrast to the common perception that game theory emphasizes the role of choice, it in fact becomes most valuable, perhaps, when used to explore the forces that constrain human behavior.

1.3 Conviction

Thus far two forms of comprehension have been explored. The first is apprehension. The second—explanation—establishes the logical links that render the behavior one seeks to explain a necessary outcome. A major point of this essay is that the two forms of understanding are complements rather than substitutes: to endorse the one form of comprehension is to underscore as well the importance of the other.

The process of comprehension cannot terminate at explanation, however. More needs to be achieved before the researcher can accord credence to her account or elicit conviction from others. The account must also find confirmation. It must yield outcomes that are consistent with the data and, in particular, data other than that from which it was first derived.

To address the process of confirmation, we move from the world of the ethnographer and formal theorist to the world of the methodologist. Two methodologies warrant special attention: the making of "small-N" comparisons—the controlled use of case studies—and the use of "large-N" methods—the statistical analysis of quantitative data.[5]

In addressing the process of confirmation, it is useful to marshal an example. Doing so allows us to revisit the relationship between immersion and explanation and to understand when a research program achieves a resting point: the point of conviction, where the researcher comes to believe an explanation to be true and when she is able to demonstrate its validity to others.

2 By Way of Illustration

From the mid-1970s to the late 1980s, I inhabited the world of coffee. I begin with a discussion of fieldwork I conducted in the coffee zones of East Africa and the search for explanations of the economic behavior of the peasants in that region.

2.1 Introduction to the Field

The district of Meru runs down the north-eastern slopes of Mount Kenya; that of Mengo straddles Kampala, the capital of Uganda. In the course of my research into coffee production in East Africa, I found, as have others, that many farmers failed to

---

[5] The best treatments remain King, Keohane, et al. (1994); Przeworski and Teune (1970); and Geddes (2003).

produce what they technically could produce—given their access to land, labor, and capital—had they been the maximizers of profits. In addition, I found the kinds of tensions often recorded in studies of peasant communities (e.g. Redfield 1960; Wolff 1966; Scott 1976): fear of neighbors, jealousy, and a commitment to sharing, be it of beer or food, time or companionship, or of hardship or an unexpected windfall.

Many had looked at such behavior and posited cultural roots for it. Writing in the 1980s, Goran Hyden (Hyden 1981), for example, attributed to villagers in East Africa an "economy of affection" in which leisure is highly prized and the benefits of companionship valued more highly than private gains. Those who fail to abide by the norms of the community, by this argument, are sanctioned and become the objects of gossip, rumor-mongering, and, quite possibly, violence.

Appeals to culture provide a possible explanation for the behavior of the coffee growers. "Soaking and poking," however, I encountered reason to believe that the behavior of the coffee growers represented a choice. Rather than being driven by cultural norms and therefore inflexible, their behavior represented, I came to believe, a strategic response to the forces about them, and was therefore susceptible to change.

In both Kenya and Uganda coffee production takes place within a thicket of public institutions: cooperative societies, agricultural banks, government departments, and research centers. Among the most powerful of these is the coffee board: a monopsonist that purchased coffee from farmers at a price that it set. To the coffee growers, the coffee board was the tax man. In conversations in homesteads or over beer, many growers, I learned, felt were they to produce more, they would simply be more heavily taxed.

Experience in the field thus suggested an alternative to a "cultural" understanding of the peasantry in eastern Africa. A strong preference for leisure could indeed dissuade farmers from profit maximization. But it appeared more plausible that their behavior represented a strategy: in the face of the behavior they anticipated from the government and their peers, it was reasonable for farmers to choose leisure over productive activity.

2.2 The "Small-N" Road to Conviction

I now faced the task of convincing myself that the explanation "worked." Fortunately, for me at least, both Kenya and Uganda had recently undergone changes in political regimes. I therefore could employ temporal comparisons to test my argument. In Kenya, power had shifted from Jomo Kenyatta, who was from the coffee-growing regions, to Daniel Arap Moi, who was not. In Uganda, a military invasion had driven Idi Amin into exile. I therefore had the opportunity to use data from political shocks to test my ideas about the behavior of farmers.

Jomo Kenyatta had been a friend of the coffee farmer. While president, he had allied with GEMA—a powerful brotherhood of wealthy persons from the Gikuyu, Embu, and Meru communities (Widner 1992) within the Central Province of Kenya. Many members of this elite not only possessed coffee estates but also occupied offices in the agencies that governed the coffee industry. Because the interests of those in power so closely aligned with those of the small producers, the latter believed that the former would act in good faith.

When Kenyatta died in 1978, Daniel Arap Moi became president. Coming from Rift Valley Province, Moi did not belong to GEMA; indeed, he feared it. In an effort to weaken the political power of the Central Province, he labeled GEMA "tribal" and disbanded the organization. Placing political hatchet-men in key legal positions, he used the power of the state to attack, rather than to support, the agencies that superintended the production of coffee (Bates 1997). When I conducted my research in Meru, I therefore encountered an industry that had been shorn of political protection. From my research I learned that the transfer of power had marked the beginning of the decline—both economic and political—of coffee production. An industry that had prospered under Kenyatta began to stagnate under Moi. And farmers that had once aggressively sought to maximize chose instead to "make do."

Uganda too had experienced a change of presidents: Milton Obote, backed by Tanzania's armed forces and an alliance of other politicians from Uganda, had driven Idi Amin from the State House into exile. As they positioned themselves to compete for power in the new political order, several members of this alliance had recruited their own armies. Into a world in which villagers already feared the encroachment of their neighbors, there now circulated an abundant supply of weapons. When I arrived in the field, Mengo had become militarized. From the maelstrom of conflict in Mengo I emerged convinced that African coffee growers not only chose between leisure and income, as cultural accounts would have it. They also chose between income maximization and military activity: if prosperous, one has to be prepared to fight in order to defend one's property. There were few signs of the economy of affection in Mengo.[6]

At the start of my fieldwork in eastern Africa, I therefore found reason to doubt "cultural" explanations of the behavior of villagers. While such explanations might account for the reluctance of coffee producers to maximize their incomes, they implied that such behavior was invariant over time. A theory that viewed their behavior as the product of choice implied that what was a best response under one state of the world might well not be under another, and their conduct would therefore change. As the world about the coffee growers changed, I found, so too had their behavior. Changing from the "accumulators"[7] of the Kenyatta years to the sullen satisficers of those under Moi, those in Kenya demonstrated that they could indeed change the way in which they managed their farms.

The peasants of Mengo also changed their behavior and in so doing challenged the cultural account. Once characterized as practitioners of the economy of affection, they became violent. They became attackers and defenders, opportunists and heroes, patriots and traitors, as their villages were swept into the currents of the war that lasted from the overthrow of Idi Amin to the installation of Yoweri Museveni.

---

[6] For a formalization of this argument, see Bates, Greif, et al. (2002).

[7] A phrase employed by local intellectuals to characterize prosperous peasants. See, for example, Kitching (1980).

Having been encouraged through conversation and conviviality to conceive of farmers as rational actors, I could conceive of the games they played with the government and with those about them. I could use the logic of games to infer how, behaving rationally, they would choose, given their beliefs about the conduct of others. In the world they occupied, backward induction would lead the farmers to consume leisure rather than expend costly effort in the production of coffee, and thus account for their economic choices. In a world of peace, it led them to adhere to the "economy of affection." In a world at war, their best response was to fight. I could thus comprehend their political behavior as well. By taking advantage of change over time, I was able to make comparisons that provided evidence supportive of my account.

But the evidence did not yet satisfy. For one, the data employed to test the explanation were drawn from the same sample as had been used to construct it. Moreover, if the explanation were powerful, then there should be additional opportunities for confirmation. For if powerful, the explanation should generate additional implications which would be amenable to testing. I therefore changed my location in the world of coffee and I changed the topic of my research. Moving from Africa to Latin America, I focused on the politics of policy making rather than on the economics of farming.[8]

3 Moving out of Sample

To my surprise, I found that while coffee was produced in Colombia by small farmers, the government of Colombia did not treat coffee producers in a predatory manner. In contrast to the conduct of governments in Amin's Uganda, Moi's Kenya, and other portions of Africa, the government of Colombia instead offered farmers low taxes and high-quality services and helped the industry to maximize its export earnings. Peasant producers were treated as if powerful, not marginal in Colombia's political economy.

Retaining the premise of rationality in choice, I attempted to account for this difference by taking counsel from relevant theories. Some (e.g. Olson 1971) addressed the politics of interest groups; others (e.g. Downs 1957) the politics of party competition. Both moved from citizen preferences to public policy outcomes, basing their reasoning on rationality in choice and the incentives that shape strategic choices in political settings. In Africa in the 1970s and 1980s, few governments tolerated "multipartyism:" most were single-party or military regimes. In this authoritarian environment, organized interests dominated the policy process. In Colombia, by contrast,

---

[8] A major reason for this move was to seek respite from the violence I had encountered in post-Amin Uganda. Moving to Colombia, I soon learned that violence was not an African problem; it was a development problem.

two major parties competed for votes and governments secured power by winning electoral majorities. By the logic of collective action, should policy result from competition among organized interests, farmers—being numerous and disorganized—should lose out. In the context of electoral politics, numbers become an advantage; and should other conditions prevail (see below), they could become politically pivotal and so gain a political advantage. The comparison of policy making in Africa and Latin America thus provided a test of the rational choice approach by providing a test of the theories of policy making to which it gives rise.

What I had found throughout Africa was a systematic pattern of political expropriation; the explanation appeared to lie in the logic of interest groups. The core of the political economy of most African states consisted of the government, urban-based industry, and organized labor; peasant agriculture occupied the periphery. The first set of interests was concentrated geographically, which lowered the costs of organization; the second was dispersed and thus faced higher costs of organization. Urban-based industries tended to be economically concentrated as well, with a few large firms dominating the market; by contrast, the agricultural industry remained virtually atomistic in composition and no single producer could reasonably aspire to influence prices. While urban-based firms possessed incentives to organize, for farmers, the incentives were weak (see Olson 1971 and Bates 1981).

What I encountered in Colombia, however, was the politics of party competition. The logic governing this process would be the logic of majority rule in spatial settings, which implied that if properly located in the political space that defined electoral politics, peasants could extract favorable policies from candidates competing for office.

My intuition thus suggested that the roots of policy differences lay in the structure of political institutions. Whether that intuition would yield an explanation depended, among other things, on the structure of issue space in Colombia and on the location of coffee growers within it. To explore this possibility, I turned to archival sources. I reviewed the issues that divided the two parties: the nature of property rights, the position of the Catholic Church, and the power of the central government. Positions on these issues proved to be correlated, I found, rendering the problem one-dimensional and giving rise to the possibility of equilibrium outcomes.[9] Politicians from the coffee zones, I further noted, had repeatedly proven willing to break from the left wing of the Conservative Party to join governments from the right wing of the Liberal Party—and vice versa—thus making and breaking governments. The structure of party competition in Colombia thus appeared to render coffee farmers pivotal. Politicians ambitious for office would indeed possess strong incentives to advocate policies designed to secure their backing. While the politics of interest groups may have reduced the power of farmers in Africa, in Colombia, at least, the politics of electoral competition magnified it.

Drawing new data from outside of the original sample and confronting the logic of rational choice in a domain other than that in which I had first applied it, I gained

---

[9] As a test, I presented this formulation to seminars attended by the most learned students of Colombian history. The stress was that of a doctoral examination; so too the sense of relief at having passed.

increased confidence in my explanation of the behavior of East Africa's peasants. But to convince others, I recognized, I needed more: I needed data that would enable me to control statistically for the impact of variables that I might have been unable to control when making "small-N" comparisons. I therefore began to look for "large-N" data that would yield unbiased tests of my ideas and ones in which I could have high levels of confidence.

3.1 The "Large-N" Road to Conviction

From the late 1940s to the mid-1970s, party competition in Colombia ceased, first yielding to military rule and then to a national front in which the parties shared power at every level—and in every branch—of government. In the mid-1970s, party competition resumed.

In Colombia, as in Africa, coffee exports are taxed. But in Colombia, unlike in Africa, a major portion of the tax is rebated to the coffee producers who employ it to build roads and to provide electricity, schools, and clinics in the coffee zones. The percentage rebated to the coffee farmers varied over time, however. Using time series data from 1939–84, I was able to relate the percentage rebated to the structure of political competition. To a degree significantly greater than would be likely by chance, I found, when governments were chosen as a result of party competition, the percentage of the revenue which coffee growers were able to retain increased on average over 12 percentage points; when they were not—as when the military held power—the percentage fell by over 20 percentage points. By controlling for other possible determinants of revenue collection and the kinds of errors to which time series data, by their nature, can give rise, I was able to test my argument linking political institutions to government policies toward agriculture.

Armed with the lessons drawn from the Colombian case, I then returned to the study of Africa. There I joined a team of researchers and gathered data on government policies and political institutions for forty-six African nations over a twenty-six-year period (1970–95). Included in these data were measures of policy choice. Governments that to a high degree substituted public bureaucracies for private markets we labeled the creators of "control regimes;" the policies of those that refrained from such intervention we labeled "symptom free." The data on political institutions recorded whether the governments were based on no-party, single-party, or competitive-party systems.

Over the full set of African cases for the period 1970–95 there was a close statistical association between the existence—or non-existence—of political competition and the choice of policy regimes (Table 7.1).

Because I was now employing statistical methods, I was able to control for the impact of unobserved variables. In contrast to small-N investigations, by introducing fixed effects into a statistical model, I was able to eliminate the impact of features not captured in the model that might influence policy choice in one country but be absent in another. And by controlling for period effects, I was able to control for

Table 7.1 Fixed effects logit estimates

	1 Control regime	2 Syndrome free	3 Control regime	4 Syndrome free
No party	1.030 (2.53)	−0.169 (−0.35)		
Single party	2.730 (6.25)	−1.869 (−3.75)		
Military government			2.286 (5.44)	−0.644 (−1.29)
1975–9	1.212 (3.02)	−4.600 (−4.18)	0.475 (1.16)	−3.977 (−4.57)
1980–4	1.222 (3.01)	−4.124 (−4.8)	0.303 (0.73)	−3.440 (−4.41)
1985–9	−0.149 (−0.4)	−1.013 (−2.28)	−1.228 (−3.01)	−0.552 (−1.12)
1990–4	−2.509 (−6.41)	0.925 (2.59)	−1.228 (−3.01)	1.792 (4.23)
>1995	−2.579 (−4.00)	1.222 (2.04)	−3.749 (−7.94)	2.432 (3.49)
No. Observations	675 17	525 19	620 14	499 16

Note: Z-scores in parentheses. In computing standard errors, clustered by country.

variables that would affect policy making in all countries and that varied with time: the debt crisis, for example, or the oil price shocks of the 1970s—or changes in the price of coffee.

My research had thus focused on public policy toward farmers. Immersion convinced me that coffee producers in eastern Africa were canny strategists. Based on this premise, I was able to account for their economic behavior and the political fate that befell them. To convince myself and others, however, I had to demonstrate that the logical implications of my account were consistent with observable data and, in particular, data other than that which gave rise to the original interpretation. Drawing from the experience of another continent, I was able to show that differences in political institutions indeed related to the fate of the coffee industry and in ways that the logic would suggest. By drawing data from the politics of the coffee industry, I was able to increase my confidence in my analysis of the economics of peasant production. And by moving from small-N comparisons to data more amenable to statistical treatment, I was able to impart greater credibility to my account.[10]

4 CONCLUSION

In this essay, I have sought to present a strategy for comparative research. At the beginning is immersion: a deep study of a time and place. The movement from insight to explanation is marked by the production of theory. The resultant explanation may be logically coherent, consistent with the observations that inspired it, and faithful to the original intuition. But to be convincing, the explanation has to be demonstrated. It has to find empirical confirmation.

To comprehend the political world about us, we therefore need to engage in qualitative research, to mobilize theory, to make small-N comparisons, and to employ statistical methods. Each task provides an element of what we need to know in order to comprehend. Only when all have been deployed can our efforts come to rest, our intellects feeling satisfied.

REFERENCES

ACHEN, C. 1986. *The Statistical Analysis of Quasi-experiments.* Berkeley and Los Angeles: University of California Press.

AMIT, V. 2000. *Constructing the Field: Ethnographic Fieldwork in the Contemporary World.* London: Routledge.

BARRY, B. M., and HARDIN, R. 1982. *Rational Man and Irrational Society? An Introduction and Sourcebook.* Beverly Hills, Calif.: Sage Publications.

BATES, R. H. 1981. *Markets and States in Tropical Africa.* Berkeley and Los Angeles: University of California Press.

—— 1997. *Open Economy Politics.* Princeton: Princeton University Press.

—— GREIF, A. et al. 1998. *Analytic Narratives.* Princeton: Princeton University Press.

—— —— et al. 2002. Organizing violence. *Journal of Conflict Resolution,* 46 (5): 599–628.

BRAUDEL, F. 1980. *On History.* Chicago: University of Chicago Press.

BRIZUELA, B. M. 2000. *Acts of Inquiry in Qualitative Research.* Cambridge, Mass.: Harvard College.

DIXIT, A. K., and SKEATH, S. 2004. *Games of Strategy.* New York: W. W. Norton.

DOWNS, A. 1957. *An Economic Theory of Democracy.* New York: Harper and Row.

ECKSTEIN, H. 1975. Case study and theory in political science. In *Handbook of Sociology,* ed. N. Smelser. Beverly Hills, Calif.: Sage.

[10] See also Varshney (1993, 1995).

Fenno, R. F. 1966. *The Power of the Purse: Appropriations Politics in Congress*. Boston: Little Brown.

—— 1990. *Watching Politicians: Essays on Participant Observation*. Berkeley: Institute of Governmental Studies University of California at Berkeley.

Geddes, B. 2003. *Paradigms and Sand Castles*. Ann Arbor: University of Michigan Press.

Geertz, C. 1993. *The Interpretation of Cultures: Selected Essays*. London: Fontana Press.

George, A. L., and Bennett, A. 1998. *Case Study and Theory Development*. Cambridge, Mass.: MIT Press.

Hyden, G. 1981. *No Shortcuts to Progress*. Berkeley and Los Angeles: University of California Press.

King, G., Keohane, R., et al. 1994. *Designing Social Inquiry*. Princeton: Princeton University Press.

Kitching, G. 1980. *Class and Economic Change in Kenya*. London: Yale University Press.

McAdam, D., Tarrow, S., et al. 2001. *Dynamics of Contention*. New York: Cambridge University Press.

Olson, M. 1971. *The Logic of Collective Action*. Cambridge, Mass.: Harvard University Press.

Przeworski, A., and Teune, H. 1970. *The Logic of Comparative Social Inquiry*. Malabar, Fla.: R. E. Kreiger Publishing.

Redfield, R. 1960. *The Little Community, and Peasant Society and Culture*. Chicago: University of Chicago Press.

Scott, J. C. 1976. *The Moral Economy of the Peasant*. New Haven: Yale University Press.

Sekon, J. 2003. Revisiting Case Selection. Cambridge, Mass.: Department of Government, Harvard University, typescript.

Stinchcombe, A. L. 1968. *Constructing Social Theories*. New York: Harcourt Brace & World.

Varshney, A. ed. 1993. *Beyond Urban Bias*. London: Frank Cass and Company.

—— 1995. *Democracy, Development and the Countryside*. Cambridge: Cambridge University Press.

Wedeen. L. 2002. Conceptualizing culture: new possibilities for political science. *American Political Science Review*, 96: 713–28.

Widner, J. 1992. *The Rise of a Party State in Kenya: From "Harembe!" to "Nyayo."* Berkeley and Los Angeles: University of California Press.

Wolff, E. R. 1966. *Peasants*. Englewood Cliffs, NJ: Prentice-Hall.

CHAPTER 8

....

COLLECTIVE
ACTION THEORY

....

ELINOR OSTROM

In my Presidential Address to the American Political Science Association, I asserted that "the theory of collective action is *the* central subject of political science" (Ostrom 1998, 1). I made this bold assertion because collective action problems pervade the study of comparative politics at all levels from local neighborhoods through international regimes. The empirical literature includes studies of widely different types of collective action occurring at multiple levels including: the evolution of institutions to facilitate long-distance trading patterns (Greif, Milgrom, and Weingast 1994); the organization of community water enterprises (Hicks and Peña 2003); the problems of gaining international cooperation (Snidal 1985; Keohane and Ostrom 1995); studies of protest, civil war, and revolution (Lichbach 1995; McGinnis and Williams 2001; McGinnis 2007); the provision of national defense (Wallner 2002); international assistance (Gibson et al. 2005); the inability of the US Congress to limit spending (Shepsle and Weingast 1984); and voting (de Matos and Barros 2004).

The term "social dilemma" refers to a setting in which individuals choose actions in an interdependent situation. If each individual selects strategies based on a calculus that maximizes short-term material benefits to self, individuals will take actions that generate lower joint outcomes than could have been achieved. In other words, a social dilemma can be analyzed as a game where the Nash equilibrium for a single iteration of the game yields less than the socially optimal outcome. The reason that such situations are *dilemmas* is that at least one outcome yields higher returns for *all* participants, but rational participants making independent choices are not predicted to achieve this outcome. A better optimal outcome could be achieved if those involved "cooperated" by selecting strategies other than those prescribed by the Nash equilibrium. Since the suboptimal joint outcome is an equilibrium, no one is independently motivated to change their choice, given the predicted choices of all others.

While empirical evidence generates some optimism that collective action can be achieved in some settings, the *problem* of collective action remains: How can participants in social dilemmas avoid the temptation of suboptimal equilibria and move closer to optimal outcomes?

Developing a coherent theory of collective action is a real challenge. At the individual level, individuals do take costly actions that effectively take the interests of others into account. Shivakumar (2005) and Gellar (2005) provide evidence of local and regional groups that are successfully engaging in collective action in Somaliland and in Senegal where little cooperation occurred earlier. On the other hand, individuals may callously ignore or viciously harm others depending on the setting in which they find themselves (see Fiske, Harris, and Cuddy 2004).

Thus, an important task for all social scientists is achieving a more coherent synthesis of theoretical work that posits variables affecting the likelihood of undertaking diverse forms of collective action leading to positive or negative results for others. We must be able to explain success as well as failure of efforts to achieve collective action. Further, we need to recognize that forms of collective action differ in regard to the distribution of benefits and harms to those in a group and those who are external to it. Mobs, gangs, and cartels are forms of collective action as well as neighborhood associations, charities, voting, and organizing political parties.

In this chapter, I propose to focus on three broad topics. First, I will examine the growing and extensive theoretical literature positing a host of structural variables presumed to affect the likelihood of individuals achieving collective action to overcome social dilemmas.[1] None of these structural variables, however, should really make any difference in the probability of successful collective action if we continue to treat the *model* of rationality that has proved successful in explaining behavior and outcomes in competitive market settings as a universal *theory* of human behavior. Thus, the second major section of the chapter will examine how a theory of boundedly rational, norm-based human behavior is a better foundation for explaining collective action than a model of maximizing material payoffs to self. If one posits that individuals can use reciprocity and reputations to build trust in dilemma situations, then one can begin to explain *both* successful and unsuccessful efforts to overcome social dilemmas through collective action. The third section of the chapter will then examine the linkage between the structural measures discussed in the first section and the core individual relationships discussed in the second. In conclusion, I will reflect on the challenge that political scientists face in testing collective action theory in light of the large number of variables posited to affect outcomes.

---

[1] In this chapter, I do focus primarily on theoretical literature rather than the vast empirical literature on collective action since I was asked to write a chapter on collective action *theory* and many of my other work focuses on diverse bodies of empirical research (Ostrom 1990, 2005).

1 Structural Variables Predicted to Affect the Likelihood of Collective Action

A rich array of theoretical speculations, formal game-theoretic models, and computer models of evolutionary processes have generated a long list of structural variables that are frequently postulated to affect the likelihood that a set of participants will be able to achieve outcomes greater than the deficient Nash equilibrium—or, the cooperators' dividend (Lichbach 1996). Let us first focus on structural variables that do not essentially depend on a situation being repeated. These include:

(1) the number of participants involved;
(2) whether benefits are subtractive or fully shared (i.e. public goods vs. common-pool resources);
(3) the heterogeneity of participants;
(4) face-to-face communication; and
(5) the shape of the production function.

Then, we will focus on situations where repetition of the situation makes possible the impact of additional structural variables including:

(6) information about past actions;
(7) how individuals are linked; and
(8) whether individuals can enter or exit voluntarily.

Let us turn to a brief discussion of these eight major variables and how they are posited to affect the possibility of collective action and the size of benefits achieved.

1.1 Situations Where Repetition is Not Relevant

Among the variables that are posited to affect the likelihood of participants overcoming a social dilemma are five variables considered to be important whether or not the situation is repeated: the number of participants, whether benefits are subtractive or fully shared, their heterogeneity, whether they can communicate, and the shape of the production function they face.[2]

1.1.1 *The Number of Participants Involved*

In his influential book *The Logic of Collective Action*, Mancur Olson (1965) argued that as the size of a group increased, the probability of a group achieving a public good decreased and the extent of non-optimality increased. Olson posited two reasons for this hypothesis. First, as group size increases, the noticeability of any

---

[2] This section draws on Ostrom (2001).

single input to the provision of a public good declines. It is then easier for the individual to think that their own free riding will not be noticed and thus it will not affect the likelihood that the good will be provided. Second, coming to an internal agreement about coordinated strategies in larger groups involves higher transaction costs. Thus, a core theoretical hypothesis has been that the number of participants will likely reduce the probability of achieving any form of collective action or at least diminish the amount of joint benefits that could be achieved.

On the other hand, some theorists have generated the opposite prediction from those based on the work of Olson (1965). In an effort to understand the phenomenon of age grade organization[3] that was so frequently used in most of Africa as a means of providing public goods—particularly defense—Bates and Shepsle (1995) developed a formal model of a three-period, overlapping generations, public good game. A corollary of this model generates a prediction that the provision of public goods is *positively* correlated with group size since the more individuals in an age set, the easier it is to produce any particular level of a public good. Agrawal (2000) posits a curvilinear relationship between size of group and collective action.

The impact of group size has been subject to considerable theoretical debate. Chamberlin (1974) pointed out that differences in group size frequently affect other key variables including the marginal impact of an individual's contribution of a fixed amount (see also Frohlich and Oppenheimer 1970; Pecorino 1999). Thus, how size might affect the likelihood of cooperation depends on how other structural variables are affected by the size of a group.

1.1.2 *Subtractive versus Fully Shared Benefits*

In Olson's original analysis, he included all dilemmas where it was difficult to exclude potential beneficiaries, whether or not they had contributed. Unfortunately, Olson's analysis confounded situations where the consumption of benefits by one individual subtracted benefits from others with situations where consumption was non-subtractive in nature (characterized as having full jointness of supply—see Ostrom and Ostrom 1999). In a public good environment, increasing the number of participants tends to bring additional resources that could be drawn on to provide a benefit that will be jointly enjoyed by all. It is because of the additional resources available in a larger group and the non-subtractability characteristic of public goods that Marwell and Oliver (1993, 45) conclude that when "a good has pure jointness of supply, group size has a *positive* effect on the probability that it will be provided."[4]

Goods that are subtractable in nature are better defined as common-pool resources (CPRs) (Ostrom, Walker, and Gardner 1992). Social dilemmas related to CPRs share with public good provision the problems of free riding, but they also include the problems of overharvesting and crowding. In a CPR environment, an increase in the number of participants, holding other variables constant, is negatively related to achieving social benefits.

---

[3] All males in such cultures born between a predetermined number of years become one age set and advance together through several assignments including warrior.

[4] This helps to explain the findings of Bates and Shepsle (1995) above.

Weissing and Ostrom (1991) analyzed a formal game examining the impact of the number of individuals involved in a CPR game where each player has an opportunity to take a legal amount of water from an irrigation system or steal water and the choice between monitoring or not the behavior of others in the system. When all other variables are analytically held constant, an increase in the number of players increases the rate of stealing at equilibrium. However, many variables are affected by increasing the number of participants. The value of water at the margin for irrigators is likely to increase (thus making stealing more attractive). The impact of one person's stealing may be spread out over more individuals and thus the loss to any one farmer of someone else stealing water may be less severe at the margin (thus making monitoring less attractive). An increase in the number of participants may also mean a larger system where more water is available and the consequences listed above would then not follow. Thus, in a CPR environment, whether size has a positive impact, a negative impact, or any impact, is dependent upon how other variables are affected by a change in the number of participants.

1.1.3 *The Heterogeneity of Participants*

Participants can be heterogeneous in many ways. Olson (1965) argued that if there were one or a few individuals who had much stronger interests in achieving a public good (in other words, they faced different payoff functions), the probability of a group achieving a public good increased even though the good was still likely to be underprovided.[5] Others have speculated that heterogeneity in assets, information, and payoffs are negatively related to gaining a cooperators' dividend due principally to increased transaction costs and the conflict that would exist over the distribution of benefits and costs to be borne. In fact, the literature contains many arguments that point to heterogeneity as a serious deterrent to cooperation (Hardin 1982; Johnson and Libecap 1982; Libecap and Wiggins 1984; Isaac and Walker 1988; Kanbur 1992; Bardhan 1993; Seabright 1993). E. Jones (2004) reasons that the presence of wealthy participants may encourage trust in them early in a process of collective action and encourage the formation of cooperatives. Inequality in distribution of benefits may, however, reduce trust and cooperation later in the process. The impact of heterogeneity on levels of collective action achieved frequently interacts with the shape of the production function for a good and thus will be discussed further below.

1.1.4 *Face-to-Face Communication*

Given that non-cooperative game theory predicts that communication will make *no* difference in the outcome of social dilemmas, the repeated findings of a strong positive effect that communication has on the outcomes of collective action

---

[5] Closely related to the concept of a privileged group is the international relations theory of hegemonic stability (Kindelberger 1973; Keohane 1984). Hegemonic stability theory posits that heterogeneity promotes cooperation because large actors are endowed with more resources (including the power to coerce others) and are better able to produce a public good such as international peace whose benefits are provided to all whether they contribute or not. The theory predicts that when there are a limited number of larger states dominating international relations the collective good of peace is more likely to be provided.

experiments is a major theoretical puzzle (Sally 1995). The result has been replicated so many times, however, that contemporary scholars have to take it seriously.

Frohlich and Oppenheimer (1998) explain the effectiveness of communication in general related to the needs of individuals in such settings to express the desire to each other that they should forgo their immediate self-interest for the benefit of the group. In other words, communication is used for "moral suasion." And, being able to look others directly in the eye while discussing such moral issues is substantially better than relying on written communication. Kerr and Kaufman-Gilliland (1994) conclude that communication in general helps a group gain a sense of "solidarity" and that face-to-face communication enhances the likelihood that individuals will keep their promises to cooperate. In general, the efficacy of communication appears to be related to the increased trust that individuals acquire when promises are made to them in a face-to-face setting. When they are in a repeated situation, they use the opportunity for communication to discuss deviations from promises made in a highly critical and moralistic tone (Ostrom, Gardner, and Walker 1994; Valley, Moag, and Bazerman 1998).

1.1.5 *The Shape of the Production Function*

All social dilemmas involve individuals who could take actions that produce benefits for others (and themselves) at a cost that they themselves must bear. The production function that relates individual actions to group outcomes may take any of a wide diversity of forms (see Figure 8.1). One possible form is a step function (b in Figure 8.1), in which actions by up to k participants make no difference in the benefit function, but actions by k or more participants discontinuously shift the benefit functions upward. Russell Hardin (1976) was among the first to argue that when the shape of the production function for a public good was a step function, solving social dilemmas would be facilitated since *no* good would be provided if participants did not gain sufficient inputs to equal or exceed the provision point (k). Until the benefit is actually produced, it is not possible to "free ride" on the contribution of others. In these settings, individuals may assume that their participation is critical to the provision of the good. This type of production function may create an "assurance problem" rather than a strict social dilemma. For those who perceive their contribution as critical, not contributing is no longer the unique Nash equilibrium.

Closely related to this attribute of the production function itself are sharing formulas that may be developed by participants to make each person of the entire group, or a designated minimal contributing group, feel that their contribution is critical (van de Kragt, Orbell, and Dawes 1983). By agreeing that each person will contribute a set proportion of what is believed to be the total cost of obtaining a good, the individuals in such a minimal contributing set face a choice between contributing and receiving the benefit (assuming others in the minimal contributing set also contribute), or not contributing and receiving nothing.

Strict step functions or discrete goods are relatively unusual production functions. Marwell and Oliver (1993) conduct an extensive analysis of monotonically increasing,

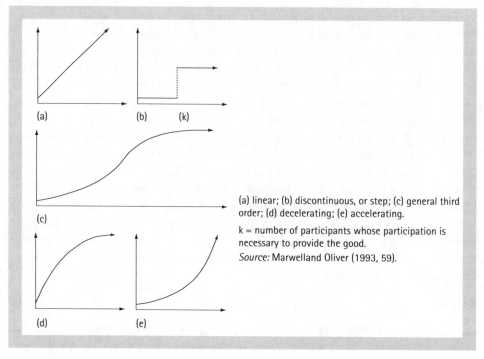

(a) linear; (b) discontinuous, or step; (c) general third order; (d) decelerating; (e) accelerating.

k = number of participants whose participation is necessary to provide the good.

Source: Marwelland Oliver (1993, 59).

Fig. 8.1 General types of production functions

linear and non-linear production functions relating individual contributions and the total benefits produced. Linear production functions are used extensively in n-person PD and public good games where the prediction is that a homogeneous group will contribute zero resources. Marwell and Oliver focus on non-linear functions and distinguish between third-order production functions that are decelerating and those that are accelerating. In the decelerating case (*d* in Figure 8.1), while every contribution increases the total benefits that a group receives, marginal returns decrease as more and more individuals contribute. When contributions are made sequentially, the initial contributions have far more impact than later contributions. The example they use to illustrate such a production function is calling about a pothole in a neighborhood where a city administration is sensitive to citizen support (1993, 62). The first call brings the pothole to the attention of city officials and puts it on the list of things to be repaired (raising the probability of repair from zero to perhaps .4 or higher). The second call increases the probability of repair still further, but not as much as the first call. Later calls continue to increase the probability but with a smaller and smaller increment.

With an accelerating production function (*e* on Figure 8.1), initial contributions make small increments and later contributions yield progressively greater benefits. "Accelerating production functions are characterized by *positive interdependence*: each contribution makes the next one more worthwhile and, thus, more likely" (1993, 63). Protest activities where mass actions are needed in order to gain a positive response involve accelerating functions. A strike involving only a few workers is unlikely to produce the level of benefits yielded by a strike involving a very large proportion of the workers of a firm or in an industry.

The theoretical predictions depend sensitively on the particular shape of the production function, on whether all participants are symmetric or have different levels of assets, on the sequence in which individuals contribute, and on the information generated by each action. For homogeneous groups facing decelerating curves, which Marwell and Oliver assert characterize many field situations involving large numbers of potential beneficiaries, getting over the initial period where the returns to participants are negative defeats collective action before it can generate sufficient inputs to gain net benefits. Thus, collective goods that have a decelerating production function are unlikely to be provided by large groups of relatively homogeneous individuals acting independently, or if provided, they will be provided as Olson predicted at a suboptimal level. The prediction for homogeneous groups and accelerative functions is also gloomy. The key is whether the initial contributions are made and this is somewhat less likely with a homogeneous group than with a heterogeneous group who may have some members with high levels of interest and who would be more interested in contributing the initial inputs.

1.2 Repetition of Interactions

With repeated interactions, at least three more structural variables are posited to affect the level of cooperation achieved in social dilemma situations: the level of information generated about past actions, how individuals are linked, and voluntary entry and exit.

1.2.1 *Information about Past Actions*

The amount of information that an individual can obtain about the earlier actions of others can make a substantial difference when choosing strategy in a repeated game. In a two-person game where individuals know the structure of the game and learn accurate information about the outcomes achieved, the behavior of the other individual is also known automatically. As soon as more than two individuals are involved, accurate information about outcomes alone is no longer sufficient to inform one player about the actions of others. In families and small neighborhoods, where interactions are repeated, reputations for always voting or always contributing to political campaigns can be built over time and group members can build up a level of trust about other participants (Seabright 1993). Cooperation can grow over time in such settings. In large groups, the disjunction between an individual's actions and reputations is more difficult to overcome. In some situations, individuals can observe the actions of others and thus know what each individual did in the previous rounds. Various ways of monitoring the actions of participants increase or decrease the availability and accuracy of the information that individuals have concerning the particular actions of known individuals (or types of players) in the past (Janssen 2004).

1.2.2 *How Individuals are Linked*

Sociologists and social psychologists have stressed the importance of how individuals may or may not be linked in a network when confronting various types of social dilemmas (Granovetter 1973; Cook and Hardin 2001).[6] They have posited that individuals who are linked in a network where A contributes resources to B, and B contributes resources to C, and C contributes resources to A—or any similar unidirectional linking—are more likely to contribute to each other's welfare than individuals whose resource contribution goes to a generalized pool from which all individuals obtain benefits. The reason given for this expectation is that individuals in an undifferentiated group setting can expect to free ride for a longer period of time without reducing their own benefits than when contributions have to be delivered to someone in the chain of relationships in order for benefits to eventually come to them. Anyone in the chain who stops contributing faces a higher probability (so the argument goes) of the chain of benefit-enhancing contributions stopping and their losing out on obtaining a positive benefit. Creating a particular type of network may change the structure of the game from an n-person PD to an Assurance Game (Yamagishi and Cook 1993).

1.2.3 *The Possibility of Choosing Whether to Play or Not (Entry and Exit)*

Orbell and Dawes (1991) and Hauk and Nagel (2001) have argued that when individuals have a choice as to whether to play social dilemma games with others, and they can identify the individuals with whom they have played and have a memory of past history, individuals will choose partners so as to increase the frequency with which cooperative outcomes are achieved. This gives individuals a third choice in a social dilemma game. Besides deciding whether to cooperate, they can decide whether to "opt out." If one player opts out, the decision round ends, and everyone receives a zero payoff. All players have an effective veto over the entire play of the game.

Janssen (in press) has developed an agent-based model of a two-person, prisoner's dilemma in which individuals can cooperate, defect, or withdraw. Each agent carries generalized symbols (such as wearing long hair or dressing in a particular manner) that can be identified by others. The symbols are used by participants to remember which type of player cooperated in the past. This enables agents to gain or lose trust that the other participant will cooperate depending on the symbols of those who cooperated or defected in the past. Given this capacity to recognize trustworthiness in others *and* the capacity to withdraw from playing a game at all, cooperation levels rise over time and reach relatively high levels in populations composed of 100 players. With 1,000 players, cooperation levels are lower unless the number of symbols that can be used to recognize trustworthy players is increased—a somewhat counter-intuitive result (see also Hauert et al. 2002).

---

[6] If the linkage structure is that of a pure hierarchy, it is presumed by many theorists that the dilemma disappears through the exercise of command and control mechanisms.

2 Towards a More General Theory of Human Behavior

As is by now obvious from the above discussion, the earlier image of individuals stuck inexorably within social dilemmas has slowly been replaced in some theoretical work with a recognition that individuals face the *possibility* of achieving results that avoid the worst outcomes and, in some situations, may even approximate optimality for themselves. It is still possible, of course, that groups who successfully overcome internal collective action dilemmas generate high costs for others. Cartels and gangs are a threat to us all. The clear and unambiguous predictions of earlier theories have been replaced with a broad range of predictions including some that are far more optimistic. The theoretical enterprise has, however, become more opaque and confused.

This is a particularly challenging puzzle for scholars who yearn for theories of behavior that explain outcomes in all types of setting. To have one theory—rational choice theory—that explains how individuals achieve close to optimal outcomes in markets, but fails to explain voting or voluntary contributions to political campaigns, is not a satisfactory state of knowledge in the social sciences. Simply assuming that individuals are successfully socialized into seeking better group outcomes does not explain the obvious fact that groups often fail to obtain jointly beneficial outcomes (Dietz, Ostrom, and Stern 2003).

When it is used successfully, the rational choice model is largely dependent for its power of explanation on how the structure of the situations involved is modeled (Satz and Ferejohn 1994). In other words, the context within which individuals face social dilemmas is more important in explaining levels of collective action than relying on a single model of rational behavior as used in classical non-cooperative game theory (see Orbell et al. 2004). In highly structured and competitive environments, predictions generated from the *combination* of a model of the situation and a model of complete rationality are well supported empirically. As Alchian (1950) demonstrated long ago, competitive markets eliminate businesses that do not maximize profits. Further, markets generate limited, but sufficient, statistics needed to maximize profits. The institutional structure of a market rewards individuals who make economically rational decisions and who can then be modeled as if they were determinate, calculating machines.

A broader theory of human behavior views humans as adaptive creatures (Jones 2001) who attempt to do as well as they can given the constraints of the situations in which they find themselves (or the ones that they seek out) (Simon 1955, 1957, 1999). Humans learn norms, heuristics, and full analytical strategies from one another, from feedback from the world, and from their own capacity to engage in self-reflection. They are capable of designing new tools—including institutions—that can change the structure of the worlds they face for good or evil purposes. They adopt both short-term and long-term perspectives dependent on the structure of opportunities they face. Multiple models are consistent with a theory of boundedly rational human behavior, including a model of complete rationality when paired with repetitive, highly competitive situations.

2.1 Heuristics and Norms

Many situations in life do not generate information about all potential actions that one could take, all outcomes that could be obtained, and all strategies that others could take. One simply assumes this level of information when using a model of complete rationality. In most everyday situations, individuals tend to use heuristics—rules of thumb—that they have learned over time regarding responses that tend to give them good (but not necessarily optimal) outcomes in particular kinds of situations. In frequently encountered, repetitive situations, individuals learn better and better heuristics that are tailored to the particular situation. With repetition and sufficiently large stakes, individuals may learn heuristics that approach best-response strategies (Gigerenzer and Selten 2001).

Many theorists interested in collective action have focused on the potentially positive effects of participants adopting simple heuristics to use when they are in a social dilemma situation. Morikawa, Orbell, and Runde (1995), for example, examine the efficacy of using the simple heuristic of "expect others to have the same dispositions as yourself." They conduct a computer simulation where each actor in a population of 10,000 actors is matched to another actor. Those simulated actors whose payoff is above the mean are multiplied by two, while those whose payoff is below the mean are eliminated from the simulation. From their simulations, they predict that the heuristic is of most value to individuals who are moderately disposed to cooperate rather than holding either of the extremes. Their simulation also generates the prediction that the heuristic will be most valuable when social dilemmas occur among those in close proximity and that the probability of there being some very cooperative groups of agents increases with the size of the population.

In addition to learning instrumental heuristics, individuals also learn norms. By norms, I mean that the individual attaches an internal valuation—positive or negative—to taking particular types of action. Analytically, individuals can be thought of as learning norms of behavior that are relatively general and fit a wide diversity of particular situations. Crawford and Ostrom (2005) refer to this internal valuation as a delta parameter that is added to or subtracted from the objective costs of an action or an outcome. Andreoni (1989) models individuals who gain a "warm glow" when they contribute resources that help others more than they help themselves in the short term. Knack (1992) refers to negative internal valuations as "duty." The strength of the commitment made by an individual to take particular types of future actions (telling the truth, keeping promises) is reflected in the size of the delta parameter. After experiencing repeated benefits from their own and from other people's cooperative actions, individuals may resolve that they should always initiate cooperation in the future.[7] Or, after many experiences of being the "sucker" in such experiences, an individual may resolve never to initiate unilateral cooperation and to punish non-cooperators whenever feasible.

James Cox and colleagues posit that individual behavior in a particular setting is affected by an individual's initial emotional or normative state and then by direct experience with others in a specific setting (Cox 2004; Cox and Deck 2005). The underlying norms and direct experience in a particular setting combine to affect orientations toward reciprocity. "Instead of beliefs or type estimates we use emotional states based on actual experience: my attitude toward your payoffs depends on my state of mind, e.g. kind or vengeful, and your actual behavior systematically alters my emotional state" (Cox, Friedman, and Gjerstad 2004, 1).

Fairness is also one of the norms used by individuals in social dilemma settings. The maximal net return to a group may be obtained in a manner that is perceived to be fair or unfair by those involved—using the general concept that "equals should be treated equally and unequals unequally" (see Isaac, Mathieu, and Zajac 1991). When participants are symmetric in regard to all strategically relevant variables, the only real fairness issue relates to the potential capability of some to free ride on others (Dawes, Orbell, and van de Kragt 1986). When participants differ, however, finding an allocation formula perceived by most participants as fair is far more challenging (Rawls 1971). In both cases, however, theorists have argued that when participants think that a proposal for sharing costs and benefits is fair, they are far more willing to contribute (Isaac, Mathieu, and Zajac 1991).

Since norms are learned, they vary substantially across individuals, and within individuals across the different types of situations they face, and across time within any particular situation. As Brennan and Pettit (2004) stress, however, norms that help to solve social dilemmas need to be shared so that individuals who act contrary to the norm fear the reduction in esteem likely to occur. Once some members of a population acquire norms of behavior, they affect the expectations of others. When interacting with individuals who are known to use retribution against those who are not trustworthy, one is better off by keeping one's commitments.

2.2 Contingent Strategies and Norms of Reciprocity

Many theorists posit that one can explain behavior in social dilemmas better if one assumes that individuals enter situations with an initial probability of using reciprocity based on a calculated strategy that reciprocity leads to higher outcomes *or*

---

[7] Whenever games are repeated, the discount rates used by individuals also affect the adoption of norms including that of reciprocity. In settings where individuals do not strongly discount outcomes that will occur in the distant future, they can realize the benefits of cooperation over a long series of plays—thus offsetting the initial material advantage of not cooperating. As the future is more strongly discounted, however, the calculation made by an individual focuses more on the immediate material payoffs. Thus, a delicate relationship exists between the discount rates used by individuals, the size of the potential benefit to be achieved, and the willingness of individuals to accept the norm of reciprocity (Abreau 1988; Axelrod 1984; Curry, Price, and Price 2005).

based on a norm that this is how one should behave (Fehr and Gächter 2000; Bolton and Ockenfels 2000; Falk, Fehr, and Fischbacher 2002; Panchanathan and Boyd 2004). In either case, individuals learn to use reciprocity based on their prior training and experience. The more benefits that they have received in the past from other reciprocators, the higher their own initial inclinations. The more they have faced retribution, the less likely they estimate that free riding is an attractive option. Their trust that others will also be reciprocators is highly correlated with their own norms but is affected by the information they glean about the reputation of other players and their estimate of the risk of extending trust given the structure of a particular situation.

By far the most famous contingent strategy—tit-for-tat—has been the subject of considerable study from an evolutionary perspective. In these analyses, pairs of individuals are sampled from a population who then interact with one another repeatedly in a PD game. Each individual is modeled as if they had inherited a strategy including the fixed maxims of always cooperate, always defect, or the reciprocating strategy of tit-for-tat (cooperate first, and then do whatever the others did on the last round). Axelrod and Hamilton (1981) and Axelrod (1984) have shown that when individuals are grouped so that they are more likely to interact with one another than with the general population, and when the expected number of interactions is sufficiently large, reciprocating strategies such as tit-for-tat can successfully invade populations composed of individuals following an all-defect strategy. But the size of the population in which interactions are occurring must be relatively small for reciprocating strategies to survive potential errors of players (Bendor and Mookherjee 1987). Boyd and Richerson (1988) have examined a model where more than two individuals are sampled from a large population to interact repeatedly in an n-person prisoner's dilemma. They conclude that increasing the size of the relevant population reduces the probability that selection will favor reciprocating strategies unless tight subgroups are formed that rarely interact across subgroup boundaries.

Reciprocating strategies continue to limit what individuals can do who face others who do not cooperate. The only way of "punishing" defection is to defect oneself, which may lock participants into the deficient equilibrium. Punishment in field settings usually involves some action other than defecting oneself on an agreement. Since punishing someone else usually involves a cost for oneself and produces a benefit for everyone, it is a second-order social dilemma (Oliver 1980; Yamagishi 1986).

Hirshleifer and Rasmusen (1989) partially tackled this problem by modeling the problem as a two-stage game with a cooperation stage followed by a punishment stage where both are repeated many times. With a costless punishment strategy, they demonstrate that a strategy of cooperating, punishing non-defectors, and then punishing those who did not punish defectors is a subgame perfect equilibrium. Hirshleifer and Rasmusen find that the strategy of cooperate and then punish any defectors will increase to a polymorphic equilibrium in large populations if (1) defectors respond to punishment by a single player by cooperating thereafter and (2) the long-run benefits to the punisher exceed the costs they pay for punishing someone else. This strategy survives with strategies that initially defect but cooperate if punished and under some conditions with strategies that cooperate but do not punish. Increasing group size does reduce the probability that this strategy will induce cooperative behavior due to increases in the cost of punishing a larger set.

Boyd and Richerson (1992) build a two-stage evolutionary model based on Hirshleifer and Rasmusen's model of a large population from which groups of size n > 2 are selected. The first stage is an n-person PD where an individual selects cooperate or defect. In the second stage, any individual can punish any other individual at a cost to the punisher and to the punished. The same group continues for the next round dependent on a probability function. Strategies are modeled as if they were inherited. They allow errors to occur in the execution of a cooperative strategy, but all other strategies are executed as intended. After the rounds of interaction are completed, the more successful strategies are reproduced at a higher rate than the less successful strategies.

In the Boyd and Richerson (1992) model, an increase in group size requires an offsetting linear increase in the number of interactions to achieve similar levels of collective action (see also Richerson and Boyd 2005). They also find that moralistic strategies "which punish defectors, individuals who do not punish noncooperators, and individuals who do not punish nonpunishers can also overcome the problem of second-order cooperation" (1992, 184). When moralistic strategies are common, defectors and cooperators who do not punish are selected against due to the punishment directed at them. "In this way, selection may favor punishment, even though the cooperation that results is not sufficient to compensate individual punishers for its costs" (ibid.). These moralistic strategies can stabilize any behavior—a result that is similar to the famous "folk theorem" that any equilibrium can be stabilized by such punishing strategies as the grim trigger. Yamagishi and Takahashi (1994) explore in an evolutionary simulation whether linking sanctioning to cooperative actions so that cooperators punish defectors and defectors do not punish other defectors solves the problem of aggressive moralistic strategies or meta norms. When these strategies are linked, they find close to 100 percent cooperation.

Several of the heuristics or strategies posited to help individuals gain larger cooperators' dividends depend upon the willingness of participants to use retribution to at least some degree. In tit-for-tat, for example, an individual must be willing to "punish" a player who defected on the last round by defecting on the current round. As mentioned above, the grim trigger is a strategy that cooperates with others until someone defects, and then defects the rest of the rounds (Fudenberg and Maskin 1986). In repeated games where substantial joint benefits are to be gained from mutual cooperation, the threat of the grim trigger is posited to encourage everyone to cooperate. A small error on the part of one player or exogenous noise in the payoff function, however, makes this strategy a very dangerous one to use in large environments where the cooperators' dividend is substantial.

Güth and Kliemt (1995) show that retributive emotions can survive in evolutionary stable ways if it is possible for players to know in advance whether the person with whom they are playing is characterized by a "strong conscience" or a willingness to impose punishments if cooperation is not selected. Bester and Güth (1994) examine the possibilities for "altruism" or what would be better described as "other regarding" preferences to evolve over time in a population facing social dilemmas. Using an indirect evolutionary approach in which preferences become endogenous, they show that including another in one's utility function depends on the favorable response of the other to cooperative moves. Family members, in particular, are more likely to have other family members in their utility functions, but their argument differs from the kin selection argument. The evolution of what they call "altruism" within a family is not linked to genetic transmission but rather to the fact that family members are better informed about each other. Signaling concern for others by giving to charity, for example, may also increase the likelihood that such preferences can survive and multiply in a population of non-related individuals. Further, the evolution of preferences that include benefits to others is more likely to emerge in populations where individuals are not anonymous and can use symbols to identify their type (Ahn, Janssen, and Ostrom 2004).

2.3 The Core Relationships: Reputation, Trust, and Reciprocity as They Affect Cooperation

In situations where individuals can acquire a reputation for using positive and negative reciprocity and being trustworthy, others can learn to trust those with such a reputation and begin to cooperate—as long as others also cooperate (Fukuyama 1995). Thus, at the core of an evolving theoretical explanation of successful or unsuccessful collective action are the links between the trust that one participant (P_i) has in the others ($P_j \ldots P_n$) involved in a collective action situation, the investment others make in trustworthy reputations, and the probability of all participants using reciprocity norms (see Figure 8.2). When some individuals initiate cooperation in a repeated situation, others learn to trust them and are more willing to adopt reciprocity themselves, leading to higher levels of cooperation. And, when more individuals use reciprocity, gaining a

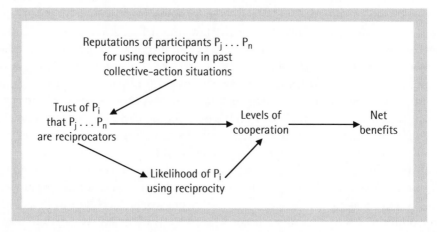

Fig. 8.2 The core relationships at the individual level affecting levels of cooperation in a social dilemma

reputation for being trustworthy is a good investment as well as an intrinsic value. Thus, reputations for being trustworthy, levels of trust, and reciprocity are positively reinforcing. This also means that a decrease in any one of these can generate a downward cascade leading to little or no cooperation.

3 Linking Structural Variables to the Core Relationships

Instead of explaining cooperation directly from the material incentives facing individuals in social dilemmas, the task we now face is how to link external structural variables to an inner core of individual-level variables—reputation, trust, and reciprocity—as these in turn affect levels of cooperation and net benefits achieved. We already understand some of the potential linkages. For example, one can confidently posit that in a small, homogeneous group interacting in a face-to-face meeting to discuss producing a public good with an accelerating production function, the costs of coming to an agreement will tend to be low and the probability that individuals keep their promises will be high. Previous gossip will have identified which members of the group could be trusted to keep agreements and efforts to exclude untrustworthy participants would be undertaken. The combined effect of the structural variables in this example on reputation, trust, and reciprocity is likely to overcome short-term, material benefits that individual partici-pants are tempted to pursue. In a different context—a large, heterogeneous group with no communication and no information about past trustworthiness who jointly use a common-pool resource—individuals will tend to pursue short-term material benefits and potentially destroy the resource.

Thus, using a broader theory of human behavior that includes the possibility that participants use reciprocity and cooperate in social dilemmas when they trust others to do the same enables scholars to generate testable hypotheses based on combin-ations of structural variables as they interact to increase or decrease the likelihood of cooperation and net benefits occurring (see Weber, Kopelman, and Messick 2004 for a similar effort). It is not possible, however, to link all of the structural variables identified above in one definitive causal model given the large number of variables and that many of them depend for their impact on the value of other variables. For now, it is possible to illustrate this general approach with the framework shown in Figure 8.3 where the structural variables discussed above are linked in a general way to the core relationships.

One cannot assign a fixed direction of relationships in this approach, however, given that the sign depends on the configuration of other variables in a particular focal social dilemma. A small group with extreme heterogeneity in the benefits to be obtained from a collective action, for example, is an entirely different group than a

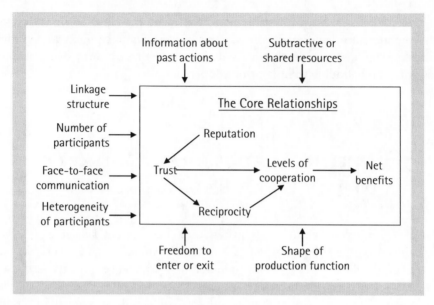

Fig. 8.3 A framework linking structural variables to the core relationships in a focal dilemma arena

small group of relatively homogeneous players. Further, in a small group with extreme heterogeneity, face-to-face communication may lead to exacerbated conflict rather than reduction in conflict and agreement on new sets of rules. Instead of one large, general causal model, one can develop specific scenarios of causal direction, such as those posited above, that can be tested (see Ostrom 1998). Thus, an important next step in the development of collective action theory is more careful attention to how structural variables interact with one another. One cannot posit simple explanations based upon an assumption that size alone makes a difference, that heterogeneity alone makes a difference, that a step-level production function alone makes a difference, or the capacity to exit alone makes a difference—all proposed by some scholars as the primary variable one needs to examine. It is the combination of these variables that evokes norms, helps or hinders building reputations and trust, and enables effective or destructive interactions and learning to occur. What is important about this simple and general framework is recognition that at any one time multiple variables affect the core variables of reputation, trust, and reciprocity.

Further, the variables linked together on Figure 8.3 are not an exhaustive set of all structural variables posited to affect collective action—they are the set that appears to be most frequently mentioned in the general literature reviewed above. Many of these variables are posited to affect other intermediate variables—such as transaction costs and the development of shared norms—that in turn affect the probability of cooperation.

Still other variables are identified in more specialized work. Agrawal (2002) has, for example, identified over thirty variables posited by scholars studying collective action related to organizing the governance of common-pool resources. Many of the variables he identifies have interactional effects. Agrawal (2002, 68–70) develops several causal chains to connect a subset of these variables together for testing in field and laboratory settings. Some of the variables identified by Agrawal relate to the likelihood of participants changing the rules that affect the structural variables that, in turn, affect the core relationships.

4 Conclusions

A key lesson of research on collective action theory is recognizing the complex linkages among variables at multiple levels that together affect individual reputations, trust, and reciprocity as these, in turn, affect levels of cooperation and joint benefits. Conducting empirical research on collective action is thus extremely challenging. There is no way that one can analyze the entire "spaghetti plate" of variables that have been identified and their interactions in a single empirical analysis. The reason that experimental research has become such an important method for testing theory is that it is a method for controlling the setting of many variables while changing only one or two variables at a time (Camerer 2003). In addition, one can self-consciously examine the interaction of several variables over a series of carefully designed experiments—something that is almost impossible to do in field research.

Conducting case studies in similar environments that differ in regard to one or two key variables is also an important strategy, but difficult to design (Alston 2005). Large-n research on collective action is a challenge both in terms of obtaining accurate and consistent data, but also because of the large number of variables that potentially affect any one type of collective action (Poteete and Ostrom 2004). Instead of looking at all of the potential variables, one needs to focus in on a well-defined but narrow chain of relationships—as recommended by Agrawal (2002). One can then conduct analysis of a limited set of variables that are posited to have a strong causal relationship (for examples, see Gibson, Williams, and Ostrom 2005; Hayes and Ostrom 2005). Thus, the theory of collective action is not only one of the most important subjects for political scientists, it is also one of the most challenging.

References

ABREAU, D. 1988. On the theory of infinitely repeated games with discounting. *Econometrica*, 80 (4): 383–96.

AGRAWAL, A. 2000. Small is beautiful, but is larger better? Forest-management institutions in the Kumaon Himalaya, India. Pp. 57–86 in *People and Forests: Communities, Institutions, and Governance*, ed. C. Gibson, M. McKean, and E. Ostrom. Cambridge, Mass.: MIT Press.

AGRAWAL, A. 2002. Common resources and institutional sustainability. Pp. 41–85 in *The Drama of the Commons*, National Research Council, Committee on the Human Dimensions of Global Change, ed. E. Ostrom, T. Dietz, N. Dolšak, P. C. Stern, S. Stonich, and E. Weber. Washington, DC: National Academy Press.

AHN, T. K., JANSSEN, M., and OSTROM, E. 2004. Signals, symbols, and human cooperation. Pp. 122–39 in *The Origins and Nature of Sociality*, ed. R. W. Sussman and A. R. Chapman. New York: Aldine de Gruyter.

ALCHIAN, A. A. 1950. Uncertainty, evolution, and economic theory. *Journal of Political Economy*, 58 (3): 211–21.

ALSTON, L. J. 2005. The "case" for case studies in political economy. *Political Economist*, newsletter of the section on political economy, American Political Science Association, 12 (4): 1, 8, 10.

ANDREONI, J. 1989. Giving with impure altruism: applications to charity and Ricardian equivalence. *Journal of Political Economy*, 97: 1447–58.

AXELROD, R. 1984. *The Evolution of Cooperation*. New York: Basic Books.

—— and HAMILTON, W. D. 1981. The evolution of cooperation. *Science*, 211: 1390–6.

BARDHAN, P. 1993. Analytics of the institutions of informal cooperation in rural development. *World Development*, 21 (4): 633–9.

BATES, R. H., and SHEPSLE, K. A. 1995. Demographics and institutions. Paper presented at the Frontiers of Economics Conference (in honor of Douglass C. North), Washington University, St Louis.

BENDOR, J., and MOOKHERJEE, D. 1987. Institutional structure and the logic of ongoing collective action. *American Political Science Review*, 81 (1): 129–54.

BESTER, H., and GÜTH, W. 1994. Is altruism evolutionarily stable? Working Paper. Tilburg: Tilburg University, Center for Economic Research.

BOLTON, G. E., and OCKENFELS, A. 2000. ERC: a theory of equity, reciprocity, and competition. *American Economic Review*, 90: 166–93.

BOYD, R., and RICHERSON, P. J. 1988. The evolution of reciprocity in sizable groups. *Journal of Theoretical Biology*, 132: 337–56.

—— —— 1992. Punishment allows the evolution of cooperation (or anything else) in sizable groups. *Ethology and Sociobiology*, 13: 171–95.

BRENNAN, G., and PETTIT, P. 2004. *The Economy of Esteem*. Oxford: Oxford University Press.

CAMERER, C. F. 2003. *Behavioral Game Theory: Experiments in Strategic Interaction*. Princeton: Princeton University Press.

CHAMBERLIN, J. 1974. Provision of collective goods as a function of group size. *American Political Science Review*, 68: 707–16.

COOK, K. S., and HARDIN, R. 2001. Norms of cooperativeness and networks of trust. Pp. 327–57 in *Social Norms*, ed. M. Hechter and K.-D. Opp. New York: Russell Sage Foundation.

COX, J. C. 2004. How to identify trust and reciprocity. *Games and Economic Behavior*, 46: 260–81.

—— and DECK, C. 2005. On the nature of reciprocal motives. *Economic Inquiry*, 43 (3): 623–35.

—— FRIEDMAN, D. and GJERSTAD, S. 2004. A tractable model of reciprocity and fairness. Working Paper. Tucson: University of Arizona, Department of Economics.

CRAWFORD, S. E. S., and OSTROM, E. 2005. A grammar of institutions. Pp. 137–74 in *Understanding Institutional Diversity*, ed. E. Ostrom. Princeton: Princeton University Press. Originally published in *American Political Science Review*, 89 (3) (1995): 582–600.

CURRY, O. S., PRICE, M. E., and PRICE, J. G. 2005. Is patience a virtue? Individual differences in discount rates and cooperativeness. Paper presented at the 17th meeting of the Human Behavior and Evolution Society, Austin, Tex.

DAWES, R. M., ORBELL, J. M., and VAN DE KRAGT, A. 1986. Organizing groups for collective action. *American Political Science Review*, 80 (4): 1171–85.

DE MATOS, J. A., and BARROS, P. P. 2004. Social norms and the paradox of elections' turnout. *Public Choice*, 121 (1–2): 239–55.

DIETZ, T., OSTROM, E., and STERN, P. 2003. The struggle to govern the commons. *Science*, 302 (5652): 1907–12.

FALK, A., FEHR, E., and FISCHBACHER, U. 2002. Appropriating the commons: a theoretical explanation. Pp. 157–92 in *The Drama of the Commons*, National Research Council, Committee on the Human Dimensions of Global Change, ed. E. Ostrom, T. Dietz, N. Dolšak, P. C. Stern, S. Stonich, and E. Weber. Washington, DC: National Academy Press.

FEHR, E., and GÄCHTER, S. 2000. Fairness and retaliation: the economics of reciprocity. *Journal of Economic Perspectives*, 14 (3): 159–81.

FISKE, S. T., HARRIS, L. T., and CUDDY, A. J. C. 2004. Why ordinary people torture enemy prisoners. *Science*, 306: 1482–3.

FROHLICH, N., and OPPENHEIMER, J. 1970. I get by with a little help from my friends. *World Politics*, 23: 104–20.

—— —— 1998. Some consequences of e-mail vs. face-to-face communication in experiment. *Journal of Economic Behavior and Organization*, 35: 389–403.

FUDENBERG, D., and MASKIN, E. 1986. The folk theorem in repeated games with discounting or with incomplete information. *Econometrica*, 54 (3): 533–54.

FUKUYAMA, F. 1995. *Trust: The Social Virtues and the Creation of Prosperity*. New York: Free Press.

GELLAR, S. 2005. *Democracy in Senegal: Tocquevillian Analytics in Africa*. New York: Palgrave Macmillan.

GIBSON, C. C., ANDERSSON, K., OSTROM, E., and SHIVAKUMAR, S. 2005. *The Samaritan's Dilemma: The Political Economy of Development Aid*. Oxford: Oxford University Press.

—— WILLIAMS, J. T. and OSTROM, E. 2005. Local enforcement and better forests. *World Development*, 33 (2): 273–84.

GIGERENZER, G., and SELTEN, R., eds. 2001. *Bounded Rationality: The Adaptive Toolbox*. Cambridge, Mass.: MIT Press.

GRANOVETTER, M. 1973. The strength of weak ties. *American Journal of Sociology*, 78: 1360–80.

GREIF, A., MILGROM, P., and WEINGAST, B. R. 1994. Coordination, commitment, and enforcement: the case of the merchant guild. *Journal of Political Economy*, 102: 745–77.

GÜTH, W., and KLIEMT, H. 1995. Competition or co-operation: on the evolutionary economics of trust, exploitation and moral attitudes. Working Paper. Berlin: Humboldt University.

HARDIN, R. 1976. Group provision of step goods. *Behavioral Science*, 21: 101–6.

—— 1982. *Collective Action*. Baltimore: Johns Hopkins University Press.

HAUERT, C., DE MONTE, S., HOFBAUER, J., and SIGMUND, K. 2002. Volunteering as red queen mechanisms for cooperation in public good games. *Science*, 296: 1129–32.

HAUK, E., and NAGEL, R. 2001. Choice of partners in multiple two-person prisoner's dilemma games: an experimental study. *Journal of Conflict Resolution*, 45: 770–93.

HAYES, T. M., and OSTROM, E. 2005. Conserving the world's forests: are protected areas the only way? *Indiana Law Review*, 37 (3): 595–617.

HICKS, G. A., and PEÑA, D. G. 2003. Community acequias in Colorado's Rio Culebra watershed: a customary commons in the domain of prior appropriation. *University of Colorado Law Review*, 74 (2): 387–486.

HIRSHLEIFER, J., and RASMUSEN, E. 1989. Cooperation in a repeated prisoner's dilemma with ostracism. *Journal of Economic Behavior and Organization*, 12: 87–106.

Isaac, R. M., Mathieu, D., and Zajac, E. E. 1991. Institutional framing and perceptions of fairness. *Constitutional Political Economy*, 2 (3): 329–70.

—— and Walker, J. M. 1988. Communication and free-riding behavior: the voluntary contribution mechanism. *Economic Inquiry*, 26 (4): 585–608.

Janssen, M. A. 2006. Evolution of cooperation when feedback to reputation scores is voluntary. *Journal of Artificial Societies and Social Simulation*, 9 (1): online, **http://jasss. soc.surrey.ac.uk/9/1/17.html**

—— In press. Evolution of cooperation in a one-shot prisoner's dilemma based on recognition of trustworthy and untrustworthy agents. *Journal of Economic Behavior and Organization*.

Johnson, R., and Libecap, G. 1982. Contracting problems and regulation: the case of the fishery. *American Economic Review*, 72: 1005–23.

Jones, B. D. 2001. *Politics and the Architecture of Choice: Bounded Rationality and Governance*. Chicago: University of Chicago Press.

Jones, E. C. 2004. Wealth-based trust and the development of collective action. *World Development*, 32 (4): 691–711.

Kanbur, R. 1992. Heterogeneity, distribution and cooperation in common property resource management. Background Paper for the World Development Report. Mimeograph.

Keohane, R. O. 1984. *After Hegemony*. Princeton: Princeton University Press.

—— and Ostrom, E., eds. 1995. *Local Commons and Global Interdependence: Heterogeneity and Cooperation in Two Domains*. London: Sage.

Kerr, N. L., and Kaufman-Gilliland, C. M. 1994. Communication, commitment and cooperation in social dilemmas. *Journal of Personality and Social Psychology*, 66: 513–29.

Kindelberger, C. P. 1973. *The World in Depression*. Berkeley and Los Angeles: University of California Press.

Knack, S. 1992. Civic norms, social sanctions, and voter turnout. *Rationality and Society*, 4: 133–56.

Libecap, G., and Wiggins, S. 1984. Contractual responses to the common pool: prorationing of crude oil production. *American Economic Review*, 74: 87–98.

Lichbach, M. I. 1995. *The Rebel's Dilemma*. Ann Arbor: University of Michigan Press.

—— 1996. *The Cooperator's Dilemma*. Ann Arbor: University of Michigan Press.

McGinnis, M. 2007. *Strategies for Improving Global Response to Conflict: Lessons from the Horn of Africa*. Bloomington: Indiana University, Workshop in Political Theory and Policy Analysis.

—— and Williams, J. T. 2001. *Compound Dilemmas: Democracy, Collective Action, and Superpower Rivalry*. Ann Arbor: University of Michigan Press.

Marwell, G., and Oliver, P. 1993. *The Critical Mass in Collective Action: A Micro-social Theory*. New York: Cambridge University Press.

Morikawa, T., Orbell, J. M., and Runde, A. S. 1995. The advantage of being moderately cooperative. *American Political Science Review*, 89 (3): 601–11.

Oliver, P. 1980. Rewards and punishments as selective incentives for collective action: theoretical investigations. *American Journal of Sociology*, 85: 356–75.

Olson, M. 1965. *The Logic of Collective Action: Public Goods and the Theory of Groups*. Cambridge, Mass.: Harvard University Press.

Orbell, J. M., and Dawes, R. M. 1991. A "cognitive miser" theory of cooperators' advantage. *American Political Science Review*, 85 (2): 515–28.

—— Morikawa, T., Hartwig, J., Hanley, J. and Allen, N. 2004. "Machiavellian" intelligence as a basis for the evolution of cooperative dispositions. *American Political Science Review*, 98 (1): 1–15.

OSTROM, E. 1990. *Governing the Commons: The Evolution of Institutions for Collective Action.* New York: Cambridge University Press.

—— 1998. A behavioral approach to the rational choice theory of collective action. *American Political Science Review*, 92 (1): 1–22.

—— 2001. Social dilemmas and human behavior. Pp. 21–41 in *Economics in Nature: Social Dilemmas, Mate Choice and Biological Markets*, ed. R. Noë, J. Van Hooff, and P. Hammerstein. Cambridge: Cambridge University Press.

—— 2005. *Understanding Institutional Diversity.* Princeton: Princeton University Press.

—— GARDNER, R. and WALKER, J. 1994. *Rules, Games, and Common-Pool Resources.* Ann Arbor: University of Michigan Press.

—— WALKER, J. and GARDNER, R. 1992. Covenants with and without a sword: self-governance is possible. *American Political Science Review*, 86 (2): 404–17.

OSTROM, V., and OSTROM, E. 1999. Public goods and public choices. Pp. 107–18 in *Polycentricity and Local Public Economies: Readings from the Workshop in Political Theory and Policy Analysis*, ed. M. McGinnis. Ann Arbor: University of Michigan Press. Originally published as pp. 7–49 in *Alternatives for Delivering Public Services: Toward Improved Performance*, ed. E. S. Savas. Boulder, Colo.: Westview Press, 1977.

PANCHANATHAN, K., and BOYD, R. 2004. Indirect reciprocity can stabilize cooperation without the second-order free rider problem. *Nature*, 432: 499–502.

PECORINO, P. 1999. The effect of group size on public good provision in a repeated game setting. *Journal of Public Economics*, 72: 121–34.

POTEETE, A., and OSTROM, E. 2004. Heterogeneity, group size and collective action: the role of institutions in forest management. *Development and Change*, 35 (3): 437–61.

RAWLS, J. 1971. *A Theory of Justice.* Cambridge, Mass.: Harvard University Press.

RICHERSON, P. J., and BOYD, R. 2005. *Not by Genes Alone: How Culture Transformed Human Evolution.* Chicago: University of Chicago Press.

SALLY, D. 1995. Conversation and cooperation in social dilemmas: a meta-analysis of experiments from 1958–1992. *Rationality and Society*, 7: 58–92.

SATZ, D., and FEREJOHN, J. 1994. Rational choice and social theory. *Journal of Philosophy*, 91 (2): 71–87.

SEABRIGHT, P. 1993. Managing local commons: theoretical issues in incentive design. *Journal of Economic Perspectives*, 7 (4): 113–34.

SHEPSLE, K. A., and WEINGAST, B. R. 1984. Legislative politics and budget outcomes. Pp. 343–67 in *Federal Budget Policy in the 1980's*, ed. G. Mills and J. Palmer. Washington, DC: Urban Institute Press.

SHIVAKUMAR, S. 2005. *The Constitution of Development: Crafting Capabilities for Self-Governance.* New York: Palgrave Macmillan.

SIMON, H. A. 1955. A behavioural model of rational choice. *Quarterly Journal of Economics*, 69: 99–188.

—— 1957. *Models of Man.* New York: Wiley.

—— 1999. The potlatch between political science and economics. Pp. 112–19 in *Competition and Cooperation: Conversations with Nobelists about Economics and Political Science*, ed. J. Alt, M. Levi, and E. Ostrom. New York: Russell Sage Foundation.

SNIDAL, D. 1985. Coordination versus prisoner's dilemma: implications for international cooperation and regimes. *American Political Science Review*, 79: 923–47.

VALLEY, K. L., MOAG, J., and BAZERMAN, M. H. 1998. A matter of trust: effects of communication on the efficiency and distribution of outcomes. *Journal of Economic Behavior and Organization*, 34 (2): 211–38.

van de Kragt, A., Orbell, J. M., and Dawes, R. M. 1983. The minimal contributing set as a solution to public goods problems. *American Political Science Review*, 77 (1): 112–22.

Wallner, K. 2002. The provision of public goods in international relations: a comment on "goods, games, and institutions." *International Political Science Review*, 23 (4): 393–401.

Weber, J. M., Kopelman, S., and Messick, D. M. 2004. A conceptual review of decision making in social dilemmas: applying a logic of appropriateness. *Personality and Social Psychology Review*, 8: 281–307.

Weissing, F. J., and Ostrom, E. 1991. Irrigation institutions and the games irrigators play: rule enforcement without guards. Pp. 188–262 in *Game Equilibrium Models II: Methods, Morals, and Markets*, ed. R. Selten. Berlin: Springer-Verlag.

Yamagishi, T. 1986. The provision of a sanctioning system as a public good. *Journal of Personality and Social Psychology*, 51 (1): 110–16.

—— and Cook, K. S. 1993. Generalized exchange and social dilemmas. *Social Psychology Quarterly*, 56 (4): 235–48.

—— and Takahashi, N. 1994. Evolution of norms without metanorms. Pp. 311–26 in *Social Dilemmas and Cooperation*, ed. U. Schulz, W. Albers, and U. Mueller. Berlin: Springer-Verlag.

PART III

STATES AND STATE FORMATION
POLITICAL CONSENT

CHAPTER 9

WAR, TRADE, AND STATE FORMATION

HENDRIK SPRUYT

1. INTRODUCTION

ONLY a few decades ago the study of the state lay moribund in political science, banished to the realm of historical scholarship. Behavioralism, methodologically individualist in its epistemological approach, sought to understand the political process by micro-level analyses. Pluralism in turn extolled the virtues of an American polity in which social actors rather than governmental action accounted for political outcomes.

In reaction to those dominant perspectives some scholars called for a renewed interest in the role of the state and state formation (Nettl 1968; Tilly 1975). Political science, and particularly the subfields of comparative politics and international relations, embraced those calls with vigor. The scholarship examining the causal connections between state formation, regime type, and state failure is today so vast that any discussion must, by necessity, constitute a bird's eye overview.

The scholarship on state formation has concentrated on several key features of the modern state, particularly its immense capacity to mobilize and tap into societal resources, and its ability to wield coercive force. In classic Weberian parlance, the state is that "compulsory political organization" which controls a territorial area in which "the administrative staff successfully upholds the claim to the monopoly of the legitimate use of physical force in the enforcement of its order," (Weber 1978, i. 54). Inevitably accounts stressing this feature of modern statehood focus on the importance of warfare and the monopolization of warfare by the state.

The Weberian definition also draws attention to related but distinct dimensions of state formation: the formation of a rationalized-legal administration; the rise of extractive capacity by a central government; and the legitimacy of such authority. The modern state transformed personalistic rule and ad hoc justification of authority to depersonalized, public governance based on the rule of law (Collins 1986). With this transformation came the claim that government could, far more intrusively than pre-modern governments, regulate many aspects of social and political life. Its ability to mobilize populations for economic growth and warfare went thus hand in hand with its ability to raise revenue (Levi 1988; Webber and Wildavsky 1986). Logically, scholars who adopt those economic and administrative foci are particularly interested in tracing how the institutional structures of the state were affected by economic changes, such as trade and the advent of capitalism, and how the state in turn influenced class structure, capitalist development, and the provision of public goods (North 1981).

The formation of the modern state inevitably involved the creation of new legitimizations of authority and power. Nascent political elites in early states either displaced or sought to control kinship structures, ethnic ties, and religious authority and to forge a new identification with the authority of the state and the holder of public office (Anderson 1991). Modern states recast and channeled individual loyalties to the extent that modern states could affect every level of individual and social life—unlike the capstone governments of older polities which extended over vast geographic areas without affecting their societies in any great measure (Gellner 1983).

Besides an exponential increase in governmental capacity, modern states differ from precursors in another important way: modern state authority is defined uniquely as territorial rule with fixed geographic boundaries. Thus, at the crossroads of the study of international relations and comparative politics, another body of literature has focused particularly on the territorial aspects of modern authority (Kratochwil 1986; Ruggie 1986; Spruyt 1994). How did the notion of territorial, sovereign states displace authority structures that were universalistic in ambition (empires), based on theocratic justification (as the aspirations to forge a unified Christian Europe), or based purely on market exchanges (as trading city-networks)? This territorial aspect of statehood arguably preceded the other characteristics associated with modern states, as rational administration, fiscal ability, and national loyalty. Indeed, from purely a territorial perspective, states preceded nations and high-capacity modern administrations by several centuries.[1]

Inevitably the study of any one of these features of state formation will implicate other aspects. Monopolization of violence can only occur if governments are deemed at least partially legitimate. Moreover, the successful monopolization of violence itself will correlate with the ability of central governments to establish some modicum of efficient administration as well as the ability to raise revenue. Thus, while each aspect of statehood may be studied in its individual form as an ideal type, any analysis must involve other dimensions of state formation. As a consequence, regardless of the particular feature of the state that one wishes to study, causal explanations will inevitably have to account for the specific dynamics of warfare, economic transformation wrought by trade and finance, and ideological aspects of state legitimization.

---

[1] The territorial aspect of statehood is thus closely connected to the notion of sovereignty. See Benn (1967); Hinsley (1986). For a recent critique that the importance of sovereignty has been overstated, see Krasner (1999).

The particular modalities of state formation, in terms of its twin features (governmental capacity and territorial definition), will determine the type of regime. Some governments will try to mobilize their societies by contractual agreement or vest their claims to legitimacy in popular approval. Others might seek alternative modes of mobilization and support.

This essay makes several claims. First, a serious student of state formation, regardless of the geographic area of interest, should take European state formation as its referent point.[2] It is that particular conceptualization of authority that succeeded in displacing rival forms of political organization in Europe and which was then transplanted globally (Giddens 1987; Strang 1991). Moreover, methodologically, such a comparative study serves to demonstrate maximum contrast in values on the causal variable (van Evera 1997). State formation outside of Europe was greatly affected by external pressure, a vastly different international milieu (both in term of security and economics), and proceeded in a highly compressed chronology. Highlighting the key causal dynamics in the European case will thus serve to demonstrate how the external and the internal aspects of state development interacted in a vastly different manner outside of Europe.

Second, the study of European state formation serves as a useful template to generate causal hypotheses regarding regime development in general. Understanding how European state formation influenced the propensity for absolutist or constitutionalist forms of government will shed light on regime transitions elsewhere, particularly given the variation in historical trajectories. The variation on the independent variables, obvious when contrasting European and non-European cases, allows us to deductively generate rival expectations about state formation and regime type. For example, Lisa Anderson (1987) has taken such an approach to study state formation in North Africa and the Middle East. Victoria Tin-bor Hui has compared early imperial Chinese state formation with the European experience (2004).

Jeffrey Herbst (2000) is undoubtedly correct in asserting that the literature on state formation has focused excessively on the European experience. But even he bases his account of state construction in Africa by juxtaposing the African experience with European trajectories, and by utilizing theories of European state formation, such as those of Charles Tilly.

This chapter thus starts with a brief account of European state formation. It distinguishes the generative factors behind the transformation of late medieval forms of government to new types of authority from the selection and convergence among these distinct types.[3]

The essay then turns to a discussion of how the process of state formation had effects on the type of regime that emerged in various states. That is, while the next section of this chapter provides for an overview of how sovereignty and territoriality were established as key features of authority in Europe, the following section discusses how state formation implicated the rise of absolutist or constitutionalist forms of rule. The fourth part highlights how accounts of state formation in Europe currently inform the study of

[2] Two of the best overviews of European state formation are Badie and Birnbaum (1983) and Poggi (1978). For a more extensive discussion of state formation and regime type, see Bendix (1978).

[3] For a more extensive discussion, see Spruyt (1994); Tilly (1990).

state development in newly emerging countries, and identifies particularly intriguing avenues for further enquiry. The manner in which non-European regions diverged from the European experience profoundly affects their contemporary status as effective or failed states, and the likelihood that democratic transitions will be successful.

2 CAUSAL DYNAMICS OF STATE FORMATION

2.1 War Making as Generative Cause

Early state formation in Europe correlated with changes in the frequency and modes of warfare (Bean 1973; Tilly 1975). Starting roughly in the early fourteenth century, military developments began to disadvantage the mounted cavalry and challenge the social and political organization of feudalism.

First, massed infantry (at battles such as Courtrai) and English longbow archers (as at Agincourt) booked resounding successes against heavy cavalry. Thus, relatively unskilled troops of socially low position could, with the right organization and if sufficient in number, defeat more highly skilled knights. The result was a shift to the greater use of infantry soldiers which individually were less expensive to equip than mounted knights. By some calculations, the costs of equipping a knight with armor and horse required roughly the labor of 500 commoners. However, given the larger aggregations of fighting men that were required for successful combat, the new military style required overall greater outlay. Whereas armed feudal service was based on personal ties (resembling a form of artificial kinship) and for a relatively short period of time (forty days per year was the norm), the emerging style of warfare called for larger numbers of paid troops. At the end of the Hundred Years War, the French thus moved towards a standing army.

The successful deployment of massed infantry was followed by the introduction of gunpowder. Given the rudimentary arms of the time, its effects were first felt with the introduction of siege artillery (McNeill 1982). Even in its nascent form such artillery proved capable of destroying the most advanced fortifications of that time, as demonstrated by the Ottoman conquest of Constantinople in 1453. Advances in artillery thus sparked a defensive reaction towards building ever more advanced and thus more expensive fortifications, employing the *trace italienne*.

All these developments in military technology in turn necessitated greater centralization, administration, and central revenue.[4] Such revenue could be gained by internal mobilization and taxation. Alternatively, rulers could pursue territorial conquest and geographic efficiencies of scale.

Military developments thus begot institutional innovation. Institutional innovation in turn corresponded with greater effectiveness on the battlefield and the opportunity to

---

[4] The historical record is clear on this point; for a brief synopsis, Ames and Rapp (1977); Bean (1973). Rasler and Thompson (1985) demonstrate how war making led to state expansion in the modern era.

expand one's realm. This in turn ratcheted up competition among rival lords and kings making the successful conduct of war the key feature of early modern administration. Between 1500 and 1700 many of the great powers were continuously at war or on a war footing (Parker 1979, 1988).

Charles Tilly (1985) has compared this process of state formation to a protection racket. While various lords competed for the loyalty (and thus revenue) of their subjects, kings tended to be the most efficient providers of protection and thus displaced lesser lords, leading to the Weberian characterization of the state as having a monopoly on violence. Tilly's account thus melds a description of a broad exogenous change—the change in the nature of warfare—with a contractarian explanation for the rise of central authority. Central authority provided protection in exchange for revenue.

Tilly is no doubt correct in arguing that early states devoted most of their revenue to waging war (see, for example, Brewer 1989). Moreover, his account is particularly appealing in providing a methodological individualist explanation, a micro-level account, for a larger structural, macro-level phenomenon. Many other accounts working in a similar vein have contented themselves with descriptive narratives chronicling the evolutionary progress to the modern state. Not only does Tilly's account provide for a plausible explanation it also logically entails that the modalities of contracting between subjects and ruling elites should lead to different forms of authority, which Tilly rightly noted in his earlier work (1975) and for which he tried to account in his later book (1990).

Yet several problems remain with accounts stressing solely the importance of warfare. Some historians, particularly those associated with the Princeton school pioneered by Joseph Strayer, locate institutional innovation before the great revolutions in military technology (Strayer 1965). Norman administrative structures and French royal practices met with considerable success during the thirteenth century. Clearly the subsequent process of state development had many more centuries to come, but it does raise questions regarding military changes as the primary or only dynamic.

Second, the contractarian account does not fully convince. Tilly argues that kings were the most efficient providers of protection, but if subjects (consumers) were indifferent between the providers for protection, one would expect many warlords to have been able to rise to kingship given the weak position of kings. (If kings were already more powerful than the other lords, the explanation would be tautological and insufficient.) Yet historically this seldom occurred. Dynastic lineages were quite durable. In other words it leaves the attraction of the king as contractarian party to provide protection or other public goods unexplained.

Finally, Tilly alternates between an explanation based on relative factor endowments and a coalitional explanation of political strategy. Polities endowed with capital (urban centers) forced political elites to enter into contractual arrangements with the cities. Towns were not inclined to surrender their liberties and revenues to authoritarian rule, and thus capital-intensive mobilization occurred in north-western Europe and northern Italy. Tilly then classifies mobilization in areas lacking rich capital endowments as coercive. In so doing he assumes that areas rich in either labor or land would both show a similar political strategy of mobilization along authoritarian lines. Empirically, it might be the case that aspiring political elites forged alliances with landowning aristocracy, as happened with the Prussian Second Serfdom (Rosenberg 1943–4). Theoretically, however, one need not a priori preclude an elite–peasant bargain against landowners if labor were abundant. Indeed, to some extent North and Thomas's (1973) and North's (1981) account of the decline of the feudal order is based on a shift in relative factor endowments diminishing the ability of landowners to coerce the peasantry. Put another way, concluding that capital abundance might correlate with constitutionalist government, does not logically require one to conclude that capital scarcity must correlate with coercive forms of rule.

2.2. Economic Transitions and the Rise of Trade as a Generative Factor

A rival account acknowledges the changes in the military milieu of the late medieval period, but stresses instead the economic changes that marked the end of feudalism and the gradual emergence of politically consolidated states and incipient capitalism. These economic changes pre-dated the military revolution of this period, and made possible the subsequent emergence of large-scale mercenary warfare. This economic perspective on the rise of the territorial state can in turn be distinguished in neo-Marxist views and neo-institutionalist analyses.

Neo-Marxists and neo-institutionalists are in broad agreement with regard to economic change being the causal factor behind the demise of personalized feudalistic rule. From the eleventh century on, a variety of factors eroded the economic foundations of feudalism and precipitated the beginning of early (merchant) capitalism. They differ, however, in the role played by the state in this process.

(Neo-)Marxist analyses and neo-institutionalists concur on the rise of trade as a harbinger of early capitalism (Anderson 1974a, 1974b; North and Thomas 1973).[5] Urbanization and the growth of trade led to the emergence of a social group that was politically and socially disadvantaged in the feudal structure. These burghers (burg dwellers, from which bourgeoisie) made their living by production and trade and thus stood outside the traditional barter, personalized exchange that formed the basis of the feudal economy. Indeed, burghers were politically free from servile bonds unlike the peasantry (city air makes free, as the medieval adage had it).

In the neo-Marxist account, however, the state performed the role of arbiter of class tensions. The advent of early capitalism thus dovetailed and necessitated the growth of a state apparatus. A royal–urban alliance, and in some cases a royal–peasant alliance, brought the feudal, decentralized order to its end.

Neo-institutionalists recognize the role of urbanization and the emergence of new economic groups that opposed the existing feudal order. However, the state does not act in a predatory fashion, as an agent of the ruling class (the emerging bourgeoisie), but emerges out of contracts between ruler and subject, and the ruler's desire for personal gain, by maximizing societal welfare.

---

[5] In historical scholarship, this argument was popularized as the Pirenne thesis (Pirenne 1952).

Douglas North and Robert Thomas (1973) pioneered such explanations, suggesting that changes in weather, agricultural innovations (such as crop rotation and the deep plough), increased trade flows, diminished invasions, and demographic shifts altered the relative power of social groups possessing land, labor, and capital. These environmental shifts thus transformed the balance between the factors of production. The resulting change in relative bargaining power of the various factors in turn influenced political outcomes. Thus, the decline of population following the plague of 1353 (and there were numerous outbreaks of the disease) created a supply shortage of labor, enhancing the bargaining position of the peasantry vis-à-vis the possessors of land (the aristocracy). This eroded the feudal economy based on indentured agriculture.

A more fully articulated neo-institutionalist perspective emerges in North's later work (1981, 1990). This perspective takes an explicitly contractarian approach. The ruler exchanges protection for revenue. Efficiencies of scale in the provision of this public good lead to consolidation in one provider. Secondly, the ruler acting in this monopoly position allocates property rights to maximize the revenue of society at large, and, by taxation, thus yield more revenue for the individual ruler. However, the ruler's monopoly is not absolute. Rivals within the state might emerge as more efficient (or less extortionist) providers of public goods. Or rival states might provide exit options to the constituents (North 1981, 23).

Neo-institutional explanations thus emphasize a potential communality of economic interests between the monarchy and the emerging mercantile groups. As far as military protection goes mercantile groups would be indifferent between who provided protection. However, kings were more attractive as contracting parties than local feudal lords, given efficiencies of scale. Moreover, mercantile groups favored greater standardization of weights, measures, and coinage; the weakening of feudal obligations; clearer definition of property rights; and written legal codes. Given royal interests in maximizing revenue, such standardization, monetization of the economy, and legalization of royal rule (by the introduction of Roman law) were as dear to the king as they were to urban interests.

Neo-institutional accounts, therefore, share the neo-Marxist interpretation of a royal–urban alliance as a key explanation for the emergence of more rationalized, centralized, and territorially defined rule. It differs in placing less emphasis on the state as a coercive mechanism to remedy the inefficiencies of feudalism and repress the labor force. It stresses instead the role of the state as an institutional solution to the transaction and informational hurdles that hampered the feudal economy.

2.3 The State as Ideological Revolution

A third account of early state formation places particular emphasis on ideology. The move towards depersonalized, rationalized administration could only occur against the backdrop of a dramatic shift in collective beliefs.[6] On the one hand this entailed

---

[6] See, for example, Corrigan and Sayer (1991). Pizzorno (1987) suggests the state assumed many of the ideological roles claimed by institutionalized religion.

the emergence of a sense of individuality. Thus Macfarlane's (1978) observation regarding the emergence of individualism in twelfth-century England has an important bearing on the rise of early capitalism (and the early state). John Ruggie (1993) has similarly noted the changes in perception giving rise to a sense of mechanical, ordered structure. Changes in artistic perception coincided with, and were indicative of, changes in perceptions of right political order—an order which could emerge by rational design rather than religious mandate. Rather than presuppose a contractarian environment, an examination of ideological shifts clarifies the conditions under which humans came to understand themselves as atomistic individuals (rather than members of larger social entities), and how they came to see themselves as contracting parties of ruler and subject (rather than being part of some preordained order).[7] What methodological individualist accounts take as a given (in either seeing war or economic changes as altering the terms of the contract between rulers and ruled), ideological reflections pry apart and problematize.

The emergence of the early state, consequently, meant that the feudal collective consciousness was abandoned. In classical feudal theory, political order was modeled on that of heaven (Duby 1978). As such, a tri-level political order was the most desirable. At the pinnacle stood "those that prayed." Those that fought, the military aristocracy, should serve those that prayed. Peasants and commoners, "those who worked," in turn were inferior to both of the other castes and occupied the lowest rung. The notion of territorial authority based on contract challenged such concepts of preordained station.

The emergence of individual states also challenged the notion that Europe, being the domain of Christianity, should constitute one political community. In the feudal perspective the pope as its leader would be served by the vicar of God, the emperor, who formed the sword and right hand of the spiritual elements.

In practice, however, the centuries-long conflict between emperor and pope, and the subsequent victory of monarchy over either of those two conceptualizations, meant that the religious views of a theocratic imperial Europe came to naught. The territorial conceptualization of authority won out over alternative logics of legitimization. States emerged out of the stalemate for European dominance of emperors and popes.[8]

3 DIVERSITY AND SELECTION

Any generative account of institutional change runs the risk of functionally linking, in a post hoc manner, causal explanations of institutional demise to the specific institutional outcome that is the focus of that particular scholar. But in liminal

---

[7] Neo-institutionalists as North (1981, 45–58) also draw attention to ideology, but do so largely from a functional perspective, seeing ideology as a device to overcome collective action problems, rather than as creating preferences and identity.

[8] Not coincidentally the Investiture Struggle empowered territorial kings (Tierney 1964).

moments when old orders are shattered and space opens up for institutional innovation, agents rarely agree on the type of innovation they should bring about. Individuals have diverse preferences. They might be risk averse, or ignorant of the long-term consequences of their choices. Initial choices might have unintended consequences in the long run (Thelen 2004).

Thus generative accounts of state formation require some account for selection among the diversity of agent choices. At the sunset of the feudal order various alternative forms for structuring political authority were possible, as Tilly (1975) noted. The imperial claim to reconstitute a hierarchically governed European space surfaced in various guises. German emperors claimed to revive the Roman Empire. Later, Spanish rulers sought to expand their authority under the imperial banner with similar theocratic ambitions. Such theocratic claims were only gradually set aside by agreements as the Treaty of Augsburg (1555) and the Peace of Westphalia (1648).

Additionally, city-states, city-leagues, loose confederal entities (such as the Swiss federation), and odd hybrid states (such as the Dutch United Provinces) held center stage throughout late medieval and early modern European history.[9] Such authorities often held competing claims to rule over a given geographic space. For example, many cities throughout northern Europe held dual allegiance to the territorial lord in their vicinity and the city-leagues of which they were members.

The explanations for the convergence to a system of sovereign entities, which claimed exclusive jurisdiction within recognized borders, tend to parallel the analytic approaches of the end of feudalism. Accounts focusing on changes in military affairs tend to emphasize selection. Neo-institutionalists in turn stress the efficiency of institutional design, combining selection mechanisms with individual preferences. Those stressing ideational changes draw attention to sovereignty as a social construct.

Thus, accounts that stress the importance of war emphasize selective mechanisms in Darwinian terms. Indeed, some of these views lean towards strong-form selection. Given a particular environment selection will be harsh, trending towards convergence on a singular surviving type. Sovereign, territorially defined organization with strong central administrations thus defeated and eliminated less efficient and less effective forms of governance. In the study of international relations, realists tend to favor this view of environmental selection, although they may blend such agent-less accounts with intentional mimicry of successful practice and socialization (Waltz 1979).

Strong-form selection, however, is a rarity even in biology. Odd types and less efficient designs often continue to exist in niches. So too, multiple institutional forms often exist side by side in the political realm. Path dependence, entrenched interests, and jury-rigged institutional solutions that agents devise in the face of challenges to the existing institutions, all militate against simple selective mechanisms.

---

[9] In an interesting article Knudsen and Rothstein 1994 argued that Denmark and Scandinavia differed from both the "Western" mode of state formation (based on strong urban centers and free peasantry) and the "Eastern" mode (based on weak towns and serfdom), presenting us with two hybrid types. In a bold claim Putnam (1983) argues that the medieval development of Italian city-states explains many of the institutional features of the Italian landscape today, suggesting that scrutiny of past state development sheds light on the present.

Consequently, neo-institutionalists often blend selective mechanisms and deliberate agent choices. Rather than simply note the competitive advantage of states they ask why such advantages existed in the first place, or why certain polities did not opt for more efficient arrangements, as, for example, by changing manifestly inefficient property rights. Neo-institutional explanations thus account for the advantage of sovereign territorial organization in terms of its success in reducing transaction and information costs, and the provision of public goods in general (North 1981; Spruyt 1994). The system of sovereign, territorial states did not emerge simply by blind selection but equally by individual choices. Rulers were cognizant of their limitations to rule, given exit options for their constituents. Internal and external rivalry also led rulers to opt for more efficient designs. They made conscious decisions to delimit spheres of jurisdiction in domestic and international realms.

Finally, perspectives that emphasize sovereign territoriality as an ideational construct tend to sociological and anthropological explanations for why this form displaced rival types. Sociological institutionalism, in particular, sees the convergence toward the state as a process of mimicry and social imprinting (Thomas et al. 1987). Polities tend to interact with like types of government. At the same time newly emerging polities will style themselves self-consciously to conform to the existing "organizational field" (DiMaggio and Powell 1983). The existing set of practices is taken for granted by those wishing to be deemed legitimate states.

4 State Formation and Regime Type

Competition, individual strategic choice and mimicry affected not only the displacement of non-territorial forms of rule, but they also had a direct bearing on the types of regimes that emerged. Variation in intensity and modes of warfare, as well as the differential impact of trade and modernization, affected the development of absolutism and constitutionalism.

As Otto Hintze (1975) noted, frequent and intense warfare will tend to correlate with authoritarian government. The need to mobilize resources by the state will lead to a high degree of government intervention in society. Frequent geopolitical conflict will require manpower and financial resources in order to secure the survival of the polity. Rather than rely on militias and incidental service, the state will prefer to develop standing military forces.

Those military forces, however, can serve a dual purpose. Not only will they serve to protect the state from external enemies, they can be used to repress internal dissent. Thus, frequent and intense warfare will give birth to a garrison state, justified by external threats, but equally capable of stifling constitutionalist movements. The Prussian Great Elector and the Junkers forged their alliance in reaction to the mortal threats posed by Sweden, Austria, and Russia, but equally used this coalition to establish a Second Serfdom without constitutional guarantees (Rosenberg 1943–4).

Hintze also noted that land-based forces had different internal effects than naval forces. Those polities that were fortunate enough to have geographic advantages and who could rely on maritime power for their external defense (such as Britain) need not suffer the same fate as countries that needed to maintain large standing armies. Although the government might still require considerable burdens from the population in terms of taxation, naval forces could not be as easily deployed for internal repressive purposes. Heavy taxation would thus have to be obtained by consent rather than coercion.

Charles Tilly (1990) and Brian Downing (1992) have expanded on these insights. Tilly observed that the ready availability of financial resources might mitigate the tendency towards absolutism. Although all European states were heavily involved with frequent, organized warfare from roughly the late fifteenth century onward (Parker 1988), garrison states only emerged where urban centers were poorly developed. Although, as noted earlier, Tilly confuses his descriptions of political strategies with a description of relative factor endowments, he is correct in noting the relative absence of absolutist forms of government on the European core axis that ran roughly from the European north-west to northern Italy. The states that formed this core axis had strong urban communities whose consent was required for war. Thus, these polities emerged as constitutionalist forms of government.

Downing rightly adds that other intervening variables might affect the causal relation between war and regime type. The availability of external capital (through colonies, or allies), as well as geographic features that facilitate defense (the Swiss mountains, for example), may complicate the picture. Defense of the state, even if surrounded by belligerent actors, need not necessarily lead to a garrison state. Rather than internal mobilization the state may secure its existence by judicious management of its external relations.

Downing's account thus draws attention to how warfare and economic milieu intertwine to affect regime type. Where trade flourished urban centers were vibrant. This allowed the state to raise large sums of capital for warfare, while at the same time the strong urban centers demanded participation in how this money would be allocated.

War making and economic transition interacted also with the creation of early capitalism by mercantilist practices. Although Machiavelli realized (and before him Cicero) that money was the sinews of power, power in turn provided one with markets and commodities. War making and economic change thus pointed towards greater government intervention and absolutist rule in the classical mercantilist style. Indeed, all states, including Britain and the Netherlands (the later champions of liberal trade), engaged in such mercantilist practices during their formative phase.

The particular timing of state development may further affect the impact of external competition on regime type. Taking Germany and Russia as templates, Gerschenkron argued that late state formation required not merely the centralization of political authority and definition of territorial boundaries, but also an activist government to catch up with more advanced economies (Gerschenkron 1962). Modernization from the "top down" thus correlated with authoritarianism.

Taking his cue from Gerschenkron and Hintze, Thomas Ertman (1997) submits that geopolitical competition, combined with the periodization of state building, sheds light not only on regime type but also on the state's administrative infrastructure. The latter can be patrimonial or administrative-bureaucratic. The timing of the onset of competition and the pre-existing strength of local assemblies affect subsequent outcomes on regime type and administrative structure.

All things being equal geopolitical competition prior to 1450 should lead to patrimonial administration and absolutism in Latin Europe, but constitutionalism and patrimonialism in Britain, due to the strength of local assemblies. With the later onset of geopolitical competition and strong local assemblies in Hungary and Poland, we should expect bureaucratic constitutionalism in Eastern Europe. However, this did not happen, says Ertman, due to the independent effect of parliament, reversing the expected outcomes in the British and East European cases.

His discussion usefully opens up the analysis beyond regime type or administrative structures. However, one may wonder whether the account succeeds. Thus whereas Tilly, Hintze, Downing, each in their own way, try to account for the relative strength of local assemblies, Ertman takes this variation as a starting point, and then argues that this variation in turn had subsequent effects on the emergence of absolutism versus constitutionalism. However, when he introduces the strength of parliament as having an independent effect on the outcomes observed the account gains a tautological flavor.

Finally, neo-institutional accounts of state formation have also weighed in the discussion of state formation and regime type. Neo-institutionalists suggest that less hierarchical regimes have salutary internal and external consequences. Internally, less hierarchical governments tend to foster economic development when the government has credibly tied its own hands (North and Weingast 1989). Since entrepreneurs need not fear government predation, their private incentives to pursue economic gain parallel public objectives. Externally, governments that tie their own hands can more credibly commit to international obligations. Since the sovereign is accountable to its domestic public it cannot retreat from international agreements (Cowhey 1993; Martin 2000). Democratically accountable governments thus have a competitive advantage over rival types.

Neo-institutionalists in a sense thus reverse, and alter, the causal linkage of conflict and regime type. Whereas Hintze, Downing, and others focus on the consequences of warfare on regime type, neo-institutionalists might well concentrate on the effect that regimes have on rulers' ability to mobilize society for war. Thus rulers that are constitutionally bound might be more able to raise revenue from their population, or from other states, in times of war (D'Lugo and Rogowski 1993). Similarly, given audience costs and their ability to credibly commit, democratic regimes make states more attractive as allies and trading partners.[10]

---

[10] On the relevance of audience costs for credibility, see Fearon (1994).

5 STATE FORMATION AND STATE FAILURE IN THE MODERN ERA

The literature on state formation in Europe thus presents a variety of analytic angles to clarify how sovereign territoriality became the constitutive rule for the modern state system, why some states developed as constitutional or absolutist regimes, and how some states created rational administrative structures which others lacked. However reflecting on the European historical trajectory generates theoretical lenses through which to view contemporary developments elsewhere. Nowhere is this more pertinent than in the newly independent states that emerged in the latter part of the twentieth century.[11]

Indeed, since the end of the Second World War the number of independent states has multiplied almost fourfold. Decolonization in Africa and Asia created new entities in the shadow of erstwhile maritime empires while the end of communist domination in Eastern Europe and the fragmentation of the USSR added another two dozen polities in the 1990s. While the new polities have emerged in a state system in which the adherence to the principle of sovereign territoriality is a sine qua non for international recognition, these new states face a dramatically different environment than the early European actors.

Consequently, most of the independent states that emerged in the twentieth century readily accept territorial sovereignty as a constitutive rule of international relations (although it is perhaps challenged by certain religious principles in Islam). State capacity and rational, bureaucratic administration, however, have been found critically wanting, burdened as many of these states are by patrimonialism, weak economies, and rampant organized corruption. This weak administrative infrastructure has affected their ability to monopolize the means of violence within their borders; their ability to develop viable domestic economies; and their ability to provide public goods to their populace. Combined with borders that have been superimposed on heterogeneous populations, rulers inevitably lack legitimacy.

5.1 The Changed Security Environment

The new states of the post-1945 era emerged in a completely different security environment than the states of early modern Europe. Rather than emerge out of the cauldron of geopolitical conflict that for centuries typified the European landscape most of these entities gained independent status by fiat. Even in the USSR, conflicts that emerged in

---

[11] There is also a growing body of literature that has started to examine non-European state formation prior to European colonial expansion. Tin-bor Hui (2004) thus argues that state formation during China's Warring States period (656–221 BC) looked markedly different than war making and state making in Europe. Carolyn Warner notes how some states in West Africa had emerged as viable territorial entities with considerable state capacity before European encroachment (Warner 1998).

the wake of the Union's collapse were primarily conflicts within the newly independent states, secessionist conflicts, not inter-republic wars.[12]

Many of these states consequently acquired independence after colonial powers withdrew and by subsequent international recognition, but they did not undergo the process that accompanied traditional state formation (Jackson 1987). Although some colonies fought wars of liberation, compared to the centuries of European geopolitical strife, these wars did not require long-term mobilizational strategies. As a result, these nationalist conflicts did not enhance state capacity. In the words of Joel Migdal, while the governments of such newly independent countries affect many spheres of social life, they lack the ability to direct these societies. Weak states confront strong societies (Migdal 1988).

Interstate war, in general, is increasingly considered an aberration. The international community considers war an illegal means of pursuing foreign policy objectives (Zacher 2001). Thus, the United Nations only legitimizes force under specific conditions. Furthermore, for much of the Cold War the bipolar environment stifled conflict. Many wars of the post-1945 era were internal conflicts, or conflicts between the lesser powers. In addition, nuclear weapons and the balance of power made great power conflict unwinnable. Finally, territorial aggrandizement has become more difficult and is no longer a prerequisite for the accumulation of wealth (Spruyt 2005).

For these reasons, warfare has declined in frequency and has become virtually obsolete in Europe and the Americas. Arguably, the likelihood of interstate war, although not improbable in Asia and Africa, has declined even there. The lack of frequent, intense conflict has retarded the development of strong states in regions such as Africa (Herbst 1989). Given a low population density and high costs of creating an administrative infrastructure, pre-colonial African states largely concentrated state resources in a key core area with state control receding further away from the core. Boundaries were permeable. The current international system, however, recognizes the imperially imposed borders to mark the extent of (ascribed) state authority. African political elites have embraced these borders in an attempt to expand their own power and mediate external pressures. Tellingly, Herbst criticizes this artificiality: "the fundamental problem with the boundaries in Africa is not that they are too weak but that they are too strong" (Herbst 2000, 253).

In some areas the state lacks a monopoly of violence altogether. Instead, multiple groups vie with each other for internal control of the state (Reno 1998). Some of these groups might provide some public goods, resembling the beginnings of proto-states in late medieval Europe. "Shadow states" thus emerge in lieu of recognized public authority. In many cases, however, rulers tend to pursue more particularistic gains favoring narrow clienteles or ethnic communities. Warlordism, trafficking in drugs or conflict diamonds, and ethnic conflicts emerge in their wake.

The absence of an actor who holds a monopoly on the legitimate exercise of force has led to the introduction of private actors who possess means of violence (Singer 2003). As Avant (2005) points out, the consumers and suppliers for these private

---

[12] The former Yugoslavia or India and Pakistan might be construed as exceptions.

actors come from a wide array of actors. Thus, whereas European states saw a gradual monopolization of violence and the gradual eradication of armed private actors (Thomson 1989, 1990), some areas in Africa are witnessing the opposite trend.

The internal features of weak and failed states might contradict some expectations from international relations. Whereas this literature has largely studied patterns of international interaction by examining developed states, weaker states in the developing world might not follow expected patterns of balancing and bandwagoning (David 1991; Lemke 2003).

5.2 The Economic Environment and Late State Formation

These newly emerging states also face a different economic environment than early European states. Not only has the direct link between warfare and state making been severed, but it has weakened the traditional mercantilist junction of state making and modernization. The barriers to interstate war thus hinder the ability of emerging states to create, and mobilize, consolidated internal markets, and at the same time pursue state revenue by external aggrandizement.

Mercantilist state making has been further impeded by the spread of liberal capitalism. American hegemony explicitly yoked the creation of the Bretton Woods system to the denunciation of mercantilist practice and imperial preference. While primarily intended to delimit the protectionist and interventionist practices of the European great powers, this subsequently had consequences for their erstwhile colonies.

Globalization of trade and capital markets has also led to pressures for convergence. If strong states, such as France, had to give way due to international capital flight in the early 1980s (Garrett 1992), such constraints must hold a fortiori for less developed countries. How much latitude states still have to pursue neo-mercantilist strategies and thus link economic development and state making, as late developing European states could (Gerschenkron 1962; Hall 1986), is an ongoing matter of debate. Arguably the East Asian states succeeded in state development because they found means to utilize protectionist measures and industrial policy to their benefit (Johnson 1982; Amsden 1989; Deyo 1987). Richard Stubbs (1999) submits that the East Asian states managed to develop during the Cold War by a classical linking of preparation for war (due to the communist threat) and economic development (partially with support of American capital and aid.). Neo-mercantilist economic policy, state development, and authoritarian government went hand in hand. Indeed, there is some evidence that the more successful developing states in the 1990s, such as China, resisted the "Washington consensus" that preached the virtues of less government intervention and liberal trade (Wade 2003).

Given the apparent success of the East Asian "tigers" one inevitably must ask why state making and interventionist economic policy making did not lead to state capture and rent seeking by elites in that region, and why the developmental state has had less success elsewhere (Haggard and Kaufman 1995). In comparing two Middle Eastern states (Turkey and Syria) with South Korea and Taiwan, David

Waldner claims that premature incorporation of popular classes during the state-building process had an adverse effect on economic development (Waldner 1999). South Korea and Taiwan, by contrast, managed to hold back participation and distributive pressures. Thus rather than see differential external factors as causes for successful economic takeoff and state formation, this alternative line of enquiry explains variation by different internal trajectories of coalition building.

Other newly emerging states have followed alternative paths of economic mobilization. In the standard European developmental path, internal mobilization for war and economic development often meant a tradeoff for the ruler between mobilization and participation. In common parlance, taxation required representation. Absolutist rulers could only circumvent the connection by making potential opponents of royal centralization tax exempt. The lack of taxation of the aristocracy thus correlated with the absence of effective parliamentary oversight in pre-revolutionary France, Spain, and Prussia.

Some of the newly independent states that possess considerable natural resources, however, can obtain resources without making such tradeoffs. Rents accruing from natural resources, particularly in natural gas and oil, allow governments to provide essential public goods, or side payments to potential dissidents, without having to make concessions. The rentier state literature thus argues that rentier economies show an inverse correlation with democracy (Anderson 1986; Chaudhry 1997; Dillman 2000; Karl 1997; Vandewalle 1998). The standard rentier argument was developed with particular reference to the Middle East, but the argument has been applied to other states as well. Intriguingly, the notion of rents might also be extended to other export commodities, or even foreign aid.[13]

But there is some debate whether rentier states inevitably lead to societal acquiescence. In one perspective, rentier economies might generate the very conditions that precipitate dissidence. Because governments selectively allocate rents to select groups, the presence of considerable financial resources makes it worthwhile for the excluded group to mobilize its constituency to challenge the existing authority (Okruhlik 1999).

In another intriguing line of enquiry, some scholars have examined the relation between economic context and the state through formal models. This has yielded interesting observations with regards to efficient state size and the number of states in the international system. Alesina and Spolaore (1997) start from the premiss that public goods provision is more efficient in larger units. Thus, a fictitious social planner could maximize world average utility by designing states of optimal size with an equilibrium number of units. Several factors, however, will offset the benefits of large jurisdictions. First, heterogeneous populations will make uniform public goods provision more costly. Second, given diverse preferences and the declining efficiency of provision the further one resides from the center of the country, democratic rulers will not be able to create optimal redistributive systems as efficiently as rulers who can unilaterally maximize utility. Third, an international liberal trading scheme will decrease the costs for small jurisdictions.

---

[13] For a good overview of some of this literature, see Cooley (2001).

They have extended this line of analysis to the provision of security as a public good (Alesina and Spolaore 2005). A geopolitical hostile environment creates benefits for large jurisdictions, as security provision will be more efficient. With declining international competition such benefits will recede and the number of nations will expand.

International relations scholars have made similar observations, albeit from different analytic perspectives. Michael Desch (1996) thus argued, following realist views in international relations scholarship, that the durability of alliances and territorial integrity were heavily dependent on the presence of external threat. Events since the end of the Cold War seem to have borne such expectations out. Moreover, if Alesina and Spolaore are correct, the attempts to foster democratic regimes in many of the new states will not necessarily lead to economically efficient outcomes. Finally, their analysis comports well with Herbst's (2000) argument. The artificial borders of many African states, which thus comprise many diverse ethnic communities, have coincided with inefficient economic outcomes and the suboptimal provision of public goods.

5.3. Legitimizing the State in Newly Emerging Polities

The preceding observations have serious consequences for rulers seeking to legitimize their rule and the existing territorial borders. The ideological legitimation of the sovereign, territorial state in Europe involved a threefold process. First, it required the triumph of rule based on territoriality. The idea of a theocratic, universalist non-territorial organization based on a Christian community had to be displaced in favor of territorial identification. Already by the fourteenth century kings had started to challenge papal claims to rule. And by the sixteenth century, by the principle *cuius regio, eius religio*, territorial rulers came to determine the dominant religious identification of their state.

Second, the state had to contend with alternative forms of identification and loyalty—ethnic community, clans, kinship structures, and trans-territorial loyalties (as with feudal obligations). National language, public education, compulsory military service, and other strategies were enlisted to "forge peasants into Frenchmen" (Weber 1979; Posen 1993). The emergence of national armies and citizenship went hand in hand. In exchange for public goods provision and protection, citizens had to do more than pay taxes; they had to serve with life and limb to defend the national community (Levi 1998). The creation of a nation to identify with the particular territorial space, consequently, involved a destruction of local variation and identification and a reconstruction of a national citizen.

Third, in the process of contractual bargaining or even by coercive imposition of authority over time, the state acquired a taken-for-granted character. The greater the contractarian nature of the state, the greater the ability of the state to acquire legitimacy. But even authoritarian states, once they had attached legitimate rule to the disembodied state, rather than a particular dynastic lineage, could count on popular support in moments of crisis, such as war.

Few of these processes are at work in the newly independent states of the last decades. Territorial identification has not uniformly displaced trans-territorial affinity based on language and religion. For example, whether the idea of territorially demarcated authority is compatible with theocratic organization in the Muslim world still remains a matter of debate (Piscatori 1986). The interplay of trans-territorial claims to rule varies by historical legacy, the particular manifestation of the dominant religion on the ground, and even individual rulers' calculations. Even within the same country territorial rulers themselves have at particular junctures championed trans-territorial affinities while their successors denied such claims. In Egypt, Nasser invoked pan-Arab loyalties, while Sadat proved more an Egyptian nationalist. While many Middle East rulers (Gause 1992) have largely abjured the trans-territorial claims of their early independence, the legitimacy of their authority remains contested.

The newly independent states of the former Soviet Union have not been immune either. Some scholars have suggested an attraction of pan-Turkic identification (Mandelbaum 1994). Others see legitimization problems which look similar to those of the Middle Eastern states given the tensions between secular rulers, often the direct heirs of the Communist Party cadres, and religious authorities.

In many newly independent states local affinities of tribe, ethnic community, clan, and kin dominate any sense of national citizenship. In the Middle East and North Africa, states such as Tunisia and Egypt, which were historically relatively autonomous entities prior to colonial subjugation, have had a longer track record of melding local identity with territory (Anderson 1987). Other states, such as on the Arabian peninsula, have had to contend with various alternate loci of identification, some of which were fostered by colonial rule. Similarly, in the newly independent states of Central Asia, traditional loyalties, like clan networks, continue to provide means of representation vis-à-vis state authorities as well as means for demanding state distribution towards such networks (Collins 2004).

This pattern holds equally in Africa as in many states of Asia. Even where nationalist elites gained their independence by force of arms rather than by metropolitan retreat, these elites have not always been successful in creating a national identity. For instance, although the Indonesian army obtained considerable popular support in its struggles with the Dutch, the national project has largely been seen as a Javanese one. Ethnic and regional tensions have thus resurfaced in such places as Borneo, Atjeh, and Ambon.

In Eastern Europe and the former Soviet area as well, nationalist elites have had mixed success. Czechoslovakia and Yugoslavia dissolved altogether, while Romania, Hungary, and many of the former Union republics continue to face multiple challenges. Within the former Soviet Union, the Baltics, who could fall back on a prior historical legacy of independence, have fared better in muting virulent tensions.

As said, these states emerged due to a mixture of imperial collapse, metropolitan withdrawal, international delegitimization of empire, and nationalist resistance. In very few instances were elites involved in contractarian bargaining with social actors. Nationalist alliances were often agreements of convenience rather than durable quid pro quo exchanges as in European state formation. The internal features of successful state making were absent and thus logically the means through which rulers could justify their authority.

This is not to say that national elites in all newly emerged states are doomed to failure. Although public goods provision might be suboptimal in heterogeneous populations, and although there are reasons to fear deleterious overall effects of ethnic diversity on economic growth, strategic choices to mitigate the effects of ethnic cleavages can bear fruit. For example, there is some evidence that nation-building efforts in Tanzania, despite a highly heterogeneous population, and despite limited resources, have met with considerable success. In Tanzania, the government chose a national language policy, reformed local governments following independence, distributed public expenditures equitably, and adopted a national school curriculum. As a result public school expenditures show far less correlation with ethnicity and the nation-building project as a whole has been relatively successful. In Kenya, conversely, public goods have been distributed far less equitably and nation building has stalled (Miguel 2004). Taking Tanzania as a "less likely case" for successful nation building, given its low level of economic development and its ethnic diversity, suggests that deliberate state strategies might yield modest success even under difficult circumstances.

6 INSTITUTIONAL LEGACIES OF EMPIRE

There is, given the observations above, a broad consensus that late state formation outside of the Western experience, and particularly in the developing countries, occurs in a vastly different environment and will thus diverge from the European model. In addition to a different geopolitical and economic milieu, the newly independent states differ from the European trajectory in that many of them emerged in the wake of imperial disintegration and retreat. The study of emerging states thus sparked enquiry into the institutional consequences of imperial rule.

The former Soviet space and Eastern Europe have proven particularly fertile ground for comparative political studies. Given the relative similarity of background conditions (particularly in the former USSR), these states lend themselves to cross-case analyses regarding institutional choice and the consequences of institutional type (Laitin 1991; Elster 1997). What kinds of institutions emerged during this third wave of democratization? With scarcely more than a decade gone by, it appears evident that many polities in Eastern Europe and the former Soviet Union have opted for strong presidential systems (Easter 1997).

One hardly needs to mention that the consequences of presidential and parliamentary systems remain a matter of debate within the comparative politics literature. Those in favor of parliamentary forms of government argue that presidential systems lend themselves to abuse of power and are poorly equipped to deal with multiethnic societies (Lijphart 1977; Linz 1996; Skach and Stepan). Presidential systems will thus be prone to eroding democratic rights and to limiting parliamentarian opposition. Conversely, others argue that parliamentary systems might be as prone to abuse and winner-take-all policies as presidential systems (Mainwaring and Shugart 1997). Comparative study of these states in the years ahead will be a fruitful avenue of enquiry to test these rival arguments.

Eastern Europe and the former Soviet republics also provide a laboratory for the study of economic transition. Shortly after independence, proponents of "shock therapy" held sway.[14] Economists suggested that a successful, rapid transition to a capitalist system was feasible. Subsequent analysis, partially on the basis of comparisons with Western European state formation and economic development, remained far more skeptical. Political and social conditions that had accompanied takeoff in Western Europe seemed absent. Paradoxically, states which seemed to have inherited fewer institutional and material resources from the USSR, such as the Ukraine, proved to be more successful in their transition than Russia itself, which could build on the state capacity left from the USSR (Motyl 1997).

Finally, this region has provided generalizable theoretical insights about institutional arrangements and territorial fragmentation. Valerie Bunce suggests in her comparative analysis of Czechoslovakia, Yugoslavia, and the USSR that civil–military relations and ethnofederal institutions are key elements that may contribute to territorial dissolution (Bunce 1999).[15] More recent research, however, suggests that ethnofederal solutions might not have such adverse consequences and might be able to deal with heterogeneous populations. A balance between the core region and other units might be critical for the stability of the ethnofederal arrangement (Hale 2004).

The Soviet ethnofederal system also had some unique features that contributed to its demise. The Soviet titular elite policy officially linked particular nationalities to territorial entities but also created incentives for the agents (the titular elites) to disregard commands from the principal (the Communist Party), particularly when oversight mechanisms declined while at the same time rewards from the center diminished. Steven Solnick utilizes such a principal–agent framework to contrast Chinese territorial integrity during its economic transition with the collapse of the USSR (Solnick 1996).[16] Randall Stone (1996) has argued that lack of oversight and information problems plagued principal (USSR) and agents (the East European states) as well—seriously distorting their pattern of trade.

Finally, scholarship has also turned to the question whether colonial legacies show commonalities across time and space, despite widely divergent historical and cultural trajectories. A growing body of research has started to compare the states of Central Asia and African states (Beissinger and Young 2002; Jones-Luong 2002). These states share various features in common that do not bode well for their subsequent development. They share poverty, a history of institutionalized corruption, patrimonial institutions,

---

[14] One such proponent was Anders Aslund (1995).

[15] Other accounts that look at the particular nature of Soviet ethnofederalism are Brubaker (1994); Roeder (1991); Suny (1993).

[16] For another account using a neo-institutionalist logic, see Nee and Lian (1994).

and weak state development due to imperial domination. Nevertheless some of these states have embarked on modest democratic trajectories (such as Kyrgyzstan) while others remain authoritarian (such as Uzbekistan). Similarly, some sub-Saharan states show modest economic success (such as Botswana) while others evince abject failure (such as Zimbabwe). Cross-regional comparison, therefore, might allow greater specification of the causal variables for state failure, economic takeoff, and democratic reform.

To conclude, the study of the state is alive and well. Indeed, there has been a dramatic revival of studies of state formation, the linkage between state formation and regime type, as well as of state failure. It is also clear that subfield boundaries fade into the background in the study of such substantive macro-level questions. While the integration of subfields has been most manifest within comparative politics and international relations, other subfields may contribute greatly as well. American politics, in its nuanced understanding of institutional choices and their consequences, can shed light on how electoral reforms might enable or constrain economic growth and democratic reform. Questions of citizenship, identity politics, and legitimacy inevitably involve political philosophy.

Aside from multidisciplinarity, the study of the state must be historical. For better or for worse, it is the European state system which has been superimposed on the rest of the world. The differences in historical environment and the divergent trajectories not only shed light on the problems confronting the newly independent states of the last half-century, but possibly point the way to remedies which might start to address the dire effects of state failure.

References

ALESINA, A., and SPOLAORE, E. 1997. On the number and size of nations. *Quarterly Journal of Economics*, 112 (4): 1027–56.

—— —— 2005. War, peace, and the size of countries. *Journal of Public Economics*, 89: 1333–54.

AMES, E., and RAPP, R. 1977. The birth and death of taxes: a hypothesis. *Journal of Economic History*, 37: 161–78.

AMSDEN, A. 1989. *Asia's Next Giant: South Korea and Late Industrialization.* New York: Oxford University Press.

ANDERSON, B. 1991. *Imagined Communities.* New York: Verso.

ANDERSON, L. 1986. *The State and Social Transformation in Tunisia and Libya, 1830–1980.* Princeton: Princeton University Press.

—— 1987. The state in the Middle East and North Africa. *Comparative Politics*, 20 (1): 1–18.

ANDERSON, P. 1974a. *Passages from Antiquity to Feudalism.* London: Verso.

—— 1974b. *Lineages of the Absolutist State.* London: Verso.

ASLUND, A. 1995. *How Russia Became a Market Economy.* Washington, DC: Brookings Institution.

AVANT, D. 2005. *The Market for Force: The Consequences of Privatizing Security.* New York: Cambridge University Press.

BADIE, B., and BIRNBAUM, P. 1983. *The Sociology of the State.* Chicago: University of Chicago Press, 1983.

BEAN, R. 1973. War and the birth of the nation state. *Journal of Economic History*, 33 (1): 203–21.

BEISSINGER, M., and YOUNG, C. eds. 2002. *Beyond State Crisis? Postcolonial Africa and Post-Soviet Eurasia in Comparative Perspective.* Washington, DC: Woodrow Wilson Center Press.

BENDIX, R. 1978. *Kings or People.* Berkeley and Los Angeles: University of California Press.

BENN, S. 1967. Sovereignty. Pp. 501–5 in *The Encyclopedia of Philosophy,* vol. vii/viii. New York: Macmillan.

BREWER, J. 1989. *The Sinews of Power.* New York: Alfred Knopf.

BRUBAKER, R. 1994. Nationhood and the national question in the Soviet Union and post-Soviet Eurasia: an institutionalist account. *Theory and Society,* 23: 47–78.

BUNCE, V. 1999. *Subversive Institutions.* New York: Cambridge University Press.

CHAUDHRY, K. 1997. *The Price of Wealth: Economies and Institutions in the Middle East.* Ithaca, NY: Cornell University Press.

COLLINS, K. 2004. The logic of clan politics: evidence from Central Asian trajectories. *World Politics,* 56 (2): 224–61.

COLLINS, R. 1986. *Weberian Sociological Theory.* Cambridge: Cambridge University Press.

COOLEY, A. 2001. Booms and busts: theorizing institutional formation and change in oil states. *Review of International Political Economy,* 8 (1): 163–80.

CORRIGAN, P., and SAYER, D. 1991. *The Great Arch.* New York: Blackwell.

COWHEY, P. 1993. Elect locally—order globally: domestic politics and multilateral cooperation. Pp. 157–200 in *Multilateralism Matters,* ed. J. Ruggie. New York: Columbia University Press.

DAVID, S. 1991. Explaining Third World alignment. *World Politics,* 43 (2): 233–56.

DESCH, M. 1996. War and strong states, peace and weak states? *International Organization,* 50 (2): 237–68.

DEYO, F. ed. 1987. *The Political Economy of the New Asian Industrialism.* Ithaca, NY: Cornell University Press.

DILLMAN, B. 2000. *State and Private Sector in Algeria.* Boulder, Colo.: Westview Press.

DiMAGGIO, P., and POWELL, W. 1983. The iron cage revisited: institutional isomorphism and collective rationality in organizational fields. *American Sociological Review,* 48: 147–60.

D'LUGO, D., and ROGOWSKI, R. 1993. The Anglo-German naval race as a study in grand strategy. In *The Domestic Bases of Grand Strategy,* ed. R. Rosecrance and A. Stein. Ithaca, NY: Cornell University Press.

DOWNING, B. 1992. *The Military Revolution and Political Change.* Princeton: Princeton University Press.

DUBY, G. 1978. *The Three Orders.* Chicago: University of Chicago Press.

EASTER, G. 1997. Preference for presidentialism: postcommunist regime change in Russia and the NIS. *World Politics,* 49 (2): 184–211.

ELSTER, J. 1997. Afterword: the making of postcommunist presidencies. Pp. 225–37 in *Postcommunist Presidents,* ed. R. Taras. New York: Cambridge University Press.

ERTMAN, T. 1997. *Birth of the Leviathan.* New York: Cambridge University Press.

FEARON, J. 1994. Domestic political audiences and the escalation of international disputes. *American Political Science Review,* 88: 577–92.

GARRETT, G. 1992. International cooperation and institutional choice: the European Community's internal market. *International Organization,* 46 (2): 533–60.

GAUSE, G. 1992. Sovereignty, statecraft and stability in the Middle East. *Journal of International Affairs,* 45 (2): 441–69.

GELLNER, E. 1983. *Nations and Nationalism.* Ithaca, NY: Cornell University Press.

GERSCHENKRON, A. 1962. *Economic Backwardness in Historical Perspective.* Cambridge, Mass.: Harvard University Press.

GIDDENS, A. 1987. *The Nation-State and Violence.* Berkeley and Los Angeles: University of California Press.

HAGGARD, S., and KAUFMANN, R. 1995. *The Political Economy of Democratic Transitions.* Princeton: Princeton University Press.

HALE, H. 2004. Divided we stand: institutional sources of ethnofederal state survival and collapse. *World Politics,* 56 (2): 165–93.

HALL, P. 1986. *Governing the Economy.* Cambridge: Polity Press.

HERBST, J. 1989. The creation and maintenance of national boundaries in Africa. *International Organization,* 43 (4): 673–92.

—— 2000. *States and Power in Africa.* Princeton: Princeton University Press.

HERZ, J. 1976. *The Nation-State and the Crisis of World Politics.* New York: David McKay.

HINSLEY, F. H. 1986. *Sovereignty.* Cambridge: Cambridge University Press.

HINTZE, O. 1975. *The Historical Essays of Otto Hintze,* ed. Felix Gilbert. New York: Oxford University Press.

HUI, V. 2004. Toward a dynamic theory of international politics: insights from comparing ancient China and early modern Europe. *International Organization,* 58 (1): 175–205.

JACKSON, R. 1987. Quasi states, dual regimes, and neo-classical theory: international jurisprudence and the Third World. *International Organization,* 41 (4): 519–49.

JOHNSON, C. 1982. *MITI and the Japanese Miracle.* Stanford, Calif.: Stanford University Press.

JONES-LUONG, P. 2002. *Institutional Change and Political Community in Post Soviet Central Asia.* New York: Cambridge University Press.

KARL, T. 1997. *The Paradox of Plenty: Oil Booms and Petro States.* Berkeley and Los Angeles: University of California Press.

KNUDSEN, T., and ROTHSTEIN, B. 1994. State building in Scandinavia. *Comparative Politics,* 26 (2): 203–20.

KRASNER, S. 1999. *Sovereignty: Organized Hypocrisy.* Princeton: Princeton University Press.

KRATOCHWIL, F. 1986. Of systems, boundaries and territoriality: an inquiry into the formation of the state system. *World Politics,* 39 (1): 27–52.

LAITIN, D. 1991. The national uprisings in the Soviet Union. *World Politics,* 44 (1): 139–77.

LEMKE, D. 2003. African lessons for international relations research. *World Politics,* 56 (1): 114–38.

LEVI, M. 1988. *Of Rule and Revenue.* Berkeley and Los Angeles: University of California Press.

—— 1998. Conscription: the price of citizenship. Pp. 109–47 in *Analytic Narratives,* ed. R. Bates, A. Greif, M. Levi, J. Rosenthal, and B. Weingast. Princeton: Princeton University Press.

LIJPHART, A. 1977. *Democracy in Plural Societies.* New Haven: Yale University Press.

LINZ, J. 1996. The perils of presidentialism. Pp. 124–42 in *The Global Resurgence of Democracy,* ed. L. Diamond and M. Plattner. Baltimore: Johns Hopkins University Press.

MACFARLANE, A. 1978. *The Origins of English Individualism.* Oxford: Blackwell.

MCNEILL, W. 1982. *The Pursuit of Power.* Chicago: University of Chicago Press.

MAINWARING, S., and SHUGART, M. 1997. Juan Linz, presidentialism, and democracy: a critical appraisal. *Comparative Politics,* 29 (4): 449–71.

MANDELBAUM, M. ed. 1994. *Central Asia and the World.* New York: Council on Foreign Relations Press.

MARTIN, L. L. 2000. *Democratic Commitments: Legislatures and International Cooperation.* Princeton: Princeton University Press.

MIGDAL, J. 1988. *Strong Societies and Weak States.* Princeton: Princeton University Press.

MIGUEL, E. 2004. Tribe or nation? Nation building and public goods in Kenya versus Tanzania. *World Politics,* 56 (3): 327–62.

MOTYL, A. 1997. Structural constraints and starting points: the logic of systemic change in Ukraine and Russia. *Comparative Politics,* 29 (4): 433–47.

Nee, V., and Lian, P. 1994. Sleeping with the enemy: a dynamic modeling of declining political commitment in state socialism. *Theory and Society*, 23 (2): 253–96.

Nettl, J. P. 1968. The state as a conceptual variable. *World Politics*, 20 (4): 559–92.

North, D. 1979. A framework for analyzing the state in economic history. *Explorations in Economic History*, 16: 249–59.

—— 1981. *Structure and Change in Economic History*. New York: W. W. Norton, 1981.

—— 1990. *Institutions, Institutional Change and Economic Performance*. Cambridge: Cambridge University Press.

—— and Thomas, R. 1973. *The Rise of the Western World*. Cambridge: Cambridge University Press.

—— and Weingast, B. 1989. Constitutions and commitment: the evolution of institutions governing public choice in 17th century England. *Journal of Economic History*, 49: 803–32.

Okruhlik, G. 1999. Rentier wealth, unruly law, and the rise of opposition: the political economy of oil states. *Comparative Politics*, 31 (3): 295–315.

Parker, G. 1979. Warfare. Ch. 7 in *New Cambridge Modern History*, vol. xiii, ed. P. Burke. Cambridge: Cambridge University Press.

—— 1988. *The Military Revolution*. New York: Cambridge University Press.

Pirenne, H. 1952/1925. *Medieval Cities*. Princeton: Princeton University Press.

Piscatori, J. 1986. *Islam in a World of Nation-States*. New York: Cambridge University Press.

Pizzorno, A. 1987. Politics unbound. Pp. 26–62 in *Changing Boundaries of the Political*, ed. C. Maier. Cambridge: Cambridge University Press.

Poggi, G. 1978. *The Development of the Modern State*. Stanford, Calif.: Stanford University Press.

Posen, B. 1993. Nationalism, the mass army, and military power. *International Security*, 18 (2): 80–124.

Putnam, R. 1983. Explaining institutional success: the case of Italian regional government. *American Political Science Review*, 77 (1): 55–74.

Rasler, K., and Thompson, W. 1985. War making and state making: governmental expenditures, tax revenues and global war. *American Political Science Review*, 79 (2): 491–507.

Reno, W. 1998. *Warlord Politics and African States*. Boulder, Colo.: Lynne Rienner.

Roeder, P. 1991. Soviet federalism and ethnic mobilization. *World Politics*, 43 (2): 196–232.

Rosenberg, H. 1943–4. The rise of the Junkers in Brandenburg-Prussia, 1410–1653. *American Historical Review*, Part I, 49 (1): 1–22; and Part II, 49 (2): 228–42.

Ruggie, J. 1986. Continuity and transformation in the world polity. Ch. 6 in *Neorealism and its Critics*, ed. R. Keohane. New York: Columbia University Press.

—— 1993. Territoriality and beyond: problematizing modernity in international relations. *International Organization*, 47 (1): 139–74.

Singer, P. 2003. *Corporate Warriors: The Rise of the Privatized Security Industry*. Ithaca, NY: Cornell University Press.

Skach, C., and Stepan, A. 1993. Constitutional frameworks and democratic consolidation: parliamentarism versus presidentialism. *World Politics*, 46 (1): 1–22.

Solnick, S. 1996. The breakdown of hierarchies in the Soviet Union and China: a neoinstitutional perspective. *World Politics*, 48 (2): 209–38.

Spruyt, H. 1994. *The Sovereign State and its Competitors*. Princeton: Princeton University Press.

—— 2005. *Ending Empire: Contested Sovereignty and Territorial Partition*. Ithaca, NY: Cornell University Press.

Stone, R. 1996. *Satellites and Commissars*. Princeton: Princeton University Press.

STRANG, D. 1991. Anomaly and commonplace in European political expansion: realist and institutionalist accounts. *International Organization*, 45 (2): 143–62.

STRAYER, J. 1965. *Feudalism*. New York: Van Nostrand Reinhold.

STUBBS, R. 1999. War and economic development: export-oriented industrialization in East and Southeast Asia. *Comparative Politics*, 31 (3): 337–55.

SUNY, R. 1993. *The Revenge of the Past*. Stanford, Calif.: Stanford University Press.

THELEN, K. 2004. *How Institutions Evolve: The Political Economy of Skills in Germany, Britain, the United States, and Japan*. New York: Cambridge University Press.

THOMAS, G., MEYER, J., RAMIREZ, F., and BOLI, J. 1987. *Institutional Structure: Constituting State, Society and the Individual*. Beverly Hills, Calif.: Sage.

THOMSON, J. 1989. Sovereignty in historical perspective: the evolution of state control over extraterritorial violence. Pp. 227–54 in *The Elusive State*, ed. J. Caporaso. Newbury Park, Calif.: Sage.

—— 1990. State practices, international norms, and the decline of mercenarism. *International Studies Quarterly*, 34 (1): 23–48.

TIERNEY, B. 1964. *The Crisis of Church and State, 1050–1300*. Englewood Cliffs, NJ: Prentice Hall.

TILLY, C. 1975. *The Formation of National States in Western Europe*. Princeton: Princeton University Press.

—— 1985. War making and state making as organized crime. Pp. 169–87 in *Bringing the State Back in*, ed. P. Evans, D. Rueschemeyer, and T. Skocpol. Cambridge: Cambridge University Press.

—— 1990. *Coercion, Capital and European States, AD 990–1990*. Cambridge: Basil Blackwell.

VAN EVERA, S. 1997. *Guide to Methods for Students of Political Science*. Ithaca, NY: Cornell University Press.

VANDEWALLE, D. 1998. *Libya since Independence: Oil and State-Building*. Ithaca, NY: Cornell University Press.

WADE, R. 2003. What strategies are viable for developing countries today? The WTO and the shrinking of development space. *Review of International Political Economy*, 10 (4): 621–44.

WALDNER, D. 1999. *State Building and Late Development*. Ithaca, NY: Cornell University Press.

WALTZ, K. 1979. *Theory of International Politics*. New York: Random House.

WARNER, C. 1998. Sovereign states and their prey: the new institutionalist economics and state destruction in 19th-century West Africa. *Review of International Political Economy*, 5 (3): 508–33.

WEBBER, C., and WILDAVSKY, A. 1986. *A History of Taxation and Expenditure in the Western World*. New York: Simon and Schuster.

WEBER, E. 1979. *Peasants into Frenchmen: The Modernization of Rural France, 1870–1914*. Stanford, Calif.: Stanford University Press.

WEBER, M. 1978. *Economy and Society*, 2 vols. Berkeley and Los Angeles: University of California Press.

ZACHER, M. 2001. The territorial integrity norm: international boundaries and the use of force. *International Organization*, 55 (2): 215–50.

....

CHAPTER 10

COMPLIANCE, CONSENT, AND LEGITIMACY

RUSSELL HARDIN

....

In political theory and in political discourse more generally, the family cluster of terms, compliance, consent, and legitimacy, can be used as strictly positive, descriptive terms, but the latter two tend to be given a normative slant, perhaps more often than not. Strangely, it is the last of these that is most commonly treated as prima facie normative, although it has a distinctively different status that can make it not suited to normative claims. It is citizens who comply and who consent, but it is usually states or laws that are said to be legitimate. In general in any society with even a modicum of plural values, a state or a regime or a particular government that is legitimate to some is likely be illegitimate to others, so that the attribute of legitimacy does not fully apply to states or regimes. Very often it is little more than a psychological assertion of some citizens that their state or government or regime is legitimate *to them* or in their eyes.

The fundamental, modal relationship of citizens to their governments most of the time is acquiescence, which may fall substantially short of compliance in the political equivalent of working to rule or going slow on the job or of the child's grudgingly slow chewing of anything green. When a nation is under attack, there may be a surge of loyalty as citizens rally round the flag, so that at least many citizens then go well beyond mere acquiescence. In wartime, indeed, the goals of both the citizenry and the government are narrowed to focus on winning or surviving the war, so that there

* I wish to thank Diana Marian for a very useful commentary on a draft and for her research assistance.

is genuinely substantial harmony of interests. The British regime was plausibly legitimate in the eyes of almost everyone in the United Kingdom during the Second World War. Contrariwise, during unusually tumultuous times of rebellion and demonstration within a society mere acquiescence may already be in question, as in the 1960s in several Western democracies. Moreover, in general it is extremely difficult for a populace to organize against its own government if that government is functioning moderately well in maintaining order, so that it can concentrate its efforts at control on a relatively small number of dissidents.

The most difficult and fraught of these terms is legitimacy, not least because the other terms in this family are relatively clear by comparison. But it is also probably true that it is more complicated just because it is inherently a system-level concept whose import depends on individual-level assessments. Consent and compliance are only causally related to system-level issues; they are not conceptually implicated at that level as legitimacy is.

In contemporary systematic arguments, we typically ascribe legitimacy to a regime on one of three possible grounds: how it came into existence, what it does for us, or our relationship to it both historically and now. The first of these once was often about some god's part in establishing our government, but in the liberal democratic states of our time, this theocratic claim is an irrelevant consideration, although it may be asserted in certain, especially Islamic, states even today. In recent centuries, the most common argument of political philosophers is that legitimacy turns on the consent, somehow defined, of the governed.

The second ground is typically more or less a welfarist concern with what the regime does for its citizens (as in what is sometimes referred to as a benefit theory of obligation to government or to obey the law). This is perhaps the most common view of those who are concerned with evaluating regimes around the world, especially when the evaluators are not primarily normative political theorists. For example, Western criticisms of many regimes in the Third World are that they do not serve their people well.

The third ground is the most common issue in the Weberian tradition of relating legitimacy to authority and domination. In this tradition, we look to how government works and maintains itself rather than to how it comes to power or what it specifically does for us. On such an account, Stalin's regime in the Soviet Union had considerable legitimacy. And all of the post-war regimes of West Europe have great legitimacy.

Consent seems to have entered vernacular political philosophy as the natural, even necessary grounding for political authority. It is a sad fact that there is apparently no systematic account of vernacular views in political and legal philosophy. Because all of the theories canvassed here are about impacts and effects on the general populace, we need to know and understand vernacular views. If we are to say why people do obey, our normative theories are likely less relevant than are popular views for answering our queries. Many leaders in any democratic regime and even in an authoritarian regime might hope to convince their populace that they are backed by consent and not merely tolerated through acquiescence (Weber 1922/1978, 213). After the narrowest margin of victory by any president ever to be re-elected in the

United States, President George W. Bush declared that he now had political capital and that he would use it to accomplish the things that his supporters wanted from government. Not only was his own margin slight, the margin in the House of Representatives was very narrow, so that party discipline became strenuous and even vicious to keep the majority intact and in line.[1]

1 Conceptual Background

In social and political theory there may be no more confused and confusing literature than that on legitimacy. The term is used in ways that are positive and normative and sometimes there is a silent move from the positive to the normative. Such a move violates David Hume's (1739–40/2000, 3.1.1.27) dictum that we cannot infer normative conclusions from mere facts. If we want to reach normative conclusions, we must begin at least in part with normative assumptions. The most common positive use of the term legitimacy is the simple claim that officers of the legal system followed extant rules and procedures in reaching a conclusion, as in a criminal trial. The decision, if arrived at by proper procedures, is said to be legitimate. This means, of course, only that it is legitimate within the relevant legal system. In another legal system, a strictly analogous outcome could be illegitimate. One might say further that the decision reached in this way is right or correct, but this adds nothing to saying, positively, that it is legitimate. One might also say that it is good to follow extant procedures. But this normative claim wants normative justification. Against any such claim, we might agree that a certain legal system is itself a bad system and that following its procedures would be morally bad even though legitimate. Hence, positive legitimacy can be normatively bad.

In political theory, the more common claim is that a regime is legitimate or illegitimate. This is analogous to saying that a legal system, not the decisions taken within it, is legitimate or illegitimate. And yet, a standard way to establish a claim that a particular regime is legitimate is to show that it followed or was created by procedures that are somehow morally compelling in their own right. Probably the most common justification in modern political theory, especially since John Locke (1690/1988, ch. 8), is that the regime was created through consent of the people, usually through a so-called social contract. I wish to argue that any such justification is inadequate and that likely no regime is or perhaps has ever been legitimate in such a sense. Those who assert that a regime is legitimate therefore do little more than assert their approval of the regime.

---

[1] It is sometimes supposed that there will be a minimum winning coalition in a legislative body. Strangely, however, parties are commonly more extreme and more disciplined when they have a narrowly minimum winning coalition than when they have an easy majority. A true ideolog therefore should want to keep a majority coalition small in order to be more successful in demanding party discipline.

To borrow a term from twentieth-century moral theory, such supporters are emotivists in political theory. Or, in some cases, they assert that the regime works to support or abide by some moral theory that they approve. This last defense of a regime is the only genuinely normative theory, but it clearly starts up front as a normative theory and there are few defenders of such a position other than some of the utilitarians and perhaps Hume. Since very few moral theorists in philosophy today are utilitarian, there are almost no extant contemporary defenses of the legitimacy of political regimes that could count as successful moral defenses. Among specifically political philosophers, by far the most common claims are essentially emotivist and are therefore empty of any compelling argument. "I like it" is not a compelling argument unless we are choosing, for example, flavors of ice cream. What works for ice cream does not work for constitutional regimes.

Political debate about the legitimacy of various constitutional moves often turns on whose side you are on, as in the debates about the legitimacy of secession of states from the USA in the decade or so before the Civil War. There was no definitive constitutional provision on the issue. That fact was used as evidence by partisans of both sides. For Abraham Lincoln, no provision meant it was not an option and this view was reinforced by the general cast of the origins of the nation, which suggested that the states were folded into and therefore superseded by the nation. For southerners such as John C. Calhoun (1853/1992), no provision meant secession was not forbidden, and their view was strengthened by the general cast of the origins of the nation, which suggested that the states had had to agree to union and might therefore now choose to opt out of the nation because they no longer agreed. The constitutional prohibition against secession was de facto established by the victory of the North in coercing the southern states to stay in the Union. That is not a particularly compelling moral principle.

There is no standard normative definition of legitimacy. A claim of legitimacy could be normative because it is based in utilitarian, Kantian, consent, or other moral principles. Or it could be grounded in religious principles, as in the work of Thomas Aquinas (see Finnis 1998) or Sayyid Qutb (1990). Or it can simply be ad hoc, as in emotivist assertions. But one can assert the legitimacy of a regime without claiming a moral defense of it. The Weberian account of legitimacy—that the government is well established and it works in some important sense—is arguably not moral and it is arguably the best positive theory of legitimacy that we have.

2 Theocratic Legitimacy

Traditionally, in Europe from the medieval period until the time, roughly, of Hobbes, the standard ground for claiming legitimacy was to assert the divine right of monarchs, as though to claim that God had chosen the leader. The palpable silliness of this claim did not seem to get in the way of asserting it or, possibly, even believing it as Filmer (1680/1949) seems to do. Strangely, God seems to have chosen occasional usurpers to overthrow previously anointed monarchs. As long as there was a hier- archically organized Church with the power to rule over some aspects of civil and political life, the countless failures of the theocratic view could be officially ignored. But that view was irreparably broken when monarchs began to be executed by mere people. Filmer attempted to explain away the difficulties but did so in a way that largely surrendered his theological grounding of authority. He reduced obligation to obedience to whoever is in power, implicitly including Cromwell, the usurper (Daly 1979, 104–23). This is oddly not far from the position of Weber.

The main body of Christian theological philosophy of government was natural law theory, especially represented by Thomas Aquinas (1225?–1274). Much of his argu- ment for the goodness of monarchs and their service of the common good is bland and unconvincing. Indeed, in keeping with his era, it is more assertion, often from analogies to, for example, architecture, than argument. But occasionally all of the later visions of political obligation come into his remarks. For example, he presages Weber's views in his granting that some laws "have their binding force not only from reason, but [also] from their having been laid down." Reason would be from their fit with natural law. But natural law clearly is inadequate to give us the details of our laws, just as architectural theory is inadequate to determine the details of a building beyond its general shape and methods of construction. Hence, many of our laws have their force "from human law alone" (Finnis 1998, 267). Aquinas also, of course, argues that the point of government is to secure peace, although this notion has religious overtones and is not strictly the social order that concerns Hobbes or Hume. But it does include "a sufficiency of at least the necessities of life" (1998, 227).

The eventual move from the theocratic and theological to the democratic ground- ing of legitimacy was arguably the most important political development of the past millennium in Europe. In effect, the religious divisions caused by the Reformation wrecked any hope of grounding politics in religious principles (Curley 1994, pp. xlv– xlvi). Protestantism, if it was to be intellectually coherent, virtually required basing government in consent or some other individual-level principle. The core move from Catholicism to Protestantism is the lodging of judgement on what to believe in the individual believer, even to the point of producing Bibles in the vernacular for the people to read and interpret for themselves. Among the things they could discover from their own reading was that much of the liturgy and hierarchy of the Church was extra-biblical and even corrupt.

The political significance of the move to Protestantism is that even earthly political judgement must be taken down to the level of the individual citizen. For example, it is especially important to realize that there can be no laws by revelation. As Hobbes asks, "*how can a man without supernatural revelation be assured of the revelation received by the declarer? and how can he be bound to obey them?*" (Hobbes 1651/1994, 26.40, emphases in the original). In essence, how can I trust your claim of revelation? In the 1668 Latin edition of *Leviathan* Hobbes additionally says that "since it is nothing but revelation made to an individual man, it obliges only him to whom it is made" (31.3 n.). He goes on to assert this principle at demonstrative length so that we cannot miss the point. The claim that each of us must follow the dictates revealed directly to ourselves alone is virtually a defining principle of Protestantism, which therefore demanded new principles for grounding compliance with government policies and demands and for asserting the legitimacy of any government.

It is less often noted that this claim is devastating to the Catholic Church. The leadership of the Church through many centuries opposed various independent strains of thought not only on scripture but also on governance of the Church and its flock. This leadership is men who proclaim themselves to be especially qualified to ascertain true doctrine. They have no objective proofs of their qualifications and therefore they are subject to Hobbes's dismissal of revelation. In Hobbes's time, however, it was reasonable to suppose that religious diversity must produce social disorder. He therefore argues that the sovereign ought to establish the content of public religion and forms of worship while leaving individuals to believe whatever they believe in private.

While rejecting theocratic arguments, Hobbes provides two direct accounts of a government's legitimacy: consent and successful rule, as spelled out in his analyses of commonwealths by institution (contract) or acquisition (power). His central moral concern with making citizens better off is the ground principle for another account that is generally consistent with either of the other two accounts. These three accounts remain today as our chief approaches to assessing legitimacy and justifying compliance.

3 Contractarian Legitimacy

Possibly the most commonplace contemporary defense of the legitimacy of some government is from the view that the society is constituted by a broad social contract to which citizens have in some sense consented. The putative analogy with ordinary legal contracts supposedly gives the social contract metaphor great force. In particular, if contractarian arguments are compelling, they yield a very important principle for governing a society. If the contractual arrangements to which we consent entail the use of coercion to get us to do what we agreed to do, then a fundamentally important part of the behavior of real governments is justified by our prior consent to be coerced in certain circumstances. In an ordinary contract at law, you and I essentially do voluntarily submit ourselves to the possibility of later coercion to force one or the other of us to live up to our contract. Without the threat of coercive legal backing, we would never enter into many contracts in which the stakes are moderately to very high. If we can generalize from such ordinary contracts to the social contract, then we can rationally justify coercion as what the citizens have agreed to (Hardin 1990). In particular, our agreement to a social contract would entail our acceptance of an obligation to obey the law and to be subject to coercion if we do not obey.

Of course, if the social contract is not analogous to a standard contract at law in this respect, then it does not offer this solution to the problem of justifying coercion of citizens by government. Unfortunately, traditional contractarian political theory was more or less gutted by Hume's (1748/1985) critique that it was virtually inconceivable that anything approaching broad consent had been the ground on which any political regime had ever been constructed. His critique is scathing. Sheldon Wolin (1988) partially echoes this view in saying that citizenship is, in fact, a matter of birthright and that consent therefore plays no role in justifying any citizen's membership in the community. Wolin thinks that the contract doctrine is not only ahistorical in Hume's sense that there may never have been a consensual creation of government but even more in the sense that the idea of a contracting moment is to obliterate history and to start from scratch, as he says John Rawls (1971/1999) does in his theory of justice (Wolin 1988, 18).

"Our (or the) social contract" is now a term of ordinary discourse and its meaning has been substantially degraded. For example, people may be said to violate the social contract when they litter or they fail to vote. The supposed violators might ask just where is the contract that lays out such detailed requirements on behavior. Academic successors to the contractarian tradition now speak of contractualism, by which they mean reasonable agreement (Barry 1995; see further Hardin 1998). In this conception, agreement actually drops out and is replaced by a rationalist account of what constitutes reasonable. Some contract. This is, of course, not very different from Rawls's own move to establish principles of justice behind the veil of ignorance, where there is in fact *only one representative person, who must therefore come to a rationalist view of what those principles must be* (Rawls 1971/1999, 139/120)—not an agreed view in the sense in which parties to a contract might agree on the terms of their exchange. As has been true more generally in academic philosophy, moral philosophy dominates political philosophy and, indeed, the main advocate of reasonable agreement applies the notion primarily to moral theory (Scanlon 1999, ch. 5; 1982, 115 n.).

It is often supposed that an attraction of contractarian thinking is that it rests on procedures that are morally compelling, procedures that themselves might be consensual independently of the results that follow from using them. Actual proponents of the modern versions of such theory have excluded procedures almost entirely, so that there is only a rationalist moral principle, usually not stated, to support any contract. The slow alteration of the meaning of contract into something utterly contrary to contract finally leaves us with no grounding for popular government—unless one wishes merely to assert, as a deontological moral principle, that the rationalist project or its conclusion is morally right. Strangely, however, the project so far has no reasonably agreed upon conclusion. What agreements it reaches are largely metatheoretical.

There are many forerunners of the basic idea of contractarian theory, which is that the people somehow consent to their rulers. The conflict between bottom-up consent and top-down rule played out over many centuries. Francis Oakley (1983, 316) says that "theories of consent pertaining now to legitimacy rather than legality, authority rather than power" began to enter the debates. Marsilius of Padua (1342/1956) was probably the leading figure with his *Defensor Pacis*, which was understandably condemned by the pope, whose position of primacy was, Marsilius says, only a historical accident and not a God-given status (ii, ch. 18). Marsilius argues that government should follow from election, not from hereditary succession. The purpose of government is to maintain the peace so that citizens may have good lives; and the government must be subject to law.

It is ironic that Thomas Hobbes's (1651/1994, 26.6 and 29.9) vision of law as requiring a supreme power—a sovereign that is not subject to the civil laws, that is above the law—survives until our own day despite this attack from Marsilius. Indeed, it breathes fire in the positive law theory of Jeremy Bentham (1789/1970), John Austin (1832/1954), Hans Kelsen (1934/1967), and H. L. A. Hart (1961/1994). Their approach is definitionalist. Bentham, who could be called the greatest definitionalist, and his successors start by—and often never get beyond—*defining* law or a legal system, *the concept of law*. Their claim for a sovereign then seemingly becomes part of the definition of a legal system despite the fact that modern legal systems clearly do not work that way.

Hume, the great empiricist and even pragmatist, writing four centuries after Marsilius, would have to say that this move of the positive law theorists is contrary to sense because we first have to know how such a system can be made to work. Ought implies can, and if an apparently wonderful rationalist system, with a sovereign dictating all the rules, cannot work, we should take no interest in it. It is pointless to define law without connecting it to the human world it is to govern. From very different perspectives, Marsilius and Hume both dismiss the hierarchy that Hobbes and his followers insist on as though it were part of the nature of law and order. As Hume says, a political ruler survives in office through opinion, which is the convention of acquiescence by various officers of the law (Hume 1741/1985, 32–3). That is to say, there must be others in the government who are mobilized by their loyalty or at least acquiescence before the ruler. Hence, the ruler is not all-powerful—and could not possibly be.

Hobbes is somewhat misfit with the definitionalists because he establishes his case with arguments from the sociological possibilities of law and order. Unfortunately, his social science is inadequate to his task and he concludes, for reasons of his nascent political sociology, that we must have an all-powerful sovereign not subject to legal or other restraints. With a far richer social scientific understanding of these issues, Hume supposes that we can constrain government through conventions that are analogous to the conventions that government uses to mobilize its own power to control us (Hardin forthcoming, ch. 4). This suggests that social order is the result of a dual convention on the part of the governors and on the part of the obedient citizens. But if such a convention works, then it can also work to constrain law givers who can readily be made subject to their own laws in violation of Hobbesian and positive law principles.

Marsilius (1342/1956, ii, ch. 20) opposes the hierarchists' view primarily from normative considerations, although he also plants the seeds of the Hobbesian and Lockean position on individual belief: that individuals must be treated as autonomous judges of scriptural truth because one cannot be forced to believe anything. Our beliefs are not under the control of our wills.[2] Marsilius insists that, when there is disagreement about scriptural meaning, it must be resolved by the whole body of Christians or by representatives they have elected. Protestantism cannot be far away if the hierarchical Church cannot suppress Marsilius and other such independent thinkers. In essence, the claim of the Church and of monarchs almost everywhere is that those at the top of the hierarchy of order are rightfully there and must be obeyed. They must be obeyed because they supposedly have greater wisdom and also of course because they have power.

The doctrine of consent is a full-scale attack on this hierarchist view, especially on its epistemic bases, and it eventually carries the day in Europe and increasingly now in many other parts of the world.[3] Sadly, however, its victory does not turn on its coherence. Collective consent is one of the most perversely incoherent notions in all of political philosophy. In arguments from consent to the legitimacy of a regime, there is a potential fallacy of composition, because, as noted earlier, it is unlikely that all citizens in a real society would consent to the same things in their political regime. The pluralism of any major democratic nation today encompasses groups that are fundamentally hostile to the regime. They generally acquiesce because doing so serves their interest but not because they are fond of or committed to the regime.

They acquiesce in large part because the regime has the power to suppress them if they do not. The acquiescence of most citizens contributes to the government's power, enabling it to use its limited resources against those who acquiesce less readily. This is a weaker claim than Hart's supposition that "if a system of rules is to be imposed by force on any, there must be a sufficient number who accept it voluntarily. Without their voluntary co-operation, thus creating *authority*, the coercive power of government and law cannot be established" (1961/1994, 196/201). This claim seems to be an overstatement, unless acceptance means nothing more than mere acquiescence, which often is enough for the dual coordination that defines a state's power over its citizens.[4] Numerous occupying forces have surely survived through the successful use of coercion without significant support from the occupied societies.

---

[2] Hobbes says that our beliefs are not subject to commands (1651/1994, 26.41). Against enforcing religious belief, Locke (1689/1950, 18) says that "such is the nature of the understanding that it cannot be compelled to the belief of anything by outward force." Locke's claim is dismissed by his contemporary Jonas Proast (1690/1984, 4–15) with the surprisingly more subtle argument that force can be used to get someone to read and consider religious views and thereby to open the possibility that they might change their minds. Proast thinks Locke's concern with the use of compulsion to change one's belief directly is a correct but largely irrelevant consideration. On the other hand, Proast too optimistically supposes that the truth of Christianity must virtually be obvious to anyone who reads in it. The views of a majority of Europeans suggest that he is badly wrong.

[3] Although the Catholic Church remains a few centuries behind broader developments in Europe.

[4] Such a reading would not fit well in what is a discussion of law and morals (Hart 1961/1994, ch. 9). Hart's discussion, however, is highly nuanced and subtle.

Incidentally, note that contemporary social scientists often join with the legal positivists when they insist that we start any enquiry by first defining what we mean by such terms as institution, government, and power. This is analogous to what Austin, Kelsen, and Hart do. They begin with the operationalization of the largest, most complex, most inclusive social concepts in their realm: law and legal system. Against this move, one might imagine Ernst Mach, the physicist and early proponent of positivist operationism in science, starting with the operationalization of nature or matter instead of distance or the atom (see further Hardin 2001, 71–6). Physics would have been stopped dead in its tracks if scientists had been controlled by this impossible vision. Social scientists under the sway of this vision often fly off into grandiose theorizing.

4 CONSEQUENTIALIST LEGITIMACY

In most of the literature on legitimacy, there is at least some allusion to the mutual advantage of government that brings social order. That is the general principle behind Marsilius' judgements of the system of his time. It is also one of two principles that Rawls attempts to square in his theory of justice; Rawls speaks of his citizens as being "mutually disinterested" (1971/1979, 13/12).[5] Mutual advantage is also a deep concern of Hobbes, for whom the order brought by any sovereign, almost no matter how draconian, is better than the disorder in Hobbes's awful state of nature or civil war.[6] But its greatest exponent is Hume, who insists that, psychologically, we approve of government and its actions to the extent we can empathize with their good effects on people, including ourselves. In all of these theorists' accounts, mutual advantage is essentially welfarist. It is not strictly about economic benefits, although these may be and commonly are an important consideration.

Hume states the vision of mutual advantage often. In his summary comparison of justice and various personal virtues and vices, he says of justice that its distinguishing feature is that it serves the mutual advantage, and not merely the utility or interest of particular individuals. The whole scheme "of law and justice is advantageous to the society and to every individual" (Hume 1739–40/2000, 3.3.1.12; see also 1752/1985a, 255). The final phrase, "and to every individual," merely defines "mutual advantage," which is Hume's central motivating social principle. We all want the mutual advantage to be served because we all gain thereby. Brian Barry rightly characterizes Rawls's theory of justice as being a blend of mutual-advantage and egalitarian elements. He attributes to "Rawls as well as Hume the idea that justice represents the terms of

---

[5] The other principle is egalitarianism. And the blending of these two is a matter of fairness through the Difference Principle.

[6] This may often be the only determinate claim one can make for any particular mutual-advantage resolution: that it is better than the world with no resolution.

rational cooperation for mutual advantage under the circumstances of justice" (Barry 1989, 148).

Both Hobbes and Hume suppose that any extant government is likely to be better than what would happen if we try to change the government, because the change is apt to involve a chaotic and destructive period of transition. For them, this is not a conservative reluctance to see change or a mere prejudice in favor of the status quo, but is a genuinely theoretical concern about causal relations. For Hobbes the hostility to changing the form of government would apply to a democratic as well as a draconian monarchical government. The problem is the costs and difficulty of recoordinating from a present regime to a new one. For Hume the problem is recoordinating to create a new convention to replace a present convention.

Hume generally does not make any normative argument in favor of a form of government beyond its serving mutual advantage, which includes the protection of individual liberties and the consequent enabling of economic creativity and progress. What Hume wants in general is explanation of this achievement, not justification. One could make mutual advantage a normative principle, as it is in Rawls's theory of justice. But for Hume and Hobbes mutual advantage is entirely functional in that it motivates action because it satisfies the interests of every one of us to some degree. They could happily accept the view of Marsilius that the most import-ant role of government is the *defensor pacis*, the defender of a peace in which all citizens may prosper.

Hume explicitly argues for mutual advantage not because it is utilitarian but because it is the aggregate implication or version of self-interest. It is a value only in the sense that it gives each of us what we want in comparison to some other state of affairs. It is just self-interest in the sense that I get the improvement in my own state of affairs only through the mutual-advantage move that also makes others better off (Hume 1739–40/2000, 3.3.1.12). I therefore can be motivated for the mutual advantage entirely from my own interests. *If I view the fates of all others with at least mild sympathy and I also see that the improvement in their fates is coupled with improvement in my own, then I have very strong reason to support a mutual-advantage move for all of us.* Moreover, because I know that others will not favor special treatment of me that is not coupled with mutual advantage, I am likely to see any mutual-advantage move as about as good a public choice as I can expect. This does not guarantee my compliance with policies of the regime, but it adds to the likelihood of my compliance, not least by adding to the incentives I have for compliance.

In discussions of these arguments, by far the most common query or challenge is to pose a particular case in which a person is a loser from the application of the law, the rules of property, or some other convention that is justified by an argument from mutual advantage. Such an objection is based on a fundamental misconception. The argument for a mutual-advantage convention is that having the overall system, for example, of law makes us better off than we would have been without the system of law. This is an ex ante argument. The formulation of the commonplace objection is wrong-headed in that it typically supposes a one-off example. To be a credible objection it must be formulated as a whole-cloth rejection of the idea that the chaos of an unordered society would be preferred by some people over a well-ordered society. Ex ante it is virtually inconceivable that this is true. Even a devoted criminal must prefer a society that is well enough organized to produce enough to steal. Outside a productive society, crime definitely does not pay.

What is true, of course, and what might be objectionable, is that any change of current rules or institutions is likely to have losers who would have been better off keeping the old rules or institutions. But if the possibilities for change are themselves part of the old system, this objection does not work either. For example, one can object that replacing the former Soviet system with a developing market economy and an open democracy has produced many losers. That is true—indeed, a large fraction of those over the age of 50 at the time of the initial change must still be losers well over a decade later and must have little hope of ever being winners. But one probably cannot design the institution that would have guaranteed the permanent stability of the prior system, which, as static as it may have been, was inherently subject to endogenous change, such as economic collapse that would have made far more losers.

5 AUTHORITY AND DOMINATION

The largest single literature in the social sciences on legitimacy is possibly that which builds on and contributes to Max Weber's definition of authority as the legitimate use of power. This definition seemingly makes authority a normative term. But it leaves the troublesome problem of how we define legitimacy. Weber comes very close to defining it as consistent with the capacity to stay in power; if we suppose that legitimacy is a normative term, this is an ought-from-is conclusion. In the view of many, consent makes legitimate, as though consent is both a positive and a normative term. This view is from the theorist's stance outside the system. From within the system, Weber argues that citizens' belief in the legitimacy of their government makes compliance with its rule easier, whatever they might mean by the term legitimacy, and their meanings might be highly varied. In any case, consent to government is bound up in submission to government. The actual causal relations in a real society in the age of liberal government are a tangled mess.

Consider the particularly stark set of causal relations implicit in the view that power makes legitimate. Arthur Stinchcombe (1968) straightforwardly defines government legitimacy as a function of power, or rather of the nesting of power in larger and more encompassing units as the challenges to authority become larger and larger. A local criminal might call on the city's Mafia to back him up. The local cop calls on the city's police force for back-up. Eventually, the Mafioso runs out of higher powers before the police do, and the police, in winning this showdown, establish their legitimacy. Although the specifically nested form that the power takes in this account is important, legitimacy is essentially power, and there is no need to invoke or assert normative terms. Here legitimacy is a positive term, as it is when it is applied internally to law. Marsilius wants normative considerations to trump the hierarchy of power in the Church. For Stinchcombe, the story stops at hierarchical power. On his account, in a time when the Mafia dominated Sicilian life with impunity, the government of Sicily was not legitimate and did not have much authority. That of Idi Amin in Uganda was legitimate in Stinchcombe's sense, unless there was some international power to trump his rule. Emotivist popular opinion would presumably reverse these two to say the government of Sicily was legitimate while that of Uganda was illegitimate. It would be easy empirically to establish Stinchcombe's case but hard to craft a compelling notion of legitimacy that would capture the popular view of these two cases.

By cutting out a couple of the causal connections, Stinchcombe gives an account that is descriptively coherent if not normatively compelling. If we try to go much further to investigate the motivations of people, we cannot expect to find a single coherent account of legitimacy and compliance. You may find a present government or one of its major policies legitimate in the sense that you happily consent to it, while I do not consent but only resentfully submit to the government's power to do what it wills with respect to me. To claim much more than this is to assert a fallacy of composition. Each of us, or say John C. Calhoun and Abraham Lincoln, might have and use the same notion of legitimacy, but the objects that make for our judgements differ enough that we, taken as a group, do not have a coherent notion of the legitimacy of our particular government.

There is no coherent, singular collective notion here. Recall the opening remark that, of the triumvirate of compliance, consent, and legitimacy, it is the last of these that is most commonly seen as a normative term. But it is clear that the last of these is severely undercut by the fallacy of composition inherent in associating our individual stances with the kind of collective stance that claims that some government or legal system is legitimate. Legitimacy in this systemic sense is likely to be an emotivist term, not a descriptive term and not a coherent normative term. We can do research on the extent and varieties of consent and compliance in some society. But we will find it much harder even to define a researchable notion of legitimacy for a government unless, out of all the conceptions considered here, our notion is essentially that legitimacy is the preponderance of power, as in Stinchcombe's purely positive conception. Moreover, in Weber's conception of legitimacy, for anyone to say that a regime is legitimate they must be able to say that some large fraction of the populace believe it is legitimate (although, again, their beliefs might have highly varied grounds).

Weber's account appears to be ambiguous. He could be saying that popular belief in a regime's legitimacy makes it legitimate; or he could be saying that what a regime needs in order to maintain social order is the widespread belief in its legitimacy (independently of whether it is legitimate). Weber gives us no clear account of how or why people do come to believe a regime is legitimate. They just do "come to see domination as valid or binding" and this belief becomes an internalized structure or norm[7] that guides further behavior (Swedberg 2005, 148). All of this sounds credible, although Weber does not say how we could establish it as factual. Rather, in his sometimes casual treatment of factual claims, Weber (1922/1978, 213) merely says, "experience shows that in no instance does domination voluntarily limit itself to the appeal to material or affectual or ideal motives... in addition every such system attempts to establish and to cultivate the belief in its legitimacy." Jürgen Habermas (1975/1973, 99) dismisses this assertion as essentially not verifiable: "It is meaningless to probe behind the factual grounds of validity. The fiction that one could do so if necessary... can be comprehended only from a functionalist point of view, that is, by treating validity claims as functionally necessary deceptions."[8]

Weber (1922/1978, 214) invokes a strange logic: "Naturally, the legitimacy of a system of domination may be treated sociologically only as the probability that to a relevant degree the appropriate attitudes will exist, and the corresponding practical conduct ensue... What is important is the fact that in a given case the particular claim to legitimacy is to a significant degree and according to its type treated as 'valid': that this fact confirms the position of the persons claiming authority and that it helps to determine the choice of means of its exercise." That is to say, a regime is legitimate if the populace behave as though it is. More fully, we the populace must think it is legitimate and we must react to it by doing what we think it can legitimately demand from us. Weber turns legitimacy into a systemic concept and he defines it circularly in terms of itself, or at least in terms of our perception of itself. It is legitimate if we believe it is legitimate. If we put this definition into the second place in which "legitimate" occurs, we get an infinitely recursive formula that would be of no use. And yet, because Weber's claim is a sociological and not simply a logical claim, it is not beyond our understanding.

Incidentally, it is important to note that Weber's legitimacy does not strictly depend on consent. You might meaningfully say you do not consent to our government even though you agree that it is legitimate in something like Weber's sense. You could even say you think the regime is heinous but that it is legitimate. Hence, Weber's vision is not a back door entry into normative evaluation as determined by consent. Weber explicitly allows for such a stance. He says, "It is by no means true that every case of submissiveness to persons in positions of power is primarily (or even at all) oriented to this belief [in the regime's legitimacy]." For example, "people may submit from individual weakness and helplessness because there is no acceptable alternative" (Weber (1922/1978, 214). This need not even mean that there is in principle no acceptable alternative. There may be. But it might be unreachable without unbearably high costs of collective action to move us to the better alternative, as in the arguments of Hobbes and Hume opposing rebellion. When southerners in the USA thought the US regime was illegitimate, they paid dearly for trying

---

[7] When Weber speaks of a convention, he typically means what we today would call a norm (Swedberg 2005, 53).

[8] The immediate object of Habermas's critique is Niklas Luhmann, but Weber stands in the background as the original proponent of the view being criticized.

to reject it. Anyone with foresight into the outcome of that conflict might therefore have insisted that the then-current regime was legitimate.

Weber might have cut short the debate between Lon Fuller (1958) and H. L. A. Hart (1958) over the legitimacy of laws such as those against informers in Nazi Germany. Independently of whether those laws were moral, they were legitimate in Weber's sense. That is very close to the position that Hart takes. The central difference is that Weber does not merely argue from the procedural account of how those laws came to be but from the strict legitimacy of the regime that promulgated them, with legitimacy defined psychologically as the beliefs of the populace and the rulers. For domination based on rational grounds, legitimacy rests on "a belief in the legality of enacted rules and the right of those elevated to authority under such rules to issue commands (legal authority)" (Weber 1922/1978, 215). We do not have surveys of citizens in Nazi Germany to tell us what they thought of the regime, but there were referendums in parts of Central Europe in which those people voted in favor of annexing their areas into the German nation. We can also presumably suppose that the regime in Germany was more commonly perceived as legitimate by relevant citizens than was the Nazi occupation government of Czechoslovakia.

Hart's view is not in Weber's sense here psychological. Indeed, Hart seems to judge a legal system from afar or from on high, as though there were a truth of whether a particular system follows his definition, and that truth need not be—and likely is not—known to us the citizens. Moreover, that truth is not one that guides the actual role holders in the legal system, because they need not agree on the system's fit with Hart's (1961/1994) concept of law. In this sense, his "positive" theory of law is perversely idealist. What we the citizens think or believe is much more nearly what Weber supposes. We suppose that, in some meaningful sense, our governors and the officers of our legal system just do have the power to tell us what to do in many contexts. We might even suppose that this is a reasonable fact, but we need not grant any such thing. We may do little more than acquiesce in their rule; and in democracies we might even vote for them despite disliking much of what they are likely to do in office. We have very little choice in the matter.

A purely philosophical analysis of legitimacy is of even less interest to how the real world of politics works than is a purely definitional account of law and a legal system. To understand the role of any notion of legitimacy in the world of real politics requires social science and introspection that is not ordinarily part of the normative philosophical enterprise, although it often probably should be. It requires a grasp of what real people can and might think. Or, often, *it requires assessing what they do even absent any articulate understanding on their part, so that what they say they think may be irrelevant to how they and their system work.* Weber's account is a mess with its confusing logic (or illogic) and its undefended empirical claims. But this may be a saving grace in part, because people and their belief systems are a mess.

Maybe Weber's analysis fits ordinary, messy people whose understandings of their own world are confused, illogical, factually ungrounded, and vague beyond measure. Weber's account is, not least for this reason, more realistic than either the procedural or the consequentialist theories of legitimacy for ongoing, well-established states.

Norms and conventions beyond norms explain a large part of ordinary obedience to established legal systems and states. Indeed, for many people these may explain the entirety of such obedience. We just continue to do what we have more or less always done, and if anyone challenges us by saying that our regime is illegitimate, we will be dismissive rather than analytical in our reply. We will not be prepared to respond if we are challenged to be analytical and precise in our account of the legitimacy of our regime. In the end, we are as circular as Weber: We obey our regime because that's what we do.

6 Concluding Remarks

Those who run the positive and normative senses of legitimacy together often go on to suppose that citizens have a duty to obey the law because, after all, the law is right or good or, in an older and fading tradition, because the populace consented to it.[9] On a Weberian account of domination, no duty follows, although it may be in the interests of virtually all citizens to comply with directives of any government that is competent to enforce its policies. But Weber seems to associate normative claims with his account as, for example, when he writes of "legitimate domination." We can nevertheless take his non-normative claims seriously in their own right without bringing in moral requirements. Habermas (1975/1973, 101–10) also seems to have a normative view in his discussion of "justifying normative-validity claims." In his account, under certain circumstances agreement is right making.

Consider an example. It might be hard to claim legitimacy for some of the successor regimes of Eastern Europe after 1989 on Weber's account or on the consent account, although for most of the citizens of any of these nations, the consequentialist or welfarist account might fit very well. After a couple of decades, the Weberian account might begin to fit and might even displace the welfarist account almost entirely as the generation of those who made the transition is displaced by a younger generation that has no such comparative experience.[10] Hence, claims for legitimacy would shift from potentially normative to merely descriptive. Descriptively, Weber's account must fit virtually every regime that has been in power for a generation or so without civil war. The US regime was therefore not legitimate for southerners in the decade or two after the US Civil War but it was legitimate for northerners from a couple of decades after the beginnings of the US constitutional regime. It continues to be legitimate for virtually everyone in the USA today.

---

[9] Richard Flathman (1993, 528) asserts the contrary: that all other claims for legitimacy have faded and that consent has returned to the fore as the main consideration.

[10] Arguably, no account can entirely omit welfarist considerations because no theory of legitimacy should allow a totally parasitic regime that utterly ignores its populace.

Hobbes says that laws are laws only by sovereign will, "not by virtue of the prescription of time" (Hobbes 1651/1994, 26.9). This is presumably a definitional claim for him, but sociologically it is often false. Age gives legitimacy to laws and to regimes and the authority of laws from the distant past may constrain a government. Indeed, the British government is constrained by distant past conventions that do not even have the formal force of law, that are not even always written down (Marshall 1984). British citizens all attained adulthood after most of those conventions were in place, and citizens expect them to have force, indeed binding force.

It is important to keep very clear that this quasi-Weberian sense of the legitimacy of a regime that has been in place for a generation is a positive, not a normative, conception. It might be true that, say, the US regime is good today, but that is not a relevant consideration for the concept of legitimacy except insofar as its goodness motivates some Americans to defer to it as legitimate. Such deference might enable the regime to govern more easily. As Richard Swedberg (2005, 148; also see 64) says, "To exclusively base a political regime on interests or violence tends to create instability, while the regime becomes stable if it is seen as valid or binding." The larger the fraction of the citizenry who defer to a government, the smaller the effort the government must expend to achieve its policies and programs. This is likely to be true for any conception of legitimacy, including all of those canvassed here.

Hobbes and Hume oppose rebellion or revolution against even a bad regime.[11] If they were party to later concerns with legitimacy, they might even say that bad regimes are generally legitimate up, perhaps, to the point at which rebellion might be justified. Weber could not suppose that every extant regime is legitimate in his sense, and if popular belief is that a regime is not legitimate, he would have to allow for disobedience to it, even to the point of revolution. He might agree with Hobbes that revolution would be too costly to make sense for the current generation. It might be good for later generations that our generation suffers the costs of bringing about a change, but that is not part of Weber's concern with legitimacy.

Although legitimacy in this conception is a positive term, it is nevertheless motivating for citizens. Once the regime or the law has a well-established character, we may begin to expect it to maintain that character and our responses to it might push it along well-established lines. We may even begin to think it is right that it follow those lines, but what is more important causally is that we act in ways that reinforce its character.

In general, piecemeal notions such as legitimacy and consent do not have independent moral status. Their morality depends, case by case, on other considerations and is, in particular, subordinate to more general moral principles and theories. Efforts to make legitimacy a coherent and compelling normative term generally fail, largely for Hume's reason. Many positive facts about the world and our behavior in it do not yield a moral conclusion. We can bring morality with us to analyze our world, but we cannot find it in that world. The only useful conceptions of legitimacy are

---

[11] Although Hume (1752/1985*b*, 506) praises the results of the Glorious Revolution of 1688, which happened a couple of decades before he was born.

grounded in positive facts, including facts of consent and compliance. We may know what it means to say that some action within a system of law or within a government is legitimate. But for us to conclude that the action is good or right, more is needed. If we can further say that the system of law or government in which the action is legitimate is itself good or right, then we can presumably conclude that the action is good or right.

Many writers hold consent or agreement to be a right-making consideration (for example, see Gauthier 1986; Habermas 1975/1973). We should say that consent is itself neither right nor wrong, good nor bad, but if we consent to X, then X has therefore some claim to being right. Consent is not normatively definitive even then, however, because we might consent to do some awful thing, and our consent does not make it right. Legitimacy has a similarly equivocal quality. Moral and political philosophers might therefore be wise to let these terms pass to social scientists, for whom they have positive value as positive terms and for whom it is not necessary that they have specifically normative content. We might normatively judge regimes and policies from our usual moral theories and we are likely to find our moral judgements not well correlated with positive legitimacy.

Political scientists might also want in general to have a notion of legitimacy that predicts the behavior of the populace (as in Rogowski 1974). An emotive account that is likely to be very inarticulate is also likely to be a good fit with popular views. This is, of course, an objective and not a normative claim. An emotive account could apply to the legitimacy of an utterly immoral regime, such as that of Hitler. A partial analog of this issue is in the mass of recent work on so-called trust in government. Almost no one trusts government in the ways that they trust good friends and close relatives. It is to the latter that any coherent account of trust must be directed. Abstracting from that context to supposed trust in government is to move into the emotive realm. For example, shortly after the terrorist attacks of September 2001, Americans professed a much higher level of trust in their government than they had shortly before the attacks. This response can hardly make sense objectively as a response to the trustworthiness of that government, because that was the government that had refused to hear of preparations for terrorist attacks, that told one of its own officers to drop the issue, and that rejected FBI worries about recent immigrants who were learning how to fly but not how to land commercial aircraft.

Trust is a frequently abused term and here it seems to have meant nothing other than the rally-round-the-flag syndrome. Citizens who assert great trust in their government are probably only asserting their strong approval of it or loyalty to it. That can be useful information for our explanations of their behavior, but it has little or none of the appeal of trust in a friend (Hardin 2002, ch. 7). Similarly strong emotive assertions of the legitimacy or rightness of a regime can be very important in enabling the regime to carry out its policies and in explaining some of the behavior of citizens. But an emotive theory is a theory of the psychological nature of moral beliefs or responses; it is not a moral theory. Legitimacy and consent are similarly not moral principles. And their objective content at the popular level is likely to be essentially emotive.

REFERENCES

AUSTIN, J. 1832/1954. *The Province of Jurisprudence Determined.* New York: Noonday.

BARRY, B. 1989. *Theories of Justice.* Berkeley and Los Angeles: University of California Press.

—— 1995. *Justice as Impartiality.* Oxford: Oxford University Press.

BENTHAM, J. 1789/1970. *An Introduction to the Principles of Morals and Legislation,* ed. J. H. Burns and H. L. A. Hart. London: Methuen.

CALHOUN, J. C. 1853/1992. *A Disquisition on Government.* Pp. 3–78 in *Union and Liberty: The Political Philosophy of John C. Calhoun,* ed. R. M. Lence. Indianapolis: Liberty Fund.

CURLEY, E. 1994. Introduction to Hobbes's *Leviathan.* Pp. viii–xlvii in *Leviathan,* by T. Hobbes. Indianapolis: Hackett.

DALY, J. 1979. *Sir Robert Filmer and English Political Thought.* Toronto: University of Toronto Press.

FILMER, R. 1680/1949. *Patriarcha: A Defence of the Natural Power of Kings against the Unnatural Liberty of the People.* In *Patriarcha and Other Political Works of Sir Robert Filmer,* ed. P. Laslett. Oxford: Oxford University Press.

FINNIS, J. 1998. *Aquinas: Moral, Political, and Legal Theory.* Oxford: Oxford University Press.

FLATHMAN, R. E. 1993. Legitimacy. Pp. 527–33 in *A Companion to Contemporary Political Philosophy,* ed. R. E. Goodin and P. Pettit. Oxford: Blackwell.

FULLER, L. L. 1958. Positivism and fidelity to law. *Harvard Law Review,* 71: 630–72.

GAUTHIER, D. 1986. *Morals by Agreement.* Oxford: Oxford University Press.

HABERMAS, J. 1975/1973. *Legitimation Crisis,* trans. T. McCarthy. Boston: Beacon Press.

HARDIN, R. 1990. Rationally justifying political coercion. *Journal of Philosophical Research,* 15: 79–91.

—— 1998. Reasonable agreement: political not normative. Pp. 137–53 in *Impartiality, Neutrality and Justice: Re-reading Brian Barry's* Justice as Impartiality, ed. P. J. Kelly. Edinburgh: Edinburgh University Press.

—— 2001. Law and social order. *Philosophical Issues,* 11: 61–85.

—— 2002. *Trust and Trustworthiness.* New York: Russell Sage Foundation.

—— Forthcoming. *Hume: Political Theorist.* Oxford: Oxford University Press.

HART, H. L. A. 1958. Positivism and the separation of law and morals. *Harvard Law Review,* 71: 593–629.

—— 1961/1994. *The Concept of Law,* 2nd edn. Oxford: Oxford University Press.

HOBBES, T. 1651/1994. *Leviathan,* ed. Edwin Curley. Indianapolis: Hackett.

HUME, D. 1739–40/2000. *A Treatise of Human Nature,* ed. D. F. Norton and M. J. Norton. Oxford: Oxford University Press. Cited in the text by book, part, section, and paragraph numbers.

—— 1741/1985. Of the first principles of government. Pp. 32–6 in *David Hume: Essays Moral, Political, and Literary,* ed. E. F. Miller. Indianapolis: Liberty Classics.

—— 1748/1985. Of the original contract. Pp. 465–87 in *David Hume: Essays Moral, Political, and Literary,* ed. E. F. Miller. Indianapolis: Liberty Classics.

—— 1752/1985a. Of commerce. Pp. 253–67 in *David Hume: Essays Moral, Political, and Literary,* ed. E. F. Miller. Indianapolis: Liberty Classics.

—— 1752/1985b. Of the Protestant succession. Pp. 502–11 in *David Hume: Essays Moral, Political, and Literary,* ed. E. F. Miller. Indianapolis: Liberty Classics.

KELSEN, H. 1934/1967. *Pure Theory of Law.* Berkeley and Los Angeles: University of California Press.

LOCKE, J. 1689/1950. *A Letter Concerning Toleration.* Indianapolis: Bobbs-Merrill.

—— 1690/1988. *Two Treatises of Government*, ed. P. Laslett. Cambridge: Cambridge University Press.

MARSHALL, G. 1984. *Constitutional Conventions: The Rules and Forms of Political Accountability*. Oxford: Oxford University Press.

Marsilius of Padua. 1324/1956. The *Defensor Pacis* [The Defender of Peace], trans. A. Gewirth. New York: Columbia University Press.

OAKLEY, F. 1983. Legitimation by consent: the question of the medieval roots. *Viator*, 14: 303–35.

PROAST, J. 1690/1984. *Letters Concerning Toleration*. New York: Garland.

QUTB, S. 1990. *Milestones* [Ma'aallim Fittareek], trans. A. Z. Hammad. Indianapolis: American Trust Publications.

RAWLS, J. 1971/1999. *A Theory of Justice*. Cambridge, Mass.: Harvard University Press.

ROGOWSKI, R. 1974. *Rational Legitimacy: A Theory of Political Support*. Princeton: Princeton University Press.

SCANLON, T. M. 1982. Contractualism and utilitarianism. Pp. 103–28 in *Utilitarianism and Beyond*, ed. A. Sen and B. Williams. Cambridge: Cambridge University Press.

—— 1999. *What We Owe to Each Other*. Cambridge, Mass.: Harvard University Press.

STINCHCOMBE, A. L. 1968. *Constructing Social Theories*. New York: Harcourt, Brace.

SWEDBERG, R. 2005. *The Max Weber Dictionary: Key Words and Central Concepts*. Stanford, Calif.: Stanford University Press.

WEBER, M. 1922/1978. *Economy and Society: An Outline of Interpretive Sociology*, trans. E. Fischoff et al., 2 vols. Berkeley and Los Angeles: University of California Press.

WOLIN, S. 1988. Contract and birthright. Pp. 12–30 in *Crisis and Innovation: Constitutional Democracy in America*, ed. F. Krinsky. New York: Blackwell.

CHAPTER 11

....

NATIONAL IDENTITY

....

LIAH GREENFELD
JONATHAN EASTWOOD

1 NATIONALISM AND NATIONAL IDENTITY: DEFINITIONAL ISSUES

....

THE study of national identity must begin with a preliminary investigation of the question of identity as such, given that many of the features of an instance of a type are dependent on the nature of the type itself. At the level of the individual, identity can be understood as an aspect of one's cognitive map that concerns the configuration and structure of one's self in relation to the social world. The cognitive map is the image of the social order held by a given social actor, and is differentiated into a variety of subcomponents: images of the broader social order, conscious and semi-conscious expectations of behavioral norms, conceptions of morality and justice, and so forth. Identity is an aspect, rather than a subcomponent, of the cognitive map due to its inextricable connection to most of the components of the cognitive map itself. One's identity is bound up with one's image of the world, one's ethical outlook, and so forth.

There is, for this very reason, a human need for identity that is tightly connected to the human need for order more generally (Shils 1975; Berger and Luckman 1967; Geertz 1977). Human beings are not born with a biologically pre-programmed blueprint for order and must, therefore, construct it themselves. This functional need is satisfied by culture (the aforementioned "cognitive map" is simply a typified, internalized form of the cultural blueprint for social order). Basic human functioning is dependent on each social actor's having a relatively clear, relatively unproblematic conception of self, and one of the primary manifestations of *anomie* (that is, the breakdown of order at the social structural level) at the level of existential experience is the breakdown of the experience of the self.

The identity of an individual has multiple layers, the salience of which varies both between cultures (that is, between its typical experience in multiple cultures) and in the same individual depending on his or her horizons of experience in one culture. Thus, various aspects of one's multilayered identity are cast into relief by one's immediate environment, by conversations, interactions of other sorts, and even potentially by intervention at the biological level (given that identity, rooted in the human brain, is supported by/rests on certain biological structures).

The identity of a typical individual is (like all of individual consciousness, as Durkheim 1965, pp. lvi, 1–10 so capably demonstrated) inextricably bound to that individual's culture: to the intersubjective universe of meaning that he or she inhabits. Culture itself, a fundamentally symbolic emergent phenomenon best conceived of as a process, is by its very nature constantly undergoing self-transformation. This constant self-transformation is manifested, for obvious reasons, not only in culture's externalized symbolic forms but also in the conscious experience (and thus the lived identity) of individuals. Yet when we speak of identities, we mean the publicly manufactured common troughs from which individual identity is constructed, and our goal here is not to examine national identity at the psychological level.

For heuristic purposes identity can be divided into types in a different way. Different identities have different orientations towards key spheres or modes of human activity. Thus, we can speak of "political identity" as a subtype of identity that is oriented towards politics: that is, political identity is one's identity in relation to the distribution of power (or the structure of relationships of domination) in a given community. It is to be stressed that no *central* form of identity can be a political identity alone. Central identity is one which orients one's behavior in all spheres of one's activity, underlying and directing the dictates of more specific identities, such as sexual identity, professional identity, one's identity as a parent, and so forth. For example, the behavior of an American woman would differ from the behavior of a woman "in general" (which, in fact, is impossible to postulate), which would be different from the behavior of a medieval Christian woman. The same is true of an American socialist and a Russian socialist identity (with the difference deriving from the difference in national identity). National identity, as will be shown below, is indeed a political identity but it is not limited to this.

While generalizations about given cultural moments always obscure some of the rich detail of the process itself, it is nevertheless possible to mark out distinguishing features of different moments in the cultural process which correspond to the main ways in which that process constitutes the central identities of its participants. Thus, one can speak of certain cultures as being essentially "religious," and one of the principal factors in making such a determination is the nature of the typical identity in such a society. An essentially religious society is one whose common "world-image" (to use Weber's term) is based on the conception of there being some other, "transcendental" world which is somehow superior to or otherwise more important or fundamental than this one (that is, than the "empirical" world conceived of as lacking independent meaning, "mundane" or "earthly"). This transcendental world need not be imagined as a particular place—like the notion of heaven in the Christian world—and indeed cultural configurations like Buddhism that do not necessarily conceive of the transcendental in spatial terms are just as "religious" by this definition as any other. A religious identity—which is the central form of identity in any essentially religious culture—is one somehow linked with or oriented towards this other, transcendental world. This linkage may take the form of the medieval Christian who regarded himself as being placed on earth in a brief preliminary "test" of sorts with consequences for his fate in the other world, for the Hindu whose expected path of multiple reincarnation is aimed towards the achievement of Nir-vana, or the Buddhist who aims at the dissolution of the self through ritualized activity and meditation. One's self-understanding, in all of these contexts, is essentially tied to life strategies oriented toward this other world.

National identity is not religious identity (just as national culture is not religious culture) and as we will see national identity inverts the central characteristic of religious identity just discussed: national identity is an identity of this, empirical, literally earthly world.

What is distinctive about national identity? First, it is connected, like all identities, to a specific "world-image," in this case to the "national" image of the world. This image of the world has three principal characteristics that set it off from the images of the world (and corresponding identities) that preceded it: first, as noted above, it is essentially secular. It is focused on this empirical world and presents it as ultimately meaningful: for it, it is empirically, sensually experienced human life that matters most. As the national image of the world extends itself over time, claims that the concerns of "this world" should be made subservient to another become more and more marginalized, even among many ostensibly religious persons. The second critical characteristic of the national image of the world is that it represents the human world as divided into concrete communities, coextensive with the mass of the population or "the people," which are themselves imagined (in ideal form anyway) as being fundamentally unstratified. In short, the national image of the world is an egalitarian image of the world. National identity is inseparably bound to the notion that all of one's co-nationals are *in some meaningful sense* equal to oneself. The final definitive characteristic of national identity is the related notion of popular sover-eignty. The national image of the world is one for which the legitimate bases of political authority lie in the nation—or people—itself. For this reason (as well as the second), national society is the source or cultural blueprint of modern forms of democracy (in both Tocqueville's sense of the word and in the sense that it is used in contemporary parlance). Each of these three definitive characteristics of national identity and the national image of the world are related in ways that should strike the reader as intuitively apparent.[1]

---

[1] For a more detailed discussion of this definition see Greenfeld (1992).

Nationalism (the form of culture characterized by national identity's salience) is the most fundamental image of the social order in modernity and as such represents the specific form of modern social consciousness and can be treated as a cultural "blueprint" for various features of social and political organization in the modern world. This does not mean, of course, that we embrace a naive constructivist or an idealist position: there is no suggestion here, as will be seen below, that nationalism emerges independent of pre-existing structural patterns in society or that it independently transforms social and political structures without those structures being in some way problematized by a variety of conditions or factors. This is not the place to recount the multitude of cultural, economic, social, and political implications of nationalism and national identity (which include, among other things, a rationalized system of law, and, in most nationalisms, an economy oriented towards sustained growth[2]) but two principal implications—one pertaining to the social structure and one pertaining to the character of political institutions—call for some consideration here.

The fundamental social implication of nationalism is an open system of social stratification (that is, a status system in which upward and downward social mobility is possible and even encouraged). This means that national identity is, as has been noted above, one for which the members of the association in question are understood to be in some crucially important sense equal. As will be seen in the section below, the precise respect in which members of the nation are considered equal varies from nation to nation, from type to type. Yet the very presumption of such base-level equality implies open stratification. Another way to put this is to say that national identity is linked to a meritocratic understanding of the social order.

Scholars have long noted the characteristically high rates of social mobility in modern societies, yet the realization that this was essentially linked to nationalism is a relatively recent one (and is by no means even now the consensus among theorists of nationalism). It was long assumed—given the predominant, structuralist philosophy of social science that has reigned, with notable exceptions, since the institutionalization of sociology and political science—that the rise of open stratification could simply be explained as a function of the immersion of occupational structures in capitalist markets. We do not dispute the relevance or significance of capitalism in this connection, only the suggestions that (a) it is natural and (b) it has acted on the system of stratification directly and without the influence of any ideational or cultural forces and should therefore be considered the primary cause. Capitalism would, of course, be strained by a closed system of stratification within which men and women of talent were not free to pursue the economic ends that they saw fit, and the granting of positions of economic significance or responsibility on the bases of hereditary right is a formula for poor economic performance and ultimately failure. It is thus probably correct that the rise of capitalism contributed to the opening of stratification and it would be folly to deny that the dynamics of the capitalist economy have an enormous impact on the patterns by which individuals move up and down in the social hierarchy.

[2] See Greenfeld (2001*b*).

Yet it was the notion that the social order was composed of equal individuals and the corresponding idea that status was to be achieved and not assigned at birth that was ultimately responsible for the breakdown of the society of orders and, more important for our purposes, it is this conception of the social order that underlies and maintains open stratification. A radical decline in the consensus view with regard to the legitimacy of open stratification would have an enormous impact. Open stratification, so closely linked with national identity, is itself responsible for many of the crucial features of modern social and political life, particularly because it is the main structural determinant of (or, alternatively, is best considered itself a form of) *anomie*.[3]

The very fact that nationalism perpetuates and in a sense institutionalizes anomie due to its clear prescription for an open system of stratification means that national identity is tightly bound to several notable experiential characteristics of modern life. First, it is closely connected with the pre-eminent place that *ambition* and *envy* hold in the modern emotional repertoire, and indeed is clearly a significant element in the rise of all cultural formations—such as the modern novel—that correspond to this. Open stratification also sets the stage for characteristically modern bases for and expressions of political discontent. Expectations are consistently raised and, due to the meritocratic understanding of the social order that is explicitly prescribed by most nationalisms, their frustration is in some cases politically incendiary.[4]

The primary and fundamental political implication of nationalism and national identity is the state: that is, nationalism implies state-centered politics. At first glance this might seem an unduly radical claim. Have there not been states ever since the point at which agriculture was sufficiently developed to allow for the maintenance of a non-laboring political class? Or did we not arrive at the state the very moment when medieval and early modern kings wrested control from the nobility and established themselves as truly *sovereign*? Were there not patrimonial states, etc.?

Many commentators uncritically accept Max Weber's seeming definition of the state as the central, territorially based political institution that holds a monopoly on the legitimate use of force, relying on comments he made in "Politics as a vocation" which seem to limit his definition of the state to this quality. Weber's method of definition in the passage from which this interpretation is drawn departs from his standard practice. Normally, Weber attempts (as do his consistent followers) to define a given institution in relation to the central human propensity that it serves. That is, the institution is defined in relation to the end that it seeks or towards the satisfaction of which it is oriented. Weberian sociologists of science, such as Robert Merton and Joseph Ben-David, focused on the institution of science in just this way, as the structured activity oriented to the satisfaction of the curiosity of certain individuals about the empirical world, following on a number of comments Weber makes in "Science as a vocation" (Weber 1958; Ben-David 1971; Merton 1938).

---

[3] See Durkheim (1984, 1979).

[4] For a more detailed discussion of these issues see Greenfeld (forthcoming). See also Greenfeld and Eastwood (2005).

The state, however, Weber here says cannot be defined in relation to the ends it seeks, presumably because it is purely instrumental. Power itself is not an end (recall that power is just the probability that a given actor will achieve his or her ends). Thus Weber defines the state by the means at its disposal, and its distinctive means is the use of legitimate violence.

Yet a consideration of other passages in his work generally accorded less attention yields the realization that the most important characteristic of the state is its *impersonality*, that is, the fact that it is entirely independent for its existence and legitimacy of the individuals who staff and run it, including the head of state, who holds an *office*.[5] This is the feature that most clearly distinguishes the political institution we know as the state from a governmental institution similar to the one at the head of which stood Louis XIV. As Weber wrote in a footnote in "Basic sociological terms," "the concept of the state has only in modern times reached its full development" and therefore

it is best to define it in terms appropriate to the modern type of state, but at the same time, in terms which abstract from the values of the present day, since these are particularly subject to change. The primary formal characteristics of the modern state are as follows: It possesses an administrative and legal order subject to change by legislation, to which the organized activities of the administrative staff, which are also controlled by regulations, are oriented. This system of order claims binding authority, not only over the members of the state, the citizens, most of whom have obtained membership by birth, but also to a very large extent over all action taking place in the area of its jurisdiction. It is thus a compulsory organization with a territorial basis. Furthermore, today, the use of force is regarded as legitimate only so far as it is either permitted by the state or prescribed by it. (Weber 1968, 56)

Of particular significance here is the linkage of the administrative and legal order in question to *legislation*, and the fact that, by this definition, *all* of the state's administrators are subject to its regulations: none stand above or outside of them. At first glance this very impersonality seems independent of nationalism, but it is, in fact, a function of nationalism's principle of popular sovereignty, since the ultimate source of political authority is the imagined will of the nation itself, and since, in a national society, the leaders rule (whether or not this is institutionalized in a formal-democratic way) in the name of and by the mandate of the people.[6] In short, impersonality means in actual practice the delegation of authority by the holder of sovereignty (the nation) and therefore *representation* of one form or another. Thus we can understand why the only form of monarchy compatible with national identity historically has been the constitutional monarchy.

---

[5] We do not mean to define the state solely in terms of its impersonality: this is only one of the central, distinguishing characteristics (i.e. the state is not defined simply as an impersonal political structure, since myriad impersonal political structures that clearly are not states could be listed). The state does, indeed, as Weber observed, exercise a monopoly on the legitimate use of force in a given territory.

[6] For an extended discussion of nationalism's relationship with the state see Greenfeld (1996).

2 HISTORICAL EXPLANATIONS FOR THE RISE OF NATIONALISM

There has been nothing approaching consensus among historians of nationalism about the causes of the emergence of national identity (which is not surprising since they have disagreed on the definition of the *explanandum*). Perhaps the most fundamental disagreement is between approaches that we might call sociological structuralism and cultural constructivism. The question of the nature of nationalism and national identity (i.e., how these terms are defined) is tightly bound up with the question of the causes of the emergence of these phenomena which, in turn, cannot truly be separated from the questions of when nationalism and national identity emerged. Anthony Smith has conveniently provided a map of the terrain of scholarship on the subject, suggesting that theories of nationalism's emergence can be understood as falling under three paradigms: primordialism (nationalism has always been with us and, for the most radical primordialists in evolutionary psychology, is biologically hardwired into us), perennialism (which seemingly holds that nationalism is not biologically based and therefore an eternal part of our nature but that it has nevertheless been with us in many forms for many centuries), and modernism (which, of course, holds that nationalism is a modern phenomenon, though "modernist" theorists do not agree about the dating or even the basic nature of modernity) (Smith 1986, 7–12).

From the perspective of evolutionary psychology, nationalism really requires no explanation whatsoever. It is indistinguishable from any sense of territorial or instinctual group feeling that might be found in any type of society (including animal societies), essentially similar to the emotive bases of tribal social solidarity. To the extent that an explanation is offered by such theorists, it falls under the category of armchair evolutionary theorizing: nationalism as understood in this way must have been evolutionarily selected precisely because it enhanced the reproductive success of those humans who had such feelings. This explanation is essentially similar to the way that Richard Dawkins (1976) and others have attempted to explain altruism. This approach has found very few adherents in comparative politics research and indeed it seems hard to imagine it making major contributions to our understanding of nationalism in today's world, if ever. Less biologically-based versions of primordialism (indeed, more influential in the field of comparative politics) can be found as well, such as in the work of Walker Connor (1994).

As noted above, a related set of views, labeled "perennialism" by Anthony Smith, seem to differ only as a matter of degree from primordialism. Perennialism, according to Smith, is the view that "the units and sentiments found in the modern world are simply larger and more effective versions of similar units and sentiments traceable in much earlier periods of human history; and that, given the characteristics of human beings, their propensity to kinship and group belonging and their need for cultural symbolism for communication and meaning, we should expect nations and nationalism to be perennial and, perhaps universal" though not necessarily "natural" (Smith 1986, 12). For some, it is hard to see precisely what separates perennialism from primordialism, or, rather, the difference seems to be merely a matter of degree.

The majority of scholars of nationalism, however, have been "modernists," and the majority of these have attempted to explain the rise of nationalism through one or another form of structuralism. The first, and simplest, version of the structuralist explanation for the rise of nationalism is that nationalism is to be understood in terms of the functions it served in relation to the capitalist world economy. Thus, some scholars have argued that nationalism (here generally not defined—and certainly never defined as in this chapter—or understood simply as a variety of group sentiment or even cultural chauvinism) arose in order to cause certain social actors to behave in certain ways necessary for the extension and world dominion of capitalism. For example, classical Marxist theory understands nationalism to serve the basic functional need of dividing the proletariat, thus delaying the possibility of collective class solidarity until the moment when productive forces (and the "pauperization" and "immiseration" of the working class) have developed sufficiently for revolution to take place.[7] Other scholars have claimed (in circular fashion) that national sentiment is functional in relation to the emergence of national markets and/or for the creation of national industries. Thus for these scholars the emergence, development, and ongoing maintenance of nationalism and national identity are best *explained* by these allegedly served functions. It should be stressed that not all champions of these views consider themselves to be Marxists, and that they may disagree with Marx about many other issues, but the fact remains that this conception of national identity and its historical origins owes to Marx its greatest debt. For example, Eric Hobsbawm, a self-proclaimed Marxist, offers an account remarkably similar to that provided by Ernest Gellner, who did not identify himself in such terms.[8]

The second major version of structuralist theories of nationalism is found in the group of those which understand nationalism's emergence not directly in relation to capitalism but in relation to the state. For these theorists, nationalism was seen by statesmen of the eighteenth and nineteenth centuries as a suitable basis for social solidarity and they deliberately (for some theorists this process is more conscious

---

[7] It is, presumably, for this reason that "the struggle of the proletariat with the bourgeoisie is at first a national struggle" since "the proletariat of each country must, of course, first of all settle matters with its own bourgeoisie." One of the two main ways in which Marx distinguishes the Communist Party from other left-wing parties of the time is that "they point out and bring to the front the common interests of the entire proletariat, independently of all nationality" (Marx 1978, 482–4). Alternatively, Marx famously wrote of the obsolescence of nationalism. See Marx (1978, 476–77). It is at least in part to deal with this "anomaly for Marxist theory" that Benedict Anderson wrote *Imagined Communities*. See Anderson (1991, 3).

[8] The similarities in their accounts are striking, and have been explicitly noted by Hobsbawm. First, he accepts and employs Gellner's definition of nationalism and then goes on to proclaim that "If I have a major criticism of Gellner's work it is that his preferred perspective of modernization from above makes it difficult to pay adequate attention to the views from below." In short, the difference between Gellner and Hobsbawm's accounts is fundamentally a matter of perspective or emphasis: both see industrial modernity as nationalism's cause. See Hosbawm (1990, 9–11).

than for others) staked out legitimizing strategies for the state by attempting to foment nationalism. Several things should be noted here. First, the fact that a given social theory focuses on or otherwise takes account of "the state" does not make that theory any less structuralist than those theories which treat cultural phenomena as rising out of capitalist economic development not mediated by a state. This is due to the fact that most of these theorists (though, it should be noted, not all[9]) see the state itself as arising out of capitalist economic processes.[10] Thus for the majority of state-centric nationalism theorists the state only serves to mediate between the forces of capitalist economic development and political identity, a concept which retains a place in a category which owes much to the old Marxist idea of the "superstructure." There is less of a difference between those who "bring the state in" and those who "leave it out" than is ordinarily supposed.

Benedict Anderson's scholarship and the many derivative works to which it has given rise might be taken to constitute a third category. For Anderson, of course, national identity is understood to be distinctive in that a nation is an "imagined community" and one which is imagined to be "sovereign" and evidencing "deep, horizontal comradeship" (Anderson 1991). Given Anderson's stress on the imagined qualities of nationalism (as should be clear from the above discussion, all identities are imagined, even those whose members all encounter each other in face-to-face situations) many interpreters have read his work as a variety of constructivism. Yet there is one independent variable, or depending upon where one looks in his text perhaps two independent variables, in Anderson's explanatory account of the rise of nationalism. The first, and most obvious, is the amalgam of factors which Anderson refers to as "print capitalism," by which he means the spread of communicative media on a mass scale for profit. Anderson argues that not only does print capitalism allow for the possibility of the spread of nationalism, but that it is indeed its fundamental cause: the media produced by print capitalism, through bringing people together communicatively, themselves produce the imagined communities in question (one wonders why it is to be expected, if this is the case, that media would naturally lead to the emergence of communities imagining themselves to be "sovereign," or indeed where the sense of "horizontal comradeship" would come from). In any case it is not hard to see that print capitalism is simply a stage in the development of capitalism itself, and so, viewed from this angle, Anderson's account should be considered a variation on the first category of structuralist theory mentioned above. The other independent variable that appears in Anderson's account in certain passages is at least superficially quite different. In key places, the structures of political-administrative systems are decisive. This is particularly true in his treatment of Latin America, where he argues that the very administrative units of the Spanish

---

[9] John Breuilly, for example, is suspicious of such attempts to ultimately trace nationalism back to economic processes 1994).

[10] For Gellner, for example, nationalism was a product of "an objective need for homogeneity," since "a modern industrial state can only function with a mobile, literate, culturally standardized, interchange-able population." See Gellner (1983, 46).

colonial system created "imagined communities" which quickly became national in character.

An alternative approach looks not to some preordained "first cause" such as capitalist economic development or the state to explain the rise of national identity but instead takes a genuinely Weberian view of the subject. By this we mean neither that it takes Weber's actual view of nationalism,[11] which, though suggestive, was rather limited and perhaps ultimately misleading, nor that, as is so often the pretext for someone's being labeled a "neo-Weberian," that he or she simply discusses some things, like the state, that Weber also discussed. Instead, we mean that we make no a priori determination with respect to causality (indeed we posit multicausality in social life) and we expect to find reciprocal interaction between ideas (like the idea of national identity) and so-called structural features of society. We attempt to understand the emergence and spread of national identity in relation to the consciousness of the individuals who turned to it. What sorts of cognitive problems did these individuals have that were solved by constructing a new image of the social world?

As noted above, status and identity are themselves intricately connected. The status structure can be conceptualized as the skeleton of the cognitive map noted above. The human need for order is, of course, a need for order not just in human society itself but in the very image of the cosmos, but social order is indeed fundamental, and is centrally satisfied by the ascription of status.[12] It is for this reason that disruptions in social structure—specifically in the status hierarchy—coincide with identity problems at the individual level, a hypothesis left unconsidered by Christopher Lasch (1991) in his attempt to explain the rise of a "culture of narcissism," which is, after all, a society plagued by a preoccupation with problematic identity.

Empirical research has strongly indicated that nationalism and national identity are likely to be turned to by social strata in pre-national societies whose old status positions are suddenly problematized. In short, the national image of the world and the identity that accompanies it are likely to be selected by such groups precisely because they seem to resolve status-related problems. The reason that nationalism seems likely to resolve such issues is its egalitarianism: precisely because it clearly stipulates that all national members are equal, it serves as a condemnation of a status situation that the stratum in question experiences as *unjust* (and provides a language for the expression of this sense of injustice).[13] This is not to make any normative

[11] See Weber (1995, 21–5).

[12] The authors do indeed mean to assert that the need for order is "primordial." This view should not be confused with the perspective of "primordialism" within the world of scholarship on nationalism: we take nationalism, like all forms of culture, to be one possible response to this primordial need, and by no means a universal one, as should be clear from other parts of this discussion.

[13] Nationalism is inherently egalitarian, but this does not mean (a) that its egalitarian ideals are everywhere fully realized; (b) that all nationalisms conceive of equality in similar terms (e.g. for some, equality may be conceptualized in terms of equal civil rights, in others, an equal share in the dignity of a "glorious" but authoritarian society); or (c) that nationalism cannot, in turn, be used to foster inequality between members and non-members. What is more, no matter how egalitarian nationalism may be, it cannot do away with stratification and the distribution of power, and nationalism, therefore, provides the legitimizing framework for some level of political inequality in all national societies.

claim about the actual experiences of such groups: to *condemn* those responsible for the plight of the French aristocracy under Louis XIV or of Indian intellectuals under the British Empire is not a social scientific exercise. Instead, the important issue is the *sense* of injustice, which is in each case connected to the unsettling of established hierarchical privileges.

According to this research tradition, nationalism was born precisely in response to such an upsetting of traditional hierarchies. Because nationalism and national identity are ideas, and not "natural" phenomena produced mechanistically in relation to a given level of social development, they were born, and in a single time and place (indeed, though we will never be able to trace it this far, the ideas logically must have been first *imagined* by a single individual, one who surely had no conception of how radically these ideas would transform the world). Nationalism and national identity were born in early sixteenth-century England, and constituted a novel conceptual strategy for dealing with a profound sense of status inconsistency among both the remnants of the old aristocracy and, more important, new social climbers who increasingly filled the bureaucracy and aristocracy of Tudor England in the years following the Wars of the Roses. It should not be forgotten that the self-understanding of the *Society of Orders* was one for which it was entirely unnatural (and probably *wrong*) for such social mobility to take place. To imagine this we must conceptually step outside of our own culture which (being a national culture, which by definition prescribes open stratification) to recall that social mobility and "self-actualization" more generally were not always celebrated and indeed were out and out condemned. It must have been very difficult for the upwardly mobile in Tudor England to make sense out of their experience. The word "nation," which in the context from which it was applied in this cultural moment meant "an elite," when applied to the mass of the population, bestowed upon these individuals a status that accounted for their life experience as upwardly mobile social climbers. It did so precisely through imputing to them a new identity—*national identity*—akin, more or less, to the ennoblement of the entire population (to the extent that this new identity could be translated into the terms of the old world) (Greenfeld 1992).

The development of nationalism and national identity was, for reasons that should by now be clear, uneven, and therefore an account which paints its advance in Europe and elsewhere with broad brushstrokes (i.e. as having proceeded at the same pace across the continent) is certain to be misguided. For a considerable period of time, England remained the *only* society that properly speaking can be said to have possessed *national identity*, though through intercultural contact others encountered the idea and one might find, in the seventeenth century, the occasional French, Spanish, or German "nationalist." More often, however, to the extent that the term "nation" was used in these societies, it retained its traditional meaning as a "community of birth" and, more fundamentally, did not constitute the core identity of its so-called members: in fact, it was entirely peripheral to their self-understanding and, due to its very thinness, could not have been otherwise.

When it did travel to other societies it always entered, as noted above, by way of strata themselves experiencing one or another form of status inconsistency.

In France, this was the aristocracy, which famously had been emasculated by the crown, most notably under Louis XIV (though, for interesting psychological reasons, this became even less bearable when the emasculating monarch was not such a formidable figure). Here, the issue was less a need to justify social mobility than a desire to shore up a rapidly declining status position by any means necessary, even if that meant destroying the old order entirely (Greenfeld 1992). It might at first glance seem paradoxical that individuals whose interests clearly were to shore up their traditional status would turn to such a revolutionary doctrine as nationalism, but this seeming paradox is resolved when one considers just how revolutionary this doctrine was. Novel ideas contain many qualities that are unseen by those who turn to them; one of the reasons why, as Weber and Merton noted, unintended consequences are so notable in the sweep of history.[14] These suffering aristocrats seem to have only seen (a) that the national image of the world was one that rationalized their opposition to absolutist encroachment on their traditional privileges and (b) it *seemed* to offer a new basis for their status insofar as that status could be justified in relation to their service to the nation (and English society, clearly proclaiming itself a nation, seemed to have allowed for a preferable status situation for its elites). The reader knows what became of them.

Similar patterns can be detected in other cases: even those in which the victory of national identity was not always as decisive as it had been in France. Nationalism in Spain seems also to have initially appealed to portions of the aristocracy (along with some members of the socially mobile *letrado* bureaucracy) and in those parts of Latin America where national identity first emerged it was likewise among the old elite families whose traditional status had been called into question by, among other things, the reforming policies of the Spanish Bourbons.[15]

In Germany the case was a bit different, precisely because status inconsistency was generated by different forces and among a different social group, the intellectual class, produced by the explosion of German universities in the eighteenth century and the relative paucity of posts for the graduates of those universities, productive of a form of status inconsistency well captured by the *Bildungsroman*, most notably *Anton Reiser* (Greenfield 1992).

Much of the globe became national only in the twentieth century, and though this is not the place for a recounting of the spread of national identity in that era, the hypothesis that its true importation into each society rested upon a given stratum's experience of status inconsistency is a live one likely to yield fruitful further research. It is worth noting that colonialism played a decisive role in this spread, and for a number of reasons. First, the colonial system produced a variety of carriers of the national idea. Second, colonialism frequently thrust segments of colonial populations into precisely the sort of status inconsistency that made nationalism attractive to those segments.

---

[14] See Merton (1936).   [15] See Eastwood (2006).

3 TYPES OF NATIONALISM AND THEIR POLITICAL IMPLICATIONS

Perhaps the most important contribution that theoretically informed empirical research on nationalism can make to the subfield of comparative politics is the construction of a typological scheme for nationalisms. It is quite obvious that not all instances of national identity are the same, and indeed common and divergent patterns of national identification can be discerned.

Typologies of nationalisms have been with us for some time. Historically, most of these typologies have been dichotomies and attempted to distinguish between so-called "eastern" and "western" nationalisms, the former being most especially those of Russia and Central and Eastern Europe and the latter those of Western Europe and the United States. This typology, so transparently a reflection of the bifurcation of the world that culminated in the Cold War, saw "eastern" nationalisms as having long histories and as being authoritarian or even totalitarian in their politics. "Western" nationalisms, which were largely confined to England and France (and in some cases the United States) were to be preferred. The classical formulation of this account is found in the work of the great historian Hans Kohn, in *The Idea of Nationalism* and in *Nationalism: Its Meaning and History.* As Kohn wrote,

In the Western World, in England and in France, in the Netherlands and in Switzerland, in the United States and in the British dominions, the rise of nationalism was a predominantly political occurrence; it was preceded by the formation of the future national state, or, as in the case of the United States, coincided with it. Outside the Western world, in Central Europe and Eastern Europe and in Asia, nationalism arose not only later, but also generally at a more backward stage of social and political development...nationalism, there, grew in protest against and in conflict with the existing state pattern...Because of the backward state of political and social development, this rising nationalism outside the Western world found its first expression in the cultural field.[16]

Critics have argued that these categories (perhaps precisely because they are not always employed as ideal types) have a tendency to essentialize and reduce actual

---

[16] Kohn (1944, 329). See also the discussion in Smith (1971, 196–8). It goes without saying, of course, that a wide variety of alternative typologies of nationalism not of this sort have been with us since long before even Kohn's work. Max Sylvius Handman, in 1921 (another era, like the 1990s, in which national identity was on everyone's minds), constructed a four-part typology, dividing nationalisms into the following four categories: "oppression-nationalism, irredentism, precaution-nationalism, and prestige-nationalism." In some ways building on this typology, Louis Wirth drew a conceptual map that placed "hegemony nationalism," such as those characteristic of the unification movements in Italy and Germany in the 19th century, characterized by a desire for "continuity of territory, similarity of language, and kinship of culture;" "particularistic nationalism," which "is based upon the secessionist demand of national autonomy;" "marginal nationalism," such as that "characteristic of border territories and populations such as Alsace, Lorraine, Silesia, Schleswig, the Saar and the Rhineland, the Italo-Austrian and Swiss frontier, and similar strategic areas in Europe;" and "the nationalism of minorities" (Wirth 1936). See also Plamenatz (1973). Gellner admits to basically retaining a version of Plamenatz's typology, though he adds a third type: "diaspora nationalism." See Gellner (1983, 101).

national groups to caricatures. Nevertheless, such distinctions have found their way in many forms into more recent theorizing.

The language of "eastern" and "western" nationalisms has largely been discarded, yet we can see that even in Kohn's early work one finds them expressed in new terms: "cultural" nationalisms and "political" nationalisms. So named, of course, this typology forces the analyst who employs it into logical contradiction. All nationalisms and instances of national identity are "cultural" (for precisely the reasons discussed above). Likewise, all are inherently political: that is, they have massive repercussions for the distribution and operation of power in their societies.

This distinction between "cultural" and "political" nationalisms has become widespread. It is particularly notable in the work of John Hutchinson, who, in fact, argues that cultural nationalism is political, lamenting that "little attention has been paid to the role of cultural nationalism in the formation of nations since the eighteenth century."[17] Often times, this distinction is presented as a similar dichotomy between "civic" and "ethnic" nationalisms, "civic" meaning "political" and "ethnic" standing for "cultural."

The authors of this chapter prefer the more recent typology of Liah Greenfeld. In *Nationalism: Five Roads to Modernity*, she argued that a typology of national identities is best constructed along two axes, significantly complicating the above picture. The x axis measures the way in which a given nation imagines its relationship with its members.[18] On one end of the axis, the individualistic pole, a nation is imagined to be nothing more than a collection of discrete individuals. The other end of the axis, the collectivistic pole, designates those nations which exist as reifications of the groups of individuals that make them up. That is, collectivistic nations imagine themselves to be "super-agents" that exist over and above their individual members, collective beings of a certain sort. This latter sort of nationalism can be conceptually difficult to grasp among social scientists who (rightly) have been trained as methodological individualists. Here we yet again see confirmation of Max Weber's declaration that we must attempt to understand social reality in terms of the perceptions of its participants, rather than our own.

The y axis in this typology measures the criteria for membership in the nation. At one pole we find *civic* nationalism, for which membership is coterminous with citizenship (the nation is thus seen as a form of *association* that one can join and from which one can depart). At the other pole we find *ethnic* nationalism, for which membership in the nation is determined by the possession of ascriptive (usually phenotypic) characteristics, most often imagined to be possessed by the nation's members as a result of their genetic inheritance. Such national membership, it should be emphasized, is within its own terms not a matter of choice (though, of course, it is not logically inconsistent for members of civic nations to "choose" to belong to such an ethnic nation as well).

These two axes would seem to yield four theoretically possible types of national identity, but it is important to note that individualistic-ethnic nationalism is logically

---

[17] Hutchinson (1987*a*). See also his (1987*b*).   [18] Greenfeld (1992). See also Greenfeld (2001*a*).

contradictory and therefore rarely if ever found (though we should not assume from the outset that outlying individual social actors will conceive of their own national membership in such terms, given the well-demonstrated human tolerance for unnoticed logical inconsistency). It is a contradiction in terms because individualistic nationalism presupposes the very associational character of the nation found in civic nationalism. In nations imagined as ethnic, the essence of the nation is not in its individual members but in what is common to them (and which lies beyond their control). In nations imagined as civic, in contrast, the essence of the nation is associational, which means individualist conceptions of the nation are possible though not inevitable. Most collectivistic nationalisms are ethnic, for reasons to be discussed below, though there are a fair number of collectivistic and civic nations, including some of the nations of Latin America as well as the paradigmatic case: France.

This typology can be distinguished from the seemingly similar emphasis upon civic and ethnic distinctions in the work of Rogers Brubaker who, in his study of French and German citizenship, essentially repeats the old typology noted above. As Brubaker writes,

If the French understanding of nationhood has been state-centered and assimilationist, the German understanding has been *Volk*-centered and differentialist. Since national feeling developed before the nation-state, the German idea of the nation was not originally political, nor was it linked with the abstract idea of citizenship. This prepolitical German nation, this nation in search of a state, was conceived not as the bearer of universal political values, but as an organic cultural, linguistic, or racial community—as an irreducibly particular *Volksgemeinschaft*. (Brubaker 1992, 1)

It should of course not be missed that Brubaker here falls back into the same "political"/"cultural" categorization scheme. Perhaps more important, his dichotomous typology does not consider the important dimension of the individualistic-collectivistic axis (to be fair, of course, Brubaker does not set out to provide a typological theory of nationalisms as such, but instead relies on such an implicit typology for his study of French and German citizenship).

Finally, it should be noted that these different types do have different political implications. Collectivistic nationalisms (whether civic or ethnic) have a tendency towards authoritarian politics (or, it might be better to say that at the general level collectivistic nationalism is the most common form of potentially authoritarian political culture). This does not mean that ethnic nationalisms are "fated" to give rise to authoritarian politics or that other factors do not apply. It just points to the clear and demonstrable correlation of collectivistic nationalism with authoritarian politics (Greenfeld and Chirot 1994).

Likewise, *ethnic* and collectivistic nationalisms are more conducive to ethnic violence than civic nationalisms of any kind.[19] Again, this is not to suggest that all or even most nations that conceive of themselves in ethnic terms engage in such violence, but that the likelihood of ethnic violence is higher in such cases. This is not

[19] See Greenfeld and Chirot (1994), as well as Chirot (1996), for a detailed discussion of the relationship between ethnic-collectivistic nationalism and various forms of large-scale violence.

just because conceptualizing human differences in ethnic terms is a logical prerequisite for acting on ethnic distinctions, but also because ethnic nationalisms *tend* historically to have been formed in relation to *ressentiment* against the west, conceived here not as a geographic unit but as an idea (thus German ethnic nationalism was formed as an anti-western nationalism).

4 CONCLUSION

According to the perspective outlined here, national identity is *the* central identity in the modern world (just as the nationalism is that world's cultural blueprint), holding a position roughly equivalent to the Christian identity that prevailed in medieval Europe. It implies those features of social and political life that commentators have regarded as central to modernity, most especially the open system of social stratification and the state (understood as an essentially impersonal, representative political institution). National identity's emergence is best understood in relation to macro-level status dynamics, specifically to status inconsistency, though there is no necessary connection between the two variables (that is, in historical terms the development of national identity is only one among many possible responses to status inconsistency). Finally, national identity can be divided into three distinct types (individualistic-civic, collectivistic-civic, and collectivistic-ethnic), which have a variety of implications for comparative politics and which can help to explain specific instances of authoritarianism, inter-ethnic violence, and other phenomena.

This perspective suggests myriad possibilities for future research, of which we will mention two. Some of this is in the area of specific case studies. Despite the massive amount of writing on nationalism in anthropology, history, sociology, and political science in recent years, an astonishing number of cases in virtually all world regions are not fully understood. Much of this has to do with the until-recent hegemony of a sociologically structuralist paradigm for studying nationalism. From the point of view of the authors of the present chapter, while many studies carried out in this paradigm are suggestive and yield fruitful insights, as full-scale explanations of the emergence of nationalism they suffer from the weaknesses they have inherited from their foundational texts. This may be particularly true in the area of postcolonial nationalism studies, where an explicit focus on elite status dynamics can be expected to open doors to useful research.

Another area within comparative politics in which the theoretical perspective presented here might be applied is in the empirical study of the relationship between types of nationalism and democratization practices.[20] Do given types of nationalism

---

[20] We refer here not to democracy in Tocqueville's sense, which is built into nationalism by definition, but instead to formal liberal-democratic political practices typically studied by contemporary social science.

and national identity within certain world regions vary in terms of the receptivity to democratization processes they engender? This could most easily be incorporated in studies coming from what is most often labeled a "political culture approach," and the relative (though by no means total) inattention to types of nationalisms in contemporary studies of political culture should be remedied.

References

ANDERSON, B. 1991. *Imagined Communities: Reflections on the Origins and Spread of Nationalism.* London: Verso.

BEN-DAVID, J. 1971. *The Scientist's Role in Society: A Comparative Study.* Englewood Cliffs, NJ: Prentice-Hall.

BERGER, P., and LUCKMAN, T. 1967. *The Social Construction of Reality: A Treatise in the Sociology of Knowledge.* Garden City, NY: Anchor Books.

BREUILLY, J. 1994. *Nationalism and the State.* Chicago: University of Chicago Press.

BRUBAKER, R. 1992. *Citizenship and Nationalism in France and Germany.* Cambridge, Mass.: Harvard University Press.

CHIROT, D. 1996. *Modern Tyrants.* Princeton: Princeton University Press.

CONNOR, W. 1994. *Ethnonationalism: The Quest for Understanding.* Princeton: Princeton University Press.

DAWKINS, R. 1976. *The Selfish Gene.* New York: Oxford University Press.

DURKHEIM, E. 1965. *Rules of Sociological Method,* trans. S. Solovay and J. Mueller. New York: Free Press.

—— 1979. *Suicide: A Study in Sociology,* trans. J. A. Spaulding and G. Simpson. New York: Free Press.

—— 1984. *The Division of Labor in Society,* trans. W. D. Halls. New York: Free Press.

EASTWOOD, J. (2006). *The Rise of Nationalism in Venezuela.* Gainesville: University Press of Florida.

GEERTZ, C. 1977. Religion as a cultural system. Pp. 87–125 in *The Interpretation of Cultures,* by C. Geertz. New York: Basic Books.

GELLNER, E. 1983. *Nations and Nationalism.* Ithaca, NY: Cornell University Press.

GREENFELD, L. 1992. *Nationalism: Five Roads to Modernity.* Cambridge, Mass.: Harvard University Press.

—— 1996. Nationalism and modernity. *Social Research,* 63 (1): 3–40.

—— 2001*a*. Etymology, definitions, types. Pp. 251–65 in *Encyclopedia of Nationalism,* vol. i, ed. A. Motyl. New York: Academic Press.

—— 2001*b*. *The Spirit of Capitalism: Nationalism and Economic Growth.* Cambridge, Mass.: Harvard University Press.

—— 2005. When the sky is the limit: busyness in contemporary American society. *Social Research,* 72 (2): 315–38.

—— and CHIROT, D. 1994. Nationalism and aggression. *Theory and Society,* 9: 79–130.

—— and EASTWOOD, J. 2005. Nationalism in comparative perspective. Ch. 12 in *Handbook of Political Sociology,* ed. Thomas Janoski et al. New York: Cambridge University Press.

HOBSBAWM, E. 1990. *Nations and Nationalism since 1780: Programme, Myth, Reality.* New York: Cambridge University Press.

HUTCHINSON, J. 1987a. Cultural nationalism, elite mobility, and nation-building: communitarian politics in modern Ireland. *British Journal of Sociology*, 38 (4): 482–501.

—— 1987b. *The Dynamics of Cultural Nationalism: The Gaelic Revival and the Creation of the Irish Nation-State*. Boston: Allen & Unwin.

KOHN, H. 1944. *The Idea of Nationalism*. New York: Macmillan.

LASCH, C. 1991. *The Culture of Narcissism: American Life in an Age of Diminishing Expectations*. New York: W. W. Norton and Company.

MARX, K. 1978. The manifesto of the Communist Party. Pp. 469–500 in *The Marx–Engels Reader*, ed. R. C. Tucker. New York: W. W. Norton.

MERTON, R. K. 1936. The unanticipated consequences of purposive social action. *American Sociological Review*, 1 (6): 894–904.

—— 1938. *Science, Technology, and Society in Seventeenth-Century England*. Bruges: Saint Catherine Press.

PLAMENATZ, J. 1973. Two types of nationalism. Pp. 22–37 in *Nationalism: The Nature and Evolution of an Idea*, ed. E. Kamenka. London: Edward Arnold.

SHILS, E. 1975. Charisma, order, and status. Pp. 256–75 in *Center and Periphery: Essays in Macrosociology*, by E. Shils. Chicago: University of Chicago Press.

SMITH, A. 1971. *Theories of Nationalism*. London: Duckworth.

—— 1986. *The Ethnic Origins of Nations*. Cambridge: Blackwell.

WEBER, M. 1958. Science as a vocation. Pp. 129–56 in *From Max Weber*. Oxford: Oxford University Press.

—— 1968. Basic sociological terms. Pp. 3–26 in *Economy and Society*, by M. Weber, vol. i. Berkeley and Los Angeles: University of California Press.

—— 1995. The nation. Pp. 21–6 in *Nationalism*, ed. J. Hutchinson and A. D. Smith. New York: Oxford University Press.

WIRTH, L. 1936. Types of nationalism. *American Journal of Sociology*, 41 (6): 723–37.

C H A P T E R   1 2

....

ETHNICITY AND ETHNIC CONFLICT

....

ASHUTOSH VARSHNEY

"UNTIL recently," wrote Donald Horowitz in 1985, "the field of ethnic conflict has been a backwater of the social sciences."[1] This statement is to be taken seriously. Horowitz's *Ethnic Groups in Conflict* was a seminal text. For the first time in scholarly history, a book on ethnic conflict covered a whole variety of topics, ranging from concepts and definitions to those spheres of institutional politics (party politics, military politics, affirmative action) in which the power of ethnicity had become obvious and could no longer be ignored. Some important social science arguments had emerged earlier, especially on the relationship between ethnicity and nation building,[2] ethnicity and modernity,[3] ethnicity and consociational democracy (Lijphart 1969; 1977), and migration and ethnic conflict (Weiner 1978). But each of these works covered a specific problem at hand. *Ethnic Groups in Conflict* covered a wide array of topics under the umbrella of ethnicity, becoming thereby the founding text of the field.[4]

Over two decades have passed since then. There has been such an explosion of research on ethnicity and ethnic conflict that the field can no longer be called a "backwater of the social sciences." Especially since the end of the Cold War, the rise of ethnicity has coincided with the weakening of the customary left–right ideological

---

[1] As stated in the introductory chapter of Horowitz (1985, 13).

[2] For example, Brass (1974); Connor (1972); Geertz (1963); Shils (1957); Smith (1979).

[3] For example, Rudolph and Rudolph (1968); and Deutsch (1966).

[4] For whatever it is worth, it may be noted that according to "Google scholar", as of February 1, 2007, Horowitz's *Ethnic Groups in Conflict* had been cited 807 times. Some works on nationalism have been cited more, but none more on ethnicity or ethnic conflict.

axis in politics the world over, both in the developed and developing world. As a research field, too, ethnicity has become a growth industry, straddling a variety of disciplines, topics, and methods, and attracting a large number of scholars.

But have we made progress? And if so, in what ways? In a widely read evaluation of the field, published in 1998, Brubaker and Laitin were negative about the progress made:

Notwithstanding the increasing scholarly interest in ethnic and nationalist violence, there is no clearly demarcated field of social scientific inquiry addressing the subject, no well-defined body of literature, no agreed-upon set of key questions or problems. It is not simply that there is no agreement on how things are to be explained; more fundamentally, there is no agreement on what is to be explained, or whether there is a unitary phenomenon (or a coherently related body of phenomena) to be explained. Rather than confronting competing theories or explanations, we confront alternative ways of posing questions, alternative approaches to or "takes" on ethnic and nationalist violence, alternative ways of conceptualizing the phenomenon, and situating it in the context of wider theoretical debates.[5]

Two things should be noted about this evaluation. First, it relates only to ethnic and nationalist violence, not to the whole field of ethnicity. The latter term now covers topics as varying as ethnic identity formation, ethnic movements and protests, ethnic voting and ethnic parties, ethnic heterogeneity and allocation of public goods, ethnic diversity and economic growth rates, and ethnic riots, pogroms, and civil wars. No essay can cover all of these topics adequately. I will confine myself to only two topics: ethnic identity and ethnic conflict. I will distinguish them especially from national identity and nationalism on the one hand, and civil wars on the other. These latter topics are covered elsewhere in this volume. I will use arguments about nationalism and civil wars only to the extent that they clarify my analytic overview of the literature on ethnic identity and conflict.

Second, what Brubaker and Laitin find troubling may, in part, be viewed as a reflection of the field's age. As King, Keohane, and Verba (1994) argued, the younger fields are like a double-edged sword. Typically, they do not have a body of theory that most scholars agree with, but the returns to entry may be great. In the established fields, strong theory exists and progress is typically marginal. In younger fields, big theoretical strides can be made.

Has the field made great strides since Brubaker and Laitin wrote their evaluation? I argue below that progress has been substantial. I also argue that wide acceptance of two concepts—mechanisms and variations—has driven the evolution of research, especially in the last ten years.

In earlier times, scholars often used to leave theory building to a link, or affinity, between structural conditions and the rise of ethnic conflict or nationalism. Gellner (1983) is the most illustrative, and well-known, example of this tendency. Gellner essentially theorized that the rise of the industrial age required nationalism, as linguistic standardization became necessary for communication between citizens and the rural masses left their village particularities behind, moving to unknown

---

[5] This essay is reproduced as Brubaker and Laitin (2004), where the section I have cited is on p. 92.

cities in search of industrial employment. Given the social science norms of the 1990s, a critique was easy to launch. The fact that industrialization *required* nationalism did not mean that it would happen. Why should need create its own fulfillment? At the very least, we need an account of the organizations, movements, or leaders that would undertake the task of converting objective needs into actual outcomes.

The idea of variance, similarly, has made advances possible. Theorizing about ethnic violence used to be based on establishing commonalities across the many cases of violence (or sometimes based on an in-depth case study or two).[6] By the mid-1990s, following the popularity of King, Keohane, and Verba (1994), this came to be called "selection bias," and deemed inadmissible for theory construction.

Selection on the dependent variable, it was later recognized, was not entirely without its uses. It could, for example, knock down an existing theory, if the generalizations based on similar cases led to an argument opposed to the existing theoretical orthodoxy. But in and of its own, it was not enough to generate a new valid theory.[7] Outcome variation was a better principle to follow for theory construction. Most research in the field has followed this principle over the last decade.

Despite these advances, Brubaker and Laitin are right in one sense. Cumulation has been quite slow. Very few theories have been fully knocked over. A more rapid "creative destruction" is likely to take place in the future, especially because testing has become a norm in the field.

Existing arguments about ethnic identity and/or ethnic conflict can be divided up into five traditions of enquiry: essentialism, instrumentalism, constructivism, institutionalism, and realism. There are theories within each tradition. I will concentrate on the first four traditions in this chapter, *concentrating on the core idea of each tradition and how it has evolved over time.*

I will leave out realism. Brought in from the field of international relations, realism is driven by the concept of security dilemma. Realists argue that when an existing state collapses, relations between ethnic groups begin to resemble those between states in the international system, the difference between defensive and offensive ethnic mobilization disappears, and neighbors kill neighbors to ensure that they are not possibly killed in the future. Such situations are more applicable to civil wars, excluded from the purview of this essay, and discussed elsewhere in this volume.

Section 1 is conceptual. Given the number of terms moving imprecisely about in the field, clarity about what we mean by the various terms is necessary for constructing a clear analytic domain. Section 2 surveys explanations provided in the four traditions of enquiry, analyzes the inadequacies or merits of arguments within each tradition, and reviews the evolution of arguments. Section 3 presents conclusions.

---

[6] For example, the arguments about conflict in Horowitz (1985) were based on the commonalities principle. In his more recent work, Horowitz has taken note of variance and dealt with it. See Horowitz (2001, ch. 12).

[7] See Varshney (2006) and Laitin (2006). It should also be noted that the search for commonalities is quite valid if one is identifying the characteristics of the phenomenon or problem at hand.

1 Concepts

1.1 What is Ethnicity?

Following Horowitz (1985), ethnicity as a term designates a sense of collective belonging, which could be based on common descent, language, history, culture, race, or religion (or some combination of these). Some would like to separate religion from this list, letting ethnicity incorporate the other attributes. From the viewpoint of political identities and group solidarity, this separation is a semantic quibble. It becomes critical, however, when ethnicity and religion clash (East and West Pakistan before 1971, Kashmiri Hindus and Muslims, Irish Protestants and Catholics, black and white American Christians).[8]

How is a nation different from an ethnic group? An ethnic group may do without a state of its own; a nation implies bringing ethnicity and statehood together. Nationalism therefore becomes a principle that "the political and the national unit should be congruent" (Gellner 1983, 1). This congruence may be satisfied in a federal arrangement, or may head for nothing short of sovereignty.

In official as opposed to academic terminology, another term "nationality" is also used, particularly in the former Soviet bloc. In this three-tiered classification, a nation is a group with a political and territorial home; a nationality is a large ethnic group without such a home (but with cultural rights pertaining to language and sometimes religion); and an ethnic group is a smaller collectivity, different from a nationality but not large enough to be called a nationality. In the post-1945 Yugoslavia, Croats, Macedonians, Serbs, Slovenes, and Montenegrins were called nations; Albanians, Hungarians, Bulgarians were nationalities; and Austrians, Greeks, Jews, Germans, and Poles were "other nationalities and ethnic groups." In the 1971 constitution, Muslims of Yugoslavia were promoted from a nationality to a nation.

For a transition from an ethnic group to nationhood, territorial concentration remains central. Dispersed ethnic groups typically demand affirmative action (preference in jobs, education, political representation) and protection of language, religion, and culture. National demands for sovereignty or federalism normally come from territorially concentrated ethnic groups (Québécois, Basques, Sikhs, Kashmiris, Bengali Muslims, Eritreans, Filipino Muslims, Sri Lanka Tamils, Acehnese).

This does not, however, have to be so. The Basques in Spain have had a separatist movement; the Catalans, though territorially concentrated, have not. Tamil Nadu in India saw signs of separatism till 1962; its neighbors Kerala, Karnataka, and Andhra Pradesh never did. All of these are linguistically cohesive, territorially concentrated, and culturally distinctive states. In other words, a conjunction of territorial concentration and ethnicity may be a necessary condition for nationalism, though it is manifestly not sufficient.

---

[8] See, however, a new proposal in Chandra (2006).

When the national demand goes beyond a federal arrangement of power, the pre-existing larger territorial nationalism is challenged: ethnicity begins to seek territoriality and therefore nationhood. Given that territoriality in the current state system also generally tends to define citizenship, a challenge to the existing notion of citizenship is also posed. Three sacrosanct principles of the nation-state system, thus, become vulnerable: territoriality, citizenship, and sovereignty. Since the number of territorially based ethnic groups is currently larger than the number of nation-states, the existing nation-state system must be considered vulnerable. Some ethnic conflicts may not remain simply ethnic; they may eventually take steps towards separatist nationalism.

1.2 Conflict and Violence

A distinction between violence and conflict is also necessary. In an ethnically plural society, where freedom of expression is not curtailed, some conflict on identity-based cleavages is typically to be expected. Indeed, such conflict may mark all multiethnic polities, authoritarian or democratic. As compared to an authoritarian polity, a democratic political system may simply have a more open expression of such conflicts. In pursuit of political order and stability, authoritarian polities may push ethnic discontent under the surface and induce long phases of ethnic silence, but a coercive outlawing, or forcible containment, often increases the odds of an accumulated outburst, when an authoritarian system starts liberalizing, or when its legitimacy begins to unravel.

Indonesia is an excellent example. During the Suharto era (1966–98), on ethnocommunal issues the government had a so-called SARA policy. SARA was an acronym for ethnic (*suku*), religious (*agama*), racial (*ras*), and inter-group (*antargolongan*) differences. These differences were neither to be mobilized, nor discussed in the public realm. In the 1980s, Suharto's Indonesia came to be widely viewed as a stable and well-ordered society. However, by 1998, as the system began to lose its legitimacy, horrendous group violence took place on ethnocommunal lines (Bertrand 2004). The former Yugoslavia is another example, although it remains unclear whether ethnic rivalries there were contained more by laws or by an ideological system which, much like the former Soviet Union, sought to create a new communist identity overriding the ethnic and national identities that had so hobbled the Balkans in the first half of the twentieth century.

In contrast, conflicts are a much more regular feature of pluralistic democracies, for if different ethnic groups exist and the freedom to organize is available, there are likely to be struggles over: which language should be used in schools and employment; whether migrant ethnic groups should be allowed entry into the country and/or given restricted rights; whether different groups should be under one civil law for marriages, divorce, and property inheritance, or multiple family laws should be derived from the diverse religious or customary codes; whether religious dress can be allowed in public spaces; whether some groups should be given the benefits of affirmative action, how, and to what extent; whether the allocation of public resources favors some ethnic groups more than others. India and the United States are good illustrations of how democracies frequently witness such conflicts. Democracy is no guarantee that ethnic conflicts will not flare up. Indeed, some argue that democracies might give politicians incentives to play the ethnic card (Snyder 2000; Wilkinson 2004).

The conceptual issue is whether conflict is violent, or it is pursued within the institutionalized channels of the polity. When ethnic protest is channeled through parliaments, assemblies, and bureaucracies, or when it takes the form of strikes and non-violent demonstrations on the streets, it is an expression of conflict to be sure, but it is not a form of ethnic violence. Such institutionalized conflict, which can be quite healthy for a polity in many ways, must not be equated with riots, pogroms, and civil wars. The explanations for violent and non-violent conflict may also be different.

1.3 Types of Violent Conflict

One more conceptual clarification concerns the various forms of violent conflict. Collective violence, not individual violence or homicides, is at issue here. Collective violence can be defined as violence perpetrated by a group on another group (as in riots and pogroms), by a group on an individual (as in lynchings), by an individual on a group (as in terrorist acts), by the state on a group, or by a group on agencies of the state (as in civil wars).

The most widespread collective violence is typically divisible into three forms—riots, pogroms, and civil wars. Riots refer to a violent clash between two groups of civilians, often characterized as mobs. While, in riots, the neutrality of the state may be in doubt, the state does not give up the principle of neutrality. In pogroms, typically a majority community attacks an unarmed minority, and the principle of neutrality is for all practical purposes dropped by the state. The state administration either looks away, or sides with the attacking group. In civil wars, the state not only abandons the principle of neutrality, but it either becomes a combatant fighting an armed rebel group, or is physically unable to arbitrate between two armed groups fighting each other (Kalyvas 2006).

The key difference between pogroms and civil wars is that in the former, the target group—typically a minority—is hapless and unarmed, whereas in civil wars both combating sides are armed. Riots or pogroms typically precede civil wars, as in Sri Lanka in the 1980s, but all riots and pogroms do not lead to civil wars. Unlike Sri Lanka, the massive 1969 Malay–Chinese riots in Malaysia did not culminate in a civil war, nor for that matter have the Muslim–Christian riots of northern Nigeria in the 1990s led to a civil war there.[9]

---

[9] The last civil war in Nigeria took place in the late 1960s. It had nothing to do with Muslim–Christian divisions. It was ethnically driven.

2 TRADITIONS OF EXPLANATORY ENQUIRY

2.1 Essentialism

Essentialism is the oldest tradition of enquiry in the subfield of ethnicity and has been seriously under attack of late. It emerged at a time when the early enthusiasm, witnessed at the birth of the newly decolonized nations after the Second World War, had begun to ebb. In country after country, the story seemed to be similar. Nation building encountered serious ethnic resistance from within. Why was that so? Why could smaller ethnic identities not be subsumed under larger country- or state-level identities that governments were ostensibly seeking to create?

The first scholarly response was simply that the decolonized states were new, but ethnic, or communal animosities—sometime also called national animosities—were old and, therefore, deeply historically rooted. The primordialism of ethnic groups was a stronger bond and a more powerful motivator of human conduct than the pull of civic ties being forged by the new states (Geertz 1963; Shils 1957). This view found its most systematic exponent in Connor (1972, 1994). As late as the early 1990s when, as discussed later, the constructivist attack on essentialism was at its full cry and only journalists were willing to use the term "ancient hatreds" (Kaplan 2003), Connor was willing to argue that "man is a national," not rational, "animal," and at the core of nationalism lay the notion of "shared blood" or "shared ancestry" (Connor 1994).

Essentialism in this form had three primary weaknesses. The first had to do with variations. If ethnic antagonisms were so deep-rooted, why did ethnic violence rise and fall at different times? Yugoslavia may have come apart with a nearly all-consuming violent thud in the 1980s and 1990s, but there was a long stretch of peace during the socialist period. Do institutional designs not change human motivations? Did violence at the time of Yugoslavia's break-up show that in times of state collapse, ethnic antagonisms flare up, or that ethnic hatreds *caused* the collapse of Yugoslavia? Another type of variation is interspatial. Why did the same groups live peacefully in some places, but not in others? Hindu–Muslim violence often flared up in certain parts of India, not all over India (Varshney 2002; Wilkinson 2004).

Second, a lot of ethnic conflict in the world had nothing to do with old hostilities at all. Rather, older inhabitants of a land clashed with a relatively new migrant group, with little or no long history of contact. Can one establish the "primordial" or "ancient" roots of Chinese–Malay violence in Malaysia? The Chinese, after all, arrived in Malaysia mostly in the nineteenth and twentieth centuries. Similarly, it was primarily in the nineteenth and twentieth centuries that the Chinese came to Indonesia, and the Ibos flowed to northern Nigeria. Yet the anti-Chinese violence in Indonesia and the anti-Ibo violence in the Hausa-dominated northern Nigeria in the twentieth century was as ferocious as that between Hindus and Muslims, both older groups, in India.

The third attack on essentialism emanated from what came to be called the constructivist school. To talk about nations having primordial animosities, the constructivists argued, was wrong. In arguments that over time shook the foundations of essentialism and became mainstream wisdom, constructivists argued that nations were constructed only in modern times (Anderson 1983). Before the rise of modernity, most human interactions were on a small scale. Only ecclesiastical and dynastic communities spread beyond the local and the regional. The implication was that religious or dynastic animosities could be said to be pre-modern, even primordial, but *ethnic* animosities had local or regional protocols. By bringing far-flung people into the frame of human consciousness, it is modernity that changed the meaning of ethnicity and also led to nationhood. To speak of primordial ethnic or national antagonisms was historically false.

Essentialism, however, did not fully disappear, as was predicted and expected. These attacks—variations, modern provenance of conflicts, and constructivism—led to a fresh honing of arguments. Accepting the inadequacies of a Connor-style argumentation, Petersen (2002) recast essentialism with psychological theories about emotions.

On "ancient hatreds," he argued:

Most academics dismiss the "ancient hatreds" argument. They show how violent interethnic "histories" are often fabrications, inventions that serve the interests of rabble-rousing elites. If "ancient hatreds" means a hatred that has produced uninterrupted ethic warfare, or an obsessive hatred consuming the daily thoughts of great masses of people, then the "ancient hatreds" arguments deserves to be readily dismissed. However, if hatred is conceived as a historically formed "schema" that guides action in *some situations*, then the conception should be taken more seriously. (Petersen 2002, 62–3, emphasis mine)

In short, the existence of hatred did not require a proof about its ancient origins. Even if hatred had non-ancient origins, it could profoundly shape human behavior. Human nature was quite capable of expressing hatred. In what might be called a neo-essentialist twist, Petersen turned an argument about primordial hatreds into an argument about *human nature*:

the motivation to participate in or support ethnic violence and discrimination [is] ... inherent in human nature. Until we realize that the capacity to commit ethnic violence lies within all of us we are in danger of constantly being surprised at the emergence of forces from the "dark ages." (Petersen 2002, 1)

Petersen built four models, based on four different kinds of emotions: fear, hatred, resentment, and rage. Fear as an emotion guides individuals in situations of security threats; hatred in conditions of historical grievance; resentment in settings of status discrepancies; and rage simply expresses a desire to "lash out" due to accumulated emotions, but without a specific target. A prediction was made with respect to how each emotion would work, and a test devised in Eastern Europe. Petersen's general argument, finally, was that resentment born out of status reversals explained most of the ethnic violence in twentieth-century Eastern Europe during periods of state collapse (during and after the First and Second World Wars, and at the end-game of communism). Hatred, fear, and rage explained fewer cases of violence, but they were also present.

Emotions have been, on the whole, neglected in social science theories about ethnic conflict. It is now clear that the field will have to engage Petersen's neo-essentialist arguments. One potential line of engagement is obvious. What is the role of institutions in reining in, or redefining, emotions? Why do these emotions explode in times of state collapse, not when state authority is firmly anchored? Does that variation indicate something about our deep-seated human nature, or about the causal role of institutions, in the outbreak of ethnic violence? A second question is about whether state collapse, even in Eastern Europe, necessarily leads to horrendous violence. Laitin (1998) argues that new identity formation after the end of communism was peaceful in the Baltic republics and Kazakhstan. What accounts for such dramatic variation?

2.2 Instrumentalism

The core idea of instrumentalism is that ethnicity is neither inherent in human nature nor intrinsically valuable. Ethnicity masks a deeper core of interests, which are either economic or political. Ethnicity is useful for gaining political power or for drawing resources from the state. That is why it is deployed so often in multiethnic societies. Conflicts take place because leaders strategically manipulate ethnicity for the sake of political power, or for extracting resources from the state (Bates 1974, 1983; Chandra 2004; Hechter 1986; Rabushka and Shepsle 1972).

This line of reasoning runs into several difficulties.[10] Even if we accept that leaders gain by mobilizing ethnicity and that is why they deploy ethnic symbols and idioms in politics, why should the masses come along? Why do leaders in multiethnic societies so often think that ethnicity is the means to power or for extracting resources from the state, not mobilization based on economic or ideological programs? Second, if the masses were also instrumental, would ethnic collective action not be crippled by free rider problems? One can perhaps understand why it would be instrumentally rational for someone to join an ethnic movement when it is close to capturing power, but why would ethic mobilization begin at all? A fuller account or inclusion of "selective incentives" (Olson 1965) or "commitment" (Sen 1973) is required. Third, if ex-ante odds are quite high that ethnic mobilization or protest would lead to violence by another group, or to punitive action by the state, why should anyone participate in ethnic mobilization at all? Why would instrumentally rational people take such high risks? One could propose that people are coerced into participating in ethnic mobilization, but that would have to be demonstrated, not assumed.

In different ways, some of the more widely noted instrumentalist scholarship of the last decade and a half seeks to address these problems (Hardin 1995; Fearon and Laitin 1996; Collier and Hoeffler 1998, 2004; Collier, Hoeffler, and Sambanis 2005). Extending the idea of "focal points" originally proposed by Schelling (1963), Hardin argues that the central strategic problem in ethnic mobilization is one of

---

[10] These criticisms are based on Horowitz (1985, 2001), and Varshney (2003).

coordination, not one of collective action. In the latter, it is rational to "free ride," but in coordination games, it is rational to cooperate so long as others are cooperating. A "charismatic leader," a "focus," is what one needs to reinforce expectation about the behavior of others.

To understand this point better, it is worth recalling the famous Schelling example:

When a man loses his wife in a department store without any prior understanding on where to meet if they get separated, the chances are good that they will find each other. It is likely that each will think of some obvious place to meet, so obvious that each will be sure that the other is sure that it is obvious to both of them.[11]

The "lost and found" section of the department store, argued Schelling, could serve as one such obvious place, but not if there were many "lost and found" sections in the store. "Prominence" or "uniqueness" distinguished a focal point. That is why it could be used to facilitate the development of mutually consistent expectations. Seen this way, ethnicity could serve as a "focal point," and ethnic mobilization would simply require coordination of expectations. Ethnicity did not have to be intrinsically valued for it to be politically useful.

Though ingenious, this resolution has its own difficulties. Two come to mind immediately (Varshney 2003). First, why is ethnicity-based mobilization akin to a coordination game, but class-based mobilization a form of collective action saddled with free rider problems? Hardin's answer is that ethnicity provides "epistemological comforts of home," but that restates the problem. Why should ethnicity provide these comforts, not class or party? After all, the Marxists-Leninists had believed for much of the twentieth century that the Communist Party would be home to the new socialist man, replacing ethnicity or nationhood. Second, why should it be easier to mobilize ethnicity, despite the risks of injury, incarceration, or death? Saying ethnic mobilization is a mere coordination problem does not square with the well-known risks of ethnic conflict. In short, can one really explain ethnic preferences in an entirely instrumental way, or is recourse to the psychological or cultural foundations of ethnicity necessary?

Fearon and Laitin (1996) respond to these difficulties by restricting the domain of instrumental rationality, even while using instrumentalist assumptions for developing their core argument. Instead of asking why there is so much ethnic conflict and violence in the world, they first note that the incidence of ethnic violence is lower than is normally believed. Instead of engaging in killings, many ethnic groups, in fact, live in peace. There is a gap between actual violence and what is theoretically possible.

What would explain inter-ethnic peace and cooperation? Relying on the notion of ethnic groups as information networks, they game-theoretically generate a powerful and unexplored idea as an equilibrium solution: "in-group policing."[12] Faced with provocation or attacks, a group could restrain its members from hitting back, and

---

[11] Schelling (1963, 54). We are, of course, talking about the pre-cellphone days.

[12] It should be noted that "in-group policing" remains a deductive idea, still to be systematically and empirically tested. The fear of "spiraling" produces the other equilibrium solution, meaning individuals of one group could be expected to attack the other group indiscriminately in response to an attack, which could lead to escalating violence, which in turn would induce cooperation.

rely on similar restraining exercised by the other group. This is possible because each ethnic group has better information about its own members than about those of the other group, which in turn can allow each group to check who the in-group "opportunists" are, meaning those who would use the provocation to retaliate.

Does this mean that explanation of ethnic conflict requires no recourse to psychological theories of grievance? Careful not to make universalistic claims, Fearon and Laitin explicitly lay out the limits of their theory:

> We should emphasize . . . that we are not offering a full causal theory of either ethnic peace or ethnic violence. We specify what we believe are important causal mechanisms that appear to have been systematically neglected . . . But we do not pretend that our formulation or . . . mechanisms we identify tell the whole causal story. A richer story would surely include . . . narratives of interethnic injury. It might also include the motivations stemming from indignities suffered by peoples who are considered of lower rank and who seek to overturn a rigid social ordering. (Fearon and Laitin 1996, 715)

In short, an instrumental use of ethnicity—in this case, ethnicity as a communication and information device rather than an intense form of group attachment—may explain part of the phenomenon of violence, but historical indignities and injuries may well be relevant. Exploring a variety of conflicts in different settings should begin to show which motivations are present where. This argument leads to the possibility that ethnic conflict could have pluralistic microfoundations.

Let me now turn to another new argument. Collier and Hoeffler (1998, 2004) are associated with the famous "greed versus grievance" framing of ethnic violence. Though they concentrate only on civil wars, an extreme form of ethnic conflict, their argument is worth considering here. The strength of their belief in instrumentalism has evolved in an educative manner.

Based on a large-N statistical model, Collier and Hoeffler (1998) first argued that social scientists had been wrong to believe that civil wars were the consequence of accumulated grievances of a victimized or targeted ethnic group in society. A grievance-based argument was simply equal to accepting the discourse of rebels. Instead, a greed-based model had an infinitely better fit with data.

They model rebellion as an industry in which looting generated profits. Leaders of rebellions are driven by a desire to amass fortunes, and the masses join them, for in poor societies with very few economic opportunities, the opportunity costs of participation in a rebellion are low and the benefits—in the form of a share of the loot—quite substantial. Given their geographical concentration, natural resources are an especially "lootable commodity." Civil wars predominantly erupt in economies highly dependent on natural resource extraction.

This was, arguably, the sharpest framing of the instrumentalist view ever witnessed in the field. And the notion that both models—greed and grievance—were tested with a large-N dataset added a new punch. Instrumentalist arguments used to be about ethnic mobilization, something decidedly less violent than civil wars, and large-N datasets were rarely, if ever, used for testing.

However, as the Collier–Hoeffler argument evolved, its sharpness and universality steadily diminished. When the dataset was enlarged, coding further finessed, and model specifications changed, they concluded that "we cannot reject one model in favor of the other" and "while the (greed) model is superior, some elements of the grievance model are likely to add to its explanatory power" (Collier and Hoeffler 2004, 577). Still later, the findings of the statistical model were subjected to carefully chosen case studies because even if the statistical model "predicted all cases of civil war onset perfectly, it would still not be able to tell us much about the process through which these outcomes (war or peace) are generated. By contrast, analyzing the process—the sequence of events and the interaction of variables in the (statistical) model over time—is the comparative advantage of case study designs.... Qualitative analysis can help us sort out the endogenous from the exogenous variables in the model" (Collier Hoeffler, and Sambanis 2005, 2).

What, then, was the final conclusion? "The distinction between greed and grievance," they argued, "should be abandoned for a more complex model that considers greed and grievance as inextricably fused motives for civil war" (Collier, Hoeffler, and Sambanis 2005, 2).

Just as pure essentialism could not survive empirical scrutiny, pure instrumentalism also could not. Future work in this tradition is likely to be highly domain specific. Instrumental uses of ethnicity do exist and will continue to. But one will have to be clear about the kinds of questions for which either instrumentalist assumptions can be made, or instrumentalist claims can be sustained. Not all forms of ethnic behavior, or ethnic conflict, can be linked to instrumental rationality.

2.3 Constructivism

Constructivism is the new conventional wisdom in the field of ethnicity and nationalism. Its central idea is that our ethnic and national identities are constructs of the modern epoch. This claim is relatively straightforward for national identities, for work across a whole range of traditions shows that nations were born with the rise of the industrial age.[13] Political units took the form of city-states or empires before that.[14]

But the argument is also made with respect to ethnic identities (Hobsbawm and Ranger 1983; Mamdani 1996; Vail 1989; Suny 2001). The claim is not that there were no Turks, Han Chinese, Tibetan, Zulus, or Scots in pre-modern times. Rather, in pre-modern times, mass identities were locally or regionally based. Only some kinds of identities—for example, the aristocratic or ecclesiastical—were extra-local or extra-regional. Modernity transformed the meaning of ethnic identities by bringing *the masses* into a vastly expanded framework of consciousness and meanings.

Three kinds of mechanisms have generally been identified to show how this came about—technological, ideational, and, in the former colonies, colonial policies, institutions, and practices. Anderson's *Imagined Communities* (1983), arguably the

---

[13] However, see Kedourie (1993).
[14] For the link between nations and modernity, see, among others, Greenfeld (1992).

most influential text in the field of ethnicity and nationalism, calls attention to the rise of "print capitalism"—the arrival of the printing press and capitalism—as the basic mechanism through which local identities were transformed into larger national identities.[15] The boundaries of the political community typically depended on the spread of the vernacular and the decline of "truth languages" such as Latin or Sanskrit.

The second mechanism that constructivists now routinely embrace relies on the arguments made by Taylor (1994) about how modernity brought about *ideational* changes in human life. In pre-modern times, one's identity—who am I?—was given by one's place in the traditional social structure. People accepted ascriptive social hierarchies, or their "stations" in life. In modern times, hierarchies may exist, but ascriptive hierarchies are not easily accepted. In pre-modern times, the notion of *honor*, reserved only for a few, marked relations between people of different ranks. Modernity has introduced us to the notion of *dignity*, to which all regardless of rank are entitled. Finally, the pursuit of dignity is dialogical, not monological—that is, it takes place in interaction with others. Our identity is

partly shaped by recognition or its absence, often my misrecognition of others, and so a person or groups of people can suffer real damage, real distortion, if the people or society around them mirror back to them a confining, demeaning, or contemptible picture of themselves. Nonrecognition or misrecognition can inflict harm, can be a form of oppression, imprisoning someone in a false, distorted and reduced mode of being. (Taylor 1994, 25)

Though acceptable and internalized in the past, much of ethnic or national assertion in the modern world is about resisting such "confining, demeaning or contemptible" pictures that the dominant groups—through colonial rulers and state bureaucracies—have often relayed to the subordinate groups. The keyword here is dignity, not material self-interest.[16]

Given the heavy reliance on historical detail, constructivism first flourished in the discipline of history (Weber 1976; Hobsbawm and Ranger 1983; Vail 1989). In comparative politics, Anderson (1983) was the first to make the constructivist argument. Some others also joined in, especially concentrating on the structure of colonial rule and colonial policies. Laitin (1986) explained why in Yoruba politics in Nigeria, religious cleavage was missing, even though both Islam and Christianity dominated the religious landscape. He argued that for reasons of their own, the British did not allow religion to be the basis of politics in Yorubaland, electing instead to emphasize tribal cleavages. By the time they left, the tribal cleavages were so deeply institutionalized that they became the political common sense of Yorubaland. Chatterjee (1986) argued that the images of Indians British rulers created and propagated,

---

[15] According to "Google scholar", as of February 1, 2007, Anderson's *Imagined Communities* had been cited over 6,300 times, followed by Gellner's *Nations and Nationalism* (1,449 times), and Taylor's *Multiculturalism and the Politics of Recognition* (1,205 times). All three texts are covered in this chapter.

[16] Technical change—in the form of print capitalism—is the centerpiece of Anderson (1983), but Taylor's ideational change is often implicit in his arguments about the birth of nationalism in the former colonies. "Creole pioneers" felt humiliated in Spanish America, rebelling against the Spanish rulers (Anderson 1983, ch. 4).

once they conquered India, led to the development of nationalism in India. These three examples notwithstanding, constructivism remained on the margins of how ethnicity was studied in comparative politics in the 1980s and for much of the 1990s. Constructivism's rise in other disciplines, especially history, far preceded its incorporation in political science.

Although it is by now customary to state that constructivism has become the dominant mode of argumentation about ethnicity within political science as well, one of its key weaknesses ought to be noted. Constructivism accounts for identity formation well, but it does not do a good job of explaining ethnic conflict. Often, a distinction between identities and conflict is not drawn. The key constructivist idea on conflict is that each society has a historically constructed "master cleavage"— Protestant versus Catholic in Northern Ireland, Hindu versus Muslim in India, black versus white in the USA—and political entrepreneurs can easily insert local, often trivial, incidents, events and rumors into the "master narrative," creating inflammable situations and instigating violence (Brass 1997, 2003). In social scientific terms, a causal role is thus assigned to master narratives and political entrepreneurs.

The problem is that the master cleavage is typically at the national level and political entrepreneurs are also available throughout the length and breadth of a country, but ethnic violence tends to be highly locally, or regionally, concentrated. In the 1960s, racial violence in the USA was heavily concentrated in northern cities; southern cities, though intensely politically engaged, did not have riots (Horowitz 1983). A mere eight cities in India, holding less than 6 percent of the country's population, accounted for just a little less than half of all deaths in Hindu–Muslim riots during 1950–95 (Varshney 2002). Between 1990 and 2003, fifteen districts of Indonesia, in which less than 7 percent of the nation's population lived, had close to 85 percent of deaths in all forms of group violence short of secessionary wars (Varshney, Panggabean, and Tadjoeddin 2006).

How can one explain local variations with a nation-level constant ("master cleavage," "master narrative") and the countrywide ubiquity of political entrepreneurs? The answer perhaps lies in (a) how local structures of some kind discourage political entrepreneurs from inserting local incidents into the master narrative; or (b) how political entrepreneurs are unable to instigate violence even when they insert local events into the larger narrative; or (c) how the presence of local or regional narratives counters the power of a master narrative (Varshney 1997). Constructivist arguments about violence are thus far built on case studies of violence, not on a comparison of peaceful and violent cases. Selection bias has led to significant weaknesses; studying variations has explanatory promise.

A final question about constructivism remains. Are constructivism and instrumentalism merely two sides of the same coin? Chandra (2001) has argued that divisions in the field of ethnicity and nationalism should simply be viewed as those between essentialists and constructivists. According to her, Geertz (1963) is an example of essentialism, and constructivist arguments include not only those made by Anderson (1983) and Laitin (1986), reviewed above, but also those made by Bates (1974), included here as an example of instrumentalist reasoning. To recall, the latter argument is that ethnicity is a conduit for extracting resources from the state; nothing more need be said or assumed. According to Chandra, what distinguishes constructivism is the notion that "ethnic groups are fluid and endogenous to a set of social, economic and political processes" (Chandra 2001, 7).

The instrumentalist and constructivist approaches are undoubtedly opposed to the primordialist view of ethnicity, but that is where the similarity ends. According to instrumentalist reasoning, ethnic identity is not valuable in and of itself; it is basically a mask for a core of "real" interests, political or economic. As interests change, masks also do, making ethnic groups "fluid." One should, therefore, expect the same people to pick different sides of their multiple identities at different times and at different places.

This view should not be equated with constructivism. Constructivism is not about the radical *short-run* fluidity of identities. It is about the *long-run* formation, and the consequent *stickiness*, of identities. In Anderson's case, the argument is epochal: he discusses how the birth of print capitalism in modern times created national identities. Weber (1976) shows how peasants were turned into Frenchmen *over more than a century* after the French Revolution—through a conscription army and public schools. Colley's argument is about how "Britishness" emerged out of "Englishness," "Scottishness," and "Welshness" *over more than a century* (1707–1837), and how the presence of France as a "Catholic enemy" and a colonial empire especially blunted the historically rooted intensity of English–Scottish rivalries (Colley 1993).

Each of these scholars demonstrates how *new* identities came about, but it does not follow that they view identities as radically *fluid*.[17] That identities are constructed does not mean that they do not become internalized and institutionalized, and acquire meaning.

Constructivism is basically about the long-run stickiness, instrumentalism about the short-run fluidity.[18] While equally opposed to primordialism, they are fundamentally different in their assumptions, explanatory ambition, and methodological impulse.

---

[17] One should also note that Laitin (1986) was profoundly opposed to an instrumental view of ethnic identity formation, though his positions changed later (Fearon and Laitin 1996; Laitin 1998). Consider the following arguments in the earlier book:

Rational choice theorists . . . cannot tell us if ultimately butter is better than guns; it can tell us that at a certain point the production of a small number of guns will cost us a whole lot of butter, and at that point it is probably irrational to produce more guns. Within a political structure, individuals constantly make marginal decisions. (Rational choice) theories can give us a grasp on how individual political actors are likely to make choices within that structure.

(Rational choice) theory cannot, however, handle *long-term and non-marginal* decisions. When market structures are themselves threatened, and people must decide whether to work within the new structure or hold on to the old—without an opportunity for a marginal decision—microeconomic theory is not applicable. . . . Structural transformations—changing the basic cleavage structure of a society—are not amenable to the tools of microeconomic theory. (Laitin 1986, 148–9)

Identity choice was not a marginal, but a structural decision. Instrumental rationality, therefore, was inapplicable.

[18] The relationship between the long-run stickiness of some identities and short-run fluidity of others may have to be sorted out, but that is another matter altogether. The two should not be conflated.

2.4 Institutionalism

If constructivism has come to shape the literature of the formation of ethnic *identities*, institutionalism has long dominated the arguments about ethnic *conflict* in comparative politics. The core idea here is that the designs of political institutions—consociational or majoritarian polities, proportional representation or first-past-the-post electoral systems, federal or unitary governments—explain why some multiethnic societies have violence, and others, peace.

Ethnic pluralism, it is argued, requires political institutions distinct from those that are suitable for ethnically undivided societies. A mechanical transfer of institutional forms regardless of whether a society is marked by deep ethnic divisions can cause ethnic violence. The foundations of such arguments go all the way back to John Stuart Mill in the nineteenth century. Mill had claimed that common loyalty to a political center was a precondition for a democracy to function. A multiethnic society was likely to have many loyalties, not one. Only under the tutelage of a more politically advanced ethnic group can order be maintained and ethnic violence avoided. Tutelage was necessary until a civic consciousness towards a political center, not to an ethnic group, emerged.

Nobody can suppose that it is not beneficial to a Breton or a Basque of the French Navarre to be brought into the current of ideas and feelings of a highly civilized and cultivated people—to be a member of the French nationality... than to sulk on his own rocks, the half-savage relic of past times, revolving in his own little mental orbit, without participation or interest in the general movement of the world. The same remark applies to the Welshman or the Scottish Highlander, as members of the British nation. (Mill 1990, 385–6)

Colonial tutelage is no longer popular, but the arguments about whether multiethnic societies should have majoritarian democracies continue to be debated. Lijphart (1977) and Horowitz (1985, 1991)have defined the field. Lijphart continues to argue in favor of consociationalism, in which each ethnic group's political and cultural affairs are left to its elite, and inter-ethnic compromises are made only at the elite level. Horowitz argues against it, suggesting that the electoral system should make it impossible for political parties to win power unless they appeal across ethnic groups, not lock them in a permanent intra-ethnic embrace. The former is more likely to lead to peace, the latter to violence.

This debate has greatly advanced our understanding of ethnic conflict.[19] However, it has left one big problem unresolved. The Lijphart–Horowitz arguments have basically been about national-level institutions. Using national-level concepts, we certainly explain why country A, rather than country B, tends to have more ethnic violence, but we cannot understand the regional or local variations within the same country. For institutional explanations to be relevant to local or regional variance, the electoral designs or institutions must themselves vary locally or regionally.

The neo-institutionalist work of recent vintage goes in the direction of uncovering local institutional variations. Varshney (2002) argues that local variation in conflict is

[19] For a review, see Reilly (2001).

best explained by whether local civic organizations, including political parties, exist and whether they integrate ethnic communities or segregate them. Wilkinson (2004) argues that in a first-past-the-post electoral system, it is the effective number of parties and the need for minority support—both of which can vary regionally and/or locally—that determine whether ethnic violence will occur or peace will obtain.

A second new development in the literature is the focus on the relationship between institutions and identity choice. Lijphart (2001) accepts that when consociational theory was developed in the 1960s and 1970s, an essentialist view of identities prevailed. In line with those times, he also assumed that ethnic identities were fixed, and appropriate political institutions were to be constructed in light of the fixity of ethnic identities.

The new literature shows how institutions can transform the salience of identities. Posner (2005) argues that since colonial times, Zambians have had two axes of identification: language and tribe. Zambia has four language groups and over six dozen tribes. Since independence, Zambia has also had two kinds of overarching institutions: multiparty rule and one-party rule. Under the former, Zambians embraced language as the basic political identity, and under the latter, they chose tribe. Under a multiparty system, they had to elect a constituency representative as well as the president. This meant that the political arena was national, and the larger identification (language), therefore, made sense. Under one-party system, only the constituency representative was to be elected, *not* the president. The political arena was, thus, reduced to the constituency level, and the smaller identification (tribe) became more relevant.[20]

Such reasoning, it should be noted, was implicit in Horowitz (1985). His critique of consociationalism was, in part, based on the fact that identities could change and the elite of an ethnic group, therefore, could not be expected to keep the loyalty of that group for ever. He also argued that the changing political arena would reshape the cleavages. But in the new literature, this idea is explicit. Identity choice is squarely posed as a dependent variable to be explained. As a result, we have a more self-conscious and focused explication of the institutional determinants of identity choice (Chandra 2004; Laitin 1998; Posner 2005; Waters 1990).

A marriage of constructivism and institutionalism is the third new development in the literature. To recall, a general stickiness of master cleavages is the core idea of constructivism. Institutionalism, in comparison, has begun to accept fluidity of identities, depending on the institutional context. Can historical stickiness and conjunctural fluidity be combined?

Posner (2005) begins to show how.[21] The contemporary choices between language and tribe in Zambia may be determined by whether the country has a one-party or

---

[20] It should, however, be noted that Posner's argument, though presented as one about identity choice, could as easily be constructed as an argument about electoral choice. It is not the Zambian identities that changed with the alteration in the party system, but only how Zambians voted.

[21] Posner argues that he is, in effect, combining constructivist, institutional, and instrumental-rational arguments. The last does not appear to be true. Technically speaking, an instrumental-rational view requires that (a) the microfoundations be defined in terms of self-interest, which is not affected by "framing;" and (b) given those microfoundations, collective action problems be resolved, for group

multiparty rule, as noted above. But colonial history, argues Posner, had already deeply institutionalized only two identities: linguistic and tribal. This was because of the administrative and recruitment policies and census practices of British rulers and companies. Several other axes of identification were conceivable.

The innovative marriage of constructivism and institutionalism on identity formation/choice faces some tougher challenges ahead. Van Evera (2001) has posed the important question of whether identities can be fluid, *if formed or deepened by violent conflict.* In other words, is Zambia an easy case? In Zambian history, is there anything like India's Hindu–Muslim violence at the time of partition, Malaysia's Malay–Chinese violence 1945–69, Sri Lanka's Sinhala–Tamil violence since 1977, and the several descents into ethnic warfare in the Balkans? Van Evera claims that if violent conflict constructs, or deepens, identities, they cannot be easily reconstructed. Future research under the marriage of constructivism and institutionalism may have to respond to this challenge.

3 CONCLUSION

Three conclusions can be drawn from the arguments above. First, if one thinks of cumulation in Popperian terms—as progress through a systematic disconfirmation of theories—then only two theoretical ideas have been knocked over in the last ten to fifteen years. No one seriously argues any more that ethnic identity is primordial, nor that it is devoid of any intrinsic value and used only as a strategic tool. Pure essentialists or pure instrumentalists do not exist any longer. Nor is it likely that they will re-emerge, given the force of empirical evidence. Second, the traditions which produced these theories, however, continue. Innovation within has taken place, or a new set of unresolved problems promises innovation. Essentialism has moved towards an argument about human nature, especially in conditions of state collapse. Instrumentalism has sought to restrict its domain, or begun to think of models in which "greed and grievance" will be "inextricably fused." Constructivism has to sort out whether subnational and local variations in conflict can be explained within its own guiding assumptions and principles. Institutionalism has to ascertain whether identities are fluid only under some circumstances, and how fluid they are. Third, the field has become methodologically highly self-conscious and sophisticated and that is only to be welcomed. However, methodological disputes or

action is, by definition, riddled with free rider problems. The fact that colonial rulers created some institutions and rules, to which the subjects responded, is equal to a framing-induced response, which takes Posner's argument towards cognitive rationality, whose roots lie in psychology, not towards instrumental rationality, whose roots lie in economics. Moreover, Posner assumes group action based on the meanings assigned by the colonial rulers. The free rider problem is not resolved. Posner's argument, thus, combines constructivism and institutionalism, but does not bring in instrumentalist reasoning in its technical sense. To see what is theoretically at stake here, see Sen (2002); Taylor (2006); Varshney (2003).

methodological advances alone will not generate significant progress.[22] Some of the most creative work in the future is likely to be problem and puzzle driven and may well emerge from border crossings and mixed approaches. Of course, not all borders can be crossed. It is, for example, not clear whether essentialism and instrumentalism can ever be brought together without grotesque internal inconsistencies. But border crossings between constructivism and institutionalism have been initiated, and should certainly be more easily possible. The results could be highly instructive.

REFERENCES

ANDERSON, B. 1983. *Imagined Communities*. London: Verso.

BATES, R. 1974. Ethnic competition and modernization in contemporary Africa. *Comparative Political Studies*, 6 (4): 457–84.

—— 1983. Modernization, ethnic competition, and the rationality of politics in contemporary Africa. Pp. 153–71 in *State versus Ethnic Claims: African Policy Dilemmas*, ed. D. Rothchild. Boulder, Colo.: Westview Press.

BERTRAND, J. 2004. *Nationalism and Ethnic Conflict in Indonesia*. Cambridge: Cambridge University Press.

BRASS, P. R. 1974. *Language, Religion and Politics in North India*. Cambridge: Cambridge University Press.

—— 1997. *Theft of an Idol*. Princeton: Princeton University Press.

—— 2003. *The Production of Hindu–Muslim Violence in Contemporary India*. Seattle: University of Washington Press.

BRUBAKER, R., and LAITIN, D. 2004. Ethnic and nationalist violence. In *Ethnicity without Groups*, ed. R. Brubaker. Cambridge, Mass.: Harvard University Press.

CHANDRA, K. 2001. Cumulative findings in the study of ethnic politics. *APSA-CP*: 7–25.

—— 2004. *Why Ethnic Parties Succeed*. New York: Cambridge University Press.

—— 2006. What is ethnic identity and does it matter? *Annual Review of Political Science*, 9: 397–424.

CHATTERJEE, P. 1986. *Nationalist Thought and the Colonial World*. Minneapolis: University of Minnesota Press.

COLLEY, L. 1993. *Britons*. New Haven: Yale University Press.

COLLIER, P., and HOEFFLER, A. 1998. On the economic causes of civil war. *Oxford Economic Papers*, 50: 563–73.

—— —— 2004. Greed and grievance in civil war. *Oxford Economic Papers*, 56: 563–95.

—— —— and SAMBANIS, N. 2005. The Collier–Hoeffler model of civil war onset and the case study research design. Ch. 1 in *Understanding Civil War: Evidence and Analysis*, ed. P. Collier and N. Sambanis. Washington, DC: World Bank.

CONNOR, W. 1972. Nation-building or nation-destroying? *World Politics*, 24 (3): 319–55.

—— 1994. *Ethnonationalism*. Princeton: Princeton University Press.

DEUTSCH, K. 1966. *Nationalism and Social Communication*. Cambridge, Mass.: MIT Press.

FEARON, J., and LAITIN, D. 1996. Explaining interethnic cooperation. *American Political Science Review*, 90 (4): 713–35.

[22] For a recent methodological debate in the field, see the symposium on David Laitin's work *Qualitative Methods* (2006).

GEERTZ, C. 1963. The integrative revolution: primordial sentiments and civil politics in the new states. Pp. 105–57 in *Old Societies and New States*, by C. Geertz. New York: Free Press.

GELLNER, E. 1983. *Nations and Nationalism*. Ithaca, NY: Cornell University Press.

GREENFELD, L. 1992. *Nationalism: Five Roads to Modernity*. Cambridge, Mass.: Harvard University Press.

HARDIN, R. 1995, *One for All*. Princeton: Princeton University Press.

HECHTER, M. 1986. Rational choice theory and the study of race and ethnic relations. Pp. 264–79 in *Theories of Race and Ethnic Relations*, ed. D. Mason and J. Rex. Cambridge: Cambridge University Press.

HOBSBAWM, E., and RANGER, T. eds. 1983. *The Invention of Tradition*. Cambridge: Cambridge University Press.

HOROWITZ, D. L. 1983. Racial violence in the United States. In *Ethnic Pluralism and Public Policy*, ed. N. Glazer and K. Young. Lexington, Mass.: Lexington Books.

—— 1985. *Ethnic Groups in Conflict*. Berkeley and Los Angeles: University of California Press.

—— 1991. *A Democratic South Africa?* Berkeley and Los Angeles: University of California Press.

—— 2001. *The Deadly Ethnic Riot*. Berkeley and Los Angeles: University of California Press.

KALYVAS, S. 2006. *The Logic of Violence in Civil War*. New York: Cambridge University Press.

KAPLAN, R. D. 2003. *Balkan Ghosts*. New York: St Martin's Press.

KEDOURIE, E. 1993. *Nationalism*, 4th expanded edn. Oxford: Blackwell.

KING, G., KEOHANE, R., and VERBA, S. 1994. *Designing Social Inquiry*. Princeton: Princeton University Press.

LAITIN, D. D. 1986. *Hegemony and Culture*. Chicago: University of Chicago Press.

—— 1998. *Identity in Formation*. Ithaca, NY: Cornell University Press.

—— 2006. Ethnography and/or rational choice. *Qualitative Methods*, 4 (1): 26–33.

LIJPHART, A. 1969. *The Politics of Accommodation*. Berkeley and Los Angeles: University of California Press.

—— 1977. *Democracy in Plural Societies*. New Haven: Yale University Press.

—— 2001. Constructivism and consociational theory. *APSA-CP* 12 (1): 11–13.

MAMDANI, M. 1996. *Citizen and Subject*. Princeton: Princeton University Press.

MILL, J. S. 1990. *Three Essays*. New York: Oxford University Press.

OLSON, M. 1965. *The Logic of Collective Action*. Cambridge, Mass.: Harvard University Press.

PETERSEN, R. D. 2002. *Understanding Ethnic Violence*. New York: Cambridge University Press.

POSNER, D. 2005. *Institutions and Ethnic Politics in Africa*. New York: Cambridge University Press.

Qualitative Methods. 2006. Symposium: ethnography meets rational choice. 4 (1): 2–33.

RABUSHKA, A., and SHEPSLE, K. 1972. *Politics in Plural Societies*. Columbus, Oh.: Merrill.

REILLY, B. 2001. *Democracy in Divided Societies: Electoral Engineering for Conflict Management*. Cambridge: Cambridge University Press.

RUDOLPH, L., and RUDOLPH, S. 1967. *The Modernity of Tradition*. Chicago: University of Chicago Press.

SCHELLING, T. 1963. *The Strategy of Conflict*. New York: Oxford University Press.

SEN, A. 1973. Rational fools. *Philosophy and Public Affairs*, 6 (4): 317–44.

—— 2002. *Rationality and Freedom*. Cambridge, Mass.: Harvard University Press.

SHILS, E. 1957. Primordial, personal, sacred and civil ties. *British Journal of Sociology*, 8 (2): 130–45.

SMITH, A. 1979. *Nationalism in the Twentieth Century*. New York: New York University Press.

SNYDER, J. 2000. *From Voting to Violence*. New York: W. W. Norton.

SUNY, R. G. (2001). Constructing Primordialism. *The Journal of Modern History*, 73 (3): 862–96.

TAYLOR, C. 1994. *Multiculturalism and the Politics of Recognition*. Princeton: Princeton University Press.

TAYLOR, M. 2006. *Rationality and the Ideology of Disconnection.* New York: Cambridge University Press.

VAIL, L. ed. 1989. *The Creation of Tribalism in Southern Africa.* Berkeley and Los Angeles: University of California Press.

VAN EVERA, S. 2001. Primordialism lives! *APSA-CP* 12 (1): 20–2.

VARSHNEY, A. 1997. Postmodernism, civic engagement and ethnic conflict: a passage to India. *Comparative Politics,* 30 (1): 1–20.

—— 2002. *Ethnic Conflict and Civic Life.* New Haven: Yale University Press.

—— 2003. Nationalism, ethnic conflict and rationality. *Perspectives on Politics,* 1 (1): 85–99.

—— 2006. Recognizing the tradeoffs we make. *Qualitative Methods,* 4 (1).

—— PANGGABEAN, R. and TADJOEDDIN, Z. 2006. Creating datasets in information-poor environments: patterns of collective violence in Indonesia. Paper presented at the annual meetings of the American Political Science Association.

WATERS, M. 1990. *Ethnic Options.* Berkeley and Los Angeles: University of California Press.

WEBER, E. 1976. *Peasants into Frenchmen.* Stanford, Calif.: Stanford University Press.

WEINER, M. 1978. *Sons of the Soil.* Princeton: Princeton University Press.

WILKINSON, S. 2004. *Votes and Violence.* New York: Cambridge University Press.

PART IV

POLITICAL REGIMES AND TRANSITIONS

CHAPTER 13

MASS BELIEFS AND DEMOCRATIC INSTITUTIONS

CHRISTIAN WELZEL

RONALD INGLEHART

1 INTRODUCTION

ONE of the central questions in comparative politics is "What determines the emergence, survival, and development of democracy?" Since its inception, political culture research has been inspired by this question and has claimed to provide a profound answer: the fate of democracy depends on ordinary people's intrinsic commitment to democratic principles.

This premise involves two assumptions. First, one assumes that mass tendencies in individual-level beliefs differ from one population to another, providing meaningful descriptions of a population's political culture. Second, one assumes that mass beliefs are relevant in shaping the emergence, survival, and functioning of political systems. This relevance claim constitutes the major justification of most political culture research: unless mass beliefs affect political systems, there is little point in analyzing them. But even though this is the field's most fundamental claim it has rarely been demonstrated or even investigated. In fact most research has been limited to analyzing orientations and beliefs at the individual level.

This chapter addresses this puzzle in three steps. To begin with, we outline why political culture studies have been reluctant to analyze the aggregate effect of mass beliefs on democracy. As we will show, this has much to do with the widespread assumption that the impact of mass beliefs on democracy can be inferred from individual-level findings. In the next step we will illustrate that this assumption represents an "individualistic fallacy," arguing that the impact of mass beliefs on democracy can only be analyzed at the aggregate level, for democracy only exists at this level. In the final step we report findings from recent studies, which demonstrate that mass beliefs have indeed an aggregate effect on the emergence and survival of democracy. We relate this insight to other approaches in the comparative study of democracy, embedding it in a broader theory of democratic development.

2 CONGRUENCE THEORY

The claim that mass beliefs are system relevant was formulated long ago. When Aristotle asked in *Politics* why some polities have oligarchic orders while others have democratic ones, he sought the answer in the prevailing mentality of a given polity: a democratic order, for example, flourishes when the prevailing mentality is one of moderation and mutual respect, so that citizens consider each other as equals. More than 2,000 years later similar arguments were advanced by Charles de Montesquieu (1748) in *De l'esprit des lois* and Alexis de Tocqueville (1843) in *De la démocratie en Amérique*, both of whom speculated that political systems in which power is subject to popular control are most likely found among publics with a liberal-minded spirit.

All of these works assume that there is a natural link between two different types of societal-level phenomena: *institutional system properties* characterizing a society's political system, and *psychological mass tendencies* describing a population's dominant orientations. In modern times, Eckstein (1966) framed this *mass-system linkage* in terms of congruence theory, claiming that the political system's authority patterns must be congruent with the authority orientations that guide people in their daily activities. Otherwise the system will lack acceptance and become unstable. A democratic order, for example, will be fragile if it is imposed on an authoritarian-minded population.

The failure of democracy in Weimar Germany is a significant illustration of this pattern. Certainly, deficiencies in institutional design helped the Nazis to abuse democratic procedures, but these deficiencies do not explain why the Nazis were able to gain mass support in the first place. Along with others, Bracher (1971/1955) concluded that democracy failed in Weimar Germany because it was a "democracy without democrats." The assumption underlying this statement is that democracy was incongruent with the authoritarian-minded spirit of most Germans, a legacy of Prussian militarism under the Kaisers. The authoritarian mentality did not suffice to guarantee the failure of democracy in Weimar Germany. But it made the arrangement so vulnerable that it broke down under the impact of the Great Depression.

3 DEMOCRATIC AND AUTHORITARIAN PERSONALITY

Empirical research on belief systems began with psychological studies of personality types. Adorno et al. (1950) identified an "authoritarian personality," which these authors saw rooted in threat perceptions that nurture low self-esteem, misanthropy, and dogmatic rigidity. In a complementary way, Lasswell (1951) explored the qualities of the "democratic character," which emanates from "freedom from anxiety" and consists of an open ego, confidence in human potentialities, and above all self-esteem. Succinctly put: "The failure of democracy is the failure to develop social relations that allow for high levels of self-esteem" (Lasswell 1951, 521).

Likewise, Maslow (1988/1954) argued that two essential facets of a "self-actualizing" orientation–emphasis on individual autonomy and a sense of human equality—constitute a democratic orientation, "indeed a democratic orientation in the deepest possible sense" (Maslow 1988/1954, 167). For people who rely on their own judgement and see others as equals are unlikely to accept absolute authority and are not easily mobilized against other groups of people. Thus, an emancipative orientation that combines individualistic and humanistic attitudes makes people immune to authoritarian and xenophobic temptations, diminishing the support basis of demagogues and autocrats.

In the same vein, Rokeach (1960) held that authoritarianism and xenophobia are allied in a "closed" belief system, which is anchored in existential threats. By the same token, liberalism and altruism go together in an "open" belief system, anchored in existential security (Rokeach 1960, 72). Asking with which political systems these orientations are most compatible, it is evident that open beliefs are more compatible with democracy, while closed beliefs are more compatible with authoritarian rule (Rokeach 1973). Triandis (1995, 50–60) made a similar assumption. He classified societies in which open beliefs prevail as "individualistic cultures" and societies in which closed beliefs are dominant as "collectivist cultures," claiming that individualistic cultures have a stronger affinity to democracy than collectivist ones. All of this work points to the conclusion that a population's prevailing psychological outlook is a selective force in the emergence and survival of political regimes, helping to delegitimize incompatible regimes and legitimize compatible ones.

4 A PSYCHOLOGICAL THEORY OF DEMOCRATIC DEVELOPMENT

Political scientists are largely unaware of these early psychological approaches. This is a serious deficiency as these approaches provide the building blocks of a comprehensive theory of democracy in two ways. First, they identify types of psychological orientations that constitute a selective force in the evolution of political systems. Second, they link these orientations with social conditions that determine which orientations tend to become dominant in a society. Putting these two aspects together leads to a comprehensive theory of democratic development.

First, social configurations that induce existential pressures (e.g. precarious economic conditions, crime and war, conflated cleavages, and extreme social polarization) are conducive to closed belief systems. Existential pressures tend to close people's minds because they make people feel vulnerable, leading them seek for protection under the shield of group cohesion, absolute authority, and dogmatic rules. By the same token, social configurations that induce more secure existential conditions (e.g. economic prosperity, physical security, cross-cutting cleavages, and moderate social polarization) nourish open belief systems. Permissive existential conditions tend to open people's minds because they lower anxiety, diminishing the need for protection that nurtures group closure, absolute authority, and dogmatic rules. This gives people more room to emphasize autonomy, liberty, tolerance, and trust. Hence, processes such as economic modernization that bring more favorable existential conditions tend to shift a society's belief system from a more closed to a more open outlook (Inglehart 1977, 1990, 1997).

Second, belief systems affect the legitimacy of institutional settings, with closed belief systems legitimizing authoritarian systems and open belief systems legitimizing democratic ones. Thus, if closed mass beliefs change into open ones, a given authoritarian system comes into conflict with mass beliefs. The system becomes illegitimate. Other conditions being equal, this makes an institutional change to democracy more likely because open beliefs provide the motivations guiding people to support pro-democracy movements and join freedom campaigns. Conversely, economic breakdowns or social crises tend to close people's minds in ways making them more receptive to authoritarian solutions. In any case, belief systems should constitute a major selective force in the evolution of political systems.

Dahl (1973) advanced another variant of this assumption, arguing that the psychological orientations he considers conducive to democracy (tolerance and moderation) emerge under specific social conditions: middle-class-dominated, meritocratic market societies. This type of societies, which already existed in pre-industrial freeholder or merchant communities, is characterized by relatively equal opportunities (in terms of market access) and existential autonomy (in terms of individual property). Equal opportunities and existential autonomy nurture a sense of human equality and choice, eliminating the need for absolute authority and group closure. Dahl, like Lipset (1959), saw libertarian-egalitarian orientations embedded in social configurations that feature meritocracy, existential autonomy, and relatively equal opportunities. And like Lipset, he saw these libertarian-egalitarian orientations as the psychological ground on which democracies emerge, survive, and flourish. Taken together these reflections provide the model of regime selection depicted in Table 13.1.

This model differs from recent versions of modernization theory (Przeworski and Limongi 1997) and resource distribution theories (Vanhanen 2003; Boix 2003) in that

Table 13.1 A psychological model of regime selection

	Authoritarian track	Democratic track
Objective social conditions	Pressing and polarized	Permissive and balanced
	⇓	⇓
Subjective orientations	Closed mass beliefs	Open mass beliefs
	⇓	⇓
Selective force in favor of	Authoritarian regimes	Democratic regimes

it includes mass beliefs. Including mass beliefs as an intervening variable between socioeconomic conditions and democratization is completely logical. Democratization cannot be achieved by socioeconomic conditions themselves as it always needs collective actions to install democracy; but such actions in turn need motivational forces driving them to seek a particular outcome such as democracy. Mass beliefs provide these motivational forces. Thus, people's prevailing beliefs translate socioeconomic conditions into the collective actions that attain, sustain, and deepen democracy.

Although the building blocks of this model have been available for many years, it has not been tested empirically until recently. This is partly a legacy of how the influential civic culture study conceptualized the link between mass beliefs and democracy.

5 THE LEGACY OF THE CIVIC CULTURE STUDY

Studies of personality types helped to identify the psychological orientations giving people a predisposition to support democratic or authoritarian rule, respectively. But these psychological studies did not measure how widespread these orientations are among given populations, so no assessment of an entire society's democratic "maturity" was possible.

This deficiency was a starting point of the civic culture study by Almond and Verba (1963), which conducted representative national surveys of orientations that were thought to be crucial for the persistence of democracy. This was done in five countries allowing for cross-national comparisons of political culture. A number of important political culture studies followed this example, such as the Political Action study (Barnes and Kaase et al. 1979), the Continuities in Political Action study (Jennings and van Deth 1989), and the Beliefs in Government series (Kaase and Newton 1995). These studies stimulated the emergence of long-term cross-national survey programs, the first of them being the Eurobarometer, followed by the International Social Survey Program, Latinobarometer, the New Europe Barometer, the Afrobarometer, the East Asia Barometer, the Asiabarometer, and the Comparative Study of Electoral Systems. Finally, the European Values Study led to the emergence of a genuine World Values Survey that has now measured mass beliefs in more than eighty societies worldwide.

The civic culture study covered only five countries, which is too small a number to permit statistically significant analyses of the linkage between mass beliefs and variation in political systems. But we now have data from scores of societies, covering the full range from authoritarian to democratic regimes, which makes it possible for the first time to test the central claim of the political culture school—that cross-national variation in mass beliefs affects democracy.

Despite a massively widened database, statistically significant tests of whether and to what extent mass beliefs affect democracy are still very rare (exceptions include Muller and Seligson 1994; Inglehart 1997, ch. 6; Welzel, Inglehart, and Klingemann 2003; Seligson 2002; Hadenius and Teorell 2006; Welzel and Inglehart 2006; Welzel 2006). This is partly a legacy of the way in which the civic culture study conceptualized the link between mass beliefs and democracy.

The civic culture study champions a "civic allegiance" model emphasizing orientations that support democratic systems when they are already in place. These orientations include satisfaction with participative opportunities, policy outcomes, and a given democratic system at large. The fixation on allegiance led to a neglect of orientations that motivate people to *oppose* a given system and to demand democracy when it is not in place. This has left a lasting imprint on political culture studies to date, which are still more concerned with attitudes that help to consolidate democracy than with attitudes motivating popular pressure to democratize. As a consequence, the political culture approach has been ill equipped to shape the field of comparative democratization studies—despite an improved database. In a sense the civic culture tradition has distracted studies of mass beliefs too far from the older psychological studies. It became forgotten that this work identified the orientations that can motivate popular pressure to democratize.

Why did the civic culture study not conceptualize mass orientations in light of their potential to motivate pressures to democratize? A plausible answer is that when Almond and Verba were writing no "societal-led" democratization was observable. Societal-led transitions to democracy seemed to have been a unique feature of the handful of early democracies in Western Europe and North America where democratization had started with the liberal revolutions of the eighteenth century. When Almond and Verba were writing, the most salient cases of democratization (Germany, Italy, and Japan) were post-war democracies in which democratization was not a societal-led but rather an "externally monitored" process (Karl and Schmitter 1991). In this light it seemed that mass orientations that—in theory—could motivate popular pressure to democratize are practically irrelevant when the question of whether a society becomes democratic or not is decided by external events such as wars and military intervention. In such cases, mass orientations can affect the survival but not the attainment of democracy.

But externally monitored democratization played virtually no role in the massive third wave of democratization (Huntington 1991). Apart from Grenada, all of the third wave transitions were of the societal-led type, in which internal forces played the crucial role. But a lingering tendency to consider mass orientations as democracy consolidating, but not democracy inducing, has inhibited the political culture school in the study of democratization. Insensitivity to the individualistic fallacy is another reason for this inhibition.

6 OVERLOOKING THE INDIVIDUALISTIC FALLACY

Most political culture studies examine the individual-level determinants of attitudes that are assumed to have an impact at the societal level. Scholars who analyze support for democracy do this because they assume that more widespread support makes democratic systems more stable. But even though this is an aggregate-level assumption, scholars do not test it at this level. Instead they estimate individual-level effects on support for democracy, as if knowing what increases support for democracy at the individual level is the same as knowing what stabilizes democracy at the aggregate level (Seligson 2002).

Almond and Verba (1963, 186) set a precedent for this practice, opening chapter 8 of the civic culture study by claiming to analyze "how civic competence and participation affect a political system." Although this addresses an aggregate-level question in which the dependent variable is a society's political system, Almond and Verba actually analyze how system support at the individual level is shaped by people's sense of subjective competence and self-reported political participation. This example was followed in scores of subsequent studies, all of which assume that when one knows what increases support for democracy at the individual level, one also knows what strengthens democracy at the aggregate level. The assumption that one can draw aggregate-level conclusions from individual-level findings pervades the entire political culture literature.

The fact that this assumption is widespread does not make it true. In fact it is false. Knowing what increases incomes at the individual level does not tell us what increases incomes at the aggregate level. If making profit through corruption increases incomes at the individual level, one cannot conclude that more corruption will increase national income levels. Concluding that the way things operate at one level of analysis, tells us how they function at another level, is a mere leap of faith that cannot be taken for granted until the conclusion has been tested.

This was demonstrated long ago by Robinson (1950) who showed that the relationship between two variables can vary in strength, significance, and sign at different levels of analyses. Robinson concluded that no inference from one level of analysis to another level is validated until it has been tested. This is true for cross-level inferences in both directions: the "ecological fallacy" consists in falsely assuming that a relationship found at the aggregate level also exists at the individual level. But the reverse form of reasoning is also unwarranted: the "individualistic fallacy" consists in falsely assuming that a relationship found at the individual level also exists at the aggregate level (Alker 1969).

There is widespread awareness of the ecological fallacy but research in mass beliefs is remarkably unaware of the individualistic fallacy. In fact, the prevailing conception of the ecological fallacy is itself an exemplification of the individualistic fallacy.

7 MISCONCEPTIONS OF THE ECOLOGICAL FALLACY

The prevailing conception of the ecological fallacy has made scholars very hesitant to analyze aggregate-level effects of individual-level attitudes. Unfortunately, this is unnecessary as the prevailing conception of the ecological fallacy is itself fallacious. Consider one of the most widely cited notions of the ecological fallacy problem: Przeworski and Teune's (1970, 73) dictum that an aggregate-level relation that is not reflected at the individual-level within each aggregate unit is spurious. This claim implies that an aggregate-level relation is meaningless if it does not show up in the same way among individuals within the units of aggregation.[1] Scholars still use this dictum as authority to invalidate aggregate-level findings by demonstrating that the same relations are not present at the individual level (Seligson 2002). Let's consider an example showing why this method is flawed.

There was a significant aggregate-level relation between the Nazi vote and the unemployment rate in late Weimar Germany, such that people in regions with higher unemployment rates were more likely to vote the Nazis. But Falter (1991) has shown that within a given region, unemployed people were *not* more likely to vote for the Nazis than people who had jobs. If one applied Przeworski and Teune's dictum to this case, one must conclude that the region-level relation between unemployment and the Nazi vote is meaningless because there is no corresponding relation among individuals within the regions. This is a strong cross-level inference: one deduces the non-validity of an existing relation at the aggregate level from the non-existence of the same relation at the individual level—which is a pure form of the individualistic fallacy (for another exemplification of this flaw, see Hadenius and Teorell 2006).

The failure in this conclusion is to overlook that social phenomena, such as unemployment, do not have to influence the behavior of an individual as a *personal* attribute of this individual itself; they can also influence the behavior of an individual

---

[1] To avoid misunderstandings, we do not claim that there is no such thing as an ecological fallacy. We only claim that a widespread notion of it is wrong.

as an aggregate attribute of the population in which the individual lives. In this case the relation is invisible at the individual level *within* populations. It only becomes obvious when aggregate-level variation between populations is taken into account. To be concrete, individuals were not more likely to vote for the Nazis if they themselves were unemployed. For this reason there was no individual-level relation between unemployment and the Nazi vote within regions. But individuals were more likely to vote for the Nazis if unemployment in their region was high because regional unemployment created anxiety affecting all individuals in the same region, regardless of whether they had themselves been unemployed or not. Thus, regional populations with higher aggregate unemployment had higher aggregate vote shares of the Nazis.

The fact that a phenomenon such as unemployment affects individual behavior as an aggregate attribute of the surrounding population, not as a personal attribute of the individuals themselves, does not make this phenomenon spurious. The fact that unemployment affected voting behavior as an aggregate attribute rather than a personal property does *not* invalidate unemployment as a cause of a rising Nazi vote share. It simply illuminates the mechanism through which unemployment became effective. In this case this was largely an *ecological* mechanism: aggregate unemployment, not individual unemployment, shaped people's behavior.

8 AGGREGATE RELATIONS BETWEEN INDIVIDUAL-LEVEL BELIEFS

Analyzing four waves of individual-level data from the World Values Survey, Inglehart and Welzel (2005) identified a broad syndrome of emancipative orientations, which they labeled "self-expression values." This syndrome resembles what Rokeach (1960) called an open belief system or what Maslow (1988/1954) characterized as a "self-actualizing" orientation, and approximates what Lipset (1959) and Dahl (1973) described as libertarian-egalitarian orientations. According to Lasswell (1951) this syndrome is rooted in a "general belief in human potentialities"—a belief that integrates individualistic and humanistic attitudes into an overarching emancipative orientation. Through an aggregate-level factor analysis based on 140 national surveys, this emancipative orientation becomes manifest in five attitudes (factor loadings on common dimension in brackets): emphasis on human freedom reflected in liberty aspirations (.87), an affinity to civic action reflected in self-reported participation in petitions (.84), a sense of self-esteem reflected in life satisfaction (.82), tolerance of nonconformity reflected in acceptance of homosexuality (.78) and an open-minded attitude to others reflected in generalized trust in people (.61).[2]

---

[2] For measurement details see the Internet Appendix to Inglehart and Welzel (2005) at **www.world valuessurvey.org/publications/humandevelopment.html** under "Variables" (#49).

Two components of this syndrome, liberty aspirations and life satisfaction, are very weakly related at the individual level within populations, showing correlations as low as $r=.01$ in a number of national samples. But at the aggregate level we find a highly significant $r=.67$ correlation between liberty aspirations and life satisfaction: populations in which more people value liberty are on average more satisfied with their lives. But people are not more satisfied with their lives than the average of their population when they also are more liberty-minded than average. It is not people's own liberty-mindedness that affects their life satisfaction. Instead, the effect is ecological: populations in which an emphasis on liberty is widespread create a liberal climate that affects all individuals in that population, increasing the mean level of life satisfaction. Thus, esteem of liberty does not impact on life satisfaction as a personal characteristic, but as an aggregate property of one's society.[3] Ecological effects of this sort are invisible among individuals within the same aggregate unit; they become manifest only when one varies the aggregate units. The fact that many characteristics affect individuals as aggregate attributes of their population, not as their personal attributes, is not an ecological *fallacy* but an ecological *reality*.

Some relations are entirely ecological and *only* exist at the aggregate level. Democracy, for example, exists only at the aggregate level, so the assumption that the beliefs of individuals affect democracy can only mean that aggregations of these beliefs affect democracy. But this has rarely been demonstrated.

9 MASS BELIEFS IN DEMOCRATIZATION RESEARCH

Among hundreds of articles in comparative survey research dealing with democratic attitudes, only a handful have analyzed the linkage between mass beliefs and democracy at the aggregate level. Among the few exceptions is Putnam's (1993) study in which he demonstrates a strong aggregate-level relation between democratic performance and generalized trust. But this aggregate analysis, convincing as it is, is limited to regions within one nation, Italy. Very few comparable studies have been done on a multi-country basis, the exceptions including work by Paxton (2002) and Norris (2002).

The lack of studies analyzing the aggregate effects of beliefs is particularly obvious in one of the most important fields of comparative politics: the study of democratization. The study of democratization has been dominated by two approaches: an actor-centered approach focusing on collective actions that bring democracy, and a

---

[3] In a regression analysis in which individual life satisfaction is the dependent variable (measured on a 1 to 10 scale) and in which an individual's own liberty aspirations as well as its population's aggregate liberty aspirations are introduced as predictors ($N=241,125$), aggregate liberty aspirations show a clearly stronger effect than individual liberty aspirations (the beta coefficients are .296 and .012).

structural approach emphasizing socioeconomic configurations that condition democratization processes. Neither of these approaches pays much attention to mass attitudes. This is surprising, since the political participation literature, the social movement literature, and the mobilization literature all have demonstrated that attitudes operate as a major intervening force between socioeconomic conditions, on one hand, and collective actions on the other hand (Klandermans 1984; McAdam 1986; Verba, Schlozman, and Brady 1995). These studies make it clear that socioeconomic conditions cannot translate into collective actions unless these conditions help produce the attitudes that *motivate* these actions. Socioeconomic conditions structure societies but cannot by themselves generate specific actions. Conversely, collective actions do not take place without motivational forces that channel them towards specific goals. Thus, any explanation of democratization is incomplete if it does not include the motivational forces through which objective socioeconomic conditions translate into concrete collective actions (Huntington 1991, 69).

These considerations point to a model in which democratization is explained by (1) given socioeconomic conditions being conducive to (2) specific patterns of mass beliefs that (3) motivate the collective actions that ultimately bring democratization.

The most comprehensive analyses to test this model were carried out by Welzel and Inglehart (Welzel, Inglehart, and Klingemann 2003; Welzel and Inglehart 2005, 2006; Inglehart and Welzel 2005; Welzel 2006). Their findings confirm this model in three respects. First, they show that there is an ecological syndrome of emancipative orientations whose attitudinal components resemble what Lasswell, Rokeach, and Maslow, respectively, described as "democratic," "open," and "self-actualizing" orientations. This syndrome integrates individualistic and humanistic attitudes into an emancipative ethos tapping liberty aspirations, tolerance of nonconformity, affinity to civic action, trust in people, and a sense of self-esteem. The components of this syndrome vary consistently between populations, with populations that score high on one of these orientations scoring correspondingly high on the others as well.

Second, this syndrome of emancipative orientations is rooted in social configurations that lower existential pressures and bring more permissive living conditions, giving people a stronger sense of security and autonomy. Economic modernization contributes to this process as it increases people's material resources, intellectual skills, and social opportunities to network with other people as they choose. This nurtures a sense of human autonomy that leads people to emphasize emancipative ideals, giving rise to mass self-expression values. Accordingly, a summary indicator of a population's material resources, intellectual skills, and social networks taken from Vanhanen (1997)[4] predicts very well how large a share of a population

---

[4] Vanhanen measures the availability of material resources using data on the share of family farms in the agrarian sector and the deconcentration of production property outside the agrarian sector. To measure intellectual skills he uses literacy rates and tertiary enrollment ratios. We interpret his measure of occupational complexity (based on urbanization and the size of the non-agrarian sectors) as an indicator of network diversity, assuming that more complex societies have more diverse networks. Vanhanen combines these three measures of resources, skills, and networks in a summary indicator that he calls "power resources." We use his measures of this index for around 1993 (see Vanhanen 1997, 42–63).

emphasizes emancipative ideals. As the partial plot in Figure 13.1 illustrates, the fact that permissive conditions give rise to emancipative orientations is not a Western phenomenon, restricted to Protestant societies as a cultural relativist might suspect. For the effect holds even when one controls for the strength of a society's Protestant tradition.[5]

Third, emancipative mass orientations are conducive to democratization, especially the rise of "effective" democracy, as opposed to mere electoral democracy: the extent to which a society emphasizes emancipative ideals explains fully 80 percent

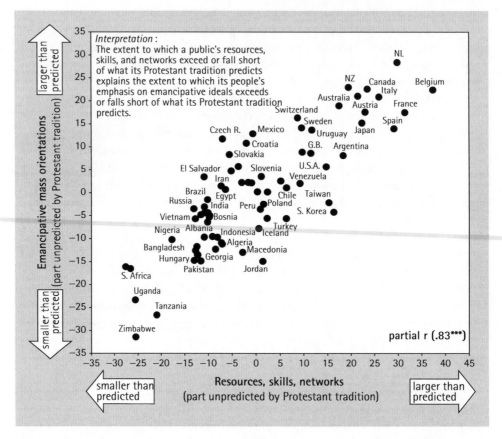

Fig. 13.1 The effect of resources, skills and networks on emancipative orientations controlling for the protestant tradition

Note: Resources, skills, and networks cover a period in the early 1990s. Emancipative orientations cover the period 1989–1999. The control variable (Protestant tradition) covers the early 1990s.

[5] As a proxy for the strength of the Protestant tradition we use the percentage of denominational Protestants per country (data are from the early 1990s taken from the Britannica Book of the Year 1998).

of the variance in effective democracy.[6] One might suspect that the causal order of this effect runs in fact into the opposite direction, so that widespread emancipative orientations are produced by previous democracy. But this is not the case as the partial plot in Figure 13.2 indicates. Controlling for the level of democracy measured before emancipative orientations,[7] these orientations still show a significantly positive effect on subsequent levels of effective democracy. Interestingly, emancipative mass orientations have an even stronger effect on democracy than has explicit mass support for democracy. The reason for this is that emancipative orientations indicate an intrinsic commitment to the principles of liberty and tolerance that are inherent in the concept of democracy without naming it. By contrast, support for the mere word democracy can easily be inflated by lip service without involving deeper commitments to democratic freedoms. Thus, emancipative orientations give people a firmer motivation to stand up for democratic freedoms than does explicit support for democracy (Inglehart and Welzel 2005, 270).

We assume that emancipative mass orientations affect democracy because these orientations motivate the mass actions that help sustain or attain democratic freedoms. Evidence for this is available for self-reported participation in civic mass action. When one separates participation in civic actions from emancipative orientations, treating self-reported activities such as demonstrations, boycotts, and petitions as a dependent variable, emancipative orientations show the strongest effect on these activities, both at the individual and aggregate level (Welzel, Inglehart, and Deutsch 2005, 136). Interestingly, the individual-level impact of emancipative orientations on civic action varies with the distribution of individual resources in a society, as a multi-level model shows. Although there is a significant fixed effect of emancipative orientations on civic actions that holds under all context variations (including authoritarian systems), it is also true that the strength of the effect grows with more widespread resources and freedom. In other words, emancipative orientations always translate into civic actions, but they do so more easily when more resources are available.

---

[6] Our measure of "effective" democracy deflates measures of democratic freedom taken from Freedom House. It deflates democratic freedom to the extent to which corrupt governance practices lower the quality of this freedom (corruption measures taken from the World Bank). Thus, a society's effective level of democracy can be low for either of two reasons: either there is no democratic freedom, so there is nothing to deflate; or there is democratic freedom but corrupt governance practices deflate it seriously. In both cases, citizens are hindered to effectively practice democratic liberties, a perspective under which it does not matter for which of the two reasons effective democracy is low. Note that the societies' "effective" levels of democratic freedom are more closely related to emancipative mass orientations than is true for "raw" levels of democratic freedom. India, for instance, is in no way an outlier with respect to its effective level of democracy, which is located where the Indians' emancipative orientations predict it should be. Also, societies do not bounce in their effective levels of democratic freedom as they sometimes do in their raw levels of democratic freedom when a democratic constitution is adopted or abandoned (Welzel and Inglehart 2006). For measurement details see the Internet Appendix to Inglehart and Welzel 2005 at **www.worldvaluessurvey.org/publications/humandevelopment.html**, under "Variables" (#21).

[7] For this matter we use a summary democracy score combining the Freedom House scores and the Polity IV scores covering the years 1984–8. This period ends one year before the period covered by emancipative orientations starts.

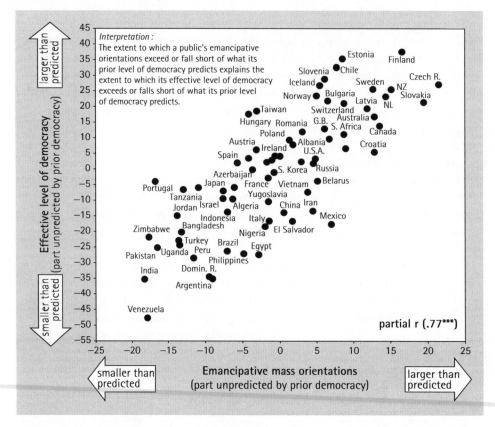

Fig. 13.2 The partial effect of emancipative orientations on effective democracy controlling for prior democracy

Note: The measure of effective democracy covers the years 2000–2004. Emancipative orientations cover the period 1989–1999. The control variable (prior democracy) covers the period 1984–88.

Unfortunately, the linkage between mass orientations and actions cannot be systematically analyzed with regard to *observed* mass activities because standardized data on observed actions are not available in the same differentiation as data on mass orientations. But some illustration is possible using the threefold classification by Karatnycky and Ackerman (2005). These authors have shown that whether a non-democracy converts into democracy, whether such a transition will end in incomplete democracy only or lead to complete democracy, and whether a fall back into non-democracy happens, all depends on how much the public is involved in pro-democratic civic actions. To demonstrate this, Karatnycky and Ackerman have classified mass involvement in pro-democratic civic actions as "weak or absent," "moderate," and "strong." Using this classification, the box plot in Figure 13.3 shows that pro-democratic mass actions are indeed linked with emancipative mass orientations. Emancipative orientations are least widespread where pro-democratic mass activities are weak or absent and most widespread where these activities are strongest.

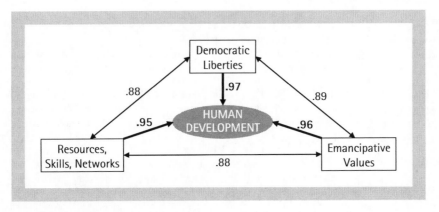

Fig. 13.3 The human development dexus

Note: Numbers on bidirectional arrows are correlation coefficients (r). Numbers on one-directional ARROWS are factor loadings on common underlying dimension. N=74.

Regardless of how exactly the causal mechanisms operate, the crucial point is that (1) people's resources, skills, and networks, (2) their emancipative orientations, and (3) their democratic liberties go so closely together that they indeed reflect just one underlying dimension of cross-national variation. This is illustrated in Figure 13.4. We call this underlying dimension "human" development. For the common theme underlying each of its three components—freedom of choice—constitutes a genuinely *human* potential (Sen 1999). Since making autonomous choices is a universal potential of our species, societies do not differ in this human potential, regardless of cultural traditions. What differs is how much space societies allow for the human potential to develop. As Table 13.2 illustrates, this space is measured in three major dimensions of social reality: socioeconomic conditions, cultural belief systems, and political institutions. Within this framework, democracy is just one out of three major manifestations of human emancipation, all three of which tend to co-evolve very closely.

10 Mass Beliefs and Institutions

The psychological make-up of given populations is a central aspect of social reality: societies are run by believing, thinking, and striving people. Political culture research measures and analyzes this aspect of reality through standardized cross-national surveys. It focuses on the very core of democracy, the people.

The political culture approach differs in important ways from institutional approaches. Institutional approaches have tended to ignore attitudes, assuming that human motivations do not differ—or if they do, they do so only as a response to different incentives set by institutions. Thus, under given institutional settings, human motivations are seen as constant, so that it is unnecessary to measure them.

Table 13.2 The human development (HD) of societies

	Socioeconomic dimension	Cultural dimension	Institutional dimension
HD takes place when:	**Resources, skills, and networks** empower people *means-wise.*	**Emancipative ideals** empower people *motivation-wise.*	**Democratic liberties** empower people *rights-wise.*
HD determines:	the extent **able** to pursue	to which **willing** self-chosen	people are **entitled** priorities
HD enlarges people's:	**Capabilities** of	**Aspirations** for Self-determination	**Entitlements** to
HD results in:	**Human**	**empowerment**	
	(diminishing external constraints on intrinsic human choice)		

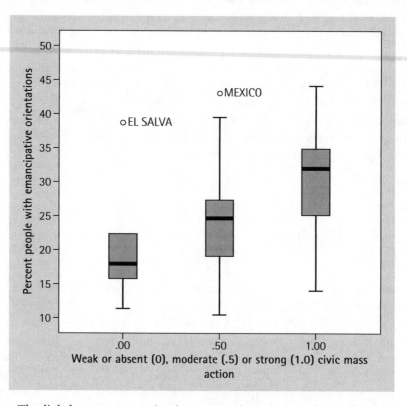

Fig. 13.4 The link between emancipative mass orientations and pro-democracy mass action

The political culture approach, by contrast, assumes that human motivations can and do differ, independent of institutional incentives. Because institutional incentives are *extrinsic* to people, these incentives do not override people's *intrinsic* motivations. But precisely because of this, what institutions offer can easily come into conflict with what people want. This is why motivational forces sometimes nurture pressures for institutional change, as when rising emancipative orientations motivate social pressures to democratize an authoritarian regime.

11 CONCLUSION

We started from the puzzle that the most central premise of the political culture school—that mass beliefs affect democracy—has rarely been tested, outlining some of the reasons why this is so. Besides the fact that suitable data have not been available until recently, a neglect of attitudes that motivate pressures to democratize in combination with the belief that individual-level findings allow for conclusions about the state of democracy at the aggregate level, all inhibited the political culture school to demonstrate that mass tendencies in individual-level beliefs have aggregate effects on democracy. We argued that this is an unnecessary deficiency, going back to psychological studies that already identified the emancipative orientations that are most likely to motivate popular pressures to democratize. Then we reported findings from a series of recent cross-national studies that have analyzed the effects of mass beliefs on the broadest possible basis. These findings indicate that emancipative mass orientations have indeed a positive effect on democracy and are themselves nurtured by socioeconomic modernization. These findings locate democracy in a broader theory of human development, the underlying theme of which is human emancipation. As an emancipative achievement, democracy flourishes most in an emancipative environment, of which emancipative beliefs are a central component. We conclude that for the first time in the history of comparative politics there is systematic evidence demonstrating that the political culture school's most central claim is correct: mass beliefs do affect democracy.

REFERENCES

ADORNO, T., FRENKEL-BRUNSWICK, E., LEVINSON, D., and SANFORD, R. N. 1950. *The Authoritarian Personality*. New York: Wiley.

ALKER, H. R., Jr. 1969. A typology of ecological fallacies. Pp. 69–86 in *Quantitative Ecological Analysis in the Social Sciences*, ed. M. Dogan and S. Rokkan. Cambridge, Mass.: MIT Press.

ALMOND, G. A., and VERBA, S. 1963. *The Civic Culture: Political Attitudes in Five Western Democracies*. Princeton: Princeton University Press.

ANDERSON, C. J., and TVERDOVA, Y. V. 2001. Winners, losers, and attitudes about government in contemporary democracies. *International Political Science Review,* 22 (4): 321–38.

—— et al. 2005. *Losers' Consent.* Oxford: Oxford University Press.

BARNES, S. H., KAASE, M., et al. 1979. *Political Action: Mass Participation in Five Western Democracies.* Beverly Hills, Calif.: Sage.

BELLAH, R. N. et al. 1996. *Habits of the Heart. Individualism and Commitment in American Life.* Berkeley and Los Angeles: University of California Press.

BOIX, C. 2003. *Democracy and Redistribution.* New York: Cambridge University Press.

BRACHER, K. D. 1971/1955. *Die Auflösung der Weimarer Republik* [The Dissolution of the Weimar Republic], 5th edn. Königstein: Deutsche Verlagsanstalt.

BRATTON, M., and MATTES, R. 2001. Support for democracy in Africa: intrinsic or instrumental? *British Journal of Political Science,* 31: 447–74.

—— —— and GYMIAH-BOADI, E. 2005. *Public Opinion, Democracy, and Market Reform in Africa.* New York: Cambridge University Press.

CHANLEY, V. A., RUDOLPH, T. J., and RAHN, W. M. 2000. The origins and consequences of public trust in government: a time series analysis. *Public Opinion Quarterly,* 64: 239–56.

CINGRANELLI, D., and BOOTH, R. 2004. *CIRI Data Set.* Downloadable at **http://ciri.binghamton.edu/index.asp**

CONVERSE, P. E. 1970. Attitudes and non-attitudes. Pp. 168–89 in *The Quantitative Analysis of Social Problems,* ed. E. R. Tufte. Reading, Mass.: Addison-Wesley.

CROZIER, M., HUNTINGTON, S. P. and WATANUKI, J. 1975. *The Crisis of Democracy.* New York: New York University Press.

DAHL, R. A. 1973. *Polyarchy: Participation and Opposition.* New Haven: Yale University Press. 1st edn. 1971.

DALTON, R. J. 2004. *Democratic Challenges, Democratic Choices.* Oxford: Oxford University Press.

DIAMOND, L. 1999. *Developing Democracy: Towards Consolidation.* Baltimore: Johns Hopkins University Press.

—— 2003. Can the whole world become democratic? Center for the Study of Democracy. Paper 03–05.

DOORENSPLEET, R. 2004. The structural context of recent transitions to democracy. *European Journal of Political Research,* 43: 309–36.

ECKSTEIN, H. 1966: *A Theory of Stable Democracy.* Princeton: Princeton University Press.

ELKINS, Z. 2000. Gradations of democracy? Empirical tests of alternative conceptualizations. *American Journal of Political Science,* 44: 293–300.

ETZIONI, A. 1993. *The Spirit of Community.* New York: Crown Publishers.

FREEDOM HOUSE. 2005. *Freedom Ratings.* Dataset downloadable at **www.freedomhouse.org**

FALTER, J. 1991. *Hitlers Wähler* [Hitler's Voters]. Munich: C. H. Beck.

GASIOROWSKI, M. J., and POWER, T. J. 1998. The structural determinants of democratic consolidation: evidence from the Third World. *Comparative Political Studies,* 31: 740–71.

GIBSON, J. L. 1997. Mass opposition to the Soviet putsch of August 1991: collective action, rational choice, and democratic values. *American Political Science Review,* 91: 671–84.

—— 2001. Social networks, civil society, and the prospects for consolidating Russia's democratic transition. *American Journal of Political Science,* 45 (1): 51–69.

—— DUCH, R., and TEDIN, K. L. 1992. Democratic values and the transformation of the Soviet Union. *Journal of Politics,* 54: 329–71.

HADENIUS, A., and TEORELL, J. 2006. Democracy without democratic values. *Studies in Comparative International Development,* 47: 95–111.

HOFFERBERT, R. I., and KLINGEMANN, H.-D. 1999. Remembering the bad old days: human rights, economic conditions, and democratic performance in transitional regimes. *European Journal of Political Research*, 36 (1): 155–74.

HUNTINGTON, S. P. 1991. *The Third Wave: Democratization in the Late Twentieth Century.* Norman: University of Oklahoma Press.

INGLEHART, R. 1977. *The Silent Revolution.* Princeton: Princeton University Press.

——1990. *Culture Shift in Advanced Industrial Societies.* Princeton: Princeton University Press.

——1997. *Modernization and Postmodernization.* Princeton: Princeton University Press.

——and WELZEL, C. 2005. *Modernization, Cultural Change, and Democracy: The Human Development Sequence.* New York: Cambridge University Press.

JENNINGS, M. K., and VAN DETH, J. W. eds. 1989. *Continuities in Political Action.* Berlin: deGruyter.

KAASE, M., and NEWTON, K. eds. 1995. *Beliefs in Government*, 4 vols. Oxford: Oxford University Press.

KARL, T. L., and SCHMITTER, P. C. 1991. Modes of transition in Latin America, southern and eastern Europe. *International Social Science Journal*, 128: 269–84.

KARATNYCKY, A., and ACKERMAN, P. 2005. *How Freedom is Won: From Civic Resistance to Durable Democracy.* Washington, DC: Freedom House.

KAUFMANN, D., KRAAY, A., and MASTRUZZI, M. 2005. Governance matters III: governance indicators for 1996–2004. World Bank Policy Research Department Working Paper No. 2195. Washington, DC: World Bank.

KLANDERMANS, B. 1984. Mobilization and participation: social-psychological expansions of resource mobilization theory. *American Sociological Review*, 49: 583–600.

KLINGEMANN, H.-D. 1999. Mapping political support in the 1990s: a global analysis. Pp. 31–56 in *Critical Citizens: Global Support for Democratic Governance*, ed. P. Norris. New York: Oxford University Press.

——and FUCHS, D. eds. 1995. *Citizens and the State.* Beliefs in Government 1. Oxford: Oxford University Press.

LASSWELL, H. D. 1951. *Democratic Character.* Glencoe, Ill.: Free Press.

LEAMER, E. E. 1985. Sensitivity analysis would help. *American Economic Review*, 57: 308–13.

LEVI, M., and STOKER, L. 2000. Political trust and trustworthiness. *Annual Review of Political Science*, 3: 475–507.

LIPSET, S. M. 1959. Some social requisites of democracy: economic development and political legitimacy. *American Political Science Review*, 53: 69–105.

MCADAM, D. 1986. Recruitment to high-risk activism: the case of Freedom Summer. *American Journal of Sociology*, 92: 64–90.

MARSHALL, M. G., and JAGGERS, K. 2000. *Polity IV Project* (Data Users Manual). Baltimore: University of Maryland.

MASLOW, A. 1988/1954. *Motivation and Personality*, 3rd edn. New York: Harper & Row.

MISHLER, W., and ROSE, R. 2001. Political support for incomplete democracies: realist vs. idealist theories and measures. *International Political Science Review*, 22 (4): 303–20.

MULLER, E. N., and SELIGSON, M. A. 1994. Civic culture and democracy: the question of causal relationships. *American Political Science Review*, 88 (3): 635–52.

NEWTON, K. 2001. Trust, social capital, civil society, and democracy. *International Political Science Review*, 22 (2): 201–14.

——and NORRIS, P. 2000. Confidence in public institutions: faith, culture, or performance? Pp. 52–73 in *Disaffected Democracies: What's Troubling the Trilateral Countries?*, ed. S. J. Pharr and R. D. Putnam. Princeton: Princeton University Press.

NORRIS, P. 2002. *Democratic Phoenix: Political Activism Worldwide.* Cambridge: Cambridge University Press.

OTTAWAY, M. 2003. *Democracy Challenged: The Rise of Semi-Authoritarianism.* Washington, DC: Carnegie Endowment for International Peace.

PAGE, B., and SHAPIRO, R. Y. 1993. The rational public and democracy. Pp. 35–64 in *Reconsidering the Democratic Public,* ed. G. E. Marcus and R. L. Hanson. University Park: Pennsylvania State University Press.

PAXTON, P. 2002. Social capital and democracy: an interdependent relationship. *American Sociological Review,* 67: 254–77.

PRZEWORSKI, A., and LIMONGI, F. 1997. Modernization: theories and facts. *World Politics,* 49: 155–83.

——and TEUNE, H. 1970. *The Logic of Comparative Social Inquiry.* New York: John Wiley.

PUTNAM, R. D. 1993. *Making Democracy Work: Civic Traditions in Modern Italy.* Princeton: Princeton University Press.

——2000. *Bowling Alone: The Collapse and Revival of American Community.* New York: Simon & Schuster.

ROBINSON, W. S. 1950. Ecological correlations and the behavior of individuals. *American Sociological Review,* 15: 351–7.

ROHRSCHNEIDER, R. 1999. *Learning Democracy: Democratic and Economic Values in Unified Germany.* Oxford: Oxford University Press.

ROKEACH, M. 1960. *The Open and Closed Mind: Investigations into the Nature of Belief Systems and Personality Systems.* New York: Basic Books.

——1973. *The Nature of Human Values.* New York: Free Press.

ROSE, R. 2001. A divergent Europe. *Journal of Democracy,* 12 (1): 93–106.

ROSE-ACKERMAN, S. 2001. Trust and honesty in post-socialist societies. *Kyklos,* 54: 415–44.

SCARBROUGH, E. and VAN DETH, J. W. eds. 1995. *The Impact of Values.* Beliefs in Government 4. Oxford: Oxford University Press.

SELIGSON, M. 2002. The renaissance of political culture or the renaissance of the ecological fallacy. *Comparative Politics,* 34: 273–92.

SEN, A. 1999. *Development as Freedom.* New York: Alfred Knopf.

SHIN, D. C., and WELLS, J. 2005. Is democracy the only game in town? *Journal of Democracy,* 16 (2): 88–101.

TRIANDIS, H. C. 1995. *Individualism and Collectivism.* San Francisco: Westview Press.

VANHANEN, T. ed. 1997. *Prospects of Democracy: A Study of 172 Countries.* London: Routledge.

——2003. *Democratization: A Comparative Analysis of 170 Countries.* London: Routledge.

VERBA, S., SCHLOZMAN, K. L., and BRADY, H. E. 1995. *Voice and Equality.* Cambridge, Mass.: Harvard University Press.

WELZEL, C. 2006. Democratization as an emancipative process: the neglected role of mass motivations. *European Journal of Political Research,* 45: 871–96.

——and INGLEHART, R. 2005. Liberalism, postmaterialism, and the growth of freedom: the human development perspective. *International Review of Sociology,* 15 (1): 81–108.

————2006. Emancipative values and democracy. *Studies in Comparative International Development,* 41 (2): 74–94.

————and DEUTSCH, F. 2005. Social capital, voluntary associations, and collective action: which aspects of social capital have the greatest "civic" payoff? *Journal of Civil Society,* 1 (2): 121–46.

————and KLINGEMANN, H.-D. 2003. The theory of human development: a cross-cultural analysis. *European Journal of Political Research,* 42 (2): 341–80.

CHAPTER 14

....

WHAT CAUSES DEMOCRATIZATION?

....

BARBARA GEDDES

RESEARCH on democratization has become increasingly sophisticated during the last decade. With the completion and sharing of new datasets and the ratcheting up of training in statistics and modeling, approaches to studying democratization have changed greatly since the mid-1990s. Economic models of democratization and large-N statistical investigations of its causes play an ever larger role in its study. What we think we know about democratization has changed much less, though we have some intriguing new ideas to think about. Recent research has confirmed what we thought we knew several decades ago: richer countries are more likely to be democratic. Controversy continues about whether economic development increases the likelihood of transitions to democracy. Przeworski and his co-authors (2000) have argued emphatically that development does not cause democratization; rather, development reduces the likelihood of democratic breakdown, thus increasing the number of rich democratic countries even though it has no causal effect on transitions *to* democracy. Other careful analyses of regime change, however, continue to find a relationship between development and transitions to democracy (e.g., Boix and Stokes 2003; Epstein et al. forthcoming).

Several other empirical regularities have achieved the status of stylized facts, though all have also been challenged. Reliance on oil, and perhaps other mineral exports, reduces the likelihood of democracy (Barro 1996; Ross 2001; Fish 2002). Countries with large Muslim populations are less likely to be democratic (Fish 2002). Weiner (1987) and Payne (1993) among others have suggested that British colonial heritage contributes to better prospects for democracy later, and Barro (1996) finds support for their claims.[1]

---

[1] But Fish (2002) finds no relationship between British colonial heritage and democracy.

As with the relationship between development and democracy, controversy continues about whether these are causal relationships or correlations explained by something else. Among those who believe relationships are causal, there are disagreements about the processes through which the causes produce the outcome. Middle East experts explain the correlation between oil wealth and dictatorship as a consequence of a rentier state that can use its rents from the sale of natural resources to distribute subsidies to large parts of the population and thus to maintain popular compliance with the regime (Anderson 1987; Crystal 1995). In a parallel argument, Dunning (2006) argues that oil rents can in some circumstances be used to sustain democracy. Herb (2005), however, shows that when a measure of development that excludes the effect of oil on the economy is used in place of GDP per capita in statistical analysis of the causes of democratization, oil-rich countries fit the same patterns as other countries. The proxy measure of development has a strong positive effect on changes in democracy scores, and rent dependence, measured separately, has no effect. In short, he challenges the existence of a relationship between oil wealth and regime type. Some observers have suggested an affinity between Muslim doctrine or the attitudes of believers and authoritarianism, but Fish (2002) suggests that Muslim countries tend to be authoritarian not for the reasons usually mentioned but because of the suppression of women's rights in these countries.

In 1959, Seymour Martin Lipset argued that modernization caused democracy. He supported his claim with what was then a state-of-the-art quantitative test, a table showing a relationship between various measures of development and democracy in a cross-section of countries. In succeeding decades, analytic techniques have become much more sophisticated, more data have become available, and scholars have developed more nuanced measures of democracy. In ever more sophisticated ways, analysts have confirmed the existence of a correlation between democracy and development (Bollen and Jackman 1985; Burkhart and Lewis-Beck 1994; Gasiorowrski 1995; Barro 1996; Przeworski et al. 2000).[2] Without denigrating their contribution, which has been very great, it is still possible to note that little beyond greater certainty about that original claim has been added to the pile of knowledge we can be reasonably sure we know.

In trying to understand democratization, we have traditionally relied on descriptions of transitions in individual countries and small groups of countries or large-N statistical studies. The case studies have been very useful in providing information about particular transitions. Large-N studies typically include all countries for which information about proposed causes is available. These studies have built the current accumulation of knowledge about the relationship between development and democracy. The authors of the large-N studies have suggested various processes through which growth and the related spread of education, urbanization, and individual mobility might lead to demands for democracy, and many of these arguments have

---

[2] But see Acemoglu et al. (2005) for an empirical challenge. Acemoglu and Robinson's (2001) deductive model, however, could easily lead to a correlation between democracy and development.

been tested. A correlation between education, especially primary education, and democracy is well established (Barro 1996). Some studies have found a relationship between the income share of the middle class and democracy (Barro 1996). The results on urbanization are mixed, with some showing a negative effect on democracy. These studies have not actually modeled the process of democratization via these avenues, however. They all seem to assume that if citizens want democracy and have the required skills, they can achieve it.

Given the quality and amount of effort expended on understanding democratization, it is frustrating to understand so little. Scholars have responded by pushing the research frontier in two intriguing directions. Some have taken up Robert Barro's (1996) challenge: "Given the strength of the Lipset/Aristotle hypothesis as an empirical regularity, it is surprising that convincing theoretical models of the relation do not exist. Thus development of such a theory is a priority for future research (S182)." Modeling and testing interactions between elites, who may not want to share power, and citizens, who may want to influence distribution and therefore demand democracy as a means of gaining influence, have now moved to the top of the research agenda. Several scholars have proposed plausible deductive arguments that identify underlying causes of democratization, most of which are correlated with development, and that therefore explain the correlation. The next section discusses recent models of the process of democratization and the evidence supporting them.

A different direction has been taken by other analysts, who claim that international factors have played a much larger role in explaining democratization than earlier observers had realized. If international forces have a major effect on democratization, and especially if there is an interaction between international and domestic factors, their exclusion from statistical tests may explain some of the limited and contradictory results obtained in these tests. International influences have barely figured in the historical literature on democratization, but studies including them have produced interesting results in the last few years. The second section below summarizes recent findings about international effects on transitions to democracy.

In response to the mix of success and failure to which the study of democratization has led, I suggest that the reason results have been somewhat limited so far is that the phenomenon we label democratization actually includes several different causal processes. If the large-N studies have lumped multiple causal processes into the same statistical models, it is not surprising that only the most basic relationships have emerged. Similarly, if the models that have been proposed fit democratization in some contexts but not others, then it is also not surprising that empirical support for the models has been modest. A different approach to understanding democratization would begin by disaggregating into several distinct processes or subgroups and then theorizing different transition processes separately. In the third section I discuss some different ways to think about theoretically useful disaggregations of the process of democratization.

1 Investigating the Process: What Causes the Correlation between Development and Democracy?

In a very influential book and article, Przeworski and co-authors (1997, 2000) have argued that there is no relationship between levels of economic development and transitions to democracy. They note that transitions can occur for many reasons, not all of which are systematic. They claim that the apparent relationship results from the political stability of rich democracies. Although poor democracies sometimes collapse and return to dictatorship, rich democracies never do, which over time leads to a high proportion of rich countries among democracies. Using a different measure of democracy and a dataset covering a much longer period of time, Gleditsch and Choun (2004) also find no relationship between development and transitions to democracy after controlling for characteristics of countries' neighbors.[3]

Other analysts, however, have been unpersuaded by Przeworski et al.'s argument. In a very careful reanalysis that extends the time period back to 1850, Boix and Stokes (2003) show that development does contribute to democratic transitions, though the average effect for the whole period is small relative to the effect of development on maintaining democracy. In fact, they note that a careful reading of *Democracy and Development* shows that even Przeworski et al. (2000) find a small statistically significant effect of development on the likelihood of transitions to democracy. Boix and Stokes (2003) show that when the dataset is divided by time periods, economic development is an extremely important predictor of transition prior to 1950, but has only a small (though statistically significant) effect in the post-1950 period. Epstein et al. (forthcoming) also challenge the Przeworski et al. (2000) findings. They show that results are changed by using a trichotomous measure of democracy rather than a dichotomous one, as Przeworski et al. did. They find that development has strong predictive power for transitions into and out of the category they call partial democracy, but less effect on transitions from full autocracy to full democracy. Epstein et al.'s (forthcoming) findings should probably be interpreted as meaning that development is a good predictor of the softening or routinization of authoritarian regimes, though not necessarily of regime change.

---

[3] Pevehouse (2002) also finds no relationship between development and democratization after controlling for the average level of democracy in the members of regional international organizations that countries belong to. These findings are open to different interpretations. Since development tends to vary by region, level of development is likely to be collinear with average democraticness in neighboring countries or regional international organizations. It might be that development in a region causes democraticness in a region, thus accounting for the correlation between neighbors' regime type and the likelihood of democratization, even if neighbors have no direct influence. Alternatively, it might be that neighbors' influence is the reason for the correlation between development and democracy.

Economic development is correlated with many other trends, and one or more of those may be the causal mechanism that accounts for the apparent relationship between development and democracy. Lipset and other modernization theorists suggested that increasing education, equality, urbanization, experience of working in factories, and the weakening of traditional loyalties to tribe and village—all correlates of economic development—would result in citizens with more tolerant and participatory attitudes who would demand a say in government (Lipset 1959; Inkeles and Smith 1974). These arguments stressed the experiences and values of ordinary citizens as the bases for democracy without specifying the process through which transitions might occur or giving much attention to the possible reluctance of elites to give up power. Scholars influenced by Marx expect the middle class—which tends to grow as the economy develops—to be the carrier of the demand for democracy: "no bourgeoisie, no democracy."[4] Zak and Feng (2003) have modeled a process through which this relationship might unfold, but have not tested it.

Boix (2003), Acemoglu and Robinson (2001, 2005), and Zak and Feng (2003) argue that democratization is more likely when the income distribution—which tends to even out as countries reach high levels of development—is more equal. Boix and Acemoglu/Robinson argue that elites fear redistribution less when income distribution is relatively equal because the median voter's preference with regard to taxes will then be less confiscatory. Elites, according to Acemoglu and Robinson (2001), are willing to cede some power rather than risk the costs of revolution when they expect democracy not to lead to extremely redistributive taxation. Boix (2003) expects a linear relationship between equality and the likelihood of democratization. Acemoglu and Robinson's (2001) model suggests a non-monotonic relationship: at low levels of inequality, an increase can promote democracy by increasing the threat of revolution, but at higher levels of inequality, elites will repress rather than offering concessions because of their fear of the redistributive consequences of democratization. An empirical challenge to these arguments is that evidence of more equal income distributions in democracies is at best mixed (Bollen and Jackman 1985). There is little evidence that the current set of recalcitrant dictatorships is made up of countries with especially unequal income distributions. In the post-Second World War period, longer-lived dictatorships (excluding monarchies) have more equal income distributions than brief ones.

Boix (2003) and Rogowski (1998) argue that capital mobility, which also tends to rise with development, also contributes to democratization. When capital is mobile, it can flee in response to high taxes. Knowing that, democratic governments are expected to refrain from taxing heavily; so elites need not fear democracy. In the Boix (2003) model, elites' interests can be protected either by a relatively equal income distribution or by capital mobility. Where capital mobility is low, as in countries with predominantly agricultural economies, and income unequal, however, elites should be unwilling to negotiate democratization. The Boix and Acemoglu/Robinson arguments are discussed in more detail below.

---

[4] This is Barrington Moore's summary of Marx (1966, 416).

2 MODELS OF DEMOCRATIZATION AS STRATEGIC INTERACTIONS BETWEEN ELITES AND CITIZENS

Models of the interactions between ruling elites and others that may lead to democratization can be divided into two categories depending on their basic assumptions about who the relevant actors are and what their goals are. The Boix (2003) and Acemoglu/Robinson (2001) models described above assume that the most important division within society is between rich and poor, and that the rich form and maintain dictatorships in order to protect their assets. They also assume, as do many economic models of authoritarian politics, that the key policy decision that determines the level of redistribution is the level of taxation on domestic capital. It is assumed that the median voter, who is poor, prefers high taxes in order to redistribute wealth. The more unequal the income distribution, the poorer the median voter and thus the more confiscatory the tax rate can be expected to be in a democracy. In short, the median voter in these models has never met "Homer."[5] Elites consider changing the rules, however, because of the threat of violence or revolution. In these models politicians are perfect agents of societal interests, and political leaders do not maximize their own revenue distinct from the revenue of the elite group they represent.

An alternative conception of autocracy assumes that the most important division in society is between the rulers (sometimes simplified to a single dictator) and the ruled. They assume that rulers maximize their own income from tax revenue at the expense of both rich and poor ruled. Rulers thus set taxes at the highest rate that does not deter economic effort by citizens. In these models, rulers offer increments of democracy when doing so can increase the credibility of their promises to provide public goods and other policies that will increase economic growth and thus benefit both rulers and ruled (North and Weingast 1989; Weingast 1997; Escriba Folch 2003). Alternatively, democratic institutions may be offered as a means of directly increasing revenues (Levi 1988; Bates and Lien 1985; Rogowski 1998). Bueno de Mesquita et al. (2003) propose a more complicated set of societal divisions and actors: a leader; a ruling coalition; a "selectorate" that includes those citizens who can affect the composition of the ruling coalition; and residents, those who are taxed but politically marginal. In all these models, the ruled care about growth and the share of their own production they are allowed to keep. Taxation is not seen as a means of redistribution in favor of the poor, but rather as a means of enriching rulers. Rulers become rich by ruling; they do not rule because they were rich before achieving power. They cling to power in order to continue collecting revenue from the productive population under their control, not to protect themselves from redistributive taxation. The main

---

[5] Larry Bartels (2005) has christened the real-life low-income voter who favors more social spending but who nevertheless opposes the estate tax Homer after the famous Homer Simpson.

constraint on rulers' pursuit of wealth for themselves is the threat of declining revenue caused by capital flight or reduction in economic effort.

Both of these approaches offer some insights into the process of democratization. The Boix (2003) and Acemoglu/Robinson (2001) models are plausible simplifications of early democratizations in Western Europe and of many transitions in Latin America, but models emphasizing the conflict between rulers and ruled are more plausible when applied to recent struggles over democratization in Africa, Eastern Europe, the Middle East, and parts of Asia. These models, like large-N studies of democratization to date, have implicitly assumed that a single model will explain democratization in all times and all circumstances.

2.1 Rich Rulers versus Poor Ruled

As noted above, Boix (2003) argues that income equality and capital mobility reduce elite fears of democracy, the first because it reduces expected redistribution by popular governments and the second because it provides capital holders with an exit option if taxes become confiscatory. This is a seminal contribution to the literature on democratization because it provides plausible microfoundations for the observed correlation between development and democracy. Other laudable aspects of the research include a serious effort to test the argument and the inclusion of nineteenth- and early twentieth-century democratizations in the analysis. Virtually all other quantitative studies of democratization have looked only at the post-Second World War period because of data limitations. Boix has made a huge effort to overcome those limitations.

The Boix (2003) study has not resolved all debates, however, in part because the empirical support for the argument is somewhat ambiguous. On the positive side, income inequality has a substantial effect on the likelihood of democratization in a dataset that covers 1950–90 and thus excludes most African democratizations. We do not know if the result would change if a number of transitions in poor African countries were added. The percentage of family farms, used as a proxy for inequality in the historical tests, has a negative effect on the probability of transition, contrary to expectations. One of the measures of capital mobility, average share of agriculture as a percentage of GDP, fails to produce expected results. Other indicators used to measure capital mobility have strong effects but ambiguous interpretations.

The ratio of fuel exports to total exports, for example, is a plausible indicator of capital mobility. The correlation between reliance on oil and authoritarianism, however, is usually attributed to the oil-producing government's ability to provide transfers to large parts of the population *without* relying on taxation.[6] So how can we tell whether the reported relationship between oil dependence and democratization is caused by reduced capital mobility or the strategic use of resources by dictators to buy popular support?

---

[6] For rentier state arguments, see Anderson 1987 and Crystal (1995).

Average years of schooling is used as a measure of human capital, which is more mobile than physical capital, and Boix finds a positive relationship between education and democratization. Many other analysts have found this relationship, however, and attributed it to the propensity of more-educated citizens to demand democracy. In short, although Boix's argument is plausible and attractively simple, the empirical investigation is not definitive. The argument fits well with the stylized facts of West European democratization, however, and redistributive changes followed democratization in Western Europe as this argument would predict (Lindert 1994). Further tests of this argument deserve to be important items on the research agenda of students of democratization.

Acemoglu and Robinson's (2001) argument begins with many of the same basic assumptions about the way the world works as Boix's. It also gives a central role in resistance to democratization to elites' fear of redistribution when the starting income distribution is unequal. Its predictions are complicated, however, by limiting the threat of revolution to periods of recession. In this argument, when the rich are threatened by revolution (which only occurs during recession), they can grant redistribution without changing the political system, grant democracy as a way of making the commitment to redistribution credible, or repress. Redistribution without regime change is not credible to the poor because they know that they cannot maintain the threat of revolution after the recession is over. According to Acemoglu and Robinson, democratization is a more credible commitment to maintaining redistribution over a longer time period. (Why the poor should accept democratization as credible when even the model allows the rich to stage coups if they are dissatisfied by the later tax rate is not clear.)

The introduction of recessions, which vary in both intensity and frequency, substantially complicates making predictions about the effects of inequality on elite behavior. Equality makes democratization less threatening to elites, but how they react to inequality depends on the seriousness of the threat of revolution and the cost of repression. In this model, the likelihood of revolution depends on inequality (which increases the threat of revolution) and the intensity of recession (which decreases revolution's cost to the poor). Frequent recessions, however, increase the likelihood that the elite can credibly offer redistribution without democratization because frequent recessions allow the poor to threaten revolution often, thus enforcing the bargain. So intense recessions destabilize dictatorships leading to democratization, revolution, or repression, but frequent recessions lead paradoxically to stable authoritarianism with redistribution. The bottom line, according to Acemoglu and Robinson (2001, 957), is that "democracy is more likely to be consolidated if the level of inequality is limited, whereas high inequality is likely to lead to political instability, either in the form of frequent regime changes or repression of social unrest."

In contrast to the Boix argument, Acemoglu and Robinson expect income inequality to lead to unstable regime changes, not continued authoritarianism. One of the attractive features of the Acemoglu and Robinson model is that it explains repeated transitions between democracy and dictatorship, a phenomenon that has characterized some parts of the developing world since the middle of the twentieth century. The model seems to be a plausible simplification of events in much of Latin America and in a few other developing countries. It does not fit most of the Middle East, Eastern Europe, Africa, or Asia, where fear of redistributive taxation is not a plausible reason for resistance to democratization since substantial portions of productive assets were state or foreign owned for much of the late twentieth century. State elites who control a large portion of productive assets may certainly fear loss of power since it will dispossess them, but they will not suffer less dispossession because the income distribution is more equal. Acemoglu and Robinson do not offer systematic empirical tests of their arguments so we cannot assess their fit with the real world.

Models linking democratization to inequality seem highly plausible initially, but the empirical investigation of the relationship between regime type and income inequality does not offer strong support for their basic assumptions. Nor does empirical investigation of the relationship between democracy and redistribution. If these arguments were correct, we would expect to find the remaining dictatorships in the world more unequal on average than democracies, but Bollen and Jackman (1985) find no relationship between democracy and inequality. Przeworski et al. (2000) find a positive relationship between only one of three measures of inequality tried and transitions to democracy. They find a stronger relationship between inequality (in democracies) and democratic breakdown, which might explain any relationship that exists between democracy and equality (if one does exist), but does not support the idea that equality makes democratization more likely.

The models also assume that the main reason elites fear democracy and ordinary citizens want it is that they expect it to lead to redistribution. LIndert (1994) has shown that the expected redistribution occurred in Western Europe after the first steps toward democratization were taken, but Mulligan, Sala-i-Martin, and Gil (2003) show that contemporary democracies do not on average distribute more than dictatorships.[7] We should not be surprised by this result. Income distribution varied greatly among late twentieth-century dictatorships. Many, both communist and non-communist, expropriated traditional elites and redistributed income and opportunities through land reform, much increased public education, and industrialization policies that led to the movement of large numbers of people out of agriculture and into factories. It is hard to imagine that elites in these kinds of authoritarian regimes would be motivated by a fear of greater redistribution. They would fear loss of their own power and wealth, but not via redistributive taxation. Income equality would not reassure them.

2.2 Revenue Maximizing Rulers versus Politically Powerless Citizens

This approach to the study of democratization, which owes much to seminal articles by North and Weingast (1989) and Olson (1993), sees rulers as maximizing their own

---

[7] Boix (2003) challenges this result.

individual revenue via taxation and citizens as sharing a desire for productivity-enhancing policies and public goods, regardless of whether they are rich or poor. In this image of politics, taxes redistribute wealth from citizens to rulers, not from rich to poor. Rulers may want revenue in order to pursue wars, to buy support in order to stay in power, or for personal consumption; their reason does not affect the logic of the argument. Rulers are motivated by their desire for revenue to offer public goods and a tax rate that does not reduce investment or effort.

In some versions of this approach, societal elites or holders of capital are most affected by the ruler's policies and can do most to destabilize his rule if they are dissatisfied. Consequently, they are the ones most likely to be accommodated when the ruler offers an institutionalized form of participation in return for their cooperation. Rulers may offer representative institutions as a means of offering a credible commitment to supply desired public goods (Levi 1988; North and Weingast 1989; Escriba Folch 2003) or simply in exchange for wealth holders' contingent consent to the taxation of mobile capital (Bates and Lien 1985). As in the Boix (2003) argument, democratization becomes more likely as capital becomes more mobile, but the reason for the relationship changes. The more mobile capital, according to Bates and Lien (1985), the harder it is to tax without contingent consent and thus the more likely the ruler will offer representative institutions. Rogowski (1998) suggests a more general form of this logic in which citizens' ability to move away increases the likelihood that rulers will offer them representative institutions or good government in order to induce them to remain, along with their productive capacity, within the ruler's territory.[8] Thus these models often explain the first small steps toward democratization from absolutist monarchy.

Bueno de Mesquita et al. (2003) suggest a more complicated general framework for understanding politics in both democracy and autocracy. Their model, to reiterate, includes: a ruler supported by a winning coalition; a "selectorate," meaning those citizens who have some influence on who can join the winning coalition; and residents who play no role in selecting rulers. In democracies, the selectorate is the enfranchised population, and the winning coalition is made up of those who voted for the winning party or coalition, that is, roughly 50 percent of the selectorate. In single-party authoritarian regimes, the winning coalition is the small group of actual rulers, and the selectorate is made up of all members of the ruling party. In military regimes, the winning coalition is the junta and the selectorate is the officer corps. They do not discuss reasons for different authoritarian institutional choices.

Rulers maximize personal revenue via taxation but are constrained by the need to provide private and public goods in order to maintain the support of the winning coalition. If enough members of the ruling coalition defect because they are dissatisfied with their share, the ruler is overthrown. Citizens outside the winning

---

[8] But see Bravo (2006) for evidence that the exit of those citizens most dissatisfied with a ruler's policies may increase the probability that he survives in office—thus giving the ruler a reason to provide policies that induce the exit of those citizens most likely to join the opposition.

coalition benefit only from the public goods provided when the winning coalition is too large to be maintained by private goods alone.

Residents and sometimes members of the selectorate may hold demonstrations or join rebellions to challenge rulers who tax them too heavily or provide insufficient public goods, but rulers in this model always respond with repression. If revolutionary challengers win despite repression, the new rulers face the same incentives that other rulers do to narrow the winning coalition and keep resources for themselves. In other words, revolutions and popular uprisings in this model do not threaten redistribution or lead to democracy. Instead they lead to a seizure of power by a new leader and winning coalition who maximize their own wealth at the expense of those they exclude. One of the most useful and empirically realistic points made by Bueno de Mesquita et al. is that participation in a coup, uprising, or revolution does not guarantee the participant an improved share of power or wealth after the fall of the old regime because those who lead such movements have incentives after they win to renege on earlier promises.

Thus democracy cannot arise as a response to popular uprising in this model. Instead, it arises when the members of the winning coalition can benefit themselves by expanding its size. Members of winning coalitions are cross-pressured when it comes to the size of coalition they prefer to be part of. Their individual share of private goods is larger when the coalition is smaller, but the ruler keeps less for himself and provides more public and total private goods when the coalition is larger. In the model, the winning coalition has a tipping point at the size at which it prefers to increase further. Once that happens, democracy will eventually follow. This model, like those described above, portrays democratization as elite led. In the Bueno de Mesquita et al. (2003) model, however, winning coalition elites are motivated simply by wanting to improve their own welfare relative to that of the ruler. They are not responding either to a challenge from the excluded or to the threat of capital strike.

Models that emphasize conflict between revenue-maximizing rulers and politically powerless citizens capture elements of reality in many recent transitions in developing countries. Once the changes in the international economy provoked by the debt crisis had rendered state interventionist development strategies unsustainable, many authoritarian governments were forced to begin liberalizing their economies. In order to attract private investment to replace state investment that could not be sustained without foreign inflows, governments had to offer more predictable policies and certain public goods conducive to private investment (Roberts 2006). Like democrats, dictators' survival in office is threatened by poor economic performance. As noted by North and Weingast (1989), Acemoglu and Robinson (2001), Escriba Folch (2003), and others, policy promises made by dictators inherently lack credibility. Dictators can increase the credibility of these promises by creating institutions that give capital holders a say in policy making and that increase the constraints on the dictator's arbitrary power. Democratic institutions such as legislatures and multiparty electoral competition can create those constraints if the commitment to the institutional change is itself considered credible. If the institutions benefit both the ruler, by increasing revenues, and the ruled, by increasing productivity or welfare, then the institutional bargain is self-enforcing and thus credible. These models, in other words, provide a reason for expecting institutional bargains to be more credible than offers to provide desired policies in the absence of institutional change, which the Acemoglu and Robinson (2001) model does not.

These models thus suggest intuitions about why democratization and economic liberalization tended to vary together in the late twentieth century (Hellman 1998). Prior to the debt crisis of the 1980s, governments had a choice between relying primarily on state investment or private investment. Those that chose state investment did not have to offer credible commitments to provide public goods, predictable economic policy, or policies favorable to private investors in order to secure revenue flows, and thus the economic pressure to initiate institutional constraints on rulers' arbitrary powers was low. Since the 1980s, the state investment strategy has become unworkable except possibly in countries reliant on the export of oil or other high-priced natural resources. Consequently, governments have sought to attract private investment via capital-friendly policies, and political institutions that constrain the dictator's discretion help to make those policies credible to investors (Roberts 2006).

The emphasis on the interest differences between rulers and ruled and on redistribution in favor of rulers as a central fact of dictatorship fits well with what we know about many of the dictatorships referred to as personalistic, sultanistic, or patrimonial by different authors. These models do not accommodate the role that popular uprisings have played in many late twentieth-century democratizations, however. Moreover, most of these models are very abstract, and most tests of them have been narrowly focused or open to multiple interpretations.

Some features of late twentieth-century democratization have not found their way into models, though they have been included in large-N statistical studies. The correlation between reliance on oil exports and authoritarianism, for example, has been found repeatedly. In developing countries, oil is usually state owned or owned by foreign multinationals and taxed heavily. Whether it is state owned or not, the government draws its revenues largely from natural resource production, not from taxation on domestic wealth holders. A large mostly descriptive literature on the effects of oil on politics exists (Karl 1997; Chaudhry 1997; Anderson 1987; Crystal 1995). Yet, I know of no model that has grappled seriously with state ownership of productive resources and its effect on the struggle over democratization. All models assume a capitalist economy with private domestic investors as important actors. During the third wave of democratization, however, most transitions affected authoritarian regimes in which state investment was high. In many, foreign investment also played a large role, and revenue from foreign aid was more important than revenues from taxation in some.

International factors have also been largely absent from models of democratization. Many observers have suggested that international forces, such as the diffusion of democratic ideas and pressure from international financial institutions to democratize, have affected transitions, especially since the 1980s. Earlier quantitative studies found it hard to document these influences, but Gasiorowski (1995) and Gleditsch and Choun (2004) show that the proportion of democratic neighbors increases the likelihood of transitions to democracy in neighboring countries, lending some support to the diffusion argument. Jon Pevehouse (2002) shows that membership in regional international organizations in which most other members are democratic increases the likelihood of democratization. Since membership in democratic regional international organizations is likely to be correlated with having democratic neighbors, however, we cannot be sure whether organizations have an independent effect beyond the effect of living in a "good" neighborhood. Bueno de Mesquita, Siverson, and Woller (1992; Bueno de Mesquita and Siverson 1995) show that war affects the survival of both political leaders and regimes. Gleditsch and Choun (2004) show that wars increase the likelihood of transition from one authoritarian government to another, but neither Gleditsch and Choun (2004) nor Pevehouse (2002) shows strong evidence that wars in the neighborhood decrease the likelihood of democratization, as some have suggested. Marinov (2005) shows that although sanctions are effective at bringing down democratic leaders, they have little effect on the survival of dictators and therefore we can infer little effect on authoritarian regimes.[9] Theoretical treatments of democratization, however, continue to focus on domestic causes. It may be that the focus on domestic causes is appropriate when explaining democratizations before the Second World War, but that international influences—both economic and political—have become more pronounced over time.

3 DISAGGREGATING DEMOCRATIZATION

Assuming that there is one explanation of democratization may be the reason that scholars continue to disagree about its causes. Different analysts have deeper knowledge about some sets of cases than others, and naturally their intuitions formalized in models fit the cases they know best better than those they know less well. The findings of large-N studies differ from each other depending on specification, time period included, and cases used, leaving very basic ideas contested. Such varying results should be expected if single statistical models are being imposed on a set of disparate processes without efforts to specify how the process might differ over time or in different kinds of transitions.[10] I suggest that it would be useful to consider the possibility that processes of democratization might be different in different contexts,

[9] He does not test the effect of sanctions on economic performance, and growth is included as a control variable in the test of the effect of sanctions, so it is quite possible that sanctions do affect authoritarian survival through their effect on growth. In democracies, though, sanctions affect leadership survival even with growth controlled for.

[10] Besides the exceptions noted in the text above, a number of large-N studies have modeled factors that have changed over time. Gleditsch and Choun (2004), for example, show that the predominance of

that these differences might be systematic, and that developing a theoretical under-standing of these differences would lead to useful empirical results and a better understanding of how transitions really take place.

Two context differences that might influence the democratization process are the historical period in which it takes place and the type of regime that democracy replaces. Early democratizations took place in capitalist economies in which the rich usually held political power. Later democratizations have also occurred in countries with high levels of state ownership of productive assets, especially natural resources. State ownership makes possible both the accumulation of wealth by political leaders and also the distribution of benefits to supporters, and in some cases citizens, without the need for high taxation of private wealth holders. Rulers who have acquired wealth through access to state resources, in contrast to those who hold political power because they own private wealth, have to fear losing most of their assets if they are deposed, regardless of the income distribution or other factors that might affect future taxation.

Most transitions before the Second World War were transitions from some form of oligarchic government; many were gradual transitions from very limited suffrage to nearly universal. Post-Second World War democratizations have occurred in several quite different ways, but nearly all have involved a transition to immediate universal suffrage democracy. These have included the transition from colonial rule to uni-versal suffrage democracy at independence; transitions from universal suffrage au-thoritarianism to universal suffrage democracy; and redemocratizations in which most of the parties and political institutions of a prior democracy are reinstated at the conclusion of an authoritarian interlude. Gradual transitions from limited to almost universal suffrage have been rare during the last fifty years (cf. Huntington 1991).

If elite opposition to democracy is motivated by fear of redistributive taxation, gradual increases in suffrage should be easier than rapid ones because the median voter after a limited enfranchisement would be richer and thus demand less redis-tribution. Such institutional choices are often made during bargaining over the conditions of transition. We might expect authoritarian rulers concerned about redistributive taxation to negotiate incremental enfranchisement, but dictators with different fears might not consider universal suffrage threatening.

Various international influences on democratization have arguably had greater effects since the Second World War and perhaps greater still since the 1980s. The differences in the sources of dictators' wealth before and after the Second World War noted above are associated with a change in economic strategy that swept through the developing world between about 1930 and 1970. Nearly all developing countries initiated development strategies that increased state investment, ownership, and regulation of their economies. These strategies reduced governments' dependence

Catholicism in countries has a negative effect on prospects for democratization before Vatican II and a positive effect afterward. Gasiorowrski (1995) shows that economic crisis has different effects on the likelihood of democratization during different time periods.

on private investors and created non-tax sources of revenue, which could then be distributed along with monopolies and subsidies of various kinds in exchange for support. The ability to use state resources to expropriate traditional and foreign wealth holders and create new elites beholden to the government may have reduced pressures for democratization during the decades when this strategy remained viable.

A second change in the international economy, beginning around 1980 with the debt crisis, brought that period to an end. When foreign lending was no longer available to cover the trade and budget deficits characteristic of the state interventionist development strategy, developing country governments faced intense pressure to adopt policies conducive to attracting investment. Attracting investments depends on credible policy commitments and secure property rights. If, as various analysts have argued, dictators can use legislatures and other quasi-democratic institutions to make their policy commitments credible, the economic strategy changes brought about by the debt crisis of the 1980s should have created strong incentives toward some degree of democratization. In the post-1980 period, we see an increase in both democratizations and also the adoption of quasi-democratic institutions by authoritarian regimes (Levitsky and Way 2006).

The end of the Cold War has also changed the process of democratization. Before 1990, authoritarian regimes were supported with extensive aid and other help from both superpowers. Such aid both increased the regimes' repressive capacity (Boix 2003, 29–30) and also added to dictators' ability to buy support without redistributing from domestic producers. Since 1990, Levitsky and Way (2006) show that those authoritarian regimes with the closest linkages to the USA and Western Europe are the most likely to have democratic-looking institutions such as multiparty elections in which some real competition is allowed. Such regimes may be easier to dislodge since opposition is usually less risky and costly in them. The reduction in foreign support for dictatorships since the end of the Cold War also contributed to the increase in democratizations in the late twentieth century.

Thus, for both domestic and international reasons, we might think that a model of the early process of democratization would be different from a model of the later process. The finding by Boix and Stokes (2003) that economic development and income distribution have much stronger effects on the likelihood of democratization before 1950 than after lends support to the idea that modeling separate processes for the two time periods would be fruitful.

These cross-time differences in the causes of democratization may be caused in part by differences in the kinds of regimes from which democracies emerge. Pre-Second World War democratizations, which occurred primarily in Europe and Latin America, generally replaced governments controlled by the rich, whether these were planter oligarchies or monarchies, through electoral systems with very limited suffrage. In most of these non-democratic regimes, legislatures existed, elite parties or proto-parties competed for office, and struggles by legislatures to limit the power of monarchs or executives had played an important role in determining the shape of political institutions. Democratization tended to occur through the extension of suffrage to new groups without other large institutional changes. More citizens voted, sometimes new parties formed to attract the votes of the newly enfranchised, and elections became fairer, but parliamentary systems in Europe and separation of powers systems in Latin America accommodated the inclusion of new voters and parties.

We cannot make the same kinds of generalizations about late twentieth-century transitions. The authoritarian regimes from which late twentieth-century democratizations emerged differed from the stylized portrait in the paragraph above. Few of their rulers were born to wealthy families. Most came to prominence via either a military career or a rise to leadership in a revolutionary or nationalist party. Some contemporary authoritarian regimes have repressed all political activity, but many have held regular elections with universal suffrage. Competition for control of government has been limited by restrictions on opposition parties or manipulation of voters and playing field, not restrictions on suffrage. Some contemporary authoritarian regimes have protected the interests of the rich, but others have redistributed land, nationalized natural resources, and expropriated other wealth. Sometimes these expropriations have led to more equal income distributions and other times to an altered but equally uneven distribution with wealth concentrated in the hands of the dictator's family and supporters. In the former situation, regime supporters fear the loss of power entailed by more competitive politics, not redistribution. In the latter, they fear confiscation, being brought to trial for corruption and human rights abuses, prison, and execution (Kaminski, Nalepa, and O'Neill 2006), but these dangers are not lessened by a relatively equal income distribution.

Because of these differences, late twentieth- and twenty-first-century democratizations may not only be different from earlier ones but also different from each other. If wealthy private sector elites rule countries, then they may indeed resist democratization when they expect more redistributive taxation, and their fears may be allayed by a relatively equal income distribution or capital mobility (Boix 2003). Incremental suffrage extensions may be especially easy for them to endure. If, however, ruling elites came to power either through election or revolution as the leaders of movements determined to overthrow traditional elites, then regardless of whether they actually carried out their promises or have simply stolen in their turn, their fears of being deposed seem unlikely to be allayed by factors that reduce future taxation. Instead, their fears might be allayed by enforceable bargains not to prosecute them for corruption and human rights abuses (i.e. allowing them to go into friendly exile) or institutional bargains that give them a good chance of returning to office in competitive elections in the future.

These differences do not imply a return to case studies or within-region comparisons as the main way of studying democratization, however.[11] Rather, they suggest the possibility that there are theoretically relevant differences among authoritarian

---

[11] Mainwaring and Pérez-Liñán (2003) argue that democratization in Latin America differed from the general path shown by Przeworski et al. (2000). Different models could be appropriate for different regions, as they argue, but we would only know it by comparing regions with each other. Stokes (2004) provides a thoughtful discussion of why regional differences in democratization processes might occur.

governments themselves and in the ways that they interact with the ruled that may require different explanations of how transitions from them occur. As Diamond (2002, 33) notes, contemporary authoritarian regimes differ from each other "and if we are to understand the contemporary dynamics, causes, limits, and possibilities of regime change (including future democratization), we must understand the different, and in some respects new, types of authoritarian rule." His attempt at classification, however, simply relies on drawing lines between scores on the Freedom House scale to create categories. If the relevant differences are in degrees of "not democraticness," then we do not need to theorize processes separately; we can simply include a measure of democracy in statistical models, as a number of analysts have. Unsurprisingly, they find that countries that are more democratic at time one are likely to be even more democratic at time two. We cannot tell, however, whether the analysis means that less repressive forms of authoritarianism are less stable or that democratization is often incremental, and dictatorships that have liberalized somewhat in one year often continue on that path in subsequent years. A more fruitful approach to classification would begin by thinking about how the causes of democratization seem to vary from one context to another. Then classification could be based on expectations about how those differences would be likely to unfold.[12]

Linz and Stepan (1996) take a first step toward the kind of theoretically based classification that might help explain differences in democratization processes with their classification of some authoritarian regimes as "sultanistic," meaning one individual has discretion over all important personnel and policy decisions, some as "neo-totalitarian," meaning, in effect, post-Stalinist, and so on. They expect the usual characteristics of these different kinds of authoritarian regime to have systematic effects on different aspects of democratic consolidation. These arguments have not been tested, but they do suggest plausible links between characteristics of particular kinds of authoritarianism and expected outcomes.

If post-Second World War authoritarian regimes with different kinds of leadership tend to have different institutional structures and different relationships with supporters and ordinary citizens, then we would expect them to break down differently because different institutions privilege and disadvantage different groups. A simple and intuitive way to categorize these different kinds of leadership and institutions is as professionalized military, hegemonic party, and personalistic. These regime types emerge from struggles among elite contenders with different backgrounds, support bases, and resources after seizures of power. They do not derive in an obvious way from underlying social or economic structures, and all have been compatible with a wide range of economic ideologies. All types were common in the late twentieth century, so understanding something about how they break down might help to explain why post-1950 democratizations have been different from those that came

---

[12] Some early descriptions of democratization classified transition processes themselves using categories such as from above, from below, by transaction, and so on. What I suggest here might build on these earlier ideas but differs from them in that the classifications of differences would be rooted in basic features of authoritarian regimes.

before. In the real world, there are of course lots of borderline cases, but we can use the simple types to develop theories and empirical expectations.

On average, governments ruled by the professionalized military are more fragile than other kinds of authoritarianism (Gasiorowrski 1995; Geddes 2003).[13] They are more easily destabilized by poor economic performance because factionalization over how to respond to crisis causes many officers to want to return to the barracks in order to reunify the armed forces. Because of officers' dread of factionalism, the first moves toward liberalization often arise within the military elite, as noted by O'Donnell, Schmitter, and Whitehead (1986). Since military rulers usually decide to return to the barracks rather than being forced out, transitions from military rule tend to be negotiated and orderly. Negotiation is more likely to lead to democracy than is violent overthrow, and the successors to professionalized military regimes are nearly always elected in competitive elections. Thus the fall of a military regime usually results in a democracy, though it may not last.

In contrast to the military, several scholars have noted the robustness of hegemonic party regimes. Geddes (2003) shows that regimes ruled by dominant parties last substantially longer than other non-monarchic forms of authoritarianism.[14] Gandhi and Przeworski (2006) argue that dictators supported by single parties survive longer in office. When dominant or single-party regimes face severe challenges, they try to hang on by changing institutions to allow some participation by moderate opponents—thus isolating and rendering less threatening more extreme opponents (Lust-Okar 2005; Magaloni 2006). When they see the writing on the wall, they put great effort into negotiating electoral institutions that will benefit them when they become ex-authoritarians competing in fair elections (Geddes 1995; Magaloni 2006). If members of a dominant party regime cannot maintain their monopoly on power, they prefer to be replaced by a democracy since they have a good chance of being able to continue their political careers as democratic politicians. Replacement by an opposing authoritarian regime is likely to exclude them from the political game at best. Consequently dominant party governments negotiate their extrications through elections. The elections that end the rule of hegemonic parties most often initiate a democracy, but sometimes they result in a new hegemonic party regime. This happens because the new ruling party can sometimes make use of institutions originally devised to help the previous ruling party.

Regimes in which power has been personalized under one individual, however, are more likely to be replaced by a new dictatorship than by a democracy (Hadenius and Teorell 2005). Personalistic dictators are less willing to negotiate leaving office because they face a greater likelihood of assassination, prosecution, confiscation, or exile than do the leaders of other kinds of authoritarianism. Transitions from personalist dictatorship are seldom initiated by regime insiders; instead, popular

---

[13] For the logic underlying this argument and some of the evidence supporting it, see Geddes (2003).

[14] Hadenius and Teorell (2005) find different survival rates than do most other scholars because their coding rules do not allow them to distinguish between what most other analysts would identify as a regime change and smaller institutional changes that occur while a regime, in the usual sense of the word, remains in power.

opposition, strikes, and demonstrations often force dictators to consider allowing multiparty elections (Bratton and van de Walle 1997). Personalistic dictators are more likely to be overthrown in revolutions, civil wars, popular uprisings, or invasions (Skocpol and Goodwin 1994; Geddes 2003). Linz and Chehabi (1998) have described the difficulties of democratization following what they call sultanistic regimes. Several observers have suggested that transitions from personalist rule are more affected by international factors, such as pressures from international financial institutions and invasion by neighboring or ex-colonial countries, than are other kinds of authoritarianism. International financial institutions pressured a number of African dictators to agree to multiparty elections (Bratton and van de Walle 1997).

For these reasons, the process of transition from personalized dictatorship should not be modeled as an elite-led bargain. Transitions from personalized dictatorship are less likely to result in democracy, but sometimes they do. A model that focused on such transitions would help us to understand the special circumstances that lead to this outcome. Neeman and Wantchekon (2002) have proposed that democracy occurs when neither of two contending forces can defeat the other. They address situations in which opposition to dictatorship has developed into civil war, but the model might be generalizable to non-violent forms of political conflict. Models that explain transitions to democracy from personalized dictatorship should be on the democratization research agenda, as should models that include foreign pressures.

There may be other fruitful ways of disaggregating the democratization process. My point in this section has not been to argue that there is one true way to break the process into theorizable parts, but rather that we have considerable evidence that not all democratizations occur in the same way and that these differences are systematic not random. The identification of democratization as one "thing" is an artifact of our use of normal language to describe the process. If the current state of empirical knowledge allows us to see that there are theoretically important differences in democratization processes depending on when they happened, what kinds of dictatorship were being replaced, or something else, we should not expect a single model to capture all the processes well. Nor should we combine all democratizations in the same statistical tests without making an effort to specify cross-time or other theoretically relevant differences.

4 CONCLUSION

Recent empirical research on democratization has confirmed the relationship between economic development and democracy. Most research also agrees that countries with oil and mostly Muslim populations are less likely to be democratic, though these conclusions have been challenged by some analysts. It has also confirmed that countries with highly educated populations are more likely to be democratic.

The explanations for these correlations remain contested. Przeworski et al. (2000) argue that economic development causes democratic stability not democratization. Boix and Stokes (2003), however, show that economic development had a substantial impact on democratization before the Second World War and continues to have a smaller effect. Middle East scholars have described a process through which oil rents are translated into popular acquiescence to authoritarianism, but Herb (2005) argues that oil wealth leads to a misspecification of statistical tests of the effect of economic development on democratization in oil-rich countries, not to a special kind of rentier authoritarianism. Most observers have attributed the apparent affinity between Islam and authoritarianism to traditional values widely held by individual Muslims, but Fish (2002) claims that the treatment of women in Muslim societies hinders democratization.

These empirical regularities with contested interpretations bring two tasks to the forefront of the research agenda in the study of democratization: empirical studies aimed explicitly at testing different causal mechanisms; and the creation of carefully specified models to explain democratization. Some progress is being made on both fronts. Fish (2002) tests his argument about the treatment of women. Herb (2005) attempts to disaggregate the effects of rentierism from the effect of economic development as a way of testing the rentier state argument. Boix (2003) tests his argument that income equality and capital mobility increase the likelihood of democratization. None of these tests is fully persuasive, but they are very useful steps in the direction of identifying causal mechanisms. Boix (2003), Acemoglu and Robinson (2001, 2005), Zak and Feng (2003), North and Weingast (1989), Weingast (1997), Bates and Lien (1985), Neeman and Wantchekon (2002), and others have proposed formal models of democratization that offer a number of useful insights. Most of these models have been proposed as universal explanations of democratization, but when examined carefully, most turn out to be useful simplifications of democratization or elements of it in one specific context.

I suggest that we take seriously our own research showing systematic differences in the process of democratization across time and type of authoritarianism. Other differences in the process may also be theoretically important. We might make progress faster, both empirically and theoretically, if we identified clear domains for our arguments about the causes of democratization rather than assuming that just because we cover many processes of democratization with one word we should also uncritically model it as one process regardless of what we know about historical and other differences.

REFERENCES

ACEMOGLU, D., and ROBINSON, J. 2001. A theory of political transitions. *American Economic Review*, 91: 938–63.
———— 2005. *Economic Origins of Dictatorship and Democracy.* New York: Cambridge University Press.

—— Johnson, S., Robinson, J. and Yared, P. 2005. Income and democracy. NBER Working Paper 11205.

Anderson, L. 1987. The state in the Middle East and North Africa. *Comparative Politics*, 20: 118.

Barro, R. 1996. Determinants of democracy. *Journal of Political Economy*, 107: S158–S183.

Bartels, L. 2005. Homer gets a tax cut: inequality and public policy in the American mind. *Perspectives on Politics*, 3: 15–31.

Bates, R., and Lien, D. 1985. A note on taxation, development, and representative government. *Politics and Society*, 14: 53–70.

Boix, C. 2003. *Democracy and Redistribution.* Cambridge: Cambridge University Press.

—— and Stokes, S. 2003. Endogenous democratization. *World Politics*, 55: 517–49.

Bollen, K., and Jackman, R. 1985. Economic and non-economic determinants of political democracy in the 1960s. Pp. 27–48 in *Research in Political Sociology*, ed. R. G. Braungart and M. M. Braungart. Greenwich, Conn.: JAI Press.

Bratton, M., and van de Walle, N. 1997. *Democratic Experiments in Africa: Regime Transitions in Comparative Perspective.* Cambridge: Cambridge University Press.

Bravo, J. 2006. The political economy of recent Mexico–U.S. migration: a view into Mexican sub-national politics. Ph.D. dissertation. Duke University.

Bueno de Mesquita, B., and Siverson, R. M. 1995. War and the survival of political leaders: a comparative study of regime types and political accountability. *American Political Science Review*, 89: 841–55.

—— —— and Woller, G. 1992. War and the fate of regimes: a comparative analysis. *American Political Science Review*, 86 (3): 638–46.

—— Smith, A., Siverson, R. M. and Morrow, J. D. 2003. *The Logic of Political Survival.* Cambridge, Mass.: MIT Press.

Burkhart, R., and Lewis-Beck, M. 1994. Comparative democracy: the economic development thesis. *American Political Science Review*, 88: 903–10.

Chaudhry, K. 1997. *The Price of Wealth: Economies and Institutions in the Middle East.* Ithaca, NY: Cornell University Press.

Crystal, J. 1995. *Oil and Politics in the Gulf: Rulers and Merchants in Kuwait and Qatar.* Cambridge: Cambridge University Press.

Diamond, L. 2002. Thinking about hybrid regimes. *Journal of Democracy*, 13: 21–35.

Dunning, T. 2006. Does oil promote democracy? Regime change in rentier states. Presented at Annual Conference of the International Society for New Institutional Economics, Boulder, Colo.

Epstein, D., Bates, R., Goldstone, J., Dristensen, I., and O'Halloran, S. Forthcoming. Democratic transitions. *American Journal of Political Science.*

Escriba Folch, A. 2003. Legislatures in authoritarian regimes. Working Paper 196, Instituto Juan March de Estudios e Investigaciones.

Fish, M. S. 2002. Islam and authoritarianism. *World Politics*, 55: 4–37.

Gandhi, J., and Przeworski, A. 2006. Authoritarian institutions and the survival of autocrats. Unpublished MS. Emory University.

Gasiorowski, M. 1995. Economic crisis and political regime change: an event history analysis. *American Political Science Review*, 89: 882–97.

Geddes, B. 1996. The initiation of new democratic institutions in Eastern Europe and Latin America. In *Institutional Design in New Democracies*, ed. A. Lijphart and C. Waisman. Boulder, Colo.: Westview.

—— 2003. *Paradigms and Sand Castles: Theory Building and Research Design in Comparative Politics.* Ann Arbor: University of Michigan Press.

GLEDITSCH, K. S., and CHOUN, J. L. 2004. Autocratic transitions and democratization. Prepared for presentation at the International Studies Association, Montreal.

HADENIUS, A., and TEORELL, J. 2005. Learning more about democratization: persistence and fall of authoritarian regimes 1972–2003. Prepared for presentation at the APSA.

HELLMAN, J. 1998. Winner take all: the politics of partial reform in postcommunist transitions. *World Politics*, 50: 203–34.

HERB, M. 2005. No representation without taxation? Rents, development and democracy. *Comparative Politics*, 37: 297–317.

HUNTINGTON, S. 1991. *The Third Wave: Democratization in the Late Twentieth Century*. Norman: Oklahoma University Press.

INKELES, A., and SMITH, D. H. 1974. *Becoming Modern: Individual Change in Six Developing Countries*. Cambridge, Mass.: Harvard University Press.

KAMINSKI, M., NALEPA, M., and O'NEILL, B. 2006. Normative and strategic aspects of transitional justice. *Journal of Conflict Resolution*, 50: 292–302.

KARL, T. 1997. *The Paradox of Plenty: Oil Booms and Petro-States*. Berkeley and Los Angeles: University of California Press.

LEVI, M. 1988. *Of Rule and Revenue*. Berkeley and Los Angeles: University of California Press.

LEVITSKY, S., and WAY, L. 2006. Competitive authoritarianism: origins and evolution of hybrid regimes in the post-Cold War era. Presented at APSA, Philadelphia.

LINDERT, P. 1994. The rise of social spending, 1880–1930. *Explorations in Economic History*, 31: 1–37.

LINZ, J., and CHEHABI, H. E. eds. 1998. *Sultanistic Regimes*. Baltimore: Johns Hopkins University Press.

—— and STEPAN, A. 1996. *Problems of Democratic Transition and Consolidation: Southern Europe, South America, and Post-Communist Europe*. Baltimore: Johns Hopkins University Press.

LIPSET, S. M. 1959. Some social requisites of democracy: economic development and political legitimacy. *American Political Science Review*, 53: 69–105.

LUST-OKAR, E. 2005 *Structuring Conflict in the Arab World: Incumbents, Opponents and Institutions*. Cambridge: Cambridge University Press.

MAGALONI, B. 2006. *Voting for Autocracy: The Politics of Party Hegemony and its Decline*. Cambridge: Cambridge University Press.

MAINWARING, S., and PÉREZ-LIÑÁN, A. 2003. Levels of development and democracy: Latin American exceptionalism, 1945–1996. *Comparative Political Studies*, 36: 1031–67.

MARINOV, N. 2005. Do economic sanctions destabilize country leaders? *American Journal of Political Science*, 49: 564–76.

MOORE, B. 1966. *Social Origins of Dictatorship and Democracy: Lord and Peasant in the Making of the Modern World*. Boston: Beacon Press.

MULLIGAN, C., SALA-I-MARTIN, X., and GIL, R. 2003. Do democracies have different public policies than non-democracies? National Bureau of Economic Research.

NEEMAN, Z., and WANTCHEKON, L. 2002. A theory of post Civil-War democratization. *Journal of Theoretical Politics*, 14: 439–64.

NORTH, D., and WEINGAST, B. 1989. Constitutions and commitment: evolution of the institutions governing public choice in 17th century England. *Journal of Economic History*, 49: 803–32.

O'DONNELL, G., SCHMITTER, P., and WHITEHEAD, L. 1986. *Transitions from Authoritarian Rule: Tentative Conclusions about Uncertain Democracies*. Baltimore: Johns Hopkins University Press.

OLSON, M. 1993. Dictatorship, democracy, and development. *American Political Science Review*, 83: 567–76.

PAYNE, A. 1993. Westminster adapted: the political order of the Commonwealth Caribbean. In *Democracy in the Caribbean*, ed. J. Dominguez, R. Pastor, and R. DeLisle Worrell. Baltimore: Johns Hopkins University Press.

PEVEHOUSE, J. 2002. Democracy from the outside-in? International organizations and democratization. *International Organization*, 56: 515–49.

PRZEWORSKI, A., and LIMONGI, F. 1997. Modernization: theories and facts. *World Politics*, 49: 155–83.

—— ALVAREZ, M. E., CHEIBUB, J. A. and LIMONGI, F. 2000. *Democracy and Development: Political Institutions and Well-Being in the World, 1950–1990*. Princeton: Princeton University Press.

ROBERTS, T. 2006. An international political economy theory of democratic transition. Unpublished MS. UCLA.

ROGOWSKI, R. 1998. Democracy, capital, skill, and country size: effects of asset mobility and regime monopoly on the odds of democratic rule. Ch. 4 in *The Origins of Liberty: Political and Economic Liberalization in the Modern World*, ed. P. Drake and M. McCubbins. Princeton: Princeton University Press.

ROSS, M. 2001. Does oil hinder democracy? *World Politics*, 53: 325–61.

SKOCPOL, T., and GOODWIN, J. 1994. Explaining revolutions in the contemporary Third World. Pp. 301–44 in *Social Revolutions in the Modern World*, ed. T. Skocpol. Cambridge: Cambridge University Press.

SMITH, B. 2004. Oil wealth and regime survival in the developing world. *American Journal of Political Science*, 48: 232–46.

STOKES, S. 2004. Region, contingency, and democratization. Presented at Conference on Contingency in the Study of Politics, Yale University.

WEINER, M. 1987. Empirical democratic theory. Pp. 3–34 in *Competitive Elections in Developing Countries*, ed. M. Weiner and E. Ozbudun. Durham: University of North Carolina Press.

WEINGAST, B. 1997. The political foundations of democracy and the rule of law. *American Political Science Review*, 91: 245–63.

WHITEHEAD, L. 1996. Three international dimensions of democratization. Pp. 3–25 in *The International Dimensions of Democratization: Europe and the Americas*, ed. L. Whitehead. Oxford: Oxford University Press.

ZAK, P., and FENG, Y. 2003. A dynamic theory of the transition to democracy. *Journal of Economic Behavior and Organization*, 52:1–25.

CHAPTER 15

....

DEMOCRACY AND CIVIC CULTURE

....

FILIPPO SABETTI

WHAT sets Hobbes's *Leviathan* apart from almost all other explorations of the constitution of order among thinkers of his time is his lack of attention to culture. Hobbes's exception confirms the rule that most Enlightenment writers combined political and economic analyses with moral and cultural considerations. Since then, many analysts have continued this combined tradition of enquiry—from Tocqueville in his discussion of mores and habits of the heart in shaping and fostering a democratic republic in the United States, to more recent efforts to understand how and what cultural beliefs, common knowledge, and mental models shaped coordination mechanisms in and across different societies since medieval times (e.g. Berman 1983, 2003; Chwe 2003; Greif 1994). That culture is, indeed, a foundational attribute of society *and* a foundational concept for social science is hard to dispute (Eckstein 1996). The human condition makes it so. This very fact, however, tends to frustrate efforts to understand the relationship between culture and the organization of society. Several central questions continue to plague efforts: Why does the major link in the relationship between culture and action remain contentious and often unconvincing, despite widespread agreement in the literature about their relationship? How can we gain a better grasp of what we mean when we say that culture matters in politics? What kind of data and what kind of tests would give greater confidence to conclusions?

In the past few decades, comparative political behavior has become a very data-rich field of research. Measurement problems aside, we now have accumulated a

* I am grateful for comments on earlier drafts to Carles Boix, Mark Graber, Raymond Grew, Erik Kuhonta, Brian Loveman, Alfio Mastropaolo, Michael McGinnis, Elinor Ostrom, Dietlind Stolle, and Georg Vanberg. The chapter draws on research supported by the Social Sciences and Humanities Research Council of Canada and the Earhart Foundation.

robust body of comparative survey evidence on voter–elite linkages in established democracies in both North America and Western Europe. But, in spite of Almond and Verba's path-breaking work, *The Civic Culture* (1963), professional interest in explaining democratic outcomes with cultural variables has not fared well. By the 1980s, cultural accounts had become, by all measures, more sophisticated than their 1960s counterparts, but the promised renaissance of political culture did not occur. In fact, the very call for such a renaissance succeeded more in generating controversy than in gaining new practitioners. A turning point was the publication of Robert D. Putnam's *Making Democracy Work* (1993). By advancing a more structuralist perspective, this work expanded traditional understanding of the impact of culture on politics and unleashed social capital research into its current widespread and lively phase of development. By 2001, the number of citations to articles and books using the concept of social capital had already escalated to 220 from two citations in 1991 (Ostrom and Ahn 2003, p. xi). The concept of social capital can now be found in "every corner of the social science" (Ostrom and Ahn 2003, p. xi) and of historical studies (Rotberg 1999/2001).

The renaissance sparked by Putnam's work was completely unexpected. We take as evidence a decadal review of the state of comparative politics published in 1993, which paid little or no attention to civic culture (Rogowski 1993, esp. 443–4). A subsequent review essay on "The civic culture at 30" summed up the state of research this way: "work on the civic culture today has an aura of working anomalies in Ptolemaic astronomy," while Putnam's "stunning breakthrough" gives much promise to political culture research (Laitin 1995, 169, 171). Hence we confront another round of questions: Why did the cumulative contribution to understanding democracy derived from political culture research remain so problematic? Why has it progressed so unexpectedly with social capital? What is left of "civic culture" in social capital? Does this new approach offer better prospects for advancing, or even ending, the quest for democracy's necessary or sufficient conditions, or will it continue to be "a waste of time," as some predict (Tilly 2004a, 9, 35, 39)?

This chapter aims to take stock of the state of research on democracy and culture by providing answers to these sets of questions. In assessing what has been done and, in the process, suggesting what remains to be done, the chapter seeks to improve understanding of the relationship between culture and action, and between political culture and democratic outcomes.

The discussion is divided in five parts. The first section explores the way the literature has dealt with the possible meanings of culture and political culture and their relationship to action. The second section suggests why there has been little cumulative contribution to democracy derived from political culture research. The third section traces how efforts to rethink how and why we approach the subject matter in certain ways led many analysts to break out of established epistemological demarcations, and, as a result, reinvigorated the tools of investigation and research on democracy and civic culture. The subject of the fourth sections draws from answers to two questions: What benefits has social capital research produced to date in comparative politics? Why does the conceptualization of social capital continue to be debated? The conclusion briefly summarizes the discussion and explores the implications of improved tools of investigation for future research.

1 FROM CULTURE TO CIVIC CULTURE

The work of anthropologists Kroeber and Kluckhohn (1952/1963) on the general history of the word culture is often cited to point out a marked collective ambiguity in the meaning and use of culture. Their work lists more than 164 meanings of culture classified under a variety of headings: descriptive, historical, normative, psychological, structural, genetic and residual definitions. What all these definitions have in common is a conception of culture as the by-product of the human search for the meaning of life, or as the critical and systematic development of human experience. Culture as an abstract generalizing concept or "data container" includes symbols, ideas, beliefs, norms, customs, and knowledge. Relational, cognitive, and environmental mechanisms such as socialization, language, and adaptation coexist making it possible for objective (logically consistent or contradictory) features of culture to become common knowledge, and to be transferred through learning to give rise to complex systems of human artifacts as well as predictability, or limitation of possibilities, in human behavior. The locus of culture is both in society and in individuals as cultural values and customs exist in hearts and minds, and the closest we can get to grasping them is in their public expression as human behavior and institutions. The disagreement about culture turns on what we mean when we say that culture matters in the study of comparative politics.

It is not hard to appreciate why *The Civic Culture* by Gabriel Almond and Sidney Verba (1963) remains a path-breaking study. Its normative concerns can be found in classic works from Montesquieu to Tocqueville. Discussion about the social prerequisites of democracy has also contributed to maintain political culture on the research agenda (Lipset 1994). At the time when the work of Almond and Verba appeared, confidence in Anglo-American political institutions was high, and so their research seemed to elevate Anglo-American political ideas and practice to some kind of cross-national inspirational model. It also served to reinvigorate scholarly arguments against both Marxist materialism and structural functionalism.

Almond and Verba defined political culture as "the psychological or subjective orientations toward politics" studied quantitatively. They sought to do three things all at once. By focusing on citizen orientation, they transformed the concept of political culture into something more deeply seated than public opinion and more sharply focused than the concept of culture. By seeking knowledge of what facilitates, or impedes, democratic stability, they aimed to build a theory of civic culture linking political culture to the political process. By showing that that it was technically

possible to study citizen orientations quantitatively and cross-nationally, they ensured that the significance of their study remained well after the (Cold War) period
when the research was conceived.

Before long, researchers followed and expanded the empirical and normative
meaning of the concept to include values, symbols, norms, attitudes, as well as
orientations. The blurring of the analytical distinction between social and psychological components of political culture enhanced its popularity but made it difficult
to ground preference formation in a theory of motivation about how and why people
make choices that affect political life. As a result, it became difficult to speak of a
single political culture approach and to assess the claims of the various approaches.

By the end of the 1960s, a leading contributor to political culture was compelled to
acknowledge that "the term 'political culture' is capable of evoking quick intuitive
understanding, so that people often feel that without further and explicit definition
they can appreciate its meaning and freely use it." That carried "the considerable
danger that it [would] be employed as a 'missing link' to fill in anything that cannot
be explained in political analysis" (Pye 1968, 204). By the end of the 1970s, an
assessment of the state of the research on measuring, and comparatively analyzing,
the mass-level political cultures of societies—the linkage between the behavior of the
individuals and the behavior of systems—led some analysts to speak of a cause in
search of effects (Elkins and Simeon 1979). Others suggested that it was democracy
that produces civic culture and not the other way around (Barry 1978, 51–2). In
developing a game-theoretic approach to the political foundations of democracy,
Barry Weingast suggested more recently that there is something to the argument
developed by Almond and Verba, if only in the form of expectations (civic culture as
shared norms) that may be operating between governmental elites and citizens to
constrain public officials (Weingast 1997, 254).

In the late 1970s, Almond and Verba revisited and sought to update their cross-
national study (1980). There was little doubt that many of the questions raised in 1963
were still pertinent for comparative politics: "What shapes individual political
beliefs? Which beliefs are politically significant? How do political beliefs affect
political systems? How does historical experience affect what people think about
politics?" (Verba 1980, 409). But questions about the soundness of the conception of
democracy and the methodology of the original study as well as questions about the
validity of the inferences drawn from the earlier findings made it difficult to update
or replicate the original work (see also Street 1994).

The problem of how multiple components of a single variable can be linked to
political behavior remained, in spite of some renewed attempt to overcome it
through a culture theory of the kind suggested by Aaron Wildavsky and colleagues
(Wildavsky 1987; Thompson, Ellis, and Wildavsky 1990). Wildavsky aimed to construct a cultural theory that would permit the understanding of culture's effects on
action in any country, any time, and any place. Even those sympathetic to such an
attempt have not found it persuasive (Laitin 1988; Ostrom and Ostrom 1997). A
general Culture Theory is not possible in part because different systems of societal
order require different theories to understand the diversity of structured human

interaction. No general culture theory can explain norms, attitudes, behavior, or political outcomes based on different and even opposing conceptions of culture and politics.

We still lack a persuasive way to shore up political culture as a concept and the cultural approach as a means to acquire knowledge. A literature review (Reisinger 1995) of the various approaches and methodologies summed up the challenges this way:

(1) How to define the concept;
(2) how to disentangle subcultures (for example, elite or regional political culture in countries like Canada) from a society's overall political culture;
(3) how to integrate the many individual-level orientations of which the concept is composed;
(4) how to create a societal-level variable from individual-level components;
(5) assuming the foregoing have been resolved, how to measure the concept;
(6) how to derive hypotheses about individual political behavior from the subjective orientations under study; and
(7) how political culture interacts with institutions and other attributes of a polity to produce a propensity for certain types of political outcomes.

The conclusion was that political culture was little more than a rubric "under which different authors focus on different individual orientations, employ different measures and different methods of aggregating the orientations, then test different propositions about the links between those individual orientations and politics" (Reisinger 1995, 329). What, then, have we learned from political culture research after roughly four decades of research? What kind of cumulative research program has been built?

2 THE CHALLENGE OF CUMULATIVE KNOWLEDGE

A 1999 collection of essays exploring global support for democratic governance (Norris 1999) carried on its front cover praise by Gabriel Almond as "the Civic Culture study 40 years later." But the collection contradicted somewhat Almond's claim. The essays showed that systematic evidence for the relationship between civic culture and democracy was complex to obtain and difficult to interpret.

At the start of the new millennium, even Britain, once a model of civic culture, seemed to have adopted a more skeptical political culture, as a recently conducted citizen audit on democracy and participation reported (Seyd and Whiteley 2002). This research raised doubts about the view advanced by Almond and Verba that "general social trust is translated into politically relevant trust" (1963, 285). The British public was reported to be distrustful of the political elite at all levels of government, though not distrustful of interpersonal trust. Contrary to the conventional wisdom that interpersonal trust translates into political trust, the two kinds of trust were found to be largely unrelated to each other (Seyd and Whiteley 2002; also Hall 1999, 432–33). The case of Britain is by no means exceptional. A review of several cross-national studies of social and political trust in several democracies noted that "(T)here is not a close or consistent association between social and political trust, between social trust and political behaviour, or between activity in voluntary associations and political attitudes of trust and confidence. The links, where they exist, tend to be weak and contingent" (Newton 1999, 185).

The strongest advocate of the political culture approach to the study of democracy has remained Ronald Inglehart. He defined civic culture as a coherent syndrome of personal life satisfaction, political satisfaction, and interpersonal trust and support for the existing political order. Anticipating Putnam's argument somewhat, Inglehart suggested that high and low levels of civic culture appear to be stable and enduring even over centuries. He spared no effort to design tests aimed at giving greater confidence to his conclusions. Yet his claim—that over half the variance in the persistence of democratic institutions can be attributed to the effects of political culture alone (Inglehart 1990, 41)—is problematic in both methods and findings. Five broad categories of issues continue to stand in the way of cumulative knowledge.

Much of the research on democracy, the crisis of democracy, and democratization over the past thirty years or so records little or nothing about the relationship between democratic outcomes and civic culture. This may be attributable to the reluctance of researchers to invest time and energy in tackling the meanings of the concepts of democracy and civic culture, in deciding what methodology to use for choosing dependent and independent variables, each involving composite factors, and in assessing their relative importance and relationship. Other reasons can be attributed to the swings in the pendulum of fads and fashion that engage North American scholarly attention, or to a widespread misunderstanding, or high expectation, of what causal analysis can actually accomplish in social science (Kitschelt 2003, 51–2). Some analysts may even regard as futile, or a waste of time, the search for either uniform conditions or repeated sequences of democratization and de-democratization (Tilly 2004a, 9, 35, 39). Whatever the reasons may be, little or no notice has been taken of the presumed importance of political culture for democratic processes in much of the comparative politics literature.

Neither studies of consociational democracy (Lijphart 1977), accounts of elitist accommodation in (re)established democracies (DiPalma 1990), nor research on the survival of democracy in European societies (Budge and Newton 1997) take real notice of political culture. What allows democracies to emerge from dictatorships and survive in most countries, and endure in places like India, cannot be easily accounted for in terms of the variables privileged by Inglehart (see Boix and Stokes 2003; Przeworski et al. 1996; Varshney 1998). In fact, there was no place for civic culture explanations in recent surveys on a number of generalizations actually achieved concerning democratization within their geographical and temporal reach (Bunce 2000, 2003).

When the relationship between democracy and civic culture is carefully considered, a second set of problems emerges: whether it is possible to treat individual dispositions as the fundamental causes of social processes. This criticism does not just apply to culturalists; it also applies to phenomenologists, behaviorists, and methodological individualists as well. Democratization and de-democratization cannot, it is argued (Tilly 2004a, p. xi), be understood through the "reconstruction" and "aggregation" of individual dispositions just before their point of action. Another stream of literature highlights another type of disagreement about the causal link. Inglehart's causal model is based on an assumption of unidirectional causation—that civic culture has an effect on democracy and that democracy does not have an effect on civic culture (Inglehart 1988, 1990, 1997; Inglehart and Welzel 2004)—that has left many comparativists unconvinced. Heated debate has not helped to give confidence in the testing of competing explanations and conclusions (Jackman and Miller 1996a, 1996b; Muller and Seligson 1994). The question still remains: whether it is possible, and if so how, to design statistical tests which give greater confidence to particular conclusions (see also Mahoney and Rueschemeyer 2003, 23–4).

Third, culturalists like Inglehart do not help their argument by calling up support from Max Weber and Edward C. Banfield. Most historians do not take seriously Max Weber's thesis about the Protestant ethic and the spirit of capitalism. Weber's thesis "appears to be a social misconstruction" (Hamilton 1996, 88). At best, Weber's thesis remains a hypothesis (Hamilton 1996, 88). It is possible that an opposite causal direction was at work—that the rise of capitalism stimulated the appearance of Protestantism (Hamilton, 1996, 92).

Banfield's "amoral familism" is such a powerful indictment of people that most comparativists have been reluctant to generalize it beyond southern Italy; they also seldom call up Banfield's account of the people in his "unheavenly city." The indictment of Montegrano villagers is not true. Banfield ignored the presence of horizontal bonds of reciprocity, trust, solidarity, and ad hoc mutual aid and exchanges of services that went beyond relationships with one's own kin, which were and remain very much part of the local way of life. His predictive hypothesis cannot account for the long-enduring secondary associations and community organizations throughout the village's long history as far back as medieval times. If, indeed, the people at the time of Banfield's research were "prisoners," they were prisoners more of the institutional rules that governed their agricultural and communal activities than of their local culture, about which Banfield has surprisingly little to say (Sabetti 2000, ch. 8).[1]

Fourth, another stream of research suggests that it is easier to reach more convincing conclusions about the relationship between democracy and civic culture when the constitutional, collective choice, and operational dimensions of political systems are approached separately. That is, it is possible to be "critical citizens" about some dimensions of political life without rejecting constitutional democracy or the entire system. In the United States and in Canada, as in Western Europe, public opinion

---

[1] A laudable attempt to compare the civic values of Italians and Italian-Americans runs afoul of the same conceptual and empirical problems (Rice and Feldman 1997).

polls have found overwhelming support for the underlying framework of democratic systems of government (contributions in Norris 1999; Pickup et al. 2004). There has been little or no reported "crisis of democracy" at that level of analysis. Public confidence in the running of governmental, administrative, and street-level public institutions is another matter. Though researchers (Norris 1999, 266) suspect that a supportive political culture is necessary for the consolidation and operation of democratic government, they cannot give exact measures of regime support, in part because it is difficult to treat the political orientations of citizens exogenous to the way governments themselves work. The reported incongruence gap between system support and specific support—namely that critical citizens view the running of political institutions with distrust and disdain, but still believe in constitutional democracy—may not be a gap at all if we keep in mind the multiple design criteria of federal systems.

Finally, it is hard to avoid the conclusion that the scholarly community does not know much more than it did three or four decades ago as a result of political culture research. The challenge of cumulation is also the challenge of the way democracy and civic culture have been conceptualized to inform, direct, and constrain empirical research (Johnson 2003). A chief strength in Putnam's *Making Democracy Work* lies precisely in the fact that it tapped a rich vein of thinking and research aimed at respecifying democracy and civic culture as conceptual variables, thereby offering better and stronger prospects to build a cumulative research program.

3 RESPECIFYING KEY VARIABLES[2]

A renewed interest in understanding how we think, and why we seem obliged to think in certain ways, led several social scientists and intellectual historians to explore the conceptual history of democracy and civic culture beyond their usual epistemological demarcations. The result is a broad range of theoretical enquiries and detailed empirical cases suggesting respecification of both conceptual variables. The rest of this section brings these advances together to suggest the work that has been done to reinvigorate the study of democracy and civic culture.

3.1 Respecifying Democracy

Prevailing explorations of the relationship between democracy and civic culture rest largely on questionable definitions of democracy. Sometimes, a minimalist, Schum-

---

[2] I am following here David Laitin (2002, 632) when he suggested that, often, even small respecifications of a dependent variable can have a large repercussion for the explanatory significance of the independent variable.

peterian, definition has prevailed; in other times, democracy has been equated with political stability; other times still, comparativists have used democracy as a synonym for government performance. What unites most analyses of democracy is a state-centric, national view of democracy. To be sure, there are variations in the conception of what a democratic state is, particularly for post-communist East European states (Grzymala-Busse and Jones-Luong 2002, 531–2). But the central government—that is, the ensemble of national electoral, legislative, administrative, and judicial institutions that makes up the state—has been generally presumed to have the capacity to make policies that will govern society. There is more to democracy than such prevailing views.

Going against French liberals of his time, Tocqueville used the American experience to challenge the entrenched European view of the state and to shift the focus of concern to local democracy, away from national democracy and state-centric conceptions. Since then, a rich literature has accumulated beyond the American case to suggest that democracy is not something that emanates only from the top. It is also a bottom-up process of self-governance. This process occurs when individuals who participate in an ongoing pattern of relationships can and do devise some of their own rules to govern those relationships within particular domains. Agents of constitutional/institutional choice are not confined to national rulers, governments, or constituent assemblies but include individuals acting in a collective capacity at multiple scales to secure future goods or to tackle particular policy problems.

Reframing the meaning of democracy to include processes of self-governance makes available for study many patterns of associative interaction and integration across time and space. They include such entities as free cities, neighborhood associations, corps like town councils, rural parishes, provincial estates and parliaments, fraternities such as mutual aid societies, artisanal and commercial guilds, local and provincial undertakings for the creation and maintenance of civic assets ranging from churches to bridges, as well as the body of self-enforcing rules that emerged, first as the Amalfitan Table and later as the Customs of Barcelona, for regulating market transactions and business associations involving local, regional, and long-distance trade (e.g. Berman 1983, chs. 11–12). The economic expansion of Sicily and its export-oriented agricultural market that put the island ahead of many other parts of Western and northern Europe in late medieval times cannot be properly understood until we appreciate the trust networks that underpinned the Sicilian political and institutional structures that regulated access to markets (Epstein 1992, ch. 4). Accounts of the *ancien régime* origins of democratic liberty in France (Bien 1994; Bossenga 1991), the vitality and perils of small-town democracy in Habsburg Spain (Nader 1990), and the remarkable resilience of institutions for collective action in the Italian Alps (Casari and Plott 2003) reveal a new world for comparative historical analysis constituted by multiple political orders, with horizontal and vertical bonds existing simultaneously and sequentially on the same plane—in effect, multi-level governance involving reciprocal relations between civic culture and democracy. The standard view, reiterated by Charles Tilly (2004a, 36, 66, 82), that nothing remotely resembling democracy existed in Iberia and the rest of Europe before the nineteenth century is not tenable.

It is true that the strength of such local ventures in European history did not often equate with the liberties of the people they were supposed to serve. Probably no civic asset can meet twenty-first-century standards of democratic practice. Most excluded women; decision-making procedures were often susceptible to manipulation by inner circles and wealthy people. Attempts to sustain multi-level governance among an array of overlapping but uncoordinated undertakings are never easy. Even when such undertakings were long enduring, as in the case of governing the commons in many parts of the world and the irrigation networks in Valencia and the Po River valley, they did not all work alike. Yet these weaknesses, and gaps in knowledge, do not detract from the main argument: namely, that democracy as the processes of self-governance among all sorts of institutions was antecedent to, and coterminous with, the development of national democracy. Recent studies of American political development provide additional theoretical ground for the argument (Orren and Skowronek 2004). The political order that emerged in the United States was typically composed of numerous institutions that functioned relatively autonomously of each other; some institutions may have been quite democratic, others not, and many functioned based on very different democratic norms.

However imperfect and tumultuous by twenty-first-century standards, "the existence and practices of such groups [and institutions] are nonetheless relevant to the story of democracy," for, as some analysts suggest in a survey of democracy's place in world history, "if one insists on perfect democracy in a community before conceding its relevance to the history of democracy, then democracy has no history and never will" (Mulhberger and Paine 1993, 27–8). This history helps to shed light on important questions in comparative historical analysis: How is it possible for ordinary people living in hierarchically ordered regimes characterized by principles of privilege and absolute monarchy to learn to deliberate collectively on matters of common concerns, often through long-enduring institutions for collective action? How did ordinary people manage to construct their lives through civic associative activities, to engage in the everyday practices of self-governance, and to develop a sense of civic selfhood, apart from a logic of state formation, or alongside the formal regime? Where and how did they learn to turn to, and interiorize, such ideas?

When we turn to the contemporary world, the domain of "democratic governance" is more complex and expansive than what we usually imagine it to be. As a rule, most people live in multi-organizational arrangements grounded in complementary or competing forms of democratic ideas and practices—representative institutions for national politics and more participatory forms at other levels (Mansbridge 1980). A flourishing body of scholarship concerned with the evolution of institutions of collective action governing common property resources, from the Philippines to Norway, supports three conclusions: (1) "a group of individuals can organize themselves voluntarily to retain the residuals of their own efforts" (Ostrom 1990, 25); (2) "effective and long-lasting constitutions are frequently negotiated at a micro-level rather than at the macro-level of an entire political system" (Ostrom 1989, 2); and (3) "the proportion of successful self-organized systems increases to the extent that central governments invest in general institutional facilities that enhance the capabilities of self-governing practices or forms of collective action with democratic qualities" (Ostrom 1992). Translated into the concern of this chapter, a more fitting exploration of the relationship between democracy and civic culture needs to go, in Jane Mansbridge's words, "beyond adversary democracy" (1980) and recognize the richness of democratic forms of governance, without diminishing what Adam Smith, among others, recognized: the importance of the role of national governmental arrangements in ensuring defense, the rule of law, and the protection of property rights.

The preceding discussion has profound implications for comparative research. First, a state-centric conception of democracy is too narrow to explore the relationship between democracy and civic culture, as the state is not always the all-encompassing apex of problem solving in democratic societies. Second, multi-level governance involving citizen participation, civic engagement, subnational institutions, and other forms of collective undertakings has a long history pre-dating national states and national elections. Democratic institutional diversity is true in Europe and North America as in other parts of the world, even though social structures may be much more hierarchical outside the Western world and therefore may not exhibit the same depth of social associations and societal democracy. Third, comparativists need to be more attentive to the fact that robust democratic governance can result where people participate in the practice of problem solving, including the design of subnational institutions and other forms of collective action. Fourth, contrary to what many analysts since Tocqueville have assumed, there is no automatic correspondence between daily democratic practices in civil society and the macro-political order. The practice of democracy in civil society can generate a civic culture, without automatically effacing authoritarian structures in macro-political orders. Finally, respecifying the concept of democracy brings to light the possibility that more complex linkage mechanisms can exist between democracy and civic culture than those stipulated by the standard civic culture argument. These implications for comparative analysis acquire more force when joined together with new advances in understanding civic culture.

3.2 Respecifying Civic Culture

Working often independently of one another, a rich mix of political scientists, game theorists, historians, sociologists, and other social scientists has generated considerable literature going beyond the standard meaning of civic culture. Three advances are especially important for our purpose. One strand deals with trust.

Originally, trust was considered a critical dimension of the syndrome of positive attitudes or political orientations that went into the making of civic culture (Almond and Verba 1963). Unfortunately, the comparative literature of the 1970s did not seriously engage in further explorations of trust. Credit must go to Diego Gambetta (1988) for placing trust on the research agenda again, across the entire range of social, economic and political life. Since then, interest in trust has mushroomed.

One problem, brought to light by Tilly (2004b), is that much of this literature has generally neglected to draw attention to the fact that people have created and recreated trust networks as endogenous mechanisms for sustaining networks for markets, interpersonal credit, and other forms of economic and social organization. The interactive process required to integrate these trust networks in public, national politics was, however, rarely available, often unstable, and generally hostile (Tilly 2004b). Support for this view can be called up from research in different parts of the world. A few illustrations should suffice.

Going beyond the formal institutions of government, some analysts have uncovered dense trust networks in the form of local and civic organizations in the history of Latin American democracy (Forment 2003). These networks have been characterized as a form of "civic Catholicism" to distinguish them in a provocative way from political models developed for the north Atlantic world and too hastily universalized. Civic Catholicism was stronger in Mexico than in Peru, but its basic outlines were similar in both nations to the point of treating it as constitutive of democratic life in Spanish America in the same way that Protestantism and Republicanism were constitutive of modern democracy in Britain, the Dutch Republics, and the United States. The critical problem in Latin America—explored more in depth in other studies—is that trust could not extend to macro-political orders grounded, as they were, in "constitutions of tyranny" (Loveman 1993). What happened in Quebec with a somewhat similar kind of civic Catholicism helps to understand what kind of macro-political order complements democratic trust networks. Research has discovered that Catholic Action youth movements of the 1930s and other such organizations played a central role in formulating the religious ideology underlying the Quiet Revolution in the 1960s (Gauvreau 2005). This is why recent research has placed in sharp relief the Catholic origins of the transformation of the Quebec vision of society and state. The relative success of Quebec's own brand of civic Catholicism came to depend on the constitution of Canadian federalism.

Trust networks developed in the Sicilian countryside with the rise of Christian Democracy in the 1890s suggest some important, and not just temporal, differences from the civic Catholicism found in the New World. The steadily increasing improvements that followed in Sicily with the spread of Christian Democracy in the late 1890s drew attention to the as yet unremedied problem of absence of law and order in the countryside. The lesson in working together that had been learned through church-sponsored associations was extended by some villagers to overcome the problem of public security in the countryside. This is how the mafia in Villalba, often described as the capital of the mafia, emerged in the late 1890s (Sabetti 1984/2002, 103). This development lends support to Gambetta's view that private protection has been a distinguishing feature of the Sicilian mafia (1993), but not necessarily to his treatment of the mafia as the price of public mistrust. The emergence of the Villalba mafia by the late 1890s had more to do with the spirit of community problem solving that had been learned by working together in voluntary associations than with the price of mistrust of formal public institutions as such (Sabetti 1984/2002, ch. 6). A chief conclusion that we can take for comparative analysis is that (mis)trust networks like the mafia are not constant; they are variable and do not endure for ever, even among the same population (see also Sabetti 2006).

The Russell Sage Foundation Series on Trust is especially indicative of the range of interdisciplinary work that is currently being done: from explorations of trust and governance (Braithwaite and Levi 1998) to experimental research involving the cognitive, biological, and evolutionary foundations of trust (Ostrom and Walker 2003). What emerges is that trust is "a holding word" with several faces (Levi 1998, 78). There are indeed notions of trust and trustworthiness that spring from shared identity, emotional connectedness, or moral standards that are not additive terms in a subjective utility model. But there is also trust (or distrust) that is rationally grounded, of a form that Russell Hardin calls "encapsulated interest" (Hardin 1998). While analysts may differ about what weight to attach to various kinds of beliefs, norms, and knowledge, they tend to share the view that citizens and government officials will trust each other when there are mutual benefits in doing so. Research from ten post-communist countries in Eastern Europe and the former Soviet Union strongly support the superiority of institutional explanations of the origins of political trust, especially micro-level explanations, while providing little support for either micro-cultural or macro-cultural explanations (Mishler and Rose 2001). Still, the effects of the act of trust are normatively ambiguous: "trust may be good when it leads to socially productive cooperation, but it can equally lead to exploitation of the trusting by the trusted, confirm a person's sense of inability to make good judgments, or produce support for unjust or morally retrograde rulers" (Braithwaite and Levi 1998, 377). We are left with an institutional challenge: "how to attain the social advantages of trust while avoiding its undesirable effects" (Braithwaite and Levi 1998, 377).

These conclusions bring renewed appreciation to what Tocqueville recognized in his work on the old regime and the French revolution (Tocqueville 1856/1956, pt. 2 ch. 3, 50–1, and pt. 2, ch. 6, 67–71): that a chief attitude or orientation toward the political among citizens is the outcome of their encounters with people in positions of authority, rather than the product of, say, some ("French" or "Mediterranean") culture as such; and that a system of centralized government and administration tends to impede rather than promote public trust.

A second respecification of civic culture derives from the study of the history of the concept itself. Since the critique by Pateman (1980), the critical literature has been enriched by efforts coming from comparative sociologists and postmodernist writers. These efforts are summarized and extended in more recent works (e.g. Bridges 1997; Somers 1995a, 1995b). We draw on these to sketch the basic argument.

The concept of civic culture formulated by Almond and Verba was definitional, not relational, something which is also evident in Almond's account (1980) of the intellectual history of the concept. By contrast, the *civic* culture of communities is the civic culture that emerges from human interaction as people confront concrete instances of coming to terms with their own environment. Almond and Verba's formulation denies, or skips over, the processes by which people develop over time and through interaction the capacities proper for citizenship in particular communities, and in relation to the larger world. It draws on the vocabulary and world view of a culture of citizenship embedded in the Enlightenment project, but defined exclusively in terms of a universalist world view that requires uniform application (of the kind suggested by Talcott Parsons). It rejects the cognitive and moral validity of culturally particularized beliefs that emanate from, and are adapted to, local ecological niches. Civic culture properly understood is not "context free" or "institution free" *à la* Banfield. It is a configuration of relational representations and practices that exists as a contentious—structural and contingent—social phenomenon. Before we start treating civic culture as an independent variable we need to appreciate how much of a dependent variable it really is (Somers 1995*a*, 134).

This way of understanding civic culture poses several challenges. First, it serves as a useful reminder that the concept as used since Almond and Verba represents only one strand of the liberal political tradition. This strand, often termed "rationalist liberalism" (Levy 2003), has, since Voltaire, tended to view local communities and mediating institutions as allied to arbitrariness, superstition, and local tyranny, standing in the way of direct relations between the state and the citizens. Second, it draws attention to another strand of liberalism, often termed "pluralist," that views local communities and mediating institutions as allied to freedom and self-government, against the entrenched view of the European state. Thinkers like Acton, Cattaneo, and Tocqueville are notable exponents of this tradition. Third, the tension between rationalism and pluralism is embedded in liberalism from its very beginning and cannot be resolved by definitional fiat. Fourth, just as economic progress and well-being can derive from non-Western values, such as those that have been ascribed to Japan, so economic progress and well-being in Western societies can equally be ascribed to multiple strands, and not just one strand, of liberalism. Finally, a history of the concept reminds analysts that a civic culture emerges from the way people in different communities use knowledge in the art of associating together to craft institutions of self-governance, to engage in joint activities, or to resolve joint and collective problems. In brief, civic culture is endogenous to the practice of political democracy itself.

A third, parallel but complementary, development in the 1980s is associated with attempts to rethink the meaning of capital beyond Marx's surplus value, and physical and human capital (Lin 1999, 28–30). Working at the interstice of social science and rational choice theory, James Coleman went beyond the first generation of collective action theory to suggest that social capital was another kind of capital created "through changes in the relations between persons that facilitate action." This way "a group within which there is extensive trustworthiness and extensive trust is able to accomplish much more than a comparable group without that trustworthiness and trust" (Coleman 1988, 100–1). The conceptual history of social capital suggests that the term recaptures insights present in social science since the beginning of the discipline (Farr 2004; Portes 1998, 1–3; Woolcock 1998). Often, the concept was present, among social scientists and ordinary people, without the term (Parker Follett 1924; Sabetti 1984/2002, 98–104). But what makes Coleman's conceptualization and treatment of social capital truly original is that his was also a way (1) to account for anomalies in collective action that could not be explained by the rational choice theory, (2) to bridge theoretical and disciplinary divides with other approaches, and still (3) to be consistent with rational choice.

4 SOCIAL CAPITAL: A NEW APPROACH TO CIVIC CULTURE RESEARCH?

Not surprisingly, some of the first applications of Coleman's conceptualization of social capital can be found among practitioners of rational choice theory (Ostrom 1992). With the publication of Robert D. Putman's *Making Democracy Work* (1993) and his subsequent explorations for the United States, the concept gained widespread recognition and application. Putnam defined social capital as "features of social organization such as networks, norms and social trust that facilitate coordination and cooperation for mutual benefit" (1995, 67).

Social capital research has spread so fast that it is not possible to do justice here to the huge literature that has accumulated. Already by 1998, the literature spanned several substantive fields: economic development; family and youth behavior problems; schooling and education; community life; work and organization; democracy and governance; and general cases of collective action problems (Schneider et al. 1997; Woolcock 1998, 193–4 n. 20). Since then, it has expanded to understand how to bridge ethnic divisions in the Balkans (Pickering 2006), to extend the analysis of Italian industrial districts beyond that originally provided by Putnam (Farrell and Knight 2003), to identify the role of formal and information institutions in developing countries (Chopra 2001), and to examine the gendered use of social capital as an instrument for facilitating women's political engagement, knowledge, and representation in Western democracies (O'Neill and Gidengil 2006). These developments are all the more remarkable if we consider that "the achievements of *Making Democracy Work* are as impressive as its problems" (Tarrow 1996, 396; see also Sabetti 2000, ch. 9). So alongside the excessive praise and the ubiquitous citations, profound disagreement has emerged in the literature as to how social capital might matter (e.g. Adam and Roncevic 2003; Szreter 2002; Stolle and Hooghe 2004). The disagreement cannot be settled here. But it is possible to provide some orientation as to the richness of the debate.

Recalling some of the shortcomings in Putnam's work, some critics (e.g. Koelble 2003, 209–10) have raised the question of the efficacy of a method of analysis if it tells us little that is accurate or if it repeats what we already know through other methods. An initial answer is that any method of analysis, no matter how good it may be, does not carry with it foolproof assurances that it will be used properly. The strength of Putnam's work is that it tapped rich veins of research aimed at respecifying civic culture and democracy and, as a result, moved comparative research on democracy and civic culture in new directions—leaving to others to apply, and learn from, the lessons of his work. After all, there is only so much that a single book can do.

Already by 1996, it was possible to see some general results that have by now become widespread aspects of comparative research: (1) social scientists and historians have added social capital to the list of key variables they consider in trying to explain social, political, and economic phenomena; (2) students of political culture have been forced to expand their accounts of the impact of culture to accommodate Putnam's more structuralist perspective; (3) following Putnam's example, there is renewed appreciation among researchers of the need to integrate quantitative and qualitative data in their analyses; (4) the policy community, from the World Bank to city hall, has been particularly energized by the findings of *Making Democracy Work*; and, perhaps, more importantly, (5) in social capital, historians, political scientists, anthropologists, economists, sociologists, and policy makers have found a common language within which to engage one another in open and constructive debate about some of the most pressing issues of our time (Boix and Posner 1996; see also Rotberg 1999/2001; Woolcock 1998). All this without denying the dark side of social capital in the form of what Margaret Levi calls "unsocial capital" (Levi 1996; see also Armony 2004).

There is much conceptual debate about which factors are forms of social capital and which are mere consequences of it. Putnam claimed to have made small changes in the original definition offered by Coleman. Starting from the point of view that capital always involves multiple forms, Ostrom and Ahn express no surprise that multiple forms of social capital can exist: it is "counterproductive ... to assume that the concept of capital has a fixed set of innate meanings" (2003, p. xxv). They select three broad forms of social capital that are particularly important for the study of collective action: trustworthiness, networks, and formal and informal rules (2003). A careful review of the varied definitions of social capital shows what positive implications they have had for the measurement of the concept, for its data sources, for what constitutes the dependent variable, and for conclusions and implications in different settings (Krishna 2002). But this view is by no means widely shared.

Culturalists have tended to focus on the attitudinal components of social capital, casting them as exogenous and durable, not subject to change in the short-to-medium term. Structuralists and institutionalists have responded by challenging the presentation of causal arrows and treating attitudinal components like trust as endogenous. "Political structures and political context" are critically important, and "can go a long way toward shaping both the kinds of organizations represented in society and their impact on the behavior and attitudes of citizens" (Edwards and Foley 1998, 128). "Social capital may be caused by how government institutions operate and not by voluntary associations," which is leading to an entire new stream of research on an institutional theory of social capital (Rothstein 2001, 207; see also Szreter 2002; Rothstein and Stolle forthcoming). Other researchers have stressed that, "rather than emanating from a culture of trust, social capital is a public-good by-product of organizations" (Jackman and Miller 1998, 55). One way to differentiate opposing ways of looking at social capital has been put this way: "considering trust endogenous encourages us to ask which arrangements provide incentives for trust. Considering trust exogenous, however, means that we take levels of trust as given and not subject to change in the short-to-medium term" (Jackman and Miller 1998, 51).

These contradictory conclusions can be found in Putnam's own evolving position. While he calls up Banfield in support of his argument for Italy, he is less reluctant to do so for the case of the United States; he supports historical determinism for Italy but not for the United States. Thus the decline of social capital reported in *Bowling Alone* "directly contradicts the logic of *Making Democracy Work*. In Putnam's Italian model, the kind of overnight deterioration of civic virtue that he proposes regarding America would be inconceivable—once civic virtue is in place it is incredibly durable over centuries" (Lehman 1996, 25). But, according to others (e.g. Skocpol and Fiorina 1999), Putnam's analysis of the American case continues to be insensitive to the role of government.

Two related issues suggest that it is still too premature to reach firm conclusions. One issue has to do with how social capital is generated. An examination of American data for the period 1972–94 has led some analysts to suggest that social capital is "as much a consequence of confidence in institutions as the reverse" (Brehm and Rahn 1997, 1018; see also Schneider et al. 1997). More recent research designed expressly to get at the question of how the attitudinal components of social capital are generated reports that the development of civic attitudes is shaped by governmental public policy and political institutions as well as by social interaction (Hooghe and Stolle 2003). But this is only a first progress report of research on the sources of social capital.

The other issue has to do with the fact that, for all the research undertaken, we still do not know exactly how social capital existing among members of community organizations affects the performance of governmental institutions. This was a problem in Putnam's original research on Italy (Sabetti 2000, 114). In 1996, Carles Boix and Daniel Posner (1996) presented four models of how social cooperation at the level of community might translate into good government performance. Their suggestion—that the articulation of societal demands, bureaucratic efficiency, civic virtues, and elite accommodation might get at how government performance can become a direct reflection of the cooperation it receives from its citizens—has not been acted upon to reach firm conclusions. Research tracing the roots of development and democracy in India reveals, however, the importance of local political entrepreneurs, other than more traditional and hereditary heads of village groups, for acting as catalyst agents in linking effective collective action and superior goal performance (Krishna 2002). In the absence of such social animators, social capital can remain a latent resource and unrealized potential for mutually beneficial collective action. How social capital is generated and made "active" for democratic outcomes is a promising area of research.

5 CONCLUSION

Despite the multicentury preoccupation with democracy and civic culture, before and after Hobbes, the study of the relationship between civic culture and democratic outcomes remains problematic, if not in its infancy. In the late 1950s and early 1960s a new generation of social scientists sought to place the study of the relationship on solid empirical grounds, only in the end to set the political culture approach on a degenerative path. Just around the time when this path had reach the point of self-destruction, social capital research emerged, with new tools of investigation and a body of new case research necessary for theory building and testing. This unexpected development reinvigorated the study of civic culture and democracy.

While the development caught most comparative political scientists by surprise, it had been in the making for quite some time, as this chapter suggests. What sets social capital research apart from the old civic culture research is more deliberate efforts than in the past to delve into the interior of the body politics, so to speak, and to understand the sources and dynamics of what pieces fit together to create and maintain healthy democracies. By combining an interdisciplinary perspective with adequate attention to variations and specificities of social capital in relation to other types of capitals, there is hope that we can untangle the complex relationship between democracy and civic culture. This new advance will probably not end the quest for democracy's necessary or sufficient conditions. Charles Tilly may be right. But, if the research generated by social capital, to date, is an indication of the outline of research that can be done, the quest will not be "a waste of time."

REFERENCES

ADAM, F., and RONCEVIC, B. 2003. Social capital: recent debates and research trends. *Social Science Information*, 42 (2): 155–83.

ALMOND, G. 1980. The intellectual history of the civic culture concept. Pp. 1–36 in *The Civic Culture Revisited*, ed. G. A. Almond and S. Verba. Boston: Little & Brown.

—— and VERBA, S. 1963. *Civic Culture*. Princeton: Princeton University Press.

—— —— eds. 1980. *Civic Culture Revisited*. Boston: Little & Brown.

ARMONY, A. C. 2004. *The Dubious Link: Civic Engagement and Democratization*. Stanford, Calif.: Stanford University Press.

BARRY, B. 1978. *Sociologists, Economists and Democracy*. Chicago: University of Chicago Press.

BERMAN, H. 1983. *Law and Revolution*, vol. i. Cambridge, Mass.: Harvard University Press.

—— 2003. *Law and Revolution*, vol. ii. Cambridge, Mass.: Harvard University Press.

BIEN, D. D. 1994. Old regime origins of democratic liberty. Pp. 23–71 in *The French Idea of Freedom*, ed. D. Van Kley. Stanford, Calif.: Stanford University Press.

BOIX, C., and POSNER, D. 1996. Making social capital work: a review of Robert Putnam's *Making Democracy Work: Civic Traditions in Italy*. Paper no. 96–4. Cambridge, Mass.: Harvard University, Weatherhead Center for International Affairs.

—— and STOKES, S. C. 2003. Endogenous democratization. *World Politics*, 55: 517–49.

BOSSENGA, G. 1991. *The Politics of Privilege: Old Regime and the Revolution in Lille*. New York: Cambridge University Press.

BRAITHWAITE, V., and LEVI, M. eds. 1998. *Trust & Governance*. New York: Russell Sage Foundation.

BREHM, J., and RAHN, W. 1997. Individual-level evidence for the causes and consequences of social capital. *American Journal of Political Science*, 41 (3): 999–1023.

BRIDGES, T. 1997. *The Culture of Citizenship: Inventing Postmodern Civic Culture.* Washington, DC: Council for Research in Values and Philosophy.

BUDGE, I., and NEWTON, K. 1997. *The Politics of the New Europe.* Harlow: Addison Wesley Longman.

BUNCE, V. 2000. Comparative democratization: big and bounded generalizations. *Comparative Political Studies,* 33: 703–34.

—— 2003. Rethinking recent democratization: lessons from the postcommunist experience. *World Politics,* 55: 167–92.

CASARI, M., and PLOTT, C. R. 2003. Decentralized management of common property resources: experiments with a centuries-old tradition. *Journal of Economic Behavior & Organization,* 51: 217–47.

CHOPRA, K. 2001. Social capital and development: the role of formal and information institutions in a developing country. Paper. Delhi: University Enclave, Institute of Economic Growth.

CHWE, M. S.-Y. 2003. *Culture, Coordination and Common Knowledge.* Princeton: Princeton University Press.

COLEMAN, J. 1987. Norms as social capital. Pp. 133–55 in *Economic Imperialism: The Economic Approach Applied Outside the Field of Economics,* ed. G. Radnitzky and P. Bernholz. New York: Paragon House.

—— 1988. Social Capital in the Creation of Human Capital. *American Journal of Sociology,* 94 (supplement): S95–S120.

DI PALMA, G. 1990. *To Craft Democracies: An Essay on Democratic Transitions.* Berkeley and Los Angeles: University of California Press.

ECKSTEIN, H. 1996. Culture as a foundation concept for the social sciences. *Journal of Theoretical Politics,* 8 (4): 471–97.

EDWARDS, B., and FOLEY, M. W. 1998. Civil society and social capital beyond Putnam. *American Behavioral Scientist,* 42 (1): 124–39.

—— —— and DIANI, M. eds. 2001. *Beyond Tocqueville: Civil Society and the Social Capital Debate in Comparative Perspective.* Hanover, NH: Tufts University Press of New England.

ELKINS, D. J., and SIMEON, R. E. B. 1979. A cause in search of its effect, or what does political culture explain? *Comparative Politics,* 11: 127–45.

EPSTEIN, S. R. 1992. *An Island for Itself: Economic Development and Social Change in Late Medieval Sicily.* New York: Cambridge University Press.

FARR, J. 2004. Social capital: a conceptual history. *Political Theory,* 32: 6–33.

FARRELL, H., and KNIGHT, J. 2003. Trust, institutions, and institutional change: industrial districts and the social capital hypothesis. *Politics & Society,* 31: 537–66.

FORMENT, C. A. 2003. *Democracy in Latin America: Civic Selfhood and Public Life in Mexico and Peru.* Chicago: University of Chicago Press.

GAMBETTA, D. ed. 1988. *Trust: Making and Breaking Cooperative Relations.* Oxford: Blackwell.

—— 1993. *The Sicilian Mafia: The Business of Private Protection.* Cambridge, Mass.: Harvard University Press.

GAUVREAU, M. 2005. *The Catholic Origins of Quebec's Quiet Revolution, 1931–1970.* Montreal: McGill-Queen's University Press.

GREIF, A. 1994. Cultural beliefs and the organization of society: a historical and theoretical reflection on collectivist and individualist societies. *Journal of Political Economy,* 102 (5): 912–50.

GRZYMALA-BUSSE, A., and JONES-LUONG, P. 2002. Re-conceptualizing the state: lessons from post-communism. *Politics and Society,* 30: 529–54.

HALL, P. 1999. Social capital in Britain. *British Journal of Political Science,* 29: 417–61.

HAMILTON, R. F. 1996. *The Social Misconstruction of Reality: Validity and Verification in the Scholarly Community*. New Haven: Yale University Press.

HARDIN, R. 1998. Trust in government. Pp. 9–27 in *Trust in Governance*, ed. V. Braithwaite and M. Levi. New York: Russell Sage.

HOOGHE, M., and STOLLE, D. eds. 2003. *Generating Social Capital. Civic Society and Institutions in Comparative Perspective*. New York: Palgrave.

HOWARD, M. M. 2002. The weakness of postcommunist civil society. *Journal of Democracy*, 13: 157–69.

INGLEHART, R. 1988. The renaissance of political culture. *American Political Science Review*, 82: 1023–230.

—— 1990. *Culture Shift in the Advanced Industrial Countries*. Princeton: Princeton University Press.

—— 1997. *Modernization and Postmodernization*. Princeton: Princeton University Press.

—— and WELZEL, C. 2004. What insights can multi-country surveys provide about people and societies? *APSA-CP Newsletter*, 15: 6–11.

JACKMAN, R. W., and MILLER, R. A. 1996a. A renaissance of political culture? *American Journal of Political Science*, 40: 632–59.

—— —— 1996b. The poverty of political culture. *American Journal of Political Science*, 40: 697–716.

—— —— 1998. Social capital and politics. *Annual Review of Political Science*, 1: 47–73.

JOHNSON, J. 2003. Conceptual problems as obstacles to progress in political science: four decades of political culture research. *Journal of Theoretical Politics*, 15 (1): 87–115.

KITSCHELT, H. 2003. Accounting for postcommunist regime diversity: what counts as a good cause? Pp. 49–88 in *Capitalism and Democracy in Central and Eastern Europe: Assessing the Legacy of Communist Rule*, ed. G. Ekiert and S. E. Hanson. New York: Cambridge University Press.

KOELBLE, T. 2003. Ten years after: Robert Putnam and making democracy work in the post-colony or why mainstream political science cannot understand either democracy or culture. *Politikon*, 30: 203–18.

KRISHNA, A. 2002. *Active Social Capital: Tracing the Roots of Development and Democracy*. New York: Columbia University Press.

KROEBER, A. L., and KLUCKHOHN, C. 1952/1963. *Culture: A Critical Review of Concepts and Definitions*. New York: Vintage Books.

LAITIN, D. 1988. Political culture and political preferences. *American Political Science Review*, 82: 589–93.

—— 1995. The civic culture at 30. *American Political Science Review*, 89: 168–73.

—— 2002. Comparative politics: the state of the subdiscipline. Pp. 630–59 in *Political Science: State of the Discipline*, ed. I. Katznelson and H. V. Milner. New York: Norton.

LEHMAN, N. 1996. Kicking in groups. *Atlantic Monthly*, 277: 22–6.

LEVI, M. 1996. Social and unsocial capital. *Politics & Society*, 24: 45–56.

—— 1998. A state of trust. Pp. 77–101 in *Trust & Governance*, ed. V. Braithwaite and M. Levi. New York: Russell Sage.

LEVY, J. 2003. Liberalism's divide, after socialism and before. *Social Philosophy and Policy Foundation*, 278–97.

LIJPART, A. 1977. *Democracy in Plural Societies: A Comparative Exploration*. New Haven: Yale University Press.

LIN, N. 1999. Building a network theory of social capital. *Connections*, 22 (1): 28–51.

LIPSET, S. M. 1994. The social rerequisites of democracy revisited: 1993 presidential address. *American Sociological Review*, 59: 1–22.

LOVEMAN, B. 1993. *The Constitution of Tyranny: Regimes of Exception in Spanish America.* Pittsburgh: University of Pittsburgh Press.

MAHONEY, J., and RUESCHEMEYER, D. 2003. Comparative historical analysis: achievements and agendas. Pp. 3–40 in *Comparative Historical Analysis in the Social Sciences,* ed. J. Mahoney and D. Rueschemeyer. New York: Cambridge University Press.

MANSBRIDGE, J. 1980. *Beyond Adversary Democracy.* New York: Basic Books.

MISHLER, W., and ROSE, R. 2001. What are the origins of political trust? Testing institutional and cultural theories in post-communist societies. *Comparative Political Studies,* 34: 30–62.

MULHBERGER, S., and PAINE, P. 1993. Democracy's place in the world. *Journal of World History,* 4 (1): 23–45.

MULLER, E. N., and SELIGSON, M. 1994. Civic culture and democracy: the question of causal relationship. *American Political Science Review,* 88: 635–52.

NADER, H. 1990. *Liberty in Absolutist Spain.* Baltimore: Johns Hopkins University Press.

NEWTON, K. 1999. Social and political trust in established democracies. Pp. 169–87 in *Critical Citizens: Global Support for Democratic Governance,* ed. P. Norris. New York: Oxford University Press.

NORRIS, P. ed. 1999. *Critical Citizens: Global Support for Democratic Governance.* New York: Oxford University Press.

O'NEILL, B., and GIDENGIL, E. eds. 2006. *Gender and Social Capital.* New York: Routledge.

ORREN, K. and SKOWRONEK, S. 2004. *The Search for American Political Development.* New York: Cambridge University Press.

OSTROM, E. 1989. Microconstitutional change in multi-constitutional political systems. *Rationality and Society,* 1: 11–50.

—— 1990. *Governing the Commons: The Evolution of Institutions for Collective Action.* New York: Cambridge University Press.

—— 1992. *Crafting Institutions for Self-Governing Irrigation Systems.* San Francisco: ISC Press.

—— and AHN, T. K. eds. 2003. *Foundations of Social Capital.* Northampton, Mass.: Elgar.

—— and WALKER, J. eds. 2003. *Trust and Reciprocity: Interdisciplinary Lessons from Experimental Research.* New York: Russell Sage.

OSTROM, V., and OSTROM, E. 1997. Cultures: frameworks, theories and models. Pp. 79–89 in *Culture Matters: Essays in Honor of Aaron Wildavsky,* ed. R. Ellis and M. Thompson. Boulder, Colo.: Westview Press.

PARKER FOLLETT, M. 1924. *Creative Experience.* New York: Longmans, Green & Co.

PATEMAN, C. 1980. The civic culture: a philosophic critique. Pp. 57–102 in *The Civic Culture Revisited,* ed. G. Almond and S. Verba. Boston: Little & Brown.

PICKERING, P. 2006. Generating social capital for bridging ethnic divisions in the Balkans: case studies of two Bosniak cities. *Ethnic and Racial Studies,* 29: 79–103.

PICKUP, M., SAYERS, A., KNOPFF, R., and ARCHER, K. 2004. Social capital and civic community in Alberta. *Canadian Journal of Political Science,* 37: 617–45.

PORTES, A. 1998. Social capital: its origins and application in modern sociology. *Annual Review of Sociology,* 24: 1–24.

PRZEWORSKI, A., ALVAREZ, M., CHEIBUB, J. A., and LIMONGI, F. 1996. What makes democracies endure? *Journal of Democracy,* 7 (1): 39–55.

PUTNAM, R. D. 1993. *Making Democracy Work.* Princeton: Princeton University Press.

—— 1995. Bowling alone: America's declining social capital. *Journal of Democracy:* 65–78.

PYE, L. 1968. Political culture. Pp. 218–25 in *International Encyclopedia of the Social Science,* ed. D. W. Sills. New York: Macmillan.

REISINGER, W. M. 1995. The renaissance of a rubric: political culture as concept and theory. *International Journal of Public Opinion Research,* 7 (4): 328–52.

RICE, T. W., and FELDMAN, J. L. 1997. Civic culture and democracy from Europe to America. *Journal of Politics*, 59: 1143–72.

ROGOWSKI, R. 1993. Comparative politics. Pp. 431–49 in *Political Science: The State of the Discipline II*, ed. A. W. Finifter. Washington, DC: American Political Science Association

ROTBERG, R. I. ed. 1999/2001. *Patterns of Social Capital: Stability and Change in Historical Perspective*. New York: Cambridge University Press.

ROTHSTEIN, B. 2001. Social capital in the social democratic welfare state. *Politics & Society*, 29 (2): 207–41.

—— and STOLLE, D. Forthcoming. An institutional theory of social capital. In *Social Capital: A Reader*, ed. J. van Deth and D. Castiglione. Oxford: Oxford University Press.

SABETTI, F. 1984/2002. *Village Politics and the Mafia in Sicily*. Montreal: McGill-Queen's University Press.

—— 2000. *The Search for Good Government: Understanding the Paradox of Italian Democracy*. Montreal: McGill-Queen's University Press.

—— 2006. The mafia misunderstood—again. *Journal of Modern Italian Studies*, 11 (2): 232–9.

SCHNEIDER, M., TESKE, P., MARSCHAL, M., MINTROM, M., and ROCH, C. 1997. Institutional arrangements and the creation of social capital: the effects of public school choice. *American Political Science Review*, 91: 82–93.

SEYD, P., and WHITELEY, P. 2002. Is Britain still a civic culture? Paper prepared for the Annual Meetings of the British Group of the American Political Science Association Meetings, Boston.

SKOCPOL, T., and FIORINA, M., eds. 1999. *Civic Engagement in American Democracy*. Washington, DC: Brookings Institution Press.

SOMERS, M. 1995a. What's political or cultural about political culture and the public sphere? Toward an historical sociology of concept formation. *Sociological Theory*, 13: 113–44.

—— 1995b. Narrating and naturalizing civic society and citizenship theory: the place of political culture and the public sphere. *Sociological Theory*, 13: 229–74.

STOLLE, D. 2003. Sources of social capital. Pp. 19–42 in *Generating Social Capital: Civic Society and Institutions in Comparative Perspective*, ed. M. Hooghe and D. Stolle. New York: Palgrave.

—— and HOOGHE, M. 2004. Review article: inaccurate, exceptional, one-sided or irrelevant: the debate about the alleged decline of social capital and civic engagement in western societies. *British Journal of Political Science*, 35: 149–67.

STREET, J. 1994. Political culture: from civic culture to mass culture. *British Journal of Political Science*, 24: 95–113.

SZRETER, S. 2002. The state of social capital: bringing back in power, politics and history. *Theory and Society*, 31: 573–621.

TARROW, S. 1996. Making social science work across space and time: a critical reflection on Robert Putnam's *Making Democracy Work*. *American Political Science Review*, 90: 389–97.

THOMPSON, M., ELLIS, R., and WILDAVSKY, A. 1990. *Cultural Theory*. Boulder, Colo.: Westview Press.

TILLY, C. 2004a. *Contention and Democracy in Europe 1650–2000*. New York: Cambridge University Press.

—— 2004b. Trust and rule. *Theory and Society*, 33: 1–30.

TOCQUEVILLE, A. DE 1856/1956. *The Old Regime and the French Revolution*. Garden City, NY: Doubleday.

VARSHNEY, A. 1998. Why democracy survives. *Journal of Democracy*, 9 (3): 36–50.

VERBA, S. 1980. On revisiting the civic culture: a personal postscript. Pp. 394–410 in *The Civic Culture Revisited*, ed. G. Almond and S. Verba. Boston: Little Brown.

WEINGAST, B. 1997. The political foundations of democracy and the rule of law. *American Political Science Review*, 91: 245–63.

WILDAVSKY, A. 1987. Choosing preferences by constructing institutions: a cultural theory of preference formation. *American Political Science Review*, 81: 3–21.

WOOLCOCK, M. 1998. Social capital and economic development: toward a theoretical synthesis and policy framework. *Theory & Society*, 27: 151–208.

CHAPTER 16

DICTATORSHIP: ANALYTICAL APPROACHES

RONALD WINTROBE

1 INTRODUCTION

THIS chapter surveys work on authoritarianism which takes an "economic" or rational choice approach. The assumption that dictators themselves are rational can certainly seem controversial for the likes of Hitler, Stalin, Pol Pot, or even Saddam Hussein. Such leaders and their actions are routinely labeled "fanatical" for their behavior, many aspects of which were extremely bizarre and cruel. But to assume that dictators are rational does not mean they have the same goals as most people. It just means that, whatever their goals, which we take as given, they choose the best means to implement them consistent with available information.

That economic methods are used also does not mean that behavior was guided by economic goals. Nor does it mean we assume that the economy is the most important aspect of a dictator's performance. It would be silly to suggest that Hitler or Pol Pot were motivated by money or personal consumption, and other goals—power or ideology—have been the most important ones for many dictators. But rational choice can be just as useful in understanding the behavior of people who are motivated by power or ideology rather than wealth.

Of course, some dictators *are* simply motivated by personal consumption and their indulgences have become legendary, including the palaces of the Shah of Iran, the Mercedes Benzes of the typical African dictator, or the shoes for Imelda Marcos (the wife of Ferdinand Marcos of the Philippines). I call these people *tinpots* to denote their small-scale aspirations. The small-time dictator or "traditional auto-crat" (as Jeanne Kirkpatrick 1982, following Friedrich and Brzezinski 1965, called this type) is one of the classic images of dictatorship.

At the opposite extreme from tinpots are *totalitarian* dictators, apparently motiv-ated solely by power or ideology, and the classic works on totalitarianism—especially Arendt's *The Origins of Totalitarianism* (1951)—continue to be worth reading today for their picture of the nightmare of life under regimes (Nazi Germany and Russia under Stalin) with seemingly unlimited power over their citizens.

For economists, the same idea of a regime in which all power and the capacity to do anything emanates from the center entailed a rather different picture in the Soviet case at least: the bumbling bureaucracy. The system of central planning implied a staggering amount of room for information distortion and cumulative error, epitomized by the classic Soviet cartoon of a group of Soviet managers gazing with satisfaction at a single enormous nail and congratulating themselves on overfulfilling the plan, which was expressed in tons.

Rational choice analysis of the limits of dictatorial power suggests that neither image was correct (see Section 2 below). It was not and could not have been true that, as a Nazi official[1] once boasted, "the only time an individual had a private life was when he was asleep." Nor could the Soviet system have worked entirely as suggested by the "command economy" construct without collapsing much earlier than it did.

The wave of authoritarianism in Latin America in the 1970s gave birth to a different construct—the "bureaucratic authoritarian" model (O'Donnell 1980), in which authoritarian political systems were thought to arise in order to implement capital deepening. In turn the species—along with later variants such as the Pinochet regime in Chile — can be recognized as simply another variant of a classic type—*tyranny*—used in ancient times to describe a form of rule in which the leader implements particularly unpopular policies and stays in power through repression.

Finally there is the evanescent image of the benevolent dictator or *timocrat*.[2] There is very little evidence that a regime like this ever existed, but economists are particularly vulnerable to this idea because economic theory says there is a right way to run an economy and the idea of acting as the *éminence grise* (even if not acknowledged!) for a benevolent dictator is always a difficult temptation for the economist to resist. Indeed the concept, if not the persona,[3] is embedded in the social welfare function of economic theory.

These four images occur over and over in the literature on dictatorship. But while there has always been and continues to be work on particular regimes, rational choice has been applied to understand autocracy only recently, beginning in the 1980s with the works of North (1981) and Tullock (1987). Douglas North (1981) pointed out that the structure of property rights in a society which maximize the rents or the returns

---

[1] Robert Ley.

[2] The term "timocracy" denoting a government where the ruler loves his people is borrowed from Plato's Republic.

[3] Sometimes, as in Olson and McGuire (1996), the identity of the two concepts is made explicit.

to the ruler was not necessarily the best system from the point of view of maximizing the wealth or welfare of that society. Tullock (1987) focused on, among other things, the problem of autocratic succession, and the attempts of the autocrat to secure his tenure in office and avoid a coup.[4]

No formal model of dictatorship appeared until the 1990s when two were produced, one focusing mainly on the behavior of dictators (Wintrobe 1990, 1998) and one comparing the economics of dictatorship with democracy (Olson 1993; Olson and McGuire 1996; Olson 2000). More recently, a new theme in this second vein has emerged, that dictatorships redistribute less than democracies and for that reason may be capable of higher economic growth. The notion goes back to Tocqueville, but in modern form it has been revived by Barro's empirical work (1996a, 1996b). A third theme, which has preoccupied much of the literature in history and political science, is that of the origins of dictatorship, and in particular why a democracy sometimes collapses and dictatorship appears (see, for example, Linz and Stepan 1978). This subject is treated only implicitly here, mainly on the ground that very little rational choice analysis of it has been done until very recently (Boix 2003; Acemoglu and Robinson 2005), and it is surveyed elsewhere in this handbook.[5] So this survey focuses on two main issues: the behavior of dictators, and the comparison of their economic performance and redistributive tendencies with the democracies. I focus on analytic work and on econometric testing. Work on particular regimes and non-analytic work is unfortunately ignored due to lack of space.

The next section deals with behavior. It first outlines my model and then proceeds to more recent contributions, including important developments within the North framework. Section 3 proceeds in the same way with the comparison between democracy and dictatorship, beginning with the Olson model and then proceeding to more recent work on economic performance and on redistribution. Throughout I focus on theory and evidence, not on policy implications, though the latter are briefly mentioned at various points in the text. The final section concludes.

2 THE BEHAVIOR OF DICTATORS

2.1 The Dictator's Dilemma

The classic view of the difference between democracy and dictatorship in political science (e.g. Friedrich and Brzezinski 1965) is that dictators stay in power through repression. Dictators rule by commands and prohibitions. The police monitor

---

[4] Kurrild-Klitgaard (2000) extends Tullock's framework and tests it with a case study of coups against monarchs in Denmark in the period 935–1849.

[5] See the chapters on "transitions" in this volume and the survey by Acemoglu and Robinson in the volume on political economy.

compliance and there are sanctions for disobedience. Dictators who use the political apparatus to run the economy are analyzed the same way in economics: the "command economy" model has been and still is the basic tool for analyzing the economies of the former Soviet Union.

However, rule by repression alone creates a problem for the autocrat. This is the Dictator's Dilemma (Wintrobe 1990, 1998)—the problem facing any ruler of knowing how much support he has among the general population, as well as among smaller groups with the power to depose him. The use of repression breeds fear on the part of a dictator's subjects, and this fear breeds a reluctance on the part of the citizenry to signal displeasure with the dictator's policies. This fear on their part in turn breeds fear *on the part of the dictator*, since, not knowing what the population thinks of his policies, he has no way of knowing what they are thinking and planning, and of course he suspects that what they are thinking and planning is his overthrow. The problem is magnified the more the dictator rules through repression and fear. The more his repressive apparatus stifles dissent and criticism, the less he knows how much support he really has. The natural state of the dictator who rules by fear is paranoia. The issue was first (to my knowledge) discussed in the ancient Greek philosopher Xenophon's dialogue *Hiero or Tyrannicus*, in which the tyrant complains:

we know as a matter of course that those who serve through fear try by every means in their power to make themselves appear like friends... And what is more, plots against tyrants spring from none more than from those who pretend to love them most. (Xenophon, reprinted in Strauss 1963/1991, 5)

Dictators throughout history have been afflicted by paranoia. Stalin is typical. Alan Bullock reports that "His suspicions never slept" (1991, 358). A contemporary victim is Saddam Hussein. His (plastic) surgeon, Ala Bashir, reports in his book *The Insider: Trapped in Saddam's Brutal Regime* (2005) Saddam speaking to him as follows:[6]

If your dog is young and small, you can hit it and kick and punish it in various ways. But when it is big and strong you have to think twice before punishing it. It might bite you. So imagine what it is like to be surrounded by one hundred dogs. (Saddam to Ala Bashir, on his own bodyguards; Bashir 2005, 155)

To solve this problem, dictators do not rule by repression alone but through loyalty and political exchange. Like democratic politicians, they try to implement the policies their people want in order to obtain support for their rule. But, again, like democratic politicians, there is no legal way to enforce these "political exchanges." What guarantees one party that the other party will not cheat or renege in a political exchange? An interest group cannot sue a politician for breaking his promise, and a politician cannot sue an interest group for switching its support to his opponents. The general solution to this problem of preventing cheating on exchange in product markets is a "trust" or "loyalty premium"[7] So the dictator invests in the

---

[6] I am indebted to Brendan O'Leary for this item.

[7] For the general argument on how trust premia deter cheating, see Shapiro (1983) on product markets or Shapiro and Stiglitz (1984) on wage premia ("efficiency wages") in labour markets. The application to politics and dictatorship is in Wintrobe (1990 or 1998, ch. 2).

loyalty of his supporters by "overpaying" them, particularly those in a position to bring the regime down, such as the military. The loyalty premium can take the form of subsidized ("efficiency") wages or capital projects, pork barrel projects, the distribution of goods and services at subsidized prices, and so on. The recipients provide loyal support in return.

In sum, in order to stay in office, the dictator not only represses his opponents, he *redistributes* to keep his supporters loyal. So while there is always a class of people who are repressed under a dictatorship, there is also, in any successful dictatorship, another class–*the overpaid*. As far as the people in the middle are concerned, the sad thing is that they can side with either group. The general population may be unhappy that their civil liberties may be taken away, but other aspects of the regime may compensate for this as far as they are concerned.

That dictatorships use two instruments—repression and loyalty—to stay in power suggests a useful classification of regimes. Four types can be distinguished: tinpots, tyrants, totalitarians, and timocrats. Thus, totalitarian regimes combine high repression with a capacity to generate loyalty. Under tyranny, the regime stays in power through high repression alone and loyalty is low. A tinpot regime is low on both counts. And timocracy implies that loyalty is high even at low levels of repression. These correspond to the four types or *images* mentioned which I suggested in the introduction[8] have tended to recur over and over in the literature on dictatorship.

Wintrobe (1998) shows how the different types of regimes can each be derived from a more general framework. The model also provides answers to some other conundrums about dictatorship, including the question, raised most forcefully by Hannah Arendt (1951), of what limits a dictator's power. We first analyze the workings of a tinpot regime, then look at totalitarian regimes, and then show how each of the different types in fact just represent solutions (equilibrium levels of power and repression) of a more general model.

2.2 Equilibrium Loyalty and Repression in a Tinpot Regime

First, assume that the relationship between the inputs of loyalty and repression and their output (power) can be represented by the production function

$$\pi = \pi(L,R) \tag{1}$$

This production function is represented by a set of iso-powerlines, where higher iso-powerlines denote higher power. One of these is shown in Figure 16.1.

Secondly, assume that the amount of loyalty available to the dictator is, like any capital good, fixed in the short run, but variable in the long run. On the other hand, the level of repression is variable in the short as well as in the long run.

The objective function of a tinpot dictator is to maximize consumption only. In Figure 16.1, the tinpot dictator seeks no more power over the population than represented by the lowest iso-powerline in the figure, π_{min}. At any lower level of power, the

---

[8] For details, see Wintrobe (1998, ch. 1).

tinpot will be deposed. Should the tinpot obtain more resources than required to attain $\pi = \pi_{min}$ (resource constraints will be discussed shortly) he does not spend them on repression or loyalty, but on his own personal consumption or that of his family. Since the tinpot always remains on π_{min} (as long as he stays in office), it immediately follows that there is an inverse relationship between the amounts of L and R demanded by the tinpot: An increase in R results in a fall in the level of L demanded.

Now consider the supply of loyalty to a tinpot dictator. I assume that while the tinpot may have a monopoly of formal political office, he does not monopolize political power in the country, but faces opposition in the sense of potential alternatives to his government. Citizens and interest groups may establish (possibly covert) ties with these potential opposition leaders. If the level of political repression is increased, people become more afraid of dealing with opposition groups, and their incentive to remain loyal to the regime increases. So the aggregate supply of political loyalty is initially positively related to the level of repression, as depicted by the L curves in Figure 16.1. If the supply of loyalty is L_0, equilibrium is at E_0, with loyalty and repression L_0 and R_0 in the figure.

The budget line in Figure 16.1 refers only to expenditures associated with staying in office, i.e. expenditures on loyalty and repression. Any surplus is spent by the dictator—on palaces, Mercedes Benzes, and so on. A tinpot is interested only in consumption, and maximizes consumption subject to the constraint of staying in office. In a sense, he can be thought of as maximizing "profits"—total tax revenue minus expenditures necessary to stay in office. We can derive the equilibrium tax rate

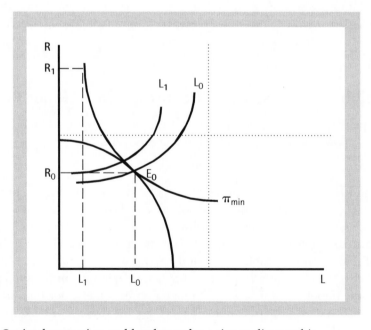

Fig. 16.1 Optimal repression and loyalty under a tinpot dictatorship

for a tinpot if we further assume that the tinpot's *total* budget (i.e., not just expenditures on loyalty and repression but also including government resources diverted to the dictator's personal consumption) arises solely from a proportional revenue—maximizing income tax.

Taxes have two negative effects from the dictator's point of view. They reduce work effort—and therefore income. The fall in income depends on η—the elasticity of income with respect to the tax rate (as in Brennan and Buchanan 1980's analysis of Leviathan). But, in addition, higher taxes displease the dictator's subjects, and may tempt them to withdraw their loyalty. To maintain it, the dictator will need to offer a higher "price" (P_L), in the form of rents or other subsidies, for their loyalty.

The tinpot may therefore be described as choosing a tax rate to maximize "profits"—the difference between total revenue and the total costs of staying in office, taking both of these negative effects of taxes into consideration.

Let t = the tax rate and Y_0 = total income; P_R and P_L are the prices of repression and loyalty, respectively. Then the tinpot maximizes profits Z, as in

$$\text{Max } Z = tY_0(1-\eta t) - P_R R - P_L L \tag{2}$$

subject to the constraint of staying in office:

$$\pi = \pi_{\min} - \pi(L,R) \tag{3}$$

where $\pi_{\min}$ represents the minimum power necessary to stay in office. This yields the first-order condition for t:

$$Y_0(1-2\eta t) = [\partial P_L/\partial t]L \tag{4}$$

In (4) the left-hand side is the marginal revenue from an increase in the tax rate, taking into account the loss in work effort and therefore income, and the right-hand side is the marginal cost of raising taxes. The latter is the result of the fact that the increase in tax rates reduces loyalty, and the dictator can only maintain it by increasing the price paid for it ($\partial P_L/\partial t > 0$). Equation (4) differs from the Brennan and Buchanan revenue-maximizing tax rate which is simply $t^* = 1/2\eta$. The difference is due to the fact that our tinpot has to worry about staying in office. No such concern arises for Brennan and Buchanan's Leviathan, who is assumed to have no difficulty in staying in office even at confiscatory tax rates.

2.3 A Totalitarian Regime

At the opposite extreme from a tinpot is a totalitarian regime. In a totalitarian regime I assume that the dictator uses the instruments of repression and loyalty to maximize power over the population under his or her control. The classic historical examples are Nazi Germany and Stalin's Russia in the 1930s, as analyzed by Arendt (1951) and others. This conception of totalitarian regimes is useful in that it places them at the opposite extreme from tinpots. Most real-world dictatorships undoubtedly lie somewhere in between.

What is the constraint on the totalitarian Leader's maximization of power? So long as the aggregate supply of loyalty curve is upward sloping, the dictator can increase his or her power over the population by increasing the level of repression. Consequently if the supply of loyalty L were upward sloping throughout its range, the only possible equilibrium would be a corner solution involving the perfect repression of the population. However, theoretical considerations suggest that there is a conflict between perfect repression and the maximization of power over the population.

To see this, note that as the regime becomes more extreme and the level of repression increases, genuine loyalty to the regime begins to dry up, as people become increasingly worried that they will not be repaid for their loyalty but become a victim of the regime's repression instead. Consequently, at sufficiently high levels of repression, the aggregate supply of loyalty curve bends backwards as depicted in Figure 16.2. Equilibrium is at the highest possible level of power consistent with the supply of loyalty, or at E in Figure 16.2.

The two types of regime differ in their response to external shocks such as a decline in economic performance or the imposition of sanctions. Thus the tinpot regime will raise repression in response to either of these two events, while the totalitarian will lower it. This provides a key to policy.

2.4 The Limit to the Dictator's Power (and Budget)

The analysis so far rests on a simplification which it is time to make explicit: it shows the equilibrium levels of loyalty and repression for a fixed price of loyalty P_L. But the

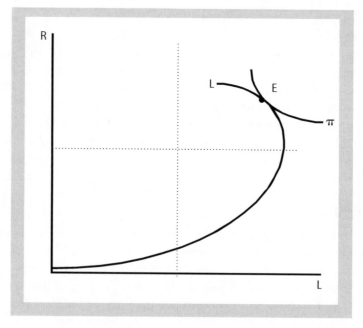

Fig. 16.2 A totalitarian dictatorship

price of loyalty, P_L, is a variable under the dictator's control. An increase in P_L would bring forth a larger supply of loyalty, L, for any given level of R, i.e., it would shift L to the right (not shown).

A second simplification is that rulers either maximize consumption (tinpots) or power (totalitarians or tyrants). To generalize the approach, and to show the true limits to a dictator's power, suppose now that all dictators have the *same* utility function,[9] whose arguments are consumption (C) and power (π).

$$U = U(\pi, C) \tag{5}$$

The dictator is constrained in two ways. The first constraint is the costs of accumulating power. This is governed by the prices of repression and loyalty, P_R and P_L. These, in turn, depend on the political institutions of the regime: is there a mass party? Are the police and the army subservient to it? And so on. This constraint is illustrated by the upward-sloping curve $\pi(B-C)$ curve in Figure 16.3, implying a positive relationship between the dictator's *total* budget B, minus expenditures on C, and the level of π obtained. This curve shows how the dictator can convert *money* into *power*.

Note that there are "diminishing returns" to these expenditures. Diminishing returns to the accumulation of loyalty imply that successive increases in P_L will increase L by less and less. With a fixed price of loyalty P_L the limit to repression is that the supply curve of loyalty bends backwards after some point. But if P_L can be increased this limit no longer applies. If there is no limit to the dictator's capacity to

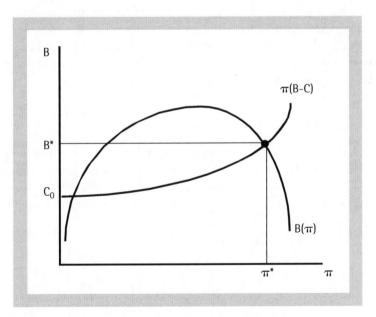

Fig. 16.3 Equilibrium power and budget in the general model

[9] Tinpots and totalitarians emerge as the special cases at either extreme where U_c or $U_\pi = 0$.

raise P_L, there is no obvious limit to the dictator's power, loyalty, or level of repression.

The question then is, is there any limit to the dictator's resources? It would be arbitrary to specify that the dictator's power is limited by a revenue-maximizing tax, as we did in equation (4). For, so long as the dictator has sufficient power, he can raise more funds by imposing new tax bases and by finding other ways to raise money. In short, if there is no limit to his power, there is no limit to his resources either. It follows that the limits to resources and to power must be simultaneously determined.

So let us turn to the second constraint, which is the ruler's capacity to use his power to increase revenue, as summarized by the $B(\pi)$ curve in Figure 16.3. This curve describes the relationship between the exercise of political power, and its consequences for the dictator's budget, i.e. the conversion, in effect, of *power* into *money*. There are many ways for a government to convert power into money: the most obvious are through taxation, regulation, or the provision of public goods which raise national income.

It seems reasonable to assume that, initially, the power-to-money curve $B(\pi)$ must be positively sloped: starting from very low (or zero) levels of power the provision of basic public infrastructure or the imposition of simple taxes at low rates must raise revenue. But after some point, further exercise of power must ultimately lower the budget by reducing the efficiency of the economy, therefore lowering national income and tax revenue.

Equilibrium in Figure 16.3 is at the intersection of the $B(\pi)$ and $\pi(B-C)$ curves, or at E_0, implying a (total) budget of B^*, and power equal to π^*.[10] Neither resources nor power alone limit the dictator's power. Diminishing returns to the accumulation of either one simultaneously determine the limits to both power and money. The nature of this equilibrium may be stated briefly: beyond E_0, either the dictator cannot obtain enough power to support a further increase in his budget, or, alternatively, he cannot obtain enough money to support an increase in power.

The equilibrium is also shown in equation

$$B(\pi) = P_\pi \pi(B-C) + C. \qquad (6)$$

The left-hand side of (6) shows the dictator's budget B as a function of power (π), i.e. it shows how the dictator's power may be used to obtain money (budget). The right-hand side shows how the funds are "spent:" either on consumption, C, or accumulating power π via the money-to-power relation $\pi(B-C)$, with each unit of π multiplied by P_π—the "price" of power in terms of money.

Maximizing (5) subject to (6) gives

$$\frac{U_c}{U_\pi} = \frac{1}{P_\pi\left(1-\frac{1}{E_\pi}\right) - B_\pi} \qquad (7)$$

where E_π is the elasticity of power with respect to its price.

---

[10] See Wintrobe (1998, ch. 5) for a proof.

Equation (7) shows that the ruler will choose the combination of C and π where the marginal rate of substitution between these two is equal to the ratio of their marginal costs. And once either the level of π or the budget B is set, the dictator chooses the optimum R and L (where their marginal productivities in producing power are equal to their marginal costs, as shown in Figure 16.1). So this analysis jointly determines the dictator's optimal levels of, C^*, π^*, B^*, and R^*, L^*.[11] In turn, changes in the capacity to raise revenue or to repress dissent, the supply of loyalty, the dictator's consumption, or any other exogenous variable entering into the equilibrium depicted by equations (5) and (6) or (7) and Figures 16.1 or 16.2 will change the levels of these variables, often in predictable ways, as we will see in the next subsection.

Note that the analysis just described also determines whether a dictator is a tinpot, totalitarian, or tyrant. That is, the different types are not exogenous but are endogenously determined by the variables in equation (7) or Figure 16.3 and Figure 16.1 or 16.2. To see this point, look at Figure 16.1. The light dotted lines in the figure divide the space into four regions, which correspond to the four types: tinpot, totalitarian, etc. Because equilibrium π^* and B^* are low, R and L are low, and the regime is a tinpot. But had equilibrium π^* and B^* been higher, equilibrium could have occurred in any of the other three quadrants, and the regime would be totalitarian, tyrant, or timocrat.

Thus the classification of regimes just describes different solutions to the general model. To illustrate, compare Stalin's Russia and Pinochet's Chile. Repression was high under both regimes but the most reasonable depiction of Pinochet is that he was a tyrant while Stalin is a classic totalitarian. Why? There was no mechanism in the Pinochet regime for the mass distribution of rents like the Communist Party in the former Soviet Union. So the slope of the money into power curve $\pi(B-C)$ in Figure 16.3 would be relatively steep in the case of Pinochet, flat for Stalin. Alternatively E_π in equation (7), the elasticity of power with respect to its price, is high for the former, low for the latter. Secondly, the freeing of markets in Chile meant that the use of political power to interfere with markets would reduce their efficiency, so the power-into-money curve $B(\pi)$ would turn downwards at a low level of π, (B_π would turn negative in equation (7)). The Soviet system, on the other hand, may have been inefficient economically, but since the economy was largely demonetized and controlled by the Party, *at the margin* an increase in the power of the Party helped the economy ($B_\pi > 0$). Both dictators were undoubtedly motivated by power ($\frac{U_c}{U_\pi}$ low), but the working of the Soviet system required a totalitarian leader, while the Chilean experiment needed a tyrant.

2.5 An Application: Revolution

A central question in revolutionary theory (and for dictators seeking to remain in power) is the relationship between the level of repression under a regime and the

---

[11] A comprehensive exposition of the general model is in Wintrobe (1998, ch. 5).

likelihood of revolution. Recently there has been a lot of interesting work, mainly by sociologists, but also by economists and political scientists, on this issue (e.g. Rasler 1996; Opp and Ruehl 1990; Khawaja 1993). These models are often rational choice in spirit but then incorporate social interactions, both among revolutionary groups and between them and the wider society. Thus the models incorporate bandwagon effects, model of critical mass, information cascades, and critical threshold models.[12] Each of these social interactions describes a chain reaction in which the initial participation of small numbers triggers the participation of much larger numbers over time, sometimes (as in East Germany or Iran) bringing down the government.

Another strand in the literature concerns the effects of repression on dissidence. Opp and Ruehl (1990) have argued that, while repression clearly has a direct negative effect in impeding protest, it has an indirect effect which may stimulate protest in the longer run if repression leads to micromobilization processes that raise incentives for protest.

Obviously the relationship between repression, dissidence, and the likelihood of revolution is complicated. To sort them out, we need a model. In the Wintrobe model outlined in the last section, so long as $\pi > \pi_{min}$, the dictatorship has enough power to remain in office and there is no revolution. However, a change can occur which reduces the effectiveness of the reward or punishment mechanisms. If the change involves a deterioration in the dictator's capacity to accumulate power or to raise resources, this means that the equilibrium budget and power fall (either the $\pi(B-C)$ or the $B(\pi)$ curve would shift back in Figure 16.3). If they fall far enough, the system no longer has sufficient power to stay in office, i.e. there is a revolution. Such a revolution is "rational" in the sense that the dictatorship no longer has the capacity to defend itself. Thus the essential reason for a revolution is that a change or a series of changes occurs which weakens the state. In turn, the weaker the state becomes, the more that any *individual* potential dissident will come to believe that successful revolution is possible. Hence the free rider problem at the individual level also tends to be solved, since the essential condition for rational participation in rebellion is more likely to be fulfilled when the probability of successful revolution increases.

It follows that to calculate the effects of increased repression on the population, it is crucial to know the state of the regime or what type of regime we are dealing with. In the Iranian revolution, it seems reasonable to suppose that we are dealing with a tinpot. Among the indicators of this we may consider that repression was generally low, there was no mass party, and the main purpose of the regime seemed to be to finance the lifestyle of the Shah and his family (see the description in Arjomand 1986 and elsewhere).

Suppose then that the loyalty on the part of the population fell during the 1970s, as the economic performance of the regime deteriorated throughout that period.[13] If the regime was a tinpot, it was in danger of collapsing, as a fall in loyalty would

---

[12] The first paper applying economic theory to revolution is Roemer 1985.

[13] A downward shift in the supply of loyalty curve in Figure 16.2 generally implies a new tangency at a lower level of R (not shown). For more details, see Wintrobe 1990, or 1998, ch. 3.

reduce power below the minimum level of power required to stay in office. The Shah's optimal response to the deterioration of economic conditions and the emergence of protest was therefore to raise repression. Thus repression should immediately have been raised to R_1 in Figure 16.1 in order to stay in office.

In the long run, this action will *expand* the supply of loyalty (along curve L_1) and the regime can eventually relax repression somewhat and still remain in office. These further adjustments are not analyzed here.[14] But the important point is that, as long as the regime is a tinpot, *the optimal response to a fall in loyalty is to expand repression in the short run.*

There is also a general theoretical point to be made. As long as repression is low to begin with, it is difficult to argue that an increase in repression will lower power by so much that it will destroy the regime. This implies that the supply of loyalty is backward bending (negatively sloped) even at low levels of repression. But if that were generally the case, no dictatorship could survive for very long. As soon as repression was raised sufficiently, micromobilization responses implying a fall in loyalty (increase in dissidence) would occur and the regime would collapse. But there have been many stable and long-lasting dictatorships in the real world.

Consequently, the model does not support the analyses of Rasler (1996) and others that the result of increased repression will simply cause a micromobilization of protest and result in regime downfall. Indeed, others have suggested that, on balance, the Shah relaxed repression over this period (Arjomand 1986), and a number of events that occurred and are discussed by Rasler are consistent with this interpretation. Thus, mobilization occurred because the regime appeared weak, and its inconsistent policies on repression in response to the various crises over the period (admirably analyzed by Rasler) reinforced this belief.

What about a totalitarian leader? In general, the optimum response to a fall in loyalty is to relax repression.[15] The totalitarian leader is in no immediate danger of being deposed, since power is normally more than sufficient to stay in office. To illustrate, repression had indeed been steadily relaxed in Eastern Europe in response to the deteriorating functioning of the bureaucratic economy throughout the 1970s and 1980s without precipitating a revolution. But the regimes were steadily weakened, and ready for collapse when the Hungarian regime dismantled its border controls in 1989. Revolution was only necessary in East Germany and elsewhere because neither the regime nor the leaders of the various reform movements were willing to recognize that fact and negotiate their demise.

2.6 Evidence

An interesting test of Wintrobe's theory was done by Schnytzer and Sustersic (1997). They used membership in the Communist Party (League of Communists in Yugoslavia) over the period 1953–88 as an index of support for the communist

---

[14] See the reference in the previous footnote.   [15] Wintrobe (1990, or 1998, chs. 3 and 10).

regime. They assume that jobs, or the likelihood of obtaining promotion, were important sources of rents provided by the Party to its members. The relative value of these rents would increase with the level of unemployment. So, on Wintrobe's theory we should expect membership to be positively correlated with unemployment. Similarly, the political exchange model predicts that LCY membership should be inversely correlated with the level of real wages. The results strongly supported these predictions in the two provinces where the Communist Party was strongest (Serbia and Montenegro). There was little emprirical support for them in Slovenia and Macedonia, where the Communist Party was weakest. In mixed provinces (Bosnia-Herzegovina and Croatia) the results were intermediary between these extremes, as one might expect.

Islam and Winer (2004) test Wintrobe's theory of non-democratic regimes using a large sample of both non-democratic and democratic countries. Countries are classified into different regime types using the combined values of the Gastil indices of political freedom and civil liberties. Hypotheses concerning the relationship between economic growth and the combined value of the indices are then tested over the period 1967–92. The results indicate clearly that the relationship between an index of civil and political freedoms and economic growth varies substantially across the three regime types. Other aspects of the theory are partially confirmed. In particular, positive growth leads to a reduction in the degree of freedom in totalitarian regimes (that attempt to maximize power), and negative growth (falling levels of per capita real income) appears to reduce freedom in tinpot regimes (that just attempt to maintain power), as predicted by the Wintrobe theory. On the other hand, positive growth in tinpots and negative growth in totalitarians also reduces freedom, contrary to the theory. In the case of tinpots, the absolute value of the effect on the index of freedom appears to be bigger for negative than for positive growth, as predicted by Wintrobe's model. Some results concerning differences across regimes in the effect of schooling on freedom are also provided. Schooling increases freedom in democracies and tinpots, but not in totalitarian regimes, possibly because in those regimes schooling has an "indoctrination" element.

A comprehensive test of a variant of the political exchange model vs. the command model was tested on Soviet data. Lazarev and Gregory (2003) use the recently opened Soviet archives to study the allocation of vehicles (automobiles plus trucks) in 1933 by top decision makers in the highest agency of Soviet government, the Council of People's Commissars. Relatively few of these goods were produced at that time, they were priced well below equilibrium, and they were highly sought after by consumers ranging from the bureaucratic elite to individual enterprises. Lazarev and Gregory extracted from the texts of petitions, letters of support, allocation orders, and correspondence in 1933 a total of 557 observations. For each case they identify the number of vehicles requested, the number granted, and the attributes of the petitioner, including its level, location, branch, etc. as well as the characteristics of the petition and the type of argumentation used.

Two hypotheses are compared on this data: the "command" or "central planning" hypothesis, and a political exchange model. The economic planning model suggests that successful petitions would be based on the production capacity of the claimant, and consider economic reasons used to substantiate the claim. The "political gift exchange" model suggests that the process would involve the distribution of vehicles "in return for loyalty" (Lazarev and Gregory 2003, 8). "What is important is whether the petitioner is able to contribute directly to [the Dictator's] hold on power through an input of loyalty" (2003, 10). Successful petitions would be those made by Party, civilian administration, army, and control organs, those relatively high in the territorial Party hierarchy, those with celebrity status, and those with close connections to the Dictator and to his immediate circle.

The results strongly supported the political exchange model. Petitioners with close political connections had the best chance of success. None of the attributes of the economic planning model, namely major industrial branch, support by planner, economic reasoning, enter the estimated model with the expected sign or significance. Most striking are the *negative* effects of support by planner, economic reasoning, etc. Indeed, the authors conclude that "the political gift exchange model not only dominates in the retail allocation of vehicles but . . . the pattern of decision-making exhibits an anti-economic component" (2003, 13).

The main predictor of revolution in the Wintrobe model is the weakness of the state. Goldstone et al. (2004) use a "state failure" approach to understanding the origins of revolution. Using the POLITY IV dataset, they classify regimes over the period 1955 to 2001 into six types; full democracies, weak full democracies, strong and weak partial democracies, autocracies, and autocracies that allow some competition. They conclude that

The most unstable and dangerous regimes are partial democracies, regimes that combine elections and some other elements of democracy with significant aspects of authoritarian rule. These regimes are in fact far more prone to experience revolutions, ethnic wars, genocides, and violent regime changes than any other kinds of regimes . . . . Economic factors do affect stability. Countries with lower levels of infant mortality, and with economies more open to international trade, do have lower rates of political crises. However, *these effects are generally an order of magnitude smaller than the institutional effects of regime type.* That is, the impact of "getting the institutions right" on the risks of violent political crisis is generally five to ten times as large as the impact of levels of poverty or trade. (Goldstone et al. 2004, 431–2)

In turn, why did the dictator introduce elements of democracy? It is not clear whether the regimes are unstable because they are partial democracies or they are partial democracies because they are unstable. But either way, the main predictor of revolution is the weakness of the state.

2.7 New Work on Repression: Dynamics, Ideology, and Genocide

The theory of repression has been extended by Philip Verwimp (2001), who attempts to understand the behavior of the Habyarimana regime in Rwanda, and in particular to explain the origins of the tragic genocide that took place there. The paper applies

Wintrobe's model in a new way (by using the price of coffee as an index of the capacity of a dictatorial regime to generate loyalty) and it extends the model to explain genocide. Verwimp suggests that the Habyarimana regime, frustrated by its loss of power, attempted to split the population along ethnic lines and set one group against the other, at the end by rewarding Hutus for the extermination of Tutsis. Thus the genocide is interpreted as the attempt by the regime to remain in power by accentuating the ethnic split of the population into two groups, ultimately singling out one for extermination by the other.

Spagat (2001) studies the optimal strategy for a dictator hanging on to power by choosing how much repression to apply in every period. State variables are the amount of "hate" and "fear" in society which are both increasing in the amount of repression from the previous period. Hate, fear, and a random shock determine the quantity of repression required for the dictator to survive. Spagat shows that in every period there are only two possible optimal choices: the minimal repression necessary to retain power (which he calls "no demonstration") or the maximum possible repression ("demonstration"). The state space can be divided into two regions separated by an increasing function such that "no demonstration" is optimal in one and "demonstration" in the other. It is difficult to know how variables such as hate and fear can be operationalized, but other implications can be derived from this way of thinking (see Spagat 2002 discussed below).

Bernholz (2001) models the evolution of totalitarian regimes. In the model there are "believers" who are convinced that others have to be converted to the supreme values of their ideology for their well-being and, possibly, enemies of their creed whose presence is obnoxious to them. Believers spend resources on winning new converts and to win the secular power of the state. Whether they succeed in this endeavor depends on the costs of converting new believers and on the amount of resources they are prepared to spend for this purpose, given their incomes and their propensity to consume. Their chances of success are greater if a crisis occurs, an event which is usually outside of their control. Once secular power has been secured, the resources of the state can be used to win more converts, to drive into exile or to kill inconvertibles, and to try to reach the imperialistic aims implied by the ideology. If the latter is not the case, the regime may turn into a mature "ideocracy" after having reached its domestic aims. This would for instance be the case if all inconvertibles were removed and all the rest of the population been converted. In this case no further terror and/or repression characteristic of totalitarian regimes are required. If the ideology *by its nature* implies ambitious imperialistic aims, for instance the domination of the whole globe by the believers, it is highly probable that these aims cannot be reached. As a consequence either a war is lost and this leads to the removal of the totalitarian regime, or the ends have to be adapted to maintain the credibility of the ideology. But then the totalitarian state may again turn into a mature ideocracy, if the ideology has been reinterpreted to remove its unrealistic imperialistic aims. Or the change of the ideology weakens the regime in such a way that it loses its proselytizing character altogether, and turns into an ordinary auto-cratic regime.

2.8 The Irony of Absolutism

Another important analysis of the behavior of dictators and of the limits on their power is provided by "the irony of absolutism." The "irony of absolutism" is described in a series of works by North, Weingast, Root, and others (e.g., North 1981; North and Weingast 1989; Root 1994). In North's (1981) model of the monarchy, the king maximizes revenue, and the central problem is that the structure of property rights which is appropriate for this purpose is not usually that which is efficient from the economic point of view. More subtly, there is a tradeoff between power and revenue. As Root describes the "Irony of Absolutism," absolute power gave the king the capacity to repudiate debts, but

Creditors took into account the king's reputation for repudiating debts and therefore demanded higher interest rates than would otherwise have been needed to elicit loans. Actually, *because he was above the law, the king had to pay more for loanable funds than did his wealthy subjects.* In short, the Crown had a problem asserting its credit because it had a history of reneging on commitments. (Root 1994, 177, Italics added)

North and Weingast suggest that this problem gave rise to the Glorious Revolution in England, in which power over the Treasury was devolved on parliament. In this way the king could credibly commit to repay. No such devolution of power occurred in France. The result was that the English king solved the problem of how to raise funds and could finance his army and other expenditures while the French king did not, bringing about the chronic shortage of revenue that was one of the factors leading to the French Revolution.[16]

Congelton (2002) extends North and Weingast's analysis of "The Irony of Absolutism." He suggests a generalized template, "king and council," for looking at these issues. In practice one rarely observes pure forms of dictatorship that lack a council, or pure forms of parliament that lack an executive. All kings share power. Generally government policies emerge from organizations that combine an executive branch of government, "the king," with a cabinet or parliamentary branch, "the council." Congelton provides an explanation for this regularity: The bipolar "king and council" constitutional template has a number of properties which give it great practical efficiency as a method of information processing and collective choice. First, a council generally has a wider array of direct experience and/or knowledge than the king does, and therefore is in position to be a better estimator of "policy consequences" than the king alone tends to be. Second, a bipolar design can reduce losses from conflict in cases where significant power centers other than the king exist. Third, a king and council template which provides agenda control to the king tends to reduce the extent to which majoritarian cycles may arise in the council. Fourth, the king and council templates allow gradual evolutionary shifts of power between the executive and parliament as circumstances change without the necessity of violent conflict. Finally, insofar as a form of majority rule is used by the council and is stable,

---

[16] Note that the irony of absolutism is incorporated into equation (6) above: it means that after some point $B_\pi < 0$, i.e. that an increase in the autocrat's power π reduces budgetary revenue B. This is also shown in Figure 16.3, where the slope of the $B(\pi)$ curve turns negative after some point.

the recommendations of council tend to be both robust as estimators and moderate in their policy recommendations.

3 DEMOCRACY VS. DICTATORSHIP

One deep concern has been the possibility that autocratic forms of economic organization might be superior to democratic ones in terms of economic growth or efficiency. This has been a recurring nightmare, beginning in the twentieth century with the fear of communism as an economic system, followed by admiration and fear of Hitler's juggernaut in the 1930s, and extending in more recent years to the threats from "Japan, Inc.," "Asian values," South Korea and Chile, and now the "free market communism" of China. So there has been a lot of research asking the question: Which is better for the economy, democracy or dictatorship?

The problem in answering it is that the economic systems under autocracies vary so much. Those who believe there is some simple formula for distinguishing the economy of dictatorship from that of democracy should think for a moment about, say, the economies of Nazi Germany, Papa Doc's Haiti, Pinochet's Chile, and the former Soviet Union.

Nevertheless, at least four broad hypotheses have been advanced: (1) the idea of the dictator as a stationary bandit (Mancur Olson); (2) Tocqueville's idea that democracies redistribute more than dictatorships; (3) a U-shaped curve where democracies grow faster than dictatorships as long as they are not " too" democratic (Barro); (4) the contest for power (Wintrobe). We take them in turn.

3.1 The Mystery of the Stationary Bandit

The most prominent theoretical idea in this literature is undoubtedly Olson's concept of an autocrat as a "stationary bandit"—at one point he refers to it as "the other invisible hand"—that guides rulers. Olson's new and surprising point is that the dictator's interest in maintaining the wealth of the society that he preys upon leads him to use his power to at least some extent in the public interest. For example, McGuire and Olson assert that

whenever a rational self-interested actor with unquestioned coercive power has an encompassing and stable interest in the domain over which the power is exercised, that actor is led to act in ways that are, to a surprising degree, *consistent with the interests of society and of those subject to that power*. It is as if the ruling power were guided by a hidden hand no less paradoxical for us than the invisible hand in the market was for people in Adam Smith's time. (McGuire and Olson 1996, 73, italics in the original)

In Olson's 1993 article and (2000) book, this concept is approached through a criminal metaphor. Each theft reduces the wealth of society and therefore the amount available for the thief to steal. Does this lead the thief to curtail his activity, in order to preserve the wealth of his prey? For the typical criminal, the answer is "no" because his interest is too narrow. The wealth of the society on which he preys is like a public good to the typical small-scale criminal, his effort to preserve it would have only a minuscule effect, and so he is better off free riding rather than attempting to conserve it. On the other hand, the Mafia and other criminal organizations which have a monopoly on crime in their area do have a sufficiently *encompassing* interest to take the effects of their thefts on the wealth of society as a whole. Thus Olson suggests that they typically do not steal at all but engage in protection instead, charging the citizens a fee to ensure the safety of their victims both from others and from the protectors themselves.

This metaphor then becomes the foundation for the origins of government. The logic is the same as that just outlined with respect to government by a "roving" vs. that by a "stationary" bandit: the stationary bandit, unlike the roving one, has an encompassing interest in preserving the wealth of the society from which he steals, and therefore limits his "theft" (taxes) and even provides public goods—both to the point where the marginal benefit to him is sufficient to account for his costs in terms of forgone income. The history of the forms of government is then simple to derive: autocracy (the stationary bandit) arises out of anarchy as the bandit(s) with the greatest capacity for violence takes over the area and substitutes an encompassing for a narrow interest; democracy arises out of dictatorship when autocracy is overthrown and none of the individuals or leaders involved in the coup has sufficient power to make themselves autocrats.

The dictator redistributes income to himself by raising taxes, and also by spending money on government services to the extent that these raise national income and therefore, in turn, tax revenue, above the cost of providing them. Now, it is well known that at some point, tax *rates* can be raised too high from the point of view of maximizing tax *revenue*. Similarly, government services can be expanded beyond the point where they contribute to the net revenues of the autocrat. Various reciprocal conditions for the autocrat's optimum can be derived. For example, the optimum tax rate is just the rate which maximizes revenue

$$t^* = 1/2\eta \tag{8}$$

Where t* is the optimal tax rate, and η is the elasticity of work effort with respect to the tax rate.

Conditions like this were originally derived by Brennan and Buchanan (1980). Indeed, equation (8) can be recognized as the special case of a tinpot dictator discussed above, but one who is completely secure in office and therefore does not have to worry about the possibility that he may be deposed.

Similarly, the optimum level of government services for the income-maximizing autocrat is

$$Y'(G) = 1/t^* \tag{9}$$

where G is the level of government services, Y'(G) is the rate at which income (Y) grows as G expands.[17] To give a simple illustration, suppose the optimal tax

[17] Olson and McGuire 1996 give slightly more complicated versions of these conditions. The present formulation is taken from Mueller (2003, 408).

rate for an autocrat is two-thirds. At this optimum, the proportionate social loss from the autocrat's redistribution to himself is $1/t$ or $3/2$. Then the autocrat provides the public good where the marginal social product is $3/2$ times his marginal social cost (McGuire and Olson 1996, 77).

These formulas for the autocrat can then be compared to those for a democratic government and for other types of government. The general idea is that a democratic government is more "encompassing" than an autocrat and therefore the democracy chooses lower tax rates.

In the end, just two variables are necessary to compare and analyze governments:

(i) how encompassing (breadth of self-interest) is the interest of the ruler;
(ii) how long (time horizon) is his interest.

Thus, in the same way that dictatorship is superior to anarchy because the dictator has a more encompassing interest in the society he rules, so democracy is superior to dictatorship because democratic majorities are more encompassing than the interest of the dictator. Similarly, dictators or democracies with long time horizons have more of an interest in preserving or enhancing the wealth of the society they rule than those who govern only for the short term.

To sum up, McGuire and Olson say that "it is nonetheless remarkable how much of the encompassing interest of the secure autocrat leads him to take account of the welfare of his subjects . . . the degree of overlap between the interests of the autocrat and his subjects is startling" (McGuire and Olson 1996, 80).

Some evidence is presented in Keefer et al. (1996), who argue that any incentive an autocrat has to respect property rights comes from his interest in future tax collections and national income and increases with his planning horizon. They find an empirical relationship between property and contract rights and an autocrat's time in power.

Now, one difficulty with Olson's analysis is that, comparing dictatorships, the *worst* regimes in human history have been precisely those such as Nazi Germany, Soviet Russia, or Pol Pot's Cambodia which appear to have been the most encompassing. All these regimes took an interest in the lives of all of their citizens (and thus were encompassing[18]). The reason is simple: it was those regimes which wanted to remold the citizens and the societies under their rule and therefore intervened most dramatically and thoroughly into the lives of their citizens. But whether it is their record on the environment or their infamously brutal treatment of minorities, it is an understatement to suggest that the historical record of these regimes offers little that is to be admired. So the theory appears to be capable, not just of misleading with respect to the understanding of autocratic regimes, but of "getting it wrong" in a spectacular fashion.

---

[18] Indeed, Olson himself (2000) uses this term to describe Stalin's regime. See the discussion of Congleton's (forthcoming) paper below, which shows more precisely how a dictator whose rule is encompassing but who is *insecure* in office tends to make life worse for his subjects than an equally insecure but more narrowly based ruler.

The same problem appears with respect to the second variable, the time horizon of the dictator. In Olson's model, the longer the time horizon, the better, i.e. the more the dictator tends to rule in the social interest. But regimes with a long time horizon have been precisely those in which the leaders had a tighter grip on power, and hence were more capable of molding the society and the individuals within it, i.e. the "mobilizational" regimes, as those of Stalin, Hitler, and Pol Pot have been sometimes called by political scientists. Those where the regime is just interested in looting the society typically have a shorter time horizon.

In short, from the point of view of citizens of these regimes, especially the peasants under Stalin, the Jews under Hitler, the blacks under apartheid in South Africa, and so on, it would no doubt have been better if their bandits had been less stationary!

At the same time, there is clearly a kernel of truth in the stationary bandit concept. So the question then appears to be why the theory seems to be so misleading in certain respects, and a number of papers have been published which try to either single out which aspect of it is responsible for it going off the rails where it does, and whether the theory can be modified to shed these implications and preserve and possibly expand on the undoubted kernel of truth in it. The subjects include the comparison between dictatorship and anarchy (Moselle and Polak 2001), adaptation of the model to include war and foreign conquest (Wilke 2002), and the issue of the dictator's security in office (Congleton forthcoming). We take each in turn.

Moselle and Polak (2001) challenge the alleged superiority of dictatorship over anarchy. In their model, the existence of a state can result in lower levels of both output and welfare than would occur under anarchy. This occurs if the state is "predatory" in the sense that the rulers extract taxes from the population for their own ends. In this framework, even a weak state can be bad for output and welfare and a "corrupt" state that makes side deals with bandits can be especially bad.

Wilke (2002) argues that "the basic mistake" of McGuire and Olson is to identify the reign of a stationary bandit as a peaceful reign. He shows that "belligerent stationary bandits" (e.g. Alexander the Great, Hannibal, Napoleon, Hitler, Stalin) might involve their subjects in costly, mistaken, and fruitless wars, something that neither a roving bandit nor a democracy would do. As Wilke puts it, "The introduction of war into the dictatorship-model shows a further major advantage of democracy: people are protected from subjective and often biased assumptions of autocratic rulers concerning the probability of winning 'their' war" (Wilke 2002, 331).

Another (explicit) assumption in Olson's analysis is that the dictator is perfectly secure in office. I suspect one important problem with Olson's framework is the lack of emphasis on competition. Once the struggle for power is assumed away, many of the most interesting aspects of the behavior of dictators become idiosyncratic features of their preferences, and hence largely unpredictable, instead of being derived from the principle of competition. Thus the wars among the monarchies, etc., are all just aspects of "princely consumption." And how would the model explain Stalin's war against the peasantry, Hitler's treatment of the Jews, and the persecution of minorities in other dictatorships? On the bandit model, the only way to understand these forms of behavior is that dictators have some monopoly power, and that they use this power to implement their preferences which happen to be weird preferences. The reason for this is that the model does not deal with the competitive struggle to acquire and maintain dictatorial powers. So the behavior of the dictator cannot be understood as motivated by competition or survival in office but simply as consumption.

A new paper (Congleton forthcoming) develops this point with a general model in which society is made up of interest groups. Some of these support the dictator, others support opposition groups. As in the Wintrobe political exchange model the dictator uses repression and loyalty to maintain his hold on power. The difference is that in Congleton's model groups are clearly either supporting or oppositional. This gives rise to some novel predictions. There are two extreme polar cases. At one extreme, the dictator who is completely secure in office sets tax rates to maximize total revenue, as in Olson's model. However, unlike the Olson model, the dictator here is assumed to be able to discriminate among individuals with different "work ethics" (elasticity of work effort with respect to tax rate) and implements so-called Ramsay taxes, in which those who are most sensitive to an increase in taxes are taxed least, and so forth. Thus tax preferences might be provided to exporters and industries dependent on foreign capital because those markets are often competitive and sensitive to tax rates. The Ramsay system minimizes the deadweight losses from taxation. At the other extreme, the dictator who is completely *in*secure, and totally preoccupied with staying in office, implements taxes which are the opposite of Ramsay taxes! The decisive factor is the "elasticity of support" rather than work effort. The more likely a group could switch to supporting the opposition, the lower its tax rates will be.

Of particular interest is that the dictator's security interest may be said to be encompassing in that it includes consideration of all politically relevant groups. But, as Congleton notes,

the welfare of many opposition groups is *inversely related to the dictator's own expected welfare*. Uncertainty elicits malice rather than benevolence towards such groups. Moreover, the more numerous are the members of such opposition groups, the smaller and more concentrated the truly encompassing *security interests* of the dictator tend to be, and, consequently, the more repressed and poorer is the average resident of the country. (Congleton Forthcoming, 19, italics in the original)

In general, the greater the weight of security relative to income in the dictator's calculus, the greater the difference between the taxation of supporters and opponents. And the more uncertain is a dictator's tenure of office, the more repressive and discriminatory a dictatorial regime tends to be. So in this way of thinking, the heart of the problem is the assumption of perfect security in office. The more secure the dictator, the closer he resembles the Olsonian ideal, and the more insecure, the more he departs from it.

Congleton's model is an important advance. Still the conclusion is odd. In economic life, the first theorem of welfare economics says that it is competition, under certain circumstances, which aligns the private interest with the public interest. In the economics of politics, competition normally has the same beneficial effect, pushing parties towards the median voter's preferences, as in Downsian models, or forcing interest groups towards relatively efficient policies as in interest group models (Becker 1983; Austen Smith 1997). Why should things be different in dictatorships? And can it really be true that the less opposition a dictator faces, the better off his subjects will be?

3.2 Tocquevillian Models

Another, both older and newer, approach to comparing dictatorship with democracy is the Tocqueville hypothesis. This is the idea that democracies redistribute more than dictatorships. The logic is that if the franchise is extended more widely, i.e., to the poor and the property-less, they will vote for higher taxes and more redistribution. In Meltzer and Richards's (1981) well-known formulation, the lower the income of the median voter relative to mean income, the more redistribution would take place as a result of the electoral process. In turn, economic growth suffers.

Barro (1996a, 1996b) looks at the effect of democracy on growth via redistribution. He stresses the advantages of dictatorship, i.e. the autocrat, unlike the democratic politician, is capable of shutting down or simply ignoring the redistributory demands of interest groups characteristic of democracy (Barro 1996b, 2). His empirical work suggests that more democracy raises growth at low levels of political freedom but depresses growth when a moderate amount of freedom has already been attained. However, the effect of an increase in political freedom on economic growth is not very large and the overall effect "not statistically different from zero" (Barro 1996b, 6). Barro's results are only obtained once certain variables are held constant, including free markets, the rule of law, and small government consumption. So, really, again, only certain *kinds* of dictatorship are being discussed.

De Haan and Sturm (2003) ask a related question, namely whether democracy or autocracy is more conducive to economic freedom. Thus it is sometimes argued that only an authoritarian government is in a position to to introduce liberalization measures that initially may involve massive layoffs and cuts in entitlements. Chile, South Korea, and Taiwan introduced democracy only after economic reforms were implemented successfully. On the other hand, it has been argued that only governments with some legitimacy will be able to implement and sustain policies with high short-term costs. Thus, Keefer et al. (1996) found that, in general, democracies provide greater security of property rights and contractual rights than autocracies. De Haan and Sturm examine the relationship between economic and political freedom, focusing on developing countries. Their dependent variable is the (change in the) economic freedom indicator as measured by Gwartney, Lawson, and Block (1996) over the period 1975–95. Focusing on the relationship between this and various indicators for democracy, they find a *positive* relationship between democracy and economic freedom.

Przeworski and Limongi (1993) review a large number of studies, and find that about half show democracy growing faster than dictatorships, while the other half find the opposite. Przeworski et al. (2000) find that basically there is no difference between the rates of growth in dictatorships vs. democracies in their comprehensive examination of the performance of these two kinds of regimes in 141 countries over the forty years or so after the Second World War. But the same study confirms the importance of politics on economic growth. They show that changes in office (political instability) and other forms of unrest such as strikes, demonstrations, and riots reduce economic growth substantially under dictatorship, whereas while these are more frequent under democracy they do not cause a reduction in the rate of growth there (Przeworski et al. 2000, 192–3).

Sen (1999) calls the general idea that dictatorship is better suited to economic development than democracy the Lee thesis, after Lee Kwan Yew, the autocratic but economic efficiency-minded ruler of Singapore for many years. Sen raises many questions about Lee's ideas and suggests instead that democracy is intrinsically important to the process of development. In particular, Sen's observation that famines only seem to occur under dictatorship is provocative. However, no general theoretical model is presented which compares democracy with dictatorship.

Two other contributions address the problem of why some dictatorships, most notably regimes in East Asia and Chile, appear to be pro-growth while in others the autocrat is "predatory" and simply plunders the economy. Robinson (1997) argues that the likelihood of predatory behavior may be positively related to the extent to which a regime is encompassing and values the future. He develops a model in which whether or not a state is predatory hinges on the relationship between development and the distribution of political power. Development may be inconsistent with the preservation of the political status quo if it causes centers of power to emerge who are rivals to the dictator. Predatory behavior is also more likely the lower the level of income and the more unequal the society. To put it bluntly, from the dictator's point of view, ruining the economy can sometimes be a good thing! And the regimes of Mobutu and Papa Doc, who both did this, were extremely long-lived. A democratic politician cannot hope to profit in the same way.

Michael Spagat's (2002) paper addresses this problem by suggesting that there is a "bifurcation point" or level of capital below which it does not pay the dictator to try and develop the economy, and above which the dictator pursues rapid growth in order to maximize his personal consumption over time. He develops this idea in a simple formal model. A particularly novel feature of it is that there is an endogenous probability of a political catastrophe which removes the dictator from power, and this in turn depends on the dictator's capacity to satisfy certain groups which depends on the level of the capital stock. Hence a dictator's economy sometimes grows faster than a social planner's might, as capital accumulation wards off the possibility of catastrophe. The authors use simulation analysis to show the existence of bifurcation and to show how it depends on various parameters, and they provide some empirical evidence using Gastil data of the existence of bifurcation, and of their basic prediction that the variance of growth rates in dictatorship is higher than that under democratic regimes.

Perhaps the basic flaw of Tocquevillian models is exposed in a recent paper by Lee (2002). Tocqueville's hypothesis is based on two simple propositions: (1) a society conferring decisive power on the poorer fraction of the population has an incentive to tax at higher rates; and (2) higher taxes choke off investment and therefore growth. Implicitly, however, the assumption is made that the fiscal policy is "paternalistic," i.e., every citizen receives an equal transfer regardless of the regime. Many oligarchies and autocracies, on the other hand, are characterized by a significant *redistribution bias* towards the ruling elite (to satisfy their demands for palaces, military adventures, and so forth). In every country but a perfect democracy, there is some fraction of the population which does not share in the redistribution of tax revenues. So any regime can be defined as a pair p,r where p is the fraction of the population which does not have the right to vote, and r the fraction which does not share in the redistribution of tax revenues. In a perfect democracy, $(p, r)=0$, and in a perfect autocracy $(p,r)=(1,1)$.

Now, a less democratic regime may wish to tax at lower rates because the participation bias p is higher. This is the "Tocqueville effect:" the decisive voter is richer, and wants lower taxes. But it also tends to have a greater redistribution bias r—Lee calls this the "Olson effect"—as the rich can now exploit the poor more than before and taxes become more regressive. So the autocracy could easily impose *higher* taxes than a more democratic regime. In general, as Lee shows, it is difficult to predict what will happen as the results depend not only on the values of p and r but also on the degree of inequality in the society and the productivity of fiscal policy. But the main point is that there is no theoretical reason to believe that democracies have higher taxes than dictatorships.

Mulligan, Gil, and Sala-i-Martin (2004) test to see how policies differ between democracy and dictatorship. Their findings are that democracies redistribute slightly *less* than economically and demographically similar non-democracies. (2004, 61), and that non-democracies collect almost 4 GDP percentage points less than non-communist democracies in taxes. Following what they refer to as the "barriers to entry approach" in which the suppression of political competition is an important activity for dictators because it helps them maintain their position, they explain this as a "markup," part of which could be spent on limiting political competition.

Other than that they find very little difference between democracies and non-democracies with respect to economic and social policies. One problem here is that democracies and development strongly covary and, as this is not controlled for in the estimations, it is not surprising that democracy underperforms.

With respect to variables that can be interpreted as limiting competition for public office they do find significant differences. These include the use of the death penalty, the level of military spending, civil liberties, censorship of the press, and the regulation of religion. By far the largest coefficient is for military spending. Partly this can be explained vis-à-vis the "democratic peace" literature in political science (that democracies do not appear to make war against other democracies), but the military can also be used to shore up a dictator's position in office.

One possible flaw in this, and in much of the other empirical work comparing democracy with dictatorship, is that dictatorships (in this case, non-democracies) are simply lumped together. To illustrate, it is easy to imagine that tinpots and tyrants spend less on social and economic services than the democracies do, while totalitarian regimes spend more. Thus totalitarian regimes like Castro's Cuba spend more on schooling and health than many democracies do, while Papa Doc's Haiti spent less. Hence there is no theoretical reason to expect that a catch-all category like "non-democracies" would have different levels of expenditure on social services than democratic governments do. The only prediction is that the variance of spending on these items would be higher in the non-democracies.

In contrast to economic models which consider the incentives of a ruler, *once he is in office*, Wintrobe (2002) focuses on the conditions under which the ruler obtains power, and how he can be deprived of it. Among the most obvious and commonly considered types of political system—democracy, dictatorship, anarchy, and heredi-tary monarchy—*only* democracy appears to possess a relatively low-cost procedure or mechanism which makes it possible to transfer political power on a regular and systematic basis, where the transfer is accepted by those who lose power as well as those who gain it, and which offers some possibility that these reallocations will tend to shift power into the hands that can use it most effectively.

If democracies can transfer power at relatively low cost, does power typically transfer from lower to higher valued uses? How does democracy compare to dicta-torship in this respect? One difference is that in dictatorship, some of the costs of inefficient policies can be shifted to fall on those who are repressed. A nice illustra-tion of this is the effect of sanctions against Saddam Hussein, discussed by Kaempfer, Lowenberg, and Mertens (2004). The sanctions generated rents, and these were appropriated by those who are close to Saddam. The losses from the sanctions were borne by those who were opposed to the regime, and this in turn weakened their capacity to oppose it, leading to his further entrenchment in power. To put it simply, the sanctions against Saddam Hussein did not necessarily weaken his hold on power at all.

Another issue is the relative influence of producer vs. consumer groups under dictatorship vs. democracy. Ever since the work of Downs, it has been a standard proposition in the economics of politics that democracy favors producer groups over consumer groups (Downs 1957; Stigler 1971; see also Becker 1983). The main reasons advanced are that since these groups are small, it is relatively easy for them to overcome the free rider problem, and since their per capita benefits would be large from any subsidy, they have a substantial interest in applying pressure to obtain it. On the other hand, consumer groups are large, and the per capita benefit from any subsidy would be small.

I pointed out above that dictators cannot survive in office on the basis of repression alone but need support as well. Which groups can be expected to support dictators? Consumer groups, environmental groups, and other groups with a large number of potential supporters, each of which has a small stake in issues like the prices of goods or the state of the environment, have difficulty surviving or forming under autocracy. There are typically no laws protecting human rights under dictatorship. Without such laws, it is difficult for large groups—such as consumers—to organize. There is no free press to call attention to pricing or environmental or labor abuses and to aid in the formation of a mass membership and there are no independent courts in which to sue violators. In brief, the usual weapons of mass organizations—publicity and the courts—are more easily countered by a dictator than a democratic politician.

On the other hand, the weapons of small producer groups such as cash donations actually thrive in the closed environment and tame courts of a dictatorship. In exchange, dictators obviously have much to offer producers for their support including tariffs, subsidies, and other rents, fewer problems from labor unions, and the removal of unfavorable regulations. So the possibility of a trade of rents for support between the dictator and the small, concentrated interest group is actually *enhanced* under dictatorship, just as trades with representatives of broader public opinion are diminished. This implies that *producers typically have more power under dictatorship than democracy.*

This provides an alternative explanation for Barro's evidence cited above: that the rate of growth is slightly higher under dictatorship than democracy at low levels of dictatorship and lower at high levels of repression. Since producers especially benefit from economic growth, their greater political weight under dictatorship implies that dictators would emphasize this policy. Note, however, that this growth comes as the result of the greater influence of producer groups and is not necessarily a Pareto improvement. Thus the growth could arise to the detriment of the environment, the consumer, etc. Moreover, at high levels of repression, this positive effect on growth is increasingly overwhelmed by the information problems generated by the Dictator's Dilemma, which increasingly hamper growth and ultimately strangle it.

Finally it is worth pointing out that an extension of the theory of property rights used in this analysis provides a simple economic justification of human rights. Economic efficiency justifies the ownership of private property on the ground that property should be allocated to the party who is most highly motivated to maximize its value. Who is it that can be counted to manage or take care a piece of property best? The owner. Human rights give this privilege of "ownership" of the individual to that individual himself or herself. Under dictatorship, it resides with the sovereign. But the dictator, as Sen suggested (1993), tends to regard the people under his rule as "stock" and cannot be expected to care for their lives the way they would themselves. Perhaps this explains Przeworski et al.'s striking result that average lifespan is systematically lower under dictatorship (see Przeworski et al. 2000, ch. 5).

4 CONCLUSION

At the risk of oversimplifying, it might be worthwhile to summarize the picture or image of dictatorship which emerges from the rational choice theories and evidence on dictatorship discussed in this chapter.

To begin with, there is considerable support for the idea that dictatorships operate by political exchange rather than solely by repression and command. Dictatorships make trades with their constituents, much in the way that politicians in democracies do. This is the basic idea behind the "Dictator's Dilemma" and it is not inconsistent with the "Stationary Bandit" perspective. And it fits with the evidence based on microdata on the allocation of resources in the former Soviet Union, with the anti-cyclical behavior of membership in the Communist Party of Yugoslavia, with the evidence that on average, the economic and social policies of the non-democracies do not differ that much from democracies, and with the evidence that there is, if anything, greater redistribution in non-democracies than democracies.

The political exchange perspective also means that dictators seek the loyal support of interest groups, especially among the military and other groups which have the strongest capacity to depose them, but also among broader elements of their population. The traditional emphasis on the free rider problem, if correct, would indicate that dictators need worry only about the possibility of a palace revolt, but in the light not only of the experience of the last quarter of the twentieth century but of new models of critical mass, bandwagon effects, and so on which provide a rational choice role for the masses in revolution, this picture no longer seems valid.

At the same time, the evidence seems uncontroversial that dictatorships do make extensive use of the tool of repression. They spend more on the military than democracies do, abrogate civil liberties, make more use of imprisonment and the death penalty, restrict freedom of worship, and so on. There is also some support for the idea that dictatorships tend to tax their populations more heavily than democracies do, the surplus paying for the extra military expenditures. This point does not contradict the idea of political exchange just discussed. Dictators prefer to rule on the basis of support, but where they believe they are unlikely to get it they use repression. So the dictator is like a democratic ruler in some ways, but he has a more complex (and more cruel) calculation to make. This point was neglected in models which stressed the identity of interest between a democratic ruler and a dictator. Recent work which introduces repression and war into these models makes them more interesting, even if it weakens their controversial implications about the beneficence of dictatorial rule.

Thirdly, there seems to be little support for the idea that democracies redistribute more than dictatorships. The idea is flawed in that it is based on looking at how a theoretical democracy would behave but pays no attention to what a dictator would do. In particular it takes no account of the redistributory tendency of dictatorships. For example, there is no reason to believe that the rent seeking, corruption and related tendencies decried of modern democracies are any less a feature of dictatorships; quite the opposite. But they may take different forms, as appears to have been the case in South Korea. Both theoretically and empirically, the idea that democracies redistribute more than dictatorships seems flawed. And the search for a benevolent form of dictatorship which implements the economic policies favored by the current wisdom of economists has always been and continues to be a mistake in my view.

There is some empirical evidence that dictatorships can be usefully classified into two types. The general idea that not all dictatorships are the same could be expanded on. More specifically, every regime works in a particular way, and while a general framework of a phenomenon is fundamental, models of particular types of regime could be further developed within this general picture. For example, very little work has been done on theocracy, especially given the exploding importance of religion in contemporary politics. Another important area here is the nature of new forms of dictatorship such as the current Chinese communist-capitalist regime.

One promising development is the attention being paid to some of the specific problems of the contemporary (and the old!) world like genocide, famine, and war, and to show their deep connection in some form to authoritarianism. Work on revolution could also be integrated more deeply into the study of authoritarian rule.

From the policy point of view, the idea that dictatorships typically rule with more support from their populations than is commonly believed has deep implications for the feasibility of deposing dictatorships. However attractive the idea of liberating a population from the repressive rule of an autocrat may seem, the point about support means that this task is not going to be as simple as one would believe based on a model of dictatorship which says that dictatorships rule by repression alone. It also complicates the task of the replacement of the regime by a more democratic one. The record of success by the Western powers here, from the Bay of Pigs to the recent invasion of Iraq, is poignant testimony to this point.

REFERENCES

ACEMOGLU, D., and ROBINSON, J. A. 2005. *Economic Origins of Dictatorship and Democracy.* New York: Cambridge University Press.

ARENDT, H. 1951. *The Origins of Totalitarianism.* New York: Harcourt, Brace, Jovanovich.

ARJOMAND, S. A. 1986. Iran's Islamic revolution in comparative perspective. *World Politics,* 38 (3): 383–414.

AUSTEN SMITH, D. 1997. Interest groups. Pp. 296–321 in *Public Choice: A Handbook,* ed. D. Mueller. New York: Cambridge University Press.

BARDHAN, P. 1990. Symposium on the state and economic development. *Journal of Economic Perspectives,* 4: 3–7.

BARRO, R. 1996a. Democracy and growth. *Journal of Economic Growth,* 1: 1–27.

—— *Getting It Right.* 1996b. Boston: MIT Press.

BASHIR, A. 2005. *The Insider: Trapped in Saddam's Brutal Regime.* London: Abacus.

BECKER, G. 1983. A Theory of Competition among Interest Groups for Political Influence. *Quarterly Journal of Economics,* 98: 371–400.

BERNHOLZ, P. 2001. Ideocracy and totalitarianism: a formal analysis incorporating ideology. *Public Choice,* 108 (1–2): 33–75.

BOIX, C. 2003. *Democracy and Redistribution.* New York: Cambridge University Press.

BRENNAN, G. and BUCHANAN, J. 1980. *The Power to Tax: Analytic Foundations of a Fiscal Constitution.* Cambridge: Cambridge University Press.

BULLOCK, A. 1991. *Hitler and Stalin: Parallel Lives.* London: HarperCollins.

CONGLETON, R. 2002. From dictatorship to democracy without revolution. Paper delivered at the American Economic Association Meetings, Atlanta.

—— Forthcoming. How encompassing is a dictator's interest? Interest groups, targeted repression, and economic development. *Public Choice.*

DE HAAN, J., and STURM, J.-E. 2003. Does more democracy lead to greater economic freedom? New evidence for developing countries. *European Journal of Political Economy*, 19 (3): 547–63.

DOWNS, A. 1957. *An Economic Theory of Democracy*. New York: Harper.

FEARON, J. D. 1995. Rationalist explanations for war. *International Organization*, 49: 379–414.

FREEDOM HOUSE. Annual 1978–2001. Freedom in the world: the annual survey of political rights and civil liberties. *Freedom Review*. New York: Freedom House.

FRIEDRICH, K., and BRZEZINSKI, Z. 1965. *Totalitarian Dictatorship and Autocracy*. Cambridge, Mass.: Harvard University Press.

GOLDSTONE, J., GURR, T., MARSHALL, M., and VARGAS, J. 2004. It's all about state structure: new findings on revolutionary origins from global data. *Homo Economicus*, 21 (2), special issue on "The rationale of revolutions," ed. Mario Ferrero.

GWARTNEY, J., LAWSON, R., and BLOCK, W. 1996. *Economic Freedom of the World, 1975–1995*. Vancouver: Fraser Institute.

HAGGARD, S. 1990. *Pathways from the Periphery: The Politics of Growth in the Newly Industrializing Countries*. Ithaca, NY: Cornell University Press.

HARRISON, M. 2002. Coercion, compliance and the collapse of the Soviet command economy. *Economic History Review*, 55: 397–433.

ISLAM, M., and WINER, S. L. 2004. Tinpots, totalitarians (and democrats): an empirical investigation of the effects of economic growth on civil liberties and political rights. *Public Choice*, 118: 289–323.

KAEMPFER, W., LOWENBERG, A., and MERTENS, W. 2004. International economic sanctions against a dictator. *Economics and Politics*, 16: 29–51.

KANG, D. C. 2002a. Bad loans to good friends: money politics and the developmental state in South Korea. *International Organization*, 56: 177–207.

—— 2002b. *Crony Capitalism: Corruption and Economic Development in South Korea and the Philippines*. New York: Cambridge University Press.

KEEFER, P., CLAGUE, C., KNACK, S., and OLSON, M. 1996. Property and contract rights under democracy and dictatorship. *Journal of Economic Growth*, 1 (2): 243–76.

KHAWAJA, M. 1993. Repression and popular collective action: evidence from the West Bank. *Social Forum*, 8: 47–71.

KIRKPATRICK, J. 1982. *Dictatorship and Double Standards: Rationalism and Realism in Politics*. New York: Simon and Schuster.

KURRILD-KLITGAARD, P. 2000. The constitutional economics of autocratic succession. *Public Choice*, 103: 63–84.

LAZAREV, V., and GREGORY, P. 2003. Commissars and cars: a case study in the political economy of dictatorship. *Journal of Comparative Economics*, 31: 1–19.

LEE, W. 2002. Is democracy more expropriative than dictatorship? Tocquevillian wisdom revisited. *Journal of Development Economics*, 921: 1–45.

LINZ, J., and STEPAN, A. 1978. *The Breakdown of Democratic Regimes*. Baltimore: Johns Hopkins University Press.

McGUIRE, M., and OLSON, Jr., M. 1996. The economics of autocracy and majority rule: the invisible hand and the use of force. *Journal of Economic Literature*, 34: 72–96.

MELTZER, A. H., and RICHARDS, S. F. 1981. A rational theory of the size of government. *Journal of Political Economy*, 89: 914–27.

MOSELLE, B., and POLAK, B. 2001. A model of a predatory state. *Journal of Law, Economics and Organization*, 17: 1–33.

MUELLER, D. 2003. *Public Choice III*. New York: Cambridge University Press.

MULLIGAN, C. B., GIL, R., and SALA-I-MARTIN, X. 2004. Do democracies have different public policies than nondemocracies? *Journal of Economic Perspectives*, 18: 51–74.

NISKANEN, W. A. 1997. Autocratic, democratic and optimal government. *Economic Inquiry*, 35: 464–79.

NORTH, D. C. 1981. *Structure and Change in Economic History.* New York: W. W. Norton.

—— and WEINGAST, B. 1989. Constitutions and commitment: the evolution of institutions governing public choice in seventeenth century England. *Journal of Economic History*, 49: 808–32.

O'DONNELL, G. 1980. Tensions in the bureaucratic authoritarian state and the question of democracy. Pp. 285–31 in *The New Authoritarianism in Latin America*, ed. D. Collier. Princeton: Princeton University Press.

OLSON, M. 1993. Democracy and development. *American Political Science Review*, 87: 567–75.

—— 2000. *Power and Prosperity: Outgrowing Communist and Capitalist Dictators.* New York: Basic Books.

—— and McGUIRE, M. 1996. The economics of autocracy and majority rule: the invisible hand and the use of force. *Journal of Economic Literature*, 34: 72–96.

OPP, K. D., and RUEHL, W. 1990. Repression, micro-mobilization, and political protest. *Social Forces*, 69: 521–47.

PRZEWORSKI, A., and LIMONGI, F. 1993. Political regimes and economic growth. *Journal of Economic Perspectives*, 7: 51–70.

—— ALVAREZ, M. E., CHEIBUB, J. A., and LIMONGI, F. 2000. *Democracy and Development: Political Institutions and Well-Being in the World 1950–1990.* New York: Cambridge University Press.

RASLER, K. 1996. Concession, repression, and political protest in the Iranian revolution. *American Sociological Review*, 61: 132–52.

ROBINSON, J. 1985. When is a state predatory. MS. USC.

ROEMER, J. 1985. Rationalizing revolutionary ideology. *Econometrica*, 53 (1): 85–108.

ROOT, H. 1994. *The Foundation of Privilege: Political Foundations of Markets in Old Regime France and England.* Berkeley and Los Angeles: University of California Press.

SCHNYTZER, A., and SUSTERSIC, J. 1997. Why join the party in a one-party system: popularity vs. political exchange. *Public Choice*, 94: 117–34.

SEN, A. 1993. Political rights and economic needs. The John M. Olin Lecture in Law and Economics at the University of Toronto Law School.

—— 1999. *Development as Freedom.* Oxford: Oxford University Press.

SHAPIRO, C. 1983. Premiums for high quality products as returns to reputations. *Quarterly Journal of Economics*, 98: 659–79.

—— and STIGLITZ, J. E. 1984. Equilibrium unemployment as a worker discipline device. *American Economic Review*, 74: 433–44.

SPAGAT, M. 2001. Political instability and growth in dictatorships. MS. Royal Holloway College London.

—— 2002. The dynamics of repressive dictatorships. Paper presented at the American Economic Association meetings, Atlanta.

STIGLER, G. 1971. The theory of economic regulation. *Bell Journal of Economics*, 2: 2–21.

STRAUSS, L. 1963/1991. *On Tyranny.* London: Free Press.

TULLOCK, G. 1987. *Autocracy.* Dordrecht: Martinus Nijhoff.

VERWIMP, P. 2001. The political economy of coffee and dictatorship in Rwanda. *European Journal of Political Economy*, 19: 161–81.

WILKE, T. 2002. The investment theory of wars: belligerent dictators in the McGuire/North model of autocracy. *Public Choice*, 112: 319–33.

WINTROBE, R. 1990. The tinpot and the totalitarian: an economic theory of dictatorship. *American Political Science Review*, 84: 849–72.

—— 1998. *The Political Economy of Dictatorship*. New York: Cambridge University Press.

—— 2001. How to understand, and deal with dictatorship: an economist's view. *Economics of Governance*, 2: 35–58.

—— 2002. The contest for power: property rights, human rights, and economic efficiency. Paper presented at the American Economic Association meetings, Atlanta.

—— 2004. Rational revolutions. *Homo Economicus*, 21 (2), special issue on "The rationale of revolutions," ed. Mario Ferrero.

PART V

POLITICAL INSTABILITY, POLITICAL CONFLICT

CHAPTER 17

....

RETHINKING REVOLUTIONS: A NEO-TOCQUEVILLIAN PERSPECTIVE

....

STEVEN PINCUS

"THERE is no part of history better received than the account of great changes and revolutions of states and governments," wrote the Anglican cleric Gilbert Burnet in the middle of the seventeenth century. This was so, he claimed, because "the variety of unlooked for accidents and events, both entertains the reader and improves him" (1681, sig (b)r). Another early commentator on revolutions emphasized that revolutions were not only entertaining but difficult to interpret. "When great revolutions are successful their causes cease to exist," explained Alexis de Tocqueville, "the very fact of their success has made them incomprehensible" (1983, 5). Little has changed in the century and a half separating us from Tocqueville. Revolutions continue to fascinate and to baffle. In the late 1970s Theda Skocpol observed that "during the last two decades theories of revolution have sprung up thick and fast in American social science" (1979, 8). The pace of scholarship on the subject of revolution has only accelerated since Skocpol wrote those words.

 * I am grateful for the very helpful comments, criticisms, and suggestions of: Haydon Cherry, Arvind Elangovan, Bryan Garsten, Phil Gorski, Evan Haefeli, Alan Houston, Meg Jacobs, Friedrich Harz, Krishan Kumar, Emilio Kouri, Jim Livesey, Claudio Lomnitz, Bill Sewell, Chuck Walton, Alice Wolfram, and the editors of this volume, Carles Boix and Sue Stokes.

Revolutions continue to fascinate and amaze because each new revolution seems to raise doubts about the previous generation of sophisticated theorizing. Unfortunately, each new revolution has encouraged scholars to develop ever-more elaborate explanations, with new variables and new sets of possible outcomes. Each new account of revolutions is more complex than the last. Along with new causes have come new distinctions in the typology of revolutions. We now hear of political revolutions, social revolutions, great revolutions, lesser revolutions, Third World revolutions, and twentieth-century revolutions. This essay, inspired by insights offered by Alexis de Tocqueville and other early commentators on revolutions, attempts a more parsimonious explanation for the causes of revolutions *tout court*, and suggests some new directions in explaining their outcomes.

1 DEFINING REVOLUTION

Revolutions are relatively rare and distinctive events. They fundamentally transform states and societies. "A revolution," suggests Samuel Huntington, "is a rapid, fundamental, and violent domestic change in the dominant values and myths of a society, in its political institutions, social structure, leadership, and government activity and policies." Revolutions are thus distinguishable from violent leadership changes in which social and political structures remain as they were. They are also separable from wars of independence in which the former colony's social and political structures remain but the locus of sovereignty is shifted.[1] Useful as Huntington's definition is, it needs to be qualified and amplified. The rapidity of revolutions must be measured in years not in months. "Revolutions," as Jeff Goodwin has pointed out, "are best conceptualized not as events, but as processes that typically span many years or even decades" (2001, 4). Revolutions, also, possess a common ideological element: a self-conscious commitment to epochal change. Revolutionary actors insist that their achievement, or their aspirations, represent a fundamental temporal break from the past. "True revolution," as Isaac Kramnick notes, "seeks a new beginning" (1972, 31). So for Richard Price, the American Revolution "opens a new prospect in human affairs, and begins a new era in the history of mankind" (1784, 2). Almost a century earlier the English polymath John Evelyn had described England's Glorious Revolution as spawning "a new creation."[2] It was this same conception of a temporal break that prompted the French Jacobins to construct a new calendar in 1793.

---

[1] Huntington (1968, 264). While I share Charles Tilly's concerns about the causal analysis in Huntington's account, I find his assertion that by Huntington's definition "one might reasonably argue that no revolution has ever occurred" peevish. Tilly (1973, 433). Huntington's definition is not too far removed from that offered by Thomas Paine: see Paine (1792, 5).

[2] John Evelyn to John Evelyn Jr., 18 December 1688, British Library, Evelyn MSS, JEJ 1.

Revolutions, thus, constitute a structural and ideological break from the previous regime. They entail changes to both the political and socioeconomic structures of a polity. They involve an often violent popular movement to overturn the previous regime. Revolutions change the political leadership and the policy orientations of the state. And, revolutionary regimes bring with them a new conception of time, a notion that they are beginning a new epoch in the history of the polity.

Class conflict, then, is incidental to the causes of revolutions. Despite the central role that class struggle plays in some influential accounts of revolutions, and the role that class divisions clearly played in some revolutions, to insist that class struggle is constitutive of revolution would be to narrow unnecessarily the field of analysis. The French Revolution of the late eighteenth century, once the classic case of class-based social revolution, is no longer thought to have had the class basis that Skocpol among others assumed.[3] Other twentieth-century revolutions, such as the Iranian and Mexican Revolutions, would also appear to be excluded from a definition of revolution that places class struggle at its center. Such a narrow definition of revolution would seem to have little social scientific value. Revolutions must involve popular movements; those popular movements need not be class based.

Nor is it useful to distinguish between social and political revolutions. Events that "transform state structures but not social structures" are civil wars, rebellions, or *coups d'état*; they are not revolutions.[4] Revolutions must involve both a transformation of the socioeconomic orientation and of the political structures. That transformation must take place through a popular movement, and the transformation must involve a self-consciousness that a new era has begun. The distinction usually drawn in the literature between social and political revolutions, it seems to me, is a normative not an analytical one. Scholars draw a bold line between social and political revolutions because they admire some revolutionary outcomes and disdain others. Analytical language has been used to disguise political preferences.

2 MODERNIZATION AND REVOLUTION

Why, then, do revolutions happen? Social scientists and historians have not been at a loss for explanations. As books and articles have proliferated, so have the stories scholars have told about the causes of revolutions. Despite the richness of the literature, it is possible to discern two types of explanations that now dominate the discussion, both associated with prominent social scientists. The first explanation of

---

[3] Skocpol (1979, 4). For current state of play, see Livesey (2001, 3–14); Kaplan (1995, especially 99–108); Spang (2003, especially 120–4). All of the authors are critical in their own ways of the revisionist consensus, yet none tries to revive the kind of "class struggle" narrative provided by Skocpol. One of the opening salvos in the assault on the class struggle interpretation was fired by the British academic Colin Lucas (1973), who receives only incidental treatment in the discussions of Livesey and Kaplan.

[4] This distinction is drawn by Skocpol (1979, 4); Foran (2005, 8); Arendt (1963, 64).

revolution is that the old regime is overturned by modernizers. The second analysis specifies that the old regime is done in by a new social group, a class that seizes power and overturns the structures of the state and society. For all of their differences, both explanations of revolution are modernization stories.

"Revolution," Huntington declares, " is characteristic of modernization. It is one way of modernizing a traditional society." In particular Huntington argues that revolution "is most likely to occur in societies which have experienced some social and economic development and where the processes of political modernization and political development have lagged behind the processes of social and economic change." Although Huntington distinguishes between a Western and an Eastern pattern of revolution, in both cases, as Tilly perceptively points out, "the immediate cause of revolution is supposed to be the discrepancy between the performance of the regime and the demands being made upon it. . . . Which in turn occurs as a more or less direct effect of rapid social and economic change."[5]

The class struggle explanation for revolution differs from the classic modernization story in two fundamental ways. Whereas the classic modernization story focuses on a generalized transition from a traditional to a modern society, the class struggle model highlights the transition from one mode of economic production to another. "The conception of social revolution used here," Theda Skocpol emphasizes, "draws heavily upon Marxist emphases on social structural change and class conflict" (1979, 13). And, whereas the classic modernization story focuses exclusively on internal domestic transitions, Skocpol, in particular, highlights the international context. "Modern social revolutions have happened only in countries situated in disadvantaged positions within international arenas," she points out. "The realities of military backwardness or political dependency have crucially affected the occurrence and course of social revolutions" (1979, 23). This situation of comparative backwardness is itself inextricably tied to modes of production. "All modern social revolutions," says Skocpol, "must be seen as closely related in their causes and accomplishments to the internationally uneven spread of capitalist economic development and nation-state formation on a world scale" (1979, 19). It is in this sense that Skocpol argues that "revolutionary crises developed when the old-regime states became unable to meet the challenges of evolving international situations" (1979, 47).

Despite these important interpretative, analytical, and (one suspects) normative differences, these two dominant explanations for revolution share a great deal. Both are fundamentally stories about modernization. Both emphasize that revolutions occur in societies in which social and economic modernization has made the state appear to be outmoded, to be an *ancien régime*. Despite the differences in approach, Skocpol shares with Huntington the notion that "epochal modernizing dynamics in part cause and shape revolutionary transformations."[6]

In contrast to both the classical modernizing and class struggle perspectives, I suggest that revolutions occur only when states have embarked on ambitious

---

[5] Huntington (1968, 264–74); Tilly (1973, 435). For an earlier modernization story, see Johnson (1966, 61–2). For a description of the broader family of modernization stories, see Goodwin (2001, 17).

[6] Skocpol (1979, 24). The point I am making is also emphasized by Goodwin (2001, 19–20).

state modernization programs. Revolutions do not pit modernizers against defenders of an old regime. Instead revolutions happen when the political nation is convinced of the need for political modernization, but there are profound disagreements on the proper course of state innovation. For all of the emphasis that the approaches of Huntington and Skocpol place on "political and institutional factors," I suggest, they have missed this crucial point (Huntington 1968, 275; Skocpol 1979, 5). State modernization is a necessary *prerequisite* for revolution. The extent and nature of modernizing social movements may encourage state modernization, they may help to shape the nature of the revolutionary process, but they do not spark revolution unless state modernization is already under way.

3 DEMOGRAPHY AND REVOLUTION

Before laying out the case that state modernization is a necessary prerequisite to revolution, it is important to acknowledge that there has been one powerful analysis of revolutions that does not stress modernization. Jack Goldstone, in his widely discussed *Revolution and Rebellion in the Early Modern World*, has advanced an altogether different thesis. "Revolutions," Goldstone insists, "are not provoked by a battle between the past and the future, or between good and evil; they are instead provoked by imbalances between human institutions and the environment." The key factor in promoting state breakdown, according to Goldstone, has nothing to do with social or economic modernization. "The motivation for change," Goldstone insists, "came from ecological shifts in the relation of the population size to agricultural output, which produced diverse conflicts between elites and states, among elite factions, and between popular groups and authorities" (1991, pp. xxiv, 27, 37). In Goldstone's breathtaking analysis, which traverses the early modern world from Europe to East Asia, traditional Malthusian crises, not modernizing economies, promote state breakdown and revolution.

The demographic explanation for revolutions and state breakdown relies on an important empirical claim. Goldstone suggests that there was "state breakdown not merely in Europe but on a world wide scale, clustered in two marked 'waves,' the first culminating in the mid-seventeenth century, the second in the mid-nineteenth, and separated by roughly a century, from 1660 to 1760, of stability" (1991, 3). The periods of instability were periods of demographic growth, the period of stability was one of population stagnation. "If population decline restores a traditional balance of people and resources," Goldstone explains, "traditional institutions may be revived" (1991, p. xxv).

While innovative and interpretatively exciting, Goldstone's analysis fails to make sense of the early modern world that is his focus. Monumental state breakdowns and revolutions occurred during his "century of stability" of 1660–1760. Goldstone dismisses England's Glorious Revolution of the later seventeenth century as "not really a revolution."[7] This view contrasts with that of classic commentators and recent scholarship. Karl Marx thought the Glorious Revolution marked "the first decisive victory of the bourgeoisie over the feudal aristocracy" (1973, 308). The great Tory jurist Sir William Blackstone agreed that it was the Glorious Revolution, "the happy revolution," that marked the decline of feudalism in England and the full establishment of England's "civil and political liberties."[8] The Glorious Revolution was a popular and violent event in which both the nature of English governance and the socioeconomic orientation of the regime were radically transformed. Not only did the new regime alter its foreign, imperial, economic, and religious policies, but subsequent commentators—whether supportive or critical of the revolution—almost universally described the Revolution as a new beginning in English history.

England was not the only European state to undergo a state breakdown, a state transformation, or a revolution in the century of so-called stability. The United Provinces of the Netherlands were convulsed by violent and spectacular state upheavals. In the face of military reverses at the hands of the French in the summer of 1672, a wave of popular protests and riots swept across the wealthiest state in Europe. The rioters eventually forced the great republican leader John De Witt to resign from office in early August. Then, on 20 August, De Witt and his brother Cornelius were ripped limb from limb on the streets of The Hague. The result was to make William of Orange Stadholder in July 1672, "transforming the structure of power." Popular political violence had changed the Netherlands from a republican into a quasi-monarchical regime (Israel 1995, 796–806; Geyl 1939, 345–400; Rowen 1978, 840–84).

Scandinavia, too, suffered state breakdowns between 1660 and 1760. Between 1660 and 1683, Frederik III and Christian V transformed Denmark from an elective monarchy into one of the most absolute states in Europe. Frederik III, in the wake of Denmark's disastrous military defeat by the Swedes 1657–60, "staged a coup" to ensure that the monarchy would become hereditary in 1660. In the following decades "the old oligarchical social order" was replaced "by a meritocracy in which the talented could reach the top irrespective of their social origins." The Danish Law of 1683 created "order and transparency in every aspect of life." The Danish political and social order had been permanently transformed.[9] Despite its victory over Denmark, the Swedish state was also dramatically transformed after 1680. In the Swedish case, in fact, it was not so much defeat and comparative backwardness, but anxiety that Sweden did not have the resources to maintain its hard-won status as a great power that provoked the transformation from an elective to an absolute monarchy (Upton 1998, 10; Roberts 1967, 230). In 1680 Charles XI formally achieved the status of

---

[7] Goldstone (1991, 318). Skocpol dismisses that revolution as "a political revolution" (1979, 141, 144, 294). Interestingly both Goldstone and Skocpol agree with the interpretation advanced by Margaret Thatcher in a speech delivered on 7 July 1988: House of Lords Record Office, WMT/22/Part I.

[8] Blackstone (1765–9, i. 397–8, iv. 435). For two very different accounts of the revolution that emphasize that the Glorious Revolution was a revolutionary transformation with both social and political aspects, see Hill (1961, 4–5); Pincus (2006, 1–33); Pincus (forthcoming).

[9] Jespersen (1994, 40–6). Contemporaries made the same point. See Molesworth (1692).

absolute monarch. In the words of one scholar, Charles XI "effected a revolution in the power of the monarchy." The Swedish Diets lost the power to limit his authority. He was then able to restructure radically the Swedish army, the Swedish navy, and Swedish finances. Significantly, the transformation of the Swedish state, which some interpreted as a royal coup, involved a massive transfer of resources from "private hands to the public domain." In essence the Swedish nobility was emasculated (Roberts 1967, 233, 247–9; Upton 1998, 31–89). Swedish state and society had been transformed.

Northern Europe was not the only region that underwent state breakdown in the so-called era of stability. The Spanish state was spectacularly transformed in a pan-European war, the War of the Spanish Succession. Europeans from London to Vienna and beyond were convulsed by the downfall of the Spanish Habsburg monarchy. Spain devolved into civil war. The Bourbon monarchy that emerged from the war altered the nature of the Spanish state. The new state generated a new "bureaucratic elite" and "a shift in power towards the central government." After 1714 the new Spanish royal line engaged in a further set of state reforms (Lynch 1989, 37, 60).

The demographic explanation for revolution and state breakdown asserts that states are at risk of upheaval only during periods when population growth outstrips economic resources. During periods of population stability, there should be state stability. However, the period of population stability, 1660–1760, was an era of frequent and dramatic state breakdown and revolution throughout Europe. We must therefore look elsewhere for the causes of revolution.

4 THE KEY FACTOR: STATE MODERNIZATION

The key factor, I claim, in explaining revolutions was neither population pressure nor socioeconomic modernization. In some cases both factors may have played a role. Instead the key factor was state modernization. In all revolutions, I suggest, the old regime had ceased to exist prior to the revolution. Revolutions, then, do not pit modernizing elements against defenders of the traditional order. Instead revolutions occur only after the regime in power has set itself on a modernizing course. Revolutions are the often-violent working out of competing modernization programs.

Scholars have long perceived empirical problems with both the classic and class struggle versions of the modernization story. Charles Tilly, for one, has pointed out that the historical record suggests "no direct relationship [between] the pace of structural change" and revolution. Indeed, Tilly notes the evidence suggests a negative relationship: "rapid change, diminution of political conflict." "Large-scale structural changes" indirectly affect "the probabilities of revolution," Tilly concludes, but "there is no reliable and regular sense in which modernization breeds revolution."[10] Social and economic transformation, social modernization, may lead to political changes, but not to state breakdown. Rather, state modernization makes a regime ripe for revolution.

By state modernization, I should make clear, I mean a self-conscious effort by the regime to transform itself in fundamental ways. State modernization will usually include an effort to centralize and bureaucratize political authority, an initiative to transform the military using the most up-to-date techniques, a program to accelerate economic growth using the tools of the state, and the deployment of techniques allowing the state to gather information about and potentially suppress social and political activities taking place in a wide range of social levels and geographical locales within the polity. Frequently state modernizers deploy the same rhetoric of creating new beginnings that we normally associate with revolutionaries.

Louis XVI's France, Tocqueville long ago suggested, was a classic case in which attempts to modernize the state made the regime ripe for revolution. "Experience teaches us," writes Tocqueville, that "the most perilous moment for a bad government is one when it seeks to mend its ways" (1983, 176–7). Tocqueville was generalizing from his knowledge of the French case. There, in the decades prior to the Revolution, "modern institutions" had emerged "within the shattered framework of the feudal system" (1983, 57–8). So extensive were the programs of state modernization that "the whole nation seemed to be in the throes of a rebirth" (1983, 171). Far from being a reactionary, Louis XVI was a determined reformer. "During his entire reign Louis XVI was always talking about reform," notes Tocqueville, "and there were few institutions whose destruction he did not contemplate" (1983, 188). In the later eighteenth century the French state was becoming increasingly centralized, "more systematic in its methods and more efficient" (1983, pp. viii–ix, 32, 60). In 1787 Louis XVI initiated a "wholesale remodeling of the entire administration" (1983, 194, 201). In 1788 the king "issued an edict overhauling the entire judicial system" (1983, 193). In response to France's demoralizing and devastating defeat in the Seven Years War (1757–63) "the government had become more energetic, had launched into a host of activities to which until then it had not given a thought" (1983, 178–9). The point is not that Louis XVI's regime anticipated all of the changes later brought about by the revolutionaries, nor that Louis XVI was a misunderstood radical, but that Louis XVI was a modernizer. His activities shifted the terrain of political discussion and activity. The Revolution was the violent working out of competing modernization programs.

The French Revolution was not the first example of this phenomenon. A century earlier, England had been convulsed with a similar revolutionary pattern. James II and the English political nation were also concerned that recent military setbacks,

---

[10] Tilly (1973, 432, 447). It should be noted that Skocpol has claimed a fundamental compatibility between her claims and Tilly's because they share a belief "that the mass, lower-class participants in revolution cannot turn discontent into effective political action without autonomous collective organization and resource to sustain their efforts" (Skocpol 1994, 241). However, the evidence presented by Tilly in this essay seems to raise more fundamental questions about the relationship between class definition and and revolution than Skocpol allows.

this time against the Dutch, had rendered his kingdom a second-rate power. James II also benefited from an expansion of English foreign trade that enabled him to modernize and expand the English army, to massively increase the state bureaucracy, and to impose central control on local government. James also developed a wide-ranging and efficient surveillance system, deploying numerous informers in England's coffee houses, taverns, and churches. He used the newly created post office to open letters, so he could keep tabs on the country's political pulse. He also used extensive political surveys to assess political sentiment, and to facilitate the removal of political dissidents and replace them with loyalists. The revolutionaries who overthrew James implemented an alternative modernization program. The post-revolutionary regime was also determined to modernize, centralize, and augment the state. But that regime did so with a very different economic strategy—one committed to developing England's manufacturing sector rather than seeking to expand the agrarian sector through territorial acquisition—a different foreign policy, and a profound commitment to religious toleration.[11]

Twentieth-century revolutions followed the same pattern as those of the seventeenth and eighteenth centuries. State modernization was a necessary prerequisite to revolution. The Mexican Revolution was preceded by a period of extensive state modernization. Mexico's president Porfirio Diaz had initiated a series of reforms that the historian Friedrich Katz has christened the "Porfirian road to modernization" (Katz 1986, 64). Diaz modernized the Mexican army along Prussian lines, making it into a career open to talents (Knight 1986, i. 18). Diaz's finance minister, José Limantour, "balanced the budget, reformed the treasury, abolished internal tariffs and overhauled the country's banking institutions" (Knight 1986, i. 23; Katz 1986, 56). All of this work required a significant augmentation of the Mexican administration. As a result the size of the state bureaucracy "greatly increased" (Katz 1986, 38). Diaz also used his power to bring Mexico's opposition press "under control" (Katz 1986, 35). Diaz's achievement was to create a "national ruling class" that ran "a strong, centralized regime" (Katz 1986, 56; Knight 1986, i. 15).

The Russian and Turkish Revolutions of the early twentieth century both followed attempts to modernize the state, though, in both cases, the state modernization was in part forced upon the old regime. In Russia, the tsars had already taken steps towards emancipating the serfs in the nineteenth century. By the early twentieth century state reforms "had managed to turn the state administration into a uniform and modern institution" (Sohrabi 1995, 1392). Russian defeat in the Russo-Japanese War and the subsequent 1905 Revolution quickened the pace of state modernization. Tsar Nicholas created the Duma, a national elected parliament, and legalized political parties and trade unions. He had at his command the largest standing army in Europe. And before the Revolution that began in October 1917 Nicholas had initiated "a major program of social reform" (Fitzpatrick 1982, 15–16, 31–6).

Sultan Abdulhamid II similarly embarked on a series of state reforms prior to the Turkish Revolution of 1908. Aware that the European powers were anxiously

---

[11] The evidence for this is laid out in Pincus (forthcoming).

awaiting the opportunity to carve up the once formidable Ottoman Empire, the sultan reluctantly but actively pursued a policy of modernization. He greatly expanded the state school system and the railway network. He initiated a wide-ranging program to modernize the Turkish army along German lines (Akmese 2005, 19–21). Prior to the Revolution of 1908, then, the Sultan "had managed to create major modernized sectors within the Ottoman military and bureaucracy, sectors that began to operate on the basis of legal/rational rules of conduct" (Sohrabi 1995, 1391).

State modernization was also a precursor to the Chinese Revolution.[12] In this case, China's defeat at the hands of the Japanese (1895), followed by the Boxer Rebellion (1899–1901), had encouraged a series of rapid and far-reaching reforms. Large sections of the military were reformed in the Western tradition. In 1905, the classical Confucian examination system was abandoned, making possible wide-ranging educational reforms. According to Jonathan Spence, "government control of the economy was also strengthened, as more state-directed but merchant-run companies were founded and the railway network was gradually extended" (1982, 90–1). In September 1906, the government proclaimed that a constitution and a further series of administrative reforms were being prepared. In early twentieth-century China, Michael Gasster concludes, all parties "were advocates of political modernization." The conflict that would soon rise to the level of revolution "concerned the form of modern government China should have and the method by which modern government should be introduced" (Gasster 1968, 75, 81).

The Iranian Revolution of 1979, so problematic for scholars who understand revolutions to be about the triumph of modernization or the ultimate victory of the peasant class, was yet another example of an ambitious state modernizer paving the road to revolution.[13] Shah Mohammad Reza Pahlavi was the architect of a thoroughgoing modernization program. His army of over 400,000 men was supplied with thoroughly modern weapons, advisers, and technologies. His vast "bureaucracy managed such diverse functions and enterprises as the oil industry, the steel industry, ports, railroads, and even atomic energy." The Shah, of course, had also fine-tuned a secret police force that was widely feared and despised (Razi 1987, 454). According to one commentator the Iranian Revolution was "a political struggle set in motion by the centralization and modernization of the state."[14] The revolutionaries were not reactionaries. They had different visions for a modern Iran. This reflected the broad base of the opposition to the Shah, including, in addition to the clergy, "the bazaar merchants, the tribes, the intellectuals, the technocrats, the students, the industrial workers, the usually timid civil servants, and in the end even a segment of the armed

---

[12] This point has been made by Skocpol as well (1979, 77).

[13] Arjomand (1988, 191). Theda Skcopol has admitted that the Iranian Revolution poses some fundamental problem for her interpretation: "Rentier state and Shi'a Islam in the Iranian Revolution," in Skocpol (1994, 240–3, 245–7).

[14] Arjomand (1988, 194). He describes the modernization program on pp. 71–4.

forces" (Razi 1987, 455–6). Even the ultimately triumphant Islamists could be said to have a vision of a modern Islamic republic.[15]

The Cuban Revolution of 1959 would at first glance appear to pose the greatest interpretative problems. Most commentators suggest that Fulgencio Batista's vulnerability stemmed in large part from his desire to deprofessionalize the army. Yet even Batista was an aggressive, if quirky, state modernizer. Batista's recipe for political survival included promoting rapid economic growth, which he fostered in part "by the state's development banks" (Domingnez 1998, 125). He had, in the view of another commentator, "embarked on an industrialization program" (O'Connor 1970, 29). Batista, who had emerged as Cuba's leading political figure in 1933, had developed an immense state bureaucracy in which one in nine Cubans was employed by the state. Of course, one element of Batista's modernizing state—as in all the other examples of state modernization—was an arm of political repression. As many as 20,000 Cubans may have been killed by the state between 1952 and 1959 (Foran 2005, 60). Fidel Castro rose to power offering an alternative vision of Cuban modernization.

Why should state modernization be a necessary step on the road to revolution? The answer is both sociostructural and ideological. State modernization necessarily brings a huge swath of people into contact with the state. Modernizing states tend to create vast new centralized bureaucracies. Tax collectors, local governors, postmasters, secret policemen all descend into the localities as never before. This new contact with the state in everyday life encourages those for whom national politics was previously distant and largely unimportant to care deeply about the state's ideological and political direction. By creating a demand for information and a means of supplying it, modernizing states create newly politicized peoples. Modernizing state institutions also employ large new sectors of the population.[16] Modernizing armies and bureaucracies not only make large groups of state employees, they educate these new employees in new methods, new world views, and, in many cases, teach them to embrace a national rather than regional or local identity. It is for this reason that many revolutions involve radical cadres from within the modernizing institutions, such as the Young Turks in early twentieth-century Turkey, or the army deserters led by the future duke of Marlborough in late seventeenth-century England. Modernizing states create new political publics.

By announcing a break with the past, modernizing states create an ideological opening. In order to explain and justify state expansion, state transformation, and the necessary intrusions in everyday life, modernizing states have to proclaim and explain their new direction. In so doing, they are compelled to concede the need for radical change. Potential revolutionaries are no longer obliged to explain to a potentially skeptical or conservative populace why change is necessary. Revolutionaries are left with the far less imposing task of explaining why the state's chosen modernization path is doomed to failure or deleterious. Modernizing states necessarily stir up

---

[15] Ali Shariati who has been called "the ideologist of the revolt" blended "Islam with modern ideas" (Keddie 2003, 200, 227). Arjomand has highlighted some modern elements of the Iranian Revolution, the establishment of the Majles, the "keen interest in technology," and "the commitment to rural development and improvement of the lot of the peasantry" (1988, 206–7).

[16] That this creates revolutionary potential seems to be the point developed by Boix (2003, 28).

wide-ranging debates about the means and ends of modernization. Modernizing states create the ideological space for a modernizing opposition.

Modernization of the old regime was not one step in an ineluctable progression to revolution. States did not necessarily modernize in response to revolutionary pressures. The Russian Romanovs and the Chinese Q'ing may have modernized their states in unsuccessful attempts to thwart revolution. But in other cases the regime was responding to other pressures. James II modernized the English state apparatus at the apex of his domestic popularity. The great state reforms proposed by Louis XVI were a response not to domestic discontent but to a perceived competitive disadvantage in the face of British power. The ambitious programs of state development embarked upon by Diaz in Mexico and Pahlavi in Iran were not counter-revolutionary programs. In both cases the agendas appear to have more to do with international status than with silencing a well-defined revolutionary opposition. State modernization projects were more likely to spawn revolutionary responses than they were to be themselves desperate attempts to react to revolutionary demands.

What are the differences between my account and previous ones? Most theorists of revolution have emphasized the creation of social movements with the potential to overthrow the old regime. I argue by contrast that the origins of revolution are to be found in the state modernization that begins within the old regime, a modernizing program that makes the old regime into a modern state. This account contrasts with that of Huntington, who claims that "revolutions are unlikely in political systems which have the capacity to expand their power and to broaden participation within the system" (1968, 275). It is precisely the state's capacity to broaden contact that creates new politicized groups. Although I share with Skocpol the view that international developments may place extreme pressure on old regimes, I do not agree with her suggestion that "the repressive state organizations of the pre-Revolutionary regime have to be weakened before mass revolutionary action can succeed" (Skocpol 1994, 241). In the English, Cuban, or Iranian cases, the repressive elements of the state were strengthening rather than weakening at the moment of the revolution. In fact, it is the expanding power of the state that often creates desperation to act before resistance becomes futile. I disagree, in turn, with Jeff Goodwin that revolutionary movements develop on the periphery of states that are "organizationally incoherent and militarily weak especially in outlying areas of society" (Goodwin 2001, 26). It is precisely the modernizing state's actions to extend its authority more deeply into society that politicize and mobilize people on the periphery. State modernization, not state breakdown—increasing state strength not impending state weakness—is a presage of revolution.

5 WHEN DOES STATE MODERNIZATION GIVE RISE TO REVOLUTION?

Of course, not all state modernization programs gave rise to revolutions. The ambitious and extensive reformulations of the state in Sweden and Denmark created more stable rather than more volatile regimes. Louis XIV pursued a remarkable program of state modernization that centralized his power, limited the possibility for judicial opposition, created a variety of new state industries, and modernized both the army and the navy. The outcome was not revolution but a golden age of French government.[17] Similarly. the Meiji Restoration in Japan (1868) "established a system of universal education, formed a modern army and navy, and recruited an efficient administrative bureaucracy both nationally and locally."[18] In this case, too, the new state was not overturned by a revolutionary movement, but rather created an effective military machine.

Why, then, did some state modernizations lead directly to revolution, while others produced a stable and efficient state? In answering this question I am on shaky ground. Because most scholars have focused on the social prerequisites for revolution, rather than on state modernization, there is not a wealth of scholarship on which to draw. The work of historians, because not usually comparative, is largely unhelpful in this regard.

The best explanation for why some modernizing regimes suffer revolution and others enjoy stability and political success is that offered by Carles Boix. "Given some uncertainty about the technology of repression in the hands of the wealthy," Boix posits, "revolutions and some forms of armed conflict should erupt with some positive probability" (2003, 93). This suggests that revolutions are more likely in situations in which the modernizing regime is not clearly perceived to have a monopoly of the forces of violence. This may happen when the modernization program has been so rapid as to create the perception of administrative weakness, as in the case of late eighteenth-century France or late seventeenth-century England. Or it may happen when the regime has proven unable to repress fledgling opposition movements, as in Cuba and China. When the modernizing state quickly demonstrates its control of resources and disarms the opposition, as in seventeenth-century Denmark and Sweden, or late nineteenth-century Japan, revolutions do not occur.

Ideology must play a role as well. Opposition groups can be silenced either by physical repression or by high levels of ideological consensus. Louis XIV was almost certainly aided in his massive modernization project by his successful self-representation as the leader who would allow France to achieve universal dominion (Burke 1992). In general when regimes are able to marshal patriotic rhetoric in such a way as to depict successfully their political opponents as enemies of the nation, they are much more likely to avoid revolution. Naturally should the patriotic language be cause or consequence of international conflict, military victory becomes essential to remaining in power. Would the Russian Revolution have happened if the tsar's armies had been victorious in the First World War?

---

[17] There has been much dispute over the nature of French absolutism in the 17th century, but most commentators agree that Louis XIV vastly increased state power in France. See Collins (1995, 79–124); Parker (1983, 118–36).

[18] Huber (1981, 1); Beasley (1990, 54–69); Norman (1975, 114–15). Huber describes the Meiji Restoration as a service revolution. However, as Beasley points out, the Meiji Restoration failed the usual standard of revolution. There was no mass popular movement, there was no new conception of time. The popular debate was not about establishing a new political order. The Meiji Restoration seems to me a classic example of thoroughgoing state modernization.

6 OPEN AND CLOSED OUTCOMES

Why did some revolutions generate relatively open regimes, while others produced more repressive, closed societies? Why did some revolutions, like the Glorious Revolution and the American Revolution, create more competitive political cultures, while the Russian and Chinese revolutions created less pluralistic regimes?

This, of course, is a modification of the classic question posed by Barrington Moore in *Social Origins of Dictatorship and Democracy*. Why, Moore asks, did some states become democracies, other states fascist, while still others became communist? The answer that Moore provides is rich in historical detail and analytical subtlety. But it can be neatly summarized. Moore suggests that in England, France, and the United States, "capitalism and democracy" was achieved "after a series of revolutions." These revolutions, Moore concludes, were "bourgeois revolutions." This is because "a vigorous and independent class of town dwellers has been an indispensable element in the growth of parliamentary democracy." "No bourgeois, no democracy," Moore crisply puts it (1966, 3–155, 413, 418). In Germany and Japan, by contrast, Moore sees the development of capitalism without democracy. Economic modernization happens in those countries without "a strong revolutionary surge" culminating ultimately in "fascism." In these cases, in contrast to England, France, and the United States, modernization was brought about by a strong "landed upper class." While Moore refers to this model of "revolution from above," he makes it clear that these are revolutions without revolutionary activity. Modernization happened without "popular revolutionary upheaval" (Moore 1966, 413, 433). The cases Moore describes in this category are what I have called state modernization projects that are not followed by revolution. Finally, communist revolutions, those that occurred in China and Russia, were revolutions that had "their main but not exclusive origins among the peasants" (Moore 1966, 413).

For all of Moore's historical sophistication and analytical acumen, his account is ultimately not persuasive. Both the French Revolution and the English Civil War were followed by periods that could hardly be called democratic. Napoleon certainly celebrated the image of the Frenchman, and he did codify French law, but Napoleon's pursuit of the old French goal of universal dominion was not based on the political support of a democratic regime. The English Civil War, which was quickly followed by the execution of Charles I in 1649, did not lead seamlessly to parliamentary democracy. Charles II and especially James II (1685–8) created a strong absolutist state that had to be overthrown by a violent popular revolution in 1688. Had Napoleon not been defeated, had James II been able to crush the revolutionaries in 1688, the path to parliamentary democracy would have been far less smooth in both countries. A strong bourgeoisie does not ineluctably produce parliamentary democracy. Nor does state transformation from above necessarily lead to fascism. Both Denmark and Sweden experienced state modernization led by an absolutist king. Yet, both countries are now more closely associated with social democracy than fascism. One is left persuaded that there are some basic truths in Moore's analysis but that the argument depends heavily on feats of historical gymnastics.[19]

An alternative answer to the question of why some revolutions give rise to more democratic regimes while others give rise to more authoritarian ones has been advanced by Hannah Arendt. For Arendt, the reason why the French Revolution ultimately followed "a disastrous course" while the American Revolution created a democratic society had everything to do with the aims of the revolutionaries (1963, 215). From "the later stages of the French Revolution up to the revolutions of our own time," laments Arendt, "it appeared to revolutionary men more important to change the fabric of society... than to change the structure of the political realm" (1963, 25). Revolutions focused on social rather than political questions inevitably produced authoritarian regimes. This was because, as in the French Revolution, the revolutionary energy was diverted away from attention to freedom. "The direction of the French Revolution was deflected almost from its beginning from this course of foundation [of freedom] through the immediacy of suffering," Arendt posits, "it was determined by the exigencies of liberation not from tyranny but from necessity." It was this logic, according to Arendt, that "helped in the unleashing of a stream of boundless violence" (1963, 92).

Arendt's explanation for the varying political outcomes of revolution is even more pessimistic than Moore's. Like Moore, Arendt relates her outcomes to "Historical stages" (Moore 1966, 414). Whereas Moore suggests that the democratic and fascist stages have passed, Arendt posits that ever since the French Revolution, revolution-aries have sought to remedy social rather than political problems. Nevertheless, there are significant historical problems with Arendt's analysis. Social issues *were* part and parcel of England's Glorious Revolution, the revolution that paved the way for parliamentary democracy. That social issues played a prominent role in England's later seventeenth-century revolution is hardly surprising since it was John Locke (1632–1704) who, in Arendt's view, invented the central idea of social revolutionaries: the notion that "labour and toil" were not the activities "to which poverty con-demned those were without property," but "were, on the contrary, the source of all wealth" (Arendt 1963, 23). Locke's notion that labor created property made wealth potentially infinite; therefore it would be humanly possible to eliminate poverty. It was precisely this ideology that motivated many of the revolutionaries of 1688–9 to transform England from an agrarian to a manufacturing society, from a society bounded by limited raw materials to a society fueled by the limitless possibilities of human creation (Pincus 2005). Even more damaging for Arendt's argument is the fact that her quintessential political revolution, the American Revolution, had a social dimension. Tim Breen's recent work has placed the "consumer boycott" at the center of his account of the American Revolution. "The American Revolution

---

[19] Boix has modified Moore's argument by distinguishing political outcomes in weakly industrialized and strongly industrialized countries (Boix 2003, 40). While I find Boix's argument more analytically satisfying, and I share his enthusiasm for resuscitating the questions posed by modernization theorists, he is asking a fundamentally broader question than I am. He is asking about "democratic transitions;" I am asking more narrowly why some revolutions give rise to more democratic regimes, and why others give rise to more authoritarian ones.

was," Breen argues, "the first large-scale political movement to organize itself around the relation of ordinary people to manufactured consumer goods" (2004, pp. xvi–xviii). Colonial subjects in North America were turned into revolutionaries when British taxes deprived them of the consumer goods that had made them feel civilized. Social questions were at the heart of the concerns of America's revolutionaries.

Why then did some revolutions create democratic states while others gave birth to authoritarian societies? The answer, I suspect, has a great deal to do with economic structures of the societies in which the revolutions took place. The French Revolution, like all other revolutions, as Tocqueville noted, "created an atmosphere of missionary fervor and, indeed, assumed all the aspects of religious revival" (1983, 12–13). Revolutionaries are certain of their own position. They voluntarily brook no compromises. Faced with political resistance, revolutionaries left to their own devices are willing to force people to be free. However, when the revolutionary states are economically dependent on foreign trade for their survival, these states are in turn dependent on the merchant communities. Merchant communities demand free flows of information to conduct their trade, and are thus hostile to authoritarian regimes that monopolize information. It was the economic and political clout of the foreign trading communities, I suspect, that prevented England after 1688 and the United States in the early national period from adopting one-party rule. In states that were relatively economically self-sufficient—France under Napoleon, China, and the Soviet Union—relatively authoritarian regimes with a single dominant party triumphed. Iran has been able to remain a closed society because of the state's control of the vast oil revenues. Cuba, though not economically self-sufficient, was a special case. In its formative years the Castro regime was able to depend on a single trading partner, the Soviet Union.

In a sense, I am offering a refinement of Barrington Moore's thesis. It is not so much that the lack of a bourgeoisie means no democracy. Iran had a robust bourgeoisie, Cuba a significant one. Rather, unless the survival of the state depends on the economic activities of the bourgeoisie—especially those involved in foreign trade—there will be no democracy. Because revolutionary states have a tendency towards missionary zeal, they find it difficult to accommodate ideological opposition. Democracy persists only when the state has insufficient resources to survive unless it negotiates with the bourgeoisie and international economic interests. It is not the size or quality of the bourgeoisie that matters. It is their economic power. Scholars interested in explaining the political outcomes of revolutions should focus less on the class composition of the revolutionary society, and more on the financial structure of the state within that society.

7 CONCLUSION

The methodological and interpretative stakes in the analysis I have been tracing are profound. If state modernization is a prerequisite for revolution, then scholars have been asking the wrong sorts of questions. Instead of offering a bewildering set of causal factors that trigger revolutions,[20] or as in the older literature a broad menu of preconditions and precipitants,[21] scholars should disaggregate the study of revolutions into three separate questions. First, why did states modernize? Here, it seems to me the kind of analysis of the international context proposed by Skocpol is most useful. Second, why did some modernizing states and not others undergo revolutions? The answer to this question is still not well understood. Third, why did revolutions that pitted competing models of the modern state against one another have different political outcomes? Again, this is an important question to which the answers are not well known. The smorgasbord of causal factors offered by students of revolution fails to distinguish among these questions. I suspect that the answer to the first question has very much to do with the international political context, the second has much to do with the ideological and economic resources of the state, and the third is best answered by understanding the degree to which the country in question can achieve economic self-sufficiency.[22]

Whatever the answers to these questions, I have shown that the prevailing models for explaining revolutions have wrongly assumed that revolutions occur when an old regime is incapable of adjusting to changed circumstances. Instead, I show, revolutions happen only when the old regime commits itself to state modernization. "One of the most evident uniformities we can record," offers Crane Brinton almost as an afterthought in his preliminary discussion, "is the effort made in each of our societies to reform the machinery of government" (1938, 39). Similarly, in her analysis of the Russian Revolution, Sheila Fitzpatrick concludes that "there was progress" in the political realm before 1917. "But," she suggests, that very progress "contributed a great deal to the society's instability and likelihood of political upheaval: the more rapidly a society changes (whether that change is perceived as progressive or regressive) the less stable it is likely to be" (1982, 16). These historical insights should inform the way we think about revolutions. Revolutions are not struggles to overturn traditional states. They occur only after regimes have determined, for whatever reasons, to initiate ambitious modernization programs. Revolutions, then, pit different groups of modernizers against one another.

References

AKMESE, H. N. 2005. *The Birth of Modern Turkey*. London: I. B. Tauris.
ARENDT, H. 1963. *On Revolution*. London: Penguin Books.

---

[20] This approach was pioneered by Thomas Paine (1796, 33). It has continued through the work of Foran (2005, 18).

[21] That literature is summarized and critically reviewed by Stone (1966, 164 ff).

[22] I should emphasize that the primary contribution of this essay is not to provide definitive analytical solutions. My method here is necessarily speculative. But, I hope by redefining and disaggregating the important questions surrounding the causes and consequences of revolutions to make it possible to arrive at some more definitive answers. Those answers, I insist, must make sense of the gamut of revolutions from the Glorious Revolution of 1688–9 to the Iranian Revolution of 1979 and beyond.

ARJOMAND, S. A. 1988. *The Turban for the Crown*. Oxford: Oxford University Press.

BEASLEY, W. G. 1990. *The Rise of Modern Japan*. London: Weidenfeld and Nicolson.

BLACKSTONE, W. 1765–9. *Commentaries on the Laws of England*. Oxford: Clarendon Press.

BOIX, C. 2003. *Democracy and Redistribution*. Cambridge: Cambridge University Press.

BREEN, T. H. 2004. *The Marketplace of Revolution*. Oxford: Oxford University Press.

BRINTON, C. 1938. *The Anatomy of Revolution*. New York: W. W. Norton & Co.

BURKE, P. 1992. *The Fabrication of Louis XIV*. New Haven: Yale University Press.

BURNET, G. 1681. *The History of the Reformation of the Church of England*, part I, 2nd edn. London: T. H. for Richard Chiswell.

COLLINS, J. B. 1995. *The State in Early Modern France*. Cambridge: Cambridge University Press.

DOMINGUEZ, J. 1998. The Batista regime in Cuba. Pp. 113–31 in *Sultanistic Regimes*, ed. H. E. Chehabi and J. J. Linz. Baltimore: Johns Hopkins University Press.

FITZPATRICK, S. 1982. *The Russian Revolution*. Oxford: Oxford University Press.

FORAN, J. 2005. *Taking Power: The Origins of Third World Revolutions*. Cambridge: Cambridge University Press.

GASSTER, M. 1968. Reform and revolution in China's political modernization. In *China's Revolution*, ed. M. C. Wright. New Haven: Yale University Press.

GEYL, P. 1939. *Orange and Stuart 1641–1672*, trans. A. Pomerans. New York: Charles Scribner's Sons.

GOLDSTONE, J. A. 1991. *Revolution and Rebellion in the Early Modern World*. Berkeley and Los Angeles: University of California Press.

GOODWIN, J. 2001. *No Other Way Out*. Cambridge: Cambridge University Press.

HILL, C. 1961. *The Century of Revolution*. Edinburgh: Thomas Nelson and Sons.

HUBER, T. M. 1981. *The Revolutionary Origins of Modern Japan*. Stanford, Calif.: Stanford University Press.

HUNTINGTON, S. 1968. *Political Order in Changing Societies*. New Haven: Yale University Press.

ISRAEL, J. I. 1995. *The Dutch Republic: Its Rise, Greatness and Fall 1477–1806*. Oxford: Clarendon Press.

JESPERSEN, K. 1994. *History of Denmark*, trans. I. Hill. Houndmills: Palgrave.

JOHNSON, C. 1966. *Revolutionary Change*. Boston: Little, Brown & Co.

KAPLAN, S. L. 1995. *Farewell, Revolution: The Historians' Feud: France, 1789/1989*. Ithaca, NY: Cornell University Press.

KATZ, F. 1986. Mexico: restored republic and Porfiriato, 1867–1910. Ch. 1 in *Cambridge History of Latin America*, vol. v, ed. L. Bethell. Cambridge: Cambridge University Press.

KEDDIE, N. R. 2003. *Modern Iran: Roots and Results of Revolution*. New Haven: Yale University Press.

KNIGHT, A. 1986. *The Mexican Revolution*. Cambridge: Cambridge University Press.

KRAMNICK, I. 1972. Reflections on revolution. *History and Theory*, 11 (1): 26–63.

LIVESEY, J. 2001. *Making Democracy in the French Revolution*. Cambridge, Mass.: Harvard University Press.

LUCAS, C. 1973. Nobles, bourgeois and the origins of the French Revolution. *Past and Present*, 60: 84–126.

LYNCH, J. 1989. *Bourbon Spain 1700–1808*. Oxford: Basil Blackwell.

MARX, K. 1973. The East India Company. In *Karl Marx: Surveys from Exile, Political Writings*, vol. ii, ed. D. Fernbach. London: Penguin Books.

MOLESWORTH, R. 1692. *Account of Denmark*. London: Timothy Goodwin.

MOORE, B., Jr. 1966. *Social Origins of Dictatorship and Democracy*. Boston: Beacon Press.

NORMAN, E. H. 1975. *Origins of the Modern Japanese State*. New York: Pantheon Books.

O'CONNOR, J. 1970. *The Origins of Socialism in Cuba*. Ithaca, NY: Cornell University Press.

PAINE, T. 1792. *Rights of Man*. London.

——1796. *The Decline and Fall of the English System of Finance*, 2nd American edn. New York.

PARKER, D. 1983. *The Making of French Absolutism*. London: Edward Arnold.

PINCUS, S. C. A. 2005. Whigs, political economy and the Revolution of 1688–89. In *Cultures of Whiggism*, ed. D. Womersley. Newark: University of Delaware Press.

——2006. *England's Glorious Revolution 1688–89*. Boston: Bedford/St Martin's.

——Forthcoming. *The First Modern Revolution*. New Haven: Yale University Press.

PRICE, R. 1784. *Observations on the Importance of the American Revolution*. London.

RAZI, G. H. 1987. The nexus of legitimacy and performance: the lessons of the Iranian Revolution. *Comparative Politics*, 19 (4): 453–69.

ROBERTS, M. 1967. *Essays in Swedish History*. London: Weidenfeld and Nicolson.

ROWEN, H. H. 1978. *John de Witt, Grand Pensionary of Holland, 1625–1672*. Princeton: Princeton University Press.

SKOCPOL, T. 1979. *States and Social Revolutions*. New York: Cambridge University Press.

——1994. *Social Revolutions in the Modern World*. Cambridge: Cambridge University Press.

SOHRABI, N. 1995. Historicizing revolutions. *American Journal of Sociology*, 100 (6): 1383–447.

SPANG, R. 2003. Paradigms and paranoia: how modern is the French Revolution? *American Historical Review*, 108 (1): 119–47.

SPENCE, J. D. 1982. *The Gate of Heavenly Peace*. London: Penguin Books.

STONE, L. 1966. Theories of revolution. *World Politics*, 18 (2): 159–76.

TILLY, C. 1973. Does modernization breed revolution? *Comparative Politics*, 5 (3): 425–47.

TOCQUEVILLE, A. DE 1983. *The Old Regime and the French Revolution*, trans. S. Gilbert. New York: Anchor Books.

UPTON, A. F. 1998. *Charles XI and Swedish Absolutism*. Cambridge: Cambridge University Press.

CHAPTER 18

....

CIVIL WARS

....

STATHIS N. KALYVAS

1 WHAT IS A CIVIL WAR AND WHY STUDY IT?

....

WHEN domestic political conflict takes the form of military confrontation or armed combat we speak of civil war. This is a destructive development: the mean number of deaths in the 146 civil wars that took place between 1945 and 1999 is 143,883 (Sambanis 2004b). Besides direct fatalities, civil war causes many more indirect ones through mass dislocation, epidemics, famines, and the degradation of the state apparatus. Economic costs are also massive, both directly and indirectly. Economic development is stalled or, even, reversed.

Civil war is a phenomenon prone to serious semantic confusion, even contestation. The description of a conflict as a civil war carries symbolic and political weight since the term can confer or deny legitimacy to a warring party. Indeed the very use (or not) of the term is part of the conflict itself. This is why euphemisms are so common. Civil war is often described through such terms as *Troubles*, *Emergency*, or *Situation*, while rebels are typically described as bandits or, more recently, terrorists (and some civil wars are presented as being instances of the "war on terror"). This sort of semantic and political contestation accounts, in great part, for the fact that the systematic study of civil wars is a rather recent development.

Besides the effects of political contestation, the study of civil war suffered from conceptual competition by cognate phenomena such as revolution and ethnic conflict. Until recently, the study of revolutions was privileged by researchers. This may have reflected a normative preference, or at least sympathy, for social revolutions, whereas civil war is hardly held as a desirable outcome. In the early 1990s, the

* I am grateful for helpful comments and suggestions by Ana Arjona, Laia Balcells, Nicholas Sambanis, Elisabeth Wood, and the volume's editors.

violence that broke out following the break-up of the Soviet Union and Yugoslavia caused renewed focus on "ethnic conflict." The realization that both social revolution and ethnic conflict were part of a broader concept, formerly known as rebellion and now defined as civil war, ushered in a new era of research in the mid-1990s. It is commonplace to state that the study of civil war by political scientists has since boomed. It is much less commonplace, however, to ask why this boom has occurred in the first place.

The boom in the study of civil war has three sources. First, development econo-mists specializing in the study of African economies and funded primarily by the World Bank sought to make the case that civil war was a major impediment of economic development. Second, the quasi-disappearance of interstate wars led scholars of international relations and international security specializing in the study of war to shift their focus to the one instance of war practiced today, namely civil war. Third, the resurgence of ethnic conflict during the early post-Cold War years led students of ethnicity, including sociologists and comparativist political scientists, to focus on all types of intrastate conflict, rather than ethnic conflicts alone.

These three "sources" of interest in civil war correspond to three roughly distinct styles of research: an economics, an international relations (IR), and a comparativist style. While recognizing the complexity of the issue and acknowledging that the causes of civil wars are multiple, economists have primarily stressed the impact of natural resources, IR scholars have pointed to ethnic antagonism, and comparativists have focused on state capacity.

Several definitions of civil war exist, but they converge around the same key dimensions of the phenomenon. Civil war can be defined as armed combat taking place within the boundaries of a recognized sovereign entity between parties subject to a common authority at the outset of the hostilities (Kalyvas 2006). This definition stresses two key features: the militarization of conflict, requiring at least two com-peting sides (including a relatively large rebel organization with military equipment and full-time recruits) and differentiating civil war from communal riots, terrorism, crime, and genocide; and a domestic challenge directed against the authority of the current holder of sovereign authority, which distinguishes it from interstate war.[1] In fact *internal war* (Eckstein 1965) would be a more precise term, but civil war is the dominant term because of its common usage.

Definitional consensus conceals considerable disagreement about operationaliza-tion and, hence, divergence in coding practices. A major issue is the definition of internal conflicts crossing the threshold of war. Studies have relied on various fatality thresholds, primarily inspired by the coding rules used in the first major dataset of wars, the Correlates of War (COW), which is also the basis on which most subse-quent datasets were built. Disagreements include whether fatality counts are absolute

---

[1] The size of the rebel organization may vary but cannot be reduced to a few dozens of clandestine combatants.

or relative ("per capita"), whether they are cumulative over time or yearly, whether fatalities include battle-related deaths only or civilian deaths only (or both), and the distribution of fatalities between competing sides. Coding decisions are crucial in determining the onset and termination of civil wars and distinguishing between a single ongoing but intermittent war or a succession of several distinct ones. The problem is exacerbated by inconsistencies in coding within the same datasets, problematic categories (e.g. "extra-systemic wars"), and the well-known unreliability of fatality data from civil wars: most civil wars take place in impoverished countries where record-keeping bureaucracies are lacking. There is also debate about the usefulness of relying on a dichotomous characterization (war versus peace) versus a continuous conceptualization that would better capture intensity levels, and whether civil war is an independent phenomenon (conceptually speaking) as opposed to being a single "value" of the larger phenomenon of political violence.

2 MACRO FINDINGS AND DEBATES

The main method used to identify the determinants of civil war is the statistical analysis of data on all country-years since 1945. The pool of independent variables that have been identified as potential determinants of civil war onset includes the level of economic development, political instability, ethnic heterogeneity, the presence of plentiful natural resources, a history of conflicts, war-prone and undemocratic neighbors, high infant mortality, small military establishments, political regimes that are neither dictatorships nor democracies ("anocracies"), mountainous terrain, large population, diasporas, oil production, and various geographic and time effects (the Middle East and North Africa and the 1960s turn out to be significant). Several econometric models have identified a number of factors as potential determinants of civil war onset. Collier et al. (2003, 53–4) summarize a great part of the findings in the following way: "Countries with low, stagnant, and unequally distributed per capita incomes that have remained dependent on primary commodities for their exports face dangerously high risks of prolonged conflict. In the absence of economic development neither good political institutions, nor ethnic and religious homogeneity, nor high military spending provide significant defenses against large-scale violence. Once a country has stumbled into conflict powerful forces—the conflict trap—tend to lock it into a syndrome of further conflict."

For all its succinctness, this statement conceals several disagreements of emphasis and interpretation. The effect and interpretation of natural resources, geography, ethnic heterogeneity, regime type, inequality, or diasporas has been widely debated (Cederman 2004; Sambanis 2001). Divergence between econometric specifications, estimation methods, measurement procedures, and datasets makes it very hard to evaluate in a definitive way the effect of each variable and arrive at a definitive theory of civil war onset.[2] Endogeneity remains a major concern. Unfortunately, the identification of instruments remains either extremely difficult or limited, both chronologically and geographically (Miguel, Satyanath, and Sergenti 2004). Perhaps more importantly, several competing and observationally equivalent underlying causal mechanisms account for the observed effect of perhaps the most important variable, poverty. To mention just two, poverty is consistent with both low opportunity costs for joining a rebellion and high grievances and desire for social redress—i.e. opportunity and intention to rebel.

Nevertheless, it is possible to bundle different sets of variables into three types of theoretical arguments, loosely linked to the three styles of analysis outlined above. The story told by international relations scholars stresses ethnic heterogeneity, development economists emphasize the role of natural resources; and comparativist scholars point to the role of state capacity. According to the first version, civil war is primarily an expression of nationalist aspirations and ethnic disputes; the second version stresses civil war as a phenomenon taking place in countries that suffer the curse of plentiful natural resources, and the third one points to weak states as the main prediction of civil war.

Disputes between ethnic groups and nationalism figure prominently in the descriptive and theoretical literature but occupy a minor place in the recent econometric one. Various scholars (Wimmer and Min 2006; Toft 2003; Sambanis 2001; Posen 1993) have pointed at the role of ethnic divisions in leading to civil war. Their arguments focus on (ethnic) group dynamics and group demographies. There are at least three stylized stories (and likely several more). According to the first one, state collapse creates a "security dilemma:" in the absence of a state conflict uncertainty about the intentions of the other group inevitably leads to conflict. Since neither group knows the other's intentions, each has an incentive to build up defensive capabilities to protect itself from an attack by the other group. However, since most defensive capabilities can be used offensively, defensive build-up can appear as signaling aggressive intentions (Posen 1993; Water 1997). According to the second one, civil war is caused by a "commitment problem" that arises when two groups find themselves without a third party that can credibly guarantee agreements between them (Fearon 1998). The third story argues that civil war is caused by ethnic secessionists wishing to carve their own separate state via their capacity to articulate a military challenge based on existing ethnic networks reinforced by patterns of (ethnic) population concentration in specific territory (Toft 2003). Using a global dataset including fixed geographical territories from 1816 to 2001 independent of the political entity in control of the territory in a specific year, Wimmer and Min (2006) expand this last argument over time and find that both interstate and civil war are closely related to the twin transformations of the rise of empires and the rise of nation-states. They also find that the rise of nation-states is related to civil war onset

---

[2] Furthermore, in his comparison of several influential datasets, Sambanis 2004*b* finds that most findings are not robust.

through political discrimination along ethnic lines and the subsequent demand of new ethnically homogeneous states.

These arguments have been found wanting by the econometric literature because the main indicator used to capture ethnic antagonism, the ethnolinguistic fractionalization index (ELF), tends to be statistically insignificant. However, the jury is still out for a number of reasons. First, ELF has been credibly criticized as inherently problematic (Posner 2004) and unable to capture (or even misrepresenting) the subtle channels through which ethnicity results in civil wars at best. Second, Sambanis (2001) claims that ethnicity should predict the causes of ethnic civil wars, not all civil wars—and argues that once this is taken into account, ethnicity is a predictor of the ethnic civil war onset. Third, it is argued that the relevant indicator is ethnic polarization rather than ethnic fragmentation. Montalvo and Reynal-Querol (2005) show that while ethnic fragmentation is an insignificant factor in civil war, ethnic polarization is highly significant. In a similar vein, Cederman and Girardin (2006) argue, and present some evidence to the effect, that the effect of ethnicity should operate through the channel of ethnic minority rule.[3] Fourth, existing ethnicity indicators have been criticized as over-aggregate. Buhaug, Cederman, and Rød (2006) are presently geo-coding ethnic demographies to produce a better index of ethnicity on the ground. Sambanis and Milanovic (2006) have been, likewise, at work to produce data using region-years as opposed to country-years.

A more general and theoretical criticism of the effect of ethnicity is that the concept of ethnic conflict is in itself flawed and that ethnicity is constructed and quite mutable (the "constructivist" claim). This is not to deny that ethnicity plays a part in conflict but that it is insufficient to look at the presence of groups (ethnic, religious, sectarian, etc.) to explain the onset of conflict, because the salience of ethnic identities can be itself the result of the conflict. In other words, the salience of ethnicity and the animosity between ethnic groups may be an outcome of the conflict rather than its cause.

Turning to the second argument, Paul Collier et al. (2003; also Collier and Hoeffler 2004) stress the effect of abundant natural resources. While poverty reduces opportunity costs for participation in rebellion, natural resources allow the financing of rebellion which may start with political aims but eventually becomes criminal organizations. The stylized story underlying these findings should be familiar to students of African politics: impoverished countries with large reserves of natural resources (particularly diamonds and oil) generate incentives for rebellion; once rebellion is on, it sustains itself precisely from these resources. Unemployed individuals participate in insurgency primarily driven by the prospect of loot.

The problems with this argument include the proxy used to capture the effect of natural resources (i.e. primary commodity exports), the opaqueness of underlying mechanisms, the lack of empirical validation for the microfoundations posited, and the theoretical assumption informing this research program (Cramer 2002).

---

[3] But see Fearon, Kasara, and Laitin (2006) for counter-evidence.

Humphreys (2005) points to a host of competing mechanisms underlying the correlation between primary commodities and civil war onset:[4] greedy rebels; greedy outsiders (natural resources as an incentive for foreign corporations and states to engage in or even foster the conflict); grievances (dependence on natural resources may cause inequality, vulnerability to trade shocks, processes of social dislocation such as forced migration, and unfair distribution of natural resources); insurgency financing; weakening of states through the "resource curse;" sparse networks. Likewise, Ross (2006) catalogs a host of additional problems of measurement error, spuriousness, endogeneity, and lack of robustness. To cite just one, it may be that poor property rights or weak rule of law cause both dependence on natural resources (through dissuasion of investment in other sectors) and civil war. Collier and Hoeffler (2004, 567) recognize the problems of observational equivalence when they point out that "primary commodities are associated with other characteristics that may cause civil war, such as poor public service provision, corruption and economic mismanagement... Potentially, any increase in conflict risk may be due to rebel responses to such poor governance rather than to financial opportunities." Qualitative studies have also pointed to the many pitfalls of assuming rather than researching causal mechanisms. For instance, Gutierrez (2004) shows that given the lack of material selective incentives, the sanctions against plundering, and the harsh demands that the Colombian FARC imposes on its members, this group does not fit the "criminal rebels" thesis despite its strong dependence on an illicit natural resource, coca. A related problem is the tendency that characterizes this line of research, of extrapolating insights and intuitions from contemporary African civil wars to the full set of civil wars, past and present.

In response to these criticisms there have been several attempts to disaggregate natural resources. For example, Lujala, Gleditsch, and Gillmore (2005) propose indicators of natural resources endowment that distinguish lootable from non-lootable natural resources; they specifically distinguish between two types of diamonds (primary or non-lootable and secondary or lootable) and test whether they are diversely associated with civil war onset and incidence. Ross (2006) follows a similar disaggregation course. He constructs more accurate and exogenous measures of oil, diamond, and other mineral wealth, distinguishing non-fuel rents per capita, fuel onshore rents per capita, fuel offshore rents per capita, primary diamonds production per capita, and secondary diamonds production per capita. Results, however, remain inconclusive.

Last, a third story points to the role of (repressive) state capacity, as proxied by GDP per capita, along with conditions favoring rural insurgency, as proxied by an indicator of mountainous terrain (Fearon and Laitin 2003). Both grievances and greed may motivate leaders and followers, but unless they are able to exploit the weakness of the state, they are unable to translate their preferences into civil war. In other words, potential insurgent leaders are more likely to launch rebellions when

---

[4] Including the two mechanisms proposed by Collier et al. (greedy rebels and insurgency financing).

they have a better chance of success. One such condition is a state's inability to fund sufficient police and administrative presence in its hinterlands. The stylized story is one of weak states that police mountainous peripheries poorly and, when rebellions erupt, badly. If a limited rebellion erupts and the state responds with indiscriminate violence, it may feed it rather than stop it. More generally, Fearon and Laitin (2003, 88) have argued that the civil wars of the post-1945 period have structural roots, in the combination of the military technology of guerrilla warfare and decolonization, which created an international system numerically dominated by fragile states with limited administrative control of their peripheries. Hironaka (2005) provides a similar account, stressing the long-term effects of decolonization. Like the previous arguments, this one faces the problem of assuming, through the statistical significance of a "mountainous terrain" indicator, rather than demonstrating its causal mechanism. As pointed out above, poverty can be an indicator of greed, grievance, and state capacity.

Furthermore, GDP per capita is highly correlated with variables, such as population density or urbanization, which may account for both the weakness of counterinsurgent effort and low state capacity (Kocher 2004). The interpretation of the "rough terrain" variable as signaling low state capacity is also open to questioning since it remains unclear whether countries with rough terrain experience civil wars in precisely those areas (Sambanis 2004a).

Obviously, these three arguments do not exhaust the theoretical accounts of civil war onset. Though presently unfashionable, grievances also attract theoretical and empirical attention (Regan and Norton 2005). Various accounts of grievance have been proposed. Boix (2004) finds that civil wars are caused by a combination of inequality and capital mobility, while Gurr (1970) argued in the past that relative deprivation through the mechanism of rising expectations, rather than inequality and poverty, causes rebellion and revolutions. Obviously, the problems with grievances as a determinant of civil war onset is that they seem to be much more prevalent than civil war and that they are very hard to measure directly. Ultimately, it is difficult to escape the conjecture that one has to look for combinations of demand for, and supply of, rebellion (or intention and opportunity).

To illustrate some of the complexities in figuring out and sorting out competing causal mechanisms, I discuss below the issue of the relation between a country's rural dimension and civil war onset.

3 THE RURAL DIMENSION

Civil war is associated with a social dimension that is poorly understood and inadequately studied: the rural dimension. Poor societies tend to be rural and insurgencies tend to begin and are fought primarily in the rural countryside (Tong 1991; Brustein and Levi 1987). In contrast, the types of political violence experienced by developed Western democracies tend to take the form of terrorism in primarily urban settings. Mass ethnic riots seem to be an outlier in this respect as they seem to affect primarily urban areas of poor countries (Varshney 2003; Wilkinson 2004).

However, the causal salience of the rural dimension is simultaneously consistent with several causal mechanisms of civil war onset, including grievances resulting from unequal land distribution, worsening land distribution, or crop failure; the ability of insurgents to hide among rural populations without being denounced because of local norms of solidarity and honor; higher levels of tolerance among rural people to threats of violence; a tradition of peripheral rebellion reinforced by norms of reciprocity which leads to mass participation in anti-state activities ranging from contraband smuggling and banditry to full-fledged rebellion; the fact that an economy based on subsistence farming tends to favor armed resistance more than one based on wage labor, and a pattern of human ecology whereby the dispersion of population settlements in rural environments impedes policing: it is easier to enforce a curfew in a town than in a large rural area because taxing and monitoring hundreds, or even thousands, of hamlets exposes small army detachments to ambush (Kitson 1960, 12; Escott and Crow 1986, 376; Gambetta 1993, 109; Tone 1994, 162–6; Nordstrom 1997, 99; Horton 1998, 126; Kocher 2004).

A large literature developed mostly in the 1970s, but currently marginalized, has addressed the politics of mass rural rebellion. It is primarily structural, in that it seeks to link forms of ownership and land distribution to the emergence of large-scale peasant rebellion, though some authors have focused on local and individual micro-mechanisms (Stinchcombe 1961; Moore 1966; Wolf 1973; Paige 1978; Popkin 1979; Anderson 1993). According to Scott (1976), peasants rebel motivated by grievances originated in a combination of economic and political structural conditions; peasant behavior is thought to be determined by a set of values related to the right of subsistence and the right and duty of reciprocity that are rooted in the "existential situation" that peasants face. One prediction of this literature is that countries with large numbers of landless peasants, be they agricultural workers or sharecroppers, are likely to spawn violent political unrest. A contradictory prediction is that small landowners may be the source of violent agitation. There are many variations pointing to particular groups such as squatters or migrants (Anderson 1994). Finally, some arguments point to crop types as the relevant dimension. An intriguing implication is that globalization can exacerbate rural conflict by setting wealthy tariff-protected farmers from the West against poor peasants of the developing world (Kirschenmann 2003).

Theorization of the relation between inequality (in general) and violence has a long tradition, but only recently has there been some, admittedly broad, empirical testing of this conjecture (Boix 2003). The evidence is mixed. On the one hand, land property patterns are very hard to measure and are, therefore, usually excluded from econometric studies; on the other hand, the case study evidence is inconclusive (Wood 2003; Wickham-Crowley 1992).

State capacity arguments assume that the rural dimension proxies for processes primarily related to irregular war rather than pre-war grievances. Rural areas tend to be difficult to police in the first place, which is why insurgencies are likely to be concentrated there. Though grievances may still matter, they cannot result in violent mobilization alone because they are likely to be repressed. Put otherwise, state repression is off the equilibrium path.

This insight allows the reinterpretation of some findings that take ideology or ethnicity as the main causal variables of violence. For example, Gulden (2002) finds that in Guatemala over half of the army killings took place in municipalities in which the Mayas made up between 80 and 90 percent of the population; based in part on this finding, he claims that this instance of mass violence constitutes genocide. However, these municipalities are mostly rural and located far from centers of government control. They could have just as easily been targeted because they were located in areas of guerrilla presence as because they were Mayan. This raises the issue of endogeneity of grievances: did the guerrillas pick their location based on the presence of Maya grievances or did they educate the Mayas who just happened to live in terrain that favored insurgent activity about their plight? Empirical evidence supplied by Stoll (1993, 87) allows a partial separation of the two: the army's repression did not focus on areas where indigenous organizations (and presumably grievances) were strong but guerrillas had little presence, but rather in areas where the guerrillas were trying to organize despite weak indigenous organizations. In fact, the four areas of greatest government violence follow the insurgents' swath as it moved south to cut the Pan-American Highway. Trejo (2004) provides additional fine-grained evidence from Mexico, linking the action of the Catholic Church among indigenous communities and the Zapatista insurgency.

An important insight from in-depth studies that goes in a similar direction is that geography may trump pre-war allegiances—an insight that would question the grievances causal mechanism. For example, during the American Civil War, Confederate guerrillas were strong in the Appalachians, the Cumberlands, and the Ozarks—in the very areas within the Confederacy which most Union sympathizers inhabited (Beckett 2001, 11); following their defeat in the cities, the Chinese communists staged a comeback from backward and isolated "border areas" where their pre-war support was minimal if not non-existent (Schran 1976); the urban populations in the German-occupied Soviet territories were more likely than rural ones to dislike the occupying authorities, partly because of their closer earlier identification with the Soviet regime and partly because of the more miserable conditions of life and work in the towns; yet, "paradoxically, the partisan movement was largely a rural phenomenon" (Dallin, Mavrogordato, and Moll 1964, 335). The French communist FTP guerrillas were very successful in the rural areas that exhibited very limited pre-war communist support (Kedward 1993, 131). Likewise, the Renamo insurgency against the Frelimo government in Mozambique developed in the same areas where the Frelimo anticolonial insurgency had been strong; in contrast, areas that supported the Portuguese incumbents during the anticolonial war tended to side with the Frelimo incumbents during the Renamo insurgency (Nordstrom 1997, 98–9; Geffray 1990, 41). A high-ranking American officer serving in the Dominican Republic in 1921 argued that the construction of roads would stifle the insurgency: "A highway would bring the people more in contact with the Capital, thus giving the Central Government an opportunity to control political conditions" (in Calder 1984, 164).

Further confirming the importance of military resources in generating control and hence collaboration is the oft-noted propensity of villages located near central roads to collaborate with incumbents (Sansom 1970, 60–1; Kriger 1992, 208). Whereas "modernizing" villages near main roads in Vietnam had been among the first to respond to revolutionary appeals, they were also more likely to be controlled by the government and "as the risks of political action escalated during the middle and late 1960s, the gap between political attitudes and behavior widened, and many revolutionary sympathizers became inactive when the dangers became too great or, in some cases, adopted a clandestine role so deeply hidden that it often amounted to a temporary cessation of revolutionary activities" (Elliott 2003, 589). The availability of external support for insurgents turns the combination of terrain and proximity to borders into a strong predictor of insurgent control, especially when it comes to ethnic insurgencies (Toft 2003).

The Nicaraguan case allows a type of natural experiment, insofar as it is possible to compare the behavior of the Sandinistas in their successive roles as insurgents and, later, as incumbents. This comparison suggests that popular allegiances were often endogenous to the exercise of territorial control. During the "contra" phase of the war, the (incumbent) Sandinistas firmly controlled the towns but were absent from the mountains: "The only Sandinista presence in the mountains would be a military one" (Horton 1998, 137). As a result, people in those areas supported the contras. In contrast, many mountainous zones, which now collaborated with the contras, had supported the Sandinista guerrillas in the 1970s, even when they were urban activists who had fled the cities for the countryside (1998, 21–2). The opposite is true of the towns, which were controlled by the (Somozista) incumbents in the first phase of the war and the Sandinista (incumbents) in the second one. In Horton's (1998, 21) words: "Hundreds of Sandinista Army soldiers were stationed in the town of Quilalí and *as a result* the town itself always remained firmly under FSLN control" (emphasis mine). In other words, whereas the Sandinistas *qua insurgents* based themselves in inaccessible rural terrain, they found themselves limited to cities when, *qua incumbents*, they faced the contra insurgency.

The issues illustrated by the discussion point to the importance of studying closely the interaction of military, social, and political dynamics of civil wars. At the same time, it is important to recognize that even if individual civil wars can be bundled under the same conceptual category, there may be significant differences between subcategories. For example, Sambanis (2001) has suggested that ethnic civil wars may have different causes than non-ethnic civil wars. The same insight can be derived with regard to state capacity. The fact that there is a civil war in a given country signals (in a tautological sense) that the incumbent state is *somehow* weak or lacks state capacity. But what does state weakness or insufficient state capacity mean exactly? Consider the Russian state during the late 1990s, facing the Chechen insurgency, the Turkish state of the 1980s, facing a Kurdish insurgency in its eastern periphery, the Liberian state which was facing several peripheral insurgencies during the early 1990s, and the fledgeing Bosnian state, which was facing the Serb secessionist challenge throughout its territory in the early 1990s. All these states were fighting civil wars, and they were all "weak" by the mere fact that they had been unable to prevent these civil wars from erupting. Yet, no one would seriously contend that Russia, Turkey, Liberia, and Bosnia were equally weak.[5]

4 TYPE OF ONSET AND WARFARE

A way to address this problem is, perhaps, to introduce a measure of induction and distinguish between types of civil war. The problem, of course, is to do so in a way that is informed by either theory or solid empirics, rather than current events.[6] For example, Fearon (2004) sets out to distinguish between five types of civil wars in order to explain different patterns of duration. Fearon identifies three types of brief civil wars (civil wars arising out of military coups and popular uprisings, anticolonial wars, and wars arising out of the collapse of the Soviet Union and Yugoslavia) and one type of long civil war (peripheral insurgencies relying on guerrilla warfare) with two particular subtypes ("sons of the soil wars," i.e. wars between peripheral ethnic minorities and state-supported migrants of a dominant ethnic group, and conflicts where the rebel group has access to natural resources). This distinction has undoubtedly an important heuristic value, but mixes analytical criteria (the war's origins) with more contextual criteria (the collapse of the Soviet Union and Yugoslavia).

Wars can be classified in many ways: some stress the primary actors involved (e.g. international or domestic), their goals (e.g. offensive or defensive), their world views and societal projects ("greed and grievance"), and so on. A popular way to classify civil wars is by stressing the war's "master cleavage." This is the basis, for instance, of the distinction between ethnic and non-ethnic wars. The problem is that uncovering one master cleavage turns out to be much more difficult than seems at first sight because civil wars are highly complex process, where one cleavage potentially hides another (Kalyvas 2003). Of course, complexity is part and parcel of most political and social phenomena and the goal of social scientific explanation is to reduce complexity. However, the problem is magnified in civil wars. Consider the following description of the civil war in Sudan by the journalist Deborah Scroggins (2004: 79–80):

---

[5] Furthermore, states such as Burkina Faso or Equatorial Guinea would certainly be classified as "weak" by country experts, yet they somehow manage to avoid civil wars. A problem faced by state capacity arguments is to explain how weak states manage to remain stable much more frequently than they face military challenges.

[6] As is the case with the popular distinction between "new" and "old" civil wars (Kaldor 1999) which was inspired by journalistic accounts of ongoing civil wars and a superficial reading of the historiography of past civil wars (Kalyvas 2001).

I have often thought that you need a...kind of layered map to understand Sudan's civil war. A surface map of political conflict, for example—the northern government versus the southern rebels; and under that a layer of religious conflict—Muslim versus Christian and pagan; and under that a map of all the sectarian divisions within those categories; and under that a layer of ethnic divisions—Arab and Arabized versus Nilotic and Equatorian—all of them containing a multitude of clan and tribal subdivisions; and under that a layer of linguistic conflicts; and under that a layer of economic divisions—the more developed north with fewer natural resources versus the poorer south with its rich mineral and fossil fuel deposits; and under that a layer of colonial divisions; and under that a layer of racial divisions related to slavery. And so on and so on until it would become clear that the war, like the country, was not one but many: a violent ecosystem capable of generating endless new things to fight about without ever shedding any of the old ones.

In other words, to analyze the civil war in the Sudan as just (or primarily) an ethnic or a religious war is problematic. An alternative is to rely on analytical criteria based on dimensions of the conflict that combine origins and dynamics. A relevant distinction in this respect is between civil wars associated with processes of state implosion at the center and those associated with peripheral challenges. This distinction has the advantage of combining the criterion of origin with that of warfare, which is essential in understanding the way in which the war is organized and sustained.

A common empirical observation in the literature on civil wars is that most of them are fought by means of irregular ("guerrilla") warfare rather than conventional warfare. A few civil wars mix irregular and conventional warfare (e.g. Russia, China, Vietnam), while a very small number are fought fully or predominantly as conventional wars (e.g. Spain). All in all, conventional civil wars are "rare instances appearing only under specific and rather exceptional circumstances" (Derriennic 2001). In contrast, almost all interstate wars are fought conventionally.[7] In short, there is a high degree of overlap between civil and non-conventional war on the one hand, and interstate and conventional war, on the other. It follows that the study of civil war must incorporate the dimension of warfare. This is, to a degree, the insight that provides the main microfoundation for the state capacity story (Fearon and Laitin 2003).

The distinction between irregular and conventional war is common and widely accepted, though the terminology varies. Like all distinctions, it is an ideal-typical one with the two types' edges blending into each other. Conventional warfare entails face-to-face confrontations between regular armies across clear frontlines. This type of warfare requires a commonly shared perception of a balance of power between the two sides in the sense that they are both willing to face each other conventionally, across clearly defined frontlines. In the absence of some kind of mutual consent (which entails some reasonable belief in future victory), no conventional battle can take place (Beaufre 1972). On the other hand, irregular war is a type of warfare that requires a choice by the strategically weaker side "to assume the tactical offensive in

---

[7] The very few irregular interstate wars consist mostly of low-intensity border skirmishes, such as the Libya–Chad war and the war between Belize and Guatemala (Harkavy and Neuman 2001).

selected forms, times, and places" (Simons 1999, 84)—in other words to refuse to match the stronger side's expectations in terms of the conventionally accepted basic rules of warfare. A stylized description of irregular war goes as follows: the state (or *incumbents*) fields regular troops and is able to control urban and accessible terrain, while seeking to militarily engage its opponents in peripheral and rugged terrain; challengers (rebels or *insurgents*) hide and rely on harassment and surprise. Such wars often turn into wars of attrition, with insurgents seeking to win by not losing while imposing unbearable costs on their opponent. There are many variations to this stylized scenario, involving outside intervention or assistance that may lead the insurgents to gradually switch from irregular war to conventional war (e.g. China); conversely, the progressing deterioration of the state may force incumbents to opt for irregular war as well (e.g. Sierra Leone).

In short, irregular warfare is a manifestation of military asymmetry between actors—both in terms of their respective power and their ensuing willingness to fight on the same plane: the weaker actor refuses to directly face the stronger one. The main empirical indicator of irregular war is the dearth of large-scale direct military confrontations or "set battles" and the absence of frontlines. Irregular war is not wedded to a specific cause (revolutionary, communist, or nationalist) but can be deployed to serve a very diverse range of goals. Of course, asymmetry is not an exclusive feature of irregular war; it is also compatible with other forms of violence, including the "terrorist" use of indiscriminate violence.

While asymmetry is predominantly expressed in irregular war, the converse is not the case, as often implied: symmetry (or parity) is not synonymous with conventional war. Rather, it is possible to point to a type of warfare that often gets confused with irregular war, which can be dubbed "symmetric non-conventional warfare" (Kalyvas 2005). This type of warfare is often described as "primitive" or "criminal" war and entails irregular armies on both sides in a pattern resembling pre-modern war. Hence the following conjecture: conventional civil war emerges either out of failed military coups or secession attempts in federal or quasi-federal states);[8] irregular war results from peripheral or rural insurgencies (which may or may not be secessionist in intent); and "symmetric non-conventional warfare" takes place in civil wars that accompany processes of state implosion. State implosion can be sudden or gradual; a way to identify this process is by examining the state of the government army and whether it has become indistinguishable from rival militias in terms of loose organization and fractured chain of command.

In a different formulation, it could be hypothesized that conventional and "symmetric non-conventional" wars tend to result from processes of state implosion, whereas peripheral or rural insurgencies are the likely products of processes whereby the authority of the central state is challenged.

More specifically, conventional civil wars take place when an existing army splits either because of a failed coup (e.g. Spanish Civil War) or because a unit of a federal

---

[8] By "quasi-federal" states, I mean states that have devolved a substantial degree of their military authority, particularly through the creation of extensive local and regional militias.

or quasi-federal state, which can claim control over a substantial part of the state's armed forces, attempts to secede (e.g. the American Civil War, the Biafran War). High levels of external support or external intervention in favor of the rebel side may turn an irregular war into a conventional one: this was the case during the late phases of the Chinese Civil War and the Vietnam War.

Second, irregular civil wars emerge incrementally and often slowly from the periphery. They entail a slow and patient process of state building by the rebels. Geography plays a key role in their onset and dynamics. Examples include civil wars in Malaya, Mozambique during the Portuguese colonization, Kashmir, Aceh (Indonesia), and elsewhere.

Last, "symmetric non-conventional" wars are much less studied and understood; in fact, they are often bundled with rural guerrilla wars. These wars are fought on both sides by irregular armies following a process of state implosion. This entails the disintegration of the state army and its replacement by rival militias which typically equip themselves by plundering the arsenal of the disbanded army. This type of warfare differs from conventional civil war because it lacks regular armies. At the same time, it differs from irregular war because it often displays clear frontlines. The presence of frontlines, which takes various forms (including roadblocks and checkpoints), has been stressed in many descriptions of symmetric non-conventional wars. At the same time, warfare often consists of roving militias raiding "enemy" territory along with killing and plundering. Of course, indiscriminate violence by regular armies in other types of war often takes the same form (think of the counter-insurgency operations of the German and Japanese armies in occupied countries during the Second World War). In symmetric non-conventional wars, however, this becomes the main form of warfare by all sides. Examples include the Lebanese Civil War, the wars in Congo-Brazzaville, Somalia, Liberia, Sierra Leone, and many civil wars that erupted in the wake of the Soviet Union's collapse (Derluguian 2005). In some cases, these wars are concluded when a faction manages the transition from "roving" to "stationary bandit," thus becoming a state builder. A fruitful direction of future research along these lines would consist of relating these types of civil war with various outcomes (onset, duration, types of settlement, violence, etc.). For example, it could be hypothesized that conventional civil wars are likely to be longer than coups but shorter than irregular wars; or that third-party intervention is much easier in asymmetric, non-conventional wars compared to irregular ones. Likewise, it would seem that "greed" arguments better capture the dynamics of asymmetric non-conventional wars while state capacity arguments correlate with irregular wars. Ethnic animosity arguments could correspond to all three types of war: conventional war if minority ethnic groups are well represented in the state's army, irregular war if minority ethnic groups are concentrated in the country's periphery, or asymmetric non-conventional war if the war follows a process of state collapse.

In sum, there is a possible relation between the process of civil war onset and the form of warfare characterizing the war. If this characterization holds it could be consequential from both a theoretical and a policy perspective. Clearly, we need a better understanding of warfare, not just onset, especially given the host of dynamics spawned endogenously by civil war.

5 FUTURE RESEARCH AGENDAS

Three highly stylized types of arguments attempt to account for the onset of civil war. All three point to important causal factors and all have a measure of empirical backing: ethnic antagonism, the presence of natural resources, and weak states may all increase the risk of a civil war, especially in poor states. At the same time, each argument faces considerable challenges from alternative methods of statistical estimation, different or improved measures, new data, and novel theoretical and conceptual insights. Sambanis's (2002, 217) assessment is still correct: in spite of a recent boom in research, civil war still "represents the most poorly understood system failure in the domestic political process."

Even when the findings of large cross-national studies are statistically significant and econometrically sound, the likelihood that a country identified as being at risk will experience a civil war in a given year remains very small, which limits the direct policy relevance of this research. More importantly, the actual causal pathways through which the long-term risk of civil war turns into its realization remain unspecified, unknown, and/or untested. Likewise, the stylized facts about the many facets of civil war that motivate econometric stories are usually untested and sometimes false (Cramer 2002). For example, Kalyvas and Kocher (2006) have provided systematic data strongly suggesting that rebels do not always or necessarily face a collective action problem, as is axiomatically assumed in the literature. Because incumbents frequently respond to the flare-up of rebellion with massive indiscriminate violence individual peasants living in targeted areas may find it rational to join the insurgents.

Most importantly, civil wars are deeply "endogenous" processes (Kalyvas 2006). Collective and individual preferences, strategies, values, and identities are continuously shaped and reshaped in the course of a war, while the war itself aggregates all kinds of cleavages from the most ideological to the most local. Popular loyalty, disloyalty, and support cannot be assumed as exogenous and fixed. Hence, theories which assume actors and preferences to be frozen in their pre-war manifestations and rely on this assumption to explain various aspects of civil wars, such as their onset, duration, or termination, will be likely biased. This bias is reinforced by the tendency to deduce pre-war actors, preferences, and identities from "master narratives" of civil war. To be sure, such narratives simplify the complexity of civil wars. However, the fact that civil wars are also state-building processes means that their "master narratives" are likely to be contaminated by the war's outcome: they will be distorted and their ambiguities and contradictions will be erased. Often the hegemony of such narratives is so powerful that even researchers that collect detailed accounts tend to disregard or downplay their findings because they do not fit into existing frames.

Last, civil wars are an example of multifinality: it may well be that not all civil wars are caused by the same set of factors. Significant divergences in the ways in which civil wars are conducted can be linked to processes of state implosion as opposed to processes of peripheral challenge. If this is the case, then different types of civil war may emerge from different combinations of causal factors.

These problems help structure the future research agenda. First, research on civil wars will increasingly move toward the specification and testing of disaggregated causal pathways and mechanisms. Second, micro–macro relationships will be studied less through cross-national statistical analyses and more through integrated research designs that make intensive use of fine-grained subnational data—quantitative as well as qualitative. Third, both these trends call for opening up the black box of civil war and exploring the complex ways in which a military challenge is articulated, emerges successfully, and is countered—i.e. the microfoundations of civil war including processes of recruitment and violence. Questions such as rebel recruitment, peasant collective action, rebel rule, peripheral state and rebel organization, peripheral state and rebel financing, dynamics of violence will be studied in increasingly sophisticated ways combining ethnographic, archival, and econometric methods (Kalyvas 2006; Arjona and Kalyvas 2006; Humphreys and Weinstein 2005). At the macro level, we are likely to see more studies that embed civil wars into macro-historical processes, but in ways that incorporate insights and findings from both the emerging micro-level literature and older, overlooked literatures including work on peasant rebellion (Wimmer and Min 2006; Hironaka 2005; Derluguian 2005; Boix 2004). These trends all point toward studies that are multi-method, take history seriously, use sophisticated empirical strategies coupled with high-quality data, and are characterized by more theoretical and empirical depth. In short, the indeterminacy of current findings signals less a declining research program and more the emergence of an exciting research agenda.

References

ANDERSON, L. E. 1993. Agrarian politics and revolution: micro and state perspectives on structural determinism. *Journal of Theoretical Politics*, 5: 495–522.

——1994. *The Political Ecology of the Modern Peasant: Calculation and Community*. Baltimore: Johns Hopkins University Press.

ARJONA, A., and KALYVAS, S. N. 2006. Preliminary results from a survey of demobilized fighters in Colombia. Unpublished paper.

BEAUFRE, A. 1972. *La Guerre révolutionnaire: les formes nouvelles de la guerre*. Paris: Fayard.

BECKETT, I. F. W. 2001. *Modern Insurgencies and Counter-Insurgencies: Guerrillas and their Opponents since 1750*. London: Routledge.

BOIX, C. 2003. *Democracy and Redistribution*. New York: Cambridge University Press.

——2004. Inequality, capital mobility, and political violence. Unpublished paper.

BRUSTEIN, W., and LEVI, M. 1987. The geography of rebellion: rulers, rebels, and regions, 1500 to 1700. *Theory and Society*, 16: 467–95.

BUHAUG, H., CEDERMAN, L.-E., and RØD, J. K. 2006. Modeling ethnic conflict in center—periphery dyads. Unpublished paper.

CALDER, B. J. 1984. *The Impact of Intervention: The Dominican Republic during the U.S. Occupation of 1916–1924*. Austin: University of Texas Press.

CEDERMAN, L.-E. 2004. Articulating the geo-cultural logic of nationalist insurgency. Unpublished paper.

——and GIRARDIN, L. 2006. Beyond fractionalization: mapping ethnicity onto nationalist insurgencies. Unpublished paper.

COLLIER, P., and HOEFFLER, A. 2004. Greed and grievance in civil war. *Oxford Economic Papers*, 56: 563–95.

——ELLIOTT, V. L., HEGRE, H., HOEFFLER, A., REYNAL-QUEROL, M., and SAMBANIS, N. 2003. *Breaking the Conflict Trap: Civil War and Development Policy*. Washington, DC: World Bank and Oxford University Press.

CRAMER, C. 2002. *Homo Economicus* goes to war: methodological individualism, rational choice, and the political economy of war. *World Development*, 30: 1845–64.

DALLIN, A., MAVROGORDATO, R., and MOLL, W. 1964. Partisan psychological warfare and popular attitudes. Pp. 197–337 in *Soviet Partisans in World War II*, ed. J. A. Armstrong. Madison: University of Wisconsin Press.

DERLUGUIAN, G. M. 2005. *Bourdieu's Secret Admirer in the Caucausus: A World System Biography*. Chicago: University of Chicago Press.

DERRIENNIC, J.-P. 2001. *Les Guerres civiles*. Paris: Presses de Sciences Po.

ECKSTEIN, H. 1965. On the etiology of internal wars. *History and Theory*, 4: 133–63.

ELLIOTT, D. W. P. 2003. *The Vietnamese War: Revolution and Social Change in the Mekong Delta, 1930–1975*. Armonk, NY: M. E. Sharpe.

ESCOTT, P. D. 1978. *After Secession: Jefferson Davis and the Failure of Confederate Nationalism*. Baton Rouge: Louisiana State University Press.

——and CROW, J. J. 1986. The social order and violent disorder: an analysis of North Carolina in the Revolution and the Civil War. *Journal of Southern History*, 52: 373–402.

FEARON, J. D. 1998. Commitment problems and the spread of ethnic conflict. Pp. 107–26 in *The International Spread of Ethnic Conflict*, ed. D. A. Lake and D. Rothchild. Princeton: Princeton University Press.

——2004. Why do some civil wars last so much longer than others? *Journal of Peace Research*, 41: 275–301.

——KASARA, K., and LAITIN, D. D. 2006. Ethnic minority rule and civil war onset. Unpublished paper.

——and LAITIN, D. D. 2003. Ethnicity, insurgency, and civil war. *American Political Science Review*, 97: 75–86.

GAMBETTA, D. 1993. *The Sicilian Mafia: The Business of Private Protection*. Cambridge, Mass.: Harvard University Press.

GEFFRAY, C. 1990. *La Cause des armes au Mozambique: anthropologie d'une guerre civile*. Paris: Karthala.

GULDEN, T. R. 2002. Spatial and temporal patterns in civil violence: Guatemala 1977–1986. Center on Social and Economic Dynamics, Working Paper No. 26.

GURR, T. R. 1970. *Why Men Rebel*. Princeton: Princeton University Press.

GUTIERREZ, F. 2004. Criminal rebels? A discussion of war and criminality from the Colombian experience. *Politics and Society*, 32: 257–85.

HARKAVY, R. E., and NEUMAN, S. G. 2001. *Warfare and the Third World*. New York: Palgrave.

HIRONAKA, A. 2005. *Neverending Wars: The International Community, and the Perpetuation of Civil War*. Cambridge, Mass.: Harvard University Press.

HOFHEINZ, R. 1969. The ecology of Chinese communist success: rural influence patterns, 1923–45. Pp. 3–77 in *Chinese Communist Politics in Action*, ed. D. Barnett. Seattle: University of Washington Press.

HORTON, L. 1998. *Peasants in Arms: War and Peace in the Mountains of Nicaragua, 1979–1984*. Athens: Ohio University Center for International Studies.

HUMPHREYS, M. 2005. Natural resources, conflict, and conflict resolution: uncovering the mechanisms. *Journal of Conflict Resolution*, 49: 508–37.

—— and WEINSTEIN, J. 2005. Handling and manhandling civilians in civil war. *American Political Science Review*, 100: 429–47.

KALDOR, M. 1999. *New and Old Wars: Organized Violence in a Global Era*. Stanford, Calif.: Stanford University Press.

KALYVAS, S. N. 2001. "New" and "old" civil wars: a valid distinction? *World Politics*, 54: 99–118.

—— 2003. The ontology of "political violence": action and identity in civil wars. *Perspectives on Politics*, 1: 475–94.

—— 2005. Warfare in civil wars. Pp. 88–108 in *Rethinking the Nature of War*, ed. I. Duyvesteyn and J. Angstrom. Abingdon: Frank Cass.

—— 2006. *The Logic of Violence in Civil War*. New York: Cambridge University Press.

—— and KOCHER, M. A. 2006. How free is "free riding" in civil wars? Violence, insurgency, and the collective action problem. Unpublished paper.

KEDWARD, H. R. 1993. *In Search of the Maquis: Rural Resistance in Southern France 1942–1944*. Oxford: Oxford University Press.

KIRSCHENMANN, F. 2003. The current state of agriculture: does it have a future? Pp. 101–20 in *The Essential Agrarian Reader: The Future of Culture, Community and the Land*, ed. Norma Wirzba. Lexington: University Press of Kentucky.

KITSON, F. 1960. *Gangs and Counter-Gangs*. London: Barrie and Rockliff.

KOCHER, M. A. 2004. Human ecology and civil war. Ph.D. thesis. University of Chicago.

KRIGER, N. 1992. *Zimbabwe's Guerrilla War: Peasant Voices*. Cambridge: Cambridge University Press.

LUJALA, P., GLEDITSCH, N. P., and GILLMORE, E. 2005. A diamond course? Civil war and a lootable resource. *Journal of Conflict Resolution*, 49: 538–52.

MIGUEL, E., SATYANATH, S., and SERGENTI, E. 2004. Economic shocks and civil conflict: an instrumental variables approach. *Journal of Political Economy*, 112: 725–53.

MONTALVO, J. G., and REYNAL-QUEROL, M. 2005. Ethnic polarization, potential conflict and civil war. *American Economic Review*, 95: 796–816.

MOORE, B. 1966. *Social Origins of Dictatorship and Democracy: Lord and Peasant in the Making of the Modern World*. Boston: Beacon Press.

NORDSTROM, C. 1997. *A Different Kind of War Story*. Philadelphia: University of Pennsylvania Press.

PAIGE, J. M. 1978. *Agrarian Revolution: Social Movements and Export Agriculture in the Underdeveloped World*. New York : Free Press.

POPKIN, S. L. 1979. *The Rational Peasant: The Political Economy of Rural Society in Vietnam*. Berkeley and Los Angeles: University of California Press.

POSNER, D. N. 2004. Measuring ethnic fractionalization in Africa. *American Journal of Political Science*, 48: 849–63.

POSEN, B. 1993. The security dilemma and ethnic conflict. *Survival*, 35: 27–47.

REGAN, P. M., and NORTON, D. 2005. Greed, grievance and mobilization in civil wars. *Journal of Conflict Resolution*, 49: 319–36.

ROSS, M. 2006. A closer look at oil, diamonds, and civil war. *Annual Reviews of Political Science*, 9: 265–300.

SAMBANIS, N. 2001. Do ethnic and nonethnic civil wars have the same causes? A theoretical and empirical inquiry (part 1). *Journal of Conflict Resolution*, 45: 259–82.

—— 2002. A review of recent advances and future directions in the quantitative literature on civil war. *Defence and Peace Economics*, 13: 215–43.

—— 2004a. Using case studies to expand economic models of civil war. *Perspectives on Politics*, 2: 259–79.

—— 2004b. What is civil war? Conceptual and empirical complexities of an operational definition. *Journal of Conflict Resolution*, 48: 814–58.

—— and MILANOVIC, B. 2006. Explaining the demand for sovereignty. Unpublished paper.

SANSOM, R. L. 1970. *The Economics of Insurgency in the Mekong Delta of Vietnam*. Cambridge, Mass.: MIT Press.

SCHRAN, P. 1976. *Guerrilla Economy: The Development of the Shensi-Kansu-Ninghsia Border Region, 1937–1945*. Albany: State University of New York Press.

SCOTT, J. C. 1976. *Moral Economy of the Peasant: Rebellion and Subsistence in Southeast Asia*. New Haven: Yale University Press.

SCROGGINS, D. 2004. *Emma's War*. New York: Vintage.

SIMONS, A. 1999. War: back to the future. *Annual Reviews of Anthropology*, 28: 73–108.

STINCHCOMBE, A. L. 1961. Agricultural enterprise and rural class relations. *American Journal of Sociology*, 67: 165–76.

STOLL, D. 1993. *Between Two Armies: In the Ixil Towns of Guatemala*. New York: Columbia University Press.

TOFT, M. D. 2003. *The Geography of Ethnic Violence: Identity, Interests, and the Indivisibility of Territory*. Princeton: Princeton University Press.

TONE, J. L. 1994. *The Fatal Knot: The Guerrilla War in Navarre and the Defeat of Napoleon in Spain*. Chapel Hill: University of North Carolina Press.

TONG, J. 1991. *Disorder under Heaven: Collective Violence in the Ming Dynasty*. Stanford, Calif.: Stanford University Press.

TREJO, G. 2004. Indigenous insurgency: protest, rebellion, and the politicization of ethnicity in 20th century Mexico. Ph.D. dissertation. University of Chicago.

VARSHNEY, A. 2003. Nationalism, ethnic conflict, and rationality. *Perspectives on Politics*, 1: 85–99.

WALTER, B. 1997. The Critical Barrier to Civil War Settlement. *International Organization*, 51: 335–64.

WICKHAM-CROWLEY, T. P. 1992. *Guerrillas and Revolution in Latin America: A Comparative Study of Insurgents and Regimes since 1956*. Princeton: Princeton University Press.

WILKINSON, S. I. 2004. *Votes and Violence: Electoral Competition and Ethnic Riots in India*. New York: Cambridge University Press.

WIMMER, A., and MIN, B. 2006. From empire to nation state: explaining wars in the modern world, 1816–2001. *American Sociological Review* (forthcoming).

WOLF, E. R. 1973. *The Peasant Wars of the Twentieth Century*. New York: Harper and Row.

WOOD, E. J. 2003. *Insurgent Collective Action and Civil War in El Salvador*. New York: Cambridge University Press.

CHAPTER 19

CONTENTIOUS POLITICS AND SOCIAL MOVEMENTS

SIDNEY TARROW
CHARLES TILLY

On 29 January 2001, the magazine *Time Asia* worried in print about whether the extra-institutional removal of Philippine President Joseph Estrada, for all its popular support, would actually undermine the Philippines' fragile democracy in the longer run. The whole process had begun within institutional channels but quickly poured into the streets. In November 2000 the Philippine Congress had voted to impeach Estrada for taking kickbacks from gamblers and dipping into tobacco excise taxes for his own enrichment. The twenty-two-member Senate then took over as impeachment court. Although demonstrations against Estrada and public demands for his resignation soon began, the main action remained in the Senate until 16 January. On that day, senators voted 11–10 against opening an envelope said to contain evidence that Estrada had indeed received illegal payments. Senate president Aquilino Pimentel, in the minority of 10, immediately resigned his post.

Pimentel's resignation was a signal for the anti-Estrada mobilization to move to the streets. In *Time Asia*'s vivid account:

This has been called the pager revolution for good reason: within minutes of the Senate vote, text messages had flashed through Manila ether telling anti-Estrada Filipinos to GO TO EDSA.

Hundreds of thousands converged on the capital, following directions to, as one message put it, WEAR BLACK TO MOURN THE DEATH OF DEMOCRACY. Said another text message, EXPECT THERE TO BE RUMBLES. (*Time Asia* 2001, 3)

EDSA stands for Epifanio de los Santos Avenue, a central Manila thoroughfare where, in 1986, praying nuns had faced down the tanks of Philippine president Ferdinand Marcos, helping drive him out of office. That set of confrontations had gained fame as People Power. Accordingly, participants and observers soon began calling the events of January 2001 People Power II. Crowds, bands, and banners filled Manila's streets in a resonant call for the president's resignation. After holing up in the presidential palace for four days, Estrada left in disgrace, but without a formal resignation, on 20 January. A few headlines from the Manila daily *Philippine Star*, excerpted in Table 19.1, convey the turmoil. Looking back at these events ten days later, *Time Asia* fretted about two contradictory possibilities: first, that the popular mobilization of January would set the precedent for new disorders once Estrada's successor, Gloria Macapagal Arroyo, tried to govern; second, that in fact an extra-legal deal within the Filipino elite had engineered the entire crisis, with street demonstrations no more than a convenient smokescreen for high-level maneuvers. After all, Philippine business had long opposed the populist Estrada (a famous film actor), Macapagal Arroyo had resigned her cabinet post well before the impeachment proceedings began, rumors of a military coup started to circulate early in December, former president Corazon Aquino and Cardinal Jaime Sin (both major figures of People Power I) had early announced their support for Estrada's resignation, the defection of Estrada's top military officers finally persuaded him to give up the presidential palace, and supporters of Estrada soon took to the streets in their turn, a working-class force to battle the mainly middle-class demonstrators against the embattled president (Rafael 2003, 422). Far from expressing a unanimous popular will, the removal of Estrada clearly divided the Filipino population.

What was happening here? Students of social movements habitually emphasize movement actions *against* institutions, but the constitutional crisis that produced Estrada's departure from office in January 2001 began *within* institutional politics. But did all that commotion in Manila's streets provide nothing but camouflage for the decisive political steps taken by an establishment that had already decided to rid itself of an inconvenient figurehead and that would manipulate his successor as well? Or was it an episode of social movement politics? Or were both a part of the broader set of phenomena that we call *contentious politics*?

To place political phenomena like the Philippines' turmoil of January 2001 in theoretical perspective, we need first to make clear what we mean by "contentious politics;" we then relate it to the more familiar concept of the "social movement." We will then shift from this essentially static typology to ways of studying the dynamics of contention. We move from there to an examination of democracy, violence, and some questions about the future of social movements.

Table 19.1 Selected headlines from the *Philippine Star*, December 2000 – January 2001

12/1	Anti-Estrada Forces Launch Civil Disobedience Plan
12/8	Anti-Estrada Protesters Prevented from Marching to Senate
12/8	US Expresses Concern Over Coup Rumors Amid Estrada Trial
12/11	Estrada Woos Church, Left: Commutes All Death Sentences to Life, Frees Political Prisoners
12/18	Edsa Rally Set Today
12/24	Acquittal to be Met with Massive Civil Disobedience
1/9	Rallyists Maul Senate Driver
1/10	Protesters to Defy Senate Rally Ban
1/16	Malacañang [presidential palace] Ready to Crush Anarchy
1/18	Edsa II to Erap: Resign
1/19	Edsa Protesters Form Human Chain
1/19	Nationwide Work Stoppage Set Today
1/19	Estrada Loyalists Chase Students with Clubs
1/20	Estrada Government Collapses
1/20	Rallyists Clash in Makati
1/21	3 Hurt, 6 Nabbed in Mendiola Clash
1/21	US Recognizes GMA [Gloria Macapagal Arroyo] Government

1 CONTENTIOUS POLITICS

Isn't all of politics contentious? According to a strict reading of our definition, certainly not. Much of politics—the majority, we would guess—consists of ceremony, consultation, bureaucratic process, collection of information, registration of events, educational activities, and the like. Registering to vote, attending associational meetings, reading and publishing newspapers, asking officials for favors, and similar actions constitute the bulk of political life; they usually involve little if any collective contention. The *contentious* politics that concerns us is episodic rather than continuous, occurs in public, involves interaction between makers of claims and others, is recognized by those others as bearing on their interests, and brings in government as mediator, target, or claimant.

Isn't "contentious politics" just another way of saying "social movements"? We think not. Although movements and other forms of contentious politics share many mechanisms and are part of the political process, broadly conceived, as we use the term, the social movement emerged in a particular historical and social context—Western Europe and North America in the late eighteenth and early nineteenth centuries—and has properties that distinguish it from civil wars, strike waves, revolutions, and political violence (Tilly and Tarrow 2006, chs. 6 and 7).

Disaggregating movements from within the more general term "contentious politics" will help to focus on these differences, on the conditions that give rise to movements, and to the transitions between movements and other forms of contention. Or so we will argue in this chapter.

The January 2001 episode in the Philippines had many of the characteristics usually associated with social movements—protesters, rousing speeches, People Power. But these properties are characteristic of other phenomena too: strike waves, riots, ethnic conflict, civil wars, even elections. This broader range of phenomena is what we call "contentious politics:"

- *contentious* in the sense that they involve the collective making of claims that, if realized, would conflict with someone else's interests;
- *politics* in the sense that governments of one sort or another figure in the claim making, whether as claimants, objects of claims, allies of the objects, or monitors of the contention.[1]

By contentious politics we mean:

episodic, public, collective interaction among makers of claims and their objects when (a) at least one government is a claimant, an object of claims, or a party to the claims and (b) the claims would, if realized, affect the interests of at least one of the claimants.

Roughly translated, the definition refers to collective political struggle.

Of course, each term in such a definition cries out for further stipulations. The term "episodic," for example, excludes regularly scheduled events such as votes, parliamentary elections, and associational meetings—although any such event can become a springboard for contentious politics. Again, we take "public" to exclude claim making that occurs entirely within well-bounded organizations, including churches and firms. Despite obvious parallels between some struggles occurring inside and outside these boundaries, we concentrate here on those having manifestly political ramifications. The distinction matters because the involvement, however peripheral, of governments greatly increases the likelihood of intervention of coercive agents such as police and, on the average, increases the stakes of the outcome.

Is this subset of politics too sprawling and amorphous to constitute a coherent field of enquiry? We are betting against that supposition. Let us put the matter with two illustrations from our earlier work with sociologist Doug McAdam. In the 1850s the acrimonious debate in Congress over the slavery dispute in Kansas took place inside an institution but was patently contentious and occasionally violent, and thus belongs within the same definitional universe as the so-called Mau Mau rebellion of Kenya in the 1950s, mounted against the institutions of British colonialism (McAdam, Tarrow, and Tilly 2001). Both qualify, in our terms, as *episodes of contention.*

---

[1] We wish to express our gratitude to our collaborator, Doug McAdam, with whom we developed many of the ideas reflected in this chapter and who inspired our common work (see McAdam, Tarrow, and Tilly 2001; Tarrow and McAdam 2005; Tilly and Tarrow 2006). We also recognize the Mellon-Sawyer Seminar at the Center for Advanced Study in the Behavior Sciences out of which all of this work came. For a companion volume, see Aminzade et al. (2001).

We do not claim that congressional disputes and anticolonial movements are identical, or that they conform to a single general model. They obviously differ in a host of consequential ways. Yet we group them within the same field of contentious politics because we think the study of political contention has fragmented excessively, spawning a host of distinct topical literatures—revolutions, social movements, industrial conflict, international war, civil war, interest group politics, nationalism, democratization—dealing with similar phenomena by means of different vocabularies, techniques, and models and mainly proceeding in cordial indifference to each other's findings.[2] While focusing in this chapter on movements, we want to make clear that they constitute only a subset of contentious politics and engage in activities both contentious and otherwise—some of them within institutions.

Our work challenges any rigid boundary between institutionalized and non-institutionalized politics. The underground war waged by Richard Nixon that resulted in the botched Watergate break-in and the resulting impeachment inquiry stemmed, in large part, from Nixon's hostility to the anti-war movement and other movements of the New Left. Similarly, Mau Mau had its origins, not in some spasm of anticolonial violence, but in a circumscribed conflict involving a set of four legally constituted political actors: Kenya's colonial authorities, British officials, Kenyan nationalists, and Kenya's white settler community. Virtually all broad social movements, revolutions, and similar phenomena grow from roots in episodes of institutional contention. But even as we employ the distinction, we insist that the study of politics has too long reified the boundary between official, prescribed politics and politics by other means. As an unfortunate consequence, analysts have neglected or misunderstood both the parallels and the interactions between the two.

Boundaries between institutionalized and non-institutionalized politics are hard to draw with precision. Take the coalition that formed around opposing President Reagan's nuclear arms policy in the 1980s; both its strength and its ultimate defeat were due to the fact that it crossed the boundary between institutional groups and those outside of institutions. Newly formed movement organizations like the Nuclear Weapons Freeze Clearinghouse (NWFC) combined with established peace organizations, on the one hand, and with congressional Democrats, on the other, to form a coalition that convinced the government to start an arms control process (Meyer 1990). Only by crossing the formal boundary between institutional and non-institutional politics can we understand the dynamics of such episodes of contentious politics.

More important, the two sorts of politics involve similar causal processes. For example, the study of coalitions has almost always been operationalized within legislative institutions. But coalitions occur widely in the disruptions of rebellions, strikes, and social movements (Rochon and Meyer 1998; Levi and Murphy 2004). The same is true for strategic interaction and identity struggles, which occur widely both in the politics of established institutions and in rebellions, strikes, and

---

[2] A partial exception is the study of social revolutions, in which there are clear connections to the study of social movements, as explored, for example, by our colleague Jack Goldstone (1998).

movements. As long as the same mechanisms and processes can be identified in institutional and non-institutional politics, we argue, they should be studied irrespective of institutional boundaries.

Of course, institutions both constrain and enable contentious politics and different kinds of regimes produce different configurations of contention. Regimes consist of regular relations among governments, established political actors, challengers, and outside political actors, including other governments. The connections among contention, political power, and institutions appear both in turbulent periods and in the more routine politics of both authoritarian regimes and settled democracy (Tilly and Tarrow 2006, ch. 3). The concept of *political opportunity structure* and changes in these opportunities help to guide scholars through these variations and their dynamics.

Political opportunity structure refers to features of regimes and institutions that facilitate or inhibit a political actor's collective action and to changes in those features. Drawing on the research of many scholars in what has been called "the political process tradition," we identify six properties of regimes that are crucial features of opportunity structure:

- the multiplicity of independent centers of power within the regime;
- its relative closure or openness to new actors;
- the instability or stability of current political alignments;
- the availability of influential allies or supporters;
- the extent to which the regime represses or facilitates collective claim making;
- decisive changes in these properties.

Threats also vary in different opportunity structures and most people who mobilize do so to combat threats or risks (Goldstone and Tilly 2001). But threats and opportunities co-occur and most people engaging in contentious politics combine response to threat with seizing opportunities. For example, in Iraq under the American occupation regime, the Sunni population saw construction of a new constitution as a threat to its power; yet while its federal structure gave the Shia and Kurdish areas control over Iran's oil revenues, it also provided institutional autonomy to all three groups. Both threats and opportunities shift with fragmentation or concentration of power, changes in a regime's openness or closure, instability of alignments, and the availability of allies.

2 PERFORMANCES AND REPERTOIRES OF CONTENTION

Contentious politics features enormous variation in its issues, actors, interactions, claims, sequences, and outcomes from time to time and place to place. But it also displays great regularities in the ways that contention unfolds. Similar mechanisms and processes produce distinctive political trajectories and outcomes depending on their combinations and on the social bases and political contexts in which they operate. We can begin to capture some of the recurrent, historically embedded character of contentious politics by means of two related theatrical metaphors: *performances and repertoires*.

Contentious performances are relatively familiar and standardized ways in which one set of political actors makes collective claims on some other set of political actors. Presentation of a petition, taking of a hostage, or mounting of a demonstration constitutes a *performance* linking at least two actors, a claimant and an object of claims. Innovation occurs incessantly on the small scale, but effective claims depend on a recognizable relation to their setting, on relations between the parties, and on previous uses of the claim-making form. The demonstration, the petition, and the internet-based call to action have become *modular performances*, generic forms that can be adapted to a variety of local and social circumstances.

The most common performance in modern contentious politics is *the demonstration*: the orderly passage through public space of an organized collectivity on behalf of some claim, identity, or program (Tilly and Tarrow 2006, 12–16). From the late eighteenth century to our time, the orderly passage of demonstrators through urban space to present a claim has been used by people demanding almost anything from the right to vote to the demand that others be denied that right, to the right to practice a trade, to the demand that others be kept out of one, from the right to abortion to the right to life (Favre 1990; Fillieule 1997; Grimsted 1998; Kinealy 2003; Pigenet and Tartakowsky 2003; Tartakowsky 1997, 2004). Despite their common properties, such modular performances can be adapted to different contexts and draw on the languages, symbols, and practices of local circumstances.

Contentious performances sometimes clump into *repertoires* of claim-making routines that apply to the same claimant–object pairs: bosses and workers, peasants and landlords, rival nationalist factions, and many more. *Contentious repertoires* are arrays of performances that are currently known and available within some set of political actors. In the past, repertoires contained ritual shaming, *charivari*, the pulling down of houses, forced illuminations, grain seizures, and the like (Tilly 1978, 1995; Tarrow 1998). These days strikes, slowdowns, lockouts, contract negotiations, grievance hearings, and third-party mediation all belong to the claim-making repertoires that connect bosses and workers.

The theatrical metaphor of the repertoire calls attention to the clustered, learned, yet improvisational character of people's interactions as they make and receive each other's claims. Claim making usually resembles jazz and street theater rather than ritual reading of scripture. Like a jazz trio or an improvisatory theater group, people who participate in contentious politics normally have several pieces they can play, but not an infinite number (Sawyer 2001). Like familiar jazz tunes, the pieces evoke and express specific emotions, recall memories of previous encounters, and thus establish continuity between political actors' pasts and presents.

Repertoires vary from place to place, time to time, and pair to pair. But on the whole when people make collective claims, they innovate within limits set by the repertoire already established for their place, time, and pair. Exactly how people draw on contentious repertoires varies greatly. We can see the influence of *weak repertoires* when formerly authoritarian regimes give way to semi-democratic or pluralistic regimes. At the other extreme from weak repertoires, *ritual political performances* sometimes occur. Think of May Day, the international day of workers' rights. It began in July 1889, the centenary of the French Revolution, when a congress of trade unionists met in Paris to propose that "a great international demonstration should be convoked, on the same day all over the world, to put governments on notice to reduce the workday to eight hours" (Tartakowsky 2004, 14). Over the next few decades, this contentious claim settled down into a regular and ritualized demonstration of popular power, spread across the globe, and brought millions of workers onto the street and into the parks and squares for what became a ritualized festival of labor.

When people intervene in such events to make collective claims, they bend them back from ritual toward *strong repertoires*. In Europe, some workers used the First of May to go on strike or to place insurgent demands on the agenda. Similarly, in the United States, student protesters sometimes interrupt the ritual of a college commencement, turning it temporarily into a demonstration. So doing, they generally adapt chants, signs, symbols, and actions that are familiar from other settings. Over historic time and in most places, strong repertoires have usually prevailed. This is not to say that strong repertoires never change, but only that changes normally occur through innovation at the margins. Nevertheless, some periods of history overflow with new performances and new variants of old ones. We may be living in just such a period, when the explosion of suicide-based attacks and the broad and rapid diffusion of internet-based calls to action mark a period of dramatic repertoire change.

3 SOCIAL MOVEMENTS

A social movement consists of

> *a sustained challenge to power holders in the name of a population living under the jurisdiction of those power holders by means of public displays of that population's worthiness, unity, numbers, and commitment.*

As it developed in the West after 1750, the social movement emerged from an innovative, consequential synthesis of three elements: *campaigns, repertoires of association,* and *public self-representations:*

A *campaign* is a sustained, organized public effort making collective claims on targeted authorities. Unlike a one-time petition, declaration, or mass meeting, a *campaign* extends beyond any single event—although social movements often include petitions, declarations, and mass meetings. A campaign always links at least three parties: a group of self-designated claimants, some object(s) of claims, and a public of some kind. The claims may target governmental officials, but the "authorities" in question can also include owners of property, religious functionaries, and others whose actions (or failures to act) significantly affect the welfare of many people. Not the solo actions of claimants, object(s), or public, but interactions among the three, constitute a social movement. Even if a few zealots commit themselves to the movement night and day, furthermore, the bulk of participants move back and forth between public claim making and other activities, including the day-to-day organizing that sustains a campaign.

Associational repertoires. People have always come together in associations. But in the past, many of these associations were vertical—i.e., they were linked to notables—or all-encompassing—i.e., religious communities. The special-purpose association brought people together around concrete, often contingent aims and produced its own repertoire of organizational routines—the lockbox holding both funds and dues; the membership card, the trade union branch. During the twentieth century, special-purpose associations and cross-cutting coalitions in particular began to do an enormous variety of political work across the world (Burstein 1999). Organizations participating in social movements, furthermore, sometimes move into these other political spheres: conducting political campaigns, establishing labor unions, creating durable interest groups, becoming religious sects, or forming separatist communities (Kriesi 1996).

Some movement organizations are patently "insiders"—that is, their actions are wholly or mainly determined by institutional routines. Consider the European Environmental Bureau: it is heavily subsidized by the European Commission, maintains lavish offices in Brussels, and offers expert testimony to the European Parliament and the Environmental Directorate (Rucht 2002). That is an extreme case of movement co-optation. But even movement "outsiders" are tied to the logic of institutions; the celebrated "Battle of Seattle" in 1999 and the sequence of international protests that followed it were aggressively transgressive in what they did and what they claimed, but they depended on the scheduling of international meetings, on the interaction of demonstrators and the authorities, and on the weight of the most institutionalized sector of the labor movement. Institutions offer the framework within and around which both "insiders" and "outsiders" interact.

Movements often leave associational residues behind them long after their campaigns have ended (Rupp and Taylor 1987)—what we call "social movement bases" (Tilly and Tarrow 2006, ch. 6). Consider the American women's movement: while the peak of its public activity subsided after the 1970s (Costain 1992) its activists created a panoply of stable institutions, organizations, women's study programs, and cultural understandings that reached into corners of society which few would consider "social movements" (Katzenstein 1998; Mansbridge and Flaster 2005). These social movement bases, while they often remain latent, can become available as bases for future mobilization when, as often happens in contentious politics, new alignments and new axes of conflict trigger them to become manifest.

Public self-representation. Movement participants make concerted public representations of worthiness, unity, numbers, and commitment on the part of themselves and/or their constituencies (Tilly 2004). For example:

- *worthiness:* sober demeanor; neat clothing; presence of clergy, dignitaries, and mothers with children;
- *unity:* matching badges, headbands, banners, or costumes; marching in ranks; singing and chanting;
- *numbers:* headcounts, signatures on petitions, messages from constituents, filling streets;
- *commitment:* braving bad weather; visible participation by the old and handicapped; resistance to repression; ostentatious sacrifice, subscription, and/or benefaction.

For social movements, creating a self-representation goes much deeper than creating an image. Because they are creating a collective actor, movements do an enormous amount of identity building through their interaction with significant others (Melucci 1988; Tilly and Tarrow 2006, ch. 4). Interaction occurs first among those within the inner core of the movement—whom we can call "activists." But it also takes place with sympathizers on the margins of the movement, with opponents, and with key third parties like the media, the police, and public authorities. In an important sense, the task of a movement's activists is to turn sympathizers into participants, turn indifferent onlookers into sympathizers, and neutralize opponents. Demonstrations or other forms of collective action bring together actors who know little or nothing of one another at the outset, but who sometimes emerge from their interaction as a unified actor with a collective identity, with boundaries that separate them from others, and with a set of unified claims against common targets. In doing so they become constituted political actors.

Campaigns, associational repertoires, and public self-representations vary enormously from one movement to another, but movements connect those properties in logical ways. Consider two examples: In the 1830s, the American antislavery movement launched a long and varied campaign against both slaveholders and public authorities through forms of association and public action that drew heavily on the repertoire of the evangelical revival of the previous decade, presenting itself as righteous, unified, numerous, and stalwart (Young 2007). Similarly, in the 1990s a political Islamist movement developed among young Muslims in Western Europe and throughout the Muslim world. They campaigned for a return to Islamic tradition through the wearing of the headscarf; they organized themselves through religious schools, political parties, and clandestine cells; and they presented themselves publicly as worthy, unified, numerous, and deeply committed to their Islamic faith (Singerman 2004; Wiktorowicz 2004). But while the antislavery movement increasingly entered institutional politics, Islamists' actions expanded into a variety of types of contentious politics.

4 Dynamics of Contention

Thus far, our argument has been largely static. Yet it has drawn from what has been called the "political process" tradition in social movements studies (McAdam,

McCarthy, and Zald 1996). But despite the label "process," this tradition is lodged in a structuralist ontology. First in a social structural mode (e.g., "movements are the product of structural imbalances") and then in a political structural mode ("movements are the result of political opportunities" and "mobilizing structures"), scholars from the 1960s through the 1980s—including ourselves—tended to see movements as the direct outcomes of structural constants and variations. That tradition has to some extent been challenged by, and has fruitfully absorbed some aspects of, the 1990s' "cultural turn" (Morris and Mueller 1992; Goodwin and Jasper 2004). Growing out of a European tradition of study of the "new" social movements in the 1970s and extending to the United States in the 1980s, this new approach criticized the instrumental bias in the political process tradition. Its proponents called for the reinsertion of discourse, collective identity, framing, and emotion into the study of social movements (Aminzade and McAdam 2001; Gamson 1992; Melucci 1988; Rochon 1998).

By the end of the 1990s the more digestible parts of this "cultural turn" had been absorbed into the mainstream of empirical research on contentious politics. In a first move away from structuralism, scholars integrated the concept of "framing" into the canon, combining it with both opportunity structures and mobilizing structures to form a triad of explanatory factors for movement collective action (McAdam, McCarthy, and Zald 1996). But this triad was still largely static: although its proponents (including the present authors) believed that opportunities, mobilizing structures, and frames change, producing new movements and affecting movement dynamics, how they act on collective action was left largely unspecified. For example, from the first, analysts identified a robust correlation between individuals' involvement in social networks and recruitment into movements (Diani and McAdam, eds. 2003). But the specific mechanism linking networks and recruitment was not clear: was it access to information, solidarity, mutual confidence building, or social control? Unless the mechanisms linking these factors to social movements were specified, research into movement dynamics would remain wholly correlational.

With respect to mobilization of social movements, the raw materials were available to construct a mechanism-based process model (McAdam 1999, preface). With respect to "framing", David Snow and his collaborators had already done path-breaking work on mechanisms like "frame bridging" and "frame transformation" (Snow et al. 1986; Snow and Benford 1992). But with respect to other important contentious processes, like identify formation, polarization, scale shift, and diffusion, analysts were more likely to list the factors that they saw producing these outcomes than to specify their constituent mechanisms.

In the course of our work on contentious politics, we discovered the necessity of taking strategic interaction, consciousness, and historically accumulated culture into account. We treat social interaction, social ties, communication, and conversation not merely as expressions of structure, rationality, consciousness, or culture but as active sites of creation and change. We have come to think of interpersonal networks, interpersonal communication, and various forms of continuous negotiation—including the negotiation of identities—as figuring centrally in the dynamics of contention. This has led us away from the search for general models that purport to summarize whole categories of contention and toward the analysis of smaller-scale causal mechanisms that recur in different combinations with different aggregate consequences in varying historical settings.

5 MECHANISMS AND PROCESSES

Let us first distinguish between social mechanisms and processes and then relate them to one another in social movement politics:

Mechanisms. We see mechanisms as delimited events that change relations among specified sets of elements in identical or closely similar ways over a variety of situations. They can operate at the individual level—as in the well-known "self-fulfilling prophecy" (Hedström and Swedberg 1998, 12–13). These are what we call *dispositional mechanisms.* Scholars coming from a rational choice persuasion tend to privilege dispositional mechanisms like changes in preferences (for example, see Weingast 1998).

Mechanisms can also be seen at the level of externally generated shifts between the structure or process of concern and surrounding structures and processes, for example, resource depletion (McCarthy and Zald 1977). These are what we call *environmental mechanisms.* The classical social movement approach gave pride of place to environmental mechanisms, such as resource depletion, population change, and the imposition of international factors on domestic politics.

A third form of mechanisms—*relational mechanisms*—is mechanisms that alter connections among people, groups, and interpersonal networks. We see relational mechanisms as particularly central to movement dynamics because they describe the variety of ways in which challengers alter their connections both to insiders and to contentious politics in general. Consider the mechanism that we call *brokerage*: the linking of two or more previously unconnected social sites by a unit that mediates their relations with one another and/or with yet other sites. Two actors might have almost complete identity of views, class backgrounds, and organizational templates, but in the absence of third parties who can bring them together, they may never be able to form a movement coalition.

Environmental. dispositional, and relational mechanisms combine. In *Dynamics of Contention,* for example, we examined how the onset of the American Civil War occurred against the background of an *environmental* mechanism—the massive antebellum shift of population and voters to the West. This contributed to and combined with a *cognitive* mechanism—the growing *disposition* of northerners to see southern vs. northern westward expansion as a zero-sum game. Both were manifest through a *relational* mechanism—the brokerage of a coalition between free-soil seeking westerners and antislavery northerners by a political party—the new Republican party (McAdam, Tarrow, and Tilly 2001, ch. 6).

Mechanisms seldom operate singly. They typically concatenate with other mechanisms into broader processes (Gambetta 1998, 105) or form a sequence of mechanisms so closely linked that they form a robust process. *Processes* are regular sequences of such mechanisms that produce similar (generally more complex and contingent) transformations of those elements. There are no uniquely social movement processes, but some recur so frequently in contentious politics that we find them in a wide variety of episodes of contention. Here are four that we have found especially useful in examining contentious politics:

- *Mobilization* consists in a number of interacting mechanisms, starting from the environmental ones that have been broadly labeled "social change processes" passing through cognitive and relational mechanisms such as attribution of opportunity and threat, social appropriation, framing of the dispute and arraying of innovative forms of collective action. In his reconstruction of the American civil rights movement, Doug McAdam arrays these mechanisms in a sequential, interactive process of mobilization (McAdam 1999, preface).
- Another family of mechanisms is what we call *political identity formation*. The establishment of political identities involves changes in the awareness within the persons involved as well as within other parties to those identities that they constitute an identity, but it also involves alterations in connections among the affected persons and groups. In her innovative work with global justice activists, Donatella della Porta sees the formation of a transnational political identity growing out of a sequence of international protest events and local and regional social fora (della Porta 2005).
- A third group of mechanisms is found in movement *coalition formation*, in which weak social and political actors combine in order to face powerful, entrenched opponents. Margaret Levi and Gillian Murphy define coalitions as *collaborative, means-oriented arrangements that permit distinct organizational entities to pool resources in order to effect change*. In their work on the "Battle of Seattle" they identify two overlapping coalitions, one of which was aimed at demonstrating broad unity of labor, environmentalists, and civic groups against the World Trade Organization, and the second to defend the civil rights of arrested protesters against the Seattle Police (2006).
- A fourth group of mechanisms is found in the process of *polarization*. By polarization we mean widening of political and social space between claimants in a contentious episode and the gravitation of previously uncommitted or moderate actors towards one, the other, or both extremes. When it occurs, polarization is an important accompaniment to contentious episodes because it vacates the moderate center, impedes the recomposition of previous coalitions, produces new channels for future ones, fills even the most pragmatic of policy issues with ideological content which can block their solution, and can lead to repression, armed conflict, and civil war. We examined such a process of polarization in the struggle between Jacobins and Girondins in the French Revolution (McAdam, Tarrow, and Tilly 2001, ch. 10).

Examining these four processes makes possible a more dynamic account of social movement trajectories than is found in either classical structural accounts or the newer "cultural turn" and rational choice accounts of contentious politics. We see movements emerging through the mobilization of objective and constructed claims on behalf of a variety of represented actors on the part of movement entrepreneurs. Because they are weak and their claims diverse, these figures fashion new identities around these claims and bridge their interests in movement coalitions.

But as our initial story from Manila illustrated, these moves do not occur in a political vacuum. The shaping of powerful movement coalitions around the claims of challengers can trigger two other processes. First, the desire for broadened support brings the movement into contact with insiders who sympathize with its claims, see in it opportunities for advantage, or both; this can lead either to movement co-optation or to divisions in the political class that weaken the position of elites and, at the extreme, can bring about a situation of divided sovereignty. Second, to the degree that they threaten opponents, mobilization and coalition formation frequently give rise to opposing movements and coalitions, and to a process of polarization between the movement and a counter-movement (Meyer and Whittier 1994). When that counter-movement is embraced by authorities, the original movement is weakened, perhaps fatally.

The struggle over legal abortion in the United States reveals many of these tendencies. Movement emergence in the 1960s was followed by a process of coalition formation that involved new and practiced actors from both outside and inside the American political establishment. This led both to the inclusion of the movement in the mainstream and to early success, in the form of the *Roe* v. *Wade* Supreme Court decision of 1972. This was followed by its partial demobilization and by the formation of a powerful counter-movement in the form of the Pro-Life coalition, which gained the support of competing sectors of the elite, religious institutions, and, ultimately, of the administration of George W. Bush.

6 CONTENTION, MOVEMENTS, AND DEMOCRACY

Contention and social movements bear paradoxical relationships to democracy. Considered as sheer frequency of public, collective claim making, on the whole contention greatly increases with democratization. Many more groups and much higher proportions of the citizenry join in making collective claims of one sort or another. Social movements, moreover, thrive in democracies. They benefit from the (always incomplete) rights to associate, to assemble, and to speak that expand with democratization. But democracies also contain contention dramatically, significantly decreasing the frequency and intensity of collective violence in public politics. The path to and from democracy, furthermore, usually passes through heightened contention, including revolution, civil war, and violent inter-group competition. Consider just the cases of Ireland and the United States: both arrived at today's public politics of widespread contention and frequent social movements through hard-fought civil wars.

Democracies channel contention. They do so by facilitating claims that follow the forms of electoral politics and legislative representation, tolerating claims that fall within the rules of association, assembly, and speech, but vigorously repressing claims that take place outside the standard repertoire. In democracies, specialized police forces distinct from the war-fighting armed forces generally take on the responsibility of channeling contention into a regime's facilitated and tolerated forms. They do so not only by policing assemblies and public spaces, but also by monitoring and subverting collective actors they (or their political mentors) identify as threatening to act outside acceptable channels.

Three pressing questions arise from this complexity.

First, what causes the broad but still incomplete correspondence between social movements and democratic institutions?

Second, to what extent and how does democratization itself cause social movements to form and prosper?

Third, under what conditions, and how, do social movements actually advance democracy?

Why the broad correlation between democracy and social movements? It results in part from a simple fact: the same processes that promote democratization also promote social movements. Those processes include (a) increases in the numbers and connections among potential political participants, for example through urbanization and grouping of workers in large organizations; (b) equalization of resources and connections among potential political participants, for example through broad public education and access to mass media; (c) insulation of public politics from existing social inequalities, for example through the formation of cross-class political coalitions and parties; (d) integration of interpersonal solidarities into public politics, for example through shared military service and veterans' benefits. These promoters of democracy also facilitate social movements by breaking down segmentation, patron–client politics, and localism in favor of wide-ranging connections among dispersed people who share the same interests.

Yet democratization itself also promotes social movements directly. It does so most obviously by broadening and equalizing rights within public politics: not only rights of association, assembly, speech, and electoral participation, but also rights built into laws whose enforcement one group of citizens or another may find unsatisfactory. In a complementary way, democracy typically expands citizens' *obligations*— obligations to answer census takers, perform military service, attend school, and so on. Those obligations likewise become matters of public, collective contestation by means of campaigns, social movement performances, and public displays.

In addition, democratization promotes the formation of institutions that in their turn facilitate or participate in social movements: political parties, labor unions, trade associations, non-governmental organizations, lobbies, and government agencies (for example agricultural ministries) committed to support of specific constituencies rather than of the general public. In all these regards, de-democratization reverses the causation, inhibiting social movements where once they thrived. Spain under Franco and Italy under Mussolini provide telling examples of the social movement's decline in de-democratization, as do the many Latin American countries that temporarily fell under authoritarian rule during the 1960s and 1970s.

With this mixed record, we might wonder whether social movements themselves promote democratization. Under some circumstances, they do. They do so when they activate the democracy-promoting processes listed earlier:

- increasing the numbers and connections among potential political participants, e.g. by drawing previously inactive people into public causes;
- equalization of resources and connections among potential political participants, e.g. by carrying on programs of public education and supporting participation of disadvantaged population segments;
- insulation of public politics from existing social inequalities, e.g. by organizing coalitions across ethnic, racial, religious, and class lines;
- integration of interpersonal solidarities into public politics, e.g. by drawing in whole groups of friends and relatives.

It follows that narrowly based movements, movements on behalf of parochial privileges, and movements to exclude others from politics threaten democracy to the extent that they prevail. Democracy maintains a precarious balance between movements that sustain and threaten its survival. This is why social movements changed and engendered changes as they shifted from north to south.

7 NORTH AND SOUTH IN CONTENTIOUS POLITICS

The social movement repertoire developed in Western Europe and the United States through the familiar processes of national state building, parliamentarization, and industrialization. Does this mean that movements are a parochially "northern" phenomenon? Yes and no: "yes," because movements emerged out of the atmosphere favorable for campaigning, associating, and public presentation of liberalizing Western states and themselves advanced their democratization; but "no" because—once invented—the movement form itself became modular and diffused around the world. After its invention in Western Europe, it diffused westward and southward through print and the telegraph, the railroad and the steamship, colonialism and the reaction to it, immigration, and the brokerage carried out by movement missionaries (Tarrow 2005, ch. 6). Consider nationalism, with Benedict Anderson (1991): a theory that first grew out of the French and American revolutions became a modular expression of a wide variety of claims and changed shape as it encountered indigenous traditions, new forms of organization, and other doctrines with which it merged.

Social movements came up against the very different structures of opportunity and constraint in the (usually) less liberal states and societies they encountered in the east and south. Consider what happened to the social democratic model as it diffused from Western and Central to Eastern Europe in the late nineteenth century. What had already evolved into democratically run mass movements with distinct and open trade union, political party, and civil society structures in the West gave way to semiclandestine cellular structures led by professional revolutionaries as they moved eastward. When Lenin asked "What is to be done?" and answered with the formula of the vanguard party, he was calling for nothing less than the transformation of the Western social movement into something that could survive both tsarist repression and the indifference of a largely peasant society.

Diffusion and adaptation of the social movement repertoire was not unidirectional from north and west to south and east: Leninism once again provides an example. Once invented in the east, the vanguard model did move westward, competing with its Western social democratic progenitor and—in the form of fascism and National Socialism—defeating social democracy along with democracy altogether. Diffusion from east to west could also revitalize Western movements. The peculiar mix of Indian cultural elements and strategic reasoning that produced Gandhian non-violence was "dislocated" and theorized by interpreters in the West, helping to produce successes of the American civil rights movement and the practice of non-violence in the post-socialist states of Serbia, Georgia, and Ukraine (Chabot 2002).

India aside, the conditions that gave rise to the social movement in the West have seldom been approximated elsewhere. And this means that other forms of contentious politics—from civil wars to religious-based insurgency—have been far more common in those parts of the world. Consider what has happened to the Islamist movement that first developed in South Asia, Saudi Arabia, and Egypt in the first part of the last century (Kepel 2002). As these movements began to gain support, repressive regimes forbade political association and mobilization by means of formal organizations other than a few state-authorized political parties. So doing, they increase the reliance of ordinary people on informal networks as vehicles for survival and influence (Singerman 1995, ch. 3). The impoverishment of formal public life drove activism underground (Singerman 2004, 148–9) from where it has given rise to the most feared transnational movement in the world today.

Nominally Islamic regimes had little choice, however, but to tolerate (and keep a wary eye upon) ostensibly non-political Islamic organizations such as medical clinics, schools, charities, and cultural societies (Wiktorowicz 2001, 83). The same regimes, nevertheless, generally face covert opposition by networks of Islamists: activists who seek to impose strict religious rule over states they regard as having secularized and/or sold out to the secular West. Few Islamists plunge as deep into opposition as Osama bin Laden and al-Qaeda, but many share bin Laden's hope for a purified Islamic world.

As a consequence, Islamists themselves combine concealment and dissimulation; they keep their organized networks underground, but they infiltrate tolerated Islamic organizations, seeking both to influence those organizations and to recruit promising believers into their own networks. Jordan's Salafi enthusiasts gain most of their new members from existing circles of pious but politically inactive Muslims (Wiktorowicz 2001, 134–5). Faced by political repression and toleration of non-political expression, political Islamism gave rise to the pattern of political violence we see today.

8 POLITICAL VIOLENCE AND SOCIAL MOVEMENTS

Given our view that social movements are engaged in sustained and largely public campaigns in democracies or democratizing polities, how do we regard the political violence that has spread across the world over the last decade, and especially since September 11, 2001?

As compared with civil wars, genocide, and ethnic combat, social movements produce whatever effects they have chiefly by non-violent means. They call attention to the presence of organized political actors and their claims mostly without significant physical damage to persons or property. When collective violence arises in social movements, it occurs principally in three circumstances: when activists struggle with police and other professional guardians of public order; when activists of a given persuasion and competing or hostile activists confront each other; and when groups committed to direct action use or break away from non-violent movement gatherings such as demonstrations and public meetings to outbid former comrades.

The dynamics of the relationship among non-violent movements, state repression, and political violence is poorly understood, mainly because students of political violence have largely limited themselves to a correlational logic (Collier and Hoeffler 2004; Fearon and Laitin 2003). They have shown that environmental factors like mountainous terrain, the presence of natural resources, and low GNP per capita are all closely connected to the outbreak of civil war; what they have not shown are the mechanisms that escalate non-violent contention into terrorism or civil war.

This is a dynamic that the study of contentious politics can help students of civil war, ethnic conflict, and other forms of violent conflict to uncover (Sambanis and Zinn 2005). For example, working with Italian data from the 1960s and 1970s, della Porta and Tarrow argued that state repression, competition and outbidding, and declining mass support were the major mechanisms that produced the Red Brigades and other advocates of armed struggle (1986). And expanding the civil war datasets developed by Gurr and others, Sambanis and Zinn pinpoint certain forms of repression, modeling, and opportunity structure as the factors that produce civil wars out of non-violent secessionist movements (2005, 36).

Three questions deserve much more attention: (1) What determines the frequency with which repression, inter-movement competition, and outbidding arise in different sorts of movements and settings? (2) what are their impacts on the overall effects of social movements? (3) Under what conditions and by what processes do participants in other more frequently violent forms of contentious politics such as terror and militia activity turn to social movement activity, and vice versa? Superior answers to these questions would clarify the futures of both collective violence and social movements.

9 FUTURES OF CONTENTIOUS POLITICS

Our confidence in the strong—though not deterministic—relationship of democracy and social movements obliges us to close with very brief comments on three current issues in social movement research:

First, are we entering a "movement society," one in which the classical social movement repertoire has become so omnipresent that the distinction between social movements and institutional politics has largely dissolved?

Second, what can we say about the outcomes of social movements? Faced by the overwhelming force of modern states, under what conditions can they produce political and social change?

Third, given the origins of the social movement in national politics, how does the process of globalization that some have seen weakening the power and autonomy of the national state affect the strategy and future of the social movement?

These three remain open questions on which analysts divide, and on which insufficient evidence is so far available. Let us sketch the questions without proposing definitive answers to them.

10 THE MOVEMENT SOCIETY

Even in relatively democratic polities only a minority of citizens ever participates directly in the campaigns, performances, and displays of social movements. Despite that fact, participants and students of social movements—overlapping categories—often claim that the distinction between movements and institutions is disappearing. The distinction dissolves, goes the argument, as every interest group grabs the package of associations, meetings, petitions, demonstrations, and public statements; as holders of power contain, manipulate, or subvert movements; as specialists and specialized organizations displace the militants of yesteryear; and as movements lose their impact on politics to mass media, opinion polls, and amply financed electoral campaigns. With two or three demonstrations a day in Washington DC alone, after all, national politicians can hardly find social movement activities novel or exciting. According to this view, social movements are becoming just one more form of political expression, and a decreasingly effective one.

In a contrary view, participants and observers of transnational movements often claim that a fundamentally new era is just beginning for social movements. International coordination is becoming easier, goes the claim, for three reasons. First, the world is simply becoming more connected, which means that advocates of environmental preservation, justice, or women's rights occupy greater common ground with their counterparts in other world regions, and have less and less chance of changing the conditions that concern them without international coordination. Second, international institutions such as the World Bank and the United Nations wield increasing influence worldwide, but by doing so provide grounds for widely separate advocates to coordinate their use of their international facilities or their advocacy of new international policies. Third, ramifying communication networks—most recently via the internet—dramatically lower the costs of communication and coordination across world regions. Future movements, go the most ambitious interpretations, will largely dispense with local face-to-face organizing in favor of vast, worldwide, often virtual mobilization. If this view is correct, the next movement society will not develop nationally, but internationally.

These disagreements matter. They pivot on causes and effects as well as simple descriptions. Is it true that democratic political systems eventually tame and institutionalize social movements, so that they eventually lose some of their effectiveness? Like the local shaming ceremony and the military *coup d'état*, are performances in the classic social movement repertoire passing into history as new social processes generate new forms of collective claim making? Is internationalization actually producing major changes in the character of social movements across the world? Do huge, one-day, worldwide mobilizations produce discernible effects on international policies and institutions? To what extent and how, in any case, do social movements produce their effects on power holders and public policies?

11 OUTCOMES OF CONTENTIOUS POLITICS

Textbooks on social movements almost invariably describe their subject as organized attempts to bring about social change. As far as it goes, such a characterization is unobjectionable, but it leaves open a number of important issues:

First, what kind of change do movements seek to bring about? In his magisterial book *The Strategy of Social Protest* (1975), William Gamson enumerates two main kinds of efforts: to bring about group acceptance and to advance group goals. He might have added that some movements seek personal development, while others try to affirm collective identities.

Second, under what conditions do movements succeed? Gamson elaborates that they are more likely to succeed when they have centralized organizations, make only modest claims, do not use violence, and do not seek to displace rulers. But Gamson neglects to ask what elites are doing while movements make efforts to achieve their goals. States can facilitate or repress movements; offer opportunities for access or deny them; even sponsor or create movements that match state goals.

Finally, posing the question of movement success as the outcome of a binary relationship between states and challengers ignores what other actors contribute or how they detract from movement goals. These can include institutional elites, political parties, interest groups, and counter-movements. The success of movement efforts cannot be seen as the two-person game. In other words, movements are part of a broader parallelogram of forces in which they may not be the major players and in which the results may look very different than the goals they set out with. This takes us to our final set of reflections on the future of contentious politics—the effects of globalization.

12 GLOBALIZATION AND CONTENTIOUS POLITICS

Any time a distinctive set of social connections and practices expands from a regional to a transcontinental scale, some globalization is occurring. Each time an existing transcontinental set of social connections and practices fragments, disintegrates, or vanishes, some deglobalization occurs. Only when the first sort of process is far outrunning the second does it clarify matters to say that humanity as a whole is globalizing. On balance, the period since the Second World War qualifies. Despite some localizing counter-trends, internationalization of capital, trade, industrial organization, communications, political institutions, science, disease, atmospheric pollution, vindictive violence, and organized crime have been producing a net movement toward globalization since the middle of the twentieth century.

Some connections between globalization and shifts in contentious politics across the world since the middle of the twentieth century are fairly clear, but others remain highly debatable. The rising integration of national economies into world trading circuits combined with the increasing intervention in national economies by financial institutions such as the International Monetary Fund has greatly increased the frequency and similarity of popular responses to fiscal austerity and threats to previously protected industries across the world. Civil wars have largely displaced interstate wars worldwide under the triple influence of:

- multiplication in the sheer number of low-capacity states whose survival as distinct entities (if not necessarily under present management) the international community guarantees;
- world trade in contraband such as arms, drugs, and diamonds that supports militias and rebel armies almost regardless of the popular support they command;
- emigrant diasporas (some involved in the movement of contraband) supplying aid to opponents of existing regimes.

But other questions about the impact of globalization remain hotly contested and worthy of systematic research.

First, as the question of "social movement society" has already forced us to ask, does globalization more or less automatically connect potential activists across the world, present them with similar challenges, and thus move social movement collective action away from local and national concerns? The best evidence we have is that involvement in global economic networks is not a country's best predictor of participation in transnational contention; far more influential are the nature of the domestic political system and the degree of that country's involvement in international institutions (Smith 2004; Tarrow 2005).

Moreover, metaphors of the "network society" aside (Castells 1996), there are enormous cultural gaps, differences in interests and values, and high transaction costs involved in trying to connect activists across borders (Tarrow 2005, ch. 9). Even in Western Europe, where we might expect to find the greatest shift to the supranational level, the vast majority of contentious acts remain couched at the domestic level, even those that target European institutions (Imig and Tarrow 2001).

Third, should we infer that "global" social movements will displace militia activity, inter-ethnic conflict, and nationally oriented party politics in the near future? Some students of globalization regard all forms of transnational contention as "global social movements" but we demur. If, as we have done, we define the social movement as a sustained challenge to power holders in the name of a population living under the jurisdiction of those power holders by means of public displays of that population's worthiness, unity, numbers, and commitment, than many forms of transnational contention do not qualify as movements. That does not make them less meaningful; it only means that they lack the characteristics that have made the social movement a specific form in the contentious politics of the modern world. Our task is to examine whether new forms of contentious politics are emerging across borders.

Most important, to what extent and how does globalization affect the capacities of individual states across the world to control and respond to political action within their territories? If, for example, global networks are reducing state capacities, will that process accelerate the internationalization of contentious politics? In the 1990s, a "global civil society" view developed according to which states were being simultaneously eroded by the forces of economic globalization and by the cross-border connections of civil society groups (see e.g. Anheier, Glasius, and Kaldor 2005). In the wake of September 11, 2001 and the Iraq War, we are not convinced that states are losing their grip.

Social movements as we know them have only existed for two centuries or so. Contentious politics and political institutions, however, have been with us since humans first created states close to 10,000 years ago. Social movements may not survive the current wave of internationalization, but contentious politics and political institutions will continue to evolve. In studying the interplay of social movements, contentious politics, and institutions, we are examining the future—and the perils—of democratic participation.

REFERENCES

AMINZADE, R., and McADAM. D. 2001. Emotions and contentious politics. In Aminzade et al. 2001: 14–50.

—— et al. 2001. *Silence and Voice in the Study of Contentious Politics*. Cambridge: Cambridge University Press.

ANDERSON, B. 1991. *Imagined Communities: Reflections on the Origin and Spread of Nationalism*. London: Verso.

ANHEIER, H., GLASIUS, M., and KALDOR, M. eds. 2005. *Global Civil Society 2004/5*. London: Sage Publications.

BURSTEIN, P. 1998. Interest organizations, political parties, and the study of democratic politics. Ch. 3 in *Social Movements and American Political Institutions*, ed. A. Costain and A. McFarland. Boulder, Colo.: Rowman and Littlefield.

CASTELLS, M. 1996. *The Rise of the Network Society*. Oxford: Blackwell Publishers.

CHABOT, S. 2002. Transnational diffusion and the African-American reinvention of the Gandhian repertoire. Pp. 97–114 in *Globalization and Resistance: Transnational Dimensions of Social Movements*, ed. J. Smith and H. Johnston. Lanham, Md.: Rowman and Littlefield.

COLLIER, P., and HOEFFLER, A. 2004. Greed and grievance in civil war. *Oxford Economic Papers*, 56: 563–95.

COSTAIN, A. 1992. *Inviting Women's Rebellion: A Political Process Interpretation of the Women's Movement*. Baltimore: Johns Hopkins University Press.

DELLA PORTA, D. 2005. Multiple belongings, flexible identities, and the construction of "another politics": between the European social forum and local social fora. Pp. 175–202 in *Transnational Protest and Global Activism*, ed. D. della Porta and S. Tarrow. Lanham, Md.: Rowman and Littlefield.

—— and TARROW, S. 1986. Unwanted children: political violence and the cycle of protest in Italy. *European Journal of Political Research*, 14: 607–32.

DIANI, M., and McADAM, D. eds. 2003. *Social Movements and Networks: Relational Approaches to Collective Action*. Oxford: Oxford University Press.

FAVRE, P. ed. 1990. *La Manifestation*. Paris: Presses de la Fondation Nationale des Sciences Politiques.

FEARON, J. D., and LAITIN, D. D. 2003. Ethnicity, insurgency, and civil war. *American Political Science Review*, 97: 91–106.

FILLIEULE, O. 1997. *Stratégies de la rue: les manifestations en France*. Paris: Presses de la Fondation Nationale des Sciences Politiques.

GAMBETTA, D. 1998. Concatenations of mechanisms. In *Social Mechanisms: An Analytical Approach to Social Theory*, ed. P. Hedström and R. Swedberg. Cambridge: Cambridge University Press.

GAMSON, W. A. 1975. *The Strategy of Social Protest*. Homewood, Ill.: Dorsey Press.

—— 1992. The social psychology of collective action. In *Frontiers in Social Movement Theory*, ed. A. Morris and C. McClurg Mueller. New Haven: Yale University Press.

GOLDSTONE, J. A. 1998. Social movements or revolutions? On the evolution and outcomes of collective action. In *From Contention to Democracy*, ed. M. Giugni, D. McAdam, and C. Tilly. Boulder, Colo.: Rowman & Littlefield.

—— and TILLY, C. 2001. Threat (and opportunity): popular action and state response in the dynamics of contentious action. In *Silence and Voice in Contentious Politics*, ed. R. Aminzade et al. Cambridge: Cambridge University Press.

GOODWIN, J., and JASPER, J. M., eds. 2004. *Rethinking Social Movements: Structure, Meaning, and Emotion*. Lanham, Md.: Rowman and Littlefield.

GRIMSTED, D. 1998. *American Mobbing, 1828–1861: Toward Civil War*. New York: Oxford University Press.

HEDSTRÖM, P., and SWEDBERG, R. 1998. *Social Mechanisms: An Analytical Approach to Social Theory*. Cambridge: Cambridge University Press.

IMIG, D., and TARROW, S. 2001. Mapping the Europeanization of contention: evidence from a quantitative data analysis. In *Contentious Europeans: Protest and Politics in an Emerging Polity*, ed. D. Imig and S. Tarrow. Lanham, Md.: Rowman and Littlefield.

KATZENSTEIN, M. F. 1998. *Faithful and Fearless: Moving Feminist Protest Inside the Church and the Military*. Princeton: Princeton University Press.

KEPEL, G. 2002. *Jihad: The Trail of Political Islam*. Cambridge, Mass.: Harvard University Press.

KINEALY, C. 2003. Les Marches orangistes en Irlande du Nord: histoire d'un droit. *Le Mouvement social*, 202: 165–82.

KRIESI, H. 1996. The organizational structure of new social movements in a political context. In *Comparative Perspectives on Social Movements*, ed. D. McAdam, J. McCarthy, and M. Zald. Cambridge: Cambridge University Press.

LEVI, M., and MURPHY, G. 2004. Coalitions of contention: the case of the WTO protests in Seattle. *Political Studies*, 54 (December 2006): 651–70.

McADAM, D. 1999. *Political Process and the Development of Black Insurgency, 1930–1970*, 2nd edn. Chicago: University of Chicago Press.

—— McCARTHY, J. and ZALD, M. N., eds. 1996. *Comparative Perspectives on Social Movements*. New York: Cambridge University Press.

—— TARROW, S. and TILLY, C. 2001. *Dynamics of Contention*. New York: Cambridge University Press.

McCARTHY, J., and ZALD, M. N. 1977. Resource mobilization and social movements: a partial theory. *American Journal of Sociology*, 82: 1212–41.

MANSBRIDGE, J., and FLASTER, K. 2005. "Male chauvinist", "feminist," "sexist," and "sexual harrassment": different trajectories in feminist linguistic innovation. *American Speech*, 80: 56–279.

MELUCCI, A. 1988. Getting involved: identity and mobilization in social movements. Pp. 329–48 in *From Structure to Action: Comparing Social Movements across Cultures*, ed. B. Klandermans, H. Kriesi, and S. Tarrow. Greenwich, Conn.: JAI Press.

MEYER, D. S. 1990. *A Winter of Discontent: The Nuclear Freeze and American Politics*. New York: Praeger.

—— and WHITTIER, N. 1994. Social movement spillover. *Social Problems*, 41: 277–98.

MORRIS, A. D., and MUELLER, C. M., eds. 1992. *Frontiers of Social Movement Theory*. New Haven: Yale University Press.

PIGENET, M., and TARTAKOWSKY, D. eds. 2003. Les Marches. *Le Mouvement social*, 202, entire issue.

RAFAEL, V. L. 2003. The cell phone and the crowd: messianic politics in the contemporary Philippines. *Public Culture*, 15: 399–425.

ROCHON, T. R. 1998. *Culture Moves: Ideas, Activism, and Changing Values*. Princeton: Princeton University Press.

——and MEYER, D. S., eds. 1998. *Coalitions and Political Movements: The Lessons of the Nuclear Freeze*. Boulder, Colo.: Lynne Rienner.

RUCHT, D. 2002. The EU as a target of mobilisation: is there a Europeanisation of conflict? Pp. 163–94 in *L'Action collective en Europe*, ed. R. Balme, D. Chabanet, and V. Wright. Paris: Presses de Sciences Po.

RUPP, L. J., and TAYLOR, V. 1987. *Survival in the Doldrums: The American Women's Rights Movement, 1945 to the 1960s*. New York: Oxford University Press.

SAMBANIS, N., and ZINN, A. 2005. From protest to violence: an analysis of conflict escalation with an application to self-determination movements. Unpublished paper. Yale University Department of Political Science.

SAWYER, R. K. 2001. *Creating Conversations: Improvisation in Everyday Discourse*. Cresskill, NJ: Hampton Press.

SINGERMAN, D. 1995. *Avenues of Participation: Family, Politics and Networks in Urban Quarters of Cairo*. Princeton: Princeton University Press.

——2004. The networked world of Islamist social movements. Pp. 143–63 in *Islamic Activism: A Social Movement Theory Approach*, ed. Q. Wiktorowicz. Bloomington: Indiana University Press.

SMITH, J. 2004. Exploring connections between global integration and political mobilization. *Journal of World-Systems Research*, 10: 255–85.

SNOW, D. A., and BENFORD, R. D. 1992. Master frames and cycles of protest. In Morris and Mueller 1992: 133–55.

——ROCHFORD, B., Jr., WORDEN, S., and BENFORD, R. 1986. Frame alignment processes, micromobilization, and movement participation. *American Sociological Review*, 51: 464–81.

TARROW, S. 1998. *Power in Movement: Social Movements and Contentious Politics*. New York: Cambridge University Press.

——2005. *The New Transnational Activism*. New York: Cambridge University Press.

——and McADAM, D. 2005. Scale shift in transnational contention. Pp. 121–50 in *Transnational Protest and Global Activism*, ed. D. della Porta and S. Tarrow. Lanham, Md.: Rowman and Littlefield.

TARTAKOWSKY, D. 1997. *Les Manifestations de rue en France, 1918–1968*. Paris: Publications de la Sorbonne.

——2004. *La Manif en éclats*. Paris: La Dispute.

TILLY, C. 1978. *From Mobilization to Revolution*. Reading, Mass.: Addison-Wesley Pub. Co.

——1995. *Popular Contention in Great Britain, 1758–1834*. Cambridge, Mass.: Harvard University Press.

——2004. *Social Movements, 1768–2004*. Boulder, Colo.: Paradigm Publishers.

——and TARROW, S. 2006. *Contentious Politics*. Lanham, Md.: Paragon Press.

Time Asia. 2001. People Power Redux. 29 January, **www.time.com/time/asia/magazine/2001/0129/cover1.html**, viewed 14 August 2003.

WEINGAST, B. 1998. Political stability and civil war: institutions, commitment, and American democracy. Pp. 148–93 in *Analytic Narratives*, ed. R. Bates et al. Princeton: Princeton University Press.

WIKTOROWICZ, Q. 2001. *The Management of Islamic Activism: Salafis, the Muslim Brotherhood, and State Power in Jordan.* Albany: State University of New York Press.

——ed. 2004. *Islamic Activism: A Social Movement Theory Approach.* Bloomington: Indiana University Press.

YOUNG, M. 2007. *Bearing Witness against Sin: The Birth of American Social Activism.* Chicago: University of Chicago Press.

C H A P T E R   2 0

....

MECHANISMS OF GLOBALIZED PROTEST MOVEMENTS

....

MARK I. LICHBACH

HELMA G. E. DE VRIES

1 INTRODUCTION

....

WHILE architects built the post-Cold-War world, popular movements against neo-liberal globalization and against war mobilized protesters around that world. For example, worldwide demonstrations on November 30, 1999, during the Battle of Seattle, and February 15, 2003, before the US invasion of Iraq, involved millions of protesters in dozens of countries. Academic theorists have tried to explain how different kinds of macro-level global institutions activated the mechanisms behind the global protests, one of the newest forms of contentious politics.

- *Economics*. Thomas Friedman analyzed the losers of neo-liberal globalization and Chris Chase-Dunn the structural deficits of the world system.
- *Culture*. Ben Barber stressed pre-modern backlash and Ron Inglehart postmodern and postmaterial angst.
- *Society*. Margaret Keck and Kathryn Sikkink located activist non-governmental organizations (NGOs) and Manuel Castells an emergent global civil society.

- *Politics*. Sid Tarrow discovered the complex internationalism of an emerging world polity, Michael Hardt and Antonio Negri American hegemony and empire, David Held a global democratic deficit, and Dani Rodrik state-level democratic incapacity.

Activist thought has also enriched our understanding of global economics, culture, society, and politics. Protester reflections have clarified several institution–mechanism–protest linkages.

The literature on contentious politics, which explores meso-level processes of mobilization, can also be drawn upon to explain the global protests. Doug McAdam, Sidney Tarrow, and Charles Tilly's Synthetic Political Opportunity Theory or SPOT analyzes political opportunities, mobilizing structures, and cultural frames. Mark Lichbach's Collective Action Research Program or CARP analyzes market, community, contract, and hierarchy mobilization processes.

Finally, the micro-level or survey literature on political behavior can also be tapped. Sidney Verba's theory of political participation examines protesters' decision calculi, individual resources, recruitment or institutional resources, psychological engagement, and issue intensity.

This chapter draws together these intellectual resources. We offer a survey of theories of contentious politics that aims to explore their applicability to the new phenomenon of global protest movements (GPMs). Our theme is that macro global institutions drive meso mobilizing processes that micro recruit individuals into GPMs. Using general theories of contentious politics focused at the macro, meso, and micro levels of analysis, we derive competing explanations about the mechanisms used to mobilize GPMs.

We also suggest that differences between GPMs may be attributed to their differential usage of mobilizational mechanisms, and thus that these mechanisms may also account for the successes and failures of the various new manifestations of contentious politics. When mobilizational mechanisms are refracted through the lenses of academic theories and activist thoughts about globalized protest, we can develop and test hypotheses that distinguish GPMs and other forms of contention. Our main goal is in fact to compare and contrast the mechanisms involved in different GPMs as well as contentious politics more broadly. This comparison allows us to refine our understandings of how these mechanisms work in explaining globalized collective action as well as other forms of contention.

Using macro, meso, and micro processes to analyze protest involves an investigation of resources, relationships, and values in protests, protester coalitions, and protesters. Compared to non-protesters, movement participants in various GPMs have differential access to certain sets of resources, relationships, and values. Resources include education and socioeconomic well-being. Contacts and networks created by participation in parties, interest groups, and social movement organizations constitute relationships. Values are attitudes and beliefs (e.g. having postmodern values or favoring globalization). We expect that protest locations, groups in protest coalitions, and protesters are more likely to be characterized by the high availability of these resources, relationships, and values. These features seem to differentiate protests, coalitions, and protesters in GPMs, and may play a role in inspiring globalized collective action.

While the exploration of GPMs is nascent in the field of contentious politics, and many of the theories which have been used to explain globalized collective action have also been applied to understand other forms of contention, we argue that dynamics of contention are best accounted for using such a multi-level theoretical framework. One must explore the linkages between macro-level targets, meso-level organizing, and micro-level political behavior. One must compare and contrast the mechanisms behind different GPMs as well as other forms of contentious politics. And one must consider activist thought, which provides activists' perspectives on GPMs, in addition to traditional academic theories. Our framework is summarized in Table 20.1.

Academics and activists thus show how macro, meso, and micro explanations of protest suggest alternative mechanisms of contention. By specifying how abstract mechanisms work in concrete situations, the theories can help us compare and contrast disparate GPMs and other types of contention. Future research should investigate linkages between movements' differential mobilizational success and differences in their strategic use of mobilizational mechanisms. To do so, researchers must pick and choose among the mechanisms of our multi-level framework, to which we now turn.

Table 20.1 Model of the mechanisms explaining the mobilization of globalized protest

Macro-level	Economic mechanisms (economic, world systems)
	Culturalist mechanisms (cultural backlash, postmodern value changes)
	World society mechanisms (empowered non-state actors)
	World polity mechanisms (complex internationalism)
	US hegemony explanations (opposition to US hegemony)
	Neo liberal institutional trilemma mechanisms (democratic deficit)
Meso-level	SPOT mechanisms (PO, MS, CF)
	CARP mechanisms (contract, community, hierarchy)
Micro-level	Political behavior mechanisms (resource accumulation, associational recruitment, psychological involvement, issue intensity)

2 MACRO-LEVEL MECHANISMS

According to McAdam, Tarrow, and Tilly, contentious politics refers to "episodic, public, collective interactions among makers of claims and their objects when (a) at least one government is a claimant, an object of claims, or a party to the claims and (b) the claim would, if realized, affect the interests of at least one of the claimants" (2001, 5). Contentious politics thus includes many forms of political struggle, concerning issues of interstate conflict, civil war, revolution, repression, ethnic conflict, genocide, politicide, human rights, riots, strikes, demonstrations, protests, civil disobedience, dissent, and everyday resistance. Contentious events can be violent or non-violent, and their scope can be domestic, transnational, or global. These forms of contention are interrelated, and although some speculate they are driven by similar causal mechanisms, they are often studied in isolation. Tarrow (2005) has made considerable inroads in his seminal attempt to generalize across episodes of transnational contention.

GPMs involve a series of globally coordinated, simultaneous demonstrations on key dates of action, occurring at dozens or even hundreds of protest venues located on most every continent. Compared to the recent anti-war and global justice protests, GPMs have occurred previously, but not with the same degree of global coordination, simultaneity, and inclusiveness geographically. Compared to the waves of contention in the late eighteenth century, 1830, 1848, 1918–19, the late 1920s and early 1930s, 1968, and 1989–91, the recent protests were more global than merely transnational; occurred in most continents as opposed to just some continents; involved a higher degree of cross-national collaboration and temporal simultaneity; focused on the global nature of protest as a primary tactic; and were low on violence.

In the last decade, GPMs against globalization and against war have thus mobilized protesters around the globe in new ways. Namely, on November 30, 1999, the principal day of international action during the Battle of Seattle protests against the World Trade Organization (WTO), coordinated protest occurred in many countries, including the United States, the United Kingdom, Canada, Iceland, Ireland, Portugal, France, Switzerland, the Netherlands, Germany, Italy, Greece, Czech Republic, Turkey, Israel, Pakistan, India, South Korea, the Philippines, and Australia (Laskey 2001, 84–90). More recently, an even more mobilized and globalized anti-war movement has arisen, with many dates of globally coordinated protest involving hundreds of protest locations, between 2001 and the present. One of the most mobilized and geographically globalized anti-war protests occurred on February 15, 2003, involving an estimated "12 million people" by "interconnected social movements on every continent" (Solnit 2004, p. xxiii).

It is natural to explain macro-level phenomena with macro-level variables. GPMs may be explained with mechanisms that focus on several aspects of the global order: economic markets, world systems, cultural values, world society, world polity, US hegemony, and the neoliberal institutional trilemma. These macro-level explanations are systemic influences that both academics and activists point to as sources of global contention.

2.1 Economic Mechanisms

2.1.1 *Economic Issues*

Political economists stress the material basis of protests and thus theorize about activists who mobilize unions with material grievances. Accordingly, academics posit an economic issues structural mechanism suggesting that GPMs are, at root, a protectionist reaction to global markets experiencing economic globalization and heightened domestic economic pressures. While the economic benefits of neo-liberal globalization are a diffuse public good, the economic costs are concentrated on the losers who take action. According to this approach, distributional impacts explain how the dissidents mobilize in GPMs.

Since the losers under economic globalization are seen as the opponents of neo-liberal globalization, the economic issues mechanism leads us to expect globalized collective action in locations where the losers of globalization are clustered; where the unemployed are concentrated; and where neo-liberal reforms are implemented with the greatest domestic problems and least popularity. Protesters are moreover expected to have grievances focused on domestic problems related to neo-liberal policies. Common material concerns are likely used to solidify coalitions, and coalitions are expected to include groups representing material interests. Finally, protesters are expected to be affected negatively by globalization; to have a negative view of globalization and neo-liberal reform; and to have relationships with individuals representing material interests through union or interest group memberships.

2.1.2 *World Systems*

While the economic market explanation of the protests focused on the agency of the "losers" of economic globalization, the world systems argument is that the international system has a long history of counter-hegemonic projects and antisystemic movements. Hence, the world systems mechanism finds proponents amongst the activists who focus on the systemic problems posed by the global market. According to the world systems structural mechanism, resistance has always been globalized and protest often comes in waves and affects many countries at the same time. For example, there is a long history of protest against capitalism because people claim that it ignores social welfare, destroys cultures, damages the environment, and hurts human rights and democracy.

The world systems mechanism thus focuses on the structure of the new global market—the globalization of material interests (Chase-Dunn 1989). The present international political economy consists of a set of interlinked country-level economies that create global markets in land, labor, and capital. Problems of production—trade, finance, immigration, migration, communications, transportation, growth, poverty, inequality, diseases, epidemics, and the environment—are all now global. Thus, it is not possible for a country to isolate itself from global economic trends (e.g. technology), cycles (e.g. booms and busts), and shocks (e.g. oil crises).

According to world systems theories, economic globalization, guided by policies of neo-liberal globalization, has produced destabilization, exploitation, and dependency, which eventually beget materially based movements and protests. The neo-liberal Washington consensus—the type of pure capitalism sometimes advocated by the International Monetary Fund (IMF) and World Bank (WB)—generates many problems that spur protests (Rodrik 1997, 1999, 2001). The dark side of neo-liberal economic globalization is, first, that globalization produces interdependent economies that are vulnerable to the global trends, cycles, and shocks that destabilize political economies. Unregulated capital movements, for example, lead to booms and busts which can bring down whole countries. Some further suggest that globalization produces relative deprivation (inequality and economic stratification); absolute deprivation (unemployment and poverty); and structural dependency (special vulnerabilities of marginalization and exploitation that produce underemployment, resource depletion, population growth, urbanization, natural disasters, disease, and epidemics). These phenomena fuel populist movements. And the more neo-liberal the policies, the greater the resistance: globalization leads to the reduction of the welfare state that ends the social safety net.

World systems theories, in sum, posit that dissidents involved in GPMs are participants in yet another counter-hegemonic, anti-systemic movement, currently using global resistance to oppose a global market which has increasingly globalized interests. As Multilateral Economic Institution (MEI) meetings increase, MEI protest campaigns and mobilizations are expected to increase. Protests are expected to occur in locations where people have gained less through globalization or been more hurt by global markets. Protesters are expected to have grievances focused on domestic problems related to the system's prescribed neo-liberal reforms. Groups representing material interests are expected to be important members of protest coalitions. Protesters are expected to have negative attitudes toward globalization.

2.1.3 Economic Threat Attribution

A third related global economic mechanism, the economic attribution of threat, is sometimes used by activists to frame grievances so as mobilize participants. Some activists suggest that economic problems due to neo-liberal reforms and the global economic system are hurting people (Faraclas 2001, 67). Activists appeal to material interests by suggesting that in this global economic system the haves are trying to control the have-nots: "The few (the wealthy and mobile elites) are once again attempting to control the many, that is the diversity group" (Hawthorne 2001, 87). Hence, important labor unions like the AFL-CIO have even endorsed global justice protests and formed coalitions with global justice groups (Danaher and Burbach 2000, 9; Njehu and Ambrose 2001, 49–50). By connecting reforms sought by global economic institutions to concrete domestic economic problems, unions were drawn into global justice protest coalitions (Brecher, Costello, and Smith 2000, 55; Starr 2000, 83, 89). Activists also try to mobilize participants by drawing the connection between the global economic system and military interventions. Wolfwood (2001, 87) states,

Globalization and militarization are inseparable. The North Atlantic Treaty Organization (NATO) bombed Yugoslavia so that multinational corporations can have access to state-owned mines and oil pipelines, and so that foreign-armed thugs can use Yugoslavian territory for the international drug trade, one of the top ten commodities traded globally.

Both academics and activists thus advance economic explanations of mobilization. Academics endorse structural mechanisms, such as the economic issues mechanism and world systems mechanism, that tend to explain events using larger social structures. In contrast, activists put forth attribution mechanisms that relate events to people's claims and grievances and they try to use such frames strategically. However, most activists tend to focus on other explanations of protest, and academics concur that poor people rarely hit the streets during globalized resistance. Economic mechanisms behind GPMs are thus often considered more peripheral than other explanations that activists and academics put forth. We now turn to these alternatives.

2.2 Pre-modern Fundamentalism and Postmodern Relativism as Culturalist Mechanisms

2.2.1 *Cultural Backlash*

Culturalists argue that specific values and value change have led to GPMs. Some culturalist explanations of these protests stress a cultural backlash mechanism or protectionist reaction to the globalization of identities (Barber 1995). Western, and especially American, values are increasingly hegemonic and have come to define social and cultural identities around the entire world. Global pop culture is thus becoming consumer cosmopolitanism: a common global lifestyle of taste, fashion, and talk in which people define their identity and express themselves symbolically through their material possessions. The New World Order, which connects individuals everywhere at all times, is destroying the autonomy and cohesion of states, societies, and local communities—their cultures, civil societies, markets, democracies, and bureaucratic state institutions.

One possible backlash to this cultural onslaught is the death of politics—alienation, withdrawal, depoliticization, fatalism, nihilism, cynicism, defeatism, and immobilism. Another possible backlash involves the revival of politics. GPMs are thus about a reactionary defense of pre-modern, fundamentalist values against the universal and global logic of the market, the West, the United States, and bourgeois culture. The defensive or protectionist reaction to these purported globalisms and universalisms is diversity and fragmentation: Jihad, fundamentalisms, and particularisms. In the New World Order, resistance thus relies on local traditions to define themselves in opposition to global neo-liberal values. Globalization re-invigorates older forms of solidarities (interests and identities) as weapons to deal with globalization. Traditional religious and ethnic cultures have thus produced fundamentalist backlash to dominant Western values and policy orientations. Glob-alized resistance to global order therefore occurs because of backlash to the globally dominant path of development—neoliberalism.

The results are economic nationalism and autarky, populistic rhetoric and racial chauvinism, anti-internationalism and isolationism. We would therefore expect some protesters to have protectionist grievances focused on promoting traditional values. As Western values have penetrated formerly isolated pre-modern cultures, various kinds of movements have arisen. Thus, we would expect some protests to occur in locations with recently increased Western influence and heightened percep-tion of the threat posed by Western values.

2.2.2 *Opposition to Authority, Cosmopolitanism, Heterogeneous Identities, and Relativism*

The other cultural explanation of GPMs is that they are a product of a movement toward postmodern values in activist segments of industrialized and Third World societies. Postmodernists claim, or advance the metanarrative, that metanarratives are breaking down. Today's world is therefore characterized by heterogeneity and fragmentation—multiple modernities or postmodernity—in which the self seeks several different moral causes. No longer is society preoccupied with materialism, but now that a certain level of material welfare has been reached, people have the luxury of focusing on other, more idealistic, ends. Postmodern values are evident in decreased trust of and skepticism toward authority; increased protest and other forms of active political participation; decreased conventional participation; decreas-ing religiosity; increasing support of progressive ideals; and increased grouping of such issues as peace, human rights, the environment, women's rights, and gay rights (Inglehart 1997). Thus, people with postmodern values are more likely to hold a multiplicity of grievances and to select a multiplicity of targets. Some anarchists radically opposing globalization may draw from postmodern relativism—anarchically opposing all manifestations of power, or all forms of authority. Other protesters, opposing war or globalization, may be less radical and draw from the issues which have been grouped together and made salient during postmodernity as well as its popularization of active political participation and distrust of authority.

Academics suggest several postmodern mobilizational mechanisms that relate societal change to activism: opposition to authority, cosmopolitanism, heteroge-neous identities, and relativism. The opposition to authority mechanism suggests that people are more likely to participate politically via protest when they are opposed to authority. The cosmopolitanism mechanism suggests that people are more likely to mobilize around a set of ideals they claim as universal and universally valid. The heterogeneous identity mechanism suggests that protesters are more likely to develop several ideals and become active in several social movements because identities are more fragmented and unstable, and emergent in social situations like protests. The relativism mechanism suggests that people's actions and attitudes are not a constant but rather evolve relative to their cultural and historical context; thus, individuals are likely to adapt as their context becomes more opposed to traditional authority, as multiple ideals become linked, and identity becomes increasingly fluid. These several societal changes are likely to lead an individual to become more engaged in progressive collective action.

Postmodern mobilizational mechanisms thus suggest that multi-issue idealistic activists who are unconcerned with materialism are likely to mobilize into GPMs. More protests are expected at locations where postmodern values are most commonly held. Coalitions are likely to involve groups working on disparate ideals, and the recognition of common ties across these ideals is likely to be a key factor in binding the coalitions together. Protesters are expected to hold less modern and more postmodern values than the general population, to mobilize for various idealistic causes, to frame their opposition in a way that connects several idealistic causes, to oppose traditional authority, and to engage in active political participation.

2.2.3 *Postmodern Ideals Framing*

Activists indeed use a postmodern ideals framing mechanism to mobilize. Many argue vehemently that they are motivated by a common set of progressive ideals and not by common material interests. As Danaher and Burbach (2000, 10) state,

In contrast to the money cycle that is the central organizing principle of the corporate elites, the movement is organized around the life cycle (human rights and protecting Mother Nature).... we challengers focus our core values on the quality of relations among people and between people and the environment.

The wide array of progressive values that activists see as interconnected under this umbrella include "environmental concerns, human rights, hostility to patriarchy, and a vision of human community based on unity of diverse cultures seeking an end to poverty, oppression, humiliation, and collective violence" as well as nuclear weapons and apartheid (Brecher, Childs, and Cutler 1993, p. ix; Callinicos 2003, 134). Moreover, activists emphasize their mutual distrust of state authority as well as their relative valuation of progressive ideals over material interests (Danaher and Mark 2003, 1). Activists acknowledge that protesters from the industrialized north tend to be well-off and white, and they argue that minorities and the disenfranchised are too preoccupied with their own material problems to protest for these ideals (Barlow and Clarke 2002, 214–15). Activists' postmodern ideals framing mechanism coincides nicely with academics' postmodern values arguments about mobilization which suggest that protesters are more likely to have a postmodern world-view: to link various social causes together as progressive ideals; to place more value on these ideals than on material needs; to distrust traditional authority; and to participate politically by protesting rather than voting.

Quite a few protesters discuss multi-issue linkages and engage in collective action for these disparate issues. Further, many activists emphasize their predilection for these ideals over material interests. Postmodern structural mechanisms like opposition to authority, cosmopolitanism, heterogeneous identities, and relativism have much overlap with postmodern ideals framing. Academics look at cultural changes structurally, describing a societal transition in which materialist values are giving way to postmodern values and certain kinds of activism are increasing. While some academics are still skeptical about the mobilizational power of value change, this perspective is increasingly popular in activist circles. Activists are concerned with mobilizing individuals in collective action, and hence they respond to societal changes by adapting their framing and adopting postmodern ideals. Therefore, the postmodern values perspective is increasingly central for activists.

2.3 World Society Mechanisms

World Society explanations maintain that a globalized civil society has facilitated GPMs (Florini 2000). These explanations suggest that globalization is triumphant over the state—that it has even rendered the state obsolete. Neo-liberalism thus tosses problems away from states and markets and passes them on to individuals and groups. Deconstructing the state gives an opening to civil society. Hence, non-governmental organizations in civil society (NGOs) are organized to protest against the state about the market and to counter the market by organizing cooperative communities. The "end of sovereignty" or "sovereignty at bay" has thus given way to world society—bottom-up global governance through the growth of transnational civil society. This global civil society or global community is a borderless world composed of NGOs, international non-governmental organizations (INGOS), multinational corporations (MNCs), and international organizations (IOs). As they become increasingly dense, these create organizations in global civil society: layered sets of networks and connections that are not defined by spatial location and geographic context and that are often connected to formal intergovernmental relations.

2.3.1 Empowered Non-state Actors

The decline of the state has been accompanied by the rise of non-state actors, such as GPMs, which have built global civil society. The empowered non-state actor structural mechanism has meant new forms of collective action and solidarity. The movement is not traditionally organized and thus is not institutionalized or centralized, and it is not a political party but a network, a set of local and global connections. Castells (1997), Melucci (1996), and Keck and Sikkink (1998) thus suggest that networks combine unities and disunities, permanence and impermanence, the global and the local. There is also a transnational public sphere of global communications; the internet has produced global bandwagons of dissent. Hence, the globalization of interests, identities, and institutions creates a variety of economic, social, cultural, and political grievances that are mobilized via the internet. Due to internet-based resistance, virtual activism, and cyberpolitics, protest is now a global-wide phenomenon that comes in waves and affects many countries simultaneously. GPMs thus build upon existing transnational advocacy networks which, in turn, build upon transnational civil society.

An equally dramatic global force in instant communication is worldwide television. Global TV has collapsed space and time, deterritorialized states, and, some argue, created a borderless and distanceless Marshall McLuhan global village that manifests interconnectedness, interrelatedness, integration, and interdependence. Since people know in real time how events in one locale affect events in other locales, local news becomes the subject of worldwide concern. The individual citizen of the world connects to global events, relates to all people, and has a consciousness of a global *problématique*. The human community becomes the focal point, and activists think and frame issues globally while acting locally.

The empowered non-state actor mechanism thus posits that participants in an oppositional civil society are mobilizing globally to advocate that states take an active role in globalization. As the threats globalization poses to states' power become increasingly salient, MEI protest campaigns are expected to increase in frequency. Most MEI protests are expected to occur at locations where an oppositional civil society is especially strong and active or where neo-liberal reforms have coincided with domestic problems and may have heightened perceptions of weakened state power tied to globalization. Grievances at these protests are expected to concern state problems resulting from neo-liberal reforms. The key actors in protest coalitions are expected to represent global or cosmopolitan identities who complain of inadequate state responses to globalization. At times when the salience of weakened state power coinciding with Western-centric globalization is heightened, protest is expected to spike. Protesters are expected to be more active in civil society and more opposed to globalization and war than the general population.

2.3.2 *Global Civil Society Recruitment*

Similarly, activists suggest a global civil society recruitment mechanism, arguing that a global civil society is developing which is opposing threats to state sovereignty and fighting for accountability (Brecher, Childs, and Cutler 1993, p. ix). During the Seattle WTO protests, the strength and oppositional activity of these groups became evident (Wolfwood 2001, 147). Both the 50 Years Is Enough Network and the World Social Forum drastically increased in size (Brecher 2003, 204; Danaher and Burbach 2000, 8). An astounding 51,300 participants attended the second World Social Forum in 2002, and attendance has more than doubled in more recent Social Forums (Brecher 2003, 204). Besides emphasizing democracy and democratic reforms, these activists advocate global civil society as a solution to global problems (Brecher, Costello, and Smith 2000, 42). This argument about the mobilizational power of global civil society is made by both activists and academics.

World Society mechanisms of collective action focus on the mobilizational structures that are presented by an increasingly globalized civil society. Academics emphasize the empowered non-state actor mechanism which suggests how structural changes in society may influence protest turnout. Activists put forth a global civil society recruitment mechanism, since they are focused on using new global structures to get people to hit the streets. Most activists and academics are focused on global civil society as only one piece of the mobilizational puzzle, which explains how organizers reach out to people but does not necessarily explain the grievances that successfully draw participants to a protest.

2.4 World Polity Mechanisms

2.4.1 Complex Internationalism

The globalization of institutions is creating targets and political opportunities for GPMs. As interdependence increases, as the power of international institutions deepens, and as the scope of global governance broadens, civil society networks grow. These non-governmental associations take advantage of the political opportunities afforded by international institutions and their meetings, especially in providing information and advocacy of particular issues. However, sometimes these organizations also have ties to groups that use demonstrations and public appeals to advance grievances which target these international institutions and their meetings. According to Tarrow, internationalism provides structured opportunities for interactions between these groups which facilitate transnational activism and coalition formation (2005). GPMs are thus part of the conflictual process of globalization, just as national protests were part of the conflictual process of building nation-states. GPMs are thus a part of global governance, institutions, democracy, and representation.

Tarrow (2005, 7) advances the complex internationalism mechanism. Internationalism is defined as "a dense, triangular, structure of relations among states, nonstate actors, and international institutions, and the opportunities this produces for actors to engage in collective action at different levels of this system" (2005, 25). Tarrow diminishes the causal impact of globalization, which he sees as "a source of claims and a frame for mobilizations" as well as "a source of interest, ideology, and grievances" (2005, 7, 19).

Rather, Tarrow accentuates how transnational contention is influenced by "states' domestic structures," "the international institutions that they have created," and "the processes that link 'the local with the global' " (2005, p. xiii). Tarrow argues that internationalism "provides an opportunity structure within which transnational activism can emerge" since it "offers a focal point for resistance to [globalization], and provides opportunities for the formation of transnational coalitions and movements" (2005, 7–8). Tarrow distinguishes between globalization as just one of many sources of values, interests, and ideals vis-à-vis internationalization as an institutional framework structuring actors' relations, stating,

Like the movement that Polanyi identified in the Industrial Revolution, globalization creates new social victims and transforms the role of states; and like the expanding national state in the nineteenth century, internationalization constrains and creates opportunities for citizens to engage in collective action, both in resistance to globalization and around other issues. (2005, 19)

The end result of internationalism's structured opportunities for relations producing transnational coalitions and movements are the increasingly transnational but domestically based actors whom Tarrow describes as rooted cosmopolitans (2005, 43). Tarrow states, "Through the use of both domestic and international resources and opportunities, domestic-based activists—citizens and others—move outward to form a spectrum of 'rooted cosmopolitans' who engage in regular transnational practices" (2005, 35). Transnational activists, on the other hand, are a subset of rooted cosmopolitans, "people and groups who are rooted in specific national contexts but who engage in contentious politics activities that involve them in transnational networks of contacts and conflicts" (2005, 29). What distinguishes transnational activists from rooted cosmopolitans is "their ability to shift their activities among levels" and to take "advantage of the expanded nodes of opportunity of a complex international society" (2005, 29, 43).

According to Tarrow, the international political opportunity space structures the relations of transnational contenders in such a way as to change the participatory versus oppositional roles of groups he calls "NGO insiders" and "social movement outsiders" (2005, 29). Insiders are known for "gravitating to international institutions and taking part in highly institutionalized service and advocacy activities" as well as "lobbying and collaborating with international elites to the point of co-optation" (2005, 29, 45). In contrast, outsiders "challenge these institutions and organizations," "challenge international institutions' policies and, in some cases, contest their existence" (2005, 29, 45).

On the one hand, Tarrow cites the rise in activists who "face both inward and outward," and argues that the "distinction between 'insiders' and 'outsiders' may be blurring" (2005, 47). Key in Tarrow's argument is the increasing insider–outsider cooperation "around international institutions, conferences, and processes" that he observes (2005, 48, 211). On the other hand, Tarrow also suggests that, eventually, internationalization may be leading insider participation to be supplanted by outsider opposition, as "participation in international protests may even resocialize insiders into outsiders" and outsiders' "numbers seem to be increasing" (2005, 48).

In sum, Tarrow (2001, 234) looks for a larger political system within which GPMs fit. Political opportunities for GPMs are provided by the composite polity (e.g. multilateral economic institution meetings and international events) (Tarrow 2001, 242–4). As interdependence increases, both multilateral economic institutions and the international actions of governments of particular states (including their heads of government and key cabinet members) are likely targets for globalized opposition.

World polity theories suggest that those who perceive international institutions and their meetings as political opportunities are likely to mobilize. As annual MEI meetings increase and are increasingly perceived as focal points, protest campaigns are expected to increase. Since Tarrow sees globalization as one of many interests, ideals, and values around which transnational activists mobilize, he would likely expect similar rates of protests at meetings of institutions directly linked to the Washington Consensus and its neo-liberal agenda (e.g. the IMF/WB) vis-à-vis the meetings of other international institutions about which transnational activists have grievances. MEI protest campaigns are expected to increase over time. Protests are expected in locations where MEI meetings are held and where there is easy access to MEIs. Spikes in globalized protest events are expected to coincide with important MEI meeting dates.

2.4.2 *Attribution of Opportunity*

As they target the political opportunities multilateral institutions present for protest, activists in effect posit an attribution of opportunity mechanism. After targeting one international institution, they find other institutions to target, expanding their target repertoire from the WTO to the WB and IMF, for instance (Danaher and Burbach 2000, 8). Further, some MEIs offer NGOs opportunities to participate in their meetings (Wolfwood 2001, 147). Other institutions that present political opportunities for the protesters to mobilize include the GATT, NAFTA, and FTAA (Global Exchange and Public Citizen 2001, 20–1, 131).

Using the attribution of opportunity mechanism, activists thus focus on international institutions as targets. Similarly, via the complex internationalism structural mechanism, academics focus on the various mobilizational opportunities created by these globally empowered institutions, both creating extra-institutional targets for collective action as well as as an intra-institutional NGO support. Both activists and academics recognize that the world polity is only part of the explanation—it is a set of targets that draw out protest participants, but it is not a complete explanation of the ways in which organizers are able to mobilize people into action. In sum, activists blame international institutions and academics study the political opportunities that these institutions create for mobilizers.

2.5 US Hegemony Mechanisms

2.5.1 *Opposition to US Hegemony*

Academics advance the opposition to US hegemony structural mechanism, suggesting that GPMs might be explained as opposition to the American quest for global hegemony during the current unipolar moment of American power. Under Pax Americana or empire, global institutions are designed by the United States to manage conflict, assure legitimacy, attain consensus, and maintain authority (Hardt and Negri 2000, 15). The globalized resistance strikes at the global order—this total system. As Hardt and Negri thus suggest, there is really one struggle against one enemy, and all struggles are really part of this one struggle: "each struggle, though firmly rooted in local conditions, leaps immediately to the global level and attacks the imperial constitution in its generality" and "the only strategy available to the struggles is that of a constituent counterpower that emerges from within Empire" (2000, 56, 59). In the face of totalizing power, nothing is therefore outside the system. The common center tries to create homogeneity out of heterogeneity. The opposition to US hegemony mechanism thus suggests that opposition, while firmly rooted in local conditions, directly attacks the global order and hence identifies a common enemy that all can fight against, uniting all struggles. These struggles are simultaneously economic, political, and social—the struggles over personal lives and political power. The struggles themselves are constitutive of—help construct—new public spaces for discourse and new forms of community. The resulting struggles and crises are met by the center's efforts to resolve conflicts and restore a global equilibrium to its conceptions of peace and justice.

American hegemony theories thus suggest that opponents of American global hegemony or empire seeking are likely to mobilize against the current global order, which they see as a by-product of American hegemony. Thus, globalized protests are expected to be more likely as US policy appears exceptionally hegemonic (e.g. when the United States is taking unilateral action). Globalized protest participants are expected to have unfavorable attitudes toward US hegemony or toward US policies that can be construed as hegemonic or empire seeking.

2.5.2 *US Hegemony Target Attribution*

Similarly, activists put forth US hegemony target attribution mechanisms. Opposition to American policies that appear hegemonic, empire seeking, or unilateral is another way in which activists frame their dissent. In formulating and framing grievances, activists even rely on some academics who emphasize Empire or US Hegemony as an explanation of conflict (Hardt and Negri 2003, 118). While activists tend to make connections with US hegemony in their grievances about war or about globalization, academics tend to make these linkages to US hegemony in their elaboration of targets. For instance, activists oppose a globalization that perpetuates Western hegemony (Brecher, Childs, and Cutler 1993, p. xiv). Alternatively, globalization is opposed as a part of "US imperialism's drive to maintain its hegemony" or unilateral US action (Brecher 2003, 206; Callinicos 2003, 139). Thus, activists and academics alike have emphasized how state actions that appear to perpetuate Western or US hegemony have tremendous mobilizational power.

Both activists and academics connect dissent with opposition to US or Western hegemony. Academics' opposition to US hegemony structural mechanism focuses on likely American or Western oppositional targets whereas activists' US hegemony target attributional mechanism tends to emphasize these connections between activists' grievances about war and globalization. Thus, both activists and academics suggest that US hegemony helps to explain global dissent, but both employ other perspectives to explain the processes by which dissent is mobilized.

2.6 Neoliberal Institutional Trilemma Mechanisms

2.6.1 *Global Democratic Deficit*

While the world polity explanation of the protests focused on the agency of the international institutions, the neo-liberal institutional trilemma offers a deep, structural explanation. This perspective focuses on the interplay of institutions that produce a global democratic deficit. The basic idea is that given independent states, international economic integration begets democratically active civil societies that protest economic globalization. These three institutions—international institutions in global orders, developmental coalitions in embedded states, and protest coalitions in democratic civil societies—affect the globalization of protest through the agency of the people involved. These institutions, in other words, add up to the issue of global governance and hence are the interrelated parts of a larger structural understanding of GPMs.

We have three interrelated institutions that manufacture three interrelated public goods: states embedded in the global order create national economic prosperity, which is supported by international institutions that create world peace and by democracy that creates stable civil societies. Neo-liberals thus have three desiderata: world peace or external security, economic prosperity or the growth of wealth, and domestic stability or internal order. Institution builders thus face a Machiavellian state (elites interested in maintaining and expanding their power) in a Hobbesian world (anarchy of states) and thus must build an international order, a political economy, and an authority system (Hobbes 1651/1988; Machiavelli 1514/1961). Looked at from the point of view of the people rather than the powerful, citizens demand that governments supply institutions to maximize external security (peace not war), maximize efficiency (growth not stagnation), and minimize social control (representation not repression).

We shall call the problem displayed in Figure 20.1 the Neo-liberal Institutional Trilemma (NIT), or the impossible trinity of an integrated global economy (strong MEIs), independent states (strong developmental coalitions that can make and implement national economic policies), and active civil societies (conventional democratic politics that allows protectionist groups to influence the state). The problem is that while states want international institutions to promote economic efficiency, mass publics demand that their governments safeguard them, and neither international institutions nor the governments which have ceded sovereignty and agreed to economic integration managed by international institutions can be held accountable as easily. Rodrik (2001, 347–65) thus formalizes Ruggie's (1982, 1991) arguments about embedded liberalism as follows:

- If we want democratically active civil societies, we can have either integrated national economies or independent states.
- If we want integrated national economies, we can have either independent states or democratically active civil societies.
- If we want independent states, we can have either integrated national economies or democratically active civil societies.

Neo-liberals therefore can have two things but not all three at once. Hence, there are two important tradeoffs:

- For a given level of integrated national economies, the more independent the states, the less active the democratic civil societies.
- For a given level of independent nation-states, the more integrated the national economy, the less active the democratic civil society.

And here is where the global democratic deficit mechanism and thus anti-globaliza-tion protest becomes relevant: *Neo-liberalism is not the best of all possible worlds because*

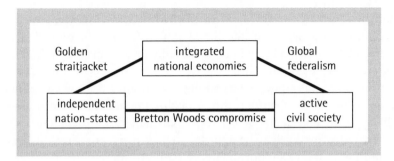

Fig. 20.1 The Neoliberal Institutional Trilemma (Ruggie; Rodrik)

people are complaining about its institutions. The Battle of Seattle, for instance, was a fight about the WTO and global governance.

More specifically, while the neo-liberal global order might lead to peace (although critics claim that competition among capitalist states is more likely than cooperation among them), and while it might even lead to prosperity (although critics claim that in the race to the bottom, the rich get richer and few benefits trickle down to the poor), the neo-liberal global order has produced political instability because it generates redistributive conflicts over the democratic nature of its institutions.

Thus, the Neo-liberal Institutional Trilemma asserts that neo-liberal rhetoric about democracy exceeds the neo-liberal grasp because neo-liberal globalization puts democracy in a golden straitjacket, constructed by international and state institutions, that forces political parties to the median voter while opening up civil society to the proliferation of special interests. In a democracy, that is, neo-liberalism contracts political (electoral) space (openness to international trade forecloses Keynesian macroeconomic policies and welfare state social policies) while neo-liberalism expands social (civil society) space (issues of trade, neo-liberalism, and capitalism involve more and more constituencies). The spread of democracy, at least a rhetorical part of NIT, has also contributed to the rise of civil society through the call for participation, accountability, and transparency. As cosmopolitan and international consciousness rise, the policy agenda widens even further as more voices demand access.

Neo-liberal Institutional Trilemma theories thus suggest that protest is likely in democracies with integrating economies: in globalized democracies where international economic integration coincides with threats to state independence or in globalizing democracies where state independence coincides with poor international economic integration. Further, in the former, globalized, and largely northern countries, protesters are likely to make claims that focus on threats to state sovereignty and civil society caused by the integration of national economies, whereas in the latter, globalizing, and largely southern countries, protesters are likely to focus on inequality and exclusion in the global market. The highest level of protest is most likely when the NIT is most salient: in globalized democracies during crises when states' power is noticeably lessened or in the globalizing democracies when poor international economic integration causes domestic problems like increased unemployment, decreased wages, and increased prices. For instance, unilateral military intervention by a hegemon like the USA is likely to incite northern protest because it makes state sovereignty in a globalized world seem weaker; and domestic economic crises like those in Latin America during the 1990s are likely to spur southern protests because they make southern exclusion from the global market in a globalizing world more salient. Further, globalized democracies' protest coalitions are less likely to involve material interests than globalizing democracies' protest coalitions. Protesters are likely to be opposed to neo-liberal globalization, to support national autonomy, and to support inclusive economic development.

2.6.2 *Attribution of Threat to Democracy*

Activists have also connected protest with the pursuit of democracy, using the threat to democracy attribution mechanism. Activists argue they are targeting a global economic system which threatens the sovereignty of the people and claim that they desire democratic institutional changes in these MEIs (Danaher and Burbach 2000, 11). Dissent is framed as a struggle for democracy, as depicted in the following quotes: "[Most civil society groups] are all fighting for fundamental democratic rights" and "[The anti-corporate insurrection] is a rebellion that seeks to reclaim democracy" (Barlow and Clarke 2002, 207; Danaher and Mark 2003, 2). Further, Norberg-Hodge indicates how economic integration is tied together with threats to sovereignty and problems of dependence, arguing that "economic globalization" is leading to the "erosion of democracy" (2001, 180–2). The solution, according to the activists, rests with empowering the people as the ultimate political authority or combating threats to democracy (Brecher, Costello, and Smith 2000, 42; Danaher and Mark 2003, 2). Activists therefore emphasize threats to democracy as a problem and suggest democratic reforms and democratic power to the people as solutions. Academics, on the other hand, focus on groupings of structures of economic integration and democratic civil society that facilitate activists' dissent.

Activists and academics are thus connecting problems during economic integration with threats to democracy. Further, both suggest that the solutions lie in people power, dissent, and democratic reforms. While academics put forth the global democratic deficit structural mechanism, focusing on how increasing integration in democratic states leads to dissent, activists suggest the threat to democracy attribution mechanism which connects economic globalization and democracy through grievances and solutions.

3 MESO-LEVEL MECHANISMS

GPMs also may be explained by meso-level mechanisms that specify the processes that mobilize dissident movements. Contentious politics theories come in rationalist and structuralist variations (Lichbach 1997, 1998a, 1998b). The structuralist approach provides the better transition from global macro theories and the rationalist approach the better transition to the micro-political behavior approach. As shown earlier in Table 20.1, this section discusses meso mechanisms and processes, such as political opportunities or communal linkages, that cut across the global economy, society, culture, and polity.

3.1 SPOT Mechanisms

The structuralist's explanandum is "contentious politics:" the "collective action" and "collective mobilization" of "contenders" for power. SPOT-Strategic Political Opportunity theory—skillfully weaves several strands of resource mobilization and political process arguments into a "broad framework" (Tarrow 1994, 2) that explains contentious politics. This synthesis argues that GPMs are "triggered by the incentives created by political opportunities, combining conventional and challenging forms of action and building on social networks and cultural frames" (Tarrow 1994, 1). Tarrow thus argues that three structural mechanisms are crucial:

- *PO. Politics, defined in terms of political opportunities.* The polity is structured in four ways: "the relative openness or closure of the institutionalized political system," "the stability of that broad set of alignments that typically undergird a polity," "the presence of elite allies," and "the state's capacity and propensity for repression" (McAdam, McCarthy, and Zald 1996, 10). PO are therefore "consistent—but not necessarily formal or permanent—dimensions of the political environment that provide incentives for people to undertake collective action by affecting their expectations for success or failure" (Tarrow 1994, 85). Political processes, institutions, and alignments thus set the context for the strategic interaction of a movement with its allies and opponents in civil society and the state.
- *MS. Society, defined in terms of mobilizing structures.* Civil society is structured along class, status, gender, ethnic, religious, and racial lines. These partially overlapping systems of stratification "link leaders with the organization of collective action—center with periphery—permitting movement coordination and allowing movements to persist over time" (Tarrow 1994, 136). Elite–mass linkages include "informal as well as formal [vehicles] through which people mobilize and engage in collective action" (McAdam, McCarthy, and Zald 1996, 3). Dissident MS thus include communities and associations rooted in civil society.
- *CF. Culture, defined in terms of cultural frames.* Culture is structured by shared meanings, symbols, and discourses. Social movements are thus constituted by the culture in which they operate. Structuralists also think of culture in another way (Lichbach 1995, 450 n. 5). Movements strategically frame meanings, symbols, and discourses so as to define grievances, pose solutions, and advance their "cognitive liberation" (McAdam 1982). CF therefore involves the "conscious strategic efforts by groups of people to fashion shared understandings of the world and of themselves

that legitimate and motivate collective action" (McAdam, McCarthy, and Zald 1996, 6). Culture, as much as politics and society, structures resistance to authority.

While McAdam, Tarrow, and Tilly (2001) have recently emphasized and expanded a more dynamic set of mechanisms, the root of SPOT theories still suggests that global protesters take advantage of perceived political opportunities, make use of civil society organizational and recruitment networks, and commonly frame their grievances to mobilize supporters. As political opportunities posed by annual MEI meetings increase, MEI protest campaigns and protest mobilization are expected to increase. Protests are expected to be more likely in locations where MEI meetings are more frequent and access to MEIs is more readily available. On dates of key MEI meetings and international events, protest is expected to spike. Protesters are expected to take advantage of many political opportunities for action, joining several social movements and engaging in various forms of active political participation at higher rates than the general population. Globalized protests involving disparate social movements are expected when a diverse, structured civil society is involved in mobilization. Protesters are expected to be more involved in civil society than the general population. When unifying frames are used to mobilize people to action, larger numbers of people with diffuse grievances are expected to be mobilized, and various interests are expected to be represented at the protests. Successful coalitions are expected to include material interests, social identities, global ideals, and students. Unifying frames are expected to help draw together disparate social movements. Finally, globalized protest participants are expected to share certain standpoints, which are used as common frames during mobilization.

3.1.1 Focal Points and Political Opportunities

Using a political opportunities mechanism, activists argue that MEIs, MEI meetings, international events, unpopular US unilateralism, unpopular neo-liberal reforms, and concrete domestic problems tied to global events offer useful and interrelated focal points during mobilization (Barlow and Clarke 2002). The WTO, WB, IMF, multinationals, GATT, NAFTA, FTAA, and Structural Adjustment Programs are included amongst the targets of mobilizers (Global Exchange and Public Citizen 2001, 20–1, 131). Thus, activists tend to view political opportunities as a mobilizational mechanism.

While academics also argue that protesters mobilize using political opportunities, the different macro theories offer different predictions of the focal points that will be used. World polity and SPOT political opportunities theories suggest that protesters will take advantage of the political opportunities for mobilization presented by international institutions and international events. World systems theories suggest that protesters will target the institutions that promote the global market and domestic problems tied to the global market. US hegemony theories suggest that protesters will likely target meetings and events that are tied to US hegemonic acts. The Neo-liberal Institutional Trilemma suggests that events which make threats to state autonomy salient in globalized democracies, or which make international economic integration salient in such states, are likely to be focal points.

3.1.2 *Pre-existing Organizations and Mobilized Structures*

Activists argue that pre-existing organizations are important mobilizing structures. Included amongst such groups are "not only conventional NGOs, but also local social movements, foundations, the media, churches, trade unions, consumer organizations, intellectuals" (Brecher, Costello, and Smith 2000, 83–4). Even labor has been drawn into these coalitions, with the AFL-CIO endorsing the April 2000 WB/IMF demonstrations and smaller unions also taking a stand (Brecher, Costello, and Smith 2000, 56). Protests are more successful, according to activists, when organizations are grouped in coalitions. According to Klein (2001, 149),

the protests are themselves made up of "coalitions of coalitions," to borrow a phrase from Kevin Danaher of Global Exchange. Each anti-corporate campaign is made up of many groups, mostly NGOs, labor unions, students and anarchists. They use the Internet, as well as more traditional organizing tools, to do everything . . . The groups remain autonomous, but their internal coordination is deft . . .

The resultant networks

have become the main vehicle through which the campaigns of globalization from below have been organized. . . . Network participants can be highly diverse and may disagree on many matters, as long as they accept the network's defining frame of the issues that it addresses. (Brecher, Costello, and Smith 2000, 84)

Thus, activists emphasize associational networks' capacity to become mobilizing structures for protests.

Likewise, academics argue that organizers pull together pre-existing organizations in their diverse communities to mobilize followers. Various theories offer predictions about which preexisting organizations are likely to be important mobilizers. World society, political behavior, and SPOT mobilizing structures theories suggest that pre-existing organizations in civil society will be targeted for mobilization. Economic and world systems theories suggest that material interests and unions, in particular, will be key in mobilization. Pre-modern values and US hegemony theories suggest that groups working to preserve traditional values and groups opposed to the United States will be important mobilizers. Postmodern values theories suggest that groups with progressive ideals that engage in multi-issue organizing are likely to succeed in mobilization. The Neo-liberal Institutional Trilemma suggests that groups with broad progressive ideals are likely targeted by organizers in globalized democracies, whereas organizers in globalizing democracies are likely to target pre-existing groups that are more narrowly concerned with material interests.

3.1.3 *Strategic Frames and Cultural Frames*

Activists use cultural frames strategically as mobilizational mechanisms. To mobilize more participants, they seek links between strategic issues as well as connections between global and local grievances. Activists allow for "infinitely expandable systems" of NGO and "affinity group networks" (Klein 2001, 149–50). Activists make clear that they value a set of ideals and not material interests so as to attract other ideal-oriented groups (Danaher and Burbach 2000, 10). To attract new NGOs or affinity groups, activists emphasize the interconnections between different issues. For instance, they look for "links between human rights, environmental, and indigenous concerns" (Prokosch and Raymond 2002, 52). Callinicos (2003, 134) argues that these issue linkages distinguish today's GPMs, stating,

It is this sense of the interconnection of different issues through the systemic logic of capitalism that defines the anti-capitalist movement by contrast with the earlier campaigns that concerned themselves with more specific (though hugely important) issues such as nuclear weapons, apartheid, and even the environment.

Further, activists also attract new participants by linking country-level or local issues with global targets. Globalized protest activists are encouraged to seek links with domestic issues (Heckscher 2002, 237). Similarly, Barlow and Clarke (2002, 217) argue that local issues should be connected with global targets, stating,

The purpose of these networks would be to organize local campaigns of resistance and alternatives. Emphasis would be put on highlighting the links between local community issues and NAFTA, the FTAA, and the operations of corporate governance institutions like the WTO, the IMF, and the World Bank.

Thus, activists strategically frame issues so as to mobilize greater numbers of organizations, affinity groups, and individuals.

Further, academics argue that organizers reframe selective incentives strategically, to create global public goods out of local public goods. Various theories suggest which strategic frames will be used during mobilization. Political behavior issue intensity and SPOT cultural frames theories suggest that strategic frames will target issues that certain segments of the public strongly oppose. Economic and world systems theories suggest that strategic frames will target neo-liberal globalization, institutions, and policies. Pre-modern values and US hegemony theories suggest that strategic frames will target threats to traditional values and US hegemonic action. Postmodern values suggest that strategic frames will target threats to progressive ideals and emphasize the connections amongst various ideals. The Neo-liberal Institutional Trilemma suggests that strategic frames will target broader ideals in globalized democracies and more narrow, material interests in globalizing democracies.

3.2 CARP Mechanisms

The rationalist approach to contentious politics asks: Were the protesters in Seattle and activists involved in other GPMs rational? Or even better, how were they rational? Rationalists suggest that the members of the protest coalition, just like the people who are constructing the neo-liberal institutions that the protesters oppose, were quite rational actors. After discussing the rationality of the rebels, we discuss their global rebel's dilemma.

3.2.1 *Rational Rebels*

First, many of the protesters against globalization knew what they were saying. Evidence gleaned from interviews with elite activists indicate that many protesters were knowledgeable about the substantive issues and that they wanted to communicate their ideas through various forms of grassroots education. Activist websites, moreover, often reflected recent academic criticisms of MEIs (Anderson 2000; Haggard 2000). Thus, the leading activists were certainly not ignorant, irrational, or opportunist looters or vandals.

Second, the evidence shows that the protests at the Battle of Seattle were not spontaneous but well planned. Major protest-supporting organizations, such as the Direct Action Network (DAN) and the Ruckus Society, developed detailed maps indicating where the WTO delegates would reside and where and when the major events would take place. The actual distribution of contentious activity, moreover, showed carefully built interconnections among action phases of the events. Moreover, the protesters were strategically mobile, moving to specific locations to block particular paths of delegate traffic, aided by cellphones and pagers.

Dissidents put together their diverse protest coalition by organizing immediately before the episode, and in fact an ongoing campaign against neo-liberal globalization had been in existence years before the episode. In the middle of November the DAN and the Ruckus Society were holding training sessions for a variety of social movement activists. Students, churches, labor unions, and environmentalists were similarly organized. Further, before the Battle of Seattle a number of important social movement organizations labeled themselves as "global." Examples include the San Francisco-based human rights and economic justice group Global Exchange and the Nader-influenced Citizen's Global Trade Watch. Other groups in Seattle such as the Committee in Solidarity with the People of El Salvador (CISPES) had many years of experience working on international solidarity/human rights issues that focus on a particular country or region.

3.2.2 *A Global Rebel's Dilemma*

While the diverse nature of the Seattle coalition is understandable, its contradictions—the collective action problems of combining people with different material interests, social identities, and global ideals so that they can act on a global scale—are immense. How did anti-WTO activists mobilize and sustain their diverse rainbow coalition?

This is a puzzle because the rationalist or Olsonian approach tells us that collective action among dissidents in several different nations is much more difficult to organize than collective action among dissidents in a single nation. Size works against collective action, and the largest possible dissident community is a global one. This perspective thus would predict that a worldwide movement, or one that attempts to secure the cooperation of movements in many different countries, runs up against incredibly difficult mobilization problems. International mobilizing efforts, the theory says, inevitably fade away.

Rational dissidents involved in the GPMs must solve the biggest Rebel's Dilemma (Lichbach 1995) of them all: Citizens of the world unite! The activists are trying to solve the problems of collaborating with others around the globe who do not share their national culture or even language, in the face of resource costs and political risks. And what is particularly amazing about this GPM is not that it operates across countries (many INGOs do that), nor that it is a network of policy wonks who work on an issue area across countries (many transnational advocacy networks do that). What is amazing is that this GPM mobilizes citizens across different countries for protesting—a demanding form of INGO collective activism that is exceedingly rare. Yet, compared to protest against a state, the benefits are more diffuse, the chances of success more remote, and the role of the individual less significant. And compared to other global actors—states who can mobilize coercive power, firms who can mobilize economic power, and even INGOs who can regularly interact with intergovern-mental organizations (IGOs)—an activist GPM is resource poor. GPMs are in fact less politically efficacious than national ones that are part of national deliberation over the government's policy in which the movement can influence citizens to join interest groups and political parties. Indeed, the growth of international institutions might actually work against the growth of local resistance because of weakened political opportunity structures.

Hence the puzzle of globalized local resistances—in spite of formidable collective action problems, resistance occurs at the same time and in the same ways in many different states. What accounts for simultaneous (albeit sometimes small in number and often uncoordinated) resistances? What enables so many similar challenges to the global order from "below" to turn up in so many countries at the same time?

Work on the Rebel's Dilemma, or the problem of free riding and non-participation in protest and rebellion (Lichbach 1992; Moore 1995), was sparked by economists (Tullock 1971) and sociologists (Gamson 1990) who drew upon Olson's (1965) idea that the norms of instrumental rationality, especially in the market-oriented struc-tures of the modern world, promote self-interest and therefore could work against the collective good. Hence, the fundamental assumption of the collective action research program (CARP) is that collective endeavors often involve public good and Prisoner's Dilemma elements. The famous deduction and prediction of collect-ive action (CA) thinking is therefore the Five Percent Rule: less than 5 percent of the supporters of a cause become actively involved in the cause and non-activists outnumber activists nineteen to one. CA, in other words, is the rare exception and not the general norm.

However, can we explain the 5 percent who do participate in CA? Solutions to the CA problem vary on a deliberative and an ontological dimension, as displayed in Table 20.2 (Lichbach 1995, 21). Prior discussions may or may not occur between the actors involved in a CA problem, and solutions to the CA problem may thus result in either unplanned or planned order. The entities involved in a CA problem may be individuals only or institutions; structures, and/or relationships may pre-exist indi-viduals and therefore help impose order; and thus solutions to the CA problem may thus result in either spontaneous or contingent order. Combining dimensions produces the classic distinctions of social thought: the market, community, contract, and hierarchy mechanisms.

Of these four sets of solutions, market mechanisms of social order and CA may be thought of as the baseline. The other three sets of solutions vary the context in which the baseline model is placed. Community mechanisms explore how common belief systems solve Olson's problem, contractual mechanisms study the ways in which mutual agreements produce CA, and hierarchy mechanisms examine how hierarchies structure CA. Mobilization by market implies that individuals are driven by a variety of individual-level forces. Mobilization by hierarchy, in contrast, involves pre-existing dissident organizations that explicitly mobilize their followers. Mobilization by contract and community involves more self-organization by dissidents. Pure contract implies a self-governing arrangement that produces protest. Pure community implies a multifunction self-governing arrangement that has been mobilized into protest. These ideal types may be used to investigate how actual cases of protest are structured. Lichbach (1995) fits approximately two dozen sets of solutions to the CA problem into this typology of the organizational forms behind CA. CA theorists thus wager on a few driving causal mechanisms or CA models and investigate how instrumental rationality and self-interest are embodied in these spheres of group action.

CARP theories suggest that protesters take advantage of perceived focal points, pre-existing associational networks, selective incentives for particular groups, and strategic frames to mobilize masses. Increases in annual MEI meetings are expected to be accompanied by corresponding increases in MEI protest campaigns and mobilizations. Protests are expected in locations where MEI meetings are more common and MEIs are more accessible. Globalized protest participants are expected to take advantage of many focal points for action, engaging in several social movements and more actively engaging in various forms of active political participation than the general population. When networks are used in mobilization, protest coalitions are expected to consist of groups representing different interests, including material interests, social identities, global ideals, and students. Globalized protest participants are expected to be part of such networks and network associations. When selective incentives and a federal group structure are offered to mobilize pre-existing organizations in their diverse communities, protest coalitions are more likely to become globalized and to tie together disparate social movements. Common frames are required to tie together a federal group structure of groups mobilized

Table 20.2 Solutions to the collective action problem

		Deliberation	
		Unplanned order	Planned order
Ontology	Spontaneous order	Market	Contract
	Contingent order	Community	Hierarchy

using selective incentives. Reframing particularized grievances in universal terms is also expected to yield rainbow protest coalitions successful in mobilizing globally.

3.2.3 *Planning and Contract*

Activists seeking to mobilize large-scale GPMs tend to organize conferences. The use of such conferences already occurred in "dozens of packed meetings" during the Battle of Seattle (Wolfwood 2001, 147). Later, the World Social Forum was organized so that civil society organizations from all around the world could meet and plan (Barlow and Clarke 2002, 203). As Brecher (2003, 204) states,

> The World Social Forum (WSF) in Porto Alegre, Brazil, has emerged as a global assembly for globalization from below's discussion and networking. In 2002, the second WSF brought together 51,300 participants, including 15,230 delegates representing 4,909 organizations from 131 countries.

Activists thus use planning conferences as mobilizational mechanisms.

Further, academics suggest that international conferences of dissident organizations help coordinate organizers' activities. Several theories suggest which groups are likely to play instrumental roles in planning. World society, political behavior civil society, and SPOT mobilizing structures theories suggest that representatives of civil society are likely to constitute the key participants of international planning conferences. Economic and world systems theories suggest that representatives of material interests such as unions are likely important conference attendees. Pre-modern values and US hegemony are likely to suggest that organizations working to preserve traditional values and organizations opposed to US hegemony are likely to supply key conference attendees. Postmodern values theories suggest that groups with progressive ideals that engage in multi-issue organizing are likely to constitute instrumental conference attendees. The Neo-liberal Institutional Trilemma suggests that globalized democracies are more likely to have large-scale conferences of varied dissident organizations, whereas globalizing democracies are likely to involve small-scale meetings of narrowly defined and materially oriented dissident organizations.

3.2.4 *Networks and Community*

Activists rely on virtual networks to build transnational linkages (Brecher, Childs, and Cutler 1993, pp. xv–xvi). Even the labor movement has started engaging in "transnational electronic networking" (Brecher, Childs, and Cutler 1993, p. xvi). By interacting online, movements are transformed and become stronger. Independent Media Centers (IMC) are part of one such global network that has "sprung up in at least forty different countries worldwide, connected by the internet" (Brecher, Childs, and Cutler 1993, pp. xvi–xvii; Graeber 2003, 328). IMC have become very powerful mobilizers. As Graeber (2003, 328) states, "However, despite some remarkable triumphs (during Genoa, the IMC home page, **www.indymedia.org**, was getting more hits than CNN's), this is still but a faint challenge to those who control what gets put on television." Activists thus recognize the mobilizational power of virtual networks. Academics also suggest that the organizers use the internet to lower the transaction costs of bringing together a diverse set of groups in global civil society. Various theories predict which groups are likely to be instrumental in mobilizational networks, as mentioned in our earlier discussion of planning conferences.

3.2.5 *Selective Incentives and Hierarchy*

Selective incentives are frequently offered by activists, as they try to mobilize local groups into transnational action by connecting local problems to global problems in protest grievances and targets. As Barlow and Clarke state, "Emphasis would be put on highlighting the links between local community issues and NAFTA, the FTAA, ... the WTO, the IMF, and the World Bank" (2002, 217). Activists use strategies like "framing issues in such a way that their salience to a potential ally is clear" (Brecher, Costello, and Smith 2000, 93). One activist recommends,

Likewise, it's important to be aware of how the structural adjustment programs of the World Bank have parallels in our own country from cuts in education to lack of affordable health care and housing.... Seek allies among local education, labor, and environmental groups... (Heckscher 2002, 237)

Thus, activists use selective incentives as a mobilizational mechanism. Some activists are paid, some paid positions are opened to movement members, and patrons and sponsors of the movement subsidize some transportation costs and donate housing for the demonstrators. To create global public goods out of local public goods, activists need to reframe selective incentives. Protesters thus rely on long-standing opposition to state-led development coalitions. Similarly, protesters use a federal group structure that creates an umbrella for the groups. Finally, the dissidents pull together pre-existing organizations in their diverse communities to mobilize followers via linkages among trade issues and thus offer selective incentives and local public goods to keep the various groups happy.

4 Micro-level Mechanisms

GPMs may in the end be explained by micro-level mechanisms which catalog the mobilization of individual protesters. While CARP offers a thin rationalist explanation of the protesters' actions, political behavior theories examine deeper motivations, perceptions, and expectations. Four sets of factors are typically involved.

4.1 Resource Accumulation and Access

Academics suggest that the resource accumulation mechanism helps explain protest participation in GPMs. Resources are often used to predict participation, replacing earlier explanations that focused on socioeconomic group memberships as participatory predictors (Verba et al. 1993, 453). Participation is often well predicted by individually based socioeconomic resources like education, income, time, and political interest (Leighley and Nagler 1992, 734; Verba et al. 1993, 493). Other predictors that have been used to operationalize resources include money, command of English, and civic skills (Verba et al. 1993, 492). Various types of participation differ in terms of time and monetary commitments, and thus the impact of resources differs depending on participation type (Brady, Verba, and Schlozman 1995, 285). According to the resource accumulation mechanism, socioeconomic resources are expected to predict protest participation, with protest more likely to occur in locations that have higher resources and protesters more likely to have high levels of resources.

Activists suggest a similar resource access mobilizational mechanism. Money, time, and internet access are recognized as resources that facilitate dissent. In fact, Martinez (2000, 76) suggests that minorities' lesser access to resources dampens their participation in much global justice mobilizing. Accordingly, she reports that activists attribute the absence of people of color to minorities' lesser internet access and "the likelihood of brutal police repression," "lack of funds for the trip, inability to be absent from work during the week, and problems in finding child care" (Martinez 2000, 76).

4.2 Associational Recruitment and Involvement

The associational recruitment mechanism is offered by other scholars to explain protest participation in GPMs. Such scholars focus on a broadened definition of resources, emphasizing institutionally based resources obtained through associational activity or mobilization (Leighley 1995, 197; Verba et al. 1993, 492). Putnam, for instance, argues that a decline in civil society involvement may be related to participatory declines in politics (2000, 342). These involvements are alleged to have participatory benefits, teaching civic skills and the value of participation in public life as well as helping to forge relationships (Putnam 2000, 19, 339; Verba et al. 1993, 492). The participatory benefit of these skills, values, and relationships seem to vary across participation types (Brady, Verba, and Schlozman 1995, 285). In some studies, the participatory impact of civic engagement rivals that of economic predictors (Ayala 2000, 99). According to this associational recruitment mechanism, protest is likely to occur in locations with high associational activity and protesters are likely to be active associational members.

An associational involvement mobilizational mechanism is also posited by activists. As we have argued when discussing world society, virtual networks, and conference planning, local organizations are very important mobilizers. Knoche states, "Local organizations in communities, workplaces, and schools are the building blocks of any radical transformation of our society" (2004, 289). Carlsson points out that groups must strategically institutionalize themselves if they wish to engage in sustained action (2004, 236). There are many ways in which associational involvement can mobilize participants, as they interact with other group members, change their values, learn about new issues, and gain access to better information and resources that facilitate dissent (Milstein 2004, 280–1).

4.3 Psychological Involvement and Social Transformation

Third, some political behavior scholars emphasize the participatory impact of prior political activity, and its potential for psychological transformation and attitudinal change. In some research, politically relevant attitudes better predict participation than economic factors (Katosh and Traugott 1982, 374–5; Oliver 1999, 204). Political participation predicts certain types of protest and may thus help to explain participation in GPMs (Bean 1991, 272).

A social transformation mobilizational mechanism is also suggested by activists. Crass exemplifies this mechanism with a description of Baker's model of organizing in the early twentieth century, stating,

She believed that a movement fighting for social transformation must also be transforming the individuals involved. She believed that people grew and developed through collective work to challenge oppression. She wasn't just talking about the ways that people see the world, but also the place they see themselves in the world; from being acted upon by forces of oppression to acting in the world for social justice. This shift involves learning politics and skills, but also a sense of self and being prepared to act. (2004, 443)

Thus, political knowledge and skills develop with movement interaction, and likely predict later participation in the movement. Similarly, Crass explains that one objective of protest is psychological growth and empowerment: "For Baker, direct action was about achieving immediate goals, but it was also deeply connected to developing a sense of power in the people involved" (2004, 432). Milstein also suggests that as activists are exposed to each other, a movement will grow, new alliances will develop, and identities will morph (2004, 281). She suggests that affinity groups "come together as friends or because of a common identity, or a combination of the two," in which "our unity needs to take precedence over our diversity" (2004, 280). Hence, activists come together because of a shared identity and bonds, and these identities and bonds grow with greater exposure.

4.4 Issue Intensity, Discontent, and Issue Consensus

The issue intensity and discontent mechanism consists of a fourth grouping of factors some academics use to predict participation in GPMs. Much controversy surrounds the impact of these issues. In predictions of conventional participation, issue standpoints seem to play a small role (Bean 1991, 253; Carmines and Layman 1997, 304–5, 308; Goren 1997, 406). In contrast, unconventional participation and political violence seem to be predicted by issue intensity and discontent (Bean 1991, 270, 271; Conover, Gray, and Coombs 1982, 328; Gurr 1968, 250). In particular,

Conover, Gray, and Coombs found that oppositional issue standpoints seemed to predict participation more than supportive issue standpoints (1982, 328). Thus, the issue intensity and discontent mechanism would suggest that protest would be expected in places where people are discontented with government policies, and protesters are expected to be opposed to governmental policies.

Activists suggest an issue consensus framing mechanism. Groups come together because they care about or share discontent over some overlapping issues (Milstein 2004, 280). They share some common values, favoring collective responsibility over corporatization; local economics over the global economy; diversity over monoculture; real democracy over proxy decision making; global justice over corporate rule; community over empire; and systemic change over the System (Reinsborough 2004, 179). Besides sharing these values, there are specific issues on which groups of protesters share standpoints: opposition to neo-liberal globalization as proposed by various MEIs and opposition to US military intervention in Afghanistan and/or Iraq (Solnit 2004, pp. xxii–xxiii; Bello 2004, 22; Klein 2004, 249).

Political behavior theories thus suggest that GPMs are mobilized via the resource accumulation, associational recruitment, psychological involvement, and issue intensity and discontent mechanisms. Protesters are expected to be active members of civil society. Participatory benefits are expected for active associational participants. Accordingly, protesters also are expected to be ardent in their engagement in various forms of active political participation. Globalized protest participants are expected to be more actively engaged in several forms of active participation than the general population. Protesters are also expected to share certain values and to be more discontented with the state and its policies than the general population.

5 CONCLUSION

Our macro perspective drew on international relations theories and studied GPMs as transnational actors with transnational causes—global culture, society, market, and politics. Our meso perspective drew on contentious politics theories and explored meso-level processes of mobilization into protest. According to Synthetic Political Opportunity Theory or SPOT (McAdam, Tarrow, and Tilly 2001) these mechanisms and processes involve the structuring power of institutions (called political opportunities), the organizing power of society (called mobilizing structures), and the actor formation power of the environment (called cultural framing). More concretely, transnational contention involves mechanisms in which actors frame issues globally, externalize claims, internalize contention from abroad in their societies, shift the scale of conflict from domestic to international, form transnational coalitions, adopt insider–outsider coalitions, send boomerangs abroad for help, and adopt defensive transnationalism. We also drew on the meso-level processes of market, community, contract, and hierarchy of the Collective Action Research Program or CARP (Lichbach). Our micro perspective drew on theories of political behavior and examined the components of protesters' decision calculi—individual resources, recruitment or institutional resources, psychological engagement, and issue intensity. We argued, in sum, that macro global institutions drive meso mobilizing processes that micro recruit individuals into GPMs.

Academic theories and activist thought allowed us to compare and contrast the mechanisms behind GPMs. We suggest that future research center on exploring the relationships between movements' differential mobilizational success and differences in their strategic use of mobilizational mechanisms. We argue that forms of contention are differentiated by their reliance on these multi-level mechanisms. In the remainder of the conclusion, we show how future research might proceed. We compare the anti-globalization and anti-war GPMs, speculating on how inter-movement differences in mobilization may be attributed to moderate versus radicalized usage of mobilizational mechanisms. Macro-level targets, meso-level organizing, and micro-level political behavior are all important and interrelated pieces of the puzzle in accounting for contentious politics, we argue, and the judicious application of selected parts of our framework can be useful in explaining different concrete phenomena.

The less mobilized anti-globalization movement seems to be characterized by more radical variants of mobilizational mechanisms which are less appealing to masses cross-nationally. For global justice activists, economic justice is at the crux of their concerns, as the global market and the entire structure of the world system are targeted. Some segments in the anti-globalization movement focus on protecting traditional values and communities against Westernization. The anti-globalization movement is opposed to authority; has a more cosmopolitan world-view (with international concerns, targets, and grievances); is characterized by heterogeneous coalitions with multiple and fluid individual identities; and seems to take a more relativist approach, permitting their identity a lot of leeway to evolve in response to contextual change. Ideals are framed in a postmodern fashion, focusing on the interconnectedness of many disparate ideals. Non-state actors who are radical and decentralized and recruitment styles that are anarchic seem to characterize the anti-globalization movement. Further, anti-globalization activists seem to use many targets at both the international and domestic level; focus their US-centered opposition on US empire seeking; are opposed to the capitalist system that the US economy plays such an important role in supporting; and focus on the democratic threat posed by international institutions and the global market. As to meso-level mechanism usage by the anti-globalization movement, focal points are abstract and less domestically grounded; fringe organizations are more active; frames appeal to more radicalized ideals, involve extremist tactics, and are not so domestically grounded; smaller, issue-specific or regionalized conferences and smaller, more fragmented networks are involved; and abstract selective incentives that are not domestically grounded are offered to potential recruits. Finally, in terms of micro-level mechanisms, the anti-globalization movement seems to have more participants who are younger, not working full time, still in school, and with a lot of free time; unstructured recruiting seems to be used to target fringe associations; the movement comes from a long-standing protest participation tradition and many consider lobbying or institutional participation as "selling out;" and absolutist hard-core positions on issues of war and globalization are taken by many.

In contrast, the more mobilized anti-war movement seems to be characterized by more mainstream variants of mobilizational mechanisms which are more appealing to large numbers of people in different contexts. Economic concerns are less central for the bulk of the anti-war movement, as they take a measured approach, acknowledging the benefits of the current global market structures, but try to connect disparate policies they oppose to economic policies. Protecting traditional values seems less of a concern for the anti-war movement, and they rather seem to embrace progressivism. The anti-war movement is more respectful of authority and seems more likely to conditionally oppose it; has strong national roots; is characterized by homogeneous coalitions with fewer and more stable individual identities; and seems to take a less relativist approach, pretty unresponsive to contextual changes. The anti-war movement uses more modern framing, focusing on single issues, and does not try to tie together so many disparate issues. Civil society groups that are reformist and more centralized seem more likely to get involved, and block recruitment seem to characterize the anti-war movement. Additionally, anti-war activists focus on largely domestic targets; focus their US-centered opposition on particular US policies and not so much on US hegemony; and focus more on the democratic threat posed by domestic policies than on the global democratic deficit. As to meso-level mechanism usage by the anti-war movement, focal points are more concrete and domestically oriented; mainstream organizations are the focus; frames are domestically grounded, oriented toward liberalism, and involve conventional tactics; larger, more globalized conferences and larger, more centralized networks are involved; and selective incentives that are more concrete and domestically anchored are offered to potential recruits. To conclude, as to the anti-war movement's usage of micro-level mechanisms, more participants who work full-time, are wealthier, are educated, and have less free time seem to be involved; structured recruiting of conventional associations seems to be used; the movement seems to originate in a more conventional participation tradition, levying institutional tactics as well as protest tactics; and more nuanced positions on issues of war and globalization, taking different conditions into account, seem to be taken.

We thus suggest that macro, meso, and micro mechanisms are used in a more radical fashion by the less mobilized GPM against globalization, and in a more moderate fashion by the more mobilized GPM against war. Multi-level mechanisms can also be useful in understanding other forms of contention, and other successes and failures in mobilizing collective action. Hence, we suggest a research agenda that involves applying these different mechanisms to compare and contrast the successes and failures of other movements in contentious politics. In this endeavor, academic and activist thought should be consulted.

REFERENCES

ANDERSON, S. 2000. In focus: IMF: reform, downsize, or abolish. **www.cc.columbia.edu/sec/ dlc/ciao/pbei/fpif/anso1.html**

AYALA, L. J. 2000. Trained for democracy: the differing effects of voluntary and involuntary organizations on political participation. *Political Research Quarterly*, 53 (1): 99–115.

BARBER, B. R. 1995. *Jihad vs. McWorld*. New York: Random House.

BARLOW, M., and CLARKE, T. 2002. *Global Showdown: How the New Activists Are Fighting Global Corporate Rule*. Toronto: Stoddart.

BEAN, C. 1991. Participation and political protest: a causal model with Australian evidence. *Political Behavior*, 13 (3): 253–83.

BELLO, W. 2004. Global capitalism versus global community. Pp. 17–26 in *Globalize Liberation: How to Uproot the System and Build a Better World*, ed. D. Solnit. San Francisco: City Lights Books.

BRADY, H. E., VERBA, S., and SCHLOZMAN, K. L. 1995. Beyond Ses: a resource model of political participation. *American Political Science Review*, 89 (2): 271–94.

BRECHER, J. 2003. Globalization today. Pp. 199–210 in *Implicating Empire: Globalization and Resistance in the 21st Century World Order*, ed. S. Aronowitz and H. Gautney. New York: Basic Books.

——CHILDS, J. B. and CUTLER, J. eds. 1993. *Global Visions: Beyond the New World Order*. Boston: South End Press.

——COSTELLO, T. and SMITH, B. 2000. *Globalization from Below: The Power of Solidarity*. Cambridge: South End Press.

CALLINICOS, A. 2003. The anti-capitalist movement after Genoa and New York. Pp. 133–50 in *Implicating Empire: Globalization and Resistance in the 21st Century World Order*, ed. S. Aronowitz and H. Gautney. New York: Basic Books.

CARLSSON, C. 2004. Radical politics: assuming we refuse, let's refuse to assume. In *Globalize Liberation: How to Uproot the System and Build a Better World*, ed. D. Solnit. San Francisco: City Lights Books.

CARMINES, E. G., and LAYMAN, G. C. 1997. Value priorities, partisanship, and electoral choice: the neglected case of the United States. *Political Behavior* 19 (4): 283–316.

CASTELLS, M. 1997. *The Information Age: Economy, Society, and Culture*, 3 vols. Oxford: Blackwell.

CHASE-DUNN, C. 1989. *Global Formation: Structures of the World-Economy*. Cambridge: Basil Blackwell.

CONOVER, P. J., GRAY, V., and COOMBS, S. 1982. Single-issue voting: elite–mass linkages. *Political Behavior*, 4 (4): 309–31.

CRASS, C. 2004. Looking to the light of freedom: lessons from the civil rights movement and thoughts on anarchist organizing. Pp. 427–45 in *Globalize Liberation: How to Uproot the System and Build a Better World*, ed. D. Solnit. San Francisco: City Lights Books.

DANAHER, K., and BURBACH, R. eds. 2000. *Globalize This! The Battle against the World Trade Organization and Corporate Rule*. Monroe, Me.: Common Courage Press.

——and MARK, J. 2003. *Insurrection: Citizen Challenges to Corporate Power*. New York: Routledge.

FARACLAS, N. G. 2001. Melanesia, the banks, and the BINGOs: real alternatives are everywhere (except in the consultants' briefcases). Pp. 69–76 in *There is an Alternative: Subsistence and Worldwide Resistance to Corporate Globalization*, ed. V. Bennholdt-Thomsen, N. Faraclas, and C. Von Werlhof. Victoria: Spinifex Press.

FLORINI, A. M. ed. 2000. *The Third Force: The Rise of Transnational Civil Society.* Washington, DC: Carnegie Endowment for Peace.

FRIEDMAN, T. L. 2000. *The Lexus and the Olive Tree: Understanding Globalization.* New York: Anchor Books.

GAMSON, W. A. 1990. *The Strategy of Social Protest,* 2nd edn. Belmont, Calif.: Wadsworth.

GLOBAL EXCHANGE and PUBLIC CITIZEN. 2001. The global rule makers: undermining democracy around the world. In *Global Uprising: Confronting the Tyrannies of the 21st Century,* ed. N. Welton and L. Wolf. Gabriola Island: New Society Publishers.

GOREN, P. 1997. Political expertise and issue voting in presidential elections. *Political Research Quarterly,* 50 (2): 387–412.

GRAEBER, D. 2003. The globalization movement and the new New Left. Pp. 325–37 in *Implicating Empire: Globalization and Resistance in the 21st Century World Order,* ed. S. Aronowitz and H. Gautney. New York: Basic Books.

GURR, T. 1968. Psychological factors in civil violence. *World Politics,* 20 (2): 245–78.

HAGGARD, S. 2000. *The Political Economy of the Asian Financial Crisis.* Washington, DC: Institute for International Economics.

HARDT, M., and NEGRI, A. 2000. *Empire.* Cambridge, Mass.: Harvard University Press.

———— 2003. Globalization and democracy. Pp. 109–21 in *Implicating Empire: Globalization and Resistance in the 21st Century World Order,* ed. S. Aronowitz and H. Gautney. New York: Basic Books.

HAWTHORNE, S. 2001. The clash of knowledge systems: local diversity in the wild versus global homogeneity in the marketplace. Pp. 79–84 in *There is an Alternative: Subsistence and Worldwide Resistance to Corporate Globalization,* ed. V. Bennholdt-Thomsen, N. Faraclas, and C. Von Werlhof. Victoria: Spinifex Press.

HECKSCHER, Z. J. 2002. Lessons for the World Bank bond boycott. In *The Global Activist's Manual: Local Ways to Change the World,* ed. M. Prokosch and L. Raymond. New York: Thunder's Mouth Press.

HELD, D. 1995. *Democracy and the Global Order: From the Modern State to Cosmopolitan Governance.* Stanford, Calif.: Stanford University Press.

HOBBES, T. 1651/1988. *Leviathan.* London: Penguin.

INGLEHART, R. 1997. *Modernization and Postmodernization: Cultural, Economic, and Political Change in 43 Societies.* Princeton: Princeton University Press.

KATOSH, J. P., and TRAUGOTT, M. W. 1982. Costs and values in the calculus of voting. *American Journal of Political Science,* 26 (2): 361–76.

KECK, M. E., and SIKKINK, K. 1998. *Activists beyond Borders: Advocacy Networks in International Politics.* Ithaca, NY: Cornell University Press.

KLEIN, N. 2004. Moving through the symbols. Pp. 249–62 in *Globalize Liberation: How to Uproot the System and Build a Better World,* ed. D. Solnit. San Francisco: City Lights Books.

KLEIN, R. 2001. Globalized bodies in the twenty-first century: the final patriarchal takeover? Pp. 91–105 in *There is an Alternative: Subsistence and Worldwide Resistance to Corporate Globalization,* ed. V. Bennholdt-Thomsen, N. Faraclas, and C. Von Werlhof. Victoria: Spinifex Press.

KNOCHE, T. 2004. Organizing communities: building neighborhood movements for radical social change. Pp. 287–312 in *Globalize Liberation: How to Uproot the System and Build a Better World,* ed. D. Solnit. San Francisco: City Lights Books.

LASKEY, M. 2001. The globalization of resistance: N30 international day of action. Pp. 83–91 in *The Battle of Seattle: The New Challenge to Capitalist Globalization,* ed. E. Yuen, G. Katsiaficas, and D. Burton Rose. New York: Soft Skull Press.

LEIGHLEY, J. E. 1995. Attitudes, opportunities, and incentives: a field essay on political participation. *Political Research Quarterly*, 48 (1): 181–209.

——and NAGLER, J. 1992. Individual and systemic influences on turnout: who votes? 1984. *Journal of Politics*, 54 (3): 718–40.

LICHBACH, M. I. 1992. Nobody cites nobody else: mathematical models of domestic political conflict. *Defence Economics*, 3 (4): 341–57.

——1995. *The Rebel's Dilemma*. Ann Arbor: University of Michigan Press.

——1997. Contending theories of contentious politics and the structure-action problem of social order. *Annual Review of Political Science*, 1: 401–24.

——1998a. Competing theories of contentious politics: the case of the civil rights movement. Pp. 268–84 in *Social Movements and American Political Institutions*, ed. A. Costain and A. McFarland. Boston: Rowman and Littlefield.

——1998b. Contentious maps of contentious politics. *Mobilization*, 2: 87–98.

MCADAM, D. 1982. *Political Process and the Development of Black Insurgency, 1930–1970.* Chicago: University of Chicago Press.

——MCCARTHY, J. D., and ZALD, M. N., eds. 1996. *Comparative Perspectives on Social Movements: Political Opportunities, Mobilizing Structures, and Cultural Framings.* New York: Cambridge University Press.

——TARROW, S., and TILLY, C. 2001. *Dynamics of Contention.* Cambridge: Cambridge University Press.

MACHIAVELLI, N. 1514/1961. *The Prince.* London: Penguin.

MARTINEZ, E. B. 2000. Where was the color in Seattle? Looking for reasons why the Great Battle was so white. Pp. 74–81 in *Globalize This! The Battle against the World Trade Organization and Corporate Rule*, ed. K. Danaher and R. Burbach. Monroe, Me.: Common Courage Press.

MELUCCI, A. 1996. *Challenging Codes: Collective Action in the Information Age.* Cambridge: Cambridge University Press.

MILSTEIN, C. 2004. Reclaim the cities from protest to popular power. Pp. 277–86 in *Globalize Liberation: How to Uproot the System and Build a Better World*, ed. D. Solnit. San Francisco: City Lights Books.

MOORE, W. H. 1995. Rational rebels: overcoming the free-rider problem. *Political Research Quarterly*, 48 (2): 417–54.

NJEHU, N. N., and AMBROSE, S. 2001. How the A16 protests were organized. Pp. 46–53 in *Democratizing the Global Economy*, ed. K. Danaher. Monroe, Me.: Common Courage Press.

NORBERG-HODGE, H. 2001. Local lifeline: rejecting globalization-embracing localization. Pp. 178–88 in *There is an Alternative: Subsistence and Worldwide Resistance to Corporate Globalization*, ed. V. Bennholdt-Thomsen, N. Faraclas, and C. Von Werlhof. Victoria: Spinifex Press.

OLIVER, J. E. 1999. The effects of metropolitan economic segregation on local civic participation. *American Journal of Political Science*, 43 (1): 186–212.

OLSON, M. 1965. *The Logic of Collective Action: Public Goods and the Theory of Groups.* Cambridge, Mass.: Harvard University Press.

PROKOSCH, M., and RAYMOND, L. 2002. *The Global Activist's Manual: Local Ways to Change the World.* New York: Thunder's Mouth Press.

PUTNAM, R. D. 2000. *Bowling Alone: The Collapse and Revival of American Community.* New York: Simon and Schuster.

REINSBOROUGH, P. 2004. Decolonizing the revolutionary imagination: values crisis, the politics of reality, and why there's going to be a common-sense revolution in this generation. Pp. 161–211 in *Globalize Liberation: How to Uproot the System and Build a Better World*, ed. D. Solnit. San Francisco: City Lights Books.

RODRIK, D. 1997. *Has Globalization Gone Too Far?* Washington, DC: Institute for International Economics.

——1999. *The New Global Economy and Developing Countries: Making Openness Work*. Washington, DC: Overseas Development Council.

——2001. Governance of economic globalization. Pp. 347–65 in *Governance in a Globalizing World*, ed. J. S. Nye and J. D. Donahue. Washington, DC: Brookings Institution Press.

RUGGIE, J. G. 1982. International regimes, transactions and change: embedded liberalism in the postwar economic order. *International Organization*, 36: 379–415.

——1991. Embedded liberalism revisited: institutions and progress in international economic relations. Pp. 202–34 in *Progress in Postwar International Studies*, ed. E. Adler and B. Crawford. New York: Columbia University Press.

SOLNIT, D. 2004. The new radicalism: uprooting the system and building a better world. Pp. xi–xxiv in *Globalize Liberation: How to Uproot the System and Build a Better World*, ed. D. Solnit. San Francisco: City Lights Books.

STARR, A. 2000. *Naming the Enemy: Anti-Corporate Movements Confront Globalization*. London: Zed Books Ltd.

TARROW, S. 1994. *Power in Movement: Collective Action, Social Movements and Politics*. Cambridge: Cambridge University Press.

——2001. Transnational politics: contention and institutions in international politics. *Annual Review of Political Science*, 4: 1–20.

——2005. *The New Transnational Activism*. Cambridge: Cambridge University Press.

TULLOCK, G. 1971. The paradox of revolution. *Public Choice*, 11: 89–100.

VERBA, S., LEHMAN SCHLOZMAN, K., BRADY, H., and NIE, N. H. 1993. Race, ethnicity and political resources: participation in the United States. *British Journal of Political Science*, 23 (4): 453–97.

WOLFWOOD, T. J. 2001. Seattle: a convergence of globalization and militarization. Pp. 146–52 in *There is an Alternative: Subsistence and Worldwide Resistance to Corporate Globalization*, ed. V. Bennholdt-Thomsen, N. Faraclas, and C. Von Werlhof. Victoria: Spinifex Press.

PART VI

MASS POLITICAL MOBILIZATION

CHAPTER 21

THE EMERGENCE OF PARTIES AND PARTY SYSTEMS

CARLES BOIX

With the exception of a few Swiss cantons where all voters assemble in annual assemblies or *Landsgemeinde* and some New England towns where neighbors debate and vote in open meetings, all contemporary democracies are representative democracies. Direct democracy is simply impractical in today's world. States are too large in territory and population for a sizeable fraction of the citizenry to debate together and directly any political question at hand in a meaningful, sustained manner. The range and complexity of most issues that fall under public consideration is such that no citizen can master them even if she were to invest all her time in politics. As in the sphere of economic life, where agents work and produce in a highly specialized manner, contemporary politics has given way also to the idea of division of labor in all its dimensions. Instead of deciding directly, voters choose, through regular elections, a number of politicians to set policy and govern them. In other words, they fully delegate the power to make decisions and to supervise those decisions to their representatives for a given period of time, that is, until new elections are held. In turn, those future elections are roughly the only, albeit probably imperfect, mechanism to discipline policy makers to act on behalf of the voters' interests.

The very scale of contemporary polities and the electoral and parliamentary dynamics of representative democracies have in turn prompted politicians to create or join electoral and legislative "teams" or parties, that is, stable organizations through which politicians coordinate their political activity across electoral districts, in parliamentary assemblies, and in executive or governmental committees. In the parliamentary arena the coordination in parties reduces the transaction costs associated with crafting and passing laws. Moreover, partisan coordination probably enhances the ability of the legislature to hold the executive accountable. In the electoral arena, parties can gather and employ in a more efficient manner the financial and human resources politicians need to inform and mobilize voters. By easing the process of candidate selection and forcing the strategic coordination of voters on their members, they increase their electoral odds of victory. Finally, the creation of a pattern of stable cooperation among some legislators should confer on them a clear advantage over their opponents in terms of presenting a stable program and of defending their record in a clear-cut manner before voters.[1]

Unsurprisingly, political parties are a pervasive phenomenon in representative democracies. Factional coordination or the stable cooperation of political representatives came into being shortly after the formation of the first modern assemblies: in the United States since the 1780s, in France in the first year of the French Revolution, in Britain through the opposition of Tories and Whigs. As the electorate expanded and elections became clean and truly competitive mechanisms of selection, those factions developed into gradually more cohesive machines—disciplining their members in favor or against the government, presenting voters with a unified program, and taking care to bring voters to the ballot box. Modern parties, as both electoral and legislative machines, emerged in the late 1820s and early 1830s in Jacksonian America. In Belgium and Switzerland unified Liberal (or Radical) parties were founded in the late 1840s. In Britain, Liberals finally cohered as a parliamentary party in the 1850s. By the 1880s both they and the Conservatives were unified national organizations for all purposes. In the last third of the nineteenth century Catholics and social democrats launched highly centralized, mass parties in continental Europe. By the time the First World War started almost all electoral contests and parliamentary struggles pivoted around well-organized parties in all representative democracies.

1 THE QUESTION: WHAT PARTIES? WHICH PARTY SYSTEMS?

Although the coordination of politicians into parties, that is, into vote-seeking and governing teams of candidates and parliamentarians, has been a universal, almost lawlike phenomenon in contemporary democracies, the ways in which politicians have organized and voters have responded to partisan appeals have varied widely over time and across countries. On the one hand, political parties differ in their internal architecture: how hierarchical they are; the strength of their parliamentary wing vis-à-vis the party apparatus; the number, extraction, and commitment of their

---

[1] The functions performed by parties were extensively discussed in the sociological and structural literature of the 1960s and 1970s (LaPalombara and Weiner 1966; Sartori 1976). This research was recast in rational and institutional terms, which I follow here, in the 1990s (Cox and McCubbins 1993; Aldrich 1995).

membership; or their cohesiveness, ranging from loose, almost ad hoc coalitions of interests, to tightly disciplined organizations whose members never deviate from the official position of the party (Duverger 1954; Panebianco 1988).

On the other hand, parties vary in their external dimension or attributes, that is, in their articulation in the electoral market. First, they diverge in their ideological orientation and their programmatic goals—in other words, they differ in the set of promises they make to electors and, constrained by world conditions, in the decisions they make.[2] Second, they differ in the size of their electoral support and parliamentary representation as well as in the stability with which they hold their voters.

The programmatic stance of any party and, to a lesser degree, its electoral strength are a function of the choices made by its members about which goals they will pursue and how they should advance them. But the electoral support of any party depends also on the ideological commitments and political strategies adopted by other political competitors in two ways. First, parties draft their electoral platforms partly in response to the programmatic (and policy) choices other parties make on issues such as the provision of public goods, the control of education, and the conduct of foreign policy. Second, voters eventually vote on the basis of the alternative positions taken by the different parties in the electoral market. In other words, both the size and the political stance of parties are the outcome of the strategic interaction of different politicians and their organizations in their quest for electoral success. From this point of view, it then makes sense to talk about the system of parties or "party system" in any country—that is, about the national profile, in terms of number, size, and ideological preferences, of parties.

In the following section I summarize the two main competing explanations of party systems, the historical-sociological literature and the neo-institutionalist research agenda, and evaluate their strengths and limitations. In the next two sections I then suggest a method of restructuring the way in which we should think how parties emerged that integrates, in a broad analytical framework, both approaches.[3]

2 CURRENT THEORETICAL LITERATURE

2.1 Sociological Accounts

In a path-breaking study published in 1967, Lipset and Rokkan emphasized the heterogeneity of interests and social groups to explain the emergence of different party systems in Western Europe in the nineteenth and early twentieth centuries (Lipset and Rokkan 1967).

---

[2] A recent and important strand of literature distinguishes today between (strictly) programmatic and clientelistic parties (Kitschelt et al. 1999; Stokes 2005). Here I do not make this distinction—I take "clientelistic" parties to have as their program the distribution of particularistic goods to their supporters.

[3] Most of this section relies heavily on Boix (2006b).

More specifically, they claimed that the number and relative strength of different parties across European nations was determined by two crucial historical events: a national revolution, that is, the construction of modern, secular nation-states; and the industrial revolution. As the state elites engaged in the construction of a single administrative apparatus, a centralized bureaucracy and a national standardized culture, they faced the resistance of two social groups—the members of territorial peripheries that opposed the process of centralization and the Catholic Church, which was in danger of losing its properties, educational structures, and in some instances its direct influence over state policy. In turn, the industrial revolution, with the emergence of manufacturing firms and the parallel growth of cities, generated two additional dimensions of conflict: between countryside and cities (mostly around trade policy) and, within the latter, between the owners of capital and workers.

The capital–labor conflict eventually emerged in all countries—and acquired full political significance with the full extension of universal suffrage. By contrast, the specific nature and the strength of the other three kinds of conflict (territorial, religious, and rural–urban) varied across Europe (and, by default, although Rokkan and Lipset do not treat them, in the former settler colonies governed through democratic institutions). The type of political parties that formed varied across countries as a function of those dimensions of conflict. To name a few examples, religious conflict was considerable in most Catholic countries as well as in those countries where there was a significant Catholic majority. But it was fundamentally absent in Scandinavia. Trade policy played a central role in the latter and in most large states but not in countries such as Belgium or the Netherlands.

In addition to the variation in the nature and size of social interests, party systems were also shaped by the sequence of alliances made by the political elites (and counter-elites) of each country. In those countries where the Reformation triumphed and the state controlled the national Protestant Church, the central conflict hinged around trade issues and the opposition of land versus town. In Britain landholders and the established Church coincided in the Conservative Party against a Liberal Party based on urban interests and Nonconformist Protestants. In Scandinavia, the urban center confronted the landed areas (and, in some cases, the dissident churches). Catholic countries experienced in turn a split between clerical and anticlerical parties and each of these was intertwined with the land–urban cleavage in different forms. Those countries sitting on the border between Protestant and Catholic Europe, that is, Germany, the Netherlands, and Switzerland, combined both worlds—with the electoral support of each party clustered in particular geographical areas.

2.2 Limits of the Sociological Account

The work of Lipset and Rokkan has spawned a substantial sociological literature bent on understanding the interests and sectors that supported each party.[4] Yet it has also

---

[4] For a recent summary of the literative see Caramani (2004).

prompted in due time important criticisms. Here I first discuss and reject what we may want to call a radical critique of the sociological approaches to party formation. I then introduce an amended theory of interest-based party politics—one in which institutional environments and the sequence of entry in elections are decisive to understanding the final form of party systems.

In its most radical stance, some critics of the sociological approach question entirely the assumption that voters have a set of pre-existing preferences that politicians represent in a direct, immediate manner. They contend, instead, that identities and political preferences do not exist as objective data waiting to be channeled and mobilized by certain parties and that it is in fact politicians and parties that shape identities. Their argument comes in two main forms. Some scholars claim that political preferences effectively do not exist—voters are an ignorant set, at most endowed with private motives or passions, which an ambitious politician articulates around some ideological principle to serve his own private interests. Others acknowledge that voters' preferences (over some policies or issues) may exist but immediately assert that they are too many to serve any practical purpose for the researcher interested in predicting why certain groups and ideas became mobilized in the electoral arena. Since any political identity may emerge, as little attention as possible should be paid to the idea of pre-existing "electoral spaces." In both accounts, politicians are not ideologically motivated actors that seek to represent certain interests and implement their policy preferences. They are, instead, vote-maximizing entrepreneurs who, calculating which types of issues may increase their electoral support, choose what groups to politicize and mobilize and in what ways. Mainly cultivated in the study of ethnic conflict and national identity, this radical critique of the sociological theories of identity formation and mobilization has gathered steam in recent years to explain the formation of new cleavages in democratizing nations in the former communist bloc and the Third World.[5]

It is interesting to notice that this "constructivist" critique partakes of one of the central tenets and weaknesses of the darling of Keynesian macroeconomics theory— the pre-rational expectations model of business cycles. To justify the possibility of expanding demand and lowering unemployment without incurring any accelerating inflation, until the 1960s Keynesian economists assumed that workers were ignorant or plainly irrational individuals who would not push for higher wages in response to the manipulation of economic aggregates by a smart, strategic government. Naturally, their models crumbled under the monetarist and rationalist critiques they received in the 1970s. Similarly, political constructivists generally present voters as fools that can be easily manipulated by politicians. Yet they are logically inconsistent in how they build their theory: whereas they break the central tenet of instrumental rationality for voters, they do not for political elites, which they assume to be fully strategic in their behavior.

An amended interest-based theory of party systems. If we accept that both voters and candidates are rational agents, that is, they are capable both of defining their interests—immediately or, over time, by learning, through trial and error, what their

---

[5] For a forerunner of these arguments, see Sartori (1968), who insisted on the autonomy of politics to explain party formation over purely sociological accounts.

interests are—and of acting upon them—selecting their representatives according to some welfare-enhancing criteria in the case of voters and crafting viable candidacies to win elections in the case of politicians—some sociological theory of elections has to be brought back in again. Politicians do not operate in a vacuum: their electoral promises and their policy-making decisions need to make sense in the context of the everyday practices and preoccupations of voters to give the former a reasonable change to succeed at the ballot box. For politicians to successfully mobilize voters on the basis of certain ideas or programs, voters must sense some (material or ideational) affinity with the electoral platform they are offered. In short, to explain party systems we need to understand the type and distribution of preferences of voters, that is, the nature of the policy space.

Still, even if interests matter, the sociological approach is in need of considerable amendment. Sociological approaches forget to characterize the conditions (of a temporal, organizational, or institutional kind) that determine the ways in which politicians choose to coordinate in parties. In other words, the sociological literature has been too quick in positing an automatic relationship between interests and political action. Instead, interests should be thought of as being latent variables that may or may not crystallize in the form of parties. As shown by the spatial literature of elections that flourished in the 1960s and 1970s and has overtaken the discipline since the publication of Rokkan and Lipset's work, political parties cannot be seen as the unmediated reflection of social and economic interests for at least three reasons.[6] First, voters care about multiple issues—and their positions on the latter are not necessarily correlated in the same direction. For example, most farmers favor agricultural subsidies and this may lead to the formation and electoral success of an agrarian party. But not all farmers necessarily behave as such at the ballot box—a fraction of them may cast their vote for a non-agrarian party that promises policies, such as universal health care or the introduction of teetotaler laws, about which they care first and foremost. Thus, in a multidimensional space, parties can structure a winning coalition by appealing to very different types of voters. Second, parties may break a straightforward relationship between the economic position of voters and the policy that would result from automatically satisfying their interests through the construction of broader policy bundles (higher public spending on education to compensate for trade openness). Workers employed in import-competing firms should be prone to vote for protectionist parties. But they may end up voting for a free trade candidate if the latter credibly promises compensatory mechanisms (such as vocational training) to adjust to future global shocks (Boix 2006a). Finally, most decisions of voters about whom to support are mediated by their beliefs about the effects that certain policies will have on their welfare. Thus, a substantial portion of the low-income voters may end up voting for conservative parties if they believe that low taxes and laissez-faire policies, which in principle reduce the amount of net transfers they will receive from the state and weaken any

---

[6] This literature shows that positing an automatic translation of interests to parties would be wrong even in a world in which institutions did not exist or did not force voters to coordinate and act strategically. I deal with the impact of institutions later, in Section 2.3.

protective regulations in the labor market, are the best mechanism to generate growth and raise their income in the long run.

The non-sociological traits of Lipset and Rokkan. Before I consider in detail the organizational and institutionalist literature that has developed to complement or even replace sociological explanations of party formation, let me note that Lipset and Rokkan did something that many of their direct followers (and, particularly, most of their summarizers) have failed to do: they acknowledged that a purely "society-centered" rendition of the process of party formation would be insufficient.[7] Accordingly, they stressed both the temporal and the institutional factors at play in the formation of parties: they insisted on the rules that governed participation and representation during the nineteenth century; and they emphasized that parties were ultimately the result of choices made by elites about what groups they would ally with.

Still, their non-sociological arguments were cast at too high a level of generality. It is true that they postulated a set of "cleavages" and they derived from them several actors or groups (in the administrative, economic, territorial, and religious arenas) of universal application to explain Western Europe. And they even described the types of alliances (or, more precisely, the restrictions on the alliances) that could be struck among those different groups. But, beyond several specific historical descriptions of the patterns of political representation for particular countries, they never specified the ways in which those groups (alone or in a coalition with other groups) became organized in certain institutional networks and party organizations across countries. Writing before the literature on social choice and spatial models became ingrained in the scientific study of politics, they paid little attention to the derivation of elite strategies from their ultimate preferences. And they did not specify the ways in which electoral rules and organizational capacity mattered for electoral purposes.

2.3 Organizational and Institutional Explanations

If the electoral arena is often crowded with multiple issues (i.e. if it is a multidimensional political space) and if there is an uncertain link between voters' interests and the policy instruments that must be adopted to satisfy them, then sociological explanations must give way to models that emphasize the ways in which institutional structures determine the nature of partisan representation.

Within this institutionalist literature, there are in turn two broad schools of thoughts. On the one hand, several scholars emphasize the role of political elites and organizations in choosing what constituencies to mobilize and under what banner. Przeworski and Sprague (1986) investigate the decision of socialist parties to contest elections and the means through which they managed an electoral tradeoff between appealing to their natural constituencies as working-class parties (at the risk of never attaining an absolute majority in parliament) and moderating their platforms to attract middle-class voters.

---

[7] Kitschelt (this volume) is a clear attempt to correct the standard and strictly sociological interpretation of Lipset and Rokkan.

Kalyvas (1996) locates the emergence and growth of Christian Democratic parties in the decisions of church elites and the organizational capabilities of the Catholic lay movement.

On the other hand, strict institutionalist scholars have shown that electoral and constitutional rules determine the number of candidates and parties through two channels. First, electoral rules, and particularly plurality rule, encourage the strategic behavior of both elites and voters, forcing their coordination around those candidates that appear viable to avoid wasting votes and resources. More specifically, single-member districts lead to the concentration of ballots onto two candidates. As the magnitude of the district rises, the number of viable candidates rises as well. Generally speaking, in districts with M seats, the number of viable candidates, that is, the number of candidates that will receive votes, will not exceed $M+1$ (Duverger 1954; Cox 1997).

Second, national institutions matter as well in how they shape party coordination for a simple reason: electoral laws may determine the extent of coordination at the district level but they cannot account for the process of party coordination across districts. In his path-breaking study of nineteenth-century British parliamentary politics, Cox (1987) attributed the formation of a two-party system to (the combination of plurality rule and) the growth of government as a cabinet fully responsible before parliament (and capable of employing the threat of elections to exact the loyalty of its supporters). Shugart and Carey (1992) have shown that presidentialism also shapes the number of candidates. In presidential systems where the president is elected through plurality rules, the number of electoral candidates is close to two. This is particularly true when the legislature is also elected using plurality law. If the legislature is chosen according to proportional representation (a frequent case in Latin America), the number of presidential candidates slightly exceeds the Duvergerian prediction: it is likely that having many congressional parties increases the chances that more than two will launch their own candidate in the presidential contest. In presidential systems with a run-off election the constraining effect is much milder: the number of presidential candidates fluctuates around four. The type of presidential election affects the structure of party systems in the legislature as well. If the president is elected through plurality and both presidential and legislative elections are held at the same time, the number of congressional parties is small—between 2.1 and 3.1 depending on the electoral system for the election of congress. Otherwise, the type of presidential election has no impact on the congressional party system. More recently, Chhibber and Kollman (2004) have emphasized the federal or centralized nature of the state to explain the final number of parties.

2.4 The Limits of Institutionalism

Institutional accounts face two important limits. First, the type of rules in place cannot be employed to predict the spatial location, ideological commitments, and nature of electoral support of the parties that will compete in the electoral arena—particularly if elections take place in multidimensional spaces. Plurality rule may generate two-party systems. But whether two competing parties end up being socialist and conservative, liberal and clerical, free trader and protectionist, or any other combination is independent of the electoral law in place.

Second, institutional models cannot easily account for change. Strict institutionalists think of institutional rules as some sort of self-sustaining equilibrium. According to this account, plurality rule generates a two-party system in which the two parties have no interest in lessening the constraining effects of the electoral law. Proportional representation fragments the electoral arena into several partisan structures and the actors that profit from this fragmentation veto any attempt to tighten the requirements to elect any representative. To put it more generally, strict institutionalists see the political actors as wholly endogenous to the institutional structure in which they make choices—as a result, because policy makers are themselves the outcome of a particular incentive structure, they should have little interest in changing the rules of the game that sustain them.[8]

There is much truth in this view of institutions as relatively stable mechanisms. But constitutional settings in general and electoral laws in particular are themselves the choice of political actors. And these political actors are not wholly endogenous to the institutional rules in place. Shocks exogenous to electoral laws (for example, the formation of an industrial working class) and the option new actors have to develop strategies of action external to the electoral game (for example, forming unions that contest elections at a later point) have the capacity of altering the institutional equilibrium in place.

3 A Theory of Party System Emergence: Analytical Steps

Given the insights and limitations of the models reviewed so far, a more systematic explanation of the emergence of party systems must be based on the integration of two theoretical steps. The first step is strictly analytical and consists in describing the structure of incentives within which voters vote and politicians decide to run for office. Depicting the institutional mechanisms of any representative democracy, that is, the ways in which elections, government formation, and policy making work, will let

---

[8] Most explanations of the choice of institutions either depict institutions as efficient solutions to collective action and time consistency problems (Knight 1992) or simply refer to them as self-reinforcing equilibria (Putnam 1993). The adoption of proportional representation has been related to the trade requirements of small countries (Rogowski 1987) or to its capacity to manage political conflict in heterogeneous societies (Katzenstein 1985; Lijphart 1977). Political parties have been purported to solve coordination failures (Aldrich 1995; Cox 1987). Still, efficiency theories have clear difficulties in accounting for cross-temporal and cross-national variation and, particularly, in explaining the choice of suboptimal institutions, the pervasive existence of instances of political stagnation, and the breakdown of political regimes. As a matter of fact, the predominance of these rather functionalist approaches is doubly surprising given a central insight of analytical institutionalism: that, precisely because they shape political equilibria, institutions are themselves the outcome of political strategies (Riker 1986).

us predict, at a most general or abstract level, the ways in which voters and politicians act to maximize the probability of reaching their objectives—given the institutional rules in which they operate. This can done by drawing upon the very extensive contemporary literature on elections, spatial theory, and strategic coordination (driven by electoral rules) to describe the workings of representative government.

The second step is historical. Starting from the incentive structure that shapes the behavior of voters and parties, we need to describe and make sense of the sequence of historical events through which politicians coordinated in parties, choosing particular programs and electoral strategies, and voters then rallied around them. Such an approach should show why certain parties emerged at certain historical junctures; why others did not or, if they did, failed at the ballot box; and, finally, why they chose particular electoral institutions which, in turn, shaped the number and type of viable parties.

These two steps are complementary. Without analytical foundations, the historical description of party systems and elections would remain an amorphous, variegated set of facts. With some partial (and very laudable) exceptions, most of the scholarly literature on this problem still has this character. Conversely, without any attention to the historical sequence at work, we would be unable to account for the dynamics of institutional change that were at the heart of the process of party formation we want to explain. And therefore we would be unable to sort out which variables preceded which events and how. As discussed before, this lack of attention to history (and, more precisely, timing) handicaps most of the formal work on electoral systems and party systems. The findings that institutional structures covary with the number of parties are mostly correlations that tell us little about the way in which institutions and parties unfolded over time and how actors shaped the mechanisms of democratic representation.

Consider now in more analytical detail the way in which democratic elections work. As summarized in Figure 21.1, in any election, some citizens first decide to advance their candidacy (jointly with a particular electoral platform or list of policy promises). Voters then cast their ballots and only a few candidates become elected, that is, only a few gather a sufficient number of votes (where sufficient is defined by the electoral law in place) to get into public office. After elections, the elected representatives convene to form government and set policy until new elections take place. These policies, which may well include the procedures to select candidates in future elections (i.e. the electoral laws), purportedly have an impact on the well-being of citizens (and politicians) and should affect how the next election is fought and how voters will decide again.

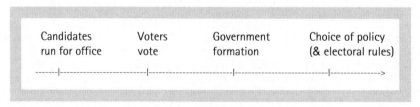

| Candidates run for office | Voters vote | Government formation | Choice of policy (& electoral rules) |

Fig. 21.1 The temporal sequence of representative democracies

Given this temporal structure, where elections lead to some policy outcomes which may have some welfare effects on the electorate, the decision of voters to cast their ballot for a given candidate depends in turn on two things. In the first place, voters generally vote for the candidate who makes promises (or who, in case she is running for re-election, brings in certain accomplishments) that are relatively closer to their ideal policies or goals than the positions adopted by the remaining politicians. Yet, in the second place, the decision of voters to support a politician is conditional on them considering her a viable candidate, that is, on believing that she has reasonable chances of winning (and probably of affecting the choice of policy). More precisely, voters vote for a candidate if they (individually) expect that she will muster enough support from other voters to be elected to office. Thus, voters may decide to eschew the candidate they like most but believe very unlikely to win and instead concentrate their support on a less preferred but electorally "safer" politician (to defeat a third and even less preferred candidate).

Given the mechanisms that define the behavior of voters, we can turn to see how politicians will behave—that is, under what conditions and in what ways they will decide to run for office. First, candidates will tend to pick policies that are attractive to a sufficient section of the electorate (to go on and win the seat they are contesting). Second, politicians will only contest an election (and therefore parties will only be launched) if they can appear as viable candidates, that is, only if voters will take them as serious alternatives worth voting for.

From the structure of incentives of voters (electing welfare-maximizing representatives) and politicians (being recognized as useful and viable candidates and then being elected), there follow three main components or building blocks on which we should construct a theory of party system formation: the preferences of voters; their information and beliefs (about what other voters will do and the chances of politicians to get elected); and, finally, the electoral institutions through which votes are aggregated and candidates elected.

First, since elections discipline politicians to act on behalf of the electorate, a theory of party system formation must depart from an account of the distribution of the voters' preferences, that is, of the electoral space in which parties compete. Parties cannot deviate too much from the demands of their voters because they risk being heavily punished in the electoral arena. Still, knowing the profile of the electorate would seldom be enough to predict the nature of the party system in any given country for reasons I discussed before: only on rare occasions do voters have full information about the policies of parties; and they may have positions in multiple dimensions that may make them susceptible to many different types of political appeals. All in all, however, the types and numerical distribution of voters act as the main determinants of how parties position themselves in the electoral market.

Second, since the expectations voters have about the electoral chances of different candidates may be as central as (or sometimes even more central than) the interests of voters in determining their vote, we need to pay attention to the mechanisms that determine those beliefs and therefore that shape both the strategic coordination of politicians and the instrumental vote of voters. Two points are in order here.

The existence of expectations (and the corresponding strategic behavior that follows from them) confers some considerable advantage on those politicians that entered at the beginning of the sequence of elections relative to later entrants. That is, in an empty electoral arena, where there still is little information (provided by past elections) about who may be the best candidate around which to coordinate to defeat the least preferred politician, strategic considerations may play a minor role in voters' minds. By contrast, once some parties become established as the main electoral contenders, voters are suddenly much more constrained in their behavior. The main parties constantly appeal to their own electoral viability, as already proven in previous elections, in opposition to new, perhaps more preferred but as yet untested candidates, to maintain the allegiance of voters.

This electoral advantage, which comes from having some recognizable label, some organization, and some reputation at winning elections, has an additional and very important consequence. It gives parties the capacity and time to adjust policy promises and particular candidates to shifts in the electorate or in the preferences of electorates so that they can remain strongly competitive in the electoral arena. In short, the combination of being an early entrant and exploiting the strategic calculations of voters explains why we see so much persistence in party labels over time, even under periods of considerable ideological and social flux. Thus, for example, in spite of several wars, the transformation of the economy away from traditional smokestack industries, and substantial changes in social values, Democrats and Republicans have split the American electorate for over a century. Similarly, Conservatives and Labour have alternated in power in London for about eighty years. It has been by exploiting the strategic coordination of voters and gradually adjusting policies over time that these parties have systematically deterred the entry and consolidation of many third political forces.

This discussion on the stability of party systems leads us in turn to a second point, namely the conditions that precipitate the breakdown of the prevailing party system. At first sight, new parties seem to emerge whenever the electoral market changes abruptly—either because substantial numbers of new voters participate in the polls (due to a change in franchise rules) or when the interests of significant portions of the electorate change (for example, after massive migrations to the city or sudden political realignments precipitated by war). Yet, by and large, the formation and consolidation of new parties takes place only when their candidates are able to break the "expectations" advantage that the existing parties tap into to sustain their leading position. This can only happen if the entering parties enjoy sufficient organizational strength to mobilize their electors and move them away from the old equilibrium (in which they voted or are going to vote for one of the old parties because it was viable) to a new equilibrium (in which they support the new party). As the historical section discusses in more detail, the irruption of socialist parties in Europe followed the decision of trade unions to shift their support away from (left-leaning) liberal politicians to social democratic candidates.

Finally, since the decision of voters over whom to vote for (and, in fact, of politicians to form a party) is strongly affected by the institutional rules that specify the translation of votes into seats, we need to examine the nature and selection of the electoral laws to understand the formation of party systems. In the international system, actors (the states) do not choose the rules of the game—in fact, there are hardly any, except for some informal cooperation within a general condition of anarchy. In markets, firms only partially (if at all) define the rules of competition. By contrast, in representative democracies, politicians set the very rules according to which they will be selected. And they generally draft them to maximize their electoral chances. This simple fact forces us to tackle the causes underlying the choice of the rules of the game. In other words, a theory of party formation would be incomplete if we did not pay attention to the incentives that make politicians maintain the legal status quo (something that happens most of the time) or alter it (something that occurs very rarely and with substantial consequences).

4 Historical Account

In this section I apply the analytical building blocks discussed to interpret the historical sequence through which party systems emerged in the West—starting with a gradual process of political liberalization in the early nineteenth century and culminating with the full incorporation of its citizens in the first half of the twentieth century.

4.1 Initial Conditions

At the starting point of their process of democratization, most countries shared a very similar system of political representation—which we may want to think of as a pre-party system of representation. First, their electorates were very small, for two alternative reasons. In the overwhelming majority of instances, the regulation of the franchise conditions was extremely restrictive—limited to propertied men. In those exceptional cases in which the franchise was much more open, only a small portion of the citizenry turned out to vote. Second, the election of representatives was conducted through small, mostly single-member, districts and based on majoritarian rules. Third, electoral competition was extremely decentralized. Candidates, who were minimally coordinated (if at all) with other politicians across the nation, ran for office on local issues and relied very strongly on personal networks and clienteles in their own constituency. In many cases the idea of competition itself was spotty—candidates ran unopposed in one-third of the British constituencies in the early 1830s, in one-third of the Belgian and Danish districts in the 1850s and 1860s, and in almost a quarter of the Swiss ones in the 1890s. All in all, elected politicians acted as the delegates of local, territorialized interests in what may have often looked like a diplomatic mission in the central parliament. For example, in the early nineteenth century, the vast majority of parliamentary Acts in Britain had a private nature, that is, they authorized or regulated local business, permits, or works (Cox 1987).

4.2 The Growth of States and Electorates

This state of things changed dramatically under the impact of both the construction of unified and modern states and the gradual expansion of the franchise.

As the central state grew or attempted to grow in size and political relevance, mainly in response both to intensifying military competition between sovereign states and to the emergence of an industrial economy (at home or abroad), its decisions (and the administrative machinery it deployed to apply them) acquired an acute distributive profile in the national arena. It is true that national politics had already been crucial to the lives and businesses of a broad swath of the population (or at least to its elites). But up until then their impact had a mostly sporadic or episodic character—mainly around certain critical, well-defined historical convulsions such as wars and religious persecutions. By contrast, by the middle of the nineteenth century, policies devised in the capital systematically affected the interests of everyone in the country. National governments were now adjudicating over a growing number of decisions for the whole territory and therefore were capable of creating true winners and losers at the national level. And this in turn encouraged all the territorial interests represented in parliament to coordinate across territories and representatives either to support the government in place and its policies or to oppose it in a persistent and effective manner.

Besides the heightened role of the state, the gradual expansion of the franchise also spurred the formation of political parties as cohesive parliamentary and electoral machines. Larger electoral districts forced politicians to establish mechanisms to canvass the vote. To compete effectively against the traditional elites that were elected on the basis of a personal vote, the new parties that sprang up in the late nineteenth century to mobilize Catholics and socialist voters had to rely on broad organizations to collect their dues and sustain their candidates.

As shown by Cox (1987), legislative cohesion of British parliamentary parties grew systematically in the nineteenth and reached very high levels by the early twentieth century. Although parliamentary data for other countries in that period are scanty, by the last third of the nineteenth century most countries had several tightly organized parties. The example of Gladstone, who transformed the British Liberal Party into a truly electoral machine in the 1860s, and of the religious mass parties in continental Europe, which obtained impressive electoral results in the 1870s and 1880s, simply forced the old liberal and conservative parliamentary platforms to adapt as well and to become modern partisan organizations.

4.3 Voters' Preferences: The Franchise and the Space of Competition

In response to the nationalization of political life, politicians coordinated into permanent parliamentary (and, later, electoral) parties according to two key factors: first, the space of electoral competition, that is, the economic and religious preferences of voters;

and, second, the sequence and pattern of electoral mobilization. I deal with the first factor in this subsection. I discuss the timing of mobilization in the next subsection.

Two main political conflicts structured the space of electoral competition. On the one hand, the electorate divided over the regulation of economic life by the state. On the other hand, voters often split on the role the state should have on education and the creation of a common national culture.

The economy. A sustained fall in transportation costs (due to new technological advances) in combination with generalized international competition (intensified by the French revolutionary wars) spurred states to assert their control over the economic life of their territory. This implied breaking old local autonomies and corporations, abolishing internal barriers to trade, and eventually building a unified domestic market. Hence, once a national economic space had been established and the state had taken charge of setting the level of tariffs and taxes and the provision of public services, economic policy making turned into the object of systematic contestation between the different economic interests in society.[9]

The impact of economic interests on the *initial* electoral alignment of parties was mediated by the very limited franchise that prevailed in most countries in the first half of the nineteenth century as follows. Since only those individuals with property voted, electoral conflict along the income ladder (over redistributive policies), that is, between upper, middle, and working classes, was very light if not completely absent. Political contestation crystallized instead over the distinctive trade interests of the urban manufacturers in opposition to those of the propertied classes in the countryside. In a way, this coincided with the existing local or territorial representation of interests—rural and urban interests were respectively clustered in different geographical areas and therefore the process of partisan coordination proceeded naturally from the agglomeration of representatives from contiguous districts. (As indicated later, the broadening of the electorate contributed to shift the structure of the electoral space toward more class-based politics.)

The nationalization of religion and culture. Prompted by the ideas of the French Revolution, the wars of the turn of the nineteenth century, and the demands of industrialization, the state engaged in the creation of a homogeneous public culture and, in many instances, in the formation of a unified nation—mainly through the extension of equal political rights and the control and uniformization of the educational system. This hastened a divisive political battle over the delivery of education between the state and non-national churches (either the Catholic Church or non-state Protestant confessions) and, in a few instances, between the state and some national minorities.

Whereas the urban–rural dimension of conflict (mostly associated with trade issues) was almost universal across countries, the educational, religious, and territorial battles

---

[9] The construction of a unified economy was part and parcel of the politics of the time and was likely to contribute to the nature of the party system that finally emerged (for example in Switzerland). But I take the process of unification as mostly fixed, preceding (and mostly exogenous to) the processes of partisan coordination I am examining here. This assumption seems reasonable since all states eventually unified their economies—when they did not they eventually failed and disappeared (this is a way to read the absorption of all the smallish states that ended up in Germany and Italy).

broke out in some countries only. Whether they did was a function of the relation between the state and the existing church or churches in each country. The religious dimension of conflict did not appear in those countries where there was a single national church. There the state controlled its whole administrative apparatus and the provision of education. There was no organized opposition—in fact, there was little reason to expect it since the state did not discriminate (as it did in countries with a plurality of churches besides the official church) among its citizens for religious beliefs.

Religion only became a central matter of contention in those countries with several churches besides the official, state-sponsored church. This happened both in Protestant countries, like Britain, where church-goers were divided between Anglicans and Nonconformists, or the Netherlands, which had several Protestant churches (on top of a substantial Catholic minority), and in Catholic countries, where the Church controlled most of the existing educational structure. (This line of explanation departs strongly from the standard theory put forth by Lipset and Rokkan 1967, who distinguished between Protestant countries, with hardly a religiously defined electoral divide, and Catholic ones, with a marked clerical–anticlerical cleavage. The problem with their explanation is that religious conflict was not confided to Catholic nations. It was notorious in several Protestant countries as well.[10])

The existence of a restrictive franchise had a much smaller impact on altering the way in which the religious question affected the construction of electoral coalitions. Religious differences often cut across income levels and economic sectors—that is, in many instances religious practice and affiliation varied independently of class or profession. In those circumstances, religious and educational disagreements continued to play a key role in both the elections and parliament.[11]

4.4 The Sequence of Mobilization: From Dimensions of Conflict to Party Systems

Two initial parliamentary parties. At the initial stages of the process of coordination, that is, when most instances of collaboration happened at the parliamentary or congressional stage (while individual candidates still run as independents in their respective districts), the need to support (or oppose) a national government and pass

---

[10] Lipset and Rokkan actually noted this for Norway—but then made reference to the territorial, periphery nature of Norwegian fundamentalism to explain this exception away. Still, their explanation cannot encompass the cases of Britain, where Nonconformism was one of the pillars of the Liberal Party in the middle of the 19th century, and the Netherlands, where the formation of the CHU and ARP cannot be accounted for. The religious cleavage faded away in Britain in the early 20th century—but the territorial cleavage it marked still persists today. In the Netherlands, it did not disappear until the 1970s.

[11] Still, the impact of the franchise was not always negligible. In several cases the structure of the franchise biased the weight of different religious denominations at the ballot box. For example, because most Welsh Nonconformists were disenfranchised till the electoral reform of 1868, the Liberal Party did not control Wales until the last third of the 19th century. Similarly, the very restrictive electoral franchise in place in Belgium until 1893 put the Catholic party at a permanent disadvantage at the polls. This was a well-known fact to Liberals, who tried to tinker with it even more as the Catholic challenge grew over time.

national policies impelled politicians to coordinate in two parliamentary (and generally loose) parties—generally speaking, conservative and liberal.[12]

In one-dimensional electoral spaces, these parties proved stable even as they grew tighter in their parliamentary cohesion and stronger in their organizational capacity over time. In a few instances, one-dimensional spaces were the result of only having one dimension of conflict. This was the case of Sweden in the 1880s, where the religious-educational question hardly mattered and its population was culturally homogeneous. After a modern parliament replaced the old four-chamber system, the fall of agriculture prices in the 1870s spurred a bitter conflict between protectionists and free traders, each one clustered geographically. After the former suffered a temporary split, both forces crystallized into liberal and conservative parties. One-dimensional competition also happened in countries with several electoral dimensions that nonetheless were relatively well correlated—the case of Belgium, at least before the introduction of near universal male suffrage in 1893, where rural districts were overwhelming Catholic while urban constituencies were strongly anticlerical.

The religious question and the entry of third candidates. In those countries where both the economic and the religious issues were salient in the electoral arena, the dominant position of liberals and conservatives was certainly weaker—particularly given that the religious issue was sustained by a certain organizational network that could be mobilized at any time against any of the existing candidates. This mobilization, and the corresponding collapse of two-party systems, happened in Germany, the Netherlands, and Switzerland, where Catholic and Protestant parties launched successful electoral campaigns in the second third of the nineteenth century. But all other two-party systems, like the British one, did remain in place until the final expansion of the universal suffrage in the early twentieth century (and the growth of socialism).[13]

The roots of electoral stability of liberals and conservatives (or the lack of it) were mostly of an institutional and organizational kind. As discussed in the analytical section above, in the context of majority rules, which were in place across all countries in the nineteenth century, voters had very few incentives to desert the existing party, such as the liberal party, in favor of a more preferred alternative, such as a radical candidate, unless they had strong assurances that, by doing so, they would not split the left-wing majority and make the victory of a conservative politician possible. In this coordination game, the liberal party (as well as any other dominant parties in their respective districts) enjoyed an electoral advantage that allowed it to remain in power and to contain internal splits and external threats with considerable

---

[12] The tightness of these coalitions was a function of the institutional structure of the country (the French Third Republic, where the structure of the legislature was based on strong committees, had very loose parties) and the emergence of well-organized competitors in the electoral arena (which prompted competitors to strengthen their internal organizations).

[13] As discussed in the following section, the number of dimensions did not predict the number of parties. This has instead been the position of a substantial part of the literature that followed Lipset and Rokkan (1967). Taagapera and Shugart (1989), for example, claim that the number of parties is simply the number of dimensions minus one. Lijphart takes a similar position conditional on the degree to which dimensions of conflict overlap or not. Lipset and Rokkan (1967) develop a broad theory of cleavages and interests—but their discussion on the ways in which these cleavages or groups become represented is informal and particular to each country they examine.

success. A third party could only contest the elections as a truly credible alternative and therefore convince enough voters to simultaneously move away from the old parties if it could rely on a strong organizational basis or, more often, on some parallel, "pre-partisan" organization that could convince all their members that (given the context of majoritarian rules) everyone else in that organization would vote for that new party simultaneously.

In those countries in which liberal and conservative politicians had clashed (and coalesced in separate parliamentary factions) around the religious dimension early in time, that is, where educational and church-related issues had crystallized into the main partisan and electoral alignment, one of the two parties relied or came to rely on the network of religious organizations. As a result, no third party could exploit (or, in fact, had any incentive to exploit) the latter.[14] This was the case of Belgium, where educational matters and church policy defined all elections since the 1840s, in France, where voters split along clerical–anticlerical lines from the French Revolution (Tackett 1986) throughout the 1970s (Converse and Pierce 1986), and in the southern German states (before German unification). In all these cases, conservative candidates (and their successors in the form of a Catholic party in Belgium) counted on a dense network of Catholic associations and practices. In a reverse way, this was also the instance of Britain. There the first phase of partisan competition (after the first electoral reform of 1832) grew out of the trade (and therefore territorial) divide in the 1840s. Yet in the late 1850s and early 1860s religious issues, which had been relevant in a sporadic manner in the first third of the nineteenth century, came to the forefront of electoral politics as Gladstone decided to appeal to and integrate the Nonconformist electorate and its organizations into the Liberal Party to defeat the Tory Party. Accordingly, the politicization of the religious dimension did not result in a new party. It was simply subsumed within the already existing (and increasingly more disciplined) two parliamentary parties. (Naturally, once politicians started targeting a large and therefore heterogeneous portion of the electorate, they had to face considerable electoral and political tensions within the party. The British Liberal Party, for example, picked its support from urban employers and skilled employees in export-oriented firms, Nonconformists, and non-church-goers. Similarly, many Catholic parties in continental Europe included rural voters, urban middle classes, and a sizeable chunk of the working-class electorate—particularly after the introduction of universal suffrage. Their leaders had to manage considerable factional conflict through legislative logrolling and the creation of compensatory mechanisms to buy disgruntled voters. The stability and coherence of these parties were less than robust. From time to time parties suffered from dramatic breakdowns and parliamentary realignments like the 1885 split between Gladstonian Liberals and Liberal Unionists in Britain or the temporal split between moderate and radical free traders in Sweden from 1893 to 1899. Yet, all in all, they enjoy truly remarkable levels of electoral continuity.)

By contrast, the initial divide between liberals and conservatives collapsed in Prussia (before 1870) and unified Germany (after 1870), the Netherlands, and Switzerland. In

---

[14] Moreover, there were generally no organizational networks of a rural versus urban kind that could be employed to galvanize voters on that dimension. Even then there were some exceptions, such as the farmers' parties that appeared in Germany in the late 1890s and Scandinavia in the early 20th century.

all these instances, Liberals moved toward a strong anticlerical position in the second half of the nineteenth century. In turn, Conservatives, representing the Protestant elites that had built those countries—by war in Germany and Switzerland—could not appeal to Catholic voters in a credible manner. In those circumstances, the existing religious networks could be and were easily mobilized to break the bipartisan status quo (Kalyvas 1996).

The entry of socialist parties. In the late nineteenth and early twentieth centuries the party system in advanced democracies witnessed a new wave of transformations as a result of the growth of socialist parties. This change derived from the combination of two factors: a broader and changing electorate and the decision of unions to sponsor challengers against liberal incumbents.

As voting rights were eventually extended to hitherto unenfranchised citizens at the turn of the twentieth century, the electoral space evolved accordingly. The past dominant divide between rural and urban districts which characterized the electoral politics of the nineteenth century now became subsumed within a broader space where income differentials mattered substantially. This transformation of the electoral space opened a window of opportunity for socialist, that is, non-liberal left-wing parties. As summarized in Table 21.1, the Belgian, British, and Swedish socialist parties only became a relevant force after the introduction of universal or quasi-universal male suffrage.

Table 21.1 Socialist parties and electoral success

		Extent of male suffrage	
		None or partial	Universal
	No	Britain before 1900	USA
		Belgium before 1870s	[Canada]
		Norway before 1900	France till 1900s
		Sweden before 1900	New South Wales before 1890s
			Switzerland before 1900
Unions shift support to socialist parties			
	Yes	Britain 1900–18	Australia
		Belgium 1870s–1893	Britain after 1918
		Italy before 1918	Belgium after 1893
		Norway 1899–1900	France partially after 1905
		Sweden 1900–11	Germany after 1871
			Italy after 1918
			Norway after 1900
			Sweden after 1911
			Switzerland in 1900s

But this condition was in itself insufficient. Without the proper organizational tools, socialist candidates could hardly derail any liberal or progressive incumbents. As with the case of other political issues, the existing majoritarian electoral laws truly deterred the entry of third candidates. In nineteenth-century France, Switzerland, and the United States, male universal suffrage did not result in the emergence of any socialist party in parliament. In Norway, where the proportion of enfranchised men grew from 21 percent in 1879 to 90 percent in 1900, Liberals and Conservatives continued to receive together over 95 percent of the votes during that period. It was only after trade unions, historically allied to the liberals, decided to break with the latter that socialist parties emerged as a real threat to the old party system at the turn of the twentieth century. The emergence of strong social democratic parties across Europe is well correlated with the decision of unions to stop supporting liberal candidates: in the early 1870s in Germany, in the 1880s in Belgium, in 1899 in Norway, in 1900 in Britain, and in the early 1900s in Sweden. By contrast, without union endorsement, socialist parties fared dismally. Before the formation of the Labour Representation Committee in Britain, several socialist candidates ran for office yet failed in a resounding manner in the 1890s in London. Unable to secure the support of unions, the American Socialist Party peaked at between 3 and 6 percent of the national vote in the 1910s, was barely represented in Congress, and fizzled out in the inter-war period. Similarly, although male universal suffrage was in place in Switzerland from the middle of the nineteenth century, the Swiss Socialist Party did very poorly among working-class voters before the union movement shifted its political alliances away from radical liberal candidates in 1908.

4.5 Electoral Institutions and the Resulting Party System

The scholarly literature on electoral systems has shown that the type of electoral laws and the nature of party systems are strongly correlated (Duverger 1954; Taagepera and Shugart 1989; Cox 1997). Plurality and majority rules come hand in hand with two-party systems. Proportional representation laws tend to generate multiparty systems.

Majoritarian systems—particularly plurality rule—reinforce two-party systems for two reasons. Because, as described before, the election of the top vote-getter in a single district compels voters to coordinate strategically around the top two candidates, that electoral system dissuades any parliamentarians from splitting from their own party (even in the wake of substantial policy disagreements). Moreover, it also makes it very hard for any new political force to attract the support of enough voters to become a robust alternative to the established parties. Thus, the top two parties in votes (and seats) should have no incentives to change the electoral system. Absent a massive electoral realignment, due either to a strong organizational network that breaks up the existing partisan duopoly or to a political crisis of historical proportions, the status quo does not change and majoritarian rules and bipartisan systems remain in place indefinitely.

Proportional representation has similar self-sustaining tendencies. By lowering the threshold to elect a candidate, it often pushes the party system to higher levels of fragmentation. Naturally, once there are several parties, none of them has any incentive to re-establish plurality rule because that change could well mean their electoral demise. Therefore, substituting plurality rule for proportional representation will only be implemented under extraordinary circumstances and by actors external to the old party establishment.[15]

A quick look at the evolution of electoral laws since the emergence of representative democracies shows that electoral systems hardly change over time. Plurality and two-round majority laws remained in place across the West during the nineteenth century. Starting in several Swiss cantonal elections in the late nineteenth century and in Belgium in 1899, most countries adopted proportional representation mechanisms in the first two decades of the twentieth century. Majoritarian electoral regimes only remained in place in Britain, its settler colonies, inter-war France, Japan, and Spain. After 1920 the reform of existing electoral systems again happened very rarely.[16]

The dramatic transformation of the electoral system in most first-wave democracies in the early twentieth century resulted from the rapid growth of socialism. Without the rapid emergence of a credible socialist machine, electoral rules did not change. The two main parties splitting the national vote had no incentive to change the rules that maintained their electoral advantage. At most, they simply adjusted their electoral platforms in response to the changing interests of voters and to potential third-party challenges. In the United States, Republicans and Democrats easily weathered the (eventually abortive) appearance of a socialist party in the early twentieth century. In Canada Liberals and Conservatives kept receiving most of the votes until the 1930s.

By contrast, wherever labor and socialist parties became credible alternatives at the ballot box, the majoritarian system actually multiplied their threat very quickly: it made it possible for socialists to transform themselves into one of the top two parties at the expense of one of the old parties. Still, the emergence of socialism acted as a necessary but not a sufficient condition of electoral reform. Proportional representation was not introduced whenever one of the old parties retained a dominant position in the non-socialist camp (and therefore attracted all non-socialist voters). This was the case of Britain, where the Liberals split into two factions after the First World War and the Conservatives, emerging as the safest alternative to block socialism, eventually absorbed anti-Labour liberals. By the mid-1920s, as it was clear that the Liberals were fast becoming a marginal force, neither Labour nor the Tories entertained anymore the idea of dropping the plurality system. Proportional representation did not become law either whenever the non-socialist parties coalesced to form a single political organization—this happened in Australia, where free traders and protectionists merged to form the Anti-Socialist Party in the mid-1900s.

Proportional representation replaced the old electoral system in those countries in which the socialist party was strong and none of the non-socialist parties could act as

---

[15] This is the case of the French electoral reform of 1958 and in the Italian one in the early 1990s.

[16] Shifts from plurality to proportional representation or vice versa took place only, and very rarely, after the Second World War and in the early 1990s (with the collapse of dominant party hegemonies in Italy and Japan). France and Greece are the only countries which have experienced systematic volatility in their electoral systems throughout the 20th century.

the focal point around which non-socialist voters could rally to defeat socialism—either because the non-socialist parties were too balanced in votes and voters could not determine which one had an electoral advantage or because their political disagreements over other issues such as trade or religion were so intense that they blocked any type of instrumental vote.

REFERENCES

ALDRICH, J. H. 1995. *Why Parties? The Origin and Transformation of Party Politics in America.* Chicago: University of Chicago Press.

BOIX, C. 2006a. Between protectionism and compensation: the political economy of trade. In *Globalization and Egalitarian Redistribution,* ed. P. Bardhan, S. Bowles, and M. Wallerstein. Princeton: Princeton University and Russell Sage Foundation.

—— 2006b. The birth of party democracy: the formation of party systems in advanced democracies. Unpublished MS.

CARAMANI, D. 2004. *The Nationalization of Politics: The Formation of National Electorates and Party Systems in Western Europe.* Cambridge: Cambridge University Press.

CHHIBBER, P., and KOLLMAN, K. 2004. *The Formation of National Party Systems: Federalism and Party Competition in Canada, Great Britain, India, and the United States.* Princeton: Princeton University Press.

CONVERSE, P. E., and PIERCE, R. 1986. *Political Representation in France.* Cambridge, Mass.: Harvard University Press.

COX, G. W. 1987. *The Efficient Secret: The Cabinet and the Development of Political Parties in Victorian England.* New York: Cambridge University Press.

—— 1997. *Making Votes Count: Strategic Coordination in the World's Electoral Systems.* New York: Cambridge University Press.

—— and McCUBBINS, M. D. 1993. *Legislative Leviathan: Party Government in the House.* Berkeley and Los Angeles: University of California Press.

DUVERGER, M. 1954. *Political Parties.* New York: Wiley.

KALYVAS, S. 1996. *The Rise of Christian Democracy in Europe.* Ithaca, NY: Cornell University Press.

KATZENSTEIN, P. 1985. *Small States in World Markets: Industrial Policy in Europe.* Ithaca, NY: Cornell University Press.

KITSCHELT, H., MANSFELDOVA, Z., MARKOWSKI, R., and TOKA, G. eds. 1999. *Post-Communist Party Systems: Competition, Representation, and Inter-party Cooperation.* Cambridge: Cambridge University Press.

KNIGHT, J. 1992. *Institutions and Social Conflict.* Cambridge: Cambridge University Press.

LAPALOMBARA, J., and WEINER, M. eds. 1966. *Political Parties and Political Development.* Princeton: Princeton University Press.

LIJPHART, A. 1977. *Democracy in Plural Societies.* New Haven: Yale University Press.

LIPSET, S. M., and ROKKAN, S. 1967. *Party Systems and Voter Alignments.* New York: Free Press.

PANEBIANCO, A. 1988. *Political Parties: Organization and Power.* Cambridge: Cambridge University Press.

PRZEWORSKI, A., and SPRAGUE, J. 1986. *Paper Stones: A History of Electoral Socialism.* Chicago: University of Chicago Press.

PUTNAM, R. 1993. *Making Democracy Work.* Princeton: Princeton University Press.

Riker, W. H. 1986. *The Art of Political Manipulation*. New Haven: Yale University Press.

Rogowski, R. 1987. Trade and the variety of democratic institutions. *International Organization*, 41: 203–24.

Sartori, G. 1968. Political development and political engineering. In *Public Policy*, ed. J. D. Montgomery and A. O. Hirschman. Cambridge: Cambridge University Press.

—— 1976. *Parties and Party Systems: A Framework for Analysis*. Cambridge: Cambridge University Press.

Shugart, M. S., and Carey, J. 1992. *Presidents and Assemblies: Constitutional Design and Electoral Dynamics*. New York: Cambridge University Press.

Stokes, S. 2005. Perverse accountability: a formal model of machine politics with evidence from Argentina. *American Political Science Review*, 99 (3): 315–25.

Taagapera, R., and Shugart, M. S. 1989. *Seats and Votes: The Effects and Determinants of Electoral Systems*. New Haven: Yale University Press.

Tackett, T. 1986. *Religion, Revolution, and Regional Culture in Eighteenth-Century France: The Ecclesiastical Oath of 1791*. Princeton: Princeton University Press.

CHAPTER 22

PARTY SYSTEMS

HERBERT KITSCHELT

THE concept of party system, while ubiquitous in political science texts, hardly receives systematic treatment, if handbooks by Greenstein and Polsby (1975) and Goodin and Klingemann (1996) are the reference points (cf. Epstein 1975; Pappi 1996). In a similar vein, all editions of the American Political Science Association's *Political Science: The State of the Discipline* (1983, 1993, 2002) discuss parties only within the micro-political context of individual political behavior and preference formation, but have no room for party systems. In the most recent volume, party systems appear only in Fiorina's (2002) article centered exclusively on US parties.

The subject of political party systems may be too complex and heterogeneous to deserve coherent treatment in key political science handbooks. Therefore entire handbooks have been devoted to the study of parties and party systems (cf. Katz and Crotty 2006). Or the proliferation of party system typologies in the 1950s and 1960s may have led to a "confusion and profusion" (Sartori 1976, 119) not even resolved by Sartori's own last-ditch effort. Or comparative politics at least in America has turned its attention so decisively toward comparative political economy, political regime change, and ethnocultural identity politics as to ignore the study of parties and party systems.[1] Nevertheless, party system attributes continue to play a critical role in treatments of political economy and public policy. The substantive alignments of interests and the competitiveness of party systems representing such interests are critical variables in studies of political economy, public policy, and democratic regime survival.

In this article, I first conceptualize party systems separate from parties in analogy to Waltz's (1954, 1979) treatment of international systems separate from states(Section 1). I then identify systemic properties of party systems for the comparative-static analysis

---

[1] Not by chance, these are the three prominent themes of comparative politics singled out by Laitin 2002 in his overview of the comparative politics subfield.

of competition (Section 2). Subsequently, I probe into the historical-evolutionary competitive dynamic of party systems (Section 3). Here historical-comparative analysis comes into its own beyond the study of formal properties of party systems and competition. My contribution refrains from discussing party systems as independent variables that may account for outputs and outcomes of democratic politics, as this subject is covered in other handbook chapters.

1 THE CONCEPT OF PARTY SYSTEM

Waltz (1954) distinguished three analytical levels or "images" of international politics. The first deals with human behavior, the motivations and actions of individual policy makers and members of societies. The second focuses on processes of group decision making internal to state organizations, as they produce binding collective decisions about foreign policy. The third examines state strategies as a consequence of "systemic" features. The system is conceived as a set of interacting units (Waltz 1979, 40). In a system, the action of *each* participant entity is affected by the actions of *all others*. Systemic theory must hence "show how the systems level, or structure, is distinct from the level of interacting units" (ibid.). In game-theoretic language, systemic features map the structure of the game, as defined by actors' resources, preference schedules, and feasible moves that translate into positive or negative outcomes contingent upon the other players' moves. If preferences are fixed and exogenous, equilibrium states of a system are entirely determined by systemic features concerning the numbers of players, the rules of movement, and resources distributed among the actors. As in economic markets, hegemonic or oligopolistic configurations permit actors to coordinate around different equilibria (relative prices, states of war and peace in the system) than competitive markets with many suppliers and purchasers.

Also party system theory identifies numbers of players, distributions of resources and capabilities among them, and permissible rules of movement to arrive at predictions that hold true regardless of internal idiosyncrasies of the individual elements. Equilibria concern the number of sustainable players, their profile of payoffs, and their relations of alliance and conflict among each other. These then translate into practices of creating and maintaining government executives, extracting and allocating scarce resources to constituencies, and maintaining or abandoning democracy more generally. Even if such systemic propositions are successful, however, they may require qualifications and further specifications based on knowledge about the internal behavior of individual parties, thus setting limits to a purely systemic analysis.

At least tacitly the "three images" of international relations theory have always been a staple also of comparative party system theory, as Sorauf's (1964) distinction between "party in the electorate" (individual behavior and orientations), "party as organization" (polities as organizations), and "party systems" suggests. Party systems theory is driven by a particular parsimony of focus: Net of idiosyncrasies characterizing individual actors (citizens, politicians) and modes of intra-party decision making, does the structure and dynamics of party systems causally account for identifiable outputs and outcomes of the political process?

Let me begin by outlining first and second image assumptions without which no useful hypotheses about third image (systemic) features and processes can be derived. Just as international systems presuppose historically distinctive first and second image features (cf. Ruggie 1989; Spruyt 1994), also party "systemness" and "systemic processes" take place only when certain lower order conditions are satisfied.

First image assumptions about individual actors (citizens, politicians). Systemic strategic interactions among parties presuppose that at least some citizens compare candidates and parties for electoral office with respect to some of the rewards they offer citizens. If all citizens abstain from voting, vote in a random fashion, or vote based on immutable affective collective group affiliations rather than the comparative alignment of principals' and potential agents' preferences, then there can be no systemic processes. In the sense of Lupia and McCubbins (1998) or Erickson, MacKuen, and Stimson (2002), at least some voters must be "rational information misers" whose strategic choices (voting or non-voting, supporting one candidate/party rather than another) are contingent upon the expected behavior of other voters and of electoral candidates who offer to serve as their agents in legislatures and executives.

In a similar vein, the candidate agents ("politicians") in the electoral polity must strategically act so as to take the preferences and strategic options of at least some principals (voters) and rival candidates into account in their own choice of a course of action. Just as states in international relations theory are postulated to seek survival, politicians seek (re)election to political office—executive office, and as a second best legislative office—as the baseline objective, whatever other goals they may pursue beyond that (personal rents, glory, policy, or targeted benefits for constituencies). Whether and how they pursue these higher-order objectives is endogenous to the competitive situation, characterized by the rules of the game, the stances of their competitors, and the demands of the voters. It is these constraints that prevent politicians in some circumstances from becoming just utterly cynical self-regarding rent maximizers and predators.[2] In some circumstances, the pursuit of executive office may presuppose that politicians credibly commit to collective goods producing public policies.

Systemic processes in electoral democracies presuppose the *existence of an "electoral market"* in which choices of principals and agents are contingent upon each other. There must be some "elasticities" between supply and demand. Where empirically this condition is not met, systemic party theory is inapplicable. Principals may lack material and cognitive resources to participate in an electoral market, e.g. in extremely poor countries, or they may be so committed to a particular political agent ("party identification") as to pre-empt systemic processes, e.g. in ethnically highly divided polities.

---

[2] On systemic conditions for the choice of parties' and politicians' preferences, see Strom 1990a.

Second image assumptions about constituent entities of the party system (collective agents). In mass democracies with universal franchise, principals and agents can act effectively in electoral markets only through intermediary vehicles of coordination that help them to overcome collective action problems, to facilitate the flow of information in the market, and to simplify the range of service options based on which principals and politicians may enter direct or indirect contracts with each other. Political parties, the constituent elements of a party system, may provide some or all of such services (Aldrich 1995). Party is here used in a generic sense as a set of politicians pooling resources, not necessarily the label that demarcates parties in a legal-institutional sense. The effective locus of coordination may sometimes be factions within party labels or coalitions combining party labels (Morgenstern 2004). To simplify matters, parties are henceforth the effective collective agents, not necessarily the legal labels.

Parties may help to overcome collective action problems by reducing voters' costs of information gathering and candidates' costs of information distribution in the run-up to the electoral choice. Parties may also reduce problems of "social choice" that surface in unstable and cycling majority decisions in legislatures and governments by bundling and binding sets of politicians with different individual preference schedules to work together in pursuit of a single collective preference schedule ("party program").[3] There may be other vehicles of collective mobilization that contribute to the articulation and aggregation of interests, such as social movements and interest groups. Only in a very few limitational empirical cases, such as Papua New Guinea, does democracy appear to exist without parties in the generic sense of a system of collective agents intermediating in the electoral process. At the other end of the spectrum, where most parties exhibit some durability and capacity to coordinate citizens and politicians time and again, we speak of party system institutionalization (Huntington 1968, ch. 7; Mainwaring and Scully 1995). It is akin to what Sartori (1968, 288–97; 1986, 55–6) has called a "structured" party system and Mair (1997, 213–14) refers to as "systemness" through "closure," namely the identity of interacting corporate units (parties) over some extended time period.

2 VARIETIES OF PARTY SYSTEMS

Party system theory aims at predicting strategies of the competitors and preferably identifying equilibria of such strategies. The critical elements are the number of competitors and the "currency" of competition for voter support, namely the policy issues and issue bundles politicians promise to enact to shore up electoral support. Theories typically assume an indirect exchange between voters and politicians.

---

[3] On the theory of party formation, see especially Aldrich (1995); Cox and McCubbins (1993, chs. 4 and 5); and Snyder and Ting (2002). Whether or not they solve collective action and social choice problems, as Aldrich 1995 postulates, however, is a contingent process (see below).

Citizens surrender their vote at the beginning of the electoral term in exchange for the winning politicians implementing campaign promises during the electoral term. Democratic accountability operates indirectly because of (1) the time elapsed between election and policy delivery; (2) the benefits and costs of policy accruing to all voters, regardless of whether they supported winners; and (3) voters speaking their verdict over the record of governing politicians (and the opposition) retrospectively at the end of the electoral term and taking that evaluation into account in their prospective assessment of politicians' promises for the subsequent electoral term.

The policy-based "responsible partisan" model, however, is only one special case of principal–agent relations within a broader set of mechanisms expressing democratic accountability. Before turning to the key elements of the common models of party competition—numbers of competitors and numbers of dimensions of competition—let us therefore distinguish modes of democratic accountability in terms of different principal–agent exchanges (Section 2.1). Moreover, and related to this point, critics have argued that responsible partisan models home in on a highly constrained view of the currency of competition, namely policy positions rather than a variety of valence goods broadly conceived (Section 2.2). Once the special place of positional issue competition has been characterized, we then can turn to numbers of players and dimensions of policy issues as structural properties of party systems (Sections 2.3 and 2.4). Finally, for all party systems we can distinguish greater or lesser intensity of competition or "competitiveness" (Section 2.5).

2.1 Modes of Democratic Accountability

Why do voters support parties and how can politicians in calculated fashion appeal to voters for support? Party systems theories focus on mechanisms that involve rational deliberation, as opposed to affective psychological attachments, such as party identification, voter identification with the objective traits of candidates (gender, ethnicity), or the personal inspirational ("charismatic") qualities of a candidate. Inasmuch as support based on such criteria treats them as tracers of candidates' cumulative policy records and policy commitments, such as in Fiorina's (1977, 1997) felicitous phrase of party identification as the "running tally" of a party's past record, of course, they are incorporated into theories of party competition.

Among rational modes of accountability, let us distinguish between indirect and direct exchange between voters (as principals) and politicians (as their agents). In the indirect policy exchange, citizens surrender their vote in accordance with the responsible partisan model. The exchange is indirect because it involves an inter-temporally long drawn out process between the principal delivering the vote and the agent putting authoritative measures into place that allocate costs of benefits to all members of abstract categories of voters, regardless of whether individual members of each category actually voted for the decision maker or not. Politicians may have only a general sense of where their supporters are located in society.

They are unable to pinpoint, monitor, or sanction their voters. In contrast to this indirect "policy" exchange, in direct, targeted, "clientelistic" exchange, individuals and small groups of voters obtain immediate gratification in exchange for their vote or suffer negative consequences in case of supporting the loser. The currency of exchange here involves gifts or money, public sector jobs, public housing, privileged access to social policy transfers, favorable regulatory rulings, or procurement contracts that allow firms to hire workers who supported the winning party and candidate.[4] Clientelistic politics comes with direct or indirect social mechanisms permitting politicians to monitor and even sanction the electoral behavior exhibited by small groups.

Numerous theories have tried to account for the relative prominence of clientelistic exchange relations in party competition (cf. Scott 1969; Schmidt et al. 1977; Shefter 1994; Kitschelt 2000a; Piattoni 2001; Keefer 2005; Kitschelt and Wilkinson 2006). Increasing affluence and eradication of poverty may make the relative value of clientelistic inducements meaningless for voters and heightens their sensitivity to the opportunity costs of such practices, e.g. in political production of collective goods. Net of development, clientelism hinges upon the economic viability of state-owned, state-subsidized, or state-regulated firms and entire sectors. Eonomic entities operating under a state-provided "soft budget" umbrella are more amenable to crony appointments and thus clientelism. The presence of mobilized and electorally vocal ethnocultural groups in divided societies furthermore tends to fuel clientelistic practices (cf. Horowitz 1985; Chandra 2004; Wilkinson 2004). Furthermore, all these factors may interact with the competitiveness of a party system (see below). Greater competitiveness may fuel more intensive efforts by politicians to engage in either clientelistic and/or programmatic policy competition.

Whether electoral and executive institutions affect the balance of clientelistic and programmatic competition in party systems, however, is a matter of disagreement. Electoral rules that require candidates to carve out narrowly circumscribed electoral constituencies with whom candidates have direct dealings may induce clientelistic exchange (cf. Katz 1980; Ames 2001). But it is easy to find examples of closed-list multi-member district electoral systems where most parties have practiced clientelism, such as Venezuela (–1999) and Austria, or programmatic parties in open list preference voting systems (cf. Samuels 2004).

2.2 Valence or Positional Competition

Critics of conventional theories of party competition have introduced another useful distinction that can be related to modes of democratic accountability: that between valence and positional issues or party offers (Stokes 1963). Citizens' preference

---

[4] Clientelism always involves material incentives to turn out the vote, not just a monetary transfer by a rich citizen to a party in exchange for economic favors. Such material provisions, of course, make it easier for politicians to establish clientelism.

distribution over some salient, prized good is highly skewed so that most citizens want more rather than less of a good (honest politicians, competent management of the economy...). Parties do not take "positional" stances over whether or not to supply some good, but whether they can credibly supply that good better or to a greater extent than their rivals. Each party claims to have "more" attractive candidates and technical advisers, demonstrate "greater" competence in producing collective goods (such as facilitating economic stability and growth, protecting the environment, preventing terrorism), and/or distribute "more copious" targeted benefits to anyone who is asking for them.

Positional competition, by contrast, assumes a broad distribution of voter preferences over the merits of the parties' offers of goods or services. Parties may then promise different things to different voters on the same dimension (see Section 2.3). Positional offers mostly concern policy issues and bundles thereof. But critics of positional theory claim that for voters valence issues trump positional issues most of the time. Retrospective economic voting, for example, has to do with the perceived "competence" of a party's politicians in delivering good economic performance, such as low inflation and high growth. Moreover, non-policy modes of principal–agent relations also operate in the realm of valence competition. In clientelistic politics, parties compete for votes by advertising themselves as suppliers of the most copious, reliable, and expediently delivered targeted benefits. And competition with a candidate's personal charisma may turn on widely desired qualities such as leadership, compassion, or youthful dynamism.

Nevertheless, there is no one-to-one relationship between modes of democratic accountability and the prevalence of valence or positional offers in party competition. With respect to candidate qualities, while no voter would want incompetent politicians, some citizens may prefer compassion and careful deliberation as a quality of political leadership over decisiveness and expedient action. In a similar vein, descriptive representation of electoral constituencies (by means of the candidate's gender or ethnicity) may be a "positional" strategic move in diverse constituencies where candidates with different ethnocultural markers are competing for political office. Also clientelistic exchange may evolve according to a positional dynamic. There may be electoral situations with highly diversified constituencies that make it attractive for some parties to embrace clientelism and imply that one of its correlates, corruption, should be treated leniently, whereas other parties take the opposite position.

Most importantly, however, one might directly contradict Stokes (1963) and actually assert that most policy issue appeals are at least implicitly positional rather than valence based. Whereas many ultimate objectives in political life may be of the valence type, politics is about the choice of means to obtain those ends, and here one may be firmly in the realm of positional competition because of cognitive and evaluative disagreements. People may have different assessments about the causal efficacy of a policy means to reach an end, given the complexity and uncertainty surrounding causal relations in social life. People may also disagree on the distributive implications that the choice of policy means involves. Politicians may use valence codes—such as fighting crime, reducing inflation, or creating jobs—to pursue a distributive agenda. For politicians it is part of the art of herethetics (Riker 1986) to conceal the distributive implications of their own appeal to valence issues, but to highlight those of their opponents' valence issue frames. It is important to realize the limits of valence competition because the *Party Manifestoes Project*, as the most comprehensive and systematic enterprise to register the programmatic appeals of political parties, was at least initially based on the supremacy of a valence-based characterization of party competition (cf. Budge, Robertson, and Hearl 1987; Budge et al. 2001).

Figure 22.1 summarizes the relationship between accountability mechanisms and the prevalence of valence or positional competition. Empirically, I claim the following testable regularities. Political candidate appeals play out in most instances into valence competition and only rarely as positional competition. Clientelistic accountability works mostly as valence competition among parties (who can deliver the most and most reliably? alternatively: Who is the "cleanest" in rejecting clientelistic inducements?). Under certain conditions of economically highly stratified constituencies with great disparities of income, clientelism may become a matter of positional competition, with some parties defending and others attacking it.

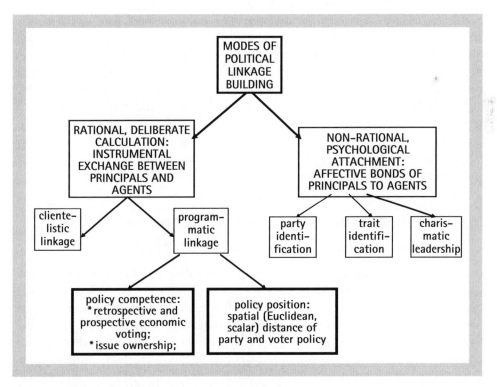

Fig. 22.1 Modes of Political Linkage in Democracies

2.3 Numerical Properties: Fractionalization, Effective Number, and Volatility

From early on, party systems have been divided into two-party and multiparty systems (cf. Duverger 1954; Downs 1957), ultimately giving way to a proliferation of numerical criteria (Mair 1997, 200–6). Most prominent may have been Sartori's (1976) further distinction between moderate and polarized multiparty systems dependent on the presence of "anti-system" spoiler parties. But since the 1970s typologies of party systems have fallen out of favor to the advantage of a variable-based, finer instrument to gauge the size of party systems. It is the measure of party system fractionalization (Rae 1967), or its mathematical inversion proposed by Laakso and Taagepera (1979), the "effective number of parties," whether calculated in terms of voter support for parties (ENVP) or size of parliamentary parties (ENPP). The basic idea here and in further mathematical iterations of the measure (Molinar 1991) is to combine the number and the size distribution of parties in a polity in a single coefficient of fragmentation that sums up the parties in a polity weighted by their size. Fractionalization measures employ partisan labels as their unit of counting. Such measures are meaningful only as long as parties can be treated as unitary collective actors (cf. Morgenstern 2004).

The same qualification applies to a widely used structural parameter of party systems in the temporal dimension, the volatility of party systems. The volatility index summarizes the percentage differences of electoral support obtained by the same parties in two subsequent elections (usually divided by two to give a maximum value of 100) (cf. Pedersen 1983). It is almost self-evident that fractionalization and volatility are closely related. But where several parties are close to each other and operate as one "bloc" in legislatures and elections, a party-based volatility index may seriously overstate volatility by not focusing on the "inter-bloc" volatility of party systems (cf. Bartolini and Mair 1990). The differential conceptualization of volatility may have major consequences, if one employs the concept to gauge the stability and consolidation of party systems over time (e.g. Mainwaring and Scully 1995; Roberts and Wibbels 1999).

2.4 Policy-Based Programmatic Party Systems: Social and Political Divides, Cleavages, Competitive Dimensions

In addition to numbers of players, spatial-positional theories of programmatic party systems consider the number of dimensions on which parties compete, something that empirical comparative analysis often refers to as "cleavages." Because of the variability of language that prevails in this literature, it is important to draw clear terminological distinctions. There are lines of division running through every society generated by social, political, economic, and cultural group interests and sentiments of deprivation. If such divides of traits, affiliations, and opinions are durable we may call them *cleavages* (Rae and Taylor 1970), particularly if they mutually reinforce each other (Bartolini and Mair 1990). They are separate from mere "divisions" that denote more fleeting group divides typically associated with a single point decision (e.g. to take an example from Europe: driving on the left or the right side of the road). Cleavages tend to have the qualities of social *entrapment and closure*. Individuals face costly barriers to enter and to exit a social or political category and the rewards and deprivations associated with membership. Therefore they tend to organize as that category in order to acquire or defend certain economic, political, or cultural resources, rights, and privileges.

Only few of these divides ever translate into collective action to change the allocation of gratifications, let alone the very specific and challenging form of party politics. A *political partisan divide* appears where parties represent different sides of a social divide. Statistically, such partisan mapping of divides can be detected with techniques of factor and discriminant analysis as well as regression analysis, with party choice as the dependent variable, especially multinomial logistic models. The number of social divides that map onto the party system may be larger than the number of partisan divides, if there are several reinforcing divides captured by the same party alternatives. Thus, if all working-class voters are also secular and all non-working-class voters are religious, there will be no separate religious and class partisan political divides, even if parties map both issues onto the party system. Conversely, where group memberships on social divides cross-cut each other *and* are mapped onto parties, they tend to generate multiple partisan divides.

From the perspective of office-seeking strategic politicians, what matters for their strategic moves to win elections may be neither social nor even partisan divides, but only the minimal set of *competitive divides or "competitive dimensions"* in a party system. These are only those divides on which voters display some *elasticity of partisan choices,* responding to modifications of the competing parties' appeals and offers. By contrast many political divides are a matter of political identification rather than competition (cf. Sani and Sartori 1983). In this instance, group membership predicts the propensity to favor a party, but there is no open electoral market in which voters would change their partisan choice, were competing parties to modify their appeals on the given political dimension. In case of a competitive dimension, a critical subset of rational voters is responsive to parties' changing electoral appeals. These elasticities are elusive to measure, as they would require a panel data design. A weak tracer of the competitive status of a dimension is the salience of the underlying issues for voters and parties.

Table 22.1 summarizes the terminological conventions introduced in the preceding paragraphs. An example might illustrate the usefulness of the distinctions in anticipation of the stylized historical sketch provided later (Section 2.4). In Belgium, until the 1950s, there were two cross-cutting political partisan divides that were both competitive, a social class-based one pitting the working-class socialists, at one extreme, against the cross-class Christian Democrats in the center and the business-oriented liberals at the other extreme, and a religious divide separating a secular socialist-liberal sector from a Catholic Christian Democratic camp. Over time, the religious divide lost its competitiveness and became a pure partisan

Table 22.1   The organization of issue opinions in democratic party competition

CENTRALITY OF DIVISIONS FOR THE ORGANIZATION OF THE PARTY SYSTEM?	DURABILITY OF ISSUE DIVISIONS?	
	LOW: "DIVIDES"	HIGH: "CLEAVAGES"
LOW: IDEOLOGICAL DIVISIONS AT THE SOCIETAL LEVEL	SOCIAL and "IDEOLOGICAL" DIVIDES	SOCIAL and "IDEOLOGICAL" CLEAVAGES
INTERMEDIATE: PARTISAN DIVISIONS AT THE POLITICAL LEVEL	POLITICAL PARTISAN DIVIDES (transitory)	POLITICAL PARTISAN CLEAVAGES
HIGH: COMPETITIVE DIMENSIONS	COMPETITIVE DIVIDES (transitory)	COMPETITIVE CLEAVAGES

identification divide. As a parallel movement since the 1950s a hitherto politically unmapped, but long-standing ethnocultural divide over language and region began to articulate itself on the plane of party competition, but much more so in Flanders than in Wallonia. By the 1990s, a realigned socioeconomic distributive divide, the ethnolinguistic divide, and a newly arising libertarian-authoritarian divide over political governance all surface in Belgian party competition, particularly in Flanders. At the same time, the old socioeconomic working class versus business divide as well as the religious divide had lost their capacity not only to shape party competition, but even to maintain a partisan identification divide.

Does the number of parties reflect the number of cleavages in a party system (Taagepera and Grofman 1985; Lijphart 1999, 81–3)? While there may be some tendency that a proliferation of societal divides boosts the number of political partisan divides and the latter boosts the number of competitive dimensions, this is far from a foregone conclusion. The relationship between numbers of parties and positional divides in a polity is theoretically problematic and empirically untested because existing research has taken insufficient care in conceptualizing political divides and competitive dimensions.

In many instances, but not in the Belgian example above, political parties reduce the number of active dimensions of electoral competition to one or two only. The literature offers several not necessarily exclusive reasons for a reduction in the dimensionality in party competition. In all instances, the baseline assumption is that parties cannot simply cherry-pick issues and refrain from taking a stance on the full scope of salient issues, except if they are very small niche parties. This is so because party politicians are elected in territorial districts to represent constituencies over an uncertain and unlimited range of issues in legislatures where they have only very limited agenda control, as is evidenced by the necessity to vote on a state budget that covers a bewildering range of issues.

First, where institutional barriers to entry favor a two-party system, politicians in the established parties have powerful incentives to prevent internal party divisions through cross-cutting issues and therefore map positions on new and salient issues on the existing divides (Stimson 2005). Second, general cognitive limits of politicians' and citizens' information processing of political alternatives give a strong advantage to parties that can articulate their positions in a very low-dimensional space of ideological alternatives (cf. Downs 1957; Hinich and Munger 1994; Lupia and McCubbins 1998). Third, the evolution of social structure and the effects of policies, such as the growth of the welfare state, on the distribution of preferences in society might facilitate a bundling of political preferences around a very low-dimensional space (Kitschelt 1994). None of these hypotheses suggests that there is a logically compelling constraint according to which particular issue positions fit together.

2.5 The Competitiveness of Party Systems

Party systems are more "competitive," when (1) there is great uncertainty of electoral outcomes and (2) uncertainty matters, i.e. small variances in parties' electoral support translate into large variance in their legislative representation and/or bargaining power over executive appointments, patronage, or policy. Where competitiveness is intense, politicians make greater efforts to mobilize support and voters pay more attention to politics (campaign contributions, turnout, information processing).

In two-party systems, competitiveness has often been measured as the ex-ante closeness of two candidates in the electoral race, i.e. the expected margin of victory. But this operationalization is not sufficiently general and does not take the "stakes" of the electoral contest into account. Do voters and candidates make a great effort, if the alternatives on offer are essentially the same?

Competitiveness of a party system is intense, if the following five conditions prevail (see Figure 22.2).[5] (1) For strategic politicians, marginally greater support translates into large increases in bargaining power over legislative majorities (coalitions) and executive office appointments. "Majoritarian" democracy with single-member districts and plurality formula that tend to manufacture single-party unified majority government, at least under parliamentarism, and lack of outside institutional veto points, thus giving high institutional leverage to legislative or executive coalitions, tends to increase the competitiveness of elections (cf. Lijphart 1999; Powell 2000; Tsebelis 2002). (2) Where more than two effective contenders prevail, politicians shore up competitiveness if they configure around *identifiable alternative parties or party blocs* vying for political power.[6] On the side of voters, preference distribution must make all actors perceive the outcome as both (3) close (low margin of victory between party blocs) and (4) open in the sense that there is

---

[5] For a related discussion of electoral competitiveness, also there referred to as "executive responsiveness," see now Franklin (2004, 112–14).

[6] For a discussion of identifiability and its operationalization see Strom (1990b, 47, 73–5).

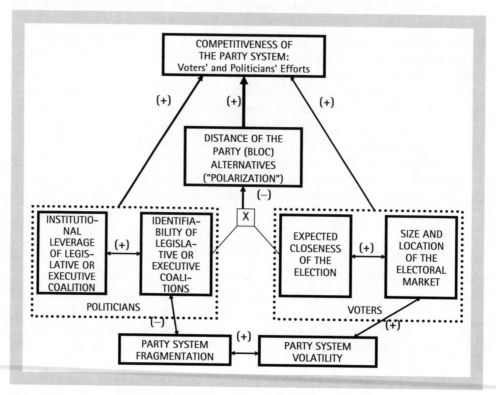

Fig. 22.2 Variables Influencing the Competitiveness of Party Systems

a sizeable electoral market of floating voters situated between the electoral alternatives and responsive to small modulations of candidates' appeals.

Even if these four conditions are met, competitiveness is intense, however, only if also (5) the "stakes" of the competition are high, i.e. the disparity of the cost–benefit allocation by rival camps of politicians is great. Politicians raise or lower the stakes in part as a function of conditions (1) through (4), but as the next section will show, these relations are far from unambiguous. On the face of it, one might expect the median voter theorem to hold: Where two identifiable blocs compete to win majority status that endows great institutional leverage on the winner and there is an electoral market between the competitors in a close race, both camps of politicians actually *reduce* the stakes by offering *similar* cost–benefit allocations in case of victory, and these commitments are most pleasing to the median voter. As we shall see, there are complications that contradict this logic of countervailing forces between strong competitiveness at the level of majority formation and weak competitiveness of majority action ("stakes").

Given the complexity of the conditions that affect the competitiveness of elections both from the perspective of politicians' as well as voters' incentives to make an effort in the electoral contest, simple measures such as party system fragmentation and volatility cannot serve as empirical tracers of competitiveness. Nevertheless, they have often been employed for such purposes, although they only indirectly affect some of the conditions that determine competitiveness. Moreover, the causal links attributed to such measures are debatable at best. While party system fragmentation has often been considered to boost electoral competitiveness by increasing uncertainty of electoral victory, the opposite may be true because fragmentation tends to reduce the identifiability of governing coalitions. Party system volatility may be a tracer of the size of the electoral market, but not necessarily of its location (between rival camps?). Moreover, following Bartolini and Mair (1990) for the task of predicting politicians' and voters' strategic choices in the party competition, volatility would have to be measured at the level of party blocs rather than individual labels, a practice rarely followed in the literature.

3 COMPARATIVE STATICS: STRATEGIC CHOICE IN PARTY SYSTEMS

Most theories of party system competition work with the assumption that (1) principal–agent relations concern indirect programmatic exchange about (2) positional issues and offers. Strategic choices vary according to the number of competitors and the relevant competitive dimensions of party systems only. The key objective is to find equilibria contingent upon numbers and dimensions of competition such that no strategic actor could alter her choice without lowering her payoff. Because formal research over half a century has found that the identification of equilibria under such conditions is elusive, more recent theorizing has relaxed model assumptions, including those about principal–agent relations and positional issues, to obtain equilibrium predictions. Alternatively, the quest for equilibria has been abandoned altogether and been replaced by agent-based modeling in computer simulations.

3.1 Simple Spatial Theory: The Elusiveness of Equilibria

The most simple case and the starting point of the literature is Downs's (1957) median voter theorem according to which two parties will both choose policy appeals proximate to the position of the median voter. To derive this equilibrium, one must postulate among many other things (1) office-motivated politicians with (2) perfect knowledge of the situation (including voter preferences), (3) not having to fear the entry of additional competitors, (4) relying on the selfless support of political activists whose objectives are perfectly aligned with that of the candidates, (5) competing in a unidimensional space of voter distribution for the support of rational voters who (6) have explicit preference schedules and knowledge of the situation, (7) must not abstain, and (8) cast their vote for the party whose announced position is closest to their personal ideal point (9) at the very moment of the election. In a similar vein, under highly restrictive conditions of unidimensional competition, some formal theories can show that in systems with four or more candidates rivals disperse over the competitive space and generate an equilibrium distribution.[7]

Relaxing any one or several of the numerous assumptions necessary to derive the median voter theorem, however, reveals its fragility (for an overview: Grofman 2004). This dovetails with the empirical observation that even in unidimensional two-party competition often enough the positions of the competitors diverge rather than converge. Also equilibrium conditions in multiparty and/or multidimensional competition are fragile and elusive. Shepsle (1991) sees no promise to find equilibria when both more than one competitive dimension or more than two candidates are allowed and certain other reasonable assumptions apply. In a survey, one of the most prolific contributors to spatial theorizing of party competition concludes "that simple theoretical generalizations about the structure of competition are unlikely to be forthcoming" (Ordeshook 1997, 266). Theories that try to gain empirical relevance have therefore made additional assumptions or abandoned the search for equilibria. In both instances, the key aspiration is to account for both conditions of party dispersion as well as stability, even if the size of electoral districts (M) and the electoral formula would permit larger party systems with more entry (cf. Cox 1997: $M+1$ as outer bounds of the size of party systems).

3.2 Complex Spatial Theory: Equilibria under Special Conditions

Because of the proliferating literature, I confine myself to listing a few prominent proposals to relax spatial-positional theories of competition. I sidestep valence-based issue theories of competition (Budge and Farlie 1983), as I am convinced that issues are always positional, when choices are properly framed. "Valence" comes into play, however, through non-issue considerations of candidate attractiveness, party identification, including the competence of both to deliver selective benefits or "good" public policy, and here we get to two prominent recent proposals to account for stability and dispersion of party positions in two- and N-party systems.

First, Adams, Merrill, and Grofman (2005) develop a spatial model in which ingredients of (1) voters' non-policy partisan predilections (including identification), (2) discounting of the candidates' credibility or effectiveness in delivering on their promises, and (3) voters' ability to abstain bring about stable equilibria of programmatically dispersed parties in unidimensional or multidimensional spaces. The non-policy partisan preferences are key, while discounting and the option to abstain only amplify their effect on the dispersal of the partisan vote. The logic is clear. If voters identify with a party for non-policy reasons, they support it even if its current issue positions are further removed from the voter's ideal point than those of a

---

[7] See especially Enelow and Hinich (1990) and Shepsle (1991).

competitor. While plausible, the trouble with this argument is that "non-policy" factors involve a whole host of variables that must be unpacked and that indirectly often may have a subtle policy base, for example when the influence of people's occupation or party identification may amount to a long-term assessment of a party's policy commitments.

Second, Schofield (2003, 2004) has refined a valence model of competition in which strategic parties disperse over a programmatic issue space so long as their advantage or disadvantage in capturing voters on an additional valence dimension, incorporating their candidates' reputation for competence and leadership, gives them flexibility in their programmatic appeals. While formally elegant, in empirical terms this proposal may generate a post hoc opportunistic account of party system strategic dispersal. Just as in Adams et al.'s (2005) investigation, given the flexibility of the key independent variable, researchers will always be able to locate some sort of valence factor, if dispersal of parties occurs.

Third, starting with May (1973) and Robertson (1976) through Aldrich (1983) and Schlesinger (1984) to McGann (2002) and Miller and Schofield (2003), theorists have introduced preference heterogeneity among the principals who select a party's electoral candidates and office holders. If such candidates rely not only on voters, but also on party "activists" who contribute labor and capital to mobilize voters without being candidates themselves, then the aspirations and preferences of the latter may matter for the strategic appeals of the former. To preserve the electoral credibility of their party, leaders may need to give activists some voice in the strategic decision-making process, thus demonstrating that unity around a set of objectives is more than tactical lip service of a few leaders, but a broadly shared commitment (Caillaud and Tirole 2002). But party activists tend to be ideologs who join a party to express programmatic preferences rather than to win elections (cf. Panebianco 1988). To secure indispensable activist input, candidates may be compelled to adopt issue positions distinctly removed from their optimal voter issue appeal. Whether or not activists hold such radicalizing positions, however, may depend on the format of the party system and on societal preference mobilization around a class of issues (cf. Kitschelt 1989a). In multiparty systems where dissatisfied activists can join competing party labels it is less likely that activists express systematically different views than instrumental for the pursuit of votes and office.

Fourth, a long line of modeling has postulated that electoral candidates are not just office, but also policy seeking, and therefore diverge from their spatially optimal vote-getting programmatic appeal. The most encompassing and complex elaboration of that perspective can be found in Roemer (2001) who shows that even in the two-party case the presence of policy-motivated candidates, faced with uncertainty over voters' preferences in a two-dimensional policy space and the task to build a winning coalition among three different intra-party factions around a winning joint electoral strategy, will yield equilibrium positions that clearly set the competitors apart from each other.

Fifth, voters may be strategic and not vote based on the proximity between their own policy ideal points and that of individual parties, but that of likely future partisan coalitions (Kedar 2005). In that case more extreme parties may gain larger shares of votes and yield a more polarized spectrum of alternatives. Voters support more radical parties than is warranted by their own policy ideal points in the expectation that these have to bargain policy compromises with moderate collaborators that ultimately bring the center of policy gravity of a coalition government close to the voters' sincere ideal points. A further modification of this point may be a model of lexical voting (Kitschelt and Rehm 2005). If parties, constrained by their past record of action, do not substantially diverge from each other on a highly salient policy dimension so that voters are basically indifferent between the partisan alternatives, in a manner of "lexical" ordering in their choice among parties voters may focus on a second, third, or n-th dimension of competition just as long as partisan alternatives on that dimension are stark and salient for the voters.

Sixth, voters may not act on a simple spatial rationale in which they gauge the Euclidean distance, weighted by salience, between their own ideal policy schedules and those of the partisan competitors, but support parties in a "directional" fashion based on whether they take a pronounced position on the "correct" side of a political issue, thus giving parties an incentive to disperse their issue positions (cf. Rabinowitz and McDonald 1989). A huge theoretical and empirical literature surrounds this proposal that ultimately appears to conclude that both spatial and directional elements enter voters' calculation, but that empirically the directional component only adds a vanishingly small modification to the basic spatial set-up of voting behavior (cf. Merrill and Grofman 1999).

3.3 Agent-Based Modeling of Party Competition

As a backlash against formal theory, but also voicing unease with purely historical narratives of party competition, a new computational approach of agent-based modeling of political behavior has tried to gain theoretical insights in the comparative statics and dynamics of party systems (cf. Kollman, Miller, and Page 1992, 1998). Critical assumptions are here that voters and politicians have very limited knowledge-processing capacity and therefore act on simple rules rather than on a survey of everyone's preferences and strategic options. Because voters vote spatially, but process little information, parties can only slowly move in the issue space without wrecking their reputation. Following Laver (2005), parties act on simple rules of thumb, such as that of "hunter" who repeats appeals that have increased electoral support recently and modifies them, if elections were lost, or that of "predator" who always moves toward the electorally strongest party. In a two-dimensional space with randomly distributed voters, such conduct may yield a gradual gravitation of the partisan actors to the center region of the space, but with no party moving directly dead center and continuous oscillation of positions that prevents stable equilibria.

The advantage, but also downside, of agent-based computational models is that an infinite number of modifications and complications can be introduced without knowing the epistemological advantage of each move in the enterprise. Do we achieve a theoretical explanation of observable behavior if the simulation results of a certain model specification coincide with empirical patterns? What if many different specifications reproduce the same empirical patterns? What this suggests is that agent-based modeling must be combined with empirical research that lends robustness to the behavioral assumptions employed in the computer simulations. In this sense, Laver's model could be enriched by a simple calculus of voters' abstention or participation in elections, contingent upon the observed parties in the vicinity of voters.

3.4 Entry of New Parties

Formal spatial theories have scored only very limited success in accounting for party entry (for a critique, see Laver and Schilperoord 2005, 8–9). More promising may be a recent non-spatial game-theoretical model with incomplete information where a potential entrant interacts with an established party, although it makes questionable assumptions about the distribution of incumbent and challenger (private) knowledge in the game and generates rather mixed empirical results (Hug 2001).

The informal, empirical literature has implicitly been driven by a behaviorally constrained quasi-spatial framework of competition in which the entry and exit of parties is seen as a result of an interplay between demand and supply (cf. Hauss and Rayside 1978; Harmel and Robertson 1984; Kitschelt 1988, 1995a). Induced by socio-logical and political-economic developments, new political demands become salient that established political parties are not willing to service. This intransigence may result from an interaction of (1) the reputation of an established party that can be changed only slowly at considerable electoral cost combined with (2) the electoral tradeoffs involved in modified programmatic appeals. While a new issue appeal may attract new electoral constituencies only gradually, established voters may be alien-ated quickly, plunging an established party into an electoral crisis. Barriers of entry to new challengers, as erected by electoral systems, mass media access, or party finance, may make it more or less comfortable for existing parties to ignore new political demands. Computational models can capture both the strategic immobility of established parties as well as the barriers to entry encountered by new parties (cf. Laver and Schilperoord 2005).

While much of the informal and computational literature on party entry implicitly subscribes to a spatial model of party competition, though with relaxed rationality endowments for voters and politicians, critics have modified this perspective through salience models. Meguid (2005) argues that new niche parties may arise if a party antagonistic to its claims nevertheless raises the salience of the issue by engaging in an adversarial strategy in the hope to hurt an existing competitor who prefers to dismiss the issue because it might internally divide and make it lose some of its current party constituencies, if the issue were to become salient. Meguid tries to endogenize the dimensions of party competition itself. In a more radical fashion this was anticipated by Riker's (1982, 213–32) theory that a permanent loser party on an existing dimension of party competition may try to create a new competitive dimension in the party system that internally divides the hegemonic party and creates an opening for a new party or an old loser to displace it electorally. Riker's historical reference point is the rise of the Republicans with the slavery issue. The example also shows, however, the limits of a voluntarist theory in which strategic politicians can "manufacture" salient issue dimensions. As Weingast's (1998) alternative account of the slavery issue in party competition suggests, politicians may create new parties and alignments only when political-economic conditions enable them to count on an exogenous process in which sufficiently large constituencies develop new political claims that are not mapped onto the existing party system.

4 HISTORICAL DYNAMICS OF PARTY SYSTEMS

Students of the historical dynamics of party systems, the trailblazer of which was Lipset and Rokkan's (1967) article about the emergence and persistence of political cleavages in Western Europe, implicitly build on and apply many elements explicitly modeled in spatial theories of party competition and in models of party entry and exit. Thus there is no contradiction between the formal or informal general analytical literature on party competition, on one side, and the comparative-historical analysis of party system evolution. As socioeconomic, political, and cultural conditions create new divides of interests and values in society, different issue bundles will be mapped onto the arena of party competition, contingent upon the institutional constraints and strategic opportunities politicians see in the game of jockeying for votes, political office, and control of public policy. Ideally, the general analytical and the historical-comparative literatures on party systems complement and cross-fertilize each other. Whereas the former is mostly a comparative-static analysis of strategic moves when the political preferences of voters and party politicians are given, but the number of partisan players is either exogenous or endogenous, the latter fills this ahistorical framework with flesh and blood by identifying the sociological, political-economic, and cultural developments that shape preferences as well as the institutional and strategic conditions that influence the set of political strategies seen as feasible by the political actors.

4.1 Classical Analysis of Party System Formation in Western Europe

Lipset and Rokkan (1967) analyze the development of European party systems from the nineteenth to the mid-twentieth century against the backdrop of the twin challenges of the national and industrial revolutions that began to take place since the seventeenth century. But in no way is their analysis one of sociological determinism (Sartori 1968). First of all, the historical conditions that shaped the mobilization of societal divisions were shot through with political action. The development of parties and party systems takes place against the backdrop of strategic political choices and interactions among conflicting elites in the process of building territorial states, subduing religious associations under state authority, coping with the reticence of agrarian elites against relinquishing political control, and including the growing working-class movements in institutionalized politics. Second, they emphasize the complex and varied political process of electoral enfranchisement and institution building both as consequence and as cause of party system formation. Agrarian and religious divides therefore do not naturally flow from sociological conditions, but result from a complex strategic interaction among political elites.

The finest examples of post-Lipset–Rokkan comparative historical analysis capturing the interrelations of demand and supply conditions in the formation and realignment of European party systems are probably the works of Luebbert (1991), Kalyvas (1996), and Bartolini (2000). Luebbert emphasizes the different strategic conflict between socialist, liberal, and conservative parties in the mobilization of agrarian constituencies to account for different pathways of party systems in the inter-war period. Kalyvas (1996) highlights the strategic calculations of the Catholic Church and of Catholic lay politicians involved in the formation of confessional parties since the late nineteenth century. And Bartolini (2000) develops an all-inclusive landscape of demand and supply conditions that have shaped the mobilization of the class cleavage in European politics as the last and therefore residual line of conflict strategic politicians had to wedge into already party systems already constituted along other divides.

These books render a more subtle and empirically plausible picture of party formation than two analytically leaner, but historically far less insightful perspectives. Przeworski and Sprague's (1986) intentionally voluntarist account of partisan class politics emphasizes strategic politicians and their capacity to shape the terms of working-class formation, although the empirical analysis is compelled to concede the powerful role of pre-existing cross-nationally varying cultural diversity, corporatist interest intermediation, and socioeconomic development of blue-collar electoral constituencies. At the opposite end of the spectrum, Rogowski (1989) offers an economically determinist account of political coalitions and partisan cleavages in Europe and around the world based on relative scarcities of domestic land, labor, and capital in world markets and resulting group interests over trade openness or protectionism under conditions of an expanding or a contracting world economy. While yielding important novel insights, the analysis overstates the importance of external economic exposure for the formation of political divides and competitive dimensions, probably because it lacks an analysis of the conditions under which collective mobilization of economic interests and their translation into party competition takes place.

4.2 The Transformation of Party Politics in Post-Industrial Democracies

Lipset and Rokkan's (1967) famous dictum about the "freezing" of European party systems in the 1920s was hugely overrated in the literature. What started out as a simple observational suggestion in the conclusion to a lengthy comparative-historical analysis of European political cleavage formation was subsequently blown up into a fundamental theoretical and empirical claim about the nature of mature, institutionalized party systems. The empirical observation of relative party system stability in Europe over some period of time, however, did not compel Lipset and Rokkan to deny that such systems may get caught up in a profound process of systemic dealignment and realignment (cf. Mair 1997, 4). At least three different themes in the comparative literature about the transformation of party systems in affluent post-industrial democracies deserve highlighting.

First, inspired by Lipset and Rokkan's work, many scholars have probed into continuity or decline of existing European political cleavage structures. Studies of aggregate party system volatility usually found only moderate increases (cf. Maguire 1983; Shamir 1984; Bartolini and Mair 1990). But individual-level voting analysis shows a strong, though cross-nationally variable decline in conventional class voting (cf. Franklin, Mackie, and Valen 1992). On the one hand, this gave rise to a perspective that postulates a "dealignment" of voters from parties (Dalton, Flanagan, and Beck 1984; Dalton 2004). Post-industrialization has made especially educated citizens distrustful of parties and prepared to engage in a variety of forms of political interest mobilization that sidestep the electoral process. That trend is associated with declining voter turnout, disjointed single-issue voting, and vanishing partisan identification, resulting in a detachment of economic and social structures of conflict from partisan-level divides.

As a second theme contradicting the dealignment perspective, other scholars have emphasized the emergence of new partisan divides and competitive dimensions with post-industrial economic structure. Realignments of political-economic interests with the implosion of the manual working class, the differentiation of educational-professional skills, and the rise of a vast non-profit sector of social services, often configured around the welfare state, create new opportunities for political parties to realign political divides and competitive dimensions (cf. Brooks, Nieuwbeerta, and Manza 2006; Evans 1999; Knutsen 2006; Manza and Brooks 1999). Again, partisan divides and competitive dimensions are no direct reflection of underlying social change, but result from the strategic positioning of parties and their ability to craft electoral coalitions (cf. Kitschelt 1994; Kitschelt and Rehm 2005). These party system changes may not so much signal a demise of economic-distributive politics, as diagnosed in the postmaterialism literature (Inglehart 1990, 1997), as a novel fusion of economic interest alignments and demands about political and cultural governance.

The combination of economic and non-economic interests by entrepreneurial politicians faced with cross-nationally varying strategic configurations among existing parties is also at the heart of a burgeoning literature on new party formation and success in post-industrial democracies. While this literature initially focused on a libertarian left (cf. Kitschelt 1988, 1989*b*; Redding and Viterna 1999), much more attention has recently been devoted to the rise of extreme rightist parties in many European polities and Anglo-Saxon settler democracies. While there is widespread agreement on the socioeconomic transformations that bring about electoral constituencies available for such parties (primarily manual laborers at different skill levels and traditional small business owners, such as farmers, craftsmen and shopkeepers, men with low skills more generally) and pit them against other groups impervious to rightist political appeals (primarily highly trained professionals, particularly women and especially in the social service sector), it is more contentious how political opportunity structures have affected the nature of the radical right's appeals and its electoral success (cf. Kitschelt 1995*a*; Lubbers, Gilsberts, and Scheepers 2002; Norris 2005). Central controversies concern the extent to which the radical right incorporates liberal market economics into its menu of political appeals (cf. Cole 2005; Ivarsflaten 2005; Kitschelt 1995*a*; Schain, Zolbergi and Hossau 2002), the causal efficacy of electoral laws in promoting or preventing the rise of new radical rightist parties (Carter 2005; Golder 2003; Jackman and Volpert 1996; Norris 2005; Veugelers and Magnan 2005) and the role the convergence and similarity among conventional left and right parties in their policies and governing practices has played for the success of new rightist parties (Carter 2005; Ignazi 2003; Kitschelt 1995*a*; Meguid 2005; Norris 2005; van der Brug, Fennema, and Tillie 2005; Veugelers and Magnan 2005).

A further interesting question of realignment concerns the way divisions over European integration have inserted themselves into national party systems (cf. Gabel 1998; Hix 1999; Marks and Wilson 2000; Marks, Wilson, and Ray 2002; Marks and Steenbergen 2004). In many countries, it is unlikely that European integration becomes a competitive dimension in the sense specified above (cf. Mair 2000). Beyond that, contextual conditions related to the perceived and anticipated consequences of EU integration for national political economies may bring about a rather diverse insertion of the EU issue into domestic politics (cf. Bringar, Jolly, and Kitschelt 2004; Ray 2004; Scheve 2000).

A third and final theme concerns the extent to which citizen–politician relations in contemporary post-industrial polities can still be conceived within a principal–agent framework. Some have argued that the transition to capital-intensive campaign strategies with an overwhelming role for the mass media and increasingly funded by public party finance has created unaccountable "party cartels" impervious to voter demands (Blyth and Katz 2005; Katz and Mair 1995, reprinted in Mair 1997), while others have invoked the power of competition and voter exit to contradict that thesis (Kitschelt 2000*b*). In other words, does the undeniable tendency of voters to express greater dissatisfaction with parties than in previous decades indicate that there is a crisis of political representation precipitated by unaccountable elites, or are these misgivings by-products of weaker economic performance and structural economic change that opens opportunities for partisan realignment?

4.3 Party Systems in New Democracies of the Developing World

Whereas comparative literature on Western OECD polities worries about the erosion of relations of democratic accountability, students of democracy in developing countries are preoccupied with the reverse question of whether accountability relations and "institutionalized" party systems will ever emerge in the first place. Particularly students of Latin American and post-communist politics have been impressed by the high volatility of many parties and party systems signaling difficulty in establishing lasting relations between voters and political agents (cf. Mainwaring and Scully 1995; Mair 1997, ch. 8; Roberts and Wibbels 1999; Rose and Munro 2003). In countries where party systems have developed some staying power, it is not programmatic politics based on indirect exchange, but clientelistic principal–agent relations that appear to dominate the scene and adapt to new constituencies and political challenges, whether in South and South-East Asia (cf. Kohli 1990; Chandra 2004; Chhibber 1998; Krishna 2002; Sachsenröder 1998; Wilkinson 2006), in Latin America (Fox 1994; Gibson 1997; Levitsky 2003) or post-communist Eastern Europe (Hale 2006; Kitschelt et al. 1999). The persistence or demise of clientelistic conditions does not simply depend on economic poverty and unequal asset distribution in a polity, but also on the strategic incentives generated within the arena of party competition to switch to a different accountability relationship (cf. Kitschelt and Wilkinson 2006). Also weak performance of public sector enterprises or of publicly regulated companies that are often shot through with clientelistic exchange relations may affect how democratic political accountability relations evolve.

Upon closer inspection, within each region of the developing world the current state of party system consolidation and the practices of principal–agent relations varies widely. Both in post-communist Europe as well as in Latin America a number of party systems have quite clearly structured programmatic political cleavages and rather stable competitive partisan divides, particularly if we follow Bartolini and Mair's (1990) focus not on the volatility of individual parties, but on party blocs with roughly similar appeals within a cleavage system. A growing literature has examined the extent and the nature of political cleavages and competitive party divides in the post-communist region (cf. Bielasiak 2002; de Waele 2004; Evans and Whitefield 1993, 2000; Kitschelt 1992, 1995b; Lewis 2000; Pridham and Lewis 1996; Tavits 2005; Whitefield 2002). Particular attention has been devoted to the insertion of the former communist ruling parties into democratic partisan politicis (cf. Bozoki and Ishiyama 2002; Grzymala-Busse 2002). Controversies surround both the descriptive characterization of the political divides and competitive dimensions as well as the explanation for more or less programmatic structuring. Is it a consequence of political experiences of the past ("legacies") in each country, of democratic institutions (such as electoral systems and relations between the executive and the legislature), or of the momentous political-economic reforms that generate new divides between interests?

Comparative scholarship on Latin America has asked closely parallel questions. Some authors have ventured to identify the historical origins, profile, and durability of political cleavages in at least some party systems (Dix 1989; Coller and Collier 1991; Coppedge 1998). Others have focused on general patterns of stability and change in Latin American party systems in order to explore the causes of democratic party system institutionalization (cf. Dix 1992; Mainwaring and Scully 1995; Geddes 2003). In Latin America, just as in Eastern Europe, those party systems appear more consolidated and structured around mechanisms of programmatic accountability in which there had been other episodes of democratic competition before the current spell of democratic competition beginning in the 1980s. Such episodes of broad political mobilization enabled people to gain political experience and sometimes even to "lock in" certain political economic achievements, such as the beginnings of a welfare state, that provided a focal point to crystallize electorates around programmatic alternatives, particularly in an era of conomic reform and market liberalization.

There is a curious asymmetry, however, when comparing Eastern Europe and Latin America. In Latin America party system consolidation and programmatic structuring tend to have undergone the greatest erosion in the 1990s and since 2000 precisely in countries with historically more established party systems. This erosion is greatest in Venezuela, followed by Argentina, but also present to a lesser extent even in Costa Rica, Uruguay, Mexico, and Chile. At the same time, Latin American countries with always inchoate party systems show few signs of changing that state of affairs. In Eastern Europe, by contrast, the polities with the most promising historical priors for party system institutionalization around programmatic accountability are also those that have achieved the comparatively greatest institutionalization. But even many less hospitable places have shown signs of moving toward patterns of programmatic accountability.

In Eastern Europe and also in South and South-East Asia sustained economic growth for at least the past decade and often longer has most certainly benefited the gradual establishment of robust structures of representation. In Latin America, by contrast, the demise of import-substituting industrialization strategies in the 1980s and the inability of political elites to embrace a definite new strategy of political-economic development, as evidenced by anemic growth and repeated monetary stabilization crises, may have contributed not only to the region's continuing economic hardship, but also the fragility of its democratic party systems.

5 CONCLUSION

My review of the party system literature has been highly selective, driven by my personal research interests in the area and an effort to stress certain agenda points for future research. Thus I believe more emphasis has to be placed on the comparative study of the varieties of mechanisms that may govern the relationship between principals and agents in democratic party systems. I also believe that in the study of the "dimensionality" of party competition, more attention needs to be paid to the distinction between social, political, and competitive partisan divides. Third, and intimately linked to the previous point, the competitiveness of party systems deserves better conceptualization and more intensive study than in the past. Conversely, I submit that too much significance has been attached to certain relatively easily measured macro-level properties of party systems, such as party system fragmentation, polarization, and volatility, none of which are good measures of party system competitiveness.

My treatment of party systems has ignored, however, any discussion of the concept as independent variable. After all, we might develop concepts and theorems of party systems not for their own sake, but as fruitful tools to study the consequences of party competition for a variety of political and economic processes. Among them I would count the formation of legislative and executive majorities, the resulting process of policy formation and implementation, and ultimately the consequences of party system dynamics for the stability and survival of the political regime form itself. Since these topics are treated elsewhere in this volume, I could do without a detailed discussion in this entry on party systems. At the same time, a more sophisticated conceptualization of party systems, particularly of mechanisms of democratic accountability and partisan competitiveness, may perform wonders in improving the causal efficacy of explanations that employ party system attributes to predict political economic developments and political regime trajectories.

References

ADAMS, J., MERRILL, S., III, and GROFMAN, A. 2005. *A Unified Theory of Party Competition*. Cambridge: Cambridge University Press.

ALDRICH, J. 1983. A Downsian spatial model with party activism. *American Political Science Review*, 77: 974–90.

—— 1995. *Why Parties? The Origin and Transformation of Party Politics in America*. Chicago: Chicago University Press.

AMERICAN POLITICAL SCIENCE ASSOCIATION. 1983. *Political Science: The State of the Discipline. 1983*, ed. S. M. Lipset. Washington, DC: APSA.

—— 1993. *Political Science: The State of the Discipline. 1993*, ed. A. W. Finifter. Washington, DC: APSA.

—— 2002. *Political Science: The State of the Discipline. 2002*, ed. I. Katznelson and H. Milner. New York: W. W. Norton.

AMES, B. 2001. *The Deadlock of Democracy in Brazil*. Ann Arbor: University of Michigan Press.

BARTOLINI, S. 2000. *The Political Mobilization of the European Left, 1860–1980: The Class Cleavage*. Cambridge: Cambridge University Press.

—— and MAIR, P. 1990. *Identity, Competition and Electoral Availability. The Stability of European Electorates 1885–1985*. Cambridge: Cambridge University Press.

BIELASIAK, J. 2002. The institutionalization of electoral and party systems in postcommunist states. *Comparative Politics*, 34: 189–210.

BLYTH, M., and KATZ, R. 2005. From catch-all politics to cartelisation. *West European Politics*, 28: 33–60.

BOZOKI, A., and ISHIYAMA, J. eds. 2002. *The Communist Successor Parties of Central and Eastern Europe*. Armonk, NY: M. E. Sharpe.

BRINEGAR, A., JOLLY, S., and KITSCHELT, H. 2004. Varieties of capitalism and political divisions over European integration. Pp. 62–89 in *Dimensions of Contestation in the European Union*, ed. G. Marks and M. Steenbergen. Cambridge: Cambridge University Press.

BROOKS, C., NIEUWBEERTA, P., and MANZA, J. 2006. Cleavage-based voting behavior in cross-national perspective: evidence from six postwar democracies. *Social Science Research*, 35: 88–128.

BUDGE, I., and FARLIE, D. 1983. *Explaining and Predicting Elections*. London: Allen and Unwin.

—— ROBERTSON, D. and HEARL, D., eds. 1987. *Ideology, Strategy and Party Change: Spatial Analyses of Post-War Election Programmes in Nineteen Democracies*. Cambridge: Cambridge University Press.

—— KLINGEMANN, H.-D., VOLKENS, A., BARA, J., and TANENBAUM, A. (with group of further co-authors). 2001. *Mapping Policy Preferences: Estimates for Parties, Electors, and Governments 1945–1998*. Oxford: Oxford University Press.

CAILLAUD, D., and TIROLE, J. 2002. Parties as political intermediaries. *Quarterly Journal of Economics*, 117: 1453–89.

CARTER, E. 2005. *The Extreme Right in Western Europe: Success or Failure?* Manchester: Manchester University Press.

CHANDRA, K. 2004. *Why Ethnic Parties Succeed: Patronage and Ethnic Headcounts in India*. Cambridge: Cambridge University Press.

CHHIBBER, P. K. 1998. *Democracy without Associations*. Ann Arbor: Michigan University Press.

COLE, A. 2005. Old right or new right? The ideological positioning of parties of the far right. *European Journal of Political Research*, 44: 203–30.

COLLIER, D., and COLLIER, R. 1991. *Shaping the Political Arena*. Princeton: Princeton University Press.

COPPEDGE, M. 1998. The evolution of Latin American party systems. Pp. 171–96 in *Politics, Society, and Democracy*, ed. S. Mainwaring and A. Valenzuela. Boulder, Colo.: Westview Press.

COX, G. 1997. *Making Votes Count*. Cambridge: Cambridge University Press.

—— and McCUBBINS, M. 1993. *Legislative Leviathan: Party Government in the House*. Berkeley and Los Angeles: University of California Press.

DALTON, R. J. 2004. *Parties without Partisans: Political Change in Advanced Industrial Democracies*. Oxford: Oxford University Press.

—— FLANAGAN, S., and BECK, P. A. 1984. *Electoral Change in Advanced Industrial Democracies: Realignment or Dealignment?* Princeton: Princeton University Press.

DE WAELE, J.-M. ed. 2004. *Les Clivages politiques en Europe centrale et orientale*. Brussels: Édition de l'Université de Bruxelles.

DIX, R. 1989. Cleavage structures and party systems in Latin America. *Comparative Politics*, 22: 23–37.

—— 1992. Democratization and the institutionalization of Latin American political parties. *Comparative Political Studies*, 24: 488–511.

DOWNS, A. 1957. *An Economic Theory of Democracy*. New York: Harper and Row.

DUVERGER, M. 1954. *Political Parties*. London: Methuen.

ENELOW, J. M., and HINICH, M. eds. 1990. *Advances in the Spatial Theory of Voting.* Cambridge, Mass.: Cambridge University Press.

EPSTEIN, L. D. 1975. Political parties. Pp. 229–78 in *Handbook of Political Science, iv: Non-Governmental Politics,* ed. F. I. Greenstein and N. W. Polsby. Reading, Mass.: Addison-Wesley.

ERICKSON, R. S., MACKUEN, M. B., and STIMSON, J. A. 2002. *The Macro-Polity.* Cambridge: Cambridge University Press.

EVANS, G. ed. 1999. *The End of Class Politics? Class Voting in Comparative Context.* Oxford: Oxford University Press.

——and WHITEFIELD, S. 1993. Identifying the bases of party competition in eastern Europe. *British Journal of Political Science,* 23: 521–48.

——— 2000. Explaining the formation of electoral cleavages in post-communist democracies. Pp. 36–68 in *Elections in Central and Eastern Europe: The First Wave,* ed. H. D. Klingemann, E. Mochmann, and K. Newton. Berlin: Edition Sigma.

FIORINA, M. 1977. An outline for a model of party choice. *American Journal of Political Science,* 21: 601–25.

——1997. Voting behavior. Pp. 391–414 in *Perspectives on Public Choice,* ed. D. C. Mueller. Cambridge: Cambridge University Press.

——2002. Parties, participation, and representation in America: old theories face new realities. Pp. 511–41 in *Political Science: The State of the Discipline,* ed. H. V. Milner and I. Katznelson. New York: Norton.

FOX, J. 1994. The difficult transition from clientelism to citizenship. *World Politics,* 46: 151–84.

FRANKLIN, M. 2004. *Voter Turnout and the Dynamics of Electoral Competition in Established Democracies since 1945.* Cambridge: Cambridge University Press.

——MACKIE, T., and VALEN, H. eds. 1992. *Electoral Change: Responses to Evolving Social and Attitudinal Structures in Western Democracies.* Cambridge: Cambridge University Press.

GABEL, M. 1998. Political support for European integration: an empirical test of five theories. *Journal of Politics,* 60 (2): 333–54.

GEDDES, B. 2003. *Paradigms and Sandcastles.* Ann Arbor: University of Michigan Press.

GIBSON, E. 1997. The populist road to market reform: policy and electoral coalitions in Mexico and Argentina. *World Politics,* 49: 339–70.

GOLDER, M. 2003. Explaining variation in the success of extreme right parties in Western Europe. *Comparative Political Studies,* 36 (4): 432–66.

GOODIN, R. E., and KLINGEMANN, H.-D. eds. 1996. *A New Handbook of Political Science.* Oxford: Oxford University Press.

GREENSTEIN, F. I., and POLSBY, N. W. eds. 1975. *Handbook of Political Science, iv: Non-Governmental Politics.* Reading, Mass.: Addison-Wesley.

GROFMAN, B. 2004. Downs and two-party convergence. *Annual Review of Politics,* 7: 25–46.

GRZYMALA-BUSSE, A. M. 2002. *Redeeming the Communist Past: The Regeneration of Communist Parties in East Central Europe.* Cambridge: Cambridge University Press.

——2003. Redeeming the past: communist successor parties after 1989. Pp. 157–81 in *Capitalism and Democracy in Central and Eastern Europe,* ed. G. Ekiert and S. E. Hanson. Cambridge: Cambridge University Press.

HALE, H. 2006. Correlates of clientelism: political economy, politicized ethnicity, and post-communist transition. Forthcoming in *Patrons, Clients, and Policies: Patterns of Democratic Accountability and Political Competition,* ed. H. Kitschelt and S. Wilkinson. Cambridge: Cambridge University Press.

HARMEL, R., and ROBERTSON, J. D. 1984. Formation and success of new parties: a cross-analysis. *International Political Science Review,* 6: 501–23.

HAUSS, C., and RAYSIDE, D. 1978. The development of new parties in western democracies since 1945. Pp. 31–57 in *Political Parties: Development and Decay*, ed. L. Maisel and J. Cooper. Beverly Hills, Calif.: Sage.

HINICH, M., and MUNGER, M. 1994. *Ideology and the Theory of Political Choice*. Ann Arbor: Michigan University Press.

HIX, S. 1999. Dimensions and alignments in European Union politics: cognitive constraints and partisan responses. *European Journal of Political Research*, 35: 69–125.

HOROWITZ, D. 1985. *Ethnic Groups in Conflict*. Berkeley and Los Angeles: University of California Press.

HUG, S. 2001. *Altering Party Systems: Strategic Behavior and the Emergence of New Political Parties in Western Democracies*. Ann Arbor: University of Michigan Press.

HUNTINGTON, S. P. 1968. *Political Order in Changing Societies*. New Haven: Yale University Press.

IGNAZI, P. 2003. *Extreme Right Parties in Western Europe*. Oxford: Oxford University Press.

INGLEHART, R. 1990. *Culture Shift*. Princeton: Princeton University Press.

—— 1997. *Modernization and Postmodernization*. Princeton: Princeton University Press.

IVARSFLATEN, E. 2005. The vulnerable populist right parties: no economic realignment fuelling their electoral success. *European Journal of Political Research*, 44: 465–92.

JACKMAN, R., and VOLPERT, K. 1996. Conditions favouring parties of the extreme right in Western Europe. *British Journal of Political Science*, 26: 501–22.

KALYVAS, S. 1996. *The Rise of Christian Democracy in Europe*. Ithaca, NY: Cornell University Press.

KATZ, R. S. 1980. *A Theory of Parties and Electoral Systems*. Baltimore: Johns Hopkins University Press.

—— and CROTTY, W. eds. 2006. *Handbook of Party Politics*. London: Sage Publications.

—— and MAIR, P. 1995. Changing models of party organization and party democracy: the emergence of the cartel party. *Party Politics*, 1 (1): 5–28. Reprinted in P. Mair, *Party System Change: Approaches and Interpretations*. Oxford: Oxford University Press, 1997.

KEDAR, O. 2005. When moderate voters prefer extreme parties: policy balancing in parliamentary elections. *American Political Science Review*, 99: 185–200.

KEEFER, P. 2005. Democratization and clientelism: why are young democracies badly governed? World Bank Policy Research Paper 3594.

KITSCHELT, H. 1988. The rise of left-libertarian parties in western democracies: explaining innovation in competitive party systems. *World Politics*, 40: 194–234.

—— 1989a. The internal politics of parties: the law of curvilinear disparity revisited. *Political Studies*, 37: 400–21.

—— 1989b. *The Logics of Party Formation*. Ithaca, NY: Cornell University Press.

—— 1992. The formation of party systems in east central Europe. *Politics and Society*, 20: 7–50.

—— 1994. *The Transformation of European Social Democracy*. Cambridge: Cambridge University Press.

—— (in collaboration with A. J. McGann). 1995a. *The Radical Right in Western Europe*. Ann Arbor: University of Michigan Press.

—— 1995b. The formation of party cleavages in post-communist democracies: theoretical propositions. *Party Politics*, 1: 447–72.

—— 2000a. Linkages between citizens and politicians in democratic polities. *Comparative Political Studies*, 33: 845–79.

—— 2000b. Citizens, politicians, and party cartellization: political representation and state failure in post-industrial democracies. *European Journal of Political Research*, 37: 149–79.

——— Hawkins, K., Rosas, G., and Zechmeister, L. Forthcoming. *Latin American Party Systems*.

——— and Rehm, P. 2005. Work, family, and politics: foundations of electoral partisan alignments in postindustrial democracies. Paper prepared for delivery at the 2005 Annual Meeting of the American Political Science Association, Washington, DC.

——— and Wilkinson, S. eds. 2006. *Patrons, Clients and Policies: Patterns of Democratic Accountability and Political Competition*. Cambridge: Cambridge University Press.

——— and Zechmeister, E. 2003. Patterns of party competition and political accountability in Latin America. Paper prepared for delivery at the 2003 Annual Meeting of the American Political Science Association, Philadelphia.

——— Mansfeldova, Z., Markowski, R., and Toka, G. 1999. *Post-Communist Party Systems: Competition, Representation, and Inter-Party Cooperation*. Cambridge: Cambridge University Press.

Knutsen, O. 2006. *Social Class and Party Choice in Eight Countries: A Comparative Longitudinal Study*. Boulder, Colo.: Westview Press.

Kohli, A. 1990. *Democracy and Discontent: India's Growing Crisis of Governability*. Cambridge: Cambridge University Press.

Kollman, K., Miller, J., and Page, S. 1992. Adaptive parties in spatial elections. *American Political Science Review*, 86: 929–37.

——— ——— ——— 1998. Political parties and electoral landscapes. *British Journal of Political Science*, 28: 139–58.

Krishna, A. 2002. *Active Social Capital: Tracing the Roots of Democracy and Development*. New York: Columbia University Press.

Laakso, M., and Taagepera, R. 1979. Effective number of parties: a measure with application to western Europe. *European Journal of Political Research*, 12: 3–27.

Laitin, D. 2003. Comparative politics: the state of the subdiscipline. Pp. 630–59 in *Political Science: The State of the Discipline*, ed. H. V. Milner and I. Katznelson. New York: W. W. Norton.

Laver, M. 2005. Policy and the dynamics of party competition. *American Political Science Review*, 99: 263–82.

——— and Hunt, B. W. 1992. *Policy and Party Competition*. London: Routledge.

——— and Schilperoord, M. 2005. The birth and death of political parties. Draft prepared for *Philosophical Transactions of the Royal Society B*. Edinburgh, 30 July–5 August.

Levitsky, S. 2003. *Transforming Labor-Based Parties in Latin America*. Cambridge: Cambridge University Press.

Lewis, P. G. 2000. *Political Parties in Post-Communist Eastern Europe*. London: Routledge.

Lijphart, A. 1999. *Patterns of Democracy*. New Haven: Yale University Press.

Lipset, S. M., and Rokkan, S. 1967. Cleavage structures, party systems, and voter alignments: an introduction. Pp. 1–64 in *Party Systems and Voter Alignments: Cross-National Perspectives*, ed. S. M. Lipset and S. Rokkan. New York: Free Press.

Lubbers, M., Gijsberts, M., and Scheepers, P. 2002. Extreme right-wing voting in Western Europe. *European Journal of Political Research*, 41: 345–78.

Luebbert, G. 1991. *Liberalism, Fascism, or Social Democracy: Social Classes and the Political Origins of Regimes in Interwar Europe*. New York: Oxford University Press.

Lupia, A., and McCubbins, M. 1998. *The Democratic Dilemma: Can Citizens Learn What They Need to Know?* Cambridge: Cambridge University Press.

McGann, A. J. 2002. The advantages of ideological cohesion: a model of constituency representation and electoral competition in multi-party democracies. *Journal of Theoretical Politics*, 14: 37–70.

MAGUIRE, M. 1983. Is there still persistence? Electoral change in western Europe, 1948–1979. Pp. 67–94 in *Western European Party Systems: Continuity and Change*, ed. H. Daalder and P. Mair. Beverly Hills, Calif.: Sage.

MAINWARING, S., and SCULLY, T. 1995. Introduction: party systems in Latin America. Pp. 1–35 in *Building Democratic Institutions: Party Systems in Latin America*, ed. S. Mainwaring and T. Scully. Stanford, Calif.: Stanford University Press.

MAIR, P. 1997. *Party System Change: Approaches and Interpretations*. Oxford: Oxford University Press, 1997.

——2000. The limited impact of Europe on national party systems. *West European Politics*, 23: 27–51.

MANZA, J., and BROOKS, C. 1999. *Social Cleavages and Political Change: Voter Alignments and U.S. Party Coalitions*. Oxford: Oxford University Press.

MARKS, G., and STEENBERGEN, M. eds. 2004. *European Integration and Political Conflict*. Cambridge: Cambridge University Press.

——and WILSON, C. 2000. The past in the present: a cleavage theory of party response to European integration. *British Journal of Political Science*, 30: 433–59.

————and RAY, L. 2002. National political parties and European integration. *American Journal of Political Science*, 46: 585–94.

MAY, J. D. 1973. Opinion structure and political parties: the special law of curvilinear disparity. *Political Studies*, 21: 135–51.

MAYHEW, D. R. 2000. Electoral realignments. *Annual Review of Political Science*, 3: 449–74.

MEGUID, B. 2005. Competition between unequals: the role of mainstream party strategy in niche party success. *American Political Science Review*, 99: 347–60.

MERRILL, S., III, and GROFMAN, B. 1999. *A Unified Theory of Voting: Directional and Proximity Spatial Models*. Cambridge: Cambridge University Press.

MILLER, G., and SCHOFIELD, N. 2003. Activists and partisan realignment in the United States. *American Political Science Review*, 97 (2): 245–60.

MOLINAR, J. 1991. Counting the number of parties: an alternative index. *American Political Science Review*, 85: 1383–91.

MORGENSTERN, S. 2004. *Patterns of Legislative Politics*. Cambridge: Cambridge University Press.

NORRIS, P. 2005. *Radical Right: Voters and Parties in the Electoral Market*. Cambridge: Cambridge University Press.

ORDESHOOK, P. 1997. The spatial analysis of elections and committees: four decades of research. Pp. 247–70 in *Perspectives on Public Choice*, ed. D. C. Mueller. Cambridge: Cambridge University Press.

PANEBIANCO, A. 1988. *Political Parties: Organization and Power*. Cambridge: Cambridge University Press.

PAPPI, F. U. 1996. Political behavior: reasoning voters in multi-party systems. Pp. 255–74 in *A New Handbook of Political Science*, ed. R. E. Goodin and H.-D. Klingemann. Oxford: Oxford University Press.

PEDERSEN, M. 1983. Changing patterns of electoral volatility in European party systems, 1948–1977: explorations in explanation. Pp. 29–66 in *Western European Party Systems: Continuity and Change*, ed. H. Daalder and P. Mair. Beverly Hills, Calif.: Sage.

PIATTONI, S. ed. 2001. *Clientelism, Interests, and Democratic Representation*. Cambridge: Cambridge University Press.

POWELL, G. B. 2000. *Elections as Instruments of Democracy: Majoritarian and Proportional Visions*. New Haven: Yale University Press.

PRIDHAM, G., and LEWIS, P. eds. 1996. *Stabilizing Fragile Democracies: Comparing New Party Systems in Southern and Eastern Europe.* London: Routledge.

PRZEWORSKI, A., and SPRAGUE, J. 1986. *Paper Stones.* Chicago: University of Chicago Press.

RABINOWITZ, G., and McDONALD, S. E. 1989. A directional theory of issue voting. *American Political Science Review*, 83: 93–121.

RAE, D. W. 1967. *The Political Consequences of Electoral Laws.* New Haven: Yale University Press.

—— and TAYLOR, M. 1970. *The Analysis of Cleavages.* New Haven: Yale University Press.

RAY, L. 2004. Don't rock the boat: expectations, fears, and opposition to EU level policy-making. Pp. 51–61 in *Dimensions of Contestation in the European Union*, ed. G. Marks and M. Steenbergen. Cambridge: Cambridge University Press.

REDDING, K., and VITERNA, J. 1999. Political demands, political opportunities: explaining the differential success of left-libertarian parties. *Social Forces*, 78: 491–510.

RIKER, W. 1982. *Liberalism versus Populism.* San Francisco: Freeman.

—— 1986. *The Art of Political Manipulation.* New Haven: Yale University Press.

ROBERTS, K., and WIBBELS, E. 1999. Party systems and electoral volatility in Latin America: a test of economic, institutional, and structural explanations. *American Political Science Review*, 93: 575–90.

ROBERTSON, D. 1976. *A Theory of Party Competition.* New York: Wiley.

ROEMER, J. 2001. *Political Competition: Theory and Applications.* Cambridge, Mass.: Harvard University Press.

ROGOWSKI, R. 1989. *Commerce and Coalitions.* Princeton: Princeton University Press.

ROSE, R., and MUNRO, R. 2003. *Elections and Parties in New European Democracies.* Washington, DC: Congressional Quarterly Press.

RUGGIE, J. G. 1989. International structure and international transformation: space, time, and method. Pp. 21–35 in *Global Changes and Theoretical Challenges*, ed. E.-O. Czempiel and J. Rosenau. Lexington, Mass.: D. C. Heath.

—— 1993. Territoriality and beyond: problematizing modernity in international relations. *International Organization*, 47: 139–74.

SACHSENRÖDER, W. 1998. Party politics and democratic development in East and Southeast Asia: a comparative view. Pp. 1–35 in *Political Party Systems and Democratic Development in East and Southeast Asia*, vol. i, ed. W. Sachsenröder and U. E. Frings. Ashgate: Aldershot.

SAMUELS, D. 2004. From socialism to social democracy: party organization and the transformation of the Workers' Party in Brazil. *Comparative Political Studies*, 37: 999–1024.

SANI, G., and SARTORI, G. 1983. Polarization, fragmentation and competition in western democracies. Pp. 307–340 in *Western European Party Systems. Continuity and Change*, ed. H. Daalder and P. Mair. Beverly Hills, Calif.: Sage.

SARTORI, G. 1968. The sociology of parties: a critical review. Pp. 1–25 in *Party Systems, Party Organisation and the Politics of the New Masses*, ed. O. Stammer. Berlin: Institut für Politische Wissenschaften.

—— 1976. *Parties and Party Systems: A Framework for Analysis.* Cambridge: Cambridge University Press.

—— 1986. The influence of electoral systems: faulty laws or faulty method? Pp. 43–68 in *Electoral Laws and their Political Consequences*, ed. B. Grofman and A. Lijphart. New York: Agathon Press.

SCHAIN, M., ZOLBERG, A., and HOSSAU, P. eds. 2002. *Shadows over Europe: The Development and Impact of the Extreme Right in Western Europe.* Houndmills: Palgrave Macmillan.

SCHEVE, K. 2000. Comparative context and public preferences over regional economic integration. Paper presented at the Annual Meeting of the American Political Science Association. Washington, DC.

SCHLESINGER, J. 1984. On the theory of party organization. *Journal of Politics*, 46: 369–400.

SCHMIDT, S. W., GUASTI, L., LAND, C. H., and SCOTT, J. C. eds. 1977. *Friends, Followers, and Factions*. Berkeley and Los Angeles: University of California Press.

SCHOFIELD, N. 2003. Valence competition in the spatial stochastic model. *Journal of Theoretical Politics*, 15: 371–83.

—— 2004. Equilibrium in the spatial "valence" model of politics. *Journal of Theoretical Politics*, 16: 447–81.

SCOTT, J. C. 1969. Corruption, machine politics, and political change. *American Political Science Review*, 62: 1142–58.

SHAMIR, M. 1984. Are western party systems "frozen"? A comparative dynamic analysis. *Comparative Political Studies*, 12: 35–79.

SHEFTER, M. 1994. *Political Parties and the State: The American Historical Experience*. Princeton University Press.

SHEPSLE, K. 1991. *Models of Multiparty Electoral Competition*. Chur: Harwood Academic Publishers.

SNYDER, J. M., Jr., and TING, M. M. 2002. An informational rationale for political parties. *American Journal of Political Science*, 46: 90–110.

SORAUF, F. J. 1964. *Party Politics in America*. Boston: Little, Brown.

SPRUYT, H. 1994. *The Sovereign State and its Competitors*. Princeton: Princeton University Press.

STIMSON, J. 2005. *Tides of Consent: How Public Opinion Shapes American Politics*. Cambridge: Cambridge University Press.

STOKES, D. 1963. Spatial models of party competition. *American Political Science Review*, 57: 368–77.

STROM, K. 1990a. A behavioral theory of competitive political parties. *American Journal of Political Science*, 34: 565–98.

—— 1990b. *Minority Government and Majority Control*. Cambridge: Cambridge University Press.

TAAGEPERA, R., and GROFMAN, B. 1985. Rethinking Duverger's law: predicting the effective number of parties in plurality and PR systems: parties minus issues equals one. *European Journal of Political Research*, 13: 341–53.

TAVITS, M. 2005. The development of stable party support: electoral dynamics in post-communist Europe. *American Journal of Political Science*, 49 (2): 283–98.

—— 2006. Party systems in the making. the emergence and success of new parties in new democracies. *British Journal of Political Science* (forthcoming).

TSEBELIS, G. 2002. *Veto Players*. Princeton: Princeton University Press.

VAN DER BRUG, W., FENNEMA, M., and TILLIE, J. 2005. Why some anti-immigrant parties fail and others succeed: a two-step model of aggregate electoral support. *Comparative Political Studies*, 38: 537–73.

VEUGELERS, J., and MAGNAN, A. 2005. Conditions of far-right strength in contemporary Western Europe: an application of Kitschelt's theory. *European Journal of Political Research*, 44: 837–60.

WALTZ, K. 1954. *Man, the State, and War: A Theoretical Analysis*. New York: Columbia University Press.

—— 1979. *Theory of International Politics*. Reading, Mass.: Addison-Wesley.

WEINGAST, B. 1998. Political stability and civil war: institutions, commitments, and American democracy. Pp. 148–93 in *Analytical Narratives*, ed. R. H. Bates, A. Greif, M. Levi, J.-L. Rosenthal, and B. R. Weingast. Princeton: Princeton University Press.

WHITEFIELD, S. 2002. Political cleavages and post-communist politics. *Annual Review of Political Science*, 5: 181–200.

WILKINSON, S. I. 2004. *Votes and Violence: Electoral Competition and Ethnic Riots in India*. Cambridge: Cambridge University Press.

——2006. Explaining changing patterns of party–voter linkages in India. Pp. 110–40 in *Patrons, Clients and Policies*, ed. H. Kitschelt and S. I. Wilkinson. Cambridge: Cambridge University Press.

CHAPTER 23

....

VOTERS AND PARTIES

ANNE WREN

KENNETH M. MCELWAIN

1 REALIGNMENT OR DEALIGNMENT IN THE PARTY–VOTER NEXUS

....

POLITICAL parties assume a prominent position in comparative studies of electoral and legislative behavior in advanced industrialized democracies. Unlike the electoral system, parliamentary committees, or other pervasive political institutions, parties are rarely defined—in either structure or function—by the national constitution.[1] Nevertheless, political parties can be found in essentially all democratic—and some autocratic— polities. Indeed, many studies of party politics lead with E. E. Schattschneider's famous quote, "Political parties created modern democracy and modern democracy is unthinkable save in terms of parties" (1942).

The reasons given for the relevance of political parties are manifold, but early studies focused on the parties' utility in the electoral process, particularly how they helped voters structure their preferences at the ballot box. As modern governments faced a widening and increasingly complex array of policy issues in both the pre-war and post-war periods, citizens were seen as being unwilling (or unable) to gather and process all the facts necessary to make an informed decision about which candidate to vote for (Campbell et al. 1960). Political parties—particularly those with long legacies and organized bases of support—simplified this process by providing an

---

[1] There are notable exceptions, including Germany where the German Basic Law explicitly specifies the legal rights, functions, and structure of parties.

informational heuristic about the policy platforms of those parties' candidates (Downs 1957). An American factory worker with strong labor union ties could infer how a Democratic Party candidate would vote in Congress without knowing very much about the candidate, herself. Again, in the words of Schattschneider, "The parties organize the electorate by reducing their alternatives to the extreme limit of simplification" (1960).

In addition to acting as informational cues, political parties played a crucial organizational and legislative role. Many parties—particularly on the left—maintained a large membership base, through which they recruited election candidates, distributed information, and aggregated interests to produce a coherent policy platform (Aldrich 1995; Dalton and Wattenberg 2000). They have also been the primary players in parliamentary decision making and coalition formation. Political parties coordinated like-minded members of parliament into cohesive legislative blocs, and, through the various carrots and sticks at their disposal, rewarded or sanctioned politicians based on their adherence to the party's long-term goals (Laver and Schofield 1990; Cox and McCubbins 1993; Bowler, Farrell, and Katz 1999).

In their classic treatment, Lipset and Rokkan (1967) describe the deeply embedded relationship which formed between voters and the early mass parties. Those parties which successfully organized in the period at, or before, the extension of mass suffrage enjoyed a first-mover advantage in the relationships which they built with the new electorates. The scale of this advantage was such that observed party systems in Western Europe displayed high levels of continuity between the 1920s and the 1960s, in spite of the turbulent political events which occurred in Europe during this period. As a result, these authors famously argue, the structure of electoral cleavages had become "frozen" so as to reflect the structure of ideological conflict in these countries at the time of the mass parties' foundation.

Parties' organizational strategies were particularly important in strengthening the affective relationships between parties and voters during this period. The incorporation of significant segments of the electorate into the grassroots networks of the main political parties, or into closely associated organizational groups such as trade unions, facilitated the inculcation of lasting political identities.[2] As a result, voters exhibited considerable stability in their voting behavior, as their decision making relied heavily on the informational shortcuts provided by trusted political organizations. Elections essentially became contests over which party could develop the largest mass organization, and the vote shares of established parties tended to be relatively stable.

Even as Lipset and Rokkan described this deeply embedded linkage between parties and voters, however, there were indications of upheaval in the electoral landscape. Figure 23.1 shows trends in the total vote shares of parties established before 1960—in other words, parties which were in existence during the peak periods

---

[2] See Przeworski and Sprague (1986) on the organizational strategies of electoral socialist parties and their relation to the trades union movement; see Kalyvas (1996) on the relationship between Christian Democratic parties and Catholic social organizations.

of the "frozen cleavage" hypothesis—from the 1960s on.[3] The figure is composed of two panels, one containing annualized data and showing all data points; the second showing the average for each period between elections, or "election count," across all countries.[4] Using both year and election count allows us to differentiate between political outcomes that are a function of factors that affect countries contemporaneously (i.e. by year), or whether they vary by the frequency and natural cycle of electoral competition (i.e. by election count). Regardless of the measure, we can see that there is a strong quadratic relationship between time and the performance of established political parties.[5] The total vote share of these parties has declined at an increasing rate since the 1960s, indicating the stronger electoral presence of relatively new parties.

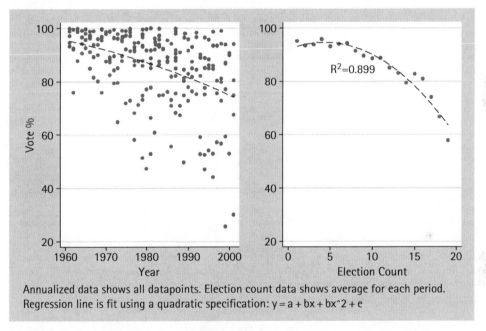

Annualized data shows all datapoints. Election count data shows average for each period. Regression line is fit using a quadratic specification: y = a + bx + bx^2 + e

Fig. 23.1 Total vote % of parties established before 1960

[3] Electoral data here and in other figures are compiled from the following countries: Australia (1946–2004); Austria (1945–2002); Belgium (1946–2003); Denmark (1945–2001); Finland (1945–2003); French 5th Republic (1958–97); (West) Germany (1949–2002); Greece (1974–2004); Iceland (1946–2003); Ireland (1948–2002); Italy (1948–2001); Japan (1946–2003); Luxembourg (1954–2004); Malta (1947–2003); the Netherlands (1946–2003); Norway (1945–2001); Portugal (1976–2002); Spain (1977–2004); Sweden (1948–2002); and United Kingdom (1945–2005). Data taken from Gorvin (1989) and Caramani (2000).

[4] For example, the observation for election count "1" is the average vote share across all sampled countries in the first election held in the period under consideration. The election count figure restricts data to cases where election count is less than twenty; because only Australia, Denmark, and Japan have had that many elections in the post-war period, including those cases could bias results based on factors specific to those countries. All figures in this chapter restrict election count to less than twenty.

[5] The fitted values are quadratic predictions of total vote % based on a linear regression of total vote % on election count and election count squared. The quadratic prediction is calculated using the "twoway qfit" function on Stata 9.

Additionally, numerous studies have found evidence of increasing instability in voter–party relationships. Panel surveys of individual voters show that the level of party switching and ticket splitting has been rising (Clarke and Stewart 1998; Dalton, McAllister, and Wattenberg 2000). Similarly, formal membership in political parties has been falling in recent decades (Scarrow 2000), as has voter turnout—particularly in the 1990s (Wattenberg 2000). These changes have had a significant effect on election outcomes: there have been more new parties entering the political arena (Hug 2001; Tavits 2006), and, perhaps most significantly, fluctuations in the vote and seat shares of political parties have become more volatile (Mair 1997; Clarke and Stewart 1998; Dalton, McAllister, and Wattenberg 2000). Figure 23.2 displays trends in electoral volatility in the post-war period, using the Pedersen Index which measures net changes in parties' vote shares from election to election (Pedersen 1979).[6] The figure again uses two different time scales: one that plots every election by year, and a second that displays average volatility by election count. The scatter plots show that electoral volatility has increased over time at a fairly steady rate.[7]

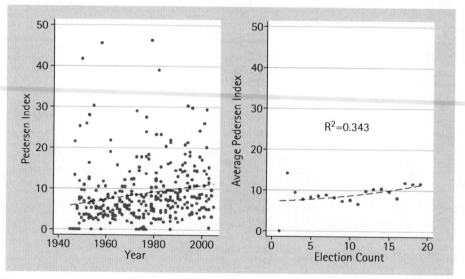

Fig. 23.2 Electoral volatility over time

[6] The Pedersen Index measures net changes in vote share using the formula: $0.5^* \sum (|V_{i,t} - V_{i,t-1}|)$, where V_i = vote share of each party i, and t = current election. There is some disagreement in the literature over how to calculate net vote share for new political parties. For example, if Party A and Party B merge to create Party C, should volatility be calculated as $V_{C,t} - V_{(A+B),t-1}$ or simply as V_C? Similarly, should fringe parties that are often tabulated in the "other" category be ignored altogether or treated as one bloc? In this chapter, we use the total vote share of Party C as the value of vote swing, and—following Lijphart 1994—ignore fringe parties altogether. This choice is motivated by the difficulty of keeping full track of which parties are merging/splitting in any given election, especially where different factions of the original party are amalgamated into separate parties.

[7] While the line of best fit is calculated using a quadratic regression, the slope appears to be constant over time, indicating that volatility is increasing linearly.

These disparate trends in the data are indicative of changes in the nature of the relationship between parties and voters in advanced industrial democracies. The question is how we are to understand these transformations. A useful theoretical guideline is provided by Otto Kirchheimer (1966), who predicted three interconnected changes to the party–voter linkage: a reduction in the party's adherence to stringent ideologies, a de-emphasis in the party's electoral reliance on particular social classes or denominations, and the strengthening of the party leaders' organizational authority over individual party members. In recent years, the comparative politics literature has identified change along each of these dimensions. Here, we broadly group these indicators into two subcategories, each with different implications for the future.

On one side of the party–voter nexus is a gradual shift in the distribution and content of the electorate's *policy preferences*, and the powerful challenge that this poses to the continuing popularity of existing political parties. In Lipset and Rokkan's framework, the primary electoral cleavage which emerged in all states derived from the industrial revolution: the historical ideological confrontation between capitalism and socialism, and the class conflict between workers and the owners of capital.[8] In the electoral arena, this conflict focused increasingly on practical policy debates on the appropriateness and scope of government intervention in the economy, with parties of the left advocating high levels of welfare redistribution and state intervention in the economy, while parties of the right advocated the welfare-maximizing properties of free market outcomes.

In recent years, however, some authors have pointed to the increasing political salience of distributional conflicts which cannot be easily understood in traditional "left–right" terms, as the world's most economically developed democracies become more oriented towards service production, and more integrated into international economic networks (Rodrik 1997; Iversen and Wren 1998). Others argue that at high levels of economic development and security, the salience of distributional conflict itself declines, making way for "postmaterialistic" concerns about quality of life issues such as the environment and personal autonomy (Inglehart 1977, 1997). These changes in preference are forcing a transformation in the *expressive content* of political parties, particularly in the range of policies that governments pursue. Where parties cannot adjust their policy platforms to the evolving concerns of voters, we can expect electoral volatility to continue—at least until new parties emerge to take their place.

Of perhaps more significance in the long run, however, is the *organizational* and *institutional* transformation of political parties in general, and the fraying of the connective tissue binding voters to parties in particular. In the idealized form, the mass party model was once efficient because deeply embedded party–voter linkages benefited both sides of the transaction. Voters could rely on parties to inform them about current policy debates and simplify choices between candidates at the polls. Political parties could listen to their grassroots networks to get a sense of prevailing

---

[8] The pattern of secondary cleavages, on the other hand—reflecting historical conflicts over religion, territorial issues, or rural–urban divides—varied from country to country depending on their individual history.

winds in public sentiment, and more importantly, benefit electorally from having a readily mobilized voting bloc. Two, largely exogenous changes in the electoral environment have challenged this mass party structure: improvements in the educational level of voters, and innovations in marketing and advertising technology, particularly public opinion polls and the television. Armed with these new tools, voters can now gather political information cheaply through non-party sources, and parties no longer have to maintain a massive grassroots organization to mount an effective national campaign (Dalton and Wattenberg 2000). In other words, it is argued that the usefulness of mass party organizational strategies has declined for both politicians and voters, creating incentives on both sides for their abandonment.

Although these two trends are not mutually exclusive, the primacy of either one draws different implications for the future of the party–voter linkage. Whereas the inability to match changes in the electorate's policy preferences is problematic for *existing parties*, changes in political capabilities represent a fundamental shift in the density of ties connecting voters to *all political parties*. The former leaves the door open for eventual ideological *re*alignment and long-term electoral stability, while the latter predicts greater fluidity in voter–party allegiances and permanent electoral *de*alignment. Table 23.1 depicts the causal logic and observable implications of both hypotheses in greater detail.

In this chapter, we re-evaluate the literature on re- vs. dealignment and offer our own predictions regarding the future of the party–voter linkage. In the next section, we discuss the argument that socioeconomic and demographic shifts are causing the worsening performance of traditional parties. The old guard has purportedly failed to adapt to the evolving concerns of voters, leaving them vulnerable to electoral attack from new entrants. Section 3 describes recent changes in parties' organizational structures and their implications for the electoral performance of traditional parties, and the stability of electoral outcomes more generally. In Section 4 we report the results of a statistical analysis designed to investigate the effects of electoral competition and organizational change on the performance of traditional mass parties. Section 5 presents our conclusions and some directions for future research.

Table 23.1   Realignment vs. dealignment

Theory	Stimulus	Short-term implication	Response	Long-term implication
Realignment	Change in voter preferences	Growing ideological gap between voters and ESTABLISHED parties	Established parties adopt new policy platforms; Where slow, new parties take their place	Stabilization of vote fluctuations
Dealignment	Change in voter/party capabilities	Weaker affective and organizational ties between voters and ALL parties	Change in party organization: declining relevance of party activists and more "national" or centrist policies	Continuing vote fluctuations; declining voter turnout

To tip our hand early, we believe that the empirical ledger is tilted in favor of dealignment. The indications are that recent increases in electoral instability are symptomatic of more than a short-term readjustment of the party system to changing electoral preferences—although there is little doubt that such an adjustment is occurring. Rather they stem from underlying changes in the organizational structure of political parties themselves. We also note, however, that trends in electoral volatility do not seem to have much effect on the stability of government composition more generally. As such, the broader political implications of increased electoral instability may be less significant than is sometimes claimed.

2 CHANGES IN THE POLICY PREFERENCES OF VOTERS

In standard theories of parliamentary behavior, voter preferences are assumed to be exogenous and fixed, while parties are reactive "second movers" who strategically choose policy platforms which maximize their political appeal. Early spatial models latched onto the idea of "issue congruence," wherein voters select political parties which advocate policies that are closest to their own preferences, and parties respond by crafting platforms which cater to the largest number of voters. Under certain conditions— most notably unimodal, left–right voter preferences and a first-past-the-post electoral system—parties should converge around the median voter and adopt centrist platforms (Downs 1957). More recent models of "directional" voting, on the other hand, assume that voters generally have vague policy preferences, and that their choices are determined by the direction and intensity of a party's promises—leading to ideological divergence, rather than convergence, among parties (Rabinowitz and Macdonald 1989; Iversen 1994). Under both models, however, the *mechanism* of ideological formation is identical: parties advocate policies which allow them to capture the largest segment of voters (Stokes 1999).

For much of the late nineteenth and twentieth centuries, the primary ideological cleavage in electoral competition formed along the left–right economic dimension. Socialist parties forged close alliances with labor unions and emphasized workers' interests—particularly lower unemployment and economic security—in their policy platforms. Conservative parties, on the other hand, maintained strong ties to capital owners and tended to advocate conditions better suited for business development and capital investment. While the ideological separation between the two groups was not hard and fast, numerous studies have found empirical evidence of distinctive partisan patterns in the policy outputs of governing parties which relate to the preferences of these parties' core constituencies (Hibbs 1977; Alesina and Rosenthal 1995).

Beginning in the 1970s, however, there has been a gradual shift in the distribution of policy preferences within the electorate. Most critical is the declining salience of the left–right economic cleavage as traditionally understood. This has occurred partially as a function of demographic changes. There is evidence that the social anchors of traditional partisanship have been eroding since the 1970s, with white-collar workers and a "new middle class" of service sector workers replacing farmers and laborers as the key socioeconomic segments of the electorate (Mair, Muller, and Plasser 2004). These changes have been associated with a decline in traditional class-based voting in many countries (Clark and Lipset 2001).

Alongside these demographic trends are changes in the debate over issues of economic organization, and in the range of alternatives under consideration. With the collapse of communism in Eastern Europe, debates over the relative merits of capitalism and socialism have been replaced by discussions as to how best to manage the national economy in an internationally integrated economic environment. The increased openness of capital markets in particular has placed significant restrictions on national governments' abilities to pursue independent fiscal and monetary policies (Simmons 1998; Boix 2000). In many countries, responsibility for monetary policy has been delegated to politically independent central banks in an effort to counteract inflationary pressures (Grilli, Masciandoro, and Tabellini 1991). For national governments in EU member states, meanwhile, the constraints on independent action have been made even tighter by the establishment of an independent European Central Bank and the adoption of a single currency. The balance of evidence from numerous empirical studies suggests that while these constraints have been insufficient to remove distinct patterns of partisanship in economic policy making, the size of these effects has declined in recent decades (Wren 2006).

Empirical evidence also suggests that on economic issues, party ideologies are showing signs of convergence. Using data from the Comparative Manifesto Project, Budge, Robertson, and Hearl (1987) posit that electoral manifestos are converging towards the center on the left–right economic scale. Caul and Gray (2000) find that the left–right distance between major parties has declined in ten out of fifteen advanced democracies, and that this centralization has been most pronounced in majoritarian electoral systems, where centripetal pressures on policy are most powerful. Closer analysis adds the important caveat that this trend is not unilinear: Volkens and Klingemann (2002) show that the ideological distance between parties decreased 1940–60, increased 1970–80, and has been decreasing again since the late 1980s. In general, however, both the degree of polarization (the salience of the left–right spectrum) and the range of ideology (distance between the leftmost and rightmost parties) appear to have been higher in the 1940s than in the 1990s. Ezrow (2005) suggests that this gradual centralization may be a vote-maximizing strategy, as centrist parties tended to win slightly more votes between 1984 and 1998.

As parties moderate their ideologies, the scope of policies offered to voters has narrowed. The moderation of party platforms has, in turn, led to more centrist *governments*. Figure 23.3 displays diachronic trends in the ideological composition of the first cabinet that forms after an election, relative to the last cabinet in power before the election. While government turnover also occurs between elections, examining ideological change *across* elections allows us to see how the initial shake-up in parliamentary seats affects which actors seize power. Governments are coded "1," "2," or "3," depending on whether a majority of the cabinet's portfolio is held by right-wing, centrist, or left-wing parties, respectively.[9] The graphs on Figure 23.3 separate data points into cases where the government preceding the election was leftist, centrist, or rightist (pre-ideology), and tracks changes in the direction of the next government's ideology (post-ideology). The data indicate a clear trend towards more centrist governments, particularly since the 1970s. In other words, both conservative and socialist governments are veering to the center, while centrist governments are holding steady.

The decline in the salience of the left–right economic divide (as traditionally defined) has also allowed room for secondary cleavages to increase in electoral significance. This change was predicted by Inglehart (1977, 1987, 1997), whose early work identified a "value change" in advanced industrial societies associated with the increased prosperity and economic security in the post-Second World War era. With their material needs met by economic development and the expansion of the welfare state, younger generational cohorts are purportedly prioritizing "lifestyle" issues such as the environment and individual liberty over more traditional material concerns. Importantly, Inglehart's work with public opinion data shows that these

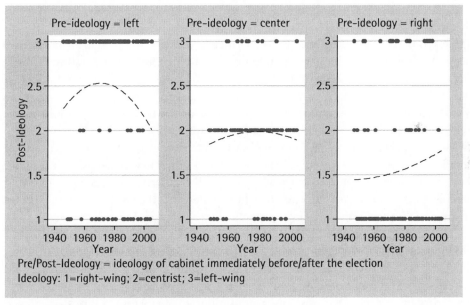

Pre/Post-Ideology = ideology of cabinet immediately before/after the election
Ideology: 1=right-wing; 2=centrist; 3=left-wing

Fig. 23.3 Trends in Cabinet Ideology Across Elections

[9] More formally, the ideological balance of cabinet is coded as: 1=conservative parties control at least 51% or superplurality of cabinet positions; 2=centrist parties control at least 51% OR there is a left–right alliance where each side controls at least 33% of cabinet; 3=leftist parties control at least 51% or superplurality of cabinet. Superplurality is defined as holding more portfolio positions than the other two factions combined, e.g. not counting independents, % of left >% center +% right. Data on government composition and political party ideology are taken from Woldendorp, Keman, and Budge 2000 and the Comparative Political Data Set (Armingeon et al. 2005).

value changes tended to persist even as the post-war cohort aged, indicating the existence of a permanent shift in the electoral landscape (1987, 1997).

There are grounds for arguing that Inglehart's thesis—that the salience of "material" issues in advanced industrial democracies is declining—is overstated. Iversen and Wren (1998), for example, point out that the transition to a services-based economy confronts societies with stark new sets of distributional choices which cannot be easily understood in terms of traditional economic cleavages between "left" and "right." Similarly, several authors point to the increased significance of political conflict over globalization and, in particular, over perceived tradeoffs between economic openness, employment, and welfare state protection in Western democracies (Rodrik 1997). Kitschelt (1994, 1995) argues that electoral cleavages over "non-economic" issues of the environment or immigration are actually intimately linked with new sets of economic cleavages in post-industrial societies. The traditional left–right economic divide has shifted to incorporate this new dimension so that it now ranges from "left-libertarian"—concentrated among workers who are relatively sheltered in the new economic environment and who tend to espouse "postmaterial" values—to "right-authoritarian"—concentrated among those who perceive their welfare and economic security as threatened by recent economic changes, particularly economic openness.[10]

Traditional parties have been sluggish in their response to these socioeconomic changes, leaving open policy space for new parties to capture. While the entry of new parties into the political arena is by no means a novel trend, the proportion of elections with new parties has certainly been on the rise in recent decades. Of fifty-one elections during the 1950s, 27.5 percent saw at least one new party compete.[11] While this ratio held steady through the 1970s, it began to rise sharply in the 1980s, when 30.0 percent of elections had at least one new party, and even more in the 1990s, when 47.3 percent of elections saw new competition.

The new parties which have emerged in recent decades can be divided into three broad categories, centered around issues which were either new or neglected by existing parties. First are what Kitschelt (1994) calls left-libertarian parties, represented most notably by the Ecologists or Greens, whose emergence correlates with the rise of postmaterialist concerns over environmental degradation and nuclear energy.[12]

The second grouping is the New Radical Right, a mostly European phenomenon closely associated with emerging concerns over immigration from developing countries. The New Radical Right's electoral strategy is to capture policy space left empty by the increasing centralization of the traditional parties' platforms (Kitschelt 1995). While these parties—represented most (in)famously by Le Pen's Front National in France,

[10] Benoit and Laver (forthcoming), in their recent expert survey covering forty-seven countries, also find evidence that the "left–right" dimension is increasingly interpreted in terms of ecological as well as economic issues in many countries.

[11] There is some disagreement in the literature over how to code a genuinely new party—particularly whether one should count the merger of two parties into one as a new entity (Hug 2001; Tavits 2006). Here, we do not discriminate between types of parties, and count all splits, mergers, and genuinely new parties. The one caveat is that we only count parties that win at least 1% of the vote or one seat in parliament.

[12] There are also several new socialist and communist parties, which are seen as competitors to traditional social democrats on both the left–right and libertarian–authoritarian dimensions.

Haider's FPO in Austria, and Pim Fortuyn in the Netherlands—are best known for their xenophobic stance towards immigrants, their overall electoral strategy is more nuanced, as they adopt firm conservative principles in support of market liberalism which appeal to independent shop owners and conservative businessmen.

The third category is regionalist parties, which espouse greater political independence of their territories from the central government without necessarily staking ideological positions on the left–right debate. Found most commonly in fragmented polities, De Winter (1998) argues that the best predictor of regional party success is the level of linguistic fractionalization—think Belgium and Spain—and to some extent, regional wealth—richer regions generally want more autonomy.

Figure 23.4 shows diachronic trends in the entry of new political parties, looking at parties with discernible ideological trends that tilt left and right, as well as those that are largely centrist. The left–right categorization is based not only on traditional class conflicts, but also on a libertarian–authoritarian dimension including environmentalism on the left and immigration on the right. Regionalist parties with distinct positions on the left–right cleavage are included within this taxonomy, but those that primarily advocate regional autonomy are excluded, since the particulars of regional political competition tend to be very country specific.

Figure 23.4 offers some interesting insights. First, the steady increase in the number of left-libertarian parties is driving the rise in the total number of new parties. In the post-war period, leftist parties constituted 52 percent of new parties which entered electoral competition. This resonates with Inglehart's (1987) argument that postmaterialist voters tend to line up on the left side of the ideological spectrum, thereby prompting the entry of proportionately more leftist parties over time. Second, centrist parties show the least amount of diachronic fluctuation in the number of new entries. Restricting the data to

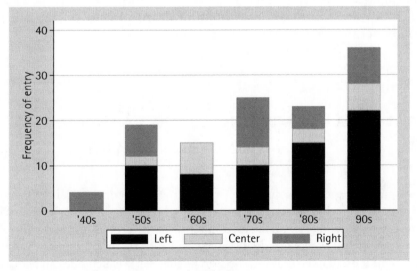

Fig. 23.4 Frequency of new party entry by ideology

between 1950 and 2000, the average number of new centrist parties per decade is 4.4, with a maximum of seven (in the 1960s) and a minimum of two (in the 1950s). The frequency of entry by new right-wing parties, on the other hand, displays the greatest level of instability. There was an average of 6.2 new conservative parties per decade between 1950 and 2000, but this ranged from zero new parties in the 1960s to eleven in the 1970s.

The increase in the number and ideological distribution of new parties provides some support for the hypothesis that the faltering performance of traditional parties stems partly from their failure to adapt to socioeconomic change. In line with Inglehart's hypotheses, it appears that old-guard parties, competing for centrist votes in traditional "left–right" terms, have been most consistently vulnerable to attack from new left parties with platforms focused on postmaterialist issues. It remains to be seen whether increases in the number of new right parties observed in the 1990s—associated with increased distributional concerns over economic globalization, and immigration more specifically—will persist in the coming decades.

Changes in vote preferences, however, cannot fully account for patterns of electoral volatility over the last few decades. Under the mass party model, the socialization of voters into enduring political identities ensured that changes in vote share would occur only when there were radical demographic shifts in the primary constituencies of the established parties. Given that shifts of this magnitude transpire slowly, we would expect the associated vote fluctuations to be relatively low and stable, at least to the extent that the voter–party linkage remains strong. At the same time, if new political parties have been successfully capturing disenfranchised voters, then their entry should lower volatility over time. However, as we saw from the scatter plots in Figure 23.2, electoral volatility has in fact increased at a fairly steady rate over the past forty years. This suggests that what we are observing is not simply preference divergence between voters and parties, but rather a more permanent *organizational* detachment between the two. In the next section, we discuss the more fundamental changes which are occurring in the nature of the party–voter linkage and their implications for the performance of the traditional parties.

3   ORGANIZATIONAL CHANGES TO THE PARTY–VOTER LINKAGE

The demographic explanation discussed in the last section cannot explain why existing parties cannot simply inculcate new members into their fold. The obstacles to this kind of strategic flexibility may be understood in terms of the *organizational rigidity* of the mass party model. If voters are tightly embedded into the institutional structure of specific political parties, the only question on polling day is which side can better coax their partisans to show up. In effect, election outcomes turn on shifting patterns in unionization or disparities in regional population growth. While the mass party organization may have been an effective means of political mobilization in an era where parties could not accurately monitor trends in popular sentiment and voters had little access to political information, this institutional structure severely limited the ideological flexibility of parties and the political choices of voters.[13]

Over time, however, the organizational structure of political parties, themselves, has begun to change. At the grassroots level, membership in political parties has been in steady decline in the last three decades (Katz and Mair 1992). Comparing fourteen advanced-industrialized democracies, Scarrow (2000) finds that most countries have seen a decline in party enrollment since 1960—both in absolute terms and as a ratio of the electorate—and that this downturn has been particularly pronounced since the 1990s. While parties often inflate membership figures for marketing purposes, Scarrow also cites public opinion poll data to demonstrate that self-reported party membership has experienced a steep fall.

These findings complement the literature on the diminishing affective ties between parties and voters. Using Eurobarometer surveys, Dalton, McAllister, and Wattenberg (2002) show that while the proportion of "very" and "fairly involved" partisans have stayed fairly constant over time, many "weak" sympathizers are turning into political independents. Examining majoritarian political systems, Clarke and Stewart (1998) detect what they call a "dealignment of degree:" while the percentage of voters with strong partisan ties is declining, they are turning into weak partisans or independents, not into supporters of other parties. On a broader comparative scale, Dalton, McAllister, and Wattenberg (2000) find an increase in the *reported* willingness of voters to split tickets between parties when there are multiple elections for different levels of government at stake. In general, the evidence points to voters abandoning partisan allegiances altogether, rather than permanently switching their allegiances to different parties.

This transformation is most pronounced among younger generations, who have grown up outside the mass party organization. Dalton (2000) makes the crucial point that the proportion of youths professing strong partisan attachments has been falling far faster than for older demographic groups. Inglehart (1987) argues that the strength of partisan attachments tend to increase with age, but only amongst voters who form attachments while they are young. If this is true, then the growing ranks of disaffected youth imply even weaker party–voter linkages down the road.

Underlying this transformation are two exogenous changes to the electoral marketplace—better education and new technology—which have allowed parties and voters to divest themselves of the mass party model. Both factors have altered the extent to which voters need parties to gain information about political events on the one hand, and how much parties rely on their grassroots membership on the other. While preference changes represent a shift in the ideological congruence between voters and parties, organizational changes are a function of shifts in the *capability* of the two actors, and the extent to which both sides depend on one another to maximize political goals.

---

[13] See Mair, Muller, and Plasser (2004) for more on country-specific causes and effects of party responses to increasing electoral volatility.

From an organizational standpoint, the two key societal functions of parties have been to educate voters about policies (Duverger 1954) and simplify choices among candidates (Downs 1957). Whereas this role was valuable when workers lacked the means to gather and process political information, improvements in educational attainment and the proliferation of media outlets provide new, non-party sources of information to voters. With near-universal literacy in advanced industrialized democracies, almost everybody can follow events in newspapers, and even more easily through television, radio, and the internet. The growing pluralism in information dissemination frees voters from blindly following party cues, while also increasing the odds that voters will learn information which parties may prefer to edit out, such as poor government performance or bribery scandals.

In addition to voters no longer needing parties, parties can now mount effective national campaigns without being bound to the preferences of partisan activists. While grassroots party members once provided invaluable manpower during election campaigns (Aldrich 1995), the proliferation of television ownership since the 1970s and internet access more recently allows party elites to bypass these middlemen altogether and launch media advertisements to tap a wider audience (Farrell 2002). Indeed, Dalton, McAllister, and Wattenberg (2002) find that in almost all countries, fewer and fewer people are participating in actual campaign activities. This new organizational mobility allows parties to better adapt to the shifting ideological concerns of the electorate at large.

The influence of new technology is also reflected in the greater centralization of political parties, particularly in the coordination of electoral campaigns. One measure is the growing identification of the party label with the party *leader*. Looking at the ratio of mentions of candidates compared to parties, Dalton, McAllister, and Wattenberg (2000) find that the media now refers to leaders more frequently than to parties. Indeed, most countries now prominently feature televised party leader debates before the election (Farrell 2002).

A second change is the way in which policy platforms are crafted and disseminated during campaigns. Whereas the mass party organization used to be a crucial medium through which party elites gathered information about the policy preferences of voters, the increasing availability and reliability of opinion polls make it possible for parties to collect data from a wider segment of the electorate. The sophistication of advertising tools also allows parties to "sell" or "market" platforms based on the salient issues of the day, rather than articulating only those issues which have been popular in the past (Farrell and Webb 2000). The professionalization of campaign managers and the quantitative increase in staffers at party headquarters are symptoms of this evolution. Whereas mass parties once served as important networks connecting a vast membership organization to the elites, this more recent trend represents the transformation of parties into professional campaign agencies for individual political candidates, particularly the party leader.

One important side effect of the decline of the mass party model has been the decline in levels of voter turnout across advanced industrial democracies. Under the mass party model, party leaders could count on grassroots activists to drum up support and convince voters to show up on election day. There has, however, been a sharp decline in actual turnout figures, particularly since the 1980s. While turnout averaged 84.6 percent in the 1950s with a minimum of 71.3 percent, it has fallen to 77.3 percent since 2000 with a minimum of 59.5 percent. This drop-off stems in part from the declining mobilizational capacity of established parties. Figure 23.5 examines turnout as a function of the proportion of total votes garnered by political parties that had competed in that country's first post-war election. The correlation between turnout and the vote share of established parties is 0.293, and as the quadratic regression line indicates, there is a strong positive relationship between the two. Turnout tends to be higher when established parties dominate the electoral process; put differently, turnout is directly related to the electoral salience of these parties.

4 ELECTORAL COMPETITION, ORGANIZATIONAL CHANGE, AND THE PERFORMANCE OF TRADITIONAL PARTIES

The comparative politics literature thus provides us with two sets of hypotheses to account for the decline in vote share of traditional parties. The first focuses on socioeconomic and demographic changes in advanced industrial societies, suggesting that the failure of traditional parties to adapt to these changes and to the increased salience of new issues may be hampering their ability to compete effectively. The

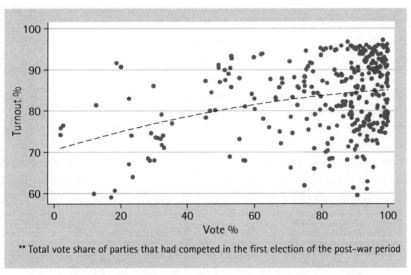

** Total vote share of parties that had competed in the first election of the post-war period

Fig. 23.5 Relationship between turnout and the vote share of established parties

second highlights a more fundamental change in parties' political and organizational roles. As new technologies play an increasingly important role as conduits of information between parties and voters, and as voters' levels of education and independently acquired political knowledge increase, the need for mass party organizations has declined. In this view, the faltering electoral performance of traditional parties and increasing volatility in voting behavior are symptomatic of a generalized decline in the relevance of the existing party model.

Disentangling the causal weight of these disparate factors is no mean feat, given that vote volatility, turnout, party membership, and new party entry all vary closely with time. We attempt to investigate these effects through a regression analysis, using *Pre-1960 Vote*, or the total vote share of all parties that had been in existence before 1960, as the dependent variable. Because pre-1960 parties were in existence during the peak periods of the "frozen cleavage" hypothesis, they represent those parties that traditionally had the strongest mass organization base. The statistical model employed is a pooled OLS regression with panel-corrected standard errors and panel-specific AR1 (autoregressive process of order 1) autocorrelation.[14] Each case in the dataset is one election in a given country after 1960, which yields a total of 220 cases among twenty advanced-industrialized democracies. The model uses "country" and "election count" as the panel and time variables, respectively.

We include two lagged variables that pertain directly to changes in the electoral and organizational viability of pre-1960 parties. To capture electoral volatility, we include *Lag Pedersen*, which is the Pedersen Index measure for vote fluctuation in the *last* period. If electoral volatility is due to vote trading between established parties, then higher values of vote fluctuation should *not* affect the collective vote shares of pre-1960 parties. On the other hand, a negative coefficient would indicate that diachronic increases in electoral volatility are in fact due to post-1960 parties stealing votes from pre-1960 groups. *Lag turnout* is a continuous variable for the proportion of the total electorate which cast a ballot in the *previous* election. Because pre-1960 parties traditionally won votes by mobilizing their grassroots membership, lower turnout may indicate a decline in their organizational capacity. If turnout is not tied to the organizational capacity of any subset of parties, however, decreasing turnout should not adversely affect pre-1960 parties any more than it does post-1960 parties. We use the lagged rather than the contemporaneous measures for both *Pedersen* and *Turnout*, because of endogeneity concerns over cause and effect.[15]

Another important independent variable is *New party count*, a discrete measure which tabulates the number of new parties that entered that given election. If it is true that the decline in the electoral performance of traditional parties reflects, in part, their failure to adapt to socioeconomic change—i.e. if new parties are capturing voters that value new policy issues neglected by traditional parties—then we should

---

[14] The AR1 specification indicates the inclusion of a lagged dependent variable.

[15] For example, vote swings of pre-1960 parties are direct, empirical components of the measure for current electoral performance, making contemporaneous values a "tainted" measure when explaining the dependent variable. The correlation between turnout and lagged turnout is 0.904, while the correlation between Pedersen and Lagged Pedersen is 0.218.

see new party entry have a negative impact on the vote share of the established parties. On the other hand, if new parties generally have little influence on overall patterns of electoral competition or are simply trading votes with one another, then their entry should have insignificant effects on the old guard's performance.[16]

A series of other variables capture trends in electoral instability. We include the dichotomous variable *Coalition* which equals "1" when a coalition government immediately preceded the election. This follows a simple empirical observation by Rose and Mackie (1983) that parties in coalition governments generally do worse in the subsequent election than those in single-party governments. While all government parties lose votes on average, the effect is stronger for coalition parties, because their supporters often see the policy deals made to support coalition governments as an abandonment of the party's electoral manifesto. *Parliamentary turnover* is a discrete variable that counts the number of changes in cabinet composition between the last to current elections. We predict that government parties will be penalized by voters should they be unable to maintain a stable cabinet.

We also include two measures for political institutions. *Electoral change* is a dichotomous variable that equals "1" where the electoral system was altered prior to the election. This is recorded when there is a change in: (1) the electoral formula (e.g. switch from plurality to PR and vice versa, or changes in the type of PR rule); (2) the mean district magnitude (change of more than 10 percent); and (3) the legal threshold of representation. Changes to the electoral system alter the framework of electoral competition and, as such, should have a negative effect on *Pre-1960 vote*, as institutional change should disproportionately harm parties which have nurtured their organizational base to maximize efficiency under the status quo system.

Effective threshold is a continuous variable that measures the effective threshold of representation, a composite index of various electoral rules which represents the difficulty of winning a seat under that electoral configuration (Lijphart 1994).[17] One of the difficulties of winning votes in plurality systems (which have higher thresholds) is that voters tend to behave more strategically by not casting ballots in favor of doomed parties, even if they prefer the doomed party to more prominent, established alternatives (Duverger 1954; Cox 1997). In theory, a higher effective threshold should allow older parties to do better, since inertial effects in favor of the status quo party system are stronger.

Finally, dummy variables for *Decade* are also included in the model to distinguish between factors that affect all countries at the same point in time, and those that affect countries at certain periods in their political maturation (as captured by the *Election count* time factor). Crucially, *Decade* also allow us to disentangle the impact of the other independent variables from a simple time trend.

[16] While models of strategic party entry generally predict that new parties should only compete when the odds of success are good, empirical studies have found that most new parties tend to do quite poorly. As of yet, there is no robust model on the correlates of initial party success (Hug 2001; Tavits 2006).

[17] The effective threshold is calculated by averaging (1) the threshold of exclusion, which is the maximum percentage of votes that a party can obtain without being able to win a seat, and (2) the threshold of inclusion, which is the minimum percentage of votes that a party can win and still gain a seat. The threshold of exclusion ($Texcl$) $= V/M+1$, where $V=$vote share and $M=$number of seats in the district. The threshold of inclusion ($Tincl$) is the higher of either (1) the legal threshold of representation, or (2) $Tincl = 100/2M$, where M=average district magnitude (Lijphart 1994).

Table 23.2 displays the regression results from the pooled OLS regression. The overall model fit is excellent, with an R-squared of 0.97. The analysis yields some interesting observations regarding the electoral competition between new and older parties, as well as the organizational capacity of the older parties themselves.

First, we can see that the entry of new parties decreases the vote share of parties that had been around before 1960, suggesting that new entrants are indeed competing successfully on new issues. The coefficient on the *New party count* variable is negative, with each additional party lowering the vote share of pre-1960 parties by 3.58 percent.

Second, the increase in electoral volatility has been more damaging to traditional parties than to newer parties. The negative coefficient for *Lag Pedersen* indicates that electoral volatility has a negative effect on the vote share of traditional parties as a group. A one standard deviation increase in *Lag Pedersen* decreases *Pre-1960 vote* by 1.85 percent. These estimates indicate that instability in election outcomes is due to older parties losing voters to newer parties, rather than simple horse-trading between established parties.

Third, the *Lag turnout* variable has a positive coefficient, such that a 10 percent decrease in turnout in the previous period decreases the vote share of established parties by 1.5 percent. This finding again points to the significance of changes in the organizational structure of traditional parties. The implication is that older parties are losing votes faster than newer parties due to their declining ability to mobilize voters on election day.

Turning to the other variables, we can see that, as expected, *Coalition* is negative while *Parliamentary turnover* is positive, although only *Coalition* is statistically significant at conventional levels. The coefficients of both institutional variables—*Effective threshold* and *Electoral change*—have signs in the predicted direction, although their substantive impact is low. The difference between the most permissive and most restrictive thresholds—0.67 in the Dutch system of nationwide PR vs. 35 under British-style single-member plurality—only equates to an increase in the vote share of pre-1960 parties by 3.5 percent. The most likely explanation for the small coefficient is that the AR1 variable (lagged *Pre-1960 vote*) already incorporates the effects of electoral threshold on voter behavior in the previous time period, and because electoral threshold rarely changes over time, the lagged variable understates the true impact of this measure. Similarly, electoral rule change, which should theoretically wreak havoc on election outcomes, only decreases *Pre-1960 vote* by 1.89 percent. This may reflect the fact that electoral rules are generally altered at times and ways that favor incumbent government parties, many of which are pre-1960 groups (McElwain 2005). The decade dummies are all significant and positive, with the size of the coefficient becoming larger the further back one goes in time. Since there were fewer "new" parties in 1960 than in 1990, it is not surprising that older parties did progressively worse as the years wore on.

In sum, this simple analysis produces a few important findings. The entry of new parties has had a significant negative impact on the vote share of parties established before 1960. The traditional parties, as a group, appear to face a genuine electoral threat from the new competitors organized around new electoral issues, which we described in Section 3. Their faltering electoral performance, therefore, may be partly

Table 23.2 Estimating the electoral performance of established political parties (1960–2002) (model: pooled OLS regression, correlated panels corrected standard errors (PCSEs))

Variable	Vote % of pre-1960 parties		Descriptive statistics		
	β	(SE)	Min/max	Mean	S.D.
New party count	− 3.576[c]	0.563	0/5	0.483	0.856
Lag Pedersen	− 0.273[c]	0.091	0/46.35	8.852	6.793
Lag turnout	0.149[a]	0.089	59/97.2	83.583	8.880
Coalition	− 2.585[b]	1.316	0/1	0.562	0.497
Parliamentary turnover	0.535	0.435	0/6	0.727	1.080
Electoral change	− 1.888[a]	1.056	0/1	0.103	0.305
Electoral threshold	0.102[a]	0.061	.67/35	11.074	11.319
1960s	11.925[c]	2.748	# of cases:	45	
1970s	8.966[c]	2.514		60	
1980s	7.239[c]	2.589		60	
1990s	3.289	2.342		55	
Constant	70.988[c]	7.711			
Wald	147.81				
N	220				
R^2	0.965				

Notes: Group variable: country (20); time variable: election count (1–24).
Panel-specific AR(1) auto-correlation; sigma computed by pairwise selection.
[a] $p < 0.1$.
[b] $p < 0.05$.
[c] $p < .01$.

attributed to a failure to compete successfully on new policy dimensions. At the same time, the close relationship between the decline in voter turnout and the electoral performance of the established parties indicates that organizational change—and in particular the scaling back of the grassroots organizations of mass parties—has also had a critical role to play. Finally, and of considerable interest, is the finding that the increase in electoral volatility has not affected all parties proportionately, but rather has had a particularly negative impact on traditional parties.

How should we interpret these results? On the one hand, we might expect to observe increased electoral volatility as a side effect of electoral realignment. That is, if party systems are currently undergoing a period of adjustment in response to socioeconomic changes, then we should see a short period of increased volatility followed by a return to vote stability as the system returns to equilibrium, when once-established parties adjust their policy platforms or new parties take their place. On the other hand, if increased electoral volatility is in fact a symptom of more fundamental changes in party organizations, and in the nature of the voter–party relationship, then there is no reason to expect a reduction in volatility over time. Indeed, the statistical analysis shows support for both positions: new parties are entering the electoral arena and taking votes away from established parties, but at the same time, political mobilization—the hallmark of the "mass party model"—is declining overall and harming the electoral bottom line of the old guard.

Adjudicating between these two forces is a challenging task for future research, and lies beyond the scope of this essay. We can, however, investigate some empirical indicators which allow us to discern "trends within trends." Specifically, while electoral volatility may be on the rise, we can examine whether the *rate* of increase is high or low; put differently, are increases in volatility accelerating or holding steady? We conduct a simple test by comparing Pedersen Index values at time (t) with lagged Pedersen values at time (t−1). The correlation between the contemporaneous and lagged values is only 0.218, indicating that vote fluctuations in one time period do not allow us to infer a great deal about fluctuations in the next period. The standard deviation for $Pedersen_{(t)} - Pedersen_{(t-1)}$ is much larger (8.553) than the mean (0.504), attesting to the high instability in electoral volatility. Figure 23.6 analyzes the rate of change in electoral volatility by displaying the difference between the contemporaneous and lagged measures, excluding elections that followed a major electoral rule change.[18] The data suggest that the rate of increase in electoral fluctuations is holding steady over time, giving us no reason to believe that

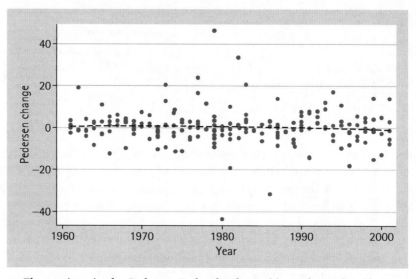

Fig. 23.6 Fluctuations in the Pedersen Index [Pedersen(t)−Pedersen(t−1)]

[18] Including cases following electoral rule change does not significantly change results, but this operationalization better captures natural trends in electoral volatility independent of *institutional* volatility.

electoral volatility will decline any time soon. Importantly, there is no indication of electoral stabilization *despite* the increasing number of new political parties (described in Figure 23.4). Based on the limited data available here, what we seem to be observing is steady *dea*lignment, rather than cyclical realignment.

5 CONCLUSIONS

Parties play a crucial role in parliamentary politics, and its purported decline—operationalized here and in other works by an electoral volatility index—has been the focus of numerous studies of electoral and legislative behavior. Scholars have identified two parallel trends in the linkage between parties and voters. First, voters are showing weaker partisan identification with political parties, and there appears to be a widening gap between the policy preferences of voters and the electoral manifestos of parties. Second, improvements in educational attainment and innovations in media technology are strengthening the political capability of both parties and voters, making it unnecessary or undesirable for both groups to be locked into a mass party structure. These two changes are interconnected, one symptom of which is the increasing centralization of party platforms in favor of the median voter: the availability of advertising tools allows parties to tap a national audience for votes (capability change), but is also exacerbating the ideological distance between parties and voters (preference drift).

These two explanations have different implications for the future of the party–voter linkage. If preference change is the main culprit for electoral instability, we should see an eventual decline in vote volatility once existing parties realign and adapt to the evolving policy preferences of voters, or when new parties emerge to take their place. If electoral instability is driven by changes in the political capability of voters and parties, however, then the organizational ties between the two groups will continue to fray, and current vote fluctuations can be interpreted as a precursor to permanent partisan *dealignment*.

In this essay we have analyzed the causal weight of these divergent hypotheses. The literature suggests that new parties typically take advantage of ideological niches left unoccupied when older parties veer to the political center, leading to the proliferation of parties espousing "postmaterialist" values. Our statistical analysis confirms that older parties are progressively losing votes to newer groups, but equally important, that established parties are failing to ensure that their supporters turn out on polling day. Coupled with the fact that trends in electoral volatility—the rate of change in vote fluctuations—have held steady over time, the preponderance of evidence seems to point to long-term dealignment rather than temporary realignment.

While cross-national regressions are one way to study the effects of new parties on electoral competition, to truly understand the salience of new political parties, we must develop a better understanding of how they are structured internally. In theory, new parties should be organized in a way that best matches the preferences and capabilities of voters at the time of that party's inception; the organizational structure of older parties, on the other hand, may reflect historical baggage from the incentive structure of previous time periods. To play devil's advocate, if successful new parties develop a mass organization rather than a catch-all structure, we could infer that the full mobilization model of older parties is still relevant and that recent trends in electoral volatility do not necessarily indicate dealignment.

One way of settling this debate is to develop a "life-cycle model" of political parties. While there has been intriguing new research on *when* parties form, there is less information about what determines their initial success, how their organizational structure changes over time, and what factors explain their lifespan. This requires comprehensive data on the membership rolls, internal by-laws, ideological composition, and electoral strategies of new parties, but also of established parties which are currently dominant but were once young themselves. Most studies of electoral and party politics begin in the post-war period (as we do), but it is difficult to understand the evolution of new parties without knowing how parties which were small at their inception gradually became larger.

This distinction between small and large parties is more than just a matter of votes, since the organizational foundations of electoral success differ between parties of different size. Kirchheimer (1966), for example, argues that only large, nationally competitive political parties should adopt a catch-all structure, since smaller parties espousing relatively extreme or new ideological positions would be better off allying closely with the niche bloc of voters that care passionately about these issues. Maintaining a mass organization structure becomes problematic only when the ideological diversity within the party expands or the membership balloons to an unmanageable size, but new parties, particularly postmaterial groups, are still relatively small. As such, it is difficult to infer how they will adjust their organizational foundation should they become successful, especially if Inglehart is correct in predicting an expanding voter base with postmaterialist values.

Finally, while electoral volatility is an interesting phenomenon in its own right, it is by no means clear whether this should lead to a more fundamental change in party politics. On the one hand, the demobilization of mass parties, the increasing salience of postmaterialist values, and/or changes in the content of ideological debates over the economy may all change the issues discussed and policies legislated in parliament. On the other hand, instability in the electorate does not necessarily indicate instability in government composition and formation. The entry of new parties may diminish the electoral salience of established parties, but are these new parties increasingly entering government or causing more rapid turnovers in government composition?

This query lies at the heart of Peter Mair's distinction between party change and party *system* change. Party changes occur when the vote distribution between existing parties with similar ideological positions fluctuates, such as when socialist and communist parties trade votes. This does not change the overall pattern of political competition, however, since the left vs. right cleavage is preserved. Party *system* change, on the other hand, entails a shift in the cleavage structure of politics or in patterns of government formation. For example, if a dominant centrist party loses votes to both left- and right-wing parties, the ideological basis of political competition becomes more polarized. Alternatively, when a majoritarian party that competes against a coalition of smaller parties splits, creating a new system where two latent coalitions are vying for power, the basis of government formation is altered. A good example is Ireland in the late 1980s, when the Progressive Democrats split from Fianna Fáil, weakening the latter's claim of being a viable majoritarian party and setting up coalition alternatives of Fianna Fáil-PD vs. Fine Gael-Labour. In general, party change appears to be more frequent than party system change, leading Peter Mair to argue that electoral volatility is not fundamentally altering the foundation of political competition (Mair 1997; Mair and Mudde 1998).

Figure 23.7 gets at this distinction between party change and party system change by displaying trends in the frequency of cabinet turnover between elections.[19] Cabinets are far from stable in parliamentary systems: opposition parties can orchestrate a government coup by passing a vote of no confidence, or the cabinet may dissolve itself strategically to redistribute ministerial portfolios and spread the wealth among more MPs (Mershon 2002). One of the implications from the literature on electoral volatility is that the prevalence of new parties should decrease government longevity, since newer parties lack the expertise and long-standing relations with other parties that make it possible to keep governments intact. The left panel of Figure 23.7 shows, however, that

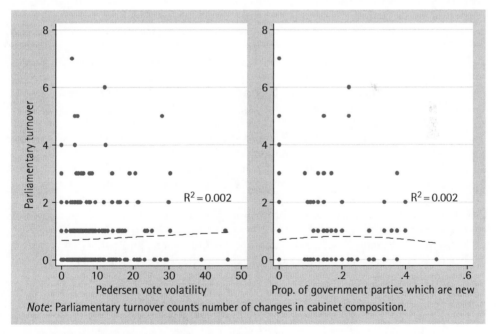

Note: Parliamentary turnover counts number of changes in cabinet composition.

Fig. 23.7 Components of government stability

[19] Cabinet change is recorded whenever the executive is replaced or a new party enters/leaves the existing cabinet. This coding follows Woldendorp, Keman, and Budge (2000).

government stability is independent of *electoral* stability, as measured by vote volatility. The right panel depicts the relationship between the proportion of total government parties that are new (defined as never having been in government) and cabinet stability, and this, too, indicates that government stability is independent of new party entry.

While there are other ways to measure government effectiveness—examining policy outputs and macroeconomic performance come to mind—this figure suggests that the doom and gloom surrounding normative evaluations of electoral volatility may be overblown. Indeed, to the extent that older parties still occupy most cabinet positions, the decline in their relative vote shares may simply signify the desire to shed electoral fat, or organizational capacity that is irrelevant to legislative power. Restated, the question is whether parties are becoming leaner and meaner vs. thinner and weaker. While the relative stability in government composition speaks to the former, we trust future research to better explicate the causes and effects of changes to the party–voter linkage.

References

ALDRICH, J. H. 1995. *Why Parties? The Origin and Transformation of Political Parties in America*. Chicago: University of Chicago Press.

ALESINA, A., and ROSENTHAL, H. 1995. *Partisan Politics, Divided Government, and the Economy*. Cambridge: Cambridge University Press.

ARMINGEON, K., LEIMGRUBER, P., BEYELER, M., and MENEGALE, S. 2005. Comparative political data set 1960–2003. Institute of Political Science, University of Berne.

BENOIT, K., and LAVER, M. Forthcoming. *Party Policy in Modern Democracies*. London: Routledge.

BOIX, C. 2000. Partisan governments, the international economy, and macroeconomic policies in OECD countries, 1964–93. *World Politics,* 53: 38–73.

BOWLER, S., FARRELL, D. M., and KATZ, R. S. 1999. Party cohesion, party discipline, and parliaments. Ch. 1 in *Party Discipline and Parliamentary Government,* ed. S. Bowler, D. M. Farrell, and R. S. Katz. Columbus: Ohio State University Press.

BUDGE, I., ROBERTSON, D., and HEARL, D. eds. 1987. *Ideology, Strategy, and Party Change: Spatial Analyses of Post-War Election Programmes in 19 Democracies*. Cambridge: Cambridge University Press.

CAMERON, D. 1984. Social democracy, corporatism, labor quiescence, and the representation of economic interest in advanced capitalist society. Pp. 143–78 in *Order and Conflict in Contemporary Capitalism,* ed. J. H. Goldthorpe. Oxford: Clarendon Press.

CAMPBELL, A., CONVERSE, P. E., MILLER, W. E., and STOKES, D. E. 1960. *The American Voter*. Chicago: University of Chicago Press.

CARAMANI, D. 2003. The end of silent elections: the birth of electoral competition, 1832–1915. *Party Politics,* 94: 411–43.

—— 2000. *The Societies of Europe: Elections in Western Europe since 1815*. London: Macmillan Reference Ltd.

CAUL, M. L., and GRAY, M. M. 2000. From platform declarations to policy outcomes: changing party profiles and partisan influence over policy. Pp. 208–37 in *Parties without Partisans: Political Change in Advanced Industrial Democracies,* ed. R. J. Dalton and M. P. Wattenberg. Oxford: Oxford University Press.

CLARK, T. N., and LIPSET, S. M. 2001. *The Breakdown of Class Politics: A Debate on Post-Industrial Stratification.* Baltimore: Johns Hopkins University Press.

CLARKE, H. D., and STEWART, M. C. 1998. The decline of parties in the minds of citizens. *Annual Review of Political Science*, 1: 357–78.

COX, G. 1987. *The Efficient Secret: The Cabinet and the Development of Political Parties in Victorian England.* Cambridge: Cambridge University Press.

—— 1997. *Making Votes Count: Strategic Coordination in the World's Electoral Systems.* Cambridge: Cambridge University Press.

—— and McCUBBINS, M. D. 1993. *Legislative Leviathan: Party Government in the House.* Berkeley and Los Angeles: University of California Press.

DALTON, R. J. 2000. The decline of party identifications. Pp. 19–36 in *Parties without Partisans: Political Change in Advanced Industrial Democracies*, ed. R. J. Dalton and M. P. Wattenberg. Oxford: Oxford University Press.

—— McALLISTER, I., and WATTENBERG, M. P. 2000. The consequences of partisan dealignment. Pp. 37–63 in *Parties without Partisans: Political Change in Advanced Industrial Democracies*, ed. R. J. Dalton and M. P. Wattenberg. Oxford: Oxford University Press.

—— —— —— 2002. Political parties and their publics. Pp. 19–42 in *Political Parties in the New Europe: Political and Analytical Challenges*, ed. K. R. Luther and F. Muller-Rommel. Oxford: Oxford University Press.

—— and WATTENBERG, M. P. 2000. Unthinkable democracy: political change in advanced industrial democracies. Pp. 3–18 in *Parties without Partisans: Political Change in Advanced Industrial Democracies*, ed. R. J. Dalton and M. P. Wattenberg. Oxford: Oxford University Press.

DE WINTER, L. 1998. Conclusion: a comparative analysis of the electoral, office and policy success of ethnoregionalist parties. Pp. 204–47 in *Regionalist Parties in Western Europe*, ed. L. De Winter and H. Tursan. New York: Routledge.

DOWNS, A. 1957. *An Economic Theory of Democracy.* New York: Harper and Row.

DUVERGER, M. 1954. *Political Parties: Their Organization and Activity in the Modern State.* New York: Wiley.

EZROW, L. 2005. Are moderate parties rewarded in multiparty systems? A pooled analysis of Western European elections, 1984–1998. *European Journal of Political Research*, 44: 881–98.

FARRELL, D. M. 2002. Campaign modernization and the west European party. Pp. 63–84 in *Political Parties in the New Europe: Political and Analytical Challenges*, ed. K. R. Luther and F. Muller-Rommel. Oxford: Oxford University Press.

—— and WEBB, P. 2000. Political parties as campaign organizations. Pp. 102–28 in *Parties without Partisans: Political Change in Advanced Industrial Democracies*, ed. R. J. Dalton and M. P. Wattenberg. Oxford: Oxford University Press.

GORVIN, I. ed. 1989. *Elections since 1945: A Worldwide Reference Compendium.* Chicago: St James Press.

GRILLI, V., MASCIANDORO, D., and TABELLINI, G. 1991. Political and monetary institutions and public financial policies in the industrialized countries. *Economic Policy*, 13: 341–92.

HIBBS, D. 1977. Political parties and macroeconomic policy. *American Political Science Review*, 71: 1467–87.

HUG, S. 2001. *Altering Party Systems: Strategic Behavior and the Emergence of New Political Parties in Western Democracies.* Ann Arbor: University of Michigan Press.

INGLEHART, R. 1977. *The Silent Revolution: Changing Values and Political Styles among Western Publics.* Princeton: Princeton University Press.

—— 1987. Value change in industrial societies. *American Political Science Review*, 814: 1289–303.

—— 1997. *Modernization and Postmodernization: Cultural, Economic, and Political Change in 43 Societies.* Princeton: Princeton University Press.

IVERSEN, T. 1994. The logics of electoral politics: spatial, directional, and mobilizational effects. *Comparative Political Studies*, 272: 155–89.

—— and WREN, A. 1998. Equality, employment, and budgetary restraint: the trilemma of the service economy. *World Politics*, 50: 242–56.

KALYVAS, S. N. 1996. *The Rise of Christian Democracy in Europe*. Ithaca, NY: Cornell University Press.

KATZ, R., and MAIR, P. eds. 1992. *Party Organizations: A Data Handbook on Party Organizations in Western Democracies, 1960–1990*. London: Sage Publications.

—— —— 1995. Changing models of party organization and party democracy: the emergence of the cartel party. *Party Politics*, 11: 5–28.

KIRCHHEIMER, O. 1966. The transformation of the western European party systems. Pp. 177–200 in *Political Parties and Political Development*, ed. J. LaPalombara and M. Weiner. Princeton: Princeton University Press.

KITSCHELT, H. 1994. *The Transformation of European Social Democracy*. Cambridge: Cambridge University Press.

—— 1995. *The Radical Right in Western Europe: A Comparative Analysis*. Ann Arbor: University of Michigan Press.

KORPI, W., and SHALEV, M. 1979. Strikes, industrial-relations and class conflict in capitalist societies. *British Journal of Sociology*, 302: 164–87.

LANGE, P., and GARRETT, G. 1985. The politics of growth: strategic interaction and economic performance in the advanced industrial democracies, 1974–1980. *Journal of Politics*, 473: 792–827.

LAVER, M., and SCHOFIELD, N. 1990. *Multiparty Government: The Politics of Coalition in Europe*. Ann Arbor: University of Michigan Press.

LEWIS-BECK, M. 1988. *Economics and Elections: The Major Western Democracies*. Ann Arbor: University of Michigan Press.

—— and STEGMAIER, M. 2000. Economic determinants of electoral outcomes. *Annual Review of Political Science*, 3: 183–219.

LIJPHART, A. 1994. *Electoral Systems and Party Systems: A Study of Twenty-Seven Democracies 1945–1990*. Oxford: Oxford University Press.

LIPSET, S. M., and ROKKAN, S. eds. 1967. *Party Systems and Voter Alignments*. New York: Free Press.

McELWAIN, K. M. 2005. Manipulating electoral rules: intra-party conflict, partisan interests, and constitutional thickness. Doctoral dissertation. Stanford University.

MacKUEN, M. B., ERICKSON, R. S., and STIMSON, J. A. 1992. Peasants or bankers? The American electorate and the US economy. *American Political Science Review*, 863: 597–611.

MAIR, P. 1990. Introduction. Pp. 1–22 in *The West European Party System*, ed. P. Mair. Oxford: Oxford University Press.

—— 1997. *Party System Change*. Oxford: Oxford University Press.

—— and MUDDE, C. 1998. The party family and its study. *Annual Review of Political Science*, 1: 211–29.

—— MULLER, W. C., and PLASSER, F. eds. 2004. *Political Parties and Electoral Change: Party Responses to Electoral Markets*. London: Sage Publications.

MERSHON, C. 2002. *The Costs of Coalition*. Stanford, Calif.: Stanford University Press.

PEDERSEN, M. N. 1979. The dynamics of European party systems: changing patterns of electoral volatility. *European Journal of Political Research*, 71: 1–26.

POWELL, G. B., and WHITTEN, G. D. 1993. A cross-national analysis of economic voting: taking account of the political context. *American Journal of Political Science*, 372: 391–414.

PRZEWORSKI, A., and SPRAGUE, J. 1986. *Paper Stones: A History of Electoral Socialism*. Chicago: University of Chicago Press.

RABINOWITZ, G., and MACDONALD, S. E. 1989. A directional theory of issue voting. *American Political Science Review*, 83: 93–121.

RODRIK, D. 1997. *Has Globalization Gone Too Far?* Washington, DC: Institute for International Economics.

ROSE, R., and MACKIE, T. T. 1983. Incumbency in government: asset or liability? Pp. 115–37 in *Western European Party Systems: Continuity and Change*, ed. H. Daalder and P. Mair. Berkeley, Calif.: Sage Publications.

SCARROW, S. E. 2000. Parties without members? Party organization in a changing electoral environment. Pp. 79–101 in *Parties without Partisans: Political Change in Advanced Industrial Democracies*, ed. R. J. Dalton and M. P. Wattenberg. Oxford: Oxford University Press.

SCHATTSCHNEIDER, E. E. 1942. *Party Government*. New York: Farrar and Rinehart.

—— 1960. *The Semisovereign People: A Realist's View of Democracy in America*. Fort Worth: Harcourt Brace Jovanovich College Publishers.

SIMMONS, B. 1998. The internationalization of capital. Pp. 36–69 in *Continuity and Change in Contemporary Capitalism*, ed. H. Kitschelt, P. Lange, G. Marks, and J. Stephens. Cambridge: Cambridge University Press.

STOKES, S. C. 1999. Political parties and democracy. *Annual Review of Political Science*, 2: 243–67.

STROM, K. 1990. *Minority Government and Majority Rule*. Cambridge: Cambridge University Press.

TAVITS, M. 2006. Party system change: testing a model of new party entry. *Party Politics*, 121: 99–119.

VOLKENS, A., and KLINGEMANN, H.-D. 2002. Parties, ideologies, and issues: stability and change in fifteen European party systems 1945–1998. Pp. 143–68 in *Political Parties in the New Europe: Political and Analytical Challenges*, ed. K. R. Luther and F. Muller-Rommel. Oxford: Oxford University Press.

WATTENBERG, M. P. 2000. The decline of party mobilization. Pp. 64–76 in *Parties without Partisans: Political Change in Advanced Industrial Democracies*, ed. R. J. Dalton and M. P. Wattenberg. Oxford: Oxford University Press.

WOLDENDORP, J., KEMAN, H., and BUDGE, I. 2000. *Party Government in 48 Democracies 1945–1998: Composition-Duration-Personnel*. Dordrecht: Kluwer Academic Publishers.

WREN, A. 2006. Comparative perspectives on the role of the state in the economy. In *Oxford Handbook of Political Economy*. Oxford: Oxford University Press.

CHAPTER 24

PARTIES AND VOTERS IN EMERGING DEMOCRACIES

FRANCES HAGOPIAN

POLITICAL parties are the most important agents of political representation in modern democracies. They choose *which* voters to mobilize and *how* to mobilize them. They may seek to construct broad, loosely defined coalitions, or build support among groups with fixed linguistic, territorial, or occupational identities. They may offer voters material goods, jobs, or divisible and excludable benefits for their communities, candidates possessing charisma or other desirable personal qualities such as honesty, competence, or a strong work ethic, or a shared religion, ethnicity, social class, or set of ideas about government and society. They may, in short, appeal to voters through clientelism, patronage, or the pork barrel, personalism, or performance, or on the basis of identity, program, or ideology. Which strategies parties choose, and what explains these choices and their short- and long-term success, are the subjects of this chapter.

Several themes in the party–voter relationship are common to advanced and emerging democracies. In both, parties develop strategies to attract voters, frame policy proposals on salient issues, and present themselves as competent and pragmatic governors that share the identities and values of voters. But in many other ways, there are stark differences between the two sets of countries that afford an opportunity to address a broader set of questions about parties and their voters than we typically do in advanced democracies. In emerging democracies, where partisanship is often weak, parties are ephemeral, and party systems, properly speaking, barely exist at all, we may ask not merely what accounts for a shift in the vote share of a particular party but also how partisan cleavages emerge, on what bases parties choose to mobilize voters, and why parties are sometimes able to form stable bonds with voters where these have been elusive or unable to prevent them from loosening where they were once strong. At the same time, we face the theoretical challenge of tackling such questions with paradigms developed on the basis of the politics of industrial democracies that do not necessarily travel well. New democracies begin from a different starting point with respect to the timing of the emergence of social class voting bases and professional bureaucracies, follow episodes in which antecedent party activity was suppressed, or are attempting to lay roots in societies in which poverty and inequality are egregious, associational life weak, international economic constraints on the scope of domestic policy hard, and global communication reaches into even the most remote rural areas.

At present, we lack a general theory of how parties mobilize voters in the context of the extreme electoral fluidity of many emerging democracies. Unlike in the advanced industrial societies, where stable partisanship is understood to have arisen from sociological (especially socioeconomic, religious, or regional) categories, either organically (Lipset and Rokkan 1967) or abetted by party agency (Sartori 1969), and been reinforced by programmatic appeals, in emerging democracies where electors are poor and salient divisions within the electorate are lacking, it is assumed that parties offer voters cash payments, patronage jobs, or pork barrel projects for their communities, or that their candidates make strong personalistic appeals. In a vicious cycle, such parties lack coherence, fail to define clear programs of government, and are not rooted in the electorate, leading to weakly institutionalized and unstable party systems. Institutional configurations that place a premium on the individual reputations of candidates, which are common in many emerging democracies, are widely believed to augment the likelihood that the party–voter relationship will be unstable.

This chapter contends that such portraits of the party–voter relationship in emerging democracies are too limited, and that in order to develop better theory, we need to think more broadly about the ways in which transitions to democracy and market economies enter into the strategic calculations of parties and their representatives, alter the balance of power of key institutional and social actors, and create new issue divides that may reshape inter-party competition and transform the basis of voter mobilization. Stronger programs that appeal to more clearly defined constituencies may allow patronage-based parties to transform themselves into programmatic ones, and the decision to collude over difficult policy choices may drive once programmatic parties to develop personalistic or clientelistic linkages with voters, and their constituencies to become indistinguishable from one another.

In the sections that follow, I first describe the weak and unstable nature of the linkages between parties and voters in new democracies. Looking deeper into the thesis that the nature of the linkage may hold a clue to the stability of partisanship,

I ask the prior question of what explains partisan cleavages and party choices about which voters to mobilize. In the third section, I review familiar institutionalist and structural explanations for how parties mobilize voters. Fourth, I offer an alternative framework for understanding the mobilization strategies that parties choose that begins with an understudied strategic aspect of the party–voter relationship—the way in which inter-party competition, voter demand, and strategies for representation are linked. Finally, I assess the state of our theory and knowledge about parties and voters in emerging democracies, and offer a brief research agenda for the future.

How parties mobilize voters matters. When they do so on a clientelistic basis, governments are often unable to pass legislation responding to national emergencies (Ames 2001), elites develop an interest in blocking economic development, and public goods may go underprovided (Brusco, Nazareno, and Stokes 2004, 84).[1] An absence of programmatic differences and policy alternatives can also lead to a collapse of citizen participation and interest in politics (Hagopian 2005), and when voters fail to connect with parties, the survival of parties may be seriously jeopardized (Crisp 2000), the legitimacy of democracy in the eyes of citizens and political elites may be diminished (Kitschelt et al. 1999, 1), and democracy may become unstable (Lipset 2001, 5). At the other extreme, parties with strong identities and polarizing ideologies can exacerbate political conflict, hinder necessary policy compromise, and also threaten democracy.

1 Mobilizing Voters in Emerging Democracies: The Magnitude of the Challenge

Today's emerging democracies in Latin America, Central and Eastern Europe, Asia, and sub-Saharan Africa were swept up in the third wave of democratization (Huntington 1991) that began in the southern European countries of Portugal, Spain, and Greece in 1974. In Latin America, there were only three democracies in 1978; today, there are but two authoritarian regimes, Cuba and Haiti. Of the twenty-seven countries that emerged from communist rule in east central Europe and the former Soviet Union, only seven were rated categorically as "not free" by Freedom House in 2004. In Asia, South Korea, Taiwan, Thailand, the Philippines, and Mongolia have joined India as full democracies, while Turkey, Sri Lanka, Bangladesh,

---

[1] This is so because clientelist parties benefit from underdevelopment and the maldistribution of income given that the cost to parties of vote buying rises as incomes rise, and voters will support clientelist over programmatic parties because they will receive the public goods offered by a programmatic party whether or not they vote for it, but will receive the clientelist inducements only for voting for a clientelist party.

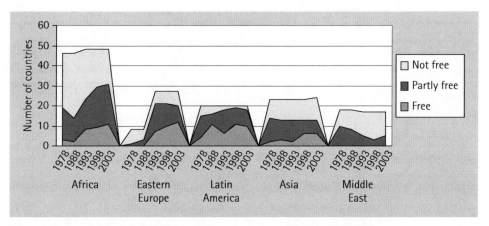

Fig. 24.1 Freedom House ratings of emerging democracies, 1978–2003

Malaysia, Singapore, Indonesia, East Timor, and Nepal have extended some political rights and civil liberties. In sub-Saharan Africa, only Botswana, Senegal, Zimbabwe, Namibia, and Mauritius held regular elections before 1990; by 1998 only four countries had *not* held some sort of competitive contest during the 1990s (Gibson 2002, 202) (Figure 24.1). These countries are self-evidently an internally diverse lot. They include former military regimes, communist regimes, and personalistic dictatorships of varying tenure. Prior to their most recent authoritarian episode some were democracies with party systems and systems of voter mobilization that could plausibly be resurrected, whereas others had little or no prior experience with democracy, no tradition of political parties, and only a very weak civil society. Gross national income per capita averaged $3,280 in Latin America, but only $450 in sub-Saharan Africa and $460 in South Asia in 2002 (World Bank 2004).

In few emerging democracies today is the relationship between parties and voters strong and stable. From Russia to Brazil, only a minority of voters identifies with parties. In 1994, the mean percentage of party identifiers in seven central and Eastern European countries was 27 and in three former Soviet republics, 15; many were so opposed to political parties that they did not intend to vote (Rose 1995, 552, 554). More recently, 37 percent of Eastern European and one-third of voters in all emerging democracies express an attachment to a party; in Asia, less than one-quarter do (Table 24.1). Even if the self-reporting of identification with parties in mass surveys is not the best way to measure partisanship and partisanship may not be as weak as appears,[2] clearly voters in emerging democracies are less attached to parties than in the industrial democracies. The average rate of electoral volatility, or the net change

---

[2] Brader and Tucker (2001, 71–2) question that partisanship in new democracies can and should be measured by party identification alone. Using the Russian case, they develop an alternative approach that identifies nascent partisanship by ascertaining (1) loyalty or stability in a voter's party choice over time; (2) consistency between a voter's party preference and her other, political evaluations; and (3) a correspondence between the interests and beliefs of the attached voter and the appeals or programs of her party.

Table 24.1 Partisanship and electoral volatility in emerging and industrial democracies

Regional means	Mean electoral volatility, lower chamber[a]	Party identification[b]
Southern Europe[c]	12.8	44.1
Eastern Europe[d]	44.0	37.3
Latin America[e]	30.0	27.7
Asia[f]	22.8	23.1
Sub-Saharan Africa[g]	28.4	–
Emerging democracy mean	30.6	34.7
Industrial democracy mean[h]	12.5	47.5

[a] Mean electoral volatility scores for sub-Saharan African countries calculate net change in party votes over at least two elections (Kuenzi and Lambright 2001), and in other regions for countries classified as "free" or "partly free" by Freedom House after 1978 that as of 2003 had had at least three consecutive lower chamber elections (Mainwaring and Torcal 2006).
[b] Rates of party identification derived from responses to two questions: "Do you usually think of yourself as close to any particular political party?" and if the respondent answers "yes," "What party is that?" The two-question format produces lower levels of partisan identification than a single question, but accurately measures cross-national variation in partisanship. Survey years are reported below in parentheses.
[c] Spain (2000), Portugal (2002); Greece (mean electoral volatility score only).
[d] Belarus (2001), Czech Republic (1996), Hungary (1998), Lithuania (1997), Poland (1997), Romania (1996), Russia (2000), Slovenia (1996), Ukraine (1998); Bulgaria, Estonia, and Latvia (mean electoral volatility only).
[e] Brazil (2002), Chile (1999), Mexico (2000), Peru (2001); Argentina, Bolivia, Colombia, Ecuador, and Venezuela (mean electoral volatility only).
[f] South Korea (2000); Taiwan (1996); Thailand (2001) (party identification only); India (mean electoral volatility only).
[g] No sub-Saharan African countries were included in the CSES data. Thirty countries are included in the mean legislative volatility score.
[h] Australia (1996), Denmark (1998), Germany (1998), Japan (1996), the Netherlands (1998), Norway (1997), Sweden (1998), Switzerland (1999), United Kingdom (1997), United States of America (1996); Canada (1997), Israel (1999), New Zealand (1996) (party identification only); Belgium, France, and Italy (mean electoral volatility only).
Sources. Electoral volatility: Mainwaring and Torcal 2006, 27–8; Kuenzi and Lambright 2001, 449. Party identification: Samuels 2006, 5 (original source, Comparative Study of Electoral Systems, available at www.umich.edu/cses).

in the party vote from one election to the next, for all emerging democracies—30.6—is two and one-half times higher than in the advanced industrial democracies today, nearly seven times higher than it was in the United States from 1948 to 1996, and three and one-half times higher than it was in thirteen European democracies 1885–1995 (Bartolini and Mair 1990, 68, cited in Roberts and Wibbels 1999, 576). Average rates of electoral volatility for lower Chamber elections have reached 44.0 in Eastern Europe; 30 in Latin America; 22.8 in India, South Korea, and Taiwan; and 28.4 in thirty countries in sub-Saharan Africa that had had at least two multiparty elections in the 1990s. In only five African nations—Botswana, Gambia, Namibia, Senegal, and South Africa—are party systems institutionalized with regular party competition and stable parties in the electorate, and do citizens and organized interests perceive that parties and elections determine who governs (Mainwaring and Scully 1995; Kuenzi and Lambright 2001, 461, 442).

Electoral volatility in emerging democracies is driven in part by the rising supply of parties, but upstart parties would not experience even fleeting success at the polls if voter attachments to parties were stronger. Parties of patronage, which characteristically are linked to voters only loosely, are alleged to be far more prevalent in these democracies than parties of program. Anecdotally, clientelist and patronage politics were viewed as fundamental to partisan politics in the Philippines, Indonesia, Burma, and Malaysia (Scott 1972), Côte d'Ivoire and Senegal (Lemarchand 1972), and Mexico, Brazil, Colombia, and much of Latin America (Mainwaring and Scully 1995), but there has been little systematic research about the past and current importance of clientelism and patronage in part because such particularistic forms of party–citizen linkage are easier to charge than prove. The frequency of vote buying may be gleaned from national election surveys, where these exist and the right questions are asked, but the full extent of patronage and pork barrel projects is notoriously harder to measure, especially at the level of parties and party systems.[3] We also do not know if personalism is as widespread as believed. On the one hand, in Korea the personal and moral character of individual political leaders, not their affiliation with a political party or policy orientations, is what has mattered most to voters in every election survey since 1954 (Shin 1999, 187–8). But in Russia, where prevailing stereotypes also allege that personalism is the magnet attracting voters, assessments of personal qualities of candidates played a less prominent role in state Duma elections in 1995 than "transitional partisanship"—partisan affinity in favor of the socialist, nationalistic, governmental, or liberal parties, and in the presidential elections of 1996, citizens' issue opinions mattered most, and assessments of the personal qualities of the candidates was the least significant predictor of voting (Colton 2000, 218, 222).

The weakness of party–voter relationships is not merely a result of the newness of democracy. In nineteen new democracies, there is no statistically significant tendency toward diminishing electoral volatility over the course of four electoral periods (Mainwaring and Torcal 2006, 12), a finding that belies the standard assumption that partisanship will stabilize, according to Converse's classic socialization model (1969, 167), over a period of essentially about two and one-half generations. Moreover, despite claims that partisan loyalties are more difficult to cultivate when people gather information from the media and not from party operatives, at least one observer has dismissed the role of the media in suppressing partisanship, finding that in Korea the better people are informed, the more likely they are to develop an attachment to a political party (Shin 1999, 184–5). Similarly, there is little evidence for the "neo-corporatist" thesis, which maintains that when associational life is dense,

---

[3] Such surveys exist for only a handful of countries, including Argentina, Brazil, and Mexico. It is difficult, but possible, to investigate the budget amendments introduced by individual deputies, as Ames 2001 has done for Brazil.

citizens who have alternative channels of representation need not rely on political parties to defend their interests to the state (Schmitter 1992). Not only do examples abound of *symbiotic* relationships between parties and their social networks, including Peronist neighborhood associations in Argentina (Levitsky 2003) and the local volunteer firefighting brigades of the Polish Peasants' Party (Grzymala-Busse 2002, 125), but again in Korea, those more active in civic affairs are slightly *more* attached and favorably oriented toward parties than their less active peers (Shin 1999, 184).

In new democracies, analysts also assume that in the absence of strong party identities, retrospective evaluations of government performance will weigh heavily in the voting decisions of citizens, with high electoral volatility significantly correlated to poor performance of the economy (Mainwaring and Torcal 2006). There is no conclusive evidence that this was so in Russian presidential and legislative elections in the mid-1990s. In the state Duma election of 1995, retrospective evaluations of government performance were the least powerful predictor of voting behavior (Colton 2000, 218). In presidential elections, they mattered more, but not as much as citizens' issue opinions. In Latin America, poor government performance did erode support for incumbents and provoked high levels of electoral volatility from 1982 to 1990 amid economic crisis conditions characterized by high inflation, stagnant economic growth, and severe exchange rate depreciation (Remmer 1991). In Latin America's "lost decade" of the 1980s in a process that Coppedge (2001, 186) calls "political Darwinism," several parties that could not adapt to economic crisis conditions vanished from the political scene while others that could—personalist parties, governing parties to the right of center (that were successful in controlling inflation), and left-of-center parties in the opposition—survived. Yet, if voters in these emerging democracies were primarily retrospectively evaluating government performance, then we should expect electoral volatility to have diminished appreciably with the stabilization of prices and the resumption of economic growth in the 1990s. In fact, electoral volatility rates were *higher* in the 1990s than they were during the 1980s (23.2 and 19.6, respectively) (Roberts and Wibbels 1999, 577). A recent cross-regional study (Seligson and Tucker 2004) affirmed that votes for former authoritarian leaders appear to be correlated with authoritarian proclivities and skepticism about democracy, not the faulty performance of democratic governments.

If votes are not won and lost on the basis of media reports, the density of associational life, or yearly economic indicators, then what produces and what impedes the emergence of stable partisanship in today's new democracies? The rest of this chapter is devoted to addressing the questions of how parties decide which constituencies to target, and what determines how parties and voters are linked. But first, a caveat is in order. I proceed as though the nature of the party–voter relationship can be readily classified, but in reality, it is often difficult to distinguish a programmatic party from a non-programmatic one (both may have electoral platforms), and to establish the degree of constituency service a party's representatives must perform, and what sorts of bills they must sponsor, for a party to be considered clientelistic. Even if we could agree on the criteria for classifying this relationship, parties and individuals may *mix* strategies. In Chile, for example, highly ideological party representatives in the national legislature served as effective local brokers of clientelism in the provinces before the 1973 *coup d'état* (Valenzuela 1977), and for decades, the Argentine Peronists (Gibson 1997) and the Italian Christian Democrats made programmatic appeals to voters in some regions and clientelistic appeals to voters in others. Individual legislators often vote with their party leaders midweek and perform constituency service at the weekend. In short, we treat "programmatic," "personalistic," and "clientelistic" as discrete labels, but parties and politicians present different blends of all three, making it hard not only to fit a label to a party but also to explain why one strategy was chosen over another. It also means that different calculations may have come into play at the individual, party, and party system levels.

2 EXPLAINING PARTISANSHIP THROUGH VOTER MOBILIZATION STRATEGIES

Which constituencies do parties court? Do they seek to build heterogeneous, loose coalitions of voters, or do they target narrower but coherent groups of voters with which they expect to have a programmatic affinity, rooted for example in an economic or religious identity? Is there a relationship between who is mobilized, how they are mobilized, and how stable or successful the voter mobilization strategy is? Classically, the emergence of partisan cleavages has been explained as either springing from society's socioeconomic base (Lipset and Rokkan 1967) or as largely created by parties (Sartori 1969). For Lipset and Rokkan, four cleavages grew out of two major socioeconomic transformations—the center–periphery and religious cleavages from the national revolutions and the urban–rural and worker–capital divides from the industrial revolutions—and they shaped the European partisan landscape for decades beyond their emergence because they were deeply socially embedded. For Sartori (1969, 84, 87, 89–90), this "sociology of politics" had it backwards: Observing that some cleavages are not translated into party oppositions at all, he contended that parties were not "consequences" of class, but classes received their identities from parties. The alternatives framed by party elites explain the growing attachment of citizens to parties in the late 1970s and early 1980s in Spain (Barnes, McDonough, and López Pina 1985: 715) and the partisan cleavages that emerged after the Pinochet dictatorship in Chile (Torcal and Mainwaring 2003). Parties may be most successful in crafting partisanship when voters are not already encapsulated by well-developed social organizations (Chhibber 1999, 8, 11–13, 16).

If not every identity-based difference or even the most socially meaningful becomes a political cleavage, how do parties choose which ethnic, religious, tribal, or linguistic cleavage to make politically salient? Posner (2005) contends that because parties mobilize voters along the cleavage that will produce a *minimum winning coalition*, one with the fewest members with whom the spoils of power must be shared, this determination depends on the size of the groups a cleavage defines and whether or not the groups will be useful vehicles for political competition. In Zambia, where Chewas and Tumbukas are small minorities and not useful to mobilize as a base of social support, these two ethnic groups are allies, but just across the border in Malawi, where objective cultural differences are otherwise identical but both groups are numerically more significant and serve as viable bases for political coalition building, they are adversaries (Posner 2004). When Zambia moved from multiparty to single-party rule and back again, moreover, the effective arena of competition shifted between the national level (where broader language groups were the most salient division) and the constituency level (where tribal identities constituted the main ethnic cleavage) (Posner 2005). Chhibber (1999, 14) similarly attributed the rise of the Hindu Nationalist Party in India not to an intensification of or an increased willingness to express Hindu religiosity in Indian society, but to party appeals to a group that was not so small it was not worth courting, but also not so large that the party could not distinguish itself by endorsing a group that no other party would dare oppose.

Do politically constructed cleavages take root as deeply as those formed along the enduring fault lines of class and religion, as Lipset (2001, 7) argues? Most observers believe that programmatic or ideological linkages are more stable (cf. Mainwaring and Torcal 2006, 2), for intuitively logical reasons. Voter loyalty will not be immediately dependent upon the performance of the economy (which notoriously depends on factors beyond the control of parties and governments), the personality of candidates, or on the promise of particularistic benefits that may never arrive, but rather will be based on an attachment to a set of ideas or policy proposals that conform to a deeply rooted identity and that is likely to change only very slowly. On the other hand, where voters sell their votes to the highest bidder, or switch columns altogether based on the attractiveness of the personal qualities of particular candidates, the party is left potentially vulnerable at the polls if the goods do not arrive or when these leaders are revealed to be corrupt or pass from the scene. Unattached voters notoriously desert parties that fail in government to deliver material security and physical security from crime and politically motivated violence, especially if these were the promises on which they campaigned (Stokes 2001). Even if strong personalities are successful in office, they may undermine the development of political parties as institutions. Either way, in these cases, linkages are tenuous, party roots in society shallow, and partisanship likely to be unstable and weak.

Are personality-based and clientelist party–citizen linkages in fact an inherently unstable foundation for partisanship?[4] While the logic underpinning the assumption

---

[4] An innovative current study (Uno in progress) is studying precisely whether linkage type determines the orientation of voters to trust in parties, and party system stability, in Venezuela, Peru, and Argentina.

that personalism is an unstable basis of partisanship is unassailable, we also know that the enduring legacy of Juan and Evita Perón cemented Argentine workers for decades after their deaths to a party that turned its back on the party's core programmatic tenets. We should also not underestimate how enduring *symbolic* attachments can be to parties of national independence and revolution, such as the Algerian National Liberation Front (FLN), the Indian Congress Party, and the Mexican Institutional Revolutionary Party (PRI). It is also not self-evident that clientelism is an intrinsically unstable formula for incumbent parties. The Mexican PRI managed to stay in power for more than six decades on a foundation of vote buying and distributing pork; two of the most stable party systems in Latin America, the Colombian and the Uruguayan, were based on cross-class, catch-all parties whose original (nineteenth-century) urban–rural cleavages had long since faded and whose modern foundations clearly rested on state patronage (Collier and Collier 1991). Yet, even if these linkages may have effectively bonded voters to parties in these instances, parties that rely on these compensation mechanisms have also suffered massive voter rejection at the polls. Patronage parties become vulnerable when patronage inflation, which may follow from the logic of elections that increase the client's bargaining position (Scott 1972, 109), leads to large public deficits, inflation, and fiscal crises (cf. Mainwaring 1999, 187–90; Piattoni 2001, 25–6). When these occur, not only might voters reconsider the costs of clientelism compared with its benefits, but their tolerance also wanes for the public corruption these strategies sometimes engender.

Amid such uncertainty, we should not assume that a stable vote share necessarily rests on a consistent, programmatic strategy. A party might shore up support for its program by deploying its members to perform constituency service. Enjoying the cushion of stable partisanship, moreover, a party whose faithful were once reared on program may later convert to a clientelistic mode of mobilization. Not only can parties mix strategies, they can also change them.

3 PROGRAM, PERSONALITY, OR PATRONAGE: THE ROLE OF INSTITUTIONS AND STRUCTURES

If programmatic parties that have deeply embedded roots in civil society enjoy the electoral benefits and stability of a thick version of partisanship that only rarely breaks down, then why do parties not always make this choice? Are some parties prevented from making programmatic appeals that will eventually take root, or do they have available a better option? Shefter (1977) assumes that parties will choose patronage when they have access to state resources and an anti-patronage coalition does not exist at the time of the opening of the franchise, and Kirchheimer (1966, 184–91) that electoral competition and the hunt for votes to secure immediate electoral victories will induce major parties to shed their "ideological baggage" and become "catch-all" parties, ones that attract cross-class support and smooth over minor differences between group claims. Przeworski and Sprague (1986, 55–60), on the other hand, contend that socialist parties that too aggressively court middle-class votes necessary for an electoral majority compromise their ability to mobilize loyal working-class constituents, and cost them their identities and ultimately more votes than they will gain.

What options are open to parties when partisanship is weak and partisan cleavages inchoate? The dominant view is that the relationship that parties forge with voters is an epiphenomenon of formal democratic institutions, especially electoral rules and other institutions that control access to office or future careers (Carey and Shugart 1995). In electoral systems in which legislators gain re-election in first-past-the-post (plurality) elections in single-member districts and they owe their offices to voters, they will provide services and projects for which they can claim credit. If, on the other hand, they owe their ballot positions to party leaders and are dependent upon the reputation of their parties, as is true in closed-list proportional representation systems in which votes are pooled, then party leaders can enforce adherence to the party program. Where politicians seek to pursue their broader career interests, they might support the agendas of national and provincial party and governmental leaders who hold the power of nomination to future posts, or cultivate support among local politicians and constituents if they seek major municipal-level elective offices in the near future (Strom 1997; Jones et al. 2002; Morgenstern and Nacif 2002; Samuels 2003). Empirical support for these propositions is found in the higher rates of party discipline in contested legislative votes in countries in which election rules foster incentives for politicians to serve the party vote, such as Argentina (Jones 2002), than in those systems in which candidate selection procedures or electoral institutions encourage legislators to focus on their personal reputations in order to compete against co-partisans, like Brazil (Ames 2002), as well as from the greater propensity of legislators to initiate and work to enact targeted bills than to introduce legislation favoring programmatic or national interests (Crisp et al. 2004, 842–4).

This powerful thesis can be challenged on several theoretical and empirical grounds. First, electoral laws may determine whether voters or party leaders hold power over legislators, but they say nothing about how they wish legislators to behave. Party leaders may want to impose strict discipline on their legislative delegations at the expense of the preferences of constituents, but in other circumstances they may expect deputies to provide constituency services as a way of bolstering overall party fortunes (Carey 1996; Swindle 2002). Party leaders may even wish to prioritize policy concessions or the goal of winning future elections over maximizing their votes in the present (Cox 1997, 170). Constituents may want a handout, jobs, assistance in cutting through red tape at government agencies, or a construction project in their district, but they may also disapprove of selling their votes for such purposes and instead prefer that their representatives vote to stabilize prices, reflate the economy, invest in health care and education, and reduce crime.[5]

---

[5] Election surveys in Brazil reveal that a slim majority of voters disapprove of selling votes for food or a job.

Second, institutional theories that privilege the impact of electoral and legislative institutions on legislative behavior imply that a uniform set of incentives creates national patterns of political representation, and make no predictions about why the strategies of individual parties or legislators would vary. Such an assumption is contradicted empirically by numerous examples of partisan and individual-level differences within the same polities. Third, its strongest predictions are about choices individual politicians must make when the interests of party leaders and constituents collide. It does not really generate sufficiently clear predictions about non-zero-sum behavior, and why individual legislators might invest in their personal reputations *and* delegate authority to party leaders to solve party coordination problems and uphold the collective reputation of their parties. Fourth, the thesis is challenged to explain changes in partisan strategies of electoral competition, voter mobilization, and political representation when electoral laws and related institutional incentives have not changed. Some scholars have had more success attributing the programmatic adaptation of parties in democratic elections in Central Europe and Latin America to other political variables, such as the internal party dynamics that frame the ability of party leaders to pull their parties in new directions (Grzymala-Busse 2002; Burgess and Levitsky 2003).

Comparative scholars who apply institutionalist analysis to the problem of mobilizing voters in emerging democracies have also understudied the origins and reform of these institutions. In the historical development of the advanced democracies, electoral rules changed when the balance of strength of old and new parties shifted (Boix 1999), suggesting that institutional constraints might not be hard and the design of rules may be up for grabs. Several structural factors might influence the power balance: party constituencies can grow or shrink in an industrial revolution that swells the ranks of manual laborers at the expense of agrarian classes or in a deindustrialization that creates hard-to-organize informal sector workers. Alternatively, exogenous shocks to a party system, such as a foreign intervention or a democratic transition, might accelerate a shift in the balance of partisan electoral fortunes. Authoritarian legacies in particular might influence both the resource endowments and interests of collective actors (Kitschelt et al. 1999, 3, 11–12; Grzymala-Busse 2002, 281), which in turn may shape the rules of the game.

A second explanation for the nature of party–voter linkages locates strategies for partisan mobilization in the context of the structural conditions of a society, and particularly, its stage of development (Huntington 1968). In the early stages of socioeconomic modernization, poor voters who lack information sell their votes cheaply in exchange for the immediate delivery of material goods rather than invest them in uncertain and distant programmatic rewards, and "parties and party systems are clientelist, patronage oriented, and localist" (Kitschelt 2000, 856–7). As a society develops, the economy grows, and people move to cities, become literate, and develop modern outlooks, parties may mobilize them on an issue-oriented and programmatic basis. In richer societies with larger public sectors, voters may expect not simple gifts but patronage jobs and expensive pork barrel projects in exchange for their votes.

In fact, poor voters in poor societies sell their votes more often than their middle-class counterparts, although this practice may be less widespread than believed,[6] and it varies a great deal according to gender, age, networks of social engagement, partisan affiliation, and context. In Benin, voters in poor areas in the north were more likely to respond to clientelistic appeals than voters in the more developed areas of the south, with men less interested in public goods, and more likely to sell their votes, than women (Wantchekon 2003). In Mexico, nearly 15 percent of respondents in a 2000 Panel Study reported receiving a gift from a political party in the presidential campaign, and these rates were higher in the poorer provinces of Oaxaca and Yucatán, among older (those 50 years of age or more), male, medium-educated, lower-income, and urban voters (Cornelius 2004, 53–4). In December 2001, about 7 percent of voters and 12 percent of poor voters in Argentina reported receiving goods from political parties in the most recent election (Brusco, Nazareno, and Stokes 2004, 70). Those more likely to go to a party organizer in case of unemployment, to have received campaign handouts, and to sell their vote had links to the Peronist party, were young, lived in small towns and cities, and were given ballots by party operatives that could be more easily monitored. They were more likely to cast ballots in exchange for clientelist favors not out of a sense of gratitude or obligation or because they heavily discount the future, but because they sought even minor payoffs in a time of neo-liberal adjustment (Brusco, Nazareno, and Stokes 2004, 75, 81–2).[7]

Why are some parties better able to reap the benefits of targeting their own constituents with clientelistic resources than others? In part, parties with strong working-class roots can better take advantage of patronage than those that draw from a middle-class voting base because the utility from patronage declines monotonically with income (or skills), and transfers to higher-income voters do not provide the same returns as those to low-income voters (Calvo and Murillo 2004, 743). Incumbent parties with greater access to state patronage can also better establish clientelist linkages because their promises of particularistic benefits are more credible than those of the opposition—an expectation confirmed in elections in Benin (Wantchekon 2003). By contrast, "externally mobilized parties" with no hope of gaining access to state resources compete on program because they have no other recourse (Shefter 1977). Thus in the patronage-soaked party systems of

---

[6] In Brazil, a country assumed to be heavily driven by clientelistic voting, only slightly more than 5% of respondents to the 2002 National Election Study reported being offered something—usually cash or a job—in exchange for their vote, but it is likely most of these pertained to local elections since no more than one-fourth of these bribes were reportedly offered in the federal deputy, senator, gubernatorial, or presidential races.

[7] In Mexico, by contrast, the electoral law reform, which assured the anonymity of one's vote, led the opposition in the 2000 election to exhort voters to "take the gift, but vote as you please," and traditional PRI voters did abandon the party (Cornelius 2004, 49).

Brazil and Uruguay, the Workers' Party and the Broad Front made electoral break-throughs on the basis of party programs. Former communist parties in the Czech and Slovak Republics, Poland, and Hungary, cut off from their sources of patronage, also had to reinvent themselves and "redeem the Communist past" by inventing new programmatic appeals to convince the electorate of their commitment to new policy choices (Grzymala-Busse 2002, 124–5).

Structural explanations for clientelism partially explain the microfoundations of clientelistic behavior but do not account for the persistence of clientelist linkages and patronage politics in Belgium, Italy, Japan, and other advanced industrial societies (Kitschelt 2000). Shefter (1977) attributes cross-national differences in party strategies for mobilizing voters to the timing of suffrage extension relative to the formation of a professional career civil service and levels of industrialization: programmatic parties emerged when the civil service became professionalized before democratization and politicians could not rely on access to public sector resources to build a base for political clientelism (the German model) and where universal suffrage was achieved after industrialization, but patronage-based parties emerged where a broad-based suffrage preceded industrialization and the civil service was not insulated from politics (the US case). This thesis leaves unexplained why some countries flirted with patronage but ultimately managed to eradicate or significantly contain it (Piat-toni 2001, 19–20, 24), why clientelism became destabilized after decades of democracy (Kitschelt 2000, 858), and why parties might shift their strategies.

At their best, both institutional and structural explanations can account for existing types of party–voter linkages, but not for how and why they change. We need to explain why some catch-all, patronage-based parties can become pro-grammatic and why some programmatic parties can effectively turn to patronage; well-institutionalized parties collapse or new ones successfully enter the fray where previously one or two parties dominated; or parties associated with discredited regimes successfully reinvent themselves. We need to consider a broader range of strategic interests, and connect the micro logic of voter preferences to partisan strategic calculations about how best to win votes.

4 FROM STRUCTURES AND INSTITUTIONS TO STRATEGIES: LINKING PARTY COMPETITION, STRUCTURAL CHANGE, AND POLITICAL REPRESENTATION

In their competition with other parties, parties in emerging democracies must choose whether to compete on the basis of program, and if so, what issues to politicize for electoral gain. They may seek to broaden or reorient their electoral programs to appeal to new voters. But they must also decide how intensely to compete, that is, how much programmatic distance they should measure out between their positions and those of their rivals. Parties may ideologically polarize or sharpen their differences over key issues of policy and program in order to distinguish themselves more sharply from their proximate rivals or in order to attract a specific share of the electoral market. Or they can narrow their differences over contentious issues that divide their constituents and are certain to lose them votes. Parties may choose especially not to reopen competition over policy change that may be "given," as in Hungary (Kitschelt et al. 1999, 180) and Chile, where democratic regimes inherited market-oriented reforms that were viewed by and large as successful, treating these in effect as valence issues. Students of advanced democracies such as Jacobson (2000) assume that parties converge on policy, or polarize as US parties did in the 1980s and 1990s, in response to voter demand. In the emerging democracies, programmatic party competition, to the extent it is studied at all, is generally not treated as an endogenous reflection of the ideological or programmatic distance between party electorates, which are *assumed* to favor patronage-based programs. Yet, the emergence of new issue areas, the progress of structural change, and the fluctuating spatial distance over program may influence party strategies for mobilizing and representing voters.

Most scholars agree that the rising salience of new issues such as the protection of human rights or the environment can prompt old parties to fall out of step with their voters and new ones to pick up their orphans, or existing parties to *realign* around these issues. In emerging democracies, regime change and market-oriented reforms or the impact of globalization stand out as such defining issues. During regime transition, cleavages may be redrawn: old ones may fade and new ones may emerge. In Chile, a brutal authoritarian regime transformed a pre-authoritarian party system based on class cleavages into one divided between the supporters of the authoritarian order and their democratic opponents. In Eastern Europe, new political, economic, and religious cleavages emerged after the fall of communism between supporters and opponents of the old communist regime; the forces of market liberalism who favored dismantling social protections and state services and those that favored retaining them; and groups favoring a greater role for religious institutions and those who held firm to the secularism of the communist past and a libertarian future, and in some socioculturally divided societies, along ethnic lines (Kitschelt et al. 1999, 64; Grzymala-Busse 2002).

Most emerging democracies have also faced the need either to create markets, reform them, or adapt them to conform better to the challenges and opportunities presented by global economic integration. Economic liberalization and the turn to market-oriented economics have reshaped the context in which political representation takes place in at least three ways. First, leftist, labor-based, and centrist Christian Democratic parties whose platforms were premised on state intervention in the economy must update their party programs and even abandon long-held ideological principles. If such *aggiornamiento* risks alienating key constituencies, these parties may shift the basis of their appeals to voters from program to the provision of personal services and community resources through neighborhood-based social networks (Auyero 2001; Levitsky 2003).

Second, they have weakened clientelistic linkages between politicians and citizens. The privatization of state-owned enterprises and social services, and the deregulation of key markets and economic activities, has narrowed considerably the scope for the political use of jobs, benefits, and state regulation. Moreover, fiscal constraints have legitimized executive dominance of the budget in ways that limit partisan oppor-tunities for distributing pork through logrolling and introducing individual budget amendments. Even conceding that a politicized delivery of scarce state resources, outright vote buying, or simple constituency service might yet be an efficient electoral strategy in areas of high poverty or unemployment, parties are less likely to compete and organize consent on the basis of dispensing patronage in a time of state retrenchment than in the heyday of state intervention in the economy.

Third, market reforms have reconfigured electorates. Deindustrialization and eco-nomic liberalization have atomized society, weakened the social foundations of organizational ties and collective identities, and rendered cleavages highly fluid, thus making it difficult for parties to close off the electoral marketplace by encapsu-lating voters or articulating clearly differentiated ideologies or programs (Roberts and Wibbels 1999, 587). Unorganized and marginal urban masses are more available for catch-all, personalistic, and even "neo-populist" parties that, lacking party organiza-tion and the ability to build one, prefer a thin version of partisanship to mobilizing these groups for elections and political action (O'Donnell 1994; Roberts 1995; Weyland 1996). In such circumstances, the stability of partisanship may depend on the strength of party linkages to intermediate associations. Where parties are effectively linked with social organizations their base of support may be more durable amid economic downturns and ethnic challenges than when these linkages are in ruins.

If structural change can prompt parties to redefine their strategies for mobilizing voters, they do not do so in an automatic or predictable way, and we must be careful not to lurch from the astructuralism of institutionalism to a new form of structural deter-minism. New limits on patronage spending may motivate parties to substitute problem-solving constituency service for patronage or abandon strategies to cultivate personal votes altogether and switch to programmatic representation. If they fail to do either, they may simply pass from the scene. The erosion of a party's "natural" constituency and the loss of a credible message also insufficiently explain the *direction* and *intensity* of programmatic change. They do not dictate whether a party will lurch to the left or right, emphasize differences with their opponents on economic or cultural issues, or stress their competence in addressing valence issues. They also say little about the basis on which parties mobilize voters. Here, the connection to the strategic dimension of inter-party competition is key. Where partisan differences are sharp and the party's collective reputation and electoral appeals can therefore be based on program, party candidates have a strong incentive to uphold that program. But where such differences are negligible, candidates seeking another basis upon which to mobilize votes may cultivate a personal vote either through distributing patronage or pork or by performing constituency service. The sharpness of elite partisan cleavages, in other words, varies inversely with the extent to which party representatives cultivate a personal vote.

Such a framework helps to explain the changing nature of the party–voter relationship in several emerging democracies. Partisan electoral competition over state policy explains the transformation of India's party system from one based on two centrist, catch-all parties to one organized around social cleavages. When the state government in Uttar Pradesh in the early 1990s adopted the Mandal Commission report that introduced ethnic quotas in government employment and expanded educational opportunities for backward castes, Chhibber (1999, 135–6, 169, 218) contends, the BJP mobilized forward castes who opposed the quotas and favored a reduced role for the state in the economy. A similar dynamic is evident in Algeria. When oil revenues plummeted and the FLN government could not maintain its level of spending, the party lost its middle-class support to a religiously based party (the FIS) that redefined its program to one critical of a planning economy in order to suit middle-class economic interests. In Spain, moreover, a growing electoral challenge from the communists pushed the PSOE to modify its stance on distributive economic policy, which in turn prompted the right to shift its core programmatic appeal from the less popular social and moral issues it championed to supply-side economics and the promise of a lower tax rate (Chhibber 1999, 149–50, 203–5, 213–14). The internal coherence and widening gap in party issue positions on the economy also help to explain the strengthening of the programmatic identities of political parties in Brazil and the Czech Republic, and their narrowing in Chile may account for the increased emphasis of national legislators on personal constituency service.

The breadth of policy differences between parties and the convergence of their proposals with the demands of their constituents also help to explain the *stability* of these party–voter linkages. Wider ideological distances might lead to or reinforce partisan cleavages because ideological polarization serves to anchor parties within relatively stable and differentiated electoral constituencies, whereas depolarization, which leaves voters free to pick and choose from a variety of virtually indistinguishable policy and partisan electoral options, weakens collective identities and facilitates personality-based candidate appeals (Roberts and Wibbels 1999, 583, 586). When parties frame competing appeals and these respond to voter demand for clear policy alternatives, especially in hard times, moreover, parties may be better able to retain their partisans. Party systems that are growing stronger in Brazil and Uruguay have made such alternatives available, whereas the Venezuelan, which did not, collapsed.

5 CONCLUSIONS

This chapter asked which voters parties target in new democracies, how they mobilize them, and why. Among the dozens of emerging democracies on four continents, the relationships between parties and voters are often fragile and fluid.

In some countries parties have made a successful transition from agents of state patronage to framers of competing ideological and programmatic visions for the future; in some former one-party states, the scope of political competition has appreciably expanded, and in others, even fixed identities and stable loyalties have not immunized party systems from wrenching change. This relationship, in other words, is a dynamic one, and our theoretical explanations are of little use if they do not acknowledge this fundamental premiss. Unfortunately, most do not.

Most explanations for the continuing instability in the party–voter relationship in the emerging democracies are seriously flawed (cf. Mainwaring 1999). Persistently high rates of electoral volatility are not due merely to the insufficient passage of time, media effects, or negative evaluations of the economy and government performance. Party choices to centralize electoral and representational strategies or to allow candidates to chart their own, to mobilize voters by framing a program or distributing patronage and pork, or to catch a broad but shallow electorate or to build upon a deeply embedded social cleavage in the electorate are not predetermined by the level of economic development or the intra-party lines of accountability that derive from electoral rules and career ambitions. The legacies of authoritarian regimes and democratic transitions impact these choices, but when the influence of the old regime will be felt, and to what degree, is also theoretically unspecified.

This chapter has argued that party strategies for voter mobilization and representation respond to structural and regime change, as well as institutional incentives, but these must be located within the context of strategic, inter-party competition. Parties may mix strategies at the national, regional, or even individual level. In advancing this argument, this chapter has cast doubt on two strong presumptions in the literature on parties and voters: first, that whenever the option is open to them, parties will choose a clientelistic strategy; and second, that parties will frame programs only when they can connect to an electorate that is economically or demographically well suited to such an appeal. Parties may choose to eschew clientelism because voters may prefer public goods, especially where there are international and domestic pressures for greater transparency in government accounting and "politics as usual" is perceived to have resulted in dramatic macroeconomic failure. Alternatively, cleavages are not given in nature, and where they do not exist, parties can and do structure programmatic differences around cleavages of their own creation. As things now stand, we know far too little about the demand side of the party–voter relationship and whether politically constructed cleavages that do not match salient social divisions can endure because institutionalist analyses of intra-party accountability and its effects on policy typically treat voters as homologous units that are capable of being divided and recombined, much like Marx's metaphoric view of French peasants as potatoes in a sack (1972, 515), and structuralists assume that voters are separated by economic and subcultural divides whose boundaries parties cannot redraw. We also lack good survey data. We tend to rely on cross-national datasets that focus broadly on values and views of democracy more than on national election surveys that solicit voter positions on salient issues and the ethics of selling their votes. With rare exceptions (e.g. Kitschelt et al. 1999), we have few studies of emerging democracies that match the issue positions of parties and their electorates in the way that Converse and Pierce's landmark (1986) study did for France. Yet the accuracy of our assessments of the stability of party–voter relationships in emerging democracies depends on developing better measures of party responsiveness to voters.[8] This will be especially important if states in the future are constrained in regulating the economy, providing public sector jobs, and distributing social services by international capital mobility and a declining public tolerance for the particularistic distribution of public goods, and parties must compete on program.

Until emerging democracies stabilize, these questions will remain open. To address them, we will need to reconnect our studies of partisanship, vote-buying practices, and the spatial dimensions of party competition. Hopefully, more truly comparative research that is not only theoretically imaginative but also empirically grounded, much like the works from which I have drawn generously in this chapter, will be the currency of future debate.

REFERENCES

AMES, B. 2001. *The Deadlock of Democracy in Brazil*. Ann Arbor: University of Michigan Press.
—— 2002. Party discipline in the Chamber of Deputies. In Morgenstern and Nacif 2002: 185–221.
AUYERO, J. 2001. *Poor People's Politics: Peronist Survival Networks and the Legacy of Evita.* Durham, NC: Duke University Press.
BARNES, S. H., McDONOUGH, P., and LÓPEZ PINA, A. 1985. The development of partisanship in new democracies: the case of Spain. *American Journal of Political Science,* 29: 695–721.
BARTOLINI, S., and MAIR, P. 1990. *Identity, Competition, and Electoral Availability: The Stabilisation of European Electorates, 1885–1995*. Cambridge: Cambridge University Press.
BOIX, C. 1999. Setting the rules of the game: the change of electoral systems in advanced democracies. *American Political Science Review,* 95: 609–24.
BRADER, R., and TUCKER, J. A. 2001. The emergence of mass partisanship in Russia, 1993–1996. *American Journal of Political Science,* 45: 69–83.
BRUSCO, V., NAZARENO, M., and STOKES, S. C. 2004. Vote buying in Argentina. *Latin American Research Review,* 39: 66–88.
BURGESS, K., and LEVITSKY, S. 2003. Explaining populist party adaptation in Latin America: environmental and organizational determinants of party change in Argentina, Mexico, Peru, and Venezuela. *Comparative Political Studies,* 36: 881–911.
CALVO, E., and MURILLO, M. V. 2004. Who delivers? Partisan clients in the Argentine electoral market. *American Journal of Political Science,* 48: 742–57.
CAREY, J. M. 1996. *Term Limits and Legislative Representation*. Cambridge: Cambridge University Press.
—— and SHUGART, M. S. 1995. Incentives to cultivate a personal vote: a rank ordering of electoral formulas. *Electoral Studies,* 14: 417–39.

---

[8] Shin (1999, 191) suggests three metrics of party performance—the opportunity to participate in politics, serving the interests of the public, and offering different policies. See also Powell (2000).

CHHIBBER, P. K. 1999. *Democracy without Associations: Transformation of the Party System and Social Cleavages in India*. Ann Arbor: University of Michigan Press.

COLLIER, R. B., and COLLIER, D. 1991. *Shaping the Political Arena: Critical Junctures, the Labor Movement, and Regime Dynamics in Latin America*. Princeton: Princeton University Press.

COLTON, T. J. 2000. *Transitional Citizens: Voters and What Influences Them in the New Russia*. Cambridge, Mass.: Harvard University Press.

CONVERSE, P. 1969. Of time and partisan stability. *Comparative Political Studies*, 2: 139–71.

—— and PIERCE, R. 1986. *Political Representation in France*. Cambridge, Mass.: Belknap Press of Harvard University.

COPPEDGE, M. 2001. Political Darwinism in Latin America's lost decade. Pp. 173–205 in *Political Parties and Democracy*, ed. L. Diamond and R. Gunther. Baltimore: Johns Hopkins University Press.

CORNELIUS, W. 2004. Mobilized voting in the 2000 elections: the changing efficacy of vote buying and coercion in Mexican electoral politics. Pp. 47–65 in *Mexico's Pivotal Democratic Election: Candidates, Voters, and the Presidential Campaign of 2000*, ed. J. Domínguez and C. Lawson. Stanford, Calif.: Stanford University Press.

COX, G. 1997. *Making Votes Count: Strategic Coordination in the World's Electoral Systems*. Cambridge: Cambridge University Press.

CRISP, B. 2000. *Democratic Institutional Design: The Power and Incentives of Venezuelan Politicians and Interest Groups*. Stanford, Calif.: Stanford University Press.

—— ESCOBAR-LEMMON, M., JONES, B., JONES, M. and TAYLOR-ROBINSON, M. 2004. Vote-seeking incentives and legislative representation in six presidential democracies. *Journal of Politics*, 1: 136–56.

FREEDOM HOUSE. 2004. *Freedom in the World*. Available at **www.freedomhouse.org**

GIBSON, C. 2002. Of waves and ripples: democracy and political change in Africa in the 1990s. *Annual Review of Political Science*, 5: 201–21.

GIBSON, E. 1997. The populist road to market reform policy and electoral coalitions in Mexico and Argentina. *World Politics*, 49: 339–70.

GRZYMALA-BUSSE, A. M. 2002. *Redeeming the Communist Past: The Regeneration of Communist Parties in East Central Europe*. Cambridge: Cambridge University Press.

HAGOPIAN, F. 2005. The rising quality of democracy in Brazil and Chile. Pp. 123–62 in *The Quality of Democracy: Improvement or Subversion?*, ed. L. Diamond and L. Morlino. Baltimore: Johns Hopkins University Press.

HUNTINGTON, S. P. 1968. *Political Order in Changing Societies*. New Haven: Yale University Press.

—— 1991. *The Third Wave: Democratization in the Late Twentieth Century*. Norman: University of Oklahoma Press.

JACOBSON, G. 2000. Party polarization in national politics. Pp. 9–30 in *Polarized Politics: Congress and the President in a Partisan Era*, ed. J. R. Bond and R. Fleischer. Washington, DC: Congressional Quarterly Press.

JONES, M. 2002. Explaining the high level of party discipline in the Argentine Congress. In Morgenstern and Nacif 2002: 147–84.

—— SAIEGH, S., SPILLER, P. T., and TOMMASI, M. 2002. Amateur legislators—professional politicians: the consequences of party-centered electoral rules in a federal system. *American Journal of Political Science*, 46: 656–69.

KIRCHHEIMER, O. 1966. The transformation of the western European party systems. Pp. 177–200 in *Political Parties and Political Development*, ed. J. LaPalombara and M. Weiner. Princeton: Princeton University Press.

KITSCHELT, H. 2000. Linkages between citizens and politicians in democratic polities. *Comparative Political Studies*, 33: 845–79.

KITSCHELT, H. MANSFELDOVA, Z., MARKOWSKI, R., and TÓKA, G. 1999. *Post-Communist Party Systems: Competition, Representation, and Inter-party Cooperation.* Cambridge: Cambridge University Press.

KUENZI, M., and LAMBRIGHT, G. 2001. Party system institutionalization in 30 African countries. *Party Politics*, 7: 437–68.

LEMARCHAND, R. 1972. Political clientelism and ethnicity in tropical Africa: competing solidarities in nation-building. *American Political Science Review*, 66: 68–90.

LEVITSKY, S. 2003. *Transforming Labor-Based Parties in Latin America: Argentine Peronism in Comparative Perspective.* Cambridge: Cambridge University Press.

LIPSET, S. M. 2001. Cleavages, parties and democracy. Pp. 3–9 in *Party Systems and Voter Alignments Revisited*, ed. L. Karvonen and S. Kuhnle. London: Routledge.

—— and ROKKAN, S. 1967. Cleavage structures, party systems, and voter alignments: an introduction. Pp. 1–64 in *Party Systems and Voter Alignments: Cross-National Perspectives*, ed. S. M. Lipset and S. Rokkan. New York: Free Press.

MAINWARING, S. P. 1999. *Rethinking Party Systems in the Third Wave of Democratization: The Case of Brazil.* Stanford, Calif.: Stanford University Press.

—— and SCULLY, T. R. 1995. *Building Democratic Institutions: Party Systems in Latin America.* Stanford, Calif.: Stanford University Press.

—— and TORCAL, M. 2006. Party system institutionalization and party system theory after the third wave of democratization. Pp. 204–27 in *Handbook of Political Parties*, ed. R. S. Katz and W. Crotty. London: Sage.

MARX, K. 1972. The eighteenth Brumaire of Louis Bonaparte (orig. 1852). Pp. 436–525 in *The Marx-Engels Reader*, ed. R. C. Tucker. New York: Norton.

MORGENSTERN, S., and NACIF, B. 2002. *Legislative Politics in Latin America.* Cambridge: Cambridge University Press.

O'DONNELL, G. 1994. Delegative democracy. *Journal of Democracy*, 5: 55–69.

PIATTONI, S. 2001. Clientelism in historical and comparative perspective. Pp. 1–30 in *Clientelism, Interests, and Democratic Representation: The European Experience in Historical and Comparative Perspective.* Cambridge: Cambridge University Press.

POSNER, D. N. 2004. The political salience of cultural difference: why Chewas and Tumbukas are allies in Zambia and adversaries in Malawi. *American Political Science Review*, 98: 529–45.

—— 2005. *Institutions and Ethnic Politics in Africa.* Cambridge: Cambridge University Press.

POWELL, G. B. 2000. *Elections as Instruments of Democracy: Majoritarian and Proportional Visions.* New Haven: Yale University Press.

PRZEWORSKI, A., and SPRAGUE, J. 1986. *Paper Stones: A History of Electoral Socialism.* Chicago: University of Chicago Press.

REMMER, K. 1991. The political impact of economic crisis in Latin America in the 1980s. *American Political Science Review*, 85: 777–800.

ROBERTS, K. 1995. Neoliberalism and the transformation of populism in Latin America: the Peruvian case. *World Politics*, 48: 82–116.

—— and WIBBELS, E. 1999. Party systems and electoral volatility in Latin America: a test of economic, institutional, and structural explanations. *American Political Science Review*, 93: 575–90.

ROSE, R. 1995. Mobilizing demobilized voters in post-communist societies. *Party Politics*, 1: 549–63.

SAMUELS, D. 2003. *Ambition, Federalism, and Legislative Politics in Brazil.* Cambridge: Cambridge University Press.

—— 2006. Sources of mass partisanship in Brazil. *Latin American Politics and Society*, 48: 1–27.

SARTORI, G. 1969. From the sociology of politics to political sociology. Pp. 65–95 in *Politics and the Social Sciences*, ed. S. M. Lipset. Oxford: Oxford University Press.

SCHMITTER, P. 1992. The consolidation of democracy and representation of social groups. *American Behavioral Scientist*, 35: 422–49.

SCOTT. J. C. 1972. Patron–client politics and political change in Southeast Asia. *American Political Science Review*, 66: 91–113.

SELIGSON, A., and TUCKER, J. 2004. Feeding the hand that bit you: voting for ex-authoritarian rulers in Bolivia and Russia. Mimeo. Princeton University.

SHEFTER, M. 1977. Party and patronage: Germany, England, and Italy. *Politics and Society*, 7: 403–51.

SHIN, D. C. 1999. *Mass Politics and Culture in Democratizing Korea*. Cambridge: Cambridge University Press.

STOKES, S. C. 2001. *Mandates and Democracies: Neoliberalism by Surprise in Latin America*. Cambridge: Cambridge University Press.

STROM, K. 1997. Rules, reasons, and routines: legislative roles in parliamentary democracies. *Journal of Legislative Studies*, 3: 155–74.

SWINDLE, S. M. 2002. The supply and demand of the personal vote: theoretical considerations and empirical implications of collective electoral incentives. *Party Politics*, 8: 279–300.

TORCAL, M., and MAINWARING, S. 2003. The political recrafting of social bases of party competition: Chile, 1973–95. *British Journal of Political Science*, 33: 54–84.

UNO, S. In progress. Public support and democracy: identifying causal mechanisms for erosion of democracy in Latin America. Ph.D. dissertation. University of Notre Dame.

VALENZUELA, A. 1977. *Political Brokers in Chile: Local Government in a Centralized Polity*. Durham, NC: Duke University Press.

WANTCHEKON, L. 2003. Clientelism and voting behavior: evidence from a field experiment in Benin. *World Politics*, 55: 399–422.

WEYLAND, K. 1996. Neopopulism and neoliberalism in Latin America: unexpected affinities. *Studies in Comparative International Development*, 31: 3–31.

WORLD BANK. 2004. *World Development Indicators*. Available at **www.worldbank.org**

....

CHAPTER 25

POLITICAL
CLIENTELISM

....

SUSAN C. STOKES

IF most scholars of the topic are right, political clientelism slows economic development, vitiates democracy, and allows dictators to hold onto power longer than they otherwise would. It slows economic development by discouraging governments from providing public goods and by creating an interest in the ongoing poverty and dependency of constituents. Its vitiates democracy by undermining the equality of the ballot, allowing some voters to use their votes to communicate policy preferences while others use their votes only as an exchange for minor side payments. And it keeps dictators in power by allowing them to stage elections in which competition is stifled in which voters who would prefer to vote against the regime are kept from doing so by fear of retaliation. Given these critical effects, we need to understand clientelism's internal dynamics, its causes, and its consequences.

1 DEFINITIONS

....

1.1 Clientelism

The concept of clientelism suffers more than most from a lack of consensus about its meaning. Focusing on clientelism as a method of electoral mobilization, I define it as

* I thank Carles Boix, Valeria Brusco, Noam Lupu, and Marcelo Nazareno for their comments.

the proffering of material goods in return for electoral support, where the criterion of distribution that the patron uses is simply: did you (will you) support me?[1]

It is worth noting that "proffering of material goods" in reality sometimes takes the form of threats rather than inducements. We have the government of Singapore threatening to withhold improvements of housing in districts that elect opposition legislators (Tam 2005), Christian Democratic operatives in Naples and Palermo threatening to cite opposition-supporting grocers for health violations (Chubb 1982), and the local magnate threatening to fire citizens who vote against his favored candidates in Misiones, Argentina (Urquiza 2006), to cite just a few examples.

It is the distributive criterion of electoral support that distinguishes clientelism from other materially oriented political strategies. Consider, by contrast, what is known in the USA as *pork barrel politics*, in which benefits are paid to one or a few districts while costs are shared across all districts (Aldrich 1995, 30).[2] The implicit criterion for the distribution of pork is: do you live in my district? Or consider *programmatic redistributive politics*, in which parties in government emit public policies that withdraw resources from some groups and distribute them to others, almost always with electoral considerations in mind. The criterion for who will benefit from redistributive programs is: do you occupy a given class of beneficiaries (those who are unemployed, or have retired, or fall into a given tax bracket, etc.)?[3] Programmatic benefits therefore have a public good quality: they redistribute resources from classes of non-beneficiaries to classes of beneficiaries, but within a class of beneficiaries, particular people who qualify cannot be excluded. By contrast there is a quid pro quo aspect to clientelist redistribution: it is only available on condition that the client complies by providing political support.

My definition is not worlds apart from Kitschelt and Wilkinson's, who note that citizen–politician linkages are often "based on direct material inducements targeted to individuals and small groups of citizens whom politicians know to be highly responsive to such side-payments and willing to surrender their vote for the right price." This they call a "patronage-based, voter-party linkage" (2007, 10). But alternative (or at least different) definitions abound. One defines "patron–client relationships" more generically as a "vertical dyadic alliance . . . between two persons of unequal status, power or resources each of whom finds it useful to have as an ally someone superior or inferior to himself (Landé 1977, p. xx). The "dyadic" part of the definition underscores the face-to-face quality of clientelism; the "alliance" part emphasizes the repeated character of the relationship.

Other students of clientelism define it narrowly as an exchange of a public sector job for political support (see e.g. Robinson and Verdier 2003, 2)—what many call

---

[1] A different phenomenon, which would be labeled *campaign finance* or *corruption* (depending on a country's laws), is when private actors give money to politicians and parties in exchange for legislative concessions and other favors. In this relation, the flow of money is the reverse of the flow in clientelism: it goes not from politician to private actor but from private actor to politician.

[2] Safire notes that the phase "probably is derived from the pre-Civil War practice of periodically distributing salt pork to the slaves from huge barrels" (1993).

[3] These distinctions are conceptual, not empirical: a politician who deploys clientelist strategies may simultaneously provide public and programmatic-redistributive goods (see Magaloni, Diaz-Cayeros, and Estérez 2006).

patronage. Still others define it in terms of what it is that patrons and clients exchange. According to James Scott, the relation is an "instrumental friendship in which an individual of higher socioeconomic status (patron) uses his own influence and resources to provide *protection or benefits*, or both, for a person of lower status (client) who, for his part, reciprocates by offering *general support and assistance*, including personal services, to the patron" (1972, 92, emphasis mine). Whitaker makes a similar point in his discussion of politics in emirates, writing that in clientelist relations, "patronage, economic security, and protection can be exchanged for personal loyalty and obedience" (cited in Lemarchand 1977, 102).

Scott's definition raises the question: under what conditions would a client not simply purchase protections and benefits in the market, rather than eliciting them from someone whom he knows personally and who is of a higher status than he? Markets may not exist or be well developed for the kinds of protections or benefits sought. Or these protections and benefits may be available on the market but their potential consumer (the client) has insufficiently plentiful resources (income) to secure them from an impersonal seller. The low-income, limited-assets client has other resources in greater abundance: time, a vote, insertion into networks of other potential supporters whom he can influence, and the like. We do not have to get very far into definitions of clientelism before we are reminded of the material poverty of the client.

Scott's definition also focuses our attention on the clients' interest in securing security and protection. In many polities security and protection are provided by the state as a public good. Hence, taking Scott's two points together, all else equal we would expect patron–client ties to be prevalent in societies with widespread poverty and with a relatively weak and ineffective state apparatus.

1.2 Vote Buying and Patronage

Having explored definitions of clientelism (and offered my own), I now do the same for the related concepts of patronage and vote buying. In my usage, patronage and vote buying are subclasses of clientelism. Whereas clientelism involves the dyad's inferior member giving electoral support broadly construed, including her own vote and efforts to secure for the patron the votes of others, vote buying is a more narrow *exchange of goods (benefits, protections) for one's own vote*. In contrast, again, to pork and programmatic redistribution, the criterion for selecting vote sellers is: did you (will you) vote for me?

Patronage, in turn, is *the proffering of public resources (most typically, public employment) by office holders in return for electoral support*, where the criterion of distribution is again the clientelist one: did you—will you—vote for me? Hence patronage is distinct from the broader category of clientelism. In clientelism, the more powerful political actor may or may not hold public office, and therefore may or may not be able to credibly promise to secure public resources (as opposed to, say, party resources) for the client. In patronage, the patron holds public office and distributes state resources. This definition concurs with those of others, such as

Mainwaring, who defines patronage as "the use or distribution of state resources on a nonmeritocratic basis for political gain" (1999, 177). The clientelism–patronage distinction corresponds to Medina and Stokes's (2007) one between *economic monopoly* over goods which the patron controls independent of the outcome of an election, and *political monopoly* over goods that he controls only if he retains office. An example of an economic monopoly is a grain elevator in a rural community, access to which its owner can limit to those who voted or will vote for him, whether or not he wins the election. An example of a political monopoly is public employment, which a patron can use to reward or punish voters only in the case that he wins.

Whether a relationship is of more general clientelism or of patronage—whether it is based on an economic or a political monopoly—is consequential. Under a political monopoly, voters who wish to throw a patron out of office may face a collective action problem: his exit represents a public good, yet the voter who votes against him when a majority of others does not risks suffering the patron's retaliation. Each voter minimizes her risk and maximizes her payoff when she votes for the unpopular patron but all other voters (or at least a majority) vote against him. Yet because all voters face this same incentive, the unpopular patron remains in power.

An implication is that, in polities in which patronage or political monopoly is widespread, one cannot infer a party's (or its program's) popularity from its electoral successes. Mexico's PRI offers an example of a ruling party that remained in power and continued to win elections, probably long after its underlying popularity had been severely eroded (see Magaloni 2006).

2 Two Waves of Studies of Clientelism

The post-war literature on clientelism comes basically in two waves, the first one inspired by the emergence of new nations, the second by the democratization of large swaths of the developing world. The papers gathered and reissued in Schmidt, Scott, Landé, and Gausti's influential 1977 reader, *Friends, Followers, and Factions*, had first appeared in print between 1950 and 1974, the bulk of them during the ten years after 1964. Important monographs appeared in the 1980s (such as Judith Chubb's studies of clientelism and patronage in southern Italy), and the theoretical ground for studies of clientelism began to shift in the late 1980s and 1990s.

After a hiatus of several decades, studies of political clientelism are again legion. In addition to reappearance in journals and monographs, after 2007 we will have not one but three major new collections on related topics.[4] The two waves of writings differ in many ways: in the political regimes studied (the early wave was indifferent to regimes, the second focused mainly on clientelism under democracy); in the basic conceptual

---

[4] They are Piattoni (2001); Schaffer (2007); Kitschelt and Wilkinson (2007).

categories employed; in the modes of analysis used; and in their disciplinary influences. The early wave was inspired mainly by anthropology and secondarily by sociology, the later one by economics.

2.1 The Paradox of Clientelism

Relations of patron and client present us with a paradox. They entail unequal actors—slave and master, serf and lord, sharecropper and landowner, worker and manager, voter and party boss—who enter into a relationship that is both voluntary and, from the less-powerful member's vantage point, exploitative. In Kitschelt's words, clientelism "involves reciprocity and voluntarism but also exploitation and domination" (2000, 849). By extension, we would expect clientelist relations to be full of opportunities for defection and betrayal. Why does the relationship persist, even though the client might be better off severing the link? We look, then, for some social cement to keep the client and patron together.

In many early (and even some more recent) studies, the cement is a *norm*. A norm is a consequential and broadly held idea that takes the form: "*do x*" (Elster 1989). Gouldner claimed as universal a "moral norm of reciprocity" that makes two demands: "(1) people should help those who have helped them, and (2) people should not injure those who have helped them" (1960, 171). Under clientelism, superior members of dyads reinforce the norm of reciprocity by giving their inferiors ceremonial gifts, which, like spontaneous and useful gifts, (presumably) create a sense of obligation that the gift must be reciprocated. Scott reflects on the normative and psychological tenor of relations that are personalized and ongoing. The patron–client dyad is distinguished by

the *face-to-face*, personal quality of the relationship. The continuing pattern of reciprocity that establishes and solidifies a patron–client bond often creates trust and affection between the partners. When a client needs a small loan or someone to intercede for him with the authorities, he knows he can rely on his patron; the patron knows, in turn, that "his men" will assist him in his designs when he needs them. Furthermore, the mutual expectations of the partners are backed by community values and rituals. (1972, 94; emphasis in the original)

According to many norms-oriented students of clientelism, norms of reciprocity have the effect of pushing obligations from one sphere of a relationship into others. "Reciprocities that were once restricted to a specific type of exchange have thus led to cumulative or alternative exchanges among parties" (Lemarchand 1977, 106). Lemarchand cites as examples the overflow of patron–client ties in Senegal from spheres of feudal and religious obligations into clan politics; the generalizing of patron–client ties between Hutu and Tutsi in Rwanda from land ownership into cattle ownership; and the spillover of mercantile clientelism into local politics in Ibadan, Nigeria. This generalized set of obligations also spills over into relations between patron-politicians and voter-clients. Citing Wurfel, Scott notes that a Filipino politician "does favors *individually* rather than collectively because he wishes to create a personal obligation of clientship"

(1972). In sum, if the emphasis on social norms as a cement of clientelism is not ill placed, their effect is not only to keep the subordinate member of the dyad from rebelling but also to generalize his subordination.

A very different way of thinking about clientelist exchanges is that they tie the client to the patron not by encouraging a norm of reciprocity but by encouraging a fear that the flow of benefits will be cut off. Such a perspective is more consistent with turn-of-the-century (twentieth to twenty-first) sensibilities than with the sensibilities of students of clientelism in the 1960s and 1970s. But it was by no means absent from the first-wave literature. In his classic monograph *Political Leadership among the Swat Pathans*, Frederick Barth insisted that "gifts can be cancelled out by an equivalent return, and do not imply any authority of the giver over the receiver...Unilateral gift-giving...does not effectively put the recipient under an obligation to respond to the command of the giver, as does the payment of bribes or salaries." Instead, he explained, "gift-giving and hospitality are potent means of controlling others, not because of the debts they create, but because of the recipient's dependence on their continuation. A continuous flow of gifts creates needs and fosters dependence and the threat of its being cut off becomes a powerful disciplinary device" (1959, 77).

Barth's interest-oriented explanation is nearly identical to the one put forth forty years later by Brusco and her co-authors, that voters (in Argentina) comply with an implicit clientelist contract "because they anticipate that, should they not comply, they would be cut off from the flow of minor payoffs in the future" (2004, 76). (The only difference is that "satisfied men" among the Swat Pathan have incomes hundreds of times greater than those of the "hungry men" to whom they give gifts, which are therefore, from the latter's perspective, by no means "minor.")

Just as some first-wave studies posited that the cement binding clients to patrons was the client's fear of the patron's cutting off of rewards, so some second-wave studies continue to emphasize the client's normative sense of obligation to the patron. A Filipino observer explains the power of campaign gifts thus: "Once a person has granted us something, a favor, we would do everything to pay that favor back to him or her, sometimes even at the expense of ourselves" (cited in Schaffer and Schedler 2006, 32).

In a similar vein, a client of the Argentine Peronist party responded in the following way to a question about whether a local party broker asked her to attend rallies in exchange for free medicines:

No...I know that I have to go with her instead of with someone else. Because she gave me medicine, or some milk, or a packet of yerba or sugar, I know that I have to go to her rally in order to fulfill my obligation to her, to show my gratitude. (Auyero 2001, 160)

The brokers use these feelings of friendship and gratitude to harvest votes. Following a long day of handing out goods and favors at Children's Day celebrations, a Peronist broker remarked: "After what you just saw...votes will come. I don't have to go and look for them...votes will come anyway" (Auyero 2001, 82).

Yet Auyero's research shows that, in the minds of clients, the instrumentalism underlying the friendship is never far below the surface. The same client who attended rallies out of gratitude for medicine, milk, and sugar added that "if I do not go to [the Peronist broker's] rally, then, when I need something, she won't give it to me. [She would say,] 'go ask the person who went to the rally with you'" (cited in Auyero 2001, 160).

Generally, scholars have fallen into the norms or self-interest camp without subjecting their inclinations to anything like an empirical test. An exception is the study by Brusco, Nazareno, and Stokes (2004). We asked our Argentine samples whether people who received targeted goods during election campaigns felt obliged to vote for the party who had proffered the goods. Not many more answered that recipients do feel an obligation than that they do not (51 percent to 43 percent). But those who said, as a factual matter, that people do feel obliged tended to be the kind who would never receive such a handout: compared to the means for our samples they were wealthy, non-Peronist, and came from big cities. They seemed to be interpreting other people's experiences, not their own. We also asked whether people who receive goods *should* feel an obligation to reciprocate with their vote. If there is a norm of political reciprocity in Argentina saying that "gifts" demand a response, this norm has far-from-widespread acceptance: nine out of ten people whom we sampled said that recipients of campaign handouts should not feel obliged to return the favor of a handout with a vote (2004, 81). We cannot be sure that these results are not country and time specific, but they do suggest that norms of political reciprocity are not universal and are perhaps vulnerable to political mobilization against them.

3 CLIENTELISM AND COMMITMENT

The second-wave shift away from norms and toward fear of retaliation draws on economics and political economy. A series of papers in the 1980s and 1990s explained formally how parties could use individualized or targeted inducements to mobilize electoral support. The basic idea was that, rather than using public policies to effect transfers from some classes of voters to others, parties could deliver inducements to individual voters and thus bolster the parties' electoral prospects. Dixit and Londregan (1996) call this "tactical" as opposed to "programmatic" redistribution.[5] A central finding of this formal literature was that, when parties knew their constituents well and could efficiently deliver goods to those who would be most likely to return the favor with their vote, then doing so could be cost effective. Parties that practiced this strategy would target *core constituents*: voters whose needs (Dixit and Londregan 1996) or

---

[5] Their distinction does not exactly follow the one I offer above. By programmatic redistribution they mean redistribution grounded in ideological visions of redistributive justice and implemented through income (and, less commonly, wealth) taxes. Tactical redistribution (which they also refer to as "pork") is in a sense between classes of people: the examples they offer are subsidies to some industries and the location of military bases in some districts. Hence they shy away from truly individualized benefits, although their "machine case" would seem to involve individualized distribution and monitoring.

electoral predispositions (Cox and McCubbins 1986) were well known to the party and hence who presented little risk that the party would waste resources on them. (See also Lindbeck and Weibull 1987.)

Following these theoretical leads, Magaloni, Diaz-Cayeros, and Estévez (2006) posited that risk aversion is a variable quality, even of a single party over time; varying tolerance for risk could explain the mix of strategies—programmatic in some constituencies and in some periods, clientelistic in others—that parties deployed.

A difficulty with this line of theorizing about clientelism as an electoral strategy is that it deals inadequately with problems of commitment.[6] A voter who receives a bag of food with the understanding (implicit or explicit) that she will return the favor with a vote can easily renege on the deal on election day, especially when she is protected by the secret ballot. Indeed, the secret ballot was introduced to free voters of the kind of tacit coercion that vote buying entails. And the commitment problem runs in both directions: a party that before an election promises patronage in exchange for votes may well forget its promise afterwards.

To illustrate, consider a *patronage game*: members of a favored group enjoy the tactically redistributed goods, following Dixit and Londregan, only when the patronage party wins. First the voter decides whether to comply and vote for this party or defect and vote against it. Then nature makes the party either win or lose the election. If the party wins it then chooses whether to reward the voter or withhold a reward. If the party loses it cannot disburse rewards and the game ends. Figure 25.1 is the extensive form of the game. The sequence laid out there implies that the voter chooses whether to comply or defect before the outcome of the election is known (the party, if it gets to act, obviously knows that it has won).

The party gains v when the voter votes for it and assumes a loss of $-r_p$ whenever it pays a reward. By assumption, $v > r_p$: the best outcome for the party is to gain a vote without paying for it but it prefers to pay and get the vote than not to pay and forgo the vote. In this game the voter is mildly ideologically predisposed against the patronage party: its most preferred outcome is to win the reward and vote against the party but it would vote for it if necessary to win the reward. Thus it prefers the outcomes in the following order: $(r_v + d) > (r_v + c) > d > c$.

If the party wins, its dominant strategy is to withhold a reward from the voter. Whether the voter has complied or defected, the party does better denying him a reward. Knowing that the party, even if it wins, will not give a reward, the voter is always better off defecting and voting for the party which, on ideological grounds, he prefers. Hence the party never offers a reward and the voter's decision is entirely driven by its pre-redistributive preference for or against the party.

Even if the voter were ideologically inclined to vote for the patronage party, this preference, rather than the promise of patronage, would motivate the vote. The party still would do better reneging on its promise. Therefore the voter would ignore the promise and vote purely on ideology. Again, no patronage is meted out and its promise does not motivate electoral choices.

---

[6] For an exception, see Robinson and Verdier (2003).

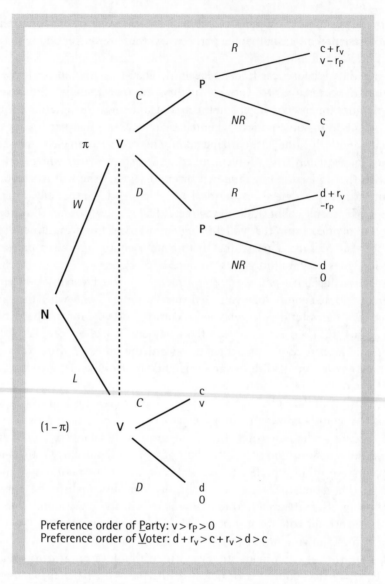

Fig. 25.1 A one-shot game between a voter and a would-be patron (rewards dependent on incumbency)

But we know that patronage and vote buying do occur and hence we need to rethink the model. Rather than the one-shot games developed in the literature, we do well to return to the insights of many students of clientelism that the relationships involved are face to face and ongoing. The "gift giving" of clientelism and patronage does not only motivate people to vote for the patron's party directly but also reinforces a social network in which patron and client are embedded. That clientelist relationships are ongoing—that the dyad is embedded in a social network—is theoretically important for several reasons. Networks provide information about their members to other members: we know whether our neighbor or co-worker votes or abstains, voices support for one party or another, and comes from a family of communists or Christian Democrats (Democrats or Republicans, Peronists or Radicals, etc.), none of which we know about strangers. Clientelist parties use operatives who are embedded in these networks and, like the Taiwanese campaign managers described by Wang and Kurzman, are "walking encyclopedia[s] of local knowledge" (2007, 94). This local knowledge allows them to make informed guesses about whether a voter to whom the party gave goods or employment actually followed through and supported the party or defected to another. Networks allow clientelist parties to sidestep the secret ballot.

The party can then use this information to reward the voter who has cooperated and punish the voter who has defected—it can hold the voter accountable for his or her vote. Yet in contrast to the kind of accountability celebrated in democratic theory, this is "perverse accountability," in which *voters* are held accountable for their actions by *parties* (Stokes 2005).

Given that patrons and clients are embedded in networks, we can model clientelism as a repeated game. The voters' preferences are given by

$$u_i = -\frac{1}{2}(v_i - x_i)^2 + r_{vi}$$

where $v_i = \{x_1, x_2\}$ is a vote for either the clientelist party or the opposition, x_i is voter i's position on the ideological spectrum, and $r_{vi} = \{0, r\}$ is the value to the voter of the reward offered by the machine in exchange for votes, relative to the value of voting according to the voter's preferences. Thus $-\frac{1}{2}(v_i - x_i)^2$ is the expressive value of voting for one of the two parties.

Table 25.1 presents the normal form of the game, and Table 25.2 simplifies the payoffs. Consider the case of a voter who is mildly opposed, on ideological or programmatic grounds, to the clientelist party. Without any inducements she will vote for its opponent, but it can offer her a reward (r) that would improve her payoff over voting against the clientelist party and not receiving the reward. That is, her preference order is:

$$\frac{1}{2}(x_i - x_2)^2 + r > -\frac{1}{2}(x_i - x_1)^2 + r > -\frac{1}{2}(x_i - x_2)^2 > \pm(x_i - x_1)^2$$

Table 25.1 Normal form of a game between the clientelist party and a voter

Voter	Party	
	Reward	No reward
Comply	$\frac{1}{2}(x_i - x_1)^2 + r, v - r$	$\frac{1}{2}(x_i - x_1)^2, v$
Defect	$\frac{1}{2}(x_i - x_2)^2 + r, -r$	$\frac{1}{2}(x_i - x_2)^2, 0$

The clientelist party, in turn, would most like to receive her vote without having to pay a reward but is willing to pay for the vote if necessary. Hence its preference order is:

$$v > v-r > 0 > -r$$

Table 25.2 makes clear that the clientelist party and the mildly opposed voter are in a prisoner's dilemma. Both would like to "cooperate" in a vote-buying arrangement, with the party paying a reward and the voter supporting the party. But if the voter supports the party then the party does better by withholding the reward, and if the party withholds the reward then the voter does better voting against it.

In the one-shot game, vote buying fails. But in the repeated game, they can cooperate to traffic in votes. They can do so by playing a grim-trigger strategy, with either side responding to a defection from the pair of strategies {vote for the clientelist, pay reward} by punishing the other side in every subsequent election in the future. The voter's minmax value, the lowest payoff that the clientelist party can hold her to, is $-\frac{1}{2}(x_i - x_2)^2$: even if she is forced to forgo the reward, she can always vote for the opposition party. The party's minmax value is 0: in response to the voter who defects, the party can at least always withhold a reward.

These minmax values allow us to define the feasible and individually rational payoffs of the two players, as illustrated in Figure 25.2. Among these payoffs is the pair that results when vote buying occurs: $-\frac{1}{2}(x_i - x_1)^2 + r, v - r$. By the folk theorems, in a repeated-play setting, if the players are patient then all feasible and individually rational payoffs enforce an equilibrium. The reason is that "when players are patient, any finite one-period gain from deviation is outweighed by even a small loss in utility in every future period" (Fudenberg and Tirole 2002, 153). Yet note also in Figure 25.2 that the vote-buying equilibrium is only one of several possible; the entire shaded area consists of feasible and individually rational payoffs.

The game outlined above generates several hypotheses:

- the greater a clientelist party's ability to directly observe an individual's vote, the more likely vote buying is to occur;
- the closer the vote comes to being fully opaque and anonymous, the less likely vote buying is to occur;

Table 25.2 Normal form of the game between the clientelist party and a weakly opposed voter with simplified payoffs

Voter	Party	
	Reward	No reward
Comply	3, 3	1, 4
Defect	4, 1	2, 2

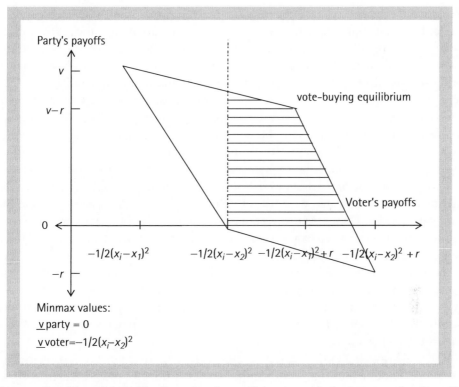

Fig. 25.2 Feasible and individually rational payoffs in repeated play between the clientelist party and a weakly opposed voter

- the closer parties are to one another ideologically, the more likely vote buying is to occur;
- the more valuable the reward or private inducement is to the voter, the more likely vote buying is to occur (Stokes 2005).

4 ARE CLIENTS CORE SUPPORTERS OR SWING VOTERS?

Clientelism as a repeated game between voters and parties embedded in social networks also tells us something about the kind of voter whom clientelist parties target. Its blandishments are wasted on loyal voters, who would support it anyway, independent of rewards, and hence cannot credibly commit to withdrawing their support should the flow of rewards be cut. Blandishments are also wasted on die-hard opposition voters. In contrast to the mild opponents discussed earlier, these die-hards' ideological distaste for the party outweighs the value of the reward; they therefore cannot credibly commit to vote for it.[7] Indifferent voters, and those who are slightly opposed to the party—whose distaste for voting for it is outweighed by the value of the reward—are the ideal targets of vote-buying efforts. The model thus predicts a marginal or swing voter strategy: parties will shower targeted rewards on people who are indifferent or slightly against them on ideological or programmatic grounds, not those who strongly support them.

A handful of studies have tested core versus swing voter hypotheses. These studies face methodological difficulties. In those using ecological data, the investigators typically consider bias in the distribution of resources toward districts that have voted heavily for the governing party in the past as evidence of a core voter strategy. Yet the voters who support the party and are then showered with public resources may have supported the party in the past because they were also, in the past, showered with resources. Hence the term "core" or "loyal" should be interpreted with caution. "Loyal" voters are those with a proven receptiveness to targeted goodies rather than those with an ideological predisposition in favor of the clientelist party. Ideally, ecological studies would control for the effect of targeted gift giving in earlier elections. Studies that rely on survey data face their own kind of endogeneity problem: does a person's self-reported friendliness toward a party cause him or her to receive handouts, or do handouts make him or her friendly? For that matter, are self-reported indifferent voters actually opponents whose opposition has been mitigated by rewards?

With these caveats in mind, empirical studies paint a mixed picture. Ansolabehere and Snyder (2002) find that US counties that traditionally provide high levels of support for the governor's party receive larger transfers from the state to local governments. They also find that a change in which party controls state government is followed by a shift in the distribution of these transfers in favor of counties that vote heavily for the new governing party.

Elsewhere in the hemisphere, several studies test core versus swing voter hypotheses with ecological data. Studying Mexico, Magaloni (2006) finds that the PRI spent lightly on social programs in regions controlled by the opposition, and spent heavily in regions in which voters would be most likely to defect by abstaining, again suggesting a marginal voter strategy. By contrast, Pérez Yarahuan (2006) finds that the ruling party favored its own electoral strongholds in the distribution of social programs and discriminated against opposition strongholds, suggesting a core strategy, at least in the 1994 election (see also Hiskey 1999). In a study of political manipulation of expenditures on an anti-poverty program in Peru, Schady (2000) finds that the Fujimori government favored "marginal" districts, ones in which the president had come close to winning or losing in his first election and in a referendum.

In Argentina, the evidence is also mixed. Weitz-Shapiro (2006) finds that toward the end of Carlos Menem's time in power and at the beginning of the De la Rúa

---

[7] Hence the preference order of the clientelist party's mild opponent is: $-1/2(x_i-x_2)^2 + b > -1/2(x_i-x_1)^2+b > -1/2(x_i-x_2)^2 > -1/2(x_i-x_1)^2$. The preference order of the die-hard opponent is: $-1/2(x_i-x_2)^2 + b > -1/2(x_i-x_2)^2 > -1/2(x_i-x_1)^2 + b > -1/2(x_i-x_1)^2$.

administration (1999–2001), the distribution of unemployment compensation funds was biased in favor of swing districts—those where margins of victory of one party or another were thin. Nazareno, Brusco, and Stokes (2006), also using ecological data, show that the smaller a party's margin of victory in past elections (or, sometimes, soon-to-occur future elections), the greater the proportion of its budget that went to expenditures on personnel. Employing survey data on campaign handouts, Stokes (2005) finds the evidence to be less decisive. Although she finds that the Argentine Peronists withheld campaign handouts from strong opponents (handouts which, according to her model, would have been a wasted on these kinds of voters), the Peronists gave inducements indifferent or marginal voters but also voters who favored the party. She speculates that clientelist parties often combine clientelist gift giving with ideological appeals: the ward-heeler who appears at a person's door with a bag of food or the offer of employment will also explain the party's programmatic advantages. Alongside their face-to-face material mobilization the parties also proselytize, and the once-indifferent voter begins to look more like a loyal constituent.

In sum, the bulk of the empirical data points toward clientelist parties targeting marginal or swing voters, but a few important exceptions find that they target core constituents. No one has accounted for this variation. Following Dixit and Londregan, Cox and McCubbins, and Magaloni and her co-authors, it may be that the key variable is risk: when politicians face ideologically diverse groups and wish to minimize their risk of wasting goodies, or when the politicians are themselves risk averse, they deploy a core voter strategy. Recent work that focuses not (following Cox's 2006 terminology) on "persuasion" (changing voters' minds about whom to vote for) but on "mobilization" (including them to vote, rather than to abstain) may shed further light on this matter.

5 Causes and Consequences

5.1 Why does Poverty Encourage Clientelism?

We saw that the very definition of clientelism points toward the poverty of the client. Indeed, it is impossible to survey the qualitative literature on political clientelism without concluding that it is a feature disproportionately of poor countries. It gets studied in the contexts of eighteenth-century Holland (Randeraad and Wolffram 2001), eighteenth- and nineteenth-century England (O'Gorman 2001), inter-war Greece (Mavrogordatos 1983), US cities in the late nineteenth century through the 1950s (Wilson and Banfield 1963; Reynolds 1988), Iceland in the 1940s and 1950s (Kristinsson 2001), southern Italy in the 1950s and 1960s (Graziano 1977; Chubb 1981, 1982), South Asia (Weiner 1967; Chandra 2004, 2007; Wilkinson 2006; Krishna 2007), South-East Asia (Landé 1965; Scott 1972), Africa (Lemarchand 1977; Wantchekon

2003; van de Walle 2007), Bulgaria (Kitschelt et al. 1999); and in Latin America from Mexico (Fox 1994; Magaloni 2006, Magaloni, Diaz-Cayeros, and Estévez 2007) to Argentina (Levitsky 2003; Calvo and Murillo 2004; Brusco, Nazareno, and Stokes 2004) and everywhere in between. We lack quantitative cross-national studies of the subject—it is hard to develop cross-nationally comparable quantitative measures of clientelism—but a mere glance at the qualitative literature shows that, while it is not an exclusive feature of the developing world (yesterday's or today's), one is much more likely to encounter it there than in the advanced democracies.[8]

Less obvious is why this is so. Without noticing that they are doing so, scholars have posited two distinct explanations for the link between clientelism and poverty. In the first and more common account, poor people value a handout more highly than do wealthy people; hence, if one is going to hand out goodies, one will target the poor (diminishing marginal utility of income—see e.g. Dixit and Londregan 1996; Calvo and Murillo 2004). In the second account, poor people are risk averse and hence value more highly a bag of goodies in hand today than the promise of a redistributive public policy tomorrow (see e.g. Desposato 2007; Wantchekon 2003; Kitschelt 2000; Scott 1976). As Kitschelt explains, "poor and uneducated citizens discount the future, rely on short causal chains, and prize instant advantages such that the appeal of direct, clientelist exchanges always trumps that of indirect, programmatic linkages promising uncertain and distant rewards to voters" (2000, 857).

Data emerging from one study cast doubt on the risk aversion explanation. Brusco, Nazareno, and Stokes (2006) find that poor Argentines were indeed more risk averse than were their wealthier compatriots. But risk aversion had no independent effect on one's propensity to sell one's vote. Comparing two equally poor voters, the more risk-averse one was no more likely to sell her vote than was the less risk-averse one.

A third account, slightly different from the others, is that not poverty per se but income inequality encourages clientelism (see e.g. Hicken 2007; Stokes 2007; Robinson and Verdier 2003). If the resources available for vote buying rise at the same rate as a country's average income, then development will not make it too expensive. But if clientelism must be paid for by a growing (upper) middle class and if its targets are themselves increasingly from the (lower) middle class, then the transfer will increasingly be as painful for those on the giving side as they are profitable for those on the receiving side, and one should encounter more resistance from the givers. Furthermore, middle-class citizens have higher opportunity costs for monitoring the activities of other voters; parties will find it more difficult to retain a presence in social networks and hence to monitor individuals' voting behavior when the distribution of voters by incomes is dense in the middle and thinner at the lower end.

Another perspective altogether is that, rather than poverty generating clientelism, clientelism generates poverty. As a strategy to stay in power, clientelist parties may develop an interest in holding back income growth. Chubb blamed underdevelopment

---

[8] Although the quantitative research has not been cross-national, we have learned much from systematic data generated by field studies (see Wantchekon 2003) and from survey research (see Brusco, Nazareno, and Stokes 2004). The latter study shows that parties were substantially more likely to try to buy the votes of poor than of wealthy Argentines.

in Italy's Mezzogiorno on clientelism and patronage carried out by the Christian Democratic Party, which wished to keep its constituents poor and dependent. Other accounts point toward the underprovision of development-enhancing public goods in polities in which office holders focus on the provision of private goods (see e.g. Robinson and Verdier 2003), and on the declining relative productivity of, and dependence on, monopolized-goods sectors as countries undergo economic development (Medina and Stokes 2007; see also Lyne 2006). Of course it may be true both that poverty causes clientelism and that clientelism causes poverty.

5.2 Institutions

Electoral rules. Some analysts find it intuitive that electoral systems that encourage the personal vote also encourage clientelism (see e.g. Hicken 2007; Kitschelt 2000). Kitschelt reasons that

Personalized contests permit candidates and constituencies to organize, monitor, and enforce direct trades of support for favors flowing from office. In multimember electoral districts, personal preference votes for individual candidates rather than entire party lists make possible personalized trades. Politicians' incentives to pursue clientelism further increase when the votes that different candidates for the same party receive individually are not pooled to calculate the seats won by the entire party and/or when the party leadership does not control the nomination of list candidates. (2000, 859)

The flaw in this account is that it elides the personalist appeal of candidates with personalized, face-to-face voter mobilization. Although the two have in common a downplaying of issues and programs, they are in other ways quite distinct. A campaign that focuses on the personal qualities of the candidate may invest in mass media appeals and rely on a highly centralized party structure. By contrast, clientelist parties and campaigns rely on an army of brokers, intermediaries, and campaign workers to monitor the actions of voters at a fine-grained level. Clientelist parties in fact are decentralized parties, and decentralization is the price that the party leadership has to pay if it is to sustain an army of brokers to, in effect, spy on voters. Were the centralized leadership, or an individual charismatic leader, able to circumvent these decentralized brokers—were they able to replace decentralized vote buying with rousing oratory or compelling ideology—they would gladly do so. The personalization of electoral campaigns is hence at odds with clientelism, and we may be on the wrong track when we link personalizing electoral rules with the prevalence of clientelism. Again, however, this dispute remains theoretical in nature, and probably will until we discover a cross-nationally robust measure of clientelism that allows us to assess the impact of electoral rules on the phenomenon.

Legal restrictions on patronage and vote buying. Today, the vast majority of democracies place legal restrictions on patronage and vote buying. They enact laws and regulations regarding the recruitment of personnel into the bureaucracy, and they prohibit vote trafficking. According to Shefter's (1977, 1994) influential analysis, patronage was strictly limited in polities in which the civil service was professionalized before the franchise was broadened, but was more widespread in polities in which mass enfranchisement pre-dated any serious efforts at civil service reform. In the latter, parties were freer to mobilize mass support by offering public employment.

Shefter's account leaves some questions unanswered. Why do civil servants professionalize early in some places and later in others? In some settings where a professionalized civil service is in place, ambitious politicians mount an effective assault on it, reversing its autonomy and turning it into a source of patronage. This was the experience, for instance, of Pakistan under Zulfikar Ali Bhutto: the country inherited an autonomous and professionalized civil service from British India but Bhutto's 1973 reform turned the Pakistani civil service into a patronage machine for his party, the PPP (see Baxter et al. 2002). In this and other instances like it, laws and regulations limiting patronage and vote buying appear malleable in the hands of politicians.

Ballots. The technology that governments and parties allow voters to use to express their electoral choices also influences clientelism. The main reason is that clientelism is greatly aided by less-than-opaque and -anonymous voting; ballots that facilitate the monitoring of voters' choices also facilitate clientelism. By the early twentieth century most countries that were independent and had democratic intervals had eliminated voice voting and gone over to the secret ballot, greatly reducing the scope for vote trafficking. Nevertheless, some ballots and balloting systems still in use today help parties infer the vote choices of individual voters. Spain, for instance, combines ticket ballots—ones containing only the names of candidates from one party's list—with the option of voting semi-publicly: Spanish voters have a choice of placing their preferred party list in an envelope in a curtained booth or doing so openly. (France and some former French colonies, as well as several other democracies, also use ticket ballots.) A handful of countries, among them Argentina, Panama, and Uruguay, use party ballots, ballots that political parties produce and in which individual candidates (for executive offices) or party lists appear on separate ballots.

Ticket and party ballots are both distinct from Australian ballots, in which all candidates or lists of candidates for a given office appear listed in the same format, and in which public agencies produce and distribute the ballots on the day before or day of the election, under controlled conditions (Converse 1972). Reynolds and Steenbergen (2005) calculate that 85 percent of countries today use Australian ballots, 15 percent what I am calling ticket and party ballots.

Party ballots may particularly facilitate vote buying not because of the format of the ballot but because parties produce them and usually can distribute them well before the election. The distribution of ballots becomes part of the process of mobilizing voters, and when parties distribute ballots along with bags of food, building materials, or other individualized inducements, the message comes across especially clearly that the favors are expected to be reciprocated with a vote. Brusco, Nazareno, and Stokes (2004) find that Argentine voters who received their ballots directly from party representatives are significantly more likely to have received campaign handouts and to report that these handouts influenced their vote.

Because it is politicians who write regulations discouraging patronage and design ballots that work against vote buying, one wonders whether these rules have an independent effect of reducing clientelism or whether they are brought to life only after other factors, such as economic development, have made clientelism less effective and hence less tempting for politicians. Still, in some settings parties compete against one another by shining a light on vote buying and electoral corruption, creating electoral incentives to carry out ballot and other institutional reforms. This dynamic has been observed in Mexico, in Taiwan, and in Argentina; in all three countries, opposition politicians admonish voters, as an Argentine politician put it, to "receive with one hand and vote with the other" (quoted in Szwarcberg 2001).

Accounts of transitions from clientelist to programmatic politics offer clues about the factors encouraging clientelism. Lehoucq and Molina (2002) attribute the decline of vote buying in Costa Rica in the 1940s to the introduction of the secret ballot and the increasing costliness of payments to voters, the latter suggestive of development as a cause of this decline.

Recall that, as illustrated in Figure 25.2, the clientelist equilibrium is only one of many possible equilibria. Schaffer and Schedler point out that, whereas markets in consumer goods are generally considered morally legitimate, "the explicit purchase of votes runs counter to present norms of democratic liberty and equality" (2006, 6). It is therefore vulnerable to ideological attacks. In Peru, a progressive military regime, followed by leftist organizers and radical clergy, encouraged people to think of themselves as citizens who should receive public services in exchange for their taxes, rather than as clients who needed to plead for special favors (Stokes 1995).

Several authors note a decline in clientelism and vote buying in Mexico with that country's gradual democratization, which culminated in 2000. A Mitofsky poll found that 5 percent of voters received a handout before the 2000 elections; the *Mexico 2000 panel study* put the number at just under 15 percent (see Cornelius 2004).[9] He interprets both numbers as a decline over past practice. Lehoucq (2006) and Cornelius give credit to Mexico's Federal Electoral Institute (the Instituto Federal Electoral, IFE), overhauled in 1994, for reducing clientelism and vote buying. Magaloni concurs, but goes a step further and analyzes the reasons why the PRI, Mexico's ruling party, was willing to grant the IFE independence. It granted this independence, in her analysis, as a way of inducing the opposition to endorse the legitimacy of elections. Fair elections with the possibility of losing were a better outcome for the PRI than illegitimate elections and the social instability that followed.

Institutional consequences of clientelism. Little research has delved into the institutional causes of clientelism, but even less into its institutional *consequences*. But in a highly original paper, Desposato (2007) studies clientelism's effects on political parties in legislatures. He reasons that parties that use clientelist strategies will behave differently in the legislature than parties that mobilize electoral support by providing public goods. Clientelist parties will work determinedly to secure public resources for distribution throughout their personal networks; when they are in opposition, they will

[9] Yet during the 2006 presidential campaign, "millions of poor Mexicans have been threatened with exclusion from health care and social assistance programs if they do not vote for various candidates [and] others, mostly in rural areas, have been given cash payoffs of $40 to $60 for their votes" (Alianza Civica, cited in *Washington Post* 2006).

display little legislative cohesion. Public-goods oriented parties will work determinedly to provide these goods and claim credit for their provision, and will display more legislative cohesion, whether in government or in opposition. Desposato compares two state legislatures in Brazil, one in a state (Piauí) where clientelism is widespread, the other in a state (Brasília) in which it is nearly absent. He finds differences in the behaviors of the legislative parties—greater frequency of roll-calls in Brasília, less cohesion of opposition parties in Piauí—that accord with his theory.

5.3 The Effectiveness of Clientelism and Patronage

Most students and casual observers of clientelism assume that it *works* as an electoral strategy—that, all else equal, a party that disburses clientelist benefits will win more votes than it would have had it not pursued this strategy. In general we do not expect parties to pursue strategies that are ineffective. And yet we have some theoretical reasons for believing that conditions are not always ripe for clientelism. In the repeated game outlined earlier, the vote-buying equilibrium is just one of many possible equilibria.

Voters who are offered patronage by an unpopular incumbent may find ways to overcome the collective action problem of voting against him or her, as they eventually did in Mexico (Magaloni 2006). And if we assume that parties sometimes lack information about the consequences of their strategies, particularly in new democracies, then we should not be surprised that they sometimes undermine themselves.[10]

A few studies have explored the electoral consequences of clientelism, most of them in the Americas. In the USA, Levitt and Snyder (1997) study the effect of pork-barrel spending (by the definition offered above) on subsequent elections for the House of Representatives. They find that an additional $100 in federal spending can increase the popular vote of the incumbent by as much as 2 percent.[11] In Peru, Roberts and Arce (1998) find a positive correlation between the Fujimori government's per capita expenditures by department on anti-poverty programs in 1994 and early 1995 and Fujimori's vote share in his 1995 (re)election.

But clientelism and patronage are not always a plus. In Argentina, Calvo and Murillo (2004) find that, in provinces governed by the Peronist party, the larger the number of public employees per thousand, the greater the Peronist vote share in subsequent elections. But in provinces governed by Argentina's other main political party, the Radicals, public employment has no significant effect on Radical vote shares. Using more disaggregated (municipal) data, Nazareno, Brusco, and Stokes (2006) find similar—and even starker—results: patronage spending by Radical mayors *depresses* their party's vote share. The same is true of spending by the federal government

---

[10] Strategic debates within parties, in the present context over whether, for instance, to pursue "air" (advertising, propaganda) or "ground" (vote buying, face-to-face mobilization) strategies, are an indication of some uncertainty about what will work and what will not.

[11] An important feature of their paper is that it deals with the fact that effort to attract federal dollars by House members is a potential omitted variable. The authors deal with this problem by introducing federal expenditures in other districts in the same state as an instrumental variable.

(controlled by the Peronists) on targeted unemployment relief programs in the late 1990s. Controlling for other factors (such as poverty), Peronist mayors could expect to receive about twice as much funding per capita as Radicals, and spending in Radical-controlled municipalities significantly *reduced* the Radical vote share in the next election. In contrast, when these same targeted funds were distributed in Peronist municipalities, local Peronists increased their vote share in subsequent elections.

Like Levitt and Snyder, Nazareno and his associates reason that mayors who knew they were in trouble heading into an election might spend more; even if the extra spending enhanced their vote share over the level it would have stayed at had they not intensified their patronage efforts, the patronage would appear, misleadingly, to depress the incumbent's support. We thus face a possible endogeneity problem: (anticipated) poor electoral performance might cause more spending, rather than spending causing poor electoral performance. To deal with this possibility, Nazareno and his co-authors employ an instrument: spending in an earlier election. Still, even correcting for endogeneity, the results hold: Radical patronage depresses the Radical vote.

Why would clientelist spending ever be bad for the party that does the spending? For some kinds of constituents—especially wealthier, more autonomous constituents—such spending may indicate inefficient, pandering governments. It is highly suggestive that the best case we have of such negative effects is spending by the Argentine Radical Party, a party of relatively middle-class constituents.

6 CONCLUSIONS

Political clientelism, the giving of material resources as a quid pro quo for political support, is best understood as part of an ongoing exchange between patron and client, with threats of defection instead of, or perhaps in addition to, norms of reciprocity sustaining it. Incorporating the old observation that patron–client linkages are face to face and ongoing allows us to model the exchange as a repeated game, and hence one that can overcome problems of commitment and defection on either side. Theoretical and empirical studies identify conditions under which both core and marginal voters will be the targets (or beneficiaries) of clientelist parties. Clientelism is intimately linked to poverty and inequality, of which it is probably both a cause and a consequence. Institutions such as personalized campaigns, ballot design, and legal restrictions may also influence whether parties deploy clientelist or programmatic strategies.

Much theoretical work and empirical research remain to be done. The affinity between poverty (inequality) and clientelism is settled fact, but the mechanisms linking the two, and the direction of causality, are not. We tend to treat clientelism as involving a dyadic link between patron and client, in an electoral context, between party and voter. But really the strategic interactions of at least three actors should be considered: party leaders, party brokers, and voters. We have some detailed empirical information on brokers, such as Wang and Kurzman's (2006) fascinating study of Kuomintang brokers in Taiwan, but the implications of their presence for theory have not been sufficiently worked out. Furthermore, we would like to know more about the interactions between parties as they strategize about which methods to pursue. Finally, our understanding of the relationship between clientelism and institutions—from macro institutions such as electoral systems to micro institutions such as ballot design—is in its infancy. Not until we achieve fuller theoretical accounts and test them with more systematically comparative data will we have the tools to tame political clientelism.

References

ALDRICH, J. H. 1995 *Why Parties? The Origin and Transformation of Political Parties in America.* Chicago: University of Chicago Press.

ANSOLABEHERE, S., and SNYDER, J. M., Jr. 2002. Party control of state government and the distribution of party expenditures. Typescript. Massachusetts Institute of Technology.

AUYERO, J. 2001. *Poor People's Politics: Peronist Survival Networks and the Legacy of Evita.* Durham, NC: Duke University Press.

BARTH, F. 1959. *Political Leadership among the Swat Pathans.* London: Athlone.

BAXTER, C., MALIK, Y. K., KENNEDY, C. H., and OBERST, R. C. 2002. *Government and Politics in South Asia.* Boulder, Colo.: Westview Press.

BRUSCO, V., NAZARENO, M., and STOKES, S. 2004. Vote buying in Argentina. *Latin American Research Review,* 39 (2): 66–88.

——— ——— ——— 2006. Clientelism and risk. Typescript. Yale University.

CALVO, E., and MURILLO, M. V. 2004. Who delivers? Partisan clients in the Argentine electoral market. *American Journal of Political Science,* 48 (4): 742–57.

CHANDRA, K. 2004. *Why Ethnic Parties Succeed: Patronage and Ethnic Head Counts in India.* Cambridge: Cambridge University Press.

—— 2007. Counting heads: a theory of voter and elite behavior in patronage democracies. Pp. 183–239 in *Patrons, Clients, and Policies: Patterns of Democratic Accountability and Political Competition,* ed. H. Kitschelt and S. Wilkinson. Cambridge: Cambridge University Press.

CHUBB, J. 1981. The social bases of an urban political machine: the case of Palermo. *Political Science Quarterly,* 96 (1): 107–25.

—— 1982. *Patronage, Power, and Poverty in Southern Italy.* Cambridge: Cambridge University Press.

CONVERSE, P. E. 1972. Change in the American electorate. Pp. 263–337 in *The Human Meaning of Social Change,* ed. A. Campbell. New York: Russell Sage Foundation.

CORNELIUS, W. A. 2004. Mobilized voting in the 2000 elections: the changing efficacy of vote buying and coercion in Mexican electoral politics. Pp. 47–65 in *Mexico's Pivotal Democratic Election: Candidates, Voters, and the Presidential Campaign of 2000,* ed. J. I. Domínguez and C. Lawson. Stanford, Calif.: Stanford University Press.

COX, G. 2006. Voters, core voters, and distributive politics. Typescript. University of California, San Diego.

COX, G. W., and McCUBBINS, M. D. 1986. Electoral politics as a redistributive game. *Journal of Politics,* 48 (2): 370–89.

DESPOSATO, S. W. 2006. How does vote buying shape the legislative arena? Pp. 144–79 in *Elections for Sale: The Causes and Consequences of Vote Buying,* ed. F. C. Schaffer. Boulder, Colo.: Lynne Rienner.

Dixit, A., and Londregan, J. 1996. The determinants of success of special interests in redistributive politics. *Journal of Politics*, 58: 1132–55.

Elster, J. 1989. *Nuts and Bolts for the Social Sciences*. Cambridge: Cambridge University Press.

Fox, J. 1994. The difficult transition from clientelism to citizenship: lessons from Mexico. *World Politics*, 46: 151–84.

Fudenberg, D., and Tirole, J. 2002. *Game Theory*, 8th edn. Cambridge, Mass.: MIT Press.

Gouldner, A. 1960. The norm of reciprocity: a preliminary statement. *American Sociological Review*, 25 (2): 161–78.

Graziano, L. 1977. Patron–client relationships in southern Italy. Pp. 360–78 in *Friends, Followers, and Factions: A Reader in Political Clientelism*, ed. S. W. Schmidt, J. C. Scott, C. Landé, and L. Guasti. Berkeley and Los Angeles: University of California Press.

Hicken, A. 2007. How do rules and institutions encourage vote buying? Pp. 68–89 in *Elections for Sale: The Causes and Consequences of Vote Buying*, ed. F. C. Schaffer. Boulder, Colo.: Lynne Rienner.

Hiskey, J. 1999. Does democracy matter? Electoral competition and local development in Mexico. Ph.D. dissertation. University of Pittsburgh.

Kitschelt, H. 2000. Linkages between citizens and politicians in democratic polities. *Comparative Political Studies*, 33 (6–7): 845–79.

—— and Wilkinson, S. eds. 2007. Citizen–politician linkages: an introduction. In *Patrons, Clients, and Policies: Patterns of Democratic Accountability and Political Competition*. Cambridge: Cambridge University Press.

—— Mansfeldova, Z., Markowski, R., and Toka, G. 1999. *Post-Communist Party Systems: Competition, Representation, and Inter-party Cooperation*. Cambridge: Cambridge University Press.

Krishna, A. 2007. Politics in the middle: mediating relationships between citizens and the state in rural north India. Pp. 298–383 in *Patrons, Clients, and Policies: Patterns of Democratic Accountability and Political Competition*, ed. H. Kitschelt and S. Wilkinson. Cambridge: Cambridge University Press.

Kristinsson, G. H. 2001. Clientelism in a cold climate: the case of Iceland. Pp. 172–92 in *Clientelism, Interests, and Representation: The European Experience in Comparative Perspective*, ed. S. Piattoni. Cambridge: Cambridge University Press.

Landé, C. H. 1965. *Leaders, Factions, and Parties: The Structure of Philippine Politics*. Yale Southeast Asia Monograph Series 6. New Haven: Yale University Press.

—— 1977. Introduction: the dyadic basis of clientelism. Pp. xiii–xxxvii in *Friends, Followers, and Factions: A Reader in Political Clientelism*, ed. S. W. Schmidt, J. C. Scott, C. Landé, and L. Guasti. Berkeley and Los Angeles: University of California Press.

Lehoucq, F. E. 2007. When does a market for votes emerge? Theoretical and empirical perspectives. Pp. 48–67 in *Elections for Sale: The Causes and Consequences of Vote Buying*, ed. F. C. Schaffer. Boulder, Colo.: Lynne Rienner.

—— and Molina, I. 2002. *Stuffing the Ballot Box: Fraud, Electoral Reform, and Democratization in Costa Rica*. Cambridge: Cambridge University Press.

Lemarchand, R. 1977. Political clientelism and ethnicity in tropical Africa: competing solidarities in nation-building. Pp. 100–23 in *Friends, Followers, and Factions: A Reader in Political Clientelism*, ed. S. W. Schmidt, J. C. Scott, C. Landé, and L. Guasti. Berkeley and Los Angeles: University of California Press.

Levitsky, S. 2003. *Transforming Labor-Based Parties in Latin America: Argentine Peronism in Comparative Perspective*. Cambridge: Cambridge University Press.

Levitt, S. D., and Snyder, J. M., Jr. 1997. The impact of federal spending on House election outcomes. *Journal of Political Economy*, 105 (1): 30–53.

LINDBECK, A., and WEIBULL, J. 1987. Balanced budget redistribution as the outcome of political competition. *Public Choice*, 52 (3): 273–97.

LYNE, M. 2007. Rethinking economics and institutions: the voter's dilemma and democratic accountability. Pp. 335–80 in *Patrons, Clients, and Policies: Patterns of Democratic Accountability and Political Competition*, ed. H. Kitschelt and S. Wilkinson. Cambridge: Cambridge University Press.

MAGALONI, B. 2006. *Voting for Autocracy: Hegemonic Party Survival and its Demise in Mexico.* Cambridge: Cambridge University Press.

—— DIAZ-CAYEROS, A. and ESTÉVEZ, F. 2007. Clientelism and portfolio diversification: a model of electoral investment with applications to Mexico. Pp. 381–429 in *Patrons, Clients, and Policies: Patterns of Democratic Accountability and Political Competition*, ed. H. Kitschelt and S. Wilkinson. Cambridge: Cambridge University Press.

MAINWARING, S. P. 1999. *Rethinking Party Systems in the Third Wave of Democratization: The Case of Brazil.* Stanford, Calif.: Stanford University Press.

MAVROGORDATOS, G. T. 1983. *Still-Born Republic: Social Coalitions and Party Strategies, 1922–1936.* Berkeley and Los Angeles: University of California Press.

MEDINA, L. F., and STOKES, S. 2007. Monopoly and monitoring: an approach to political clientelism. Pp. 150–82 in *Patrons, Clients, and Policies: Patterns of Democratic Accountability and Political Competition*, ed. H. Kitschelt and S. Wilkinson. Cambridge: Cambridge University Press.

NAZARENO, M., BRUSCO, V., and STOKES, S. C. 2006. Réditos y peligros electorales del gasto público en Argentina. *Desarrollo económico*, 46 (181): 63–86.

O'GORMAN, F. 2001. Patronage and the reform of the state in England, 1700–1860. Pp. 54–76 in *Clientelism, Interests, and Representation: The European Experience in Comparative Perspective*, ed. S. Piattoni. Cambridge: Cambridge University Press.

PÉREZ YARAHUAN, G. 2006. Policy making and electoral politics: three essays on the political determinants of social welfare spending in Mexico, 1988–2003. Ph.D. dissertation. University of Chicago.

PIATTONI, S. ed. 2001. *Clientelism, Interests, and Representation: The European Experience in Comparative Perspective.* Cambridge: Cambridge University Press.

RANDERAAD, N., and WOLFFRAM, D. J. 2001. Constraints on clientelism: the Dutch path to modern politics, 1848–1917. Pp. 101–21 in *Clientelism, Interests, and Representation: The European Experience in Comparative Perspective*, ed. S. Piattoni. Cambridge: Cambridge University Press.

REYNOLDS, A., and STEENBERGEN, M. 2005. How the world votes: the political consequences of ballot design, innovation, and manipulation. *Electoral Studies*, 25 (4).

REYNOLDS, J. 1988. *Testing Democracy: Electoral Behavior and Progressive Reform in New Jersey, 1880–1920.* Chapel Hill: University of North Carolina Press.

ROBERTS, K., and ARCE, M. 1998. Neoliberalism and lower-class voting behavior in Peru. *Comparative Political Studies*, 31 (2): 217–46.

ROBINSON, J., and VERDIER, T. 2003. The political economy of clientelism. Typescript. University of California, Berkeley.

SAFIRE, W. 1993. *Safire's New Political Dictionary.* London: Random House.

SCHADY, N. 2000. The political economy of expenditures by the Peruvian social fund (FONCODES), 1991–1995. *American Political Science Review*, 94 (2): 289–304.

SCHAFFER, F. C. ed. 2007. *Elections for Sale: The Causes and Consequences of Vote Buying.* Boulder, Colo.: Lynne Rienner.

—— and SCHEDLER, A. 2007. What is vote buying? Pp. 24–47 in *Elections for Sale: The Causes and Consequences of Vote Buying*, ed. F. C. Shaffer. Boulder, Colo.: Lynne Rienner.

SCHMIDT, S. W., SCOTT, J. C., LANDÉ, C., and GUASTI, L. eds. 1977. *Friends, Followers, and Factions: A Reader in Political Clientelism.* Berkeley and Los Angeles: University of California Press.

SCOTT, J. C. 1969. Corruption, machine politics, and political change. *American Political Science Review,* 63: 1142–58.

—— 1972. Patron–client politics and political change in Southeast Asia. *American Political Science Review,* 66: 91–113.

—— 1976. *The Moral Economy of the Peasant: Rebellion and Subsistence in Southeast Asia.* New Haven: Yale University Press.

SHEFTER, M. 1977. Party and patronage: Germany, England, and Italy. *Politics and Society,* 7: 403–51.

—— 1994. *Political Parties and the State: The American Historical Experience.* Princeton: Princeton University Press.

STOKES, S. C. 1995. *Cultures in Conflict: Social Movements and the State in Peru.* Berkeley and Los Angeles: University of California Press.

—— 2005. Perverse accountability: a formal model of machine politics with evidence from Argentina. *American Political Science Review,* 99 (3): 315–25.

—— 2007. Is vote buying undemocratic? Pp. 117–43 in *Elections for Sale: The Causes and Consequences of Vote Buying,* ed. F. C. Schaffer. Boulder, Colo.: Lynne Rienner.

SZWARCBERG, M. L. 2001. Feeding loyalties: an analysis of clientelism, the case of the Manzaneras. Typescript. Universidad Torcuato di Tella.

TAM, W. 2005. Political insecurity and clientelist politics: the case of Singapore. Typescript. University of Chicago.

URQUIZA, E. Y. 2006. Las eternas internas: política y faccionalismo en un municipio radical, 1983–1999. Pp. 57–80 in *Democracia local: clientelismo, capital social, e innovación política en Argentina,* ed. S. Amaral and S. Stokes. Buenos Aires: Eduntref.

VAN DE WALLE, N. 2007. Meet the new boss, same as the old boss? The evolution of political clientelism in Africa. Pp. 112–49 in *Patrons, Clients, and Policies: Patterns of Democratic Accountability and Political Competition,* ed. H. Kitschelt and S. Wilkinson. Cambridge: Cambridge University Press.

WANG, C.-S. and KURZMAN, C. 2007. Logistics: how to buy votes. Pp. 90–116 in *Elections for Sale: The Causes and Consequences of Vote Buying,* ed. F. C. Schaffer. Boulder, Colo.: Lynne Rienner.

WANTCHEKON, L. 2003. Clientelism and voting behavior: evidence from a field experiment in Benin. *World Politics,* 55: 399–422.

WASHINGTON POST FOREIGN SERVICE. 2006. Dirty politics "ingrained" in Mexico. June 26, p. A16.

WEINER, M. 1967. *Party Building in a New Nation.* Chicago: University of Chicago Press.

WEITZ-SHAPIRO, R. 2006. Partisanship and protest: the politics of workfare distribution in Argentina. Typescript. Columbia University.

WILKINSON, S. I. 2007. Explaining changing patterns of party–voter linkages in India. Pp. 238–97 in *Patrons, Clients, and Policies: Patterns of Democratic Accountability and Political Competition,* ed. H. Kitschelt and S. Wilkinson. Cambridge: Cambridge University Press.

WILSON, J. Q., and BANFIELD, E. 1963. *City Politics.* Cambridge, Mass.: Harvard University Press.

CHAPTER 26

....

POLITICAL ACTIVISM: NEW CHALLENGES, NEW OPPORTUNITIES

....

PIPPA NORRIS

RESEARCH on political activism compares the ways that citizens participate, the processes that lead them to do so, and the consequences of these acts. The standard paradigm was established in earlier decades by the seminal works in the social psychological tradition: Almond and Verba (1963),[1] Verba and Nie (1972),[2] Verba, Nie, and Kim (1978), and Barnes and Kaase (1979).[3]

Much empirical work comparing patterns of political participation during the 1980s tended to reflect the basic theoretical framework and predominant survey-based approach developed in earlier decades; for example, Parry, Moyser, and Day replicated their approach and core findings in Britain (1992). During the 1990s, however, several major areas can be identified where scholars have made significant advances. In the process, some of the core assumptions about the importance of individual resources and cultural attitudes made by the standard social psychological model have been subject to major refinement, or even wholesale revision. It is impossible to provide a comprehensive review of the rapidly expanding literature in the space of a short chapter, and others provide overviews of the American

---

[1] See also Almond and Verba (1980).
[2] See also Verba, Schlozman, and Brady (1995); Burns, Schlozman, and Verba (2001).
[3] See also Marsh (1977); Jennings and van Deth (1989); Adrian and Apter (1995).

literature, but here we can highlight selected developments in comparative politics and consider their implications.[4] This overview highlights four key themes which have emerged during the last decade, including (i) growing recognition of the importance of the institutional context of formal rules for electoral turnout; (ii) the widespread erosion of party membership in established democracies and questions about its consequences; (iii) the substantial revival of interest in voluntary associations and social trust spurred by theories of social capital; and lastly (iv) the expansion of diverse forms of cause-oriented types of activism, including the spread of demonstrations and protests, consumer politics, professional interest groups, and more diffuse new social movements and transnational advocacy networks. After briefly illustrating some of the literature which has developed around these themes, the chapter concludes by considering the challenges for the future research agenda in comparative politics.

1 THE STANDARD SOCIAL PSYCHOLOGICAL MODEL OF PARTICIPATION

The body of work which developed following the seminal work by Almond and Verba documented levels of participation within and across nations, and distinguished modes of political action. Empirical research draws upon multiple methods, including case studies, focus groups, experiments, and formal models, although during the last half-century the study of participation has been dominated by analysis of the sample survey. The literature established a series of well-known findings about the distribution and causes of mass activism. (i) In most democracies, voting turnout was the only mode of political participation involving a majority of citizens. (ii) Beyond this, the more demanding forms of conventional participation engaged only a small minority, including campaigning and party work, contacting representatives, and community organizing. (iii) Protest politics exemplified by demonstrations, petitions, and political strikes, regarded as a distinct form of activism, was similarly confined to a small elite. (iv) In explaining who became active, the "baseline model" developed by Verba and Nie suggested that structural resources played a significant role, notably the distribution of educational qualifications, income, and occupational status, along with the related factors of sex, age, and ethnicity. (v) Cultural attitudes, closely related to socioeconomic status and education, were also important for motivating engagement; people are more likely to participate if they feel informed, interested, and efficacious, if they care strongly about the outcome, and if they think that they can make a difference. (vi) To a lesser extent, activism was also acknowledged to be affected by institutional and social contexts, for example, Verba and Nie

---

[4] For a recent review of the extensive literature on the United States, see Schlozman (2002).

noted that levels of voter turnout were influenced by registration procedures and by affiliation with mobilizing agencies, such as labor unions and parties. But the predominance of individual-level survey analysis, based on samples representative of the general adult population within each nation, meant that the analysis of contextual effects remained underdeveloped (Books and Prysby 1988; Huckfield and Sprague 1995). These core claims became the standard textbook view from the 1960s until at least the late 1980s, with the importance of structural resources and cultural attitudes replicated and confirmed in many survey-based studies of specific nations and types of participation.[5]

Of course even during this era there was far from complete agreement within the profession about these claims; for example many of the core assumptions in social psychology about habitual forms of participation were rejected by rational choice theorists, emphasizing the conscious calculation of "costs" and "benefits," represented best by Downs (1957) and by Olson (1965).

Normative theorists were also sharply divided about the importance of civic engagement for democracy, and whether the widespread lack of public involvement documented by surveys should be accepted as a practical benchmark or whether it should be berated for undermining participatory ideals.[6] The school led by Joseph Schumpeter (1952) suggests that limited public involvement was sufficient to ensure stable and accountable government, so long as governments in representative democracies were legitimized by free and fair elections contested by rival parties and politicians at regular intervals. For proponents of this view, citizens play a critical role by having the right and opportunity to "throw the rascals out" at election, should they so desire, but not by becoming involved in day-to-day processes of public policy making. The most recent version of this thesis is developed by Hibbing and Theiss-Morse (2003) who argue that Americans do not want to be more involved in most political decisions; instead most share a widespread aversion to the messy business of political debate, compromise, and conflict resolution. The Schumpeterian perspective emphasizes that democracy is based on the values of competition and accountability as much as participation, and that the persistent social inequalities in citizen engagement generate serious flaws for direct decision making. The major policy challenge, from this perspective, is developing effective political institutions promoting party competition and leadership accountability, especially in transitional and consolidating democracies.

By contrast, those following in the footsteps of Rousseau, John Stuart Mill, and G. D. H. Cole, such as Barber (1984), advocate "participatory" or "strong" democracy. This view, which is particularly popular in the United States, regards more extensive public engagement as essential for democracy, including widespread involvement in deliberative debate, community groups, and decentralized decision making (Gutmann and Thomson 2004). Activism is thought to have multiple virtues, proponents argue, making better people, by strengthening citizen awareness, interest in public affairs, social tolerance, generalized reciprocity, and interpersonal trust, as well as fostering more responsive

---

[5] See, for example, Milbrath and Goel (1977); Bennett (1986); Conway (2000); Teixeira (1992).
[6] For a summary discussion, see Held (1996).

and effective government, by generating better decisions and more legitimate outcomes. The major policy challenge, from this perspective, lies in developing new opportunities for public deliberation and community decision making, for example through strengthening local NGOs in civil society, through the use of referenda and initiatives, as well as via other forms of community decision making involving interactive government consultation processes, neighborhood councils, and local town hall meetings.

2 ELECTORAL TURNOUT AND THE IMPORTANCE OF THE RULES

The standard socioeconomic model of voting participation developed by Verba and Nie acknowledged the role of the broader institutional context set by electoral systems and administrative procedures, but this was never given center stage. By contrast, during recent decades a growing body of comparative literature seeking to explain variations in electoral turnout, and to improve participation, has given greater emphasis to the importance of the institutional rules and legal arrangements for registration and voting, which affect both the "costs" and "benefits" of electoral activism. Comparative research on turnout has been strengthened by release of the electronic database assembled by International IDEA monitoring voter participation worldwide in national parliamentary and presidential elections since 1945 (Lopez Pintor and Gratschew n.d.). Related research collected from national electoral commissions and other official bodies has also established far more accurate information about the administrative and legal procedures involved in elections in many countries around the world, including processes of voter registration, citizenship requirements to qualify for the franchise, the use of compulsory voting, and multi-day voting, as well as public funding for campaigns and parties (Massicotte, Blais, and Yoshinaka 2004). Considerable interest has also been shown in monitoring the impact of new information and communication technologies on electoral administration, balloting, and voting, for example the use of electronic voting in Switzerland, Estonia, Austria, and the UK (Kersting and Baldersheim 2004).

Much of the more recent work on voter turnout has been concerned with estimating institutional effects, drawing comparisons across places and time, for example the impact of compulsory voting in the countries where this has been employed, and the effect of reforms to voting facilities, such as the introduction of all-mail ballots. By now a large body of literature has accumulated which confirms the importance of institutional contexts on aggregate levels of registration and voting turnout. For example Powell compared turnout in twenty-nine democracies, including the effects of the socioeconomic environment, the constitutional setting, and the party system. The study established that compulsory voting laws, automatic registration procedures, and the strength of party–group alignments boosted turnout, while participation was depressed in cases of one-party predominant systems allowing no rotation of the parties in government (Powell 1980, 1982, 1986). Jackman and Miller (1995) also examined electoral participation in twenty-two industrialized democracies during the 1980s, and confirmed that political institutions and electoral laws provided the most plausible explanation for cross-national variations in voter turnout, including levels of electoral proportionality, multipartyism, and compulsory voting.[7] Building upon this foundation, Blais and Dobrynska conducted a broader comparison by analyzing the number of votes cast as a proportion of the registered electorate in parliamentary elections in ninety-one electoral democracies from 1972 to 1995. They reported that multiple structural factors influenced turnout, including the use of compulsory voting, the voting age, the electoral system, the closeness of the electoral outcome, and the number of parties, as well as levels of socioeconomic development and the size of the country (Blais and Dobrzynska 1998; Blais 2000). Similarly Franklin, van der Eijk, and Oppenhuis (1996) compared turnout for direct elections to the European parliament and found that variations in participation among the fifteen EU member states could be attributed in large part to systemic institutional differences, notably the use of compulsory voting, the proportionality of the electoral system, and the closeness of European to national elections. Using the International IDEA database, Rose (2004) established that variations in voter turnout in post-war European national elections could be explained by the length of time in which free elections have been held, proportional representation electoral systems, the use of compulsory voting, elections held on a rest day, and the mean size of electoral districts.[8] The most recent study by Mark Franklin (2004) also emphasizes the importance of the institutional context for explaining variations in turnout among established democracies, in particular patterns of electoral competition, as well as the effects of lowering the age of the franchise.

In the United States, as well, the frequency of elections and complicated voter registration procedures have long been believed to depress American turnout, and recent research has used states as laboratories to focus attention on the impact of administrative reforms in electoral processes, including the introduction of motor vehicle license voter registration, the use of different registration closing dates, innovations in ballot design, the employment of election day or "same-day" registration, and the use of early in-person voting (Wolfinger and Rosenstone 1980; Martinez and Hill 1999; Knack 1995; Crigler, Just, and McCaffery 2004). More substantial reforms under debate in the United States include amendments to the Electoral College and to the single-member simple plurality electoral system (Hill 2002). One related controversy in this area concerns the appropriate denominator used for monitoring trends in American turnout. Many previous studies have conventionally relied upon the number of valid votes cast as a proportion of the voting age population; for example on this basis Patterson (2001) claims that, despite some fluctuations, there has been a substantial erosion of voting participation in national elections during the last three decades. Yet McDonald and Popkin (2001) suggest that any apparent erosion of voter turnout in

---

[7] See also Katz (1997).   [8] See also Norris (2004).

American presidential and congressional elections in this period is due to the growth of the ineligible population, including non-citizens and felons who are legally unable to cast a ballot, not a growth in the proportion of non-voters.[9] This reinforces the importance of drawing future cross-national comparisons where turnout is estimated based on the number of valid votes cast as a proportion of the voting age population (Vote/VAP), rather than the eligible electorate (Vote/EE). This is critical for nations where large swaths of the resident adult population are excluded from voting, whether due to limited citizenship for immigrants, partial universal suffrage (for example, excluding women), or other restrictions on voting rights for major groups (Paxton et al. 2003). At minimum, studies measuring turnout as Vote/EE need to double-check their analysis against the Vote/VAP measures to see if their main findings remain robust. It is also worth noting that the selection of starting and ending points for any analysis of time series trends is also important. We should be highly suspicious of any comparisons of electoral turnout which start the series, arbitrarily, on a particularly high point (such as the 1960 US presidential election), or which fail to acknowledge and explain significant fluctuations in the trend line which can again be best accounted for by contextual factors such as the perceived closeness of the race (including American contests, such as the 1992 and 2004 presidential elections, where turnout rises).

The flowering of new scholarship on the institutional context, much derived from aggregate statistics on voting turnout, has established that individual-level survey analysis, focused exclusively on inequalities in socioeconomic status and the distribution of cultural attitudes, is inadequate by itself. The rules of the game adopted by different countries, states, or regions can shape whether voting participation is relatively widespread across the electorate or whether it is strongly skewed towards affluent and well-educated sectors. Similarly cultural attitudes could plausibly vary systematically in different contexts, for example a sense of external efficacy could be related to actual experience of the responsiveness and performance of the political system in meeting citizens' policy concerns. The main challenge which remains, and it is a difficult challenge, is to link these approaches, so that individual-level behavior is understood within its broader institutional context. Commonly the impact of the formal rules is assumed to be relatively straightforward by generating mechanical effects, for example that compulsory voting will automatically boost turnout. Yet there remain important variations even within countries using similar electoral rules, for example among nations with proportional or majoritarian electoral systems, or among those employing compulsory voting. Some of this can be attributed to specific institutional details, for example the mean size of the district magnitude used in PR systems or the penalties attached to non-compliance. But the challenge is also to link the institutional context with individual behavior, so that we can understand what Duverger termed the "psychological" effects generated by formal rules.[10]

Further research into institutional effects on voting participation and civic engagement is also needed because this is one of the main policy challenges facing

---

[9] See also Miles (2004).

[10] The original distinction between the "mechanical" and "psychological" effects of electoral systems was made by Duverger (1954).

political science. The international community has become deeply engaged in attempts to generate free and fair elections in dozens of nations around the globe, exemplified by the transitions following the collapse of the authoritarian regime in Bosnia and Herzegovina, decolonization in East Timor, and the end of civil war in Cambodia, as well as developments in Afghanistan and Iraq (Carothers 1999). In established democracies, as well, beyond the basic electoral formula, debates have also been common about the best way to overhaul electoral procedures. This includes reforms to the legal statutes and party rules governing party eligibility and candidate nomination, the administrative process of electoral registration and voting facilities, the regulation of campaign finance and political broadcasting, and the process of election management. Established democracies have introduced a range of reforms, whether switching between d'Hondt and LR-Hare formula, adjusting the effective voting threshold for minor parties to qualify for parliamentary representation, expanding the conditions of electoral suffrage, or altering the size of their legislative assemblies (see Lijphart 1994; International IDEA 2005). In all these cases, it is assumed that electoral reform has the capacity to overcome certain problems, including issues of civic disengagement. Institutional effects are therefore worth investigating because they are theoretically important in the literature, but also because they are policy relevant for real-world problems.

3 POLITICAL PARTIES AS SHRINKING MEMBERSHIP ORGANIZATION

Established democracies simultaneously face serious challenges where many observers believe that people have grown increasingly disenchanted with political parties, indicated by rising anti-party sentiment and falling party membership. The conventional narrative of party change suggests a period of steady decline since the "golden age" of the mass party flowered in the late 1950s, a matter of considerable concern, especially in Western Europe where parties continue to be the most important intermediary institution linking citizens and the state. Work assembled by an international team led by Katz and Mair has focused new light on the internal organization of parties (Katz and Mair 1992, 1995), while Dalton and Wattenberg (2000) have recently collected the most systematic evidence about partisan trends in post-industrial societies. Following the convention established by V. O. Key (1964), the literature on parties can be divided into three hierarchical components: parties-in-elected-office, parties-as-organizations, and parties-in-the-electorate. Evidence strongly suggests that parties continue as vital sinews connecting the organs of government, and they have lost none of their function in binding together the executive and legislature for the policy-making process.[11] Yet

---

[11] See the conclusions to Dalton and Wattenberg (2001). See also Mair (1997).

many studies suggest that accumulating indications of partisan decay are becoming clear at the organizational and electoral levels (Lawson and Merkl 1988). Throughout established democracies, there is now substantial evidence from national election surveys that a glacial erosion has occurred in the strength of partisan identification in the electorate, shrinking the proportion of habitual loyalists who support their party come rain or shine.[12] Moreover, studies by Mair and van Biezen, and by Scarrow, document evidence from official records that many parties in established democracies have experienced contracting membership rolls since the 1950s, although there remain substantial variations in the levels of party membership, even within relatively similar West European democracies.[13]

Given this trend, the typical mass-branch party organization in established democracies appears to be contracting at middle level, potentially thereby limiting opportunities for political participation, weakening civil society, and lessening the accountability of party leaders to followers. Most studies assume that the shrinkage in party memberships and the erosion of party loyalties indicate problems for the health of democracy, for example that this suggests widespread public rejection of parties caused by disaffection with their performance. Yet the consequences of these developments remain unclear. As Scarrow suggests, the aggregate figures remain silent about their meaning. Parties may have been losing support and membership fees from more passive members at the periphery, but they may retain the active support of the core activists who run local branches, raise funds, deliver leaflets, select candidates and leaders, attend conventions, debate policies, and otherwise man the volunteer grassroots base in mass-branch parties.[14] Moreover the mass party is not an essential feature of all representative democracies; many countries such as France have always been characterized by elite-led party organizations run by elected officials in the legislature and in government, with minimal membership. To explore the reasons for the membership decline, surveys of members have been conducted in the major British parties, and similar initiatives have now been launched elsewhere (Seyd and Whiteley 2004). The British studies have concluded that the pressure on people's time has made party activism less desirable while, on the demand side, the major parties have less need for volunteers as fund-raisers and campaigners, reducing the incentives they offer to join (Whiteley and Seyd 2002). Public subsidies and mediated channels of campaign communication have supplemented many of the essential functions of party volunteers. In the absence of integrated cross-national surveys of party members it remains to be seen whether similar patterns are evident elsewhere. The consequence of the shrinkage in party membership for representative democracy therefore remains under debate, if parties can continue to fulfill their primary functions by competing in regular elections by offering voters a bundled choice of policies and a team of politicians, even without an intermediate layer of volunteers and activists, as a professionally managed campaign and advocacy organization.

[12] The most comprehensive reviews of the European evidence are available in Schmitt and Holmberg (1995); Dalton and Wattenberg (2001).

[13] See in particular Mair and van Biezen (2001); Scarrow (2001).

[14] For evidence of this trend in Denmark, see also Andersen and Hoff (2001).

4 SOCIAL CAPITAL, VOLUNTARY ASSOCIATIONS, AND SOCIAL TRUST

The decline of party organizations can be understood as part of a broader development affecting many of the traditional agencies used for political action. As well as parties, traditional agencies, which conventionally provided the most important social institutions for civic mobilization during the post-war era in Western Europe, included churches affiliated to Christian Democratic parties, trade unions and cooperative associations which mobilized the working class on the left, in addition to diverse interest groups and voluntary associations in civic society, exemplified by community social clubs, professional and business organizations, agricultural co-operatives, and philanthropic groups.[15] Interest in the role of voluntary organizations has been renewed by the burgeoning literature on social capital, a contemporary growth industry in political science.

Theories of social capital originated in the ideas by Pierre Bourdieu (1970) and James Coleman (1988, 1990), emphasizing the importance of social ties and shared norms to societal well-being and economic efficiency.[16] The most influential account in political science, developed by Robert Putnam, expanded this notion in *Making Democracies Work* (1993) and in *Bowling Alone* (2000) by linking ideas of social capital to the importance of civic associations and voluntary organizations for political participation and effective governance.[17] For Putnam, social capital is defined as *"connections among individuals—social networks and the norms of reciprocity and trustworthiness that arise from them"* (2000, 19). Most importantly, this is therefore understood as both a *structural* phenomenon (social networks) and a *cultural* phenomenon (social norms). This dual nature often creates problems associated with attempts to measure social capital that commonly focus on one or the other dimension, but not both. Putnam claims that horizontal networks embodied in civic society, and the norms and values related to these ties, have important consequences, both for the people in them and for society at large, producing both private goods and public goods. Moreover Putnam goes further than other contemporary theorists in arguing that social capital has significant political consequences. The theory can be understood as a two-step model of how civic society directly promotes social capital, and how, in turn, social capital (the social networks and cultural norms that arise from civic society) is believed to facilitate political participation and good governance. In particular, based on his analysis of Italian regional government, he claims that abundant and dense skeins of associational connections and rich civic societies encourage effective governance. Lastly, in *Bowling Alone* Putnam presents the most extensive battery of evidence that civic society in general, and social capital in

---

[15] For a discussion of the conceptual distinctions and theoretical frameworks in the literature, see Berry (1984). For comparative trends in membership in unions, churches, and parties see Norris (2002).

[16] For a discussion of the history of the concept, see also the introduction in Baron, Field, and Schuller (2000).

[17] The seminal works are Putnam (1993, 1996, 2000); Putnam and Feldstein (2003).

particular, has suffered substantial erosion in the post-war years in America. Putnam considers multiple causes that may have contributed towards this development, such as the pressures of time and money. But it is changes in technology and the media, particularly the rise of television entertainment as America's main source of leisure activity, that Putnam fingers as the major culprit responsible for the erosion of social connectedness and civic disengagement in the United States, with the most profound effects upon the post-war generation (Putnam 2000, 246; 1995; Norris 1996).

Putnam's work has most clearly documented the decay of traditional civic organizations and social trust in America, although dispute continues to surround the interpretation of these trends.[18] But, as Putnam acknowledges, it remains unclear whether parallel developments are evident in an erosion of traditional associational membership and social trust in similar post-industrial societies, such as Germany, Sweden, and Britain.[19] Studies in Western Europe, in post-communist societies, and in Latin America have also explored complex patterns of social trust and associational activism, along with the factors associated with strengthening social capital and civil society (Kornai, Rothstein, and Rose-Ackerman 2004; Svendsen and Svendsen 2004; Hooghe and Stolle 2003).

The cross-national evidence which is emerging remains difficult to interpret for a number of reasons. One of the limitations of comparative research on voluntary organizations is the common bias towards monitoring activism and membership in traditional voluntary associations, while failing to take account of engagement in more diffuse new social movements. Traditional voluntary associations with large memberships were usually characterized by regularized, institutionalized, structured, and measurable activities: people signed up and paid up to become card-carrying members of the Norwegian trade unions, the German Social Democratic Party, and the British Women's Institute. Traditional agencies, as well as mass-branch political parties, were characterized by Weberian bureaucratic organizations, with formal rules and regulations, full-time paid officials, hierarchical mass-branch structures, and clear boundaries demarcating who did, and did not, belong (Clarke and Rempel 1997). Active members served many functions as the voluntary life-blood of associations, such as serving on a local governing board or contributing financially to community associations, holding fundraisers, publishing newsletters, manning publicity stalls, chairing meetings, and attending socials for groups such as the Red Cross, the Parent-Teacher Association, and the Rotary Club. Some of these large-scale umbrella organizations articulated and aggregated diverse interests on behalf of their members, particularly mainstream political parties, while other public interest groups focused their energies upon narrower policy concerns and niche sectors. The immense flowering of literature on social capital has renewed attention in these organizations, for example by monitoring trends over time in the official membership rolls, as well as through cross-national surveys, notably successive waves of the World Values Survey and the 2002 European Social Survey.

By contrast, modern agencies which have evolved since the early 1960s are typified by the women's movement, the anti-globalization movement, anti-war coalitions, and the

---

[18] For critiques, see Edwards and Foley (1998); Ladd (1996); Skopol (1996); Schudson (1996); Rotolo (1999).

[19] Pharr and Putnam (2000); Putnam (2002). For other comparative work, see van Deth (1997); van Deth and Kreuter (1998); van Deth (1999, 2000).

environmental movement, as well as by diverse non-governmental organizations and multinational policy advocacy networks. These are usually characterized by more fluid boundaries, looser networked coalitions, and decentralized organizational structures. The primary goals of new social movements often focus upon achieving social change through direct action strategies and community building, as well as by altering lifestyles and social identities, as much as through shaping formal policy-making processes and laws in government (Tarrow 1994; Tilly 1978; McAdam, McCarthy, and Zald 1996; Dalton and Kuechler 1990). Observers suggest that the capacity for modern agencies to cross national borders signals the emergence of a global civic society mobilizing around issues such as globalization, human rights, debt relief, and world trade (Rosenau 1990; Lipschutz 1996; Keck and Sikkink 1998; Smith, Chatfield, and Pagnucco 1997; Kriesi, Porta, and Riucht 1998). These agencies are characterized by decentralized networked communications among loose coalitions, relatively flat "horizontal" rather than "vertical" organizational structures, and more informal modes of belonging, including shared concern about diverse issues and identity politics (Zald and McCarthy 1987; Oberschall 1993; Meyer and Tarrow 1998; Larana, Johnston, and Gudfield 1994; McAdam, McCarthy, and Zald 1996). People can see themselves as belonging simply by "turning up" or sharing political sympathies with an easy-entrance, easy-exit permeability of organizational boundaries, rather than "formally" joining through paying dues.

If new social movements have now become an important alternative avenue for informal political mobilization, protest, and expression among the younger generation, as many suggest, then this development has important implications for how we interpret and measure trends in associational life. In particular, if studies are limited to comparing membership in the traditional agencies of political participation—typified by patterns of party membership, union density, and church-going—then they will present only a partial perspective which underestimates engagement through modern agencies characterized by fuzzier boundaries and more informal forms of belonging.

5 THE RISE OF CAUSE-ORIENTED ACTIVISM

The rise of alternative organizational forms of activism is related to the growth of cause-oriented politics and the way that this has now become mainstream. Much of the traditional literature on political participation focused extensively upon forms of civic engagement which emphasize the role of citizens within representative democracy in each nation-state, including the channels influencing elections, governments, and parties. Verba and his colleagues established this framework when they drew attention to the multiple "modes" of political participation which were thought to differ systematically in their costs and benefits (Verba, Nie, and Kim 1971; Verba and Nie 1972; Verba, Nie, and Kim 1978; Verba, Schlozman, and Brady 1995). *Voting*, for example, can be described as one of the most ubiquitous political activities through regular elections, yet one that exerts diffuse pressure over elected representatives and parties, with a broad outcome affecting all citizens. *Campaign work* for parties or candidates such as leafleting, attending local party meetings, and get-out-to-vote drives, also typically generates collective benefits, but requires greater initiative, time, and effort than casting a ballot. By contrast, particularized *contacting*, such as when a constituent gets in touch with an elected representative or government official about a specific problem, requires higher levels of information and initiative, generating particular benefits for the individual but with little need for cooperation with other citizens. *Community* organizing involved local initiatives and philanthropic associations. What these traditional repertoires share is that they are focused primarily upon how citizens can influence representative democracy, either directly (through voting) or indirectly (through parties and elected officials). Verba, Nie, and Kim recognized this assumption when they defined political participation as "those legal activities by private citizens that are more or less directly aimed at influencing the selection of governmental personnel and/or the actions they take" (1978, 46). Citizen-oriented activities, exemplified by voting participation and party membership, obviously remain important for democracy, but today this represents an excessively narrow conceptualization of activism that excludes some of the most common targets of civic engagement which have become conventional and mainstream.

The early literature also drew a clear distinction between "conventional" and "protest" politics, and this terminology often continues to be used today in research. The classic study of political action in the early 1970s by Barnes and Kasse (1979) conceptualized "protest" as the willingness of citizens to engage in dissent, including unofficial strikes, boycotts, petitions, the occupation of buildings, mass demonstrations, and even acts of political violence.[20] Yet this way of thinking about activism seems dated today, since it no longer captures the essential features of the modern repertoires where many of these modes have become mainstream. In particular, during the height of the 1960s counter-culture, demonstrations were often regarded as radical acts confined to a mélange of a small minority of students in alliance with workers, with peaceful mobilization over civil rights, anti-nuclear, or anti-war protests shading into civil disobedience, street theater, "sit-ins," and even violent acts. Yet today demonstrations have become mainstream and widespread; for example the 1999–2001 World Values Survey indicates that about 40 percent of the public have participated in a demonstration in countries such as Sweden, Belgium, and the Netherlands (van Aelst and Walgrave 2001; Norris, Walgrave, and van Aelst 2004). The proportion of those who have engaged in demonstrations has more than doubled since the mid-1970s. Similar observations can be made about the widespread practice of consumer politics, while petitioning has also become far more common (Norris 2003).

As a result of these changing repertoires, it seems clearer today to distinguish between *citizen-oriented* actions, relating mainly to elections and parties, and *cause-oriented* repertoires, which focus attention upon specific issues and policy concerns, exemplified

---

[20] See also Marsh (1977); Adrian and Apter (1995).

by consumer politics (buying or boycotting certain products for political or ethical reasons), petitioning, demonstrations, and protests.[21] The distinction is not watertight; for example political parties organize mass demonstrations, and elected representatives are lobbied by constituents about specific policy issues and community concerns, as much as for individual constituency service. New social movements often adopt mixed action strategies which combine traditional repertoires, including lobbying elected representatives and contacting the news media, with a variety of alternative forms of political expression, including online networking, street protests, and consumer boycotts. Compared with citizen-oriented actions, the distinctive aspect of cause-oriented repertoires is that these are most commonly used to pursue specific issues and policy concerns among diverse targets, both within and also well beyond the electoral arena.

Of course historically many techniques used by cause-oriented activists are not particularly novel; indeed petitions to parliament are one of the earliest forms of representative democracy, and, as previous chapters in this *Handbook* discuss, periodic waves of contentious politics, radical protest, and vigorous political dissent can be identified throughout Western democracies (Tilly et al. 1975). The mid-1950s saw passive resistance techniques used by the civil rights movement in the USA and the Campaign for Nuclear Disarmament in Western Europe. Building upon this, the 1960s experienced the resurgence of direct action with the anti-Vietnam demonstrations, the student protest movements, and social upheaval that swept the streets of Paris, Tokyo, and London. New social movements expanded, particularly those concerned about women's equality, nuclear power, anti-war, and the environment. The early 1970s saw the use of economic boycotts directed against apartheid in South Africa, and the adoption of more aggressive industrial action by trade unions, including strikes, occupations, and blockades, occasionally accompanied by arson, damage, and violence, directed against Western governments (Epstein 1991). Today, collective action through demonstrations has become a generally accepted way to express political grievances, voice opposition, and challenge authorities (van Aelst and Walgrave 2001; Norris, Walgrave, and van Aelst 2005).

An important characteristic of cause-oriented repertoires is that these have broadened towards engaging in "consumer" and "lifestyle" politics, where the precise dividing line between the "social" and "political" breaks down even further. These activities are exemplified by volunteer work at recycling cooperatives, helping at battered women's shelters, or fund-raising for a local school, as well as protesting at sites for timber logging, boycotting goods made by companies using sweatshop labor, and purchasing cosmetic products which avoid the use of animal testing. It could be argued that these types of activities, while having important social and economic consequences, fall outside of the sphere of the strictly "political" per se. Yet the precise dividing line between the "public" and the "private" spheres remains controversial, as the feminist literature has long emphasized (see Pateman 1988; Phillips 1991). Cause-oriented repertoires aim to reform

---

[21] Pattie, Whiteley, and Seyd have drawn a similar distinction but they conceptualize the dividing line to lie between "collective" and "individualized" forms of activism. This seems less satisfactory as a conceptual framework, however; protests and demonstrations remain collective acts, as are new social movements, even if they bring together participants on a more ad hoc and transient basis than regular membership within parties or community associations. See Pattie, Seyd, and Whiteley (2004).

the law or to influence the policy process, as well as to alter systematic patterns of social behavior, for example by establishing bottle bank recycling facilities, battered women's shelters, and heightening awareness of energy efficiency. For Inglehart, the process of cultural change lies at the heart of this development, where the core issues motivating activists have shifted from materialist concerns, focused on bread-and-butter concerns of jobs, wages, and pensions, to greater concern about postmaterialist values, including issues such as globalization, environmentalism, multiculturalism, and gender equality.[22] In many developing societies, loose and amorphous networks of community groups and grassroots voluntary associations often seek direct action within local communities over basic issues of livelihood, such as access to clean water, the distribution of agricultural aid, or health care and schools (see Baker 1999). Issues of identity politics around ethnicity and sexuality also commonly blur the "social" and the "political." Therefore in general the older focus on citizenship activities designed to influence elections, government, and public policy-making process within the nation-state seems unduly limited today, by excluding too much that is commonly understood as broadly "political."

Another defining characteristic of cause-oriented activities is that these are directed towards parliament and government, but also towards diverse actors in the public, non-profit, and private sectors. A substantial and growing literature has compared case studies of activism within international human rights organizations, women's NGOs, transnational environmental organizations, the anti-sweatshop and anti-land mines networks, the peace movement, and anti-globalization and anti-capitalism forces (Sassen 1999; Keck and Sikkink 1998; Edwards and Gaventa 2001; Evans 2000). The targets are often major multinational corporations, including consumer boycotts of Nike running shoes, McDonald's hamburgers, and Californian grapes, as well as protest demonstrations directed against international agencies and intergovernmental organizations, such as the World Trade Organization, the World Economic Forum in Davos, and the European Commission (Keck and Sikkink 1998). This literature suggests that changes in the targets of participation reflect the process of globalization and the declining autonomy of the nation-state, including the core executive, as power has shifted simultaneously towards intergovernmental organizations like the UN and WTO, and down towards regional and local assemblies.[23] Moreover the "shrinkage of the state" through initiatives such as privatization, marketization and deregulation means that decision making has flowed away from public bodies and official government agencies that were directly accountable to elected representatives, dispersing to a complex variety of non-profit and private agencies operating at local, national, and international levels (Feigenbaum, Henig, and Hamnett 1998). Due to these developments, it has become more difficult for citizens to use national elections, national political parties, and national legislatures as a way of challenging public policies, reinforcing the need for alternative repertoires for political expression and mobilization.

[22] For details see Inglehart (1997); Inglehart and Norris (2003); Norris and Inglehart (2004).
[23] For a discussion see Held (1999); Nye and Donahue (2001); Archibugi, Held, and Kohler (1998).

6 CONCLUSIONS: THE FUTURE
RESEARCH AGENDA

The literature has been growing and diversifying during the last decade yet there are still many areas which require considerable attention. We can conclude by identifying some of the most promising directions for the future research agenda. As noted earlier, the standard view in social psychology which developed during the 1960s and the 1970s emphasized several interrelated sets of factors to explain why individual citizens participate in different modes of politics. The early work of Verba and his colleagues emphasized the influence of prior *structural resources* which people bring to politics, notably their educational qualifications, occupational status, and income, which are closely related to their ethnicity and sex, all of which facilitate participation. Education, for example, furnishes analytical skills which are useful for making sense of political issues and policy-making processes, while household income is directly relevant for the capacity to make political donations. The "baseline" resource model added *cultural attitudes*, exemplified by a sense of internal efficacy (confidence in the ability to influence public affairs), external efficacy (a sense of the system's responsiveness), civic knowledge, and political interest (such as following events in the news), which are commonly closely related to the propensity to become active. These factors remain important; indeed they continue to be included in standard accounts of participation.

Nevertheless they have been supplemented during the last decade by far greater attention to the context within which individuals act, and this approach seems likely to continue to expand. The emphasis has become less the psychological capacities and qualities inherent in individual citizens, derived from socialization processes in early childhood, than the contextual factors found within particular communities, states, elections, or countries which trigger or depress these propensities. Verba and Nie also acknowledged the broader *social context* within which individuals become active, such as the impact of trade unions and churches in mobilizing working-class communities. More recently Rosenstone and Hanson (1993) revived attention in the role of mobilizing agencies such as parties and interest groups, and there has been renewed appreciation of the way that party workers play an important role in activating voters through local campaigns. In the field of political communications, Milner (2002) and Norris (2000) have debated the role of the mass media, whether newspapers, television, and the internet are seen as encouraging or discouraging civic engagement and awareness. Huckfeldt and his colleagues have long emphasized the importance of informal social networks of personal communication which draw people into public affairs (Huckfeldt, Johnson, and Sprague 2004). Recent studies have also focused greater attention on the institutional context of the political system, notably the role of the legal rules, the electoral system, and administrative processes in determining opportunities for voting participation, and the way that patterns of party competition and the closeness of the outcome in elections stimulate turnout (Franklin 2004).

During the last decade there has been a shift in emphasis in the general body of literature comparing patterns of political participation which has given increased attention to the social processes by which organizations such as parties, associations, and community groups mobilize citizens, as well as to the broader context of the institutional rules governing forms of participation. Institutional factors have most often been studied in terms of their impact on voting turnout, where comparison of the legal context and the broader role of electoral systems has long been regarded as important, but there is a large research agenda where we need to examine how institutions also shape other dimensions of participation; for example, campaign finance laws and public funding subsidies may reduce the incentives for parties to maintain mass memberships, while laws controlling taxation and non-profit status may influence the structure of voluntary organizations and the density of associational membership in the non-profit sector.

Much work on political participation remains single nation in focus, particularly the extensive range of studies of the United States, in many ways an atypical democracy, as Lipset (1996) noted, whether in its exceptionally low level of voter turnout, the absence of mass-branch party membership, or its relatively rich patterns of voluntary activism. Comparisons within each country are typically made between groups (for example, turnout among African-Americans versus Hispanics), over time (for example, trends in electoral turnout since 1960), and occasionally across regions or states (such as the effects of registration requirements). Until recently, however, systematic multinational surveys have tended to lag behind, especially outside of Western Europe, including studies of the role of citizens in newer democracies and in authoritarian states. The development of new large-scale cross-national surveys of the electorate which have become available in recent decades, such as the Globalbarometers, are facilitating comparison of certain common forms of mass political participation, notably of voting turnout. Nevertheless few cross-national surveys exist to allow systematic analysis of the more demanding forms of participation which engage only a minority of the population, including party membership, campaign work, and associational activism. Pooling the samples contained in each of the large-scale cross-national surveys, such as the series of Eurobarometers, the International Social Survey Program, the World Values Study, and the Comparative Study of Electoral Systems, produces large enough samples to overcome some of these problems, but at the expense of thereby losing some of the ability to analyze cross-national variations in contextual effects. Moreover to establish the direction of causality suggested by analytical models there is an urgent need for longitudinal multi-wave panel surveys, although there are substantial difficulties in conducting such surveys both over time and among countries.

Another limitation is that comparative research also continues to focus primarily upon "traditional," "conventional," or "civic" forms of activism, understood as those acts where citizens are primarily seeking to influence elected officials and the policy-making process in representative democracies within each nation-state. By contrast, far less comparative research has examined alternative channels of political engagement, mobilization, and expression that are rapidly emerging in modern societies, including the widespread rise of demonstrations and protest politics, the growing popularity of consumer politics, and the proliferation of interest groups, more diffuse social movements, online political communities, and transnational policy networks. There remains considerable debate about the exact contours and importance of these developments, and whether these should be regarded as genuinely "new" forms of participation or reflections of older traditions. There is a broad consensus, however, that the scope of organizational agencies and the repertoire of activities under comparison has expanded and diversified over the years, and the research agenda has often failed to innovate sufficiently to capture the broader range of activities which have now become more common.

Lastly, the contemporary body of scholarship has generally proved stronger at analyzing the causes than the consequences of participation. In particular, any significant changes in the nature and level of political activism raise three important issues where we currently have few definitive answers: what is the impact of these developments for social inequality in the public sphere, if the newer forms of participation make greater demands of civic awareness and skills? What do these changes imply for the development of individual capacities, for strengthening communities, and for the quality of mass participation, for example if there has been a shift from giving volunteer time in voluntary organizations to expressing support for interest groups through financial donations? And, lastly, what do they mean at systematic level for processes of governance, the public policy agenda, and the consolidation of democracy? The difficulties of tracing the links from various specific participatory acts to the outcome in government decisions, for example how legislatures respond to expressions of public concern about patterns of public spending on welfare benefits or shifts in foreign policy, remain a classic challenge in political science. A growing body of empirical literature has been examining some of the core claims made in the normative democratic theory, notably the impact of deliberation on citizens and on decision making (Hibbing and Theiss–Morse 2003, ch. 7). Yet the broader consequences of many of the developments illustrated here remain unclear. How far newer modes of activism are either supplementing or replacing older ones, and what consequences follow for representative democracy, remains one of the central challenges facing future comparative research.

REFERENCES

ADRIAN, C., and APTER, D. A. 1995. *Political Protest and Social Change: Analyzing Politics*. New York: New York University Press.

ALMOND, G. A., and VERBA, S. eds. 1980. *The Civic Culture Revisited*. Boston: Little Brown.

—— —— 1989/1963. *The Civic Culture: Political Attitudes and Democracy in Five Nations*. Thousand Oaks, Calif.: Sage.

ANDERSEN, J. G., and HOFF, J. 2001. *Democracy and Citizenship in Scandinavia*. Basingstoke: Palgrave.

ARCHIBUGI, D., HELD, D., and KOHLER, M. 1998. *Re-imagining Political Community: Studies in Cosmopolitan Democracy*. Stanford, Calif.: Stanford University Press.

BAKER, J. 1999. *Street-Level Democracy: Political Settings at the Margins of Global Power*. West Hartford, Conn.: Kumarian Press.

BARBER, B. 1984. *Strong Democracy.* Berkeley and Los Angeles: University of California Press.

BARNES, S., and KAASE, M. 1979. *Political Action: Mass Participation in Five Western Democracies.* Beverley Hills, Calif.: Sage.

BARON, S., FIELD, J., and SCHULLER, T. eds. 2000. *Social Capital: Critical Perspectives.* Oxford: Oxford University Press.

BENNETT, S. E. 1986. *Apathy in America 1960–1984: Causes and Consequences of Citizen Political Indifference.* Dobbs Ferry, NY: Transnational.

BERRY, J. 1984. *The Interest Group Society.* Boston: Little Brown.

BLAIS, A. 2000. *To Vote or Not to Vote? The Merits and Limits of Rational Choice Theory.* Pittsburgh: University of Pittsburgh Press.

—— and DOBRZYNSKA, A. 1998. Turnout in electoral democracies. *European Journal of Political Research,* 33 (2): 239–61.

BOOKS, J., and PRYSBY, C. 1988. Studying contextual effects on political behavior: a research inventory and agenda. *American Politics Quarterly,* 16: 211–38.

BOURDIEU, P. 1970. *Reproduction in Education, Culture and Society.* London: Sage.

BURNS, N., SCHLOZMAN, K. L., and VERBA, S. 2001. *The Private Roots of Public Action.* Cambridge, Mass.: Harvard University Press.

CAROTHERS, T. 1999. *Aiding Democracy Abroad: The Learning Curve.* Washington, DC: Carnegie Endowment for International Peace.

CLARKE, T. N., and REMPEL, M. 1997. *Citizen Politics in Post-Industrial Societies: Interest Groups Transformed.* Boulder, Colo.: Westview Press.

COLEMAN, J. S. 1988. Social capital in the creation of human capital. *American Journal of Sociology,* 94: 95–120.

—— 1990. *Foundations of Social Theory.* Cambridge: Belknap.

CONWAY, M. M. 2000. *Political Participation in the United States,* 3rd edn. Washington, DC: CQ Press.

CRIGLER, A. N., JUST, M. R., and MCCAFFERY, E. J. 2004. *Rethinking the Vote: The Politics and Prospects of American Electoral Reform.* New York: Oxford University Press.

DALTON, R. 1996. *Citizen Politics,* 2nd edn. Chatham, NJ: Chatham House.

—— and KUECHLER, M. eds. 1990. Challenging *the Political Order: New Social and Political Movements in Western Democracies.* New York: Oxford University Press.

DALTON, R. J. and WATTENBERG, M. P. 2001. *Parties without Partisans: Political Change in Advanced Industrialized Democracies.* Oxford: Oxford University Press.

DOWNS, A. 1957. *An Economic Theory of Democracy.* New York: Harper & Row.

DUVERGER, M. 1954. *Political Parties: Their Organization and Activity in the Modern State.* New York: Wiley.

EDWARDS, B., and FOLEY, M. W. 1998. Civil society and social capital beyond Putnam. *American Behavioral Scientist,* 42 (1): 124–39.

EDWARDS, M., and GAVENTA, J. eds. 2001. *Global Citizen Action.* Boulder, Colo.: Lynne Rienner Publishers.

EPSTEIN, B. 1991. *Political Protest and Cultural Revolution: Nonviolent Direct Action in the 1970s and 1980s.* Berkeley and Los Angeles: University of California Press.

EVANS, P. 2000. Fighting marginalization with transnational networks: counter-hegemonic globalization. *Contemporary Sociology,* 29 (1): 230–41.

FEIGENBAUM, H. B., HENIG, J., and HAMNETT, C. 1998. *Shrinking the State: The Political Underpinnings of Privatization.* Cambridge: Cambridge University Press.

FRANKLIN, M. N. 2004. *Voter Turnout and the Dynamics of Electoral Competition in Established Democracies since 1945.* Cambridge: Cambridge University Press.

FRANKLIN, M. N., VAN DER EIJK, C., and OPPENHUIS, E. 1996. The institutional context: turnout. Pp. 306–31 in *Choosing Europe? The European Electorate and National Politics in the Face of Union*, ed. C. van der Eijk and M. Franklin. Ann Arbor: University of Michigan Press.

GUTMANN, A., and THOMSON, D. 2004. *Why Deliberative Democracy?* Princeton: Princeton University Press.

HELD, D. 1996. *Models of Democracy*, 2nd edn. Stanford, Calif.: University of Stanford Press.

—— 1999. *Global Transformations: Politics, Economics and Culture*. London: Polity Press.

HIBBING, J. R., and THEISS-MORSE, E. 2003. *Stealth Democracy: Americans' Beliefs about How Government Should Work*. Cambridge: Cambridge University Press.

HILL, S. 2002. *Fixing Elections: The Failure of America's Winner Take All Politics*. New York: Routledge.

HOOGHE, M., and STOLLE, D. eds. 2003. *Generating Social Capital: Civil Society and Institutions in Comparative Perspective*. New York: Palgrave Macmillan.

HUCKFELDT, R., JOHNSON, P. E., and SPRAGUE, J. 2004. *Political Disagreement*. New York: Cambridge University Press.

—— and SPRAGUE, J. 1995. *Citizens, Politics and Social Communication*. Cambridge: Cambridge University Press.

INGLEHART, R. 1997 *Modernization and Postmodernization: Cultural, Economic and Political Change in 43 Societies*. Princeton: Princeton University Press.

—— and NORRIS, P. 2003. *Rising Tide: Gender Equality and Cultural Change around the World*. New York: Cambridge University Press.

INTERNATIONAL IDEA. 2005. *Handbook of Electoral System Design*, 2nd edn. Stockholm: International IDEA. **www.idea.int**

JACKMAN, R. W., and MILLER, R. A. 1995. Voter turnout in the industrial democracies during the 1980s. *Comparative Political Studies*, 27: 467–92.

JENNINGS, M. K., and VAN DETH, J. 1989. *Continuities in Political Action*. Berlin: deGruyter.

KATZ, R. 1997. *Democracy and Elections*. Oxford: Oxford University Press.

—— and MAIR, P. 1995. Changing models of party organization and party democracy: the emergence of the cartel party. *Party Politics*, 1 (1): 5–28.

—— —— eds. 1992. *Party Organizations: A Data Handbook on Party Organizations in Western Democracies, 1960–1990*. London: Sage.

KECK, M., and SIKKINK, K. 1998. *Activists beyond Borders: Advocacy Networks in International Politics*. Ithaca, NY: Cornell University Press.

KERSTING, N., and BALDERSHEIM, H. eds. 2004. *Electronic Voting and Democracy: A Comparative Analysis*. New York: Palgrave Macmillan.

KEY, V. O. 1964. *Politics, Parties and Pressure Groups*. New York: Crowell.

KNACK, S. 1995. Does motor voter work? Evidence from state-level data. *Journal of Politics*, 57 (3): 796–811.

KORNAI, J., ROTHSTEIN, B., and ROSE-ACKERMAN, S. eds. 2004. *Creating Social Trust in Post-Socialist Transitions*. New York: Palgrave Macmillan.

KRIESI, H., PORTA, D. D., and RIUCHT, D. eds. 1998. *Social Movements in a Globalizing World*. London: Macmillan.

LADD, C. E. 1996. The data just don't show erosion of America's social capital. *Public Perspective*, 1: 5–6.

LARANA, E., JOHNSTON, H., and GUDFIELD, J. R. eds. 1994. *New Social Movements: From Ideology to Identity*. Philadelphia: Temple University Press.

LAWSON, K., and MERKL, P. eds. 1988. *When Parties Fail: Emerging Alternative Organizations*. Princeton: Princeton University Press.

LIJPHART, A. 1994. *Electoral Systems and Party Systems*. Oxford: Oxford University Press.

LIPSCHUTZ, R. 1996. *Global Civic Society and Global Environmental Governance.* Albany, NY: SUNY Press.

LIPSET, S. M. 1996. *American Exceptionalism.* New York: Norton.

LOPEZ PINTOR, R., and GRATSCHEW, M. n.d. *Voter Turnout Since 1945: A Global Report.* Stockholm, International IDEA. **www.idea.int**

McADAM, D., McCARTHY, J. D., and ZALD, M. N. 1996. *Comparative Perspectives on Social Movements.* New York: Cambridge University Press.

McDONALD, M. P., and POPKIN, S. L. 2001. The myth of the vanishing voter. *American Political Science Review,* 95 (4): 963–74.

MAIR, P. 1997. *Party System Change.* Oxford: Oxford University Press.

—— and VAN BIEZEN, I. 2001. Party membership in twenty European democracies 1980–2000. *Party Politics,* 7 (1): 7–22.

MARSH, A. 1977. *Protest and Political Consciousness.* Beverly Hills, Calif.: Sage.

MARTINEZ, M. D., and HILL, D. 1999. Did motor voter work? *American Politics Quarterly,* 27 (3): 296–315.

MASSICOTTE, L., BLAIS, A., and YOSHINAKA, A. 2004. *Establishing the Rules of the Game: Election Laws in Democracies.* Toronto: University of Toronto Press.

MEYER, D., and TARROW, S. eds. 1998. *The Social Movement Society: Contentious Politics for a New Century.* Lanham, Md.: Rowman and Littlefield.

MILBRATH, L. W., and GOEL, M. L. 1977. *Political Participation: How and Why do People get Involved in Politics?,* 2nd edn. Chicago: Rand McNally.

MILES, T. J. 2004. Felon disenfranchisement and voter turnout. *Journal of Legal Studies,* 33 (1): 85–129.

MILNER, H. 2002. *Civic Literacy: How Informed Citizens Make Democracy Work.* Hanover, NH: Tufts University.

NORRIS, P. 1996. Did television erode social capital? A reply to Putnam. *PS: Political Science and Politics,* 29 (3): 474–80.

—— 2000. *A Virtuous Circle.* New York: Cambridge University Press.

—— 2002. *Democratic Phoenix.* New York: Cambridge University Press.

—— 2004. *Electoral Engineering.* New York: Cambridge University Press.

—— and INGLEHART, R. 2004. *Sacred and Secular: Religion and Politics Worldwide.* New York: Cambridge University Press.

—— WALGRAVE, S. and VAN AELST, P. 2004. Who demonstrates? Anti-state rebels, conventional participants, or everyone? *Comparative Politics* (forthcoming).

NYE, J. S., and DONAHUE, J. 2001. *Governance in a Globalizing World.* Washington, DC: Brookings Institution Press.

OBERSCHALL, A. 1993. *Social Movements: Ideologies, Interests and Identities.* New Brunswick, NJ: Transaction.

OLSON, M. 1965. *The Logic of Collective Action: Public Goods and the Theory of Goods.* Cambridge, Mass.: Harvard University Press.

PARRY, G., MOYSER, G., and DAY, N. 1992. *Political Participation and Democracy in Britain.* Cambridge: Cambridge University Press.

PATEMAN, C. 1988. *The Sexual Contract.* Cambridge: Polity Press.

PATTERSON, T. 2001. *The Vanishing Voter.* New York: Knopf.

PATTIE, C., SEYD, P., and WHITELEY, P. 2004. *Citizenship in Britain: Values, Participation and Democracy.* Cambridge: Cambridge University Press.

PAXTON, P., BOLLEN, K. A., LEE, D. M., and KIM, H. J. 2003. A half century of suffrage: new data and a comparative analysis. *Studies in Comparative International Development,* 38 (1): 93–122.

PHARR, S., and PUTNAM, R. eds. 2000. *Disaffected Democracies: Whats Troubling the Trilateral Countries?* Princeton: Princeton University Press.

PHILLIPS, A. 1991. *Engendering Democracy.* Cambridge: Polity Press.

POWELL, G. B. 1980. Voting turnout in thirty democracies: partisan, legal and socioeconomic influences. Pp. 5–34 in *Electoral Participation: A Comparative Analysis*, ed. D. Rose. London: Sage.

—— 1982. *Contemporary Democracies: Participation, Stability and Violence.* Cambridge, Mass.: Harvard University Press.

—— 1986. American voter turnout in comparative perspective. *American Political Science Review*, 80 (1): 17–43.

PUTNAM, R. D. 1993. *Making Democracy Work: Civic Traditions in Modern Italy* Princeton: Princeton University Press.

—— 1995. Tuning in, tuning out: the strange disappearance of social capital in America. *P.S: Political Science and Politics*, 28 (4): 664–83.

—— 1996. The strange disappearance of civic America. *American Prospect*, 24: 34–48.

—— 2000. *Bowling Alone: The Collapse and Revival of American Community.* New York: Simon and Schuster.

—— ed. 2002. *The Dynamics of Social Capital.* Oxford: Oxford University Press.

—— and FELDSTEIN, L. 2003. *Better Together: Restoring the American Community.* New York: Simon & Schuster.

ROSE, R. 2004. Voter turnout in the European Union member countries. In *Voter Turnout in Western Europe since 1945*, ed. R. Lopez Pintor and M. Gratschew. Stockholm: International IDEA.

ROSENAU, J. 1990. *Turbulance in World Politics: A Theory of Change and Continuity.* Princeton: Princeton University Press.

ROSENSTONE, S. J., and HANSEN, J. M. 1993. *Mobilization, Participation and Democracy in America.* New York: Macmillan.

ROTOLO, T. 1999. Trends in voluntary association participation. *Nonprofit and Voluntary Sector Quarterly*, 28 (2): 199–212.

SASSEN, S. 1999. *Globalization and its Discontents.* New York: New Press.

SCARROW, S. 2001. Parties without members? In *Parties without Partisans*, ed. R. J. Dalton and M. Wattenberg. New York: Oxford University Press.

SCHLOZMAN, K. L. 2002. Citizen participation in America: what do we know? Why do we care? In *Political Science: The State of the Discipline*, ed. I. Katznelson and H. V. Miller. New York: W. W. Norton.

SCHMITT, H., and HOLMBERG, S. 1995. Political parties in decline? Pp. 95–133 in *Citizens and the State*, ed. H.-D. Klingemann and D. Fuchs. Oxford: Oxford University Press.

SCHUDSON, M. 1996. What if civic life didnt die? *American Prospect*, 25: 17–20.

SCHUMPETER, J. A. 1952. *Capitalism, Socialism and Democracy*, 4th edn. London: George Allen & Unwin.

SEYD, P., and WHITELEY, P. eds. 2004. Party members and activists. Special issue of *Party Politics*, 10 (4).

SKOCPOL, T. 1996. Unravelling from above. *American Prospect*, 25: 20–5.

SMITH, J., CHATFIELD, C., and PAGNUCCO, R. eds. 1997. *Transnational Social Movements and Global Politics: Solidarity beyond the State.* Syracuse, NY: Syracuse University Press.

SVENDSEN, G. L. H., and SVENDSEN, G. T. 2004. *The Creation and Destruction of Social Capital: Entrepreneurship, Cooperative Movements, and Institutions.* Cheltenham: Edward Elgar.

TARROW, S. 1994. *Power in Movement.* Cambridge: Cambridge University Press.

TEIXEIRA, R. A. 1992. *The Disappearing American Voter.* Washington, DC: Brookings.

TILLY, C. 1978. *From Mobilization to Revolution.* Reading, Mass.: Addison-Wesley.

—— et al. 1975. *The Rebellious Century*. Cambridge, Mass.: Harvard University Press.

VAN AELST, P., and WALGRAVE, S. 2001. Who is that (wo)man in the street? From the normalization of protest to the normalization of the protester. *European Journal of Political Research*, 39: 461–86.

VAN DETH, J. W. ed. 1997. *Private Groups and Public Life: Social Participation, Voluntary Associations and Political Involvement in Representative Democracies*. London: Routledge.

—— ed. 1999. *Social Capital and European Democracy*. New York: Routledge.

—— 2000. Interesting but irrelevant: social capital and the saliency of politics in Western Europe. *European Journal of Political Research*, 37: 115–47.

—— and KREUTER, F. 1998. Membership of voluntary associations. Pp. 135–55 in *Comparative Politics: The Problem of Equivalence*, ed. J. W. van Deth. London: Routledge.

VERBA, S., and NIE, N. H. 1972. *Participation in America: Political Democracy and Social Equality*. Chicago: University of Chicago Press.

—— —— and KIM, J. 1971. *The Modes of Democratic Participation: A Cross-National Analysis*. Beverley Hills, Calif.: Sage.

—— —— —— 1978. *Participation and Political Equality: A Seven-Nation Comparison*. New York: Cambridge University Press.

—— SCHLOZMAN, K., and BRADY, H. E. 1995. *Voice and Equality: Civic Voluntarism in American Politics*. Cambridge, Mass.: Harvard University Press.

WEBB, P., FARRELL, D., and HOLLIDAY, I. eds. 2002. *Political Parties in Advanced Industrial Democracies*. Oxford: Oxford University Press.

WHITELEY, P., and SEYD, P. 2002. *High-Intensity Participation: The Dynamics of Party Activism in Britain*. Ann Arbor: University of Michigan Press.

WOLFINGER, R., and ROSENSTONE, S. 1980. *Who Votes?* New Haven: Yale University Press.

ZALD, M. N., and McCARTHY, J. eds. 1987. *Social Movements in an Organizational Society*. New Brunswick, NJ: Transaction Books.

PART VII

PROCESSING
POLITICAL
DEMANDS

CHAPTER 27

AGGREGATING AND REPRESENTING POLITICAL PREFERENCES

G. BINGHAM POWELL, JR.

1 INTRODUCTION

By "aggregating preferences" we mean the process of considering and choosing among possible policies favored by members of the group. In a democracy the individual citizens are assumed to have preferences about the goals of public policies or about the best way of achieving those goals. Democratic preference aggregation takes equal account of all their preferences as policies are made.

There is obviously a close connection between democracy and preference aggregation. Democracy means "government by the people." Modern democracies are largely based on indirect participation in making policies through choosing representatives to govern. Insofar as representative institutions are designed to aggregate the preferences of the people as a whole, the empirical study of representative democracy will in some way involve the study of preference aggregation.

Moreover, there are strong normative connotations. Those normatively committed to democracy will be committed to representative policy-making processes that aggregate preferences to take account of what "the people" want. Some scholars define democracy itself as "necessary correspondence between acts of governance and the equally weighted felt interests of citizens with respect to those acts" (Saward 1998, 51). Such a definition implies: "No correspondence, no democracy." Others argue that the best justification for democracy is that it "provides an orderly and peaceful process by means of which a majority of citizens can induce the government to do what they most want it to do and to avoid doing what they most want it not to do" (Dahl 1989, 95). The problem of aggregating preferences is obviously close to the heart of democracy itself, whether as definition or justification.

If "the people" agree on what they want, assessing democratic preference aggregation is fairly straightforward. A representative democracy would induce making policies that correspond to what the people want. Given this expectation, empirical research could explore what specific institutions, such as different types of rules for choosing representatives, or different policy-making institutions, would be more likely to produce the democratic policies. However, "the people" are not a single entity. They are a social group. That is why their individual preferences have to be "aggregated." If there is a diversity of preferences, which is to prevail? The answer to this question turns out to be much more difficult. And, naturally, empirical research on the aggregation processes, much more complicated.

2 THE CHALLENGE OF SOCIAL CHOICE ANALYSIS

The nature of citizen preferences is, of course, a complicated topic in its own right. It is addressed in other chapters of this volume. Theories of democratic representation generally required an "enlightened" citizenry, aware of relevant considerations that shape the policy problems confronting them. Moreover, it is clear that citizens vary in the intensity with which they hold their opinions and judgements. Some theorists of democratic representation would have us take account of these intensities. In this overview of democratic preference aggregation, however, we shall assume that citizens have well-considered opinions and that their opinions should be weighted equally in the policy-making process. The question is how the diverse preferences of these citizens are to be combined to yield policies that correspond to what they want.

A fundamental problem of preference aggregation has been posed by formal studies of social choice. Social choice theorists have learned a great deal about whether and how the varied preferences of multiple individuals can be coherently and consistently aggregated into a single choice. They have found that while some configurations of citizen preferences allow meaningful democratic aggregation, others do not. From the same set of preferences among political actors, different methods or sequences of democratic aggregation may yield different substantive outcomes. To put it another way, no single alternative may command unequivocal majority support over each of the other possible choices. This finding about the implications of configurations of preferences, Arrow's "impossibility theorem" (Arrow 1951), means that we may not be able to tell whether or not a given policy choice corresponded to "what the people want." Some other outcome might have emerged from democratic procedures; that outcome might even command majority support over the given one.

Various theorists, most notably William Riker, have argued that awareness of this problem should alter our understanding of the possibilities of democracy itself:

> The populist interpretation of voting (i.e., that what the people, as a corporate entity, want ought to be public policy) cannot stand because it is inconsistent with social choice theory. If the outcomes of voting are, or may be, inaccurate or meaningless amalgamations, what the people want cannot be known. (Riker 1982, p. xviii)

Riker argues for a purely procedural assessment of democracy, in which a majority of citizens can collectively remove an incumbent government, but no policy implications can be inferred. (Also see Dahl 1956; Runciman 1969.) He warns us explicitly that "the kind of democracy that thus survives is not, however, popular rule, but rather an intermittent, sometimes random, even perverse, popular veto" (Riker 1982, 244).

Riker's analyses, and those of social choice theorists more generally, pose a serious challenge to research on preference aggregation in representative democracies. One way of understanding the research programs in comparative politics on preference aggregation is in terms of their relationship to Riker's challenge. As we shall see, whether or not they have been explicitly aware of the problem of social choice, scholars have dealt with its difficulties in several different ways, with important consequences for their inferences.

Some analysts have, in effect, followed Riker's suggestion by studying only the conditions for democratic representation, such as free elections and civil rights, eschewing entirely the problem of connecting the preferences of citizens to the policies of government. But several other approaches can also be identified. Two of these begin by using survey research to identify the preferences of citizens and examining their correspondence with the positions of policy makers. But they differ in their approaches to the multiplicity of dimensions of citizen preferences. Another approach begins with votes, rather than with preferences, and assumes that citizen's wishes are revealed sufficiently, or with unique authority, in citizens' behavior at the polls.

3 CONDITIONS FOR REPRESENTATIVE DEMOCRACY AND PREFERENCE AGGREGATION

One approach to the study of democratic preference aggregation in nation-states focuses on the *conditions* that would be necessary, although not sufficient, for large-scale representative democracy. The social choice problem is evaded by ignoring the conceptual difficulties of preference aggregation. Rather, theoretical analysis identifies institutions that seem to be necessary for democratic preference aggregation in large societies and empirical analysis focuses on the origin and maintenance of those institutions or, occasionally, the policies associated with them.

Perhaps the best-known theoretical treatment is Dahl's analysis of "polyarchy," which sketches seven institutions necessary to satisfy five criteria of the democratic process (e.g. 1989, 222). The "criteria" of voting equality, effective participation, enlightened understanding, control of the agenda, and inclusion are themselves derived as theoretical conditions necessary for democratic preference aggregation. The "institutions" of elected officials, free and fair elections, inclusive suffrage, right to run for office, freedom of expression, alternative information, and associational autonomy are argued to be empirically necessary for the realization of those criteria in large-scale democracy (1989, 221–2). Dahl is quite clear that these institutions are not sufficient to guarantee that "policies invariably correspond with the desires of a majority of citizens." For this reason among others he prefers to characterize the political systems in which they are found as "polyarchies," rather than as democracies. But he argues that "these institutions even make it rather uncommon for a government to enforce policies to which a substantial number of citizens object and then try to overturn by vigorously using the rights and opportunities available to them" (1989, 223). The approach seems consistent with Riker's "liberal" version of democracy, although more optimistic about the shortfall from "populist" ideals.

A great deal of empirical research has focused on, first, identifying the presence of these institutions in different political systems, and, second, examining the conditions that lead to them being introduced or sustained. This research has generally adopted a "process" definition of democracy and categorized empirical political systems as democratic or not (or in degree) according to the presence of these institutions and practices. Three of the best-known research programs for descriptively identifying democracies along these and similar lines are the Freedom House scales of political rights and civil liberties (**www.freedomhouse.org**), the Polity scales of democracy and authoritarianism, building on the work of Ted Robert Gurr (**www.cidcm.umd.edu/inscr/polity**), and the Prezeworski et al. classification of democracies and dictatorships (2000). Despite some differences in both definitions and empirical procedures, these studies generally identify most of the same political systems as "democracies" or "free." Some other studies, often of particular areas of the world, have suggested additions to the basic necessary institutions, such as the rule of law or equal protection of individual social relations, in order to make the other democratic institutions meaningful (O'Donnell 2004; more generally, Collier and Levitsky 1997).

The empirical expansion of "democracies," in the sense of the establishment of these institutions and processes, especially during the twenty years between 1975 and 1995, encouraged an explosion of "democratization" research. This research has investigated the economic and political conditions under which democratic regimes are introduced, "consolidated" or stabilized, and sustained (e.g. Huntington 1991; Diamond et al. 1997; Przeworski et al. 2000; Boix and Stokes 2003) or even subverted

(Schedler 2002). The connections between some of the relevant processes conditions, such as democratic elections and human rights integrity (e.g. Poe, Tate, and Keith 1999), or degree of democracy and civil war (Fearon and Laitin 2003), have also been the subject of substantial research. Some scholars have also examined the development of stable institutions that are believed to facilitate citizens' democratic choices, such as less volatile party systems (e.g. Mainwaring and Scully 1995) or citizens' understanding of the meaning of democracy (e.g. Bratton and Mattes 2001). There has also been substantial research on democracies' achievement of putatively desirable policy consequences, such as economic growth, income equality, education and life expectancy (e.g. Dreze and Sen 1989; Przeworski et al. 2000; Feng 2003), or protection of minorities from genocide (Harff 2003).

However, the vast bulk of the democratization research has eschewed investigating democratic preference aggregation itself. The social choice problem is thus evaded, even conceptually. Rather, it is assumed either that (1) sufficiently democratic preference aggregation will generally follow from introducing and/or stabilizing the institutional conditions; or that (2) those conditions are so worthy in their own right that further policy consequences are less relevant; or that (3) we already know what citizens (should) want. Most of the research programs that have directly investigated preference aggregation, attempting to link citizens' preferences with government policy, have been focused on the well-established democracies of the economically developed world.

4 MULTIPLE ISSUE CONGRUENCES AS PREFERENCE AGGREGATION

Democratic preference aggregation begins with the preferences of citizens and systematically takes account of these in choosing authoritative public policies. In a few large democracies on a few issues this may involve asking the citizens directly about their policy preferences through referendums. A number of European countries have consulted their citizens directly, for example, concerning acceptance of changes in their relationship to the European Union or the European monetary system. Only Switzerland, however, encourages fairly frequent use of referendums for ordinary policy. In most democracies at the level of the nation-state the process that links citizens and policy making is the selection of policy makers in competitive, partisan elections. Three empirical research programs in comparative politics have investigated in some depth the role of elections in aggregating citizen preferences through competitive elections. Each of these involves some means of ascertaining citizen preferences and showing how electoral competition and choosing policy makers (directly or indirectly) aggregate these. Until fairly recently, at least, these programs have not taken the final step in linking choice of policy makers to substantive public policy outcomes, which involves taking account of agency (promise keeping) and other factors shaping public policy outcomes. We return to this point in conclusion.

The research program in comparative politics that most explicitly analyzes the connections between the preferences of citizens and the positions of their policy makers is founded on the work on issue congruence in the United States. In 1963 Warren Miller and Donald Stokes used a public opinion survey to ascertain the issue positions of citizens in different US congressional districts and linked these to the preferences, perceptions, and behavior of the representatives of those districts (Miller and Stokes 1963). In this seminal paper they offered several alternative models of the empirical requirements "to ensure constituency control," addressed directly and thoughtfully the difficulties created by low levels of citizen information, considered relationships within several dimensions of public opinion, and discussed the role of political parties in the linkage process, other factors shaping the behavior of congressmen, and so forth.

Miller and Stokes saw the election as the causal connection that could require representatives to be influenced by citizen opinion. Their empirical analysis indicated, however, that in the United States the nature of this electoral connection was different in different substantive policy domains. "The representative relation conforms most closely to the responsible-party model in the domain for social welfare," where the parties usually recruited candidates differing systematically in their policy stances (Miller and Stokes 1963, 371). In this domain they noted the much greater correlations between district majorities and winners, and negative correlations with losing candidates (Miller and Stokes 1963, 359–60). In the civil rights domain, on the other hand, the representative relationship seems to be induced by congressmen's and challengers' perception and mutual anticipation of the position held by the majority of citizens in the district.

The Miller and Stokes approach aims directly at democratic preference aggregation and its consequences. Three important features are especially notable. First, their research shows how to use survey research to examine the empirical congruence between the preferences of citizens and the positions of policy makers as evidence of democratic preference aggregation. Second, they identify at least two alternative causal mechanisms of democratic competition that can create such congruence, thus embedding the correspondence itself in a theory of democratic preference aggregation induced by the institutions of representative democracy. Third, the research deals with the social choice problem in two ways: (a) within each policy area it combines issues into a one-dimensional scale; (b) it does not attempt to aggregate across policy areas. Thus, the Miller–Stokes article is content to find evidence of democratic preference aggregation in two important substantive policy areas, but not in a third, and avoids attempting a single overview of the connections between citizen preferences and policy maker positions. (Moreover, the connections established are on a dyadic constituency basis, limited to one house of the legislature, not themselves aggregated into overall correspondence between the collective citizenry and collective policy makers or chosen policy, as pointed out by Weissberg 1978. Important technical critiques of the difficulties of measuring correspondence were later published by Achen 1977, 1978.)

With some specific modifications for multiparty, parliamentary conditions, usually by taking parties, rather than geographic constituencies as the unit of congruence, applications of the Miller–Stokes approach in other countries began in the mid-1970s and have cumulated into a substantial comparative research tradition. The bulk of these studies have presented analyses within single countries: the Nether-lands (Irwin and Thomassen 1975), Italy (Barnes 1977), Germany (Farah 1980; Porter 1995), France (Converse and Pierce 1986), Australia (McAllister 1991), Britain (Norris 1995), Sweden (Holmberg 1989; Esaiasson and Holmberg 1996), New Zealand (Vowles et al. 1995, 1998), and Norway (Matthews and Valen 1999). (Also see Manion's remarkable study of semi-competitive elections in China (1996).) They tend to share at least two virtues with their Miller–Stokes exemplar. One virtue is concern with the problems of citizen opinion formation, low levels of citizen knowledge and constraint, and how to contrast these with invariably much more sophisticated and structured elite opinions. They offer great insight into the citizen context in each country and sometimes into comparative differences (often contrast-ing their results with American analyses). The second is the serious consideration of multiple political issues. They report measurable, but varying, correspondences between voters and their party representatives across different issues. They usually try to explore these through features of local electoral competition.

In addition to these single-country studies, there have been a growing number of explicitly comparative studies, beginning with Dalton's 1985 study of the representa-tiveness of candidates for the European parliament of their party voters on a variety of substantive issues. Dalton provides an excellent technical example of providing multiple measures of empirical issue representation, emphasizing closeness of voters and representatives (centrism), as well as correlations and regression coefficients, and collective correspondence. He also articulates very clearly how the "responsible party model" of voters choosing between parties offering alternative policy packages can create a theoretical model of citizen influence to underpin collective voter–representative correspondence (Dalton 1985, 278).

Clearly in the Miller and Stokes tradition is the ambitious collection of original analytic essays edited by Warren Miller himself, *Policy Representation in Western Democracies*, published shortly after his death (Miller et al. 1999). The co-authors attempt to take advantage of the availability of the emergent group of studies of citizen–legislator representation within five countries explicitly to test cross-national hypotheses derived largely from the "responsible party government" model. How-ever, they conceptualize and measure their representative relationships differently and reach diverse conclusions about, for example, the relative success of more or less structured party systems in creating correspondence on the average issue. (See e.g. Pierce 1999, 31; Holmberg 1999, 94; Thomassen 1999, 45–51; Wessels 1999, 148–51.)

In the same year Schmitt and Thomassen's *Political Representation and Legitimacy in the European Union* (1999) conceived of a model of "responsible party government," creating issue linkages through parties offering coherent policy choices, as playing a large role in their conception of the development of "European-level" representation. Their analyses of surveys of citizens and candidates in the 1994 European parliamentary elections show a very strong relative responsiveness connection between voters and representatives on the left–right scale, created apparently by voter choices and party alternatives (both national and European-level parties) consistent with the "responsible party model" conditions. There is also some relative congruence between voters and candidates on substantive European issues, shaped both by party and (more strongly) by country of origin (Thomassen and Schmitt 1997, 175; Schmitt and Thomassen 1999, 200–5). But the voters and parties are far apart in their absolute positions on the substantive issues, with most of the candidates far more pro-European on borders and common currency than their voters.

A third recent cross-national analysis in the Miller–Stokes tradition appeared in Soren Holmberg's chapter in another edited volume, comparing positions of party voters and their MPs in Denmark, Iceland, Norway, and Sweden (Holmberg 2000, 155–80). Holmberg presents dichotomized results showing agreement/disagreement of the majorities of party voters and their MPs. Refreshingly, he also reports when citizens and legislatures collectively (as opposed to voter–party dyads) have agreeing/disagreeing majorities.

Holmberg expects better correspondence between voters and party representatives on "salient and politicized issues at the center of political discourse" and finds this generally true on four issues associated with the "left–right" dimension. (Also see Thomassen 1994, 1999.) There seems to be both good absolute and good relative issue agreement. Still, even on these issues the majorities of citizens and their party representatives in Denmark, Norway, and Sweden did not correspond in fifteen of seventy-two pairs (21 percent). What is especially striking in Holmberg's data is the near unanimity of majority positions within each party's MPs. Virtually all the left and social democratic MPs took leftist positions; virtually all the Conservative and Progress MP took rightist positions. Although there is a general increase in the average support for conservative positions among citizens as we move from left to right across the parties, the citizens are generally more divided than their representatives. For many parties this implies that there is a substantial minority of voters in each party who favor positions represented in the legislature *exclusively* by representatives of other parties. (Many of the individual country studies have also shown this kind of pattern.)

Kitschelt, Mansfeldova, Markowski, and Toka's *Post-Communist Party Systems: Competition, Representation and Inter-party Cooperation* (1999) discusses issue representative of party voter–representative dyads in the new democracies of Bulgaria, Czech Republic, Hungary, and Poland in the mid-1990s (1999, 309–44). They do not forget to take account of party size in using the statistics as aggregate properties of representation for each issue (and the left–right scale) in each country. In addition to "mandate representation," they also suggest two other patterns, "polarized trusteeship" and "moderating trusteeship," that can be important alternative forms of democratic representation. Rather than assuming any of these as the correct normative baseline, they suggest the consequences of each for such aspects of democratic performance as citizen mobilization, effective policy leadership, and intensification or diffusion of political conflict (1999, 80–8, 340).

These studies in the Miller–Stokes tradition have yielded a wealth of country-specific information about preference aggregation on individual issues and in specific settings. There are also some general findings of interest, showing the possibilities and limitations of electoral competition in preference aggregation:

(1) The studies of issue preferences and partisanship repeatedly suggest that the preferences and positions of party representatives are much more structured (predictable from their partisanship across a wider range of issues) than the preferences of average citizens. In consequence, representatives' opinions on some issues will be strongly linked to their partisanship while citizens' opinions will not, potentially creating serious misrepresentation on these issues. Voters for one party may be better represented by MPs of another party. The long-run electoral dynamics of this situation are unclear. (But see Holmberg 1997 for an exploration in Sweden.)

Moreover, the greater consistency of representatives' opinions will often make them be, or appear, much more extreme than their voters. There may be high levels of relative "responsiveness," such that party representatives are differentiated from each other the same way their supporters are, but the representatives are much more consistently "left" or "right" than their respective followers. This pattern, which is what Kitschelt et al. 1999 call a "polarized trusteeship" connection, appears in many of the empirical studies (e.g. Holmberg 2000). Consistency across related issues, intensity with which preferences are held, and substantive distance from the "center" on single issues can all contribute to this pattern.

(2) The party issue congruence studies suggest that at least relative, and perhaps even absolute, issue representation (responsiveness) is greater on the issues more strongly linked to the general dimension of party competition. Indeed, this has become virtually a stylized fact (e.g. McAllister 1991; Kitschelt et al. 1999; Holmberg 2000). This simplification can ease the theoretical social choice problem, as is discussed more thoroughly in the next section.

(3) Moreover, although the comparative literature has paid less attention to issue positions that are eschewed by all the parties because unacceptable to voters generally, (as Miller and Stokes suggested was the case with the civil rights domain), it seems that they could play an important connective role. Under these circumstances we might find little relative inter-party responsiveness on the issue, as the parties do not offer contrasting choices, yet there might be close proximity of voter and representative positions. Influence would emerge from party anticipation of voter response, rather than as outcomes from voter choices. Downsian models would expect this in two-party systems. But it could also emerge in multiparty systems if few voters favor a position. Empirically, the pornography issue in Holmberg 2000's Nordic systems seems to look something like this.

Considering issues or issue dimensions separately generally avoids the theoretical social choice problem. Moreover, examining correspondence between citizens and policies on an issue-by-issue basis has some defensible features. In his thoughtful discussion of this problem, Weale points out that if there is a Condorcet winner in citizens' preferences among the possible combinations of outcomes, the examination of the issue-by-issue medians (majorities) will discover it. If there is no Condorcet winner in the multidimensional preference structure, examining issue-by-issue majorities is at least a defensible democratic procedure that does yield an outcome (Weale 1999, 146–7). It might be possible to defeat that outcome by some other combination in a straight majority vote—Arrow's paradox cannot be repealed—but for Weale that does not render majority voting as a procedure meaningless. Indeed, he argues that:

the demands of synoptic rationality involved in a comparison of alternative policy packages cannot be met in any but the most simple world. Outside very small situations citizens do not choose over logically integrated political programmes. Issue by issue we may know what the majority wants, but there is typically no way of knowing whether the intersection of these majorities, in relation to all issues, expresses a popular will. Nevertheless, the issue-by-issue median is the best approximation we shall have to a popular will. (1999, 147)

Weale also suggests that often citizens may never be aware of the potential social choice problem. On one hand, policy making is usually highly segmented into specialized communities and organizational structures. On the other hand, party competition typically reduces the very many possible specific alternatives and dimensions of choice down to a small number (1999, 146).

This last point is a somewhat uneasy consolation from the point of view of democratic design, because it hints that some policy-making rules and some electoral and party systems may reduce the numbers of alternatives more ruthlessly, or at an earlier stage in consideration, than others. This elimination might more effectively obscure potentially winning democratic combinations.

5 SINGLE DIMENSIONAL ISSUE CONGRUENCE AS PREFERENCE AGGREGATION

In Riker's attack on "populist" or "mandate" theories of democracy, he acknowledges one set of conditions under which it may be meaningful to compare "what the citizens want" with the positions and behavior of policy makers: "If, by reason of discussion, debate, civic education and political socialization, voters have a common view of the political dimension (as evidenced by single-peakedness), then a transitive outcome is guaranteed" (Riker 1982, 128).

We have already seen above that the investigations of multiple issue congruence in the Miller–Stokes tradition suggest that very often there may be a predominant dimension of party competition, to which many specific issue positions are related. Where such a single dimension emerges, it is possible, as Riker observes, to analyze the democratic nature of preference correspondence between citizens and policy makers. There is, indeed, a natural ideal of democratic preference aggregation— correspondence between the position of the median citizen and the policy makers. The median citizen position is preferred because theoretically that position can defeat any other position in a vote between the two positions. The further the policy maker from the position of the median citizen, the more citizens will be on the losing side. (This criterion does not, however, take account of intensity of preferences or, by definition, multiple issue dimensions.)

In empirical research on preference aggregation the target of such investigation is the "left–right scale" (or the "liberal–conservatism" scale in US studies), a single issue dimension that incorporates many specific issue positions and is meaningful to citizens in the society in which representation takes place. Various studies have demonstrated the emergence of such a dimension in the political discourse of mature democracies. Public opinion studies in many (but not all) countries have revealed citizens able to place themselves on a "left–right" or equivalent dimension that incorporates various specific issues and seems to evolve to incorporate newly salient ones (e.g. Inglehart 1984). Several multi-country surveys of experts showed that they were able to place political parties in such a space, which is usually shaped by issues of government and the economy, but takes on somewhat different content in different countries (Castles and Mair 1984; Huber and Inglehart 1995; Benoit and Laver 2005). All these studies involve relative positioning within the country of citizens and parties. The self-placements of party supporters have been shown to be highly related to the placements of parties by experts (Gabel and Huber 2000).

Following a slightly different approach, analysts of the large study of political party manifestos (campaign promises) in industrialized countries that reports space devoted to different substantive issues have developed a technique for placing parties in a cross-national "left–right" scale with substantively comparable positions (Budge et al. 2001). Kim and Fording have proposed a way to estimate the median voter position using those party positions and some assumptions about voters' electoral choices (1998).

If it is substantively meaningful to locate citizens and their representatives in a one-dimensional discourse, then some powerful theoretical results from abstract studies of political competition and policy making in such a single dimensional space can be brought to bear on processes of preference aggregation. As nicely summarized by Cox (1997, ch. 12), expectations about correspondence between citizen medians and policy makers can be contrasted in single-member district plurality and multi-member proportional electoral systems. (Also see Huber and Powell 1994 and Powell 2000.) In the single-member district plurality systems Duverger's law (1954) leads us to expect two-party competition in mature democracies and Downs's theory of convergence (1957) leads us to expect both parties to converge to the median voter. In multi-member proportional systems, electoral competition theory leads us to expect the parties to be distributed across the policy space as the voters are and for those distributions to be reflected fairly into the legislature. Bargaining theory then leads us to expect government and policy maker positions to be shaped heavily by the position of the median party (e.g. Laver and Schofield 1990). Thus, either system can induce, in different ways, good representational correspondence. Which system will be more likely to lead to failures in congruence of the medians depends largely on whether coordination failures in party competition and bargaining are more likely to appear at the election stage, which dominates in SMD systems, or at the legislative bargaining stage, which is essential in PR systems (Cox 1997, ch. 12).

We have already noted that a number of national and cross-national studies reported citizen–policy maker correspondence on a "left–right" dimension, as well as on various specific issues. Two recent sets of representation studies have looked empirically at preference aggregation from the point of view of such a single dimension of discourse. Both have focused on the impact of electoral rules and their consequences for congruence between the median citizen (or voter) and representatives. Powell's studies with various co-authors have estimated within each country the distance between the survey-derived median citizen self-placement and the expert-derived positions of legislature, government, and policy makers (Huber and Powell 1994; Powell 2000; Powell and Vanberg 2000; Powell 2006). These studies assume comparable distances in different countries, but do not assume substantively comparable median positions. They consistently show that the single-member district systems often fail to generate two-party convergence to the median. ("Failures" of both Duverger's law and Downsian convergence seem responsible. Also see Grofman 2004 on theoretical and empirical limitations of Downsian convergence.) These failures of convergence frequently lead to electoral victories, legislative majorities, and governments rather distant from the median voter.

Figure 27.1 shows the distance of the plurality party (horizontal dimension) and the runner-up party (vertical dimension) from the median voter in the five parliamentary SMD systems of Australia, Britain, Canada, France, and New Zealand in elections between 1950 and the late 1990s. We see that although about half of the plurality winners are within ten points of the median voter (on a hundred point scale), the other half are further away—sometimes much further. This is about the same distance from the median voter as the average plurality party under PR. There are notable differences across countries and across elections (with the large Canadian parties usually quite close to the median), but every country had at least one plurality winner over twenty points from the median. Most countries had several elections with both large parties distant from the median.

Multi-member PR systems' two-stage bargaining process seems consistently more successful in creating representative legislatures and encouraging formation of governments close to the median voter. However, such factors as pre-election coalitions and polarized large parties can pull emergent governments away from the median (Powell 2006) and create substantial variation across time and countries.

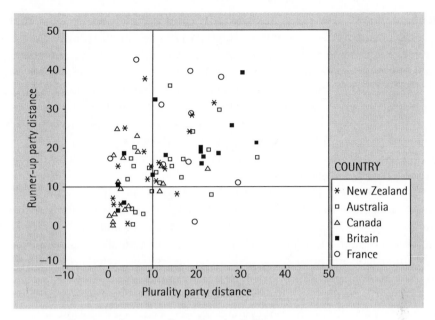

Fig. 27.1 Party distances from median voter in SMD

Interestingly, quite comparable short-term results have also emerged from analyses of the distance between the Kim and Fording-estimated median voter position and the manifesto-derived positions of legislative and governing parties (McDonald, Mendes, and Budge 2004.) McDonald and his co-authors find average short-term divergence of legislatures and governments from the median voter to be greater in the single-member district systems than in the PR systems. As they are using a longer time series and a different technique than the Powell studies (although largely the same countries), the comparable findings are encouraging. (This technique was used to derive Figure 27.1.) They are also able to discuss a variety of interesting findings from a larger time perspective.

The preference aggregation studies assuming a one-dimensional discourse are able to draw upon a rich (although not uncontroversial) body of theory and previous empirical research on party competition and government formation. Theoretically, the assumption of a discourse in a single dimension solves the social choice problem. The empirical studies have yielded interesting substantive results concerning the correspondence of medians and expected and realized conditions for correspondence failure, especially under different electoral rules. Although both of these sets of studies have focused on parliamentary systems in the industrialized democracies, there is no reason in principle why these approaches cannot be extended to democratic settings with other kinds of policy-making institutions and yet other patterns of party competition. On the other hand, it is clear that the "left–right" discourse is at best simplification of the alignment of political issues, that it is not meaningful to all voters in any country, and that in some countries it is a completely inadequate characterization of the configuration of voter preference and party competition. It is especially problematic in newer democracies or countries whose party system has become volatile.

The conditions under which such a common discourse may or may not emerge are not well understood and are an important target for future analysis. (See, e.g., Carey 2000; Kitschelt 2000.) One line of argument suggests that deliberation about policy can induce substantive agreement, or at least agreement on the dimensionality of debate, and that it is misleading to view citizens as having fixed "preferences" about policies, rather than malleable judgements about likely consequences (Weale 1999, 141–3). If this proves to be true, it is even more important to understand conditions and constraints on such a process.

The studies of left–right discourse congruence rely methodologically on some combination of citizen surveys, expert surveys, and expert coding of party manifesto statements, each of which has its particular sources of error and bias, and which are still not available in many countries. Even more seriously, the strong assumption that a single dimension discourse adequately describes citizen preferences is often disputed. Not surprisingly, an important research tradition has relied instead on the vote as a nominal expression of voter preference and analyzed the correspondence between votes and selection of policy makers as preference aggregation.

6 VOTES AS NOMINAL PREFERENCES: VOTE CORRESPONDENCE AS PREFERENCE AGGREGATION

A third major approach to the comparative study of preference aggregation is to treat citizens' votes as the only authentic revelation of their preferences, and then examine how those votes are aggregated into the selection of policy makers and coalitions for making public policy. This approach has a distinguished pedigree in comparative politics. Clearly it has much to be said for it, as the voting act appears to be a relatively "hard" piece of evidence of citizen preferences, not dependent on artificial imposition of survey questions worded in a particular way or on tapping a political discourse that citizens may not share. Insofar as fair votes weight the contribution of each citizen equally, they can claim to be quintessentially the democratic instrument. It is understandable, therefore, that analysts have invested a great deal of effort in studying the aggregation of votes. Moreover, as the simple act of voting forces the voter into taking simultaneous account of all the issues of concern to him or her and reducing them to a single choice or ranking (in a very few electoral systems), students of votes seemingly do not have to worry about the problem of themselves combining preferences across issues. Hence, they easily ignore the social choice aggregation problem.

The study of vote–seat aggregation is a highly developed area of political science research. Although Mill (1861/1958), Schattschneider (1942), and Duverger (1954) were all aware of difficulties in vote–seat aggregation under various election rules, the paradigmatic study, shaping this research for over a quarter of a century, has been Douglas Rae's *Political Consequences of Election Laws* (1967/1971). Rae's elegant little book systematically distinguished a variety of types of electoral laws, identified some of their important properties, introduced systematic measures of vote–seat disproportionality and the creation of legislative majorities, as well as the fractionalization of party systems, and performed other essential services on the way to analysis of the empirical consequences of election laws in 115 elections. Rae demonstrated that the critical feature of election rules shaping vote–seat translation in these elections was their "district magnitude" (the average number of representatives per district), which dwarfed the still significant effects of differences in computation rules and other relevant features (Rae 1967/1971, 138–40). The widely used election rule with the greatest tendency to disproportionality is the single-member district plurality rule, also known as first-past-the-post (hereafter, FPTP) used in such countries as the United States, Britain, New Zealand, and Canada. Rae's paradigmatic study also promoted implicitly the critical assumption that the party vote was a meaningful and homogeneous concept, whose aggregation into legislative seats was an important question.

Rae's landmark empirical contribution has been elaborated and developed in a variety of different kinds of studies, empirical and methodological (see Groffman and Lijphart 1986; Taagepera and Shugart 1989; Lijphart 1994; and the review in Powell 2004, especially 275–80). Such studies, and others to be found especially in *Electoral Studies*, but in many other political science journals as well, have greatly extended Rae's account of the variations in election rules and their consequences. The concept of proportionality itself contains alternative normative versions, reflected in part in different PR counting rules, as pointed out by Gallagher 1991. Specific rules are also adapted in various ways to achieve different practical purposes, including political stability and the partisan goals of the rule writers, as various studies of particular countries have elaborated.

While the analysis of election laws has dominated work on vote–seat correspondence, two other important variables have also emerged in comparative research. One of these is the geographic distribution of the votes, which is increasingly important for proportionality when the election rules have low district magnitudes, above all in single-member district systems. Naturally enough, American, British, and New Zealand scholars whose work has been primarily within such systems have long been sensitive to the role of geography, which is often ignored by scholars working in systems with large magnitude PR rules. Some insight into the source of variation is provided by the work of political geographers, who visualize the division of the country into districts as a map superimposed over a map of the distribution of preferences (e.g. Gudgin and Taylor 1979; Taylor and Johnston 1979; Taylor, Gudgin, and Johnston 1986). Some kinds of maps will produce more "wasted votes," coming from the losers in these districts, and will also produce larger seat swings from marginal vote swings. The addition of more parties can produce more wasted votes, if it means that the winners are carrying districts with less than 50 percent of the votes, or if it means that there are fewer lopsided victories of any kind. Geographically concentrated parties may not create that effect if they simply mean uneven local contests between different parties. One way of understanding gerrymandering is as a practice of drawing the boundaries to be sure there is not an even balance of winners and losers on both sides.

Lack of equality in the relationship between numbers of voters and numbers of representatives from each district may also affect disproportionality. This lack of equality may stem from the rules of representation themselves (as in the under-representation of urban districts in Spain), which is usually called malapportionment. It may also be caused by differential rates of turnout in different district, as when a labor party gains proportionately greater representation because lower turnout in urban areas means its victories are based on fewer votes. Political geographers' analyses of bias effects in two party situations suggest that they can be disaggregated into four elements: turnout, malapportionment, third party, and distributional (intentional or unintentional gerrymanders). See especially Johnston, Rossiter, and Pattie 1999 and the references therein. While this work has thus far been dominated by scholars studying Britain and New Zealand, this may be changing, as reported in Snyder and Samuels's (2001) review of malapportionment in Latin America.

Observers had also long been aware, from various perspectives, that "too many" parties is a problem for representation. Schattschneider (1942, 75 ff.) and Duverger (1954, 374) suggested the problems of more than two parties in single-member district plurality systems. Figure 27.2 shows that in the range of two to five "effective" parties, vote–seat disproportionality increases sharply as the number of parties increases in the SMD systems (solid line), whereas in this range of parties the PR systems continue to show relatively proportional outcomes (dashed line).

Taagepera and Shugart (1989) show that the effect of too many parties on proportionality is not limited to FPTP systems. Rather, disproportionality tends systematically to increase with more competing political parties. In 1997 Gary Cox in *Making Votes Count* provided an appealing theoretical framework into which to place the work on election rules, number of parties, and disproportionality. Cox draws upon a large, purely theoretical, literature on strategic voting under different voting rules, as well as upon the empirical studies, to provide a model of the "microfoundations" of Duverger's law. The work of Gibbard (1973) and Satterthwaite (1975) had demonstrated theoretically, as Leys (1959) and Sartori (1968) had suggested from empirical observation, that "strategic voting" (voting for a less preferred party or candidate because it has a better chance of winning) can be rational under any kind of voting system. One way of understanding "Duverger's law" that we expect only two parties under SMD is as successful coordination, involving party leaders and/or voters, to reduce the number of parties to match a reasonable probability of winning the only seat available in a district. Such coordination involves the strategies of party leaders, the election rules, and expectations about voters.

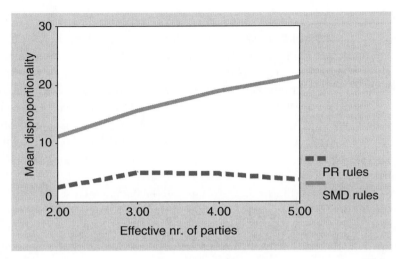

Fig. 27.2 Vote–seat disproportionality by number of parties: SMD and PR Rules

Explicitly, Cox suggests that theoretically the number of parties should be reduced to no more than the district magnitude plus one (1997, 31–2, 99 ff.).

When coordination fails, and "too many" parties compete relative to the threshold, we shall see increased levels of misrepresentation (assuming equivalent cross-district canceling effects), as we saw for the SMD systems in Figure 27.2. While any voting system will demand some coordination, the coordination task is greater and the costs of coordination failure are higher in low district magnitude systems. FPTP is the extreme case, in which a single party may receive substantial votes in many districts and yet fail to carry any of them—thus depriving many voters of representation. Cox's formulation suggested theoretically the conditions (of party objectives, information, expectations, and rules) under which coordination failures should occur–quite apart from the geographic issues.

The clear gains in our understanding of the complex interactions between election rules, geographic preferences distributions, and the number of parties are an impressive example of scientific progress. They build, moreover, on a seemingly firm foundation of preference in starting with the citizen's vote, a specific choice in the political realm made by the individual citizen. This body of research illuminates greatly the conditions under which the proportional aggregation of voter preferences, as expressed in their vote, may fail.

That granted, we should not overstate the unique authenticity of the vote as an instrument of preference revelation. Voters can only choose from among the choices offered to them. We cannot determine from the vote outcomes how those choices related to the underlying preferences of each citizen. Some voters may feel that one of the offered choices corresponds closely to the configuration of issue preferences that he or she holds; others, however, may find themselves forced to accept a package of policies that is rather distant from their ideal. The voter may also have negative preferences which are ill conveyed in the nominal act. The emergence of an extremist party as the plurality vote winner in a multiparty system may obscure the fact that two-thirds of the voters, while divided in their nominal choices, agree in opposing the extremists. (For a theoretical analysis of the disadvantage of using plurality vote winners to reflect preferences, see Weale 1999.) Voters may not even vote for their most preferred party because they feel it has no chance of winning and cast "strategic" votes to have some effect on choosing between likely winners. The degree to which these issues are problems will presumably vary according to the dispersal of voter preference packages, the variety of party alternatives, and the election rules.

Moreover, vote aggregation studies, such as vote–seat analyses, usually assume that the party or candidate choice meant the same thing to each voter. This justifies the canceling of loser's votes in one district against winner's in another to get proportional outcomes. But especially in new or highly decentralized party systems, this may not be true. The "same" party label may mean different things in different regions, for example, or the party may contain large internal factions appealing to different voters even within the same multi-member district.

For all these reasons, then, the apparently authentic datum of the nominal vote choice is more artificial and constructed, conveying less information about even party preferences, not to mention issue preferences, which are linked to parties in complex ways, than it would appear. Thus, the very real problems in using survey research to ascertain preferences are not completely circumvented by using votes. Indeed, survey research has some important advantages in providing information about preferences among multiple alternatives.

Moreover, two other problems emerge as we go from votes to policy makers. One is what normative standard of aggregation is to be used. The classic vote–seat literature, in the form it has taken since Rae's seminal work, uses proportionality as the standard. A party's seats in the legislature should correspond to its proportion of the votes won. Failing to achieve this is "disproportionality," which is measured in various ways to various degrees. But while the classic vote–seat literature uses proportionality as its standard, a case can be made for focusing on other standards, such as the responsiveness of seat changes to vote changes, with higher levels of responsiveness seen as more desirable. For example, what Gelman and King (1994) call "responsiveness" of seat changes to vote changes emphasizes amplification of the impact of party vote shifts (around the party average) on party seat shifts in the legislature. This follows in a tradition in American and British political analysis emphasizing the values of competitiveness and swing ratios. (Also see Rae 1967, 26–7, 100–1, 145.) Gelman and King explicitly contrast the American concept of responsiveness in amplifying vote shifts to the lesser responsiveness of proportionality as a value (1994, 544–5).

In one of the few studies explicitly to examine vote–seat connections from both views, Katz (1997) considers proportionality and "responsiveness" as competing democratic virtues. His comparative analysis finds that they "are influenced by much the same factors, but are inversely related" to each other (Katz 1997, 138–42).

Powell 2000 (ch. 6) follows a similar line of thought and suggests that "proportional" and "majoritarian" visions of democracy imply different relationships between votes and their legislative (or policy-making) representation. (Also see Powell with Powell 1978.)

The final difficulty with preference aggregation based on votes is getting beyond the legislative representation of votes, whether of all parties or the plurality winner, into the choice of policy makers. Here, again, advocates of proportionality in aggregation are likely to favor multiparty coalitions that maximize among policy makers, as in the legislature, the advocacy of the full range of policy alternatives. Those who favor aggregation dominated by majorities are likely to favor putting all the policy-making power in the hands of plurality vote winners (majority vote winners if possible, but empirically these are rare). Thus, vote–government correspondence can build on either proportional representation in government of all parties winning votes or on dominance of governments (and policy makers) by the plurality vote winner. In an analysis of votes, governments, and policy makers Powell finds that proportional and majoritarian (FPTP and other single-member district) systems each perform fairly well by "their own" standards of aggregation, and quite badly by the standards implied by the opposite vision (2000, ch. 6). This is consistent with Katz's finding and with the idea of a tradeoff between proportionality and responsiveness in election outcomes. (However, good responsiveness in the majoritarian systems usually requires counting the party winning the plurality of votes as entitled to unshared governing power, as very few parties win vote majorities.)

Studies of vote–government correspondence in parliamentary systems can draw upon empirical works, especially those emphasizing the role of legislative plurality parties in government formation. Rules of legislative government formation in parliamentary and mixed systems usually favor majority investiture and confidence votes, although there is substantial variation with empirical consequences. But most government formation theory and research has emphasized the positions of the parties in some kind of policy space (see Laver and Shepsle 1990), not available from nominal vote analysis, as well as party size (see Martin and Stevenson 2002). In presidential systems the votes more directly shape presidential government, although the problem of interpreting preferences remains.

Despite its problems and complexities, the research on aggregation and representation of party votes has a powerful double claim of significance. On one hand, to the extent that party votes represent nominal preferences, then the processes of aggregating party votes directly trace the aggregation of preferences. Doing so illuminates various factors, such as election laws, geographic distribution of votes, and the number of parties that shape the aggregation of millions of equally weighted votes into a small number of policy makers. It also draws our attention to alternative normative and empirical approaches in aggregation. On the other hand, even without assuming that votes directly represent preferences, the issue congruence and left–right congruence approaches, as we have seen, will still be shaped in part by the aggregation of party promises and votes as causal mechanism.

7 CONCLUDING COMMENTS

Four research programs. Four different responses to the social choice challenge. Each evades it in a different way. Democratization research examines conditions for introducing or sustaining free, democratic elections without analyzing their consequences for the correspondence of preferences and policies. Issue congruence research examines the correspondence between citizen issue preferences and representatives' positions on an issue-by-issue basis, not reconciling across different issues. Left–right issue correspondence assumes a one-dimensional preference space for citizen and party discourse, ignoring issues, voters, and party systems that cannot be encompassed in that single dimension. Election aggregation studies assume that votes are sufficient expressions of citizen preferences, ignoring constraints that may limit or distort the correspondence between preferences and votes. Thus, each falls short of a fully articulated and empirically encompassing research program of democratic preference aggregation.

Moreover, an important limitation shared by all these studies is lack of attention to issues of accountability, as the policy makers implement or neglect the policies to which they are publicly committed. They assume that the process of preference aggregation is completed with the selection of policy makers chosen by the electorate and/or committed to the citizen's preferences. There has been little investigation of the problem of faithless policy makers who may choose to implement their personal agenda or of incompetent policy makers who lack the skill to carry out their commitments. Democratic theory assumes that democratic processes will induce correspondence between acts of governance or even policy outcomes and what the citizens want. From this point of view preference aggregation is not complete until the policy makers have shown their good faith. Indeed, there is the unsettling possibility that some of the institutions that facilitate correspondence between preferences and the positions of policy makers may be inadequate, or even detrimental, for holding policy makers accountable.

There is a small, but growing, literature on the correspondence of election promises and policy efforts (e.g. Klingemann, Hofferbert, and Budge 1993; Royed 1996; Thomson 2001), as well as on the theory and mechanisms of electoral accountability (Przeworski, Stokes, and Manin 1999). A major landmark is Stokes's study of policy switching by Latin American presidents in the 1980s and early 1990s, and its electoral and policy consequences (2001). The study of corruption, increasingly recognized as a major obstacle to meaningful responsiveness to citizens in many new democracies, is also a growth industry. Eventually, these threads must be gathered into the study of democratic preference aggregation.

Yet, each of the large research programs on preference aggregation we have described has something valuable of its own to contribute to our understanding of democratic preference aggregation through competitive elections. Without introducing and sustaining the conditions for free, meaningful, and democratic elections, the other election-based analyses of preference aggregation are irrelevant. Unless election processes result in correspondence between the preferences of citizens and the positions of policy-making representatives on some specific issues, democratic aggregation has failed. Insofar as citizen preferences and party competition can be expressed in a single-dimensional political discourse, powerful theoretical tools and empirical techniques can help us understand the conditions under which democratic aggregation can succeed or fail. The aggregation of party votes into legislative and governmental representation is a critical causal mechanism for the aggregative consequences of democratic elections. These multiple research programs help illuminate each other's strengths and weaknesses. Each has made substantial progress in its own terms, avoiding the paralysis implied by Riker's rejection of the enterprise of democratic preference aggregation, and offering contributions to the larger picture. They suggest that Riker's social choice-based challenge to describing and understanding democratic preference aggregation is not unanswerable.

References

ACHEN C. 1977. Measuring representation: perils of the correlation coefficient. *American Journal of Political Science*, 21: 805–15.
—— 1978. Measuring representation. *American Journal of Political Science*, 22: 477–510.
ARROW, K. J. 1951. *Social Choice and Individual Values*. New Haven: Yale University Press.
BARNES, S. H. 1977. *Representation in Italy: Institutionalized Tradition and Electoral Choice*. Chicago: University of Chicago Press.
BENOIT, K., and LAVER, M. 2005. *Party Policy in Modern Democracies*. London: Routledge.
BOIX, C., and STOKES, S. C. 2003. Endogenous democratization. *World Politics*, 55: 517–49.
BRATTON, M., and MATTES, R. 2001. Support for democracy in Africa: intrinsic or instrumental? *British Journal of Political Science*, 31: 447–74.
BUDGE, I., KLINGEMANN, H. D., VOLKENS, A., BARA, J., and TANENBAUM, E. 2001. *Mapping Policy Preferences*. New York: Oxford University Press.
CAREY, J. M. 2000. Parchment, equilibria, institutions. *Comparative Political Studies*, 33: 735–61.
CASTLES, F., and MAIR, P. 1984. Left–right political scales. *European Journal of Political Research*, 12: 73–88.
COLLIER, D., and LEVITSKY, S. 1997. Democracy with adjectives. *World Politics*, 49: 430–51.
CONVERSE, P. E. and PIERCE, R. 1986. *Political Representation in France*. Cambridge, Mass.: Harvard University Press.
COX, G. W. 1997. *Making Votes Count: Strategic Coordination in the World's Electoral Systems*. Cambridge: Cambridge University Press.
DAHL, R. A. 1956. *A Preface to Democratic Theory*. New Haven: Yale University Press.
—— 1989. *Democracy and its Critics*. New Haven: Yale University Press.
DALTON, R. 1985. Political parties and political representation: party supporters and party elites in nine nations. *Comparative Political Studies*, 18: 267–99.
DIAMOND, L. et al. eds. 1997. *Consolidating the Third Wave Democracies*. Baltimore: Johns Hopkins Press.
DOWNS, A. 1957. *An Economic Theory of Democracy*. New York: Harper and Row.

Dreze, J., and Sen, A. 1989. *Hunger and Public Action.* Oxford: Oxford University Press.

Duverger, M. 1954. *Political Parties: Their Organization and Activity in the Modern State,* trans. B. North and R. North. New York: John Wiley.

Esaiasson, P., and Heidar, K. 2000. *Beyond Westminster and Congress: The Nordic Experience.* Columbus: Ohio State University Press.

—— and Holmberg, S. 1996. *Representation from Above: Members of Parliament and Representative Democracy in Sweden.* Aldershot: Dartmouth Publishing.

Farah, B. G. 1980. Political representation in West Germany: the institution and maintenance of mass–elite linkages. Ph.D. thesis. University of Michigan.

Fearon, J., and Laitin, D. 2003. Ethnicity, insurgency and civil war. *American Political Science Review,* 97: 75–90.

Feng, Y. 2003. *Democracy, Governance and Economic Performance.* Cambridge, Mass.: MIT Press.

Gabel, J., and Huber, J. 2000. Putting parties in their places. *American Journal of Political Science,* 44: 94–103.

Gallagher, M. 1991. Proportionality, disproportionality, and electoral systems. *Electoral Studies,* 10: 33–51.

Gelman, A., and King, G. 1994. Enhancing democracy through legislative redistricting. *American Political Science Review,* 88: 541–59.

Gibbard, A. 1973. Manipulation of voting schemes: a general result. *Econometrica,* 41: 587–601.

Granberg, D., and Holmberg, S. 1988. *The Political System Matters: Social Psychology and Voting Behavior in Sweden and the United States.* New York: Cambridge University Press.

Grofman, B. 2004. Downs and two-party convergence. *Annual Review of Political Science,* 7: 25–46.

—— and Lijphart, A. eds. 1986. *Election Laws and their Political Consequences.* New York: Agathon Press.

Gudgin, G., and Taylor, P. J. 1979. *Seats, Votes and the Spatial Organization of Elections.* London: Pion.

Harff, B. 2003. No lessons learned from the Holocaust. *American Political Science Review,* 97: 57–73.

Holmberg, S. 1989. Political representation in Sweden. *Scandinavian Political Studies,* 12: 1–36.

—— 1997. Dynamic opinion representation. *Scandinavian Political Studies,* 20: 265–83.

—— 1999. Collective policy congruence compared. Pp. 87–109 in *Policy Representation in Western Democracies,* ed. W. E. Miller. Oxford: Oxford University Press.

—— 2000. Issue agreement. Pp. 155–80 in *Beyond Westminster and Congress: The Nordic Experience,* ed. P. Esaiasson and K. Heidar. Columbus: Ohio State University Press.

Huber, J. D., and Inglehart, R. 1995. Expert interpretations of party space and party locations in 42 societies. *Party Politics,* 1: 73–111.

—— and Powell, G. B. 1994. Congruence between citizens and policymakers in two visions of liberal democracy. *World Politics,* 46: 291–326.

Huntington, S. P. 1991. *The Third Wave: Democratization in the Late Twentieth Century.* Norman: University of Oklahoma Press.

Inglehart, R. 1984. The changing structure of political cleavages in western society. Pp. 25–69 in *Electoral Change in Advanced Industrial Democracies,* ed. R. J. Dalton, S. C. Flanagan, and P. A. Beck. Princeton: Princeton University Press.

Irwin, G. A., and Thomassen, J. 1975. Issue-consensus in a multi-party system: voters and leaders in the Netherlands. *Acta Politica,* 10: 389–420.

Johnston, R. J., Rossiter, D., and Pattie, C. 1999. Integrating and decomposing the sources of partisan bias. *Electoral Studies,* 18: 367–78.

KATZ, R. 1997. *Democracy and Elections*. New York: Oxford University Press.

KIM, H. M., and FORDING, R. C. 1998. Voter ideology in western democracies. *European Journal of Political Research*, 33: 73–97.

KITSCHELT, H. 2000. Linkages between citizens and politicians in democratic polities. *Comparative Political Studies*, 33: 845–79.

——MANSFELDOVA, Z., MARKOWSKI, R., and TOKA, G. 1999. *Post-Communist Party Systems: Competition, Representation and Inter-party Cooperation*. New York: Cambridge University Press.

KLINGEMANN, H., HOFFERBERT, R. I., and BUDGE, I. 1993. *Parties, Policies and Democracy*. Boulder, Colo.: Westview.

LAVER, M., and SCHOFIELD, N. 1990. *Multiparty Government: The Politics of Coalition in Europe*. Oxford: Oxford University Press.

LEYS, C. 1959. Models, theories and the theory of political parties. *Political Studies*, 7: 127–46.

LIJPHART, A. 1994. *Electoral Systems and Party Systems: A Study of Twenty-Seven Democracies, 1945–1990*. New York: Oxford University Press.

MCALLISTER, I. 1991. Party elites, voters and political attitudes: testing three explanations of mass–elite differences. *Canadian Journal of Political Science*, 24: 237–68.

MCDONALD, M. D., MENDES, S., and BUDGE, I. 2004. What are elections for? Conferring the median mandate. *British Journal of Political Science*, 34: 1–26.

MAINWARING, S. P., and SCULLY, T. R. eds. 1995. *Building Democratic Institutions: Party Systems in Latin America*. Stanford, Calif.: Stanford University Press.

MANION, M. 1996. The electoral connection in the Chinese countryside. *American Political Science Review*, 90: 736–48.

MARTIN, L., and STEVENSON, R. 2002. Government formation in parliamentary democracies. *American Journal of Political Science*, 45: 33–50.

MATTHEWS, D. R., and VALEN, H. 1999. *Parliamentary Representation: The Case of the Norwegian Storting*. Columbus: Ohio State University Press.

MAY, J. D. 1973. Opinion structure of political parties: the special law of curvilinear disparity. *Political Studies*, 21: 136–51.

MILL, J. S. 1861/1958. *Considerations on Representative Government*, ed. C. V. Shields. Indianapolis: Bobbs-Merrill.

MILLER, W. E., and STOKES, D. 1963. Constituency influence in Congress. *American Political Science Review*, 57: 165–77.

——et al. 1999. *Policy Representation in Western Democracies*. Oxford: Oxford University Press.

NORRIS, P. 1995. May's law of curvilinear disparity revisited. *Party Politics*, 1: 29–47.

O'DONNELL, G. 2004. Quality of democracy: why the rule of law matters. *Journal of Democracy*, 15: 32–46.

PIERCE, R. 1999. Mass–elite issue linkages and the responsible party model of representation. Pp. 9–32 in *Policy Representation in Western Democracies*, ed. W. E. Miller. Oxford: Oxford University Press.

POE, S. C., TATE, C. N., and KEITH, L. C. 1999. Repression of the human right to personal integrity revisited. *International Studies Quarterly*, 43: 291–313.

PORTER, S. R. 1995. Political representation in Germany: effects of candidate selection committees. Ph.D. thesis. University of Rochester.

POWELL, G. B. 2000. *Elections as Instruments of Democracy: Majoritarian and Proportional Visions*. New Haven: Yale University Press.

——2004. Political representation in comparative politics. *Annual Review of Political Science*, 7: 273–96.

POWELL, G. B. 2006. Election laws and representative government. *British Journal of Political Science*, 36: 291–315.

—— with POWELL, L. W. 1978. The analysis of citizen–elite linkages: representation by Austrian local elites. Pp. 197–218 in *The Citizen and Politics: A Comparative Perspective*, ed. S. Verba and L. W. Pye. Stamford, Conn.: Greylock.

—— and VANBERG, G. 2000. Election laws, disproportionality and the left-right dimension. *British Journal of Political Science*, 30: 383–411.

PRZEWORSKI, A., STOKES, S. C., and MANIN, B. 1999. *Democracy, Accountability, and Representation*. New York: Cambridge University Press.

—— ALVAREZ, M. E., CHEIBUB, J. A. and LIMONGI, F. 2000. *Democracy and Development*. New York: Cambridge University Press.

RAE, D. 1967/1971. *The Political Consequences of Electoral Laws*. New Haven: Yale University Press.

RIKER, W. H. 1982. *Liberalism against Populism*. San Francisco: W. H. Freeman.

ROYED, T. J. 1996. Testing the mandate model in Britain and the United States. *British Journal of Political Science*, 26: 45–80.

RUNCIMAN, W. G. 1969. *Social Science and Political Theory*. London: Cambridge University Press.

SARTORI, G. 1968. Political development and political engineering. Pp. 261–98 in *Public Policy*, ed. J. D. Montgomery and A. O. Hirschman. Cambridge: Cambridge University Press.

SATTERTHWAITE, M. A. 1975. Strategy-proofness and Arrow's conditions. *Journal of Economic Theory*, 10: 1–7.

SAWARD, M. 1998. *The Terms of Democracy*. Oxford: Blackwell Publishers.

SCHATTSCHNEIDER, E. E. 1942. *Party Government*. New York: Holt, Rinehart and Winston.

SCHEDLER, A. 2002. Democracy without elections: the menu of manipulation. *Journal of Democracy*, 13: 36–50.

SCHMITT, H., and THOMASSEN, J. 1999. *Political Representation and Legitimacy in the European Union*. Oxford: Oxford University Press.

SNYDER, R., and SAMUELS, D. 2001. Devaluing the vote. *Journal of Democracy*, 12: 146–59.

STOKES, S. C. 2001. *Mandates and Democracy: Neoliberalism by Surprise in Latin America*. New York: Cambridge University Press.

TAAGEPERA, R., and SHUGART, M. S. 1989. *Seats and Votes: The Effects and Determinants of Electoral Systems*. New Haven: Yale University Press.

TAYLOR, P. J., GUDGIN, G., and JOHNSTON, R. J. 1986. The geography of representation. Pp. 183–92 in *Election Laws and their Political Consequences*, ed. B. Grofman and A. Lijphart. New York: Agathon Press.

—— and JOHNSTON, R. J. 1979. *The Geography of Elections*. New York: Holmes and Meier.

—— and LIJPHART, A. 1985. Proportional tenure vs. proportional representation. *European Journal of Political Research*, 13: 387–99.

THOMASSEN, J. 1994. Empirical research into political representation. Pp. 237–64 in *Elections at Home and Abroad*, ed. M. K. Jennings and T. E. Mann. Ann Arbor: University of Michigan Press.

—— 1999. Political communication between political elites and mass publics: the role of belief systems. Pp. 33–58 in *Policy Representation in Western Democracies*, ed. W. E. Miller. Oxford: Oxford University Press.

—— and SCHMITT, H. 1997. Policy representation. *European Journal of Political Research*, 32: 165–84.

THOMSON, R. 2001. The programme to policy linkage: the fulfillment of election pledges on socio-economic policy in the Netherlands, 1986–1998. *European Journal of Political Research*, 40: 171–97.

VOWLES, J., AIMER, P., CATT, H., LAMARE, J., and MILLER, R. 1995. *Towards Consensus? The 1993 Election in New Zealand and the Transition to Proportional Representation*. Auckland: University of Auckland Press.

————BANDUCCI, S., and KARP, J. 1998. *Voters' Victory? New Zealand's First Election under Proportional Representation*. Auckland: University of Auckland Press.

WEALE, A. 1999. *Democracy*. New York: St Martin's Press.

WEISSBERG, R. 1978. Collective versus dyadic representation in Congress. *American Political Science Review*, 72: 535–47.

WESSELS, B. 1999. System characteristics matter: empirical evidence from ten representation studies. Pp. 1137–61 in *Policy Representation in Western Democracies*, ed. W. E. Miller. Oxford: Oxford University Press.

CHAPTER 28

ELECTORAL SYSTEMS

REIN TAAGEPERA

1 How Electoral Systems Matter

WHO governs? Electoral systems matter in democracies because they affect the answer to this question. The rules for allocating assembly seats on the basis of popular votes can make a party with 25 percent electoral support a major player in the assembly or reduce it to a mere 5 percent of the seats.

An electoral system consists of electoral laws and the skills people exert in using them. Laws can be promulgated overnight, but it takes several electoral cycles for politicians and voters to learn how to handle these laws to their best advantage. Electoral system is intertwined with party system. Even the earliest election in a new democracy is bound to produce some constellation of parties in the representative assembly.

As an example, the plurality rule for seat allocation often tends eventually to produce a two-party system (the famous Duverger's law to which I will return). However, many more parties may run rather successfully in many elections before two major parties are winnowed out. Strong regional variations may block the process indefinitely. In such a multiparty system the electoral *laws* may be similar to those in two-party systems, but the electoral *system* arguably differs, because voters maintain options beyond two parties.

My overview focuses on electoral rules, because the impact of this institutional part of electoral systems is relatively well understood not only qualitatively but also with some quantitative rigor. But we should remember that historical and cultural factors may produce different outcomes on the basis of the same electoral rules. Apart from electoral rules in a narrow sense, other institutional factors also contribute to the electoral system. In particular, the number of seats in a representative assembly will be seen to affect representation.

Electoral systems affect politics, but they are also products of politics. They can be altered by political pressures. After an initial bow to this two-way causality, most researchers treat electoral laws as causes of party systems rather than results. But how often does plurality allocation rule *result* from an initial two-party constellation rather than *producing* it? If the dawn of democracy in a given country finds the decision makers divided into two parties, they may wish to choose the plurality rule so as to block entry of new competitors. If, on the contrary, the initial decision makers are split into many parties, they may wish to play it safe and adopt proportional representation (PR) so as to reduce their risk of total elimination.

Only recently has this issue been addressed systematically (Boix 1999; Benoit 2004; Colomer 2005). Party systems do tend to precede and determine the electoral laws. Once in place, though, the electoral rules thus chosen help to preserve the initial party constellation. To avoid causal implications, we may reword Duverger's law, saying that "seat allocation by plurality rule tends to go with two major parties."

Electoral studies are a relatively mature field of study, located at the core of political science:

Although there are many concerns of political science that do not center around elections, the study of democratic practices—to which elections indisputably are central—is certainly one of the most crucial topics for the discipline as a whole. The study of elections is more than the study of electoral systems, and the study of electoral systems is more than "seats and votes", but the numerical values of seats and votes for individual political parties and candidates are among the most important quantitative indicators that we as political scientists employ in our work. (Shugart 2006)

For political scientists electoral rules offer a further attraction: the possibility of institutional engineering. For the given votes, one can calculate the extent to which different electoral rules would have altered the composition of the representative assembly, and propose changes in rules. Of course, under different rules voters might have voted differently; for instance, a shift from plurality to PR may encourage voters to shift to third parties. Actual changes in electoral rules are infrequent, because they usually require agreement by representatives chosen under the old rules—and why should they change rules that got them elected? Still, compared to political culture as well as institutions firmly stipulated in constitutions, electoral rules may well be the feature most conducive to institutional engineering.

The quantitative nature of many features of electoral systems—the numbers of seats and votes, precise allocation algorithms, and the like—may attract those political scientists who yearn to discover quantitative regularities akin to those that have paid off so handsomely in natural sciences. For the same reason, electoral studies may repel those who consider the study of politics an art rather than a science, or at most a science that thrives on richness of details rather than broad generalizations. Any general scientific laws in politics, if they exist at all, are bound to be hidden, submerged in considerable random scatter in data, given that students of politics are largely reduced to non-repeatable observations *in vivo* instead of repeatable laboratory tests. This scatter may easily be construed as absence of general laws. My overview, however, presents evidence that some logical models can be constructed for electoral systems and that they lead to specific quantitative predictions which are confirmed empirically by *averages* of many electoral systems.

This review first covers the typology and comparative study of electoral systems, focusing on the rise of the "Duvergerian agenda." The central part presents recent advances in the macroscopic dimension of this agenda. Advances in the broader agenda of electoral studies are covered in the last major section. I conclude with a provocative issue: to what extent can electoral studies supply a "Rosetta Stone" to political science in general? These issues are expanded on in a forthcoming book (Taagepera 2008).

2 THE STUDY OF ELECTORAL SYSTEMS

2.1 Basic Typology

Elections can apply to one position (president), a few (local council), or many hundred (parliament). Voters may have to voice unqualified support for one or several candidates ("categorical ballot"), or they may be able to rank candidates ("ordinal ballot"). Even with only one position at stake, the rules may require a mere plurality of votes to win, or an absolute majority. For the purpose of generating a majority, candidates may be eliminated sharply (a two-candidate run-off) or gradually (e.g. by dropping the candidate with the fewest votes).

Multi-seat bodies offer even wider options. Seats may be allocated in districts where the number of seats (district "magnitude," M) can vary from one (single-member districts, SMD) to the total number of seats in the assembly (S). Voters may vote for party lists ("closed lists"), individual candidates within lists ("open" or "preferential" lists), or for specific candidates. In single non-transferable vote (SNTV), M candidates with the most votes win seats, while in single transferable vote (STV) the one with the fewest first-preference votes is dropped and such votes are reassigned according to next preferences. On the basis of list votes, all seats may go to the plurality winner (e.g. in US Electoral College elections in a given state), but most often they are distributed by some PR rule, such as d'Hondt or Sainte-Laguë divisors or simple (Hare) quota and largest remainders.

This overview cannot do justice to the enormous variety of electoral rules that have or could be used, much less explain their detailed procedures. The application of SNTV, STV, divisor, quota, and various other seat allocation rules is explained in any monograph on electoral systems worldwide, such as Lijphart (1994), Reynolds and Reilly (1997), Katz (1997), Farrell (2001), and Norris (2004). The most widespread electoral rules are multi-seat List PR and single-seat plurality, often called first-past-the-post (FPTP).

The *simplest family of electoral systems* is the one where a total of S seats are allocated to closed lists in a single round, in districts of equal magnitude M and according to a PR formula (which for $M=1$ effectively boils down to FPTP). Two parameters, M and S, suffice to specify such a simple system. The seat allocation formula also affects the outcome, especially when M ranges from 2 to 5. D'Hondt gives a slight edge to larger parties, compared to simple quota and largest remainders. Still, changes in magnitude matter markedly more, unless one shifts to a semi-proportional or plurality formula.

Apart from FPTP elections that involve no primaries (e.g. UK), perfectly simple electoral systems are rare. In practice, district magnitudes vary across the country, and the ballot may be ordinal. There may be primaries or several rounds, legal thresholds of representation, or transfer of some votes and seats to a higher tier that uses different rules. Voters may have several votes that apply in different ways. Thus, the German mixed member proportional (MMP) rule asks voters to cast a vote for a candidate in an SMD and also for a party in essentially nationwide PR allocation, which compensates for the disproportionality introduced at the SMD level. In the superficially similar "parallel" rule in Japan, no such compensation occurs.

The impact of seat allocation rules on the conversion of votes into seats is easiest to investigate for simple systems. The contrast between plurality and PR allocation rules is extreme in the case of a nationwide single district ($M=S$). Here plurality rule would assign all S seats in the assembly to the winning list, while PR rules would produce highly proportional outcomes. As the electorate is divided into increasingly smaller districts ($M<S$), the contrast between the outcomes of plurality and PR rules softens, until they yield the same outcome in the case of FPTP ($M=1$).

2.2 Comparative Studies

The study of electoral systems began with advocacy pieces, such as Mill (1861), for specific sets of rules. It reached a major analytical landmark with Duverger (1951, 1954) who first clearly announced what came to be called Duverger's law and hypothesis: FPTP tends to go with two major parties ("law"), while multi-seat PR tends to go with more than two major parties ("hypothesis"). As district magnitude increases from $M=1$ to $M=S$, the number of parties actually tends to increase gradually, at a decreasing rate, when PR is used.

Note that the Duverger statements (law and hypothesis) involve only one parameter, district magnitude. This means they address only the systems I have called simple. They say nothing about elections with run-offs, tiers, legal thresholds, ordinary ballots, or any other complications.

What produces the outcomes noted by Duverger? Low district magnitudes (and $M=1$ in particular) arguably put a squeeze on the number of parties in two ways. The "Duverger mechanical effect" means that, in an FPTP district, only the two largest parties tend to win, so that votes for third parties are effectively wasted. The "Duverger psychological effect" means that voters tend to abandon such third parties in the next elections. With reduced votes, third parties win still fewer seats and are gradually eliminated, unless they have local strongholds.

Duverger highlighted the possibility of systematic relations between electoral rules and political outcomes. The search for such regularities has been called the "Duvergerian agenda" (Shugart 2006), and it arguably has formed the core of the field of electoral studies during the late 1900s. This search looks for answers, preferably quantitative, to questions like: How does the electoral system shape the party system? To what extent are voters' choices affected by electoral rules? And what are the processes that cause the relationships? The very idea of the existence of systematic relationships between electoral rules and political consequences remains controversial, but it keeps revolving.

Among the dozens of monographs and hundreds of articles that have advanced the field, at least the following must be mentioned, along with an inevitably superficial characterization of some main achievements. Rae (1967) coined the term "magnitude" and applied it to systematic worldwide analysis. Riker (1982) streamlined the argument for Duverger's statements and effects. Taagepera and Shugart (1989) showed that, with PR, the number of parties continues to increase with increasing magnitude even beyond $M=2$ or 3. Lijphart (1994) introduced the notion of effective threshold to construct simple analogs for actual more complex systems. Cox (1997) elucidated the various forms of strategic coordination that underlie the elusive "psychological effect."

The state of the field has been covered lately in monographs and edited works by Katz (1997), Reynolds and Reilly (1997), Farrell (2001), Norris (2004), Colomer (2004), and Gallagher and Mitchell (2006). Lijphart (1999) and Powell (2000) have analyzed the role of electoral systems as a core part of democratic institutions. Shugart and Carey (1992) and Jones (1995) have studied their impact on presidential regimes.

Specific geographic areas, electoral rules, and/or social groups have been addressed in more detail by Reynolds (1999) on southern Africa, Grofman et al. (1999) on SNTV in East Asia, Bowler and Grofman (2000) on STV, Shugart and Wattenberg (2001) on MMP, Grofman and Lijphart (2002) on PR in Nordic countries, Darcy, Welch and Clark (1994) and Henig and Henig (2001) on women's representation, and Rule and Zimmerman (1994) on women and minorities.

The ability to carry out analyses of worldwide scope has depended on availability of electoral data. Among data collections, Mackie and Rose (1991, 1997) has been the major workhorse regarding long-established democracies. Nohlen, Krennerich, and Thibaut (1999), Nohlen, Gotz, and Hartmann (2001), and Nohlen (2005) have completed the gap for Africa, Asia-Pacific, and the Americas, respectively. A comparable collection for East Central Europe (Nohlen and Kasapovic 1996) seems to be available, as yet, only in German.

2.3 The Duvergerian Agenda and Beyond

The Duvergerian agenda means explaining the results and causes of Duverger's mechanical and psychological effects. It includes micro and macro aspects. A micro dimension underlies the psychological effect, which involves the individual decisions of voters, party leaders, and contributors in what Cox (1997) calls strategic coordination. Reed (1991) observed that in Japanese SNTV elections, $M+1$ "serious" candidates tend to run in a district with M seats. Cox (1997, 99) presented the $M+1$ rule as a direct generalization of Duverger's law and tested it in various ways.[1]

The long-standing macroscopic approach tries to make use of the restrictions imposed by electoral rules (low district magnitude, in particular) to explain the number and size distribution of parties, as well as the degree of disproportionality of seats to votes.[2] The number of political cleavages or "issue dimensions" is also taken into account, to the extent it can be estimated independently of party differences. Shugart (2006) considers the macro dimension of the Duvergerian agenda the "core of the core" of electoral studies.

As far as the study of simple electoral rules for parliamentary elections is concerned, advances since 1980 have been such that Shugart (2006) feels that "the agenda of proportionality and number of parties is largely closed" and needs only fine-tuning. But it is always risky to call an agenda closed.[3] True, the "core of cores" has been investigated to the point where meaningful spin-offs have become possible toward systematic investigation of more complex electoral systems, intra-party impact of electoral rules, and the effects of "second-order" rules such as closed vs. open lists. But this need not mean that the core issues are resolved. In the following I shall focus on the recent findings in the macro-Duvergerian realm and on what remains to be done. Thereafter, I will briefly review various other directions.

3 THE MACRO-DUVERGERIAN AGENDA

3.1 The Macro-Duvergerian Core Idea

The broad idea underlying the Duvergerian statements is that, on the average, *the distribution of party sizes depends on the number of seats available.* Directly, this means the number of seats in the electoral district. Single-member districts restrict the

---

[1] Here $M+1$ applies to the number of viable candidates or lists, depending on the electoral rules. The distinction between candidates and lists is blurred at low M, where few parties expect to win more than one seat. In the Netherlands, however, where all 150 assembly seats are determined in a single nationwide district (i.e. $M=150$), 151 viable candidates seems an understatement, while the number of "viable" parties (those who win or narrowly fail to win at least one seat) is closer to square root of M plus 1, which for the Netherlands is about 13.

[2] The most widespread measure of the number of parties is the Laakso and Taagepera 1979 "effective number of parties" (ENP), defined as $N = 1/\Sigma p_i^2$, where p_i is the i-th party's fractional share of the total votes or seats. The most widespread and mutually competing measures of deviation from proportionality are Loosemore and Hanby 1971's $D = 1/2\Sigma|v_i - s_i|$ and Gallagher 1991's $Gh = [1/2\Sigma(v_i - s_i)^2]^{1/2}$, where v_i and s_i are vote and seat shares, respectively, of the i-th party.

[3] Around 1900, just prior to the birth of relativity and quantum mechanics, many considered physics a closed field, and the head of the US Patent Office recommended closing the Office, given that everything that could possibly be invented already had.

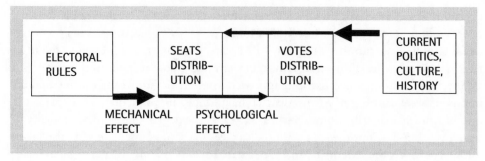

Fig. 28.1 The opposite impacts of current politics and electoral rules

number of parties more than do multi-seat districts. However, the total number of seats in the representative assembly must also matter, because more seats means more room for variety.[4] It is possible to have more than ten parties in a 500-seat assembly, but not in the ten-seat national assembly of St Kitts and Nevis. At the same district magnitude, a larger assembly is likely to have more parties, all other factors being the same.

Concomitantly, the seat share of the largest party is also affected by the number of seats available. In a single-member district, the largest party is bound to have 100 per cent of the single seat available. As district magnitude is increased, the largest share can only decrease, to make room for an increasing number of parties. The same applies to the largest share in the entire assembly. A larger assembly is likely to have more parties, and this puts more pressure on the largest share. Extending this reasoning to the second largest share and so on suggests that, with all other factors being the same, the entire distribution of party sizes should depend on the number of seats available, *on the average*. I will shortly present some empirical evidence.

Do other factors matter, such as a country's historical tradition and culture, and the moment's political events? Of course they do. For individual elections, votes come first, based on current politics and, more remotely, on the country's peculiarities. They will determine the seats, in conjunction with the mechanical effect of the electoral rules. But for the average of many elections, the causal arrow reverses its direction (see Figure 28.1). Through the mechanical effect, electoral rules pressure the distribution of seats to conform to what best fits in with the total number of seats available. Through the psychological effect, the electoral rules eventually also impact the distribution of votes, possibly counteracting culture and history. As a result, the average of many elections in many countries that use similar electoral rules may produce a predictable pattern.

I will first present empirical evidence that these ideas do reflect reality. Then I will present the theory that logically leads to these outcomes.

---

[4] Thus the percentage of blacks in the houses of US states tends to be higher than in the respective senates, although the electorates and electoral rules are basically the same. The only difference is that houses usually have more members (Grofman and Handley 1989).

3.2 Empirics of Simple Electoral Systems

3.2.1 *The Largest Seat Share*

The seat share of the largest party matters politically. A larger share supplies a firmer grip in a cabinet or, if the largest party is excluded, a stronger base for opposition. Even a cursory inspection of data shows that the largest share (s_1) tends to increase with decreasing M—as is implicit in Duverger's statements. Inspection also shows that for FPTP ($M=1$) the largest share increases with decreasing assembly size (S). The largest share typically surpasses 65 percent in tiny island countries where assemblies have only ten to thirty seats. We hypothesize that s_1 decreases with increasing M as well as with increasing S.

Figure 28.2 shows the largest seat share (s_1) graphed against the "seat product" MS of district magnitude and assembly size. (A modified version has been published in Taagepera and Ensch 2006.) Both variables are on logarithmic scales. All those elections in Mackie and Rose (1991, 1997) were included where electoral rules are relatively simple so that M can be defined. The straight line shown is NOT the best fit line but represents the *theoretical prediction* based on a logical quantitative model to be presented soon: $s_1 = (MS)^{-1/8}$. It is visibly close to the best fit, as confirmed by tests in Taagepera and Ensch (2006). Note that the equation encompasses presidential elections ($M=S=1$ and $s_1=1$) as a special extreme case, a conceptual "anchor point." No other combination of M and S seems to produce a less scattered picture than the one based on the seat product MS.

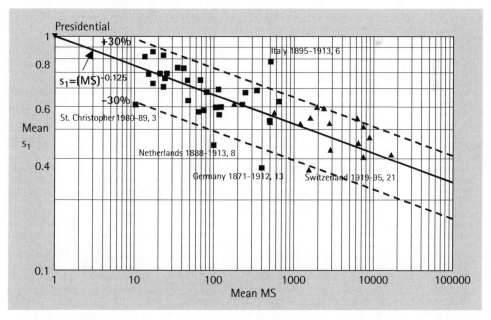

Fig. 28.2 Seat shares of the largest party (s_1) vs. the product of district magnitude (M) and assembly size (S) for 46 fairly simple systems. Squares: $M=1$; Triangles: $M > 1$

3.2.2 *Other Seat Shares, for Given Largest Share*

The largest seat share sets limits for all the other shares. None of them may exceed the largest, and their sum must equal $1-s_1$. As the largest share increases, all other shares are affected. It makes sense to graph the average second-largest share (s_2) at given largest share versus this largest share itself, in what has been called the Nagayama triangle format (Reed 2001). The logically allowed area for s_2 is the triangle underneath the line $s_2 = s_1$ when $s_1 < 0.5$, and underneath $s_2 + s_1 = 1$ when $s_1 > 0.5$.

The process can be repeated for the third-largest party and so on. This is done in Figure 28.3, for averages of many elections with the same largest share, about 350 elections in all. (A modified version has been published in Taagepera and Allik 2006.)

The resulting pattern looks complex but still offers regularities. As the largest share increases the shares of next-ranking parties at first increase, at the expense of still smaller parties, but then they successively begin to decrease. The curve for second-ranking party soon separates itself from those of third parties, so that the two largest parties stand out from the crowd. Amazingly, it will be seen that this complex pattern can be reproduced with a logical quantitative model.

We have seen previously that the largest share depends on the product MS, on the average. Here the average share of the i-th ranking party, at given s_1, is seen to depend on the largest share. Therefore, the average seat shares of all i-th ranking parties depend on the seat product MS in the case of simple electoral rules where M can be defined—albeit it is a quite intricate relationship. Taken together, Figures 28.2 and 28.3 represent a complete empirical description of average seats distribution based on the Duvergerian idea, for simple electoral systems: The average distribution of seat shares of parties depends on the number of seats available—in the electoral district (M) and in the representative assembly (S).

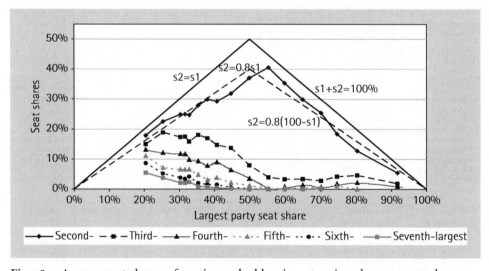

Fig. 28.3 Average seat shares of parties ranked by size, at a given largest party share

3.2.3 Duration of Cabinets

The duration of cabinets obviously matters in politics. If we succeeded in connecting this duration to electoral rules it would confirm that the Duvergerian idea has far-reaching political consequences. The smaller the largest party, the more fragile the cabinet can be expected to be, all other factors being the same. Since the largest seat share decreases with increasing MS, cabinet duration should also decrease with increasing MS, on the average. We are now so many steps removed from direct impact of electoral rules that various other factors may well blur the effect of electoral systems.

Figure 28.4 shows cabinet duration (C) graphed vs. the seat product MS. Both are on logarithmic scales. Included are those twenty-five out of the thirty-six stable democracies studied by Lijphart (1999) for which average M can be defined. The dashed line is the best linear fit, with $R^2 = 0.33$. Cabinet duration clearly does decrease with increasing MS.

More important, the thick line represents the *theoretical prediction* based on a logical quantitative model to be presented soon: $C = 42\mathrm{yrs.}/(MS)^{3/8}$. It is visibly not the best fit, and R^2 drops to 0.19. As a theoretical prediction *not based on any actual data*, it is nonetheless quite successful, as the predicted line does pass through the center of the data cloud. The dotted lines indicate the zone within a factor of 2 of the prediction. Out of twenty-five countries, nineteen are within this zone. Once we control for the observed effect of electoral rules, other factors that affect cabinet duration may emerge more clearly and thus may be more amenable to analysis.

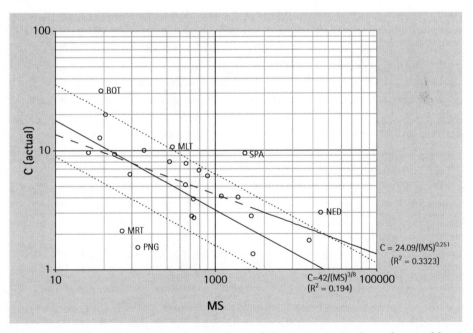

Fig. 28.4 Coalition duration vs. the product of district magnitude and assembly size (from Taagepera and Sikk 2004)

3.3 The Theory of Simple Electoral Systems

3.3.1 *What are Logical Quantitative Models?*

The next stage is to construct logical quantitative models to account for the empirical observations above. What are logical quantitative models? The answer is best introduced by a simple example, which actually will be the first step in explaining the dependence of the largest seat share on electoral rules.

Consider an electoral district with 100 seats, such as the Netherlands actually had in 1918–52, nationwide. How many parties are likely to win seats, and what is the likely average number of seats per party? At least one party must win seats and no more than 100 can. Also the average number of seats per party can range from 1 (when 100 parties win 1 seat each) to 100 (when one party wins all the seats). In the absence of any other information, if we had to give an answer, we would minimize maximum error by guessing at the mean between the logical limits. There are logical reasons to use the geometric mean (see Taagepera 1999). Hence we would guess at 10 seat-winning parties with an average of 10 seats each.

Actually, 8 to 17 parties won seats in the Netherlands; the geometric mean for the nine elections was 10.4 parties winning seats. This case illustrates the observation that a guess based on conceptual limits can be appreciably off for an individual election but still can be close for the average of several elections.

Why not use the good old arithmetic mean? It would lead to a logical inconsistency. The arithmetic mean of 1 and 100 is 50.5. But an average of 50.5 parties winning an average of 50.5 seats per party would amount to a total of 2,550 seats rather than 100! Looking for logical inconsistencies is another tool for constructing logical quantitative models. In the present case only the geometric mean avoids inconsistency.

The resulting general formula for a single district of magnitude M is that the number of parties expected to win at least one seat is around $p' = M^{1/2}$ (Taagepera and Shugart 1993). Note that for SMD ($M=1$) this equation yields $p' = 1$, as it certainly should.

This is an example of a logical quantitative model. Such models use logical reasoning to produce more specific quantitative predictions than merely directional ("If x goes up then y will go down"). The approach used here depended on making the most out of conceptual lower and upper bounds, but this approach is of course not the only one. The models reflect the averages of large numbers of cases. They are probabilistic in the sense a single case has a 50–50 probability of being higher or lower than the prediction.

Logical quantitative models arguably form the backbone of disciplines such as theoretical physics, and they figure in other sciences. Political science has neglected their potential, possibly because the advent of computers has fed the false hope that throwing raw data into regression and factorial analysis will uncover the secrets of social mechanisms, without further effort on our part. This is not the way developed sciences have proceeded (Coleman 2007; Colomer 2007). Statistical approaches are the more fruitful when guided by logical quantitative models.

3.3.2 The Largest Seat Share

Consider an assembly of S members elected in districts of magnitude M. If $p' = M^{1/2}$ parties win seats in a district, the number (p) of parties that win seats in the entire assembly must be at least $M^{1/2}$—this is the lower limit on p. The upper limit is $S^{1/2}$, because this is how many parties would be expected to win seats if the entire assembly were elected in a single nationwide district. The guess based on the geometric mean of the extremes is

$$p = (MS)^{1/4}.$$

This is the number of seat-winning parties, those who have at least one seat in the assembly. Note that this is where the seat product MS first appears as a central characteristic of a simple electoral system.

The average fractional share for a seat-winning party would be $1/p$. The largest share (s_1) must at least equal this average and at most fall slightly short of the total (1). The guess based on the geometric mean of the conceptual extremes is

$$s_1 = (MS)^{-1/8}$$

(Taagepera and Shugart 1993). This is close to the best fit in Figure 28.2. The equation above also predicts that the product of s_1 and $(MS)^{1/8}$ should equal 1.0000. The actual geometric mean for 46 fairly simple systems (30 at $M=1$ and 16 at $M>1$) is 1.0097 (Taagepera and Ensch 2006)—only 1 percent off.

Such a high degree of agreement is surprising and possibly unsettling. The model is based only on the limitations imposed by two institutional inputs—assembly size and district magnitude. True, in the absence of any other knowledge, $s_1 = (MS)^{-1/8}$ would be the best guess we could make. But don't we really know more? Doesn't politics make any difference? What about the Duverger mechanical and psychological effects?

The answer to the last question is that the mechanical effect considers how *vote* shares in *an individual election* are distorted to make the seat shares more conform to what the institutions want to impose (cf. Figure 28.1). The psychological effect, in turn, considers how *vote* shares later adjust themselves to the dictates of institutions. These effects have relatively little impact on the *average* distribution of *seats* over a long time period.

But still, political factors could conceivably exist that boost or shrink the largest party's seat share, compared to what blind probabilities offer. For instance, a bandwagon effect might boost the largest shares in all countries. It may be disappointing to find there are no universal political factors that affect the largest seat share. Deviations from the main trend in Figure 28.2 suggest such factors may exist at the national level. With a sufficiently large number of countries, however, such national factors just seem to cancel out.

3.3.3 Other Seat Shares, for Given Largest Share

Here, specifically political factors finally do enter, largely in the form of strategic coordination stressed by Cox (1997). Recall the way the largest share was previously estimated. We can estimate the second-largest share, for the given largest share, using the same approach. The second-largest share cannot be larger than the largest. It also cannot be more than what is left over by the largest, nor can it be smaller than this leftover divided by the remaining number of seat-winning parties.

Once the mean guess for the second-largest party is calculated, we can proceed to the third-ranking party, and so on. Then we can graph those other shares against the largest share, the way it was done in Figure 28.3. The resulting pattern, however, differs markedly from the empirical one (Taagepera and Allik 2006), meaning that sheer probabilities do not suffice here.

The next step in model building is to assume that, even in PR systems, a certain share of potential small party supporters do not vote for them, for various reasons. Strategic sequencing (Cox 1997, 194) may be the main mechanism, along with various other strategic considerations plus sheer dearth of information on the existence and programs of small parties.

How large must a party be before it stops being a "small" party that loses support and becomes a "large" party that starts to benefit from the transfers? The watershed is found to be around the inverse of the fractional share of the largest party. For $s_1 = .25$, the four largest parties profit. For $s_1 = .5$, only two do. When we assume that about one-half of the potential small party supporters shift to larger parties and correct the purely probabilistic models for this shift (Taagepera and Allik 2006), then the result is close to the empirical picture shown in previous Figure 28.3.

What has been achieved and what remains to be done? First, the empirical pattern in Figure 28.3 was graphed, and it begged for an explanation. Second, a model was constructed that approximates the pattern observed. Thus, even such an apparently complex empirical pattern is not beyond our present explanatory ability. Questions remain. How would the empirical picture in Figure 28.3 look, if seats were replaced by votes? How would it look if list PR and FPTP were graphed separately? Above all, empirical evidence on size distribution of parties should be used to examine the processes that cause abandonment of smaller parties. The Duvergerian agenda is far from completed.

3.3.4 *Duration of Cabinets*

It would be a major payoff for the Duvergerian agenda if the duration of cabinets could be logically connected to electoral systems. The first step is to connect this duration to the number of parties, by introducing the notion of communication channels. N parties have $N(N-1)/2$ potential tension channels among them. Adding intra-party tensions, the total can be approximated as $N^2/2$. The average duration of cabinets may be expected to be inversely proportional to the number of tension channels. If so, then the *average* duration of cabinets (C) would be related to the number of parties through $C = k/N^2$, where k is a constant to be determined empirically.

When the number of parties is taken as the effective number of assembly parties ($N = 1/\Sigma s_i^2$) the agreement of the form $C = k/N^2$ with actual duration is extremely good for thirty-five out of the thirty-six democracies studied by Lijphart (1999, 132–3), the exception being Switzerland with its unusual institutional set-up (Taagepera 2003).

The constant is found to be around $k=42$ years, a value which reminds one of the maximum duration of a political career. Thus

$$C=42 \text{ years}/N^2.$$

The next step is to connect the effective number N to the fractional seat share of the largest party (s_1). It can be shown that N cannot be less than $1/s_1$ nor larger than $1/s_1^2$. Hence, on the average, N could be expected to be around $N=s_1^{-3/2}$. Combined with the previous findings $s_1=(MS)^{-1/8}$, the result is

$$N=(MS)^{3/16}.$$

Finally, combining with $C=42$ yrs./N^2, we obtain $C=42\text{yrs.}(s_1^3)$ and

$$C=42 \text{ years}(MS)^{-3/8}.$$

This predicted curve passes close to the center of the cloud of data points in Figure 28.4.

Thus, a logical quantitative connection between cabinet duration and electoral rules has been established. The value of the constant at 42 years is of course established empirically, but this is typical for physics laws too. For instance, the gravitational constant G in the universal law of gravitational force, $F=Gmm'/r^2$, is empirically determined. The main point is that the functional relationship (inverse square) between C and N is confirmed. However, it could be improved upon.[5]

3.3.5 From Votes to Seats and Back to Votes

As one looks at *individual elections*, votes come first and seats come last. It made sense, therefore, in the early electoral studies to take the votes as given and try to explain the seats in terms of votes. The realization that the institutional impact on the *average of many elections* operates in the opposite direction (cf. Figure 28.1) makes us focus first on the seat share distribution. This has been done with some success in the preceding pages. It is now time to ask: What can average seat share distributions tell us about the averages of vote shares? I will first review what can be found by going from votes to seats and then proceed to the reverse approach. Explanation of seats in terms of votes has been presented in some detail in Taagepera and Shugart (1989, 142–98). The main findings are the following.

Henri Theil (1969) expressed the mechanical effect of FPTP on the transformation of vote shares into seat shares through a logical quantitative model: $s_i/s_j=(v_i/v_j)^n$, where s_i, s_j, v_i, and v_j are the seat and vote shares, respectively, of parties i and j. The crucial observation was that, among all functions of the form $s_i/s_j=f(v_i/v_j)$, this is the only one that does not lead to inconsistencies in the presence of more than two parties. Here we have another case where winnowing out inconsistencies leaves only

---

[5] While cabinet duration is well correlated with the effective number of parties, the latter's connection to the largest seat share through the approximation $N = s_1^{-3/2}$ is imperfect. A more precise way to connect N to s_1 is being worked out (Taagepera 2008) and would improve the fit. Cabinet duration data for countries with very small assemblies would also help, so as to extend the range of MS in Figure 28.4.

one acceptable form. Exponent n reflects the degree of proportionality. For $n=1$ we have perfect PR. For $n>1$, larger parties are overrepresented, while for $n<1$ smaller parties would be overrepresented.

The equation above can be transformed into $s_i = v_i^n / \Sigma v_i^n$, where the summation is over all parties that receive votes. In this form, the seat share of any party can be directly calculated, when all the vote shares are given–provided that the value of proportionality index n is given.

Theil (1969) left the value of n open, but it had been observed ever since 1900 that this index is around 3 in parliamentary elections with FPTP. This was expressed in the empirical "cube law:" $s_i / s_j = (v_i / v_j)^3$. Now, as a thought experiment, reduce the number of seats available gradually to 1. Next, go in the opposite direction and increase it to equal the number of voters. It becomes clear that proportionality index n must decrease with increasing number of seats (S) but increase with increasing number of voters (V). The only simple form that satisfies certain logical requirements is $n = logV/logS$.

The "cube law" emerges because all democratic assemblies tend to follow a *cube root law of assembly sizes*: $S = V^{1/3}$. This law derives from a model that minimizes the number of communication channels that make demands on a single representative. It follows that $logV/logS=3$ applies approximately. The number of voters can be approximated by total population (P): $S = P^{1/3}$. The seat–vote relationship can be extended to multi-seat PR by positing $n = (\log V / \log S)^{1/m}$.

Combined with Theil's $s_i / s_j = (v_i / v_j)^n$ or $s_i = v_i^n / \Sigma v_k^n$, the resulting "law of minority attrition" covers the basic pattern of a wide variety of elections, from direct and indirect presidential elections to parliamentary elections with simple electoral rules. It also extends to women's "rubber ceiling" and various other situations where the share of minorities decreases the smaller the total number of positions available. All the preceding is explained and annotated in Taagepera and Shugart (1989, 142–98).

The awareness of the tendencies expressed in the "cube law" probably has contributed to its demise in more recent elections, as parties have learned to counteract this natural tendency by concentration of resources into the most profitable districts (see graphs in Blau 2004).[6] But as a first approximation, the law of minority attrition still holds.

The equation $s_i = v_i^n / \Sigma v_k^n$ enables us to estimate seat shares, once the actual vote shares in a given election are given. Now it is time to reverse direction. The former equation leads to $v_i = s_i^m / \Sigma s_k^m$, with $m = 1/n = logS/logV$. Once the average seat shares are estimated from institutional inputs, we can use the latter equation to estimate the average vote shares over many elections with simple electoral rules (Taagepera 2001). Some methodical problems remain with this approach (Taagepera 2008), but the principle is clear.

To the extent the vote shares are estimated, we can use the seat and vote shares to estimate the deviation from proportionality, using any of the standard indices. This

---

[6] When does our understanding of the world alter the world itself? In quantum mechanics, the observation of an elementary particle inevitably alters either its position or momentum (the famous principle of indeterminacy), but the problem fades in macroscopic physics. Micro-organisms respond to the invention of antibiotics by mutations that increase their resistance. Awareness of the law of gravitation helped humans to devise ways to circumvent its impact and build airplanes. When political science develops laws that describe simple political phenomena, politicians can be expected to look for loopholes. They can match aeronautical engineers in inventiveness.

would complete the macro-Duvergerian agenda of explaining the number and size distribution of parties, as well as the degree of disproportionality between vote and seat shares, in terms of restrictions imposed by electoral systems.

Figure 28.5 shows the current stage of apparent near-completion of the macro-Duvergerian agenda. Dashed arrows indicate looser links that may need further work. Random error increases at each additional step away from institutional inputs. Moreover, deviation from proportionality involves subtractions of almost equal

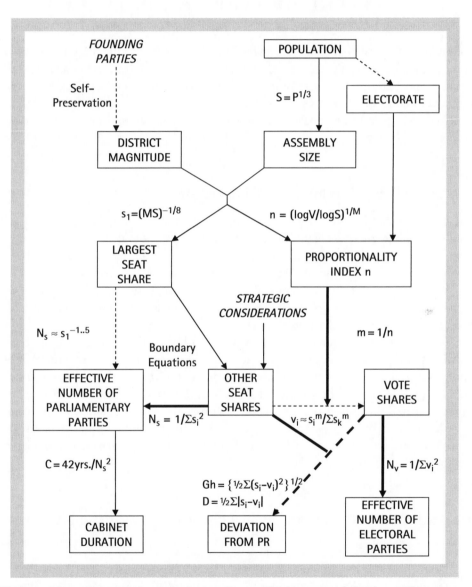

Fig. 28.5 Macro-Duvergerian agenda, as of 2007. Thick arrows: definitions. Thin arrows: logical quantitative models. Dashed arrows: looser connections.

quantities, an operation that boosts random error. It remains to be seen whether a quantitative connection to electoral rules can emerge above this background noise, but work in progress (Taagepera 2008) shows promise.

4 THE BROADER AGENDA

Although the Duvergerian macro-agenda is far from completed, it has been investigated to the point where meaningful spin-off has become possible toward systematic investigation of more complex electoral systems, intra-party effects of electoral rules, and the effects of "second-order" rules such as closed vs. open lists. Any advances in the macro dimension also present new challenges to the micro dimension. In the following survey, I owe much to the recent overview of electoral systems by Matthew Shugart (2006).

4.1 The Micro Dimension of Duverger

The processes that lead to the Duvergerian average patterns of distribution of seats need to be made more explicit. The mechanical and psychological effects are entangled, and Benoit (2002) has argued that the strength of the mechanical effect has been often overstated due to "prefiltering" by psychological considerations. The psychological effect itself risks being a catch-all term for rational choices of varied types by individual actors in individual elections. The actors include not only voters but also party leaders and campaign contributors.

Cox (1997) achieved a major advance with his aforementioned notion of "strategic coordination," which may or may not materialize so as to offer an optimal number of candidates or lists. Cox concludes from his testing of the aforementioned "$M+1$ rule" that the quality of voter information decreases with district magnitude. Blais (2000) has investigated the limits of rational choice approaches to the decision to vote or not to vote. This chapter lacks space to cover the still broader agenda of strategic considerations by candidates, voters, and parties which, in turn, depend on the ideological distribution of parties.

4.2 Cultural and Geographical Determinants of the Number of Parties

Besides institutions, the number of politicized social cleavages or "issue dimensions" also affects the number of parties. In the absence of distinct issues, parties will not form even if the electoral rules offer few restraints. However, impressionistic estimates of the number of issue dimensions risk become tautological, as they are affected by the known number of parties. To counteract this risk, Ordeshook and Shvetsova (1994) introduced ethnic heterogeneity as a measurable proxy for issues. This may be an underestimate, as it overlooks non-ethnic cleavages, but it represents an advance toward objective measurement. The interaction of cleavages and district magnitude has been confirmed by Ordeshook and Shvetsova (1994) as well as Amorim Neto and Cox (1997) and Cox (1997, 208–21).

Once one agrees on which ethnic groups are distinct, their effective number can be measured essentially the same way as it is done for parties. However, the location of these groups also matters. A group uniformly dispersed across the country may contribute less to heterogeneity than does a group of equal size concentrated in a border area where it forms the majority of the population. More generally, geographical location of support for different parties interacts with the effect of electoral rules in determining their strength in the assembly (Gudgin and Taylor 1979; Johnson 1981; Eagles 1995), along with turnout differences and malapportionment (Grofman, Koetzle, and Brunell 1997).

4.3 Effect of Unequal District Magnitudes

Compared to more complex electoral systems, uneven M has been considered a minor deviation from simple systems, yet it can significantly alter the survival chances of small parties. Imagine a country with 100 FPTP districts in sparsely inhabited countryside plus a 100-seat district in the capital city region. The average district magnitude is $M=2.0$, but the effect is vastly different from that of 100 districts with two seats each. In the latter, a two-party system is likely, with limited openings for a third party. In the former, in contrast, the 100-seat district would enable some ten parties to win seats, even while most of them will not win any FPTP seats. Even less drastic discrepancies in district magnitudes can increase the number of parties, compared to more uniform distributions with the same mean M.

Furthermore, uneven distribution of district magnitudes can bias party representation, for the same overall votes, as Monroe and Rose (2002) have shown, using Spanish data. Parties with strong rural support can make a clean sweep in small rural districts and also obtain representation proportional to their small fraction of votes in large urban districts. In contrast, parties with strong urban support will obtain no more than proportional representation in the cities while wasting most of their votes in the countryside.

4.4 Two-tier PR

Two-tier PR systems come in two forms: parallel and compensatory. The outcomes can be quite different, yet the two are often confused. Take the example where voters cast votes in 100 FPTP districts and also in a 100-seat nationwide district. With parallel rules, the FPTP seats may go to two major parties, while all parties win their proportional share in the nationwide tier. In total, the third parties win about one-half of their proportional due in seats, while the two large parties are overpaid accordingly. With compensatory rules, in contrast, nationwide proportionality is restored (usually subject to a legal threshold of votes), which means that the major parties lose whatever advantage they obtained in the FPTP districts.

Elklit and Roberts (1996) have stressed this "two-tier compensatory member" electoral rule as a separate category, more often called mixed member proportional (MMP). The volume edited by Shugart and Wattenberg (2001) updates our knowledge about the particularities of this approach that avoids malapportionment problems, yet preserves the benefits of local representation.

Several countries have recently adopted two-tier PR, either as parallel allocation (e.g., Italy and Japan) or MMP (e.g. New Zealand and Scotland), offering political scientists the equivalents of crucial experiments among and within countries. In New Zealand the shift from FPTP to MMP has reduced disproportionality, as expected (Gallagher 1998), but may not have reduced the adversarial nature of politics characteristic of FPTP (Barker and McLeavy 2000). Note that reduction in disproportionality results directly from a softened mechanical effect, which is instantaneous, while political style is a cultural aspect that may need more time to set in. In Japan the shift from SNTV to FPTP and PR in parallel arguably makes the system more disproportional (Gallagher 1998), and the dominant Liberal Democratic Party has maintained its grip.

Italy's shift from list PR to FPTP and PR in parallel highlights a little-noted aspect of Duvergerian effects in FPTP districts: they tend to favor formation of two major blocs, but those blocs need not be unified parties. In Italy, parties form two blocs to contest the SMD, while maintaining their separate identities thanks to the nationwide part of elections (Katz 1996). Thus Duverger's law is observed to work at the district level (Reed 2001), while the nationwide landscape remains almost as fractured as it was under list PR.

4.5 Preferential-list PR

It matters more than one may think whether voters vote for parties or for individual candidates (Grofman 1999). Shugart (2006) observes that the literature implicitly has equated PR with closed lists (which are part of my definition of simple electoral rules), even while preferential (open) lists (PL) may be more prevalent in practice.

In fact, PL can be used even in the FPTP framework, as Uruguay has done for presidential elections (Shugart 2006). Several candidates, possibly belonging to separate but allied parties, form open lists, where voters vote for a specific candidate. The single seat goes to the list that achieves plurality and, within the list, to the candidate with the most votes. It so to say combines primaries with general elections. Thus, FPTP as usually understood may look like closed-list PR applied to SMD, but it is more akin to SNTV in SMD. In both SNTV and standard FPTP a party is penalized for presenting an excessive number of candidates

The study of PL remains underdeveloped. It comes in a bewildering number of subtly different forms, with possibly important consequences. The attempts at classification of various closed-list, preferential-list, quasi-list, and non-list rules by Shugart (2006) may offer a road map.

4.6 The Intra-party Dimension

For given vote shares, electoral rules affect not only which parties win seats but also who gets those seats within the party. In list PR, parties may wish to appeal to various constituencies by including women, ethnic minorities, etc., and some of them may win. For the single candidate in standard FPTP, parties tend to prefer males of dominant ethnicity. Hence the percentage of women tends to be higher in assemblies elected by PR (Rule 1981). PR may also promote higher intra-party turnover (Darcy, Welch, and Clark 1994; Henig and Henig 2001).

Matland and Taylor (1997) document a finer distinction: Even in multi-seat closed list PR, parties tend to place males at the top of the list when they expect to win only one seat. Preferential lists may enable women to win even when the party leadership does not expect it.

A candidate's ability to win depends on party label and also on the "personal vote" his or her own image can attract. Carey and Shugart (1995) reasoned that the incentive to cultivate a personal vote should increase with increasing district magnitude in open-list PR but decrease in closed-list PR. Indeed, the larger the district magnitude, the less incentive for personal activity closed lists can offer, given the low probability that such activity by the n-th ranked candidate can increase the number of seats won by the party exactly from n-1 to n. In open-list PR (and also SNTV), personal activity can put a candidate ahead of fellow candidates, the more so when more seats are at stake. The two contrary trends fuse at $M=1$, where the single candidate is the party's face in that district. Two indirect tests have confirmed this conjecture. As M increases, the frequency of initiating bills of a local character goes up for PL but down for closed list (Crisp et al. 2004). So does the probability that the candidate is born in the district and is experienced in elected office (Shugart, Valdini, and Suominen 2005).

Further examples of the incidence of general election rules on intra-party politics are given in Shugart (2006). Little is as yet known about them, because intra-party data are more voluminous and harder to come by than inter-party election data.

5 Are Electoral Systems a Rosetta Stone for Political Science?

As advances in sciences bring new answers they also engender new questions. The broader agenda for the study of micro-Duvergerian processes, complex electoral systems, and intra-party impact of electoral rules visibly has reached a stage where the territory is still being mapped and further intricacies are being discovered. Its predictive ability is far from completion. In contrast, the macro-Duvergerian agenda that focuses on the simplest electoral systems has seen a breakthrough, since 1990, in quantitative prediction of the average impact of electoral systems on the distribution of seats among parties. Extension to distribution of votes and prediction of disproportionality is in sight. This breakthrough is based on logical quantitative models. To the extent that the theory of simple systems is complete, gradual extension to more and more complex systems can proceed.

Electoral systems are inextricably intertwined with party systems. The number and strengths of parties are largely measured in terms of election results—votes and seats. Cohesion and ability to get one's way in negotiations may be more meaningful but are harder to measure. Thus the effective number of parties, usually based on election figures, remains perhaps the most widely used single index in political science, despite its well-known shortcomings. It pops up whenever the party system is included as a possible factor in explaining or affecting any political phenomenon.

Such penetration of other subfields made Taagepera and Shugart (1989) ask whether electoral studies could offer some branches of political science the equivalent of what the Rosetta Stone did for the deciphering of Egyptian hieroglyphs.

Compared to other political phenomena, electoral systems deal with fairly hard numbers: number of votes, seats, electoral districts, and so on. Thus these studies are especially amenable to methods used in more established scientific disciplines.... Votes might be to the quantitative development of political science what mass has been for physics and money for economics: a fairly measurable basic quantity. (Taagepera and Shugart 1989, 5)

In developed sciences quantitative expressions interlock. The same quantities recur in various different equations. A constant measured in one context is used in a different one. These numerical values are stepping stones. In comparison, quantitative knowledge in political science has largely been fractured. The numerical values of coefficients found in a regression analysis are rarely used for further analysis. These numerical values are end points.

Figuratively, quantitative relations in physics are like railroads in Europe—they interlock. Those in political science are like many railroads in Africa—isolated tracks starting in port cities and ending in the bush.

Except for simple electoral systems. Here the product of district magnitude and assembly size leads to the number of seat-winning parties, which leads to the largest seat share, which leads to the effective number of parties (cf. Figure 28.5). Here we have the beginnings of an interlocking network of equations which, through the duration of cabinets, promises to extend beyond the realm of electoral and party systems.

Besides such "colonization" potential, the success of logical quantitative models in electoral studies offers a supplementary methodological approach for other subfields. More approaches are available for quantitative study of politics than regression and factor analysis on the one side and rational choice on the other. Some other sciences have been served well by thought experiments based on the notions of boundary conditions and extreme cases, continuity of change between those limits, elimination of logical inconsistencies, etc. They could have their uses in political studies too.

Henry E. Brady (2004) has claimed that "Rather than look for the universal covering laws that are true in all times and places, political scientists should be cognizant of history and context." The "rather than" is a superfluous limitation because we can follow both approaches intertwined. For instance, one need not claim $s_1 = (MS)^{-1/8}$ as "true in all times and places" in order to make it a useful comparison standard for actual election outcomes. The methods that have worked in electoral studies will not open all doors in political science, but this is not needed. It suffices if they open some.

REFERENCES

AMORIM NETO, O., and COX, G. W. 1997. Electoral institutions, cleavage structures, and the number of parties. *American Journal of Political Science*, 41: 149–74.

BARKER, F., and McLEAVY, E. 2000. How much change? An analysis of the initial impact of proportional representation on the New Zealand parliamentary party system. *Party Politics*, 6: 131–54.

BENOIT, K. 2002. The endogeneity problem in electoral studies: a critical re-examination of Duverger's mechanical effect. *Electoral Studies*, 21: 35–46.

—— 2004. Models of electoral system change. *Electoral Studies*, 23: 363–89.

BLAIS, A. 2000. *To Vote or Not to Vote? The Merits and Limits of Rational Choice Theory*. Pittsburgh: University of Pennsylvania Press.

BLAU, A. 2004. A quadruple whammy for first-past-the-post. *Electoral Studies*, 23: 431–53.

BOIX, C. 1999. Setting the rules of the game: the choice of electoral systems in advanced democracies. *American Political Science Review*, 93: 609–24.

BOWLER, S., and GROFMAN, B. eds. 2000. *Elections in Australia, Ireland, and Malta under the Single Transferable Vote: Reflections on an Embedded Institution*. Ann Arbor: University of Michigan Press.

BRADY, H. E. 2004. Introduction [to symposium: two paths to a science of politics]. *Perspectives on Politics*, 2: 295–300.

CAREY, J. M., and SHUGART, M. S. 1995. Incentives to cultivate a personal vote: a rank ordering of electoral formulas. *Electoral Studies*, 14: 417–39.

COLEMAN, S. 2007. Testing theories with qualitative and quantitative predictions. *European Political Studies*, 6: 2 (forthcoming).

COLOMER, J. M. 2004. *Handbook of Electoral Systems Choice*. London: Palgrave.

—— 2005. It's parties that choose electoral systems (or Duverger's law upside down). *Political Studies*, 53: 1–21.

—— 2007. What other sciences look like. *European Political Studies*, 6: 2 (forthcoming).

COX, G. W. 1997. *Making Votes Count: Strategic Coordination in the World's Electoral Systems*. Cambridge: Cambridge University Press.

CRISP, B. F., ESCOBAR-LEMMON, M. C., JONES, B. S., JONES, M. P., and TAYLOR-ROBINSON, M. M. 2004. Vote-seeking incentives and legislative representation in six presidential democracies. *Journal of Politics*, 66: 823–46.

DARCY, R., WELCH, S., and CLARK, J. 1994. *Women, Elections, and Representation*. Lincoln: University of Nebraska Press.

DUVERGER, M. 1951. *Les Partis politiques*. Paris: Le Seuil.

DUVERGER, M. 1954. *Political Parties: Their Organization and Activity in the Modern State.* London: Methuen.

EAGLES, M. ed. 1995. *Spatial and Contextual Models in Political Research.* London: Taylor and Francis.

ELKLIT, J., and ROBERTS, N. S. 1996. A category of its own: four PR two-tier compensatory member electoral systems. *European Journal of Political Research,* 30: 217–40.

FARRELL, D. M. 2001. *Electoral Systems: A Comparative Introduction.* London: Palgrave.

GALLAGHER, M. 1991. Proportionality, disproportionality and electoral systems. *Electoral Studies,* 10: 38–40.

—— 1998. The political impact of electoral system change in Japan and New Zealand. *Party Politics,* 4: 203–28.

—— and MITCHELL, P. eds. 2006. *The Politics of Electoral Systems.* Oxford: Oxford University Press.

GROFMAN, B. 1999. SNTV, STV, and single-member district systems: theoretical comparisons and contrasts. In Grofman et al. 1999: 317–33.

—— and HANDLEY, L. 1989. Black representation: making sense of electoral geography at different levels. *Legislative Studies Quarterly,* 14: 265–79.

—— KOETZLE, W., and BRUNELL, T. 1997. An integrated perspective on the three potential sources of partisan bias: malapportionment, turnout differences, and the geographic distribution of party vote shares. *Electoral Studies,* 16: 457–70.

—— and LIJPHART, A. eds. 2002. *The Evolution of Electoral and Party Systems in the Nordic Countries.* New York: Agathon.

—— LEE, S.-C., WINCKLER, E. A., and WOODALL, B. eds. 1999. *Elections in Japan, Korea, and Taiwan under the Single Non-Transferable Vote.* Ann Arbor: University of Michigan Press.

GUDGIN, G., and TAYLOR, P. J. 1979. *Seats, Votes and the Spatial Organization of Elections.* London: Pion.

HENIG, R., and HENIG, S. 2001. *Women and Political Power: Europe since 1945.* London: Routledge.

JOHNSTON, R. J. 1981. *Political, Electoral and Spatial Systems.* London: Oxford University Press.

JONES, M. P. 1995. *Electoral Laws and the Survival of Presidential Democracies.* Notre Dame, Ind.: Notre Dame University Press.

KATZ, R. S. 1996. Electoral reform and the transformation of party politics in Italy. *Party Politics,* 2: 31–53.

—— 1997. *Democracy and Elections.* Oxford: Oxford University Press.

LAAKSO, M., and TAAGEPERA, R. 1979. Effective number of parties: a measure with application to West Europe. *Comparative Political Studies,* 23: 3–27.

LIJPHART, A. 1994. *Electoral Systems and Party Systems.* Oxford: Oxford University Press.

—— 1999. *Patterns of Democracy: Government Forms and Performance in Thirty-Six Countries.* New Haven: Yale University Press.

LOOSEMORE, J., and HANBY, V. J. 1971. The theoretical limits of maximum distortion: some analytic expressions for electoral systems. *British Journal of Political Science,* 1: 467–77.

MACKIE, T. T., and ROSE, R. 1991. *The International Almanac of Electoral History.* London: Macmillan. Previous editions: 1974, 1982.

—— —— 1997. *A Decade of Election Results: Updating the International Almanac.* Glasgow: Centre for the Study of Public Policy, University of Strathclyde.

MATLAND, R. E., and TAYLOR, M. M. 1997. Electoral system effects on women's representation: theoretical arguments and evidence from Costa Rica. *Comparative Political Studies,* 30: 186–210.

MILL, J. S. 1861. *Considerations on Representative Government.* New York: Harper and Brothers.

MONROE, B. L., and ROSE, A. G. 2002. Electoral systems and unimagined consequences: partisan effects of districted proportional representation. *American Journal of Political Science*, 46: 67–89.

NOHLEN, D. ed. 2005. *Elections in the Americas: A Data Handbook*. Oxford: Oxford University Press.

—— GOTZ, F., and HARTMANN, C. eds. 2001. *Elections in Asia and the Pacific: A Data Handbook*, vols. i and ii. Oxford: Oxford University Press.

—— and KASAPOVIC, M. 1996. *Wahlsysteme und Systemwechsel in Osteuropa*. Opladen: Leske & Budrich.

—— KRENNERICH, M., and THIBAUT, B. eds. 1999. *Elections in Africa: A Data Handbook*. Oxford: Oxford University Press.

NORRIS, P. 2004. *Electoral Engineering: Voting Rules and Political Behavior*. Cambridge: Cambridge University Press.

ORDESHOOK, P., and SHVETSOVA, O. 1994. Ethnic heterogeneity, district magnitude, and the number of parties. *American Journal of Political Science*, 38: 101–23.

POWELL, G. B. 2000. *Elections as Instruments of Democracy: Majoritarian and Proportional Visions*. New Haven: Yale University Press.

RAE, D. W. 1967. *The Political Consequences of Electoral Laws*. New Haven: Yale University Press.

REED, S. R. 1991. Structure and behavior: extending Duverger's law to the Japanese case. *British Journal of Political Science*, 29: 335–56.

—— 2001. Duverger's law is working in Italy. *Comparative Political Studies*, 34: 312–27.

REYNOLDS, A. 1999. *Electoral Systems and Democratization in Southern Africa*. Oxford: Oxford University Press.

—— and REILLY, B. 1997. *The International IDEA Handbook of Electoral System Design*. Stockholm: International Institute for Democracy and Electoral Assistance.

RIKER, W. H. 1982. The two-party system and Duverger's law: an essay on the history of political science. *American Political Science Review*, 76: 753–66.

RULE, W. 1981. Why women don't run: the critical contextual factors in women's legislative recruitment. *Western Political Quarterly*, 34: 60–77.

—— and ZIMMERMAN, J. F. eds. 1994. *Electoral Systems in Comparative Perspective: Their Impact on Women and Minorities*. Westport, Conn.: Greenwood.

SHUGART, M. S. 2006. Comparative electoral systems research: the maturation of a field and new challenges ahead. Pp. 25–55 in *The Politics of Electoral Systems*, ed. M. Gallagher and P. Mitchell. Oxford: Oxford University Press.

—— and CAREY, J. M. 1992. *Presidents and Assemblies: Constitutional Design and Electoral Dynamics*. New York: Cambridge University Press.

—— VALDINI, M. E., and SUOMINEN, K. 2005. Looking for locals: voter information demands and personal vote-earning attributes of legislators under proportional representation. *American Journal of Political Science*, 49: 437–49.

—— and WATTENBERG, M. P. eds. 2001. *Mixed-Member Electoral Systems: The Best of Both Worlds?* Oxford: Oxford University Press.

TAAGEPERA, R. 1999. Ignorance-based quantitative models and their practical implications. *Journal of Theoretical Politics*, 11: 421–31.

—— 2001. Party size baselines imposed by institutional constraints: theory for simple electoral systems. *Journal of Theoretical Politics*, 13: 331–54.

—— 2003. Arend Lijphart's dimensions of democracy: logical connections and institutional design. *Political Studies*, 51: 1–19.

TAAGEPERA, R. 2008. *Predicting Party Sizes: The Logic of Simple Electoral Systems*. Oxford: Oxford University Press (forthcoming).

—— and ALLIK, M. 2006. Seat share distribution of parties: models and empirical patterns. *Electoral Studies*, 25: 696–713.

—— and ENSCH, J. 2006. Institutional determinants of the largest seat share. *Electoral Studies*, 25: 760–75.

—— and SHUGART, M. S. 1989. *Seats and Votes: The Effects and Determinants of Electoral Systems*. New Haven: Yale University Press.

—— —— 1993. Predicting the number of parties: a quantitative model of Duverger's mechanical effect. *American Political Science Review*, 87: 455–64.

—— and SIKK, A. 2004. Institutional and cultural determinants of cabinet duration. Unpublished.

THEIL, H. 1969. The desired political entropy. *American Political Science Review*, 63: 21–5.

CHAPTER 29

....

SEPARATION
OF POWERS

....

DAVID SAMUELS

1 INTRODUCTION

....

EVEN as broad international processes of globalization dominate mass consciousness in today's world, national political leaders continue to engage in heated debates—some of which even result in bloodshed—over what some consider incidental details of institutional design. Truly, in a world in which institutions did not matter, Iraq's Sunnis, Shiites, and Kurds might simply pick a constitution out of a hat and live happily ever after. Yet such a notion is ludicrous. Individuals and social groups fight over institutional design because one's political position within an institutional matrix carries *symbolic* importance as well as *substantive* importance in terms of "who gets what" out of politics.

For better or worse, scholars have largely ignored institutions' symbolic importance to political actors and focused on debating the degree to which institutions affect outcomes such as economic growth or political stability. Perhaps the most fundamental institutional difference across the world's democracies is whether the executive and legislative powers are fused or separate. Intelligent people have explored the question of the "best" constitutional design since antiquity: Aristotle was perhaps the first comparativist, sending his acolytes-cum-graduate students into the field to gather comparative constitutional "data." Yet it was the nightmare of Weimar Germany's collapse into Nazi terror that sparked interest in this question for twentieth-century scholars (Hermens 1941). For many scholars, the failure of democracy in many countries during the Cold War (1945–90), particularly in Latin America, provided additional confirmation that the separation of powers can affect democracy's potential to flourish (e.g. Linz 1990).

Scholarly interest in the separation of powers gained added impetus during the so-called "third wave" of democratization, which began in the 1970s and ran through the end of the Cold War. Shugart and Carey's *Presidents and Assemblies*, published in 1992, represents a scholarly milestone as the first attempt to synthesize scholarly knowledge about the separation of powers. Their book set the research agenda and encouraged scholars to investigate important questions such as the extent to which the separation of powers affects the likelihood of democratic collapse, whether certain institutions are more likely to promote democratic consolidation, and whether regime type matters for policy output and governability.[1]

This chapter addresses the question of "what difference does the separation of powers make?" Scholars have suggested that the difference between fused or separate powers affects myriad political "outputs," and I will not pretend that this essay covers every conceivable question. Instead, following a brief section that defines the differences between democratic regimes, I explore four key questions about the extent to which the separation of powers "matters":

(1) To what extent does the separation of powers affect the relative "decisiveness" and "resoluteness" of the political process?
(2) What impact does the cabinet have on political process and output across democratic regimes?
(3) Does the separation of powers contribute to regime crises and/or collapse?
(4) In what ways does the separation of powers affect how we think about democratic representation and accountability?

I concentrate on these questions because they home in on comparativists' central theoretical and empirical concerns, the "big issues" in the study of politics: the nature and consequences of the policy-making process, the chances for democracy to survive and flourish, and whether voters' opinions are heard within the tumult of democratic politics.

2 DEFINITIONS

Scholars typically identify three "versions" of the separation of powers: parliamentarism, pure presidentialism, and "semi"-presidentialism. As of 2002, of the seventy-six democracies (classified as such by receiving a "5" or better on the Polity IV combined democracy score) with a population greater than one million, thirty-one are parliamentary, while twenty-five are presidential and twenty are semi-presidential. The distinctions across democratic regimes center around the process of selecting the executive and legislative branches, and the way in which the executive and legislature subsequently interact to

---

[1] See e.g. Linz (1990, 1994); Mainwaring (1993); Stepan and Skach (1993); Sartori (1994); Jones (1995); Mainwaring and Shugart (1997a); Power and Gasiorowski (1997); Carey and Shugart (1998); Przeworski et al. (2000); Haggard and McCubbins (2001); Cheibub and Limongi (2002).

make policy and administer the government.[2] Thus Shugart and Carey (1992) specify the three differences between presidentialism and parliamentarism:

(1) Separate *origin and survival* of executive and legislative branches;
(2) *Constitutionally guaranteed executive authority* to execute the laws; and
(3) Chief executive *control over the cabinet.*

Separation of origin is defined by the process of executive selection: does it follow from a process of counting votes separately from the allocation of legislative seats (presidential) or does it follow from some process that depends on the allocation of legislative seats (not presidential)? Separation of survival is defined by the principle that ends governments: under presidentialism the terms of both the legislature and the executive are fixed and not contingent on mutual confidence, as in parliamentarism. As for constitutionally guaranteed authority, at the simplest level this means that one branch makes the laws, the other implements them. If the legislature could implement the laws without the president, the system would be some sort of hybrid regime. However, no *particular* powers are implied here.

"Semi"-presidentialism represents, as the name implies, a hybrid constitutional format. Scholars dispute the definition of semi-presidentialism and thus which countries fall into this category (see Shugart and Carey 1992; Elgie 1999; Metcalf 2000; Roper 2002), but the simplest and broadest definition is that both branches of government are directly elected (as in presidentialism), but the head of government (the prime minister) is accountable to the legislature (as in parliamentarism) (Siaroff 2003). In such systems, the president does not directly control the cabinet. Research on the consequences of semi-presidential government lag behind research on parliamentarism or pure presidentialism, because nearly all semi-presidential systems are relatively young democracies. Given this, although I compare across all three democratic regimes, much of this chapter focuses on research contrasting parliamentary and presidential systems.

Some scholars question the degree to which these institutional differences matter (e.g. Przeworski 2003). I do not claim that the separation of powers is *necessarily* associated with particular outcomes. Elsewhere, I have argued (Samuels and Shugart 2003) that the separation of powers can accommodate substantially greater *variation in governing styles and output* than a system of fused powers can. That is, separation of powers systems can resemble fused powers systems in terms of governance style and substance, or they can differ substantially. Scholars continue to seek to identify the conditions under which separation of powers systems diverge from fused systems, and seek to understand the degree to which this divergence affects the citizens who live under these systems. I now turn to the four questions mentioned above, to assess the state of our knowledge about the separation of powers and suggest how research might proceed.

---

[2] For space reasons and because I wish to focus on the impact of variation *across* democratic regimes, I do not assess debates about institutional variation *within* each regime.

3 SEPARATION OF POWERS AND GOVERNMENT "DECISIVENESS" OR "RESOLUTENESS"

Madison's notion of the separation of powers, elaborated in the *Federalist Papers*, holds that tyranny is relatively less likely under the separation of powers because such a system places the executive and legislative branches in formally different institutional environments. This generates different behavioral incentives for actors in each branch, making majority steamrolls of the minority at a minimum more difficult to coordinate. In modern political science parlance, the structure of presidentialism is designed to be *less decisive* and *more resolute* (Cox and McCubbins 2001). That is, we expect policy change to be slower and less dramatic under presidentialism, all else equal.

On the other hand, we might expect the separation of executive and legislative survival to be a recipe for unilateralism. Because a president cannot fall on a confidence vote, he or she could use the "bully pulpit" of the presidency to interfere in the legislative process, attempting to pull policy towards his or her preferred position even more than a similarly situated prime minister (PM) might (Cox and Morgenstern 2001). Even so, nothing about the core definition of presidentialism gives the president any *particular* proactive or reactive legislative powers, meaning that a president has no inherent power to *move* policy from the status quo. This highlights the critical importance of the relationship between the president and the pivotal legislator. A president with a strong legislative majority might have only slightly greater problems coordinating across branches of government than a PM with a similarly sized majority, and policy outcomes would thus be similar. Yet the separation of survival also means that such cross-branch coordination is neither encouraged nor guaranteed, *even given preference overlap between the president and his legislative majority*. Parliamentarism does not guarantee coordination, but it does encourage it: if a government breaks down under parliamentarism, it can be dissolved and a new executive can come to power with a new mandate; not so under presidentialism.

We also need to ask what happens when the position of the president and the pivotal legislator differ substantially. This situation (e.g. of minority government) occurs about twice as frequently under presidentialism as under parliamentarism.[3] Suppose that the legislative majority proposes a change in the status quo (SQ), but the president refuses to sign it into law (or vice versa). When this happens we have policy stability (perhaps leading to "stalemate" or "deadlock") and the SQ stands because the president cannot be removed from office. Deadlock is not a necessary outcome of any particular distribution

---

[3] Cheibub, Przeworski, and Saiegh 2004, found that minority governments occur in about 22% of all years under parliamentarism, and Cheibub 2002 found that minority governments occur in about 40% of all years under presidentialism. These numbers correspond with previous research (e.g. Strøm 1990*b*; Shugart 1995).

of legislative seats, in any political system. However, under parliamentarism deadlock is less likely because of the threat of removal—if the PM refuses to enact a bill parliament has passed, he is unlikely to last long as head of the government.[4] This is what Cox and McCubbins (2001, 26–7) meant by suggesting that the separation of survival makes pure presidentialism less *decisive* and more *resolute*. (See also Laver and Shepsle 1996, who suggest that the direct election of the head of government expands the independence, not the compliance, of the legislature.)

This suggests the following hypotheses:

(1) A pure presidential system is *less likely* to get from the SQ to a new policy at point P than other systems, all else equal;

(2) If P is proposed, a presidential system will move *less far in policy space* from the SQ towards P than other systems, all else equal;

(3) If P is proposed, the *time* getting from the SQ to P *will be greater* under a presidential system, all else equal;

(4) If P is proposed, the *expense* (e.g. measured in side payments) of getting from the SQ to P *will be greater* under a presidential system, all else equal.

Little research has investigated these hypotheses. These are thorny questions, because we have no way to determine a priori "how much" difference in decisiveness and/or resoluteness we should expect across regimes. Thus while Cox (2005) notes that governing majorities everywhere rarely lose votes, the data in Cheibub, Przeworski and Saiegh (2004, table 2) support the hypothesis that differences in resoluteness/decisiveness exist at the aggregate level across presidential and parliamentary systems.[5] They show that under similar levels of legislative support, parliamentary executives *always* approve their proposals with a higher rate than presidents: 82.8 percent of all executive proposals are approved under parliamentarism versus 64.1 percent of all proposals under presidentialism, indicating that constitutional structure generates a considerable degree of variation in resoluteness and/or decisiveness.

Cheibub et al. also reveal that as the degree of preference divergence between the executive and the pivotal legislator increases, presidential systems appear to be relatively *more* resolute and *less* decisive than parliamentary systems. Thus the difference in "success rates" is small under supermajority conditions—89.6 percent of all proposals for parliamentary governments are approved versus 82.6 percent for presidential governments—but are larger under single-party majority governments—89.5 percent versus 77.4 percent. The difference in success rates then increases under majority coalition government (76.0 versus 47.5 percent), minority coalition government (81.7 versus 52.5 percent), and single-party minority government (81.3 versus 65.2 percent).

---

[4] The situation may differ under semi-presidentialism, depending on the president's veto powers.

[5] The authors focused on a different question, whether minority governments are relatively less successful passing legislation than either majority or minority coalition governments in both presidential and parliamentary systems. They found this not to be true.

These numbers suggest that whatever unilateral powers a president possesses are insufficient to overcome the Madisonian inertia imposed by the separation of powers. That is, strong unilateral executive powers do not make a presidential system parliamentary because a legislature can override vetoes, quash decrees, overturn agendas, and even strip constitutional authority, without fear of the president calling new elections (Samuels and Shugart 2003).[6] Under coalition or minority government, a president might attempt a unilateral strategy and be rebuffed. Linz and other scholars fear this possibility, and suggested that parliamentarism is less problematic not only because minority governments are less frequent, but also because minority PMs can be removed if they attempt unilateral government or if deadlock emerges. In short, although presidentialism is not a *necessary* recipe for deadlock, it does allow for greater *potential* executive-legislative conflict.

Research on legislative "productivity," although useful, provides only a partial answer to the question of the relative decisiveness or resoluteness of a polity. Currently we know we know nothing about the relative similarity or difference in the *content* of proposals across democratic regimes. Given the separation of survival, presidents' and prime ministers' strategies for proposing legislation should differ, and these differences should be even larger under different levels of legislative support. As Cox and McCubbins (2004) argue, US parties' influence is most apparent not on the floor of the legislature on final-passage votes, but rather in determining what comes up for a vote or not. This is an important question for comparativists: to what extent do differences across political regimes influence the ability of political parties and/or executives to get proposals on the agenda? Perhaps the differences that Cheibub et al. highlight also exist at the proposal stage. If this is true, then the differences across political regimes in terms of resoluteness and decisiveness are even larger, and have greater real-world importance. Additional research should seek to elucidate the extent to which presidentialism increases policy resoluteness and decreases policy decisiveness, even given preference overlap between branches.[7]

---

[6] Thus high unilateral powers do not make Argentina into England: under unified government in both systems, differences in governance might not be due to regime type but to other factors (e.g. federalism). But when the executive faces legislative opposition, in Argentina we might see policy stability or deadlock *for the duration of the president's term.* In Argentina at least this seems to be associated with constitutional crisis (e.g. Alfonsín in 1989 and De la Rúa in 2001). In contrast, in the UK such a situation of divided government is unlikely in the first place and ought not to persist for long, because new elections can be called: the last "hung parliament" occurred in 1974. A similar dynamic can occur under any minority parliamentary government: *if* deadlock occurs (it might not), the government can change or elections are called.

[7] Two additional promising lines of research to mention in terms of the policy differences between presidential and parliamentary systems are related to my hypothesis that policy making is more "expensive" in presidential systems: first that the "size" of government is a function of regime type (compare Persson and Tabelleni et al. 2004 versus Boix 2005b) and, relatedly, that parliamentarism promotes "public goods" while presidentialism enhances opportunities for "rent-seeking" behavior, i.e. for corruption (Shugart 1999; Haggard and McCubbins 2001; Gerring and Thacker 2004; Kunicová 2005). Scholars have yet to come to any sort of consensus about the causal mechanisms underlying these potential differences across political regimes.

4 CABINETS: THE "MISSING LINK" IN THE STUDY OF THE SEPARATION OF POWERS

Perhaps the largest "institutionalist" literature in the study of parliamentary government focuses on cabinets. Cabinets have two purposes: (1) to build legislative support to *pass* legislation; and (2) to control the executive-branch bureaucracy that *implements* legislation. Despite the growth of research on the separation of powers, cabinets have yet to attract the same degree of scrutiny as under parliamentarism. Research is impeded by a simple lack of data on cabinet membership outside the (mostly parliamentary) countries covered by sources such as Woldendorp, Keman, and Budge (2000), although emerging scholarship should soon remedy this problem.

More importantly, the influence of the US case in the comparative study of the separation of powers has discouraged research on cabinets. In the USA, the intellectual influence of congressional scholars has relegated the cabinet to the theoretical and empirical back-burner relative to the alleged importance of *legislative* oversight of the bureaucracy. Moreover, scholars of US politics largely do not generally believe that the distribution of cabinet portfolios is directly related to the president's governing strategy and/or legislative success, as in parliamentary systems (see e.g. Bennett 1996).

Finally, Shugart and Carey's agenda-setting book paid little attention to the cabinet and directed scholars' attention elsewhere. Shugart and Carey encouraged scholars to focus on how unilateral executive powers (e.g. Carey and Shugart 1995), the electoral-institutional sources of the distribution of legislative seats (e.g. Jones 1995; Shugart 1995), or legislative politics per se (e.g. Morgenstern and Nacif 2002) affect executive–legislative relations. Given these already complex questions, the cabinet got lost in the shuffle. However, scholars have recently begun to discover the extent to which—just as in parliamentary systems—the cabinet provides a critical link between the executive and legislative branches in pure and semi-presidential systems (Deheza 1997, 1998; Thibaut 1998; Amorim Neto 1998, 2002, 2006; Altman 2000, 2001; Lanzaro 2001; Amorim Neto and Strom 2004; Almeida and Cho 2003; Roberts and Druckman Forthcoming; Amorim Neto and Samuels 2003; Carroll, Cox, and Pachón 2006).

Research on cabinet politics under different forms of democracy has the potential to shape key debates in comparative politics. For example, on the one hand, in terms of understanding coalition dynamics Cheibub and Limongi (2002, 18) suggest that "it is not true that incentives for coalition formation are any different in presidential than in parliamentary democracies." On the other hand, the president's position as formateur in pure presidential systems suggests that coalition dynamics—party decisions to enter and/or leave a coalition—should differ substantially across democratic regimes. The separation of powers gives the president the last word in policy making, whereas under parliamentarism the PM may have to concede de facto control over certain ministries to his or her cabinet partners (Laver and Shepsle 1996). Parties considering whether to join a cabinet under the separation of powers therefore have greater cause to worry that they will be unable to translate participation into real policy influence. Parties' lack of direct influence in policy making, coupled with their inability to "make and break governments," means that their expected payoff in terms of "office" and/or "policy" benefits (Strøm 1990a) should be lower in semi- and pure presidential systems relative to a parliamentary system (Samuels 2002).

This suggests that coalitions will be costlier to maintain and less stable under presidentialism. Altman (2001) indirectly confirmed this, finding that the existence of fixed terms affects the likelihood of coalition formation and maintenance. As the president's term advances, the likelihood of coalition formation decreases and the likelihood of coalition collapse increases (2001, 93). Thus, unlike parliamentary cabinets, presidential coalitions "tend to form and dissolve in synchronization with the electoral calendar corresponding to the president's term of office" (2001, 115). Theoretically, these findings suggest that the standard formal models of coalition entry and exit designed for parliamentary systems (e.g. Austin-Smith and Banks 1988) require substantial modification for presidential systems.

The impact of the separation of powers on cabinet politics, and thus on a range of other political outcomes, ranges far beyond coalition entry and exit decisions. Octavio Amorim Neto's research provides the crucial insight: under presidentialism the *size* of the coalition or the *number* of coalition members may not be the most important variables. Instead, the key variables in terms of cabinets—and thus in terms of governance outcomes—include the *proportion of partisan ministers* (versus cronies or technocrats) and the *extent to which portfolios are proportionally distributed* to coalition member parties. This argument runs counter to research that focuses on the size of and number of parties in legislative coalitions, as well as to the literature that predicts variation in policy output based on the number of "veto players" (e.g. Cheibub and Limongi 2002; Cheibub, Przeworski, and Saiegh 2004; Tsebelis 2002). Therefore, Amorim Neto's argument deserves some elaboration.

In any political system an executive's preferences about cabinet composition reflect (1) his or her policy preferences over outcomes and (2) the extent of his or her need to negotiate with other actors to obtain those outcomes. Cabinet appointment strategy is therefore a function of the degree to which the chief executive must, given his or her policy preferences, negotiate with other actors, typically legislative parties. Give this, we can array democratic regimes on a continuum of executives who are most to least dependent on legislative parties for governability: parliamentary monarchies, parliamentary republics, semi-presidential republics, and pure presidential republics.

Because prime ministers depend entirely on the confidence of legislative parties for their government's survival, they almost always appoint wholly *partisan* cabinets. For the same reason, prime ministers almost always also tend to appoint wholly *proportional* cabinets, meaning that each party in the cabinet receives portfolios in proportion to the contribution it makes to the government coalition. These are among the oldest and most solid empirical findings in political science research (e.g. Gamson 1961; Warwick and Druckman 2001).

In contrast to prime ministers, presidents do not depend on legislative confidence for their survival in office. Thus in contrast to prime ministers, presidents have greater leeway to vary cabinet partisanship and proportionality (Amorim Neto 1998, 2006).

What shapes presidents' incentives to appoint party members versus cronies or non-partisan technocrats, and whether to do so proportionally or not? For simplicity's sake let us assume that executives everywhere have only two policy-making strategies: they can seek to enact their policy goals through statutes, or through executive prerogatives. The "statutory" path requires that a proposal pass through the normal legislative process, while the "prerogatives" path may not require the involvement of the legislature. For example, some presidents can issue decrees that have the force of law.

Chief executives who know that they can only realize their goals through a statutory strategy will seek to develop a strong relationship with a legislative majority. Prime ministers must adopt such a strategy and appoint wholly partisan cabinets because they possess few autonomous prerogatives and depend wholly on legislative parties for their government's survival and for legislative success. In contrast, a directly elected executive does not depend on the legislature for survival. Thus under pure presidentialism, separation of survival and the executive's authority over the cabinet means that cabinet composition could be *more or less* related to the composition of the president's legislative coalition. On the one hand, given personal style, institutional rules, and/or the partisan composition of the legislature, presidents may believe that a "statutory" strategy is optimal, and thus that cabinet portfolios should be distributed to maximize the chances of legislative approval of statutes, as in a parliamentary system. On the other hand, if presidents decide to pursue (at least part of) their policy goals through decrees or other unilateral powers, portfolios can be filled with non-partisan technocrats, cronies, or interest group representatives.

Presidents endowed with strong unilateral prerogatives are both more likely to use those powers to achieve their goals and *relatively* less likely to cooperate with political parties. Given the separation of survival, cabinet appointment strategies are thus a function of the president's prior beliefs about the overall efficacy of the statutory versus the prerogative approach to policy making, in each ministry's policy area. The more presidents rely on statutes as a policy-making strategy, the more they will include partisans in the cabinet and the more proportional the distribution of portfolios (Amorim Neto 2006).

In semi-presidential systems, the politics of cabinet appointments differs somewhat. Here presidents can dissolve parliament, but their own survival remains secure. This tends to politically weaken the prime minister. However, both the president and the prime minister possess de facto vetoes over cabinet appointments, which weakens the president (and which contrasts with pure presidential systems). Within semi-presidential systems the relative power of the president versus the prime minister also may vary, depending on particular institutional rules: the greater the president's appointment powers, the higher the share of non-partisans in the cabinet (Almeida and Cho 2003; Amorim Neto and Strom 2004). In general, cabinet dynamics in semi-presidential systems represent a middle ground between parliamentarism and pure presidentialism.

The synthesis of Amorim Neto's argument that I have presented suggests that both the percentage of partisans in a given cabinet and the proportionality of the distribution of portfolios in the cabinet are a function not only of individual government or country attributes, but also of regime attributes. Tables 29.1 and 29.2 reveal that this is the case (see Amorim Neto and Samuels 2004 for details and additional tests).

Table 29.1 Average percentage of non-partisan ministers by regime type

Regime type	Percentage (std. dev.)
Parliamentary monarchies	0.71 (3.89)
Parliamentary republics	3.20 (10.11)
Semi-presidential republics	6.52 (14.72)
Presidential republics	29.17 (29.04)

Table 29.2 Average proportionality by regime type

Regime type	Proportionality (std. dev.)
Parliamentary monarchies	0.937 (0.127)
Parliamentary republics	0.863 (0.132)
Semi-presidential republics	0.871 (0.125)
Presidential republics	0.645 (0.266)

What are the consequences of variation in cabinet appointment strategies across democratic systems? Much research has explored the consequences—or lack thereof—of majority versus minority government, or of single versus multiparty government, both within and across democratic regimes. However, these arguments have yet to take into account the impact of variation in cabinet partisanship and proportionality. Scholars have already noted the impact of "technocratic" appointments to important ministries in many presidential systems (Bresser et al. 1993; Conaghan, Malloy, and Abugattas 1990; O'Donnell 1994; Domínguez 1997). The argument here provides a simple theoretical explanation for such appointments, which affect not only the style of governance but also its substance (an issue I take up again below, in the section on representation and accountability).

Amorim Neto (2002; see also Amorim Neto and Santos 2001) has also found a strong relationship between cabinet proportionality and the discipline of the president's legislative coalition. It follows that cabinet proportionality—and not just whether the cabinet is single party or multiparty or majority or minority—also affects the likelihood of presidential legislative success (Amorim Neto 1998). When portfolios are distributed proportionally to each party's contribution to the coalition, legislative success increases. In addition, Amorim Neto and Tafner (2002) found that cabinet proportionality is inversely related to the number of decrees that Brazilian presidents issue, confirming the hypothesized relationship between proportionality and presidents' governing strategies ("statutory" versus "prerogatives").

Amorim Neto's findings clearly contradict Cheibub and Limongi, who suggest that "the connection between coalitions and legislative effectiveness is at best dubious" (2002, 5). The connection between cabinet coalitions and legislative effectiveness is critical: When a proportional cabinet is formed, the president's legislative coalition is more disciplined, and thus the president is likely to accomplish relatively more of his legislative agenda. When the cabinet is not proportional, the opposite is more likely. Amorim Neto suggests that key factors related to cabinet appointment strategy are presidential powers and the size of the president's party. Other factors include the ideology of the president's party and national economic conditions. The connections between these variables and governance demand further investigation. Research should focus on the *way* cabinets and coalitions are pieced together, in addition to the size of the number of participants, as important explanations for variations in governance outcomes.

Another reason to encourage research on cabinets across political regimes derives from questions about bureaucratic oversight, policy effectiveness, and democratic accountability. Cabinets not only serve to build legislative support for executives' initiatives; they also indicate executives' strategy for *managing the bureaucracy* and for *implementing* legislation. The separation of powers therefore has important implications for the question of "who controls" the bureaucracy, and how. Under the separation of powers presidents control the bureaucracy largely without legislative support. Although relatively little research has addressed this topic, the separation of powers implies substantial differences in modes of bureaucratic management across democratic regimes (Moe and Caldwell 1994; Palmer 1995; Siavelis 2000; Huber and McCarty 2001; Baum 2002). For example, Huber and Shipan (2002) argue that when faced with similar policy issues, politicians in different bargaining environments will design bureaucratic control mechanisms differently. Cabinet autonomy from legislative influence can dramatically alter the bargaining environment. Differences in bargaining environments affect the quality and the type of information available to each actor, which in turn affect actors' perceptions of the benefits and costs of particular actions and strategies.

Given this, scholars using standard principal–agent theory have suggested that designing control mechanisms is more burdensome under the separation of powers, for both executives and legislators (e.g. Moe and Caldwell 1994; Palmer 1995), and that the separation of powers should result in *more detailed* bureaucratic oversight mechanisms, all else equal. This is because the separation of powers creates monitoring problems for legislators vis-à-vis the bureaucracy. Legislative parties often not only have relatively less influence over cabinet appointments under the separation of powers; a legislative majority under the separation of powers cannot bring down a government that has failed to implement legislation that the same majority passed. This ought to increase legislators' incentives in presidential systems to prefer detailed bureaucratic rules.

This is largely unexplored territory in comparative politics. For research to proceed, scholars may have to adapt principal–agent theories that have been applied in the USA and Europe (e.g. Strøm, Müller, and Bergman 2003) because such theories entail restrictive assumptions about bureaucratic capacity (Huber and McCarty 2004) and the relative strength of parties' policy-seeking goals (Samuels 2002). If bureaucratic capacity and party goals vary across democratic regimes, the design of control mechanisms should vary as well. Given dramatic changes in regulatory regimes in this age of neo-liberal reform, more research should address the question of the way in which the separation of powers may generate different incentives for bureaucratic management and thus variation in policy implementation.

In this section I have argued that cabinet politics may represent a "missing link" in the study of the separation of powers. I want to emphasize that in general, *the power to influence the cabinet is more fundamental to the policy process than any of the unilateral powers that many presidents possess*, because the legislature has no formal authority to override presidents' decisions to appoint or dismiss ministers, no matter how great the preference divergence between branches.[8] In contrast, the legislature can always annul a presidential decision to use agenda, veto, or decree powers, provided it can muster the necessary majorities to overcome these measures (Amorim Neto 1998; Cox and Morgenstern 2001). The cabinet provides a critical link between executives and legislatures, and is key to understanding bureaucracy management and policy implementation. These questions clearly demand greater scholarly attention.

5 REGIME CRISES: IS THE SEPARATION OF POWERS TO BLAME?

The breakdowns of several democracies in Latin America during the Cold War, as well as concerns about the (re)establishment of civilian government in the region democratized in the 1980s and 1990s, continue to influence contemporary debates about the relative advantages or disadvantages of the separation of powers. If it is true, as Linz (1990, 1994) and others have argued, that presidentialism facilitated the breakdown of democracy (even if it is not the proximal or only cause), can we design political institutions less prone to breakdown? Less ambitiously, can scholars at least contribute to understanding the causes of democratic breakdown and democratic success? As more and more countries adopted democracy during the "third wave" of democratization that characterized the late twentieth century, scholars, politicians, and policy practitioners around the world have continued to ask these critical questions.

Linz argued that because the executive and legislative are elected separately, they may derive their legitimacy to govern from very different sources. Moreover, conflict is more likely because fixed terms of office discourage politicians in both branches of government from moderating their stances or seeking new coalition partners. In contrast, mutual dependence in a parliamentary system heightens the incentives for cross-branch negotiation. Moreover, when such conflict emerges and persists, presidentialism lacks the exit

---

[8] There are some exceptions to this rule (e.g. censure rules in Colombia and Peru, confirmation rules in the USA, Philippines, and South Korea). However, critically, none of these rules affects the *survival* of the executive.

option of the confidence vote, which allows for a relatively smooth transition from one government to the next in parliamentary systems, without engendering a constitutional crisis. These factors generate relatively a greater likelihood of conflict between branches of government under the separation of powers, which can in turn become a regime crisis, *regardless of the distribution of partisan preferences.*

Other scholars such as Mainwaring (1993) and Jones (1995) added that conflict and its persistence are even more likely, and more likely to lead to crises, under multiparty situations, which make inter-branch negotiation more difficult and accentuate existing problems. Again, these scholars concluded that while minority and coalition governments are frequent in all democracies, parliamentarism is more flexible because the PM depends on the legislature to survive. Thus although executive–legislative conflict is not inevitable under presidentialism, it is nevertheless *more likely* as well as more likely to lead to a true crisis.

In this section I explore recent debates about the sources of regime crises under the separation of powers. Scholars agree that presidentialism experiences such crises more frequently than parliamentarism, but they disagree about the factors leading to breakdown. Adam Przeworski and his collaborators have made the most intriguing contributions to recent debates: in contrast to those who suggest that party system fragmentation contributes to regime instability, Przeworski et al. (2000, hereafter referred to as PACL for the authors' initials) reconfirm that presidentialism is more fragile than parliamentarism, but question the connection between party system attributes and presidential regime fragility.

PACL reconfirm existing research that the *absence of a majority party* in the lower house is associated with presidential regime collapse (2000, 134). However, the authors then suggest that there is no relationship between the size of the largest party and regime collapse (ibid.). Both of these arguments may be true, but they both miss the heart of the matter: the question of whether a legislative majority (of one or many parties) *is allied with or opposed to the president.* There is little theoretical basis to suppose there should be *any* relationship between the size of the largest party and regime collapse, if we do not know the political allegiance of the largest party and the other parties. PACL's attempt to relate the size of the largest party to presidential fragility therefore does little to advance our understanding of regime fragility because that particular variable begs the question of whether governance is a function of the size of the *president's* party and/or the size of the *president's* coalition.

PACL also seek to refute the notion that presidential regime collapse is correlated with legislative *fragmentation,* measured by the effective number of legislative parties (ENP). Although frequently cited, the connection between fragmentation and regime crisis has never been fully convincing because like the "largest party," ENP is context free and begs the question of the parties' allegiances. Moreover, many coalitional possibilities exist at similar levels of ENP, depending on which party is the president's and which parties are allied with the president.

For example, suppose that there are three parties with 30 percent of the seats each, and one party with 10 percent. ENP therefore equals 3.57. The smallest party is on the left, the president's party is in the middle, and the other two parties are on the right.

The president makes a deal with the party to his left, but the other two parties remain in opposition. The problem with an argument linking ENP to collapse is that it remains unclear why this particular situation is worse than one in which the president's party has 40 percent of the seats and the single other party, which refuses to deal with the president, has 60 percent of the seats. ENP here is 1.92. Perhaps these are equally problematic situations—or not—but we cannot tell by using ENP.[9] In short, PACL's argument—like other scholars'—relies on indicators that are context free and of limited theoretical value.[10]

The methodological concerns expressed here call into question the conclusions in Cheibub (2002) and Cheibub and Limongi (2002) that the combination of presidentialism and multipartism is *not* more problematic than multiparty parliamentarism, because these papers rely on similar data and arguments. For example, Cheibub (2002, 3) argues that "minority presidents, minority governments, and deadlock do not affect the survival of presidential democracies," yet his argument contradicts PACL's (2000, 134) conclusion about minority government, relies on a restricted notion of deadlock, and employs a similar argument about ENP as in PACL.

How should research proceed on these questions? Instead of using ENP or simply whether there is or is not minority government, scholars should explore the relationships between the *size of the president's party and/or coalition, the distribution of portfolios in the president's cabinet, and the extent of ideological polarization* in the legislature. The first two

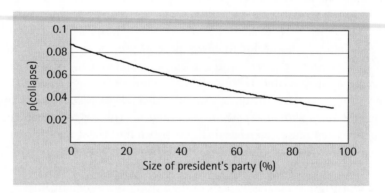

Fig. 29.1 Presidential party size and regime collapse

---

[9] There are other methodological problems with PACL's analysis. One is that forty of the 102 presidential cases where ENP>4 in PACL's dataset are from Switzerland. This case is misclassified; Switzerland is not presidential because it does not conform to the defining principle of presidentialism, separation of origin and survival. Parliament formally elects the Swiss executive council—that is, origin is not separate, although survival is. Reclassifying these forty cases eliminates a substantial proportion of the "stable regime" cases with high ENP.

[10] One could also question PACL's coding of certain cases. For example, they code Peru's democracy as collapsing in 1989 (2000, 100). Such choices make a difference when there are only twenty-four cases of presidential collapse: Peru had 2.31 ENP in 1989, but 4.10 ENP in 1992, the year that Fujimori actually shut the legislature in his *autogolpe*. PACL's strange classification helps their hypothesis, while a correct classification of Peru as democratic in 1989 would hurt their hypothesis.

are relatively easy to operationalize, while the third will inevitably rely on expert judgements. As for the hypothesized link between presidential party size and regime collapse, Figure 29.1 plots the predicted (unconditional) probability of presidential collapse in a given year against the size of the president's party.[11]

The correlation clearly supports the hypothesis. Presidential collapse is three times more likely at the lowest level of president support, where the probability is .09, than at the highest level of support, where the probability is .03 (at the median presidential party size the probability is .05). This finding returns research to a key argument in the literature: the size of the president's party and coalition remains critical for understanding the dynamics of governance in separation of powers systems. Research on presidential regime performance and survival should thus turn away from a focus on partisan fragmentation and focus on the potential interactive effects between presidential party size and location in policy space, the distribution of cabinet portfolios, and the extent and nature of ideological polarization within the legislature. Some combination of these variables may provide the key to understanding governance outcomes under the separation of powers.[12]

Although academics continue to debate the reasons why presidentialism tends to break down more frequently than parliamentarism, fortunately, regime "collapse" is far less frequent today than in decades past. This indicates an important change in civil–military relations and tolerance at the national and international level for *coups d'état* and for military governments. Yet the infrequency of regime collapse does not mean that regime *crises* remain infrequent. What causes such crises? The answer could be economic collapse, or social strain. Political institutions could also contribute. The persistence of regime crises—even if they do not result in regime collapse—forces us to take yet another look at the perennial question of the relationship between party system attributes, the separation of powers, and regime performance.

Emerging research provides new support for the hypothesis that although presidentialism is not a *necessary* ingredient for regime crisis, certain party system configurations under the separation of powers are relatively *more* likely to be associated with governance crises. Hochstetler (2005) found that from 1978 to 2004, civilian political actors mounted serious challenges to fully 42 percent of elected presidents in ten South American countries, attempting to force these leaders from office before the end of their terms. In the end, through impeachment and/or resignation, 24 percent of all presidents were actually forced from office early and, in contrast to earlier eras, were replaced by civilians instead of military leaders. Hochstetler's main purpose is to argue that street protests play a critical role in determining which presidents are forced from office. However, she also notes that a second critical factor determining both whether crises emerge and their eventual outcome is *whether the president counts on majority support in the legislature*. She found that presidents without majority support were more likely both to be challenged and to be pushed from office, as Table 29.3 shows.

---

[11] I gathered data on the size of the president's party to match the entries in PACL's dataset.

[12] See Boix (2005a) for an effort to explain the relatively greater likelihood of presidential collapse as a function of the combination of institutions and politicians' rent-seeking behavior under certain economic conditions. This research builds on theoretical insights Boix developed in previous research (e.g. Boix 2003).

Table 29.3 Frequency of challenges to presidents

	Majority	Minority	Total
Not challenged	7 (77%)	17 (53%)	24 (58%)
Challenged	2 (22%)	15 (47%)	17 (42%)
Total	9	32	41
Fell (% of total)	1 (11%)	9 (28%)	10 (24%)

Hochstetler makes three important points: First, the traditional frequency of challenges to presidential authority and legitimacy continues to this day, despite the retreat of the military from involvement in politics compared to earlier eras. Second, it is not only political elites who challenge presidents—mass protests and organized social movements play a critical role. Third, there is a causal relationship between mass protest, the distribution of partisan support within the legislature, and crises of presidentialism. These findings are limited to ten countries, but their broader implications are highly suggestive. Can we generalize Hochstetler's findings to the entire world, across all political regimes? Is pure presidentialism more prone to crises in an era when militaries are in retreat from politics the world over? Is semi-presidentialism perhaps even more vulnerable? How likely are similar crises under parliamentarism?

The frequency of serious challenges to presidential authority raises an important question: are such crises all that bad? After all, if successful, presidential challenges result in a transfer of power to civilians, not to a military junta or dictator. In an important sense, the democratic political institutions are performing as they should. Perhaps such crises resemble confidence votes in parliamentary systems more than they resemble military coups, in both the process and the outcome. On the other hand, even brief political crises are often followed by civil strife or economic hardship. We are thus left with two important research questions: whether the incidence of crises (42 percent of elected presidents in these ten countries) is *high or low* relative to the incidence of crises under other democratic regimes given similar economic and social conditions; and what the *consequences* of such crises are. If crises occur more frequently under presidentialism *and* have important political, social, and/or economic consequences, then we have identified yet another "peril of presidentialism." If the opposite is true, we have identified the mechanism by which separation of powers systems resolve deadlock situations in the absence of military willingness to enter politics.

Perhaps civil strife, strikes, deaths, or human rights violations due to suppression of political protests *do* follow presidential challenges relatively more than they follow confidence votes. Perhaps economic or social crises also follow presidential challenges and/or falls, either because the incumbent president survives but is politically weaker or because the civilian who assumes control after a president is removed from office cannot claim legitimate authority to govern. If this is true, then even with the military on the sidelines and regime "collapse" not an issue, presidentialism would remain associated with normatively bad outcomes. The question of what constitutes a "regime crisis" and what consequences follow such crises when "regime collapse" is far less frequent should challenge scholars to take a new look at presidential governance in comparative perspective.

In this section I explored recent debates about whether presidentialism contributes to the collapse of democracy. The evidence reviewed supports the view that presidentialism is not necessarily a *direct* cause of regime collapse or regime crisis, but that it may facilitate the emergence of crises and/or collapse. Moreover, evidence continues to support the notion that presidentialism and multipartism are indeed a "difficult combination." However, the links between presidentialism, multipartism, and governance remain underdetermined.

6 SEPARATION OF POWERS, REPRESENTATION, AND ACCOUNTABILITY

In previous sections I have reviewed research that supports a notion that the separation of powers affects the policy process and policy output, and also influences the chances for democracy to survive and flourish. These may all be true, but do voters know, and do they care? What difference does the separation of powers make for voters' faith in government, or their ability to influence government process or output? Do we see better or worse democratic representation under different democratic regimes, or just "different"? Can voters hold governments accountable to similar degrees or in similar ways under different forms of democratic government? Of all the research areas that I touch upon in this chapter, the question of representation and accountability is the least well explored.

Shugart and Carey (1992) suggested that presidentialism has an advantage over parliamentarism because it can maximize both national and local representation and accountability at the same time. Yet little research has assessed this hypothesis. Do voters think of presidents and legislators similarly or differently in different regimes? Do different perceptions of representation across regime types impact voters' satisfaction with democracy or with incumbent performance? To what extent does "mandate representation" (Przeworski, Stokes, and Manin 1999) differ across democratic regimes?

For example, Susan Stokes (1999, 2001) has found that minority and coalition presidents are more likely to undertake policy "U-turns" than single-party majority presidents. Complementing and building on Stokes's findings, Johnson and Crisp (2003) found that voters' ability to predict a president's future policy positions is low, but that party cohesion and party ideology are strong predictors of future *legislative* party policy behavior. Stokes's book and Johnson and Crisp's paper are notable for their efforts to systematically test for a link between citizens' preferences, as expressed through elections, and policy outcomes in a wide set of presidential systems. Still, they beg the question of whether such links are stronger, weaker, or just different *across* democratic systems.

In this regard, I have hypothesized (Samuels 2002; Samuels and Shugart 2003) that *mandate representation will be less likely under presidentialism*, because differences in executive unilateral power and separation of purpose as well as differences in party structures in presidential and parliamentary regimes encourage both voters and politicians to behave differently, leading to different conceptions of representation as well as different outcomes. This hypothesis clearly contrasts with the notion that presidential systems are "less decisive and more resolute" as discussed above; at present these remain theoretically derived yet underspecified hypotheses. Key questions of the nature and extent of democratic representation under different constitutional settings remain largely unexplored in comparative politics.

How should research proceed on the question of potential differences in democratic representation under the separation of powers? There is no research akin to the "Manifestos Project" (Klingemann, Hofferbert, and Budge 1994) that could compare across different democratic regimes to assess the extent to which parties stick to their policy platforms or violate them under different constitutional systems. Such a project would require surmounting monstrous methodological and empirical hurdles, but the payoff might be worth the cost.

Likewise, we have yet to see an effort to extend the hypotheses proffered by Powell (2000) beyond the established democracies, which only include one pure presidential system. Powell's book—and research agenda more broadly considered—is concerned with differences between "majoritarian" and "proportional" visions of democracy. Powell generally concludes that each vision of democracy performs well on its own terms, but that the "proportional" vision is superior in that it encourages relatively greater policy congruence between citizens and governments. I suggest that the distinction between proportional and majoritarian visions of democracies may be inadequate to compare across democratic regimes, because pure and semi-presidential systems can *combine* both visions of democracy (the same can be said of Lijphart's similar method of comparing across democracies). An executive election is clearly "majoritarian" in nature, while legislative elections can be either proportional or majoritarian (or even combine elements of both, with multi-level electoral systems, for example). In fact, most real-world separation of powers systems do combine elements of both visions. Given this, we may need to rethink the bases upon which we judge the "performance" of democratic institutions (Samuels and Shugart 2003). (For a promising alternative, see Carroll and Shugart 2005.)

As with representation, the nature of accountability across democratic regimes also remains largely unexplored. There exists a large literature on the "clarity of responsibility" (e.g. Powell and Whitten 1993; Anderson 2000), which suggests that accountability is more likely under relatively simpler electoral and party systems. In contrast, complex systems that obscure who is responsible for government output make it more difficult for voters to identify whom to reward or punish. Research in this vein has largely focused on European parliamentary elections. For pure presidential systems, Shugart and Carey (1992) suggested that different institutional formats can encourage or discourage electoral accountability. I attempted to empirically explore this notion in a recent paper (Samuels 2004), and found that when executive and legislative elections are not held simultaneously (a situation that cannot occur under parliamentarism), sanctioning for the state of the economy is relatively weak. In contrast, when elections are concurrent voters' capacity to reward or sanction government officials for the state of the economy increases.

Such a result qualifies Linz's (1994) critique that presidentialism's "dual democratic legitimacies" confuses voters and inhibits accountability. Despite the formal separation of powers, institutions that promote close electoral linkage between the executive and legislative branches can result in "unified democratic legitimacy." When elections are concurrent voters tend to treat the incumbent executive and his or her legislative supporters as a team, and judge them as such—regardless of whether the incumbent president is running for re-election or not. However, the electoral cycle and other institutional and party system factors can attenuate accountability, sometimes leading to a situation of relatively high "executive" accountability but relatively low "legislative" accountability for the state of the national economy.

Yet these findings left open the question of cross-regime differences in terms of electoral accountability. There are strong theoretical reasons to suppose that such differences exist. I suggest that the key difference in terms of voters' ability to hold governments accountable across democratic regimes is not the *clarity* of responsibility, but differences in the nature of *attribution* of political responsibility. Thus voters should *attribute* relatively more responsibility for outcomes to directly elected executives than to indirectly elected prime ministers. Clarity of responsibility can obscure the degree of attribution of responsibility, but if voters do not first attribute responsibility to an actor then *the complexity of the political system* is irrelevant for accountability (Samuels and Hellwig 2005).

Empirically, voters do tend to attribute relatively greater responsibility to incumbents in direct executive elections relative to parliamentary elections, as long as the election is concurrent with legislative elections (in a pure presidential system) or the election is held under unified government (in a semi-presidential system) (Samuels and Hellwig 2005).[13] Under certain conditions, voters even attribute greater responsibility to *legislative* parties under presidentialism and semi-presidentialism than under parliamentarism (ibid.). In short, under many common circumstances *stronger* electoral accountability linkages may exist *in presidential and semi-presidential systems than in parliamentary systems.*[14] This finding questions the criticism that presidentialism generally permits relatively less accountability than other forms of democracy (e.g. Lijphart 1999; Manin, Przeworski, and Stokes 1999).

---

[13] In the former, concurrence occurs about 75% of the time. In the latter, unified government occurs in about 60% of all elections.

[14] For a contrasting view, see Nishizawa (2004).

7 CONCLUSION

The constitutional separation of powers places politicians in each branch in distinctive institutional environments and endows them with particular behavioral incentives. If we believe scholarship—ancient to modern—then variation in the "degree" of separation of powers has important political consequences for governments and citizens alike. Contemporary scholars, motivated by a desire to understand what form of democracy best serves citizens' interests, continue to add to our understanding of the impact of the separation of powers. I have explored several of the key lines of research that derive from the question "what difference does the separation of powers make?" Some of my conclusions are tentative and many of the suggestions are preliminary, but I expect scholarly creativity will discover new ways to get at these important issues.

REFERENCES

ALMEIDA, A., and CHO, S. 2003. Presidential power and cabinet membership under semi-presidentialism. Paper presented at the meeting of the Midwest Political Science Association, Chicago.

ALTMAN, D. 2000. The politics of coalition formation and survival in multiparty presidential democracies: the case of Uruguay, 1989–1999. *Party Politics*, 6: 259–83.

—— 2001. The politics of coalition formation and survival in multiparty presidential regimes. Unpublished Ph.D. dissertation. University of Notre Dame.

AMORIM NETO, O. 1998. Of presidents, parties, and ministers: cabinet formation and legislative decision-making under separation of powers. Unpublished doctoral dissertation. UCSD.

—— 2002. Presidential cabinets, electoral cycles, and coalition discipline in Brazil. Pp. 48–78 in *Legislatures and Democracy in Latin America*, ed. S. Morgenstern and B. Nacif. New York: Cambridge University Press.

—— 2006. Cabinet formation in presidential democracies. *Comparative Political Studies* (forthcoming).

—— and SAMUELS, D. 2003. Cabinet partisanship and regime type in contemporary democracies. Paper presented at the annual conference of the American Political Science Association, Philadelphia.

—— and SANTOS, F. 2001. The executive connection: presidentially-defined factions and party discipline in Brazil. *Party Politics*, 7 (2): 213–34.

—— and STROM, K. 2004. Presidents, voters, and non-partisan cabinet members in European parliamentary democracies. Paper presented at the 2004 meeting of the American Political Science Association, Chicago.

—— and TAFNER, P. 2002. Governos de coalizão e mecanismos de alarme de incêndio no controle legislativo das medidas provisórias. *Dados*, 45 (1).

ANDERSON, C. 2000. Economic voting and political context: a comparative perspective. *Electoral Studies*, 19: 151–70.

AUSTIN-SMITH, D., and BANKS, J. 1988. Elections, coalitions, and legislative outcomes. *American Political Science Review*, 82: 405–22.

BAUM, J. R. 2002. Presidents have problems too: the logic of intra-branch delegation in new democracies. Unpublished Ph.D. dissertation. UCLA.

BENNETT, A. J. 1996. *The American President's Cabinet: From Kennedy to Bush.* New York: St Martin's Press.

BOIX, C. 2003. *Democracy and Redistribution.* New York: Cambridge University Press.

—— 2005*a*. Constitutions and democratic breakdowns. Unpublished paper. University of Chicago.

—— 2005*b*. The fiscal consequences of federalism. Unpublished paper. University of Chicago.

BRESSER PEREIRA, L. C., MARAVALL, J. M. and PRZEWORSKI, A. 1993. *Economic Reforms in New Democracies: A Social Democratic Approach.* New York: Cambridge University Press.

CAREY, J. M., and SHUGART, M. S. 1995. Incentives to cultivate a personal vote: a rank-ordering of electoral formulas. *Electoral Studies,* 14 (4): 417–39.

—— —— eds. 1998. *Executive Decree Authority.* New York: Cambridge University Press.

CARROLL, R., COX, G., and PACHÓN, M. 2005. How parties create electoral democracy, chapter two. *Legislative Studies Quarterly* (forthcoming).

—— and SHUGART, M. 2005. Neo-Madisonian theories of Latin American institutions. In *Regimes and Democracy in Latin America,* i: *Theories and Agendas,* ed. G. Munck. New York: Oxford University Press, forthcoming.

CHEIBUB, J. A. 2002. Minority governments, deadlock situations, and the survival of presidential democracies. *Comparative Political Studies,* 35: 284–312.

—— and LIMONGI, F. 2002. Modes of government formation and the survival of democratic regimes: presidentialism and parliamentarism reconsidered. *Annual Review of Political Science,* 5: 151–79.

—— PRZEWORSKI, A., and SAIEGH, S. 2004. Government coalitions and legislative success under presidentialism and parliamentarism. *British Journal of Political Science,* 34 (4): 565–87.

CONAGHAN, C. M., MALLOY, J. M., and ABUGATTAS, L. A. 1990. Business and the boys: the politics of neoliberalism in the Central Andes. *Latin America Research Review,* 25 (2): 3–29.

COX, G. 2005. The organization of democratic legislatures. In *The Oxford Handbook of Political Economy,* ed. B. Weingast and D. Wittman. Oxford: Oxford University Press (forthcoming).

—— and MCCUBBINS, M. D. 2001. The institutional determinants of economic policy outcomes. In Haggard and McCubbins 2001: 21–63.

—— —— 2004. Setting the agenda. Unpublished book MS. Department of Political Science, University of California, San Diego.

—— and MORGENSTERN, S. 2001. Latin America's reactive presidents and proactive assemblies. *Comparative Politics,* 33 (2): 171–89.

DEHEZA, G. I. 1997. Gobiernos de coalición en el sistema presidencial: America del Sur. Unpublished doctoral dissertation. European University Institute, Florence.

—— 1998. Gobiernos de coalición en el sistema presidencial: Américal del Sur. Pp. 151–69 in *El presidencialismo renovado: instituciones y cambio político en América Latina,* ed. D. Nohlen and M. Fernández B. Caracas: Nueva Sociedad.

DOMÍNGUEZ, J. I. 1997. Technopols: ideas and leaders in freeing politics and markets in Latin America in the 1990s. Ch. 1 in *Technopols: Freeing Politics and Markets in Latin America in the 1990s,* ed. J. I. Domínguez. University Park: Pennsylvania State University Press.

ELGIE, R. 1999. The politics of semi-presidentialism. Pp. 1–21 in *Semi-Presidentialism in Europe,* ed. R. Elgie. Oxford: Oxford University Press.

GAMSON, W. A. 1961. A theory of coalition formation. *American Sociological Review,* 26: 373–82.

GERRING, J., and THACKER, S. 2004. Political institutions and corruption: the role of unitarism and parliamentarism. *British Journal of Political Science,* 34 (2): 295–330.

HAGGARD, S., and McCUBBINS, M. D. 2001. Introduction: political institutions and the determinants of public policy. In *Presidents, Parliaments, and Policy*, ed. S. Haggard and M. D. McCubbins. New York: Cambridge University Press.

HERMENS, F. 1941. *Democracy or Anarchy?* Notre Dame, Ind.: University of Notre Dame Press.

HOCHSTETLER, K. 2005. Rethinking presidentialism: challengers and presidential falls in South America. *Comparative Politics* (forthcoming).

HUBER, J., and McCARTY, N. 2001. Legislative organization, bureaucratic capacity, and delegation in Latin American democracies. Paper presented at the conference on Brazilian Institutions in Comparative Perspective, Oxford University.

—— —— 2004. Bureaucratic capacity, delegation, and political reform. *American Political Science Review*, 98 (3): 481–94.

—— and SHIPAN, C. 2002. *Deliberate Discretion? The Institutional Foundations of Bureaucratic Autonomy.* New York: Cambridge University Press.

JOHNSON, G. B., and CRISP, B. F. 2003. Mandates, powers, and policies. *American Journal of Political Science*, 47 (1): 128–42.

JONES, M. P. 1995. *Electoral Laws and the Survival of Presidential Democracies.* Notre Dame, Ind.: University of Notre Dame Press.

KLINGEMANN, H.-D., HOFFERBERT, R., and BUDGE, I. 1994. *Parties, Policies and Democracy.* Boulder, Colo.: Westview Press.

KUNICOVÁ, J. 2005. Political corruption: another peril of presidentialism? Unpublished paper. California Institute of Technology.

LANZARO, J. ed. 2001. *Tipos de presidencialismo y coaliciones políticas en América Latina.* Buenos Aires: CLASCO/ASDI.

LAVER, M., and SHEPSLE, K. 1996. *Making and Breaking Governments: Cabinets and Legislatures in Parliamentary Democracies.* New York: Cambridge University Press.

LIJPHART, A. 1999. *Democracies.* New Haven: Yale University Press.

LINZ, J. 1990. The perils of presidentialism. *Journal of Democracy*, 1 (1): 51–69.

—— 1994. Presidential versus parliamentary democracy: does it make a difference? In Linz and Valenzuela 1994: 3–87.

—— and VALENZUELA, A. eds. 1994. *The Failure of Presidential Democracy*, 2 vols. Baltimore: Johns Hopkins University Press.

MAINWARING, S. 1993. Presidentialism, multipartism, and democracy: the difficult combination. *Comparative Political Studies*, 26 (2): 198–228.

—— and SHUGART, M. S. 1997a. Juan Linz, presidentialism, and democracy: a critical appraisal. *Comparative Politics*, 29 (4): 449–72.

—— —— eds. 1997b. *Presidentialism and Democracy in Latin America.* New York: Cambridge University Press.

MANIN, B., PRZEWORSKI, A., and STOKES, S. 1999. Elections and representation. Pp. 29–54 in *Democracy, Accountability, and Representation*, ed. A. Przeworski, S. C. Stokes, and B. Manin. New York: Cambridge University Press.

METCALF, L. K. 2000. Measuring presidential power. *Comparative Political Studies*, 33 (5): 660–85.

MOE, T. M. and CALDWELL, M. 1994. The institutional foundations of democratic government: a comparison of presidential and parliamentary systems. *Journal of Institutional and Theoretical Economics*, 150 (1): 171–95.

MORGENSTERN, S., and NACIF, B. eds. 2002. *Legislatures and Democracy in Latin America.* New York: Cambridge University Press.

NISHIZAWA, Y. 2004. Economic voting: do institutions affect the way voters evaluate incumbents? Unpublished paper. Doshisha University. Available at **www1.doshisha.ac.jp/~ynishiza/**

O'DONNELL, G. 1994. Delegative democracy. *Journal of Democracy*, 5: 55–69.

PALMER, M. 1995. Toward an economics of comparative political organization: examining ministerial responsibility. *Journal of Law, Economics and Organization*, 11 (1): 164–88.

PERSSON, T., and TABELLINI, G. 2004. *The Economic Effects of Constitutions*. Cambridge, Mass.: MIT Press.

POWELL, G. B., and WHITTEN, G. 1993. A cross-national analysis of economic voting: taking account of political context. *American Journal of Political Science*, 37: 391–414.

POWER, T. J., and GASIOROWSKI, M. J. 1997. Institutional design and democratic consolidation in the Third World. *Comparative Political Studies*, 30 (2): 123–55.

PRZEWORSKI, A. 2003. Institutions matter? Paper prepared for conference on Institutions, Behavior, and Outcomes, CEBRAP São Paulo, Brazil.

—— STOKES, S. C., and MANIN, B. eds. 1999. *Democracy, Accountability, and Representation*. New York: Cambridge University Press.

—— ALVAREZ, M. E., CHEIBUB, J. A., and LIMONGI, F. 2000. *Democracy and Development: Political Institutions and Well-Being in the World, 1950–1990*. New York: Cambridge University Press.

ROBERTS, A., and DRUCKMAN, J. Forthcoming. Measuring portfolio salience in eastern European parliamentary democracies. *European Journal of Political Research.*

ROPER, S. D. 2002. Are all semipresidential regimes the same? A comparison of premier-presidential regimes. *Comparative Politics*, 34 (3): 253–73.

SAMUELS, D. 2002. Presidentialized parties: the separation of powers and party organization and behavior. *Comparative Political Studies*, 35 (4): 461–83.

—— 2004. Presidentialism and accountability for the economy in comparative perspective. *American Political Science Review*, 98 (3): 425–36.

—— and HELLWIG, T. 2005. Democratic regimes and electoral accountability around the world. Paper presented at the 2005 meeting of the American Political Science Association, Washington, DC.

—— and SHUGART, M. 2003. Presidentialism, elections, and representation. *Journal of Theoretical Politics*, 15 (1): 33–60.

SARTORI, G. 1994. *Comparative Constitutional Engineering: An Inquiry into Structures, Incentives and Outcomes*. New York: New York University Press.

SHUGART, M. S. 1995. The electoral cycle and institutional sources of divided presidential government. *American Political Science Review*, 89 (2): 327–43.

—— 1999. Presidentialism, parliamentarism, and the provision of collective goods in less-developed countries. *Constitutional Political Economy*, 10: 53–88.

—— and CAREY, J. M. 1992. *Presidents and Assemblies: Constitutional Design and Electoral Dynamics*. New York: Cambridge.

—— and HAGGARD, S. 2001. Institutions and public policy in presidential systems. In Haggard and McCubbins 2001: 64–102.

—— and MAINWARING, S. 1997. Presidentialism and democracy in Latin America: rethinking the terms of the debate. Pp. 12–54 in *Presidentialism and Democracy in Latin America*, ed. S. Mainwaring and M. S. Shugart. New York: Cambridge.

SIAROFF, A. 2003. Comparative presidencies: the inadequacy of the presidential, semi-presidential and parliamentary distinction. *European Journal of Political Research*, 42: 287–312.

SIAVELIS, P. M. 2000. Disconnected fire alarms and ineffective police patrols: legislative oversight in postauthoritarian Chile. *Journal of Interamerican Studies and World Affairs*, 42 (1): 71–98.

STEPAN, A., and SKACH, C. 1993. Constitutional frameworks and democratic consolidation: parliamentarism versus presidentialism. *World Politics*, 46 (1): 1–22.

STOKES, S. 1999. What do policy switches tell us about democracy? In Przeworski, Stokes, and Manin 1999: 98–130.

—— 2001. *Mandates and Democracy: Neoliberalism by Surprise in Latin America.* New York: Cambridge University Press.

STRØM, K. 1990a. A behavioral theory of competitive political parties. *American Journal of Political Science,* 34 (2): 565–98.

—— 1990b. *Minority Government and Majority Rule.* New York: Cambridge University Press.

—— MÜLLER, W. C., and BERGMAN, T. eds. 2003. *Delegation and Accountability in Parliamentary Democracies.* New York: Oxford University Press.

THIBAUT, B. 1998. El gobierno de la democracia presidencial: Argentina, Brasil, Chile y Uruguay en una perspectiva comparada. Pp. 127–51 in *El presidencialismo renovado: instituciones y cambio político en América Latina,* ed. D. Nohlen and M. Fernández B. Caracas: Nueva Sociedad.

TSEBELIS, G. 2002. *Veto Players: How Political Institutions Work.* Princeton: Princeton University Press.

WARWICK, P., and DRUCKMAN, J. N. 2001. Portfolio salience and the proportionality of payoffs in coalition governments. *British Journal of Political Science,* 31: 627–49.

WOLDENDORP, J., KEMAN, H., and BUDGE, I. 2000. *Party Government in 48 Democracies (1945–1998): Composition—Duration—Personnel.* Dordrecht: Kluwer Academic Publishers.

CHAPTER 30

....

COMPARATIVE
JUDICIAL
POLITICS

....

JOHN FEREJOHN
FRANCES ROSENBLUTH
CHARLES SHIPAN

1 Introduction

....

IT is hard to think of a political system that does not trumpet its commitment to "the rule of law," based on the principle that citizens are better off when the political system establishes rules for all to follow, rather than subjecting citizens either to arbitrary rule or to anarchy.[1] By entrusting the interpretation and enforcement of laws to legal specialists, the government agrees to abide by its own laws, and the courts can rule against the government to uphold the "laws of the land." Governments in most political systems are at least rhetorically deferential to this concept.

Less universally embraced is the power of courts not only to enforce, but also to review and potentially to overrule legislative statutes. What is the justification in a democracy for a non-majoritarian body of experts to second-guess the majoritarian institutions charged with drafting the laws in a way that reflects society's interests? We explore briefly, both normatively and positively, the reasons for and against both kinds of judicial oversight.

[1] Note that "rule of law" differs from "rule by law" when a government uses laws as a tool of control (Barros 2003).

Because this chapter is comparative in focus, we spend most of our effort considering reasons for cross-national variation in judicial powers. In the United States, where an independent judiciary is now taken for granted, the state conventions were concerned that the new federal judiciary would be too powerful and insisted on adding additional procedural rights such as jury trials for civil cases. Democratic theory in Europe remained infused with the Rousseauian notion of the "sovereign assembly" far longer. The German jurist Carl Schmitt opposed judicial review on grounds that it would lead both to the judicialization of politics and the politicization of the judiciary (cited in Stone 1992). He was, of course, right about these effects. Courts undertaking judicial review make decisions with potentially large political consequences and hence make themselves unelected political actors. And from the judicialization of politics springs the politicization of the judiciary, for nowhere does the judiciary grow in importance without politicians also becoming more interested in influencing judicial appointments and processes (Ferejohn 2002). As we argue below, the differences between the US and European judiciaries have less to do with the prevailing theories of how popular sovereignty relates to jurisprudence, than with the institutional capacities of courts to act independently of political actors.

Whether the blurring of lines between the political and judicial is an evil trend to avoid, as Schmitt feared, depends on how one evaluates the countervailing benefits of courts being empowered to protect a hierarchically ordered set of legal principles. Countries that have become democracies since the Second World War have overwhelmingly embraced the idea of explicit constitutional oversight by a specially designated court, presumably because bad experiences with authoritarian rule have eroded the public's confidence in parliamentary sovereignty, or perhaps in judiciaries enforcing fascist laws (Ferejohn 2002; Ferejohn and Pasquino 2004).

Insulating courts from political manipulation is another matter. Behind the "veil of ignorance" during a period set aside for constitutional design, any group lacking certainty of future majority status may have an interest in constitutional protection of basic rights. But once in control of a legislative majority, that same group may want to reduce the power of courts to overturn duly legislated policies. Appointing judges for life can protect individual judges from being punished for rulings the government does not like, but if the political branches of government can draft new legislation that overturns court rulings or can legislatively change the composition of the court, personal security does not leave room for the courts to play a large autonomous role. Individually independent judges can function collectively as a politically dependent judiciary (Ferejohn 1999). Here, the specific institutional setting matters. Appointing judges by a legislative supermajority has the normatively desirable effect of creating a relatively non-partisan or at least an ideologically pluralistic bench. But even here, the space for autonomous court action will be determined by the rules governing court recomposition. This is an example of the more general point that rules are powerful in inverse proportion to the costs involved in coordinating against them (Hardin 2003*b*). As we will argue, the government's command of the legislative quorum required to reconstitute the court is the single best predictor of court activism regardless of the court's structure and internal composition. At the same time, this power is not sufficient; judicial independence is also affected by the broader features of the institutional and political setting.

In parts of the Third World where social conventions strain to promote socially constructive behavior under conditions of unstable political institutions, judicial independence may be both more important and more difficult to secure. Governments struggling to stay in power may relinquish control of judicial appointments and promotions, or grant judges wide jurisdictional scope, though rarely both at the same time. A government can use friendly judges to harass the opposition (Maravall and Przeworski 2003, 14). But we also know from variation in judicial independence across and within countries that shaky public support for the incumbent government sometimes gives the judiciary opportunities to rule against the government. A more nuanced understanding of the causes of judicial independence can also help us evaluate arguments about its effects.

The rest of this chapter is organized as follows. Section 2 defines more systematically what we mean by judicial independence. Section 3 presents theoretical explanations, normative and positive, for judicial independence. In Section 4 we examine judicial systems in a classificatory rather than fully empirical way, leaving open many avenues for, and we hope inspiring interest in, future research. We sketch out some of our own ideas for empirical research in Section 5. Section 6 concludes.

2 DEFINING JUDICIAL INDEPENDENCE

We take judicial independence to mean court autonomy from other actors. To the extent that a court is able to make decisions free of influence from other political actors, and to pursue its goals without having to worry about the consequences from other institutions, it is independent. The greater the level of input that these other actors have on the court's personnel, case selection, decision rules, jurisdiction, and enforcement of laws, the less independent it is. In other words, we are equating judicial independence with the court's ability to act sincerely according to its own preferences and judgements.

It is easy to conceive of courts that are at the polar ends of complete independence and utter dependence, at least in hypothetical terms; but in reality, most courts occupy a middle ground on this continuum. More difficult is to assess which factors influence the level of independence and how much weight each of these should receive. We will return to these measurement issues in subsequent sections.

2.1 Statutory Judicial Review

We start by distinguishing between two kinds of court actions to which political actors can respond. First, courts may engage in *statutory judicial review*, in which they may determine that actions by regulatory agencies or rulings by lower courts are inconsistent with existing law. Second, supreme courts or constitutional courts may be empowered to rule on the constitutionality of legislation itself. In many countries, this power of *constitutional judicial review* is given to a constitutional court that is separate from the regular judiciary and is deliberately structured to be more autonomous. But in countries such as the USA, where the Supreme Court is both an appellate court and a constitutional review body, the same court may have different levels of autonomy across these domains. Institutional hurdles for legislatures to override these different types of judicial actions, along with the legislature's ability to influence the court's personnel, will shape the level of judicial autonomy in each domain (Epstein, Segal, and Victor 2002). We consider each in turn.

If a court can determine that the rulings of regulatory agencies or other political actors (e.g. subnational governments, lower courts, etc.) are incompatible with existing law, a legislature has the option, if it has a coherent majority, to pass new legislation that overrides the court's ruling. Spatial models show how the threat of a legislative override can cause a court to implement a policy different from what it would choose if it were completely independent (e.g. Ferejohn and Shipan 1990). Consider, for example, two actors—a judiciary, denoted by J, and a parliament (or more generally, a politician) denoted by P—and a status quo point denoted by q, which represents a policy chosen by some other political actor, such as an agency. Assume that the judiciary has the option to choose a policy rather than being limited to an up or down vote; that the parliament has the opportunity to respond to the court's decision; and that the parliament will act in this policy area only once another actor, such as the court, disrupts the current equilibrium and makes the parliament worse off than it currently is (perhaps because a committee works to protect q from legislative action). Figure 30.1 presents this scenario.

If the court were independent and did not need to worry about being overridden, it would simply choose to implement J, its ideal point. But in this example—and in most political systems—the parliament will have the opportunity to respond to the court's action. Thus, if the court were to try to implement J, the parliament would respond by selecting P. The court, then, realizes that the best it can do is to move policy to P. In effect, the court is forced to take the parliament's preferences into account in order to avoid triggering an override; and to do so, it is forced to select a policy that is distant from its most preferred policy.

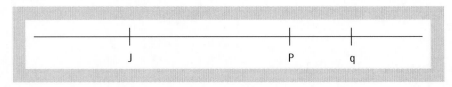

Fig. 30.1

2.2 Constitutional Judicial Review

The second kind of court action we consider, one that is weightier than judgements on agency or lower court rulings, is *constitutional judicial review*.[2] This type of review applies only to supreme courts or constitutional courts that are constitutionally authorized to review the constitutionality of legislation passed by the legislature. The strategic interaction between the judicial reviewing court and the legislature is analytically the same as what we have sketched out for overrides, except that the legislature can overturn the court's ruling only by changing the constitution itself, or by recomposing the courts to get a new ruling. Overturning constitutional review or changing the composition of courts often require supermajorities of the legislature or other cumbersome processes that are intended to give the courts more autonomy in these kinds of deliberations. Whether or not legislative coalitions are sufficiently large either to amend the constitution or to reconstitute the court determines the effective level of autonomy the court can exercise in judicial review.

In the following section we examine normative theories for why the court ought to be independent, either to enforce laws of the land, or to review the constitutionality of the laws themselves. We then return to positive analysis of the institutional and other conditions under which a court is likely in practice to be able to act autonomously from political actors.

3 Explaining Judicial Independence

3.1 Normative Theory

Even dictators, disingenuously or not, often claim that courts should enforce the "laws of the land." By allowing the government to make credible commitments not to confiscate wealth, a guardian judiciary might increase the level of private economic investment, reduce the cost of government debt, and promote economic growth (Landes and Posner 1975; North and Weingast 1989; Kerman and Mahoney 2004; Djankov et al. 2003). For these purposes, judicial independence, which allows judges to enforce contracts without the possibility of government interference, may be more important than judicial review, which typically does not protect private parties from each other.

The power of judicial review is less universally accepted, especially among democracies, because it sets the courts above majoritarian institutions in articulating and defending constitutional values above duly passed legislation. The most straightforward normative rationale is probably that everyone can be better off, from behind a veil of ignorance, when society is governed by fairly constructed constitutional principles that

---

[2] Throughout the remainder of this chapter, when we discuss "judicial review" we will be referring to constitutional judicial review, unless otherwise noted.

stipulate rights and duties, and that these might be better protected, particularly for minorities, by legal experts than by political actors supported by shifting majorities. Even without recourse to a belief in a "natural law" that is waiting for legal experts to uncover on our behalf, it is straightforward to see why a commitment to agreed-upon principles such as political equality may not be best left to political agents whose incentives are to execute that commitment selectively. The underpinning idea is that constitutional principles are more fundamental than legislation that may reflect bargains of convenience at the expense of others' political rights.

Democracies have a systematic defense against a certain kind of judicial independence in that they insist that the legislature or the people ought to have the last word on court jurisdiction. In practice, however, democracies usually support other forms of independence by granting judges lifetime or long tenure, by protecting their salaries, and by making it procedurally difficult to change the composition of the courts.

An additional public interest argument for an independent judiciary rests on the premiss that incomplete information about the future effects of legislation on outcomes would lead to excessively conservative laws were it not for the existence of an ex post check on legislative actions. To our knowledge no one has evaluated this proposition empirically. But at least hypothetically, countries with constitutional review may adopt a more risk-accepting approach to legislating without suffering from the effects of ideas gone wrong since the courts can tamp them down in fairly short order (Rogers 2001). This logic breaks down, however, if one worries about judiciaries being unaccountable to the public, particularly if judiciaries are thought have their own goals that could be out of line with the public interest.

Indeed, against arguments for judicial independence is the long-standing European concern that the legislature, as the embodiment of popular sovereignty, is the most suitable organ for making decisions in a democracy. Judiciaries can themselves be mercurial or overbearing, as some American colonists feared and as Nigerian citizens have experienced, and a better solution to the problem of protecting minority rights might be to give minorities a stronger voice in the assembly (Olowofoyeku 1989; Shapiro 2002). Others argue that legal incrementalism tends to frustrate radical reforms and naturally favors conservative causes.

This debate reduces to an empirical question about the tradeoffs entailed in a court-based versus an assembly-based protection of political and other rights, and is impossible to answer without intimate knowledge of the political institutions and processes of each country in question. We will return to these questions in the conclusion, but sidestep for now the normative debate by noting that the public good has rarely been sufficient reason for politicians to adopt any particular institutional arrangement. As Stephen Holmes quips, law does not descend upon societies from a Heaven of Higher Norms (Holmes 2003, 53). Or in Jon Elster's words, "nothing is external to society" (1989, 196). If politicians can make themselves better off by reneging, why would they choose to tie their hands? Even if long-term interaction among the same players might increase the possibility that politicians would be willing to delegate oversight authority to the courts to regularize competition, we know from the Folk Theorem that this does not preclude other equilibria. We turn now to positivist accounts that look more closely at politicians' incentives.

3.2 Political Independence

There are multiple explanations for why some judiciaries may be more politically independent or perhaps politically consequential than others.[3] Here, we focus on how political fragmentation gives courts space to take more independent action. Elected politicians have a variety of tools they can use to influence the actions of courts, such as appointing justices to their liking, passing legislation that overrides court rulings, or possibly even amending the constitution. But politicians are only able to undertake those measures to the extent that they are sufficiently coherent as a group to amass the legislative votes needed in each case. This line of argument points to political fragmentation as a crucial factor for predicting judicial independence, or to its converse, political cohesion, for predicting a weak judiciary.

According to this point of view, the more fragmented are the political actors in a political system, the more room this provides for the court. In fragmented political systems, courts have less need to worry about reprisal or override.[4] We can revisit the diagram discussed earlier to show this. Assume that, in addition to the actors presented in Figure 30.1, we now include a separate actor: an executive, denoted by E, which is distinct from the parliament. Assume also that the parliament and executive must agree on any policy in order to pass a law. In our earlier example, the court was unable to implement its most preferred policy and was forced instead to choose something that was more acceptable to the parliament. Now, however, with the executive located to the left of the court and the parliament to the right, the court is free to pursue its goals unfettered, and can implement J. It is able to do so because

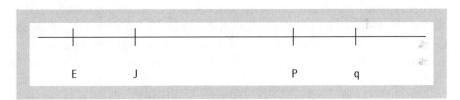

Fig. 30.2

<hr />

[3] Some scholars stress different traditions of common law versus civil law countries (for example Djankov et al. 2003), but we think this may miss deeper institutional reasons for differences in legal politics. Others model judicial autonomy as the result of deliberate delegation by legislatures (Landes and Posner 1975; McCubbins and Schwartz 1984; Graber 1993; Salzberger 1993). We think delegative models often fail to show the conditions under which an independent judiciary would be less trouble for the legislature than the problems they are supposed to solve, even in the short run. More fundamentally, they often fail to show how competing parties could agree to keep their hands off the courts. See, for example, Ramseyer and Rosenbluth (1993).

[4] Bednar, Eskridge, and Ferejohn (2001) discuss fragmentation as a cause of judicial independence, while Ferejohn 2002 takes fragmentation to be a cause of the judicialization of politics. In fragmented political systems, he argues, governments are less able to reach policy decisions and so these decisions are moved to the courts. This is clearly related to the idea that fragmentation can lead to independence—once courts act, in these systems, fragmentation diminishes the likelihood that governments will be able to respond negatively and forcefully to the court's actions. See also Chavez, Ferejohn, and Weingast (2004).

the fragmentation among the other political actors would prevent them from joining forces to overturn the court's policy choice.

In the example shown in Figure 30.2, fragmentation can occur between a legislature and an executive, much as occurs under divided government in a separation of powers system. Fragmentation, however, is not limited to divisions between an executive and a legislature, nor is it guaranteed in such systems. Fragmentation would be much lower, for example, under unified government than under divided government. And fragmentation can occur between two chambers in a bicameral system (if the upper chamber has legitimate powers), or between partners in a coalition. The point is that fragmentation can exist in a wide range of systems. Furthermore, the amount of fragmentation within a political system can vary across time with implications for judicial autonomy.

Consider now the implications of the fragmentation hypothesis for how politicians might use appointment power, legislative overrides, or constitutional revision to keep courts in line with their preferences. In many political systems, and in virtually all common law systems, elected politicians determine which justices get to serve on the courts, but in all cases, political coherence intervenes crucially in determining the effect of appointment power on court autonomy.[5] There is a wide range of possibilities, and it is important to know considerable institutional detail to understand how much coordination is possible among and within the political branches in using appointments to hold the judiciary in check. In some systems, such as Germany, responsibility is shared between federal and state-level politicians, with the Bundestag appointing half of the members of the constitutional court and the Bundesrat, representing the states, appointing the other half. Depending on the partisan composition of those units, resulting judicial appointments may be multi-partisan and beyond the ability of any coherent coalition to control.[6] In some separation of powers systems, such as the United States, this responsibility is shared by the executive and the legislature, with the result that the influence is shared and at times favors one actor or the other (Moraski and Shipan 1999). In Russia, similarly, and in France, the president and the leaders of the two legislative chambers appoint judges and members of the constitutional courts. In Mexico, on the other hand, the president heavily dominates the process and selects judges. In South Africa, a non-partisan Judicial Services Bureau recommends judges to serve on the Supreme Court; but the president then gets to choose some of these himself, and some in conjunction with the chief justice. And in many parliamentary systems, authority lies in the hands of the coalition government, though there is often a supermajority requirement for confirmation that requires a large legislative coalition to support the government's choice.[7]

To the extent that elected politicians agree on who should sit on courts, judicial independence is limited. A coherent legislative majority can also shape the processes by

---

[5] See Epstein, Knight, and Shvetsova (2001) for a thorough examination of different selection mechanisms.

[6] Furthermore, the requirement of a 2/3 supermajority for appointments effectively grants a veto over appointments to the major political parties (Vanberg forthcoming).

[7] The states in the USA provide another comparative forum for examining judicial selection mechanisms. Not surprisingly, we see a wide range of mechanisms—some judges are appointed by governors, others are appointed by the governor together with the legislature, some are selected by commissions, and others are elected, to list just some of the mechanisms in place.

which courts make decisions, thereby influencing the outcomes of judicial actions. In the USA, for example, Congress has a variety of tools with which to influence how courts review agency actions (e.g. Shipan 1997, 2000). It can give the authority for review to one court rather than another; indicate that certain actions are not reviewable by the courts; specify the grounds on which courts can make decisions; determine whether the courts must defer to agency expertise; and set deadlines for action. Another example occurs in the German system, where the Bundestag could allow the courts to review the government's environmental decision but has chosen not to do so (Rose-Ackerman 1995).[8] More generally, legislatures can alter a court's jurisdiction, and thus its discretion. And they can increase the likelihood that courts will have to hear certain types of cases by providing easier access to courts by citizens (Smith forthcoming). But if politicians are divided among themselves, these powers are muted in their effect.

Cohesiveness among the political actors who might respond to court decisions also increases their ability to use other tools to limit judicial independence. Legislatures may pass laws that limit judicial independence by influencing the courts' personnel in numerous ways—restricting judicial tenure, for example, or cutting salaries—and they will be more able to do so when fragmentation is low. At the same time, lack of fragmentation may not be sufficient to limit judicial independence. Previous legislatures may take actions that protect courts from future legislative action, by putting these things out of the reach of legislatures. Depending on whether court personnel and jurisdiction are established constitutionally or by simple legislative majority or something in between, the political independence of the judiciary can vary substantially.

In the next section, we examine how institutional rules of appointment, override, and constitutional revision shape the interaction between political and judicial actors in different types of judicial systems. The USA is somewhat atypical in not clearly specifying judicial review powers in the constitution; but it provides good material for seeing how changes in political cohesion or fragmentation affect the court's scope for autonomous action. We then consider other presidential systems, and parliamentary systems with and without constitutional courts.

4 POLITICAL FRAGMENTATION IN PRACTICE

4.1 The US Judiciary

Nowhere does the US constitution state that the judiciary shall be the guardian of the constitution to ensure that the acts of other branches are in constitutional conformity. Supreme Court Justice John Marshall asserted the court's powers of judicial

---

[8] Rose-Ackerman elaborates: "The Bundestag majority has no incentive to permit the courts to review bureaucratic policy-making. An independent judiciary could make decisions that might be embarrassing to the governing coalition" (1995, 12).

review in the landmark case *Marbury* v. *Madison* in 1803, and the other branches of government allowed this statement to stand. The irony of this case is that the court, composed of Federalist appointees, was at the time in a strategically weak position and refrained from exercising judicial review against the Jefferson administration. Thomas Jefferson's Democratic Republicans, who had won the presidency and a decisive legislative majority from John Adams's Federalists, were angry that before leaving office the Federalists had passed "midnight" legislation creating several new federal judgeships and other judicial positions, which they assigned to their partisans. Once in office, the Jeffersonians repealed the legislation creating the judgeships and refused to deliver five of the new judicial commissions that Adams had signed before leaving the White House.

Marbury, one of the Federalist appointees whose commission Jefferson blocked, sued the new government for not delivering the judicial commissions that Adams had authorized. The Democratic Republicans then repealed the Judiciary Act that had added the federal judgeships. Marshall was astute enough to know that Jefferson and his congressional majority could not only draft new legislation, but he knew that Jefferson could ignore a court order with impunity. Marshall's ruling on *Marbury* v. *Madison* was profoundly political: recognizing his weak bargaining position, he ruled that, while the Supreme Court had the right to review the constitutionality of legislative acts, the repeal of the Federalists' Judiciary Act was constitutional. Marshal established the principle and precedent of judicial review by striking down part of a congressional statute, while not taking the risk of having a court order be ignored by the president (Clinton 1994; Knight and Epstein 1996; Chavez, Ferejohn, and Weingast 2004).

The Jeffersonians allowed Marshall's bold statement about the Court's constitutional prerogatives to stand, because their concern was not with the principle of judicial review but how it might be used against them. As long as Marshall recognized the strategic reality that a united executive and legislature could withstand judicial encroachment, no further measures were required. Marshall's bold proclamation about judicial review notwithstanding, the court did not rule unconstitutional acts of the other branches until the Dred Scott decision of 1857 when Congress was deeply divided over slavery and secession.

Chavez, Ferejohn, and Weingast (2004) find, in fact, that the pattern of judicial activism and quiescence follows predictably from the degree of fragmentation or cohesion in the other branches of government. When a legislative majority stands ready to work with a president, attempts by the court to rule against legislation or executive orders would be met with new legislation and possibly worse—attempts to impeach particular justices or assaults on judicial autonomy. They identify some periods of relatively weak courts on account of legislative-executive cohesion, but these periods tend to be short and rare: a few years after the 1800 election, a few years after the Jackson election, about six years after the Civil War, and the early New Deal. Franklin Roosevelt had a sufficiently strong coalition to eventually shift the ideology of the court, although his more blatant attempt to "pack" the Supreme Court with sympathetic justices failed. As de Figueiredo and Tiller (1996) have pointed out, political alignment of the House, Senate, and president makes for weak courts. Much of the tension between the judiciary and other branches of government occurs when appointees of a previous era confront a new configuration in the political branches (Dahl 1957). Courts reduce their activism when faced with unified opposition from the other branches, and even more when appointments begin to bring the judiciary in line with the elected branches.

4.2 Presidential Systems Outside the USA

The argument about the effects of political fragmentation on judicial powers fits the US case particularly well, but it also characterizes some other presidential systems. The heyday of Argentina's high court was between 1862 and Juan Perón's presidency in 1946. Different parties controlled the presidency and legislature, and an internally heterogeneous majority party governed the legislature itself. Presidents were unable to pack the courts or purge uncooperative justices, and respected the constitutional provision that granted judges life tenure during good conduct (Chavez, Ferejohn, and Weingast 2004, 19). During this period the court overruled both the legislative and executive branches in defense of individual rights, freedom of the press, and on behalf of political dissidents. When the president's party gained control of both legislative houses between 1946 and 1983, however, the Supreme Court kept a low profile. Alfonsin's party that replaced Perón was considerably weaker on account of its minority status in the Senate, and the judiciary declared unconstitutional a number of Alfonsin's policies. Menem replaced Alfonsin in 1989 with a far stronger administration because it commanded majorities in both houses of Congress. Not surprisingly, by the fragmentation logic, the courts became docile (Iaryczower, Spiller, and Tommasi 2002; Chavez, Ferejohn, and Weingast 2004).[9]

   For other presidential systems as well, we would expect that, as a first approximation, judicial activism would be inversely related to the coherence among the political branches. The Mexican jurist Pablo Gonzalez Casanova and comparative judicial scholar Carl Schwarz have both found that the Mexican Supreme Court has a history of finding against the government with some regularity (see Hale 2000). We would want to know not only how seriously those rulings inconvenienced the government, but also if those rulings cluster in times when the government's capacity for overruling the Supreme Court is relatively low.

   The Philippine Supreme Court before Marcos declared martial law in 1972 was regarded as "one of the world's most independent, important, and prestigious supreme courts" (Tate and Haynie 1993). Presumably it was precisely because Marcos could not control the other branches of government that he used the military to shut

   [9] Helmke (2002), while providing an account that is consistent in some ways with the fragmentation story spelled out in the text, emphasizes a different angle. She argues that although Supreme Court justices nominally were guaranteed independence through lifetime tenure, from the 1930s through the 1980s, the membership of the court was routinely changed with each regime transition. As a result, justices began to behave strategically, ruling against the outgoing party and in favor of those who were soon to take office.

them down and replaced them with his friends and relatives. Needless to say, Marcos's hand-picked court was compliant, as were the courts of Bhutto's and Zia's military regimes in Pakistan (Tate 1993). But the fluctuation of court activism in tandem with the court's expectation of the president's ability to command a legislative majority seems a general pattern (Helmke 2002).

The general point is that fragmentation gives courts a certain measure of independence. When other political institutions are more fragmented, courts have less to worry about in terms of override or reprisal. As a result, they are free to challenge the government.

4.3 Judicial Powers in Old European Democracies

Given the broad public appeal of robust political and economic rights, why is judicial review not universal among democratic regimes? Our answer has two parts. Institutionally, the fusion of the legislative and executive branches in parliamentary systems removes the possible space between branches for autonomous court action to emerge on its own. But institutions represent political choices, and even parliamentary systems can choose to adopt organs of judicial review, as we will see in the following sections. As long as governments retain voter trust in their ability to uphold basic rights, the demand for institutional adjustment may remain dormant.

The effects of institutional coherence on judicial discretion are clearest in Westminster countries where a single majority party typically controls the executive. Sir Edward Coke, chief justice of the Court of Common Pleas, stated in 1610 that "in some cases the common law will control acts of Parliament and sometimes adjudge them to be utterly void" (Mezey 1983, 689). But this dictum, which found fertile soil in America's institutional environment, never became common practice in the UK.

To be sure, the Act of Settlement of 1701 that protected judges from being dismissed on grounds other than judicial malpractice introduced a measure of judicial independence. Kerman and Mahoney (2004) find that share prices increased following the Act because investors were assured that the courts were in a strong position to enforce contracts. Salzberger and Fenn (1999) find that UK judges are promoted on the basis of how frequently their opinions are reversed, rather than on the basis of how often they find against the government. But it is also true that the judiciary takes on the government only rarely, and on issues that are of relatively minor political significance (Salzberger 1993; Shapiro 2002; Chalmers 2000). This precisely what we would expect in equilibrium. With legislative and executive functions of government organized hierarchically, court rulings at odds with the legislative majority can easily be overturned.

Parliamentary countries with proportional electoral rules are more fragmented than Westminster systems in the sense that multiple parties with distinct constituencies and platforms join together to form coalition governments. Even there, however, the legislative parties in coalition operate according to "treaties" that the courts have little reason to believe they can overturn without being overruled as long as the coalition government is in power. Because the legislative and executive branches remain fused, the courts have little room for maneuver.

If the court's capacity to review legislation were high principally in presidential systems, especially under conditions of divided government, the case for the political fragmentation hypothesis would seem especially strong. Among parliamentary systems, however, variation in levels of political fragmentation alone is a poor predictor of judicial independence. In some European countries such as Switzerland, Belgium, and Luxembourg, judicial review is explicitly prohibited in the constitution. The possibility of constitutional review exists in Scandinavian countries and the Netherlands but is rarely employed. Other countries in Europe and elsewhere adopted constitutional courts during the decades after the second World War with the express purpose of protecting political and economic rights: Austria, Germany, Italy, France, Spain, and Portugal as well as Canada, Israel, Korea, South Africa, and post-communist countries in Eastern Europe. Clearly this latter is a very different path to constitutional review than the informal ebb and flow of judicial powers that can occur in politically fragmented systems.

4.4 Constitutional Courts in Europe and Beyond

In what Bruce Ackerman (1997) calls the "new beginnings" of constitutional democracy in the post-Second World War era, the choice of judicial regime seems to reflect a compromise between the American and old European models. Most new constitutions include provisions for judicial review, but within the context of a separate constitutional court that is independent of the regular judicial system and is more circumscribed by the political branches. In this section we consider only briefly why some countries have opted for the constitutional court model over the US or older European models. Our greater concern, which we sketch out here but leave in large part to future research, is with the effects of political cohesion or fragmentation on how these courts function in practice.

Ferejohn and Pasquino (2003, 250) note that "In all cases the constitutional court has developed a jurisprudence aimed at, and increasingly effective at, protecting fundamental rights." Constitutional courts have not only placed important limits on the ordinary political processes, but they have done it increasingly well. Perhaps the popularity of the courts has grown with their demonstrated effectiveness in protecting rights, and the governing coalition has less political room for undermining court autonomy.

Anti-authoritarian backlash. The European concept of the constitutional court was developed by the Austrian jurist Has Kelsen after the First World War. Unlike US-style judicial review, which Kelsen regarded as giving the US Supreme Court creeping legislative powers, Kelsen's narrower view of the court's role in guarding the constitution was potentially a better fit with the European philosophical commitment to sovereign assemblies (Kelsen 1942; Stone 1992). While Austria and Czechoslovakia adopted constitutional courts in 1920, Kelsen's ideas did not find broader resonance in Europe until after the Second World War, when all of the countries that had experienced fascist regimes established constitutional courts. Following Austria's decision to reimplement its constitutional court in 1946, Italy (1947) and the Federal Republic of Germany (1949) followed suit.

Italy and Germany seem to have adopted constitutional courts partially in response to "a deep distaste for the dismal past" (Merryman and Vigoriti 1966–7) and to guard citizens against the possibility of a political hijacking of the sort that Mussolini and Hitler had been able to pull off (Adams and Barile 1953; Cole 1959, 967).[10] As Franz Kafka memorialized in fiction, freedom from law gives totalitarianism its means to rule arbitrarily (Dyzenhaus 1998, p. vii).

In both countries, however, the legislative opposition was more eager for judicial powers than the ruling coalition. In Italy it was only after the socialists and communists gave up hope of commanding a legislative majority that they stopped dragging their feet on passing enabling legislation.[11] In both countries a legislative supermajority approves the members of the constitutional court, which ensures a broadly trans-partisan or non-partisan bench (Cole 1959, 969). To be sure, politicians have created ways of dealing with the supermajority requirement, such as the *lottizzacione* in Italy whereby the principal parties agree to split court appointments among themselves. This also occurs in Spain. While this means that the court will be multi-partisan if not non-partisan, it nonetheless remains outside the control of any single party.

The establishment of constitutional courts in Greece in 1975, Spain in 1978, and Portugal in 1982 followed a similar pattern to that of Italy and Germany. With the collapse of authoritarian regimes in those countries, there was strong public support for a judicial counterweight to potential collusion by the other branches of government. Majority parties that otherwise might have resisted this impulse might well have felt vulnerable to electoral backlash.

Decisions to adopt constitutional courts in former communist Eastern Europe and in other former authoritarian regimes look broadly similar. Following the collapse of the communist regime in the late 1980s, the Polish legislature established a new tribunal with substantially stronger powers of judicial review including the authority to issue generally binding interpretations of statutes. Between 1989 and 1994 the tribunal found unconstitutional forty of sixty statutes it reviewed (Schwartz 2000, 201–2). A simple legislative majority chooses the tribunal's members to nine-year terms it is likely that the tribunal will sometimes represent the government's coalition and at other times will represent the coalition of the previous government. This would suggest a wavelike pattern in court activism. In the early years the tribunal's rulings could be overturned by a two-thirds vote in the legislature, but in the 1997 constitution this is no longer stipulated (Rose-Ackerman 2004, 73). To overrule the court the legislature must either draft new legislation or revise the constitution, depending on the nature of the dispute.

In Hungary a group of round-table negotiators created a constitutional court in 1989, five months before the first legislative elections under the new post-communist regime.

---

[10] A large percentage of the "civil liberties cases" in Italy have involved the constitutionality of legislation enacted under Mussolini. Cole says that one-third of the first forty decisions of the court involved the constitutionality of laws and regulations of fascist vintage (Cole 1959, 980).

[11] For eight years the legislature failed to vote implementing legislation until it became clear that the Christian Democrats (DC) were consolidating their political strength (LaPalombara 1958; Volcansek 1999).

To prevent the incumbent government from dominating the court, members were to be appointed by a representative committee of the National Assembly, and approved by a two-thirds vote by the full legislature (Pogany 1993; Rose-Ackerman 2004, 76). In the early years of the new regime the court was active, striking down laws even before the first legislature began to sit. The legislature did not reappoint many of the first justices when their terms expired in 1998 and the new court has been more conservative about using natural law to decide cases where the constitution is ambiguous (Rose-Ackerman 2004, 80). It may be that the consolidation of coalition governments reduced the government's ability to organized legislative majorities to overturn bills.

In Russia, Yeltsin shut down in 1993 the constitutional court that parliament had established two years earlier, and later established one that would be easier for the president to manage. Instead of being elected by the Dumas, the court's nineteen members would be chosen by the president and approved by the Federation Council where the president has greater bargaining leverage (Remington 2002). Strong presidents have subsequently kept the court from functioning with much vigor.

In Korea, three constitutions between 1948 and 1987 paid lip service to judicial review, but the executive branch overpowered any attempts of the judiciary to exercise its constitutionally stated prerogatives. In 1988, following massive anti-government pro-tests that ended decades of autocratic rule, Korea adopted a constitutional court on the European model along with democratic reforms. There was widespread skepticism about the independence this court would exhibit, given that all nine justices are appointed by the president, though three of the nine must be from among nominees submitted by the National Assembly and three from among nominees submitted by the chief justice of the Supreme Court (West and Yoon 1992). The court seems to have understood its strategic location: it held unconstitutional fourteen of the thirty-seven pieces of legislation it reviewed between 1988 and 1991 but, as Yang notes, the court was self-restrained in dealing with politically charged cases (Yang 1993). Still the court's room for maneuver made the government uncomfortable, particularly as parties began alternating in power and the composition of the court became harder for the incumbent government to control. In the early 1990s the ruling party considered a constitutional amendment to curtail the jurisdiction of the court but backed down in the face of strong public objections.

As the apartheid regime in South Africa collapsed, a broad coalition supported judicial authority to protect political rights: not only the many whose rights had been infringed in the past, but also the outgoing whites who wanted to ensure themselves a soft political landing. In 1986, two years after declaring that a bill of rights would be inconsistent with the political tradition of the Afrikaaner, the minister of justice commissioned a study group on human rights. The 1994 constitution following the abolition of apartheid included strong provisions for judicial review (Hirschl 2000). A more representative group of judges eventually replaced the white male judges that sat on the first constitutional court. But the South African case shows that judicial powers may be strengthened not only at the instigation of newly empowered majorities, but also by outgoing governments who feel newly insecure.

The non-authoritarian cases: the legislative politics of minority protection. In some countries, such as France, Canada, and Israel, the constitutional role of courts was strengthened at the instigation of political actors who were, or expected soon to be, out of government and therefore for whom the political insulation from courts was no longer of value. As part of the minority, their interests more closely matched those of the public whose interest in constitutional protections may routinely be higher than those of the ruling government.

Post-Revolution France has oscillated between the attractions of legislative sovereignty and strong executive power, and has experimented periodically with its constitutional design to adjust the mix. The fifth Republic under Charles de Gaulle was meant to correct the problems of weak governments in the hands of unstable legislative majorities. Of judicial review, de Gaulle's opinion was that "Three things count in constitutional matters. First, the higher interest of the country… and of that I alone am judge." The other two constitutional matters for de Gaulle were political circumstances that had to be taken into account, and legalism, for which he reserved the greatest disdain (cited in Beardsley 1975, 212). The president, Assembly, and Senate each select three of the nine members of the court for nine-year terms, but the Gaullists in the early years of the fifth Republic controlled all three branches. The only way to invoke the Conseil's review powers was to appeal either to the president or to majority leaders of the parliament.

Charles de Gaulle left office in 1969 and in the hands of weaker administrations the provision for constitutional review took new shape. Once the Gaullists' legislative majority narrowed, space opened for the court to act with some autonomy. In 1971, in what is sometimes known as France's *Marbury* v. *Madison*, the court struck down a government bill that restricted freedom of political association (Morton 1988). More important was a 1974 amendment of Article 61 of the constitution, initiated by a government that saw the time was coming when it would be out of government. Passed by the requisite three-fifths legislative supermajority, the amendment extended the constitutional court's authority to rule on the constitutionality of a law upon petition by any sixty members of the National Assembly or Senate. Prior to that, only the president, the prime minister, the president of the Assembly, or the president of the Senate could refer a law to the court (Deener 1952). Since all four were usually members of the governing coalition, they were unlikely to submit one of their own laws for review. This amendment has increased the court's scope for action, as we will discuss later.

Israel's secular parties (Labor, Meretz, the Liberal Party's section of Likud, and others) established judicial review in Israel in 1992 after they had collectively lost legislative seat share in successive elections to religious and minority parties. The Shas Party alone, representing Orthodox religious residents of development towns and poor urban neighborhoods, increased its seat share from four Knesset seats in 1984 to ten in 1996 and to seventeen in 1999, making it the third largest party in the Knesset after Labor and Likud (Hirschl 2000, 109). The situation was much changed from 1949, when the Mapai, the precursor to the Labor Party representing secular middle-class voters, was an unchallenged ruling party and had no reason to delegate authority to the judiciary. The parties representing secular voters formed a coalition to establish a strong judicial oversight body that would protect their constituents' political and economic rights from encroachment by a shifting parliamentary majority (Hirschl 2000; Hofnung 1996).

4.5 Consequences: Judicial Politics in Constitutional Court Systems

What have constitutional courts done in practice, and how does their authority differ from that of supreme courts of the US type? Constitutional courts themselves vary in their scope not only by their enabling provisions but also inversely by the coherence of the political branch(es). Given supermajority rules that are typical for appointing members of constitutional courts and for changing constitutions, however, we would expect only extraordinary levels of parliamentary coherence to have an effect on constitutional court behavior.

The current French constitution, which combines presidentialism and parliamentarism, gives the court room for maneuver when the president does not control an extraordinarily large parliamentary coalition. Legislative minorities have made ample use of the amendment of 1974 that allows any group of sixty-one legislators to invite the court to review legislation. The socialists, who had opposed the amendment, regularly used the petition provision to oppose d'Estaing's government. by appealing its legislation to the Conseil. It was the conservatives' turn in the early 1980s when Mitterrand's government began trying to nationalize industries (Morton 1988). Upon appeal from parties on the right on behalf of shareholder constituents, the court's ruling added 28 percent to the government's cost of nationalization by requiring fuller compensation to the previous private owners than the government had intended (Stone 1992).

Even for coherent coalition governments, courts may have additional scope for action when the court's preferences are closer than the government's to those of the voting public's. In an argument similar to Susanne Lohmann's about how public opinion can increase the effective independence of the central bank, Vanberg (2001, forthcoming) notes that the German government is more likely to alter legislation in anticipation of a possible negative ruling of the constitutional court when its position is less popular and when the process is transparent.

5 MEASURING INDEPENDENCE EMPIRICALLY

The previous section provided a typological sketch of the workings of, and variation among, different types of judicial system, and considered some anecdotal evidence to check these claims. In this section we think about how propositions of the sort we have advanced might be tested empirically with greater rigor in future research.

As we noted earlier, one of the difficulties in grappling with the concept of judicial independence lies in measuring independence. We can identify various aspects of this concept—the ease with which a government can respond to a court ruling, for example, and the set of alternatives the government has for responding to this ruling—but identifying these aspects does not directly provide a measure that we could use in tests of independence. Furthermore, the various tools that governments can use in response to a court decision tend to exist in different combinations in different political systems, and it is not clear how much weight should be assigned to each of these tools.

What scholars can do, however, is to rely on surrogate measures. That is, rather than directly measuring independence by taking account of, and somehow adding up, its constitutive factors, we can look for a measure that reflects the behavior we would expect to find for different levels of independence. Two potential measures strike us as appropriate and useful. First, we can examine how often the court overturns the actions of the government. Second, we can examine court reactions to governmental attempts at nationalization. We consider each in turn, and then identify conditions under which these actions should be more likely to occur.

5.1 Overturning the Actions of Government

Political systems vary in the extent to which government can override judicial decisions and the ease with which governments can change the court's personnel. Both of these types of actions play an important role in establishing independence: to the extent that the government maintains dominance over the personnel on the court or can easily override its actions, we would expect to see fewer instances of the court behaving independently. And one indication that a court is behaving independently is that it is willing to overrule the government's actions. Consequently, one way to compare levels of independence across political systems is to see how often the court overturns govern-ment actions. More specifically, scholars can examine how often constitutional courts, or at least courts with constitutional powers (in countries that do not have separate constitutional courts), rule that laws passed by the government are unconstitutional.

There is, of course, a potential downside to such a measure. Courts will anticipate government reprisals; and to the extent that the court knows that the government will respond to and perhaps even push the court, it will not take actions that invite such reprisals. Put differently, in equilibrium, we might expect to find that the court never rules against the government.

While this is a valid criticism, studies of strategic anticipation have produced mixed results thus far—the jury is still out, so to speak. In one of the most comprehensive statistical examinations of this phenomenon, Segal (1997) found almost no evidence of judicial actors in the USA modifying their behavior in anticipation of future congressional actions. On the other hand, Bergara, Richman, and Spiller (2003), examining the same data, do find evidence that under certain conditions judicial actors do behave strategically by anticipating future overrides.

Rich case studies by Epstein and Knight (1998) reach a similar conclusion, as does an earlier statistical study by Spiller and Gely (1992).[12]

More importantly, two additional factors need to be taken into account. First, as we have already noted, the tools that government can use against the courts differ in severity. All impose some costs on courts, but some impose greater costs than others. Being fired, for example, is more costly than being overturned. Courts will then weigh the costs they might face against the potential benefits of reaching a policy outcome that they prefer. The ratio of these costs to these benefits is likely to be larger in political systems where the court has less independence, and smaller in countries where the courts have a great deal of independence.

Second, and related to the first point, it is possible that the court will make "mistakes" in assessing these costs and benefits and, in particular, in the likelihood of being punished for actions that it takes. Spatial models that operate under the assumption of complete information typically predict that the action being investigated will never occur— agencies never take actions that invite legislative reprisal, committees never introduce bills, and so on. At the same time, however, these models also can provide insights into the conditions under which the action in question might occur. Probably the best example of this can be found in Cameron's (2000) masterful examination of presidential vetoes in the USA Cameron begins his analysis with a perfect information model that, while providing other insights in the veto process, also predicts that, in equilibrium, vetoes will never occur, because the legislature and the president will perfectly anticipate each other's preferences and actions. He then shows how introducing uncertainty—over the location of the legislator who will be pivotal in overriding the veto, or on the president's preferences—can trigger vetoes.

In much the same way, uncertainty about the likelihood of reprisal can lead the court to underestimate the costs that it might face if it takes actions that oppose the government. If, for example, the court has a mistaken notion of the government's preferences, or if it underestimates the likelihood of government reprisals, we would expect it to be more likely to challenge the government. In effect, then, the court is making a mistake— had it known that the government would respond, and that the costs would exceed the benefits, it would not have acted. Mistakes, or uncertainty about reactions, are more likely to occur under some conditions than others, and we explore these conditions below. For now we just establish that because of this possibility, court actions overturning the government can serve as a useful measure of judicial independence.[13]

---

[12] Furthermore, numerous studies demonstrate that Congress does respond to judicial decisions (e.g. Eskridge 1991; Spiller and Tiller 1996).

[13] A significant literature in the USA focuses on the specific question of whether the Supreme Court is a partner with the elected branches of government or rather serves a counter-majoritarian function. The seminal paper in this area is Robert Dahl's (1957) "Decision-making in a democracy: the Supreme Court as a national policy-maker," in which he establishes that the Supreme Court rarely remains out of step with the other branches for very long, mainly because these other branches have the power to appoint members to the court. A long line of research has examined this question, sometimes supporting Dahl and sometimes reaching the opposite conclusion (e.g. Funston 1975; Gates 1992). Most recently, see Epstein, Knight, and Martin 2001 for how strategic behavior provides an alternative explanation for Dahl's conclusion. They argue that the Supreme Court is in step with other political actors not because of replacement, as Dahl suggested, but rather because Supreme Court justices make decisions strategically to ensure that they are not out of step.

5.2 Nationalizations

In addition to ruling on the constitutionality of laws passed by the government, courts are also called upon to rule on other actions that the government takes. One example of this occurs when the government nationalizes segments of the economy. The court can, if it chooses, strike down these actions. Particularly when the judges on the court are of different ideology, or party, or even outlook from the government—and to the extent that these judges are independent—we would expect that courts would be more likely to overturn these sorts of actions. Our knowledge of government coherence and institutional rules of court recomposition provide us with ex ante expectations of how much autonomy courts should have vis-à-vis the government. We think a fruitful line of empirical enquiry would be to see how well our expectations comport with how aggressive or quiescent courts were in protecting minority rights. How courts have responded to governments' nationalization schemes would be one such line of investigation. Again, courts may take such actions because they consider the benefits of doing so or because they have made mistakes in interpreting the preferences of other political actors. We turn next to an examination of when such mistakes will be likely to occur.

5.3 Elections and Independence

We have noted that to the extent that political actors all perfectly anticipate each other's actions, we should not expect to see any court decisions that run counter to the government's preferences. But we also argued that the court might make mistakes. It would seem useful, then, to identify the conditions under which these mistakes are most likely to occur.

Most obviously, courts are most likely to make mistakes when they are uncertain about the preferences of other governmental actors. Perhaps the highest levels of this sort of uncertainty occur right after an election, when new political actors take office. The court, accustomed to dealing with the previous political office holders, will be less certain about the exact preferences of the new politicians, and may also be uncertain about how far the new politicians will turn in order to punish the court. In other words, the courts will be uncertain about the potential costs that they will face.

Any election, of course, can increase uncertainty about preferences. But courts are more likely to be uncertain when an election leads to a major shift in party control of government. This can occur when a new party takes over in a single-majority system, with a left party being replace by one on the right, or vice versa; when an election brings new partners into a coalition; or when a shift occurs from divided to unified control of government. In any of these cases, there will be a period where the court is trying to figure out exactly what the government will or will not tolerate. And this uncertainty is likely to lead to more judicial actions that challenge the government. Hence, we should expect to find more instances of courts overturning governmental laws or ruling against nationalizations right after elections.

6 CONCLUSIONS

This essay has not attempted a comprehensive survey of the vast literatures on the nexus between politics and law, but has primarily focused instead on the narrower subject of judicial independence: what is it, how does it arise, and how do we know it when we see it? We have sketched out an argument for why judicial autonomy ought to relate inversely to the level of coherence in the political branch(es) of government, relative to the level of coherence needed to overturn the court's rulings.

Though this seems simple enough, it is harder than one might suppose to gauge judicial independence empirically because, if courts and legislatures anticipate the other's response in their own actions, there may be little conflict that erupts in public view. Without knowing the ideological position of the court or of the political coalition trying to hold judicial interference at bay, the absence of judicial findings against the government could mean either that the court had restrained itself rather than inviting legislative override, or that the legislature had incorporated the court's position in its laws rather than inviting a negative judicial ruling. In fact, if the actors have perfect information about the other's preferences and if they behaved strategically, we ought never to see legislative overrides and negative judicial rulings. One is reminded of the French constitutional court, which has explicitly incorporated consultation between the court and government with the result that laws include the anticipated reactions even before they are promulgated.

Although strategic anticipation certainly complicates empirical analysis, we nevertheless think it would be useful to take advantage of ideologically polarized or low-information situations, such as following new elections, to look for episodes of failed self-restraint. Even in France, Stone Sweet (1992) tells of conflicts between the constitutional council and the government in periods when members appointed by the previous government dominated the court. We might also expect that courts and governments might have relatively poorer information about the other's likely behavior following elections.

We have left many questions unanswered. Perhaps the most burning issue we have left on the table is what accounts for the national variation we observe in provisions for constitutional review in the first place. Political fragmentation seems to go far in explaining the correlation between divided governments and judicial autonomy. But why do some systems without particularly fragmented political systems establish constitutional courts, or for that matter, why do majorities in parliamentary systems without constitutional courts so often restrain themselves from infringing the rights of minorities? We are inclined to think that electoral competition, and the fear that majority coalitions have of losing support at the margins, is a common underpinning in the judicial politics of all democracies. Given the importance to judicial autonomy of insufficient legislative coherence for possible overrides, competitive elections are likely to be more fundamental than the trappings of "independent" courts for rule of law and minority protection in developing countries.

REFERENCES

ACKERMAN, B. 1997. The rise of world constitutionalism. *Virginia Law Review*, 83 (4): 771–97.

ADAMS, J. C., and BARILE, P. 1953. The implementation of the Italian constitution. *American Political Science Review*, 41 (1): 61–83.

BARROS, R. 2003. Dictatorship and the rule of law: rules and military power in Pinochet's Chile. In Maravall and Przeworski 2003: 188–220.

BARRY, B. 1975. Political accommodation and consociational democracy. *British Journal of Political Science*, 5 (4): 477–505.

BEARDSLEY, J. 1975. Constitutional review in France. *Supreme Court Review*, 189–259.

BEDNAR, J., ESKRIDGE, W. N., Jr., and FEREJOHN, J. 2001. A political theory of federalism. In *Constitutional Culture and Democratic Rule*, ed. J. Ferejohn, J. N. Rakove, and J. Riley. New York: Cambridge University Press.

BERGARA, M., RICHMAN, B., and SPILLER, P. 2003. Modeling Supreme Court strategic decision making: the congressional constraint. *Legislative Studies Quarterly*, 28: 247–80.

CAMERON, C. M. 2000. *Veto Bargaining*. New York: Cambridge University Press.

CHALMERS, D. 2000. The much ado about judicial politics in the UK: a statistical analysis of reported decisions of United Kingdom courts invoking EU law 1973–1998. MS. Harvard Law School.

CHAVEZ, R. B., FEREJOHN, J., and WEINGAST, B. 2004. A theory of the politically independent judiciary. MS.

CLINTON, R. L. 1994. Game theory, legal history, and the origins of judicial review: a revisionist analysis of Marbury v. Madison. *American Journal of Political Science*, 38: 285–302.

COLE, T. 1958. The West German Federal Constitutional Court: an evaluation after six years. *Journal of Politics*, 20 (2): 287–307.

—— 1959. Three constitutional courts: a comparison. *American Political Science Review*, 53 (4): 963–84.

DAHL, R. 1957. Decision-making in a democracy: the Supreme Court as a national policy-maker. *Journal of Public Law*, 6: 279–95.

DEENER, D. 1952. Judicial review in modern constitutional systems. *American Political Science Review*, 46 (4): 1079–99.

DE FIGUEIREDO, J., and TILLER, E. 1996. Congressional control of the courts: a theoretical and empirical analysis of expansion of the federal judiciary. *Journal of Law and Economics*, 39: 435–62.

DIAMOND, L. 1997. Consolidating democracy in the Americas. *Annals of the American Academy of Political and Social Science*, 550: 12–41.

DJANKOV, S., LA PORTA, R., LOPEZ-DE-SILANES, L., and SHLEIFER, A. 2003. Courts. *Quarterly Journal of Economics*, 118 (2): 453–517.

DYZENHAUS, D. 1998. Law as justification: Étienne Mureinik's conception of legal culture. *South African Journal on Human Rights*, 14: 11–37.

ELSTER, J. 1989. *Solomonic Judgements*. Cambridge: Cambridge University Press.

EPSTEIN, L., and KNIGHT, J. 1998. *The Choices Justices Make*. Washington, DC: CQ Press.

—— —— and MARTIN, A. 2001. The Supreme Court as a strategic national policy maker. *Emory Law Journal*, 50 (2): 583–611.

—— —— and SHVETSOVA, O. 2001. Comparing judicial selection systems. *William & Mary Bill of Rights Law Journal*, 10 (1): 7–36.

—— SEGAL, J. A., and VICTOR, J. N. 2002. Dynamic agenda setting on the U.S. Supreme Court: an empirical assessment. *Harvard Journal on Legislation*, 39 (2): 395–433.

ESKRIDGE, W. N., Jr. 1991. Overriding Supreme Court statutory interpretation decisions. *Yale Law Journal*, 101: 825–41.

—— and FEREJOHN, J. 1992. Theories of statutory interpretation and theories of legislatures.

FEREJOHN, J. 1999. Independent judges, dependent judiciary: explaining judicial independence. *Southern California Law Review*, 72: 353–84.

—— 2002. Judicializing politics, politicizing law. *Law and Contemporary Problems*, 65 (3): 41–68.

—— and ESKRIDGE, W. 1992. Making the deal stick. *Journal of Law, Economic and Organization*, 8 (1): 165–89.

—— and PASQUINO, P. 2003. Rule of democracy and rule of law. In Maravall and Przeworski 2003: 242–60.

—— —— 2004. Constitutional adjudication: lessons from Europe. *Texas Law Review*, 82: 1671–704.

—— and SHIPAN, S. 1990. Congressional influence on bureaucracy. *Journal of Law, Economics, and Organization*, 6: 1–21.

—— and WEINGAST, B. 1992. Limitation of statutes: strategic statutory interpretation. *Georgetown Law Journal*, 80: 565.

FOMBAD, C. M. 1998. The new Cameroonian Constitutional Council in a comparative perspective: progress or retrogression? *Journal of African Law*, 42 (2): 172–86.

FUNSTON, R. 1975. The Supreme Court and critical elections. *APSR* 69 (3): 795–811.

GATES, J. B. 1992. *The Supreme Court and Partisan Realignment: A Macro- and Microlevel Perspective*. Boulder, Colo.: Westview Press.

GRABER, M. 1993. The nonmajoritarian difficulty: legislative deference to the judiciary. *Studies in American Political Development*, 7: 35–73.

HALE, C. 2000. The civil law tradition and constitutionalism in twentieth century Mexico: the legacy of Emilio Rabasa. *Law and History Review*, 18 (2): 257–79.

HARDIN, R. 2003a. Why a constitution? In *The Federalist Papers and the New Institutionalism*, ed. B. Grofman and D. Witman. New York: Agathon.

—— 2003b. *Liberalism, Constitutionalism, and Democracy*. New York: Oxford University Press.

HELMKE, G. 2002. The logic of strategic defection: court–executive relations in Argentina under dictatorship and democracy. *American Political Science Review*, 96 (2): 291–304.

HIRSCHL, R. 2000. The political origins of judicial empowerment through constitutionalization: lessons from four constitutional revolutions. *Law and Social Inquiry*, 25: 91–149.

HOFNUNG, M. 1996. The unintended consequences of unplanned constitutional reform: constitutional politics in Israel. *American Journal of Comparative Law*, 44 (4): 585–604.

HOLMES, S. 2003. Lineages of the rule of law. In Maravall and Przeworski 2003: 19–61.

IARYCZOWER, M., SPILLER, P., and TOMMASI, M. 2002. Judicial independence in unstable environments: Argentina, 1935–1998. *American Journal of Political Science*, 46 (4): 669–706.

JACKSON, R., ATKINSON, M., and HART, K. 1977. Constitutional conflict in France: deputies' attitudes toward executive–legislative relations. *Comparative Politics*, 9 (4): 399–419.

KELSEN, H. 1942. Judicial review of legislation: a comparative study of the Austrian and the American constitution. *Journal of Politics*, 4 (1): 183–200.

KERMAN, D., and MAHONEY, P. 2004. The value of judicial independence: evidence from 18th century England. Social Science Research Network Paper. **http://ssrn.com/abstract=495642**

KNIGHT, J., and EPSTEIN, L. 1996. On the struggle for judicial supremacy. *Law and Society Review*, 30 (1): 87–120.

LANDES, W., and POSNER, R. 1975. The independent judiciary in an interest-group perspective. *Journal of Law and Economics*, 18 (3): 875–901.

LAPALOMBARA, J. 1958. Political party systems and crisis government: French and Italian contrasts. *Midwest Journal of Political Science*, 2 (2): 117–42.

LARKINS, C. 1996. Judicial independence and democratization: a theoretical and conceptual analysis. *American Journal of Comparative Law,* 44 (4): 605–26.

—— 1998. The judiciary and delegative democracy in Argentina. *Comparative Politics,* 30 (4): 423–42.

MCCUBBINS, M., and SCHWARTZ, T. 1984. Congressional oversight overlooked: police patrols versus fire alarms. *American Journal of Political Science,* 28: 165–79.

MAJONE, G. 2001. Two logics of delegation: agency and fiduciary relations in EU governance. *European Union Politics,* 2 (1): 103–72.

MARAVALL, J. M., and PRZEWORSKI, A. 2003. *Democracy and the Rule of Law.* Cambridge: Cambridge University Press.

MATTEI, U. 1997. Three patterns of law: taxonomy and change in the world's legal systems. *American Journal of Comparative Law,* 45 (1): 5–44.

MERRYMAN, J. H., and VIGORITI, V. 1966–7. When courts collide: constitution and cassation in Italy. *American Journal of Comparative Law,* 15 (4): 665–86.

MEZEY, S. 1983. Civil law and common law traditions: judicial review and legislative supremacy in West Germany and Canada. *International and Comparative Law Quarterly,* 32 (3): 689–707.

MORASKI, B. J., and SHIPAN, C. R. 1999. The politics of Supreme Court nominations: a theory of institutional constraints and choices. *American Journal of Political Science,* 43 (4): 1069–95.

MORTON, F. L. 1988. Judicial review in France: a comparative analysis. *American Journal of Comparative Law,* 36 (1): 89–110.

NORTH, D. C., and WEINGAST, B. R. 1989. Constitutions and commitment: the evolution of institutions governing public choice in 17th century England. *Journal of Economic History,* 49: 803–32.

OLOWOFOYEKU, A. A. 1989. The beleaguered fortress: reflections of the independence of Nigeria's judiciary. *Journal of African Law,* 33 (1): 55–71.

PIZZORUSSO, A. 1990. Italian and American models of the judiciary and of judicial review of legislation: a comparison of recent tendencies. *American Journal of Comparative Law,* 38 (2): 373–86.

POGANY, I. 1993. Constitutional reform in Central and Eastern Europe: Hungary's transition to democracy. *International and Comparative Law Quarterly,* 42 (2): 332–55.

PRZEWORSKI, A. 2003. Why do political parties obey results of elections? In Maravall and Przeworski 2003: 114–44.

RAMSEYER, J. M. 1994. The puzzling (in)dependence of courts: a comparative approach. *Journal of Legal Studies,* 23: 721–47.

—— and RASMUSEN, E. 1997. Judicial independence in a civil law regime: the evidence from Japan. *Journal of Law, Economics, and Organization,* 13 (2): 259–87.

—— and ROSENBLUTH, F. 1993. *Japan's Political Marketplace.* Cambridge, Mass.: Harvard University Press.

REMINGTON, T. F. 2002. *Politics in Russia.* New York: Longman.

ROGERS, J. 2001. Information and judicial review: a signaling game of legislative–judicial interaction. *American Journal of Political Science,* 45 (1): 84–99.

—— and VANBERG, G. 2002. Judicial advisory opinions and legislative outcomes in comparative perspective. *American Journal of Political Science,* 46 (2): 379–97.

ROSE-ACKERMAN, S. 1995. *Controlling Environmental Policy.* New Haven: Yale University Press.

—— 2004. From elections to democracy: building accountable government in Hungary and Poland. MS. Forthcoming from Cambridge University Press.

SAJO, A. 1995. Reading the invisible constitution: judicial review in Hungary. *Oxford Journal of Legal Studies,* 15 (2): 253–67.

SALZBERGER, E. 1993. A positive analysis of the doctrine of separation of powers, or: why do we have an independent judiciary? *International Review of Law and Economics*, 13: 340–79.

—— and FENN, P. 1999. Judicial independence: some evidence from the English Court of Appeal. *Journal of Law and Economics*, 42: 831–47.

SCHANCK, P. 1990. The only game in town: an introduction to interpretive theory, statutory construction, and legislative histories. *Kansas Law Review*, 38: 815.

SCHWARTZ, H. 2000. *The Struggle for Constitutional Justice in Post-Communist Europe*. Chicago: University of Chicago Press.

SEGAL, J. A. 1997. Separation-of-powers games in the positive theory of Congress and courts. *American Political Science Review*, 91: 28–44.

SHAPIRO, M. 2002. Judicial delegation doctrines: the U.S., Britain, and France. *West European Politics*, 25 (1): 173–99.

SHIPAN, C. R. 1997. *Designing Judicial Review: Interest Groups, Congress, and Communications Policy*. Ann Arbor: University of Michigan Press.

—— 2000. The legislative design of judicial review: a formal analysis. *Journal of Theoretical Politics*, 12 (3): 269–304.

SMITH, J. L. Forthcoming. Congress opens the courthouse doors: statutory changes to judicial review under the Clean Air Act. *Political Research Quarterly*.

SPILLER, P., and TILLER, E. 1996. Invitations to override: Congressional reversals of Supreme Court decisions. *International Review of Law & Economics*, 16 (4): 503–21.

—— and GELY, R. 1992. Congressional control or judicial independence: the determinants of U.S. Supreme Court labor-relations decisions, 1949–1988. *Rand Journal of Economics*, 23: 463–92.

STONE, A. 1992. *The Birth of Judicial Politics in France: The Constitutional Council in Comparative Perspective*. Oxford: Oxford University Press.

STONE SWEET, A. 1992. *The Birth of Judicial Politics in France*. New York: Oxford University Press.

TATE, C. N. 1993. Courts and crisis regimes: a theory sketch with Asian case studies. *Political Studies Quarterly*, 46 (2): 311–38.

—— and HAYNIE, S. L. 1993. Authoritarianism and the functions of courts: a time series analysis of the Philippine Supreme Court, 1961–1987. *Law and Society Review*, 27 (4): 707–40.

VANBERG, G. 1998. Abstract judicial review, legislative bargaining, and policy compromise. *Journal of Theoretical Politics*, 30 (3): 299–326.

—— 2001. Legislative–judicial relations: a game-theoretic approach to constitutional review. *American Journal of Political Science*, 45 (2): 346–61.

—— Forthcoming. *Prudent Jurists: Constitutional Politics in Germany*. New York: Cambridge University Press.

VAN KOPPEN, P. J. 1990. The Dutch Supreme Court and parliament: political decisionmaking versus nonpolitical appointments. *Law and Society Review*, 24 (3): 745–80.

VOLCANSEK, M. L. 1999. *Constitutional Politics in Italy*. Basingstoke: Palgrave.

WEINGAST, B. 2003. A postscript to political foundations of democracy and the rule of law. In Maravall and Przeworski 2003: 109–13.

WEST, J., and YOON, D. K. 1992. The Constitutional Court of the Republic of Korea: transforming the jurisprudence of the vortex? *American Journal of Comparative Law*, 40 (1): 73–119.

WIDNER, J. 2001. Courts and democracy in postconflict transitions: a social scientist's perspective on the African case. *American Journal of International Law*, 95 (1): 64–75.

YANG, K. 1993. Judicial review and social change in the Korean democratizing process. *American Journal of Comparative Law*, 41 (1): 1–8.

CHAPTER 31

FEDERALISM

PABLO BERAMENDI

WIDELY regarded as the solution to the problems of enlarging governments, the attractions of federalism seem to never fade away. Discussions about the allocation of power across levels of government have been at the forefront of political analysis since the dawn of modernity. And they continue to be as European democracies struggle with the scope of the process of integration, whereas state-building processes are in progress in Iraq and Afghanistan. Meanwhile, an increasing share of the world's population lives under federal rule, making ever more truthful Riker's old assessment that we live in an *age of federalism*. Along the way, decentralization of political authority has managed to keep some pedigree as a way of promoting economic prosperity and democratic governance around the world. Yet, under this appearance of unwavering attention, the understanding of the origins and workings of federalism has been subject to profound transformations, ultimately reflecting shifts of similar magnitude in the scholarly approach to the subject.

The time when comparative works on federalism were seen as "few in number and spotty in quality" (Riker 1964, 157) is long gone. Back in those days, the field was primarily made of legal analyses of constitutional designs.[1] Based on the premiss that constitutions shape and steer the life of nations, this line of work was pretty blind to the realities of politics. Today's analyses are anchored on the opposite prior. Constitutions, much like business contracts, "do not spell out the rules and procedures to be followed in every conceivable instance in precise detail" (Dixit 1997, 20). As a

* I thank Srikrishna Ayyangar, Kelly Bogart, Alberto Diaz-Cayeros, Jonathan Rodden, Mary Santy, Brian Taylor, Erik Wibbels, and the editors of this volume for their help, comments, and/or suggestions on previous versions of this chapter. All remaining errors are my responsibility.

[1] Examples of this type of approach to federalism include Wheare (1946); Bowie and Friedrich (1954); Livingston (1956); McWhinney (1962).

result, they are rewritten, manipulated by political actors who weight their preferences against the political realities of the time (Seabright 1996).

Between these two extremes, triggered by Riker's seminal contribution, the comparative politics of federalism has come a long way. The legal, and rather fragmented, analysis of constitutions has given in to a more comparative focus on different aspects of the functioning of federations. Politics has taken center stage. Similarly, the analysis of strategic interactions and their implications for the origins, evolution, and consequences of federations is clearly taking over more conventional and descriptive accounts. In the context of the economic turn in comparative politics (Levi 2000), the study of federalism has benefited from the *checks and balances* that economists and political scientists have imposed on one another. While economic models have brought to the field a much needed taste for theoretical and analytical rigor, comparativists of all kinds are adding intellectual value by shrinking the gap between theoretical premises and the stubbornness of facts. Along the way, political economists have balanced normative concerns with a more positive approximation to federal realities, shifting attention from the optimal to the actual design of federations (Rodden 2006*b*).

This chapter offers a necessarily partial review of the evolution, dominating themes, and pending tasks awaiting the comparative politics of federalism. The essay unfolds around one basic premiss, borrowed from rational choice institutionalism (Shepsle 1986). The study of institutions divides into (and combines) two levels of analysis: "In the first, analysts study the effects of institutions. In the second, analysts study why institutions take particular forms, why they are needed, why they survive" (Weingast 2002, 661). In line with this logic, the first section of the essay delimits federalism as an institution. The second section pays particular attention to the impact of federalism on democracy and the workings of the economy. Once the reasons why political actors should care about federalism have been outlined, the essay turns to the analysis of federalism as an endogenous institution, namely to the conditions under which federalism is more likely to emerge and survive. This section also brings up a number of methodological considerations on the comparative study of the origins and consequences of federalism. Finally, the essay concludes with a methodological note for caution and a discussion of the challenges that lie ahead of the field.

1 Delimiting Federalism

Federalism is a specific form of fragmentation of political power. The existence of several levels of government is a necessary, yet insufficient, condition for federalism to exist, as every state is articulated around some vertical hierarchy among different levels of government. What distinguishes federations from unitary states, unions, or confederations is the particular way in which this hierarchy is organized. In unitary states, regional or provincial officials do not have constitutional status as effective actors in a bargaining process with the center. They lack control over power or resources, and therefore have no capacity to give or take in their interaction with the center. Collective choices in a unitary state are set by whatever version of the will of the majority of citizens is produced by the electoral system. In turn, unions are "polities compounded in such a way that the constituent units preserve their respective integrities, primarily or exclusively, through the common organs of the general government, rather than through dual government structures" (Watts 1999, 11). New Zealand or pre-1993 Belgium would constitute examples of this.

As opposed to unions or unitary states, federations and confederations show an architecture of government with dual structures, driven by a process of bargaining between a number of constituent units and a center.[2] The two of them face a similar dilemma, namely how to address the combination of *self-rule* and *shared-rule* (Elazar 1987). Yet, they offer clearly distinctive solutions. Confederations emerge when constituent units join efforts to create a common government that has very limited and well-defined powers and is fiscally and electorally dependent on them. Fiscal dependence implies that the common government lacks its own fiscal base, whereas electoral dependence refers to the fact that the members of the central government are delegates of the constituent units. The United States during the period 1776–89 or the evolving European Union are two relevant examples. In contrast, the balance of power between the center and the units is substantially different in federations. In a federal system, both constituent units and the central government have constitu-tionally recognized autonomous powers to interact directly with citizens (Dahl 1983; Watts 1999). Riker defined federalism as "a political organization in which the activities of government are divided between regional governments and a central government in such a way that each kind of government has some activities on which it makes final decisions" (Riker 1975, 101). The autonomy of these two levels of government is effectively guaranteed, normally through a formal statement in the constitution and the existence of a strong judicial review system. In addition, both the center and the regions have their own fiscal bases and are directly accountable through elections. As a result, central governments in federations (as opposed to confederations) enjoy a much stronger institutional position vis-à-vis subnational governments.

While a cursory overview of existing federations reveals that national governments have more power than subnational ones, the latter are far from powerless. Thus, the question still remains as to how to strike a balance between them, i.e., how to organize *shared rule* in the presence of two strong, directly elected, levels of government. Beneath this question lies the fundamental dilemma of federalism: how to devise a set of institutions that reconcile the ability of centralized government to create economies of scale and overcome the collective action problem in certain

---

[2] It goes without saying that these negotiations (and their outcomes) require a set of guarantees that are only effective in the context of democratic regimes (Dahl 1983).

realms, and the capacity to deal with the specifics of local issues (and the informational asymmetries associated with them) in others? Granting too much power to
subnational units might jeopardize the former, whereas having too strong a central
government might jeopardize the latter. This tension was already visible in the
Federalist and the *Anti-Federalist* papers. After describing the calamities emerging
from the ill-designed constitution of United Netherlands, in which "in all important
cases not only the provinces, but the cities must be unanimous" (Federalist XX, 105),
Madison and Hamilton move on to argue that strong state governments, holding
veto powers across policy fields, bring about "contemptible compromises of the
public good" (Federalist XXII: 118).[3] In their view, there was little doubt that any
activity involving externalities across states (such as revenue collection, defense,
commerce regulations) was better handled by a properly empowered union government. In turn, the Anti-Federalist expressed the opposite fear, namely that too strong
a center was likely to usurp the power of the states, thereby eliminating the advantages of allowing "decision based on local knowledge" (Ketcham 1986).

In solving this tension, federations vary a great deal, both in terms of the set of
institutions and procedures that rule the interaction between levels of government
and the nature of the specific agreements between the center and the units, as
reflected by the levels of decentralization in different policy fields. The former are
set constitutionally and tend to be more stable and consequential than assumed by
approaches exclusively based on actors' preferences. The latter are better understood
as *congealed tastes* (Riker 1980), and are more amenable to change over time. Table
31.1 and Figures 31.1 and 31.2 illustrate this variation. In terms of the institutions
mediating the interaction between levels of government, I focus on second chambers
and different aspects of the party system. In terms of decentralization across policy
fields, I include a number of indicators of fiscal decentralization.

An important source of variation among federations is the way in which regional
interests are represented at the national level. While some countries rely upon territorial
upper chambers (USA), others make use of regularly timed conferences between the
executives (Canada) or even more informal, less structured agreements (Watts 1999;
Swenden 2004). As reflected in Table 31.1, some second chambers are directly elected
(Brazil, USA), providing a more direct representation of local constituencies, while
others are indirectly appointed by regional incumbents (Germany, Austria), thereby
facilitating a stronger influence of national political parties. Moreover, while some
upper chambers have strong powers to reshape the democratic majority (USA, Brazil),
others enjoy much more limited political capabilities (India, Spain). Federations also
differ in the extent to which national leaders are able to control the tendency of regional
incumbents to maximize the promotion of local interests. Riker (1964, 1975) distinguished between centralized (or maximum) and peripheralized (or minimum) feder-
alisms depending on the role attributed to the rulers of the federation. Figure 31.1 displays
a simplified version of Riker's index of party centralization that illustrates the differences

---

[3] For an illustration of the benefits associated with centralized policy, see Hamilton's defense of
concentrating the taxation of imports at the union level (Federalist XII, 64).

Table 31.1 Federal diversities: an overview

	Expenditure decentralization 1998–2000	Revenue decentralization 1998–2000	Vertical imbalance 1998–2000	Borrowing autonomy by subnational governments	Upper House
Argentina	42.26	39.86	–	4	Indirectly elected by local chambers until 2001. There-after, directly elected
Australia	44.40	33.21	37.7	2.5	Directly elected
Austria	31.10	24.36	34.9	1.6	Indirect election: elected by state legislatures: weighted representation
Belgium	11.03	5.79	53.6		Mixed representation: combination of directly elected, indirectly elected by linguistic councils and co-opted senators
Brazil	42.8	33.7	35.1	4.5	Direct election
Canada	58.73	52.28	20.07	2.7	Appointed: by federal government, equal representation or provinces
Germany	37.54	30.9	22.31	2.5	Indirectly elected
India	45.22	33.0	36.11	2.5	Indirect election: elected by state legislatures: weighted representation
Mexico	29.4	22.8	35.4	2.6	Direct election at the state (3 per state) level with a limited number (32) of seats selected through national proportional representation
Nigeria	29.1	20.4	–	1	Direct election
Spain	32.40	19.3	54.15	2.5	Mixed representation. About 80% elected; 20% appointed. Note, however, that senators are elected along party lines
Switzerland	46.90	43.2	24.06	3	Direct election
USA	48.61	41.6	30.99	3	Direct election

Sources: World Bank-IMF Fiscal Decentralization Database (http://www1.worldbank.org/publicsector/decentralization/fiscalindicators.htm); Rodden 2004; Watts 1999; Arzaghi and Henderson 2005.

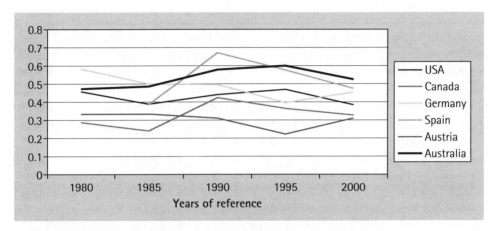

Fig. 31.1 Party centralization in six advanced federations (period averages)

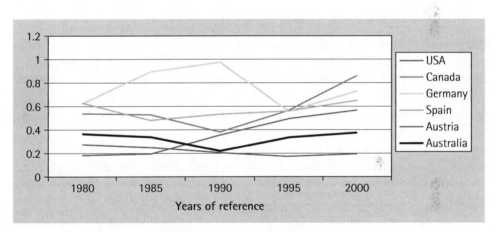

Fig. 31.2 Effective number of parties in six advanced federations: average regional deviations from national level (period averages)
Source: Author's calculations on the basis of national sources data.

in levels and trends in six advanced federations.[4] More recently, scholars have abandoned this simple dichotomy, which is based on the particular experiences of the United States, to recognize the multidimensional character of the articulation of federations (Stepan 1999). In particular, Riker's index does not tell much about how specific the patterns of political competition are in different parts of the federation. This speaks to the issue of electoral externalities. If the basic structure of political competition is similar across levels of government and electoral externalities are large, regional leaders

[4] The index is defined as the share of regional governments controlled by the same party or coalition of parties that controls the federal government.

have incentives to trade some of their local interest for a share of the political rewards to be obtained at the national level. Alternatively, the more specific the nature of political competition at the regional level, the smaller the electoral externalities will be, and therefore, the more costly it becomes to compromise with the promotion of local interests.

The issue of how to measure the scope of these externalities is still unresolved. Figure 31.2 displays an admittedly imperfect measure, based on the assumption that the *effective number of parties* (ENP, as defined in Lijphart 1999) is a reliable indicator of the structure of political competition in any given electoral unit. Figures reflect the following calculation. For each region, I first calculate the absolute value of the difference between the ENP at the regional and the federal levels. Then, the value of the distance is averaged across the regions. If the value of the index is zero or close to zero, the structure of political competition is taken to be similar across the different regions and the center. In turn, the higher the value of the index, the more diverse the electoral processes at different levels of government.[5] Again, a good deal of cross-sectional and over-time variation is observable among federations.

Finally, a third dimension of variation concerns the distribution of authority across policy fields. Table 31.1 presents a few indicators on fiscal decentralization.[6] The borrowing capacity of regions varies substantially across federations, as do the levels of expenditure and revenues decentralization. On the latter, it is important to note how similar levels of revenue decentralization mask different levels of fiscal subnational autonomy, captured indirectly by the varying degree of vertical fiscal imbalance in federations. Moreover, there is a good deal of over-time variation. For most of the twentieth century tax centralization was the dominant trend among federal democracies (Diaz-Cayeros 2004). Yet several of these federations have reversed the trend since the late 1970s, undertaking non-negligible processes of devolution of tax authority (Rodden 2004). To complicate matters further, fiscal centralization does not necessarily coincide with the centralization of policy authority, particularly in those fields in which the interaction between levels of government is done through regulatory policies (Falleti 2005; Hooghe and Marks 2003; Kelemen 2004; Rodden 2004; Schneider 2003).[7] As a result, in a context in which clear-cut distributions of authority are the exception rather than the rule,

---

[5] This indicator is open to obvious shortcomings. Suppose that two regions have a similar ENP, but only one of them has a strong nationalist party. Obviously, the nature of political competition is going to be very different in each of them. To overcome this and other limitations, Rodden and Wibbels (2005) have recently proposed to measure electoral externalities through the partial association between the support received by federal parties in national elections and the support these same parties obtain in regional elections.

[6] Expenditure (revenue) decentralization are defined as the percentage of subnational government's expenditures (revenues) out of total government expenditures (revenues). In turn, the vertical imbalance represents the degree to which subnational governments rely on transfers from the central government to finance their expenditures. Finally, the scale for borrowing autonomy captures the scope of the limitations by central governments on subnational borrowing. It ranges between 1 and 5. For sources and details, see Rodden (2004).

[7] For an innovative analysis of the distribution of regulatory powers in federations, see Kelemen (2003).

"there is no mechanical means of totting up the numbers and importance of areas of action in which either kind of government is independent of the other" (Riker 1975).

Regarding changes over time, party centralization and policy decentralization suggest that the observable equilibria between the center and the units are necessarily unstable (Bednar 2001). As Rufus Davis (1978) put it, "at best the federal compact can only be a formalized transaction of a moment in the history of a particular community." In sum, federalism constitutes a complex reality in constant flux, quite distant from the clean, binary world suggested by merely formal or constitutional typologies. As we shall see in the rest of this chapter, the history of the comparative politics of federalism is to a large extent the history of a rediscovery of these complexities as the key to a better understanding of the workings of federations, as well as the conditions under which they constitute a viable institutional choice. The next section develops this point in detail by focusing on the literature involving the political and economic consequences of federalism.

2 THE IMPACT OF FEDERALISM: COPING WITH DISILLUSION

Federalism does make a difference. It alters the set of options and constraints faced by political actors at two different levels of government, thereby modifying actors' political preferences, as well as the overall structure of incentives (Rose-Ackerman 1981). The real issue is what kind of difference federalism makes. Interestingly, had we been confronted with this question two decades ago the task would have been rather simple. Under the lead of welfare economists or public choice theorists, the answer would have read as follows: federalism breeds better democracy, better bureaucracies, and better markets. In contrast, today's answer is far less cheerful. A cumulative body of empirical and theoretical research suggests that the old expectations constituted, at least partially, a *federal illusion*. Nowadays, it is clear that the political and economic effects of federalism are complex, multidimensional, often contingent on a number of other factors, and by no means always positive. As a result, it is far less straightforward to establish what the actual consequences of federalism are. Paradoxically, this reflects a good deal of progress in a field that has been able to part ways with highly stylized, mostly normative, models of federalism to engage into a positive reconsideration of how federations actually work. In turn, this new wave of positive analyses is providing the building blocks for a much longed for, and not yet achieved, articulation of a general theory of the origins and performance of federations.

The new comparative literature on federalism is voluminous. Political scientists and economists have joined forces to produce a very rich body of research that revolves around one major theme: when it comes to the political and economic consequences of federalism, the evil is in the details. By details I refer both to the specifics of the institutional design and to the surrounding economic and social circumstances. The remainder of this section brings to task the *federal illusion* by reviewing the main contributions of the comparative politics of federalism. I will concentrate first on the relationship between federalism and democracy; thereafter I address the issue of institutional stability and the notion that federalism improves the workings of bureaucracies and markets.

2.1 Federalism and Democracy

Classical theorists commend federalism for its ability to accommodate communities of different political taste and protect political liberties at the same time. Echoing Hamilton, Madison, and Jay, Tocqueville (1835/1964) celebrated federalism as a system "created with the intention of combining the different advantages which result from the magnitude and littleness of nations." In *Democracy in America* he linked protection against foreign threats to the former and a government in which "all the efforts and resources of the citizens are turned to the internal well-being of the community" to the latter. In limiting the sovereignty of the Union, federalism would prevent large-scale governments from imposing the "tyranny of the majority" upon political liberty and good governance. Because of these two characteristics, federalism is often regarded as a facilitating condition for the establishment and duration of democracy in large, heterogeneous nations.

However, a systematic overview of the fate of large-scale, democratic federations provides a mixed picture, posing a more general, and still unresolved, set of puzzles: under what conditions does federalism facilitate democracy? Under what conditions does federalism help integrate ethnic, linguistic, or religious divides? Recent assessments range from moderate optimism to outright skepticism.[8]

Linz (1997) argues for a clear distinction between those cases in which state institutions and rule of law are consolidated before the transition to democracy begins and those in which they are not. In the former, the pre-existence of a federal structure fosters, rather than prevents, conflict, violence, and regime failure. In the latter, federalism would display its capacity to accommodate contending national identities. After coordinating a large comparison across federations, both advanced and developing, Amoretti and Bermeo (2004) lean to conclude that federalist arrangements facilitate successful accommodation. Yet, in the same volume, Bunce (2004) shows that, in the subset of post-communist regimes, democracies emerging in a pre-existing federal setting tend to be more vulnerable to the secessionist pressures of pre-existing groups. Several possible explanations have been offered to account for these differences. Bermeo (2004) suggests that federations that remain as a legacy of authoritarian regimes are less successful than federations emerging from a contractual agreement. In turn, Stepan (2001) points to the

---

[8] For earlier, generally skeptical, treatments of these issues, see Duchacek (1970); Riker and Lemco (1987); Lemco (1991).

internal articulation of power within federations. The higher the institutional leverage given to already mobilized ethnic minorities, the lower the likelihood that federations are able to prevent territorial disintegration.[9]

While suggestive, these explanations are applicable to a small subset of cases. In one of the few quantitative studies in the field, Roeder (2000) takes the most optimistic views to task. On the basis of information for 132 countries and 632 ethnic groups for the period 1955 to 1994, Roeder comes to conclude that both symmetrical and asymmetrical forms of federalism "lead to significant increases in the likelihood of ethno-national crises." Yet, further case study evidence continues to show that the specifics of how federations are designed account for their ability to contain conflict and prevent disintegration (Hale 2004; Filippov, Ordeshook, and Shvetsova 2004; Stepan 2001; Treisman 1999). Overall, the sharp contrast between different kinds of evidence suggests that the analysis of the relationship between federalism and democracy would benefit from reallocating research efforts to the theorization of processes through which federalism produces different outcomes.

How does federalism shape the incentives and strategist of reformist leaders? In turn, how does democracy affect the interaction between regional and central incumbents? How do alternative federal designs respond when multiple cleavages are politically relevant? And finally, how do alternative federal designs feed back into the incentives of different subnational groups to politicize cultural, ethnic, religious, or income differences (Fearon and Van Houten 2002)?

Recent developments in Russia and Iraq are making these questions ever more pressing. A number of scholars are focusing on the relationship between income inequality, federalism, and democracy. Boix (2003) has recently argued that insofar as it decentralizes the control over redistribution, federalism facilitates the survival of democracies with high levels of inter-regional income inequality. In turn, Hug (2005) focuses on the implications of income disparities for federal stability. A second group of scholars have focused on issues of institutional design in transitioning societies. Taylor (2005) addresses the issue of stability in hybrid federal democracies, where the conventional stabilizing mechanisms (political parties, courts) are yet to be institutionalized. Taylor points to the control over coercive power as an overlooked dimension whose organization bears importance on federal stability. Myerson (2006) focuses on electoral sequences, arguing that holding local elections first facilitates the selection of better (i.e., more responsive, less corrupted) leaders at the national level, thereby helping create a better democracy. In contrast, Filippov and Shvetsova (2005) use the Russian experience to suggest the existence of a tradeoff between federalism and democracy: in societies in transition, an ill-functioning democracy is a prerequisite for territorial integration. Local elites will contribute to stability insofar as they can keep extracting rents. Thus, as soon as political competition becomes effective, territorial integration is in peril.

---

[9] Within this framework the existence of a polity-wide (*demos enabling*) party system, able to hold the different units together throughout the transition and consolidation processes, is regarded as particularly important.

While these contributions shed light on some of the mechanisms driving the relationship between federalism and democracy, there is much to be learned about how different federal designs affect the preferences, incentives, and strategies of actors divided along multiple dimensions before any consensus is to emerge. This is particularly true in those societies in which both federalism and democracy are the object of institutional changes. Clearly, the big picture is yet to be painted.

2.2 Federalism and the Economy: towards a new consensus?

The implications of federalism for the adoption and stability of democratic regimes constitute just one aspect of the high hopes theorists put on federal institutions. As a matter of fact, the bulk of the federal illusion lies elsewhere. During the years of pluralist hegemony, the study of political institutions was not at the top of the research agenda in comparative politics. Indeed, Riker himself declared that insofar as institutions were a mere reflection of the underlying preferences in society, there was little reason to expect meaningful effects of federalism on public policy. Public economists felt differently, and in their quest to establish the optimal design of the public sector proceeded to fill the gap.

Welfare economics and Public Choice theory, while anchored on opposite, yet equally ideological assumptions, came to reinvigorate the *federal illusion*. Welfare economists were concerned mostly with market failures and the problem of externalities. In sharp contrast, public choice theorists were concerned with public sector failures and how to control the predatory, rent-seeking behavior of public officials. And yet, they came to similar conclusions about the economic benefits of federalism. For *welfare economists* (Musgrave 1997; Gramlich 1973, 1987; Oates 1972, 1991, 1999; Wildasin 1991), a decentralized institutional design works towards the goal of an optimum allocation of resources by ensuring a better fit between preferences, needs, and policies and by facilitating experimentation and innovation. Within this framework, factor mobility operates primarily as a factor of preference revelation for welfare-maximizing incumbents.[10] In turn, for *public choice theorists* (Brennan and Buchanan 1980; Buchanan 1995, 19–27; Inman and Rubinfield 1997a, 73–105; Qian and Weingast 1997, 83–92; Weingast 1993, 286–311; 1995, 1–31; Weingast, Montinola, and Qian 1995, 50–81), federalism is *market friendly* because it restrains the predatory nature of the public sector. Within this framework, factor mobility operates as a factor constraining government's predatory tendencies. By allowing voters and factors to vote with their feet across jurisdictions, federalism facilitates a better monitoring of incumbents by markets and voters.[11] As a result,

---

[10] Provided that the demand for local public services is income elastic, that these services are financed by income taxes (Oates 1972, 1991) and that there is perfect mobility, Tiebout's model predicts that communities become homogeneous in income and heterogeneous in capacities. For a critical evaluation of the benefits and shortcomings of these assumptions, see Stiglitz (1983, 17–55); Rose-Ackerman (1983, 55–85); Bewley (1981, 713–40); Zodrow (1983); Panizza (1999, 97–139).

[11] The relationship between mobility and redistribution in federal systems is a field of its own. For a more detailed treatment on the subject, see Peterson and Rom (1990); Epple and Romer (1991); Glatzer and Konrad (1994); Oates and Schwab (1988); Lejour and Verbon (1996); Christiansen, Hagen, and Sandmo (1994).

corruption is less likely to occur, the public sector is smaller (Prud'homme 1995), and markets work more efficiently. In sum, both streams of public economic theory provided the grounds for a revival of the *federal illusion* that thrived across academic departments, national governments, and international organizations.

Alas, reality did not follow suit (Rodden and Rose-Ackermann 1997). A systematic overview of the economic record of federations suggests a more complex set of empirical regularities. Federations in developing countries appear to be systematically associated with mismanagement, overspending, and market failures rather than with the virtuous properties spelled out by normative public economists (Wibbels 2000; Ziblatt and O'Dwyer forthcoming). At the other end of the spectrum, advanced federations, such as the USA or Switzerland, are vindicated as illustrations of the positive effects of federal institutions. Moreover, it is by no means clear that federalism per se leads to less redistribution (Pierson 1995; Beramendi 2003; Obinger, Leibfried, and Castles 2005).

The observable differences across federations in terms of economic performance and distribution reflect a large gap between the implicit assumptions about politics and institutions underpinning political-economic models and the actual behavior of regional and federal governments in federations (Rodden 2006; Srinivasan and Wallack forthcoming; Treisman forthcoming; Wibbels 2005a). To be sure, "it does require maturity to realize that models are to be used but not to be believed" (Theil 1971) and demanding a perfect match between any model's assumptions and each empirical experience under study quickly grows absurd. Yet, the usefulness of theoretical models in explaining the performance of federations hinges critically upon how restrictive a conception of politics comparativists are prepared to accept.[12]

The need to bridge this gap between theories and facts, between the *federal illusion* and a disappointing reality, has been the engine behind the scholarship on federalism over the last two decades. In the context of this general effort, political elites are assumed to maximize their chances to gain and retain office rather than the amount of rents they are able to extract. Moreover, scholars have come to recognize, more or less explicitly, that the best route to establish the consequences of federalism is not to focus exclusively on the underlying forces and preferences in the political system (in the old *Rikerian* way) nor to conceive of institutions as abstract entities able to reshape preferences and incentives in any given social context (in the old *institutional economics* sense), but rather in the interplay between the two of them. As a result, research efforts concentrate on two areas, namely the social and economic circumstances under which federalism operates and the political and economic implications of the specific articulation of power in federations in different contexts. The former illuminate the preferences and incentives of the major players in the federal bargain. They also speak to the effectiveness of some of the constraints highlighted by the literature, such as the actual levels of capital or labor mobility. The latter account for the interactions between federal and local governments, and how these interactions translate into policies conducive to different outcomes.

[12] For instance, conceiving of political leaders as *welfare maximizers* severely limits our ability to account for the varying degrees of economic performance in federations, as indicated by public choice theorists themselves.

2.2.1 *Social and Economic Conditions in Federations*

Governments' preferences and citizens' ability to hold them accountable are to a large extent a function of the societal and economic conditions surrounding them. Consider first the distribution of "social capital." If the principal (citizens) is poor, uneducated, or socialized in a polity where the rule of law has given way to private exchanges between patrons and clients, agents (i.e. political elites) likely hold office with the purpose of maximizing their clients' rents, as well as their own. In these contexts, civic virtues lag behind in society's pre-eminent values. As a result, the dynamics of local politics disrupts rather than facilitates the efficient working of the economy (Wibbels 2005*a*; Treisman forthcoming). In contrast, a better-educated principal, coupled with a generally endorsed set of principles guiding public life and a consolidated legal system, facilitates a different interaction between principal and agents. Electorates are more likely to punish outright rent extractions by public officials and reward good governance and economic performance. Incumbents will seek to remain in office by maximizing the satisfaction of a majority of the members of their respective *demoi*.

A second structural condition concerns the degree of asset specificity across regional economies. Asset specificity conditions the effectiveness of the constraints typically associated with labor and capital mobility as the degree of factor mobility decreases with the degree of specialization of the regional economy (Boix 2003; Beramendi 2004). In a specialized, asset-specific economy, human capital and skills are tied to the regional labor market. In addition, capital is less responsive to tax advantages and more sensible to the fit between its production needs and the characteristics of the labor force and educational system (Lucas 1990). As a result, incumbents in the richly endowed units may be less constrained by the potential externalities of decisions adopted in other jurisdictions and more constrained by the likely formation of cross-class regional coalitions. Moreover, heterogeneity among units alters the incentives of the poorly endowed units. Since capital is likely to flow from poor to rich regions, they abandon any attempt to promote economic efficiency through policy. As a result, capital mobility facilitates rather than disciplines the ability of poor units' incumbents to engage in ineffective public policy (Cai and Treisman 2005*a*). This introduces a different dimension that cuts across the level of economic development and institutionalization of civic values.

Federalism operates in a variety of contexts including advanced, specialized economies; advanced, non-specialized economies; backward, specialized economies; or backward, non-specialized economies. Insofar as federalism and decentralization link public policy to subnational political economies, the nature of the latter will be in part reflected in the economic consequences of federalism. Advanced, virtuous political economies will lead to good economic outcomes, whereas local, unconstrained, nests of corruption will perform poorly. In other words, the economic impact of adopting a federal, highly decentralized system is to a large extent context specific.

There is, nonetheless, a good deal of internal variation among both advanced and developing federations that cannot be accounted for by making references to their social and economic structures. However critical it might be, context specificity covers only half the gap between the federal illusion and the empirics of federations.

The second half concerns the interplay between incumbents' incentives and the specific architecture of power in federations. This leads us to issues of institutional design and cooperation in federations.

By introducing competition between several policy suppliers, federalism sets the stage for central and subnational governments to behave non-cooperatively. Incumbents at both levels of government seek political credit for the goods and services provided to citizens while they aim to minimize the costs incurred in satisfying citizens' demands (Migué 1997; Volden 2004, 2005; Inman and Rubinfeld 1997a). They also seek to minimize the electoral impact of unpopular policy reforms. As a result, subnational governments often incur high levels of debt to be paid by the rest of the federation through a federal bailout. More generally, federations often confront a moral hazard problem: local authorities take advantage of federal risk-sharing schemes to enact policies that increase local risks (Persson and Tabellini 1996b). Symmetrically, by decentralizing social programs without transferring the necessary resources, central governments manage to offload to regional incumbents the political costs of retrenching publicly provided social welfare.

Examples of this non-cooperative behavior plague the daily life of federations, thereby bringing back to the fore the same dilemmas confronted by Hamilton, Madison, and Jay (De Figueiredo and Weingast 2005; Inman and Rubinfield 1996): how to monitor and constrain the uncooperative behavior of subnational units without creating an overpowered, unconstrained central government? Symmetrically, how to restrain the center's power, thereby preventing it from overawing the states, without facilitating at the same time defection from the federal contract by subnational units? In pursuing a definite answer to these questions, scholars' attention has turned to two intertwined aspects of the design of federations, namely the financial self-reliance of subnational units and the different ways of institutionalizing *shared rule*.

2.2.2 *The Architecture of Power in Federations I: The Fiscal Constitution*

Financial self-reliance of subnational units combines fiscal autonomy and fiscal accountability. Fiscal accountability refers to the extent to which subnational units actually internalize the consequences of their economic behavior. As such, it presupposes high levels of fiscal autonomy, i.e. that subnational governments rely more on their own revenues and less on transfers from the federal government. Yet, the reverse is not necessarily true. Fiscal autonomy does not always imply high levels of fiscal accountability. Subject to soft budget constraints, fiscally autonomous regions may incur large debts and transfer the costs of fiscally irresponsible policies to other units in the federation. Thus, for a subnational unit to be fiscally self-reliant, hard budget constraints must be in place. If the central government bails out subnational ones from their financial obligations, macroeconomic outcomes tend to worsen while subnational units become more transfer dependent.[13] To this effect, regional transfer dependency is associated with a

---

[13] In looking at a number of countries with soft budget constraints, Wibbels (2001) illustrates how decentralized federations are less likely to generate crises in a number of macroeconomic outcomes (budget, inflation, debt) as own source revenue generation increases. See also Bardhan and Mookherjee (2006).

higher demand for bailouts (Rodden 2002) and resistance to market reforms (Wibbels 2003). There is some evidence though that, in the event of bailout by the center, subnational units lose capacity to resist institutional changes towards the hardening of budget constraints (Rodden, Eskeland, and Litrack 2003).

However, assuming that sufficiently hard budget constraints are effective, a cumulative body of literature indicates that as the fiscal autonomy (transfer dependency) of subnational governments increases (decreases), markets function better and economic outcomes improve.[14] The specialized literature sees in China an example of the benefits of fiscal autonomy, whereas, arguably, the lack of autonomy of Russian regions leads local elites to be corrupted by large national companies, thereby hampering national economic growth (Qian and Weingast 1997; Bardhan and Mookherjee 2005). Stein (1999) reports findings along the same lines: Latin American decentralization tends to produce larger governments, but this effect is particularly important in cases where vertical imbalance is high, transfers are discretional, and the degree of borrowing autonomy by subnational governments is high. More generally, both the size of government and the macroeconomic effects of expenditures decentralization are shown to be contingent on the levels of fiscal autonomy (Rodden 2003; Rodden and Wibbels 2002; Careaga and Weingast 2000). Fiscally autonomous subnational units reduce aggregate deficits and inflation rates and facilitate sustained economic growth. A compelling economic logic underlies this evidence. As greater financial self-reliance affects the extent to which subnational governments internalize the benefits of their economic progress, subnational incumbents have a strong incentive to create a market-preserving environment.

In sum, fiscal autonomy operates as a first barrier against the uncooperative behavior of subnational governments. In contrast, convoluted intergovernmental fiscal arrangements provide a natural breeding ground for political and economic opportunism. Yet, its importance notwithstanding, the economic effects of federalism and decentralization are not derived exclusively from the design of the fiscal constitution. In fact, as reflected by the recent path-breaking contributions by Wibbels (2005) and Rodden (2006), the ultimate key to the strategic interactions between different levels of government lies elsewhere, namely in the specifics of the articulation of shared rule across federations.

2.2.3 *The Architecture of Power II: The Organization of Shared Rule*

In particular, three dimensions of the distribution of power in federations are regularly mentioned as the source differences in the economic performance of federations. These are the relative strength of the national executive, the formal representation of subnational units within the national policy-making process, and the organization of party systems.

---

[14] The effectiveness of hard budget constraints is not straightforward. Legal provisions not to bail out subnational governments may not be enacted, giving way to an strategic interaction between the center and the units where the identification of bailout expectations becomes crucial. On the difficulty of empirically identifying bailout expectations and their implications for fiscal outcomes in federations see Rodden 2005.

Economists repeatedly contend that strong executives elected by national constituencies are in order if efficient national policy is to prevail over vested local interests (Inman and Rubinfield 1996; Breton 1996; Eichengreen and von Hagen 1996; Wildasin 1997; Persson and Tabellini 1996b). Yet, an excessive empowerment of the central executive provides no magic solution. For one, it defeats the very purpose of federalism in that it effectively eliminates the self-rule by constituent units. Moreover, an unrestrained national executive has plenty of incentives to overrule regional and local governments and extract a larger share of rents (De Figueirido and Weingast 2005). Furthermore, strong central governments become themselves targets for rent-seeking practices, including bailout claims (Wibbels 2005a; Rodden 2006). Thus, the issue still remains how to preserve the autonomy of local elites while limiting their incentives to distort the market at the same time.

A rich theoretical literature has focused on the importance of formal decision-making rules and procedures (Inman and Rubinfield 1997b; Cremer and Palfrey 1999, 2000).[15] The logic is simple and compelling: different designs create different sets of winners and losers depending upon the composition of preferences within each unit and the federation as a whole (Dixit and Londregan 1998). Hence, under any particular design, actors will make use of their strategic advantage to maximize the rents they are able to extract. These models complement a growing body of empirical evidence on how the organization of political representation as the institutional mechanism linking subnational specific interests to national policy making, condition the economic outcomes of federations. The recent work by Wibbels (2005a) on the determinants of market reforms in developing federations has placed the system of representation of regional interests at the center of the analysis. Given that policies are made at the national level, the fate of market reforms is in part explained by the ability of regions to use their formal representation in national institutions to obstruct or shape reforms. Wherever upper chambers play an important role in defining market reforms and/or there is a high degree of malapportionment in the lower chamber, the nature and scope of reform reflects the bargaining power of the regional coalitions for and against specific policy changes.[16]

However, the leverage granted to subnational units by the system of representation may be offset by a different mechanism mediating the interplay between national and subnational elites, namely the organization of the party system. Wibbels (2005a) analyzes the degree of partisan harmony as a mechanism that facilitates the coordination among regional and national incumbents, thereby creating the conditions for a more

[15] This literature complements a second set of theoretical models that focus on the differences between federal and unitary polities. For instance, Persson and Tabellini (1996a) have pointed out that the balance between risk sharing and redistribution depends upon the formal rules of decision making: while centralization leads to overinsurance and larger levels of redistribution, bargains among constituent units produce underinsurance and a smaller fiscal system.

[16] Reasoning along similar lines, Diaz-Cayeros et al. (2003) contend that unicameralism and parliamentarism reduce capital spending since they limit the number of independently elected politicians that must assuage their constituents through particularistic projects. In turn, Gibson, Calvo, and Falleti (2004) show that if poor, underpopulated units are overrepresented in the upper chambers, federalism severely constrains macroeconomic efficiency. Finally, Wibbels (2003) shows that strong and malapportioned senates increase the probability that a pro-bailout coalition emerges.

successful policy change. But it is Rodden's (2006) analysis of fiscal discipline in federations that analyzes more in detail the mechanisms through which the design of the party system shapes the interplay between national and subnational elites.

Under unclear divisions of authority, governments at different levels have incentives to transfer the fiscal burden of their policies to other levels. In particular, subnational governments have an incentive to incur debt and hope to be bailed out by the center whenever the financial crisis reaches its limit. Because regional governments do not know how committed to fiscal discipline the central government is, they will adjust their fiscal behavior according to their expectations regarding the central government's resoluteness. Integrated national party systems, Rodden argues, make the resoluteness of the central government more credible and facilitate the enforcement of fiscal discipline by reducing the incentives for regional incumbents to behave irresponsibly.

An integrated party system affects the incentives of subnational incumbents in two different ways. First, local elites regarded as a liability for the overall electoral profile of the party face severe consequences in terms of their own political careers. As a result, the opportunistic behavior by local incumbents is likely to be constrained and, other things being equal, economic results improve (Wibbels 2001; Rodden and Wibbels 2002; Enikolopov and Zhuravskaya 2003). Second, an integrated national party system helps solve the commitment problem between incumbents at different levels of government by intertwining their political fates. Partisan harmony and electoral coat-tails feed back on each other, facilitating the long-term cooperation between different levels of government and the party's organization. In turn, this makes the commitments between local and national elites more credible, and facilitates the renegotiation and ultimate improvement of ill-designed fiscal federal arrangements.

Overall, the effects of federalism on the economy are anything but simple.[17] Similarly, the notion that federalism restrains the development of an economically inefficient welfare state is dubious as subnational units often engage in politically profitable social spending in the hope that the actual cost is transferred to other units through a variety of centralized fiscal arrangements. Empirically, federations vary largely in terms of both the size of the welfare state and the overall levels of inequality.

In sum, depending upon external conditions and internal features, federalism may or may not discipline fiscal policy, constrain redistribution (Beramendi 2003; Obinger, Leibfried, and Castles 2005), promote corruption (Cai and Treisman 2004; Bardhan and Mookherjee 2005), or facilitate the development of a market economy. While the field has advanced significantly in mapping out different combinations between underlying conditions and observed institutional effects, some of the nuts and bolts behind these combinations are yet to be ascertained (e.g. the workings and interdependencies of the many electoral externalities existing in federations).

---

[17] The tension between competing political elites responding to different sets of incentives speaks to many other aspects of the federal illusion, such as policy experimentation. The literature on federalism and innovation is very extensive. For reviews and critiques of the classical arguments on federalism as a laboratory for policy innovation, see Rose-Ackerman (1980); Strumpf (2002); Cai and Treisman (2005b). For a recent vindication of the link between federalism and policy innovation, see Kotsogiannis and Schwager (2004). To my knowledge, a systematic empirical analysis addressing whether federalism actually leads to more and better policy innovation is still lacking.

More importantly, the new picture of federalism painted by comparative political economists begs the question of how federalism and decentralization came into existence in the first place. This is especially relevant because whatever effect federalism and decentralization trigger (given the surrounding social, political, and economic environment), it will be a long-term one due to the status quo bias of federal institutions.[18] Hence, whenever the choice to adopt a federal constitution is made or steps towards political decentralization are taken, political actors are making a decision whose implications are meant to last.

3 REVISITING THE ORIGINS OF FEDERATIONS

Largely spurred by the new style and findings of the literature on the consequences of federalism, the analysis of the origins of federalism is on its way to producing a new understanding of the processes that account for the emergence and stability of federations. From the traditional focus on a semi-open list of "conditions" for federalism, the field has moved to take on issues of endogeneity and selection, opening an entirely new set of questions. After a succinct overview on the traditional approaches to the origins of federations, this section addresses the challenges faced by this newer stream of scholarship.

3.1 Pre-Rikerian Efforts: Conditions for Federalism

Until the appearance of Riker's (1964) *Federalism*, the literature on the origins of federations was dominated by apolitical approaches. The features and circumstances surrounding past and present federations resulted in items on a list of "conditions" to be satisfied if a federation was to emerge. This line of work was very inductive in its logic. Federalism emerged as the institutional correlate of a number of cultural, historical, or even ideational characteristics of societies. The proposed lists of conditions varied in scope and detail. Deutsch (1957) centered his analysis on the level of "societal interaction" and "communication" between territories and social groups. When structural circumstances facilitate the development of these links, federalism

---

[18] After a challenging formal deconstruction of all the arguments conventionally used to either promote or warn against political decentralization, Treisman (forthcoming) indicates that "one argument did seem to be more generally valid. If political decentralization increases the number of actors whose acquiescence is needed to change policies, this will tend to entrench the status quo," provided that preferences are sufficiently heterogeneous. For instance, veto power analyses show that federalism was instrumental in preventing change in fields as diverse as the expansion or retrenchment of the welfare state (Obinger, Leibfried, and Castles 2005) or central bank independence (Treisman 2000).

as a "security community" emerged. In turn, Wheare (1946), and Bowie and Friedrich (1954) broaden the list to include conditions such as a common institutional history, the existence of a source of military insecurity, a committed leadership, or a "community of outlook based on race, religion, language or culture" (cf. Riker 1975, 115).

Riker's work departed from earlier contributions in two ways. First, his list of conditions was strictly political, including: (1) "a desire on the part of politicians who offer to bargain to expand their territorial control by peaceful means, usually either to meet an external military or diplomatic threat or to prepare for military or diplomatic aggrandizement;" and (2) "a willingness on the part of politicians who accept the bargain to give up independence for the sake of the union either because they desire protection from an external threat or because they desire to participate in the potential aggression of the federation" (1975, 114). But, second and more importantly, Riker's conditions follow from the theoretical breakthrough that the "establishment of a federal government must be a rational bargain among politicians" (Riker 1975, 116).

Herein lies the fundamental contribution by Riker to the study of the origin and functioning of federations. While it is widely acknowledged that Riker's specific predictions regarding the centrality of "a military or diplomatic threat" do not bear empirical scrutiny (Stepan 1999; Ziblatt 2006), it is equally true that by focusing on politicians' incentives, Riker deployed the foundations of all subsequent analyses of the origins and stability of federations in two important respects (Filippov 2005). First, Riker is the first to conceive politicians as strategic actors whose preferences derive from a balance between the status quo and their expectations about future institutional alternatives. Second, these institutional alternatives matter because they have distributive effects, that is to say they "produce different distributions of relative winners and losers" (Filippov 2005, 99). As a result, by conceiving the federal bargain as a choice between alternative distributive scenarios, Riker's theory rooted the terrain for a new perspective on the origins of federations and political unions.[19]

3.2 Looking Beyond the Surface: Endogenous Federal Institutions

A blooming literature on endogenous federalism and political unions develops this theme. If federal institutions and political unions are known to have discernible political and economic effects, actors derive their preferences from their expectations as to what these effects are, and what their relative position is going to be. Admittedly, they may miscalculate and make a choice on the basis of eventually wrong anticipations. But this does not imply that their expectations do not matter for the institutional choice.

A prominent example of this logic is the relationship between federalism, redistribution, and inequality (Bolton and Roland 1997; Dixit and Londregan 1998; Alesina and

---

[19] See for instance a direct application of this framework to the analysis of the process of European integration in McKay (1999).

Spolaore 2003; Beramendi 2007, 2006; Wibbels 2005*b*). This line of research places the shape and territorial specificities of the distribution of income at the core of the analysis of the determinants of political integration, fiscal and political decentralization, and the changes of institutional arrangements in currently existing federations. The core intuition is that federalism and decentralization are associated with particular distributive outcomes not because they exogenously generate them, but because distributional concerns play a fundamental role in their selection and design.

In so doing, the literature on endogenous federalism and decentralization adds a new logic to more traditional explanations of the origins of federalism and decentralization, articulated around external threats and/or internal cultural and ethnic differences (Riker 1975; Lemco 1991; Panizza 1999; Stepan 2001). More importantly, it also complements recent analyses of the logic of political and economic integration based on the need to design a more functional set of institutions to cope with the increasing mobility of factors, consumers, and taxpayers (Casella and Frey 1992; Casella and Weingast 1995). This is particularly the case in Mattli's (1999) account of regional integration. For Mattli, economic externalities explain the demand for integration, not its supply. In turn, for an effective supply of integration to emerge, pre-existing units must overcome a collective action problem motivated largely by distributional concerns. Thus, for regional integration to succeed, distributional concerns by potential losers of integration must be smoothed, or else they will have an incentive to renege. Hence, the key role of a dominant member willing to play the role of a "paymaster" to facilitate integration.[20]

The issue of endogeneity is also at the core of the recent literature on the problem of stability in federations. Formal theorists have addressed this problem by trying to establish the conditions under which federalism becomes self-enforced. That is to say, the conditions under which federalism becomes an equilibrium in which both the center and the units see it as in their interest to meet their end of the contract (De Figueiredo and Weingast 2005). Bednar (2004, 2005) conceptualizes federalism as a complex problem of public good provision in an institutional environment favorable to opportunistic behavior. Opportunism, Bednar argues, can only be contained, not eliminated, through a set of complementary institutions designed to maximize compliance. Among these institutions, particular attention is paid to constitutional safeguards, the party system, and the judiciary (see also Bednar, Eskridge, and Ferejohn 2001). Each of these institutions covers different types of opportunism, thereby reinforcing each other's effectiveness. On their own, however, they are ineffective as guarantors of federal stability. While these analyses are very illuminating of the complementarities between different federal institutions, they do not address the conditions under which these stabilizing institutions are likely to emerge.

In contrast, Filippov, Ordeshook, and Shvetsova (2004) approach stability as a distributive conflict among electorally motivated elites. In so doing, they theorize constitutional limitations as endogenous to the nature of partisan competition. Mobilization against the institutional core of the federation is contained where an

---

[20] The expansion of Structural and Cohesion Funds in Maastricht would provide an example of side payments to potential losers of the process of economic integration.

integrated party system creates political and distributional incentives for political elites to channel their demands within the system. In contrast, when political competition is vertically and horizontally unstructured, conflicts about who gets what quickly evolve into conflicts about the rules of the game. Under such circumstances, economic and political crises are the likely outcome, for political competition exacerbates ethnic divisions and economic differences. Thus, the party system operates as a mechanism that, in the face of social, ethnic, and economic basis for political conflict, ultimately contributes to either the persistence or the collapse of constitutional rules.

Yet, an additional difficulty comes from the fact that party systems themselves are endogenous to both the structure of the state and the cleavage structure within which they operate. On the basis of a comparative analysis of Latin American federations, Diaz-Cayeros (forthcoming) provides additional evidence of the difficulties of detaching institutional choices, electoral concerns, and distributive politics. His innovative analysis of the institutional dynamics of the Mexican federation reveals that the centralization of the party system and the centralization of tax policy are jointly endogenous. In this and other Latin American cases, centralization of tax policy emerges as the outcome of a bargain with local political elites. The key to the process was to allow rich regions to become richer while using centralized redistribution to buy off the support of the leaders of backward regions. This coalition between leaders of rich and poor regions alike, Diaz-Cayeros argues, was forged through the articulation of a national party system.[21]

Considered more generally, the recent literature on endogenous federalism and decentralization reverses the conventional causal line from outcomes to origins, and suggests that the observed association between federal institutions and certain outcomes responds to a process of historical self-selection. This is particularly the case when analyzing the relationship between federalism, decentralization, and income inequality, but a similar logic can be extended to different realms (Srinivasan and Wallack forthcoming; Aghion, Alesina, and Trebbi 2004). This poses a major methodological challenge. If, at least in part, federal institutions (and their effects) are self-selected, does federalism really matter? Or, to put it more moderately, when can we argue that the impact of federalism is exogenous as opposed to the outcome of a process of self-selection? Providing an answer to this question is the biggest challenge to be confronted by the comparative political economy of federalism in the years to come. I turn now to discuss alternative ways in which this challenge can be addressed.

3.3 The Way Ahead

How to cope then with issues of endogeneity and selection when analyzing the origins and consequences of federalism? A first, rather radical, take on the issue

[21] Adding further layers of complexity to the causal relation between fiscal federalism and party system, Chhibber and Kollman 2004 have exploited the experiences of Canada, India, the United States, and the United Kingdom to argue that fiscal and administrative centralization is an important cause behind the centralization of the party system.

would be to argue that whenever institutions are endogenous, their effects are self-selected and, therefore, essentially irrelevant. Insofar as federal institutions reproduce the underlying tastes of the relevant political coalition, they do not really matter per se. In addition, the identification of exogenous effects of federalism would prove a Herculean task in that, as follows from the literature on endogenous fiscal decentralization or political parties, there are simply no good instruments. Through a different route, we would revisit the early, and rather disconcerting, Rikerian assessment on the significance of federalism (Riker 1964).

A second, less sanguine approach to the problem would be to distinguish different levels of institutional analysis, and assume that some are more likely to be exogenous than others. The process generating federalism is clearly multidimensional. This chapter has identified a number of factors relevant to the origins, dynamics, and consequences of federalism that operate at three levels: external environment (ethnoterritorial mobilization, income distribution), constitutional institutions and structures (state's rights, judicial review), non-constitutional institutions (party system, fiscal federal arrangements), and the actual degree of fiscal, political, and administrative decentralization. Certainly, not all these dimensions are moving simultaneously across space and time. For instance, judicial review may help rewrite the constitutions on particular matters, but the apportionment of seats in upper chambers remains fixed (even if sometimes challenged by a minority) during long periods in the history of federations.

Being at the mercy of history (Przeworski, this volume), this lack of simultaneity leaves one window open to call partial equilibrium analysis to the rescue. An important implication of this chapter is that a general equilibrium theory of federalism is out of reach. Given the dynamic, bidirectional nature of the interplay between federalism and its environment, partial equilibrium analysis of the origins and effects of specific aspects of federalism seems to be a much more realistic and promising goal. By that I mean to exploit long-term, dynamic processes to isolate moments in which some dimensions of the problem are fixed while others (those of theoretical interest) vary. The leading intuition here is to go down the road of history in search of good instruments, that is of causal factors that lead to the adoption of federalism (or some dimension thereof) but remain genuinely unrelated to the effects federalism brings about. Insofar as it is possible to establish that the adoption of federalism or decentralization at time t is unrelated to societal, political, or economic conditions that can be taken for outcomes of federalism itself at time t+n, a solution to the problems of endogeneity and self-selection appears on target.[22]

[22] For instance, arguing beyond the classical insistence on the need for an "amalgamated security community" (Deutsch 1957; Lemco 1991), Ziblatt (2006) sees federalism as a compromise resulting from previously institutionalized, highly infrastructural political entities being able to resist coercion by larger-scale political units. In turn, O'Neill (2005) interprets state decentralization as the outcome of electoral calculations of vote-maximizing political elites at the national level. According to her, political decentralization "is most likely when the party in power believes it cannot hold on to power that is centralized in the national government but believes it has a good chance of winning a substantial portion of decentralized power through subnational elections" (2005, 5). Decentralization is then essentially an electoral strategy for parties with a long-term political perspective. Thus, insofar as electoral or geopolitical considerations actually drive the adoption of federal institutions, there is room to consider their effect on social and economic outcomes potentially exogenous. In contrast, to the extent that electoral and coalitional concerns overlap with distributional expectations, electoral strategies are no longer exogenous.

In the quest for these *moments of exogeneity,* the identification and analysis of external shocks is a promising strategy. For instance, in assessing the impact of the distribution of income on existing fiscal federal arrangements, one should look for cases in which a sudden transformation of the distribution of income is unrelated to the distributive effects of existing federal arrangements. From this perspective, the impact of the Great Depression on North American federations, or the impact of Reunification on Germany's fiscal constitution, are two historical junctures that qualify as *moments of exogeneity* where the impact of a transformation of the distribution of income on federal institutions can be cleanly analyzed.

More generally, to provide a credible case, these moments of exogeneity ought to be properly identified, both theoretically and methodologically. Theoretically, this will require to continue the blending of formal models of federalism with the taste for institutional complexities that characterizes the comparative politics of federalism.[23] In so doing, the multidimensionality of federalism becomes an asset worth exploiting.[24] Yet, to move on, a fundamental premiss ought to be accepted the fact that any given aspect of federalism is endogenous (or even self-selected) does not necessarily mean that over time it cannot generate consequences on its own. On the basis of this premiss, the relationship between the different elements of federalism among themselves, as well as with their environment, can be theorized by imposing the assumption that the other factors/dimensions are given. Recent examples of this way of proceeding include Alesina, Angeloni, and Etro's (2001), Hafer and Landa's (2004), and Volden's (2005) analyses of the joint provision of public goods in federations, Diaz-Cayeros's (2004) analysis of the impact of federalism on tax centralization, or Beramendi's (2006) study of the interplay between inequality and the representation of regional interest as determinants of fiscal decentralization. The real hurdle, however, lies in the need to set up a research design befitting the assumptions on the basis of which the theoretical relationship of interest has been identified. This brings us to methodology, where there is no perfect solution.

The best, if not the only, bet is to move away from imperfect designs through alternative routes, and hope that they all lead to the same end. Moments of exogeneity can be found in carefully constructed historical case studies, where different assumptions about what can be considered as given can be discussed in detail. But these can only complement (not replace) inferences made on the basis of a more general and systematic evaluation of the evidence. In this spirit, the quantity and quality of existing datasets on federalism and decentralization call for dramatic improvement. Despite all the progress made, the field still works with clearly contestable measurements of party system

[23] The synergies between the more normative models of market-preserving federalism and the development of comparative research on the fiscal effects of fiscal federal arrangements provide already a very good example of the benefits to be gained from breaking these boundaries. Interestingly enough, after challenging the limited applicability of market-preserving federalism, the comparative empirical literature on federalism has come to show that when the actual design of federations matches the assumptions of the model, it is indeed the case that economic outcomes are better.

[24] For instance, Falleti (2005) shows that the dynamic sequence in which different types of decentralization (fiscal, political, administrative) condition each other shapes in important ways the actual structure of power within federations.

integration, fiscal decentralization, or ethnic fractionalization, to name only a few key variables. Only by expanding the quantity and quality of data over time and space will it be possible to check the robustness of empirical findings to different assumptions about the process of generation of observables (Przeworski, this volume). In this way, theoretical and empirical advances complement each other in detaching the impact of the different dimensions of federalism from either their original causes or the conditions that shape their evolution over time. Otherwise, failure to accumulate better data will prevent scholars from providing solid answers to the leading questions in the field, thereby rendering theoretical advances an incomplete and ultimately fruitless effort.

4 CONCLUSION

The overview of the comparative politics of federalism leaves us with a paradox. While our knowledge of the workings of the different aspects of federalism and federations has expanded vastly over the last two decades, the long bemoaned goal of developing a general theory of the causes and consequences of federalism seems more of a challenge than ever. As federalism becomes less of a black box, the challenge of developing a theory able to predict both the emergence of federations and the nature and direction of its effects appears ever more gigantic.

Existing findings support conditional and probabilistic as opposed to deterministic statements on federalism and decentralization. Federalism and decentralization per se provide no magic recipe to ensure political integration or economic prosperity. Sometimes they do and sometimes they do not. In turn, this speaks to more normative concerns. The recent literature on federalism leaves no space for any federal illusion of any kind.[25] The more scholars find out about federalism and decentralization, the more cautious they become in predicting their effects or advocating their adoption. After formally highlighting the complexities involved in decentralizing government, Treisman (forthcoming) goes as far as to conclude that "decentralizing government in a particular place and time is very much a leap in the dark."

Admittedly, a good deal of the nuts and bolts of federalism and decentralization remain in the dark. But precisely for this reason it is much too early in the game to mix up the need for further insights on how federalism plays in different contexts with the impossibility of making reliable claims about the likely effects of political decentralization (or integration, for that matter). In other words, context-conditionality does not necessarily mean lack of predictability. Likewise, launching a plea for caution does not imply proclaiming an inability to engage in informed constitutional engineering. Instead of giving up that possibility altogether, a more promising route for the

---

[25] However, this should not be confused with a vindication for centralization. Even where federalism is not associated with better economic outcomes, a more centralized system might not constitute a better option given high levels of cultural, economic, and political heterogeneity.

comparative politics of federalism in the years to come is to take on the challenge of systematically disentangling the links between the specifics of the design of federations and the economic and societal conditions surrounding them. This will require both *fortuna* and *virtu*. The former is up to history and its will to provide us with enough moments of exogeneity. The latter is up to us and our ability to find the right combination of analytical tools.

REFERENCES

AGHION, P., ALESINA, A., and TREBBI, F. 2004. Endogenous political institutions. *Quarterly Journal of Economics*, 119: 565–612.

ALESINA, A., and SPOLAORE, E. 2003. *The Size of Nations*. Cambridge, Mass.: Harvard University Press.

—— ANGELONI, I., and ETRO, F. 2001. Institutional rules for federations. Unpublished paper. Department of Economics, Harvard University.

AMORETTI, U., and BERMEO, N. eds. 2004. *Federalism and Territorial Cleavages*. Baltimore: Johns Hopkins University Press.

ARZAGHI, M., and HENDERSON, J. V. 2005. Why countries are fiscally decentralizing? *Journal of Public Economics*, 89: 1157–89.

BARDHAN, P., and MOOKHERJEE, D. 2005. Decentralization, corruption and government accountability: an overview. In *Handbook of Economic Corruption*, ed. S. Rose-Ackerman. Cheltenham: Edward Elgar.

—— —— 2006. Decentralization and accountability in infrastructure delivery in developing countries. *Economic Journal*, 116: 101–27.

BEDNAR, JENNA. 2001. Shirking and stability in federal systems. Unpublished paper. Department of Political Science, University of Michigan.

—— 2004. Authority migration in federations: a framework for analysis. *PS: Political Science and Politics*, 37 (3): 403–408.

—— 2005. Federalism as a public good. *Constitutional Political Economy*, 16 (2): 189–204.

—— ESKRIDGE, W., Jr. and FEREJOHN, J. 2001. A political theory of federalism. Pp. 223–70 in *Constitutional Culture and Democratic Rule*, ed. J. Ferejohn, J. N. Rakove, and J. Riley. New York: Cambridge University Press.

BERAMENDI, P. 2003. *Decentralization and Income Inequality*. Madrid: Juan March Institute.

—— 2004. Decentralization and redistribution: North-American responses to the Great Depression. Paper presented at the Annual Meetings of the American Political Science Association, Chicago.

—— 2006. Fragmented solidarity: distributive politics on multitiered systems. M/S.

—— 2007. Inequality and the territorial fragmentation of solidarity. *International Organization*.

BERMEO, N. 2004. Conclusions: the merits of federalism. Pp. 457–86 in *Federalism, Unitarism and Territorial Cleavages*, ed. U. Amoretti and N. Bermeo. Baltimore: Johns Hopkins University Press.

BEWLEY, T. F. 1981. A critique of Tiebout's theory of local public expenditures. *Econometrica*, 49 (3): 713–40.

BOIX, C. 2003. *Democracy and Redistribution*. Cambridge: Cambridge University Press.

BOLTON, P., and ROLAND, G. 1997. The breakup of nations: a political economy analysis. *Quarterly Journal of Economics*, 112: 1057–90.

BOWIE, R. R., and FRIEDRICH, C. J. eds. 1954. *Studies in Federalism*. Boston: Little, Brown and Company.

BRENNAN, G., and BUCHANAN, J. 1980. *The Power to Tax*. Cambridge: Cambridge University Press.

BRETON, A. 1996. *Competitive Federalism*. Cambridge: Cambridge University Press.

BUCHANAN, J. 1995. Federalism as an ideal political order and an objective for constitutional reform. *Publius: The Journal of Federalism*, 25 (2): 19–27.

BUNCE, V. 2004. Federalism, nationalism and secession: the communist and postcommunist experience. Pp. 417–40 in *Federalism, Unitarism and Territorial Cleavages*, ed. U. Amoretti and N. Bermeo. Baltimore: Johns Hopkins University Press.

CAI, H., and TREISMAN, D. 2004. State corroding federalism. *Journal of Public Economics*, 88: 819–43.

—— —— 2005a. Does competition for capital discipline governments? Decentralization, globalization and public policy. *American Economic Review*, 95 (3): 817–30.

—— —— 2005b. Political decentralization and policy experimentation. Unpublished paper. Department of Economics, University of California, Los Angeles.

CAREAGA, M., and WEINGAST, B. 2000. The fiscal pact with the devil: a positive approach to fiscal federalism, revenue sharing, and good governance. Working paper. Hoover Institution, Stanford University.

CASELLA, A., and FREY, B. 1992. Federalism and clubs: towards an economic theory of overlapping political jurisdictions. *European Economic Review*, 36: 639–46.

—— and WEINGAST, B. 1995. Elements for a theory of jurisdictional change. Pp. 11–41 in *Politics and Institutions in an Integrated Europe*, ed. B. Eichengreen, J. Frieden, and J. von Hagen. New York: Springer.

CHHIBBER, P., and KOLLMAN, K. 2004. *The Formation of National Party Systems*. Princeton: Princeton University Press.

CREMER, J., and PALFREY, T. R. 1999. Political confederation. *American Political Science Review*, 93 (1): 69–83.

—— —— 2000. Federal mandates by popular demand. *Journal of Political Economy*, 108 (5): 905–27.

CHRISTIANSEN, V., HAGEN, K. P., and SANDMO, A. 1994. The scope of taxation and public expenditure in an open economy. *Scandinavian Journal of Economics*, 96: 289–309.

DAHL, R. 1983. Federalism and the democratic process. Pp. 95–108 in *Nomos XXV: Liberal Democracy*, ed. J. R. Pennock and J. C. Chapman. New York: New York University Press.

DAVIS, R. S. 1978. *The Federal Principle: A Journey through Time in Quest of a Meaning*. Berkeley and Los Angeles: University of California Press.

DE FIGUEIREDO, R. J. P., and WEINGAST, B. 2005. Self enforcing federalism. *Journal of Law, Economics and Organization*, 21 (1): 103–35.

DEUTSCH, K. 1957. *Political Community in the North Atlantic Area*. Princeton: Princeton University Press.

DIAZ-CAYEROS, A. 2004. The centralization of fiscal authority: an empirical investigation. Unpublished paper. Department of Political Science, Stanford University.

—— Forthcoming. *Federalism, Fiscal Authority and Centralization in Latin America*. Cambridge: Cambridge University Press.

—— McELWAIN, K., ROMERO, V. F., and SIEWIERSKI, K. A. 2003. Fiscal decentralization, legislative institutions and particularistic spending. Unpublished paper. Department of Political Science, Stanford University.

DIXIT, A. 1997. *The Making of Economic Policy*. Cambridge, Mass.: MIT Press.

DIXIT, A., and LONDREGAN, J. 1998. Fiscal federalism and redistributive politics. *Journal of Public Economics*, 68: 153–80.

DUCHACEK, I. D. 1970. *Comparative Federalism: The Territorial Dimension of Politics.* London: University Press of America.

EICHENGREEN, B., and VON HAGEN, J. 1996. Federalism, fiscal restraint, and European monetary union. *American Economic Review*, 86: 134–8.

ELAZAR, D. 1987. *Exploring Federalism.* Tuscaloosa: University of Alabama Press.

—— 1994. *Federal Systems of the World.* London: Longman.

ENIKOLOPOV, R., and ZHURAVSKAYA, E. 2003. Decentralization and political institutions. Unpublished paper. Moscow: Center for Economic and Financial Research.

EPPLE, D., and ROMER, T. 1991. Mobility and redistribution. *Journal of Political Economy*, 99: 828–58.

FALLETI, T. 2005. A sequential theory of decentralization: Latin American cases in comparative perspective. *American Political Science Review*, 99 (3): 327–46.

FEARON, J. D., and VAN HOUTEN, P. 2002. The politicization of cultural and economic difference. Unpublished paper. Department of Political Science, Stanford University.

FILIPPOV, M. 2005. Riker and federalism. *Constitutional Political Economy*, 16 (2): 93–111.

—— ORDESHOOK, P. C., and SHVETSOVA, O. 2004. *Designing Federalism.* Cambridge: Cambridge University Press.

—— and SHVETSOVA, O. 2005. Federalism and democracy in Russia. Paper presented at the conference Postcommunist state and society: transnational and national politics. Syracuse University.

GABSZEWICZ, J., and VAN YPERSELE, T. 1996. Social protection and political competition. *Journal of Public Economics*, 61: 193–208.

GIBSON, E., CALVO, E., and FALLETI, T. 2004. Reallocative federalism: overrepresentation and public spending in the western hemisphere. Pp. 173–96 in *Federalism and Democracy in Latin America*, ed. E. L. Gibson. Baltimore: Johns Hopkins University Press.

GLATZER, A., and KONRAD, K. 1994. Intertemporal commitments problems and voting on redistributive taxation. *Journal of Urban Economics*, 36: 278–91.

GRAMLICH, E. 1973. State and local fiscal behaviour and federal grant policy. Pp. 21–57 in *Selected Essays of Edward M. Gramlich.* Cheltenham: Edward Elgar, 1997.

—— 1987. Cooperation and competition in public welfare policies. Pp. 309–27 in *Selected Essays of Edward M. Gramlich.* Cheltenham: Edward Elgar, 1997.

HAFER, C., and LANDA, D. 2004. Public goods in federal systems. Unpublished paper. Department of Political Science, New York University.

HALE, H. 2004. Divided we stand: institutional sources of ethnofederal survival and collapse. *World Politics*, 56 (2): 165–93.

HAMILTON, A., MADISON, J., and JAY, J. *The Federalist.* Cambridge, Mass.: Hackett Publishing.

HOOGHE, L., and MARKS, G. 2003. Unraveling the central state, but how? Types of multi-level governance. *American Political Science Review*, 97 (2): 1118–40.

HUG, S. 2005. Federal stability in unequal societies. *Constitutional Political Economy*, 16 (2): 113–24.

INMAN, R. P., and RUBINFIELD, D. L. 1996. Designing tax policy in federalist economies: an overview. *Journal of Public Economics*, 60: 307–34.

—— —— 1997a. The political economy of federalism. In *Perspectives of Public Choice*, ed. D. C. Mueller. Cambridge: Cambridge University Press.

—— —— 1997b. Rethinking federalism. *Journal of Economic Perspectives*, 11 (4): 43–64.

KELEMEN, D. 2003. The structure and dynamics of EU federalism. *Comparative Political Studies*, 36 (1–2): 184–208.

—— 2004. *The Rules of Federalism: Institutions and Regulatory Policy in the EU and Beyond.* Cambridge, Mass.: Harvard University Press.

KETCHAMP, R. ed. 1986. *The Antifederalist Papers and the Constitutional Convention Debates.* New York: Penguin Books.

KOTSOGIANNIS, C., and SCHWAGER, R. 2004. Policy innovation in federal systems. Unpublished paper. Department of Economics, University of Exeter.

LEJOUR, A., and VERBON, H. A. A. 1996. Capital mobility, wage bargaining and social insurance policies in an economic union. *International Tax and Public Finance,* 3: 495–514.

LEMCO, J. 1991. *Political Stability in Federal Governments.* New York: Praeger.

LEVI, M. 2000. The economic turn in comparative politics. *Comparative Political Studies,* 33: 822–44.

LIJPHART, A. 1999. *Patterns of Democracy.* New Haven: Yale University Press.

LIVINGSTON, W. 1956. *Federalism and Constitutional Change.* Oxford: Oxford University Press.

LINZ, J. J. 1997. Democracy, multinationalism and federalism. Working Paper 103. Madrid: Juan March Institute.

LUCAS, R. E. 1990. Why doesn't capital flow from rich to poor countries? *American Economic Review,* 802: 92–6.

MCKAY, D. 1999. *Federalism and the European Union.* Oxford: Oxford University Press.

MCWHINNEY, E. 1962. *Comparative Federalism.* Toronto: University of Toronto Press.

MATTLI, W. 1999. *The Logic of Regional Integration.* Cambridge: Cambridge University Press.

MIGUÉ, J. L. 1997. Public choice in a federal system. *Public Choice,* 90: 235–54.

MUSGRAVE, R. 1997. Devolution, grants and fiscal competition, *Journal of Economic Perspectives,* 11 (4): 65–72.

MYERSON, R. B. 2006. Federalism and incentives for success. *Quarterly Journal of Political Science,* 1 (1): 3–23.

OATES, W. 1972. *Fiscal Federalism.* New York: Harcourt.

—— 1991. *Essays in Fiscal Federalism.* Cheltenham: Edward Elgar.

—— 1999. An essay on fiscal federalism, *Journal of Economic Literature,* 37: 1120–49.

—— and SCHWAB, R. M. 1988. Economic competition among jurisdictions: efficiency enhancing or distortion inducing. *Journal of Public Economics,* 35: 333–54.

OBINGER, H., LEIBFRIED, S., and CASTLES, F. eds. 2005. *Federalism and the Welfare State.* Cambridge: Cambridge University Press.

O'NEILL, K. 2005. *Decentralizing the State.* Cambridge: Cambridge University Press.

PANIZZA, U. 1999. On the determinants of fiscal centralization: theory and evidence. *Journal of Public Economics,* 74: 97–139.

PERSSON, T. and TABELLINI, G. 1996a. Federal fiscal constitutions: risk sharing and redistribution. *Journal of Political Economy,* 104 (5): 979–1009.

—— —— 1996b. Federal fiscal constitutions: risk sharing and moral hazard. *Econometrica,* 64 (3): 623–46.

PETERSON, P., and ROM, M. 1990. *Welfare Magnets: A New Case for a National Standard.* Washington, DC: Brookings Institution.

PIERSON, P. 1995. Fragmented welfare states: federal institutions and the development of social policy. *Governance,* 8 (4): 449–78.

PRUD'HOMME, R. 1995. The dangers of decentralization. *World Bank Research Observer,* 10 (2): 201–20.

QIAN, Y., and WEINGAST, B. 1997. Federalism as a commitment to preserving market incentives. *Journal of Economic Perspectives,* 11 (4): 83–92.

RIKER, W. H. 1964: *Federalism.* Boston: Little Brown and Company.

RIKER, W. H. 1975. Federalism. Pp. 93–172 in *Handbook of Political Science*, v: *Governmental Institutions and Processes*, ed. N. W. Polsby and F. I. Greenstein. Reading, Pa.: Addison-Wesley.

—— 1980. Implications from the disequilibrium of majority rule for the study of institutions. *American Political Science Review*, 74: 432–46.

—— and LEMCO, J. 1987. The relations between structure and stability. Pp. 113–34 in *The Development of American Federalism*, ed. W. H. Riker. Boston: Kluwer Academic Publishers.

RODDEN, J. 2002. The dilemma of fiscal federalism: grants and fiscal performance around the world. *American Journal of Political Science*, 46 (3): 670–87.

—— 2003. Reviving Leviathan: fiscal federalism and the growth of government. *International Organization*, 57: 695–729.

—— 2004. Comparative federalism and decentralization: on meaning and measurement. *Comparative Politics*, 36 (4): 481–500.

—— 2005. And the last shall be the first: federalism and soft budget constraints in Germany. Unpublished paper. Department of Political Science, Massachusetts Institute of Technology.

—— 2006a. *Hamilton's Paradox: The Promise and Peril of Fiscal Federalism*. Cambridge: Cambridge University Press.

—— (2006b). The political economy of federalism. In *Oxford Handbook of Political Economy*, ed. B. Weingast and D. Wittman. Oxford: Oxford University Press.

—— ESKELAND, G. and LITVACK, J., eds. 2003. *Fiscal Decentralization and the Challenge of Hard Budget Constraints*. Cambridge, Mass.: MIT Press.

—— and ROSE-ACKERMAN, S. 1997. Does federalism preserve markets? *Virginia Law Review*, 83 (7): 1521–73.

—— and WIBBELS, W. 2002. Beyond the fiction of federalism: macroeconomic management in multi-tiered systems. *World Politics*, 54 (4): 494–531.

—— —— 2005. Retrospective voting, coattails, and accountability in regional elections. Paper presented at the Annual Meetings of the American Political Science Association Meetings, Washington, DC.

ROEDER, P. G. 2000. The robustness of institutions in ethnically plural societies. Unpublished paper. Department of Political Science, University of California, San Diego.

ROSE-ACKERMAN, S. 1980. Risk taking and re-election: does federalism promote innovation? *Journal of Legal Studies*, 9: 593–612.

—— 1981. Does federalism matter? Political choice in a federal republic. *Journal of Political Economy*, 89 (11): 152–65.

—— 1983. Beyond Tiebout: modelling the political economy of local government. In Zodrow 1983: 55–84.

SCHNEIDER, A. 2003. Who gets what from whom? The impact of decentralization on tax capacity and pro-poor policy. Working Paper 179. Institute of Development Studies, Brighton.

SEABRIGHT, P. 1996. Accountability and decentralization in government: an incomplete contracts model. *European Economic Review*, 40: 61–89.

SHEPSLE, K. 1986. Institutional equilibrium and equilibrium institutions. In *Political Science: The Science of Politics*, ed. H. Weisberg. New York: Agathon.

SRINIVASAN, T. N., and WALLACK, J. S. eds. Forthcoming. *The Dynamics of Federalism*. Cambridge: Cambridge University Press.

STEIN, E. 1999. Fiscal decentralization and government size in Latin America. *Journal of Applied Economics*, 2 (2): 357–91.

STEPAN, A. 1999. Federalism and democracy: beyond the U.S. model. *Journal of Democracy*, 10 (4): 19–34.

—— 2001. *Arguing Comparative Politics*. Oxford: Oxford University Press.

STIGLITZ, J. E. 1983. The theory of local public goods twenty years after Tiebout: a perspective. In Zodrow 1983: 17–53.

STRUMPF, K. 2002. Does government decentralization increase policy innovation? *Journal of Public Economic Theory*, 4: 207–43.

SWENDEN, W. 2004. *Federalism and Second Chambers: Regional Representation in Parliamentary Federations: The Australian Senate and German Bundesrat Compared*. Brussels: PIE-Peter Lang.

TAYLOR, B. 2005. Force and federalism: controlling coercion in federal hybrid regimes. Paper presented at the conference Postcommunist state and society: transnational and national politics. Syracuse University.

THEIL, H. 1971. *Principles of Econometrics*. New York: Wiley.

TIEBOUT, C. 1956. A pure theory of local expenditures. *Journal of Political Economy*, 64: 416–24.

TOCQUEVILLE, A. DE 1835/1964. *Democracy in America*. New York: Washington Square Press.

TREISMAN, D. 1999. *After the Deluge*. Ann Arbor: University of Michigan Press.

—— 2000. Decentralization and inflation: commitment, collective action or continuity? *American Political Science Review*, 94 (4): 837–57.

—— Forthcoming. *The Architecture of Government*. Cambridge: Cambridge University Press.

VOLDEN, C. 2004. The politics of competitive federalism: a race to the bottom in welfare benefits? *American Journal of Political Science*, 46 (2): 352–63.

—— 2005. Intergovernmental political competition in American federalism. *American Journal of Political Science*, 49 (2): 327–43.

WATTS, R. L. 1999. *Comparing Federal Systems*. Institute of Intergovernmental Relations. Kingston, Ontario: Queen's University.

WEINGAST, B. 1993. Constitutions as governance structures: the political foundations of secure markets. *Journal of Institutional and Theoretical Economics*, 149 (1): 286–311.

—— 1995. The economic role of political institutions: market preserving federalism and economic development. *Journal of Law, Economics and Organization*, 11 (1): 1–31.

—— 2002. Rational choice institutionalism. Pp. 660–92 in *Political Science: State of the Discipline*, ed. I. Katznelson and H. V. Milner. London: Norton and Company.

—— MONTINOLA, G. and QIAN, Y. 1995. Federalism, Chinese style: the political basis for economic success in China. *World Politics*, 48 (1): 50–81.

WHEARE, K. C. 1946. *Federal Government*. New York: Oxford University Press.

WIBBELS, E. 2000. Federalism and the politics of macroeconomic policy and performance. *American Journal of Political Science*, 44 (4): 687–702.

—— 2001. Federal politics and market reform in the developing world. *Studies in Comparative International Development*, 36 (2): 27–53.

—— 2003. Bailouts, budget constraints, and Leviathans. *Comparative Political Studies*, 36 (5): 475–508.

—— 2005a. *Federalism and the Market*. Cambridge: Cambridge University Press.

—— 2005b. Decentralized governance, constitution formation, and redistribution. *Constitutional Political Economy*, 16 (2): 161–88.

WILDASIN, D. 1991. Income redistribution in a common labor market. *American Economic Review*, 81 (4): 757–74.

—— ed. 1997. *Fiscal Aspects of Evolving Federations*. New York: Cambridge University Press.

ZIBLATT, D. 2006. *Structuring the State: The Formation of Italy and Germany and the Puzzle of Federalism*. Princeton: Princeton University Press.

ZODROW, G. R. ed. 1983. *Local Provision of Public Services: The Tiebout Model after Twenty-Five Years*. New York: Academic Press.

COALITION THEORY AND GOVERNMENT FORMATION

KAARE STRØM

BENJAMIN NYBLADE

1 COALITION BARGAINING, GOVERNMENT FORMATION, AND REPRESENTATIVE DEMOCRACY

A COALITION is a team of individuals or groups that unites for a common purpose. For example, teams of politicians, who may all belong to one or several political parties, coalesce for the purpose of running a government. Together, these coalition members convert a wide range of social demands into a manageable set of public policies. This is only one form that coalition politics takes, but in democratic societies it is probably the most important one.

The ability of political actors to form successful coalitions is essential to representative democracy. In a democracy, no one person can legislate or exert power without

* We are grateful to Arthur Lupia and Paul L. Mitchell for their valuable contributions to other scholarship on which this chapter builds.

the support of others. Open societies typically foster a multitude of political actors who must join forces to have any hope of getting their way. Democratic rules generally require that decisions be supported by a simple or qualified majority of the people's elected representatives.

While working for a common cause, coalition members may disagree about important matters. Some disagreements stem from attempts to please distinct constituencies. For example, members who represent urbanites want policies that are different from those favored by representatives from rural regions. Conflicts can also arise when multiple members compete for important and scarce spoils or offices (e.g. that of the prime minister). How coalition members pursue their common interests and manage internal conflicts affects the fate and effectiveness of the coalitions they form.

Understanding coalition bargaining helps us grasp not only government decisions, but also who gets into government in the first place. This is particularly true in parliamentary democracies, where the government (executive) rests on the support of the parliament. Although coalition bargaining among political parties in presidential democracies can be quite important (Amorim Neto 2006; Cheibub 2002; Cheibub, Przeworski, and Saiegh 2004), it generally does not as directly affect who controls the top executive offices. Hence, the primary focus of this chapter is on government formation in parliamentary democracies.

In parliamentary regimes, government coalitions are typically formed by and through political parties. Political parties are in themselves coalitions of individual politicians who run for election under the same label. In bargaining over control of the government, however, parties tend to behave very cohesively. Hence, this chapter follows the bulk of the literature on government formation, focusing on coalition bargaining amongst unitary political parties (see Laver and Schofield 1990; Müller and Strøm 1999 for justifications of the unitary party assumption).[1] Party cohesion in parliamentary systems is driven in part precisely by the government's need to maintain parliamentary support (or at least toleration) at all times. In presidential systems, the executive is not so vulnerable, and consequently party cohesion also tends to be lower.

At every stage of a government's life cycle in parliamentary democracies, coalition decisions emerge from bargaining. Parties to such bargains have to be backward looking and forward looking at the same time. The outcomes are shaped not only by past bargains that affect the members' resources and the constraints under which they operate, but also by the fact that bargaining occurs in the shadow of future elections and under the constant threat posed by political rivals.

Bargaining theory, and more generally the game-theoretic tradition, has since Riker's (1962) seminal work been the dominant analytical framework in which coalition formation has been understood. In this chapter we show how bargaining theory has helped us understand key aspects of government formation, but also how our understanding of

---

[1] Although one growth area in the study of coalitions is in considering the importance of intra-party dynamics (Strøm 1994; Druckman 1996).

coalition bargaining has gradually moved beyond the simplistic assumptions of the first generations of such theories. We examine three specific questions in more detail: First, under what circumstances do coalition governments form? Second, what accounts for the type of government that forms? In other words, what determines whether the emerging government has minority support in parliament, whether it is a minimal winning coalition, or whether it is a surplus coalition? Finally, we consider the factors that influence whether specific parties or types of parties obtain government membership.

2 STABLE OR AD HOC COALITIONS?

The most fundamental question about coalition formation is one that is rarely raised. Coalitions can be made one issue or bill at a time, or they can be (by intention, at least) much more durable and comprehensive. What explains the choice of ad hoc versus stable coalitions? To the extent that political parties are a stable coalition of politicians, this is a question that we can drive all the way down to the level of the individual legislator. Why might politicians prefer to operate as solitary and sovereign decision makers, choosing sides from issue to issue with whatever allies might be available? And, on the other hand, why do politicians sometimes (in fact, often) submit to party authority and decide to support the policies and alliances that their party leaders favor? Similarly, the parties to which these politicians belong can form either ad hoc, free-floating coalitions, or more stable, formalized ones.

These decisions can best be understood within the framework of transaction cost politics (Dixit 1996; Strøm, Müller, and Bergman 2007). Free-floating coalitions have their advantages. They allow for more freedom, and they are more efficient in the sense that parties or legislators never have to vote for proposals they do not sincerely favor. Nor do they have to pre-commit themselves to common positions on issues that they may not even be able to anticipate. But on the other hand, compared to more stable or formalized coalitions, short-term ad hoc alliances entail a range of disadvantages, such as:

- *Increased transaction costs.* Free-floating majorities force participants to negotiate every decision anew. The time and energy needed to proceed in this manner can exhaust a party's resources and reduce its abilities to accomplish broad or multiple goals. An important part of the rationale for stable coalitions is thus that they economize on transaction costs.
- *Less policy impact and continuity.* Without a formal coalition, political decisions might not last long enough to be implemented, much less have any significant impact. In a setting without stable parties or coalitions, legislative victories may be very short-lived. Why should the majority that forms on a Tuesday morning not overturn the laws made by Monday evening's rulers? Such instability would greatly reduce the value of any decision that a governing coalition would be able to make.

After all, what is the value of governing if you have no idea whether your decisions will immediately be reversed? Such uncertainty adds another type of transaction cost.

- *Less faithful implementation.* Even if a free-floating majority were in power long enough to name its cabinet ministers, and even if its decisions were not immediately reversed, there is little reason to expect others in government to abide by these directives. Indeed, we should expect bureaucrats who dislike today's ministerial directives to disregard them if they believe that they can get away with it (see e.g. Huber 1998; Huber and Lupia 2001). In other words, just as on the high seas, the prospect of leadership instability makes mutiny more attractive.

- *Less policy credibility.* The problem of policy credibility does not end with policy implementation. For most government policies to be effective, even people outside of government must cooperate. Citizens must abide by the laws, businesses must adhere to the terms of their contracts, and countries must act within the terms of their treaties. If a government cannot credibly uphold agreements tomorrow that its leaders sign today, anyone who deals with that government has less incentive to trust or cooperate with it. In a polity governed strictly by free-floating majorities, public policy might have little long-term credibility. This might adversely affect citizens in many ways. Imagine, for example, what buying a house or investing in stocks would be like if basic property rights were subject to frequent and unpredictable change. Indeed, people attempting to base important social, political, or economic plans on government policies would likely consider free-floating majorities disastrous. Such lack of predictability could in turn cause economic inefficiencies and major social problems.

- *Less reliable voter support.* In democratic countries, politicians can bargain for a place in government *only if* citizens delegate policy-making authority to them through elections. The electoral connection—the threat that eventually voters will judge coalition members—governs their behavior. Therefore, if voters prefer a government whose actions are at least somewhat predictable, then politicians who can credibly commit themselves to something other than a transitory coalition stand to gain. Members of stable coalitions can also more easily establish "policy brand names" that reduce citizens' uncertainty about the policy consequences of voting for a particular candidate (Cox and McCubbins 1993). Indeed, stable coalitions make it easier for voters to hold government officials accountable for their actions than do free-floating majorities.

In sum, formalized, stable coalescence is a survival strategy—it enables politicians to influence government decisions, earn the trust of non-governmental actors, and maintain good long-term relations with voters while paying relatively low transaction costs. For politicians operating in parliamentary institutions, they are a collective good. To the extent that such relations and cost savings are more important than the policy freedom that free-floating coalitions could allow, stable coalitions should form.

Yet, politicians do not always choose stable coalitions. In some political systems, such as the Scandinavian countries, an environment of high information certainty and relatively low risks may be responsible for the fact that many parliamentary decisions are made through ad hoc or short-term bargaining. In presidential democracies, parties are typically less cohesive, and decision-making coalitions may often be more ad hoc (Cheibub, Przeworski, and Saiegh 2004). And in general, the fact that there may be collective benefits to be had from stable coalitions does not necessarily mean that legislators will choose to form them. Yet, even in situations in which formal executive coalitions do not form, stable legislative coalitions frequently exist (see e.g. Warwick 1994; Bale and Dann 2002). Thus, the absence of formal executive coalitions, in addition to being driven by transaction costs, also is influenced by the relative costs and benefits potential support parties can procure outside of government, particularly their ability to extract policy concessions without incurring the potentially high electoral costs of government membership (Strøm 1984, 1990b; Laver and Shepsle 1996; Mitchell and Nyblade 2006).

3 GOVERNMENT TYPE

Extreme turnover in cabinet offices is rare, although extreme stability is not the mode, either. In presidential democracies, executive terms are fixed (barring resignation, death, or impeachment), and this rigidity or predictability affects cabinet composition as well. Yet, the partisan composition of presidential cabinets may be more fluid than what is typical in parliamentary systems, since presidents may reshuffle their cabinets to increase their legislative or popular support. And in doing so, presidents will tend to be less constrained by the partisan composition of their cabinet (Amorim Neto 2006).

Given that government coalitions in parliamentary democracies tend to be fairly stable, the overriding concern among students of such governments has been to understand the type of coalition that forms. Scholars have found it useful to distinguish between governments based on the parliamentary support of the parties that participate in the government: whether these have minority support, constitute a minimal winning coalition, or have surplus members. Sometimes a single party may have a majority of seats and thus is able to govern alone. However, most parliamentary democracies, especially in Europe, feature proportional representation, which most often results in situations in which no party has a legislative majority. In such *minority situations*, it has traditionally been assumed that a majority coalition should form and that minority governments are deviations to be explained. This is because in parliamentary systems governments rest on the support—implicit or explicit—of a parliamentary majority (Müller, Bergman, and Strøm 2003).

Riker's influential work (see below) narrowed this prediction down to a minimal winning coalition. When a valuable prize is divided by a group, and the decision must be made by a simple majority rule, a minimal winning coalition maximizes the potential payoff to a majority of the group (Riker 1962). As government membership is generally considered to be a valuable prize, minimal winning coalitions should be favored.

Although minimal winning coalitions may be the "natural" outcome of bargaining, they are in fact not the most common outcome, at least in minority situations in Europe. In Table 32.1 we report some basic characteristics of coalition governments in the context where they have most often been studied: national governments in the parliamentary systems of Europe. The table reports on a sample of 424 governments formed in seventeen West European parliamentary or semi-presidential democracies from 1945 to 2000. Of these governments, only 13 percent were single-party majority governments. Twenty-two percent were single-party minority governments, while 44 percent were majority and 18 percent minority coalitions. Out of the majority coalitions, roughly three-fifths were minimal winning, whereas the rest were oversized. Thus, if we confine ourselves to minority situations, roughly 25 percent of the cabinets formed were single-party minority governments rather than formal governmental coalitions.[2] Almost as

Table 32.1   Coalition governments in Western Europe, 1945–1999

Country		Non-partisan		One party majority		One party minority		Coalitions		MWC		Surplus majority		Minority	
	n	n	%	n	%	n	%	n	%	n	%	n	%	n	%
Austria	22	0	—	4	18.2	1	4.5	17	77.3	14	63.6	3	13.6	1	4.5
Belgium	33	0	—	3	9.1	2	6.1	28	84.8	14	42.4	12	36.4	4	12.1
Denmark	31	0	—	0	—	14	45.2	17	54.8	4	12.9	0	—	27	87.1
Finland	44	7	15.9	0	—	4	9.1	33	75.0	7	15.9	20	45.5	10	22.7
France	23	0	—	1	4.3	5	21.7	17	73.9	7	30.4	8	34.8	7	30.4
Germany	26	0	—	1	3.8	3	11.5	22	84.6	17	65.4	5	19.2	3	11.5
Greece	11	1	9.1	7	63.6	1	9.1	2	18.2	1	9.1	1	9.1	1	9.1
Iceland	26	0	—	0	—	4	15.4	22	84.6	17	65.4	4	15.4	5	19.2
Ireland	22	0	—	6	27.3	6	27.3	10	45.5	5	22.7	0	—	11	50.0
Italy	51	1	2.0	0	—	14	27.5	36	70.6	4	7.8	23	45.1	23	45.1
Luxembourg	16	0	—	0	—	0	—	16	100.0	15	93.8	1	6.3	0	—
Netherlands	23	0	—	0	—	0	—	23	100.0	9	39.1	11	47.8	3	13.6
Norway	26	0	—	6	23.1	12	46.2	8	30.8	3	11.5	0	—	17	65.4
Portugal	14	3	21.4	2	14.3	3	21.4	6	42.9	3	21.4	3	21.4	3	21.4
Spain	10	2	20.0	2	20.0	6	60.0	0	—	0	—	0	—	6	60.0
Sweden	26	0	—	2	7.7	17	65.4	7	26.9	5	19.2	0	—	19	73.1
Britain	20	0	—	19	95.0	1	5.0	0	—	0	—	0	—	1	5.0
Overall	424	14	3.3	53	12.8	93	21.9	264	62.3	125	29.5	91	21.5	141	33.3

Source: Mitchell and Nyblade 2006.

---

[2] These data comes from Müller and Strøm (2000); Strøm, Müller, and Bergman (2007); and the analyses reported in this and subsequent sections draw on Mitchell and Nyblade (2007).

many coalitions deviated from our expectation by being oversized. In minority situations, then, minority governments have been the modal category, followed by minimal winning coalitions and then by surplus governments. Most countries in Western Europe have experience with all three types of government, although there is wide cross-national variation in the incidence of the various cabinet types.

4 Bargaining Theory and Government Formation

In order to make sense of these facts, let us consider the contributions of bargaining theory. The classic application of bargaining theory to political coalitions is William Riker's (1962) *The Theory of Political Coalitions*. Applying the logic of von Neumann and Morgenstern (1944) to political situations, Riker's most famous result—his "size principle"—predicts the formation of minimal winning coalitions. Using cooperative game theory, Riker modeled the formation of political coalitions as a fixed-sum bargaining game, in which participants must agree to the division of something valuable to each of them (in our case, government membership). And as Riker succinctly suggests: "In social situations similar to n-person, zero-sum games, with side-payments, participants create coalitions just as large as they believe will ensure winning and no larger" (Riker 1962, 47).

The size principle rests fundamentally on two further principles, which Riker calls the "strategic principle" and the "disequilibrium principle." Undersize ruling coalitions will have incentive to add members because the majority of parliament that is excluded from government would have both the means and incentive to upset the minority government (the strategic principle). On the other hand, members of oversized coalitions will find that the benefits of government membership are being distributed too thinly and choose to eject surplus members of the coalition (the disequilibrium principle).

Of course, coalition formation is not always strategically identical to an n-person, fixed-sum game with side payments. The degree to which coalition formation in the real world approximates Riker's model clearly varies from case to case. The greater the divergence, the less explanatory or predictive power the model may have. While reality may diverge from Riker's model in numerous ways, several are of particular interest: the payoffs, the information available to the players, and the bargaining environment in which they operate.

4.1 Payoffs

Riker assumes that the payoffs from coalition bargaining are fixed sum, which means that one player's gain must be another player's loss, and that coalition members always receive a positive payoff and non-members none. These assumptions are not always self-evident.

In the real world, parties sometimes turn down the opportunity to be a government member (e.g. the Agrarians in Sweden in 1957, the Christian People's Party in Norway in 1981, the Labour Party in Ireland on a number of occasions, see also Bale and Dann 2002), which should not occur if parties invariably derive positive utility from government membership and none from opposition. One reason why government membership may in fact be costly is that, at least in West European parliamentary democracies, government membership is more of an electoral liability than an asset (Rose and Mackie 1983; Narud and Valen 2006). Small parties that are particularly vulnerable in the electorate may have to think carefully about whether being a minor cog in a government coalition will be worth the likely electoral cost. Furthermore, it is worth the noting that the fixed-sum payoff also is violated by the fact that the durability of the government varies with the type of government formed. Majority governments, for example, generally endure longer than minority governments. So not only does the size of the shares of power depend on coalition bargaining, so too may the value of the pie that is being divided, thus further complicating the bargaining situation (see Diermeier, Eraslan, and Merlo 2002, 2003).

If the value of incumbency varies, we should expect that the more "valuable" government is, the more likely MWCs will form. This is in fact the primary force driving Riker's size principle. What could make office more or less valuable? Three such factors suggest themselves: (1) the richness of the spoils of office, (2) the policy-making opportunities that holding office entails, and (3) the expected electoral gains (or losses) resulting from incumbency (Strøm 1990b; Müller and Strøm 1999). On each of these dimensions, the value of office should be considered relative to the prospect of being in opposition (see Strøm 1990a, 42). Membership in a governing coalition is more valuable the greater the "perks" associated with it, the more it tends to positively influence electoral performance, and the more it moves policy outcomes closer to the preferences of its members (Müller and Strøm 1999). Thus, Strøm (1984, 1990a) considers two primary factors in explaining minority governments: electoral consequences and policy influence. The less governing parties are favored over the opposition in policy influence and expected electoral returns, the less attractive it is to be an incumbent, and the greater the likelihood of minority governments.

Existing scholarship has focused heavily on the second of these considerations, namely policy influence. Axelrod (1970) and De Swaan (1973) were the first scholars to give policy a more central role in the study of coalition bargaining. De Swaan assumed that policy coherence is the attribute actors attempt to maximize. Utility requires producing agreement on preferred policies and maintaining coalition harmony over time. Therefore, players prefer to join winning coalitions with the smallest possible dispersion in policy preferences ("closed minimal range" theory).[3] The general behavioral assumption is that ideologically connected coalitions will have a lower conflict of interest and a therefore a greater policy value to their members. They should therefore also be easier to form and sustain.

---

[3] De Swaan stated his central behavioral assumption as follows: "An actor strives to bring about a winning coalition in which he is included and which he expects to adopt a policy that is as close as possible, on a scale of policies, to his own most preferred policy" (1973, 88).

In recent work, most scholars have tended to move beyond the simple generalized office payoffs of Riker (1962) and Leiserson (1966), following Axelrod (1970) and de Swaan (1973) in incorporating parties' preferences over policy matters in modeling the bargaining game. These scholars frequently draw on the spatial bargaining logic of Black (1958) and Downs (1957), to emphasize the advantages of centrally located policy preferences, in unidimensional or multidimensional issue spaces (see Schofield 1993; Crombez 1996; Laver and Shepsle 1990, 1996).

These models emphasize how both relative size and central policy preferences enhance parties' bargaining power. Unlike extensions of Riker's approach, which generally explain coalition formation by focusing on the degree to which the bargaining situation conforms to their models, these models explain coalition types by focusing on the resources (seat shares) and preferences of those bargaining. Whereas these models differ in their relative emphasis on policy vs. office preferences, fundamentally they emphasize how differences in bargaining power, rather than differences in the bargaining environment, influence coalition formation.

The logic behind these bargaining power models is relatively straightforward, although in actual development they can become quite complex, as the models seek to incorporate multiple issue dimensions along with seat shares and sometimes other factors. Consider for the moment majority situations, in which, assuming that a simple majority is sufficient for winning, a single party is able to form a government by itself. While majority situations are generally ignored in most studies of government formation, they are instructive because they constitute the extreme case in which bargaining power is disproportionately concentrated in the hands of a single party. In a majority situation, by definition the majority party can form a minimum winning coalition, and it is also the median party on every issue dimension, which gives it disproportionate advantages in resource as well as office terms.

Yet, even in non-majority situations certain parties may have disproportionate bargaining power. A large, centrally located party with many potential coalition partners may be in a position to form a government on its own. In general, the costs of not coalescing can in these cases be minimized. In non-majority situations, the greater the bargaining power of the dominant player in coalition bargaining, the smaller the government is likely to be. That is to say, the concentration of bargaining power makes minority government more likely relative to MWCs and even more so relative to surplus coalition governments. This fundamental idea underlies the logic of almost all policy/size theories of coalition formation, and is most directly suggested by Crombez (1996) and Laver and Shepsle (1996).

Thus, the more bargaining power is concentrated in the hands of a single party, the less likely a coalition is to form. For example, this means that a near-majority party is more likely to form a minority government, as it only needs to pick up a few seats for each parliamentary vote. Similarly, a single party that can consistently rely on parliamentary support from allies who are not in government improves its bargaining position compared to parties that do not have any allies of this kind. Generally, large parties that are centrally located have greater bargaining power, as they have the ability to form coalitions with parties that are both on their left and their right (Laver and Schofield

1990; Crombez 1996; Laver and Shepsle 1996). In presidential systems, and especially under divided government, bargaining power may tend to be more dispersed than under parliamentary government.

4.2 Information

Riker recognized that other assumptions of his model may be even less applicable to the real world. Perhaps most important is the assumption of complete and perfect information. Real-world governments emerge from bargaining encounters in which the parties typically have much less than full information about their rivals' true preferences, what the next election may bring, and a range of other matters. The fewer and more cohesive the parties, and the longer and more consistent their track records, the more coalition bargaining situations are likely to approximate this rather stringent requirement. As the information of the players gets worse, they get more likely to hedge their bets by increasing the size of their coalitions. As Riker (1962, 88–9) suggests: "The greater the degree of imperfection or incompleteness of information, the larger will be the coalitions that coalition-makers seek to form and the more frequently will winning coalitions actually formed be greater than minimum size." Dodd (1976) tested this proposition on a sample of national governments and found supportive results.

The parties can attempt to reduce uncertainty by making credible commitments about their future actions. However, when the ability to make such credible commitments is absent or imperfect, coalition parties may have incentives to "blackmail" each other, threatening to bring down the government in order to extract concessions. To avoid this threat, a coalition may seek to add surplus actors as "insurance." In a formal model of legislative coalition formation, Carrubba and Volden (2000) predict that in order to create a more stable logroll (and avoid "blackmail" by individual members), parties create "minimum necessary coalitions," which may be larger than minimal winning. In a subsequent (2004) article, they suggest that surplus coalitions are particularly likely when the number of and diversity of actors is great, when bills are hard to pass, and when legislation tends to be costly or not very beneficial to its members. Operationally, they identify these conditions with a great number of parties and members of parliament, a bicameral system with the upper and lower house divided, a highly polarized parliament, and a small government (in the proportion of taxes relative to GDP).

In a series of publications in the mid-1980s, Eric Browne and associates (Browne, Frendreis, and Gleiber 1984, 1986) presented a more radical critique of existing coalition theory, emphasizing the importance of unforeseeable events in coalition politics. Changes of government, they claimed, could best be understood not as resulting from informed and rational bargaining among party leaders, but as the consequences of random "critical events," or exogenous shocks, that impacted on them. While few scholars have signed on to the full implications of this argument, subsequent scholarship has attempted empirically to incorporate exogenous shocks into models of cabinet duration (King et al. 1990) and theoretically to account for the effects of exogenous shocks on electoral expectations (Lupia and Strøm 1995; Diermeier and Stevenson 1999,

2000) It seems fair to expect that the exploration of informational effects will continue to be a major part of the literature on coalition politics.

4.3 Decision Rules, Institutions, and the Bargaining Environment

The third and final way in which subsequent scholarship has improved on Riker's conception of coalition politics is in its understanding of the bargaining environment, including the effects of political institutions. Fully capturing such influences required a shift in theoretical assumptions. Riker's work was based on cooperative game theory, with the specific bargaining process unmodeled. Such models generally assume that parties can make credible commitments and that the most "efficient" government will emerge. However, a substantial body of more recent scholarship has instead built on non-cooperative game-theoretic models, which focus on the incentives of individual parties and insist on a credible depiction of each stage of the bargaining process. By thus modeling the process of government formation, non-cooperative models of government formation seek to understand bargaining dynamics in ways that cooperative models cannot capture. They also offer better ways to understand the importance of institutional rules that impinge on coalition bargaining.

The range of political institutions that may affect coalition bargaining is great, and political scientists have only begun to examine such effects systematically (for surveys, see Laver and Schofield 1990; Strøm, Budge, and Laver 1994; Strøm, Müller, and Bergman 2003). Institutions help define the formal requirements that government coalitions must meet, the process by which they form, the ways in which they can make policy, and the conditions under which they can be removed and replaced.

In the first place, constitutions differ in the demands that they place on incoming governments. Some national constitutions, such as those of Germany and Spain, feature a constructive vote of no confidence, which means that no change of government is possible unless the incoming government has a positive vote of support (an investiture) from a majority of the members of parliament. Other countries have formal investiture votes but no majority requirement (Italy), whereas yet others have no investiture requirement at all (Denmark). Bergman (1993) has explored the differences between positive (in which the incoming government must garner explicit majority support) and negative (in which there is no such require-ment) parliamentarism and traced their consequences for coalition bargaining. When a formal investiture vote is required, coalitions are more likely to form. By forcing the parties in parliament to vote "Yeah" or "Nay" on each government at its very inception, investiture votes may render minority government less viable, and thereby make formal coalitions more likely to form. If there is a formal investiture vote, it is more difficult for a party tacitly to help keep a minority government in existence, yet to remain somewhat dissociated from it, so that the party can reject any responsibility for government policy and campaign against the incumbents in future elections.

Governments may also need to garner more than a simple majority in one chamber in order to "win" in coalition bargaining. In some countries the government is accountable to two chambers, so that what is a majority in one chamber may not suffice in the other. Druckman, Martin, and Thies (2005) report that the need to form a majority in a second chamber increases the likelihood of surplus coalitions.

The decision-making environment within the executive branch may also affect coalition bargaining. Thus, Laver and Shepsle (1996) build on the literature emphasizing structure-induced equilibria (Shepsle 1979; Shepsle and Weingast 1981), and argue that the set of cabinet portfolios and their respective jurisdictions decisively constrain the set of feasible policy options on which any coalition could agree, since it is difficult to prevent the holder of any given portfolio from implementing its own most preferred policy in that policy area. The data required to properly test the Laver and Shepsle model differ substantially from the type of data on government formation collected prior their work, so rigorous empirical testing of their approach has been limited (see however Warwick 1999; Laver and Shepsle 1999; Martin and Stevenson 2001). With more recent data collection efforts on portfolio allocation, however, further tests of portfolio allocation models can be anticipated. Research on Gamson's law concerning portfolio proportionality (e.g. Druckman and Warwick 2005; Warwick and Druckman 2001; Ansolabehere et al. 2005) and on the role of junior ministers (e.g. Thies 2001; Manow and Zorn 2004) has already built on this growing interest in portfolio allocation.

While most models assume that the set of relevant players includes only the parliamentary parties (or their leaders), institutional reality may be more complex. In semi-presidential democracies, governments may not only be accountable to parliament or the legislature, but also to the president, which can significantly change the bargaining environment (Amorim Neto and Strøm forthcoming). Governments may also be interested in pursuing actions that require greater support than a simple majority in parliament allows. For example, a government may wish to enact a constitutional amendment that would require a legislative supermajority. To the extent that a simple majority is insufficient to satisfy the needs of its members, the likelihood of surplus majority coalitions increases.

Moreover, institutional rules governing the process of coalition bargaining may be of crucial importance. Of particular importance may be the rules designating the formateur, the person entrusted with the task of negotiating a coalition. Baron (1991) models this process (the recognition rule), considering both fixed and probabilistic sequences, and shows how varying the formateur sequence can have a large impact on the outcome. Subsequent work has shown that formateurs tend to receive a disproportionate share of office payoffs (Warwick and Druckman 2001; Ansolabehere et al. 2005), particularly when we consider not simply their shares of ministerial portfolios, but also the relative importance of the various ministries.

5 Explaining Coalition Formation and Government Type

Bargaining models have thus tended to help improve our understanding of coalition formation by focusing on two different sets of factors: those relating to the bargaining environment and those relating to bargaining power. Both play an important role in explaining government formation in parliamentary democracies. A recent study of coalition formation in minority situations in Western Europe (Mitchell and Nyblade 2006), based on a particularly extensive set of data, finds both types of factors crucial in explaining whether ad hoc legislative coalitions or more formal executive coalitions form, and also in explaining the type of government that forms.

When government membership is more likely to cause serious costs to parties, formal executive coalitions are less likely to form. This may particularly be true when electoral volatility is high and when the previous government was terminated due to a critical event. Similarly, as opposition influence increases (when the relative benefits in policy influence of being in government decline), coalition formation becomes less likely. And in situations in which there is an inconclusive bargaining round—when parties specifically reject a potential coalition, indicating that their behavior is driven by more than simply the value placed on being in office—coalition government is less likely.

While the variables mentioned above capture the nature of the bargaining environment, the distribution of bargaining power amongst parties seems to have at least as large an impact on coalition formation. When bargaining power is disproportionately concentrated in the hands of a single party, even if that party does not have a parliamentary majority, single-party government is more likely. A consistent finding throughout the history of coalition studies is that near-majority parties are particularly likely to form minority governments (Strøm 1990a; Laver and Schofield 1990; Crombez 1996). Mitchell and Nyblade (2007) find, however, that the bargaining power of the largest party (as measured by the Banzhaf index) is an even better predictor of coalition formation than is its seat share.[4] When the largest party has particularly large bargaining power (many potential partners with whom it can form winning coalitions, while it is more difficult to form winning coalitions without the party), it is much more likely to form a government on its own. Furthermore, when the largest party is also the median party in parliament, this effect is even more pronounced. Policy centrality in itself helps favored parties avoid broad coalitions.

Although most scholarship concerns itself with predicting minority and/or surplus governments as deviations from the norm of minimal winning coalitions, one could just as easily ask what makes MWCs more likely to form. Building on Riker's work, we

---

[4] The Banzhaf Power Index measures the ability of actors with differentially weighted vote shares to influence the outcome of a vote (Banzhaf 1965). The index calculates for each voter the proportion of potential vote combinations the actor is able to "swing" (change from winning to losing), relative to the ability of other actors to swing a vote. For example, in a 100-seat legislature in which there are four parties, with 45, 26, 25, and 4 seats, if the decision rule is simple majority, the four-seat party has no bargaining power because they are unable to change the outcome of any vote, as they cannot help form any minimal winning coalition.

expect MWCs to be most likely when the bargaining environment most closely resembles a simple cooperative bargaining model. Thus, when uncertainty is low, the value of government membership is high, and the decision rule is simple majority in a single chamber of parliament, MWCs should be most likely. Furthermore, following the logic of non-cooperative bargaining models such as Crombez (1996) and Laver and Shepsle (1996), minimal winning coalitions should form when bargaining power is neither greatly concentrated in the hands of a single party (who then can form a minority government without incurring a great cost), nor so dispersed that a surplus government is formed in order to avoid the potential for blackmail. A president may complicate bargaining by dispersing bargaining power amongst more actors. So all else equal, MWCs may also be less likely in semi-presidential or presidential systems.

Empirical analysis generally supports these suggestions (Mitchell and Nyblade 2007). In minority situations, minimal winning coalitions are more likely to occur when government is valuable: when opposition influence is low, electoral volatility low, and the previous government was not ended by a "critical event." Minimal winning coalitions are also clearly related to the distribution of bargaining power in parliament. For example, when a "dimension by dimension median party" (cf. Laver and Shepsle 2000) exists that is quite small and has relatively weak bargaining power, it is especially likely to form a minimal winning coalition.

In contrast to minimal winning coalitions, minority governments have traditionally been seen as unviable and ineffective (Johnson 1975; Powell 1982). Yet, minority governments, as suggested above, need not be anomalies, and on many performance dimensions minority governments can be equal or superior to their majority counter-parts (Strøm 1985). Not surprisingly, the factors explaining minority governments are quite similar to those that explain the lack of formal coalitions, since a large majority of minority governments are not coalitions. Empirical analyses suggest that, in addition to the two major factors identified in Strøm (1984) (electoral decisiveness and opposition influence), other measures that capture the relative value of office are important as well, such as the size and bargaining power of the largest party.

Surplus coalitions, on the other hand, generally have been understood as results of the inability of parties to credibly commit to each other. A minimal winning coalition can be brought down by any one of its members. So, if the parties do not trust each other, or cannot credibly commit to supporting each other over their term in office, they may find it useful to add a surplus member, so as to make it harder for one of the members to "blackmail" the government. This argument concerning surplus governments can be traced directly to Riker (1962), has been modeled more generally in theories of legislative logrolling (Carrubba and Volden 2000), and used to explain the creation of surplus governments in parliamentary democracies specifically (Carrubba and Volden 2004). The threat of blackmail is most acute when bargaining power is broadly dispersed amongst many parties; surplus governments are more likely to form in these cases. Mitchell and Nyblade (2007) find that surplus coalitions are also less likely when government membership is not particularly valuable, for example when electoral volatility is high, and when the previous government was terminated due to a critical event or policy conflict.

In sum, both the bargaining environment and the distribution of bargaining power amongst political parties play a major role in determining the type of government formed. Minority governments are most likely to form when bargaining power is concentrated in the hands of a single party, when the costs of forming free-floating coalitions are low, and when the value parties place on being in government is not too great. Minimal winning coalitions are most likely to form when the value parties place on being in government is high relative to being in the opposition, when uncertainty is low and parties are able to credibly commit to each other, when political decisions are made by simple majority rule, and when bargaining power is neither greatly concentrated nor greatly dispersed. Surplus coalitions are most likely when bargaining is greatly dispersed amongst the various parties in parliament, when political decisions require more than a simple majority in the lower chamber of parliament, and when government membership is neither extremely costly nor extremely valuable.

6 GOVERNMENT MEMBERSHIP

From the very beginning of the academic study of coalition government, scholars have been interested in predicting not only whether coalitions form, or the type of government formed, but more specifically which parties get into government. Riker suggested that the minimal winning coalition with the smallest parliamentary support—the minimum winning coalition—should form, while Leiserson (1966) instead proposed that the minimal winning coalition with the fewest members should prevail. Empirically, neither of these specific propositions has proven particularly robust in empirical testing.

Empirical scholarship on coalition formation has had greater success predicting specific government membership by focusing less on the office-seeking models of coalition formation, and more on incorporating policy preferences. A first generation of analysis of "who gets in" in the 1970s generally came to contradictory results. Franklin and Mackie (1984) were the first to conduct multivariate tests in order to assess the relative importance of size versus policy preferences, and claimed to have reconciled the early research findings. They found that the wide discrepancy in previous studies was explained by methodological decisions such that the findings of Browne (1973) and De Swaan (1973) can be reconciled with those of Taylor and Laver (1973) "by simple adjustments of universe and weighting strategy" (Franklin and Mackie 1984, 681) and recognizing the existence of strong "country-effects." These authors go as far as to claim that in the work to date the "choice of countries is far more important than any other assumption in conditioning research findings" (Franklin and Mackie 1984, 671).[5]

---

[5] In a study of cabinet duration, Grofman similarly claims that "the principal variation in cabinet durability appears to be generated by *between-country* effects which are a function of party-system variables such as the effective number of parties" (1989, 297–8, emphasis in the original).

As statistical sophistication amongst political scientists has progressed, however, Franklin and Mackie's regression methodology has been criticized. Martin and Stevenson (2001) test a large sample of prior coalition propositions using more appropriate tools than heretofore. As they note: "The central shortcoming of [of prior approaches such as Franklin and Mackie's] is that in a regression framework...each potential coalition in a formation opportunity enters the estimation as a separate case. Thus, including countries such as Italy or Denmark, with a large number of parties at any given time, means that thousands of cases enter the estimation and completely swamp out relationships in other countries" (2001, 38). The answer, they suggest, is a maximum likelihood framework that models "government formation as an unordered discrete choice problem where each formation opportunity (not each potential coalition) represents one case and where the set of discrete alternatives is the set of all potential combinations of parties that might form a government" (ibid.). Martin and Stevenson use McFadden's conditional logit model, which is a special case of the multinomial logistic regression. Thus, potential coalitions are the discrete values that the dependent variable can take, and each potential coalition is associated with a set of size, ideology, and institutional variables that serve as the independent variables.

Martin and Stevenson find support for the effects of classic bargaining power variables (size and preference variables) as well as for bargaining environment variables such as investiture vote requirements, electoral pacts, and incumbency status. Overall, the predictive power of their models is fairly impressive (by the standards of prior work), with their best models accurately predicting the specific coalition formed (generally out of dozens or hundreds of potential coalitions) around 40 percent of the time, much greater than in previous empirical work on the subject (such as Laver and Budge 1992).

Recent work on "who gets in" builds on the Martin and Stevenson approach. Warwick (2005), with the help of an extensive expert survey, shows how information about the policy preferences of parties, beyond simple measures of their ideal points, improves our understanding of coalition politics. Warwick estimates the "policy horizons" of parties on multiple dimensions. These horizons are the points beyond which the parties are generally unwilling to compromise. Bäck and Dumont (2004) also employ the conditional logit framework as jumping-off point, using the predictions made from these models to identify cases for more intensive study. From these case studies, they seek both to identify the causal mechanisms and in turn to generate ideas for variables that could improve the predictive power of empirical models.

7   Conclusion

The study of coalition governments has been one of the most active subfields in comparative politics, and one in which progressive improvements to both our theoretical and empirical knowledge have been most obvious. The study of government formation in parliamentary democracies has been intimately linked with bargaining theory, from the original works of Riker (1962) and Leiserson (1966), to theories incorporating policy preferences such as Axelrod (1970) and de Swaan (1973), through the development of more complex models that consider both (Austen-Smith and Banks 1990) and often incorporate more of the bargaining environment, such as the influence of elections (as in Austen-Smith and Banks 1988), or other institutional and behavioral constraints on potential coalition outcomes (see Strøm, Budge and Laver 1994). Despite the advances that have been made, however, there remain significant avenues for further research.

First, there is a need for theoretic work that more carefully integrates bargaining environment (institutions) and bargaining power (size, policy) variables. Austen-Smith and Banks (1988) were pioneers in this regard, but much remains to be done. One promising line of research is that of Diermeier and his associates. Diermeier and Merlo (2000) develop a model of coalition formation in the shadow of future random shocks, following which the parties may respond by reallocating distributive benefits. Diermeier, Eraslan, and Merlo (2002, 2003) model how parties might evaluate tradeoffs between the size and durability of different types of coalitions during the coalition formation process, and how certain institutional rules and features (such as bicameralism, investiture votes, and constructive no confidence rules) may influence these tradeoffs and thus the likelihood of various types of coalitions.

Second, as in essentially every social scientific endeavor, critical measurement challenges remain. In the face of increasing evidence that policy preferences matter to coalition bargaining, coalition students were left with crude or awkward measures of such policy preferences, based either on subjective rankings or potentially on information inferred from the very behavior they sought to explain. In recent research, two primary strategies for overcoming these problems have been to generate policy estimates from expert surveys (as in Laver and Hunt 1992 and Warwick 2005), or from policy documents such as election platforms (manifestos). The latter approach can be traced back to the influence of Robertson (1976), but has been extended and regularized by the Manifesto Research Group (see Budge et al. 2001). There has been a vigorous debate about the challenges of estimating party policy positions (see Gabel and Huber 2000) and issue dimensionality (Warwick 2002; Nyblade 2004; Stoll 2005) from such data.

Finally, there are challenges in empirical tests. Studies of coalition bargaining have focused overwhelmingly on national governments in the stable parliamentary democracies of Western Europe. These data have been used, over and over again, to test and corroborate the major hypothesis of the field. There has, however, been very little testing that has gone much beyond the sample from which these propositions were derived. In future scholarship, this limitation clearly must be overcome. It is therefore most welcome to see several excellent studies of local and regional coalitions in parliamentary countries (Bäck 2003; Downs 1998), and we anticipate that the emergence of many new parliamentary democracies, especially in Central and Eastern Europe, will provide additional opportunities for rigorous tests of accepted wisdoms.

The challenges of empirical testing extend beyond issues of samples and case selection. There remain serious statistical challenges as well. For example, the conditional logit framework suggested by Martin and Stevenson (2001) rests on the statistical assumption of the independence of irrelevant alternatives (IIA), which in many cases may be problematic.[6] Additionally, as coalition formation is but one stage in the life cycle of parliamentary government (Strøm, Müller, and Bergman 2007), and parties have both memory and foresight, it might be necessary in the statistical specifications to consider the other stages of government and selection effects, as in the structural estimation approach used by Diermeier, Eraslan, and Merlo (2003).

Although these theoretic and empirical challenges remain, we remain optimistic. Given the development of coalition research over the last forty years, and the continuing activity and innovation in this field, there is no reason to believe that our understanding of coalition politics should not continue to progress rapidly in the coming decades.

References

AMORIM NETO, O. 2006. The presidential calculus: executive policy-making and cabinet formation in the Americas. *Comparative Political Studies*, 39 (10): 1292–8.

—— and STRØM, K. 2006. Breaking the parliamentary chain of delegation: presidents and nonpartisan cabinet members in European democracies. *British Journal of Political Science*, 36: 619–43.

ANSOLABEHERE, S., SNYDER, J. M., STRAUSS, A. B., and TING, M. M. 2005. Voting weights and formateur advantages in the formation of coalition governments. *American Journal of Political Science*, 49: 550–63.

AUSTEN-SMITH, D., and BANKS, J. 1988. Elections, coalitions and legislative outcomes. *American Political Science Review*, 82: 405–22.

—— —— 1990. Stable governments and the allocation of policy portfolios. *American Political Science Review*, 84: 891–906.

AXELROD, R. 1970. *Conflict of Interest*. Chicago: Markham.

BÄCK, H. 2003. Explaining coalitions. Ph.D. dissertation. Uppsala University.

—— and DUMONT, P. 2004. A combination of methods: the way forward in coalition research. Paper presented at the Annual Meetings of the American Political Science Association.

BALE, T., and DANN, C. 2002. Is the grass really greener? The rationale and reality of support party status. *Party Politics*, 8: 349–66.

BANZHAF, J. F. 1965. Weighted voting does not work: a mathematical analysis. *Rutgers Law Review*, 35: 317–43.

BARON, D. 1991. A spatial bargaining theory of government formation in parliamentary systems. *American Political Science Review*, 83: 1182–206.

BERGMAN, T. 1993. Formation rules and minority governments. *European Journal of Political Research*, 23: 55–66.

BLACK, D. 1958. *The Theory of Committees and Elections*. Cambridge: Cambridge University Press.

BROWNE, E. 1973. *Coalition Theories: A Logical and Empirical Critique*. Beverly Hills, Calif.: Sage.

—— FRENDREIS, P., and GLEIBER, D. 1984. An events approach to the problem of cabinet stability. *Comparative Political Studies*, 17: 167–97.

---

[6] A multinomial probit does not rest on the IIA assumption, and proper specification of a conditional version of this estimation technique may resolve this issue.

BROWNE, E. FRENDREIS, P., and GLEIBER, D. 1986. The process of cabinet dissolution: an exponential model of duration and stability in western democracies. *American Journal of Political Science*, 30: 628–50.

BUDGE, I., KLINGEMANN, H.-D., VOLKENS, A., BARA, J., and TANENBAUM, E. 2001. *Mapping Policy Preferences: Estimates for Parties, Electors and Governments 1945–1998*. Oxford: Oxford University Press.

CARRUBBA, C., and VOLDEN, C. 2000. Coalition politics and logrolling in legislative institutions. *American Journal of Political Science*, 44: 261–77.

—— —— 2004. The formation of oversize coalitions in parliamentary democracies. *American Journal of Political Science*, 48: 521–37.

CHEIBUB, J. A. 2002. Minority governments, deadlock situations, and the survival of presidential democracies. *Comparative Political Studies*, 35: 284–312.

—— PRZEWORSKI, A., and SAIEGH, S. 2004. Government coalitions and legislative success under presidentialism and parliamentarism. *British Journal of Political Science*, 34: 565–87.

COX, G., and McCUBBINS, M. 1993. *Legislative Leviathan*. Berkeley and Los Angeles: University of California Press.

CROMBEZ, C. 1996. Minority government, minimal winning coalitions and surplus majorities in parliamentary systems. *European Journal of Political Research*, 29: 1–29.

DE SWAAN, A. 1973. *Coalition Theories and Cabinet Formations*. Amsterdam: Elsevier.

DIERMEIER, D., ERASLAN, H., and MERLO, M. 2002. Coalition government and comparative constitutional design. *European Economic Review*, 46: 893–907.

—— —— —— 2003. A structural model of government formation. *Econometrica*, 71: 27–70.

—— and MERLO, A. 2000. Government turnover in parliamentary democracies. *Journal of Economic Theory*, 94: 46–79.

—— and STEVENSON, R. 1999. Cabinet survival and competing risks. *American Journal of Political Science*, 43: 1051–68.

—— —— 2000. Cabinet terminations and critical events. *American Political Science Review*, 94: 627–40.

DIXIT, A. K. 1996. *The Making of Economic Policy*. Cambridge, Mass.: MIT Press.

DODD. L. C. 1976. *Coalitions in Parliamentary Government*. Princeton: Princeton University Press.

DOWNS, A. 1957. *An Economic Theory of Democracy*. New York: Harper & Row.

DOWNS, W. 1998. *Coalition Government Subnational Style: Multiparty Politics in European Regional Parliaments*. Columbus: Ohio State University Press.

DRUCKMAN, J. 1996. Party factionalism and cabinet durability. *Party Politics*, 2: 397–407.

—— MARTIN, L., and THIES, M. 2005. Influence without confidence: upper chambers and government formation. *Legislative Studies Quarterly*, 30: 529–48.

—— and WARWICK, P. 2005. The missing piece: measuring portfolio salience in western European parliamentary democracies. *European Journal of Political Research*, 44: 17–42.

FRANKLIN, M., and MACKIE, T. 1984. Reassessing the importance of size and ideology for the formation of governing coalitions in parliamentary democracies. *American Journal of Political Science*, 28: 671–92.

GABEL, M., and HUBER, J. 2000. Putting parties in their place: inferring party left–right ideological positions from party manifesto data. *American Journal of Political Science*, 44: 94–103.

GROFMAN, B. 1989. The comparative analysis of coalition formation and duration: distinguishing between-country and within-country effects. *British Journal of Political Science*, 19: 291–302.

HUBER, J. 1998. How does cabinet instability affect political performance? Portfolio volatility and health care cost containment in parliamentary democracies. *American Political Science Review*, 92: 577–91.

—— and LUPIA, A. 2001. Cabinet instability and delegation in parliamentary democracies. *American Journal of Political Science*, 45: 18–32.

JOHNSON, N. 1975. Adversary politics and electoral reform: need we be afraid? In *Adversary Politics and Electoral Reform*, ed. S. E. Finer. London: Wigram.

KING, G., ALT, J., BURNS, N., and LAVER, M. 1990. A unified model of cabinet dissolution in parliamentary democracies. *American Journal of Political Science*, 34: 846–71.

LAVER, M. and BUDGE, I. 1992. *Party Policy and Government Coalitions*. New York: St Martin's Press.

—— and HUNT, B. 1992. *Policy and Party Competition*. New York: Routledge Press.

—— and SCHOFIELD, N. 1990. *Multiparty Government: The Politics of Coalition in Europe*. Oxford: Oxford University Press.

—— and SHEPSLE, K. 1990. Coalitions and cabinet government. *American Political Science Review*, 84: 873–90.

—— —— 1996. *Making and Breaking Governments: Cabinets and Legislatures in Parliamentary Democracies*. New York: Cambridge University Press.

—— —— 1999. Understanding government survival: empirical exploration or analytical models? *British Journal of Political Science*, 29: 395–401.

—— —— 2000. Ministrables and government formation. *Journal of Theoretical Politics*, 12: 113–24.

LEISERSON, M. 1966. Coalitions in politics. Ph.D. thesis. Yale University.

LUPIA, A., and STRØM, K. 1995. Coalition termination and the strategic timing of parliamentary elections. *American Political Science Review*, 89: 648–65.

MANOW, P., and ZORN, H. 2004. Office versus policy motives in portfolio allocation: the case of junior ministers. Max Planck Institute for the Study of Societies Discussion Paper 04/09.

MARTIN, L., and STEVENSON, R. 2001. Government formation in parliamentary democracies. *American Journal of Political Science*, 45: 33–50.

MITCHELL, P., and NYBLADE, B. 2007. Government formation and cabinet type in parliamentary democracies. In Strøm, Müller, and Bergman 2006.

MÜLLER, W. C., BERGMAN, T., and STRØM, K. 2003. Parliamentary democracy: promise and problems. In Strøm, Müller, and Bergman 2003: 3–32.

—— and STRØM, K. eds. 1999. *Policy, Office or Votes?* Cambridge: Cambridge University Press.

—— —— eds. 2000. *Coalition Governments in Western Europe*. Oxford: Oxford University Press.

NARUD, H. M., and VALEN, H. 2006. Coalition membership and electoral performance in western Europe. In Strøm, Müller, and Bergman 2006.

NYBLADE, B. 2004. The effective number of issue dimensions: a measure with application to West Europe. Paper presented at the Annual Meetings of the Midwest Political Science Association.

POWELL, G. B., Jr. 1982. *Contemporary Democracies: Participation, Stability and Violence*. Cambridge, Mass.: Harvard University Press.

RIKER, W. 1962. *The Theory of Political Coalitions*. New Haven: Yale University Press.

ROBERTSON, D. 1976. *A Theory of Party Competition*. London: John Wiley.

ROSE, R., and MACKIE, T. T. 1983. Incumbency in government: asset or liability? Pp. 115–37 in *Western European Party Systems: Continuity & Change*, ed. H. Daalder and P. Mair. London: Sage.

SCHOFIELD, N. 1993. Political competition and multiparty coalition governments. *European Journal of Political Research*, 23: 1–33.

SHEPSLE, K. 1979. Institutional arrangements and equilibrium in multidimensional voting models. *American Journal of Political Science*, 23: 27–60.

—— and WEINGAST, B. 1981. Structure-induced equilibrium and legislative choice. *Public Choice*, 37: 503–19.

STOLL, H. 2005. What's on the political agenda: cleavage salience and issue dimensionality in comparative perspective. Paper presented at the Annual Meetings of the Midwest Political Science Association.

STRØM, K. 1984. Minority governments in parliamentary democracies: the rationality of nonwinning cabinet solutions. *Comparative Political Studies*, 17: 199–227.

—— 1985. Party goals and government performance in parliamentary democracies. *American Political Science Review*, 79: 738–54.

—— 1990a. *Minority Government and Majority Rule*. Cambridge: Cambridge University Press.

—— 1990b. A behavioral theory of competitive political parties. *American Journal of Political Science*, 34: 565–98.

—— 1994. The Presthus debacle: intraparty politics and bargaining failure in Norway. *American Political Science Review*, 88: 112–27.

—— BUDGE, I., and LAVER, M. 1994. Constraints on cabinet formation in parliamentary democracies. *American Journal of Political Science*, 38: 303–35.

—— MÜLLER, W. C. and BERGMAN, T., eds. 2003. *Delegation and Accountability in Parliamentary Democracies*. Oxford: Oxford University Press.

—— —— —— eds. 2007. *Cabinet Governance: Bargaining and the Cycle of Democratic Politics*. Oxford: Oxford University Press.

TAYLOR, M., and LAVER, M. 1973. Government coalitions in western Europe. *European Journal of Political Research*, 1: 205–48.

THIES, M. F. 2001. Keeping tabs on coalition partners: the logic of delegation in coalition governments. *American Journal of Political Science*, 45: 580–98.

VON NEUMANN, J., and MORGENSTERN, O. 1944. *Theory of Games and Economic Behavior*. Princeton: Princeton University Press.

WARWICK, P. 1994. *Government Survival in Parliamentary Democracies*. Cambridge: Cambridge University Press.

—— 1999. Ministerial autonomy or accommodation? Contested bases of government survival in parliamentary democracies. *British Journal of Political Science*, 29: 369–94.

—— 2002. Towards a common issue dimensionality in west European policy spaces. *Party Politics*, 8: 101–22.

—— 2005. Do policy horizons structure the formation of coalition governments? The evidence from an expert survey. *American Journal of Political Science*, 49: 373–87.

—— and DRUCKMAN, J. 2001. Portfolio salience and the proportionality of payoffs in coalition government. *British Journal of Political Science*, 31: 627–49.

PART VIII

....

GOVERNANCE IN COMPARATIVE PERSPECTIVE

....

CHAPTER 33

....

COMPARATIVE STUDIES OF THE ECONOMY AND THE VOTE

....

RAYMOND M. DUCH

> How universal is economic voting? There are signs that the inclination to vote that way is hard-wired into the brains of citizens in democracies. (Norpoth 1996)

THE economic vote is the importance that the voter gives to economic performance in their decision to vote for a political party (Duch and Stevenson 2007). This economic vote is one of the rare empirical regularities that social scientists seem to agree on. As the above quote from Helmut Norpoth indicates, it has now become virtually a social science law that the economy is one of the most important influences on how individuals vote. The economic vote captures the attention of many political scientists because it provides insight into what precisely drives the individual vote decision which in turn has implications for theories of democratic accountability.

Almost fifty years of scholarly interest in the economic vote have generated four principal insights. Arguably the most important contribution of economic voting research is theoretical. The economic vote—as opposed to the "abortion" vote or the "green" vote—represents a relatively unambiguous implication of one of the leading models in the discipline: the rational model of vote choice. One of its early proponents, Anthony Downs (1957), argued that voters use information (or expectations) about party performance in office to make their vote choice. A reasonable presumption is that information about economic outcomes is particularly salient to the average voter and hence if voters are not using information about economic outcomes in a rational fashion this would cast serious doubt on the theory. But in the 1960s and 1970s modeling the voter as a utility-maximizing political "consumer" was a significant deviation from widely accepted explanations for vote choice that typically borrowed from the social-psychological literature (Berelson, Lazarsfeld, and McSee 1954; Campbell et al. 1960). Hence there was a need to develop a formal statement of how voters use information about the economy in a rational fashion to make voting decisions; a need that was nicely addressed by the likes of Kramer (1971), Barro (1973), Ferejohn (1986), and Fiorina (1978).

A second important insight is empirical evidence of economic voting. Although the greatest amount of empirical work generated over the past four decades examines the economic vote in the US case, increasing empirical attention has turned to the economic vote in non-US contexts.[1] There might be disagreement on how to demonstrate the existence of an economic vote but there seems to be a considerable consensus that it exists. These empirical efforts, particularly the comparative studies, have led to a third important insight: The economic vote varies quite significantly across countries, between elections, and even within subgroups of the population.

This instability in the economic vote is the source of a fourth important contribution of economic voting research. An unstable, or variable, economic vote does not fit well with existing theories of the economic vote and hence has led a number of scholars to question and rethink—or at least call for the rethinking of—the theory of how economic evaluations enter into the voter's utility function. Comparativists have a competitive advantage explaining contextual variation in the economic vote. The reason is obvious: While contextual variation can be explored within a single national context, such as the USA, it is likely the case that cross-national studies of economic voting will offer significantly greater payoffs than single-country studies.

In order for comparative research to make a contribution to our understanding of the economic vote it needs to address three important challenges. Most importantly, it needs to first develop a rigorous and persuasive theory that identifies the contextual factors that condition the economic vote and explains how they account for the instability in economic voting that many have identified. Much of the interesting instability in economic voting is observed in comparisons of the results of individual-level economic voting models from different countries or from different periods of time within the same country. There are now hundreds of these individual-level studies conducted over the course of the past four decades and they clearly suggest instability in economic voting. Hence, a second challenge for comparative research is leveraging this voluminous data in order to test hypotheses regarding contextual variation in the economic vote found in individual-level surveys. A third challenge is to address claims that the economic vote is a measurement artifact resulting from the endogeneity of economic evaluations. While there should be little doubt that economic evaluations are shaped by partisanship or vote

---

[1] These empirical contributions are summarized in a number of recent works including Duch and Stevenson (2007); Hibbs (2006); Lewis-Beck and Stegmaier (2000).

preference (Duch, Palmer, and Anderson 2000) there is remarkably little evidence regarding the impact of endogeneity on estimates of economic vote magnitudes. Again, with a rich and voluminous number of individual-level studies comparative scholars should be able to establish the robustness of the economic vote in the face of endogeneity.

The first part of this essay summarizes the four important contributions of economic voting research: It begins by briefly reviewing work on the American economic vote. This work has provided us with a rational sanctioning theory of the economic vote; strong empirical evidence that the economic vote exists; but clear evidence of instability in the economic vote. It then briefly reviews the comparative work on economic voting that provides even stronger evidence of instability in the economic vote—it also highlights the potential importance of institutional and political factors in explaining this variation although for the most part provides no theoretical foundation for explaining this variation.

A second section of the essay then makes the case that the comparative analysis of large numbers of individual-level voter preference studies represents a particularly promising strategy for understanding contextual variation in the economic vote. The section suggests one methodological approach for analyzing the numerous existing surveys, measuring the magnitude of the economic vote, and modeling its cross-national variation. Employing these methods I summarize evidence from Duch and Stevenson (2007) indicating that the economic vote is in fact large although unstable. In addition I provide evidence based on Duch and Palmer (2002) that these economic vote magnitudes are not a mere measurement artifact.

A third section briefly summarizes the contextual theory of the economic vote from Duch and Stevenson (2007) that builds on the assumption of instrumentally rational voters. Adopting a rationality assumption regarding vote choice implies that the voter's response to economic performance should be conditioned, in a rational fashion, by the institutional contexts. It follows from the underlying assumptions of rational vote choice models that voters are informed about the competency of different parties (both within a coalition government and in opposition) for economic performance; understand how institutional, political, and economic contexts condition their competency for economic outcomes; and incorporate strategic voting considerations into their economic vote. In addition to sketching out a rational contextual theory of the economic vote this section includes evidence for selective hypotheses derived from this theory.

1 THE THEORETICAL LEGACY OF AMERICAN RATIONAL ECONOMIC VOTING

The early American contributions to the economic voting literature were marked by the adoption of expected utility models of vote choice that favored a sanctioning view of the economic vote. Downs's *Economic Theory of Democracy* provided a theoretical foundation and vocabulary for the study of economic voting: voters are instrumentally rational actors who make vote choices based on their comparison of expected utilities for each of the competing parties. But it was Kramer's (1971) efforts to empirically assess the importance of economic well-being in voter utility functions that inspired the early economic voting research.[2] Fair (1978) took this argument a step forward by providing a formal statement of how economic performance enters the voter utility.[3] This was an important theoretical advance because it established a foundation for modeling vote choice from a rational utility maximization perspective that included economic well-being in the utility function.

As Fair (1978) emphasizes, theory is a necessary guide in determining how the economy enters into the utility function. Are voters narrowly retrospective and motivated primarily by a sanctioning reflex which is suggested by the early Kramer (1971) findings? Or do voters gather more extensive information on past economic outcomes in an effort to assess how competing potential governing "teams" might perform in the future, a selection perspective hinted at by Downs (1957) and Stigler (1973). Both perspectives share a model of individual decision making in which instrumentally rational voters are maximizing a voter utility function.

The sanctioning perspective has been widely adopted in much of the economic voting literature to date. The early path-breaking work of Kramer (1971) and Fair (1978) suggested that vote choice was shaped by the recent economic performance of incumbents rather than by comparative assessments of how competing parties might perform if elected. They concluded that the economy entered into the voter's utility function in a simple fashion: punish poor performance and reward good outcomes. V. O. Key's widely quoted characterization of the economic vote seemed well founded: "Voters may reject what they have known; or they may approve what they have known. They are not likely to be attracted in great numbers by promises of the novel or unknown" (1966, 61). Fiorina's (1981) classic work *Retrospective Voting in American National Elections* provided a more general expected utility model of voting that included economic evaluations.[4] And while both retrospective assessments and future expectations of the performance of incumbents (and challengers) figured prominently in Fiorina's models of the vote decision, Fiorina argued that future expectations are, for the most part, simple extrapolations from current trends. This provided further support for the retrospective sanctioning perspective. Hence, early in the history of economic voting this sanctioning model of voter behavior—either explicitly or implicitly— became the workhorse of models linking the economy and vote choice.

Sanctioning models presume rational voters have a relatively narrow focus: on the past and on the incumbent. Barro (1973) and then Ferejohn (1986) showed how

---

[2] That is not to say that the link between the economy and elections had not been explored. In fact Kramer (1971) does a nice job of summarizing the early efforts in this regard.

[3] As Hibbs (2006) points out, this contribution was also important because it derived an aggregate-level vote equation from this individual-level utility function that could be estimated empirically.

[4] Fiorina stopped short of providing a formal model in which retrospective economic voting emerged as rational behavior.

retrospective economic voting could be a fully rational voting strategy by building on the notion that candidates, like firms, are motivated by the maximization of rents. Voters, according to this model, are confronted with a moral hazard problem when deciding on voting for the incumbent versus opposition parties. They argue that if voters do not sanction economic performance they risk signaling to incumbents that poor economic performance would be tolerated and hence invite rent seeking on the part of self-interested political candidates. In this model voters are not engaging in the comparative assessment of utility income streams from competing political candidates—rather they simply establish a threshold performance level and re-elect incumbents that satisfy this requirement and punish those that do not (Ferejohn 1986). This leads to the *sanctioning* feature that characterizes most accounts of the economic vote. It is the concern with re-election in the future that motivates incumbents to avoid shirking their responsibilities. They anticipate that voters will sanction them if they under-perform. And in order to maintain the credibility of this threat voters punish incumbents at the polls when retrospective economic performance is substandard.

Adopting this sanctioning perspective on rational voting had important implications for the specification of economic voting models. Pure sanctioning models of the economic vote are decidedly retrospective—voters entirely discount candidate promises (so these do not enter into the utility function) and only pay attention to economic performance over the course of the incumbent's recent tenure in office.

2 THE EMPIRICAL LEGACY OF AMERICAN RATIONAL ECONOMIC VOTING

The important contribution of rational economic voting is that it inspired a rigorous deductive theory of the vote choice. Largely as a consequence of this literature, scholars have a widely accepted vocabulary for characterizing how voters use information about economic outcomes to shape their vote choice. Building on this strong theoretical foundation the economic voting field has generated overwhelming and unambiguous empirical findings from the United States that confirm the existence of a robust empirical connection between the economy and vote choice. Three different strains of research, each initiated in the 1970s, contribute to this consensus.

Mueller's (1970) classic study of presidential popularity introduced one important line of enquiry: estimating the economic vote based on aggregative-level models of presidential popularity that employed, typically, monthly readings of public approval of the chief executive with objective measures of economic performance as the independent variable (typically the actual rates of unemployment, inflation, or real GDP change). Although the detailed specification of these presidential popularity functions has been the subject of some debate, almost all estimates of presidential popularity functions confirm that the economy is a significant factor driving presidential popularity (e.g. Norpoth 1985; Beck 1991). Further, the various estimates tend to agree (roughly) on the magnitude of the effects. Beck (1991), for example, estimates that the long-run (realized over a four-year period) impact of a unit change in inflation is about a 4 percent shift in presidential popularity. Muller (1970) estimated that presidential popularity declined by about three percentage points for every percentage point rise in unemployment (Mueller's 1970, 29). While there is disagreement about the exact set of aggregate economic indicators that should appear in presidential popularity functions, there is little disagreement that *some* set of aggregate economic variables predict changes in approval and that the overall impact of usual changes in these variables is to move popularity in the range of between three and ten percentage points.

A second avenue of empirical enquiry examines how actual election outcomes depend on objective economic outcomes. One of the first of these studies was by Tufte (1978), who demonstrated, based on only eight data points, that in presidential elections from 1948 to 1978, the relationship between annual real disposable income and the vote of the president's party was practically a straight line. Subsequent researchers, using more data and refined models, confirmed Tufte's original finding (e.g. Bartels and Zaller 2001; Erikson 1990; Hibbs 2000, 2006). Bartels and Zaller (2001) evaluate a wide range of different specifications of presidential vote models and conclude that the best performing specifications are those with weighted distributed lags of real disposable income as the measure of economic performance. In particular, they point to the "Bread and Peace" model proposed by Hibbs (2000) as performing especially well.

These studies not only confirmed the existence of economic voting in the aggregate data, but tended to agree on the *magnitude* of the economic vote in US presidential elections. Specifically, a 1 percent change in annual real disposable income produces a two to four percentage point increase in support for the incumbent presidential party. These results are consistent with the magnitude of economic voting effects found by the studies discussed above, which focused on presidential popularity rather than the vote.

Early aggregate level research on the economy and elections in the United States also explored congressional contests. Kramer's (1971) influential analysis of US congressional elections from 1886 to 1964 was the first to establish that change in real disposable income over the course of the election year predicts the success of the president's party in congressional elections. This result was subsequently championed by Tufte (1975, 1979) with more recent supporting evidence from Jacobson and Kernell (1983), Lewis-Beck and Rice (1992), and Kiewiet and Udell (1998). However, unlike the results for presidential elections, this finding has been challenged by a number of scholars who failed to find a significant relationship in aggregate data (e.g. Marra and Ostrom 1989; Erikson 1990; Alesina, Londregan, and Rosenthal 1993). Nevertheless, the bulk of evidence seems to argue for the existence of economic voting in congressional elections, though the relationship is almost certainly weaker than in presidential elections.

The third strain of economic voting research traces its intellectual roots to Key (1966) who explored the impact of popular assessments of incumbent performance on the actual voting decision. Similar early efforts to use individual-level survey data to explore economic voting specifically relied on questions that asked voters about their "personal financial situation." However, the later (and most enduring) individual-level evidence for economic voting in the USA has come from questions that ask respondents about general business conditions or the country's "economic situation." Fiorina (1981) conducted an important early analysis of these survey data in which he demonstrated that economic perceptions of the national economy significantly impact vote choice in US elections (both presidential and congressional). And soon thereafter, Kiewiet (1983) confirmed Fiorina's conclusions with more data and more elaborate statistical specifications. Further, he demonstrated that assessments of general economic conditions play a more important role in shaping vote choice than pocketbook evaluations (i.e., perceptions of one's personal financial condition). Fiorina's and Kiewiet's empirical conclusions quickly entered into the lexicon of American political science and with some relatively minor qualifications or extensions have withstood extensive scrutiny (some notable examples are Alvarez and Nagler 1998; Duch, Palmer, and Anderson 2000; Markus 1988, 1992).

Unlike aggregate studies of economic voting, which are most useful for estimating a single, average magnitude of economic voting across elections, individual-level survey data, if available for several different elections, can be used to construct (and compare) estimates of the magnitude of economic voting in each election. Kiewiet (1983) was somewhat of a pioneer in this respect because he explicitly estimated economic voting for a number of different American election studies (for the period 1958 to 1980). In spite of the relatively small number of election surveys in his sample (only four of the presidential election surveys included national economic evaluations), he was able to highlight, and propose explanations for, the average difference between congressional and presidential elections (consistent with the aggregate results described above, he found economic voting to be relatively weaker in congressional elections).

As the number of these US individual election studies has increased with time, scholars have begun to document changes in the magnitude of the US economic vote from one election to the next. Fiorina, Abrams, and Pope (2003), for example, evaluate the magnitude of the presidential economic vote and speculate as to why it varies from election to election. In addition, this fairly extensive time series of individual-level US election studies has facilitated efforts to better understand the link (or lack thereof) between macro- and micro-level economic voting estimates (Erikson 2004; Duch, Palmer, and Anderson 2000).

Despite the many individual-level studies of economic voting that have been done, there is no clear consensus in the American literature on the appropriate methodology for characterizing the magnitude of the economic vote at the individual level. Kiewiet used one approach, Fiorina another, Alverez and Nagler (1998) still another. As a result, individual-level estimates of the magnitude of economic vote for presidents in the USA range broadly from election to election. For example, Kiewiet reports that a typical change in economic perceptions moves the electoral support of the incumbent by 13 percent (Kiewiet 1983, 35). In contrast, Alvarez and Nagler's (1998, 1360) estimate is close to 38 percent.[5] The lack of a uniform methodology for calculating the magnitude of the

[5] The Kiewiet (1983) result is based on moving economic evaluations for an "average" voter from "worse than a year ago" to "better than a year ago;" the Alvarez and Nagler 1998 result is based on moving national economic evaluations from worse to better.

economic vote from survey data means we do not know if estimated differences reflect real variation in the size of the economic vote or whether these differences are simply artifacts of the different methods for calculating them.

Overall, the economic vote has been subject to extensive scrutiny in the US context and the effort has borne some important insights.[6] Voting for the US president is strongly influenced by economic performance. At the aggregate level we have precise estimates of the effect of various economic aggregates on the presidential vote and on presidential approval. At the individual level, results reinforce the importance of national economic evaluations on the presidential vote, although estimates of its magnitude vary significantly and there are no agreed-upon strategies for assessing these magnitudes.

The legacy of five decades of scholarship on American economic voting provides overwhelming support for the existence of an economic vote. At the same time, though, by moving from a handful of individual-level surveys (Kiewet 1983), or eight election results (Tufte 1975), scholars have established that the magnitude of the US economic vote can vary quite significantly from one time point to the next or across different types of elections. A number of analyses of the American National Election Studies (ANES) have documented the election-on-election variability in the magnitude of the presidential economic vote (Blais et al. 2004; Fiorina, Abrams, and Pope 2003; Alvarez, Nagler, and Willette 2000; Duch, Palmery, and Anderson 2000).

This instability in the American economic vote suggests that the importance of economic outcomes might be conditioned by contextual factors, such as the competitiveness of presidential elections or variations in the economic context. Being able to specify what contextual factors enter into the vote choice model, and how, represents the most important challenge facing students of the economic vote. And I would argue that significant traction on any of these empirical and theoretical puzzles is unlikely without extending the research agenda to include cross-national studies. Cross-national studies of economic voting provide the variation in institutional, political, and economic contexts that are critical to understanding this instability.

3 The Puzzling Terrain of Comparative Economic Voting

Research on economic voting outside the US context illustrates in much starker terms its volatility. As was the case in the USA, comparative studies include aggregate

---

[6] In 1990, Erikson concluded that the relationship between economic performance and the vote is probably the most widely accepted hypothesis about voting behavior and elections—here he was obviously referring to the US case.

studies of the economy and government popularity; aggregate studies of the economy and electoral returns; and individual-level studies of economic perceptions and vote choice. Each of these three approaches to the study of economic voting suggests the presence of an economic vote but its magnitude clearly varies over time and across countries.

Comparative aggregate-level studies. The strong US aggregate-level correlations between the economy and voter preferences, illustrated by Tufte (1978) and later Hibbs (2000), have not been consistently reproduced in other national contexts. In fact, the relationships have been highly variable from country to country. For some countries aggregate studies of popularity and the economy suggest a significant relationship. This certainly seems to be the case with France where most estimates show strong aggregate economic effects (Lafay 1977; Lewis-Beck 1980; Hibbs and Vasilatos 1981) although Lecaillon (1981) is an exception. In the case of the UK, the findings have tended to confirm the presence of economic voting although again with some dissenting evidence. Goodhart and Bhansali (1970) provided the first aggregate study of popularity, demonstrating that the popularity of British governments was strongly influenced by movements in the aggregate economy (unemployment and inflation). While these early results came under criticism (e.g. Frey and Garbers 1971 and Miller and Mackie 1973), recent work seems to confirm the existence of economic voting in Britain with the debate focusing on how to specify the economic variables (objective economic variables versus subjective economic evaluations, for example) and how to control for political shocks such as the Falklands War (Whiteley 1986; Sanders, Marsh, and Ward 1991; Clarke, and Stewart 1995; Clarke, Stewart, and Whiteley 1997; Price and Sanders 1993).

Analyses of aggregate popularity and vote functions in other countries suggest considerable more variability. Estimates for Denmark were initially negative and later mixed (e.g. Paldam and Schneider 1980; Nannestad and Paldam 2000). Kirchgässner (1991) found evidence for the impact of employment on the popularity of German governments before 1982 but not after. Frey (1979) examined the fate of incumbent parties over sixty-seven years in Denmark, Norway, and Sweden and found mixed results. Similarly, Madsen (1980) in a careful study of aggregate popularity in Denmark, Norway, and Sweden found no evidence for economic voting in Denmark and Norway but does find evidence for Sweden.

Efforts to combine these various national aggregate (popularity and vote function) data and conduct comparative analyses produced mixed results. The nature and magnitude of the estimated economic voting effect varies significantly from one study to the next. Paldam (1991) analyzed electoral data from seventeen countries over the post-war period and found little evidence of economic voting in any country. Lewis-Beck and Mitchell (1990) examined aggregate data on twenty-seven elections in five European countries and found that rates of unemployment and inflation do affect the vote for governing parties. However, Chappell and Viega (2000) analyzed an expanded sample of European countries over a longer time period and found that none of the usual economic indicators had an impact on incumbent party vote share (although they did find that change in inflation rates *relative* to the European average had a significant correlation with vote share). While some of these differences might be accounted for by the sample of countries analyzed or estimation methods employed, one would be hard pressed, based on these findings, to conclude that economic vote is pervasive amongst the developed democracies.

One quite plausible explanation for this instability in these aggregate economic voting is cross-national differences in the nature of governing institutions. Powell and Whitten (1993) hypothesized that institutional "clarity of responsibility"—i.e. the extent to which political institutions allowed incumbents to diffuse responsibility for economic outcomes—might account for this contextual variation in the economic vote. Analyzing 109 elections, they interacted their index of clarity of responsibility with measures of economic performance and obtained results that led them to conclude that "the greater the perceived unified control of policymaking by the incumbent government, the more likely is the citizen to assign responsibility for economic and political outcomes to the incumbents" (Powell and Whitten 1993, 398). But the robustness of this result has been challenged by Royed, Leyden, and Borrelli (2000) who suggest that there is little support for the clarity of responsibility argument—in fact claiming that economic voting is higher for coalition as opposed to single party governments.

Comparing individual-level studies. Since as early as the 1960s, economic evaluations have become a standard item in virtually all individual-level studies of vote prefer-ences. Based on their early study of the UK electorate, for example, Butler and Stokes (1969, 392) concluded that "The electorate's response to the economy is one under which voters reward the Government for the conditions they welcome and punish the Government for the conditions they dislike."[7] However, as more individual-level studies were undertaken in other countries, a message similar to the aggregate-level country-specific studies began to emerge—the extent and nature of economic voting at the individual level was highly variable. For example, while support for economic voting at the individual level was forthcoming in France and Britain, Miller and Listhaug (1985) found little evidence for individual-level economic voting in Norway and neither did Belluci (1985) for Italy. Likewise, Nannestad and Paldam (1997), in contrast to most other results, found evidence that personal economic conditions were more important to Danish voting than evaluations of the national economy.[8]

Comparative scholars who reported negative results or that discovered evidence for unusual forms of economic voting typically attributed them to unique features of the country's political or economic context. For example, by the early 1980s Italy had experienced almost forty years of Christian Democratic rule (and so no true alternation of power). This distinguished it from most of the other western democracies and, according to Belluci (1985), may have depressed the Italian economic vote. Likewise, Miller and Listhaug (1985) speculated that the weak individual-level economic effects they found might be explained by the fact that Norway's economy is so heavily influenced by international economic trends. It might be the case, they argued, that

---

[7] As cited in Lewis-Beck (1988, 34).
[8] This result has, however, been challenged by Hibbs (1993) and Borre (1997).

voters in Norway recognize that their government has little responsibility for economic outcomes and so do not consider economic performance to be important for their vote decision. Similarity, Nannestad and Paldam (1995) suggested that Danish voters hold the government accountable for their personal economic circumstances because the extensive Danish welfare state created a connection between government policy and personal economic circumstances that did not exist in many other countries.[9]

Overall, an important result of this variability in the evidence for economic voting across countries was that it encouraged scholars to speculate about how differences in domestic politics and national economies might account for cross-national differences in economic voting. However, as Lewis-Beck and Eulau (1985) and Lewis-Beck (1988) have both emphasized, one can get relatively little leverage on the question of how political and economic context impacts economic voting by comparing the results of a relatively small number of studies that also differ dramatically in the statistical models used to produce the estimates of economic voting.

4 THE PROMISED LAND: MULTI-NATION STUDIES?

Over the past five decades there has been a proliferation of individual-level voter preference studies that allow for the kinds of comparisons advocated by Lewis-Beck. Most developed countries have been regularly generating mass public opinion surveys that include questions designed to measure the impact of economic evaluations on vote choice. With some notable exceptions (e.g. the World Values Survey, the Eurobarometer Survey, and Comparative Study of Election Systems surveys) these surveys are not standardized in the sense that they do not include a comparable set of variables measuring all of the variables that might be included in a vote choice model, for example. Nevertheless, these numerous individual-level studies often include the necessary core variables, along with appropriate control variables, that allow researchers to estimate models that explore the impact of contextual variables on individual-level relationships.

There are a number of methodological issues that arise as comparativists move from examining the economic vote employing one or a handful of national voter preference studies to modeling, simultaneously, the economic vote in 50 or 100 of these public opinion surveys. First, how do we measure the "economic vote" in such diverse settings? The economy is one of many factors that potentially affect a voter's utility for each of the candidates competing for political office. For any individual, the magnitude of the economic vote is the extent to which changes in perceptions of economic outcomes,

---

[9] Lewis-Beck (1983) previously suggested this explanation for his results about the importance of personal financial circumstances in French economic voting. And Pacek and Radcliff (1995) provide evidence of this argument employing aggregate-level data.

with appropriate controls for other theoretically relevant factors, affect the voter's utility for each of the candidates competing for office. Hence all parties competing for election have an "economic vote" since the voter's utility for any party can be positively or negatively affected by changes in economic perceptions. So, for example, a change in economic perceptions might have no impact on a voter's utility for the junior member of the governing coalition but might have a big impact on his preferences for the major party in the governing coalition. A political party's economic vote is the average of the changes in its vote probabilities for each citizen in the electorate (or in a random probability sample).[10]

Duch and Stevenson (2005) propose a strategy for estimating the economic vote for political parties in a large number of diverse public opinions surveys and then modeling the impact of context on this economic vote (what they refer to as a "two-stage strategy"). Their strategy can be illustrated with the decision to vote for or against the party of the chief executive which can be written using a logit link function as follows:

$$v_{ik} \sim Bin(\pi_{ik})$$

$$logit(\pi_{ik}) = \beta_{0K} + \beta_{1K}X_{ik} + \sum_{j=1}^{J_k} \phi_{jk}Z_{jik} \qquad (1.1)$$

In this notation, v_{ik} indicates a vote for the chief executive party by voter i in each of k election surveys where $i = 1 \ldots n_k$. Likewise, X_{ik} are retrospective economic evaluations measured at the individual level and Z_{jik} are other characteristics of individuals that shape self-reported vote choice where J_k indicates the number of these control variables associated with each k election study. The two coefficients that describe economic voting in any particular survey are β_{ok} and β_{1k} and these are allowed to vary from survey to survey. The strategy presumes a core set of variables similarly measured exists in each survey being analyzed—so in the case of economic voting, a vote choice question (typically, "if an election were held today which party would you vote for?") and a retrospective evaluation of the overall national economy (in our case the standard question as to whether respondents thought the economy had got better or worse over the past twelve months). In addition, the estimation strategy requires that a vote choice equation be specified with all of the appropriate control variables in order to ensure consistent estimates of the impact of economic evaluations on vote choice. Now the control variables, unlike the two core variables, will vary by different survey—so, for example, income might be measured differently in the French survey from that of the Dutch survey. But what is important here is simply that a properly specified vote choice model is

---

[10] Take a hypothetical electoral of three people, for example, in which it is determined that a typical improvement in the economy results in the following changes in the voters' vote probabilities for the incumbent PM Socialist Party: +2.5%; +3%; and +1.5%. The Socialist Party's economic vote would be 2.3% (the average of these three changes).

estimated for each survey—this will ensure consistent estimates of the impact of economic evaluations on vote choice.

The predicted probability that a voter i, in survey k, will vote for the party of the chief executive is the following:

$$\hat{\pi}_{ik} = \frac{e^{\hat{\beta}_{1k}(X_{ik}) + \sum_{j=1}^{J_k} \hat{\phi}_{jk} Z_{jik}}}{1 + e^{\hat{\beta}_{1k}(X_{ik}) + \sum_{j=1}^{J_k} \hat{\phi}_{jk} Z_{jik}}} \tag{1.2}$$

The coefficients from these models can be used to generate estimates, for each individual in the sample, of the impact of economic evaluations on their probability of voting for the chief executive party. The measure of the magnitude of the economic vote for this individual is simply the change in $\hat{\pi}_{ik}$ produced by a given change in her economic perceptions (say from X_{ik} to X'_{ik}):

$$EV_{ik} = \frac{e^{\hat{\beta}_{1k}(X_{ik}) + \sum_{j=1}^{J_k} \hat{\phi}_{jk} Z_{jik}}}{1 + e^{\hat{\beta}_{1k}(X_{ik}) + \sum_{j=1}^{J_k} \hat{\phi}_{jk} Z_{jik}}} - \frac{e^{\hat{\beta}_{1k}(X'_{ik}) + \sum_{j=1}^{J_k} \hat{\phi}_{jk} Z_{jik}}}{1 + e^{\hat{\beta}_{1k}(X'_{ik}) + \sum_{j=1}^{J_k} \hat{\phi}_{jk} Z_{jik}}} \tag{1.3}$$

In the Duch and Stevenson (2005) case the economic evaluation of each individual in the sample was shifted one unit in a negative direction from their actual value (the typical economic evaluation scale ranges from 1 through 3).

An estimate of the average magnitude of the economic vote for the chief executive party in the sample is obtained by calculating equation (1.3) for all individuals in the sample (i.e. using the measured values of Z_{jik} and X_{ik} setting X'_{ik} to be one category worse than X_{ik}). If the voter's economic perceptions were already at the worst category, we did not change them.[11] The economic vote for each individual was then averaged to produce an estimate of the average economic vote in the sample, EV_k. Standard errors of the predicted changes were simulated using the procedures outlined in King, Tomz, and Jason Wittenberg (2000).

Following exactly the same logic we employed multi-nomial logit to estimate the vote probabilities for each of the competing parties in the voter preference surveys we analyzed (an average of four parties per survey). Rather than an average economic vote in the sample, EV_k (based on the chief executive party vote) this gives us EV_{kp} where p indexed the specific parties in each k survey. Adopting this strategy, Duch and Stevenson obtain 678 estimates of economic vote magnitudes (one for each party in the 165 surveys analyzed).

---

[11] We also calculated the opposite change in which each voter's perceptions get one category better except those that are already the best. Comparing the results from the two measures reveals no asymmetry in economic voting—the size of the economic vote for chief executives is the same in both cases (though with opposite signs). This is in itself an important finding that corroborates previous failures to find asymmetry in individual voting models (Lewis-Beck 1988).

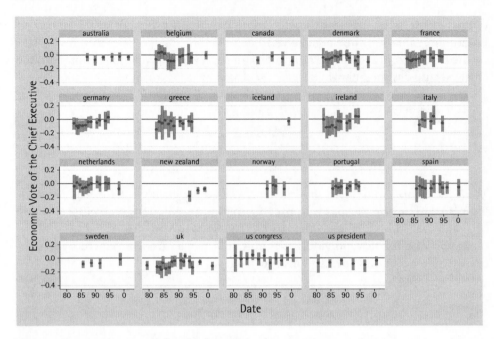

Fig. 33.1 Economic vote of the chief executive by country

Figure 33.1 provides the economic vote of the chief executive party and its standard error that Duch and Stevenson (2007) generated for 165 voter preference surveys (note that the estimates are based on a unit deterioration in economic evaluations and hence the effect on the incumbent's vote is negative). This is an important empirical result in that it confirms quite definitively that there is an economic vote in the developed democracies: The median economic vote is approximately 5 percent suggesting that typically an incumbent chief executive party can expect to gain, or lose, 5 percent of the vote because of fluctuations in retrospective perceptions of economic performance.

If we just focus on the country differences, we find an identifiable group of countries in which the *economic vote of the chief executive* is usually close to zero: Italy, the Netherlands, and US congressional elections, for example. We can also identify a cluster of countries in which the *economic vote of the chief executive* is very high: the UK, US presidential elections, Ireland, New Zealand, and Spain.

But these economic vote magnitudes also vary quite significantly over time within a particular country. For example, note that the variation in US economic voting is quite significant, rising to as high as −10 percent in 1996 but falling to almost zero percent in the 2000 election study. The French results are another example: They seem to confirm arguments regarding the impact of cohabitation on economic voting in that country (Lewis-Beck and Nadeau 2000). Note that the magnitude of the French economic vote ranges between −6 and −8 percent prior to 1987 (the first full year of cohabitation) but then falls rather precipitously to around −3 percent in 1987 and 1988. It recovers to around −5 percent in 1991 but then falls again during the next period of cohabitation, 1993 and 1994.

The second, and arguably more interesting, issue for comparativists is how to model contextual effects on the magnitude of the economic vote. In other words, how can we explain the over-time and cross-national instability in the economic vote described in Figure 33.1? From the example above, if we assume the economic vote for the chief executive party is a good proxy for overall economic voting (which Duch and Stevenson 2007 establish is in fact the case), then modeling the impact of contextual effects on its magnitudes reduces to a simple regression equation,

$$EV_k = a_0 + a_1 C_k + v_k \tag{1.4}$$

where the dependent variable is the EV_k (chief executive party economic vote) estimate generated above and measures of contextual effects (C_k) where again k indexes the particular voter preference survey from which the estimate of EV is derived. C_k, for example, could be the degree to which the national economy is subject to global influences.

There are models, though, with implications for the economic vote of particular political parties. An example would be models predicting that the vote probabilities for the senior coalition partner would be more strongly affected than those of junior coalition members by changes in economic evaluations (Duch and Stevenson 2007; Anderson 1995). Hence equation (1.4) should be extended to EV_{kp}, the economic vote of particular political parties. Accordingly, estimates of the economic vote of particular political parties based on simulated effects, employing parameters from multinomial estimation, would allow us to model the following contextual effects:

$$EV_{kp} = a_0 + a_1 C_k + a_1 P_{kp} + v_{kp} \tag{1.5}$$

where C_k is the same as above: some measure of contextual features at the country level. P_{kp} represents independent contextual variables that characterize particular parties—contention to win the prime ministership, for example. The important point here is that vote choice models need to be estimated using methods that distinguish the effects of economic evaluations on the vote probabilities for each of the major parties contending for office.

The real interesting challenge for the economic voting literature is developing theories that specify the P_{kp} and C_k terms in equation (1.5) and subjecting them to empirical tests. The remainder of this suggests theoretical and empirical avenues comparativists might take, again working within this two-stage contextual modeling strategy.

5 THE ECONOMIC VOTE: A MEASUREMENT ARTIFACT?

Instability in the individual-level measures of the economic vote poses an interesting theoretical challenge but a tractable one as I argue below. But a more problematic challenge comes from those who claim that these survey-based measures of the economic vote are plagued by serious measurement error. The implication of this challenge is that much of the individual-level variation in the economic vote seen in Figure 33.1 is measurement artifact rather than a reflection of the extent to which perceptions of objective economic outcomes shape vote choice.

Typically economic voting models treat evaluations of the economy as exogenous with the implicit assumption that they reflect some aspect of objective economic performance. But the literature on attitude formation—economic evaluations are attitudes after all—suggests that voter characteristics will affect the extent to which this "objective" information shapes their economic evaluations. One of the pioneers of the economic voting literature, Gerald Kramer (1983), suggested that individual-level analyses of economic voting are potentially problematic because individual reports of changes in economic outcomes exaggerate net changes that are politically accountable. And he pointed out that when individual-level perceptual errors correlate with partisanship or vote preference this can inflate the magnitude of the economic vote. More recently, Zaller (2004) echoed this concern, arguing that political sophisticates and partisans resist economic information from the media that is at odds with their partisanship while the economic evaluations of the less partisan are more receptive to media messages regarding economic performance. This suggests, of course, that certainly for some elements of the population, economic evaluations will be tainted by partisanship. And depending on the distribution of sophisticates and partisans in the population this could inflate or dampen the magnitude of economic voting in some contexts.

Evidence from the analysis of individual-level surveys suggests this might be a serious problem for economic voting studies. Duch, Palmer, and Anderson (2000) consider the case of economic voting in US presidential elections and conclude that national economic evaluations are strongly shaped by partisan predispositions. Erikson examines individual-level ANES survey data and concludes that "cross-sectional variation in respondent's reported perceptions of national economic conditions are largely random noise that has no bearing on political evaluations" (Erikson 2004, 5). And he argues that any observed relationship between economic evaluations and vote choice is an artifact of vote preference shaping individuals' economic perceptions. Based on their analysis of individual-level UK panel data Evans and Anderson (2006) conclude that the causal impact of vote preference on economic evaluations is stronger than the impact of these evaluations on vote choice. Finally, in their study of economic voting in four nations, Wlezien, Franklin, and Twiggs (1997) find that economic evaluations are strongly influenced by vote preference. Hence, while there is little doubt that endogeneity exists there is little consensus on its overall implications for estimates of the magnitude of the economic vote as measured at the individual level.

Following Duch and Palmer (2002) we can think about economic evaluations (X_i) in the following terms,

$$X_i = \lambda_i X^O + X_i^S + \epsilon_i$$
$$X_i^S = f(\mathbf{W}) \tag{1.6}$$

where X^O is the objective economic evaluation, X_i^S captures systematic differences due to information and subjective factors (i.e., W), and ϵ_i is the stochastic component. In this formal definition, individual-level evaluations contain two forms of "noise:" subjective considerations and random fluctuations. Both forms of noise constitute sources of non-attitudes. It is this systematic measurement error in national economic evaluations that could in fact artificially inflate the correlation between these evaluations and the dependent variable. According to Kramer (1983, 95), "we are ultimately interested only in how real economic outcomes affect voting decisions and not in economic rhetoric or perceptual imagery." The distortions of economic rhetoric and perceptual imagery might manifest themselves through X_i^S.

If we include national economic evaluations in an economic voting model without controlling for this systematic measurement error (X_i^S), the evaluations will "pick up" the direct effect of partisan predispositions, thereby producing an inflated estimate of the relationship between economic perceptions and vote choice. Note that this formal definition allows for group differences through variation in λ_i and X_i^S, and the variance of ϵ_i. Group differences in the level of economic optimism or pessimism are captured by variation in X_i^S. But there will also be group differences in the weights that individuals place on particular aspects of economic outcomes. Actual economic outcomes (X^O) can of course consist of different aspects of economic performance (growth in real disposable income, unemployment, etc.). In fact we can think of X^O as a vector of objective economic outcomes that map into (or load onto) economic evaluations (X_i) according to the weighting factor λ_i. This weighting factor could reflect differences in economic policy emphases or priorities but it could also reflect differences in knowledge or awareness of the economy.

In the conventional economic voting model, systematic measurement error in economic evaluations is defined as factors that shape X_i but are essentially unrelated specifically to economic policy outcomes—in other words the distinction between X_i^S and X^O. In the case of extreme endogeneity much of the systematic measurement error (X_i^S) that shapes X_i but is not specifically related to economic policy outcomes is highly correlated with vote choice. For example, there is considerable evidence suggesting that economic evaluations are shaped by partisanship. Because partisanship tends also to be strongly correlated with vote choice, not addressing the measurement error problem results in an inflated (or understated) correlation between economic evaluations and the dependent variable.

One conclusion some draw from this is simply to ignore individual-level analyses of the economic vote. Aggregate-level analyses of public opinion presume that aggregation eliminates the individual-level noise in mass policy attitudes (Page and Shapiro 1992; MacKuen, Erikson, and Stimson 1992). More formally, these aggregate-level analyses assume that both X_i^S and the stochastic component (ϵ_i) in equation (1.6) have zero mean. Given these assumptions and $\lambda_i = \lambda$, the mean of X_i across individuals represents a "clean" aggregate-level measure of public opinion that constitutes the latent objective evaluation. Duch, Palmer, and Anderson (2000) suggest that this may not be a panacea. They demonstrate that individual evaluations of the economy contain subjective sources of systematic variation and hence aggregation does not eliminate the individual-level noise (i.e. $E(X_i^S) \neq 0$).

Hence it is important to understand to what extent this endogeneity affects our estimate of the magnitude of the economic vote. By controlling for systematic and random measurement error in economic evaluations, we can estimate whether this error seriously affects estimates of the magnitude of economic voting at the individual level. One approach is to purge X_i, reported economic evaluations, of systematic measurement error (X_i^S) which would result in a measure of economic evaluations that included only factors contributing to meaningful fluctuations in economic evaluations (X^O) and random measurement error (ϵ_i). This would entail estimating X_i^{Purged}, which is economic evaluations purged of systematic measurement error.

Duch and Palmer (2002) suggest that the systematic component of the measurement error in economic evaluations consists of three broad factors. First, economic evaluations are shaped by partisanship. Duch and Palmer (2002) have demonstrated that national economic evaluations are to a large extent shaped by partisan predispositions—this is the case in both the American and European contexts. In addition to political partisanship, respondents may rely on personal experiences and regional economic circumstances to formulate an evaluation of the national economy. Citizens who infer national conditions from personal and local experiences are effectively evaluating the economy in a subjective rather than objective manner. Similarly, national economic evaluations may vary across individuals due to differences in levels of information and sophistication about government policy and economic outcomes. Third, social class differences may systematically shape economic evaluations. Individuals in different socioeconomic circumstances might view the same economy in a very different light (MacKuen and Mouw 1995). Similarly, citizens of different sexes and races may perceive the economy differently due to biases in their general attitudes toward the economic and political systems (on gender and economic voting, see Welch and Hibbing 1992).

Note that the coefficient (λ_i) in equation (1.6) varies across individuals. This variation results from groups of individuals placing different weight on different aspects of economic performance. These differences are captured by λ_i. This "Policy Related Variation" represents differences in economic evaluations that are grounded in self-interested differences in opinion regarding measures of economic performance and hence capture variation in economic evaluations that are grounded in meaningful policy differences, or emphases, across individuals. For example, individuals who value reducing inflation more than maintaining low unemployment (e.g. retired respondents on fixed incomes) might emphasize price stability more than job creation when evaluating the national economy.

Hence we can identify three factors contributing to systematic measurement error: party identification (PID), information, and socioeconomic status (SES). Accordingly X_i^{Purged} is estimated as follows:

$$X_i = a_1(PID) + a_2(\text{Information}) + a_3(SES) + a_4(\text{Policy}) + \epsilon_i$$

$$\hat{X}_i^s = \hat{a}_1(PID) + \hat{a}_2(\text{Information}) + \hat{a}_3(SES)$$

$$X_i^{Purged} = X_i - \hat{X}_i^s \qquad (1.7)$$

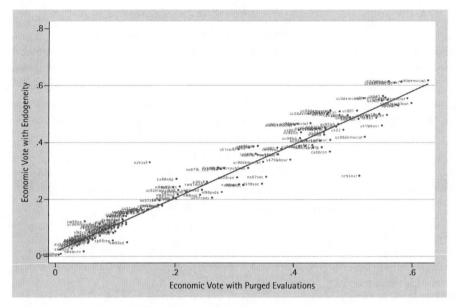

Fig. 33.2 Economic vote with purged evaluations

The estimate of vote probabilities is a modified version of equation (1.1):

$$v_{ik} \sim Bin(\pi_{ik})$$

$$logit(\pi'_{ik}) = \beta_{ok} + \beta_{1k}X^{Purged}{}_{ik} + \sum_{j=1}^{J_k} \phi_{jk}Z_{jik}. \tag{1.8}$$

The magnitude of the economic vote based on this equation is EV'_{ik}. Figure 33.2 compares the economic vote magnitudes obtain from equation (1.8) that employs economic evaluations purged of systematic subjective factors (EV'_{ik}) with the economic vote magnitude obtained from equation (1.1), employing X_i. Based on the Duch and Stevenson (2007) sample of estimated economic votes there is little evidence that systematic measurement error, due to subjective factors unrelated to the objective economy, has any significant impact on estimates of the magnitude of economic voting. Clearly there are some estimates where this is the case but overall the results suggest little difference between (EV'_{ik}) and (EV_{ik}).

We study economic voting because it provides insights into how individuals make a voting decision. Our interest here is not simply predicting election outcomes. The endogeneity debate is about whether short-term fluctuations in policy outcomes has any independent impact on subjective evaluations, or whether partisanship is an overwhelming molder of public opinion (at least as measured in public opinion polls). If individual-level measures of economic evaluations are hopelessly endogenous—the Erikson position—this is an important insight into how individuals use information to make voting decisions. It would suggest that for most voters "objective" information regarding economic outcomes is overwhelmed by partisanship, or other subjective factors, in the formation of attitudes regarding economic performance.

The evidence presented in this section though argues against this perspective. For most voters "objective" information regarding the economy does affect evaluations quite independent of the individual's partisan predispositions. There is no evidence that the economic vote measured at the individual level is hopelessly contaminated by endogeneity. This suggests that the contextual variation in the economic vote we see cross-nationally, and also over time, is not an artifact of systematic measurement error. Hence, while subjective economic evaluations certainly are affected to some degree by endogeneity, this has no systematic effect on the contextual variation in economic voting that was summarized in Figure 33.2 and is the primary concern of comparative economic voting scholars.

6 TWEAKING THE SANCTIONING MODEL

Duch and Stevenson's (2007) analysis of 163 election surveys quite clearly establish the importance of the economic vote: They identify considerable contextual variation in its magnitude; but also debunk any notion that estimates of the magnitude of the economic vote are hopelessly plagued by endogeneity. The challenge for comparative scholars is to explain this contextual variation. For the most part the approach in both the American and comparative literature has been to tweak the sanctioning model in such a fashion as to account for the "noise" that context can introduce into perceptions of economic performance.

Hibbs (2006) has pointed out that Kramer's (1983) "error-in-variables" conception of economic evaluations that is replicated in equation (1.6) can be used to model contextual variations in the signal-to-noise ratio regarding incumbent economic performance. Contexts, according to this conceptualization, vary in terms of the size of the politically relevant portion of economic outcomes. In terms of equation (1.6) this implies that the systematic measurement error (X_i^s) portion of economic evaluations (X_i) is high. When the politically relevant portion of economic outcomes (X^o) is small relative to (X_i^s), then usual survey measures of economic evaluations in the voter's preference function will contain considerable error. Hence, a particularly complex governing coalition situation or a context where relatively large exogenous shocks affect the macroeconomy would likely reduce the extent to which voter's economic evaluations reflect the politically relevant portion of economic outcomes. As Hibbs (2006) demonstrates, higher levels of error in the measure of economic evaluations will have a downward bias on its coefficient in a voting equation. Hence, contexts in which the politically relevant portion of macroeconomic outcomes is small—reflected in relatively high measurement error when overall economic evaluations are used—will be those that have a low correlation between economic evaluations and vote choice.

There is considerable evidence suggesting that variation in this signal-to-noise ratio does affect the magnitude of the economic vote. Powell and Whitten (1993) developed a measure of institutional "clarity of responsibility" that measures the extent to which political institutions allowed incumbents to diffuse responsibility for economic outcomes (the voting cohesion of the major parties, the extent to which legislative committee systems accommodated opposition party power sharing, bicameralism, coalition governments, and minority governments). Employing this index of clarity of responsibility, interacted with measures of economic performance in aggregate vote share models, the authors concluded that, "the greater the perceived unified control of policymaking by the incumbent government, the more likely is the citizen to assign responsibility for economic and political outcomes to the incumbents" (Powell and Whitten 1993, 398).

Pacek and Radcliff (1995) explored the impact of welfare state penetration on economic voting across seventeen western democracies over twenty-seven years and found that high levels of welfare spending depressed sociotropic economic voting. Hellwig (2001) analyzes a pooled sample of nine individual-level election surveys and includes contextual measures of both economic context (economic interdependence) along with the institutional variables employed by Powell and Whitten (1993). He confirms the important role that political institutions play in mediating the magnitude of the economic vote and also provides evidence of a similar mediating role for economic variables such as the extent to which national economies are integrated into the global economy. In contrast to Hellwig, Scheve (2004) finds that increased integration into the world economy has the effect of moderating exogenous shocks to a national economy which leads voters to place greater weight on the economy in their vote decision. Recent efforts by Ebeid and Rodden (2006) to explain contextual variation in economic voting across US states suggests that structural features of state economies that make them particularly vulnerable to international commodity markets reduce the magnitude of their economic vote.

On the other hand, some of the efforts to extend and empirically test the clarity of responsibility insights have resulted in fragile or unstable empirical findings. For example, Chappell and Veiga (2000) analyze 136 European parliamentary election outcomes for the period 1960–97 and find evidence that inflation (relative to European averages) shapes vote outcomes but find no support for the clarity of responsibility argument. Royed, Leyden, and Borrelli (2000) specifically challenge the robustness of the Powell and Whitten result claiming that there is little support for the clarity of responsibility argument—in fact claiming that economic voting is higher for coalition as opposed to single-party governments.[12]

More importantly though efforts to empirically test the clarity of responsibility argument suggest that context may not simply inflate the noise component (X_i^s) of economic evaluations. Empirical studies of contextual variation in the economic vote suggest voters respond in a more nuanced fashion to economic performance than is implied by the sanctioning model. An important insight in this regard comes from Anderson's (1995)

[12] Though Palmer and Whitten 2003a, and 2003b have rigorously rebutted Royed, Leyden, and Borrelli's claims.

application of the clarity notion to monthly popularity data rather than electoral data. Though he worked with only five countries, his empirical analyses indicate quite conclusively "that more responsibility in the government results in the economic variables having stronger effects on party support" (Anderson 1995, 210). Variation in the magnitude of the economic vote does not appear to be simply a function of a higher or lower noise-to-signal ratio but rather the result of voters making fairly careful distinctions regarding the competency of particular political parties for economic outcomes.

All of these, broadly speaking, comparative efforts suggest voters engage in more than the simple punishment or reward implied by moral hazard models of the economic vote. In fact I would argue that these empirical efforts, employing widely varying types of aggregate- and individual-level data, suggest the voter's signal extraction efforts are focused on determining a party's competency for economic outcomes. And, as Fearon (1999) has formally, and quite convincingly, demonstrated, once we concede that voters are engaging in competency calculations, selection motivations dominate the vote decision. This implies that merely tweaking the sanctioning model to accommodate variations in the signal-to-noise ratio or clarity of responsibility may not be sufficient for explaining contextual variation in the economic vote—an argument made recently by a number of scholars (Duch and Stevenson 2007; Fearon 1999; Cheibub and Przeworski 1999) and pursued in more detail in the next section.

7 RATIONALITY AND THE ECONOMIC VOTE RECONSIDERED

The discussion to this point has identified interesting pieces of an empirical puzzle concerning vote choice. Economic evaluations clearly matter, although more or less, depending on the political context. There is some evidence in these empirical patterns that context affects the voters' attribution of responsibility for economic outcomes to particular parties. And finally, there is evidence that voters are engaging in a signal extraction exercise, using elements of context to ascertain overall incumbent competency for economic outcomes. I would argue that the most important challenge for comparative scholars is figuring out how to assemble these pieces of the puzzle. This is a theoretical challenge that requires revisiting the micro-model of vote choice with the goal of understanding how contextual features enter into the vote choice function.

One can imagine a number of different strategies for accomplishing this goal. Duch and Stevenson (2007) propose one approach that differs from the traditional sanctioning modeling efforts described above in that it proposes a contextual model of the economic vote that presumes a rational voter who is fully informed about the political and economic context. Their approach works out a rigorous micro-model of what information is relevant, and how it is used, to inform the voting decision. They argue that in order to understand the instability in the economic vote we need to have a much clearer theory of how voters condition their economic vote on the political and economic context. Duch and Stevenson (2007) propose a model of the economic vote that builds on three important rationality assumptions: voters have rational expectations; they are fully informed about the political and economic context; and individuals are strategic, rather than sincere or expressive, voters.

Rational expectations theory implies that the same rationality assumptions should be associated with forecasts that are typically associated with static decision making. In other words rational expectations treats forward-looking decisions in the same rational fashion as static decisions, particularly in terms of how individuals use information.[13] As we saw above, the traditional economic voting model has a strong sanctioning element to it: the expected utility calculations of voters are heavily, if not entirely, determined by the retrospective assessment of incumbent performance. But if voters are behaving rationally then they should maximize their expected utilities and form *expectations* optimally, given the available information. Persson and Tabellini (1990) and Alesina and Rosenthal (1995) develop models of the economy that explicitly incorporate rational expectations and very nicely draw out the implications of rational expectations for the economic voting model. Most importantly they conclude that the rational economic vote is motivated by a concern with selection or identifying a candidate's competence for managing the macroeconomy.

Their result can be expressed in the following equation:

$$E[u_{t+1}|v_i] = \left(\frac{\sigma_\mu^2}{\sigma_\mu^2 + \sigma_\xi^2}\right)(y_{it} - \bar{y} - \mu_{it-1}) \tag{1.9}$$

$E[u_{t+1}|v_i]$ is the utility that the rational voter derives from voting for the incumbent party (i) given the observed economy; y_{it} is the rate of economic growth in period t, under incumbent party i; and $\bar{y}$ is the natural rate of growth; σ_μ^2 is the variance in the incumbent's competence shock (we can think of this as unexpected shocks to the macroeconomy that are associated with the actions of policy makers); and σ_ξ^2 is the variance in the non-political shock (we can think of this as unexpected exogenous shocks out of the control of political decision makers).

This result makes it clear when voters can extract information from fluctuations in the previous economy in order to access the current competence of an incumbent and cast an economic vote. The term $y_{it} - \bar{y} - \mu_{it-1}$ is simply observed economic performance less the parts of economic growth whose sources are known to the voter. The term captures what the incumbent has "done for the voter lately" (i.e. how the current period differs from the natural level of growth, discounted by the impact of the incumbent's known level of competence in the previous period). We can interpret the coefficient on this term, i.e. $\frac{\sigma_\mu^2}{\sigma_\mu^2 + \sigma_\xi^2}$, as the "competency signal" that voters can extract from the observed economy. This competency signal will always be positive and will approach one as the variance in the random (non-political) shocks to the economy, σ_ξ^2,

[13] Examples here include Cukierman and Meltzer (1986); Rogoff and Sibert (1988); Rogoff (1990); Persson and Tabellini (1990); and Alesina and Roubini (1999).

goes to zero. In that case, the voter knows that growth above or below the natural rate is completely due to competency shocks—consequently, deviations from the natural rate of growth will perfectly identify competent and incompetent administrations. More generally, if σ_μ^2, the variation in the competence term μ_{it}, is large relative to variation in the non-political component of growth, σ_ξ^2, then changes in the economy will provide a strong signal about the competency of the incumbent and the voter will weight the retrospective economy more heavily in her utility function. Alternatively, growth that is above or below the natural rate is a poor signal of the incumbent's competence if observed growth is more likely to result from non-political shocks than from competency shocks—i.e. if σ_ξ^2 is high relative to σ_μ^2.

The presence of the competency signal in the voter's economic expectations implies that voters will use available information to assess how much of any change in economic outcomes $(y_{it} - \bar{y} - \mu_{it-1})$ is a function of incumbent competence as opposed to being a function of exogenous shocks. This is an important result because it provides an explanation for fluctuations in the magnitude of the economic vote that is grounded in the rational actor model. As was pointed out in the previous section, the puzzle confronting comparative students of economic voting is the great variability in the magnitude of the economic vote. Much of the efforts to explain these differences has tended to focus on information shortcomings or confusion on the part of the voter. Competency models on the other hand suggest that the magnitude of the economic vote will vary because there is contextual variation in the relative importance of political as opposed to non-political, or exogenous, shocks to macroeconomic outcomes. Voters are able to tease out this information and use it to weight economic outcomes in a rational fashion.

Duch and Stevenson (2007) demonstrate that the competency signal term $\left(\frac{\sigma_\mu^2}{\sigma_\mu^2+\sigma_\xi^2}\right)$ is general enough to incorporate the major contextual factors that are typically associated with cross-national variations in the economic vote, specifically economic, political, and institutional contextual effects. How might these contexts affect the ability of citizens to distinguish exogenous from politically competent shocks to the macroeconomy? Features of the context need to systematically affect either the political competence variance or the exogenous variance terms. Whether or not one is persuaded by their theory, it nicely illustrates how theory, particularly related to individual-level reasoning on the part of voters, can, and I would argue must, inform empirical efforts to account for contextual variation in the economic vote. Hence claims regarding the impact of a particular feature of the political or economic context on the economic vote must be derived from this notion that context can either facilitate or frustrate this signal extraction challenge facing the voter. For example, what is it about concentrating responsibility in the hands of a single party that might increase the economic vote? The strength of the Duch and Stevenson (2007) theory is that this is one of a number of hypotheses that results from their competency signal model: power sharing within the governing coalition decreases the importance of the economy on vote choice only because it leads voters to attribute more weight to exogenous factors shaping the observed movements in the economy. In fact the Duch and Stevenson (2007) model explains how three major contextual variables condition the economic vote: political control of the economy; administrative responsibility; and strategic voting.

7.1 Political Control of the Economy

As I pointed out at the outset of this essay, my interest in the "economic vote" is motivated by a broader theoretical and empirical interest in how context conditions the link between voter evaluations of party performance (obviously, including governing incumbents) and vote choice. Understanding this "conditionality" is important for a range of substantive issues in political economy. This is particularly important for scholars exploring the evolving nature of political control over the economy and its implications for democratic accountability. Broad claims are often made regarding the impact on democratic accountability of globalization or of the privatization of national economies. These are arguments about how context (structural features of the economy) conditions the relationship between evaluations and vote choice. Implicit in many of these arguments is a micro-model specifying what factors shape vote choice and how the importance of these factors in the vote choice is conditioned by institutional and political contexts. Rarely are these micro mechanisms clearly specified and empirically tested. Models of contextual variation in the economic vote can be of considerable service in this regard: they focus on economic perceptions that are widely considered important to the vote choice; and they specify how voters use information about context to condition the importance of these economic evaluations in their vote choice. A case in point is arguments regarding globalization and democratic accountability.

Arguments regarding globalization and democratic governance suggest that voters are attentive to whether economic outcomes are the result of actions by electorally accountable decision makers as opposed to initiatives by economic and political actors who they cannot hold electorally accountable. These arguments presume that voters are able to determine whether a shock to the domestic economy results from actions taken by elected decision makers (a tax cut) rather than by decisions unrelated to national government officials (trade barriers imposed by a foreign entity). It implies economic voting models in which the voter is using information about this context (global influences on the domestic economy) to condition her economic vote—a more informed voter than one might observe in a typical economic voting model. The challenge here is specifying a model that explains how these contextual factors enter into the choice function of an instrumentally rational voter.

The approach adopted by Duch and Stevenson (2007) was to derive a version of equation (1.9) that incorporated the impact of institutional contexts on the competency perceived by voters. This modification distinguished between two types of decision makers, which they labeled "electorally dependent decision makers" (EDDs) and "non-electorally dependent decision makers" (NEDDs). The first of these labels (EDD) is just shorthand for referring to the elected officials that make up the national government and the bureaucracy that is responsible to them. The second label (NEDD) refers to everyone else whose decisions might impact the economy including individuals, firms, interest groups, non-electorally dependent (entrenched) bureaucrats, foreign leaders, the WTO, and many more. Competency shocks are only associated with the decisions of the EDDs (electorally dependent decision makers) while the exogenous shocks are associated with the decisions of everyone else.

Duch and Stevenson (2007) derive a vote calculus similar to equation (1.9) that incorporates the impact of institutional context on the incumbent's competency signal:

$$E\left[\sum_{l=1}^{a}\mu_{ilt+1}|v_i\right] = b\left(\frac{a\sigma_{\mu}^2}{a\sigma_{\mu}^2 + \beta\sigma_{\psi}^2}\right)\left(y_{it}-\bar{y}-\sum_{l=1}^{a}\mu_{ilt-1}\right) \qquad (1.10)$$

The voter is more likely to vote for the incumbent when the expected utility in equation (1.10) is positive. The term $y_{it}-\bar{y}-\sum_{l=1}^{a}\mu_{ilt-1}$ is the same as above, observed economic performance less the parts whose sources are known to the voter, with the difference that there is a separate utility term for each l EDD (electorally dependent decision maker) and these are summed over all a EDDs. We can interpret the coefficient on this term, i.e. $\left(\frac{a\sigma_{\mu}^2}{a\sigma_{\mu}^2+\beta\sigma_{\psi}^2}\right)$, as the "competency signal" that controls how much information about the competence of incumbents voters can extract from observed movements in the economy. The numerator of the competence signal is now the variance of the overall competence shock, which is the product of the variance of the distribution of competence shocks associated with a single decision and the number of decisions made by electorally dependent decision makers $(a\sigma_{\mu}^2)$. And in the denominator we now have a term capturing the variance of the overall exogenous shock, which is the product of the variance of the distribution of exogenous shocks associated with a single decision and the number of decisions made by non-electorally dependent decision makers $(\beta\sigma_{\psi}^2)$.

Given the assumption that σ_{ψ}^2 and σ_{μ}^2 are constant over all contexts, the impact of political and economic institutions on the strength of the competence signal (and ultimately on economic voting) must come through difference in the a and the β terms in the above equations. The numerator of the competence signal is the variance of the overall competence shock $(a\sigma_{\mu}^2)$, which implies that expanding the number of economically consequential choices that the EDD makes will increase the value of this term. More substantively, the variance in the overall competence shock should be larger in countries in which EDDs make more of the economic decisions that determine the country's growth path. Similarly, the variance in the overall exogenous shock should be larger in countries in which NEDDs make more of the economic decisions affecting growth.

When comparing the overall competency signal in different contexts the ratio of NEDDs to EDDs in each context can shape the relative size of their overall competency signals. Where a and β are from a large competency signal context (more EEDs) and a' and β' are from a small signal context (more NEEDs), Duch and Stevenson (2007) demonstrate that the ratio of NEDDs to EDDs in the large signal context must be smaller than this ratio in the smaller signal context:[14]

[14] This follows from the following:

$$\frac{a\sigma_{\mu}^2}{a\sigma_{\mu}^2+\beta\sigma_{\psi}^2} > \frac{a'\sigma_{\mu}^2}{a'\sigma_{\mu}^2+\beta'\sigma_{\psi}^2}$$

$$\frac{\beta\sigma_{\psi}}{a\sigma_{\mu}^2} < \frac{\beta'\sigma_{\psi}}{a'\sigma_{\mu}^2}$$

$$\frac{\beta}{a} < \frac{\beta'}{a'}$$

$$\frac{\beta}{a} < \frac{\beta'}{a'} \tag{1.11}$$

Determining the relative impact of political and economic contexts on the overall competency signal reduces to establishing the magnitudes of these ratios.

This result clearly identifies how global variables enter into the individual-level reasoning associated with the vote decision. Voters are able to distinguish between the relative importance, for decisions affecting domestic economic growth, of national electorally dependent decision makers as opposed to those non-electorally dependent decision makers some of which are associated with the international environment (elected officials in other countries, multinational firms, or international organizations and agreements). Globalization affects democratic governance because it shrinks the incumbent's competency signal which in turn reduces the importance of the economy in the vote decision.

A case in point is trade openness. Increased trade flows reduce the control that EDDs have on macroeconomic policy outcomes and they subject domestic economic outcomes to greater influence by NEDDs, and particularly foreign, decision makers. Aggregate demand in economies with significant dependence on export markets is subject to external demand and to prices that are determined by global markets beyond the influence of domestic policy makers. High levels of imports subject economies to inflationary (or deflationary) shocks that again are beyond the control of domestic governmental officials (Cameron 1978). The production structure in open economies is often more concentrated than in closed economies which can exaggerate the extent to which domestic economies are subject to external shocks beyond the control of incumbent policy makers (Rodrik 1998; IMF 2005). Rodrik (1998), for example, presents empirical data clearly indicting that more open economies have significantly more volatile GDP growth.[15]

Accordingly, in an open economy the number of NEDDs affecting the macroeconomy should be greater than in a closed economy (i.e. $\beta_{cl} < \beta_{op}$) while the number of EDDs should remain constant or possibly be smaller in an open economy than in a closed one (i.e. $a_{op} \leq a_{cl}$). Hence, we expect the ratio of NEDDs to EDDs will be smaller in a closed economy,

$$\frac{\beta_{op}}{a_{op}} > \frac{\beta_{cl}}{a_{cl}} \tag{1.12}$$

which suggests a lower overall competency signal in economies that are open to global economic influences. It follows, then, that a weaker competency signal in open economies will result in lower levels of economic voting.[16]

Duch and Stevenson (2007) evaluate this argument employing a measure of trade openness from the World Bank which is a ratio of total trade to gross domestic product (GDP) (World Bank 2004). Figure 33.3 presents a plot of the *economic vote of the Chief Executive* against this measure of Trade Openness (recall that a large negative economic

---

[15] See also evidence to this effect for the developing economies in Gavin and Hausmann (1996).

[16] And as Ebeid and Rodden (2006) nicely demonstrate this effect can differ at the subnational level as a function of the structural features of provincial or state economies.

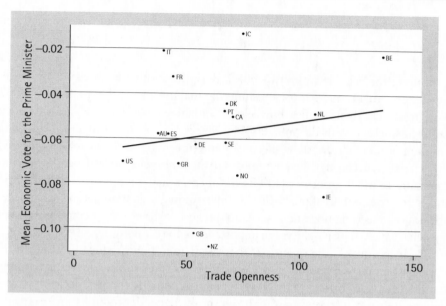

Fig. 33.3 Trade openness and average PM party economic vote

vote score indicates high levels of economic voting). First, there clearly is no evidence that the economic vote is higher in open economies as some have claimed (Scheve 2004). In fact, openness of the economy leads to a significantly smaller economic vote. This supports the contention that the competency signal in open economies is weaker than in closed economies which in turn leads to lower levels of economic voting.

The importance of measuring democratic accountability has increased with the spread of globalization, economic integration, and changes in the structural features of domestic economies. The economic vote is one of a number of types of vote choice models that can be used to gauge democratic accountability. And by providing rigorous theoretical and empirical insights into how context conditions vote choice, comparative scholars of economic voting can make extremely important contributions to this debate.

7.2 Administrative Responsibility

The previous section suggests that voters are cognizant of how responsibility for policy is shared amongst non-electorally and electorally accountable decision makers. And this has implications for the signal extraction challenge facing the typical voter and ultimately explains contextual variation in the economic vote. In many, if not most, developed democracies, administrative, or executive, responsibility is shared by more than one political party. This sharing of administrative responsibility by other legislative parties also has implications for the magnitude of the competency signal and hence the economic vote.

There is widespread acceptance in the comparative economic voting literature that the "complexity" of coalition governing situations compared to the simplicity of single-party governments accounts for at least some of the cross-national variation in the magnitude of the economic vote (Powell and Whitten 1993). But the theoretical foundation for these empirical patterns has not been well worked out aside from attributing a weak economic vote in coalition contexts to the inability of the voter to attribute responsibility. This notion that clarity of responsibility accounts for variations in the magnitude of the economic vote suggests that voters lack sufficient information or are somehow confused about policy-making responsibility. The rationality assumptions in the Duch and Stevenson (2007) model preclude any confusion or poor information on the part of voters. Rather, voters are assumed to be fully informed about how administrative responsibility is shared in the governing coalition. Hence they argue that it is not the case that voters are getting a confused or bad signal regarding competency but rather they are receiving accurate information regarding precisely how administrative responsibility is shared amongst different political parties. In their model this information regarding the proportion of administrative responsibility is summarized by the term $\lambda_{i,t}^2$ which is simply the square of the amount of *administrative responsibility* that each party holds. And one way to measure this share is in terms of percentage of cabinet seats held by a party such that in a single party majority government λ equals 1 and in a cabinet with n parties equally sharing portfolios λ equals 1/n.[17]

Duch and Stevenson (2007) derive a "responsibility" weighted competency signal that affects the voter's utility from the government's perceived economic performance in the following fashion,

$$E[\mu_{g,t}|y_{g,t}] = \left(\frac{\sigma_\mu^2 \sum\limits_{i\in g} \lambda_{i,t}^2}{\sigma_\xi^2 + \sigma_\mu^2 \sum\limits_{i\in g} \lambda_{i,t}^2} \right) (y_{g,t} - \bar{y} - \mu_{g,t-1}) \tag{1.13}$$

This result assumes that the overall competence of the government (g) in a given period is a weighted average of the competence of the incumbent parties, with weights corresponding to the amount of *administrative responsibility* that the party holds. The weight for each incumbent party at time t is $\lambda_{i,t}$, with the sum of these weights equaling one. Duch and Stevenson (2005) show that the competency shock term will be at its maximum when administrative responsibility is not shared, that is when a single party administers economic policy. The political shock term, $\sigma_\mu^2 \sum\limits_{i\in g} \lambda_{i,t}^2$, will be at its minimum when administrative responsibility is shared equally amongst each party in the cabinet.

This result generates predictions that are similar to those suggested by the "clarity of responsibility" arguments although the responsibility weighted competency signal argument developed here is grounded on the notion that voters are fully informed about how administrative responsibility is shared amongst legislative parties. Single-party majority governments would be predicted to have the highest levels of economic voting—the typical case for example, in the UK, the USA, and Canada. Coalition

---

[17] Duch and Stevenson 2007 actually examine a broader measure of administrative responsibility that includes the amount of administrative responsibility associated with opposition legislative parties but to simplify the discussion here I only examine the narrower measure based on cabinet portfolios.

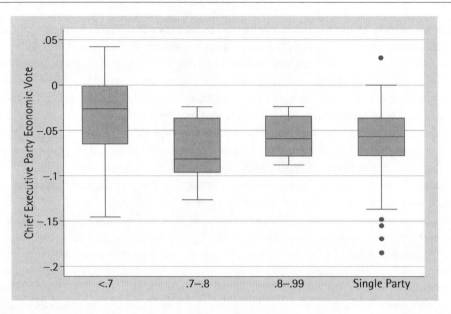

Fig. 33.4 Concentration of administrative responsibility and economic vote for chief executive party

governments, particularly those in which cabinet portfolios are equally shared by the coalition parties, are predicted to have a lower competency signal and hence lower levels of economic voting.[18] Figure 33.4, based on the chief executive economic vote magnitudes from Figure 33.1, compares the magnitude of the economic vote for four levels of concentration of administrative responsibility—the $\sum_{i \in g} \lambda_{i,t}^2$ term in equation (1.13).

There is some suggestive evidence here that contexts where there is high concentration of administrative responsibility—contexts with relatively concentrated administrative responsibility scores (greater than .7)—have relatively high levels of economic voting. Those contexts in which administrative responsibility is shared by relatively large number of parties, i.e. a concentration score falling below .7, have low levels of economic voting.

7.3 Contention and Strategic Voting

It is widely accepted that the nature of contention amongst competing candidates and strategic voting incentives, which of course vary across political contexts, have an impact on the utility of voting for particular parties contesting an election. So, for example, the likelihood that a vote for the German FDP party will affect the type of government that is formed after an election represents an important consideration when voters estimate the utility of such a vote choice. Assuming that voters are instrumentally

---

[18] Administrative responsibility can be conceptualized more broadly than parties sharing responsibility within the cabinet. It can include the influence of opposition parties in administrative responsibility through, for example, a powerful legislative committee system. Duch and Stevenson (2007) generalize the result described here to include the extent of sharing of administrative responsibility amongst all parties, both elected and opposition.

rational—an assumption consistent with much of the work on economic voting—then voters should respond strategically to electoral institutions, and to the nature of contention amongst competing parties. McKelvey and Ordeshook (1972) derive the decision-theoretic implications of this for a utility-maximizing voter:

$$E[u|v_j] - E[u|v_0] = \sum_{j' \in J} P_{jj'}(u_j - u_{j'}) \tag{1.14}$$

Where J is the set of all parties in the legislature and $E[u|v_j]$ is the expected utility from voting for party j, $E[u|v_0]$ is the expected utility from abstaining, and u_j and $u_{j'}$ are the utilities associated with parties j and j' wining the election. $P_{jj'}$ is a "pivot probability" and is defined as the probability that parties j and j' are tied for first place in the plurality race. Note that the subscript on the summation notation indicates that the sum is over all parties in the election. The voter should vote for the party for which $E[u|v_j] - E[u|v_0]$ is the largest.

This implies that the act of voting for a party can only change a voter's utility by changing the outcome of the election. The likelihood of a vote for a particular party changing the outcome of the election is captured by the probability that this vote is decisive in the contest between this party and each of the other competing parties. Consequently, the voter's expected utility for voting for a particular party is simply the sum of the ways her vote can be decisive multiplied by the utility of the outcome associated with each kind of decisive vote.

Duch and Stevenson (2007) argue that the expected utilities that voters associate with the perceived economic performance of competing parties—a standard feature of economic voting models—should be conditioned in a fashion similar to equation (1.14) by the probability of a vote being decisive. This suggests incorporating a term capturing pivot probabilities or decisiveness of each vote to the expected utility calculation described above in equation (1.9). This results in the following expected utility of voting for party j as opposed to abstaining,

$$E[u|v_j] - E[u|v_0] = b(y_{g,t} - \bar{y} - \mu_{g,t-1}) \sum_{g' \in A} (P_{j,gg'} - P_{j,g'g}) \tag{1.15}$$

In this simplified example, there are two possible outcomes: the incumbent (g) or a challenging government (g'). Here I simply assume that voters have no information regarding the expected economic outcomes associated with the challenging government which implies that $E[u_{g',t+1}] = 0$. Recall that when the $(y_{g,t} - \bar{y} - \mu_{g,t-1})$ term is positive this indicates that voters perceive a positive shock to the economy at the election period t. The last term following the summation sign on the right-hand side of equation (1.15) captures the extent to which this perceived economic performance is conditioned on strategic voting considerations. The $P_{j,gg'}$ term indicates the probability that two cabinets, g and g', are tied for selection *and* that a vote for party j will break that tie in favor of cabinet g. And the $P_{j,g'g}$ term indicates the probability that two cabinets, g and g', are tied for selection *and* that a vote for party j will break that tie in favor of cabinet g'.

If the voter perceives a positive economic shock associated with the incumbent government **g**, and a vote for party j is more likely to break a tie in favor of **g** rather than **g'**, then this positive economic shock will contribute to a positive utility for voting for j rather than abstaining. Note though that if the incumbent governing coalition (**g**) is certain to win (or the challenging coalition **g'** is certain to win) the pivot probabilities in the last expression are zero and hence the economy will not contribute to the voter's utility for casting a vote for party j as opposed to abstaining. The simplest examples come from contexts in which there is a single-party governing executive. So, for example, one would hardly expect economic evaluations to have shaped vote choice in the second round of the 2002 French presidential elections when there was no question that the incumbent President Chirac would prevail. Similarly, in the 2001 British elections, in which Labour was widely expected to win the election easily, this result suggests we should find little economic voting.

This theoretical result also has implications for the economic vote for particular parties in multiparty contexts. One implication is that the economic vote for perennial incumbent parties like the Belgian and Dutch Christian parties, the Irish Fianna Fail, or the German FDP should be depressed relative to their cabinet partners. The underlying logic here draws a distinction between the same cabinet forming over and over again versus different cabinets forming but with one, or possibly more, party always participating. It is in the latter case where we find perennial incumbent parties always entering into a coalition government. At least up until 1994, for example, no cabinet had any real chance of forming without the participation of the Dutch Christian Democratic Party (or its pre-1977 predecessors). Because a vote for parties such as these would not be pivotal in determining which government formed, the theory predicts a very low economic vote for that party.

One of the interesting implications of this strategic voting argument is that it generates predicted economic voting magnitudes that are at odds with those generated from an exclusive focus on the administrative responsibility of governing parties. The discussion in the previous section implies that the distribution of administrative responsibility should lead to higher economic voting and others, such as Anderson (1995), have suggested that a party's economic vote should be correlated with its degree of responsibility for economic outcomes in a governing coalition. But in the case of perennial governing parties that command a large number of portfolios in the governing coalition—the Dutch Christian Party and the Irish Fianna Fail, for example—the Duch and Stevenson (2007) theory predicts a very small economic vote while the party responsibility argument suggests exactly the opposite, i.e. a large economic vote. This is particularly interesting because it identifies contextual circumstances that should serve as a critical test of the Duch and Stevenson theory. There will be cases in which parties have high levels of administrative responsibility and hence are expected to have a large economic vote, at least according to those theories that favor the administrative responsibility or clarity of responsibility explanation (Anderson 1995, for example). But many of these parties that have high levels of administrative responsibility are precisely those perennial coalition partners who have pivot probabilities close to zero because voting for them will have no impact on the composition of the governing coalition.

Returning to the example of the Dutch Christian party; if we just consider how the party's share of administrative responsibility conditions the vote choice then we predict the same outcome as do theories that focus on party responsibility, i.e. a large economic vote. The Dutch Christian party after all has been an important partner in all of the governing coalitions at least until 1994. But our theory includes a strategic voting consideration: Rational voters should condition their economic vote on the probability that their vote for this party would be pivotal in determining the composition of the governing coalition. In the particular case of the Dutch Christian party, rational voters should conclude that their pivot probability is close to zero—regardless of how they vote the Dutch Christian party will likely participate in the governing coalition. Hence we predict virtually no economic vote for the Dutch Christian party while traditional responsibility arguments that ignore the strategic voting component would predict a large economic vote.

This notion that strategic voting considerations shape the economic vote for parties implies a curvilinear relationship between contention for policy-making authority and the economic vote: Parties who are both very likely and very unlikely to enter a post-election governing coalition should receive small economic votes. Those parties with moderately high levels of probability of entering a governing coalition should receive the highest levels of economic voting. We can return to the Duch and Stevenson economic vote data summarized in Figure 33.1 and explore this argument. Duch and Stevenson (2007) create a measure of contention that is simply the percentage of years dating back to 1960 that the party occupied the prime ministership (hence if the economic vote was being measured in 1988, it would be the percentage of the twenty-eight previous years that the party had held the prime ministership). I have summarized this contention measure in four groupings (parties that held the prime ministership less than 50 percent of the period back to 1960; 51–75 percent; 76–99 percent; and 100 percent). Figure 33.5 presents box plots of the economic vote magnitudes for parties in each of these four categories. The patterns here are quite consistent with the contention argument: there is a curvilinear relationship with the highest economic vote found amongst parties who have held the prime ministership between 50 and 75 percent of the years dating back to 1960. And there is little doubt here that parties that are certain to enter into a post-election governing coalition—those who held the prime ministership 100 percent of the years dating back to 1960—have the lowest levels of economic voting (the median economic vote for this group is close to zero). Moreover, this result is all the more convincing since those parties falling in this category are the ones who would be predicted to have the highest economic vote if we only considered the extent of their administrative responsibility.

A key insight from the rational vote choice literature is that voters will take into account whether their vote makes a difference in who wins or who loses elections and who gets into government. The usual understanding is that rational voters should not "waste" their vote on candidates that are sure to lose, but the same logic also applies to parties or candidates that are sure to win. Hence what matters in contexts

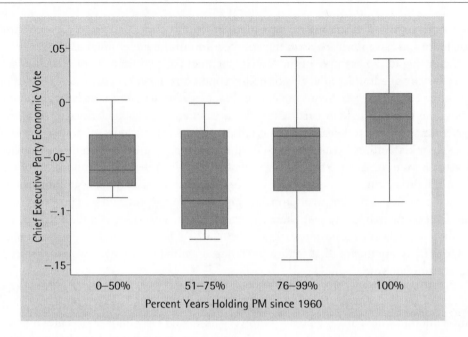

Fig. 33.5. History of holding prime ministry and the chief executive economic vote in coalition systems

with multiple parties and coalition cabinets is that the "distribution of contention" for policy-making authority will shape the incentives for strategic voting and condition the importance of economic evaluations in that decision. There will be frequent situations in which an individual's vote will have little impact on the post-election distribution of policy-making authority (because the same parties will get into government for all plausible electoral results) and hence economic evaluations will play a minor role in voting in such elections.[19]

8 SUMMARY

There is widespread recognition in the comparative voting literature that the economic vote—either at the individual or aggregate level—exhibits considerable instability cross-nationally and also over time (or from one election to the next). And

[19] A number of scholars have pointed out that contextual variation in strategic voting incentives can affect the voter's utility function such that some factors or issues matter in vote choice in one context versus another. Myerson 1993, 1999, for example, demonstrates that under Duverger's law for plurality voting, where parties compete on ideology, strategic voting considerations can lead voters to vote for corrupt candidates in spite of their preferences to minimize rent seeking and in spite of the fact that there are candidates with compatible ideological positions who lack the rent-seeking baggage.

as this essay has emphasized, explaining this variation is the principal intellectual challenge for comparative students of the economic vote. This cross-national instability in estimated effects is hardly confined to the economic vote. In fact there is considerable evidence of cross-national variation in many of the effects that are typically included in a vote choice model. The economic vote shares similar cross-national variations in its magnitude with a number of other elements of the vote choice model. Kedar (2005), for example, has made a very persuasive case for the notion that the impact of voters' issue preferences on vote choice will vary across institutional context. The impact of partisanship in vote choice models is also likely to vary quite significantly across institutional context (Huber, Kernell, and Leoni 2005; Kayser and Wlezien 2005). Class (Alford 1963) and ideology (Kim and Fording 2003) are two other obvious candidates whose effects on vote choice may vary quite significantly across contexts.

I would argue that the broad contours of the approach I've just described for modeling contextual effects on the economic vote represent a road map for comparative scholars to follow in examining how context conditions other determinants of the vote choice. In the case of modeling vote choice, comparative scholars have the benefit of a rich theoretical foundation that owes a considerable debt to students of US voting behavior. But these modeling efforts typically do not travel well outside of the US context. Hence the comparative advantage of students of comparative voting behavior is developing theoretical innovations that incorporate contextual factors into individual-level vote choice models. The challenge here is to rigorously model how contextual features condition the impact of particular variables—such as ideology, partisanship, economic perceptions, and class (for example)—on vote choice. Finally, data availability and modeling techniques make it possible to test, in a rigorous fashion, these theoretical models: There is a wealth of individual-level data from very diverse political and economic contexts that combined with advances in multi-level modeling techniques offer the possibility of innovative empirical inroads. The result will be a better general understanding of how contexts—political, institutional and economic—conditions what enters into the vote calculus and the importance that voters accord to these different considerations.

REFERENCES

ALESINA, A., LONDREGAN, J., and ROSENTHAL, H. 1993. A model of the political economy of the United States. *American Political Science Review*, 87: 12–33.
—— and ROSENTHAL, H. 1995. *Partisan Politics, Divided Government, and the Economy.* Cambridge: Cambridge University Press.
—— and ROUBINI, N. 1999. *Political Cycles and the Macroeconomy.* Cambridge, Mass.: MIT Press.
ALFORD, R. 1963. *Party and Society: The Anglo-American Democracies.* Westport, Conn.: Greenwood.
ALMOND, G. A., and VERBA, S. 1963. *The Civic Culture.* Princeton: Princeton University Press.

ALT, J., and LASSEN, D. 2004. The electoral cycle in debt is where you can't see it: fiscal transparency and electoral policy cycles in advanced industrialized democracies. Mimeo. Harvard University.

ALVAREZ, R. M., and NAGLER, J. 1998. Economics, entitlements and social issues: voter choice in the 1996 presidential election. *American Journal of Political Science*, 42: 1349–63.

—— —— and WILLETTE, J. R. 2000. Measuring the relative impact of issues and the economy in democratic elections. *Electoral Studies*, 19: 237–53.

ANDERSON, C. J. 1995. *Blaming the Government: Citizens and the Economy in Five European Democracies*. Armonk, NY: Sharpe.

BARRO, R. 1973. The control of politicians: an economic model. *Public Choice*, 14: 19–42.

BARTELS, L. M., and ZALLER, J. 2001. Presidential vote models: a recount. *PS: Political Science and Politics*, 34: 9–19.

BECK, N. 1991. The economy and presidential approval: an information theoretic perspective. Pp. 85–101 in *Economics and Politics: The Calculus of Support*, ed. H. Norpoth, M. Lewis-Beck, and J.-D. Lafay. Ann Arbor: University of Michigan Press.

BELLUCCI, P. 1985. Economic concerns in Italian electoral behavior: toward a rational electorate? In *Economic Conditions and Electoral Outcomes: The United States and Western Europe*, ed. H. Eulau and M. S. Lewis-Beck. New York: Agathon.

BERELSON, B., LAZARSFELD, P., and McFEE, W. 1954. *Voting: A Study of Opinion Formation in a Presidential Campaign*. Chicago: University of Chicago Press.

BLAIS, A., TURGEON, M., GIDENGIL, E., NEVITTE, N., and NADEAU, R. 2004. Which matters most? Comparing the impact of issues and the economy in American, British and Canadian elections. *British Journal of Political Science*, 34: 555–64.

BORRE, O. 1997. Economic voting in Danish electoral surveys 1987–1994. *Scandinavian Political Studies*, 20 (4): 347–65.

BUTLER, D., and STOKES, D. 1976. *Political Change in Britain*, 2nd College Edn. New York: St Martin's Press.

CAMERON, D. R. 1978. The expansion of the public economy: a comparative analysis. *American Political Science Review*, 72: 1243–61.

CAMPBELL, A., CONVERSE, P. E., MILLER, W. E., and STOKES, D. E. 1960. *The American Voter*. New York: Wiley.

CHAPPELL, H., and VIEGA, L. G. 2000. Economics and elections in western Europe: 1960–1997. *Electoral Studies*, 19: 183–97.

CHEIBUB, J. A., and PRZEWORSKI, A. 1999. Democracy, elections, and accountability for economic outcomes. Pp. 222–50 in *Democracy, Accountability, and Representation*, ed. A. Przeworski, S. C. Stokes, and B. Manin. Cambridge: Cambridge University Press.

CLARKE, H., and STEWART, M. C. 1995. Economic evaluations, prime ministerial approval and governing party support: rival models considered. *British Journal of Political Science*, 25: 145–70.

—— —— and WHITELEY, P. 1997. Tory Trends: party identification and the dynamics of conservative support since 1992. *British Journal of Political Science*, 27: 299–319.

CUKIERMAN, A., and MELTZER, A. H. 1989. A political theory of government debt and deficits in a neo-Ricardian framework. *American Economics Review*, 79: 713–33.

DOWNS, A. 1957. *An Economic Theory of Democracy*. New York: Harper and Row.

DUCH, R. M., and PALMER, H. 2002. Heterogeneous perceptions of economic conditions in cross-national perspective. In *Economic Voting*, ed. H. Dorussen and M. Taylor. New York: Routledge.

—— —— and ANDERSON, C. J. 2000. Heterogeneity in perceptions of national economic conditions. *American Journal of Political* Science, 44: 635–49.

—— and STEVENSON, R. T. 2005. Context and the economic vote: a multilevel analysis. *Political Analysis*, 13 (4): 387–409.

—— —— 2007. *Voting in Context: How Political and Economic Institutions Condition the Economic Vote*. Cambridge: Cambridge University Press (forthcoming).

EBEID, M., and RODDEN, J. 2006. Economic geography and economic voting: evidence from the U.S. States. *British Journal of Political Science*, 36: 527–47.

ERIKSON, R. S. 1990. Economic conditions and the congressional vote: a review of the macrolevel evidence. *American Journal of Political Science*, 34: 373–99.

—— 2004. Macro vs. micro-level perspectives on economic voting: is the micro-level evidence endogenously induced? Paper prepared for the 2004 Political Methodology Meetings, July 29–31 2004. Stanford University.

—— MACKUEN, M. B., and STIMSON, J. A. 2002. *The Macro Polity*. Cambridge: Cambridge University Press.

EVANS, G., and ANDERSEN, R. 2006. The political conditioning of economic perceptions. *Journal of Politics* (forthcoming).

FAIR, R. C. 1978. The effect of economic events on votes for president. *Review of Economic Statistics*, 60: 159–73.

FEARON, J. D. 1999. Electoral accountability and the control of politicians: selecting good types versus sanctioning poor performance. In *Democracy, Accountability, and Representation*, ed. A. Przeworski, S. C. Stokes, and B. Manin. Cambridge: Cambridge University Press.

FEREJOHN, J. 1986. Incumbent performance and electoral control. *Public Choice*, 50: 5–25.

FIORINA, M. 1978. Economic retrospective voting in American national elections: a micro-analysis. *American Journal of Political Science*, 22: 426–43.

—— 1981. *Retrospective Voting in American National Elections*. New Haven: Yale University Press.

—— ABRAMS, S., and POPE, J. 2003. The 2000 U.S. presidential election: can retrospective voting be saved? *British Journal of Political Science*, 33: 163–87.

FREY, B. 1979. Politometrics of government behavior in a democracy. *Scandinavian Journal of Economics*, 81: 308–22.

—— and GARBERS, H. 1971. Politicio-economics: on estimation in political economy. *Political Studies*, 19: 316–20.

GAVIN, M., and HAUSMANN, R. 1996. Sources of macroeconomic volatility in developing economies. MS. Washington: Inter-American Development Bank.

GOODHART, C. A. E., and BHANSALI, R. J. 1970. Political economy. *Political Studies*, 18: 43–106.

HELLWIG, T. T. 2001. Interdependence, government constraints, and economic voting. *Journal of Politics*, 63 (4): 1141–62.

HIBBS, D. A., Jr. 1993. *Solidarity or Egoism?* Aarhus: Aarhus University Press.

—— 2000. Bread and peace voting in U.S. presidential elections. *Public Choice* 104 (1–2): 149–80.

—— 2006. Voting and the macro-economy. In *The Oxford Handbook of Political Economy*, ed. B. Weingast and D. Whittman. New York: Oxford University Press.

—— and VASILATOS, N. 1981. Economics and politics in France: economic performance and political support for Presidents Pompidou and Giscard d'Estaing. *European Journal of Political Research*, 9: 133–45.

HUBER, J. D., KERNELL, G., and LEONI, E. L. 2005. Institutional context, cognitive resources and party attachments across democracies. *Political Analysis*, 13: 365–86.

INTERNATIONAL MONETARY FUND. 2005. *World Economic Outlook April 2005: Globalization and External Imbalances*. Washington, DC: IMF.

JACOBSON, G. C., and KERNELL, S. 1983. *Strategy and Choice in Congressional Elections*, 2nd edn. New Haven: Yale University Press.

KAYSER, M. A., and WLEZIEN, C. 2005. Performance pressure: patterns of partisanship and the economic vote. Paper presented at the Annual Meeting of the American Political Science Association, Washington, DC.

KEDAR, O. 2005. When moderate voters prefer extreme parties: policy balancing in parliamentary elections. *American Political Science Review*, 99 (2): 185–99.

KEY, V. O. 1966. *The Responsible Electorate*. New York: Vintage Books.

KIEWIET, D. R. 1983. *Macroeconomics and Micropolitics: The Electoral Effects of Economic Issues*. Chicago: University of Chicago Press.

—— and UDELL, M. 1998. Twenty-five years after Kramer: an assessment of economic retrospective voting based upon improved estimates of income and unemployment. *Economics in Politics*, 10: 219–48.

KIM, H., and FORDING, R. 2003. Voter ideology in western democracies: an update. *European Journal of Political Research*, 42: 95–105.

KING, G., TOMZ, M., and WITTENBERG, J. 2000. Making the most of statistical analyses: improving interpretation and presentation. *American Journal of Political Science*, 44 (2): 341–55.

KIRCHGÄSSNER, G. 1991. Economic conditions and the popularity of West German parties: before and after the 1982 government change. Pp. 103–22 in *Economics and Politics: The Calculus of Support*, ed. H. Norpoth, M. S. Lewis-Beck, and J.-D. Lafay. Ann Arbor: University of Michigan Press.

KRAMER, G. H. 1971. Short-term fluctuations in U.S. voting behavior, 1896–1964. *American Political Science Review*, 65: 131–43.

—— 1983. The ecological fallacy revisited: aggregate-versus individual-level findings on economics and elections, and sociotropic voting. *American Political Science Review*, 77: 92–111.

KYDLAND, F., and PRESCOTT, E. 1977. Rules rather than discretion: the inconsistency of optimal plans. *Journal of Political Economy*, 85: 473–90.

LAFAY, J.-D. 1977. Les Conséquences électorales de la conjoncture économique: essaie de prévision chiffrée pour Mars 1978. *Vie et sciences économiques*, 75: 1–7.

LECAILLON, J. 1981. Popularité des gouvernements et popularité économique. *Consummation*, 3: 17–50.

LEWIS-BECK, M. S. 1980. Economic conditions and executive popularity: the French experience. *American Journal of Political Science*, 24: 306–23.

—— 1988. *Economics and Elections: The Major Western Democracies*. Ann Arbor: University of Michigan Press.

—— and EULAU, H. 1985. Introduction: economic conditions and electoral outcomes in trans-national perspective. In *Economic Conditions and Electoral Outcomes: The United States and Western Europe*, ed. H. Eulau and M. S. Lewis-Beck. New York: Agathon.

—— and MITCHELL, G. 1990. Modelos transnacionales de voto economico: estudio de un conjunto de paises europeos. *Revista del Instituto de estudios economicos*, 4: 65–81.

—— and NADEAU, R. 2000. French electoral institutions and the economic vote. *Electoral Studies*, 19: 171–82.

—— and RICE, T. 1992. *Forecasting Elections*. Washington, DC: Congressional Quarterly Press.

—— and STEGMAIER, M. 2000. Economic determinants of electoral outcomes. *Annual Review of Political Science*, 3: 183–219.

McKELVEY, R., and ORDESHOOK, P. 1972. A general theory of the calculus of voting. In *Mathematical Applications in Political Science*, vol. vi, ed. J. F. Herndon and J. L Bernd. Charlottesville: University Press of Virginia.

MacKuen, M. B., Erikson, R. S., and Stimson, J. A. 1992. Peasants or bankers? The American electorate and the U.S. economy. *American Political Science Review*, 86: 597–611.

—— and Mouw, C. 1995. Class and competence in the political economy. Typescript. University of Missouri, St Louis.

Madsen, H. 1980. Electoral outcomes and macro-economic policies: the Scandinavian cases. In *Models of Political Economy*, ed. P. Whitely. London: Sage Publications.

Markus, G. 1988. The impact of personal and national economic conditions on the presidential vote: a pooled cross-sectional analysis. *American Journal of Political Science*, 32: 137–54.

—— 1992. The impact of personal and national economic conditions on the presidential vote: a pooled cross-sectional analysis. *American Journal of Political Science*, 36: 829–34.

Marra, R. F., and Ostrom, C. W. 1989. Explaining seat change in the US House of Representatives, 1950–1986. *American Journal of Political Science*, 33: 541–69.

Miller, A. H., and Listhaug, O. 1985. Economic effects on the vote in Norway. In *Economic Conditions and Electoral Outcomes: The United States and Western Europe*, ed. H. Eulau and M. S. Lewis-Beck. New York: Agathon.

Miller, W. L., and Mackie, M. 1973. The electoral cycle and the asymmetry of government and the opposition popularity: an alternative model of the relationship between economic conditions and political popularity. *Political Studies*, 621: 263–79.

Mueller, J. 1970. Presidential popularity from Truman to Johnson. *American Political Science Review*, 65: 18–34.

Myerson, R. 1993. Effectiveness of electoral systems for reducing government corruption: a game theoretic analysis. *Games and Economic Behaviour*, 5: 118–32.

—— 1999. Theoretical comparison of electoral systems. 1998 Joseph Schumpeter Lecture. *European Economic Review*, 43: 671–97.

Nannestad, P., and Paldam, M. 1995. It's the government's fault! A cross-section study of economic voting in Denmark, 1990/93. *European Journal of Political Research*, 28: 33–62.

—— and Paldam, M. 1997. From the pocketbook of the welfare man: a pooled cross-section study of economic voting in Denmark, 1986–1992. *British Journal of Political Science*, 27: 119–37.

—— —— 2000. Into Pandora's Box of economic evaluations: a study of the Danish macro VP-function 1986–1997. *Electoral Studies*, 19: 123–40.

Norpoth, H. 1985. Politics, economics and the cycle of presidential popularity. In *Economic and Electoral Outcomes*, ed. H. Eulau and M. S. Lewis-Beck. New York: Agathon.

—— 1996. The economy. Pp. 219–38 in *Comparing Democracies: Elections and Voting in Global Perspective*, ed. L. LeDuc, R. G. Niemi, and P. Norris. Thousand Oaks, Calif.: Sage.

Pacek, A. C., and Radcliff, B. 1995. Economic voting and the welfare state: a cross-national analysis. *Journal of Politics*, 57 (1): 44–61.

Page, B. I., and Shapiro, R. Y. 1992. *The Rational Public*. Chicago: University of Chicago Press.

Paldam, M. 1991. How robust is the vote function? A study of seventeen nations over four decades. Pp. 9–31 in *Economics and Politics: The Calculus of Support*, ed. H. Norpoth, M. Lewis-Beck, and J.-D. Lafay. Ann Arbor: University of Michigan Press.

—— and Schneider, F. 1980. The macroeconomic aspects of government and opposition popularity in Denmark, 1957–1978. *National Okonomisk Tidsskrift*, 118: 149–70.

Palmer, H. D., and Whitten, G. D. 2003a. Questionable analyses with no theoretical innovation: a response to Royed, Leyden and Borrelli. *British Journal of Political Science*, 33: 139–49.

—— —— 2003b. Ignorance is no excuse: data mining versus theoretical formulation of hypotheses. *British Journal of Political Science*, 33: 159–60.

Persson, T., and Tabellini, G. 1990. *Macroeconomic Policy, Credibility, and Politics*. New York: Harwood Academic.

PRICE, S., and SANDERS, D. 1993. Modeling government popularity in postwar Britain: a methodological example. *American Journal of Political Science*, 37: 317–34.

RODRIK, D. 1998. Why do more open economies have larger governments? *Journal of Political Economy*, 106 (5): 997–1032.

ROGOFF, K. 1990. Equilibrium political business cycles. *American Economic Review*, 80: 21–36.

—— and SIBERT, A. 1988. Elections and macroeconomic policy cycles. *Review of Economic Studies*, 55: 1–16.

ROYED, T. J., LEYDEN, K. M., and BORRELLI, S. A. 2000. Is "clarity of responsibility" important for economic voting? Revisiting Powell and Whitten's hypothesis. *British Journal of Politics*, 30: 669–98.

SANDERS, D., MARSH, D., and WARD, H. 1991. Macroeconomics, the Falklands War and the popularity of the Thatcher government: a contrary view. *British Journal of Political Science*, 20: 161–84.

SCHEVE. K. 2004. Democracy and globalization: candidate selection in open economies. Mimeo. Yale University.

STIGLER, G. J. 1973. General economic conditions and national elections. *American Economic Review*, 63: 160–4.

TUFTE, E. R. 1975. Determinants of the outcomes of midterm congressional elections. *American Political Science Review*, 69: 812–26.

—— 1978. *Political Control of the Economy*. Princeton: Princeton University Press.

WELCH, S., and HIBBING, J. 1992. Financial conditions, gender, and voting in American national elections. *Journal of Politics*, 54: 197–213.

WHITELEY, P. F. 1986. Macroeconomic performance and government popularity in Britain: the short-run dynamics. *European Journal of Political Research*, 14: 45–61.

WLEZIEN, C., FRANKLIN, M., and TWIGGS, D. 1997. Economic perceptions and vote choice: disentangling the endogeneity. *Political Behavior*, 19: 7–17.

WORLD BANK. 2004. *World Development Indicators*. Washington, DC: World Bank.

ZALLER, J. 2004. Floating voters in US presidential elections, 1948–2000. In *The Issue of Belief: Essays in the Intersection of Nonattitudes and Attitude Change*, ed. P. Sniderman and W. Saris. Amsterdam: University of Amsterdam Press.

......

CHAPTER 34

CONTEXT-CONDITIONAL POLITICAL BUDGET CYCLES

......

JAMES E. ALT

SHANNA S. ROSE

THE belief that politics influences economic outcomes is an old one. The scientific study of the politics of the business cycle, how economic outcomes reflect decisions made in a political context, has also been around for a while. A history of the science would point to a complex sequence of theoretical and empirical developments reflecting the desire to achieve generality and parsimony. Even so, from this broader politics of the business cycle it was a short step to the somewhat more systematic but specialized literature on "political business cycles" that studied how the cycle of elections affected aspects of the real economy like GDP growth and unemployment. The last two decades have seen the object of study—the dependent variable, if you will—shift decisively from real economic outcomes to the instruments of fiscal and monetary policy, for reasons discussed below.

A political budget cycle is a regular, periodic fluctuation in a government's fiscal policies induced by the cycle of elections. "Fiscal policies" include the magnitude, composition, and balance of public expenditures and revenues, as well as fiscal (im)balance and public debt. "Induced by the cycle of elections" can mean different things observationally, but a common theme is that some choice about fiscal policy would have been different if something about the electoral context had been different.

If the next election had been further away in time, for instance, or less competitive, fiscal policy would have been different, in a way that reflects incumbents' desires to improve their chances of electoral success.

But why might political budget cycles be "context conditional"? Don't incumbent office holders always act so as to improve their electoral chances? Put simply, they do under two conditions: they must have the incentive and the ability to manipulate policy. Or as Tufte (1978) pointed out, a politician, like a murderer, must have not only a weapon but also a motive and an opportunity. Thus, to explain systematically the relationship between differences in electoral context and differences in fiscal choice, one must ask "Under what circumstances is an action more likely to be feasible? Under what circumstances are politicians more likely to find that action desirable?" Two kinds of features predominate in contemporary thinking about these important contextual features: political institutions and voter characteristics on the one hand, and the temporal proximity and expected closeness of the election on the other.

The study of political budget cycles bears on broad questions of representation, accountability, and agency. Manin, Przeworski, and Stokes (1999) describe how "accountability" representation involves voters retaining incumbents who act in their (voters') best interests, while incumbents select the policies they deem necessary for re-election. This exemplifies the agency problem in politics: voters (principals) want politicians (agents) who will act in their best interests, but cannot perfectly monitor the agents' performance. Voters must also offer enough compensation to secure the agents' participation, and have an imperfect instrument—the vote—for exerting control. So context-conditional political budget cycles provide a lens through which to study the extent to which voters are able to select, monitor, sanction, and control politicians—and the extent to which politicians serve their own interests at the expense of voters' interests—in different political and institutional environments.[1]

This chapter investigates the contextual determinants of incumbents' ability and incentives to engineer political business cycles in the American states.[2] The states are all relatively open political economies with moderately high levels of average income, in which the rule of law is quite well established. Restricting the domain to US states holds relatively constant a wide range of socioeconomic, political, and cultural characteristics that might otherwise confound analysis. Thus, using the states as a laboratory for comparative politics has several benefits.

For instance, political science divides presidential from parliamentary regimes by the separation of legislative and executive powers. An extensive comparative politics literature focuses on the relative instability of presidential regimes. A more recent political economy literature provides conjectures and some empirical verification that presidential regimes also feature less redistribution and lower public spending, but greater accountability.[3] However, empirical studies of the separation of powers

---

[1] Disparity in the amount of information available to voters and politicians is an important intermediary variable through which institutions might affect behavior.

[2] Rose 2005 demonstrates the existence of political cycles in general spending in the American states.

[3] See, for example, Persson and Tabellini (2003).

have struggled with confounding problems, most notably the fact that presidential regimes are concentrated outside the First World. One way to learn about the impact of separated powers is to study systematically the American states, which are characterized by considerable institutional heterogeneity and yet, unlike cross-sections of countries, broadly similar constitutional settings. Indeed, in this way the states can be seen as a virtual "world sample" in which many variables can be controlled.

On the other hand, focusing on the states prevents us from directly re-examining a few findings in the literature. For instance, Adsera, Boix, and Payne (2003) suggest that an economy in which assets are more mobile (that is, an economy from which exit is a more readily available, lower-cost option) is one in which, all else equal, market-based, private responses are more likely to offset a political cycle, lowering the rents to politicians. A similar argument has been made regarding floating exchange rates (Clark 2003). Such arguments are beyond our scope, though we will examine a related question involving bond markets and constitutional restrictions.

As space considerations prevent us from examining every aspect of fiscal policy, we focus our analysis on a single dimension: the level of public spending (in real per capita terms). This emphasis is consistent with the general consensus in the literature that political budget cycles are stronger in spending than in taxes, deficits, or debt.

The remainder of the chapter proceeds as follows. We first provide a brief literature review to make clear how and why the theory of political budget cycles evolved as it did. We then describe our data and methodology. To make the paper as transparent as possible, we use throughout a single estimation method of dynamic panel analysis that has become popular in the literature. While true, it is not our point that improved methods have led to better estimates. Rather, we believe that by using one method for which we can convey some clear intuition, we can communicate the results more clearly. We next turn to the results themselves, and show that political budget cycles are more common in contexts where uncertain election outcomes make manipulation more valuable, and less common in contexts where formal rules make the cycle less desirable, if not actually infeasible. The final section offers concluding remarks.

1 CONTEXT-CONDITIONAL POLITICAL BUDGET CYCLES: THEORY AND EVIDENCE

Under what circumstances do politicians find it feasible and desirable to manipulate fiscal policy for electoral purposes? This question does not, at first glance, appear daunting; however, it immediately raises several new questions. How are desirability and feasibility related, and how does that relationship depend on the costs and benefits of alternative choices? For example, if an action is relatively infeasible, isn't it also undesirable? And vice versa: If an action is desirable, won't politicians seek to bring about (institutional) conditions under which it is feasible? If so, we need to enquire into the causes of institutional change in order to understand the circumstances under which incumbents control effective policies. The fact that feasibility involves dimensions of control and effectiveness (Franzese 2002) is yet a further source of complexity.

The questions one might ask easily outrun a scholar's ability to model systematic relationships, collect data, and estimate effects. We could go down a path of distinguishing actions and choices, asking each time under what circumstances an alternative becomes more likely, and speculating about relationships among factors. Instead, we narrow the questions down to some basic issues relating to instruments, information, and agency that come up again and again but do not have to be analyzed anew in each context. We keep the discussion intuitive to provide useful insights that readers can apply themselves in new contexts.

1.1 Issues and Arguments

Outcomes and instruments. Should one expect cycles in outcomes, like unemployment and inflation, or in instruments of policy, like spending and interest rates? The literature began with outcomes; in a seminal paper, Nordhaus (1975) showed that re-election-minded politicians who can exploit the tradeoff between inflation and unemployment known as the Phillips curve should find it optimal to expand the economy before and contract it after elections. Incumbents can profitably do this if voters are "retrospective" (or "adaptive") in the sense that they vote based on evaluations of recent economic performance; voters reward incumbents for manipulating the economy despite the fact that, after each election, output and employment return to their natural rates but inflation is higher.

Over the next two decades, the literature came to focus on electoral cycles in policy variables—particularly public spending, taxes, and deficits—rather than real variables. In one of the earliest such studies, Tufte (1978) looked for (and found) political business cycles in transfer payments. In a now-famous anecdote, Tufte pointed out that the Nixon administration, on the eve of the 1972 election, sent a letter to millions of social security beneficiaries notifying them of an increase in their monthly benefits.

This change in emphasis from outcomes to policy occurred for two main reasons. First, there was a lack of systematic empirical evidence of electoral cycles in real variables: "no one could read the political business cycle literature without being struck by the lack of supportive evidence" (Alt and Chrystal 1983, 125). One of the few studies to find strong evidence of real cycles is that of Haynes and Stone (1989); studies finding weak or no evidence of political business cycles in real outcomes include those by McCallum (1978), Lachler (1978), Golden and Poterba (1980), Lewis-Beck (1988), and Alesina, Roubini, and Cohen (1997).

A second reason (and possible explanation for the lack of evidence noted above) is that politicians do not generally control real economic variables. First, the Nordhaus model's assumption that incumbents have control over monetary policy is inconsistent with the central bank independence that characterizes the United States and many other countries (Drazen 2001, 80). Indeed, Beck (1987) finds no cycle in monetary instruments or, holding fiscal policy constant, the money supply in the United States. He concludes that while the Federal Reserve Board might accommodate fiscally induced macroeconomic cycles generated by the president and Congress, it does not generate cycles itself.[4] However, a growing literature examines the question of whether monetary cycles exist in countries with less independent central banks (see for example Clark and Hallerberg 2000) while others focus on the flexibility of the exchange rate regime (Clark and Hallerberg 2000; Dreher and Vaubel 2005). Hallerberg (2002) suggests that politicians in countries with fewer veto players prefer monetary to fiscal expansions, whereas the latter are more targetable, and thus more valuable, where there are more veto players.

Second, even when it comes to fiscal policy, incumbents typically control policy instruments that are imperfectly related to outcomes, whether because the instruments are imperfect or imperfectly understood (we return to this point below). For these reasons, it is more common today to read about cycles in fiscal policy variables such as spending, taxes, and deficits than cycles in monetary policy variables such as interest rates and monetary aggregates, or in outcomes such as growth, unemployment, or inflation. In our analysis, we assume that voters like the public goods that spending buys—even if they observe the spending imperfectly—and incumbents control the spending (perhaps also imperfectly). If re-election is valued by incumbents, then spending should rise before and fall after elections.[5]

Although it is beyond the scope of this chapter, we should note that an alternative literature starting with Hibbs (1977, 1987) and Alesina (1987, 1988) posits that politicians are partisan rather than opportunistic; thus, shifts in the real economy should follow elections in which party control changes hands. Specifically, these authors argue that left parties pursue policies associated with higher growth and lower unemployment, even at the cost of inflation, than do right parties. These and other authors (including Alt 1985; Alesina, Roubini, and Cohen 1997) find evidence of such "partisan cycles" in the United States and the OECD. Similarly, Krause (2005) finds that income growth is higher under Democratic administrations, but that Republican administrations generate larger pre-election economic expansions.

Information. If the response to Nordhaus was partly a matter of substituting instruments for outcomes, it was also partly a shift in assumptions. The earliest political business cycle models were based on the premise that voters are myopic. That is, Nordhaus argued, politicians are able to repeatedly fool voters, even though voters can easily foresee upcoming elections. More recent models of the political

---

[4] However, a few studies have found some evidence of monetary political business cycles in countries with independent central banks (see, for example, Soh 1986; Grier 1987; Lohmann 1998).

[5] If appearing competent requires more goods at less cost, then we could make the same conjectures for the deficit as for spending, and opposite conjectures (rise after, fall before elections) for revenues.

business cycle (see for example Cukierman and Meltzer 1986; Rogoff and Sibert 1988; Rogoff 1990) have abandoned this assumption in favor of the "Lucas critique" (1976), which posits that economic actors form rational expectations by optimally using all available information to forecast the future.[6] These newer models substitute an assumption of asymmetric information for voter myopia. That is, modelers typically assume that voters do not have full information about incumbents' competence. This assumption is necessary because political budget cycles only "work" if voters cannot fully distinguish between competence and electioneering. In other words, "it would be pointless for the incumbent party to try to deceive the public unless it has an information advantage" (Rogoff and Sibert 1988, 4).

In political budget cycle models, the more competent the incumbent, the less revenue she needs to provide a given level of government services. Competence may change gradually over time, as the problems facing the government—and thus the abilities required for effective public administration—evolve. Often, in these models, even if voters observe spending and taxes immediately, they can only observe the deficit or debt with a delay. As a result, voters cannot immediately distinguish deficit spending from the efficient use of revenues that indicates greater competence. Thus, politicians have an incentive to run deficits—that is, increase spending, decrease taxes, or both—before elections in an effort to signal their competence. If politicians know their own competence, they will undertake policies that effectively signal that competence in an effort to distinguish themselves from incompetent politicians. If competence is unknown to both incumbents and voters, and if incumbents only observe the state of the economy or level of debt earlier or more accurately than voters, incentives to improve re-election chances through political budget cycles still exist, and institutions can affect the value of electioneering.[7]

Agency models. Why does the political budget cycle persist? For the most part, it seems to us, simply because it is part of an agency problem, the problem at the core of modern analyses of delegation and accountability. Let us assume the following. Voters value incumbent competence, particularly as the government grows and has an increasing impact on the state of the economy, which is ultimately what voters care about. In order to select or retain more competent incumbents as their agents, voters may have to compensate them in the form of increased job security.[8] Looked at this way, the political budget cycle is an intertemporal adjustment of taxes and spending that reflects the agents' beliefs and choices about what actions increase their chances of re-election. The re-election benefit is a "rent" that the incumbent

---

[6] If voters have full information and form rational expectations, pre-election policy manipulations should not have any real macroeconomic effects as long as elections are perfectly anticipated events.

[7] Many find the equilibrium implication of the Rogoff–Sibert model, that voters correctly infer competence from observing an action that a less competent politician could not undertake, implausible. Naturally, if there were some other way to guarantee re-election of a competent politicians, voters would be happier to do without the signal. However, the implication follows from the assumption that politicians know their competence, which in the structure of the model produces a separating equilibrium, in which the less competent cannot find it worthwhile to try to do what only the competent can. Of course, if politicians themselves do not know their competence, no such equilibrium, or inference, is possible.

[8] Very accessible treatments of these issues include Przeworski (2003, chs. 4–8); Adsera, Boix, and Payne (2003).

secures (at some cost to voters) in return for managing the economy competently. In this case, if it is also true that more competent politicians find it easier to manipulate spending and taxes, then political budget cycles might be "a socially efficient mechanism for diffusing up-to-date information about the incumbent's administrative competence," albeit at the cost of increased fiscal volatility (Rogoff 1990, 22).

Thus, voters do the best they can to select good incumbents. Incumbents try to satisfy voters, and also make a little "on the side." This all happens as long as voters' control is imperfect: "if voters want to use their vote to select good politicians prospectively and to sanction the incumbents retrospectively, they must pay higher rents to the incumbent" (Przeworski 2003, 152–3). Our goal is to estimate the size of these rents, all else equal.

Empirically, the rents are the "extra" votes generated by the cycle. To estimate these extra votes, we need a model of voting which allows us to compare actual voting with "counterfactual" voting under the assumption of no political budget cycle. To have that (we do not in this chapter), we need a model of the cycle itself: an estimate of how different election-year fiscal policy is from what we might expect if there were no election at the time. We discuss these estimates below.

1.2 Situational and Institutional Conditional Effects

Considerable empirical evidence of political budget cycles has accumulated over the last two decades. For example, Alesina (1988), Keech and Pak (1989), Alesina, Cohen, and Roubini (1992), Alesina, Cohen, and Roubini (1997), and others find evidence of cycles in developed countries, and Schuknecht (1999), Block (2001), Akhmedov and Zhuravskaya (2004), Brender and Drazen (2005), and others find cycles in developing countries. However, many of these studies have found that cycles only occur during part of the sample period, or only in some categories of spending and taxes. Indeed, others have looked for cycles and been unable to find them at all (see for example Besley and Case 1995). This mixed evidence suggests that the magnitude of the cycle might depend on the "institutional, structural, and strategic contexts in which elected, partisan incumbents make policy" (Franzese 2002, 370) and which determine the circumstances under which incumbents have greater incentives and ability to create political budget cycles.

Incentives. First, consider the incumbent's incentives to manipulate public finances. In the comparative literature, some argue that the possibility of endogenous election timing affects these incentives, though in ways that might leave the observed cycle intact (see for example Smith 2004). No state allows its governor to call an early election, so we do not pursue this question here. However, at the other extreme, since the purpose of generating cycles is to increase the probability of re-election, incumbents who cannot stand for re-election might have *less* incentive to generate cycles than those who can. Indeed, testing this hypothesis motivated Besley and Case's (1995) examination of whether political budget cycles were less pronounced when US state governors faced binding term limits. However, the authors did not find an effect of the presence or absence of binding term limits, though as noted above, they actually did not find evidence of cycles in any states.[9]

But perhaps the effect of term limits is not so obvious. To the extent that parties matter, and that outgoing, term-limited incumbents want to increase their parties' chances in the next election, the re-election incentive remains intact. And to the extent that high-quality candidates from other parties coordinate on expected "open-seat" elections (see Cox and Katz 2002), the institution of term limits facilitates coordination among opponents, and the incentive grows. In that case, the effect of term limits would be to weaken the individual's motivation but strengthen the party's collective motivation; predicting the magnitude of political budget cycles becomes an empirical matter. We return to this matter below.

The incumbent's incentive to manipulate spending and taxes might also be a function of the competitiveness of elections; this idea dates back to Wright (1974), Tufte (1978), and Frey (1978). Competitiveness could be an institutional question—for instance if differences in electoral rules or the relative strength of political parties make re-election more difficult in some places than others. But more commonly competitiveness is viewed as a "strategic" variable: an election that is expected to be "closer" increases the value and thus the desirability of any action that increases the incumbent's re-election prospects.[10] Indeed, Clingermayer and Wood (1995) find a positive association between "electoral competition"—as measured by an election-year dummy variable interacted with the majority party's margin in the state legislature—and debt in the American states. However, the published result is difficult to interpret,[11] and the positive association may simply be attributable to the electoral cycle and have nothing to do with the closeness of elections. Others use opinion poll data to indicate the expected closeness of an impending election (Schultz 1995; Carlsen 1998). Below we use governor's job approval ratings data in this way.

Ability. Next consider the incumbent's ability to manipulate government finances, which might be shaped by a number of different factors. Among the institutional ones, Franzese (2002) notes that when policy control is shared among multiple policy makers, "problems of bargaining, agency, coordination, and collective action will dampen, or otherwise complicate, electioneering, especially insofar as these entities serve different constituents" (Franzese 2002, 384). In the same vein, Persson and Tabellini (2002) find that pre-election tax cuts are more pronounced in parliamentary regimes than in presidential regimes. One possible interpretation of this result is that

---

[9] This may be due to the authors' failure to control for persistence in fiscal aggregates. They use a fixed effects model, whereas most of the literature on political business cycles uses the Arrellano–Bond method, which controls for both state effects and fiscal persistence.

[10] This idea has a long pedigree. Frey (1978) argued that some of the time there is electoral pressure, while at other times incumbents are free to act ideologically. Schultz (1995) argued precisely that the worse off the incumbent ex ante, the more incentive to manipulate, in this case transfer payments in Britain. Also see Alesina and Tabellini (1990) on polarization: the more different the opponent's preferences, the greater the incentive to pull out all the stops.

[11] The authors include only the interaction term (election year times majority party margin), omitting the two variables themselves from the regression, so one cannot be sure of what are the conditional effects of each variable. See Brambor, Clark, and Golder (2005).

presidential regimes tend to have more decision makers with proposal and veto rights than parliamentary regimes.... The possibility of fiscal deadlock might accordingly be more serious, particularly in the case of divided government.... In parliamentary democracies, instead, the same majority typically controls the executive and approves the budget, and is thus better able to fine-tune fiscal policy to its electoral concerns. (Persson and Tabellini 2002, 12)

Hallerberg (2003) also describes as more effective a variety of centralized financial institutions that generate decisions involving taxes and spending. However, while more effective (competent) fiscal policy may reduce the need for political budget cycles, what makes fiscal policy easier to manage also might make it easier to manipulate. In that case centralized fiscal policy could be associated with either larger or smaller political budget cycles.

When policy control is shared, the important consideration is where the multiplicity of actors fits into the decision process. If there are multiple "veto players" (Tsebelis 2002) whose approval would be needed for decisions that underpin the political budget cycle, then the ability to manipulate will be reduced. On the other hand, the multiplicity and heterogeneous preferences of principals can inhibit their ability to coordinate on monitoring or sanctioning activities, increasing the ability of incumbents to manipulate (Ferejohn 1999). In the US states, the most obvious analog of this fragmentation, division, and multiplicity is the presence of divided government, where different parties control different branches of government.[12] Surprisingly, virtually no work has been done on the effect of divided government on the magnitude of the political business cycle; we address this question below.

Another potentially important determinant of incumbents' ability to manipulate government finances for electoral gain is the extent of the information asymmetry between politicians and voters. The incumbent's information advantage might depend on a variety of factors. Many previous studies have focused on the degree of democratization—the conjecture being that anything that brings government "closer to the people" increases transparency and reduces informational asymmetries (Hallerberg 2003, 398). For example, Brender and Drazen (2005) argue that fiscal manipulation should be more effective—and thus electoral cycles should be stronger—in new democracies, where voters are relatively inexperienced with electioneering, than in advanced democracies. In a sample of sixty-eight democratic countries over the past forty years, the authors find political budget cycles in the deficits of new but not established democracies; Persson and Tabellini (2002) and Shi and Svensson (2002) find similar results. Alt and Lassen (2006) argue that one reason political budget cycles might be more pronounced in new democracies is that they tend to be characterized by less fiscal transparency than established democracies; indeed, they find that among industrialized countries, political budget cycles are larger where fiscal institutions are less transparent.

If we think of transparency as relating to the availability of information about fiscal policy, then several factors might be important. First, there is the accessibility of

---

[12] We treat divided government as reducing the ability of incumbents to manipulate spending, because that is what arguments about coordination, veto players, and fragmentation of power stress. See Saporiti and Streb (2003). Of course, anything that reduces ability could be anticipated and thus reduce incentives.

the budget process, which determines the amount of information available to both incumbents and voters. Indeed, it is common to hear legislators complain that they are unable to understand the budget because of its complexity; multiple appropriations bills, limited access to revenue estimates, and open-ended appropriations are just a few examples of procedures that prevent incumbents from having complete information about policy. Nonetheless, incumbents generally have access to more information than does the public. A potentially important precondition for a significant flow of information to the public is a competitive media with substantial market penetration,[13] and we consider this, and the transparency of the process itself, below.

A final, and perhaps more obvious, institutional factor that might affect incumbents' ability to generate political budget cycles is the existence of fiscal rules that limit or prohibit deficits.[14] Presumably, incumbents constrained by such rules will have a more difficult time increasing spending or cutting taxes before elections. There are a variety of such rules in the American states, including referendum requirements and outright prohibitions on debt, as well as "balanced budget" rules that apply to budget proposals, legislated budgets, and spending in excess of revenues raised. Rose (2006) finds that American states with "no-carry-over" balanced budget rules—which prohibit states from carrying deficits into the next fiscal year—do not experience political budget cycles, while those without such rules do exhibit cycles. However, no-carry-over rules only appear to be effective in dampening the political business cycle if they are accompanied by borrowing restrictions. States with weaker no-carry-over rules, where politicians can close budget gaps with borrowed funds, *do* experience political business cycles. We substantiate this finding below, and suggest some reasons why balanced budget laws actually constrain policy in practice.

2 DATA, METHODOLOGY, AND RESULTS

To what extent do these political and strategic contexts affect the magnitude of the political budget cycle? To answer this question, we use panel data from forty-five American states between 1974 and 1999.[15] To keep the analysis as simple as possible,

---

[13] Alt and Lassen 2006 show that the presence of significant state-controlled media augments the political budget cycle in OECD countries, independent of budget process transparency.

[14] There is a large literature on fiscal rules and fiscal discipline, but to our knowledge no specific analysis of cycles.

[15] The sample begins in 1974 because many states had two-year gubernatorial election cycles until that year. The sample ends in 1999 because the Census Bureau temporarily discontinued its survey of state government finances in 2000–1. Arkansas, New Hampshire, Rhode Island, and Vermont are omitted from the sample because they had two-year gubernatorial election cycles during most or all of the sample period. Alaska is omitted because it is a "fiscal outlier" due to heavy reliance on severance taxes.

the key dependent variable is real per capita general expenditure, a broad measure that comprises nearly all state-level spending.[16] We create dummy variables for each year in the (four-year) gubernatorial election cycle. We then interact these election-cycle dummies with each of the six different "contextual" variables mentioned above—gubernatorial approval, gubernatorial term limits, divided partisan government, fiscal transparency, media, and fiscal rules—to see how the time profile of expenditures differs across the six contexts. Each of these key independent variables is described in greater detail below. Summary statistics for all explanatory variables are reported in Table 34.1.

Table 34.1 Summary statistics

	Mean	Std dev	Minimum	Maximum
Dependent variable				
Real per capita spending	4034.655	908.704	2471.321	7370.123
Key independent variables				
Gubernatorial approval	52.020	13.187	19	79.5
No term limit	0.367	0.482	0	1
Non-binding two-term limit	0.348	0.477	0	1
Binding two-term limit	0.207	0.405	0	1
Binding one-term limit	0.078	0.268	0	1
Divided government	0.536	0.499	0	1
Transparency index	0.467	0.167	0.111	0.904
Media density	0.235	0.041	0.160	0.327
Strict no-carry rule	0.378	0.485	0	1
Controls				
Real per capita income	22979.14	4106.3	13564.35	40594.95
Real per capita federal grants	824.486	223.893	431.103	1958.288
Unemployment rate	6.258	2.108	2.2	18
Population (millions)	5.273	5.328	0.366	33.499
Percent school aged	20.238	2.44	7.0740	27.525
Percent retirement aged	11.869	1.984	6.389	18.774
Unified Republican	0.112	0.315	0	1
Unified Democrat	0.352	0.478	0	1

[16] We could and have examined the behavior of the fiscal deficit, which equals spending minus revenues, and it is similar in most cases, though some of the patterns are less clear, as though the inclusion of revenues added "noise" to the observed cyclical behavior of spending.

2.1 Explanatory Variables

Approval. An incumbent with no chance of re-election, like an incumbent who is certain to be re-elected, has little incentive to manipulate spending for electoral purposes. Thus, we compare each of these two scenarios to the more "competitive" situation in between—moderate levels of approval. We first calculate each governor's average annual approval rating (since sometimes more than one poll is conducted per year) and then calculate the average approval rating over the four-year term.[17] We then divide each four-year gubernatorial term into three categories: low approval (less than 40 percent), medium approval (between 40 and 60 percent), and high approval (more than 60 percent). The data come from the Job Approval Ratings dataset (Beyle, Niemi, and Sigelman 2002).

Term limits. Some incumbents have no chance of re-election not because they expect to lose, but because they cannot run at all. Our coding of term-limit dummy variables divides governors into four categories. We consider governors in states without term limits who can always run, though they may in fact choose not to; those facing non-binding two-term limits (that is, who can run again, but if they win, could serve at most one more term); those facing binding two-term limits (who have been re-elected, but now cannot run); and those facing one-term limits (which, by definition, always bind, so these incumbents can never run for re-election). Leaving aside the possibility that governors act to favor party succession, we would expect larger political budget cycles in the first two groups. Data on term limits were generously provided by Tim Besley; they have been updated using the *Book of the States*.

Divided government. Our definition of divided government includes those situations in which the governor's party differs from the party that controls one or both chambers of the legislature. This definition includes independent governors. These data come from the *Book of the States*. We expect political budget cycles to be larger under unified partisan control than under divided government.

Fiscal transparency. Data on fiscal transparency come from a combination of second-ary sources (National Association of State Budget Officers and National Conference of State Legislatures) and our own survey of state budget officers. We use a simple index based on the following nine measures of transparency, each coded so that "yes" is the transparent option:[18] (1) Is the budget reported on a GAAP (Generally Accepted Accounting Principles) basis? (2) Are multi-year expenditure forecasts prepared? (3) Is the budget cycle frequency annual (as opposed to biennial)? (4) Are the revenue forecasts binding? (5) Does the legislative branch have (or share) responsibility for the revenue forecast? (6) Are all appropriations included in a single bill? (7) Does a non-partisan staff write appropriations bills? (8) Is the legislature prohibited from passing open-ended appropriations? And (9) does the budget require published performance measures? The

---

[17] We exclude from the sample governors who do not serve full four-year terms. Similar results are obtained when using only the approval rating in election years or one year prior to election years.

[18] In general, any option that increases information, justification, accessibility, or verification increases transparency. Cross-section data on these nine measures were first collected by Alt, Lassen, and Skilling for their 2002 study of the effect of fiscal transparency on the scale of government and gubernatorial approval.

index for any year is the ratio of items coded "yes" to the number of items for which data are available. For simplicity, we separate the states into three groups of equal size—those that, on average during the sample period, had high (index>0.53), medium (0.40<index<0.53), or low (index<0.40) fiscal transparency.[19] We expect bigger cycles where transparency is lower.

Media penetration. Our measure of media penetration or density is aggregate newspaper circulation per capita in each state, that is, the ratio of total newspaper circulation in a state to the population of that state.[20] The data are available only for two years, 1983 and 1995. We take the average of the per capita figures for those two years and use it as a cross-sectional measure to represent newspaper circulation over the entire sample period. We then separate the states into three groups of roughly equal size: those in which average newspaper circulation is high (circulation>0.25), medium (0.22<circulation<0.25), and low (circulation<0.22). As with transparency, if lower media penetration means less transmission of information, it should be associated with larger political budget cycles.

Balanced budget laws. Finally, following Rose (2006), we define strict "no-carry" rules as those that prohibit states from carrying deficits into the next fiscal year and are difficult to circumvent by borrowing, due to either a popular referendum requirement or prohibition on the issue of public debt.[21] Seventeen states have such strict rules, and the rules do not change in the period for which we have data. These data come from the Advisory Commission on Intergovernmental Relations and the National Association of State Treasurers.

Other controls. To ensure that our estimates of the cycle are not accidentally confounded with the effects of other state-level variables that are likely to affect fiscal policy, we include several controls. First, we control for government resources: the tax base (measured by real per capita state personal income) and real per capita grants from the federal government. Second, because economic downturns increase demand for need-based programs, we control for the unemployment rate. Third, we control for demographic variables—population size and the fraction of the population that is school aged (5–17) or elderly (over 65)—to capture demand for government services. Finally, we control for the partisan composition of government, which has been shown to affect the level of spending (see, for example, Alt and Lowry 2000). These data—and data on per capita spending—come from the Census Bureau and the *Book of the States*. Where necessary, they have been converted from fiscal to calendar years.

2.2 Estimation Issues

We estimate our quantity of interest, the magnitude of the political budget cycle, by examining the difference, across states and across cycles of elections, between

---

[19] Our results are robust to using a continuous measure of transparency.

[20] These data were generously provided by Carles Boix.

[21] In states with weak no-carry rules, on the other hand, the governor, the legislature, or a public official such as the treasurer is authorized to issue public debt.

spending in the election year (the calendar year near the end of which comes the election), and the calendar year two years after the election year (i.e. two years before the next election)—that is, the midpoint of the four-year cycle. If there is an electoral cycle in spending, then the time path of spending between elections should resemble a "V;" if there is no cycle, the path should be flat. A very simple measure of the magnitude of the cycle is the height of the "V"—that is, the difference between estimated spending at the peak and the trough of the cycle. If a contextual variable "makes no difference" empirically, the unconditional cycle that Rose (2006) identified will appear in all cases. With some adjustments, we follow the usual approach to this problem, regressing spending on controls and contextual and election cycle variables, to estimate the conditional contextual effects and quantify our uncertainty about them.

As with any panel data study, it is clearly important to control for time-invariant state-level characteristics like a "liberal culture" or a "Progressive history" that might affect fiscal policy, for example by adding fixed effects to the regression. Moreover, fiscal aggregates within a state tend to be highly correlated from one period to the next; thus, we would like to include a lagged dependent variable on the right-hand side to capture this fiscal persistence. However, it has been well known for a quarter-century that panel data models with individual fixed effects generate biased estimates in the presence of a lagged dependent variable (Nickell 1981).

We therefore employ what has become a standard approach to dealing with this problem: the general method of moments estimator developed by Arellano and Bond (1991). This method uses first differences instead of fixed effects and includes a lagged dependent variable. The use of first differences means that we analyze changes in spending, and also that each individual state-level fixed effect drops out. Unfortunately this method generates a new problem: correlation between lagged values of the dependent variable and the lagged disturbance;[22] but diagnostic tests can tell us how serious a problem this is.

In more technical terms, we use the following regression specification:

$$y_{it} - y_{i,t-1} = \beta C_{it}(E_{it} - E_{it-1}) + \lambda(X_{it} - X_{i,t-1}) + \gamma(y_{i,t-1} - y_{i,t-2}) + (\delta_t - \delta_{t-1}) + (\mu_{it} - \mu_{i,t-1}).$$

where y_{it} is per capita spending in state i and year t, E_{it} is a vector of dummy variables representing the years in the gubernatorial election cycle, C_{it} is a vector of contextual dummy variables (approval, term limits, divided government, transparency, media, or fiscal rules),[23] X_{it} is a vector of control variables representing state political and economic conditions, δ_t are year effects, and μ_{it} is a disturbance term. Since the equation is in first differences, the dependent variable measures the annual change in

---

[22] To remove this correlation between $y_{i,t-1}$ and $\mu_{i,t-1}$, the lagged levels of the dependent variable from period $t-2$ and earlier ($y_{i,t-2}, y_{i,t-3}, \ldots$) are used as instrumental variables for the difference ($y_{i,t-1} - y_{i,t-2}$). Arellano and Bond show that these lagged levels are suitable instruments if the disturbance term μ_{it} has mean zero and is not serially correlated, in which case the first difference of the disturbance term ($\mu_{it} - \mu_{i,t-1}$) has zero covariance with the levels of the dependent variables from period $t-2$ and earlier.

[23] Our measures of transparency, media, and fiscal rules do not vary over time, as explained above, and thus the contextual variable is C_i in these cases rather than C_{it}.

spending, and all time-varying variables on the right-hand side are also in annual changes. Variables that are time invariant (like state-level fixed effects) have disappeared (since they do not change) except where they are interacted with variables that do vary over time. The (differenced) year effects control for confounding due to accidental concentrations of elections in particular years. We have chosen a demanding identification strategy: thus, our estimates are likely to be a lower bound on the true magnitude of the political budget cycle.

3 ESTIMATION RESULTS

To present all of the alternative specifications and estimation techniques we have carried out would double the length of this chapter. We believe the results we present here are robust in that they show up under most specifications, and significant in that we have carried out appropriate statistical significance tests where necessary. In the cases where we find significant cycles, we are confident that the inclusion of other variables would not alter the results. For simplicity, we present a figure for each contextual variable that displays the magnitude of the cycle estimated in that case.

3.1 Incentives

Approval. We expect to observe the largest cycles under moderate levels of approval (40–60 percent) since these elections are presumably the most competitive. As Figure 34.1 shows, this prediction is borne out by the data. The cycle is largest under medium approval: the difference between real per capita spending in the election year and the

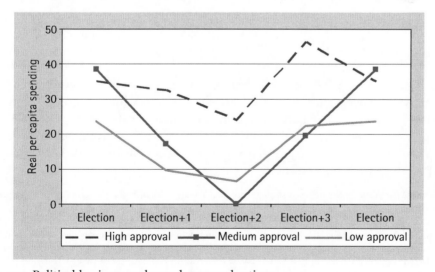

Fig. 34.1 Political business cycles and approval ratings

midpoint of the electoral cycle, all other things equal, is \$38.[24] The difference between this cycle and the high-approval cycle (\$22) is also significant at the 10% level.[25]

Term limits. We expect larger cycles when governors can run for re-election, since term-limited governors presumably have less incentive to appear competent. Contrary to this, Figure 34.2 reveals that the cycle is not significantly different under governors in states without term limits, governors facing non-binding two-term limits, and governors facing binding two-term limits. However, the cycle is slightly larger under binding one-term limits, and this difference is significant at the 10 percent level. This result is puzzling. It could be that partisan forces induce effort by these term-limited governors, as discussed above; this possibility merits further research.

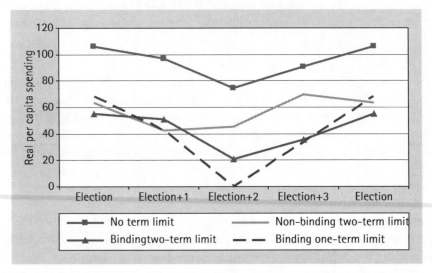

Fig. 34.2 Political business cycles and term limits

3.2 Ability

Divided government. We should observe larger cycles under unified government than under divided government if shared partisanship across branches of government increases the ability (or indeed, the incentive) to manipulate government finances. Indeed, we find evidence of a strong cycle under unified government. However, Figure 34.3 shows that the cycle is actually slightly larger under divided government, but this difference is not statistically significant.[26]

[24] The \$38 magnitude estimate is statistically significant at conventional levels. The significance test depends only on the coefficient and standard error for the election year variable, in the medium approval context.

[25] Note that the *average* level of spending appears to be highest when the governor enjoys high approval. Such differences in average levels of spending, while potentially interesting, are beyond the scope of this chapter, we are concerned only with the relative magnitudes of the cycle in different contexts. The significance test in that case is based on a test for the equality of two coefficients.

[26] In other words, the two nearly identical contextual cycles resemble the unconditional cycle.

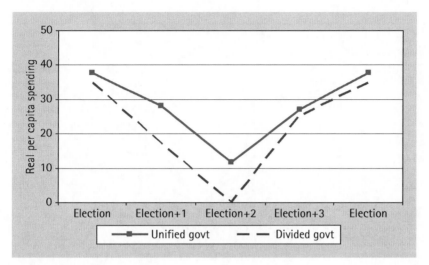

Fig. 34.3 Political business cycles and divided government

Transparency. Cycles should be larger under low transparency than under high transparency if politicians can only fool voters into believing they are competent by exploiting an information asymmetry. As predicted, the cycle is largest under low transparency ($32), followed by medium transparency ($30) and high transparency ($28), as shown in Figure 34.4. However, these differences are small and not statistically significant.

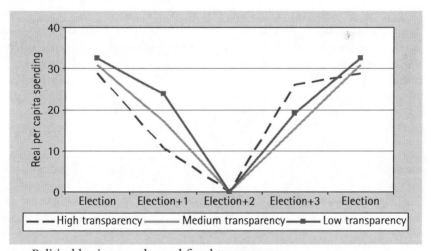

Fig. 34.4 Political business cycles and fiscal transparency

Media penetration. Along the same lines, we might expect larger cycles under low newspaper circulation than under high newspaper circulation if a strong media presence indirectly increases fiscal transparency by increasing the flow of information. Figure 34.5 shows that, as predicted, the cycle is larger ($47) under low

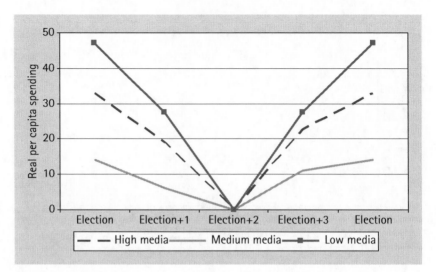

Fig. 34.5 Political business cycles and media

newspaper circulation than under medium newspaper circulation ($14); this difference is significant at the 5 percent level. Strangely, the cycle appears to be larger under high newspaper circulation than under medium circulation. However, the two conditional cycles are not statistically significantly different from one another.

Fiscal rules. Finally, we should observe larger cycles in states without fiscal rules than in those with rules if these rules are effective in limiting politicians' ability to run deficits and thus manipulate the timing of spending for electoral purposes. As predicted, the cycle is larger ($46 from peak to trough) under no rules than under rules ($6); this difference is significant at the 1 percent level. Even after including a variety of other control variables, this remains the biggest single contextual difference we find in the estimated magnitudes of political budget cycles (see Figure 34.6).

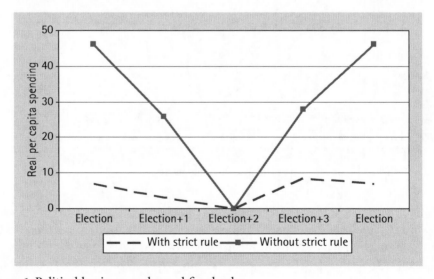

Fig. 34.6 Political business cycles and fiscal rules

4 Conclusion: Accountability and Enforcement

We began our investigation of electorally induced fluctuations in spending with two questions: "Under what circumstances is it more feasible? Under what circumstances is it more desirable?" We found some answers. On the one hand, the probability of re-election seems to be important; the expected closeness of the upcoming election, measured by moderate gubernatorial job approval, is associated with larger pre-election surges in spending. This result depends on the same mechanism identified by Schultz (1995) in the very different (national, parliamentary, European) British case. The flow of information also seems to play a role in the ability of incumbents to exploit the information advantage that underpins the political budget cycle: low newspaper circulation is associated with substantially larger budget cycles. This echoes the result Akhmedov and Zhuravskaya (2004) found in a very different place: Russian regional governments. Other results (divided government, transparency) did not come out clearly, as they had in some cross-national studies.

The clearest effect, however, was that of balanced budget laws: states that restrict politicians' ability to issue debt to cover spending shortfalls simply do not exhibit political budget cycles. But that result is both interesting and puzzling: interesting because on the whole cross-national studies have not identified similar effects, and puzzling because, while there is agreement that such laws can have real effects, it is not obvious why the laws are not evaded. Deficits are observed where no-carry-over laws exist, so why is there no evidence of a cycle in spending? Judicial sanctions for misbehavior are never observed. If the incentives for a political budget cycle are large, why are the laws adhered to?

Here is a possible answer, with some implications for the study of accountability. Transparency, we argued, allows voters to monitor incumbents' behavior. As transparency increases, the information asymmetry between politicians and voters is said to decline. But suppose the problem is not lack of information:

Information is not scarce: in fact, it is abundant. But extracting a signal—the true state of affairs—is difficult. The dimensionality problem is even more serious . . . this space will always be too large for voters to be able to control the government in all realms. (Przeworski 2003, 157)

Lowry and Alt (2001) argue that balanced budget requirements allow bond market participants to solve precisely such a signal extraction problem, and thereby

make it easier for imperfectly informed bond market investors to distinguish between political officials who choose to comply with the tradition and expectation of balance and those who do not, even without direct court enforcement. (Lowry and Alt 2001, 50)

That is, if politicians in states with no-carry rules run consecutive deficits, investors interpret their behavior as opportunism and respond sharply. Knowing that the costs will be high, incumbents avoid this behavior.

But such laws "work" not only because they aid in signal extraction but also because they allow principals to converge on the same standard of evaluation. It is important to notice that such convergence is not necessarily bad from the agent's point of view:

Agents seeking to enhance their powers have an interest in making their actions auditable in a single dimension . . . the agent is indifferent about which dimension is picked out, just so long as the [principals] coordinate on a single dimension. Thus, agent design converts the problem to one of pure coordination rather than a bargaining game. (Ferejohn 1999, 151)

Thus, agents wanting to borrow and spend could want such laws, and heterogeneous principals could find themselves better able to coordinate to enforce them. But even so,

Control of officials is . . . plagued by a coordination problem. . . . If we think of political principals as voters, with only sporadic involvement in the political process, it is difficult to be sanguine that public officials will be much restrained in their agency. (Ferejohn 1999, 150)

So this result for political budget cycles suggests two things. First, perhaps voters are not as effective as the bond market at monitoring opportunistic politicians. Even with coordination, more heterogeneity among principals is a problem, and voters are both more and less heterogeneous than market participants. Moreover, bond market monitoring occurs as a "by-product" of market participants' investment activities. Second, the mechanism to which we attribute this result also recalls other cases in the cross-national literature where investor behavior was important. Owners of mobile assets can inhibit rent seeking in the form of corruption (Adsera, Boix, and Payne 2003) while the flow of capital under floating exchange rate markets also allows market participants to inhibit political budget cycles (Clark 2003).

REFERENCES

ADSERA, A., BOIX, C., and PAYNE, M. 2003. Are you being served? Political accountability and quality of government. *Journal of Law, Economics, and Organization*, 19 (2): 445–90.

AKHMEDOV, A., and ZHURAVSKAYA, E. 2004. Opportunistic political cycles: test in a young democracy setting. *Quarterly Journal of Economics*, 1301–38.

ALESINA, A. 1987. Macroeconomic policy in a two-party system as a repeated game. *Quarterly Journal of Economics*, 102: 651–78.

——1988. Macroeconomics and politics. *National Bureau of Economic Research Macroeconomics Annual*, 3: 13–61.

——COHEN, G., and ROUBINI, N. 1992. Macroeconomic policies and elections in OECD democracies. *Economics and Politics*, 4 (1): 1–30.

——ROUBINI, N., with COHEN, C. 1997. *Political Cycles and the Macroeconomy*. New York: Cambridge University Press.

——and TABELLINI, G. 1990. A positive theory of budget deficits and government debt. *Review of Economic Studies*, 57: 403–14.

ALT, J. E. 1985. Political parties, world demand, and unemployment: domestic and international sources of economic activity. *American Political Science Review*, 79: 1016–40.

——and CHRYSTAL, K. A. 1983. *Political Economics*. Berkeley and Los Angeles: University of California Press.

——and LASSEN, D. D. 2006. Transparency, political polarization, and political budget cycles in OECD countries. *American Journal of Political Science*, 50: 530–50.

————and SKILLING, D. 2002. Fiscal transparency, gubernatorial popularity, and the scale of government: evidence from the States. *State Politics and Policy Quarterly*, 2: 230–50.

——and LOWRY, R. C. 2000. A dynamic model of state budget outcomes under divided partisan government. *Journal of Politics*, 62: 1035–69.

ARELLANO, M., and BOND, S. 1991. Some tests of specification for panel data: Monte Carlo evidence and an application to employment equations. *Review of Economic Studies*, 58: 277–97.

BECK, N. 1987. Elections and the Fed: is there a political monetary cycle? *American Journal of Political Science*, 31 (1): 194–216.

BESLEY, T., and CASE, A. 1995. Does electoral accountability affect economic policy choices? Evidence from gubernatorial term limits. *Quarterly Journal of Economics*, 110 (3): 769–98.

BEYLE, T., NIEMI, R., and SIGELMAN, L. 2002. Gubernatorial, senatorial, and state-level presidential job approval: the U.S. officials job approval ratings (JAR) collection. *State Politics and Policy Quarterly*, 2: 215–29.

BLOCK, S. 2001. Elections, electoral competitiveness, and political budget cycles in developing countries. Working paper. Center for International Development, Harvard University.

BRAMBOR, T., CLARK, W. R., and GOLDER, M. 2005. Understanding interaction models: improving empirical analyses. *Political Analysis*, 13: 1–20.

BRENDER, A., and DRAZEN, A. 2005. Political budget cycles in new versus established democracies. *Journal of Monetary Economics* (forthcoming).

CARLSEN, F. 1998. Rational partisan theory: empirical evidence for the United States. *Southern Economic Journal*, 65 (1): 64–82.

CLARK, W. R. 2003. *Capitalism, not Globalism: Capital Mobility, Central Bank Independence, and the Political Control of the Economy*. Ann Arbor: University of Michigan Press.

——and HALLERBERG, M. 2000. Mobile capital, domestic institutions, and electorally induced monetary and fiscal policy. *American Political Science Review*, 94: 323–46.

CLINGERMAYER, J. C., and WOOD, B. D. 1995. Disentangling patterns of state debt financing. *American Political Science Review*, 89 (1): 108–20.

COX, G., and KATZ, J. 2002. *Elbridge Gerry's Salamander*. New York: Cambridge University Press.

CUKIERMAN, A., and MELTZER, A. 1986. A positive theory and discretionary policy, the cost of democratic government, and the benefits of a constitution. *Economic Inquiry*, 24: 367–88.

DRAZEN, A. 2001. The political business cycle after 25 years. *National Bureau of Economic Research Macroeconomics Annual 2000*, 75–117.

DREHER, A., and VAUBEL, R. 2005. Foreign exchange intervention and the political business cycle: a panel data analysis. Unpublished MS.

FEREJOHN, J. 1999. Accountability and authority: toward a theory of political accountability. In Manin, Przeworski, and Stokes 1999: 131–54.

FRANZESE, R. 2002. Electoral and partisan cycles in economic policies and outcomes. *Annual Review of Political Science*, 5: 369–422.

FREY, B. 1978. *Modern Political Economy*. London: Martin Robertson.

GOLDEN, D., and POTERBA, J. 1980. The price of popularity: the political business cycle reexamined. *American Journal of Political Science*, 24: 696–714.

GRIER, K. 1987. Presidential elections and Federal Reserve policy: an empirical test. *Southern Economic Journal*, 54 (2): 474–86.

HALLERBERG, M. 2002. Veto players and the choice of monetary institutions. *International Organization*, 56: 775–802.

HALLERBERG, M. 2003. Fiscal rules and fiscal policy. Pp. 393–401 in *Handbook of Public Administration*, ed. B. G. Peters and J. Pierre. London: Sage.

HAYNES, S. E., and STONE, J. 1989. An integrated test for electoral cycles in the US economy. *Review of Economics and Statistics*, 71 (3): 426–34.

HIBBS, D. 1977. Political parties and macroeconomic policy. *American Political Science Review*, 71 (4): 1467–87.

—— 1987. *The American Political Economy*. Cambridge, Mass.: Harvard University Press.

KEECH, W., and PAK, K. 1989. Electoral cycles and budgetary growth in veterans' benefits programs. *American Journal of Political Science*, 33: 901–11.

KRAUSE, G. 2005. Electoral incentives, political business cycles and macroeconomic performance: empirical evidence from post-war US personal income growth. *British Journal of Political Science*, 35: 77–101.

LACHLER, U. 1978. The political business cycle: a complementary study. *Review of Economic Studies*, 45: 131–43.

LEWIS-BECK, M. S. 1988. *Economics and Elections: The Major Western Democracies*. Ann Arbor: University of Michigan Press.

LOHMANN, S. 1998. Rationalizing the political business cycle: a workhorse model. *Economics & Politics*, 10: 1–17.

LOWRY, R. C., and ALT, J. E. 2001. A visible hand? Intertemporal efficiency, costly information, and market-based enforcement of balanced-budget laws. *Economics & Politics*, 13: 49–72.

LUCAS, R. 1976. Econometric policy evaluation: a critique. *Carnegie-Rochester Conference Series on Public Policy*, 1: 19–46.

MANIN, B., PRZEWORSKI, A., and STOKES, S. eds. 1999. *Democracy, Accountability, and Representation*. New York: Cambridge University Press.

MCCALLUM, B. 1978. The political business cycle: an empirical test. *Southern Economic Journal*, 44: 504–15.

NICKELL, S. 1981. Biases in dynamic models with fixed effects. *Econometrica*, 49 (6): 1417–26.

NORDHAUS, W. 1975. The political business cycle. *Review of Economic Studies*, 42 (1): 169–90.

PERSSON, T., and TABELLINI, G. 2002. Do electoral cycles differ across political systems? Working paper. Stockholm.

—— —— 2003. *The Economic Effects of Constitutions*. Cambridge, Mass.: MIT Press.

PRZEWORSKI, A. 2003. *States and Markets*. New York: Cambridge University Press.

ROGOFF, K. 1990. Equilibrium political business cycles. *American Economic Review*, 80: 21–36.

—— and SIBERT, A. 1988. Elections and macroeconomic policy cycles. *Review of Economic Studies*, 55 (1): 1–16.

ROSE, S. 2006. Do fiscal rules dampen the political business cycle? *Public Choice*, 128: 407–31.

SAPORITI, A., and STREB, J. M. 2003. Separation of powers and political budget cycles. MS. Queen Mary University.

SCHUKNECHT, L. 1999. Fiscal policy cycles and the exchange rate regime in developing countries. *European Journal of Political Economy*, 15: 569–80.

SCHULTZ, K. 1995. The politics of the political business cycle. *British Journal of Political Science*, 25 (1): 79–99.

SHI, M., and SVENSSON, J. 2002. Political business cycles in developed and developing countries. MS. IIES.

—— —— 2003. Political budget cycles: a review of recent developments. *Nordic Journal of Political Economy*, 29 (1): 67–76.

SMITH, A. 2004. *Election Timing*. Cambridge: Cambridge University Press.

SOH, B. H. 1986. Political business cycles in industrialized democratic countries. *Kyklos*, 39: 31–46.

TSEBELIS, G. 2002. *Veto Players: How Political Institutions Work.* Princeton: Princeton University Press.

TUFTE, E. 1978. *Political Control of the Economy.* Princeton: Princeton University Press.

WRIGHT, G. 1974. The political economy of New Deal spending. *Review of Economics and Statistics*, 56 (1): 20–9.

CHAPTER 35

....

THE WELFARE
STATE IN GLOBAL
PERSPECTIVE

....

MATTHEW E. CARNES
ISABELA MARES

IN THE LAST few decades of the twentieth century, the literature examining cross-national variation in the development of policies of social protection has been one of the most dynamic fields of research in comparative politics. The sustained effort of sociologists, political scientists, and economists to understand the causes and consequences of different welfare states has generated a vast literature that is methodologically eclectic and theoretically vibrant. The accumulation of findings in this literature has fruitfully illuminated one of the most significant achievements of modern states: the ability to protect citizens from poverty in the event of sickness, old age, and unemployment.

Advanced industrialized economies have been at the center of the empirical investi-gation of policies of social protection. This was a natural starting point, due to the magnitude and importance of the welfare state in these economies, which accounts for as much as 30 to 65 percent of GDP. Based on these cases, the literature developed important insights by noting that social policies clustered in distinct "families of nations" or "worlds of welfare capitalism" (Esping-Andersen 1990; Castles 1993; Huber and Stephens 2001). Nevertheless, important theoretical disagreement continues to exist about the relative importance of different political factors in explaining the diversity of observed policies and their distributional implications.

In this essay, we argue that the most exciting research opportunities in the study of welfare states lie in examining the variation in policies of social protection in developing economies. Scholars of the welfare state need to broaden the scope of their analysis. In recent decades, policies of social protection in many developing economies have experienced a dramatic transformation. Two trends in the evolution of these policies require a systematic explanation. First, welfare states in developing countries have not unilaterally evolved towards a neo-liberal, residualistic model of social protection characterized by limited coverage and a private provision of benefits. While some Latin American countries have partially or fully privatized their old-age insurance programs, other economies—such as those of Taiwan or Korea—have enacted universal social insurance programs granting benefits to all citizens (Wong 2004). Second, we find strong variation across policy areas in the evolution and distributional implications of these policies. In distributional terms, health care policies have been more progressive than have pension policies—an outcome that holds true for policy changes both in Latin America and in East Asia.

These recent changes offer an important challenge to welfare state scholars. Are existing theories, based on the examples of advanced industrial economies, able to explain the recent transformations experienced by welfare states in developing countries? Which explanatory variables fare better than others and, if so, why? If existing explanations cannot account for the puzzling outcomes noted above, what should be the building blocks of explanations that can account for the divergence in social policy trajectories? This essay surveys the major approaches employed in study of the welfare state and evaluates the capacity of these theories to explain the bifurcated trajectory of reform experienced by social policies around the world.

1 UNDERLYING STRUCTURAL CONDITIONS: LEVELS OF INDUSTRIALIZATION AND ECONOMIC OPENNESS

The earliest studies of the emergence of social policy hypothesized that economic growth and development were key factors accounting for the emergence and expansion of modern welfare states. These processes would lead to rising industrial employment and technological capacity. This in turn, was expected to spur incentives for governments to educate their workforce and protect the aged who were no longer able to serve in industry, which, in turn would lead to higher levels of social spending (Wilensky 1975). Thus, economic development brought new social needs and the capacity to meet those needs, and welfare state development was expected to be a "by-product" of the larger process of modernization (Huber and Stephens 2001).

Quantitative tests of this hypothesis in the case of OECD economies have identified a positive correlation between variables such as the level of industrialization or economic development and aggregate social spending (Wilensky 1975). By contrast, efforts to test this hypothesis in the context of a larger universe of cases that is not only restricted to OCED economies have, so far, generated inconclusive results. The correlation between economic development and measures of aggregate spending or aggregate tax revenues is very weak and often fails to reach statistically significant levels (Adsera and Boix 2002; Mares 2005).

This line of research suggests that the growth in the level of social policy commitments in East Asian economies—such as Taiwan or Korea—is a consequence of the economic development experienced by these economies. The divergence in the trajectories of economic growth between East Asian and Latin American economies over the last few decades has also led to different labor market outcomes, which subsequently have shaped divergent social welfare systems. In Latin America, the share of industrial employment as a percentage of total employment remained stable throughout the post-war period. In Asia, by contrast, the share of population employed in industry increased over this period, which increased demands for programs that provided income support to urban industrial workers. This combination of economic growth and labor market developments laid the preconditions for differences in social spending across regions.

A major limitation of studies stressing the "logic of industrialism" is that they do not formulate precise mechanisms linking differences in the underlying structural economic variables and differences in policies of social spending. They also offer no predictions about the type of social policy chosen by countries at different levels of economic development. In other words, the question of why some countries at similar levels of economic development adopt contributory insurance, while others continue to rely on more residual, private-type social policies, remains unanswered. These explanations are also unable to account for the variation across policy areas within the same country. Thus, it is difficult to explain why Korea or Taiwan introduced universalistic protection in the area of health care but much more limited social policy provisions for old age.

A second set of arguments linking broad structural underlying factors and the size of the public sector focuses on the impact of greater economic openness. In a pioneering paper, David Cameron identified a positive relationship between the level of economic openness—measured as the aggregate flows of imports and exports as a percentage of GDP—and the size of the public sector (Cameron 1978). Cameron's findings were based on the analysis of eighteen OECD economies during the period between 1960 and 1975. To account for these results, Cameron hypothesized that in open economies, governments enact income supplements or social insurance schemes to compensate workers whose employment or income is threatened by external competition. Other scholars have supplemented these statistical findings with qualitative research on the industrial and social policies pursued by many European economies during the post-war period and have documented how these economies "complemented their pursuit of liberalism in the international economy with a strategy of domestic compensation" (Katzenstein 1985, 47; Ruggie 1982). Geoffrey Garrett and Deborah Mitchell have updated Cameron's initial findings for the period through the mid-1990s and have examined the relationship between other measures of economic openness (such as the openness of financial markets) and the size of the public sector (Garrett and Mitchell 2001) while Alicia

Adsera and Carles Boix have also considered the effect of regime type on the relationship between openness and central government receipts (Adsera and Boix 2002).

In recent years, a growing number of studies have begun to question whether the positive relationship between economic openness and the size of the public sector is robust and holds for a larger number of cases. Dani Rodrik demonstrates that the positive relationship between economic openness and the size of the public sector is not a finding that is idiosyncratic to OECD countries only (Rodrik 1997, 1998). However, in contrast to Cameron and Garrett, Rodrik argues that the appropriate measure of the external insecurity caused by trade is not the level of openness, but volatility in the terms of trade. Rodrik argues and offers some preliminary evidence that volatility in the terms of trade is associated with volatility in income, leading thus to higher demands for social insurance policies that can protect against these adverse shocks. Yet that openness can also have a contracting effect on the size of the welfare state. Under conditions of high capital mobility, governments are unable to and the result is a increase taxes on capital to compensate labor, and the result is a dampening of the rate of growth of the public sector (Rodrik 1997, 90).

While this area of research identifies an important empirical regularity, it suffers from a number of important limitations. The first is the high level of aggregation of the dependent variable. Cameron uses measures of the total revenue of governments, Rodrik uses data on government consumption, and Adsera and Boix use data on current receipts of the central government (Cameron 1978, 1244; Rodrik 1998; Adsera and Boix 2002, 239). These broad measures—lumping together all government expenditures or revenues—do not actually capture the specific expenditures that mitigate the economic dislocations resulting from changes in the terms of trade. Rodrik's argument that military expenditures, for instance, or government procurement of capital goods, play an important role in insuring against external risk is very tenuous and begs the question why some governments choose these particular expenditures rather than social expenditures to protect workers against external risk.

Second, expenditure-based measures do not capture questions of policy design that are politically salient and distributionally divisive. Gøsta Esping-Andersen succinctly expressed this objection to the use of such measures in many quantitative studies of the welfare state, stating that "expenditures are epiphenomenal to the theoretical substance of the welfare state. It is difficult to imagine that anyone struggled for expenditures per se" (Esping-Andersen 1990, 19–21).

Third, the distribution of expenditures is as important as the level of spending. What matters for the workers that have lost their jobs as a result of economic downturns is not the statistical artifact known as "per capita social policy expenditures" but the actual conditions of their social policy coverage, including the level and stipulations of social policy benefits, the stringency of eligibility criteria, etc. Countries with equal amounts of welfare spending often distribute their expenditures unevenly to various subgroups of the population or across social policy programs. Some countries might target very high levels of expenditures to narrow political clienteles, while others may distribute broadly across the entire population. Similarly, the mix between public services and social policy transfers can vary significantly across countries with similar levels of social policy expenditures. Hence, important information about the distributional implications of many social policies is simply discarded if aggregate expenditure data are used. In recent research, Mares attempts to overcome this exclusive reliance on expenditure-based measures by constructing indices that capture policy differences in the level of insurance coverage and the redistribution of risks in over 100 countries (Mares 2005, 2006b).

Can these arguments linking higher economic insecurity and larger welfare states account for the divergent trajectories experienced by welfare states in developing countries during recent decades? In an analysis of the evolution of social spending in fourteen Latin American countries over the period 1973–97, Kaufman and Segura-Ubiergo show that an increase in economic openness was associated with a decline in the level of social policy expenditures (Kaufman and Segura-Ubiergo 2001, 578). By contrast, several studies have argued that the high aggregate shocks experienced by Asian economies during the recent financial crisis contributed to increases in the size of the public sector. While these results are consistent with Rodrik's argument that openness can have an ambiguous impact on the size of the public sector, they call for a more nuanced theoretical prediction of the conditions under which one of these effects prevails.

Thus, the recent literature testing the relationship between economic insecurity and larger welfare states marks an important effort to integrate findings across developed and developing countries. Future research in this line should consider the following issues. First, more studies need to test the micro-level implications of these arguments. Is greater exposure to external risk systematically related to higher demands for social spending? How significant is its effect in predicting individual demands for social spending relative to other variables? As discussed above, at this point in the development of the literature the dependent variable is too aggregated. Future studies need to identify the range of policies that represent responses to greater openness and test the relationship between openness and social spending using more precise measures of the dependent variable. Finally, while existing research has only focused on the *demand* for social protection (and how changes in external openness affect this demand), it is also important to examine variation in the ability of policy makers to *supply* different social policies. We will return to an analysis of the variables affecting variation in supply of social protection in a subsequent section of this essay.

2 THE POWER RESOURCE PERSPECTIVE

One inherent limitation of explanations stressing broad structural differences across countries is the absence of a political mechanism linking these variables to larger public sectors or social policies characterized by broader levels of coverage and higher levels of redistribution. Beginning in the 1970s, a new direction of research—known as the power resource approach—addressed this inherent limitation. (Esping-Andersen 1985; Korpi and Shalev 1979; Stephens 1979). This perspective attributed divergence in the level of social spending to differences in the balance of power among labor-based organizations and organizations representing conservative political forces. An increase in the organizational capacity of labor-based parties or a decline in the power of employers, due to wars or depressions, was expected to lead to increases in social spending. Skocpol and Amenta concisely summarize the mechanisms through which power resources approaches argue that social policy formulation takes place:

A high proportion of wage, and eventually salaried, workers become organized into centralized unions, and those unions financially nourish a social democratic or labor party supported by the same workers in their capacities as voters. Given such working-class organizational strength in both the market and political arenas, the supposition is that taxing, spending, and administrative powers of the state can be expanded, shifting class struggles into the political arena, where workers are favored in democracy by their numbers. The model posits that the earlier and more fully the workers become organized into centralized unions and a social democratic party, and the more consistently over time the social democratic party controls the state, the earlier and more "completely" a modern welfare state develops. (Skocpol and Amenta 1986)

Initial efforts to test the predictions of the power resource perspective examined social policy developments in post-war Europe. Esping-Andersen and Korpi argued that the "political and social ghettoization of working class parties" in Germany and Austria, to a degree never experienced in Scandinavia, accounts for important variations in generosity and coverage of social insurance programs across these countries (Esping-Andersen and Korpi 1984, 203). Building on this qualitative research, a range of quantitative studies have identified a positive correlation between a variety of measures of labor strength—from union density to centralization of wage bargaining to the share of seats held by social democratic parties and aggregate social policy expenditures (Huber and Stephens 2001). Power resource scholars have also argued that a strong social democratic presence in government is not just associated with a larger public sector, but with different *types* of welfare states. In an effort to test systematically this idea, Gøsta Esping-Andersen developed an index measuring the amount to which labor policy diminishes a worker's "commodity status" and identified a positive correlation between the degree of left power and the level of decommodification (Esping-Andersen 1990, 52).

While power resource studies mark an important progress over earlier explanations, this approach suffers from a number of theoretical limitations. First, it makes relatively simplistic assumptions about the interests of workers in social insurance and does not identify sectoral (or individual-level) variables that account for the divergence among different unions or workers over the design of policies of social protection. Second, this approach postulates a zero-sum conflict among workers and employers. Workers are assumed to demand new social policies to compensate them for their disadvantaged position in the labor market (Korpi 1983). By contrast, employers are assumed to oppose any expansion of new programs. This assumption of the zero-sum distributional conflict over social policy is built into the very definition of social policy with which power resource scholars operate. As the goal of social policy is to "emancipate workers from market-dependence" through "decommodification," employers are expected to

874   MATTHEW E. CARNES & ISABELA MARES

resist all policies that weaken their absolute authority over workers (Esping-Andersen 1990). While the power resource perspective never tests the validity of these assumptions, a new wave of scholarship has demonstrated that employers' opposition to a new social policy cannot be taken for granted and that employers exhibit much greater heterogeneity in their preferences over new social policies.

Third, the power resources approach makes monolithic claims about social democratic parties, which in fact show great variation over time and across countries, and which can even be divided internally. These studies also fail to appreciate the electoral constraints under which these parties operate. However, recent work has shown that the closeness of the political competition and the identity of the challenger of left-wing parties affect both the timing and the character of policy adoption (Kitschelt 2000). Further, social democratic parties have not been univocal in calling for universal protections for all workers. During the formative years of these parties, social policy was an important source of patronage for their constituencies (Shefter 1977). On many occasions in the post-war period, these parties have concentrated their efforts on serving "insiders"—workers with secure employment who constitute the base of the party (Rueda 2005).

Finally, most of this research uses two measures of labor strength—the strength of left-wing parties and the organization of trade unions—interchangeably. However, homogeneity in the preferences and political influence of these actors cannot be assumed. Electoral calculations play an important role for left-wing parties, affecting the incentives of these parties to deliver different mixes of transfers and services. By contrast, the primary concern of unions remains the maximization of the real income of their members; social policy concerns, while important, occupy a subordinate role. In recent years, a number of studies have abandoned these earlier assumptions of substitutability between trade unions and social democratic governments. These studies have begun to examine the bargaining among these actors, the policy trade offs involved in these negotiations, and the conditions under which political exchange between unions and governments around particular social policies is sustainable. As these studies have shown, both the size of pre-existing welfare state commitments and the mix between social services and transfers affect unions' willingness to moderate their wage demands in exchange for social policy transfers (Mares 2004, 2006b). Unions' incentives to deliver moderate wage settlements decline if the tax burden increases and if the share of social policy services and transfers going to non-union members rises. Moreover, the effect of unions' wage policy on employment outcomes depends on the level of centralization of the wage-bargaining system.

As currently formulated, power resource scholarship offers only limited guidance in understanding the preferences and strategies pursued by labor-based parties in other regions of the world. How do parties trade off ideological concerns and electoral calculations? Given that labor groups are one out of many different constituencies of these parties, what role does social policy play in consolidating these heterogeneous coalitions? The policies pursued by labor-based parties in Latin America, such as the PRI in Mexico or the Peronists in Argentina, do not conform to the predictions of power resources. In the immediate post-war period, these parties rejected proposals for universalistic social policies that were advanced by representatives of their bureaucracy. Instead these parties have targeted benefits to the organized segments of their working-class base. And, as Murillo and Calvo have convincingly demonstrated, the Peronists have pursued electoral strategies premised on the provision of clientelistic private goods for their labor constituencies (Murillo and Calvo 2004).

Thus, the power resource perspective cannot adequately account for the recent changes in policies of social protection around the world. Korea and Taiwan, two countries that lacked strong social democratic parties and large and encompassing trade unions, presided over the introduction of universalistic health insurance (Wong 2004). Second, these explanations cannot account for the strong divergence across policy areas that characterizes recent reforms in both Latin America and East Asia— namely the higher redistributive bias of health care reforms. Finally, as Murillo has argued, to understand the strategies of labor-based parties in Latin America during recent decades and the conditions under which the relationship between labor-based parties and trade union movements endured, one needs to look at other variables in addition to the electoral and political strength of the labor party. These variables include the level and nature of electoral competition as well as the competition for leadership within trade unions (Murillo 2000, 2001).

3 Cross-Class Alliances

In recent years, a new wave of scholarship examining the evolution of social policies in advanced industrialized economies has provided a forceful critique of both the theoretical assumptions and empirical results of the power resource scholarship. This critique has come in two forms. One set of studies has tried to identify the interests of actors other than workers in social insurance. Other studies have challenged the assumption of a zero-sum conflict between employers and workers over the introduction of a new social policy, and have sought to specify the conditions under which employers support new social policies as well as the broader political factors that facilitate the formation of cross-class alliances.

In his study of the historical origin of social insurance in five European nations, Peter Baldwin has provided a forceful critique of the thesis linking social democratic strength and the origin of universalistic programs (Baldwin 1990). He finds that in Denmark and Sweden, universalistic, tax-financed social policies were not introduced in the post-war period, but at the turn of the twentieth century, before social democratic parties enjoyed an overwhelming political advantage. During this period, the strongest promoters of universalistic programs were political parties representing farmers and the middle classes, such as the Venstre in Denmark or the Swedish Agrarian Party. Universalistic programs were appealing to these actors for a number of reasons. They shifted the tax burden to a broader population, lowering the non-wage labor costs of many agrarian small producers. Given that the labor force in agriculture was extremely heterogeneous, including both smallholders and wage earners, this made the tax-financed, universalistic option much more attractive than a contributory policy.

This empirical challenge to the power resource perspective has important theoretical implications. Baldwin identifies other variables, in addition to class position, that shape the preferences of different actors towards social insurance. In this account of social policy development, the important political battles over the introduction of a new social policy are not fought between a perpetually disadvantaged proletariat and its capital-holding political opponents. As Baldwin points out,

> although they intersect and often coincide, the actors who do battles over social policy and social classes in the more general sense are, in fact, two distinct entities...Because the secondary redistribution undertaken by social insurance reapportions the cost of misfortune most immediately according to actuarial criteria, and not in line with the social distinctions that are important in the primary economic distribution, such actors have been first and foremost risk categories that translate only indirectly and variably into the usual definitions of class and social groups. (Baldwin 1990, 11–12)

In this account, two additional variables predict the salient cleavages over the introduction of a new social policy: the incidence of risk and the "capacity of a group for self-reliance" (which is in turn determined by the demographic outlook and economic prospects of a group). Baldwin predicts that groups characterized by a high incidence of risk and a low capacity for self-reliance will favor redistributive forms of insurance, such as contributory social insurance or universalistic social policies. In contrast, groups characterized by a low incidence of risks and a high capacity of self-reliance favor policies with narrower scope and they are often capable (and willing) to administer these policies.

By specifying the sources of others' interest in social insurance, this theoretical perspective offers important tools for the understanding of distributional conflicts over social policy in economies with weak labor movements. The gradual extension of social insurance in Korea and Taiwan—from a policy covering initially a very small number of workers in large firms to a universalistic health insurance that merged all insurance funds—posed important distributional conflicts between those sectors that were already covered by insurance and the new groups that were seeking access (Lin 1997). The relative risk profile between social policy insiders and outsiders was an important predictor of the demands formulated by these groups during the policy-making process. If sectors that already had access to insurance had a favorable risk profile as compared to groups that were not covered, they were more likely to oppose the expansion of the policy or to demand compensation from the state in the form of a subsidy or lower insurance contributions. By contrast, "insiders" were more likely to favor an extension of social insurance if "outsiders" had a favorable risk profile.

A second critique of the power resource perspective has challenged the assumption of a zero-sum conflict among employers and workers over the introduction of a new social policy, or what Peter Swenson calls the "equivalency premise of fixed class interests" (Swenson 2002, 9). As a range of new studies have pointed out, this assumption does not

fit the historical record well. Employers have not monolithically opposed the introduction of a new social policy nor have they only favored private social policies, administered
by firms. In many historical circumstances, key sectors of the business community have
favored social policies characterized by broad coverage and a wide redistribution of risks.
These examples raise two sets of questions. The first is one of preferences. What are the
sources of business interest in social insurance? What factors explain the variation in the
social policy preferences of firms? Second, once the preferences of employers were
correctly identified, these studies have provided new insights into the process of bargaining over the introduction of new social policy and the political coalitions formed during
this process.

Under what conditions are profit-maximizing firms interested in social policies? What
does social policy mean to firms? What are the institutional advantages offered by these
policies to employers? Under what conditions do these benefits outweigh the "costs"
imposed by social policies on firms, which come in the form of insurance contributions
or labor market regulations which might hinder firms' ability to deploy labor flexibly?
The new employer-centered literature has offered several answers to these puzzles. One
set of explanations has focused on employers' labor market needs. Policies with earnings-
related benefits that offer relatively higher benefits to high-skilled workers as opposed to
low-skilled workers reduce the incentives of these workers to accept jobs that do not
correspond to their skill qualifications. In this context, social policies are "instruments of
skill retention" (Mares 2003, 2005). Other studies have linked employers' support for
social insurance to their efforts to influence the competition in product markets with
other firms (Swenson 2002).

Incorporating Baldwin's earlier findings, these studies have shown that the relative
risk profile shapes not just the social policy preferences of workers but also those of
employers. The history of the introduction of social policy legislation presents numerous examples of distributional conflicts among employers between firms in high- and
low-risk sectors. Firms in industries facing a high incidence of workplace accidents have
favored the introduction of compulsory accident insurance policies. By contrast, these
proposals were strongly opposed by employers in industries with lower incidence of
accidents. Firms in industries facing high risk of unemployment have favored policies
requiring unified insurance contributions. By contrast, these proposals were opposed by
industries with a low incidence of unemployment. We see similar distributional dynamics at work in the evolution of early retirement policies in recent years. Firms with
relatively elderly workers have made intensive use of options presented by existing
policies to shed elderly workers (Mares 2003).

The recent business-centered literature has made important progress in identifying
the sources of variation in business preferences over various social policy outcomes. The
strongest predictors of the variation in the social policy preferences of firms are firm size,
skill composition of the workforce, level of competition in product markets, and relative
risk profile of the firm. While this literature successfully debunks the assumption of
monolithic business opposition to new social policy, it also pays more attention
to strategic considerations of various actors during the bargaining process over the
introduction of new policies. An important theme underpinning this literature is that

of "strategic alliances," coalitions of various actors that are formed on the second-best preference of these players. In some cases, game-theoretic analysis is employed to specify how other factors of the political environment—such as changes in the political composition of parliament—affect the strategic calculations of both unions and employers and their willingness to support policies that are their "second-best" choice (Mares 2001, 2005).

Can these business-centered explanations help us account for the variation in the trajectory of social policy reforms experienced by various countries around the world in recent decades? A strong finding of this literature is that business support for social policies is linked to the skill intensity of the workforce. Thus, it follows that in many developing countries where firms rely on low-wage labor, employers are less likely to play a proactive role supporting compulsory social insurance policies. One expects to find, however, pockets of business support for social policies in East Asian economies, where the development of a skilled workforce was a precondition of the economic development experienced by these countries (Haggard and Kaufman 2006). Business-centered approaches to social policy development are likely to have significant explanatory power in accounting for developments in this region. A number of authors have begun to examine the role played by employers in the development of the Korean welfare state and during recent policy changes (Yang 2004). Other comparative research that examines the introduction of unemployment insurance in East Asia during recent decades is trying to probe whether differences in the skill intensity of firms predict firms' support for these policies (Choung 2006; Song 2006).

4 STATE-CENTERED APPROACHES

Explanations stressing either the political resources of labor movements or cross-class alliances assigned only a tangential role to the interests and strategies pursued by state bureaucrats. For some scholars, bureaucrats mattered only "in the interstices of indifference," in other words, after other powerful societal actors had reached a consensus on the design of a new program (Baldwin 1990). For other researchers, bureaucrats were assumed to be perfect agents of their political principals. In this intellectual context, Skocpol and Evans's admonition to "bring the state back in" opened up a promising avenue of research (Evans, Rueschemeyer, and Skocpol 1985). The contribution of this literature is twofold. First, it formulates a set of explanations about the sources of policy preferences of bureaucrats. Secondly, it investigates the impact of state structures and existing policies on subsequent policy developments.

Where do the preferences of bureaucracies for different social policies come from? What factors explain this variation? A number of studies located the source of state preferences in bureaucratic actors' experience with previous policies. Margaret Weir and Theda Skocpol's analysis of the introduction of Keynesian policies in Great

Britain, Sweden, and the United States provides an illustration of this logic (Weir and Skocpol 1985). The United States and Sweden adopted policies relying on automatic adjustments in public spending to manage the employment shocks of the Depression. Weir and Skocpol seek to explain why Britain did not introduce Keynesian macroeconomic policies during the Great Depression, despite levels of labor and trade union strength that were comparable to those in Sweden. They attribute this divergence in policy to the experience of past policies. They are arguing that the experience of British policy makers with a more limited policy of unemployment insurance (introduced in 1911) led to the reluctance of British civil servants to experiment with large public scale programs that were the centerpiece of a Keynesian revival. By contrast, Swedish and US bureaucrats lacked a similar legacy and were open to a more dramatic policy shift, embracing a greater increase in expenditures on public works programs.

Other explanations for the variation in the policy preferences of bureaucrats stress ideational factors and the access to different policy ideas (Hall 1989, 1993). In Heclo's famous formulation, "state officials not only power (or whatever the verb form of that approach might be), they also puzzle" (Heclo 1974, 305). Drawing on insights from cognitive psychology, a number of scholars argue that these ideational changes are not driven by rational cost–benefit calculations of the best available alternatives. Cognitive shortcuts matter. Policy makers do not balance all relevant information, but place excessive importance on facts that are immediately available and generalize from a narrow set of observations (Weyland 2005, forthcoming). Weyland uses these insights to account for the rapid diffusion of the Chilean model of pension privatization across the world. His findings provide an account for some of the empirical regularities associated with the process of privatization—namely the simultaneous adoption of one model by contiguous countries and the gradual leveling in the number of countries adopting a change. This pattern is not exclusive to the diffusion of the recent model of pension privatization, but also applies to the earlier adoption of contributory insurance policies by most Latin American countries during the immediate post-war years and the diffusion of contributory insurance policies in Europe after Bismarck's pioneering legislation.

State-centered approaches provide important tools for the understanding of processes of social policy reform in many developing countries. Due to the weakness of trade unions, employer associations, and other societal actors in many economies, bureaucracies as agenda setters exert tremendous influence in the policy-making process (Shmuthkalin 2006). Nevertheless, these explanations have important shortcomings. While some predict continuity in preferences (due to experience with past policies), others predict very rapid change (due to bureaucrats' reliance on cognitive shortcuts); very few studies offer predictions about the set of factors that make continuity or change more or less likely. In an early seminal paper, Hall has argued that clear breaks with past policies and practices—labeled, following a Kuhnian metaphor, "third-order" policy change—is likely to be a process driven by factors external to the bureaucracy (Hall 1993). However, to date, no study has tested this insight systematically, and Weyland's recent work finds examples of dramatic changes adopted by isolated bureaucracies. Finally, almost no study has produced a set of generalizable conditions about the relative importance of the shifts in the preferences of bureacracies in explaining the adoption of new policies. In many Latin American countries, numerous proposals to privatize put forward by bureaucrats were defeated. Thus, a fuller explanation that provides more precise predictions about the timing and content of reforms requires a richer characterization of the dynamics of the policy-making process—one that incorporates other actors in addition to bureaucrats and that specifies the constraints placed by these actors on the choices of bureaucrats.

A different line of research in this literature has explored the conditions under which existing social policies have an independent causal impact on subsequent political development. Pierson's study of policy retrenchment in the UK and the USA provides an important illustration of the logic of "policy feedback" (Pierson 1994). In these countries, two right-wing politicians—Ronald Reagan and Margaret Thatcher—were engaged in a sustained effort to dismantle existing policies of income support. Their success, however, varied systematically across policy areas. As Pierson argues, differences in policy design—which affected the ability of politicians to hide unpopular measures—explain variation in policy retrenchment. Building on Pierson's initial findings, a number of other studies have begun to explore more systematically the mechanisms by which "policies create politics" (Pierson 1994, 2001, 2004; Campbell 2002, 2003). These studies have demonstrated that previous policies have an impact on the strength and mobilization of interest groups, on voter participation rates, and on the ability of policy entrepreneurs to help latent groups overcome collective action problems. In addition, a large number of studies have shown how the design of welfare states has consequences for a variety of labor market outcomes, including labor force participation rates of women and participation of the elderly in the labor market (Esping-Andersen 1990; Scharpf and Schmidt 2000).

These studies contain several insights for the study of social policy reforms in developing countries. In these contexts too, differences in the design of existing policies have affected both the preferences and the relative bargaining power of different actors during the reform process. In several economies—such as those of Argentina or Taiwan—industrial or craft unions play an important role in administering social policies. This feature of policy design has affected the preferences of these players, increasing their opposition to proposals that attempted to shift their policy responsibilities to the state. Policy makers have often relied on the threat to remove these policy responsibilities from the hands of unions, in an effort to elicit their compliance with other changes in policy, such as privatization of the pension system. Thus, while this feature of policy design has strengthened unions on some dimensions—serving as an important source of patronage—it has also weakened unions during the bargaining process, contributing to unions' acquiescence on other policy dimensions.

Theories stressing "policy feedbacks" also provide some building blocks for an explanation of the striking divergence in the trajectory of pension and health policies during the last two decades. A large number of countries in Latin America or Eastern Europe have enacted reforms that have increased the role of the second, private pillar of old-age protection, which often lowered the access of low-income sectors to benefits. By contrast, health insurance reforms have been characterized by explicit increases in the social policy expenditures targeted at the poor. Even countries with high levels of income inequality—such as Bolivia, Peru, or Columbia—have presided over the introduction of a number of programs that have subsidized health benefits for the destitute and that have increased expenditures on basic care. Differences in policy design between pensions and health care have affected distributional conflicts over the introduction of these policies and might account for the divergence in outcomes. Two differences in policy design are salient. The first is the magnitude of their public good externalities. Public health programs—such as immunization programs—generate important externalities even for groups that might be, in economic terms, net contributors to the program. This lessens the distributional conflict and increases the willingness of high-income groups to accept an increase in the amount of benefits targeted to the poor. The second important difference in policy design across pensions and health care is a difference in their time horizons. In the case of health care, today's contributions guarantee immediate access to benefits, but the lag is much longer in the case of pensions. This is also expected to affect divergence in the level of support, and hence the intensity of the distributional conflict, over the expansion of these programs. As we examine the evolution of social policies in developing countries we need to look not just at the variation in policy design but also at variation in policy implementation. Two dimensions of enforcement or implementation exert influence over subsequent changes in policy. Weakness in tax collection—which is predominantly but not exclusively a consequence of weak administrative resources of social security administrations—affects the financial sustainability of various programs. This overall weakness in state enforcement is likely to increase the attractiveness of privatization as a policy option. Yet states vary not just in their aggregate tax capacity, but also in the evenness of their tax collection. Collection of social policy contributions varies widely across different income groups. In many developing countries, social security administrations lack information about the income of small shopkeepers or other groups with precarious employment and often apply different criteria in determining the social insurance contributions of different occupations. These distributional biases in policy implementation affect the beliefs about the "fairness" of the existing social policy of other sectors and their preference over a mix of private and public benefits. Incorporating this logic, Mares has argued that differences in policy implementation affect the composition of the political coalitions supporting different policies. Observing uneven enforcement of social policies, groups that might otherwise benefit from the expansion of social insurance withdraw their support for redistributive social policies (Mares 2005, 2006b).

In sum, approaches focusing on variation in the preferences of bureaucratic officials and policy feedbacks add important elements to our understanding of the dynamics of social policy reform in recent years. They provide tools that allow us to understand both cross-regional variation and the variation across policy areas. In developing countries, the predictions of these theories have been, so far, tested with aggregate data only. Future research will have to supplement these initial findings with more detailed narratives of the bargaining process. This will allow us to test some of the predictions of strategic defection of different sectors given differential enforcement of previous policies. Finally, individual survey data—measuring not just individual support for aggregate social spending but also individual attitudes towards different mixes of private and public benefits—are needed to illuminate the variation in coalitional support for different policies.

5 CONCLUSION

We began this essay by noting the methodological eclecticism and cumulative character of the comparative welfare state literature as important strengths. The existing literature has provided important insights for our understanding of a very consequential political outcome: measures to protect workers and disadvantaged members of society through temporary or permanent economic difficulties.

Two decades ago, in a review of the field, Skocpol and Amenta called for analysts to "become unequivocally *historical* in their orientation" (Skocpol and Amenta 1986, 152, italics in original). The vast literature produced during the last two decades has followed and benefitted from this exhortation. Careful historical research—that has contextualized the preferences of key actors, but has also paid close attention to the political consequences of existing institutional configurations—has generated important insights for our understanding of the origin and consequences of social policy programs. The literature on comparative welfare states has been central to the "historical institutionalist" agenda of research and has contributed vastly to broader theoretical debates about processes of institutional change and transformation (Streeck and Thelen 2005).

In this essay, we have argued that the time has come for research on social policy to become unequivocally *comparative* in its orientation. Our understanding of variation in social policies outside of OECD economics still resembles a sixteenth-century map, with vast areas of uncharted territories. Mapping out and explaining this variation should be the goal of welfare state scholars during future decades. Existing explanations accounting for trajectories of social policy development in advanced industrialized democracies provide important building blocks in this endeavor.

REFERENCES

ADSERA, A., and BOIX, C. 2002. Trade, democracy, and the size of the public sector: the political underpinnings of openness. *International Organization*, 56 (2): 229–62.
BALDWIN, P. 1990. *The Politics of Social Solidarity: Class Bases of the European Welfare State, 1875–1975*. Cambridge: Cambridge University Press.

CAMERON, D. R. 1978. Expansion of the public economy: comparative analysis. *American Political Science Review*, 72 (4): 1243–61.

CAMPBELL, A. 2002. Self-interest, social security and the distinctive participation patterns of senior citizens. *American Political Science Review*, 96 (3): 565–74.

—— 2003. *How Policies Make Citizens: Senior Citizen Activism and the American Welfare State.* Princeton: Princeton University Press.

CASTLES, F. G. ed. 1993. *Families of Nations: Patterns of Public Policy in Western Democracies.* Aldershot: Dartmouth Publishing Library.

CHOUNG, J. 2006. The political economy of labor protection. MS. University of California San Diego.

CROUCH, C., and STREECK, W. 1997. *Political Economy of Modern Capitalism: Mapping Convergence and Diversity.* London: Sage.

ESPING-ANDERSEN, G. 1985. *Politics against Markets: The Social Democratic Road to Power.* Princeton: Princeton University Press.

—— 1990. *The Three Worlds of Welfare Capitalism.* Princeton: Princeton University Press.

—— 1999. *Social Foundations of Postindustrial Economies.* New York: Oxford University Press.

—— and KORPI, W. 1984. Social policy as class politics in post-war capitalism: Scandinavia, Austria and Germany. Pp. 179–208 in *Order and Conflict in Contemporary Capitalism: Studies in the Political Economy of Western European Nations*, ed. J. Goldthorpe. New York: Oxford University Press.

EVANS, P., RUESCHEMEYER, D., and SKOCPOL, T. eds. 1985. *Bringing the State Back in.* New York: Cambridge University Press.

GARRETT, G. 1998. Global markets and national politics: collision course or virtuous circle? *International Organization*, 52 (4): 787–824.

—— and MITCHELL, D. 2001. Globalization, government spending and taxation in the OECD. *European Journal of Political Research*, 39 (2): 145–77.

HAGGARD, S., and KAUFMAN, R. 2006. Recrafting social contracts: welfare reform in Latin America, East Asia and Central Europe. MS.

HALL, P. A. ed. 1989. *The Political Power of Economic Ideas: Keynesianism across Countries.* Princeton: Princeton University Press.

—— 1993. Policy paradigms, social learning and the state: the case of economic policy-making in Britain. *Comparative Politics*, 25 (33): 275–96.

—— and SOSKICE, D. W. 2001. *Varieties of Capitalism: The Institutional Foundations of Comparative Advantage.* Oxford: Oxford University Press.

HECLO, H. 1974. *Modern Social Politics in Britain and Sweden; From Relief to Income Maintenance.* Yale Studies in Political Science 25. New Haven: Yale University Press.

HUBER, E., and STEPHENS, J. D. 2001. *Development and Crisis of the Welfare State: Parties and Policies in Global Markets.* Chicago: University of Chicago Press.

KATZENSTEIN, P. J. 1985. *Small States in World Markets: Industrial Policy in Europe.* Cornell Studies in Political Economy. Ithaca, NY: Cornell University Press.

KAUFMAN, R. R., and SEGURA-UBIERGO, A. 2001. Globalization, domestic politics, and social spending in Latin America: a time-series cross-section analysis, 1973–97. *World Politics*, 53: 553–87.

KITSCHELT, H. 2000. Partisan competition and welfare state retrenchment: when do politicians choose unpopular policies? Pp. 265–302 in *The New Politics of the Welfare State*, ed. P. Pierson. New York: Oxford University Press.

KORPI, W. 1983. *The Democratic Class Struggle.* London: Routledge & Kegan Paul.

—— and SHALEV, M. 1979. Strikes, industrial-relations and class conflict in capitalist societies. *British Journal of Sociology*, 30 (2): 164–87.

LEVITSKY, S., and MURILLO, M. V. 2006. Variation in institutional weakness: causes and implications from a Latin American perspective. MS.

LIN, K. 1997. From authoritarianism to statism: the politics of national health insurance in Taiwan. Ph.D. dissertation. Yale University.

MADRID, R. L. 2003. *Retiring the State: The Politics of Pension Privatization in Latin America and Beyond.* Stanford, Calif.: Stanford University Press.

MALLOY, J. M. 1979. *The Politics of Social Security in Brazil.* Pittsburgh: University of Pittsburgh Press.

MARES, I. 2001. Firms and the welfare state: when, why, and how does social policy matter to employers? Pp. 184–212 in *Varieties of Capitalism,* ed. P. Hall and D. Soskice. Oxford: Oxford University Press.

—— 2003. *The Politics of Social Risk: Business and Welfare State Development.* Cambridge Studies in Comparative Politics. Cambridge: Cambridge University Press.

—— 2004. Wage bargaining in the presence of social policy transfers. *World Politics,* 57 (1): 99–142.

—— 2005. Social protection around the world: external insecurity, state capacity, and domestic political cleavages. *Comparative Political Studies,* 38 (6): 623–51.

—— 2006a. *Taxation, Wage Bargaining and Unemployment.* Cambridge Studies in Comparative Politics. New York: Cambridge University Press.

—— 2006b. The great divergence in social protection. Unpublished MS. Columbia University.

MURILLO, M. V. 2000. From populism to neoliberalism: labor unions and market reforms in Latin America. *World Politics,* 52: 135–74.

—— 2001. *Labor Unions, Partisan Coalitions and Market Reforms in Latin America.* Cambridge Studies in Comparative Politics. Cambridge: Cambridge University Press.

—— and CALVO, E. 2004. Who delivers? Partisan clients in the Argentine electoral market. *American Journal of Political Science,* 48 (4): 742–57.

PIERSON, P. 1994. *Dismantling the Welfare State? Reagan, Thatcher, and the Politics of Retrenchment.* Cambridge Studies in Comparative Politics. Cambridge: Cambridge University Press.

—— 2000. Three worlds of welfare state research. *Comparative Political Studies,* 33 (6–7): 791–821.

—— 2001. *The New Politics of the Welfare State.* Oxford: Oxford University Press.

—— 2004. *Politics in Time: History, Institutions, and Social Analysis.* Princeton: Princeton University Press.

RODRIK, D. 1997. *Has Globalization Gone too Far?* Washington, DC: Institute for International Economics.

—— 1998. Why do more open economies have bigger governments? *Journal of Political Economy,* 106: 997–1032.

RUEDA, D. 2005. Insider–outsider politics in industrialized democracies: the challenge to social democratic parties. *American Political Science Review,* 99 (1): 61–74.

RUGGIE, J. 1982. International regimes, transactions and change: embedded liberalism in the postwar economic order. *International Organization,* 36 (2): 379–415.

SCHARPF, F., and SCHMIDT, V. 2000. *Welfare and Work in the Open Economy.* New York: Oxford University Press.

SHEFTER, M. 1977. Party and patronage: Germany, England, and Italy. *Politics & Society,* 7 (4): 403–51.

SHMUTHKALIN, W. 2006. Political regimes and welfare state development in East Asia: how state leaders matter to social policy expansion in Taiwan, Thailand and China. Ph.D. dissertation. Stanford University.

SKOCPOL, T., and AMENTA, E. 1986. States and social policies. *Annual Review of Sociology,* 12: 131–57.

STEPHENS, J. D. 1979. *The Transition from Capitalism to Socialism.* New Studies in Sociology. London: Macmillan.

STREECK, W., and THELEN, K. 2005. *Beyond Continuity: Institutional Change in Advanced Political Economies.* New York: Oxford University Press.

SONG, J. 2006. Enterprise unions and the segmentation of the labor market: labor, unions and corporate restructuring in Korea, Paper presented at conference on System Restructuring in East Asia. Stanford University.

SWENSON, P. 1991. Bringing capital back in, or social-democracy reconsidered: employer power, cross-class alliances, and centralization of industrial-relations in Denmark and Sweden. *World Politics,* 43 (4): 513–44.

—— 2002. *Capitalists against Markets: The Making of Labor Markets and Welfare States in the United States and Sweden.* Oxford: Oxford University Press.

THELEN, K. 2001. Varieties of labor politics in the developed democracies. Pp. 71–103 in *Varieties of Capitalism,* ed. P. Hall and D. Soskice. Oxford: Oxford University Press.

WEIR, M., and SKOCPOL, T. 1985. state structures and the possibilities for "Keynesian" responses to the Great Depression in Sweden, Britain, and the United States. In Evans, Rueschemeyer, and Skocpol 1985: 107–63.

WEYLAND, K. 2004. *Learning from Foreign Models in Latin American Policy Reform.* Washington, DC: Woodrow Wilson Center Press.

—— 2005. Theories of policy diffusion: lessons from Latin American pension reforms. *World Politics,* 57 (2): 262–95.

—— Forthcoming. *Bounded Rationality and Policy Diffusion: Social Sector Reform in Latin America.*

WILENSKY, H. L. 1975. *The Welfare State and Equality: Structural and Ideological Roots of Public Expenditures.* Berkeley and Los Angeles: University of California Press.

WONG, J. 2004. *Healthy Democracies: Welfare Policies in Taiwan and South Korea.* Ithaca, NY: Cornell University Press.

YANG, J. 2004. Skill formation and the origin of the Korean welfare system: a reinterpretation of the authoritarian industrialization period [in Korean]. *Korean Political Science Review,* 38 (5).

....

CHAPTER 36

THE POOR
PERFORMANCE
OF POOR
DEMOCRACIES

....

PHILIP KEEFER

BECAUSE all rich countries are democratic, the opaque relationship between growth and democracy has long puzzled researchers. Opacity is less surprising, however, when one considers heterogeneity within regime types. Heterogeneity is evident when one looks at government policy choices: they vary significantly not only between rich and poor countries, but also between rich and poor, and young and old democracies. Many of these differences cannot be explained using the conceptual apparatus of the broad democracy and development literature. For example, this literature generally assumes that the main difficulty with democracy is effort by non-elite politicians to cater to non-elite constituencies by redistributing from the elites. However, in poor democracies, not only is redistribution particularly low, but corruption is particularly high, suggesting non-elite constituencies have at best a tenuous ability to hold their non-elite leaders accountable for performance.

This essay points to a recent literature on political market imperfections as an avenue to explain anomalies in the relationship between regime type and economic performance

* The findings, interpretations, and conclusions expressed in this paper are entirely those of the author and do not necessarily represent the views of the World Bank, its Executive Directors, or the countries they represent.

and, specifically, why poor democracies perform so much differently than richer democracies. Political markets are vulnerable to imperfections because citizens must rely on promises in deciding which political competitor to support. When compliance with promises cannot be observed, or where no sanctions are available to punish non-compliance, politicians are unable to exchange promises for votes and political markets cease to function. In contrast, theories of democracy and development generally assume that, for example, non-elite politicians can make credible promises to non-elite voters. However, scholars who investigate the politics of developing countries have uncovered ample evidence that this is typically not the case.

The focus here, on endogenous sources of regime performance, is not meant to downplay the potential role of external constraints on government performance. Such constraints include the restrictions that wealthy countries place on the movement of capital, goods, and labor into and especially out of poor countries, as well as external threats to national security. However, there is little evidence that these systematically explain the differences between poor and rich democracies nor that the policy choices of poor democracies identified below are the optimal response to these.

1 Poor Countries and Their Policies

Understanding the sources of policy heterogeneity across countries is an essential building block of a broader understanding of democracy, political economy, and development. This section offers ample evidence of heterogeneity in the choices of rich and poor countries and of poor democracies and non-democracies on a wide array of policy dimensions. Most of these have been linked to economic growth, including the macro-economic and market-oriented reforms of the Washington Consensus, education and public infrastructure, and the security of property rights and fiscal redistribution. Though none of them commands universal support as an explanation for economic development, no one disputes that underperformance on all of them substantially hinders development progress. Consistent with this, poorer countries make significantly different choices along these policy dimensions than richer countries; these are not easily explained by regime type. However, consistent with the ambiguous effects of democracy on growth, the policy choices of poor democracies differ little from those of poor non-democracies (Table 36.1).[1]

---

[1] For purposes of this section, a democracy is a country that exhibits competitive elections, as measured by the Database of Political Institutions (Beck et al. 2001), consistent with the idea that theories of development and democracy that place great weight on the institution of elections.

1.1 The Washington Consensus: Macroeconomic Policies and State Ownership

For most of the 1980s and into the 1990s, the bundle of policies variously characterized as the Washington or "neo-liberal" Consensus was the main response to failed growth. While the connection between these policies and growth is not universally accepted, although both poorer and richer countries largely embraced the Consensus during the 1990s, a substantial policy gap remained between the two groups of countries at the end of the 1990s.[2]

Compared to 1985, when trade volumes in rich and poor countries were 83 and 67 percent, respectively, trade volumes in 2000 were approximately 25 percent higher in both sets of countries.[3] The gap in trade volumes grew slightly: by 2000, exports and

Table 36.1 Poor democracies act like poor non-democracies

	Poor non-democracies (no.)	Poor democracies (no.)	Rich democracies (no.)
Median consumer price inflation, 1985	9.41 (40)	8.49 (13)	7.05 (40)
Median consumer price inflation, %, 2000	3.91 (38)	4.31 (32)	3.12 (60)
Mean government debt/GDP, %, 1998	71.3 (14)	53.3 (16)	47.38 (28)
Days in customs	6.8 (15)	8.15 (16)	5.23 (17)
Days to enforce a contract	410 (37)	416 (30)	331 (50)
Total government expenditures/GDP, %, 1998	.25 (21)	.23 (21)	.32 (38)
Gross sec. school enrollment (% school age children enrolled), 1998	39.8 (34)	45.7 (25)	95.8 (48)
Paved roads/total roads, 1998	44.8 (11)	38.9 (14)	69.7 (22)
Corruption (0–6, least corrupt=6), 1997	2.7 (25)	2.9 (34)	4.1 (49)
Bureaucratic quality (0–6, 6=highest quality), 2000	2.3 (28)	2.4 (30)	4.6 (51)
Rule of law (0–6, 6=highest quality), 2000	3.7 (28)	2.9 (30)	4.6 (51)

Note: Corruption, bureaucratic quality and rule of law from political risk services, *International Country Risk Guide*. All other indicators from *World Development Indicators*, World Bank.

---

[2] See Zagha (2005) for a review.

[3] Trade policies would be a better indicator of policy choices related to globalization, but country comparisons using these are misleading. One country might have low tariffs and high quotas, another the reverse; one country may tax imported consumer goods, another agricultural imports. In practice,

imports of goods and services equaled 100 percent of GDP in the 68 countries with greater than $5,385 *ppp*-adjusted per capita income and only 81 percent in the 68 countries with lower incomes.[4] Median inflation also dropped in all countries from 1985 to 2000, but again, remained approximately 25 percent higher in poorer countries in 2000. Among the 62 countries with data in 2000, median government debt was 39 percent of GDP for the richer 31 countries. Median government debt was much higher, 64 percent of GDP, for the poorer 31 countries, a substantial increase from the 45 percent of GDP that poorer countries exhibited in 1985.

Regime type seems not to have had a systematic influence on reform choices, particularly between poor democracies and non-democracies. No inflation difference was evident between poorer democracies and non-democracies in 2000; among poorer countries, regime type and trade volumes are uncorrelated in both 1985 and 2000. Only with indebtedness does democracy make a difference across the board: at least in 2000, democracies, including poorer democracies, were significantly less indebted than non-democracies.

1.2 Regulation

After the Washington Consensus, policy advice turned to second generation reforms, those aimed at distortions in the regulatory environment. Again, there is no consensus on the magnitude of regulatory effects on growth and whether the costs of regulation are outweighed by broader social benefits. However, holding aside important issues regarding the quality of growth (e.g. variations across countries in the environmental consequences of growth), there is no dispute that regulation can limit firm incentives to invest and, as a consequence, economic growth. Poor countries appear to have a strikingly different regulatory posture than rich countries and poor democracies, if anything, erect more stringent regulatory barriers than all other countries.

Data from World Development Indicators, taken from the World Bank Doing Business program (2004) and World Bank Investment Climate surveys (various dates, 2001–2004), confirm this with three indicators. Customs delays are 6.3 days in 32 poorer countries versus 3.8 in 20 richer countries; contract enforcement requires 377 days in 68 poorer countries, compared to 294 in 60 richer countries; and the median time to resolve an insolvency is 3.6 years among 64 poorer countries, but only two years among 60 richer ones. More clearly than with macroeconomic outcomes such as inflation and trade flows, these regulatory variables are more completely within the control of governments and provide a clearer indication of differences in the decisions of rich and poor country governments. One might argue that poor countries cannot afford the administrative apparatus needed to regulate efficiently. This is not convincing, however: there is no relationship between income and regulatory performance for countries with incomes per capita ranging from $500 to $10,000 (75 percent of the total).

country rankings change considerably depending on which trade policy or index of trade policies one uses (Pritchett 1991).

[4] Exports plus imports of goods and services; data from *World Development Indicators*.

Engerman and Sokoloff (2002) find in nineteenth-century Latin America that countries with competitive elections would have fewer barriers to entry and be somewhat more lightly regulated. In fact, democracies overall require about 10 percent fewer days to enforce a contract and almost a year less to resolve a bankruptcy. However, among poorer countries, competitive elections create no differences with regard to contract enforcement and bankruptcy, and are actually associated with *longer* customs delays.

1.3 The Size of Government and Redistribution

The redistributive role of government is at the core of the literature assessing the relationship between democratic institutions and growth. For example, Przeworksi and Limongi (1993) argue that elections may make it easier for the poor to redistribute income from the rich, lowering returns to investment and slowing growth.[5] Although they make the contrary argument and contend that democracy and income are positively associated, Acemoglu and Robinson (2006) also give central attention to redistribution and the security of property rights.

There is, however, little evidence that poor countries, democratic or not, engage in more redistributive activity. The total size of government is one proxy for redistribution and is notoriously small among poor countries. In 1998, 84 countries had data on consolidated central government expenditures. For the 42 poorer countries in this group, median expenditures were 24 percent of GDP; for the other 42 countries, median expenditures were a full *eight* percentage points higher.[6] One potential source of redistribution is social security; 64 countries have data on social security taxes in 1998. For the 32 poorest countries in the group, the median of the total social security taxes (paid by workers and employers) was zero. For the 32 countries with *ppp*-adjusted per capita incomes greater than $6,635, the median was six percentage points of GDP.

The association of democracy and redistribution is a subtle one. Boix (2003) and Acemoglu and Robinson (2006) argue that political and economic elites do not even permit democratization if they expect substantial redistribution. It is less surprising, therefore, that competitive elections are uncorrelated with government spending across all countries. Boix (2003) further argues that citizen demand for intergenerational transfers and unemployment payments should increase with country income, but that only in democracies should this demand become policy. Consistent with this, he finds that the interaction of democracy and log of income per capita is significant and positive (Boix 2003).[7]

---

[5] Others argue that political instability and opportunistic behavior by governments, both of which might pose graver challenges to development, might actually be mitigated by redistribution (Keefer and Knack 2002; Svensson 1998).

[6] The median *ppp*-adjusted per capita income of the group is $6,101.

[7] This result depends on the assumption that the error terms of country observations are independent over time, and is not robust to lifting this assumption (assuming clustered errors). However, the interaction of manufactured value added with democracy, an arguably more direct test of Boix's hypothesis, is significant and robust to controlling for clustered errors.

Among poorer countries, however, and inconsistent with these theories, competitive elections have a large *negative* effect on government spending. Controlling or not for per capita income, poor countries with competitive elections spend at least five percentage points of GDP less than non-democratic poor countries. Even if one stipulates that demand for redistributive spending shifts sharply with income and that elites do not permit democratization when they expect high levels of redistribution, it is surprising that poor democracies spend substantially less than poor non-democracies.

Poor countries also tax less and differently. Consistent with the arguments in Boix (2003), in 1998—when data on more than eighty countries are available—the median poor country collected total revenues amounting to 18 percent of GDP; among richer countries, the median collected 31 percent of GDP. Again, however, poor democracies collected 3.6 percent of GDP less in total revenues than poor non-democracies. Poorer countries relied significantly less on income and social security taxes and much more on non-tax revenues (2 percent of GDP in the median richer country, 3 percent in the median poorer country). However, poor democracies collected almost two percentage points of GDP *less* in income taxes than poor non-democracies.

Dozens of articles have examined Wagner's law, that citizens of richer countries demand larger government, to explain why poor countries have smaller governments. However, Wagner's law does not explain why total government spending and redistribution are insensitive to regime type—why, as the evidence here and in Mulligan, Gil, and Sala-i-Martin (2004) seems to suggest, poor democracies actually spend less than non-democracies. This phenomenon is a challenge for theories of democracy and development that is discussed further below.

1.4 Public Goods and the Composition of Government Spending

Scholars argue that policy choices regarding both human capital and infrastructure play a significant role in the growth process (see, for example, Easterly and Servén 2004). The provision of these is substantially worse in poor countries. Median gross secondary school enrollment in 1998 was 54 percentage points lower in the 59 poorer countries for which data is available than in the 59 richer countries. In 2000, 20.9 percent of the population had access to electricity in the median poorer country; 92.9 percent had access in the median richer country. The median fraction of all roads that were paved among the 69 countries with *ppp*-adjusted per capita incomes greater than $4,626 was .69 in 1999. It was only .21 in the 70 countries poorer than this.[8]

---

[8] If one restricts the comparison to the forty-nine countries with information on both public investment and paved roads, 85% of roads are paved in the median richer country, only 35% in the median poorer country.

Income does not explain lower levels of provision in poor countries. In contrast to dramatic differences in school *enrollment*, rich and poor countries exhibit only modest differences with respect to school *spending*. In 1998 (the last country for which substantial data are available) median education spending was 2.9 percent of GDP among the 39 richer countries with data and 2.6 percent of GDP in the 40 poorer countries. Consistent with the earlier findings, education spending is, if anything, lower among poor democracies than among countries lacking competitive elections.

Wages constitute the bulk of education expenditures and are correspondingly lower in poor countries. The significantly lower enrollment outcomes that result from roughly equal school spending can therefore most plausibly be attributed either to a low demand for education or to a diversion of education spending from the objective of student learning. Well-known patterns of corruption in high expenditure/low enrollment countries support the latter explanation. Foster and Rosenzweig (1996) conclude that the demand for schooling (in India) is responsive to returns to education, which is inconsistent with the former explanation.

Throughout the 1990s, public investment was actually much *higher* in poorer countries—a median 3.9 percent of GDP for the 37 poorer countries with data versus 2.8 percent for the 36 richer countries. The difference was particularly high at the beginning of the decade. In 1990, 5.1 percent of GDP was spent on public investment in the median poorer country and 2.7 percent in the median richer country. One might attribute high spending to the backward state of infrastructure in developing countries and the consequent high returns from significant investment. In this case, though, we would expect convergence over time in the quality of infrastructure in rich and poor countries. However, despite years of extra investment, the infrastructure gap is widening. From 1990, the first year for which road information is available, to 1999, the percentage of paved roads in the median richer country rose from 61.3 to 69; the median poorer country remained stagnant, at 21.

Political incentives can drive a wedge between spending and performance if expenditures on patronage and other particularistic objectives are more politically rewarding than high-quality public services. Public investment with these characteristics even has a label, "pork barrel." Evidence that particularistic motives are significant emerges from public employment spending. The median wage expense as a fraction of GDP was 4.5 percent of GDP in the 42 countries with per capita incomes exceeding $6,101 (*ppp* adjusted) but 5.6 percent of GDP in the 42 countries poorer than this.

Competitive elections have no effect on access to electricity or paved roads, nor on public investment. Among poor countries, competitive elections are significantly and *negatively* correlated with paved roads, controlling or not for income. As Feng (2003) also finds, countries with competitive elections exhibited much higher enrollments, controlling for income or not. This effect is entirely driven by rich democracies, however; 25 poorer democracies have approximately the same enrollment figures as the 34 non-democracies, again whether or not one controls for income. A strong regime effect is apparent only for wages, which drop with democracy in both rich and poor countries.

1.5 Governance: Bureaucratic Quality, Corruption, and the Security of Property Rights

Empirical investigations by many researchers conclude that rule of law, corruption, bureaucratic quality, and other governance indicators have a significant impact on growth (for an early contribution, see Keefer and Knack 1997), largely by reducing the risk-adjusted rate of return to private investment. All of these governance indicators have public good properties that link them to the policies considered earlier. A government that serves all citizens equally is, by definition, not arbitrary. When rule of law, integrity, or bureaucratic quality begin to decline, however, the tendency of governments to benefit some citizens at the expense of others grows. We would expect the same governments that underprovide education or infrastructure would also underprovide the public good of bureaucratic quality. Not surprisingly, poor countries score significantly worse than rich countries on all governance dimensions—approximately one standard deviation worse using measures from *International Country Risk Guide*.

Feng (2003) finds a positive relationship between governance variables similar to these and democracy. However, using the Database of Political Institutions measure of democracy (the competitiveness of elections) and focusing only on poor countries, there is no difference between poor democracies and non-democracies with regard to corruption or bureaucratic quality; the rule of law is actually significantly worse in poor democracies than poor non-democracies.

2 EXPLAINING AMBIGUITY IN THE DEMOCRACY–GROWTH RELATIONSHIP

A common characteristic of these policy distortions is that average citizens tend to lose and narrow interests tend to gain from them. Expedited customs procedures benefit average citizens more than policies that lead to long customs delays. Bureaucratic quality, integrity in government, and the rule of law by definition advantage average citizens more than their absence. Given that average citizens lose, competitive elections would appear to be precisely the correct institutional remedy. The correlations reported above are inconsistent with this conjecture, however: competitive elections among poorer countries are associated with policy outcomes that are no different or worse than in poorer countries without competitive elections.

Nevertheless, one of the central debates surrounding the political economy of development has turned on the role of political checks and balances and competitive elections, the institutional arrangements that essentially define democracy. That debate has, in turn, focused on two sides of the same policy coin: the extent to which democracies protect citizens against opportunistic behavior by governments and the extent to which they encourage growth-suppressing redistribution.

Political checks and balances have long been thought to be the main institutional remedy for the inability of governments to offer citizens guarantees that their investments would not be expropriated by government or by other citizens. North and Weingast (1989) explore the role of political checks and balances in the *absence* of competitive elections. They show how the financing needs of the English Crown increasingly led it to expropriate the English nobility and foreign lenders; how the efforts of the English elite to resist this led ultimately to the Glorious Revolution; and how the resulting strength of the English parliament eventually reassured buyers of English sovereign debt that the obligations would be repaid.[9]

However, other research has found limited econometric evidence supporting the claim that political checks and balances alone have a robust and large effect on the security of property rights. Keefer and Knack (1998) find statistically significant but small effects of a subjective measure of political checks and balances (*Executive Constraints* from Polity II) on the security of property rights. Keefer (2004) documents that the significant effects of an objective measure of checks and balances on growth and the security of property rights are largely attenuated when one controls for the presence of competitive elections.

As Stasavage (2003) emphasizes in his re-examination of the Glorious Revolution, the incentives of veto players matter. It might therefore be the case that elections are a necessary complement to political checks and balances, by forcing multiple veto players to satisfy a larger constituency, increasing the political costs of, for example, expropriation. Where democracy is absent, the vast majority of citizens occupy no veto gate and are protected from opportunistic behavior only as long as their interests happen to coincide with those of an elite group that does. Keefer (forthcoming) finds evidence that this is the case in the context of banking crises: elected governments are far more reluctant to recapitalize failed banks. In his study of non-democratic, post-independence African countries, Bates (1983) concludes that protection from opportunistic behavior was scant. Instead, the absence of democracy enabled favored special interests to run roughshod over the interests of the small farmer majority.

Set against these advantages of democracy, however, is the argument that democracy precipitates an increase in redistribution from political and economic elites to non-elites, stifling economic growth. Przeworski and Limongi (1993) conclude that in view of these offsetting effects, we should see no strong association between democracy and growth. Consistent with this, the early literature they review is inconclusive about the effects of democracy on growth, with many papers finding no effect. Mulligan, Gil, and Sala-i-Martin (2004) go further, simply concluding that institutions do not matter, after presenting evidence that democracies engage in *more* regressive taxation and spend *less*. They suggest that policy differences across countries are a consequence of differences in social interests. However, if institutions

---

[9] As Stasavage (2003) documents, this security emerged in those years when English merchants exercised veto power in the parliament.

were irrelevant to social policies, the effort made to change and defend institutions—measured not least in blood and money—is hard to explain.

Since the 1990s, the literature has emphasized two other possible explanations for the lack of association between democracy and growth, beyond the offsetting effects of greater security and greater redistribution. One is data: noisy measures of democracy would also mask any significant association of democracy and growth. Ambiguity persists, though, with more precise measures of democracy. The second is conceptual, recognizing that democracy is not an exogenously given characteristic of countries. Only when we take into consideration the conditions under which societies choose democracy can we make firm conclusions about whether democracy affects growth. While offering a well-documented explanation for the ambiguity of the democracy–growth relationship, this approach does not satisfactorily explain the differential performance of poor and rich democracies.

2.1 Data, Democracy, and Development

Early researchers looking at democracy and growth relied primarily on Freedom House (Gastil 1988) for its political freedoms and civil liberties indicators, and on Banks (1971) or the Polity data (Gurr, Jaggers, and Moore 1990), based on expert assessments of whether the executive in a country was constrained, political participation was open, etc. (see Bollen 1993 for a discussion). The use of these indicators has confronted two problems.

First, they already embed assessments of regime performance in their coding, creating an inherent problem of endogeneity: outcomes will naturally be better in countries where evaluators judge regimes to be better performing. This is explicitly the case with Freedom House indicators: the protection of civil liberties and political freedoms are *outcomes* of institutional arrangements rather than indicators of the institutional arrangements themselves. The Gurr, Jaggers, and Moore (1990) Polity measures of democracy are less subject to this criticism, though not free of it. For example, Polity can rate countries as exhibiting significant constraints on executive discretion even if formal political checks and balances are absent. Since theories of democracy and growth focus on the formal institutions of democracy, the use of Polity data gives rise to problems of interpretation and endogeneity.

The second difficulty is the lack of clarity regarding the weights given to different institutions (competitive elections versus political checks and balances). In Polity IV, for example, researchers cannot ascertain the weight given to competitive elections in determining whether political participation is open, one criterion for democracy in Polity IV; or whether executive constraints are fixed by institutional checks and balances or by less formal limitations on executive discretion.

In response to these difficulties, Beck et al. (2001), in the Database of Political Institutions, separately code the competitiveness of legislative and executive elections using objective criteria (whether many parties compete, with no single party or candidate getting more than 75 percent of the vote). Using these data, beginning of period competitive elections explain growth in a 1975–2000 cross-section in Keefer (2004), but only after controlling for endogeneity. Przeworski et al. (2000) assemble data beginning in 1950 that characterize countries as democratic based on equally transparent criteria: leaders are competitively elected and have changed at least once (Boix and Rosato 2001 have extended this variable back to 1800). However, estimating the effects in a panel with country and year variation since 1950, they continue to find that democracies do not grow faster. Apparently, and anticlimactically, more accurate data does not seem to unravel the puzzle of democratic underperformance.

2.2 History, Democracy, and Growth

Acemoglu, Johnson, and Robinson (2002) and Boix (2003) explain the opaque relationship between democracy and growth by arguing that democracy is chosen only when the decisive actors believe it will make them better off. That depends, in turn, on their expectations about the effects of redistribution under democracy. These expectations are shaped by the inability of actors to make credible agreements regarding future redistribution. In Acemoglu, Johnson, and Robinson (2002), elites initially control the government and economy and confront a double-edged credibility dilemma. First, they cannot credibly promise to refrain from expropriating non-elites. Non-elites therefore do not invest and growth is slow. However, elites could potentially reap large income gains if they could offer non-elites democracy and secure property rights in exchange for a credible promise from non-elites to assign elites a sufficiently high share of the resulting income gains. However, a second credibility wedge undermines this contract: the disenfranchised cannot credibly promise to refrain from massive redistribution once they take power.

Elites therefore only accept democratization when the rents they earn under the status quo are sufficiently low that the costs of redistribution are low. Under these circumstances, we should observe democracy, secure property rights, and growth going together. When elite control is lucrative, however, we should observe none of these.

This logic actually deepens the puzzle of why growth and democracy are not strongly related, since it predicts that democracies should always grow faster. In complementary analyses, though, Acemoglu and Robinson (2001) and Rosendorf (2001) allow non-elites to threaten revolution. Under these circumstances, elites sometimes concede to political openness even when they would prefer not to. If inequality is low, this leads to the earlier outcome of democracy and growth. If inequality is moderately high, their concession leads to political instability and low growth. Redistribution in such democracies is high enough that it triggers political instability as elites rise up to engage in counter-revolutions. Here, democracy and growth do not necessarily go together and regime type oscillates.

These arguments imply that prior efforts to examine the effect of democracy on growth were biased towards finding no effect by not taking into account the conditions under which elites permit democracy in the first place. The problem is not, as in Przeworski and Limongi (1993) and many others, that redistribution offsets the security of property rights under democracy, but rather that some democracies are accepted more willingly by elites than others. In those that are not, revolution and counter-revolution, political instability, and relatively high rates of redistribution are observed. If one conflates the two types of democracies, one naturally biases downwards the estimated effect of democracy on growth.

Estimations in Acemoglu, Johnson, and Robinson (2002) account for the two types of democratization empirically. First, they examine former colonies, countries where elites, backed up by a colonial power, were most likely to control democratization and where democratization was therefore largely a function of elite rents rather than of revolutionary threats from non-elites. Second, they directly control for elite rents (which discourage democratization) using settler mortality. Settlers migrate to countries where mortality is high only if rents are sufficient to offset the high risk of death. These settlers had little incentive to develop institutions that would open up political and economic participation. They find that settler mortality explains the relationship between income and democracy, as one would expect if all three variables move together (Acemoglu et al. 2005).

Engerman and Sokoloff (2002) make similar arguments and offer more direct evidence of the actions that elites took to protect their rents, finding that those Latin American countries with conditions most favorable to mining and plantation agri-culture were slowest to enfranchise voters and to offer public education. These same countries were aggressive in adopting regulations that restricted entry of the non-elite into various economic activities. Their evidence is critical in making the case that democracy, property rights, and growth should all go together and are bound together by historical circumstance.

2.3 Equality, Distribution, and Unsuccessful Democracies: Anomalies in the Late Twentieth Century

The foregoing arguments, while successful in linking theoretically and empirically historical factors to the current growth experience of democracies, have a number of other implications that are not well supported in the data. In particular, the central theoretical explanation for the poor performance of democracies in this literature is high redistribution and political instability, rooted in inequality. However, the bulk of (imperfect) evidence does not indicate that poor democracies exhibit greater income inequality and high levels of redistribution.

Slow-growing, poor democracies *do* exhibit greater instability, consistent with the democracy literature. In their table 2.7, Przeworski, et al. (2000) show thirty transitions away from democracy from 1950 to 1990, of which twenty-six were in poor democracies. Evidence from the *Database of Political Institutions* is similar. The poorer half of all countries that had competitive elections in 1980 experienced thirteen transitions out of democracy over the succeeding twenty years; the richer half only one. However, redis-tribution from the rich elite to the poorer non-elites does not seem to drive this instability. On the contrary, the earlier evidence suggests that poor democracies have *smaller* governments and engage in less redistribution than either poor non-democracies or rich countries.

Even in the politics surrounding these regime changes, redistributive concerns are hard to detect. Most democracy theories predict that redistributive, left-leaning governments take over from elite-dominated, right-leaning governments. As Table 36.2 illustrates, in the ninety-one transitions from countries with non-competitive or no elections to countries with competitive elections since 1975, in only two cases was there a transition from a right-to a left-wing government. The transition to competitive elections actually resulted in right-wing governments in more cases (thirty-one) than left-wing governments (twenty-five). Similarly, in the thirty-six transitions from competitive to non-competitive electoral systems, we would expect right-leaning governments to replace left-leaning governments. However, in fewer than half the cases (sixteen) were left-wing governments in power in the year after transition, in only one case do the data suggest a transition from a left to a right wing government, but in ten cases (not reported), the transitions are coded as being from left-wing to left-wing governments.

As with instability, measured inequality (Gini coefficients) differences across regimes are consistent with the theory: poorer democracies appear to be significantly more unequal than richer democracies. However, measured inequality is only modestly higher (four points higher) among countries that have ever experienced regime change compared to those that have never experienced it, and even this difference disappears among poorer countries. In addition, Milanovic (2000) reminds us that social conflict over redistribution is driven by market inequality, income inequality net of government redistribution, and that pre- and post-redistribution Ginis can differ substantially. Most inequality measures in cross-country databases, such as the Gini indicators from the

Table 36.2 Ideology and regime change, 1975–2004

Total changes	From democracy to non-democracy	From non-democracy to democracy
1975–2004	36	91
To left	12	25
To right	4	31
From left	16	29
From right	8	21
Left to right	2	5
Right to left	1	2

Note: Information from the Database of Political Institutions (Beck et al. 2001). A country is democratic if executive and legislative elections are coded as most competitive (LIEC=EIEC=7), and non-democratic otherwise. Ideology comes from the DPI variable coding whether the largest government party is right, left, center, or non-ideological.

World Development Indicators, are post-redistribution. Since richer democracies redistribute much more, it is possible that poor and rich democracies have similar *market* inequality. The correct inequality data may tell us that successful democracies are *more* unequal than unsuccessful democracies. Nevertheless, the absence of an obvious association among low income per capita, democracy, inequality, redistribution, and political instability motivates a search for additional explanations of the policy choices and growth record of poor democracies.[10]

3 POLITICAL MARKET IMPERFECTIONS AND HETEROGENEOUS DEMOCRATIC PERFORMANCE

If inequality and the struggle over redistribution do not fully explain the performance differences observed among democracies and the lack of impact of democratic institutions on outcomes in poor countries, what else might? A useful starting point is the observation made earlier, that policy distortions generally benefit narrow interests at the expense of broad social interests. The resources for education and public investment that do not translate into better learning or infrastructure nevertheless do flow to the benefit of recipients of patronage appointments in education ministries or to well-connected contractors. Cronies can circumvent bureaucratic obstacles that obstruct the average entrepreneur and ensure that their contracts are enforced (and their contract violations allowed) even when most cannot.

An ample literature, starting with Olson's (1965) *Logic of Collective Action*, supports an emphasis on narrow interests in explaining heterogeneity in the performance of democracies. The first strong evidence of the role of domestic politics in development focused on the role of interest groups in the policy decisions of poor countries. Bates (1981, 1983) documents the role of narrow interests in the formation of destructive agricultural politics in some African countries, Frieden (1991) shows how the characteristics of interest groups influenced country responses to debt crisis, and the analysis of the economic interests of congressional districts is a staple methodology of the American politics empirical literature. The question for the democracy and development literature is why some democracies are more permeable to special interests (elites) than others.

One answer focuses on the dynamics of political competition and political market imperfections that prevent voters from holding politicians accountable for excessive favoritism towards narrow interests or their own, private interests. Keefer and Khemani (2005) emphasize two political market imperfections, the absence of political credibility

---

[10] The earlier discussion of policy similarities between poor democracies and non-democracies offers little support for the argument that conflict between elites and non-elites revolves around issues other than redistribution, such as regulation or access to public services.

and imperfect citizen information. Where voters cannot observe political actions that affect them, or where they cannot believe the promises of political competitors, electoral competition is less efficacious, and possibly useless, in preventing politicians from catering policies exclusively to the benefit of narrow interests or themselves.

The inability of elite and non-elite politicians to make credible commitments to each other is the fulcrum of the democracy and development literature. This literature assumes away other key imperfections, however: elite and non-elite politicians *can* make credible promises to members of the elite and non-elite, respectively, who in turn can perfectly observe the actions that "their" politicians take and how these actions affect their welfare. The quality of public policy in poor democracies—little better than, or worse than, the quality of policy in poor non-democracies—calls into question the validity of this latter assumption: non-elites seem entirely unable to demand high performance from non-elite politicians.

More generally, conveying credible promises, getting credit for constituent service, and mobilizing voters are challenges that vary significantly in difficulty across countries. Bringing the nuts and bolts of political competition into the political economy of development offers a useful avenue for explaining why many democracies do poorly and, potentially, why some autocracies do well.

3.1 The Policy Consequences of Low Pre-electoral (-selectoral) Credibility

The power of political credibility to explain heterogeneous policy choices across democracies, and the similarity of the policy choices of non-democratic and democratic poor countries, depends on how one believes that citizens and politicians react to the absence of political credibility. The literature offers three possibilities: politicians and voters can do nothing to resolve the problem of credibility; voters can at least coordinate on ex post performance thresholds to discipline non-credible politicians; or politicians can actually invest in and influence their credibility. The first two have received the most attention in the literature. The last, the subject of work by Keefer and Vlaicu (2005), explicitly recognizes that the lack of political credibility is a problem not only for citizens, but also for politicians who, unable to make credible promises to citizens, cannot easily mobilize support for their candidacies.

3.1.1 *The Consequences of Non-credibility when Politicians and Citizens are Helpless to Affect it*

If neither citizens nor politicians can do anything about the lack of political credibility, even fully enfranchised citizens have no leverage over political decision makers. Since their political competitors cannot credibly promise to do better, incumbent politicians are essentially immune from challenge. Political promises, including those to redistribute income and assets, are therefore irrelevant. Stark policy predictions emerge from this view of pre-electoral credibility: governments exhibit entirely expropriatory behavior, taxing as much as possible and diverting all of the proceeds to private purposes.

As rocky as the policy landscape is in poor countries, and as plausible the claim that political competitors are not credible to voters in many democracies, it is nevertheless rare to find elected governments that are entirely insensitive to the demands of voters. Money spent on education results in some student learning; most government revenues do not end up in the Swiss bank accounts of politicians. The assumption that politicians and voters can do *nothing* about the credibility problem is clearly too extreme.

3.1.2 *The Consequences of Non-credibility when Citizens can Coordinate on Voting Rules*

Ferejohn (1986) suggests that voters coordinate on performance thresholds. If incumbents fail to meet the threshold, voters replace them regardless of who the challenger is (since challengers are non-credible, anyway). When voters are successful in this effort, governments engage in less rent seeking. Persson and Tabellini (2000) extend the Ferejohn model to demonstrate how these ex post voting rules influence the provision of public and private goods. In all cases, though they improve citizen welfare, ex post voting rules have relatively modest effects on electoral accountability.

The conditions under which ex post voting rules can be implemented are stringent, particularly the requirement that voters coordinate on a performance threshold. Keefer (forthcoming) argues, for example, that voter coordination is easiest when policy failure is quickly manifested and voter perceptions of the consequences of failure are homogeneous. However, for other policies with more subtle effects, such as education, elections impose less stringent performance requirements on politicians. Hence, it is not surprising that poor democracies, where voters are more reliant on ex post voting rules, exhibit no better education outcomes than poor non-democracies. On the other hand, in the case of banking regulation, the results of policy failure—financial crisis—are observed by all voters in a short period of time, allowing for easier coordination of performance thresholds. Consistent with the greater efficacy of ex post voting rules under these circumstances, fiscal transfers to insolvent banks are substantially less in countries that exhibit competitive elections.

However, the policy differences between richer and poorer countries cannot be explained by the conjecture that poorer countries are more reliant on ex post accountability rules. In countries in which these rules are the main device to discipline politicians, Persson and Tabellini (2000) conclude that rent seeking or corruption should be high, public good provision should be mediocre (but positive), but that transfers to narrow groups of voters should be zero. The policy record of poor democracies is especially at odds with this last prediction. On the contrary, transfers to specific groups of voters dominate electoral competition in poorly performing democracies, as one can see from the intensity of spending on wages and public investment (pork barrel).

Direct observation of political behavior in poor democracies is similarly inconsistent with the prediction that delivering goods to narrow groups of voters is unimportant in low-credibility countries. Bratton and van de Walle (1997) characterize politics in democratized Africa as "neo-patrimonial" precisely to capture the intensity with which African politicians focus on the provision of goods to narrow interests. Wilder (1999) quotes former members of the Pakistani National Assembly from the state of Punjab as saying, "People now think that the job of an MNA and MPA is to fix their gutters, get their children enrolled in school, arrange for job transfers... [These tasks] consume your whole day" (1999, 196). "Look, we get elected because we are *ba asr log* [effective people] in our area. People vote for me because they perceive me as someone who can help them" (1999, 204).

3.1.3 *The Consequences of Non-credibility when Credibility is Endogenous*

Given the large electoral gains that the acquisition of credibility can engender, it would be remarkable if politicians did *not* invest in their credibility. Keefer and Vlaicu (2005) present a model that allows non-credible politicians to pursue either of two strategies to increase the share of the electorate that believes their promises. They can invest in building up a network of voters that believes their promises (for example, by building a machine for distributing benefits, distributing money at funerals, etc.). Or they can rely on the existing client networks of patrons, making promises to patrons who, in return, make promises to clients in exchange for their votes. Where politicians follow either of these strategies, we expect to see high corruption, *high* provision of targetable goods, and low provision of non-targetable goods—precisely what we observe in poor democracies.

The clientelism literature underlines how common each of these strategies is. Scott (1972) refers to Filipino politicians who insist on doing individual favors in order to create a personal obligation and describes the 1960 elections in Burma as a competition for patrons who controlled voting blocs, rather than for the voters themselves. Stokes (2005) amply documents the Peronist party machinery in Argentina, through which individual benefits were targeted to voters. Whichever course of action politicians pursue, however, they end up making appeals to narrow groups of voters who believe their promises. This raises their preference for private goods that benefit these narrow groups relative to public goods that benefit all citizens.

Ample indirect evidence supports the argument that politicians in poorer countries are less able to make broadly credible promises to citizens. First, broad redistributive promises should be less likely in countries where political credibility is limited. Consistent with this, the Database of Political Institutions (Beck et al. 2001) records whether countries can be categorized as economically right, left, or center, or as none of these. In 2000, 72 percent of the parties in forty-six poorer countries with competitive elections could be placed in one of these categories, one standard deviation less than the 92 percent in forty-eight richer countries. Keefer (2005b) also finds that the presence of programmatic parties is associated with lower corruption, lower targeted good provision, and higher non-targeted good provision, and parties in poor democracies are less likely to be programmatic. Second, one might expect that older parties have had more opportunity to develop policy reputations regarding redistribution. One indirect way to capture policy reputation is the age of a political party. DPI figures indicate that the average number of years that a party has existed under its current name in rich democracies is twice that in poorer, forty-seven years versus twenty-three.

Bueno de Mesquita et al. (2003) recognize, as well, that limits to credibility drive policy distortions. Their approach is the converse of the one in Keefer and Vlaicu (2005), however. They allow both incumbents and challengers to credibly promise a program of taxes and public goods to all voters, but allow politicians to make credible promises of private transfers only to groups with whom they have an exogenous affinity. This gives rise to an incumbent advantage and a bias towards the inefficient provision of private goods (to these voters). Robinson and Torvik (2002) make the more plausible assumption, in a developing country context, that no politicians can make credible promises to voters. However, they also assume an exogenously given affinity that permits incumbents to make credible promises to a subset of voters, again giving rise to policy distortions.

While affinity matters in many settings, such as ethnically charged electoral climates, it is less easy to ascribe broad differences in policy performance between rich and poor countries to cross-country variation in these affinities. At the same time, as Keefer and Vlaicu (2005) argue, many of the strategies that politicians use to mobilize support are related precisely to the objective of improving the credibility of their promises to voters. Relaxing the assumption that political credibility is exogenous is necessary both to incorporate these political activities into the analysis of political competition and to generate policy predictions that are more fully consistent with observed outcomes.

4 Credibility, Democratization, and the Role of History

The evidence is persuasive that politicians in poor democracies are less able to make broadly credible promises. The policies they pursue are also consistent with a particular response to the lack of credibility: appeals to patrons and to narrow groups of voters. The credibility arguments are not only relevant to economic development, however, but also to political development and democratization. On the one hand, politicians in young democracies are on average less able to make broadly credible promises to citizens, stunting the democratization process. However, new democracies endowed with broadly credible political competitors or social structures that make political appeals to patrons relatively costly are likely to have an advantage.

Keefer (2005a) presents ample evidence that young democracies pursue policies consistent with lower levels of political credibility: greater rent seeking, more provision of targeted goods, and less provision of non-targeted goods. The more years that countries exhibit continuous elections, the greater are secondary school enrollment, the rule of law, and bureaucratic quality (non-targeted goods); the fewer are restrictions on public access to information (state ownership of newspapers, where information is a non-targeted good); the less is corruption; and the lower are the public sector wage bill and public investment, expenditures that are most easily targeted to narrow constituencies. Keefer (2004) and Persson and Tabellini (2006) also find, using different measures of democracy, different measures of accumulated democratic experience, and different time periods, that the age of democracy is a key explanatory variable for growth.[11]

The key question is whether and how young democracies consolidate. Keefer and Vlaicu (2005) show that in the absence of patrons, political competition drives politicians to invest increasingly in their own credibility, expanding the fraction of voters that believe their promises and increasing political incentives to provide non-targeted goods that benefit all citizens. However, this process is not inevitable: historical legacies, different from those emphasized in the democracy and development literature reviewed earlier, can stand in the way.

In countries where social structures make appeals to patrons relatively cheap, politicians in new democracies prefer to rely on patrons rather than to invest in their own reputation with voters. Bratton and van de Walle (1997), for example, highlight the importance of the political legacy of patrimonialism in their discussion of the emergence of democracy in Africa. A political development trap is then more likely than a virtuous circle. Patrons have no interest in non-targeted goods since it is difficult for them to convince clients that their own intervention was the key to the provision of the goods. Politicians who appeal to patrons therefore not only refrain from expanding the fraction of voters that believe their promises, they also do not provide public goods. These regimes are more likely to end early, since the lower quality of government and lack of credibility reduce citizen opposition to regime overthrow. Hence, non-credible democracies are more likely to be young.

Another possible legacy is the existence of programmatic political competitors. As Keefer and Vlaicu (2005) observe, at the time that countries such as Great Britain moved to adopt a universal franchise and competitive elections, political competitors with well-established programmatic stances already existed. In others, such as the Dominican Republic, the pre-democratic regime ruthlessly suppressed the emergence of such programmatic tendencies. Keefer (2005b) also shows that most of the countries that exhibit programmatic parties at any time during the period investigated already

---

[11] Persson and Tabellini 2006 use these findings to argue that the age of democracy increases democratic capital, the value citizens attach to democracy. Citizens are more likely to defend democracy the greater are its economic benefits; firms are more productive under democracy, but invest more only if they are confident that the democracy is stable. Hence, the more lasting is democracy, the faster is growth. The credibility arguments advanced here reach the same conclusion, but offer a more direct explanation of the policy differences between younger and older democracies.

had programmatic parties at the beginning of the period. Again, a historical legacy, this time of programmatic parties, influenced subsequent political and economic development.

5 CREDIBILITY AND PUZZLES IN THE DEMOCRACY LITERATURE

The role of credibility described here illuminates three puzzles in the democracy literature. The first is the absence of redistribution in poor democracies. In Acemoglu and Robinson (2006), for example, collective action by non-elites drives forward both democratization and pressures for redistribution. However, collective action is most likely when credible political entities exist to represent the interests of non-elites (and elites). Societies permeated by clientelism are unlikely to exhibit such collective action. In the event that they democratize, political pressures for redistribution are likely to be correspondingly weak.

Second, regime instability among poor democracies is high, but unrelated to redistributive conflict between the rich and poor. Neither is surprising when one takes into account that political competition in clientelist democracies revolves around the allocation of resources to narrow groups of voters. Fairly elected but non-credible politicians have few incentives to institute policies in the public interest. Indeed, in their emphasis on private goods directed at narrow interests, the policies of these governments resemble the crony policies of many non-democracies. Citizens, therefore, have fewer incentives to rise up to defend such democracies from regime threats and may be more susceptible to the promises of non-democratic challenger (Keefer 2006).

Third, the literature has not resolved whether democratization is driven by intra-elite or elite–non-elite conflict. Acemoglu and Robinson (2006), consistent with many others (e.g. Dahl 1971), argue that conflict between elites and non-elites drives democratization; Collier (1999) and others maintain that democratization is the product of conflict between elite groups, some of which see enfranchisement as advantageous in achieving their own interests. As Robinson (forthcoming) points out, these are analytically similar, since both predict that between-group conflict over policy drives institutional change. Political market imperfections explain why the two cases could also be hard to distinguish in practice. Both the efforts of elites to recruit non-elites, as in Collier (1999), and the efforts of non-elite leaders to form non-elite citizen coalitions, as in Dahl (1971), may run aground on the shoals of non-credibility. In those cases where these efforts fail, democratization could be quite distant from an enterprise that has engaged the masses and institutional change may indeed look like the product of conflict between small groups.

7 THE OTHER POLITICAL MARKET IMPERFECTION: INCOMPLETE INFORMATION

A substantial literature identifies significant development effects from incomplete citizen information, the other key political market imperfection to which the discussion in this essay gives short shrift. In many ways, however, the foregoing discussion applies equally to information, since the key effect of incomplete information is to prevent citizens from verifying whether politicians have fulfilled their promises. Absent verifiability, promises are empty.[12] The presence of uninformed voters distorts political decision making in at least two ways. First, politicians expend resources to sway uninformed voters, obligating themselves to special interests in the process (Grossman and Helpman 1996). Second, politicians simply ignore uninformed voters and are more corrupt (Adserà, Boix, and Payne 2003) or less apt to extend access to government programs (Besley and Burgess 2002; Strömberg 2004).

The earlier credibility discussion is relevant as well because citizen information is directly susceptible to government influence. Governments can place restraints on the press or on journalistic access to state secrets, they can favor supporters in allocating rights to media ownership, and they can censor. They can also simply own the media. This turns out to be important because in much of the research in this area, scholars have used newspaper circulation as a proxy for voter information. Newspaper circulation is certainly relevant for development: in 1995, among countries that hold competitive elections, newspaper circulation was much higher in richer than in poorer countries. However, Keefer (2005a) shows that newspaper circulation is much lower in countries in which the market share of government newspapers is higher.

The connection between the measurement of information and the earlier credibility discussion is immediate. Information is a public good. Like all public goods, therefore, it is least likely to be provided (or most likely to be restricted) when political competitors are unable to make credible promises to voters. If this is the case, newspaper circulation may capture the latent credibility of pre-electoral political promises in addition to, or instead of, exogenous variation across countries and over time in voter information. Consistent with this, Keefer (2005a) points to evidence that the negative effects of newspaper circulation on targeted expenditures of government (such as government wages) are exactly what one would predict if newspaper circulation reflected government efforts to influence access to information.

---

[12] Stokes (2001) analyzes the contrasting case in which politicians with better information than voters promise voters what voters believe is good for them, renege on their promises, and pursue policies that politicians believe are better for the voters. They suffer no negative electoral consequences because voters can verify that politicians acted in their interests.

8 CONCLUSION

After decades of research, the theme of democracy and economic development remains as important a topic of investigation as ever. The literature now has rich explanations for why some countries democratize and others do not; why democracy is associated with rapid economic development in some countries and not in others; why policy choices favor development in some democracies and not others—that is, why non-elites often fail to benefit from the policies of elected governments.

The conclusion of this essay is that the problem of credible commitment is at the core of each of these advances, but the precise role of commitment differs. The democracy and development literature points to the inability of elites and non-elites to make credible agreements with each other in order to explain why some countries have successfully democratized. These same arguments do not explain as easily performance variation among democracies. Poorly performing democracies do not seem to exhibit the inequality, redistributive tendencies, and conflict over redistribution between elites and non-elites that this literature predicts.

Other arguments, focusing on the credibility of promises from politicians to supporters (e.g., from the leaders of non-elites to the non-elite), can fill this gap: poor performance emerges in some democracies not because the conflict between elites and non-elites is more difficult to resolve, but because political competitors are unable to make credible promises to voters in the first place. History matters for this story of democratization as well, since democracies differ significantly in the extent to which they enjoy a legacy of political competitors able to make credible policy commitments to voters, or of patrimonialism that makes politicians reluctant to build up broad credibility with voters. This in turn links back to the literature focused on elites and non-elites, since it is precisely when political competitors can make credible policy commitments that we expect non-elites to be able to act collectively to force elites to give up power. Better understanding these historical links between political credibility and successful democratization is crucial to improving the success of contemporary efforts by wealthy democracies to deepen democratization among the world's poor countries.

REFERENCES

ACEMOGLU, D., and ROBINSON, J. A. 2006. *Economic Origins of Dictatorship and Democracy.* New York: Cambridge University Press.
—— 2001. A theory of political transitions. *American Economic Review,* 91 (4): 938–63.
—— JOHNSON, S., and ROBINSON, J. 2002. Reversal of fortune: geography and institutions in the making of the modern world income distribution. *Quarterly Journal of Economics,* 117 (4): 1231–94.
—— —— —— and YARED, P. 2005. Income and democracy. Mimeo. Department of Economics, Massachusetts Institute of Technology.

Adserà, A., Boix, C., and Payne, M. 2003. Are you being served? Political accountability and governmental performance. *Journal of Law, Economics and Organization*, 19: 445–90.

Banks, A. S. 1971. *Cross-Polity Time Series Data*. Cambridge, Mass.: MIT Press.

Bates, R. H. 1981. *Markets and States in Tropical Africa: The Political Basis of Agricultural Policies*. Berkeley and Los Angeles: University of California Press.

—— 1983. *Essays on the Political Economy of Rural Africa*. Cambridge: Cambridge University Press.

Beck, T., Clarke, G., Groff, A., Keefer, P., and Walsh, P. 2001. New tools in comparative political economy: the database of political institutions. *World Bank Economic Review*, 15 (1): 165–76.

Besley, T., and Burgess, R. 2002. The political economy of government responsiveness: theory and evidence from India. *Quarterly Journal of Economics*, 117 (4): 1415–51.

Boix, C. 2003. *Democracy and Redistribution*. New York: Cambridge University Press.

—— and Rosato, S. 2001. A complete data set of political regimes, 1800–1999. Mimeo. University of Chicago.

Bollen, K. 1993. Liberal democracy: validity and method factors in cross-national measures. *American Journal of Political Science*, 37 (4): 1207–30.

Bratton, M., and van de Walle, N. 1997. *Democratic Experiments in Africa: Regime Transitions in Comparative Perspective*. Cambridge: Cambridge University Press.

Bueno de Mesquita, B., Morrow, J., Siverson, R., and Smith, A. 2003. *The Logic of Political Survival*. Cambridge, Mass.: MIT Press.

Collier, R. B. 1999. *Paths Towards Democracy: The Working Class and Elites in Western Europe and South America*. New York: Cambridge University Press.

Dahl, R. 1971. *Polyarchy: Participation and Opposition*. New Haven: Yale University Press.

Easterly, W., and Servén, L. 2004. *The Limits of Stabilization: Infrastructure, Public Deficits and Growth in Latin America*. Stanford, Calif.: Stanford University Press.

Engerman, S., and Sokoloff, K. 2002. Factor endowments, inequality, and paths of development among New World economies. *Economia*, 3 (1): 41–88.

Feng, Y. 2003. *Democracy, Governance, and Economic Performance: Theory and Evidence*. Cambridge, Mass.: MIT Press.

Ferejohn, J. 1986. Incumbent performance and electoral control. *Public Choice*, 50: 5–26.

Foster, A., and Rosenzweig, M. 1996. Technical change and human-capital returns and investments: evidence from the green revolution. *American Economic Review*, 86 (4): 931–53.

Frieden, J. A. 1991. *Debt, Development and Democracy*. Princeton: Princeton University Press.

Gastil, R. 1988. *Freedom in the World: Political Rights and Civil Liberties 1987–88*. New York: Freedom House.

Grossman, G., and Helpman, E. 1996. Electoral competition and special interest politics. *Review of Economic Studies*, 63: 265–86.

Gurr, T. R., Jaggers, K., and Moore, W. H. 1990. The transformation of the western state: the growth of democracy, autocracy, and state power since 1800. *Studies in Comparative International Development*, 25: 73–108.

Keefer, P. 2004. All democracies are not the same: identifying whether institutions matter for growth. Paper presented at American Economic Association meetings.

—— 2005a. Clientelism, credibility and the policy choices of young democracies. Mimeo. Development Research Group, World Bank.

—— 2005b. Programmatic parties: where do they come from and do they matter? Paper presented at the 2005 meetings of the International Society for New Institutional Economics, Barcelona.

—— 2006. Insurgency and credible commitment in autocracies and democracies. Mimeo. World Bank Development Research Group.

—— Forthcoming. Elections, special interests and financial crisis. *International Organization*.

—— and KHEMANI, S. 2005. Democracy, public expenditures, and the poor: understanding political incentives for providing public services. *World Bank Research Observer*, 20 (1): 1–28.

—— and KNACK, S. 1997. Why don't poor countries catch up? A cross-national test of an institutional explanation. *Economic Inquiry*, 35: 590–602.

—— —— 1998. Political stability and economic stagnation. Pp. 136–53 in *The Political Dimension of Economic Growth: Proceedings of the IEA Conference Held in San Jose, Costa Rica*, ed. S. Borner and M. Paldam. New York: St Martin's Press.

—— —— 2002. Polarization, politics and property rights: links between inequality and growth. *Public Choice*, 111: 127–54.

—— and VLAICU, R. 2005. Clientelism, credibility and democracy. Mimeo. Development Research Group, World Bank.

MILANOVIC, B. 2000. The median voter hypothesis, income inequality and income redistribution: an empirical test with the required data. *European Journal of Political Economy*, 16 (3): 367–410.

MULLIGAN, C., GIL, R., and SALA-I-MARTIN, X. 2004. Do democracies have different public policies than non-democracies? *Journal of Economic Perspectives*, 18 (1): 51–74.

NORTH, D. and WEINGAST, B. 1989. Constitutions and commitment: the evolution of institutions governing public choice in seventeenth-century England. *Journal of Economic History*, 49: 803–32.

OLSON, M. 1965. *The Logic of Collective Action: Public Goods and the Theory of Groups*. Cambridge, Mass.: Harvard University Press.

PERSSON, T., and TABELLINI, G. 2000. *Political Economics: Explaining Public Policy*. Cambridge, Mass.: MIT Press.

—— —— 2006. Democratic capital: the nexus of political and economic change. NBER Working Paper W12175.

PRITCHETT, L. 1991. Measuring outward orientation in developing countries: can it be done? Policy, research and external affairs working papers, WPS 566, World Bank.

PRZEWORSKI, A., and LIMONGI, F. 1993. Political regimes and economic growth. *Journal of Economic Perspectives*, 7 (3): 51–70.

—— ALVAREZ, M. E., CHEIBUB, J. A., and LIMONGI, F. 2000. *Democracy and Development: Political Institutions and Well-Being in the World, 1950–1990*. Cambridge: Cambridge University Press.

ROBINSON, J. A. Forthcoming. Economic development and democracy: a perspective on recent research. *Annual Review of Political Science*.

—— and TORVIK, R. 2002. White elephants. CEPR Working Paper 3459.

ROSENDORF, B. P. 2001. Choosing democracy. *Economics and Politics*, 13: 1–29.

SCOTT, J. C. 1972. Patron–client politics and political change in Southeast Asia. *American Political Science Review*, 66 (1): 91–113.

STASAVAGE, D. 2003. *Public Debt and the Birth of the Democratic State: France and Great Britain 1688–1789*. New York: Cambridge University Press.

STOKES, S. 2001. *Mandates and Democracy: Neoliberalism by Surprise in Latin America*. New York: Cambridge University Press

—— 2005. Perverse accountability: a formal model of machine politics with evidence from Argentina. *American Political Science Review*, 99 (3): 315–25.

STRÖMBERG, D. 2004. Radio's impact on public spending. *Quarterly Journal of Economics*, 119 (1): 189–221.

SVENSSON, J. 1998. Investment, property rights and political instability: theory and evidence. *European Economic Review*, 42: 1317–42.

WILDER, A. 1999. *The Pakistani Voter: Electoral Politics and Voting Behavior in the Punjab*. Karachi: Oxford University Press.

ZAGHA, N. R. 2005. *Economic Growth in the 1990s: Learning from a Decade of Reform*. Washington, DC: World Bank.

CHAPTER 37

....

ACCOUNTABILITY
AND THE
SURVIVAL OF
GOVERNMENTS

....

JOSÉ MARÍA MARAVALL

1 INTRODUCTION

....

A GOVERNMENT is accountable when citizens can hold it responsible for its actions and, consequently, punish or reward it with their vote at election time. This is the core argument of why democracy may induce representation: governments can lose elections because they are accountable to citizens. The people rules because it can throw incumbents out of office if their performance does not satisfy criteria for re-election set by citizens. Electoral rewards and punishments do not take place at random: they reflect a retrospective judgement of the government by citizens at the polls. And it is the reaction of voters at election time that may ensure democratic representation when politicians anticipate such reaction and look after the interests of citizens, rather than their own, in order to survive in office.

This is, in a nutshell, what democratic accountability is about. It is a judgement of past actions of politicians, not of what the future holds. Government by the people consists only of this retrospective control of incumbents by voters every four or five

* Besides Carles Boix and Susan Stokes, I wish to thank several people for their comments on an earlier draft: Ignacio Urquizu, Andrew Richards, Sonia Alonso, Sandra León, and Henar Criado. Braulio Gómez provided competent research assistance with the dataset. I am particularly grateful to Alberto Penadés, Adam Przeworski, and Ignacio Sánchez-Cuenca for their help with this chapter.

years. This control is vertical: a relationship between agent and principal, incumbent and voters, in which elections instil in politicians, in Madison's words (1961, 352), "an habitual recollection of their dependence on the people." And as many years later Key (1966, 10) remarked, "the fear of loss of popular support powerfully disciplines the actions of governments."

This view of democracy and elections has been adopted by mainstream political science because it appears to avoid important shortcomings of alternative views on how can voters control politicians. It has thus been argued that if elections were a prospective selection of the best candidate, invested thereafter with a mandate to implement a set of policies, voters would lack any subsequent control over the selected candidate. Manin (1995, 209–14) has described how, since the end of the eighteenth century, instruments which could have made this control possible were rejected by the "founding fathers" of modern democracies: imperative mandates, binding instructions, or the immediate dismissal of representatives. Besides, post-war empirical democratic theory invalidated idealized conceptions of the democratic citizen: endless survey data showed the incidence of extended political apathy, mistrust of politicians, and powerlessness, rather than information and participation. These citizens did not vote with a sound knowledge of candidates and programs: their vote was rather the result of ideological, partisan, or class inertias. And if voters did not have good information about politics nor cared much about it, the easiest way to control incumbents was retrospective. In Riker's terms (1982, 244), "all elections do or have to do is to permit people to get rid of rulers." Instead of carefully selecting the best candidate and closely monitoring his subsequent performance in office, voters simply look back at election time and reward or punish the incumbent according to whether things have improved or not since the last election. Because incumbents fear the future verdict of citizens and want to survive in office, they do what citizens would have done had they had the same information. This is what Friedrich (1963, 199–215) called "the law of anticipated reactions."

This view of elections based on the accountability of governments is unsatisfactory in many respects. For one thing, citizens ignore the future in strictly retrospective voting: their decision is not about who is to govern them. But citizens do not just stand looking backwards, turned into pillars of salt like Lot's wife: this view does not represent well what elections are about. For another, as has repeatedly been argued (Przeworski 2003, 156–7; Manin, Przeworski, and Stokes 1999, 10–16), voters need considerable information in order to be able to attribute responsibility for past outcomes. And finally, much of the punishing is not done by voters, but by politicians. As Cheibub and Przeworski (1999, 231–5) have shown, of 310 peaceful changes of prime ministers between 1950 and 1990, 148 (48 percent) were due not to punishment by voters, but to decisions of politicians—either from the same party or from the ruling coalition. These prime ministers should have feared the intrigues of their fellow politicians just as much as the judgement of voters. Of course, it could well happen that politicians dismiss prime ministers because they simply anticipate the future verdict of voters: if this were the case, they would only act as an additional instrument to enforce accountability. But if the criteria of politicians and voters do not coincide, political survival will not only depend on the will of the people, and the incentives for an incumbent to be representative will disappear. This is the main theoretical point of the chapter, and I shall explore it with evidence on the survival of prime ministers in twenty-three parliamentary democracies,[1] from around 1945 to 2003, with 1,109 country-year observations.

2 ELECTIONS AND THE RETROSPECTIVE CONTROL OF POLITICIANS

Elections and democracy work like this. (1) Politicians compete, transmitting prospective messages about their future policies and signals about their competence. (2) Voters select those candidates closer to their ideal policy positions and more able to implement their program. (3) Politicians, once in office, adopt policies and dedicate effort to carry them through. (4) Policies and effort, under particular exogenous conditions, produce outcomes that modify the welfare of citizens. (5) At the time of the next election, voters assess retrospectively such outcomes, and attribute them to the policies and the effort of the incumbent and to the influence of exogenous conditions. (6) Voters update their preferences about policies and candidates. (7) Voters re-elect or reject the incumbent. Elections, thus, both select and assess. Citizens make a decision over their future (who is to govern them), and over their past (re-electing or getting rid of the incumbent). Madison stressed both: what elections did was "first to obtain for rulers men who possess most wisdom to discern, and most virtue to pursue, the common good of the society; and in the next place, to take the most effectual precautions for keeping them virtuous while they continue to hold their public trust" (Madison 1961, 350).

I shall discuss the second aspect of elections: whether they serve for the retrospective control of governments. That elections are just about rewarding or punishing the incumbent government was particularly emphasized by Key, who stated that the electorate was simply an "appraiser of past events, past performance, and past actions" (1966, 61). The initial model of accountability situated voters in a world of perfect information, where they knew everything at election time. Politicians had a finite horizon, so that in their final period in office incumbents were not constrained by future elections (Barro 1973). The basic problem in Barro's model was whether elections have a disciplining effect on the provision of a public good financed by taxation by a self-interested incumbent. If the prospect of re-election does not exist, politicians will choose a level of provision higher than what the representative voter

---

[1] The countries are Australia, Austria, Belgium, Canada, Denmark, Finland, France, Germany, Greece, Iceland, Ireland, Israel, Italy, Japan, Luxembourg, the Netherlands, New Zealand, Norway, Portugal, Spain, Sweden, Turkey, and United Kingdom.

would choose as optimal. With repeated elections, on the contrary, voters set a level that, if provided, leads to the re-election of the government. Otherwise, the government falls. Such a level, however, must be high enough to ensure that the incumbent does not follow its preferred alternative—which would be the outcome if losing office is not costly. The level eventually chosen by voters depends on the length of the mandate; the value of re-election for the incumbent; the rate at which the future is discounted; the difference between rents in and out of power.

Contrary to other forms of delegation, elected politicians are not offered ex ante an explicit incentive scheme in which well-defined payoffs are related to actions in the different states of the world. Rewards and punishments are ex post: in the next election, voters decide whether to continue or not delegating authority to the present incumbent. If the incumbent does not heavily discount the value of holding office in the future, it will restrain itself and look after the voters' interests. The control of the government by voters does not exist between elections.

Under conditions of perfect information, the democratic control of governments depends mostly on this intertemporal tradeoff by politicians. It will exist if incumbent politicians prefer to limit their rents today and be re-elected, rather than to maximize their rents today and be sacked in the next elections. Voters also make tradeoffs: only if they allow some rents to the incumbent will the participation constraint be overcome. Re-election depends on a voting rule: if an end-of-period welfare is achieved, the incumbent will continue in office. It will be replaced otherwise. This end-of-period welfare depends on the policies of the government and on exogenous conditions beyond its control. Perfectly informed citizens know how to assess the responsibility of the government for the outcomes, and politicians know what is required of them.

If citizens are unable to assign responsibility for changes in their welfare, elections can hardly serve to control incumbents: bad governments may survive elections and competent governments may be thrown out of office. Voters will not know actions of the government, whether what it does is in their interest or not, whether changes in their welfare are due to policies. If electoral pledges are broken voters will not know whether this is due to changed external conditions or to rent seeking. Voters can also be manipulated by politicians: the vote is a blunt instrument to reward or punish performance in a multidimensional policy space and, if distributional differences exist within the electorate, these may be played off by the incumbent.

A principal–agent framework with imperfect information has been used by Ferejohn (1986) to model a purely retrospective electoral control of governments. Incumbent politicians have an infinite horizon: there is thus no last period in which elections have no disciplining effect. The model considers only "moral hazard:" what system of incentives may prevent shirking with retrospective assessments of past performance. Voters want to maximize their welfare, and establish a threshold (κ) in their welfare as their voting rule. This threshold must be high enough to stimulate costly effort by the incumbent, but not so high that he will anticipate defeat and not supply effort. Such end-of-period welfare depends upon the effort of the government (ϵ), and upon random exogenous conditions (θ) beyond its control.

Such conditions can be represented as a probability distribution. So, the utility of voters is $\cup_v(\epsilon,\theta) = \epsilon\theta$. With incomplete information, voters cannot observe this effort nor the exogenous conditions; they are aware only of the outcome, which is the result of both θ and ϵ. Because the model is strictly retrospective, it excludes the selection of candidates as an instrument of democratic control, and therefore assumes that no differences in competence or ideology exist between "good" and "bad" politicians. Policy differences do not matter, only the effort carried out by the incumbent does. The opposition plays no active role: it is simply a clone of the incumbent. As Ferejohn (1986, 14) puts it, "the importance of challengers lies entirely in their availability. It is the existence of willing office-seekers that gives the voter whatever leverage he has on the incumbent."

The value of office (politicians wanting to be re-elected or to replace the incumbent) is what facilitates the democratic control of politicians and induces representation. If β represents the value of holding office, the incumbent's utility is $\cup^{in}(\epsilon) = \beta - \epsilon$. And $\cup^{out}(\epsilon) = 0$ is the utility out of office. To quote Ferejohn (1986, 19):

Voters have more control over officeholders when the value of office is relatively high and when the future is less heavily discounted.... An increase in the value of office can be expected not only to cost something but also to increase the level of competition for office among non-incumbents.

It is because incumbents want to be re-elected that they "try to anticipate performance-oriented voting in their choice of policies while in office" (Ferejohn 1986, 7). If is the discount rate, the incumbent will carry out effort κ/ϵ if, and only if, $\beta - \kappa/\epsilon + \delta\cup^{in} > \beta + \delta\cup^{out}$. Ferejohn concludes that, in equilibrium, the optimal threshold for re-election that maximizes voters' expected utility is $\kappa = \delta(\cup^{in} - \cup^{out})/2$. And the government will supply the effort needed for re-election when the value of exogenous conditions (θ) is greater than the value of the threshold (κ) divided by the discounted values of being in office rather than out of it. That is, when $\theta > \kappa/\delta(\cup^{in} - \cup^{out})$. If we replace κ, then $\theta > \delta\frac{\cup^{in} - \cup^{out}}{2}/\delta(\cup^{in} - \cup^{out})$, or otherwise $\theta > 1/2$. Thus, the incumbent will make the minimum necessary effort required to achieve κ when the external conditions θ are greater than 0.5 in a distribution between 0 and 1. At election time, voters assess whether the end-of-period threshold κ has been achieved or not, and consequently decide whether to keep the incumbent or throw him out.

A heterogeneous electorate can be manipulated by an incumbent. When voters have different preferences on the distribution of welfare, a government can target benefits to specific groups; while voters compete for this allocation, the government can play off these groups against one another. Suppose that there are N voters, and that each of them cares not about the aggregate outcome ($\theta\epsilon$), but about his personal welfare v_i (the sum of $v_i \ldots v_n$ equals $\theta\epsilon$). He then sets a personal welfare threshold κ_i, and votes for the government if $v_i \geq \kappa_i$. The incumbent will then distribute $\theta\epsilon$ so as to create a bare majority of voters to ensure re-election, minimizing the sum of benefits to the members of this majority; the rest of the electorate will be ignored. Any member of the minority has therefore an incentive to accept $v_i < \kappa_i$, and join the majority; otherwise he receives nothing. Eventually, every voter will downbid one another, until $\kappa_i = 0$ for all of them. The effort of the incumbent will be reduced to $\epsilon = 0$ in the limit. Thus a government will not be controlled if voters are egocentric; but only if κ is set according to criteria of aggregate welfare.

The assumptions of this strictly retrospective model are very demanding, and subsequent models have modified them in several ways. One example is Austen-Smith and Banks (1989), who introduce electoral promises in the mechanisms of accountability—not just effort, exogenous conditions, and outcomes. Theirs is a spatial voting model with two periods of office, two candidates, and a homogeneous electorate facing a problem of moral hazard. It is also a model of strict accountability, so no selection is involved: all politicians are supposed to be identical in every relevant aspect. The opposition is again a clone of the government: they are both pure office seekers, with no policy preferences. There are no term limits either: the incumbent may go on running for office. Thus, in equilibrium, voters will be indifferent between the two candidates in every election. Voters, on the contrary, are policy oriented, care about future outcomes, and want to influence the decisions of the incumbent with a retrospective voting strategy. As Austen-Smith and Banks (1989, 122) put it, "Voters in any election will attempt to deduce which of the candidates seeking office would exert the preferred amount of effort, where this preference is induced by voters' underlying preferences over policy outcomes."

End-of-term outcomes do not depend on ex ante electoral promises. But in elections the two candidates offer programs, and the result of the first election entirely depends on the program offered by the candidates (χ_{11}, χ_{12}). The new incumbent then chooses an amount of effort (ϵ), which is unobservable by voters. The legislative outcome for the first period of office is the result of effort and a random exogenous variable $(\lambda_t = \epsilon_t + \theta_t)$. Voters' retrospective strategy for controlling the government is solved backwards with sub-game perfect Nash equilibria for each period. Voters set a voting rule $\kappa(\chi)$ for the second election, which depends on how close the first-period outcome is to the initial electoral program. That is, because voters care about the credibility of electoral promises, their retrospective voting strategy is conditional on the difference between the incumbent's performance and such initial policy promises. So when candidates draft their programs for the first election anticipating this voting rule $\kappa(\chi)$, they are aware of the effort they will have to offer if they want to be re-elected. Retrospective voting in the second election ensures that voters maximize their payoffs after the first election, and render promises in electoral campaigns credible.

Another example is Persson, Roland, and Tabellini (1997), who introduce two agents, rather than one, that care about future elections: government (G) and parliament (L). Both extract rents, unobservable by voters (r_g = rents of the government; r_l = rents of the legislature). A conflict of interests exists between G and L because r_g and r_l are a zero-sum game. Voters may or may not observe the state of the world (θ), but know their consumption of public goods (c). They vote retrospectively, setting a threshold for re-election (κ) on the basis of θ if informed and of c otherwise. With separation of powers and checks and balances, G and L have separate responsibilities for the successive phases of decision making over policy, but the final decision requires the agreement of both G and L. Otherwise the status quo persists. The model uses the budget as an example: G and L must agree over its global size and its internal composition (what proportions go to r_g, r_l, and c). Because there is a distributive conflict between G and L, and the final decisions require the agreement of both (or else the status quo persists), in equilibrium the weaker agent will reveal information to voters about θ. As a consequence, voters will set the threshold κ not just on c (the consumption of public goods) but on θ; no rents from asymmetrical information will be extracted; and both G and L will be re-elected. One problem with the model is that it depends on the government and the legislature not colluding, and on the absence of parties that link the two agents.

3 SOME EMPIRICAL EVIDENCE

Retrospective models of elections have influenced a vast number of empirical studies on economic voting and political business cycles: it is because incumbents anticipate the electoral reactions to the economy that they manipulate the growth and employment rates. And voters must react to changes in economic conditions if a government is to be considered accountable. In Ferejohn's (1986, 7) words, "the performance of the economy has a major effect on the electoral fate of the incumbent executive." If the economic outcomes are good, governments would be re-elected; if the results are poor, they would lose the elections. Kiewiet and Rivers (1985, 225) thus claimed that "the proposition that voters will punish incumbents for poor performance should not be controversial." And for governments to be controlled, individual voting should be sociotropic, not egocentric—i.e. respond to general economic conditions.

A considerable amount of empirical evidence appears to support both hypotheses. Both aggregate and individual data have shown that the electoral support of governments suffers when past economic performance has been bad (see for instance Kramer 1971; Shaffers and Chressantis 1991; Lanoue 1994; Monardi 1994; Svoda 1995). And individual survey data also indicate that citizens vote according to general economic conditions, rather than to their own. But research on economic voting is not conclusive: it is not clear at all that citizens assess the past and do not think about the future when they vote; and, more generally, that good or bad economic performance is related to the electoral fate of a government.

Retrospective voting is what Fiorina expected to find in his study of national elections in the USA: "elections do not signal the direction in which society should move so much as they convey an evaluation of where society has been" (1981, 6). However, congressional and presidential elections between 1952 and 1976 showed that future expectations, and not just retrospective assessments, have a direct influence on the decisions of voters. This mixed pattern of voting is also what Lewis-Beck (1988) found in the USA as well as in Great Britain, Spain, the German Federal Republic, France, and Italy. Economic voting did indeed exist: voters' views on the economy influenced their support for the government. But such views were also about the future, not just the past. Both Fiorina and Lewis-Beck considered, however, that voters' expectations about future economic conditions were simply extrapolations from the past: "retrospective judgements have direct impact on the formation of future expectations" (Fiorina 1981, 200). This belief that retrospection influenced prospective voting was shared by many studies of economic voting (Uslaner 1989; Bratton 1994; Keech 1995).

Other studies, however, provided contrary evidence. Some concluded that voting mostly depended on expectations about the performance of the economy, rather than on the past (Kuklinski and West 1981; Lewis-Beck and Skalaban 1989; Lockerbie 1992; MacKuen, Erikson, and Stimson 1992; Price and Sanders 1995). Others have questioned the very existence of economic voting. Paldam (1991, 9) has noted the inconsistency of comparative empirical evidence: electoral rewards and punishments exist in some countries, not in others. Powell and Whitten (1993), studying 102 elections in nineteen countries between 1969 and 1988, have found that economic growth, inflation, and unemployment have no effect on electoral results. And examining the probability of electoral survival of prime ministers in ninety-nine democracies between 1950 and 1990, with 1,606 country-year observations, Cheibub and Przeworski (1999, 226–30) have concluded that past economic conditions have no effect on such probability.

If citizens do not vote influenced by past economic conditions, politicians will not be accountable for their performance in office. And if past performance is irrelevant for political survival, governments will have no incentives to launch political business cycles. When voters have adaptive expectations (Tufte 1978; Nordhaus 1975) or when expectations are rational (Cukierman and Meltzer 1986; Rogoff and Sibert 1988; Rogoff 1990; Persson and Tabellini 1990; Alesina, Roubini, and Cohen 1997), the strategy of politicians depends on whether voters retrospectively respond to changes in economic conditions. Only if politicians believe that accountability operates will they artificially expand the economy before elections.

Political business cycles involve moral hazard. Politicians are all alike: they just want to win elections. The electorate is homogeneous, and uses elections to reward competent incumbents. For Persson and Tabellini (1990), voters' expected utility depends on the growth rate and the stability of prices. With asymmetrical information, voters ignore the competence of the government, do not know the inflation rate before the elections, and observe only GDP growth and unemployment. In an economy described by a Phillips curve with a competence component, a government will artificially increase the growth and employment rates before the elections, in order to signal competence and maximize voters' utility. As a result, inflation will rise above expectations, although voters will not be aware until after the elections. With rational expectations, because voters know the incentives of incumbent politicians, wage setters anticipate this expansive strategy and the subsequent inflation: they will then increase wages. After the elections, growth will return to its natural rate but with higher inflation. In other models (Rogoff 1990), what the government manipulates is the composition of the budget. With asymmetrical information, the incumbent signals competence before the elections with visible actions (tax cuts, social transfers), at the cost of programs that can only be observed after the elections (public investment, fiscal deficits). Empirical evidence from OECD countries shows post-electoral inflationary effects of political business cycles, and no consequences on growth and unemployment rates (Alesina, Roubini, and Cohen 1997). What is a mystery is why embark on such opportunistic strategies if electoral results do not reward pre-electoral economic growth?

Several aspects of retrospective voting models are thus intriguing. For one thing, their assumptions that no selection is involved, all politicians are alike, the opposition plays no active role, and voters just deliver rewards or punishments for the past record of the government. For another, that with incomplete information voters can set a threshold for re-election based on past performance that enables them to control governments. And, as Fearon (1999) has remarked, strictly retrospective models of accountability run against widely held views of what representative politicians should be like: principled men, not just concerned with keeping their jobs. So, we shall now turn to accepting that differences among politicians may exist and that elections are also about the future.

4 THE LIMITS OF ACCOUNTABILITY

Let us start with setting the threshold for re-election. The incentives for an incumbent politician to be representative depend on such a threshold. If it is set too high, he will anticipate defeat at election time. Thus, no intertemporal tradeoff will limit rent seeking. If, on the contrary, the threshold is set too low, the incumbent will achieve it with little effort. The threshold requires that voters observe exogenous conditions: otherwise voting will be arbitrary: good governments may not survive. Suppose that the final outcome (ω), which will be judged against the re-election threshold (κ), depends on both effort (ϵ) and external conditions (θ), but voters only observe ω. If a government, upon being elected, learns that external conditions are good, it will supply little effort as long as $\omega_1(\epsilon_1\theta_1) > \kappa_1$. On the contrary, if external conditions are bad great effort will only lead to $\omega_2(\epsilon_2\theta_2) < \kappa_2$, and to electoral defeat. If voters cannot assess the relative influence of both ϵ and θ on ω, retrospective voting will not generate incentives for democratic representation.

When voters assess the influence of the incumbent's effort on their welfare, they will assign political responsibilities. This is indeed "the chief mechanism through which individuals hold actors accountable for their conduct" (Rudolph 2003a, 700). And this is why voters need information: for elections to induce representation, voters cannot be ignorant. They must know about the actions of the incumbent;

whether these actions caused the changes in their welfare; whether exogenous conditions were bad or good; whether another government and different policies would have achieved a better result. If what governments do is inconsequential for their survival, the interests of voters will not be protected by elections.

Yet, to quote Achen and Bartels (2004, 37), "a general theory of political accountability explaining when and why specific attributions or evasions of responsibility actually work is nowhere in sight." Studying the impact on US elections of natural disasters beyond the control of governments (such as a wave of shark attacks in 1916, an influenza pandemic in 1918, droughts and floods between 1896 and 2000), they argue that "retrospection is blind. When the voters are in pain they kick the government, justifying themselves with whatever plausible cultural constructions are made available to them" (Achen and Bartels 2004, 7).

Voters may react not to events, but to the answer from the government. While a government may not be responsible for natural disasters, exogenous economic shocks, or even isolated cases of corruption, it may respond promptly or not. This responsibility is much easier to assess than that associated with events and outcomes. A study of electoral reactions to the politics of the Spanish socialist government from 1982 to 1996 found that "what matters to people are not so much that cases of corruption emerge, but that once emerged the government takes measures to clarify things and demand the pertinent responsibilities. That scandals of corruption emerge is to a large measure unpredictable: the government does not have an exhaustive control on the activities of its members and the higher administrative echelons. On the contrary, the government has the capacity to react one way or the other when such cases become public" (Sánchez-Cuenca and Barreiro 2000, 74).

Institutions influence the capacity of voters to attribute political responsibilities. Empirical research has examined in particular the effects of minority and coalition governments on economic voting: clarity of responsibility becomes difficult when different parties are involved in decision making, either in government or in parliament. Powell and Whitten (1993), after examining nineteen industrial countries between 1969 and 1988, concluded that differences in economic voting were related to an "index of clarity"—the capacity to assign blame was reduced if several parties shared power, if the government had minoritarian support, if parties were not cohesive, and if the opposition controlled the legislative chamber or parliamentary committees. These conclusions have been widely discussed (Anderson 1995, 2000; Bengtsson 2004; Leyden and Borrelli 1995; Lowry, Alt, and Ferree 1998; Mershon 1996, 2002; Nadeau, Niemi, and Yoshinaka 2002; Powell 2000; Royed, Leyden, and Borrelli 2000; Rudolph 2003a, 2003b; Strom, Muller, and Bergman 2003; Whitten and Palmer 1999). But some questions remain open. Parties in a coalition are well informed about what the government does and may have incentives in providing information to citizens as long as they do not collude and keep competing against each other. Multiparty systems may offer few opportunities for "voice" and more for "exit" (Hirschman 1970; Fiorina 1981) but only if coalitions do not restrict voting against the government. Bipartisan competition and single-member constituencies may also

hamper the control of office holders (Ferejohn 1986), although single-party governments facilitate the attribution of responsibility.

In any case, if it is to be credible to politicians, the threshold for supporting the
incumbent must operate automatically, independently of who is in power. Otherwise, in order to circumvent it politicians will develop strategies of manipulation
(Maravall 1999): if effective, they will reduce the scope of accountability. Ideology is a
major instrument for such strategies. As Fiorina (1981, 194) has remarked, "If citizens
vote in accordance with habitual party identification largely devoid of policy content
and relatively impervious to change, where does electoral responsibility reside?"

Ideology is usually related to prospective, rather than retrospective, voting. When
citizens look at the past to decide what to do with the incumbent, they assess his
performance. When citizens want to select the best candidate to rule the country,
they consider his ideological proximity. Accountability is about tangible outcomes;
selection, about ideological hopes. However, as Sánchez-Cuenca (2003, 2) has noted,
"It seems odd to suppose that electorates are populated by such different creatures as
the pure ideological and the pure performance voters. More likely, voters vote out of
ideological considerations, while being sensitive to the government's performance."
The ideology of a party may help a voter to predict future policies, but ideology may
also influence retrospective voting: past policies may be seen as ideological betrayal,
or as an expression of incapacity to implement ideological promises. With data for
Great Britain, Germany, Portugal, and especially Spain, Sánchez-Cuenca shows that
the capacity of a party to preserve its supporters over time is sensitive to these
retrospective assessments of ideological reliability: "ideological voting might be
compatible with accountability when these two problems, ideological consistency
and capacity, are taken into account" (Sánchez-Cuenca 2003, 32).

If ideology is assessed retrospectively, voters will not assume that politicians are all
alike. And if politicians differ, citizens will use their vote to select the best candidate.
In Downs's (1957, 40) words, "to ignore the future when deciding how to vote . . .
would obviously be irrational since the purpose of voting is to select a future
government." If voting has to do with selection, under conditions of incomplete
information the past may be used by voters to infer expectations; past experiences
may be a useful guide for selecting a politician.

Voting then becomes a problem of adverse selection in which the past is connected
to the future. Retrospection serves to select. In Fearon's (1999) model, earlier periods
in office provide criteria to judge the quality of two candidates for office. With
incomplete information, voters have a prior belief that the probability of finding a
good candidate is a; that of a bad candidate is $1-a$. Voters cannot observe policies (χ),
just an outcome that affects their welfare (ω), and $\omega = -\chi^2 + \theta$ ($-\chi^2$ represents the
utility of policy χ for the voter, and θ is a random exogenous condition). In repeated
elections, selecting a candidate depends on a retrospective threshold: voters infer the
competence of the incumbent from outcome ω, and establish a voting rule with
threshold κ. At the time of the next election, voters update their beliefs about a (the
probability of a good candidate). If noise θ is symmetrical and unimodal, voters will
think that the government is competent if $\omega > \kappa(-\chi^2)/2$. That is, if the incumbent's

record is higher than 50 percent of the expected performance of both good and bad candidates. If the variance of noise θ increases, then the probabilities of winning of the two candidates will tend to converge. Noise θ will increase when monitoring the actions of the government becomes more difficult.

A reverse relationship between past and future may also exist: when this is the case, rather than inferred from the past, the future serves to select politicians. This is again an adverse selection problem: politicians differ in their policies, and voters have asymmetrical information on the true policy intentions of candidates. Harrington's model (1993) considers two candidates and two elections. Because they anticipate the reaction of voters to the policies implemented in office, candidates, in equilibrium, find it optimal to reveal information about their intended policies. This enhances their chances of re-election: so, if elected the first time, they stick to campaign promises.

The model works like this. In the first election, there is no incumbent to be judged retrospectively: just two candidates competing with messages (μ_1, μ_2) that offer different policies (χ_1, χ_2) within a policy space Ω. The candidates ignore the position of the median voter: they just assign a probability that he will support one of the two alternative messages. If the candidates estimate the same probability, their campaign messages will tend to converge. If messages differ, voters will identify different types of politicians: for instance, message μ_1 will be attributed to a type 1 candidate, message μ_2 to a type 2 candidate. When sending the messages, candidates will both make a guess about the position of the median voter and express their belief in the efficiency of policy χ_1 or policy χ_2. The result of the first election reveals the position of the median voter. Then, the elected politician implements policy χ within the policy space Ω: this policy may or may not correspond to that of the campaign message. If policy χ is chosen, then voters' income will be $\gamma = \omega_\chi + \theta$, in which ω_χ is a component of χ and θ is an exogenous factor. Politicians want to win elections and are dogmatic about the effectiveness of policies—they do not learn from experience. They face two decisions: (i) which message to send in the campaign, according to their beliefs in the effectiveness of policy and to the probability that the median voter will have a particular position; and (ii) which policy to follow if elected, according to promises made and to beliefs about their effectiveness in increasing voters' welfare. While they initially sympathize with particular policies, voters are uncertain about their effectiveness and cannot observe random external conditions. At the end of the period, they see the change in their welfare and update their beliefs about the effectiveness of policies.

In the second elections politicians make no new promises. The vote depends on the fulfillment of the first campaign promises and on the updated beliefs in the effectiveness of policies. Voters set a voting rule: if the incumbent has switched from his initial promises, the threshold for re-election will be higher. It can still be reached, however, if the new policy is effective enough to compensate for the betrayal. This voting rule in the second election induces politicians to transmit truthful messages in the first election campaign. At that time they do not know the position of the median voter, and are convinced of the effectiveness of their preferred policy. Thus, for a type 2 politician, it makes little sense to offer a μ_1 message in the first campaign and pretend to be a type 1 politician. If elected, he would have to behave as a type 1 politician and not be punished for betraying promises; or switch from election message μ_1, knowing that he would then be judged with more demanding criteria that would only be satisfied if the policy switch were to lead to much higher welfare. As Harrington (1993, 93–4) puts it, "future re-election considerations can induce politicians to fulfill their campaign promises... equilibria exist in which candidates reveal their true policy intentions during the campaign."

Incumbents may betray election promises for different reasons. Stokes (2003) has explained why politicians in office can switch from electoral promises and still be representative. Her model differs from Harrington's in that politicians are not assumed to be dogmatic about policies: they can learn from experience. Policy U-turns are not explained by spatial models of politics, in which politicians have no incentives to augment the difference with the ideal policy position of their voters. Prima facie all switches appear to be similar: but while some are simply due to opportunist strategies and rent seeking, others respond to what the incumbent considers to be the best interests of voters. This may happen when external conditions change, politicians revise their previous beliefs about the relative effectiveness of policies, and they conclude that the welfare of voters will be better served if promises are changed. Voters then set a more demanding voting rule (i.e. a higher threshold) for supporting the incumbent in the following elections, looking at outcomes instead of policies. So "bad" and "good" representatives can switch from initial promises, but the causes and consequences are different. Not all politicians are alike and, in order to control politicians, voters establish selective retrospective criteria.

If elections consist of a selection problem, the influence of the past over the future is clear enough. But the influence of the future is more intriguing: this is where ideology creeps in. Stokes (2001) has argued that voters may react to the economy not just assigning blame or merit for past performance, but using intertemporal and exonerative criteria as well. If the past has been bad, voters may think that it will lead to a bright future, that a tunnel had to be crossed in order to reach light. They may also believe that bad conditions were not due to the incumbent, but to the IMF, globalization, or what Harold Wilson, the British Labour prime minister, called "the gnomes of Zurich." So these voters go on supporting the government. Political reactions to the economy of 158,000 Spanish voters over a period of fifteen years show that a considerable proportion of them responded to intertemporal or exonerative considerations (Maravall and Przeworski 2001). In difficult times, more than 50 percent of the conservative (UCD) and socialist (PSOE) voters found reasons to go on supporting their governments, notwithstanding bad performance. Causality was reversed: "voters often appear to have decided, for whatever reasons, to support the government or the opposition, and only then to have chosen arguments to sustain their decision" (Maravall and Przeworski 2001, 74).

Contrary to Downs, people did not infer the future from the past. Their assessment of past conditions was realist: it coincided with objective evidence about GDP growth, inflation, and unemployment. But their expectations about the future were always much more optimistic, and this optimism was largely due to ideology. So people think about future economic conditions with political blinkers. Key (1966, 113) was right: "the average voter, like the rest of us, does not perceive a future extended with crystalline clarity from the chaos of current ambiguity." Because ideology guides thoughts about the future, and because expectations are mixed with retrospective assessments, the survival of incumbent politicians becomes a much more complex matter.

Elections can hardly facilitate the democratic control of governments if what citizens know about politics is limited and biased. First, their threshold for re-electing the incumbent will be arbitrary and create the wrong set of incentives for politicians. Second, if strictly retrospective voting is the only way to make governments accountable, it only happens in a strange world where no differences exist between politicians and where voters do not contemplate the future when electing a government. And if voters believe that differences exist among candidates and have expectations about the future, then ideology can enable politicians to avoid being held accountable.

5 Non-Electoral Threats: Voters versus Politicians

Let me restate the mainstream view: accountability and representation depend on the electoral threat that voters pose to the incumbent government. It is because politicians anticipate the reaction of voters in the next election that they will limit shirking. If democracy produces demophilia, it is because the survival of politicians in office depends on the verdict of voters at election time.

We know, however, that in parliamentary democracies prime ministers lose office in 48 percent of the cases due to conspiracies of politicians instead of decisions of voters. This was the rule in Italy between 1946 and 1994; in the French fourth Republic from 1945 to 1958; in Belgium, Finland, or Japan from 1945 onwards. Politicians being deposed by politicians is what Margaret Thatcher bitterly called a "funny old world" after her own replacement by the Conservative Party *nomenklatura* in November 1990. Such conspiracies have always been an important part of what politics is about in parliamentary democracies.

Consider the following examples, from both single-party and coalition governments, with majoritarian or minoritarian support in parliament. The first one is a replacement of a prime minister within a single-party majority government. Thatcher was brought down by a conspiracy within her own party, led by former cabinet ministers Michael Heseltine, Geoffrey Howe, and Nigel Lawson. Her party had a majority in parliament, and the Labour Party was a weak opposition under the leadership of Neil Kinnock.

Economic growth had gone down to 1.4 percent over the last two years, compared to an average of 2.3 percent in her whole period in office.[2] The popularity of Thatcher had gone down in 1990, reaching in March and April its lowest levels of her period in office, but it had gradually recovered in the spring and summer—her rates of approval had been similar in 1981, in the winter of 1982, in the spring and summer of 1986.[3] Now, elections within the party eventually led to her replacement by John Major. The conspiracy produced this reaction from Thatcher: "what grieved me was the desertion of those I had always considered friends and allies and weasel words whereby they had transmuted their betrayal into frank advice and concern for my fate" (Thatcher 1993, 855).

The second example is a change of prime minister within a single-party minority government. In January 1981, Adolfo Suárez resigned as Spanish prime minister. He had led a transition from dictatorship to democracy, obtained cross-partisan support for a constitution and an encompassing program of economic reforms (the *Pactos de la Moncloa*), and won two successive elections, forming minority single-party governments. The economy was in stagnation, with an average annual growth rate of 0.7 percent over the last two years, compared to an average of 2.8 percent for the European Community as a whole. Only one year after his last victory, different factions of his party started to conspire against him, stimulated by the Catholic Church and by the Confederation of Business Organizations (Confederación Española de Organizaciones Empresariales—CEOE): their policies over divorce, education, and the economy were very different (Powell 2001, 279–91). Splits from the party and a critical "Manifesto of the 200," signed in December 1980 by important members of the party, indicated Suárez's inability to keep UCD (Unión de Centro Democrático) together. But rather than unpopularity breeding internal dissent, it was the internal conspiracies that eroded Suárez's popularity in his final months in office.

The next two cases are prime ministers of coalition governments being replaced by politicians of their own party. Willy Brandt was the German social democratic chancellor from October 1969 to May 1975. He had brought the SPD (Sozialdemokratische Partei Deutschlands) to power, first as the minor partner of a coalition with the Christian Democrats from 1966 to 1969, then as the major partner of a coalition with the Liberal Party following the 1969 elections. Brandt won again the elections of 1972; his demise as chancellor was decided two years later by other leaders of his party—particularly by Herbert Wehner and Helmut Schmidt (Rovan 1978, 383–423). Brandt was criticized for lack of authority (*Führungschwäche*) in facing factional conflict within the SPD, mostly provoked by the Jusos (Arbeitsgemeinschaft Junger Sozialisten). Despite the 1973 oil shock, the average annual rate of growth in Brandt's last two years was 2.5 percent— higher than that of the European Community as a whole, while inflation was lower than in most European countries. The spark for the crisis was a political scandal: the discovery that Brandt's chief of staff was an East German spy, Günther Guillaume. Brandt remained leader of the SPD but was replaced in the government by Helmut Schmidt.

---

[2] Economic data for these cases are from *European Economy*, 72, 2001 (table 10, pp. 132–3). GDP data are at 1995 market prices.

[3] Satisfaction ratings are from **www.mori.com/polls/trends/satisfac.shtml**

The following example is also a replacement of a prime minister within a coalition. Only this time there were four parties in the government when Pierre Mendès-France was elected as French prime minister in June 1954, following the Dien-Bien-Phu defeat in Indo-China. Mendès-France achieved peace after a disastrous war that had lasted nearly seven years, and managed the economy with competence (Tarr 1961, 186–234). Yet he remained in power for only seven months: the opposition resided in his own party and partners in the coalition—in particular, the MRP (Mouvement Républicain Populaire)—over his position on the European Defense Community, German rearmament, and his program of economic reforms. Mendès-France resigned after being defeated in a confidence vote at the *Assemblée Nationale*, and was replaced by Edgar Faure, another leader of his party, the Parti Radical, heading the same coalition.

The last case is a prime minister being replaced by a politician from a coalition partner while his party remains in government. In Italy, Bettino Craxi headed a coalition government of five parties from August 1983 to April 1987. His party, the Partito Socialista Italiano (PSI), had joined since 1963 different coalitions headed by eleven successive Christian Democratic prime ministers. When Craxi became leader of the PSI, the socialist vote was below 10 percent and the party had one-fifth of the coalition seats in parliament. Craxi defined his strategy as responding to the imperative of *primum vivere*: the goal was to increase the political influence and the electoral support of the PSI, crushed between the two big forces of Italian politics, the DC (Democrazia Cristiana) and PCI (Partito Comunista Italiano). In the 1983 elections, the socialists managed to slightly increase their share of the vote, while the DC lost five percentage points—with 32.9 percent, its worst result since 1948 (Ercole and Martinotti 1990). Helped by the very popular socialist president of the Republic, Sandro Pertini, Craxi was accepted as prime minister by the DC and was able to survive four years in office. In this period, the average annual rate of GDP growth was 3.0 percent (the European Union average was 2.1 percent), inflation went down from 15.0 percent to 4.8 percent, the balances of trade and payments were under control. But the DC became impatient: the Christian Democrats first inflicted a parliamentary defeat on Craxi in June 1986; then forced his replacement by Amintore Fanfani heading an interim government, and finally recovered support in the 1987 elections (up to 34.3 percent). The socialists remained in coalition governments with three successive DC prime ministers until the 1994 dramatic change in Italian politics.

A plausible interpretation of such conspiracies is that "party politicians anticipate the judgement of voters when they replace their leader or decide to leave the ruling coalition" (Cheibub and Przeworski 1999, 232). This is also what Warwick (1994, 92) argued: "a desire not to be associated with economic failure encourages parties or individual parliamentarians to withdraw support for incumbent governments." If this were the case, then democratic accountability would still operate. The criteria of conspiring politicians would be the same as those of voters; Friedrich's "law of anticipated reactions" would still produce representation out of democracy. Incumbents would still be accountable to voters: fellow politicians would simply get rid of an unpopular prime minister in order to minimize electoral damage to the party or the coalition.

But suppose that this is not the true story, and that the criteria of conspiring politicians and voters do differ. The replacement of a prime minister by the ruling party or coalition would not be due to a pre-emptive strategy anticipating punishment at the polls, but to political ambitions. If this were the case, an ambitious politician would want to become prime minister when the chances of winning the following elections are good. His strategy would then be launched when electoral support is high, not low; when conditions are good, not bad.

Think of a potential challenger. His expected utility to lead the party at election time (let us call this L) is

$$EU(L) = p_e W + (1 - p_e)D.$$

The challenger must assess the probability of three possible outcomes: a successful challenge and a subsequent electoral victory (W), a successful challenge and an electoral defeat (D), and a failed challenge (F). The last alternative is the status quo (Q). Because politicians value not just public office but the leadership of the party, by hypothesis, this is the order of preferences: $W > D > Q > F$.

The expected value of challenge is

$$EU(C) = p_c[p_e W + (1 - p_e)D] + (1 - p_c)F,$$

where C is the internal challenge to the prime minister, and p_c and p_e are the probabilities of winning the internal challenge and the general elections. Challenging then depends on whether this value is larger than the value of the status quo (Q). That is, on whether

$$EU(C) > Q.$$

We assume that the value of the status quo is greater than that of a failed challenge $(Q > F)$: otherwise the challenge would always be launched for any value of the variables. As the value of the payoffs (or the probabilities) increase, so does the expected utility of challenge. So the condition of challenging is

$$p_c[p_e W + (1 - p_e)D] + (1 - p_c)F > Q. \tag{1}$$

The decision to challenge will more likely take place when any of the variables in the left hand side of the relationship increases its value. If $p_c > 0$, the inequality expressed in (1) may be formulated as a condition on the probability of electoral success:

$$p_e > \frac{1}{p_c} \frac{Q - F}{W - D} \frac{D - F}{W - D}. \tag{2}$$

As probabilities are set between 0 and 1, the challenge will not take place under certain values of the variables. For instance,

$$p_e < 1 \Rightarrow p_c > \frac{Q - F}{W - F}. \tag{3}$$

Unless the probability of success of the internal challenge is greater than the ratio $(Q - F)/(W - F)$, the probability of an electoral victory should be higher than 1 in order to have inequality (2). That is, if $p_c \leq (Q - F)/(W - F)$, the probability of an electoral victory would never be an incentive for the internal challenge.

Also if $D < Q$, the probability of an electoral victory p_e must have enough value to generate incentives to launch an internal challenge. That is,

$$p_c < 1 \Rightarrow p_e > \frac{Q - D}{W - D}. \tag{4}$$

If the probability of electoral success were smaller, the value of the internal challenge would be lower than that of the status quo, even if the challenge were to be successful. However, if $Q \leq D$, for any probability of electoral victory there would be a probability of success of the internal challenge such that this challenge would take place.

When are the probabilities of an electoral victory (p_e) a sufficient incentive to launch an internal challenge? They need not be very high. Consider a numerical example, in which the values are $W = 1$, $F = 0$, $D = 0.5$, and $Q = 0.3$. Then if $p_c \leq Q = 0.3$ the internal challenge will not be launched, in accordance to (3). But, according to (2), if p_c were to be 0.4, the challenge will be worthwhile when $p_e \geq 0.5$. If p_c were to be of 0.5, the challenge will take place when $p_e \geq 0.2$. And if p_c were to be of ≥ 0.6, the internal challenge will always be launched, independently of the probabilities of a subsequent electoral victory.

The smaller the difference in value between W and D, the more the decision to confront the prime minister will depend on p_c (the probability of success of the internal challenge). Given a value of Q, the closer the values of W and D are, the smaller the influence of p_e (the probability of an electoral victory) will be on the decision to challenge or not. To continue with the former example, if $D = 0.75$, then the challenge will always take place for any value of p_e, as long as $p_c \geq 0.4$ (never if <0.3, which is the value of Q). In fact, only when p_c is in the interval between 0.3 and 0.4 the decision to challenge or not will depend on the likelihood of winning the next elections. Below the 0.3 threshold, the challenge will never take place. Above 0.4, the influence of p_e on the decision will decrease—eventually even with a very low p_e the challenge will be worthwhile.

I shall not discuss further the conditions that facilitate the success of an internal challenge (p_c). I have argued elsewhere (Maravall 2003) that closed lists and a decentralized selection of parliamentary candidates lead to parties lasting more in office, and make the survival of prime ministers more predictable. But a conspiracy against a prime minister may be organized by the central organization of a disciplined party, as well as by factions in a divided one. As for p_e, if economic conditions influence the probability of winning the elections, strategies of politicians for replacing a prime minister will more likely take place when

$$p_e(\Delta\gamma(\theta^G)) > p_e(\Delta\gamma(\theta^B)). \tag{5}$$

θ are the good or bad economic conditions, γ the income of voters, and $p(\Delta\gamma)$ the probability of winning under increased income of voters. Even if many challenges fail, ambitious politicians are more likely to emerge when conditions are good. The consequence is that voters will punish the government at the polls when economic performance is poor; politicians, on the contrary, will replace their prime minister when the economy is growing.

The following analysis corresponds to twenty-three parliamentary democracies and 1,109 country-year observations from roughly 1945 to 2003. Table 37.1 shows the distribution of these observations according to the type of government.[4]

Table 37.1 Types of government

Parliamentary support	Composition		Total
	Coalition	Single party	
Majority	571	167	871
Minority	71	300	238
Total	642	467	1109

Prime ministers lost office in 312 occasions: in 123 cases, due to an electoral defeat (out of 329 elections); in 189 cases, to a political crisis, either within their own party (124 cases) or within a coalition (65 cases). Parties lasted longer in power than prime ministers: 7 years and 5 months on average, against 3 years and 7 months. The longest serving prime minister was Tage Erlander, who headed a social democratic government in Sweden for twenty-two years, from 1946 to 1969, and won seven consecutive elections. The party that lasted longest in office was the Democrazia Cristiana (DC) in Italy, in government for forty-eight years with twenty-six different spells of short-lived prime ministers. Governments usually lost votes between elections (−1.84 percent on average), as well as seats in 68 percent of the elections. These losses, however, did not necessarily lead to leaving office.

The contrast between votes and permanence in office is particularly clear in coalition governments. They lost fewer votes on average than single-party governments: −1.40 percent versus −2.50 percent.[5] Yet prime ministers in coalitions did not last longer in office: 3 years and 6 months, compared to 3 years and 10 months in single-party governments. Rather than on votes and seats, their political life may have depended very much on the maneuvers of their fellow politicians. If this were the case, institutions would matter for accountability: they would facilitate or hinder "clarity of responsibility." For one, responsibilities are less easily assigned in a coalition with different members.

---

[4] Both majority and coalitions are dummy variables. Majority is coded as 1, minority as 0: they indicate the parliamentary support of the incumbent, be it a coalition or a single-party government. Coalition is coded as 1, single-party government as 0: they can have either majoritatian or minoritarian support in parliament.

[5] This confirms Powell's (2000, 54) data showing that single-party governments lose more votes than coalitions. They contradict the opposite conclusion of Strom (1990, 69–70, 124).

For another, the party or prime minister that won the elections at time t does not always call the following elections at $t+1$; different coalitions may have been in power between t and $t+1$. When this happens, voters will hardly know who to reward or punish for outcomes at $t+1$. Institutions, therefore, influence the survival of governments when parliamentary politics becomes "an unprincipled game of musical cabinet chairs" (Warwick 1994, 134).

I start by examining what explains the loss of power of prime ministers and parties. I shall understand that a party loses power when it no longer has the prime minister: a spell in power may thus include different prime ministers as long as they belong to the same party. Table 37.2 uses three different regression models, largely due to the number of available observations for the predictor variables—this can be seen in the total number of

Table 37.2 The risk of losing power: prime ministers and parties

	Prime ministers			Parties		
	1	2	3	1	2	3
Event	1,035	818	399	1,011	794	386
Censored	74	73	0	98	97	13
Total	1,109	891	399	1,109	891	399
Majority	−.173[c]	−.199[c]	−.208[c]	−.126	−.128	−.086
	(.081)	(.090)	(.118)	(.082)	(.092)	(.124)
Coalition	.129[c]	.150[c]	−	.058	.020	−
	(.067)	(.074)		(.068)	(.077)	
Effective number of parties	−	−	.066[c] (.034)	−	−	.144[b] (.036)
Single-member districts	−	−	−.163 (.149)	−	−	.483[b] (.157)
Growth last two years	−.005 (.012)	.002 (.001)	−.010 (.025)	−.054[a] (.013)	−.056[a] (.015)	−.082[b] (.026)
Inflation	−	.006[a] (.001)	.060[a] (.013)	−	.007[a] (.001)	.025[c] (.011)
Political scandals	−	−	.077 (.179)	−	−	−.200 (.181)
Chi²	6.424[c]	21.956[a]	34.842[a]	20.298[a]	37.195[a]	39.655[a]
−2 log likelihood	12,752.611	9,724.142	4,080.652	12,215.934	9,232.265	3,869.950

Note: Standard errors in parenthesis.
[a] Significant at 1% or less.
[b] Significant at 5%.
[c] Significant at 10%.

country-year observations, which goes down from 1,109 to 891, and then to 399. The observations of the second model start in 1960; those of the third, in 1970. The variables correspond both to institutional features and to critical events. As King et al. (1990) demonstrated, both types of variables can be studied simultaneously in duration analyses.[6] Institutions in the first and second models are majoritarian or minoritarian, single-party or coalition governments. In the third model, coalitions were replaced by the effective number of parties:[7] both correlated strongly,[8] and the model improved with the new variable. Also single-member districts were added.[9] In the first model the only time-varying correlate was the average rate of GDP growth over the last two years in office; the level of inflation in the last year was added in the second model;[10] political scandals,[11] in the third.

The models are partial likelihood Cox regressions. They estimate the relative risk of losing office, with the assumption of proportional hazards. The hazard function, $h(t)$, is a rate that estimates the potential risk per unit time at a particular instant, given that the prime minister or the party have survived in office until that instant. Because the hazard function is not a probability it can exceed 1, and take any number from 0 to infinity.[12] What Table 37.2 shows[13] is that prime ministers, besides lasting less in power than parties, are more vulnerable to particular institutional conditions; however their survival in office is less sensitive to performance. If prime ministers have majoritarian support in parliament, their survival will be less at risk. In the three models, such risk decreases by 15.9 percent, 18.0 percent, and 18.8 percent. On the contrary, if the government is a coalition, and if the effective number of parties goes up, the risk

---

[6] Contrary to explanations that focused either on the institutional features of governments and parliaments (Blondel 1968; Taylor and Herman 1971; Laver 1974; Dodd 1976; Sanders and Herman 1977), or on critical random events (Browne, Frendreis, and Gleiber 1986).

[7] The effective number of parties is calculated according to Laakso and Taagepera (1979). It carries the same information as the Rae (1968) index of fractionalization, and is calculated from this index as $1/1-$ Rae. Rae $= 1 - \sum_{i=1}^{m} t_i^2$, where t_i is the share of the votes for party i and m is the number of parties.

[8] The correlation between coalitions and effective number of parties was .436. That between majoritarian governments and single-member districts was .194.

[9] Single-member districts were coded as 1; otherwise, as 0. Source: Huber, Ragin, and Stephens dataset (1997).

[10] Data on inflation and GDP growth are from the Michael Álvarez, José Antonio Cheibub, Fernando Limongi, and Adam Przeworski dataset, as well as from *World Development Indicators*.

[11] Political scandals refer to annual incidents of corruption, moral cases with strong public impact, or affairs relevant to national security (the Profumo case in the UK in 1963, the Günther Guillaume case in Germany in 1975). Data on survival and losses of power are from Woldendorp, Keman, and Budge (1998) as well as from **www.keesings.com**

[12] The dependent variable is thus a survival time indicator: time refers to years in office. A status indicator shows the annual observations of survival that have been censored because a prime minister or a party is still in office at the end of the study—that is, the cause of termination (elections, political crises) has not been observed. If $h_0(t)$ is the baseline hazard function (the expected risk of losing office without the predictor variables), e is the base of the natural logarithm, $X_1 \ldots X_n$ are the predictor variables, and $B_1 \ldots B_n$ the regression coefficients, then the model can be written as $h(t) = [h_0(t)]e(B_1X_1 + B_2X_2 \ldots + B_nX_n)$. The effect on the risk of losing office of the predictor variables is separated from the baseline hazard, which is assumed not to vary between cases and to depend only on duration time. The overall hazard is the product of the effect of the predictor variables and the baseline hazard.

[13] The effect of each of the different regression coefficients is $100x[exp(B)-1]$. This effect is the percentage of change in the risk (increasing or decreasing) by one unit of change in the independent variables.

increases by 12.1 percent and 16.2 percent in models 1 and 2; by 6.8 percent in model 3 (which replaces coalitions by the effective number of parties). Single-member districts, however, have no statistical significance. The higher the rate of inflation, the greater the risk: the value of the coefficient increases substantially from model 2 to model 3, both for parties and prime ministers: inflation has a greater influence on surviving in office from 1970 onwards, which is the period covered in model 3. But economic growth and political scandals[14] have no effect on the survival of prime ministers.

Parties, lasting longer in government, are somewhat more sensitive to perform-ance. Contrary to what happens to prime ministers, economic growth helps parties to stay in power: the risk of losing office decreases by 5.2, 5.4, and 7.9 percent in the three models. And, as happens with prime ministers, higher inflation rates have a negative effect on their survival. Political scandals are again irrelevant. If we look at institutional conditions, parliamentary majorities and being part of a coalition have no statistically significant effect on the risk of losing power. But this risk increases strongly under single-member districts, which are related to easier rotations in office, and also when the number of effective parties goes up. In the first case, the risk goes up by 62.1 percent; in the second, by 15.4 percent. Both correspond to model 3.

Note that in Table 37.2 the loss of power may be due to any reason—electoral defeats or political crises. I shall now focus on prime ministers—according to accountability theory, the politician who anticipates the reaction of voters at the next election. Table 37.3 shows the distribution of different causes of government termination.[15] The first is an electoral defeat: both the prime minister and his party

Table 37.3 Causes of prime ministers losing power

Causes of termination	Types of government			
	Support		Composition	
	Majority %	Minority %	Coalition %	Single party %
Electoral defeat	36.7	45.7	36.0	44.7
Replacement by PM from within the party	41.7	35.1	34.9	47.2
Replacement by PM from outside the party	21.6	19.2	29.1	8.1
Total causes of loss (N)	(218)	(94)	(189)	(123)

[14] For the period covered by model 3, I recorded seventy-two political scandals (from www.keesings.com). This number of cases can hardly explain why political scandals never have a statistically significant effect.

[15] I constructed the three different causes of termination in the country/year database using information from Woldendorp, Keman, and Budge (1998), and from www.keesings.com. In Table 37.4, each of the three causes of termination is analysed separately for the total number of country-year observations, also according to models 1, 2, and 3, which respond to the different independent variables. Censored cases reflect the years that followed the last loss of power—either due to an electoral defeat, to a replacement by another politician from the same party, or to a replacement by a politician from another party in the coalition.

leave office. The second is a political crisis: the prime minister is replaced by another politician from his own party. The third is a different sort of crisis: the prime minister is replaced by a politician from another party in the coalition, while his own party remains in government. This last cause of termination was not considered as a loss of power by a party in Table 37.2.

Table 37.4 shows the regression results for the three causes of termination. The predictor variables are the same as in Table 37.2. If we examine first the influence of institutions, it is overwhelming. Consider first majoritarian governments. They face smaller risks of losing power either through elections (a decrease of 15.6, 19.3, and 25.8 percent in the three models) or through coalition conspiracies (a fall of 48.9, 52.3, and 52.1 percent). Such risks, however, increase through internal party politics: the danger of being replaced by a comrade goes up by 61.9, 75.4, and 72.6 percent in the three models. Coalitions seem to protect incumbents from voters and from their own party comrades: the risk of replacement diminishes by 13.2 and 17.9 percent in the case of elections; by 22.5 percent and 26.9 percent in the case of internal party conspiracies. But coalitions make prime ministers more vulnerable to politicians from another party in a coalition government: the threat of losing their position goes up by 65.5 and 51.6 percent in models 1 and 2. When the effective number of parties goes up, so does the risk of being replaced by the party (which rises by 19.4 percent) or, to a greater extent, by a partner in the coalition (which increases by 25.5 percent). This is irrelevant, however, for voters: the threat of an electoral defeat does not increase. The opposite happens with single-member districts: they have a strong effect on electoral defeats, but do not matter for internal partisan replacements.[16]

If we turn now to critical events, voters do not always share the criteria of politicians for rewarding or punishing incumbents. There are two exceptions: political scandals and inflation. Neither voters nor politicians care about scandals:[17] the risk of losing power is irrelevant. When inflation goes up, the risk for prime ministers, either through elections or conspiracies, augments. The coefficient increases considerably in model 3, with observations corresponding to the post-1970 period. The maximum effect of inflation is an increase of 5.7 percent in the risk, which corresponds to an internal replacement within the party. The important difference between voters and politicians lies in the following variable: when the economy grows, the risk that prime ministers will be punished in elections decreases; the risk of successful conspiracies, on the contrary, augments. Voters see that their welfare improves and tend to reward the incumbent: the risk of losing office decreases by 5.1, 5.1, and 7.1 percent in the three models. On the contrary, politicians prefer to replace their prime ministers when conditions are good—this happens both within the prime minister's own party and among members of the coalition. The risk of an internal replacement goes up by 7.9, 8.9, and 12.4 percent in models 1, 2, and 3; that of a replacement by a coalition partner, by

---

[16] I have excluded this variable from the analysis of terminations due to coalition crises: single-member districts do not produce coalitions, and therefore no threats exist from partners in the government. The number of observations goes up from 399 to 561.

[17] Note the caveat of n. 14. Besides political scandals, I tried a corruption index from the International Country Risk Guide Corruption in the Political System. The results were also statistically non-significant.

	Survival to elections (party and prime minister)			Survival to political crises −1 (party stays, with prime minister from another party)			Survival to political crises −2 (party stays, with different prime minister from the party)		
	1	2	3	1	2	3	1	2	3
Event	983	766	364	509	353	210	809	593	315
Censored	126	125	35	600	538	351	300	298	84
Total	1,109	891	399	1,109	891	561	1,109	891	399
Majority	−.170[c]	−.214[c]	−.298[c]	−.671[a]	−.741[a]	−.736[a]	.482[a]	.562[a]	.546[a]
	(.081)	(.090)	(.124)	(.103)	(.121)	(.144)	(.095)	(.110)	(.146)
Coalition	−.142[c]	−.198[c]	—	.510[a]	.416[a]	—	−.255[b]	−.313[a]	—
	(.068)	(.078)		(.096)	(.114)		(.075)	(.087)	
Effective number of parties	—	—	.018	—	—	.227[a]	—	—	.177[c]
			(.036)			(.053)			(.044)
Single-member districts	—	—	.688[a]	—	—	—	—	—	.194
			(.159)						(.157)
Growth last two years	−.052[a]	−.052[b]	−.074[b]	.145[a]	.162[a]	.128[a]	.076[a]	.085[a]	.117[a]
	(.013)	(.016)	(.027)	(.018)	(.022)	(.030)	(.015)	(.018)	(.028)
Inflation	—	.009[a]	.022[c]	—	.005[a]	.046[a]	—	.006[a]	.056[a]
		(.001)	(.011)		(.001)	(.006)		(.002)	(.014)
Political scandals	—	—	−.260	—	—	−.105	—	—	−.063
			(.185)			(.243)			(.215)
Chi²	26.510[a]	54.469[a]	40.135[a]	125.139[a]	103.190[a]	123.231[a]	54.254[a]	61.826[a]	41.277[a]
−2 log likelihood	11,861.960	8,879.659	3,636.638	6,289.737	4,181.727	2,228.535	10,036.433	7,125.982	3,165.192

Note: Standard errors in parenthesis.
[a] Significant at 1% or less.
[b] Significant at 5%.
[c] Significant at 10%.

15.6, 17.6, and 13.6 percent, also in the three models. A growing economy whets the appetite for power: substitutes hope that they will stand a good chance of winning the next election. They may however overestimate these chances: Cheibub and Przeworski (1999, 232–3) have stated that only 30 percent of prime ministers who replaced the incumbent in the middle of a mandate win the next election.

The future of politicians who replace incumbents is less threatening in this study. Of the 189 replacements through political crises rather than elections, 86 prime ministers managed to survive the new elections (45.5 percent), while 72 (38.1 percent) were defeated. The rest (16.4 percent) did not even have an opportunity at the polls: they were themselves replaced before facing the voters. As Table 37.5 shows, if the replacement was within the party the new prime ministers stood a much better chance of surviving the elections than when the replacement took place within the coalition. Consider that of the 329 elections covered by this study, 37.4 percent ended with an electoral defeat of the incumbent.

There were therefore important differences about the future electoral prospects according to the cause of the replacement. Voters may have cared about the identity of the party: if it did not change, they remained loyal even if the prime minister had been replaced by a new one. Changes of candidates within coalitions were much riskier, regarding both voters and politicians: posterior electoral defeats and replacements by conspiracies were frequent.

Differences between voters and politicians are thus important. Politicians do not usually anticipate the verdict of voters. Warwick (1994, 75) wrote that "although government survival in parliamentary regimes depends more often on parliamentarians than voters, it may be expected that parliamentary support for governments also varies with the economic conditions that seem to matter so much to the public—after all, parliamentarians are responsible to their electorates." But this is not what the results of Table 37.4 show. When economic conditions are bad, prime ministers are threatened by voters at election time; when the conditions are good, they are threatened by fellow politicians between elections. Because the criteria of politicians for punishing incumbents do not correspond to those of voters, the incentives for incumbents to be representative are distorted in parliamentary democracies.

Table 37.5 Survival at the next elections by non-elected incumbents

	Survival %	Defeat %	Replacement before the next elections %	Total (N)
Replacement within party	62.9	33.1	4.0	100 (124)
Replacement by another party in the coalition	12.3	47.7	40.0	100 (65)
Total	45.5	38.1	16.4	100 (189)

6 CONCLUSIONS

For mainstream political science, the people rule retrospectively. According to Sartori (1987, 30, 71), "democracy is the power of the people over the people;" "in a system of representative government the people actually exercise power (political power) by being able to *control* and *change* the people in power." Because in democracies incumbents anticipate the retrospective reaction of voters in the next election, governments will look after the interests of citizens. If governments are accountable, repeated elections lead to representation.

This theory is flawed in several respects. First, it assumes that citizens can establish a threshold for re-electing the incumbent that generates incentives for governments to be representative. But for this to happen, citizens must be able to assign responsibility for past outcomes. Without information, there is no reason to think that they can discern the influence on such outcomes of actions of the government, or of exogenous conditions beyond its control. The consequence is that bad governments may survive; good ones can lose power. A minimalist theory of accountability needs to be supplemented by a theory of the information citizens need in order to sift out good from bad governments.

Two additional assumptions of the theory of retrospective accountability are particularly unconvincing. First, that all politicians are alike, and no selection is involved at election time. Second, that voters never consider the future when they cast their vote: that elections are just about delivering rewards and punishments based on retrospective criteria. Overwhelming empirical evidence shows that citizens use rational expectations trying to select the best candidate; that they consider the future as part of what elections are about. We also have evidence indicating that, when selection and the future enter into the considerations of voters, ideology influences the vote. Elections are guided not just by retrospective assessments of performance, but also by ideological hopes. For this reason, incumbent politicians find fertile ground for manipulation—that is, for handling past responsibilities and future expectations.

Finally, we know that in parliamentary democracies losses of office by prime ministers depend in one-half of the cases on decisions by politicians, not by voters. Comrades in the party or fellow politicians in a coalition may decide to get rid of the prime minister before election time. Empirical democratic theory has assumed that this decision anticipates the verdict of the next election—it minimizes punishment of the party or the coalition with a scapegoat strategy. For this assumption to stand, voters and politicians should share the same criteria for punishing prime ministers. But this is not the case. In particular, economic conditions lead to opposite reactions: when they are bad, the risk of an electoral defeat increases; when they are good, the risk of being the victim of a conspiracy goes up. If re-election is the incentive for a prime minister to be representative, such non-electoral threats undermine this incentive. Prime ministers in parliamentary democracies must spend a great deal of their time fending off conspiracies, particularly when times are good.

Elections can thus hardly lead to representation when voters are ill informed. And if conspiracies replace elections, and the criteria of politicians supplant those of voters, incentives for a government to act in the interest of citizens will be eroded. Minimalist theories do not tell us well why democracy produces demophilia.

REFERENCES

ACHEN, C., and BARTELS, L. 2004. Blind retrospection: electoral responses to drought, flu, and shark attacks. Working Paper 2004/199. Madrid: Instituto Juan March.

ALESINA, A., ROUBINI, N., and COHEN, G. 1997. *Political Cycles and the Macroeconomy.* Cambridge, Mass.: MIT Press.

ANDERSON, C. 1995. *Blaming the Government.* Armonk, NY: M. E. Sharpe.

—— 2000. Economic voting and political context: a comparative perspective. *Electoral Studies,* 19: 151–70.

AUSTEN-SMITH, D., and BANKS, J. S. 1989. Electoral accountability and incumbency. Pp. 121–50 in *Models of Strategic Choices in Politics,* ed. P. Ordeshook. Ann Arbor: University of Michigan Press.

BANKS, J., and SUNDARAM, R. 1993. Adverse selection and moral hazard in a repeated elections model. Pp. 295–311 in *Political Economy: Institutions, Competition, and Representation,* ed. W. Barnett, M. Hinich, and N. Schofield. New York: Cambridge University Press.

BARRO, R. 1973. The control of politicians: an economic model. *Public Choice,* 14: 19–42.

BENGTSSON, A. 2004. Economic voting: the effect of political context, volatility, and turnout on voters' assignment of responsibility. *European Journal of Political Research,* 43: 749–67.

BLONDEL, J. 1968. Party systems and patterns of government in western democracies. *Canadian Journal of Political Science,* 1: 180–203.

BRATTON, K. 1994. Retrospective voting and future expectations: the case of the budget deficit in the 1988 election. *American Politics Quarterly,* 22: 277–96.

BROWNE, E., FRENDREIS, J., and GLEIBER, D. 1986. The process of cabinet dissolution: an exponential model of duration and stability in western democracies. *American Journal of Political Science,* 30: 628–50.

CHEIBUB, J. A., and PRZEWORSKI, A. 1999. Democracy, elections, and accountability for economic outcomes. Pp. 222–50 in *Democracy, Accountability, and Representation,* ed. A. Przeworski, S. Stokes, and B. Manin. New York: Cambridge University Press.

CUKIERMAN, A., and MELTZER, A. 1986. A positive theory of discretionary policy, the costs of democratic government, and the benefits of a constitution. *Economic Inquiry,* 24: 367–88.

DODD, L. 1976. *Coalitions in Parliamentary Government.* Princeton: Princeton University Press.

DOWNS, A. 1957. *An Economic Theory of Democracy.* New York: Harper Collins.

ERCOLE, E., and MARTINOTTI, G. 1990. Le basi elettorali del neosocialismo italiano. In *Vent'anni di elezioni in Italia,* ed. M. Caciagli and A. Spreafico. Padua: Liviana.

FEARON, J. 1999. Electoral accountability and the control of politicians: selecting good types versus sanctioning poor performance. Pp. 55–97 in *Democracy, Accountability, and Representation,* ed. A. Przeworski, S. Stokes, and B. Manin. New York: Cambridge University Press.

FEREJOHN, J. 1986. Incumbent performance and electoral control. *Political Choice,* 56: 5–25.

FIORINA, M. 1981. *Retrospective Voting in American National Elections*. New Haven: Yale University Press.

FRIEDRICH, C. J. 1963. *Man and his Government: An Empirical Theory of Politics*. New York: McGraw-Hill.

HARRINGTON, J. 1993. The impact of reelection pressures on the fulfillment of campaign promises. *Games and Economic Behavior*, 5: 71–97.

HIRSCHMAN, A. 1970. *Exit, Voice, and Loyalty*. Cambridge, Mass.: Harvard University Press.

HUBER, E., RAGIN, C., and STEPHENS, J. 1997. *Comparative Welfare States Dataset*: www. lissy.caps.ln/compwsp.htm

KEECH, W. 1995. *Economic Politics*. New York: Cambridge University Press.

KEY, V. O. 1966. *The Responsible Electorate*. New York: Vintage Books.

KIEWIET, D. R., and RIVERS, D. 1985. A retrospective on retrospective voting. Pp. 207–31 in *Economic Conditions and Electoral Outcomes: The United States and Western Europe*, ed. H. Eulau and M. Lewis-Beck. New York: Agathon Press.

KING, G., ALT, J., BURNS, N., and LAVER, M. 1990. A unified model of cabinet dissolution in parliamentary democracies. *American Journal of Political Science*, 34: 846–71.

KRAMER, G. 1971. Short-term fluctuations in US voting behavior, 1896–1964. *American Political Science Review*, 65: 131–43.

KUKLINSKI, J., and WEST, D. 1981. Economic expectations and voting behavior in United States Senate and House elections. *American Political Science Review*, 75: 436–47.

LAAKSO, M., and TAAGEPERA, R. 1979. Effective number of parties: a measure with application to western Europe. *Comparative Political Studies*, 12: 3–27.

LANOUE, D. 1994. Retrospective and prospective voting in presidential-year elections. *Political Research Quarterly*, 14: 193–205.

LAVER, M. 1974. Dynamic factors in government coalition formation. *European Journal of Political Research*, 2: 259–70.

LEWIS-BECK, M. 1988. *Economics and Elections*. Ann Arbor: University of Michigan Press.

—— and SKALABAN, A. 1989. Citizen forecasting: can voters see into the future? *British Journal of Political Science*, 19: 46–53.

LEYDEN, K., and BORRELLI, S. 1995. The effect of state economic conditions on gubernatorial elections: does unified government make a difference? *Political Research Quarterly*, 48: 275–300.

LOCKERBIE, B. 1992. Prospective voting in presidential elections: 1956–88. *American Political Quarterly*, 20: 308–25.

LOWRY, R., ALT, J., and FERREE, K. 1998. Fiscal policy outcomes and electoral accountability in American states. *American Political Science Review*, 92: 759–74.

MACKUEN, M., ERIKSON, R., and STIMSON, J. 1992. Peasants or bankers: the American electorate and the U.S. economy. *American Political Science Review*, 86: 597–611.

MADISON, J. 1961. *Federalist Papers* no. 57. New York: New American Library.

MANIN, B. 1995. *Principes du gouvernement représentatif*. Paris: Calmann-Lévy.

—— PRZEWORSKI, A., and STOKES, S. 1999. Introduction. Pp. 1–26 in *Democracy, Accountability, and Representation*, ed. A. Przeworski, S. Stokes, and B. Manin. New York: Cambridge University Press.

MARAVALL, J. M. 1999. Accountability and manipulation. Pp. 154–96 in *Democracy, Accountability, and Representation*, ed. A. Przeworski, S. Stokes, and B. Manin. New York: Cambridge University Press.

—— 2003. The political consequences of internal party democracy. Working Paper 2003/190. Madrid: Instituto Juan March.

—— and PRZEWORSKI, A. 2001. Political reactions to the economy. Pp. 35–77 in *Public Support for Market Reforms in New Democracies*, ed. S. Stokes. New York: Cambridge University Press.

MERSHON, C. 1996. The cost of coalition: coalition theories and Italian governments. *American Political Science Review*, 90: 534–54.

—— 2002. *The Cost of Coalitions*. Stanford, Calif.: Stanford University Press.

MONARDI, F. 1994. Primary voters as retrospective voters. *American Political Quarterly*, 1: 88–103.

NADEAU, R., NIEMI, R., and YOSHINAKA, A. 2002. A cross-national analysis of economic voting, taking account of the political context across time and nations. *Electoral Studies*, 21: 403–23.

NORDHAUS, W. 1975. The political business cycle. *Review of Economic Studies*, 42: 169–90.

PALDAM, M. 1991. How robust is the vote function? A study of seventeen nations over four decades. Pp. 9–31 in *Economics and Politics: The Calculus of Support*, ed. H. Norpoth, M. Lewis-Beck, and J.-D. Laffay. Ann Arbor: University of Michigan Press.

PERSSON, T., ROLAND, G., and TABELLINI, G. 1997. Separation of powers and accountability. *Quarterly Journal of Economics*, 112: 1,163–202.

—— and TABELLINI, G. 1990. *Macroeconomic Policy, Credibility, and Politics*. New York: Harwood Academic Publishers.

POWELL, C. 2001. *España en democracia, 1975–2000*. Madrid: Plaza y Janés.

POWELL, G. B. 2000. *Elections as Instruments of Democracy: Majoritarian and Proportional Visions*. New Haven: Yale University Press.

—— and WHITTEN, G. 1993. A cross-national analysis of economic voting: taking account of the political context. *American Journal of Political Science*, 37: 391–414.

PRICE, S., and SANDERS, D. 1995. Economic expectations and voting intentions in the U.K., 1979–87: a pooled cross-section approach. *Political Studies*, 43: 451–71.

PRZEWORSKI, A. 2003. *States and Markets*. New York: Cambridge University Press.

RAE, D. 1968. A note on the fractionalization of some European party systems. *Comparative Political Studies*, 1: 413–18.

RIKER, W. 1982. *Liberalism against Populism*. Prospect Heights, Ill.: Waveland Press.

ROGOFF, K. 1990. Equilibrium political budget cycles. *American Economic Review*, 80: 21–36.

—— and SIBERT, A. 1988. Elections and macroeconomic policy cycles. *Review of Economic Studies*, 55: 1–16.

ROVAN, J. 1978. *Histoire de la social-démocratie allemande*. Paris: Seuil.

ROYED, T., LEYDEN, K., and BORRELLI, S. 2000. Is "clarity of responsibility" important for economic voting? Revisiting Powell and Whitten's hypothesis. *British Journal of Political Science*, 30: 669–98.

RUDOLPH, T. 2003*a*. Who's responsible for the economy? The formation and consequences of responsibility attributions. *American Journal of Political Science*, 47: 698–713.

—— 2003*b*. Institutional context and the assignment of political responsibilities. *Journal of Politics*, 65: 190–215.

SÁNCHEZ-CUENCA, I. 2003. How can governments be accountable if voters vote ideologically? Working Paper 2003/191. Madrid: Instituto Juan March.

—— and BARREIRO, B. 2000. *Los efectos de la acción de gobierno en el voto durante la etapa socialista 1982–1996*. Madrid: Centro de Investigaciones Sociológicas.

SANDERS, D., and HERMAN, V. 1977. The stability and survival of governments in western democracies. *Acta Politica*, 12: 346–77.

SARTORI, G. 1987. *The Theory of Democracy Revisited*. Chatham, NJ: Chatham House Publishers.

SHAFFERS, S., and CHRESSANTIS, G. 1991. Accountability and U.S. Senate elections: a multivariate analysis. *Western Political Quarterly*, 44: 625–39.

STOKES, S. 2001. Introduction: public opinion of market reforms: a framework. Pp. 1–32 in *Public Support for Market Reforms in New Democracies*, ed. S. Stokes. New York: Cambridge University Press.

STOKES, S. 2003. *Mandates and Democracy*. New York: Cambridge University Press.

STROM, K. 1990. *Minority Government and Majority Rule*. New York: Cambridge University Press.

—— MÜLLER, W., and BERGMAN, T. 2003. *Delegation and Accountability in Parliamentary Democracies*. New York: Oxford University Press.

SVODA, C. 1995. Retrospective voting in gubernatorial elections: 1982–1986. *Political Research Quarterly*, 48: 117–34.

TARR, F. de. 1961. *The French Radical Party*. Oxford: Oxford University Press.

TAYLOR, M., and HERMAN, V. 1971. Party systems and government stability. *American Political Science Review*, 65: 28–37.

THATCHER, M. 1993. *The Downing Street Years*. London: Harper Collins.

TUFTE, E. 1978. *Political Control of the Economy*. Princeton: Princeton University Press.

USLANER, E. 1989. Looking forward and looking backward: prospective and retrospective voting in the 1980 federal elections in Canada. *British Journal of Political Science*, 19: 495–513.

WARWICK, P. 1994. *Government Survival in Parliamentary Democracies*. New York: Cambridge University Press.

WATKINS, A. 1991. *A Conservative Coup: The Fall of Margaret Thatcher*. London: Duckworth.

WHITTEN, G., and PALMER, H. 1999. Cross-national analysis of economic voting. *Electoral Studies*, 18: 49–67.

WOLDENDORP, J., KEMAN, H., and BUDGE, I. 1998. Party governments in 20 democracies: an update. *European Journal of Political Research*, 33: 125–64.

CHAPTER 38

....

ECONOMIC TRANSFORMATION AND COMPARATIVE POLITICS

....

TIMOTHY FRYE

> The hardest part of the transformation, in fact, will not be the economics
> at all, but the politics. (Sachs 1993, 3)

OVER the last fifteen years the transformation of command economies has held great
attraction for scholars of comparative politics. The opportunity to explore the
impact of democratic politics, interest groups, and the European Union (EU) on
the creation of market economies in real time has attracted leading lights in
economics and political science who previously plied their talents elsewhere.[1] The
mix of scholars with deep regional knowledge and experts from other fields has
helped to make the study of the post-communist world particularly compelling.

This essay highlights how research on the transformation of command economies
has contributed to the broader literature in comparative politics. It begins by

---

[1] Among political scientists, Raymond Duch, John E. Jackson, James Gibson, Stephen Holmes, David
Laitin, Juan Linz, Alfred Stepan, and among economists, Andrei Shleifer, Jeffrey Sachs, and Joseph Stiglitz
have made important contributions to academic debate on the transformation of command economies.

depicting the great variation in economic reform across countries over the last fifteen years. From an (arguably) similar starting point in the late 1980s, countries in the region range from EU members with robust market economies to highly statist closed economies today. It then examines how regime type, interest groups, the quality of governance, and the EU have influenced economic reform. Research to date suggests that democracy has been far less of an obstacle than was previously thought; that groups gaining during the reform process may not support further reforms; that the EU can serve as a motor of economic reform; and that capable institutions, particularly states, are critical for building markets. These insights have become rather broadly accepted; however, I argue that these arguments are often lacking in microfoundations. As is often the case in comparative politics, middle-range theories are vulnerable to attack from below because they provide multiple causal paths for interpretation. In discussing each of these explanations, I try to identify ways to tighten the causal links between these middle-range factors and economic reform.

Identifying the causal link between the middle-range arguments and the outcomes at hand is important because democracy, capable states, and economic reform are highly correlated by some measures. In addition, satisfying explanations should account for the process by which outcomes are achieved rather than just for the outcomes themselves. To date, the literature on post-communist economic reform has been better at the latter than the former. Moreover, a number of scholars have expressed concerns that these middle-range factors and economic reform may spring from the same source. Thus, many questions remain about causal relationships in the study of transition economies. This problem of weak microfoundations is far from unique to the post-communist world and is a common shortcoming in the middle-range theories that dominate comparative politics.

Having taken on middle-range theories for lacking microfoundations, this essay then reviews arguments that criticize middle-range theories from a different direction: a lack of causal depth. Kitschelt (2003) has raised this methodological/ontological issue most prominently by arguing that good explanations should not only draw tight causal links based on human agency; they also should also identify more temporally distant causal factors to reduce the likelihood of tautology or banality. To this end, a number of scholars have put forward explanations for variation in economic reform in the post-communist world that focus on deeper historical causes, including the timing and nature of state building, the timing and nature of mass literacy, the role of geography and norm diffusion, as well as the legacy of communist institutions. At their best, these explanations not only identify historical factors that are correlated with contemporary economic outcomes, they also trace some mechanisms by which these historical effects have been transmitted over time. This attention to causal mechanisms offers an advance over much work in historical institutionalism. I conclude by briefly presenting my attempt to integrate temporally proximate and distant factors into an explanation for reform outcomes in the region. My argument focuses on the impact of executive partisanship, democratic institutions, and the relation of the Communist Party to national sovereignty prior to 1989.

This review essay does not include all important works on economic transformation. Far too much work has been written over the past fifteen years to shoehorn into a brief review.[2] It also does not make a case for a single method, concept, or approach as is often done in review essays. Instead it aims to clarify points of contention, identify shortcomings in the literature that merit greater attention, and to demonstrate how the transformation of command economies raises issues of general concern for students of comparative politics.

1 ECONOMIC TRANSFORMATION

Economic transformation begins with the command economy. While no two command economies were identical (just as no two market economies are identical), they did share common features. The state owned property and directed its use. Planners rather than markets set prices for most goods. Firms experienced soft rather than hard budget constraints. That is, managers were constrained more by resource shortages than by competitive pressures from the market (Kornai 1992). For all its perversities, the command economy was an equilibrium (Ericson 1992). Planners, managers, workers, and consumers responded rationally to the incentives provided by the command economy and each participant had no incentive to deviate from their strategy. Being in equilibrium, command economies were not subject to changes at the margins. They were, in Schroeder's (1979) apt phrase, "trapped on a treadmill of reform." Command economies have proven largely impervious to endogenous reform, although China and Vietnam are currently proving exceptions to this rule. The institutional innovations that underpin China's and Vietnam's ability to "grow out of the plan" are discussed later in the chapter (Naughton 1995; Qian 2003; Malesky 2005).

The twenty-seven countries of the former Soviet Union (FSU) and Eastern Europe fit most easily into the category of economies in transition and have the advantage of a roughly common institutional starting point. China, Mongolia, and Vietnam are often included in the literature as well. When comparing the three Asian economies in transition with their counterparts in the FSU and Eastern Europe, it is important to bear in mind the differences between these two groups. China and Vietnam began their transformations at much lower levels of income and retain strong one-party autocratic rule, albeit with varying degrees of competition at lower levels of

---

[2] For excellent overviews see Djankov and Murrell (2002) and Campos and Corricelli (2002). This review essay focuses on economic reform and the creation of markets rather than on economic performance, such as economic growth and inflation rates.

government. In addition, the number of goods included in the central economic plan was far less in China and Vietnam than in the command economies of the FSU and Eastern Europe (Naughton 1995). There is robust debate about the merits of drawing lessons from Asian economies in transition and applying them in the FSU and Eastern Europe, but comparisons across these groups may be quite fruitful for some questions (Qian 2003).[3]

In examining progress in the creation of market economies over the last fifteen years, one is struck by the great strides made by a number of countries, particularly given the region's hostile initial conditions, the scope of transformation, and the volatility of global markets in the 1990s. The European Bank for Reconstruction and Development (EBRD) rates progress in eight different types of economic reform on a scale where 1 equals little change from the command economy and 4.3 equals a standard equivalent to that of a developed market economy. The types of reform include large privatization, small privatization, trade liberalization, price liberalization, corporate governance reform, bank reform, securities market reform, and competition policy reform. The highest reform scores recognize the institutional variety of modern capitalist economies and do not necessarily indicate convergence on an ideal type. For the most part the scores set benchmark levels of performance found in developed market economies.

Column 1 in Table 38.1 depicts the unweighted average EBRD reform scores across all eight dimensions in the year 2004 and reveals the considerable progress that many countries have made over the last fifteen years. Poland, the Czech Republic, Hungary, Slovakia, Estonia, and Latvia have made great strides toward developing institutional frameworks that resemble developed market economies. Other countries, like Albania, Armenia, Bulgaria, Romania, Russia, and Ukraine, have struggled to introduce extensive economic reforms in some areas, but have made considerable progress in others. A final group of countries, Belarus, Uzbekistan, and Turkmenistan, have shed some elements of the command economy, but retain extensive regulation, high levels of protection, and large state sectors.

The post-communist cases remind us that reforms are multidimensional. Countries often conduct several different types of reforms simultaneously. Different types of economic reform have generally been highly correlated in the region, but variation in the rate of progress across different dimensions of economic reform is also prevalent. For example, the last three columns of Table 38.1 provide data on the reform scores for three types of reform in 2004. Column 2 indicates that most countries have significantly opened their economies to foreign trade, while Columns 3 and 4 indicate that they have made less progress in privatizing industry or improving corporate governance.[4]

---

[3] Among others see Sachs and Woo (1992), and Mau (2000) who are skeptical of such comparisons, while Naughton (1995), Stiglitz (2000), and Roland (2000) are more supportive. One difficulty in integrating studies of the two sets of countries is a lack of comparable data.

[4] Countries have made more progress in small privatization and domestic price liberalization than in other areas of reform, such as bank reform, securities market reform, and competition policy.

Table 38.1 Economic reform, 2004

	Average reform score 8 policies 1	Trade liberalization 2	Large privatization 3	Corporate governance 4
Albania	3.00	4.3	3.0	2.0
Armenia	3.06	4.3	3.3	2.3
Azerbaijan	2.71	3.7	2.0	2.3
Belarus	1.88	2.3	1.0	1.0
Bulgaria	3.41	4.3	4.0	2.7
Croatia	3.49	4.3	3.3	3.0
Czech Rep.	3.78	4.3	4.0	3.0
Estonia	3.78	4.3	4.0	3.3
FYR Macedonia	3.08	4.3	3.3	2.3
Georgia	3.04	4.3	3.3	2.0
Hungary	3.86	4.3	4.0	3.3
Kazakhstan	2.95	3.3	3.0	2.0
Kyrgzystan	3.08	4.3	3.7	2.0
Latvia	3.63	4.3	3.7	3.0
Lithuania	3.62	4.3	3.7	3.0
Moldova	2.89	4.3	3.7	1.7
Poland	3.69	4.3	3.3	3.3
Romania	3.16	4.3	3.7	2.0
Russia	2.99	3.3	3.3	3.3
Slovakia	3.70	4.3	4.0	3.3
Slovenia	3.41	4.3	3.0	3.0
Tajikistan	2.43	3.3	2.3	1.7
Turkmenistan	1.34	1.0	1.0	1.0
Ukraine	2.86	3.0	3.0	2.0
Uzbekistan	2.15	1.7	2.7	1.7
Sample Mean (std. deviation)	2.40 (76)	3.79 (.92)	3.14 (.83)	2.38 (.71)

Source: EBRD.

The impact of variation on the rate of progress across different types of economic reform has sparked debate. Some scholars have argued that economic reforms are largely complementary, that is, progress in one type of economic reform begets progress in other types of economic reform (Fischer, Sahay, and Végh 1996). For example, liberalizing trade makes it easier to liberalize domestic prices. Others have argued that variations in speed across different types of economic reform create opportunities for politicians to build coalitions of early winners from reform to support further liberalization later in the transformation (Roland 2000). This implies that variation in progress across different types of reforms may be associated with more successful reform efforts. Still others argue that variation in the progress of different types of economic reforms allows economic actors gaining from one type of economic reform to block further progress in other types of economic reform (Murphy, Shleifer, and Vishny 1992; Hellman 1998). The impact of the interaction of different types of economic reform likely depends on the specific reforms in question and more research is needed along these lines. However, even in a preliminary form this debate has helped push forward the literature on the politics of economic reform by forcing scholars to consider in more detail how different types of economic reforms may influence each other.

Over time variation tells an equally interesting story (see Figure 38.1). Some countries, like Poland, conducted extensive economic reforms at the start of the transformation and maintained a highly liberal economy throughout the post-communist era. In contrast, Belarus followed a much more gradual path of economic reform over the last fifteen years. Russia's economic reform experience is punctuated more by fits and starts. After an initial period of liberalization, Russia experienced a reversal of economic reform in 1998. Following this setback, Russia has struggled to create a greater role for markets.

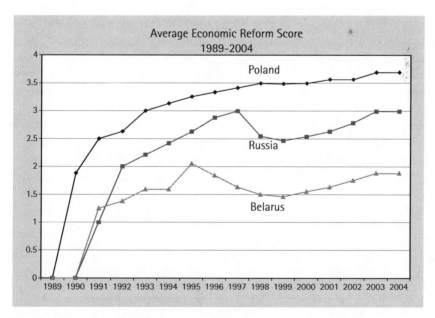

Fig. 38.1 Average economic reform score 1989–2004
Source: EBRD.

2 MIDDLE-RANGE THEORIES AND ECONOMIC REFORM: REGIME TYPE

Accounting for this variation in economic reform across countries and over time has been a central task for political scientists and economists. Most authors have emphasized middle-range theories that focus on the impact of regime type, the power of interest groups, the quality of governance institutions, and the lure of the EU. Each of these arguments has generated important insights, but they often are built on shaky microfoundations.

Guided by the conventional wisdom on the politics of economic reform emerging from studies of Latin America, initial analyses focused on regime type as a potential explanation for economic reform (Lipton and Sachs 1990; Przeworski 1991; Williamson 1994). This view emphasized that economic reforms produced concentrated costs on specific groups in the short run and dispersed benefits for society in the long run. Rulers seeking to liberalize their economies should therefore promote economic reform as rapidly as possible across a broad range of policies and insulate themselves from the inevitable populist backlash as reforms took hold. The main political challenge of economic transformation was to create institutions that would allow reform-oriented politicians to stay in power through the "valley of tears" until the economy began to rebound to their political benefit (Przeworski 1991). Countries with executives most vulnerable to popular pressure, typically via elections, should experience the slowest progress in economic reform.[5]

The emerging conventional wisdom from the post-communist world, however, challenges this argument. There is evidence that the level of democracy is positively associated with the level of economic reforms in the post-communist world. A number of works have reported high bivariate correlations between the level of democracy measured by Freedom House and the level of economic reform as measured by the EBRD's index of economic reform (Hellman 1998; EBRD 1999). Regression analysis reveals that the positive association between democracy and economic reform remains significant after introducing controls for membership in the former Soviet Union, executive partisanship, and initial levels of wealth.[6]

Despite the currency that the "democracy promotes economic reform" view has attained in recent years, it is not time to pop the champagne just yet because the microfoundations of the argument remain largely unspecified.[7] Democracy may affect economic liberalization in many ways and the causal path has yet to be

---

[5] Scholars rarely went so far as to argue that autocracies were better at conducting economic reform, but many scholars favored institutions that provided insulation from popular protest and expressed skepticism that political and economic liberalization could be mutually supportive.

[6] Time series cross-section analyses of economic reform in the post-communist world should be conducted with care given the relatively short time frame, prospect of endogeneity bias, and measurement error, but nonetheless provide considerable insight.

[7] It should be noted that democracy is far less correlated with *increases* in economic reform than with the *level* of economic reform. The correlation between the level of democracy in the year of the largest

identified. Some argue that democracy heightens accountability by giving electoral power to the losers from economic reform and thereby prevents powerful groups from hijacking the state (Hellman 1998). According to this view, accountable rulers with short tenures are less prone to capture as economic agents get fewer returns for building personalistic ties to particular rulers. However, in equilibrium, political turnover need not be associated with economic reform. The threat of losing office should deter both accountable incumbents from granting and interest groups from seeking particularistic benefits in the first place. Because the threat of turnover should be sufficient to reduce rent seeking, the empirical observation of high government turnover and extensive economic reform is not especially informative.[8]

A slightly different argument suggests that democratic states have more dispersed power, e.g. more veto points, and are therefore less prone to state capture. This may be true, but it also offers little insight into why reforms are introduced in the first place. Analyses from other regions indicate that dispersed power makes it more difficult for governments to overcome the collective action and distributional problems of introducing economic reforms, even as it may complicate the maintenance of economic reforms in later stages (Haggard 1990: Haggard and Kaufman 1995; Roubini and Sachs 1989).[9] Without some reference to the partisan preferences of the main agents of interest it is difficult to know why democratic institutions on their own are conducive to the introduction of economic reform.

Democracy may promote economic reform through the electoral cycle. There is some evidence that trade liberalization is more likely to be introduced in the year immediately following elections and is less likely to be introduced immediately before elections (Frye and Mansfield 2004). Others have found evidence of electoral cycles across different policy domains in Russia (Treisman and Gimpelson 2001), but these arguments have not been tested on a broader range of policies across countries.

Cross-national evidence from outside the region suggests that free media characteristic of democratic rule may be central to economic reform (Adsera, Boix, and Payne 2003). Using detailed receipts and videos of bribes between officials in Peru, McMillan and Zoido (2004) argue that because the size of bribes paid to the media was far larger than those paid to elected officials and bureaucrats the media are a linchpin in efforts to reduce corruption. Within Russia, regions with greater freedom of the press experience better economic performance (Yanovskiy et al. 2001). Perhaps democracy works through the freedom of the press, but this argument has not been tested across the post-communist world. More broadly, the institutions of democracy may be complements rather than substitutes and promote economic liberalization

---

increase in economic reform and the size of the increase in economic reform is .26, a relationship that falls short of statistical significance ($p = .21$). Many countries made their largest increases in economic reform early in the transformation at fairly low levels of democracy.

[8] Economic reform may be driving the level of democracy rather than vice versa (Fish 2005).

[9] Haggard and Kaufman 1995 argue that concentrated political power makes it easier to introduce economic reform, but may make it more difficult to consolidate economic reforms once they have been introduced.

only when all are present. That is, the effects of electoral pressure, dispersed power, and free media may each be necessary to promote economic reform. If this is the case, then all the pieces of democracy must be in place for it to have its desired effect on economic reform.

Two contextual factors may also make democracy more conducive to economic reform in the post-communist world than elsewhere. Democracy may be highly correlated with economic reform in the post-communist world because organized labor is so weak.[10] In Latin America, where labor has traditionally been better organized and more closely tied to political parties, the relationship between democracy and economic reform has been more tenuous. In the Latin American cases, the losers from economic reforms appear to have had greater (if far from great) success in using the institutions of democracy to block economic reforms than have their equivalents in the post-communist world. Thus, the relationship between democracy and economic reform in the region may depend on the general impotence of organized labor.

In addition, the dispersion of power typically associated with democracy may be more likely to promote economic reform in the post-communist world than in other settings. Given a status quo of highly centralized political power and an extremely statist economy at the start of the transformation, the likelihood is high that new groups entering the political sphere have more liberal economic preferences than incumbents. Thus, on balance the dispersal of power from statist incumbents is likely to increase the leverage of groups with more market-oriented preferences over policy in a post-communist setting. Using data from 1990–8, one study finds that democratic governments had open economies regardless of the concentration of political power, but that non-democratic governments with dispersed political power also had highly open economies. Only autocracies with concentrated political power retained very high levels of trade protection (Frye and Mansfield 2003).

In sum, it is not clear precisely how the level of democracy influences economic reform. Identifying the causal impact of regime type on economic reforms is important because democracy is also correlated with the presence of liberal governments, accession to the European Union, and certain historical factors as well. Here scholars of economies in transition are in the same boat as students of the democratic peace (Rosato 2003). There appears to be a correlation between the level of democracy and an outcome of interest, but the causal path is still subject to debate. More research into the process by which democracy is associated with economic reform is needed. In addition, there is a possibility that both democracy and economic reform are driven by deeper structural factors. It seems premature to embrace the emerging (and normatively pleasing) consensus that democracy and economic reform necessarily go hand in hand in the post-communist world.

---

[10] Many scholars have noted the surprising weakness of organized labor in the post-communist world. Crowley (2004) provides a nice review of this literature.

3 INTEREST GROUPS: GOOD WINNERS, BAD WINNERS, AND ECONOMIC REFORM

Scholars have also examined the role of interest groups in economic transformation. In other regions of the world, interest groups have figured prominently in explanations of economic reform in a rather straightforward fashion. Groups gaining from economic reforms received tangible benefits and pushed economic reform forward, while the losers from economic reform had to be compensated or repressed for economic liberalization to proceed (Garrett 1998; Haggard 1990). Summing up the standard view, Rodrik (1996, 29) argues that "reforms become sustainable when they generate winners with a stake in their continuation." Generating political support for economic reform was especially important in the post-communist world given that the expected beneficiaries of economic reform—firms in the private sector—barely existed in many countries at the start of the transition. This concern helped to provide an intellectual justification for rapid economic reform.[11] Many argued that privatization would benefit enterprise insiders, primarily company managers, who would then provide a constituency for further economic reform (Shleifer and Vishny 1998, 11).

Yet, evidence from the post-communist cases suggests a more nuanced view of the behavior of economic winners is appropriate. One of the biggest surprises from the literature on economic transformation is that some groups gaining from economic reform may have incentives to block further liberalization. Most prominently, Hellman (1998) argues that some economic reforms have delivered concentrated benefits to specific interest groups who are then well placed to block further reform. For example, easing restrictions on foreign trade before domestic prices are fully liberalized allows exporters to buy goods at subsidized state prices, sell them abroad at world market prices, and pocket the difference. Similarly, rapid privatization of industrial assets prior to the creation of institutions to protect property rights allows enterprise insiders to strip assets for their personal benefit. Many argue that the winners from so-called "partial reforms" have been a potent brake on the continuation of reforms.

Scholars have long recognized that groups with privileged positions in the economy can subvert the process of economic reform, but Hellman (1998) advances this notion by recognizing that the reform process itself may generate benefits to groups who then have a stake in stalling reforms. This insight, which builds on earlier work by Murphy, Shleifer, and Vishny (1992), identifies groups gaining from the transition economy as a primary obstacle to further economic reform.[12]

---

[11] Eyal, Szelenyi, and Townsley (1998) captured this problem in the aptly titled *Making Capitalism without Capitalists.*

[12] Schamis (1999) makes a similar argument for Latin America.

Others have picked up on this argument. Sonin (2003) develops a formal model that suggests that company managers grown wealthy from privatization prefer to keep the rule of law weak because they are especially well placed to use private means to protect their property, including bribing government officials and hiring private security. Hoff and Stiglitz (2004) argue that managers who take control of their enterprise through privatization face collective action and coordination problems that blunt their incentives to lobby for further institutional reform. As a group managers stand to benefit from improvements in the rule of law, but because institutional reform has distributional consequences there is no guarantee that managers will coordinate on a strategy that improves their individual lot. Indeed, managers with access to rents may prefer to delay the establishment of the rule of law until the resource is depleted.

This view has gained considerable credence, but more research on the topic is needed, particularly outside of Russia (Ganev 2001). Big winners from early rounds of economic reform are certainly the most visible opponents of further economic reform, but it is not clear that they have been the most powerful barriers to progress. In Russia, the financial crash of August 1998 dramatically weakened the political power of oligarch-controlled banks, but the last seven years have seen only slow progress in cleaning up the sector. If the oligarch banks were the biggest obstacles to reform in this sector, we might have expected more rapid progress after their decline.[13]

Similarly, if the early winners from economic reform were sufficiently powerful to capture the state, we might have expected more reversals in economic reform as early winners roll back reforms that cut against their interests. Yet reversals of economic reform have been rare and have tended to occur at low rather than high levels of economic reform. Moreover, some countries appear to have escaped the "partial reform equilibrium," an outcome that would seem unlikely given the political power of the early winners (Malesky 2005).[14] Despite these concerns, there is evidence that some groups grown wealthy off the transition economy have obstructed further reforms.

3.1 Good Winners

Not all winners, however, are bad winners. Some groups have grown rich from distortions in the reform process itself, but others have benefited from expanded opportunities to trade and have been allies in support of further economic reform. Jackson, Klich, and Poznanska (2005) find that districts in Poland that created more new private firms early in the transformation experienced higher vote shares for market-oriented parties in national elections in 1993 and 1997. This study advances

---

[13] Of course, tycoons in other sectors of the economy retain considerable influence on policy.

[14] Guriev and Rachinsky (2005) find that on average oligarchic-controlled firms in Russia obtained higher rates of profit, but it is difficult to determine whether this stronger performance is linked to characteristics of the firms or the owners' greater political power.

the debate by tracking the entry and exit of new private firms over time and by demonstrating precisely how the presence of many new private firms compels parties to favor policies that expand the market. Similarly, Fidrmuc (2000) and Tucker (2006) find that regions within countries of East Central Europe with more groups gaining from economic reform show greater support for liberal parties at the ballot box. Frye (2004) finds that managers of new private firms were especially likely to vote for pro-reform parties in parliamentary elections in Russia in 1999.

These results suggest that the reform process itself can change the balance of power among groups gaining and losing from reform in ways that are difficult to capture in a static analysis. Reforms that create robust new private sectors can generate their own constituencies in support of further liberalization, while reforms that deliver concentrated benefits to strategically placed interest groups may stall further reform. This suggests the merits of a more dynamic approach to the politics and economics of transformation than is often found in the literature.[15] In addition, these results call for a more subtle treatment of the political behavior of winners from economic reform. It would be helpful to determine the conditions under which different types of winners emerge as constituencies in support of or against further economic reform.

Perhaps more important, these results indicate that when studying political and economic change it is useful to think in terms of intertemporal contracts (Diermeier et al. 1997). Politicians and groups gaining from economic reform face a problem of credible commitment. Incumbent politicians choose policies in hopes that the beneficiaries will then provide political support. However, having received their benefits, winners may not deliver the promised political support. Indeed, having grown wealthy off the transition economy, early winners may be well placed to withhold their political support in hopes of getting a better bargain.

The problem of intertemporal change becomes more severe when we realize that public officials may also violate their end of the bargain. Having delivered selective benefits in exchange for political support, state agents may then be in a position to revoke those benefits. President Putin's campaign against several oligarchs who backed his presidential campaign in 2000 illustrates this dynamic quite well. This recognition alerts analysts to the problem of time inconsistency in conducting economic reform and raises a host of interesting questions for future research. Why does privatization "stick" in some cases, but not others? Does the fairness of privatization help make property rights secure? Are privatization deals with foreign firms easier or harder to overturn? Why do politicians who come to power respect the privatization decisions of their predecessors in some cases, but not others?

---

[15] These results portray the new private sector in a new light. Rather than being seen as marginal political actors, this view suggests that it is the small firms in the new private sector who have little lobbying power on their own but can be a force at the ballot box that are a central constituency for promoting institutional reform and democracy. This distinction is reminiscent of the oft-cited discrepancy between good bourgeois merchants and the bad bourgeois landed capitalists in Barrington Moore's *The Social Origins of Dictatorship and Democracy*. It is their limited ability to strip assets and obtain rents that gives the new private firms a stake in furthering reform and democracy.

Having received control over the enterprise, how do managers come to believe that state officials will respect their property rights?

This problem is far from unique to transition economies and is present to a greater or lesser extent in all instances of political and economic exchange. Identifying the political and social conditions that facilitate exchange between incumbent politicians and economic winners should be high on the agenda for scholars of economic transformation and comparative politics as well. In this case, the economics of transformation has highlighted a central problem of credible commitment inherent in distributional politics that is often swept under the rug.

4 GOVERNANCE, THE ROLE OF THE STATE, AND ECONOMIC REFORM

Governance and the role of the state in the economy is a third long-standing concern in comparative politics that has been central to economic transformation (Offe 1991; Grzymala-Busse and Jones-Luong 2002). Early studies emphasized scaling back the Leviathan of the communist state, but scholars soon realized that an enfeebled state did little to promote economic reform (Sachs 1994; Holmes 1996). One lesson of the post-communist transformation is the importance of capable states for building markets.

It is often stated that advocates of rapid economic liberalization ignored the reform of state institutions, but it is more accurate to note that they believed that construction of state institutions first required a stable macroeconomic environment. And they were likely right as institution building under macroeconomic instability is a dubious proposition.[16] However, it is also true that most observers were caught off guard by the rapidity of the decline of the state, the rise of the informal economy, and the great speed needed to develop the basic institutions of a market economy (Roland 2000).

Debates about the nature and capacity of state institutions to govern markets have been central to work on post-communist transformation. Three issues merit clarification. There is a widely held view post-communist states have collapsed, but in most cases states in the region retain greater capacity to tax and spend than other lower-and middle-income countries. Table 38.2 presents data from the World Bank on state tax revenue as percentage of GDP and state spending as a percentage of GDP for the year 1995 for a range of countries. On average, most post-communist states are large relative to the size of their economies and retain considerable ability to tax.

---

[16] One study finds that institutions have a stronger impact on economic growth after the first few years of transformation indicating that institutions grow in importance after macroeconomic conditions have stabilized (Campos and Corricelli 2002).

Table 38.2 Tax collection and state spending in Latin America and the post-communist world in 1995

	Tax revenue % GDP	Expenditures % GDP
Argentina	13	14
Bolivia	11	21
Brazil (1994)	20	34
Mexico	13	16
Latin America/Caribbean Average	12 (1994)	14
Albania	17	31
Bulgaria	36	42
Estonia	36	31
Europe/Central Asia average	23	31
All middle income average	12	15

Source: World Bank Development Indicators, 2005.

There is also a widespread belief that post-communist states have needed to cut spending, particularly social spending, to "free up" the market. But states with the most robust market economies have also tended to have high social spending. The lagged value of health spending per capita is positively correlated with the mean economic reform score as calculated by the EBRD (.55) (World Bank 2002; EBRD 2003).

China and Vietnam serve as outliers on this score. They have small states without generous transfer payments, but have conducted considerable economic liberalization. China is particularly interesting in this respect. Total government fiscal revenue in 1978 was about 40 percent of GDP, but by 1996 this figure had fallen to just 17 percent (Qian 2003, 320). This ratio has changed not because of drastic cuts in spending. Indeed, government revenue has doubled in this period. The decline in this figure is largely due to rapid economic growth which has led to a fivefold increase in the denominator.

Finally, governance in the post-communist world is widely thought to have been abysmal over the last decade, but several studies find that it has generally been similar to that of other middle-income countries. Murrell (2003, 1) measures governance using World Bank indicators for 1990–7 and finds that "institutional quality is roughly as expected given per capita income." Treisman (2003) uses Transparency International Indices to measure governance and reaches the same conclusion. Single-country studies produce similar findings. Despite the notorious reputation that Russia has gained for being the poster child of post-communist lawlessness, Hendley, Murrell, and Ryterman (2001) present survey evidence which suggests that legal institutions in Russia are not atypical.[17]

---

[17] By other benchmarks we might have expected governance in the region to be higher than its current level. Many authors trace the capable bureaucracies of the East Asian tigers to low levels of inequality and a highly educated workforce—factors also present early in the post-communist cases (Rodrik 2000).

Part of the debate is due to measurement problems. In the last decade, scholars have developed a range of innovative instruments to study governance and corruption, including surveys and case studies. However, as Anton Chekhov notes, "when many remedies for a disease exist, it means that the disease has not been cured."[18] This difficulty of assessing the quality of governance should not be underestimated.[19]

4.1 Blueprints and Local Knowledge

There is a consensus that "good institutions" are important, but how countries obtain them is a subject of debate. At a broad level, two camps have emerged on the sources of good institutions and the post-communist cases have been central to this discussion. The blueprint school emphasizes that we know which institutions work and there is no need to "rediscover America" as the Russian folk saying goes. The basic institutions of capitalism are well understood and can be exported with minor adaptation to local conditions. The transfer of existing institutions may spare countries the costly trials and errors that accompanied the creation of markets elsewhere. This view advocates borrowing institutions of corporate governance, bank legislation, and bankruptcy where international best practices are more or less well known (Kaufmann 2005).[20] The blueprint argument is often associated with "shock therapy" economic reform (although it need not be), because it allows for the rapid introduction of new institutions.

It is easy to caricature the blueprint school as Washington-based bureaucrats trampling on local norms to force cookie cutter solutions on experienced local public officials who have little choice but to follow instructions. But the view is somewhat more subtle and has evolved over time. Adherents to this school emphasize general principles in the design of good institutions rather than the direct transplantation of laws. The principles of transparency and accountability are treated as paramount and there is some recognition that different institutions may be available to solve governance problems.

Supporters of this view point to the influence of the European Union on economies in transition. By some accounts, the adoption of EU regulatory norms improved the quality of governance and reduced corruption in some transition economies (Mattli and Plümper 2003; Kaufmann 2005; Vachudova 2005). Why should countries experiment with new approaches when they can borrow off-the-shelf regulatory institutions and adapt them to local market conditions?

---

[18] Chekhov was a medical doctor so he knows of what he speaks. This quote is from *The Cherry Orchard*.

[19] Case studies of state institutions over time within a single country have been rare and case studies of state institutions across countries have been even less common. (See Johnson 2000; Meaney 1995; Easter 2002.)

[20] Of course, these questions are still vigorously debated by academics even as they remain broadly accepted by policy advisers (Easterly 2003).

Others have suggested that local knowledge is the building block of successful institutions (Berkowitz, Pistor, and Richard 2003; Rodrik 2000). This view is skeptical that "best-practice" institutions may be imported from other settings, in part because institutions are highly complementary. Strong institutions emerge through the ingenuity of political and economic entrepreneurs who rely on deep knowledge of local conditions (McDermott 2002). Here institutions are specific to particular contexts and emerge from path-dependent processes that use trial and error. This view is often associated with gradual approaches to economic liberalization (although it need not be), as it emphasizes experiments that may take time to evaluate.

Whether blueprints or local knowledge are relatively more important for the development of institutions, however, neglects an important insight of transformation economics—the political conditions that underpin the choice of institutions are critical. For example, Qian (2003) attributes part of China's success to the creation of "transitional institutions" that are politically feasible and efficiency enhancing, even if they fall short of the type of first-best solutions advocated by the blueprint school.[21] These institutions protect rents obtained by the politically influential, while expanding opportunities for others. The institution of dual-track pricing allowed firms to produce for the plan at one price, but sell their above-plan output at market prices. Prices were "liberalized at the margin while inframarginal plan prices and quotas were maintained." Similar was the creation of township and village enterprises (TVEs) that combined state and private ownership and ensured the local and central government a stable flow of revenue while allowing shareholders in the TVE to retain revenues above those pledged to the plan. These institutions stand at odds with the blueprint school's emphasis on broad-based price liberalization and clearly defined property rights.

In addition, the development of anonymous banking violates the blueprint school's emphasis on transparency, but has helped constrain the Chinese government in the absence of the rule of law. Anonymous banking limits information available to the government and makes predation against specific depositors more difficult. The government accepts the arrangement in part because it gains from the revenue held in banks through its controls on interest rates and capital flows (Qian 2003, 306). Thus, anonymous banking helps to decrease the capacity of the state to intervene arbitrarily in the market and thereby bolsters credible commitment. These transitional institutions work because they are well suited to China's political conditions and not because they are "best practice" institutions appropriate for mature market economies.

Shleifer and Treisman (2000) take a similar tack. They argue that privatization and tax reforms in Russia were designed to protect the rents of powerful groups, while also trying to increase efficiency at the margins. According to

---

[21] One standard approach to policy analysis is to identify economically efficient policy and then identify how politics has muddied a beautiful design. An alternative is to begin with the politically efficient policy and then identify how to adapt economic policy to bolster efficiency.

this argument, by substituting state treasury bonds for seigniorage, the Russian government preserved the rents of the politically powerful banking sector, but reduced the social costs generated by large budget deficits that had previously been financed by inflation. They argue that given the politically feasible political set of options, rulers should seek to introduce reforms that improve economic efficiency at the margins. Some have expressed concern that such an approach rewards rent seekers too generously, while defenders treat these compromises as essential costs to pay for promoting economic reform in less than ideal conditions (Stiglitz 2000; Zhuravskaya 2006).

In sum, economic transformation in the post-communist world has reinforced the importance of institutions and governance for a market economy.[22] However, the effectiveness of institutions is determined in part by incentives facing political and economic agents. More research is needed to identify more precisely why politicians supply efficiency-enhancing institutions and why powerful political actors demand them.

5 THE EUROPEAN UNION

The transformation of command economies in Eurasia, China, and Vietnam is taking place on the fringes of economic powerhouses. Most prominently, the European Union has played a powerful role in economic transformation. Eight transition economies in Eurasia joined the EU in 2004 and three more are on the doorstep. Membership in the EU provides considerable economic benefits for new member countries, and popular support for membership has been rather high. The EU has loomed large in analyses of economic reform. Roland (2000) argues that accession countries in Eastern Europe engaged in a "tournament of reform" with potential members pushing each other to enter the EU first. The power of competition and the fear of being excluded helped to spur economic reform in countries on the EU's eastern border. Vachudova (2005) argues that the possibility of accession allowed the EU to exert "passive leverage" on economic reform in East Central Europe from 1990 to 1994. As negotiations for membership began in earnest in the mid-1990s, the EU then exerted "active leverage" by pressing for specific economic reforms that were consistent with the *acquis communautaire*. In her view, the EU provided credible commitments that economic reforms would not be reversed and empowered domestic interest groups with pro-reform preferences.

---

[22] It is probably no surprise that the eminent scholar of institutions Douglass North won his Nobel Prize in 1994 as the economic transformation was under way in the former Soviet Union and Eastern Europe.

While existing arguments about the impact of the EU have made headway, the micro-logic of these arguments can be more clearly specified. There is little doubt that the potential gains to expansion were high. On the supply side, EU members sought expansion in hopes of maintaining stability on their borders, creating more secure property rights for their investments, and regulating the flow of labor from the east. On the demand side, potential members had their eyes set on EU transfer payments, high-paying jobs in member countries, and expanded export opportunities.[23] Pointing to the benefits of membership as an explanation risks the danger of functionalism. Many beneficial agreements fail to occur for a variety of reasons, particularly where distributional consequences are involved. Moreover, if the benefits of membership alone were decisive, all countries would have sought to join the EU, but governments across the region expressed varying degrees of support for accession.[24]

An additional concern in studies of the impact of the EU on economic reform is the direction of causation. Has the pull of EU membership been more powerful than the push from the economies in transition? In other words, to what extent is economic reform due to EU conditionality or to policies that countries would have pursued anyway given their partisan preferences? There was considerable debate about the merits of expansion within the EU until at least the mid-1990s (Mattli and Plümper 2002, 551). Moreover, there was vigorous debate about which countries in the post-communist world would qualify as potential members. One could argue that it was only after the countries of Eastern Europe made considerable progress in economic and political reform that the EU began to push expansion more aggressively. Alternatively, one could argue that the prospect of EU accession motivated economic reform even as the EU was lukewarm about expansion. The direction of causality between EU membership and domestic reforms likely runs both ways, which makes analysis of this process a challenge. Plümper, Schneider, and Troeger (forthcoming) address this issue using a selection model to account for the possibility that countries do not apply to the EU at random. They find that the level of democracy and market reforms influences the decision to apply to the EU, with EU conditionality playing a much larger role in promoting economic reform after a country applies for membership.

In reflecting on the impact of the EU, it may be helpful to consider some counterfactuals. Would the pull of Europe's powerful economies have been sufficient to encourage economic reform, even without the EU? What if economic reform early in the 1990s in East Central Europe went awry? Would the EU have been as supportive of enlargement? These questions cannot be answered beyond a reasonable doubt, but they point to a number of ways in which the causal logic of how the EU shaped economic reform in the region can be clarified.

---

[23] Some of these goals could have been met with policy instruments short of EU membership, such as bilateral trade agreements, free trade zones, and immigration policy.

[24] Norm-based accounts for EU membership also have difficulty accounting for variation in the strategies adopted by potential accession states. See Schimmelfennig (2001).

6 Middle-Range Theories
and Causal Depth

The types of middle-range theories presented above have made considerable headway, but are vulnerable on two fronts. First, they often lack microfoundations that offer concrete accounts of how and why policy outcomes vary across countries. Existing studies have been better at drawing correlations between middle-range factors, like regime type and state institutions, than in accounting for why these factors have the effect that they do. More attention is needed to theoretical accounts and empirical investigations that account for the decisions made by powerful economic and political agents.

In addition, a number of scholars have argued that these types of middle-range theories have tended to lack causal depth. That is, they may primarily be the reflection of deeper historical processes that are the underlying creators of market economies. Kitschelt (2003, 16) makes this case most eloquently by urging scholars to navigate between "an uncompromising structuralism that has a penchant toward excessively deep explanations without human action, on the one hand, and purely conjunctural theories that favor only the shallowest, most proximate of intertemporal social mechanisms, on the other." In specific reference to the cases at hand he notes: "causal analysis in the comparative study of post-communist politics should not be so shallow as to blur the distinction between *explanans* and *explanandum*, but it should also not be so deep as to evaporate any causal mechanism that could operate through human action, identified by preferences, skills, and expectations." With this line of argument in mind, a number of scholars have thought to push back the causal chain to find structurally deeper causes of reform outcomes in the post-communist world.

These accounts do not always seek to make sense of economic reform outcomes, but they do aim to identify the structural factors that in turn shape attempts to build market economies. For example, Kitschelt and Malesky (2000) critique institutional accounts of economic reform in the region for their neglect of the likely endogeneity of institutions themselves. They note that "the independent effect of institutions may be quite modest in many instances and vastly overshadowed by the power configurations that antedate the choice of institutions."[25] In a related argument Kitschelt (2003) suggests that the timing of state formation and the type of communist rule, whether it was bureaucratic administrative, national accommodative, or patrimonial, shapes the prospects for both democracy and economic reform. For example, the

---

[25] More specifically, they trace the constitutional choice of presidential and parliamentary institutions in the post-communist world to the extent of inter-war political mobilization, the timing of state formation, and geography. In turn, the impact of presidential and parliamentary regimes on economic reform is small and contingent on pre-existing structural conditions. Powerful presidencies may promote economic reform in highly clienteist autocratic regimes, but have more limited effects when structural conditions are not conducive to clientelism or the regime is democratic.

patrimonial communism and late state formation that marked most of the former Soviet Union gave incentives and resources to outgoing communist leaders to establish political institutions inhospitable to democracy and to pursue gradual economic reforms that reflected the interests of their constituencies. In contrast, countries like Poland and Hungary that experienced national accommodative communism entered the 1990s with more robust state institutions and human capital better suited to building a market economy and democratic political institutions. In these accounts, it is the nature of state building and the legacy of communist rule that generates institutions and human capital that travel temporally to influence the prospects for economic and political reform in the contemporary period.

Similarly, Kopstein and Reilly (2000) argue that geographic proximity to market-oriented democracies in Europe and Japan drove both the creation of democratic institutions and the extent of economic reform by spreading norms of appropriate elite behavior. They argue that "geographic proximity to the West has exercised a positive influence on the transformation of communist states." To provide a more causal account, the authors argue that geography shapes political and economic outcomes through two types of diffusion effects: neighbor effects, in which states are influenced by their neighbors, and openness effects in which states vary in their receptiveness to the "flow of ideas and the willingness and capacity of the ruling regime to allow interaction with surrounding states and to accept the influence of communication, transportation, and technology that has the potential to transform attitudes and behavior" (Kopstein and Reilly 2000, 36). The causal story here of how these diffusion effects influence economic reform is not very clear, but the larger point is well made that both economic and political reform may both be driven by geography.

Darden and Grzymala-Busse (2006) trace the outcome of the first post-communist elections, which Fish (1998) argues is a critical determinant of economic reform, to the timing of mass literacy and the content of the national curriculum.[26] They argue that the content of educational training at the timing of mass literacy shaped values and attitudes in subsequent generations in ways that map onto policy preferences in the post-communist period. They write: "What brought about the communist exit from power? We argue that the ultimate roots lie in pre-communist nationalism, fomented and fostered by mass nationalist schooling. The exit itself was the culmination of decades of nursed nationalist grievances, invidious comparisons, and carefully fostered hostility to the communist project as a foreign and inferior imposition." In a multivariate cross-section analysis, they find that the timing of mass literacy achieved via a curriculum infused with nationalist content is highly correlated with seat share of non-communist factions in the first post-communist election. One can then make the case that countries with early mass literacy under nationalist schooling

---

[26] This of course does not rule out the possibility that institutional legacies have a direct impact on economic reform. Just as political scientists have noted that the institutional legacy of the command economy shapes the prospect for democracy, economists have pointed to initial conditions and institutional legacies as important to economic outcomes (DeMelo, Denizer, and Gelb 1996).

were especially good candidates for the creation of democratic governments and market economies. This argument has the great strength of providing a means (nationalist education) by which a temporally distant factor (the timing of mass literacy) can influence a contemporary outcome (the results of the first free and fair election).

These works offer greater causal depth than has traditionally been found in the literature. They also offer the opportunity for generating instrumental variables that may help resolve some endogeneity problems. Moreover, unlike arguments that simply seek to correlate institutional or structural features of the past—years under communism or previous experience with a market economy—with contemporary outcomes, these works also try to identify the means by which temporally distant factors travel over time to influence current policy choices. These accounts, understandably, are better at identifying variations in the structural conditions that promote economic reform than at accounting for the process of economic reform once it is under way, but they do provide a needed temporal dimension to the literature.

In my own work, I try to integrate more temporally proximate and distant factors in two steps. I begin by exploring how executive partisanship interacts with democracy and the nature of political opposition before examining why countries vary in their executive partisanship.[27] I argue that despite the homogenizing pressures of the global economy, the partisanship of the executive influences the extent of economic reform.[28] Executive partisanship does not, however, exert a straightforward impact on economic reform. It interacts with the extent of political polarization and democracy to shape economic reform.[29] When political polarization is low, that is, governments face little opposition across the partisan divide in parliament, executives are able to implement their preferred policies. Liberal governments facing weak opposition from traditional ex-communist parties pursue extensive reform as in Poland, Hungary, and Estonia, while traditional ex-communist executives facing weak opposition from liberal parties pursue minimal and gradual economic reforms, as in Uzbekistan, Belarus, and Azerbaijan.

However, opposition within parliament across the liberal/traditional ex-communist divide heightens the possibility of policy reversals should the incumbent government fall. Politically polarized countries—those with a rough balance of power between liberal and traditional ex-communist factions, like Russia, Bulgaria, and Romania—face greater policy uncertainty. This polarization-induced uncertainty over future

[27] Others have argued that the partisan balance of political power shapes economic reform. In cross-sectional analysis of economic reform from 1991 to 1995, Fish 1998 finds that the seat share of the ex-communist party in the first free election is a good predictor of the level of economic reform. Aslund 2002 as well emphasizes the importance of elite partisanship for economic reform.

[28] Liberal executives with few ties to the state or party apparatus may prefer economic strategies that rely on the market because they have little control over state officials installed by the previous regime. Traditional ex-communist executives whose base of support lies in the state and party apparatus and in social groups threatened by economic reform may, in some cases, be skeptical of economic liberalization which may weaken their constituents.

[29] Here political polarization is measured by the percentage of seats held by the largest liberal (traditional ex-communist) party when a traditional ex-communist (liberal) controls the executive.

policy reduces the expected return on investment made by economic agents. With less investment and hence less tax revenue to buy political support, incumbents in a polarized environment grant more specific benefits to powerful interest groups that slow reforms in order to stay in power. The effects of this type of political polarization between liberal and traditional ex-communist factions are heightened in a democracy because political competition increases the likelihood of a change in government.

To establish the microfoundations of the argument, I use data from a 1999 survey of about 4,000 company managers in twenty countries conducted by the World Bank and the EBRD. Based on a multi-level statistical model, I find that business people in polarized political systems perceive policy as less predictable and invest at lower rates. The point here is to try to establish the path (political uncertainty) by which a middle-range variable (political polarization) influences an outcome (economic reform).

I then argue that the partisan balance of political power between liberal and traditional ex-communist factions in the post-communist world is driven by more causally deep factors. More specifically, I trace the extent of political polarization to the timing of national identify and the position of the local Communist Party within the communist bloc. In some countries, like Belarus, Uzbekistan, and Azerbaijan, the creation of a national identity came late and occurred only after the installation of communist power. In these settings, local communist leaders faced weak nationalist oppositions in the post-communist period and could rely on existing institutions to install themselves as the "defender of the nation" to stay in power. Here polarization has generally been low as traditional ex-communist leaders have largely retained their political dominance.

In other countries, like Poland, Estonia, and Hungary, national identity was created before the installation of communist power, and the local Communist Party played a subordinate role in the communist bloc. Here the local Communist Party faced a strong nationalist opposition and had little credibility with the mass public. In these countries traditional ex-Communist Party leaders quickly gave way to liberal parties who dominated the political spectrum, and again political polarization has been low.[30]

In a third group of countries, including Russia, Albania, and Romania, the creation of a national identity pre-dated communist power, but the Communist Party played a relatively autonomous role within the communist bloc. This allowed communist successor parties after 1989 to credibly claim to have made policy without being subservient to a "foreign" power. In these cases the leaders of the Communist Party had greater credibility and could claim credit for some of the achievements of the communist period, while downplaying the worst features of the period of communist rule. These themes played well with some sectors of society, but not with others, and led to a pattern of polarized politics between a liberal and traditional ex-communist camp.

---

[30] In accordance which much of the secondary literature, I treat the ex-communist parties of Poland, Hungary, Slovenia, and Lithuania as market-oriented parties (Ishiyama 1997; Grzymala-Busse 2002).

This two-pronged strategy seeks to trace the causal chain back in time to give the argument greater causal depth, but also to provide microfoundations that link middle-range factors to economic outcomes. This is far from the only strategy to explore relationships between institutional legacies and economic reform. One alternative is to make comparisons across countries with different institutions. One might gain leverage on institutional legacies by comparing economic reforms in Vietnam, China, Uzbekistan, and Kyrgyzstan (Qian 2003; Malesky 2005). All are poor, agrarian, non-democracies, but the Asian cases began reform with different institutional legacies.[31] Another useful comparison may pair Vietnam and Moldova, both of which are poor and agrarian, but the latter is surprisingly democratic (Way 2003).[32]

Finally, scholars may take advantage of case studies of theoretical outliers. For example, Ukraine and Belarus have been far less successful in conducting economic reform than their structural conditions would lead one to expect. Each began the transformation with relatively wealthy and well-educated populations located in close proximity to Europe, but have had considerable difficulty introducing market institutions. Similarly, Bulgaria's economic transformation has been far more difficult than its relatively robust democracy would suggest. Moreover, Slovakia's economic reform scores are higher under the populist Meciar than one would expect. Indeed, Slovakia's EBRD reform scores in the 1990s are almost identical to those of the Czech Republic despite the former's less promising initial conditions and more populist government.

7 CONCLUSION AND AREAS OF FUTURE RESEARCH

In sum, the post-communist cases have made important contributions to substantive debates on the creation of market economies. Studies from the last fifteen years have indicated that that democracy does not inhibit economic reform and the oft-stated tensions between democratization and economic reform have been exaggerated. In addition, the literature from the post-communist world has developed more subtle understandings of interest group politics than are commonly found in the literature on the politics of economic reform. In contrast to expectations, groups gaining from economic reform may have incentives to block rather than advance economic liberalization. The cases at hand have also found that the EU has been a key element

---

[31] The comparison is complicated by differences in the type of authoritarian rule as Uzbekistan and Kyrgyzstan are characterized by a very personalistic form of autocracy as compared to strong party rule in China and Vietnam, but may be fruitful nonetheless.

[32] Another approach is to focus on the regional level within countries that have experienced different institutional legacies. Here the frequent shifting of state borders in the past is an advantage.

of support for economic reform in some countries, but not others. Finally, the cases remind us that capable states are critical for economic liberalization.

Yet, as in comparative politics more generally, scholars have considerable room to build on these substantive insights by providing sturdier microfoundations and deeper causal chains for these arguments. Precisely how does democracy promote economic reform? When does exchange between political and economic agents stick? Under what conditions can international organizations influence policy? When do politicians support the creation of stronger state institutions? And when do private interests demand them? Answers to these questions will help draw tighter links between middle-range theories and economic reform outcomes.

In addition, there is a need for deeper arguments that trace causality back in time to ensure that the impact of middle-range theories on economic reform in the region is not solely a reflection of causally prior factors. Understanding how pre-communist and communist era legacies shape institutional choices and policy outcomes in the post-communist period has spawned a productive research agenda (Pop-Eleches 2006).

This chapter has argued that economic transformation has produced a number of empirical and theoretical insights that have challenged existing literature and contributed to areas of interest for scholars of comparative politics. Based on the logic that empirical surprises have largely shaped the research agenda in the field, it is perhaps unwise to recommend areas for future research. With this caveat, I point to three additional areas of potential interest.

7.1 Cross-regional Comparisons

Przeworski's *Democracy and the Market* set the stage for broad comparative research on economic transformation in Latin America and the post-communist world, but few works have drawn explicit comparisons between the two regions. This is unfortunate. While such comparisons raise many difficulties, interesting puzzles remain unexplored. Why does economic liberalization appear to lead to strong economic performance in the post-communist world, but not in Latin America (Aslund, Boone, and Johnson 1996; Remmer 2001)? Why is policy switching so much more prevalent in Latin America than in the post-communist world (Stokes 2001)? Why does democracy appear to have been more supportive of economic reform in the post-communist world than in Latin America? More broadly, studies that place economic transformation in cross-regional and global perspective hold promise.

7.2 Institutional Legacies

Another area for future research is to assess the impact of the institutional legacy of communist rule on economic and political transformation over time. Does the institutional legacy have a sharp impact on democracy and economic outcomes early in the transformation, but declining influence over time? If so, we might expect countries with different institutional legacies to more closely resemble each other over time. Or, is the legacy subject to increasing returns? If so, we might expect the countries of the former Soviet Union to look less like the countries of Eastern Europe in the future. In some respects this research agenda is akin to Acemoglu, Johnson, and Robinson's (2001) argument that colonial legacies established in the nineteenth century continue to separate the developed from the developing world in the last half of the twentieth century. This may help contribute to larger debates in the field about the impact of institutional legacies on economic and political outcomes.

7.3 Social Institutions and Market Economies

Scholars have paid great attention to how formal state institutions have shaped economic reform, but efforts to study the impact of social institutions on markets have been less prominent (Bruszt and Stark 1998; McDermott 2002; Ganev 2001). This is unfortunate as market economies rely on a complex mix of social institutions (networks, business associations, reputation mechanisms) as well as state institutions (courts, bureaucracies, legislatures). Several authors have examined the impact of "violent entrepreneurs"—Mafia-like organizations that provide protection in the place of a weak state—but other more benign types of social institutions have largely been left unanalyzed (Varese 2001; Volkov 2002). Do business organizations impede or promote economic reform? Why do state bodies govern some sectors, while social institutions dominate in others? Under what conditions do social networks inhibit and advance markets? The mixture of state and social institutions in protecting property rights, generating norms of behavior, and influencing the transactions costs of exchange merits more attention.

Scholars of comparative politics are only beginning to tap the potential of countries undergoing transformation from a command economy and Communist Party rule. Indeed, the transformation of command economies, like the rise of the European Union and the spectacular growth of East Asia, will likely occupy the attention of political scientists and economists alike for years to come. This essay has focused on a handful of themes of general importance for comparative politics, but this far from exhausts the potential of economic transformation for the field.

References

Acemoglu, D., Johnson, S., and Robinson, J. 2001. The colonial origins of comparative development: an empirical investigation. *American Economic Review*, 91: 1369–401.

Adsera, A., Boix, C., and Payne, M. 2003. Are you being served? Accountability and the quality of government. *Journal of Law, Economics and Organization*, 19 (2): 445–90.

ASLUND, A. 2002. Building *Capitalism: The Transformation of the Former Soviet Bloc*. Washington, DC: Brookings Institution.

—— BOONE, P., and JOHNSON, S. 1996. How to stabilize: lessons from postcommunist countries. *Brookings Papers on Economic Activity*, 1: 217–313.

BERKOWITZ, D., PISTOR, K., and RICHARD, J.-F. 2003. Economic development, legality, and the transplant effect. *European Economic Review*, 47 (1): 165–95.

BRUSZT, L., and STARK, D. 1998. *Post-Socialist Pathways: Transforming Politics and Property in East Central Europe*. Cambridge: Cambridge University Press.

BUNCE, V. 1999. The political economy of post-socialism. *Slavic Review*, 58 (4): 756–93.

CAMPOS, N., and CORRICELLI, F. 2002. Growth in transition: what we know, what we don't, and what we should. *Journal of Economic Literature*, 40 (3): 793–836.

COLTON, T. J. 2000. *Transitional Citizens: Voters and What Influences Them in the New Russia*. Cambridge, Mass.: Harvard University Press.

CROWLEY, S. 2004. Explaining labor quiescence in post-communist Europe: historical legacies and comparative perspective. *East European Politics and Society*, 18 (3): 394–429.

DARDEN, K., and GRZYMALA-BUSSE, A. 2006. The great divide: pre-communist schooling and postcommunist trajectories. MS. New Haven.

DEMELO, M., DENIZER, C., and GELB, A. 1996. From plan to market: patterns of transition. Washington, DC: World Bank Policy Research Paper.

DIERMEIER, D., ERICSON, J., FRYE, T., and LEWIS, S. 1997. Credible commitment and property rights: the role of strategic interaction between political and economic actors. Pp. 20–42 in *The Political Economy of Property Rights*, ed. D. Weimer. Cambridge: Cambridge University Press.

DJANKOV, S., and MURRELL, P. 2002. Enterprise restructuring in transition: a quantitative survey. *Journal of Economic Literature*, 40 (3): 739–92.

DUCH, R. 1993. Tolerating economic reform: popular support for transition to a market economy in the former Soviet Union. *American Political Science Review*, 93 (3): 590–608.

EASTER, G. M. 2002. Politics of revenue extraction in post-communist states: Poland and Russia compared. *Politics and Society*, 30: 599–627.

EASTERLY, W. 2003. *The Elusive Quest for Growth: Economists' Misadventures in the Tropics*. Cambridge, Mass.: MIT Press.

ERICSON, R. 1992. Economics. Pp. 49–83 in *After the Soviet Union: From Empire to Nations*, ed. T. J. Colton and R. Legvold. New York: W. W. Norton & Company. *European Bank for Reconstruction and Development Transition Report*. Various years. London: EBRD.

EYAL, G., SZELENYI, I., and TOWNSLEY, E. 1998. *Making Capitalism without Capitalists: The New Ruling Elite in Eastern Europe*. London: Verso.

FIDRMUC, J. 2000. Economics of voting in postcommunist countries. *Electoral Studies*, 19: 199–217.

FISCHER, S., SAHAY, R., and VÉGH, C. 1996. Stabilization and growth in transition economies: the early experience. *Journal of Economic Perspectives*, 10 (2): 45–66.

FISH, M. S. 1998. The determinants of economic reform in the post-communist world. *East European Politics and Society*, 12: 31–78.

—— 2005. *Democracy Derailed in Russia: The Failure of Open Politics*. Cambridge: Cambridge University Press.

FRYE, T. 2004. Markets, democracy and new private business in Russia. *Post-Soviet Affairs*, 17 (4): 309–31.

—— 2006. Partisan politics in transition economies. MS. New York.

—— and MANSFIELD, E. D. 2003. Fragmenting protection: the political economy of trade policy in the post-communist world. *British Journal of Political Science*, 33: 635–57.

FRYE, T., and MANSFIELD, E. D. 2004. Timing is everything: elections and trade liberalization in the post-communist world. *Comparative Political Studies*, 37 (4): 371–98.

GANEV, V. 2001. The Dorian Gray effect: winners as statebreakers in postcommunism. *Communist and Post-Communist Studies*, 34: 1–25.

GARRETT, G. 1998. *Partisan Politics in the Global Economy*. Cambridge: Cambridge University Press.

GIBSON, J. L. 1998. Political and economic markets: changes in the connections between attitudes toward political democracy and a market economy within the mass culture of Russia and Ukraine. *Journal of Politics*, 58: 954–84.

GRZYMALA-BUSSE, A. 2002. *Redeeming the Past: The Regeneration of Communist Parties in East Central Europe*. Cambridge: Cambridge University Press.

—— and JONES-LUONG, P. 2002. Reconceptualizing the state: lessons from post-communism. *Politics and Society*, 30: 529–54.

GURIEV, S., and RACHINSKY, A. 2005. The role of oligarchs in Russian capitalism. *Journal of Economic Perspectives*, 19 (1): 131–50.

HAGGARD, S. 1990. *Pathways from the Periphery: The Politics of Growth in Newly Industrializing Countries*. Ithaca, NY: Cornell University Press.

—— and KAUFMAN, R. 1995. *The Political Economy of Democratic Transitions*. Princeton: Princeton University Press.

HELLMAN, J. 1998. Winners take all: the politics of partial reform. *World Politics*, 50 (2): 203–34.

—— JONES, G. and KAUFMANN, D. 2003. Seize the state, seize the day: state capture and influence in transition economies. *Journal of Comparative Economics*, 31 (4): 732–50.

HENDLEY, K., MURRELL, P., and RYTERMAN, R. 2001. Law works in Russia: the role of legal institutions in the transactions of Russian enterprises. Pp. 56–94 in *Assessing the Value of the Rule of Law in Transition Economies*, ed. P. Murrell. Ann Arbor: University of Michigan Press.

HOFF, K., and STIGLITZ, J. 2004. After the big bang: obstacles to the emergence of the rule of law in transition societies. *American Economic Review*, 94 (3): 753–63.

HOLMES, S. 1996. Cultural legacies or state collapse? Pp. 22–76 in *Perspectives on Postcommunism*, ed. M. Mandelbaum, New York: Council on Foreign Relations.

ISHIYAMA, J. 1997. The sickle or the rose? Previous regime type and the evolution of ex-communist parties. *Comparative Political Studies*, 30: 299–330.

JACKSON, J. E., KLICH, J., and POZNANSKA, K. 2005. *The Political Economy of Poland's Transition: New Firms and Reform Governments*. Cambridge: Cambridge University Press.

JOHNSON, J. 2000. *A Fistful of Rubles: The Rise and Fall of the Russian Banking System*. Ithaca, NY: Cornell University Press.

KAUFMANN, D. 2005. Myths and realities of governance and corruption. *Global Competition Report*. Davos: World Economic Forum.

KITSCHELT, H. 2003. Accounting for postcommunist regime diversity: what counts as a good cause? Pp. 49–88 in *Capitalism and Democracy in Central and Eastern Europe: Assessing the Legacy of Communist Rule*, ed. G. Ekiert and S. Hanson. Cambridge: Cambridge University Press.

—— and MALESKY, E. 2000. Constitutional design and post-communist economic reform. Paper presented at the annual meeting of the Midwest Political Science Association, Chicago.

KOPSTEIN, J. S., and REILLY, D. 2000. Geographic diffusion and transformation of post-communist Europe. *World Politics*, 53 (1): 1–30.

KORNAI, J. 1992. *The Socialist System: The Political Economy of Communism*. Princeton: Princeton University Press.

LINZ, J. J., and STEPAN, A. 1996. *Problems of Democratic Transition and Consolidation: Southern Europe, South America, and Post-Communist Europe*. Baltimore: Johns Hopkins University Press.

LIPTON, D., and SACHS, J. 1990. Creating a market economy in eastern Europe: the case of Poland. *Brookings Papers on Economic Activity*, 1: 75–147.

MALESKY, E. 2005. At provincial gates: the impact of foreign direct investment on provincial autonomy and economic reform. Ph.D. dissertation. Duke University.

MATTLI, W., and PLÜMPER, T. 2002. The demand-side politics of EU enlargement: democracy and the application for EU membership. *Journal of European Public Policy*, 9: 550–74.

MAU, V. 2000. *Russia's Economic Reforms as Seen by an Insider: Success or Failure?* London: Royal Institute of International Affairs.

MCDERMOTT, G. 2002. *Embedded Politics: Industrial Networks and Institutional Change in Postcommunism*. Ann Arbor: Michigan University Press.

MCMILLAN, J., and ZOIDO, P. 2004. How to subvert democracy: Montesinos in Peru. *Journal of Economic Perspectives*, 18 (4): 69–92.

MEANEY, C. S. 1995. Foreign experts, capitalists, and competing agendas: privatization in Poland, Hungary and Czechoslovakia. *Comparative Political Studies*, 28 (2): 275–305.

MURPHY, K., SHLEIFER, A., and VISHNY, R. 1992. The transition to a market economy: the pitfalls of partial reform. *Quarterly Journal of Economics*, 107: 889–906.

MURRELL, P. 2003. Relative levels and the character of institutional development in transition economies. In *The Political Economy of Transition and Development: Institutions, Politics, and Policies*, ed. J. Fidrmuc and N. Campos. Boston: Kluwer Academic.

NAUGHTON, B. 1995. *Growing out of the Plan*. Cambridge: Cambridge University Press.

OFFE, C. 1991. Capitalism by democratic design? Democratic theory facing the triple transition in east central Europe. *Social Research*, 58 (4): 865–92.

PLÜMPER, T., SCHNEIDER, C., and TROEGER, V. Forthcoming. The politics of EU eastern enlargement: evidence from a Heckman selection model. *British Journal of Political Science*.

POP-ELECHES, G. 2006. The long arm of the past: historical legacies and political development in eastern Europe. Unpublished paper. Princeton.

PRZEWORSKI, A. 1991. *Democracy and the Market: Political and Economic Reforms in Eastern Europe and Latin America*. New York: Cambridge University Press.

QIAN. Y. 2003. How reform worked in China. Pp. 297–333 in *In Search of Prosperity*, ed. D. Rodrik. Princeton: Princeton University Press.

REMMER, K. 2001. The politics of economic policy and performance in Latin America. *Journal of Public Policy*, 22: 29–59.

RODRIK, D. 1996. Understanding economic policy reform. *Journal of Economic Literature*, 34: 9–41.

—— 2000. Institutions for high quality growth: what are they and how to acquire them. *Studies in Comparative and International Development*, 35 (3): 3–31.

ROLAND, G. 2000. *Transition and Economics: Politics, Markets, and Firms*. Cambridge, Mass.: MIT Press.

ROSATO, S. 2003. The flawed logic of democratic peace theory. *American Political Science Review*, 97 (4): 585–602.

ROUBINI, N., and SACHS, J. 1989. Government spending and budget deficits in the industrial countries. *Economic Policy: A European Forum*, 8: 101–27.

SACHS, J. 1993. *Poland's Jump to a Market Economy*. Cambridge, Mass.: MIT Press.

—— 1994. Russia's struggle with stabilization: conceptual issues and evidence. *World Bank Research Observer*, 57–80.

SACHS, J., and WOO, W. T. 1992. Structural factions in the economic reforms of China, eastern Europe, and the former Soviet Union. *Economic Policy*, 9 (18): 101–45.

SCHAMIS, H. 1999. Distributional coalitions and the politics of economic reform in Latin America. *World Politics*, 51 (2): 236–68.

SCHIMMELFENNIG, F. 2001. The community trap: liberal norms, rhetorical action, and the eastern enlargement of the European Union. *International Organization*, 55 (1): 47–80.

SCHROEDER, G. E. 1979. The Soviet economy on a treadmill of "reforms." Pp. 65–88 in *Soviet Economy in a Time of Change*. Washington, DC: Joint Economic Committee, US Congress.

SHLEIFER, A., and TREISMAN, D. 2000. *Without a Map: Political Tactics and Economic Reform in Russia*. Cambridge, Mass.: MIT Press.

—— and VISHNY, R 1998. *The Grabbing Hand: Government Pathologies and their Cures*. Cambridge, Mass.: MIT Press.

SONIN, K. 2003. Why the rich may favor poor protection of property rights. *Journal of Comparative Economics*, 31: 715–31.

STIGLITZ, J. 2000. Whither reform: ten years of transition. Pp. 27–56 in *Annual World Bank Conference on Economic Development*, ed. B. Pleskovic and J. E. Stiglitz. Washington, DC: World Bank.

STOKES, S. 2001. *Mandates and Democracy: Neoliberalism by Surprise in Latin America*. Cambridge: Cambridge University Press.

STONE, R. 2003. *Lending Credibility: The International Monetary Fund and the Post-Communist Transition*. Princeton: Princeton University Press.

TREISMAN, D. 2003. Postcommunist corruption. In *The Political Economy of Transition and Development: Institutions, Politics, and Policies*, ed. J. Fidrmuc and N. Campos. Boston: Kluwer Academic.

—— and GIMPELSON, V. 2001. Political business cycles and Russian elections, or the manipulations of "Chudar." *British Journal of Political Science*, 31: 225–46.

TUCKER, J. 2006. *Regional Economic Voting in Russia, Poland, Hungary, Slovakia, and the Czech Republic, 1990–1999*. Cambridge: Cambridge University Press.

VACHUDOVA, M. A. 2005. *Europe Undivided: Democracy, Leverage, and Integration after Communism*. New York: Oxford University Press.

VARESE, F. 2001. *The Russian Mafia: Private Protection in a New Market Economy*. Oxford: Oxford University Press.

VOLKOV, V. 2002. *Violent Entrepreneurs: The Use of Force in the Making of Russian Capitalism*. Ithaca, NY: Cornell University Press.

WAY, L. A. 2003. Pluralism and weak states: the case of Moldova. *East European Politics and Societies*, 17 (3): 454–82.

—— 2005. Authoritarian state building and the sources of political competition in the fourth wave: the cases of Belarus, Moldova, Russia, and Ukraine. *World Politics*, 57 (2): 231–61.

WILLIAMSON, J. 1994. In search of a manual for technopols. Pp. 9–48 in *The Political Economy of Policy Reform*, ed. J. Williamson. Washington, DC: Institute for International Economics.

WORLD BANK. 2002. *World Development Indicators*. Washington, DC: World Bank.

YANOVSKIY, K., KOCHETKOVA, O., MAZHUGA, A., CHERNY, D., JAVORONKOV, S., SVOIE, D., HOBSON, P., and DESJARDINS, P.-M. 2001. *Political-Economic Problems of the Russian Regions*. Moscow: Consortium for Economic Policy Research and Advice.

ZHURAVSKAYA, E. 2006. Whither Russia: a review of Andrei Shleifer's *A Normal Country*. *Journal of Economic Literature* (forthcoming).

Subject Index

Name Index

Printed and bound by CPI Group (UK) Ltd, Croydon, CR0 4YY